Basketball

Basketball

A Biographical Dictionary

Edited by

David L. Porter

Greenwood Press
Westport, Connecticut • London

Library of Congress Cataloging-in-Publication Data

Basketball : a biographical dictionary / edited by David L. Porter.
p. cm.
Includes bibliographical references and index.
ISBN 0–313–30952–3 (alk. paper)
1. Basketball players—Biography—Dictionaries. I. Porter, David L., 1941–
GV884.A1B37 2005
796.323'09'2—dc22 2004060910
[B]

British Library Cataloguing in Publication Data is available.

Library of Congress Catalog Card Number: 2004060910
ISBN: 0–313–30952–3

First published in 2005

Greenwood Press, 88 Post Road West, Westport, CT 06881
An imprint of Greenwood Publishing Group, Inc.
www.greenwood.com

Printed in the United States of America

The paper used in this book complies with the Permanent Paper Standard issued by the National Information Standards Organization (Z39.48–1984).

10 9 8 7 6 5 4 3 2 1

Contents

Preface

Basketball: A Biographical Dictionary, arranged alphabetically, features 577 basketball entries. The selection of the basketball entries proved very challenging. Before making final choices, the editor thoroughly researched several basketball encyclopedias and histories.[1] Of course, the editor assumes responsibility for any significant basketball figures inadvertently excluded from this volume.

The entries met three general criteria. First, they either were born in or spent their childhood years in the United States, though foreigners who made exceptional impacts on basketball are also covered. Second, they typically compiled impressive statistical records as players or compiled impressive records as coaches or executives. Several basketball players set collegiate or professional records. Some appeared in National Collegiate Athletic Association (NCAA) and/or National Invitation Tournament (NIT) postseason events and National Basketball Association (NBA) or American Basketball Association (ABA) playoffs. Third, they made a major impact on basketball, earning significant awards or performing for championship teams. Some have been named to the Naismith Memorial Basketball Hall of Fame or other basketball halls of fame. Many have won athletic honors, including Player of the Year, Rookie of the Year, All-America, or All-Star designation, and/or prestigious trophies, such as the Most Valuable Player, U.S. Basketball Writers Association Award, Rupp Trophy, Naismith Award, National Association of Basketball Coaches Award, Wooden Award, Associated Press Award, Broderick Award, Wade Trophy, Naismith Trophy, or Coach of the Year Award. Some excelled in Olympic competition, winning gold, silver, and/or bronze medals, and/or helped the United States in international team competitions, such as the Pan American and World Games.

Biographies usually indicate the subject's full given name at birth, date and place of birth and, when applicable, date and place of death; parental background; formal education; spouse and children, when applicable; and major personal characteristics. Authors searched diligently and persistently for this often-elusive data. In many instances, however, contributors could not ascertain the parental background and/or other of the information above. Entries feature the subject's basketball career typically include information about his or her entrance into amateur and/or professional basketball; positions played; teams played for with respective conferences or leagues[2]; points scored, rebounds made, assists made, steals made, and/or other statistical achievements; individual records set, awards and/or medals won; All-Star, tournament, playoff, and/or Olympic appearances, and personal impact on basketball. Less biographical and statistical information was available on early-twentieth century figures. Entries on coaches usually describe their teams guided, with inclusive dates; major statistical achievements; career win-loss records, with percentages; premier players coached; and coaching philosophy, strategy, and innovations.

Biographies of club executives, league officials, and referees describe their positions held, notable accomplishments, and impact on basketball.

The biographies of current players, coaches, and executives include the 2004–2005 NCAA and NBA regular seasons, the 2005 NCAA tournament, and, in most cases, the 2005 NBA playoffs and postseason honors. The book went to press during the 2005 NBA playoffs.

Brief bibliographies list pertinent sources for each biographical entry. Authors benefited from oral interviews or correspondence with biographical subjects, relatives, or acquaintances. The Naismith Memorial Basketball Hall of Fame in Springfield, Massachusetts; *The Sporting News* in St. Louis, Missouri; professional basketball teams; college and university media relations and libraries; public libraries; radio and television networks; newspapers; and magazines also provided invaluable assistance. All married female basketball players and/or coaches are listed by their most commonly known name. Appendices list biographical entries alphabetically and by place of birth and the members of the Naismith Memorial Basketball Hall of Fame.

Seventy-six contributors—members of the Organization of American Historians, North American Society for Sport History, the American Popular Culture Association, and/or other professional organizations—provided entries for this revised and expanded volume. Twenty-five people contributed completely new entries. Most authors are university or college professors with basketball expertise. School teachers, administrators, writers, publishers, editors, journalists, librarians, businessmen, lawyers, government employees, clergymen, consultants, and others also participated. Contributors are cited alphabetically with occupational affiliation following the index.

The editor deeply appreciates the enormous amount of time, energy, and effort expended by the contributors in searching for biographical information. I am especially grateful to John L. Evers, who graciously agreed to do many unassigned entries and write additional entries when last-minute cancellations occurred. Ron Briley, Lisa Ennis, Frank J. Olmsted, and Jim L. Sumner wrote at least ten new basketball entries. Biographical subjects, relatives, or acquaintances often furnished data. William Penn University librarians again provided invaluable assistance. Rob Kirkpatrick gave adept guidance and helped in the planning and writing of this volume, while Lewis Parker and Lindsay Claire furnished valuable assistance in the production stage.

My wife, Marilyn, again demonstrated patience, understanding, and support throughout the project.

NOTES

1. The principal basketball reference sources examined for the selection of new entries included Ken Shouler et al., *Total Basketball* (Wilmington, DE, 2003); Jan Hubbard, ed., *The Official NBA Encyclopedia*, 3rd ed. (New York, 2000); Mike Douchant, *Encyclopedia of College Basketball* (Detroit, MI, 1995); *Official 2004 Men's NCAA Basketball Records* (Indianapolis, IN, 2003); *The Sporting News Official NBA Register, 2003–2004* (St. Louis, MO, 2003); *The Sporting News Official NBA Guide, 2003–2004* (St. Louis, MO, 2002); *The Sporting News Official WNBA Guide and Register, 2003* (St. Louis, MO, 2003); Peter C. Bjarkman, *The Biographical History of Basketball* (Chicago, IL, 2000); and Martin Taragano, *Basketball Biographies 1891–1990* (Jefferson, NC, 1991).

Earlier volumes of the Biographical Dictionary of American Sports series list the sources used for the selection of the original entries.

2. The various professional basketball leagues and intercollegiate basketball conferences appear in the Abbreviations section.

List of Entries

Abbreviations

These abbreviations are cited in the main text and/or in the bibliography.

AA	Athletic Association
AAA	American Automobile Association
AABC	American Association of Basketball Coaches
AAHPERD	American Alliance for Health, Physical Education, Recreation, and Dance
AAU	Amateur Athletic Union
ABA	American Basketball Association
ABAOC	Amateur Basketball Association Officials Committee
ABAUSA	Amateur Basketball Association of the United States of America
ABC	American Broadcasting Company
ABL	American Basketball League
AC	Athletic Club
ACC	Atlantic Coast Conference
ACS	American Conference South
AFCA	American Football Coaches Association
AFL	American Football League
AHL	American Hockey League
AIAW	Association of Intercollegiate Athletics for Women
AIC	American International College
AL	American League (baseball)
AMA	Arena Management Association
AMC	American Conference South
ANL	American Negro League (baseball)
AOC	American Olympic Committee
AP	Associated Press
ASA	American Softball Association
ASC	American South Conference
ASL	American Soccer League
ATC	Atlantic Ten Conference
AtL	Athletic League
AuC	Auto Club
AWSF	American Women's Sports Federation
BAA	Basketball Association of America
BBC	British Broadcasting Corporation
BBO	Board of Basketball Officials

BC	Business College
BCI	Basketball Congress International
BEaC	Big East Conference
BEC	Big Eight Conference
BFUSA	Basketball Federation of the United States of America
BN	*Basketball News*
BNC	Big Nine Conference (now BTC)
BoC	Border Conference
BPAL	Baltimore Public Athletic League
BSC	Big Six (Big Seven) Conference
BSkC	Big Sky Conference
BskD	*Basketball Digest*
BT	*Basketball Times*
BTC	Big Ten Conference (also WC, formerly BNC)
BTwC	Big Twelve Conference (formerly BEC)
BuC	Buckeye Conference
BWAA	Basketball Writers Association of America
BWC	Big West Conference
BYU	Brigham Young University
CA	*Contemporary Authors*
CAB	*Cyclopedia of American Biography*
CaBA	California Basketball Association
CaBL	California Basketball League
CaCAA	California Collegiate Athletic Association
CAHL	Canadian-American Hockey League
CB	*Current Biography Yearbook*
CBA	Continental Basketball Association
CBB	*Contemporary Black Biography*
CBL	Continental Basketball League
CBOA	Continental Basketball Officials Association
CBRC	College Basketball Rules Committee
CBS	Columbia Broadcasting System
CC	Community College
CCL	Chicago Catholic League
CCNY	City College of New York
CeC	Central Conference
CIAA	Central Intercollegiate Athletic Association
CiCAA	California Collegiate Athletic Association
CIF	California Interscholastic Federation
CIT	Chicago Invitational Tournament
CL	Colonial League (baseball)
CNBRI	Commission for National Basketball Rules Interpretation
CNN	Cable News Network
ColAA	Colored Intercollegiate Athletic Association
CPL	Chicago Public League
CrC	Carolinas Conference
CtL	Connecticut League
CUSA	Conference USA
CYL	Catholic Youth League
CYO	Catholic Youth Organization

DAB	*Dictionary of American Biography*
EBL	Eastern Basketball League
ECAC	Eastern Collegiate Athletic Conference
ECBA	Eastern College Basketball Association
ECC	East Coast Conference
ECL	Eastern Colored League (baseball)
EIBL	Eastern Intercollegiate Basketball League
EIFA	Eastern Intercollegiate Football Association
EIL	Eastern Intercollegiate League
EL	Eastern League
EMBAO	Eastern Massachusetts Board of Approved Officials
EPBL	Eastern Pro Basketball League
ESPN	Entertainment and Sports Programming Network
FCA	Fellowship of Christian Athletes
FBC	Fox Broadcasting Corporation
FIBA	International Basketball Federation
FrL	Frontier League
FWC	Far West Conference
GCC	Gulf Coast Conference
GMC	Great Midwest Conference
HAF	Helms Athletic Foundation (Citizens Savings Bank)
HoF	Hall of Fame
HPER	Health, Physical Education, and Recreation
HRL	Hudson River League
IAABO	International Association of Approved Basketball Officials
IABF	International Amateur Basketball Federation
IBA	International Basketball Association
IBB	International Basketball Board
IBC	International Basketball Committee
IBCA	Illinois Basketball Coaches Association
IBFRC	International Basketball Federation Rules Committee
IBFUS	International Basketball Federation of the United States
ICC	Indiana Collegiate Conference
IHF	International Hockey Federation
IHSAA	Illinois High School Athletic Association
IL	International League (baseball)
InL	Intercollegiate League
INS	International News Service
IS	*Inside Sports*
ISL	Interstate League
ItL	Italian League
IVA	International Volleyball Association
IvL	Ivy League
JAC	*Journal of American Culture*
JC	Junior College
JSH	*Journal of Sport History*
KC	Kansas Conference
KCCA	Kansas Conference Coaches Association
KIAC	Kentucky Intercollegiate Athletic Conference
KL	Kitty League (baseball)

KSHSACSA	Kansas State High School Athletic Coaching School Association
LABC	Los Angeles Bicentennial Committee
LABF	Louisville Amateur Baseball Federation
LD	*Literary Digest*
LIU	Long Island University
LSC	Lone Star Conference
LSU	Louisiana State University
LTC	Little Three Conference
MAA	Midwestern Athletic Association
MAAC	Metro Atlantic Athletic Conference
MAC	Mid-American Conference
MBL	Metropolitan Basketball League
MBWANY	Metropolitan Basketball Writers Association of New York
MC	Metro Conference
MCC	Minnesota College Conference
MDC	Mason-Dixon Conference
MeL	Metropolitan League
MIAA	Missouri Intercollegiate Athletic Association
ML	Massachusetts League
MoVL	Mohawk Valley League
MVC	Missouri Valley Conference
MVP	Most Valuable Player
NAAD	National Association of Athletic Directors
NABA	National Amateur Basketball Association
NABC	National Association of Basketball Coaches
NABL	North American Basketball League
NACBC	National Association of College Basketball Coaches
NACDA	National Association of Collegiate Directors of Athletics
NAGWS	National Association of Girls and Women in Sport
NAIA	National Association of Intercollegiate Athletics
NAIB	National Association of Intercollegiate Basketball (became NAIA in 1952)
NASSH	North American Society for Sport History
NBA	National Basketball Association
NBACA	National Basketball Association Coaches Association
NBAPA	National Basketball Association Players Association
NBC	National Broadcasting Company
NBCA	National Basketball Coaches Association
NBCUS	National Basketball Coaches of the United States
NBDL	National Basketball Development League
NBF	National Basketball Federation
NBL	National Basketball League
NBOC	National Basketball Officials Committee
NBRC	National Basketball Rules Committee of the United States and Canada
NCAA	National Collegiate Athletic Association
NCaAA	Northern California Athletic Association
NCAB	*National Cyclopedia of American Biography*
NCBAA	National Collegiate Basketball Association of America
NCC	North Central Conference
NCCA	National Collegiate Commissioners Association
NEA	Newspaper Enterprise Association

NEBA	New England Basketball Association
NEBCA	New England Basketball Coaches Association
NEC	North East Conference
NECA	New England Conference on Athletics
NEIBT	New England Interscholastic Basketball Tournament
NEL	New England League
NFF	National Football Federation
NFL	National Football League
NFSHSAA	National Federation of State High School Athletic Associations
NHL	National Hockey League
NHSACA	National High School Athletic Coaches Association
NIAAA	National Intercollegiate Athletic Association of America
NIBL	National Industrial Basketball League
NIT	National Invitation Tournament
NJAA	New Jersey Athletic Association
NL	National League (baseball)
NNL	Negro National League (baseball)
NPBL	National Professional Basketball League
NRA	National Recreation Association
NSIC	North State Intercollegiate Conference
NWBA	National Women's Basketball Association
NWBCA	National Women's Basketball Coaches Association
NWIT	National Women's Invitation Tournament
NYAC	New York Athletic Club
NYBWA	New York Basketball Writers Association
NYHF	New York Holiday Festival
NYPL	New York Pennsylvania League
NYSL	New York State League
NYT	*New York Times*
NYU	New York University
NYWA	New York Writers Association
OBCA	Ohio Basketball Coaches Association
OC	Ohio Conference
OHSAA	Ohio High School Athletic Association
OHSGBCA	Oklahoma High School Girls Basketball Coaches Association
OSAA	Ohio State Athletic Association
OSWSA	Oregon Sportswriters and Sportscasters Association
OVC	Ohio Valley Conference
PAFB	Pan American Federation of Basketball
PAIAW	Pennsylvania Association for Intercollegiate Athletics for Women
PASE	Partners of the Americas Sports Exchange
PBL	Philadelphia Basketball League
PBWAA	Professional Basketball Writers Association of America
PCAA	Pacific Coast Athletic Association
PCAC	Pacific Coast Athletic Conference
PCC	Pacific Coast Conference
PCL	Pacific Coast League (baseball)
PEC	Pacific Eight Conference (formerly PCC)
PHSL	Public High School League
PPL	Philadelphia Public League

PRAA	Playground and Recreation Association of America
PSAL	Public School Athletic League
PSL	Pennsylvania State League
PSWA	Pennsylvania Sports Writers Association
PTC	Pac-Ten Conference (formerly PEC)
PW	*People Weekly*
RD	*Reader's Digest*
RDC	Rules Demonstration Committee
RMC	Rocky Mountain Conference
RRC	Rules Research Committee
SBC	Sun Belt Conference
SC	Southern Conference (now SEC)
SCD	*Sports Collectors Digest*
SEC	Southeastern Conference (formerly SC)
SEP	*Saturday Evening Post*
SH	*Sport Heritage*
SHSSF	Save High School Sport Foundation
SI	*Sports Illustrated*
SIBL	Senior Intercollegiate Basketball League
SIW	*Sports Illustrated for Women*
SKC	Skyline Conference
SL	*Sport Life*
SMU	Southern Methodist University
SN	*Saturday Night*
SoC	Southland Conference
SpC	Sports Club
SPHAS	South Philadelphia Hebrew Association
SpL	*Sporting Life*
SR:B	*Sports Review: Basketball*
SWC	Southwest Athletic Conference
TAAC	Trans American Athletic Conference
TCL	Tri-County League
TCU	Texas Christian University
3IL	Three Eye League
TSN	*The Sporting News*
TWBL	Turkish Women's Basketball League
UCLA	University of California at Los Angeles
UIJCC	Utah-Idaho Junior College Conference
UP	United Press
UPI	United Press International
USAB	United States of America Basketball
USAT	*USA Today*
USBA	United States Basketball Association
USBL	United States Basketball League
USBWA	United States Basketball Writers Association
USOBC	United States Olympic Basketball Committee
USOBOC	United States Olympic Basketball Officials Committee
USOC	United States Olympic Committee
USOIHC	United States Olympic Ice Hockey Commission
USPABOC	United States Pan American Basketball Officials Committee

USTFF	United States Track and Field Federation
UTEP	University of Texas at El Paso
WABA	Women's American Basketball Association
WAC	Western Athletic Conference (formerly CiCAA)
WBCA	Women's Basketball Coaches Association
WBJ	*Women's Basketball Journal*
WBNS	Women's Basketball News Service
WBT	World Basketball Tournament
WC	Western Conference (also BNC, BTC)
WCAA	Western Collegiate Athletic Association
WCAC	West Coast Athletic Committee
WCC	West Coast Conference
WCN	World Cup of Nations
WD	*Writers Digest*
WeIL	Western International League
WIAA	Wisconsin Interscholastic Athletic Association
WNBA	Women's National Basketball Association
WNIT	Women's National Invitation Tournament
WNRC	Women's National Rules Committee
WoCAA	Women's Collegiate Athletic Association
WoH	World of Hibernia
WPBL	Women's Professional Basketball League
WS	*Women's Sports*
WSC	Wisconsin State Conference
WSF	Women's Sports Foundation
WTTL	World Team Tennis League
WWA	*Who's Who in America*
WWE	*Who's Who in the East*
WWM	*Who's Who in the Midwest*
YMCA	Young Men's Christian Association

A

ABBOTT, Senda Berenson (b. March 19, 1868, Biturmansk, Lithuania; d. February 16, 1954, Santa Barbara, CA), college innovator and physical educator, was the daughter of Jewish immigrants, Albert Valvrojenski, a peddler of pots and pans, and Julia Mieliszanski. On arriving in Boston, Massachusetts in 1875, the family's surname was changed. Despite growing up in poverty, the five Berenson children were encouraged to pursue higher education. Senda's brother, Bernard, became the era's leading authority on Italian Renaissance painting. Berenson attended the Boston Girls' Latin School, but lacked physical strength to complete a full year. She enjoyed art and studied piano at the Boston Conservatory of Music, although a weak back prevented her from practicing regularly.

In 1890 Berenson began studying physical education at the newly founded Boston Normal School of Gymnastics. Under the influence of Amy Morris Homans and philanthropist Mary Hemenway (who had introduced Swedish gymnastics into the Boston public schools in the 1880s), she began developing physical stamina and vigor. Her original negative attitude toward physical activity became positive, with a conviction that it could be used to help others. Berenson left the Boston Normal School of Gymnastics in January 1892 to teach physical training at Smith College, where she, for 21 years, led women's physical education and sport. As a physical educator, she helped to organize Smith College's Gymnastics and Field Association in 1893 and introduced fencing to the college in 1895. In 1897 she became the second American woman to attend the Royal Central Institute of Gymnastic in Stockholm, Sweden. On her return to Smith College, Berenson introduced folk dance as part of the college's physical education program. In 1901 she invited Lady Constance Applebee of England to introduce field hockey to Smith College.

Berenson's most important contribution to athletics is the introduction of women to basketball. After reading about James Naismith's* newly invented game in the YMCA publication *Physical Education*, she presented basketball to the students of Smith College in the fall of 1892. In order to adapt the sport to the supposed needs of women, she modified the rules. Her ideals of athletic vigor for women were in sharp contrast to Victorian restraints of the time, but she nevertheless did not want to see women play with roughness and abandon like men. Her rules disallowed snatching the ball away from opponents, holding the ball for more than three seconds, or dribbling it more than three times. To prevent overexertion and to eliminate domination by star players, she divided the court into three divisions (line basketball), and prohibited players from crossing the lines. Berenson incorporated these regulations into the 1899 official rules, which she edited for eighteen years. These rules for women remained in use until the 1960s with only slight modifications.

Berenson stressed socialization and cooperation rather than competition and winning in sport, the standard attitudes for women's athletics in colleges until the 1960s. She opposed women's intercollegiate competition, developing instead intramural athletics that would involve many more students. From 1905 to 1917, she chaired the permanent Basketball Committee for Women, the forerunner of the NAGWS of the AAHPERD. After marrying Smith College English professor Herbert Vaughn Abbott, on June 15, 1911, she resigned from her position. She served as director of physical education at the Mary A. Burnham School in Northampton, Massachusetts, for the next ten years, traveled widely, and studied art in Europe. After her husband died in 1929, Abbott moved to Santa Barbara and resided with her sister until her death. In 1985 she was named to the Naismith Memorial Basketball Hall of Fame. She was inducted into the International Jewish Sports Hall of Fame in 1987 and the Women's Basketball Hall of Fame in 1991. *SI* listed her among the greatest sports figures of the twentieth century.

BIBLIOGRAPHY: Senda Berenson, *Basket-Ball for Women* (New York, 1901); Senda Berenson, "Basket Ball for Women," *Physical Education* 3 (September 1894), pp. 106–109; Senda Berenson, *Line Basket Ball or Basket Ball for Women* (New York, 1899); Senda Berenson Papers, Smith College Archives, Northampton, MA; Edith N. Hill, "Senda Berenson," *Research Quarterly* 12 (October 1941, Supp.), pp. 658–665; Joan Hult and Marianna Trekell, eds., *A Century of Women's Basketball: From Frailty to Final Four* (Reston, VA, 1991); Nicky Mariano, ed., *The Berenson Archive: An Inventory of Correspondence* (Cambridge, MA, 1965); L. Clark Seelye, *The Early History of Smith College, 1871–1910* (Boston, MA, 1923); Sylvia Sprigge, *[Bernard] Berenson, A Biography* (Boston, MA, 1960); Agnes C. Stillman, "Senda Berenson Abbott: Her Life and Contributions to Smith College and to the Physical Education Profession," M.S. thesis, Smith College, 1971.

Ronald A. Smith

ABDUL-JABBAR, Kareem (b. Lewis Ferdinand Alcindor, April 16, 1947, New York), college and professional player and coach, has been named in more than one media poll as the greatest pro basketball player in history. In 1989, at age 41, Abdul-Jabbar was still playing in the NBA and performed near the top of his superb game as the dominant big man in NBA history. More remarkable, he helped lead the Los Angeles Lakers to NBA titles over the Boston Celtics in 1985 and 1987 and Detroit Pistons in 1988 and was named *SI* Sportsman of the Year for 1985. Abdul-Jabbar played in the second most games (1,560) and for more minutes (57,446), scored more points (38,387), attempted more field goals (28,307), made more field goals (15,837), blocked the second most shots, (3,189), and won more MVP titles (six, 1971–1972, 1974, 1976–1977, 1980) than any player in pro basketball history. During 11 NBA seasons Abdul-Jabbar averaged 24.6 points per game. The enigmatic seven-foot two-inch, 235-pound giant, who had often seemed moody and unapproachable throughout his career, seemed to soften, relax, and approach the twilight of his career with a flair and joy that finally inspired the adulations of fans and journalists that his on-court performances had so long and so richly deserved. Abdul-Jabbar made the NBA 35th Anniversary All-Time Team (1980), the All-NBA First Team in 1971–1974, 1976–1977, 1980–1981, 1984, and 1986, and the All-NBA Second Team in 1970, 1978, 1979, 1983, and 1985. He was named one of the 50 Greatest Players in NBA History in 1996.

Alcindor was born an abnormally large baby (1 foot 10 inches) to Al and Cora Alcindor. He was the only child of a six-foot two-inch stern, uncommunicative subway policeman and a six-foot overprotective mother-housewife. By age 13, Alcindor stood six feet eight inches and weighed over 200 pounds. Recruited to play basketball at Power Memorial Academy in New York City, he dominated games from the outset. Alcindor led his school to 71 straight victories before a loss to DeMatha High School of Hyattsville, Maryland, and set New York City schoolboy records by accumulating 2,067 points and 2,002 rebounds. On graduation in 1965, over 200 college recruiters anxiously awaited his college choice that might turn their school into an instant national basketball powerhouse. Alcindor chose UCLA and Coach John Wooden*. UCLA subsequently won three consecutive NCAA championships between 1967 and 1969—his three years of varsity eligibility.

During his college career, Alcindor scored 2,325 points and averaged 26.4 points per game. Such statistics, however, do not reveal the extent to which this one player dominated the college game. He became one of a select few players in NCAA history to be named First Team All-America for all three varsity years. To ward off the bidding wars of pro scouts, Alcindor demanded that the two teams holding draft rights to him—the Milwaukee Bucks (NBA) and the New York Nets (ABA)—make one final best offer for his services. Milwaukee made that offer and paid over $1 million for him in his rookie season of 1969–1970. The wise investment saw Alcindor dominate the pro game as he had the collegiate game. He converted to the Islamic faith and legally had his name changed to Kareem Abdul-Jabbar. But his basketball abilities were never altered. Abdul-Jabbar's rookie season produced 2,361 points and 1,190 rebounds plus overnight respectability for the Bucks, as he won both league MVP and top rookie honors. By the end of his third pro season, Abdul-Jabbar had scored over 10,000 points, held two scoring titles and two MVP awards, and totaled 4,000 rebounds. He led Milwaukee in his sophomore campaign to the NBA title in only the third year of that franchise's existence. After being traded to the Los Angeles Lakers (NBA) in a historic 1975 six-player swap, Abdul-Jabbar was the spiritual leader and offensive force behind those great Laker teams of the 1980s. He eventually passed Wilt Chamberlain* as the NBA's all-time leader in many offensive categories. Abdul-Jabbar appeared in 17 NBA All-Star Games and holds the career scoring mark (251 points). Jabbar's 10-year streak of scoring in double figures in each game was ended by the Milwaukee Bucks in December 1987.

Abdul-Jabbar's personal life was often filled with tragedy amid his oncourt successes. His home and priceless collection of jazz recordings were destroyed in a 1983 fire. He has been separated from and reunited with his wife, Habiba, and their four children several times. The family members of his Muslim spiritual leader were murdered in a Washington, D.C. townhouse owned by Abdul-Jabbar. Yet through his disciplined religious life and inner strength drawn from the practice of yoga, he found personal peace and maintained his remarkable athletic career far past the age when rigorous NBA play becomes a physical impossibility. His moving 1983 autobiography, entitled *Giant Steps*, was a national best-seller, and provided a fascinating glimpse into the tumultuous world of the world's greatest basketball talent. He was elected to the Naismith Memorial Basketball Hall of Fame in 1995. Abdul-Jabbar served as assistant coach with the Los Angeles Clippers (NBA) in 2000 and coached the Oklahoma Storm (USBL) in 2002 to a 17-13 regular season record and USBL title. He scouts for the New York Knicks (NBA).

BIBLIOGRAPHY: Kareem Abdul-Jabbar and Peter Knobler, *Giant Steps: The Autobiography of Kareem Abdul-Jabbar* (New York, 1983); Kareem Abdul-Jabbar with Mignon McCarthy, *Kareem* (New York, 1990); Kareem Abdul-Jabbar file, Naismith Memorial Hall of Fame, Springfield, MA; Mike Douchant, *Encyclopedia of College Basketball* (Detroit, MI, 1995); Scott Howard-Cooper, *The Bruins 100* (Lenexa, KS, 1999); Jan Hubbard, ed., *The Official NBA Encyclopedia*, 3rd ed. (New York, 2000); Roland Lazenby, *The Lakers: A Basketball Journey* (Indianapolis, IN, 1996); *The Lincoln Library of Sports Champions*, vol. 1 (Columbus, OH, 1974); Scott Ostler and Steve Springer, *Winnin' Times: The Rise and Rise of the Los Angeles Lakers* (New York, 1986); Pat Riley, *Showtime* (New York, 1988); Gary Smith, "Now, More Than Ever, a Winner," *SI* 63 (December 23–30, 1985), pp. 78–94.

Peter C. Bjarkman

ABDUL-RAHMAD, Mahdi (b. Walter Raphael Hazzard Jr., April 15, 1942, Philadelphia, PA), college and professional player and executive, is the son of Walter Hazzard Sr. The fast, creative, six-foot two-inch, 190-pound point guard and penetrator spearheaded the 1963–1964 UCLA Bruins (PEC) college basketball team, beginning coach John Wooden's* dynasty of capturing 10 NCAA Championships in the 1964–1975 period. Willie Naulls*, a UCLA alumnus and former player, recruited Abdul-Rahmad from Overbrook High School in Philadelphia.

Abdul-Rahmad spent the 1961–1962 academic year at Santa Monica College and joined UCLA's starting lineup in 1962 to run the offense. He demonstrated so much quickness and deception that many of his passes bounced off the heads, chests, and shoulders of teammates. Naulls convinced the discouraged Abdul-Rahmad to remain at UCLA, while Wooden exhorted him to settle down and play team ball.

UCLA won the PEC title and the NCAA regionals, with Hazzard making MVP. The University of Cincinnati ousted UCLA 72-70 in the NCAA semifinals. The additions of Gail Goodrich*, Keith Erickson, and Kenny Washington, along with Wooden's adoption of a devastating full-court zone press, helped the 1963–1964 Bruins finish undefeated and defeat Duke University 98-83 for the NCAA title. Abdul-Rahmad, the Outstanding Player of the Final Four competition that year, made all America twice, participated on the 1964 U.S. Olympic team, and was named to the HAF College Hall of Fame. He was also selected to the All-1960s NCAA Tournament Team.

The Los Angeles Lakers (NBA) selected Abdul-Rahmad in the first round of the 1964 NBA draft. Abdul-Rahmad played three seasons there and performed subsequently for the Seattle SuperSonics (1967–1968), Atlanta Hawks (1968–1971), Buffalo Braves (1971–1973) and Golden State Warriors (1973). He finished his NBA career with Seattle in 1973–1974. His career included 9,087 points, a 12.6 point scoring average, and 3,555 assists. His best season came in 1967–1968, when he averaged 23.9 points for Seattle and was selected for the West All-Star Team. Although not matching his earlier collegiate exploits, Abdul-Rahmad played a useful role for his professional teams. He ranks among the select group of playmakers who have combined dramatic flair with effectiveness.

Abdul-Rahmad served as head coach of the UCLA basketball team from the 1984–1985 through 1987–1988 seasons, compiling a 77-48 overall record and 47-25 PTC win-loss record. His 1986–1987 UCLA squad won the PTC title with a 14-4 mark and finished 25-7 overall, but lost to the University of Wyoming in the NCAA West regional. Jim Harrick replaced him after UCLA struggled to a 16-14 mark in 1987–1988. Abdul-Rahmad had followed Wooden's coaching philosophy of learning fundamentals, working hard, and remaining in good physical condition. He works as a special consultant for the Los Angeles Lakers.

BIBLIOGRAPHY: Dwight Chapin and Jeff Prugh, *The Wizard of Westwood: Coach John Wooden and His UCLA Bruins* (Boston, MA, 1973); Mike Douchant, *Encyclopedia of College Basketball* (Detroit, MI, 1995); Scott Howard-Cooper, *The Bruins 100* (Lenexa, KS, 1999); Jan Hubbard, ed., *The Official NBA Encyclopedia*, 3rd ed. (New York, 2000); Neil Isaacs, *All the Moves: A History of College Basketball* (Philadelphia, PA, 1975); Ronald L. Mendell, *Who's Who in Basketball* (New Rochelle, NY, 1973); *Street & Smith's College Basketball Yearbooks, 1985–1988*; *UCLA Basketball Media Guides, 1984–1987* (Los Angeles, CA, 1984–1987); John Wooden, *They Call Me Coach* (Waco, TX, 1972).

Gustavo N. Agrait

ADELMAN, Richard Leonard "Rick" "Grizzly" (b. June 16, 1946, Lynwood, CA), college and professional player and coach, is the son of L. J. Adelman and Gladys Adelman. His parents taught and farmed early in life. His father later became building manager for the U.S. Borax Corporation.

A six-foot two-inch, 180-pound guard, Adelman excelled in basketball at St. Pius X High School in Downey, California and graduated in 1964. He attended Loyola Marymount University in Los Angeles between 1964–1965 and 1967–1968 and played basketball for the Lions. In three varsity seasons, Adelman scored 1,425 points and averaged 18.8 points.

The San Diego Rockets (NBA) selected Adelman in the seventh round (79th pick overall) of the 1968 NBA draft. Adelman spent two years in a reserve role with the Rockets before being chosen by the Portland Trail Blazers (NBA) in the 1970 NBA Expansion draft and was named team captain, the first in the club's history. In three seasons with Portland, he scored 2,422 points and averaged 10.2 points. His best season came in 1970–1971 when he averaged 12.2 points.

On September 14, 1973, Portland traded Adelman to the Chicago Bulls (NBA) for cash and a second round draft choice. The following season, he split playing time with the Bulls, the New Orleans Jazz (NBA) and the Kansas City-Omaha Kings (NBA) and retired in 1975. In seven NBA seasons, Adelman scored 3,668 points in 462 games and averaged 7.9 points. In postseason playoffs, he scored 121 points in 21 games and averaged 5.8 points.

Adelman began his basketball coaching career with Chemeketa CC in Salem, Oregon. Between 1977–1978 and 1982–1983, he led the Storm to a 141-39 win-loss record and won or shared three championships and one regional crown. Adelman moved to the professional coaching ranks in 1983 when he was named assistant coach for the Portland Trail Blazers. He remained in that position until February 18, 1989 when he replaced Mike Schuler as head coach.

Between 1988–1989 and 1993–1994, Adelman led the Trail Blazers to a 291-154 win-loss record and six consecutive NBA playoff appearances. Portland advanced to the NBA Finals twice, losing in 1990 to Isiah Thomas* and the Detroit Pistons, and in 1992 to Michael Jordan* and the Chicago Bulls.

Adelman left Portland following the 1993–1994 season to join the Golden State Warriors (NBA) and, after two losing seasons, was replaced by P. J. Carlesimo. He was named head coach for the Sacramento Kings (NBA) in September 1998. The Kings have enjoyed seven consecutive winning seasons and seven playoff appearances under the guidance of Adelman, but suffered Game 7 playoff losses three consecutive years. In 15 NBA seasons through 2004–2005, he has compiled a 708-443 regular-season win-loss record and a 68-64 playoff mark.

Adelman and his wife, Mary Kay, were married in 1973 and have four children: Kathy, R. J., Laura, and David. In 1992, Mary Kay's sister was killed in an automobile accident. The Adelmans have reared her sister's two children, Caitlin and Patrick, since 1992.

BIBLIOGRAPHY: "Rick Adelman," *Coaches*, http://www.hoopshype.com (2003); "Rick Adelman," *Coaches Bio*, http://www.nba.com (2003); Rick Adelman, *The Long Hot Summer* (New York, 1992); Ken Shouler et al., *Total Basketball* (Wilmington, DE, 2003); *TSN Official NBA Register, 2004–2005* (St. Louis, MO, 2004).

John L. Evers

AGUIRRE, Mark Anthony (b. December 10, 1959, Chicago, IL), college and professional athlete, coach, and executive, is the son of Clyde Aguirre and Mary Aguirre. Mark graduated from Westinghouse Vocational High School, where he developed his basketball prowess from 1976 to 1978. As a six-foot six-inch, 235-pound senior, Aguirre led Westinghouse to the 1978 Championship. His individual honors included being named to the All-City, All-State, and several major scholastic All-America teams, as well as the West Team for two different national high school All-Star games. Many national collegiate basketball powers sought Aguirre, who enrolled at hometown DePaul University in September 1978 to play for head basketball coach Ray Meyer*.

Aguirre's exciting play helped to catapult DePaul into national prominence, as the Blue Demons compiled a composite 79-10 win-loss record from 1978–1979 through 1980–1981. Aguirre enjoyed immediate success his freshman year, leading DePaul in scoring 21 of 32 games. He paced the nation's freshman players with a 24.0 points average, led DePaul in field goals and free throws, and established a single-season school record for total points with 767. Aguirre's 117 points led the Blue Demons to the prestigious 1979 NCAA Final Four, where he made the All-Tournament team at forward. The freshman was named an honorable mention UPI All-America.

As a sophomore, Aguirre in 1979–1980 led DePaul with 749 points and averaged 26.8 points. Aguirre's play enabled DePaul to make the 1980 NCAA Tournament, but the Blue Demons were eliminated early. DePaul won 17 consecutive contests and ranked first in the mid-season polls, with both achievements made possible by his all-around play. Aguirre earned consensus All-America honors at forward, was chosen *TSN* 1980 College Player of the Year, and made the 1980 U.S. Olympic Basketball Team, but the nation boycotted the 1980 Summer Olympic Games in the Soviet Union's capital of Moscow.

The 1980–1981 season, Aguirre's junior year, marked his last season as a Blue Demon. Aguirre led DePaul to the 1981 NCAA Tournament for the third consecutive year and paced the Blue Demons in field goals, free throws, points per game average (23.0), and total points (666). His three season total of 2,182 points established a DePaul career record, making him the first Blue Demon player to surpass 2,000 points. Aguirre, who repeated as a consensus

1981 All-America at forward, attributed his collegiate success to "forceful" Ray Meyer, saying, "He made me!"

Aguirre declared eligibility for the 1981 NBA draft. The Dallas Mavericks (NBA), a second-year expansion team, selected Aguirre first overall. Aguirre anticipated that Dallas head coach Dick Motta* would develop a winning program. In his ninth NBA game, Aguirre scored 42 points for a Dallas rookie record, but later a broken bone in his right foot sidelined him for 31 contests. In March 1982 Aguirre's shot at the buzzer against the Los Angeles Lakers enabled Dallas to capture the biggest win in franchise history. Aguirre averaged 18.7 points in 1981–1982, second on the team.

Aguirre enjoyed an outstanding career with Dallas from 1981–1982 until February 1989, when he was traded to the Detroit Pistons (NBA) for Adrian Dantley*. His Mavs records include most career points (13,930), single-season free throws (465), single-season points (2,330), single-game points (49), career field goals (5,441), career rebounds (3,244), seasons with Dallas (7), and career games with 40 or more points (22). Aguirre averaged 24.1 points for 602 Dallas regular-season games and almost 22 points per contest for 45 NBA playoff games. He was the first Maverick chosen to play in the NBA All-Star Game, playing forward for the West Team in the 1984, 1987, and 1988 All-Star Games. On the Saturday of the 1988 All-Star Game weekend, he married Angela Bowman in Chicago.

Although playing on five winning teams with Dallas, Aguirre did not perform on a major championship team until being traded to the Detroit Pistons (NBA). His role changed dramatically from the multiple record holder as starting forward at Dallas to a reserve for coach Chuck Daly's* Detroit squad. There he averaged 15.5 points for the remaining 1988–1989 games, 14.1 points in 1989–1990, and 14.2 points in 1990–1991. Aguirre played a major role in securing Detroit's NBA World Championship titles in 1989 and 1990, giving him a great sense of personal fulfillment. His 34 points in Game 4 helped the Pistons oust the Boston Celtics from the 1991 Eastern Conference semifinals. He remained with Detroit until October 1993 and retired after spending the 1993–1994 season with the Los Angeles Clippers (NBA). In 923 career NBA games spanning 13 seasons, Aguirre scored 18,458 points, averaged 20 points, and made 4,578 rebounds. He served as director of player development and scouting for the Dallas Mavericks in 1996–1997, as assistant coach for the Indiana Pacers (NBA) in 2002–2003, and assistant coach of the New York Knicks (NBA) since 2003. Aguirre and his wife, Angela, reside in Indianapolis, Indiana.

BIBLIOGRAPHY: "Aguirre's Decision: DePaul," *NYT*, April 25, 1980, p. 23; Dave Anderson, "Discovering You're No. 1," *NYT Biographical Service*, June 9, 1981, p. 771; *Dallas Mavericks Media Guide, 1996–1997* (Dallas, TX, 1996); *DePaul University Basketball Media Guide, 1978–1979, 1979–1980, and 1980–1981* (Chicago, IL, 1978–1980); *Detroit Pistons Media Guide*, 1990–1991 (Detroit, MI, 1990); *Indiana Pacers Media Guide, 2003–2004* (Indianapolis, IN, 2003); *TSN Official 2004–2005 NBA Register* (St. Louis, MO, 2004); Ronald Lazenby, *The NBA Finals* (Indianapolis, IN, 1996); *USA Today*, April 23, 1991; Gordon White Jr., "DePaul: No. 1 Ranking," *NYT*, January 27, 1980, p. 11; *Who's Who Among Black Americans* (Lake Forest, IL, 1988), p. 6.

Robert C. Saunders

AINGE, Daniel Ray "Danny" (b. March 17, 1959, Eugene, OR), college and professional athlete coach, and executive, was a six-foot five-inch, 185-pound guard who excelled in basketball for Brigham Young University (WAC) and enjoyed a solid, productive NBA career. The superb all-around athlete starred in football, basketball, and baseball at North High School in Eugene, Oregon, and in basketball and baseball at Brigham Young. Ainge's basketball honors as a senior in 1981 included making consensus All-America and winning both the Eastman and John Wooden awards. Ainge signed a long-term baseball contract with the Toronto Blue Jays (AL), compiling an undistinguished .220 batting average in 211 games, mainly as an infielder, from 1979 to 1981. The Boston Celtics (NBA) selected him in the second round of the 1981 draft as the thirty-first overall selection. Ainge sought release from his baseball contract, but the Toronto Blue Jays balked and prevailed in a court dispute. The Celtics compensated Toronto, enabling him to join Boston in December 1981.

It took some time for Ainge to blend into the Celtics' system and style because he needed to adjust to the more physical, up-tempo professional game, and he faced keen competition for playing time from other backcourt players. Eventually Ainge became an invaluable member of Boston's starting five, which battled the Los Angeles Lakers for NBA supremacy during the mid-1980s. He blossomed into a first-line player, combining poise, quickness, teamwork, discipline, and all-court scrambling ability. Opposition spectators frequently heckled Ainge, who was one of the NBA's specialists from the three-point area, for his baby-faced, boyish pout. In February 1989 the Celtics traded Ainge and Brad Lohaus to the Sacramento Kings (NBA) for Joe Kleine and Ed Pinckney in order to strengthen their inside game after losing Larry Bird* for that season. In August 1990 the Portland Trail Blazers (NBA) acquired Ainge to bolster their perimeter offense and guard rotation and consolidated their position as one of the NBA's premier teams. Portland compiled the NBA's best mark with a 63-19 record in 1990–1991 as Ainge played a valuable reserve role and placed sixth in three-point field goal percentage. The Trail Blazers lost to the Los Angeles Lakers in the Western Conference Finals in 1990–1991 and to the Chicago Bulls in the NBA Finals in 1991–1992. Ainge finished his NBA playing career with the Phoenix Suns (NBA) from July 1992 through the 1994–1995 season. He helped the Suns reach the NBA Finals against the Chicago Bulls in 1993. He held the NBA career playoff records for most three-point field goals made (172) and attempted (433) and played in the 1988 All-Star Game. Ainge's record through 15 NBA seasons included 11,964 career points in 1,042 games, an average of 11.5 points, an 84.6 percent free-throw average, and 4,119 assists. The intangibles in Ainge, who is a serious, deeply religious person, were as important as any of his statistics.

Ainge coached the Phoenix Suns from 1996–1997 through December 2000, boasting a 136-90 regular season record and 3-9 playoff mark. His best season came in 1997–1998, when Phoenix finished 56-26 for third place in the Pacific Division. In 2003, he returned to the Boston Celtics as Executive Director of Basketball Operations. The Celtics made the NBA playoffs in 2004 and 2005.

BIBLIOGRAPHY: *The Baseball Encyclopedia*, 9th ed. (New York, 1993); Peter C. Bjarkman, *The Boston Celtics Encyclopedia* (Champaign, IL, 1998); *Boston Celtics Media Guide, 1986–1987* (Boston, MA, 1986); Bob Schron and Kevin Stevens, *The Bird Era: A History of the Boston Celtics, 1978–1988* (Boston, MA, 1988); Dan Shaughnessy, *Evergreen* (New York, 1990); Ken Shouler et al., *Total Basketball* (Wilmington, DE, 2003); *TSN Official 2000–2001 NBA Register* (St. Louis, MO, 2000); *USA Today*, April 23, 1991.

Gustavo N. Agrait

ALCINDOR, Lewis F. *See* Abdul-Jabbar, Kareem

ALFORD, Stephen Todd "Steve" (b. November 23, 1964, Franklin, IN), college and professional player and coach, is the son of Samuel Alford, a former physical education teacher and assistant basketball coach, and Sharan (Masten) Alford and grew up in Monroe City, Martinsville, and New Castle, Indiana. His father, a Franklin College basketball star, served as his high school basketball coach. The six-foot two-inch, 185-pound Alford graduated in 1983 from Chrysler High School in New Castle after having tallied 37.2 points per game as a senior. New Castle reached the 1983 State tournament quarterfinals, as he was named Converse and FCA High School Player of the Year, made the All-State basketball team, and earned the State's "Mr. Basketball" accolades.

The conscientious Alford graduated from Indiana University with a Bachelor's degree in 1987 and paced the Hoosier basketball squad in scoring during his final three seasons. Under coach Bobby Knight*, he employed his outstanding jump-shooting skills to become Indiana's leading career scorer and the BTC's second highest career scorer with 2,438 points. Alford tallied 19.5 points per game for the Hoosiers, making 53.3 percent of his field goal attempts and converting 89.8 percent of his free throws. As Indiana's first freshman MVP, Alford averaged 15.5 points for the 22-9 Hoosier squad, set Indiana's field-goal percentage record (59.2), and led all NCAA Division I free-throw shooters (91.3 percent). The University of Virginia eliminated Indiana 50-48 in the East regional finals. The only college freshman selected by coach Knight for the 1984 U.S. Olympic basketball team, he converted over 64 percent of his field goals for the gold-medal U.S. squad at the Los Angeles Summer Olympic Games.

As a sophomore, Alford scored 18.1 points per game and ranked second nationally with a career-high 92.1 free-throw percentage for the struggling 19-14 NIT runner-up Hoosiers. In 1985–1986 the 21-8 Hoosiers placed second in the BTC and qualified for the NCAA tournament, as the AP and NABC All-America averaged 22.5 points. Implementation of the new three-point rule in 1986–1987 benefited Alford, who converted an impressive 53 percent and tallied 22 points per game as a consensus All-America. Indiana finished 30-4 overall, sharing the BTC title with Purdue University. At the Louisiana Superdome, he netted seven three-pointers to help Indiana edge Syracuse University 74-73 for the NCAA Championship.

The Dallas Mavericks (NBA) drafted Alford in the second round in 1987. Alford averaged 4.4 points in 169 games with the Mavericks (1987–1988, 1989–1991) and Golden State Warriors (NBA, 1988–1989). Knight lauded Alford, saying: "He's gotten more out of his abilities offensively than anybody I've seen play college basketball. He's about as good a scorer for being strictly a jump shooter as I've ever seen." Alford married Tanya Frost, a therapist, and has three children: Kory, Bryce, and Kayla.

Alford coached at Manchester College from 1991 through 1995, compiling a 78-29 record. He turned the program around, producing the school's first winning season in 1992–1993 since 1975–1976. Manchester finished 31-1 in 1994–1995, losing in the NCAA Division II Championship game.

Alford coached at Southwest Missouri State University (MVC) from 1995 through 1999, boasting a 78-48 mark. Southwest Missouri finished 24-9 in 1996–1997, making the NIT. His best season there came in 1998–1999, when Southwest Missouri fared 22-11 and reached the Sweet 16 of the NCAA tournament.

The University of Iowa (BTC) appointed Alford head coach in March 1999. He has compiled a 110-83 record there through 2004–2005 and experienced five consecutive losing seasons in the BTC. His best season there came in 2001–2002, when the Hawkeyes finished 23-12 and reached the second round of the NCAA tournament. Iowa lost to Ohio State University 81-64 in the BTC Tournament finals in 2002 and appeared in the NIT in 2002 and 2003, losing three of five contests. During 12 seasons overall, Alford has compiled a 266-159 regular-season record and has fared 3-3 in NCAA tournaments.

BIBLIOGRAPHY: Sam Alford to David L. Porter, December 7, 1989; Steve Alford and John Garrity, *Playing for Knight: My Six Seasons with Bobby Knight* (New York, 1989); *Dallas Mars Media Guide, 1991* (Dallas, TX, 1991); *ESPN Sports Almanac, 2000, 2001, 2002, 2003*; John Feinstein, *A Season on the Brink: A Year with Bobby Knight and the Indiana Hoosiers* (New York, 1987); Bob Hammel et al., *Glory of Old IU* (Champaign, IL, 2000); Austin Murphy, "Hoosier With a Hot Hand," *SI* 64 (January 6, 1986), pp. 50–51; Randy Peterson, "Hawkeyes Hire Alford," *Des Moines Register*, March 22, 1999, p. 1A; Britt Robson, "Homegrown Hoosier: The All-American-Boy Story," *Sport* 76 (February 1985), pp. 62–63; *TSN Official NBA Register, 1990–1991* (St. Louis, MO, 1990); *University of Iowa Basketball Media Guide, 2004–2005* (Iowa City, IA, 2004); *USA Today*, April 23, 1991; Alexander Wolff, "That Championship Touch," *SI* 66 (April 13, 1987), pp. 36–38.

David L. Porter

ALLEN, Forrest Clare "Phog" "Doc" "Mr. Basketball" (b. November 15, 1885, Jamesport, MO; d. September 16, 1974, Lawrence, KS), college player and coach, was the son of William T. Allen, a produce wholesaler, and Alexine (Perry) Allen a homemaker, writer, and lawyer. He played basketball when the game was in its infancy, competing on the Independence (MO) High School team. At Independence in 1903 Allen first met Dr. James Naismith*, inventor of basketball and then coach of that sport at the University of Kansas.

Allen entered the University of Kansas in 1904 and lettered in basketball from 1905 to 1907 and in baseball the latter two years. In 1905 Allen played guard and served as manager for the Kansas City AC. This basketball team won two of three games from the world champion Buffalo Germans. His team proclaimed itself the national champion because the Buffalo Germans had won both the Pan American and St. Louis World's Fair tournaments.

Allen's coaching career began at the University of Kansas in 1908 and spanned 46 years. He also coached at Baker University in Baldwin, Kansas in 1908 and 1909. After his graduation from Kansas in 1909, Allen left coaching for four years to study osteopathic medicine. He married Bessie Evalina Allen in June 1908, and they became the parents of six children. In 1912 he returned to college athletics as coach of all sports at Warrensburg Normal (now Central Missouri State University). "Doc" Allen's football, basketball, and baseball teams won numerous championships during his seven years at Warrensburg Normal. In 1919 he returned to his alma mater as director of athletics, football coach, and, principally, head basketball coach. He coached basketball there until forced to retire in 1956, when he became professor emeritus of Physical Education. At that time, the outspoken Allen referred to the university's retirement policy as the age of "statutory senility." His wife, Bessie, died on January 4, 1970.

Of all of his accomplishments, Allen cherished most having basketball added to the Olympic program. During the 1920s and early 1930s, Allen conducted virtually a one-man crusade to convince Olympic officials to include basketball in the world games. Because of his untiring efforts, the American-invented game was added to the Olympics in 1936 at Berlin, Germany. In 1952 he coached the U.S. Olympic basketball team, largely composed of the NCAA championship University of Kansas players. The Olympic team won the gold medal at Helsinki, Finland. Allen, the founder and first president of the NBCA, twice was named Coach of the Year and once Basketball Man of the Year. He was elected to the Missouri Sports, Kansas Centennial, and Naismith Memorial Basketball halls of fame. In March 1955 the 17,500-seat field house at the University of Kansas was named in his honor.

Several great athletes and coaches received their training from Allen. Allen developed coaches "Dutch" Lonborg*, Northwestern University; John Bunn*, Stanford University; Louis Menze, Iowa State University; "Frosty" Cox, University of Colorado; Dick Harp, University of Kansas; Ralph Miller*, Oregon State University; and Adolph Rupp*, University of Kentucky. His All-America players included Clyde Lovellette*, Charlie Black, B. H. Born, and Ray Evans. Allen also recruited Wilt Chamberlain* but retired before coaching him. His teams won 24 league championships, with his 1940 and 1953 squads capturing the NCAA Western titles before losing in the national finals. At Kansas, he compiled an impressive 591-219 win-loss record. His 46-year career record of 771 games won and 233 lost for a .768 percentage stood until Rupp broke it in 1968. Allen, a forceful personality and motivator, imbued his players with a winning attitude, confidence, and enthusiasm. He was an extraordinary coach who never dodged a fight or a controversy.

Allen wrote three widely read books: *My Basketball Bible* (1924), *Better Basketball* (1936), and *Coach Phog Allen's Sports Stories* (1947). He wrote hundreds of articles for magazines and became a popular speaker, whose opinions were widely sought and respected. A successful practicing osteopath, he was considered an authority on athletic injuries and treated many professional athletes. Allen dominated the game so thoroughly with his ideas and his personality that he became known as "Mr. Basketball." The first great basketball coach, he virtually found a game in a gymnasium and made it an international sport.

BIBLIOGRAPHY: Forrest C. Allen, *Coach Phog Allen's Sports Stories* (Lawrence, KS, 1947), Forrest C. Allen file, Naismith Memorial Basketball Hall of Fame, Springfield, MA; Peter C. Bjarkman, *Hoopla: A Century of College Basketball, 1896–1996* (Indianapolis, IN, 1996); Mike Douchant, *Encyclopedia of College Basketball* (Detroit, MI, 1995); "The Incredible Phog," *Kansas Alumni* 68 (March 1970), pp. 2–5; *Kansas City Star*, September 16, 1974; Larry Keith, "The Tradition," *SI* 48 (February 13, 1978), pp. 35–41; Blair Kerkhoff, *Phog Allen: The Father of Basketball Coaching* (Indianapolis, IN, 1996); Theodore M. O'Leary, "A Visit with Phog Allen," *Kansas City Star Magazine*, March 26, 1972, pp. 16–22; University Archives, Spencer Research Library, University of Kansas, Lawrence, KS.

Arthur F. McClure

ALLEN, Lucius Oliver, Jr. "The Jackrabbit" (b. September 26, 1947, Kansas City, MO), college and professional player, is the son of Lucius Oliver Allen Sr., and led Wyandote High School of Kansas City, Kansas to a 21-2 mark and a state title in basketball as a junior. Wyandote finished with a 24-0 mark and another state title his senior year. The wiry six-foot three-inch, 175-pound Allen played every position and was named second team *Parade* All-America. He averaged 25 points and 18 rebounds despite playing only three quarters a game. His state tournament rivals included Warren Armstrong (later Jabali) of Kansas City Central and Jo Jo White* of St. Louis. An above average student, he also served as vice president of his senior class.

Allen accepted a basketball scholarship to UCLA and played on the 1965–1966 freshman team, which defeated the varsity in a season-opening exhibition. Nicknamed "The Jackrabbit," he starred as a defender and scorer for great Bruin basketball teams in 1966–1967 and 1967–1968. Allen paired with playmaker Mike Warren to give UCLA a quick, heady backcourt, helping UCLA to a 30-0 record in 1966–1967 and 29-1 mark in 1967–1968, and two NCAA titles. He was named to the NCAA Men's All-Tournament teams in both 1967 and 1968. In the 1967 tourney, Allen netted 19 points in the semifinal victory over the University of Houston and 19 points in the championship win over the University of Dayton. Over the two seasons, he averaged 15.3 points and 5.9 rebounds. Academic problems sidelined him for the 1968–1969 season.

The Seattle SuperSonics (NBA) selected Allen as their first pick in the 1969 NBA draft. Allen averaged 9.8 points for the expansion franchise as a rookie. He played nine more NBA seasons, including his sixth man role with the 1971 NBA champion Milwaukee Bucks (NBA). Allen also performed for the Los Angeles Lakers (NBA), reuniting with Bucks teammate Kareem Abdul-Jabbar*, and the Kansas City Kings (NBA). For his NBA career, Allen averaged 13 points, 3.1 rebounds, and 4.5 assists. He remains one of the few basketball players to win a state high school, NCAA, and NBA championships. In 2000, Allen was named to the UCLA Athletic Hall of Fame.

BIBLIOGRAPHY: Mike Douchant, ed., *Encyclopedia of College Basketball* (Detroit, MI, 1995); Scott Howard Cooper, *The Bruins 100* (Lenexa, KS, 1999); Jan Hubbard, ed., *The Official NBA Encyclopedia*, 3rd ed. (New York, 2000); *Parade* (1965); UCLA Athletic Hall of Fame, Los Angeles, CA.

Bijan C. Bayne

ALLEN, Walter Ray (b. July 20, 1975, Merced, CA), college and professional player, moved frequently as a young man due to his father's occupation as a mechanic for the U.S. Air Force. Allen graduated from Hillcrest High School in Dalzell, South Carolina in 1993, after leading his school to a state basketball championship.

From 1993 to 1996, Allen played basketball for the University of Connecticut and majored in communication sciences. During his sophomore year, he led the Huskies in scoring, averaging 21.1 points and earning All-America status. Following his junior season, Allen opted for the NBA and was selected in the first round by the Minnesota Timberwolves (NBA). Minnesota traded his draft rights to the Milwaukee Bucks (NBA). The six-foot five-inch, 205-pound guard enjoyed immediate success in Milwaukee, averaging over 13 points and making the NBA All-Rookie Second Team in 1997.

Besides possessing a quick first step which allows him to slash toward the basket, Allen has demonstrated his three-point accuracy. He led the NBA in long range field goals attempted and made for the 2000–2001 and 2001–2002 seasons and won the Long Distance Shootout contest at the 2001 NBA All-Star Weekend. In 2000, Allen played on the gold medal–winning U.S. Olympic team. He was named to the All-NBA Third Team in 2001 and the All-NBA Second Team in 2005. He averaged 26.5 points and 4.3 rebounds in 11 playoff games, with the San Antonio Spurs eliminating the SuperSonics in the second round.

Allen starred for Milwaukee from 1996 until 2003, leading the Bucks to three NBA playoff appearances and garnering three NBA All-Star Game selections. He also participated actively in the Milwaukee community as a patron of the arts and contributor to civic causes. Allen sometimes feuded with Coach George Karl*, who criticized his star for lacking intensity. In February 2003, Allen was traded to the Seattle SuperSonics (NBA) for Gary Payton*. He paced Seattle in scoring with a 23.0 point average in 2003–2004 and a 23.9 point average in 2004–2005 and appeared in two NBA All-Star Games helping the SuperSonics make the playoffs in 2005. Allen has played in 657 regular-season games during nine NBA seasons, averaging 20.6 points, 4.7 rebounds, and 3.9 assists. He has also participated in 37 playoff games, scoring 920 points and grabbing 176 rebounds.

Allen, somewhat of a renaissance man off the court, enjoys art, golf, and acting. He played Denzell Washington's son in the 1998 Spike Lee feature *He Got Game*, receiving favorable reviews from critics. Allen has a 10-year-old daughter, who lives with her mother in Connecticut.

BIBLIOGRAPHY: Carl Fussman, "The State of the American Man," *Esquire* 135 (March 2001), pp. 130–131; Ken Shouler et al., *Total Basketball* (Wilmington, DE, 2003); "Spike and Ray," *Sport* 89 (January 1998), pp. 42–45; *TSN Official NBA Register, 2004–2005* (St. Louis, MO, 2004); L. Jon Wertheim, "Acquired Taste," *SI* 94 (February 26, 2001), pp. 50–53.

Ron Briley

ANDERSON, William Harold "Andy" (b. September 11, 1902, Akron, OH; d. June 13, 1967, Fort Lauderdale, FL), college player and coach, helped to bring college basketball into the modern era. Although considered too small for sports, he excelled in football, basketball, and track and field at Akron Central High School before graduating in 1920. He made All-City in football and basketball and set a record in the 220-yard low hurdles. Central reached the finals of the Ohio state basketball tournament once, with Anderson making the All-State team. At tiny Otterbein College in Ohio he won 11 athletic letters. These included three in football, basketball, and baseball, and two in track and field. An All-OC halfback in football, he also averaged 45 yards punting. Anderson made All-OC in basketball twice, set a college low hurdles track and field record, and led the baseball team in hitting for three consecutive seasons. The president of the junior and senior classes graduated in 1924 with a Bachelor's degree in French.

Anderson rejected a professional baseball contract from the St. Louis Cardinals (NL) because he wore glasses and instead taught and coached at Wauseon (1926) and Toledo Waite (1927–1934) High Schools. His 100-33 prep basketball record impressed the University of Toledo, which hired him in 1934. He built the Rockets into a basketball power, culminating with a third place NIT finish in 1942. In eight seasons at Toledo, he compiled a 142-41 record and developed All-Americas Chuck Chuckovits* and Bob Gerber. During this period, he coached other sports at Toledo, taught physical education at a local high school, and earned a Master's degree from the University of Michigan in 1939.

Anderson became basketball coach and athletic director at Bowling Green University in 1942 and held those posts until 1963 and 1965, respectively. His Falcon teams ranked among the best in the nation during the 1940s, routinely winning at least 20 games a season and securing five NIT bids in six seasons. In 1945 they finished second to powerful DePaul University, led by George Mikan*. Falcon All-Americas during this period were Wyndol Gray, Don and Mac Otten, and Charlie Share. Anderson pioneered the run-and-gun style of offense and the scheduling of intersectional matches from coast to coast. The slightly superstitious Anderson frequently wore the same suit to each game when the team was winning. With Al Bianchi, Jim Gerber, Jimmy Darrow, Nate Thurmond*, and Howie Komives, the Falcons won three MAC championships and made four more tournament appearances (NIT in 1954 and NCAA in 1959, 1962, and 1963). Anderson's 21-year mark at Bowling Green was 362-185.

In 1963 Anderson served as president of the NACBC and received a Doctor of Pedagogy degree from Otterbein. He participated on the honors committee of the Naismith Memorial Basketball Hall of Fame and was elected to the

HAF Hall of Fame in 1961 and the Naismith Memorial Basketball Hall of Fame in 1984.

Anderson ranked among the first college basketball coaches to reach 500 career victories (504-226), and coached 10 All-Americas. He was survived by his wife, Colinne (McClure), and three daughters.

BIBLIOGRAPHY: William Anderson file, Naismith Memorial Basketball Hall of Fame, Springfield, MA; Larry Donald, "The Bowling Green I Remember," *Basketball Times* 5–10 (April 10, 1983), pp. 10–11; Mike Douchant, *Encyclopedia of College Basketball* (Detroit, MI, 1995); Ronald L. Mendell, *Who's Who in Basketball* (New Rochelle, NY, 1973); *NYT*, June 15, 1967; Seymour Rothman, "Andy," Toledo *Blade Magazine*, January 20, 1963.

Dennis S. Clark

ANDRE, Denise Long Sturdy (b. March 22, 1951, Whitten, IA), high school player, became the most prolific scorer in Iowa girls' high school basketball history. The daughter of Raymond Dwayne Long, a linesman, and Irene Long, a postmaster, she has a twin brother, Dwayne, and other siblings, Diane, Dana, and David. Long attended Union-Whitten public schools, where she demonstrated an aptitude for sports that saved her from what she once called an unhappy childhood. Taunted by girl classmates through grade school for her ungainliness, she often played baseball with boys during the noon recess. By her freshman year, the heckling subsided to a minimum. The multitalented athlete eventually won 12 letters in three sports at Union-Whitten High School. In softball, Long pitched or played outfield while batting in the cleanup position. In track and field, she competed in the high jump, softball throw, and 440-yard run. Through basketball, however, the 5-foot 11-inch athlete left her mark in the record books and utilized the hook, jump, and set shots to score 6,250 career points in four years.

As a junior, Long led her team to the coveted 1968 Iowa State Championship. Her 93 points in a 114-66 first-round game was followed by quarterfinal and semifinal wins, in which she scored 64 and 61 points, respectively. Her scoring feats established a tournament record of 218 points for three games. In a much heralded March 16, 1968 showdown, Union-Whitten defeated Everly High School, 113-107, in the title game. The game itself was a cliffhanger, as the state's two high-scoring sharpshooters squared off. Although Everly's Jeannette Olson won the individual scoring battle, with 76 points to Long's 64, the combined talents of Denise and her cousin, Cindy Long, prevailed for a Union-Whitten win. Long established a new tournament record of 282 points for four games. She scored 1,946 points during the 1967–1968 season and averaged 62.8 points, breaking her own record average of 51.4 points established the previous year. For her efforts, she earned unanimous All-State First Team honors.

Long's senior year proved disappointing for Union-Whitten, which many picked to repeat as champions. After being eliminated in the semifinal round 73-58, Union-Whitten also lost the consolation game 89-86, despite her 79-point contribution. Still, Long established new scoring records with 1,986 points for the 1968–1969 season and a 69.6 points average. Again she was picked unanimously for All-State honors. Long's highest single-game scoring total stood at 111 points during a 1968 game. Her career average of 68.5 points included scoring 100 or more points three times.

Long became the first woman drafted into the ranks of men's professional basketball when Franklin Mieuli, owner of the San Francisco (now Golden State) Warriors (NBA), chose her as the team's thirteenth pick in the 1969 draft. Despite Mieuli's contention that Long could compete with men, NBA commissioner Walter Kennedy* voided the draft. Mieuli's next idea of a women's league to play before and during halftime of the Warrior's home games collapsed, dashing any dreams Long had of playing professional basketball except for a 40-second and one-point stint in 1979 with the Iowa Coronets for the ill-fated WPBL.

The $5,000 scholarship Mieuli provided allowed Long to enroll at the University of San Francisco for one year. After the disappointment in California, she returned to Iowa and entered the University of Northern Iowa. She withdrew after one semester to join the Overseas Crusade Team for a tour of Japan, Korea, Taiwan, Hong Kong, and the Philippines. After the tour, Long attended Marshalltown (Iowa) Community College, transferred to the University of Northern Iowa and graduated in May 1975 from Faith Baptist Bible College in Ankeny, Iowa.

As the role of celebrity overwhelmed the small-town girl, Long developed an aversion to basketball. She sought other sources of self-definition and ultimately became a born-again Christian. God took the place of basketball in the life of this high-strung young woman, who typically swallowed large quantities of Pepto-Bismol before high school basketball games. Long met fellow Christian David Sturdy at Faith Baptist Bible College and in 1974 married him across from Denise Long Park in Ankeny, Iowa in a ceremony televised by ABC's *Wide World of Sports*. They resided at Easter Lake outside Des Moines, where Denise worked as a bookkeeper for a law firm, but the couple divorced after four and one-half years. She completed a Bachelor's degree in Bible doctrine and theology from Faith Baptist in 1975, and earned a Bachelor's degree in physical education from Simpson College. Long married Lee A. Andre in June 1981. She worked as a pharmacy technician at Iowa Methodist Medical Center and earned a Bachelor's degree in pharmacy from Drake University in 1995. She is employed as a pharmacist for Osco Drug in Derby, Kansas, and resides in Rose Hill, Kansas, near Wichita.

In 1975 Long was inducted into the Iowa Girls' High School Basketball Hall of Fame. In 1982 she became the 100th member elected to the *Des Moines Register* Sports Hall of Fame. On December 11, 1984, she was the first woman athlete voted into the National High School Sports Hall of Fame.

BIBLIOGRAPHY: Janice A. Beran, *From Six-on-Six to Full Court* (Ames, IA, 1993); *Des Moines Register*, March 14–17, 24, 1968; March 13–16, 23, 1969; April 18, 1982; March 4, 2001; Jim Enright, *Only in Iowa: Where the High School Girl Athlete Is Queen* (Des Moines, IA, 1976); Janice Kaplan, "What Do You Do When You Grow Up?" *SI* 47 (July 4, 1977), pp. 30–38; Denise Long, interview with Judith A. Davidson, February 14, 1986; George Turner, Research Director, Iowa Girls' High School Athletic Union, (Des Moines, IA), interview with Judith A. Davidson, February 13, 1986.

Judith A. Davidson

ANDREAS, Lewis Peter "Lew" (b. February 25, 1895, Sterling, IL; d. June 18, 1983, Syracuse, NY), college athlete, coach, and executive, served as basketball coach for 25 years and as athletic director for 22 years at Syracuse University. The son of Harry G. Andreas and Jenny (Young) Andreas, he was introduced to sports in the Sterling public schools. After graduation, Andreas enrolled at the University of Illinois (WC) in 1916 and played freshman basketball and baseball there. With the American entry into World War I, he left Illinois to enlist in the U.S. Army. The private was assigned to Camp Crane in Allentown, Pennsylvania, and starred on its 21-0 basketball team. Andreas drove an ambulance in France, but was gassed at Soissons, France. He was discharged from the U.S. Army in May 1919 as a top sergeant.

Andreas subsequently attended Syracuse University, played end on the football team, and caught for the baseball team, among the Orangemen's best teams to date. After graduation, he taught and coached football, basketball, and baseball at Norwich (New York) High School. In his second year at Norwich, Andreas also became the school's principal. In 1925, he returned to Syracuse University as a physical education instructor, director of freshman athletics, and head basketball coach. Andreas coached basketball 25 years, from 1925 to 1943 and 1945 to 1950, producing a 364-145 record and .715 winning percentage. Only three of his quintets suffered losing records. Despite the lack of an organized championship in the 1920s, Andreas's teams uncharacteristically played a truly national schedule. During his second year in 1926, his Orangemen were named HAF National Champions. The Orangemen finished 19-1, led by three-time All-America Vic Hanson*. He also served terms as president of the NABC and ECAC and as a charter member of the NCAA Basketball Tournament Committee.

From 1927 to 1929, Andreas also coached the Syracuse football team to a 15-10-3 mark. His football teams did not excel, but he consistently scheduled the nation's finest teams, including the University of Notre Dame, Georgia Tech, University of Illinois, University of Nebraska, and University of Pittsburgh. His greatest contribution to football may have been as Syracuse's athletic director for 27 years from 1937 until 1964. During his tenure, the basketball team continued its success, a new field house was constructed, and Archbold Stadium was expanded to 40,000 seats. Andreas also fostered the development of a nationally prominent football program, featuring stars Jim Brown and Ernie Davis.

Andreas was lauded upon retirement by several coaches and athletic directors, President Lyndon Johnson, and New York Governor Nelson Rockefeller. He married Annetta Smith in 1925 and had one daughter, Elizabeth.

BIBLIOGRAPHY: Lewis Andreas clipping file, Syracuse University Archives, Syracuse, NY; Mike Douchant, *Encyclopedia of College Basketball* (Detroit, MI, 1995); Ronald L. Mendell, *Who's Who in Basketball* (New Rochelle, NY, 1973); *NYT*, May 11, 1963, p. 19; June 19, 1983, sec. 1, p. 32; *NCAA Men's Basketball Records 2004* (Indianapolis, IN, 2003).

Brian L. Laughlin

ANTHONY, Carmelo K. (b. May 29, 1984, New York, NY), college and professional player, played one year at Syracuse University and majored in selected studies in the College of Human Services and Health Professions. Anthony, the son of Mary Anthony, a custodial worker at the University of Baltimore, grew up in Baltimore, Maryland and attended Towson Catholic High School for three years. He improved his basketball skills between his freshman and sophomore seasons at a five-star summer camp. After his junior year, Anthony was named Baltimore City/County Player of the Year. To improve his game and prepare for college, he transferred to Oak Hill Academy in Mouth of Wilson, Virginia for his senior season. As a senior, Anthony led his basketball team to a 32-1 record and averaged 29 points, nine rebounds, and four assists. He was named to the McDonald's All-America East Team, a *Parade Magazine* All-America, and a *USA Today* All-America. Upon his graduation from high school, he debated between attending college and entering the NBA draft.

Anthony decided to attend Syracuse University and immediately impacted the college basketball world. As a freshman, he averaged 22 points, 10 rebounds, and two assists and led the Orangemen to the 2003 NCAA Final Four and championship game against the University of Kansas. Syracuse won the NCAA title, with Anthony being named NCAA East Regional MVP and NCAA Final Four MVP. He was selected Freshman of the Year by the USBWA, *Basketball Times*, and *TSN*, and garnered Big East Rookie of the Year honors, being one of five finalists for the prestigious Naismith Award. Anthony also has played on teams representing the United States in international play. He participated on the 2001 USA Basketball Youth Development Festival East Team and the 2002 USA Junior World Championship team. After leading Syracuse to the NCAA title as a freshman, Anthony entered the NBA draft. NBA scouts view the six-foot eight-inch, 220-pound Anthony as versatile, possessing a guard's game in a forward's body. The Denver Nuggets (NBA) selected him as the third pick overall in the 2003 NBA draft.

Anthony led Denver in scoring with 1,725 points (21.0 point average) with 498 rebounds (6.1 average) and 227 assists (2.8 average) in 82 games in 2003–2004, helping the Nuggets make the playoffs. He finished second in the NBA Rookie of the Year balloting behind LeBron James* and made the NBA All-Rookie team, edging James for highest scoring average among rookies. Anthony also became one of the youngest players in NBA history to score over 40 points in a regular-season game and was named NBA Player of the week twice. He tallied 24 points in the Game Three victory and 60 points in the first four games of the first round of the playoffs, but the Minnesota Timberwolves eliminated Denver in five games. He played on the 2004 U.S. Olympic team, which won a bronze medal. Anthony again paced the Nuggets in scoring with 1,558 points (20.8 point average) with 426 rebounds and 194 assists in 75 games in 2004–2005, lifting Denver to the NBA playoffs. He scored 96 points in five games in the first round playoff loss to the San Antonio Spurs.

BIBLIOGRAPHY: http://nbadraft.net/profiles/carmeloanthony.htm; http://www.collegesports.com/sports/m-baskbl/stories/042403aah.html; http://www.suathletics.com/carmelo; http://www.usa basketball.com/biosmen/carmelo_anthony_bio.html; *TSN Official NBA Register, 2004–2005* (St. Louis, MO, 2004).

Maureen M. Smith

ARCHIBALD, Nathaniel "Tiny" "Nate" (b. September 2, 1948, New York, NY), college and professional player and coach, is the son of "Big Tiny" Archibald, a construction worker, and Julia Archibald, a department store supervisor, was brought up in the slums of the South Bronx as the eldest of six children. Archibald became the man of the family at age 12, when his father left home. He attended New York City public schools and played basketball at DeWitt Clinton High School, where he made All-City as a senior in 1966. Archibald attended Arizona Western College in 1966–1967 and averaged 29.5 points. He played the next three years at the University of Texas-El Paso, scoring over 20 points per game his junior and senior seasons.

Nicknamed "Tiny," the six-foot one-inch guard entered the NBA in 1970 with the Cincinnati Royals (NBA) and moved with them to Kansas City-Omaha in 1972. In the Kings' inaugural season, he became the only player ever to lead the NBA in both scoring (34 points per game) and assists (11.4 per game) in the same year. That season he set an NBA record for assists with 910. Archibald played for the Kings through 1975–1976, averaging 26.5 and 24.8 points his last two seasons. In the 1976–1977 campaign, he appeared in only 34 games after being traded to the New Jersey Nets (NBA) for two players and two number one draft choices. Swapped to the Buffalo Braves (NBA), he sat out the entire 1977–1978 season with a torn Achilles tendon.

In 1978 a seven-player deal sent Archibald to Boston (NBA), where he guided the Celtics to the NBA's best record for three straight years (1979–1982) and the 1981 world championship. After a stormy relationship with coach Bill Fitch, Archibald was released by Boston at the close of the 1982–1983 season. He was signed by the Milwaukee Bucks (NBA), but suffered an early-season groin pull and sat out most of the 1983–1984 year.

Archibald, an outside shooter with great range, ranked among the greatest penetrators in the game. He used speed at the beginning and guile toward the end of his career to start fast breaks before others on the court realized it. This ability earned him many trips to the foul line, where he led the NBA in both free throws attempted and free throws made in 1971–1972 and 1972–1973, and in free throws made in 1974–1975. He made All-NBA First Team three times (1973, 1975, and 1976) and All-NBA Second Team twice (1972 and 1981). In seven NBA All-Star Games, he led his team in assists four times and scoring twice. His nine points and game-high nine assists in 1981 earned him MVP honors.

During 876 career games, Archibald scored 16,481 points (18.8 points per game) and recorded 6,476 assists. He was inducted into the Naismith Memorial Basketball Hall of Fame in 1991 and was selected one of the 50 greatest players in NBA history in 1996. A dedicated, caring individual, Archibald remembers his past. He is known in New York City for his work with youth both in and out of basketball. Archibald served as assistant basketball coach at the University of Georgia and University of Texas-El Paso from 1983 through 1989.

Archibald earned an M.A. degree in adult education and human resources development from Fordham University in 1993, and began teaching health and physical education at Public School 175/Independent School 275 in Harlem. In 1999, he helped create the Rod Strickland-Tiny Archibald Summer League for boys in New York City. In 2001, he served as head coach of the Fayetteville (North Carolina) Patriots of the newly organized National Basketball Development League (NBDL). Since January 2002 he has worked as a liaison for NBA Community Relations.

BIBLIOGRAPHY: Nate Archibald file, Naismith Memorial Basketball Hall of Fame, Springfield, MA; Peter C. Bjarkman, *The Boston Celtics Encyclopedia* (Champaign, IL, 1998); John Devaney, *Tiny, The Story of Nate Archibald* (New York, 1977); Jeff Greenfield, *Tiny Giant: Nate Archibald* (Chicago, IL, 1976); John O'Keefe, "Tiny Archibald: Basketball Hall of Famer," *Time* 152 (November 9, 1998); John Powers, *The Short Season: A Boston Celtics Diary, 1977–1978* (New York, 1979); "Return of the Man They Call Tiny," *Sport* (May 1980), pp. 56–61. Ray Sanchez, *Basketball's Biggest Upset* (El Paso, TX, 1991); *TSN Official NBA Guide, 1987–1988* (St. Louis, MO, 1987); *TSN Official NBA Register, 2004–2005* (St. Louis, MO, 2004).

Steve Ollove

ARIZIN, Paul Joseph "Pitchin' Paul" (b. April 9, 1928, Philadelphia, PA), college and professional player, is the son of Roger Arizin, a railroad mechanic for Pennsylvania Poilvsed, and Anna (Galen) Arizin. Arizin did not try out for the La Salle High School basketball team until his senior year (1946) and failed to make the squad. After enrolling at Villanova University without a scholarship, Arizin worked out at a night center to improve his skills, and made the team his sophomore year. Progressing quickly, Arizin set a single-game scoring mark of 85 points his junior year, averaged 20.1 points over an 82 game career, and led the nation with a 25.3 points-per-game average his final season. Arizin made the AP, UPI, *TSN*, HAF, Converse, and *Look* All-America First Teams, and was selected College Player of the Year as a senior in 1950. A well-rounded student, Arizin participated in the Accounting Society, Mathematics Club, and Villanova Honor Society. He graduated with a B.S. degree in accounting in 1950.

"Pitchin' Paul," the first draft choice of the Philadelphia Warriors (NBA), averaged 17 points as a rookie. The diminutive six-foot four-inch, 200-pound forward captured the scoring championship his second season (1951–1952) with a 25.4 points-per-game average and shot 48 percent from the field. He also ranked among the premier free throw shooters in the NBA with the year's longest consecutive string (19). His performance deprived George Mikan* of the scoring leadership for the first time in Mikan's illustrious career and earned Arizin a place on the All-Star First Team. Arizin married Maureen J. McAdams on October 18, 1952, and has five children, Michael, Alicia, Tim, Dennis, and Chris. Arizin's deep involvement with his family and community is reflected by membership in the Parents Society of the College of William and Mary, the Catholic Youth Organization, the Delaware County Republicans, and his co-chairmanship of the Multiple Sclerosis Liberty Bell Classic in 1973.

During his 10-year NBA career, Arizin led the league twice in scoring, made the All-NBA First Team three years, was selected the All-Star game's MVP in 1952, and led the Philadelphia Warriors to the NBA Championship over the Fort Wayne Pistons in 1956. He retired after a career spent entirely with Philadelphia in third place among the all-time NBA scoring leaders with 16,266 points for a 42 percent shooting average and a 22.8 points-per-game average and with 6,546 career rebounds. Joe Lapchick* called Arizin one of the greatest players of the modern era and described his jump shot as being "like a Renoir or a Rembrandt . . . it was perfection." In 1971 the NBA placed him on its Silver Anniversary Team. He was named one of the NBA's 50 greatest players in 1996. Additional honors include membership in the Pennsylvania Sports Hall of Fame, the HAF Hall of Fame, and the Naismith Memorial Basketball Hall of Fame (1978). After his retirement from the NBA, Arizin worked until in management positions in the Wilmington, Delaware office of IBM. The Springfield, Pennsylvania, resident has been honored by his company with numerous achievement awards and was named Delaware County Citizen of the Year in 1964.

BIBLIOGRAPHY: Paul Arizin file, Naismith Memorial Basketball Hall of Fame, Springfield, MA; Paul B. Beers, *Profiles in Pennsylvania Sports* (Harrisburg, PA, 1975); Jan Hubbard, ed., *The Official NBA Encyclopedia*, 3rd ed. (New York, 2000); Neil D. Isaacs, *Vintage NBA* (Silver Spring, MD, 1996); Ronald L. Mendell, *Who's Who in Basketball* (New Rochelle, NY, 1973); Claudia Mitroi, ed., *Philadelphia's Greatest Sports Moments* (Champaign, IL, 2000); Phil Pepe, *Greatest Stars of the NBA* (New York, 1970); *Philadelphia Inquirer*, 1948–1961, April 24, 1978; Sports Information Office, Villanova University, Villanova, PA; *TSN Official NBA Register, 2004–2005* (St. Louis, MO, 2004).

John G. Muncie

ATTLES, Alvin A., Jr. "Al" (b. November 7, 1936, Newark, NJ), college and professional player, coach, and executive, is the son of Alvin Attles Sr., and attended North Carolina Agricultural and Technical (A&T) State University. Attles proved a solid, dependable guard for 11 NBA seasons and achieved 557 lifetime victories as an NBA coach. The Philadelphia Warriors (NBA) selected Attles in the fifth round of the 1960 draft. A model of consistency and reliability. Attles spent his entire NBA playing career through the 1970–1971 season with the Warriors. The Philadelphia franchise moved to San Francisco in 1962 and played as the Golden State Warriors. Although not a star player, the tireless worker and resourceful learner possessed all-court sense and savvy and squeezed every ounce of talent from his six-foot, 185-pound frame. Attles made all nine of his shots, including eight field goals and one free throw, in Wilt Chamberlain's* 100-point game on March 2, 1962. During his NBA career, Attles scored 5,328 points for an 8.9 points average, compiled 2,463 rebounds, and recorded 2,488 assists.

As a coach with Golden State from the 1969–1970 through 1982–1983 seasons, Attles compiled a 557-518 win-loss record (.518 percent), led the Warriors to six NBA playoffs, and guided them to the 1975 NBA championship. He won acclaim for his leadership and coaching innovations and used up to 11 players in the 1975 championship series, in which the Warriors swept the heavily favored Washington Bullets in four games. Golden State, anchored by the redoubtable Rick Barry*, featured overall commitment, specific role players, and incandescent hustle and desire. The 1975 championship series marked the first time two teams headed by African American coaches had competed for a title. Attles notable achievements on the floor and from the bench were forged from steely determination and flexible understanding. Attles has served as vice president and assistant general manager of the Golden State Warriors since 1987–1988.

BIBLIOGRAPHY: Peter C. Bjarkman, *The Biographical History of Basketball* (Chicago, IL, 2000); Jan Hubbard, ed., *The Official NBA Basketball Encyclopedia*, 3rd ed. (New York, 2000); David S. Neft and Richard M. Cohen, eds., *The Sports Encyclopedia: Pro Basketball, 1891–1989*, 2nd ed. (New York, 1989); *TSN Official NBA Guide, 2004–2005* (St. Louis, MO, 2004); *TSN Official Register, 2004–2005* (St. Louis, MO, 2004).

Gustavo N. Agrait

AUERBACH, Arnold Jacob "Red" (b. September 20, 1917, Brooklyn, NY), college and professional player and coach, is the son of Hyman Auerbach and Marie Auerbach. His father, a Russian immigrant, founded a successful dry cleaning business. Auerbach captained both the handball and basketball teams his senior year at Eastern District High School in Brooklyn. He played two years both at Seth Lowe Junior College and at George Washington University, where he led the area in scoring his senior year with a 10.6 points per game average. Auerbach earned a B.A. in physical education in 1970. After coaching at St. Alban's Prep School and Roosevelt High School in Washington, D.C., he served in the U.S. Navy from 1943 to 1946. From 1946 to 1949, he coached the Washington Capitals (NBA) to an impressive 123-62 record. After a one-year stint with the Tri-Cities (NBA), he became the Boston Celtics' (NBA) coach in 1950. The five-foot, ten-inch, 170-pound Auerbach built the Celtics into a dynasty and became the first NBA coach to win over 1,000 games.

Auerbach's teams featured a high-scoring backcourt, strong defense, and tough rebounding front line. During the 1946–1947 season, the Capitals won 29 of 30 home games; other teams the same year recorded only a 57 percent home-court margin. At Boston, Auerbach recruited Bob Cousy* and Bill Sharman* in the back court and Ed Macauley*, "Bones" McKinney*, and Chuck Cooper (the NBA's first African American) in the forecourt. During the 1956–1957 season, Bill Russell* joined the Celtics with his extraordinary defensive prowess, shot-blocking finesse, and rebounding power. Russell provided the final catalyst by welding together excellent players Cousy, Sam Jones*, K.C. Jones*, Tom Sanders, and Tom Heinsohn* into one of the most formidable units in NBA history.

The Celtics in 1957 won the first of nine NBA championships under Auerbach. From 1959 to 1966, the Celtics captured eight consecutive NBA titles. Auerbach, who coached 11 consecutive NBA East All-Star teams and won 99 playoff games, was named NBA Coach of the Year in 1965 and was elected in 1968 to the Naismith Memorial Basketball Hall of Fame. In 1971 a blue-ribbon panel selected Auerbach the Silver Anniversary Coach. During his coaching career, Auerbach won 1,037 games and lost only 548 contests. Auerbach's stormy, volatile coaching style netted him over $17,000 in fines. Auerbach, a winner who stressed team unity rather than individual talents, always considered Russell superior to Wilt Chamberlain*. Russell coordinated well with the Celtics' team, while Chamberlain's teammates had to adapt to Wilt's style of play.

In his autobiography, Russell remarked: "Auerbach cannot stand the thought of losing. Anyone who has ever come to the Celtics has immediately been instilled with his philosophy. If you don't play to win, Auerbach has no place for you." Auerbach recruited players "who wanted to win" and considered himself a teacher and an excellent bench coach. According to Auerbach, "If you were a Celtic, you learned to motivate and communicate." Although Auerbach's trademark of lighting up a victory cigar angered opponents and their fans, Boston spectators eagerly awaited his ritual. On becoming general manager in 1966, Auerbach left an outstanding legacy as a coach. Auerbach had played an instrumental role in making the NBA a legitimate major pro league and helped the NBA to lower racial barriers with the highest percentage of black participants among pro sports. Auerbach served as general manager until 1984 and remains president of the Celtics, who won three NBA championships in the 1980s.

BIBLIOGRAPHY: Arnold "Red" Auerbach, *Basketball for the Player, the Fan, and the Coach* (New York, 1975); Arnold "Red" Auerbach and Joe Fitzgerald, *On and Off the Court* (New York, 1985); Arnold "Red" Auerbach and Paul Sann, *Red Auerbach: Winning the Hard Way* (Boston, MA, 1966); Arnold Auerbach file, Naismith Memorial Basketball Hall of Fame, Springfield, MA; Peter C. Bjarkman, *The Boston Celtics Encyclopedia* (Champaign, IL, 1998); Neal D. Isaacs, *Vintage NBA* (Silver Spring, MD, 1996); Bob Cousy with Ed Linn, *The Last Loud Roar* (Englewood Cliffs, NJ, 1971); Frank Deford, "A Man for All Seasons," *SI* 56 (February 15, 1982); Jan Hubbard, ed., *The Official NBA Encyclopedia*, 3rd ed. (New York, 2000); Leonard Koppett, *Championship NBA: Official 25th Anniversary* (New York, 1970); Leonard Koppett, *24 Seconds to Shoot: An Informal History of the NBA* (New York, 1968); Sandy Padwe, *Basketball's Hall of Fame* (Englewood Cliffs, NJ, 1970); Dan Shaughnessy, *The Red Auerbach Story: Seeing Red* (New York, 1994); Ken Shouler et al., *Total Basketball* (Wilmington, DE, 2003).

Lawrence E. Ziewacz

AURIEMMA, Geno (b. March 23, 1954, Montello, Italy), college coach, is the son of Donato Auriemma and Marziello Auriemma. His parents moved to the United States when he was seven years old and settled near Philadelphia. Auriemma grew up in the Philadelphia suburb of Norristown, Pennsylvania. He learned his basketball skills on Philadelphia area playgrounds and graduated from Bishop Kenrick High School in Norristown. Auriemma graduated in 1981 from West Chester University, where he earned a Bachelor of Science degree in political science. Before becoming head women's basketball coach at the University of Connecticut in 1985, he coached boys basketball at Bishop Kenrick High School, and served as assistant women's basketball coach at St. Joseph's University in Philadelphia and assistant women's basketball coach at the University of Virginia. He and his wife, Kathy, and their three children, Jenna, Alyssa, and Michael, live in Manchester, Connecticut.

Under the direction of Auriemma since 1985, the University of Connecticut women's basketball program has posted 19 winning seasons and captured five NCAA National Championships. The Lady Huskies captured the school's first national title in 1994–1995, compiling a perfect 35-0 record. The 1999–2000 Connecticut squad finished with a 36-1 record and the school's second national crown. The 2001–2002 Lady Huskies finished with a perfect 39-0 record and posted the school's third national title, while the 2002–2003 aggregate registered the school's fourth NCAA National Championship. Connecticut in 2003–2004 became only the second team in women's Division I history to win three consecutive national titles and the first Division I school with national championships in men's and women's basketball in the same season.

Connecticut has completely dominated the BEaC, winning 11 straight regular season titles through 2004 and 14 overall. The Lady Huskies have compiled a 271-29 won-loss record since 1986–1987, a 44.5 Big East Tournament record since 1989 and a 323–38 overall record the last 17 years.

Auriemma's overall 19-year win-loss record stands at 557-111, ranking him first among all active women's basketball coaches with an .834

winning percentage. He has won the Naismith National Coach of the Year Award four times (1995, 1997, 2000 and 2002), the Associated Press National Coach of the Year Award four times (1995, 1997, 2000 and 2003), the WBCA National Coach of the Year Award three times (1997, 2000 and 2002), Victor Television Sports Award three times (1995, 1996 and 2000) and six Big East Coach of the Year Awards (1989, 1995, 1997, 2000, 2002, and 2003).

Auriemma has developed five National Players of the Year: Rebecca Lobo* (1995), Jennifer Rizzotti* (1996), Kara Wolters (1997), Sue Bird* (2002), and Diana Taurasi* (2004). Internationally, Auriemma has served as an assistant coach and head coach with the USA Women's Basketball Teams in 1993, 1995–1996, and 2000–2001.

BIBLIOGRAPHY: "Geno Auriemma," *Coaches*, http://www.uconnhuskies.com (2003); "Geno Auriemma," *Father and Mother*, http://www.att.net (2003); "Geno Auriemma," *Husky Hardcores* http://www.huskyhardcores.com (2003); "Geno Auriemma," *Meet Coach Geno Auriemma*, http://www.genoauriemma.com (2003); "Geno Auriemma," *Women's Basketball*, http://www.uconnhuskies.com (2003).

John L. Evers

AZZI, Jennifer Lynn (b. August 31, 1968, Oak Ridge, TN), college and professional player, known for her frenzied and athletic style, is the daughter of Jim Azzi, a furniture store manager, and Donna Azzi, a high school English teacher, and began playing basketball at daycare. She started playing organized basketball at seven and asked for her own hoop at nine. Until Azzi and her younger sister, Susanne, entered Jefferson Junior High School, they played full court. Because their junior high team only played half court, Azzi also got involved in soccer, softball, and track and field. The game played by girls evolved into full court while both Azzi were in junior high, and they both played. The five-foot eight-inch, 147-pound Azzi continued to excel at Oak Ridge High School, averaging 19 points and earning All-America honors.

Tara VanDerveer, the head basketball coach of the Stanford University Cardinal, began recruiting Azzi in 1985. Despite her proximity to the University of Tennessee, Azzi signed with Stanford. During her four seasons from 1987–1988 through 1990–1991, the Cardinal achieved a 101-23 record, made three NCAA Tournaments, and won the NCAA title in 1990. Her individual honors included the Wade Trophy (1990), Naismith Player of the Year (1990), Kodak All-American First Team (1989 and 1990), Final Four MVP (1990), and PAC-10 Player of the Year (1989 and 1990). She averaged 13.4 points, 6.2 assists, and 3.9 rebounds per game for 122 contests.

After graduating from Stanford, with a Bachelor's degree in economics in 1991, Azzi traveled overseas, playing two seasons in Sweden and France and one in Italy. She also played with the U.S. Olympic team in the Goodwill Games, the Pan American Games, and in the Olympics, appearing on the 1996 Gold medal team. After the Olympics, Azzi cofounded the American Basketball League (ABL) and played for the San Jose Lasers from 1996 through 1999, averaging 15.0 points. When the ABL folded, she was drafted by WNBA's Detroit Shock in May 1999 and was instrumental in their playoff bid. In April 2000, Azzi was traded to Utah Starzz and averaged 9.6 points, 2.7 rebounds, and 5.0 assists per game in 2000. She finished her WNBA career with the San Antonio Silver Stars (WNBA) in 2003. In five WNBA seasons, she scored 1,288 points with 360 rebounds and 638 assists in 140 regular-season WNBA games and 6.8 points, 5.9 assists, and 2.6 rebounds in eight playoff games. She led the WNBA with a 51.4 three-point field-goal percentage in 2001. Azzi co-chairs the Promoting Achievement in School through Sports Program (PASS) and operates an adult training camp.

BIBLIOGRAPHY: Sara Gogol, *Playing in a New League* (Indianapolis, IN, 1998); Hank Hersch, "The Cardinal Rules," *SI* 72 (April 9, 1990), pp. 48–50; Anne Janette Johnson, *Great Women in Sports* (Detroit, MI, 1991); Douglas Looney, "A Cardinal Virtue," *SI* 71 (November 20, 1989), pp. 94–96; *San Francisco Chronicle* (November 14, 1996); *TSN Official WNBA Guide and Register*; WNBA website, www.wnba.com.

Lisa A. Ennis

B

BAER, Clara Gregory (b. August 27, 1863, Algiers, LA; d. January 19, 1938, New Orleans, LA), physical education professor and college pioneer, was the daughter of Hamilton John Baer and Ellen (Riley) Baer. Her mother died when Clara was only four years old. Her maternal grandmother helped her father, a broker flour merchant, take care of Clara, her sister, and two brothers. Baer received her secondary education in Louisville, Kentucky, and from 1889 to 1891 attended the Emerson School of Oratory, the Boston School of Expression, and the Posse Normal School of Physical Education in Boston. In 1891 Baer was hired to establish the first Physical Education Department at Sophie Newcomb College in New Orleans. She began the South's first teacher certification (1893–1894) and the initial four-year Bachelor's degree programs (1907) in physical education.

Baer, who introduced basketball to Newcomb College and the south in 1893, published the first women's basketball rules in 1895 under the name "Basquette," six years before the Spalding Rules by Senda Berenson Abbott*. Baer divided her court into seven divisions and allowed no dribbling, snatching, or guarding. Baer's rules, influenced by physiological principles learned from Nils Posse, permitted no two-handed passes or shots for field goals because these actions were thought to compress the chest. Baer's rules, rather than the Spalding ones, were used in Louisiana and probably other southern states until the mid-1920s. Baer also invented Newcomb Ball in 1895, carrying the college's name into almost every playground and school in the nation. Until the late 1920s, the game rivaled volleyball in popularity.

A product of her time, Baer never promoted women's sport at a highly competitive level. She did, however, play a dominant role in prompting sport for women to improve their physical and emotional health and influenced women's sport far beyond New Orleans. During summers from 1893 to 1910, she taught physical education and sport to women teachers at the Louisiana Chautauqua near Ruston, and in rural villages throughout Louisiana in summer educational institute work. She also directed the summer school of physical education at the Monteagle Sunday School Assembly in Tennessee. Because Baer trained students who lived throughout the south, she probably influenced the development of women's sport in this conservative region more than any other person. She retired from Sophie Newcomb College in 1929 after heading the Physical Education Department for 38 years.

BIBLIOGRAPHY: Clara G. Baer, *Basket Ball Rules for Women and Girls* (New Orleans, LA, 1895, 1908, 1911); Clara G. Baer, *Newcomb* (New Orleans, LA, 1895, 1911); Clara G. Baer, "The History of the Development of Physical Education at Newcomb College," National Education Association, 1914, pp. 701–704; Clara G. Baer Papers, Tulane University Archives, New Orleans, LA; *Daily Picayune*, 1891–1929, January 20, 1938; Joan S. Hult and Marianna Treckell, *A Century of Women's Basketball: From Frailty to Final Four* (Reston, VA, 1991).

Joan Paul

BAKER, Vincent Lamont "Vin" (b. November 23, 1971, Lake Wales, FL), college and professional player, is the son of James Baker, a Baptist minister and auto mechanic, and Jean

(Richardson) Baker, a quality control employee. His mother performed well in basketball, motivated him to work, and provided a formidable opponent in their workouts. Baker graduated in 1989 from Old Saybrook (Connecticut) Senior High School, where he excelled in basketball his junior and senior years. He enjoyed a good high school career and led his team to the state finals, but was not highly recruited by colleges or universities.

Baker enrolled at the University of Hartford and played four years of basketball for the Hawks. He set school records for the most career points scored (2,238) and the most blocked shots (279). Baker attained second on the school's all time list in rebounding (951), finished with a scoring average of 20.0 points and earned Honorable Mention All-America. In 1993, he earned a Bachelor's degree in mass communications. In January 1998, the university retired his jersey number.

Baker, a six-foot eleven-inch, 250-pound power forward, was selected by the Milwaukee Bucks (NBA) in the first round as the eighth pick overall of the 1993 NBA draft. He spent four years with the Bucks before being traded to the Seattle SuperSonics (NBA) in September 1997. After five seasons with Seattle, he was traded to the Boston Celtics (NBA) in July 2002.

In December 1993, Baker became a starter for the Bucks and made the NBA All-Rookie First Team that season. He was named to the NBA All-Star Team in his second season for the first of four consecutive years. He led the Bucks in scoring and rebounding for two seasons and was selected to the All-NBA Third Team in 1997.

Upon joining Seattle for the 1997–1998 season, Baker scored 1,574 points in 82 games and was voted to the All-NBA Second Team. His playing time was limited during the 1998–1999 season due to a ligament tear. Baker scored his 10,000th career point in March 2001 and blocked his 700th career shot and pulled down his 5,000th career rebound the following season. For the Boston Celtics in the 2002–2003 season, he saw limited action and only tallied 270 points. The Celtics suspended him in February 2003 and released him in February 2004 because of an alcohol-related problem. The New York Knickerbockers (NBA) signed him in March 2004. Baker appeared in 54 games in 2003–2004, averaging 9.8 points. Houston acquired him in February 2005. Baker averaged just 1.3 points in limited action in 2004–2005.

In international play, Baker played on both the 1999 gold-medal winning USA Basketball Men's Senior Team and the 2000 gold medal winning USA Men's Olympic Team in Sydney, Australia.

In 12 NBA seasons through 2004–2005, Baker has scored 11,812 points and averaged 7.5 rebounds in 783 regular season games. In 24 NBA playoff games, he has scored 316 points and averaged 13.2 points. He also posted 35 points and 24 rebounds in four NBA All-Star Games.

BIBLIOGRAPHY: Ken Shouler et al., *Total Basketball* (Wilmington, DE, 2003); *TSN Official NBA Register, 2004–2005* (St. Louis, MO, 2004); "Vin Baker," *Bio*, http://www.nba.com (2003); "Vin Baker," *Career Highlights*, http://www.nba.com (2003); "Vin Baker," *Player Info* http://www.nba.com (2003); "Vin Baker," *Seattle Supersonics*, http://www.connectionmagazine.org (2003).

John L. Evers

BANKS, Alline. *See* Sprouse, Alline Banks

BANKS, David "Davey" "Flash" "Fatty" "Pretzel" (b. 1901, New York; d. August 24, 1952, Troy, NY), professional player and coach, was the son of Samuel Banks. The five-foot eight-inch, 155-pounder, nicknamed "Flash," "Fatty," and "Pretzel," played professional basketball from 1921 to 1935 and resided in Mineola, New York until his death.

An offensive player and top shooter, Banks played for several teams (including Springfield and Holyoke, Massachusetts, Toledo, Ohio (ABL), and Troy, New York) during his professional basketball career. His career began with the Assumption Crowns (MBL) and Visitation Triangles (MBL), both Brooklyn, New York–based teams. He also spent time with the Philadelphia Sphas (EL) before joining the Original New York Celtics (ABL) in 1927.

The Original Celtics, organized by Jim Furey* in 1918 after World War I, proved the dominant professional basketball squad of the 1920s. The Celtics entered the ABL in 1926 and easily won the ABL title in 1927 and 1928. After playing 10 games in the 1928–1929 season, though, the Celtics encountered financial problems due to the high salaries paid by Furey and were disbanded. Banks joined the New York Hakoahs, a new team he helped organize in the ABL. When Furey reorganized the Celtics for the 1929–1930 season, he reunited only Banks and two other previous Celtics players. Because the Celtics once again faced financial problems, the team was turned over to the ABL. The Fort Wayne (Indiana) Hoosiers paid the ABL $3,100 for Banks's services for the remainder of the 1928–1929 season. Banks played for the Toledo Redmen (ABL) in the 1929–1930 campaign. The Celtics regrouped again in 1931 and barnstormed as independents for the next six years. The rest of the basketball world quickly caught up, however, to the underpaid, aging Celtics players.

From 1927 to 1931, Banks ranked in the top eight in ABL scoring. In 1927–1928, he tied for top honors in points per game (8.4) and ranked second in field goals (170) and total points (412). In the 1930–1931 season, although his Toledo team finished last in the NBL, Banks earned second-place honors in field goals (94), free throws (66), and total points (254).

In 1946, Banks coached the Troy Celtics (ABL). He was killed six years later in an automobile accident during which time he apparently was negotiating with the University of Notre Dame about becoming the assistant basketball coach for the 1952–1953 season.

BIBLIOGRAPHY: Glenn Dickey, *The History of Professional Basketball Since 1896* (New York, 1982); Bill Himmelman, telephone conversation with Susan J. Rayl, Norwood, NJ, October 1993; Zander Hollander, ed., *The Modern Encyclopedia of Basketball* (New York, 1973); David S. Neft and Richard M. Cohen, *The Sports Encyclopedia: Pro Basketball*, 5th ed. (New York, 1992); Murry R. Nelson, *The Originals: The New York Celtics Invent Modern Basketball* (Bowling Green, OH, 1999); *NYT*, August 25, 1952, pp. 17, 25; Robert W. Peterson, *From Cages to Jump Shots* (New York, 1990); *Troy Record*, August 25, 1952, pp. 1, 7.

Susan J. Rayl

BARKLEY, Charles Wade (b. February 29, 1963, Leads, AL), college and professional player and sportcaster, is the oldest of three sons of Frank Barkley and Charcey (Edwards) Barkley Glenn, and grew up in a small mining town east of Birmingham. His father, Frank, moved out when Charles was one year old and did not reconcile with his son until later years. The small, somewhat sickly youth lived in an extended family consisting of his young mother (whose second husband, Clee Glenn, subsequently was killed in an auto accident); his two younger brothers, Darryl and John, and his grandparents, Adolphus and "Johnnie" Edwards. Johnnie Edwards, a beautician, played a dominant role in Barkley's life for many years.

Barkley began attracting national attention while at Leads High School, although not making the varsity until his junior year. He subsequently attended Auburn University (SEC), where the six-foot five-inch, nearly 300-pound Barkley gained notoriety for his eating, rebounding, and prolific scoring. Before turning professional following his junior year, Barkley had achieved fame by scoring 25 points and making 17 rebounds as a freshman against the University of Kentucky, leading the SEC in rebounding all three years, converting 62.6 percent of his baskets, and being named 1983–1984 UPI and SEC Player of the Year. He also recorded an outstanding 25-point, 11-rebound performance in a 1982 Sports Festival game and demonstrated aggressive play at the 1984 U.S. Olympic team trials. Coach Bobby Knight* ultimately left him off that team.

The Philadelphia 76ers (NBA) selected Barkley fifth in the first round of the 1984 NBA draft and signed him after rancorous negotiations. The 76ers still were dominated by Moses Malone* and Julius Erving*, but Barkley quickly became the prototype power forward. His significant bulk, strength, quick first step, and phenomenal vertical leap enabled him to become a dominant rebounder. An exceptional all-around player, Barkley could lead the fast break, shoot from the perimeter, or guard a much taller opponent. With relatively small hands, he scored many of his points from the inside on lay-ups or on powerful, two-handed dunks.

The complex, sometimes aloof Barkley, who demonstrated uneasiness at times in the urban world of professional basketball, attracted mixed emotions from the crowds with his aggressive play, constant taunts and gestures, and problems with officials. He also carried on a tense relationship with Philadelphia management before reportedly signing an eight-year $13 million contract in 1986 and making a lucrative contract to endorse Nike basketball shoes.

The trade of Malone in 1986 and retirement of Erving in 1987 brought Barkley's emergence as the visible, vocal leader of the 76ers; Barkley remained with Philadelphia through the 1991–1992 season. The NBA saw him rank first in offensive rebounds in 1986–1987, 1987–1988, and 1988–1989, and among the top three in field goal percentage from 1986–1987 through 1988–1989. He holds single-game records for most offensive rebounds in one quarter (11) and one half (13), against New York in March 1987. Although bitter at not being selected to start until 1989, he played in the 1987–1993 and 1996 NBA All-Star Games and was named All-Star MVP in 1991. Barkley received the Schick Pivotal Player of the Year honors for his all-around excellence in the 1985–1986 and 1986–1987 seasons. Injuries sidelined Barkley for 13 games in 1990–1991, but he still ranked fourth in scoring (27.6 points per game) and field goal percentage (.570).

In June 1992, Philadelphia traded him to the Phoenix Suns (NBA). Barkley was named NBA MVP in 1993, averaging 25.6 points and 12.2 rebounds and helping Phoenix reach the NBA Finals. He shares the single-game NBA playoff records for most free throws made in one half (19) against Seattle in June 1993 and most field goals made in one half (15) against Golden State in May 1994. Barkley was traded to the Houston Rockets (NBA) in August 1996 and played his final four NBA seasons there. During 16 NBA seasons, he totalled 23,757 points (22.1 point average), 12,546 rebounds (11.7 rebound average), 4,215 assists, 1,648 steals, and 888 blocked shots in 1,073 regular season games. In 123 playoff games, Barkley tallied 2,833 points, 1,582 rebounds, and 482 assists. He won the IBM Award for all-around contributions to his team's success from 1986 through 1988, made All-NBA First Team in 1988, 1989, 1990, 1991, and 1993, All-NBA Second Team in 1986, 1987, 1992, 1994, and 1995, and All-NBA Third Team in 1996, and All-NBA Rookie Team in 1985. Barkley was named to the NBA 50th Anniversary All-Time Team in 1996, and averaged 20 points and 10 rebounds for 11 consecutive seasons. He finished with a 54 percent field goal percentage, third all-time among forwards, and retired as 18th highest scorer and 14th highest rebounder in NBA history. He competed for the gold-medal winning USA basketball teams at the 1992 Barcelona, Spain, and the 1996 Atlanta, Georgia Summer Olympic Games.

His early nicknames included "The Leaning Tower of Pizza" and "The Round Mound of Rebound," but Barkley kept his weight under control and maintained a remarkably low body fat rating. Although not involved in weight training or body strengthening, he remained among the strongest and most powerful NBA players. Barkley's grandmother persuaded him to attend Auburn during off-season to complete his Bachelor's degree. He married Maureen L. Blumhardt in 1989 and has one daughter, Christiana. Since 2001, he has been a broadcaster for Turner Sports Network.

BIBLIOGRAPHY: Charles Barkley, *Outrageous* (New York, 1992); Jan Hubbard, ed., *The Official NBA Basketball Encyclopedia*, 3rd ed. (New York, 2000); Jack McCallum, "Now Barkley Owns the Ball," *SI* 68 (January 11, 1988), pp. 36–39; Bruce Newman, "A Double Feature . . . ," *SI* 64 (March 24, 1986), pp. 32–35; Philadelphia (PA) *Inquirer*, February 1, 1987; February 10, 1989; May 17, 1989; October 8, 1989; Alan Richman, "Call Him 'Round Mound' at Your Peril," *People Weekly* 27 (April 27, 1987), pp. 76–83; Alan Richman, "Millionaire Dropout . . . ," *Jet* 72 (May 25, 1987), p. 48; Ken Shouler et al., *Total Basketball* (Wilmington, DC, 2003); *TSN Official NBA Register, 2004–2005* (St. Louis, MO, 2004); Chris Dortsch, *String Music* (Dulles, VA, 2002); Alexander Wolff, "Charles in Charge," *SI* 62 (May 13, 1985), pp. 30–31; Alexander Wolff, "The Leaning Tower of Pizza," *SI* 60 (March 12, 1984), pp. 580–600; Alexander Wolff, "On a Mission," *SI* 69 (December 12, 1988), pp. 20–25; Alexander Wolff, "3 Spot Is a Hot Spot," *SI* 69 (November 7, 1988), pp. 58–70; Alexander Wolff, "Who's Most Valuable?," *SI* 70 (April 17, 1989), pp. 42–50.

Daniel R. Gilbert

BARKSDALE, Don Angelo (b. March 31, 1923, Oakland, CA; d. March 8, 1993, Oakland,

CA), college, amateur, and professional player and scout, ranks among the pioneer African American basketball players. Barksdale graduated from Berkeley High School, where he was cut from the basketball team. At UCLA, he became the first African American to earn All-America basketball honors. The HAF and *True* magazine both placed him on their All-America basketball teams.

From 1947 to 1951, Barksdale played AAU basketball for the Oakland Bittners and Oakland Blue 'n Gold. During the 1947–1948 season with the Bittners, the six-foot six-inch, 200-pounder led the AAU in scoring with a 16.7 scoring average and finished well ahead of Vince Boryla* and Bob Kurland*. Barksdale remained the only African American AAU player. An interesting issue raised that AAU season revolved around whether he would be allowed to play in games scheduled against the Phillips 66ers in Bartlesville and Oklahoma City, Oklahoma, then a segregated state, fought efforts to desegregate its schools. No African American had played in an integrated athletic contest in the state's history. Barksdale not only performed but scored 17 points in the first game in leading the Bittners to a 45-41 victory over the Phillips 66ers. Phillips had compiled a 36-game winning streak entering the contest. Newspapers from the Midwest to California praised Barksdale as an "ambassador of goodwill for his race" and compared his performance favorably to Jackie Robinson, who had integrated major league baseball the previous year.

Because 1948 marked an Olympic year, the National AAU tournament at Denver, Colorado assumed special meaning. The top three AAU teams earned the right to enter the Olympic tournament at Madison Square Garden in New York. Barksdale led the Bittners to a third-place finish. The USOC named him to the 1948 U.S. Olympic team following the tournament, making him the first African American to receive this honor. Barksdale joined mostly Phillips 66ers and University of Kentucky Wildcats at the London, England Summer Olympic Games and helped the United States win its second gold medal in basketball.

For the next three years, Barksdale remained a dominant AAU basketball player. At the 1949 National AAU tournament, he scored 17 points to pace the Bittners to a 55-51 victory over Phillips 66 and break Phillips' string of six consecutive National AAU championships. In 1950, Barksdale led the Oakland Blue 'n Gold to the AAU tournament finals before losing to Phillips. The Oakland Blue 'n Gold joined the NIBL during his last year there in 1950–1951. He topped the NIBL in scoring and was named NIBL MVP. Although injured during the National AAU tournament, Barksdale was selected to the AAU All-America squad for the fourth successive year. Jack Carberry, the dean of Denver's sportwriters, lauded Barksdale as "the best basketball player in the amateur ranks today."

In 1951 the Baltimore Bullets (NBA) made Barksdale the fourth black NBA player. During his third NBA season, Barksdale joined the Boston Celtics (NBA) and on January 13, 1953, became the first African American player to perform in an NBA All-Star Game. Barksdale, who retired after the 1954–1955 season, scored 2,895 points and averaged 11 points in four NBA seasons.

Subsequently, Barksdale owned several Oakland, California night clubs, hosted a television show, scouted for the Golden State Warriors (NBA) basketball club, and worked as a disc jockey at several black radio stations. In 1982 he created the SHSSF to fund financially strapped athletic programs in the San Francisco Bay Area. By his death, the SHSSF had raised over $1 million to help high school sports. The Barksdales had two sons, Donald and Derek.

BIBLIOGRAPHY: *Denver Post*, 1947–1951; Jan Hubbard ed., *The Official NBA Basketball Encyclopedia*, 3rd ed. (New York, 2000); Bill Mallon and Ian Buchanan, *Quest for Gold: The Encyclopedia of American Olympians* (New York, 1984); David S. Neft and Richard M. Cohen, *The Sports Encyclopedia: Pro Basketball*, 5th ed. (New York, 1992); Ron Thomas, *They Cleared the Lane* (Lincoln, NE, 2002); *USA Today*, February 19, 1993; Alexander Weyand, *The Cavalcade of Basketball* (New York, 1960).

Adolph H. Grundman

BARLOW, Thomas Bryan "Cave Man" "Tom" (b. July 9, 1896, Trenton, NJ; d. September 26, 1983, Lakehurst, NJ), professional player, was the son of George Barlow, a grocery store owner and operator, and Catherine Barlow, and began playing basketball as a youngster. He and a brother, Charles, put up a hoop on the barn behind their house. As a Rider-Moore-Stewart Business School (currently Rider College) student, 16-year-old Barlow signed in 1912 to play pro basketball with the Trenton Tigers for $15 per game. From 1912 to 1932, Barlow played on over 10 pro teams and frequently on two or three teams simultaneously in eastern leagues. With brother Charles, Barlow opened and operated the Barlow Mills Company in Trenton, New Jersey in 1916. During World War I, Barlow served six months in the U.S. Army until the armistice was signed in 1918. During his brief military service, Barlow continued playing with the Trenton Tigers and Greenpoint (Brooklyn) in the MeL and with teams in the PSL and NYSL.

At six feet one inch and 200 pounds, the then gigantic Barlow became a strong defender, outstanding scorer and rebounder, and tough, physical player, never backing away from a fight. In 1921 Eddie Gottlieb*, one of the pioneer founders of the NBA, signed Barlow to play for the Sphas, the eventual Philadelphia Warriors. Gottlieb's team promoted pro basketball, playing all interested teams during barnstorming trips to midwestern, northern, and southeastern states. Barlow, an excellent baseball catcher, played 18 years on several semipro baseball teams as well. In 1922 New York Giants (NL) manager John McGraw tried to sign Barlow, but the latter believed basketball and mill work allowed insufficient time for a third career.

In 1926 Barlow led Gottlieb's Philadelphia Warriors to the World Basketball Championship by defeating the New York Celtics two games to one in the first pro basketball contests played in Madison Square Garden. From 1928 through 1932, Barlow again played with several teams simultaneously. With Trenton in 1928, Barlow averaged 7.3 points and placed fifth in the ABL with 274 total points. At the peak of his career, from 1926 to 1932, Barlow was the highest-paid pro player at $45 per game. Barlow retired after a particularly strenuous contest in Wilmington, Delaware in 1932. He married Mildred Kelty of Trenton in 1932, and they had two children, Thomas Jr. and Barbara. Barlow was appointed building inspector for the city of Trenton the same year and rose to building chief before his retirement in 1967. A pioneer in pro basketball, he helped to develop and promote the game. In 1981 he was inducted into the Naismith Memorial Basketball Hall of Fame.

BIBLIOGRAPHY: Thomas Barlow file, Naismith Memorial Basketball Hall of Fame, Springfield, MA; Zander Hollander, ed., *The NBA's Official Encyclopedia of Pro Basketball* (New York, 1981); Zander Hollander, ed., *The Pro Basketball Encyclopedia* (Los Angeles, CA, 1977); Robert W. Peterson, *Cages to Jumpshots: Pro Basketball's Early Years* (New York, 1990); *Trenton Times*, September 28, 1983.

Jerry Jaye Wright

BARMORE, William Leon "Leon" (b. June 3, 1944, Vienna, LA), college player and coach, is the son of Jasper Barmore and Flora McCurry. He played basketball at Ruston High School and Louisiana Tech University. Barmore made All-State and All-Gulf States Conference in high school and ranked among the best shooting guards from Ruston High and Louisiana Tech.

Barmore coached basketball at the high school level for a few years before being hired as an assistant coach for the Louisiana Tech Lady Techsters. He served as the assistant coach between 1977 and 1982 and proved instrumental in the team's 54 game winning streak. Barmore replaced Sonja Hogg as head coach and remained at Louisiana Tech for 20 seasons. He initially retired in 2000, but was persuaded to return as head coach. Barmore officially retired after the 2001–2002 season. During his 20-year tenure at Tech, he made a tremendous impact on his players and the national women's basketball landscape. The Lady Techsters won 13 conference titles (ASC, SBC, WAC) over 15 seasons. His 2000–2001 team finished 31-5, making him the first coach in Division I to record six straight seasons of 30-plus wins. His squads attained 30-plus victories in 13 seasons, competed in 20 NCAA tournaments, earned nine Final Four appearances, and played in five championship games, winning the national title in 1988.

Barmore retired with the highest winning percentage (.869) in both men's and women's college basketball, compiling a 576-87 record. He twice received the USBWA National Coach of the Year Award and coached 12 Kodak All-Americas and four Olympians. Many of his players perform in the WNBA or coach at the college level. Barmore was inducted into the Naismith Memorial Basketball Hall of Fame in 2003 as only the sixth women's coach accorded that honor. He and his wife, Rachel, have a daughter, Sharron.

BIBLIOGRAPHY: Mike Douchant, *Encyclopedia of College Basketball* (Detroit, MI, 1995); http://espn.go.com/ncw/news/2003/0509/1551650.html; http://www.latechsports.com/barmore.html; http://www.rustonleader.com/a-Barmore.htm; http://www.thenewsstar.com/html/08AC176D-CD5B-42C6-A289-3D7EE9A8827A .shtml

Maureen M. Smith

BARNETT, Richard "Dick" (b. October 2, 1936, Gary, IN), college and professional player and executive, was a six-foot four-inch, 190-pound guard noted for his unique twisting and gyrating jump shot. Barnett starred for the Tennessee State University basketball team that won three straight NAIA championships during the 1957–1959 period. He twice was named MVP of that tournament and later was selected to the All-Tournament team.

Barnett, the first-round draft choice of the Syracuse Nats (NBA) in 1959, spent his entire pro career in the NBA except for his 1961–1962 season with the Cleveland Pipers of the ill-fated ABL of the early sixties. A consistent, poised performer, he combined pure shooting with workman-like defense. Barnett was sold by Syracuse to the Los Angeles Lakers (NBA) in 1962 and was traded to the New York Knicks (NBA) in 1965. Although always a dependable starter or reserve, he peaked during his initial years with the Knicks. Barnett added all-court versatility to the exemplary, unselfish New York team as the perfect counterpart stylewise to the flamboyant Walt Frazier* in the backcourt. He proved an important cog in the championship Knicks team of 1970 and then shared in the 1973 Knicks title as a 10-minute-per-game player.

During his NBA career, Barnett appeared in 971 games, scored 6,034 baskets (45.6 shooting percentage), made 3,290 free throws (76.1 percentage), and tallied 15,358 points (15.8 points average). He played in the 1968 All-Star Game, scoring 15 points in 22 minutes. The serious, articulate, analytical Barnett, who always won the respect of teammates, opponents, and fans both on and off the court, retired after the 1973–1974 season; the Knicks retired his uniform number 12. In June 2004, he was selected commissioner of the inaugural Worldwide Basketball Association. The league of urban professionals plans to interact with schools and community groups.

BIBLIOGRAPHY: Pete Axthelm, *The City Game* (New York, 1970); Phil Berger, *Miracle of 33rd Street—The New York Knickerbockers Championship Season* (New York, 1970); Peter C. Bjarkman, *The Encyclopedia of Pro Basketball Team Histories* (New York, 1994); Lewis Cole, *Dream Team—The Candid Story of the Champion 1969–1970 Knicks* (New York, 1981); Ronald L. Mendell, *Who's Who in Basketball* (New Rochelle, NY, 1973); Ken Shouler et al., *Total Basketball* (Wilmington, DE, 2003); *TSN Official NBA Register, 1987–1988* (St. Louis, MO, 1987).

Gustavo N. Agrait

BARRY, Justin "Sam" (b. December 17, 1892, Aberdeen, SD; d. September 23, 1950, Berkeley, CA), college athlete and coach, gained fame as a highly successful basketball mentor at the University of Southern California during the 1930s and 1940s. Barry was a three-sport star in basketball, baseball, and football at both Madison, Wisconsin, High School and Lawrence College of Wisconsin. When later enrolling at the University of Wisconsin to complete his college degree, Barry did not compete in athletics. His successful coaching career was inaugurated at Madison High School and continued at Knox College of Illinois, the University of Iowa, and the University of Southern California. Barry's most permanent heritage from his Southern California coaching tenure (1930–1941; 1946–1950) was perhaps the spawning of similar careers among his disciples. Bill Sharman* (Boston Celtics star and ABA and NBA coach), "Tex" Winter (Kansas State coach), Alex Hannum* (longtime NBA coach), and other future greats achieved their start by playing and coaching under Barry. His own on-court success as a Trojans basketball mentor also should not be overlooked. Barry's Southern California teams compiled a 17-year 260-130 win-loss record. His overall collegiate record stood at 365-217. Such coaching success came on other fields of play too for the versatile Barry, who piloted the Trojans baseball squad to an NCAA championship in 1948 and also served as an assistant Trojans football coach. Ironically Barry's untimely death came on the eve of a crucial football game between the University of California and Santa Clara University that he was scheduled to scout. Barry's most lasting contribution to basketball was a personal campaign, aided by coaching rival "Nibs" Price of the University of California, that ultimately eliminated center jumps after free throws in 1936 and such jumping after all baskets during the next season. In 1978 he was elected to the Naismith Memorial Basketball Hall of Fame.

BIBLIOGRAPHY: Justin Barry file, Naismith Memorial Basketball Hall of Fame, Springfield, MA; Bill Gutman, *The History of NCAA Basketball* (New York, 1993). Neil D. Isaacs, *All the Moves: A History of College Basketball* (Philadelphia, PA, 1975); Ronald L. Mendell, *Who's Who in Basketball* (New Rochelle, NY, 1973).

Peter C. Bjarkman

BARRY, Richard Francis, III "Rick" (b. March 28, 1944, Elizabeth, NJ), college and professional player and announcer, is the second son of Richard Francis Barry II and Alpha (Stephanovich) Barry. The elder Barry had played semipro basketball and passed on his love of the game to Rick and his older brother, Dennis. Rick's talent for basketball flourished under his father's tutelage, as he became the leading scorer for his team at Roselle High School and was named to the New Jersey All-State team his senior year.

Heavily recruited by at least 25 colleges, the six-foot four and a half inch Barry (he later reached six feet, seven inches) ultimately selected the University of Miami because he knew and respected its basketball coach, Bruce Hale. Barry almost single-handedly turned the University of Miami basketball program around and transformed the Hurricanes into a national collegiate contender. He averaged 32.2 points his junior year (1963–1964) and 37.4 points his senior year (1964–1965), ranking among the nation's top college scorers and being a unanimous All-America pick in 1965. In June 1965 he graduated with a Bachelor's degree in marketing and married Pamela Hale, daughter of his college coach. They have four sons, Richard Francis IV, Jon Alan, Brent, and Drew and an adopted daughter. Jon, Brent, and Drew have played professional basketball. Barry and his wife divorced in 1979. He married Pamela Stenson in 1980 and had little contact with his children.

Barry was drafted by the San Francisco Warriors (NBA) during the first round of the NBA's 1965 draft and signed a three-year contract. Barry's first season with the Warriors proved spectacular, as he scored 2,059 points, averaged 25.7 points, and was easily selected as the NBA's Rookie of the Year in 1966. His 1966–1967 season was even better. He won the NBA's scoring title with 2,775 points (35.6 points per game), led San Francisco to the NBA championship finals (which the Warriors eventually lost to the Philadelphia 76ers), and was selected MVP in that season's All-Star Game, scoring 38 points.

Although happy with San Francisco and with one year left on his original contract, Barry signed a five-year contract with the Oakland Oaks of the newly formed ABA in 1967. Oakland gave him an annual $75,000 salary, 15 percent ownership of the team, and a five percent cut of all gate receipts over $600,000. Barry's ex-father-in-law and ex-coach, Bruce Hale, worked as general manager of the Oaks and may have influenced his decision to jump teams. In any case, his decision did not work out too well. The Warriors won a court judgment against him and prevented him from playing any pro basketball during the 1967–1968 season. On resuming his career with the Oaks in 1968–1969, however, he quickly demonstrated that his forced layoff had not diminished his abilities. Although playing in only 35 games because of a knee injury, he averaged 34 points (the highest percentage in the new ABA) and helped the Oaks into the ABA championship playoffs.

The next season saw Barry in legal trouble again. The Oakland franchise was purchased by Earl Foreman, who moved the Oaks to Washington, D.C. and renamed them the Capitals. Barry, however, refused to move and signed a new five-year contract with the Warriors (NBA) so he could stay in the San Francisco Bay area.

Court injunctions again interfered with his plans, forcing him to live up to his prior contract with Oakland/Washington. He played for the Capitals during the 1969–1970 season, averaging 27.7 points in 52 games and pacing the ABA with a .864 free throw percentage. He again led his team into the playoffs and averaged a phenomenal 40.1 points in seven games. In 1970 the Capitals moved southward and became the Virginia Squires. Barry, weary of this nomadic franchise, forced the Squires to trade him because he insulted Virginians in an interview with *SI*. Foreman traded him to the New York Nets (ABA) in exchange for $200,000 and a future first-round draft pick. He played in New York for two seasons, averaging 29.4 points in 1970–1971 and 31.5 points in 1971–1972. Although continually harassed by knee problems, he still made the ABA All-Star team and led the ABA in free throw percentages both years.

Barry left New York in 1972 and returned to the NBA by signing a six-year contract with the Golden State Warriors. During this six-season stint with Golden State, he averaged 23.9 points. Barry also led the NBA in steals in 1975 and, as usual, in free throw percentages in 1973, 1975, 1976, and 1978. He also was named NBA Playoff MVP in 1975, the year the Warriors won the NBA championship. Although growing older and suffering knee problems, Barry signed in 1978 with the Houston Rockets (NBA) as a veteran free agent for $500,000 a year. His points-per-game averaged dropped during his two seasons with the Rockets (13.5 in 1978–1979 and 12.0 in 1979–1980), as he became visibly slower on the court. But he salvaged his career by becoming a specialist at the newly implemented three-point field goal, achieving a .330 shooting percentage during the 1979–1980 season. He retired in 1980 with a lifetime 27.8 points scoring average. In 1,020 games he made 9,695 field goals (including 176 three-pointers) and 5,713 free throws for 25,279 total points. He also holds the NBA record for the most free throws made in one quarter (14 against New York on December 6, 1966).

After divorcing his second wife, Barry married Lynn November in August 1991; they had one son. Rick's autobiography, *Confessions of a Basketball Gypsy: The Rick Barry Story*, was published in 1972. Barry was elected to the Naismith Memorial Basketball Hall of Fame in 1987. In 1996, he was named one of the 50 Greatest Players in NBA history. No other player led the NCAA, ABA, and NBA in season's scoring average. After working as a WTBS cable television basketball analyst, he joined KNBC Radio in San Francisco in August 2001. Barry coached Fort Wayne (CBA) to a 25-46 mark from 1992 to 1994, New Jersey (USBL) to a 37-18 mark, and Florida (USBL) to a 16-14 mark in 1998–1999. New Jersey finished 23-6 in 1998–1999 and won the USBL Championship.

BIBLIOGRAPHY: Rick Barry with Bill Libby, *Confessions of a Basketball Gypsy: The Rick Barry Story* (Englewood Cliffs, NJ, 1972); Rick Barry file, Naismith Memorial Basketball Hall of Fame, Springfield, MA; "Rick Barry," *CB* (1971), pp. 25–27; George Diaz, "Barry Shoots from the Lip," *Orlando* (FL) *Sentinel*, June 18, 2000; *Los Angeles Times*, December 11, 1984; Bruce Newman, "Daddy Dearest," *SI* 75 (December 2, (1991); *NYT*, February 12, 1980; August 4, 1983; Alex Sachare, *One Hundred Greatest Basketball Players of All Time* (New York, 1997); Bruce Schoenfield, "Hoop is Thicker than Water," *NYT Magazine*, March 3, 1996; Ken Shouler et al., *Total Basketball* (Wilmington, DE, 2003); *TSN Official NBA Register, 2004–2005* (St. Louis, MO, 2004).

Christopher E. Guthrie

BARTOW, Gene B. "Clean Gene" (b. August 18, 1930, Browning, MO), college coach and administrator, is nicknamed "Clean Gene" because the devout Methodist does not smoke, drink, or swear. Authorities considered Bartow one of the game's best public relations men because of his sincerity and devotion. Bartow graduated from Browning High School, earned a Bachelor's degree from Northeast Missouri State University in 1953, and received a Master's degree from Washington University in St. Louis. Bartow, whom married Ruth Huffine of Galt, Missouri, and has three children, coached the Shelbina and St. Charles (Missouri) High School basketball squads to a 145-39 win-loss mark in six seasons. His 1957 St. Charles team won the state championship, defeating North Kansas City in the Class L finals.

Bartow began his collegiate basketball

coaching career at Central Missouri State University, a school that Forrest C. "Phog" Allen* had coached. After spending the 1961–1964 seasons at Central Missouri, he coached Valparaiso University (ICC) from 1964 to 1970 and led the Crusaders to 93 wins and three NCAA Tournament appearances. Bartow's emergence into the national limelight came in 1970, when he moved to Memphis State University (MVC). Bartow inherited a 6-20 team and coached the Tigers to an 18-8 record his first season. Memphis State reached the finals of the 1973 NCAA Tournament, as the NABC named Bartow national Coach of the Year. Bartow compiled an 82-32 record at Memphis State from 1970 to 1974. The University of Illinois (BTC) appointed Bartow coach for the 1974–1975 season, and struggled to an 8-18 mark. Bartow succeeded the legendary John Wooden* at UCLA, guiding the Bruins from 1975 to 1977 to 52 wins, 9 losses, two PEC titles, and an NCAA Final Four appearance in 1976. NBA teams drafted four of his UCLA players in the first round.

Bartow joined the University of Alabama-Birmingham (SBC) in 1977 and started its basketball program as coach and athletic director. He led the Blazers to national prominence by developing some remarkably successful teams. His Alabama-Birmingham basketball squad averaged 20 wins per season over its 18-year history and has qualified for postseason tournaments 10 times, appearing in the NIT in 1980, 1989, 1991, 1992, and 1993 and the NCAA Tournament from 1981 through 1987 and in 1994. University of Alabama-Birmingham (UAB) never experienced a losing season, winning 366 games altogether. Bartow's 34-year overall win-loss record stands at 647-353. From 1981 through 1987, only the University of Kentucky (SEC), University of North Carolina (ACC), and Georgetown University (BEaC) equaled Alabama's string of seven consecutive NCAA Tournament appearances. During his career, his teams averaged 19 wins per season. Several of his assistant coaches—including Lee Hunt, Larry Finch, Tony Yates, Larry Farmer, Tom Smith, and John Prince—became head coaches.

Bartow also coached numerous international amateur teams. These included the Puerto Rican national team in the 1971 and 1987 Pan American Games and in the 1972 Summer Olympic Games in Munich, Germany. Bartow also took teams to the People's Republic of China in 1973 and 1979. He serves as special adviser for the Memphis Grizzlies (NBA).

BIBLIOGRAPHY: Gene Bartow file, Central Missouri State University Archives, Warrensburg, MO; "Coaching, Friendship and Ties That Bind Hunt, Bartow," *Kansas City* (MO) *Times*, January 2, 1988; Mike Douchant, *Encyclopedia of College Basketball* (Detroit, MI, 1995); *Los Angeles* (CA) *Times*, 1975–1977; *NCAA Men's Basketball Records, 2004* (Indianapolis, IN, 2003); *UAB Basketball 1995–1996 Media Guide* (Birmingham, AL, 1995); *UCLA Basketball Media Guide, 1975–1977* (Los Angeles, CA, 1974–1976).

Arthur F. McClure

BASLOE, Frank J. (b. September 24, 1887, Budapest, Hungary; d. December 12, 1966, Herkimer, NY), sports promoter, was the son of Josef Basloe (originally Breslau), a Hungarian immigrant who operated a candy and grocery store in Herkimer, New York. Basloe attended the Herkimer school through sixth grade and embarked on his promoting career at age 16 in 1903. His basketball team consisted of Basloe, Lew Wachter, and Jimmy Williamson, who later starred for the Troy (New York) Trojans, and two Herkimer teenagers, who each received $5 a game. Basloe netted $300 on his first nine-game tour of upper New York state, soon becoming one of the most prominent managers and promoters in early professional basketball.

Over the next 10 seasons, Basloe's teams toured New York and New England annually, mostly as the 31st Separate Company (National Guard) of Herkimer. His team also captured the MoVL Championship both years in which the league operated.

In 1911 his club snapped the 111-game winning streak of the Buffalo Germans, the most famous team in professional basketball's infancy. Basloe's basketball horizons expanded to the Midwest in 1914. Basloe toured the East and Midwest each year through the 1922–1923 season, with the exception of the 1917–1918 World War I era. His teams, playing variously as the Oswego (New York) Indians and Basloe's Globe Trotters, regularly visited the Great Lakes and upper Great Plains states. Basloe's teams compiled 1,324 victories and 127 defeats and traveled nearly 95,000 miles over 19 seasons. Until the advent of the New York Original Celtics, New York Renaissance, and Harlem Globetrotters in the 1920s, his clubs reigned supreme among barnstormers.

Basloe also played semiprofessional baseball, promoted marathon runs, prize fights, and motorcycle racing, and spent one year with a comedy troupe in vaudeville. After retiring from basketball, Basloe owned a real estate business and became one of Herkimer's leading citizens.

BIBLIOGRAPHY: Frank J. Basloe, with D. Gordon Rohman, *I Grew Up With Basketball* (New York, 1952); Frank Basloe file, Naismith Memorial Basketball Hall of Fame, Springfield, MA; Sheldon Basloe, interview with Robert W. Peterson, October 6, 1987; Peter C. Bjarkman, *The Biographical History of Basketball* (Chicago, IL, 2000); Jerry Levin, interview with Robert W. Peterson, October 6, 1987; Robert W. Peterson, *Cages to Jump Shots: Pro Basketball's Early Years* (New York, 1990); Robert W. Peterson, interviews with Sheldon Basloe and Jerry Levin, October 6, 1987; Ken Shouler et al., *Total Basketball* (Wilmington, DE, 2003); Alexander Weyand, *The Cavalcade of Basketball* (New York, 1960).

Robert W. Peterson

BATTIER, Shane Courtney (b. September 9, 1978, Birmingham, MI), college and professional player, is the middle of five children of Ed Battier, a trucking executive, and Sandee Battier, a secretary. The six-foot eight-inch, 220-pound forward excelled as a student and basketball player at Country Day High School in Birmingham. He was named to the 1997 McDonald's and *Parade* All-America teams and was selected Naismith and McDonald's National High School Player of the Year.

Battier attended Duke University from 1997 to 2001. He gained a reputation in basketball as a defensive specialist in the 1998 and 1999 seasons and was named national defensive Player of the Year in 1999, 2000 and 2001, sharing the 2000 honor with the University of Cincinnati's Kenyon Martin*. Battier expanded his game in 2000, averaging 17.4 points and 5.6 rebounds. He was selected All-ACC and Second-Team AP All-America that season.

Battier enjoyed an outstanding senior season in 2001 and averaged 19.9 points and 7.3 rebounds, leading Duke to the NCAA title. He was voted MVP of the Final Four, made All-ACC, and shared the ACC Player of the Year Award with Joseph Forte of the University of North Carolina. Battier won the Wooden and Naismith awards and was selected national Player of the Year by the AP and the USBWA. He ended his Duke career with 1,984 points and 887 rebounds in 146 games and played in 131 victories, an NCAA record. Duke retired his number 31.

Battier, a versatile player, could score, rebound, and block shots. Duke coach Mike Krzyzewski* called him "a born leader, the pillar of the team." A superb student, Battier was named Academic All-America in 2000 and 2001. He graduated with a Bachelor's degree in religion and chaired the NCAA Student Athlete Council as a senior.

The Vancouver/Memphis Grizzlies (NBA) made Battier the sixth pick of the 2001 draft. Battier averaged 14.4 points and 5.4 rebounds in 2001–2002, making the NBA All-Rookie team. He averaged 9.7 points on a 4.4 rebounds in 2002–2003, 8.5 points and 3.8 rebounds in 2003–2004, and 9.9 points and 5.2 rebounds in 2004–2005. The San Antonio Spurs swept the Grizzlies in the first round of the playoffs in 2004, as Battier tallied 19 points (4.8 point average) in limited action. Through 2004–2005, he has scored 3,342 points and corraled 1,479 rebounds in 315 games. He averaged 7.3 points and 6.8 rebounds in four games in the first round playoff sweep by the Phoenix Suns.

BIBLIOGRAPHY: Tim Crothers, "The Players' Player," *SI*, 93 (November 20, 2000), pp. 90–94; Seth Davis, "Fight to the Finish," *SI* 94 (March 12, 2001), pp. 54–56; *Duke University Basketball Media Guides*, 1998, 1999, 2000, 2001, (Durham, NC, 1998–2001); Mike Krzyzewski, with Donald T. Phillips, *Five-Point Play. Duke's Journey to the 2001 National Championship* (New York, 2001); *TSN Official NBA Register, 2004–2005* (St. Louis, MO, 2004).

Jim L. Sumner

BAYLOR, Elgin Gay (b. September 16, 1934, Washington, DC), college and professional player, is the third son of John Baylor and Uzzel

Baylor. He grew up in the poor Southwest section. Because public playgrounds were closed to blacks, Baylor did not play basketball until age 14. Although inexperienced, Baylor played on the Phelps Vocational High School basketball team and made the All-City squad. He left school for a year to serve as a checker in a furniture store. At his mother's insistence, Baylor entered Springarn High School and soon established a D.C. scoring record of 68 points. Besides being the first black named to the metropolitan area All-Star team, he was selected a high school All-American.

Because of his poor academic record, major colleges and universities avoided Baylor. He obtained a scholarship to the College of Idaho, where he played both football and basketball. There he played with the silky smooth determination and pride that would be his trademark in the NBA. After his first year, however, Idaho deemphasized sports. Seattle car dealer Ralph Malone interested Baylor in Seattle University, where Baylor played for Malone's amateur team while waiting out his one year to meet eligibility requirements. During his first season, Baylor catapulted Seattle into national prominence in 1956–1957 by finishing third in national scoring and leading the nation in rebounding. Seattle compiled a 22-3 record, with Baylor making the All-West Coast All-Star Team. In the 1957–1958 season, Baylor averaged 31.5 points and grabbed 590 rebounds. He was the nation's second leading scorer and finished third in rebounding. In the NCAA finals, Baylor scored 25 points in a 84-72 loss to the University of Kentucky.

Although having another year of college eligibility, Baylor signed a contract with the Minneapolis Lakers (NBA) to help revive that franchise. If Baylor had declined the offer, Minneapolis owner Bob Short remarked, "I'd have gone out of business. The club would have gone bankrupt." He enjoyed a spectacular NBA rookie season, averaging 24.9 points and becoming only the third rookie to make the All-NBA Team. Baylor brought an artistic style to the NBA. He possessed tremendous body control, seemingly suspending himself in midair while switching direction for a better shot. Spectators praised Baylor as "poetry in motion" and "the man with a thousand moves." An awesome offensive force, Baylor possessed an outstanding medium-range jumper and superb driving ability. Although only six-feet five-inches tall and 225 pounds, he jumped well and scored many baskets on rebounds.

After the Lakers' franchise moved to Los Angeles, Baylor and Jerry West* became the best offensive tandem in NBA history. During his NBA career, Baylor scored 23,149 points in 846 games for a 27.4 points-per-game average. In 1960 he scored 71 points, becoming the first NBA player to break the 70-point barrier. Baylor made the All-NBA First Team ten times and played in 22 All-Star games. He led the Lakers in career rebounds with 11,463. Plagued by knee injuries, Baylor retired early in the 1971–1972 season. Ironically the Lakers that year won the NBA championship, an achievement Baylor never made in his distinguished NBA years. Baylor, selected to the NBA Silver Anniversary Team in 1971, was considered the greatest forward as an active NBA player. Baylor, who coached the New Orleans Jazz (NBA) to an 86-134 record from 1976–1977 through 1978–1979, was elected to the Naismith Memorial Basketball Hall of Fame in 1977. Since 1986, he has served as executive vice president and general manager of the Los Angeles Clippers (NBA). He was named to the NBA 35th Anniversary All-Time Team in 1980 and one of the 50 Greatest Players in NBA History in 1996.

BIBLIOGRAPHY: Elgin Baylor file, Naismith Memorial Basketball Hall of Fame, Springfield, MA; Frank Deford, "A Tiger Who Can Beat Anything," *SI* 25 (October 24, 1966), pp. 40–48; Merv Harris, *The Fabulous Lakers* (New York, 1972); Zander Hollander, ed., *The Modern Encyclopedia of Basketball* (Garden City, NY, 1979); Jon Hubbard, ed., *The Official NBA Encyclopedia*, 3rd ed. (New York, 2000); Leonard Koppett, *Championship NBA: Official 25th Anniversary* (New York, 1970); Leonard Koppett, *24 Seconds to Shoot: An Informal History of the NBA* (New York, 1968); Roland Lazenby, *The Lakers: A Basketball Journey* (New York, 1993); John D. McCallum, *College Basketball U.S.A. Since 1892* (Briarcliff Manor, NY, 1978); Phil Pepe, *Greatest Stars of the NBA* (Englewood Cliffs, NJ, 1970).

Lawrence E. Ziewacz

BEARD, Alana Monique (b. May 14, 1982, Shreveport, LA), college and professional player, is the daughter of LeRoy Beard and Marie Beard and graduated in 2000 from Southwood High School, where she led her basketball team to a 144-6 record and four consecutive state titles. The five-foot eleven-inch, 160-pound guard tallied 2,646 points (17.6 average), 948 rebounds (6.3 average), 513 steals (3.4 average), and 434 assists (2.9 average). A *USAT* and *Parade* Second Team All-America as a senior, Beard concluded her interscholastic career with 53 straight victories.

Coach Gail Goestenkors recruited Beard to play basketball at Duke University. Beard set a Duke career scoring record with 2,687 points (19.7 average), made 789 rebounds (5.8 average), 509 assists (3.7 average), and 404 steals (3.0 average), and compiled a .527 field goal percentage in 136 games. She became the first NCAA basketball player to attain over 2,600 points, 500 assists, and 400 steals. Besides recording 16 double-doubles, she helped Duke capture four ACC regular season and tournament championships and reach the NCAA Final Four twice.

Beard notched Duke freshman records with 509 points and 113 assists for the season and 33 points against the University of Maryland. She earned USBWA, *SIW*, *SI*, CBS Sportsline, and *WBJ* National Freshman of the Year honors, became the first freshman ever selected to the All-ACC First Team, and won ACC Freshman of the Year accolades. In 2001–2002, Beard averaged 19.8 points and 3.3 steals and led the ACC in scoring, field goal percentage, and steals. She set a Duke record with at least 20 points in eight consecutive games and helped Duke reach the NCAA Final Four. An AP, USBWA, and Kodak First Team All-America, she was named *ESPN The Magazine* Shooting Guard of the Year, and finished second for AP Player of the Year.

As a junior, Beard set Duke single-season records for points (813), field goals (294), and free throws (201). She averaged 22.0 points, 6.9 rebounds, 3.0 assists, and 2.8 steals, leading the ACC in scoring and finishing second in steals. Beard broke the Duke scoring record in January with 41 points against the University of Virginia, collected a career-best 20 rebounds in the ACC tournament championship game against the University of North Carolina, and helped Duke to a second consecutive NCAA Final Four appearance. The Victor Award winner, she was named ACC Female Athlete of the Year and repeated as an AP, USBWA, and Kodak All-America.

Beard averaged 19.7 points, 5.4 rebounds, 3.9 assists, and 2.4 steals and paced the ACC in scoring as co-captain in 2003–2004. Duke finished with a 30-4 mark, attained the number one ranking in the season's final AP poll for the first time in school history, and came within one game of the NCAA Final Four. Beard, a consensus AP, USBWA, and Kodak All-America, earned AP Player of the Year honors and garnered the Wade Trophy and first Wooden Award.

Beard's storied collegiate career included All-ACC First Team honors four years and ACC Player of the Year, Defensive Player of the Year, and All-Tournament Team recognition in 2002, 2003, and 2004. She became the first Duke's women's basketball player to have her uniform number 20 retired.

The Washington Mystics (WNBA) selected Beard as the second overall pick of the 2004 WNBA draft. She finished third in the WNBA with 69 steals in 2004, recording 437 points (13.1 point average), 143 rebounds (4.2 average), and 91 assists (2.7 average) in 34 games. She led the Mystics in scoring (16.7 point average) in the WNBA playoffs, but Washington was eliminated in the first round.

BIBLIOGRAPHY: http://goduke.collegesports.com; http://www.wbca.org; http://www.wnba.com/draft2004/prospectahnaboard.html; http://www.woodenaward.com; http://boards.espn.go.com.legi/espn/request.d11?messae & room-wnbabld-199430.

David L. Porter

BEARD, Ralph Milton, Jr. (b. December 1, 1927, Hardinsburg, KY), college and professional player, is the son of Ralph Beard Sr., a professional golfer and hardware store operator, and Pauline (Sheeran) Beard. Ralph Jr. moved with his family to Louisville, Kenturky, at age 14. His half-brother, Frank, excelled as a professional golfer. A two-time All-State basketball performer and team captain, he scored 509 points as a senior to help Male High School capture the 1946 state championship.

At the University of Kentucky from 1946 to 1949, the five-foot eleven-inch, 175-pound Beard made All-SEC for four years and All-America for three years in basketball as a ball-hawking, sharpshooting guard. The Wildcats' "Fabulous Five" also included Kenny Rollins, Wallace Jones, Alex Groza*, and Cliff Barker. At Kentucky, Beard scored 1,517 career points in 139 games and averaged 10.9 points. Coach Adolph Rupp* guided the Wildcats to 130 victories and only 10 losses in Beard's four seasons. Kentucky sparkled as SEC Champions for all four campaigns, NIT Champions and runners-up in 1946 and 1947, and NCAA National Champions in 1948 and 1949. The "Fabulous Five" participated on the U.S. basketball team that won gold medals at the 1948 London Summer Olympic Games. Madison Square Garden named Beard its MVP for college basketball for the 1948–1949 season. He was selected to the All-1940s NCAA Tournament Team.

In 1949, Beard, Groza, Jones, and Barker joined Joe Holland to form the Indianapolis Olympians (NBA), marking the first time that five players from one school had made up a professional unit and the first time that players themselves owned a team. In two NBA seasons, Beard scored 2,006 points in 126 regular-season games and averaged 15.9 points. Beard, who also averaged 16.5 points in 8 playoff games, made the All-NBA Second Team in 1949–1950 and the All-NBA First Team in 1950–1951.

In October 1951 Beard, Groza, Dale Barnstable, James Line, and Walter Hirsch of the University of Kentucky as well as 26 other players were indicted for their role in a gambling scandal. They were found guilty of controlling the margin of victory, "shaving points" in numerous college games. The court gave the 31 players suspended sentences and placed them on indefinite suspension. However, NBA Commissioner Maurice Podoloff* banned them for life because of their college gambling activities. Beard, a top amateur golfer, became a sales manager for a wholesale drug company.

BIBLIOGRAPHY: Mike Douchant, *Encyclopedia of College Basketball* (Detroit, MI, 1995); V.A. Jackson, *Beyond the Baron* (Kuttawa, KY, 1998); *Kentucky Basketball Encyclopedia* (Champaign, IL, 2000); Ronald L. Mendell, *Who Who's in Basketball* (New Rochelle, NY, 1973); David S. Neft and Richard N. Cohen, eds., *The Sports Encyclopedia: Pro Basketball, 1991–1992*, 5th ed. (New York, 1992); Bert Nelli, *The Winning Tradition: A History of Kentucky Wildcat Basketball* (Lexington, KY, 1984); Russell Rice, *Kentucky Basketball's Big Blue Machine* (Huntsville, AL, 1976); Alan Ross, *Wildcat Wisdom* (Nashville, TN, 1999); Ken Shouler et al., *Total Basketball* (Wilmington, DE, 2003); Frank Waldman, ed., *Famous Athletes of Today*, 11th series (Boston, MA, 1949), pp. 19–40.

John L. Evers

BEATY, Zelmo "Big Z" (b. October 25, 1939, Hillister, TX), college and professional player, was a six-foot nine-inch, 235-pound center who played professionally in both the NBA and ABA. He deserves more recognition as an effective, efficient player than he has received. Beaty studied at Prairie View (Texas) Agricultural and Mechanical (A&M), where his overall basketball record merited his selection to the NAIA Hall of Fame. He led Prairie View to the NAIA championship in 1962.

Drafted by the St. Louis (later Atlanta) Hawks in the NBA draft, Beaty played there in a quiet, distinguished way from 1962–1963 until 1968–1969 and averaged over 20 points in three seasons. In 1966, he ranked among the top ten in points, rebounds, and field goal percentage. He sat out the next season as his option year before joining the Utah Stars (ABA) in 1970 and quickly became one of the ABA's top players. His versatility as a pivotman is underscored by his record in two pro leagues. In the NBA, he compiled 570 games played, a .469 percent floor shooting average, a .750 free throw percentage, 5,949 rebounds, 9,107 points, and 16 points per game. In the ABA, he recorded 319 games played, a .540 percent floor shooting average, an .810 free throw percentage, 3,716 rebounds, and 6,098 points for a 19.1 points-per-game average.

Beaty's best year in the ABA came in 1972, when he scored 63 points in a game against the Pittsburgh Condors and finished eleventh in scoring (23.6 point average), sixth in rebounding (13.2 average), fourth in field goal percentage (.542), and sixth in free throw average (82.9). Beaty returned to the NBA in 1974 with the Los Angeles Lakers (NBA), who had acquired the rights to him. He retired after the 1974 season, being respected more by the players he performed against than acknowledged by the fans who saw him play. He averaged over 20 points five seasons and tallied more than 15,000 combined ABA-NBA points.

BIBLIOGRAPHY: Terry Pluto, *Loose Balls* (New York, 1990); Jan Hubbard, ed., *The Official NBA Encyclopedia*, 3rd ed. (New York, 2000); Ronald L. Mendell, *Who's Who in Basketball* (New Rochelle, NY, 1973); *TSN ABA Official Guide, 1974–1975* (St. Louis, MO, 1974); *TSN Official NBA Register, 1987–1988* (St. Louis, MO, 1987).

Gustavo N. Agrait

BECKMAN, John (b. October 22, 1895, New York, NY; d. June 22, 1968, Miami, FL), professional player, was one of the first true stars in the earliest days of basketball and was elected as a player to the Naismith Memorial Basketball Hall of Fame in 1972. He was the son of August Bechmann and Katherine Bechmann, who immigrated to the U.S. in the 1880s, Americanized their name, and settled on Manhattan's West Side. Although best known as a member of the Original Celtics (a New York-based team despite its name), Beckman began playing as a 15-year-old student for St. Gabriel's Catholic School in Manhattan in 1910.

Beckman did not attend college, but apparently next saw organized action with the Opals of the Hudson County League in 1910 and with Kingston New York (NYSL) in the 1914–1915 season. In 20 of the team's 22 games, Beckman recorded 46 field goals and 39 free throws. Statistics were kept haphazardly, with no percentages existing for either field goals or free throws. His 131 points made him tenth in NYSL scoring. His 6.6 points-per-game average was considerable in those low-scoring days. The next year (1915–1916), Beckman played for De Neri of Philadelphia in the EL, formerly known as the PBL. He played in 34 of the team's 40 games, making 88 field goals and 74 of 133 from the free throw line. With 250 points and a 7.4 points-per-game average, he finished third in the EL. In 1916–1917 he moved to Reading (EL) and scored 238 points in 38 games with 92 field goals and 54 of 94 from the free throw line. With 6.3 points per game, he ranked ninth in the EL.

The EL suspended operations because of World War I early in the 1917–1918 season. At the time, Beckman had rejoined De Neri and led the EL with 74 points in 8 games. Beckman spent the 1919–1920 and 1920–1921 seasons with Nanticoke (PSL). He was the PSL's top scorer both years, recording 101 field goals, a 9.0 points-per-game average, and 144 of 175 free throws for 346 points in 1919–1920, and 84 field goals and 193 free throws for 361 points and a 9.1 average the next season. His play impressed Jim Furey*, a New York promoter who had purchased that city's Celtics franchise, which had been dormant since World War I. Furey settled for the name Original Celtics when the previous owner would not give up the name. Furey's first team was good in 1920, but not dominant. In 1921 he acquired veteran Swede Grimstead and newcomers Beckman and Henry "Dutch" Dehnert*. They joined a nucleus of John Whitty, Pete Barry, Ernie Reich*, Joe Trippe, Eddie White, and Mike Smolick.

Beckman was considered the best free throw shooter of the era. His son, Edwin J. Beckman, recalls the early days in New York's first Madison Square Garden. There were no backboards, the court was surrounded by wire to keep the ball in play, and a shot or free throw attempt that missed the rim remained in play. "My father grew up in a rough, tough part of New York, and he loved to play basketball," Beckman said. "In that first Madison Square Garden, they put the basketball floor over a swimming pool, and the boards would come loose, causing the ball to bounce the wrong way. When they built the second Madison Square Garden, with a cement floor, the hockey surface was under the court, and sometimes ice would ooze up through the boards while a basketball game was still going on."

Beckman, listed as either five feet eight inches or an inch taller and 156 pounds, played forward. Before joining the ABL in its inaugural year, the Original Celtics barnstormed throughout the east and won 204 of 215 games one year. In the 1927–1928 season, they finished 109-11. Consequently the Original Celtics were removed from the ABL because they were too strong for the rest of the competition. Nat Holman*, a teammate and another of the game's early stars, called Beckman the greatest player he had ever known and "a tough guy who doubled as trainer, doctor, holler guy, fighter and team quarterback." Another early great, Ed Wachter* of the Troy (NY) Trojans, who often played the Original Celtics, listed Beckman on his all-time pro basketball team covering the half century from the game's founding to the early 1940s. The Original Celtics barnstormed after leaving the ABL before disbanding for good in 1941, when Beckman was nearly 46.

Beckman declined numerous coaching offers, moving from Paramus, New Jersey to Miami, Florida in 1957 to join his son and his family. On September 14, 1959, he, Dehnert, Barry, Holman, and Joe Lapchick* were inducted as a team into the Naismith Memorial Basketball Hall of Fame. For several years, Beckman served as athletic director for the Sunland Training Center, a faculty for retarded children. Beckman's wife died several years before him. He was survived by his son, Edwin, who competed in basketball, football, and boxing. One grandson, Edwin J. Beckman, played for the Kansas City Chiefs (NFL) football team for eight years and was an assistant coach for the team. Much of Beckman's basketball equipment and many of his uniforms are displayed at the Naismith Memorial Hall of Fame.

BIBLIOGRAPHY: John Beckman file, Naismith Memorial Basketball Hall of Fame, Springfield, MA; Jay Berman, interview with Edwin J. Beckman, June 15, 1987; Zander Hollander, ed., *The NBA's Official Encyclopedia of Pro Basketball* (New York, 1981); *Los Angeles Times*, June 23, 1968; Frank Menke, *Encyclopedia of Sports*, 2nd ed. (New York, 1972); William G. Mokray, *Encyclopedia of Basketball* (New York, 1963); Murry Nelson, *The Originals: The New York Celtics Invent Modern Basketball* (Bowling Green, OH, 1999).

Jay Berman

BEE, Clair Francis (b. March 2, 1896, Grafton, WV; d. May 20, 1983, Cleveland, OH), college player and coach, made college basketball in the 1930s and 1940s one of the nation's central sports attractions. He pioneered strategy and rule changes that permanently affected the game. Educated at Waynesburg (Pennsylvania) College, Ohio State University, Rider College and Rutgers University (both in New Jersey), Bee participated in basketball, baseball, and football. He combined coaching with collegiate administration and extensive publication of instructional and fictional material, including the well-known Chip Hilton sports stories for young people.

Bee suffered from tuberculosis as a youngster. His mother died from tuberculosis when he was six. He started playing basketball by age ten and studied at Massanutten Military Academy in Woodstock, Virginia. Bee spent part of his boyhood in Parkersburg and Grafton, West Virginia, and on his uncle's farm in Belleville, Kansas. Bee left high school in West Virginia for World War I service in Europe. After playing semipro football in Ohio, he enrolled at Waynesburg College in 1922. As a student manager–athlete there, he typically became involved in school administration and served as registrar at the time of his graduation in 1925. He moved to Rider College as chairman of the Accounting Department and a year later became basketball, football, and baseball coach. Bee guided his basketball squads to a 55-7 win-loss mark and his football teams to a 17-7-1 record during three seasons.

Because of his success at Rider, Bee was hired in 1931 to coach at Long Island University, then a minimal institution barely five years old. In his 20 years there (with time off for World War II service), he made Long Island University an athletic power. His squads compiled 357 wins and 79 losses in basketball, the best winning percentage for any coach in the sport. (He tried briefly and unsuccessfully to build a big-time football program, scheduling the school at Ebbets Field in Brooklyn.) His Blackbird basketball squads scored several notable achievements. From 1934 to 1936, Long Island University won 43 consecutive games. Stanford and Hank Luisetti* broke the streak in December 1936. The Blackbirds finished undefeated in 1935–1936 (25-0) and 1938–1939 (23-0) and won the NIT in 1939 and 1941. His players included luminaries of college basketball in the 1930s and 1940s such as Dick Holub, "Dolly" King, Sy Lobello, Ossie Schectman, Irv Torgoff, Danny Kaplowitz, and Julie Bender.

Bee's coaching career ended in the early 1950s, when Long Island University and other national powers like the University of Kentucky and CCNY were involved in point-shaving scandals that rocked the sports world. The deeply hurt Bee resigned. Although briefly coaching the Baltimore Bullets of the new NBA and serving as athletic director of New York Military Academy (1954–1967), Bee maintained his most vital ties with the sports world through his coaching clinics and camps. His protégés and admirers have included Frank McGuire* and Bobby Knight*, who have joined Bee's contemporaries Joe Lapchick*, Nat Holman*, and Howard Cann* in considering him a central figure in basketball development. The popular 1-3-1 zone defense and the three-second rule generally are credited to Bee.

Seton Hall and Rochester Royals (NBA) star Bob Davies* served as the model for Bee's Chip Hilton sports novels in the tradition of the All-America Boy. (Bee's NIT champions of 1941 gained the title by stopping Seton Hall's 42-game winning streak and holding Davies to four points.) Bee, who considered Davies the ideal athletic type, wrote stories that are collector's items in sports memorabilia. Elected in 1967 to the Naismith Memorial Basketball Hall of Fame, Bee contributed an introduction to Naismith's only book on his invention. Bee was blind during his last years and died at 87 of cardiac arrest, being survived by one son and one daughter.

BIBLIOGRAPHY: Clair Bee file, Naismith Memorial Basketball Hall of Fame, Springfield, MA; Peter C. Bjarkman, *Hoopla: A Century of College Basketball, 1896–1996* (Indianapolis, IN, 1996); Sandy Padwe, *Basketball's Hall of Fame* (New York, 1973); *NCAA Men's Basketball Records, 2004* (Indianapolis, IN, 2003); Mike Douchant, *Encyclopedia of College Basketball* (Detroit, MI, 1995); Zander Hollander, ed., *The Modern Encyclopedia of Basketball* (Garden City, NY, 1979); Long Island University Bureau of Sports Information, courtesy of Robert E. Gesslein, Brooklyn, NY.

Leonard H. Frey

BELLAMY, Walter Jones "Bells" (b. July 24, 1939, New Bern, NC), college and professional player, was a towering six-foot eleven-inch, 245-pound center. He graduated from J. T. Barber High School in New Bern, where he starred in basketball, and twice was selected as All-America during a remarkable college hoop career at Indiana University ending in 1961. With the Hoosiers, Bellamy established school marks for lifetime field goal percentage (.517) and single-game rebounds (33). During the summer of 1960, he played on the gold medal–winning U.S. Olympic team, considered by many the greatest amateur basketball squad ever assembled. That team included Oscar Robertson*, Jerry West*, Terry Dischinger*, Bob Boozer, Jerry Lucas*, and centers Bellamy and Darrall Imhoff. After acquiring an Olympic Gold Medal in Rome, Italy, Bellamy spent 14 seasons in the NBA. He was drafted originally on the first round by the now-defunct Chicago Packers (NBA) and was an immediate success in the pro-style game. Bellamy averaged 31.6 points in 1961–1962 for his best-ever scoring season, winning coveted Rookie of the Year honors. Between 1966 and 1972, Bellamy's NBA career included stints with the Baltimore Bullets, New York Knicks, Detroit Pistons, and Atlanta Hawks. His NBA career ended with the New Orleans Jazz (NBA) in 1974–1975. He played in four NBA All-Star contests during that span, concluding his long career as the second all-time NBA leader in field goal accuracy behind the fabled Wilt Chamberlain*. Bellamy, whose final NBA career statistics were 20.1 points per game and 13.7 rebounds per game, amassed 20,941 career points. He played 38,940 career minutes and played a record 88 regular-season games in 1968–1969, when traded from New York to Detroit. Considered a somewhat erratic player at times throughout his career, Bellamy always seemed to save top performances for the NBA's other star centers. Settling in Atlanta after his playing days, Bellamy served as a Georgia delegate to the 1984 Democratic National Convention. The quiet, somewhat eccentric Bellamy was nicknamed "Bells" around the NBA for his habit of talking continuously to himself (whom he addressed as "Bells") and to his opponents during the course of on-court action. In 1993, he was elected to the Naismith Memorial Basketball Hall of Fame.

BIBLIOGRAPHY: Walt Bellamy file, Naismith Memorial Basketball Hall of Fame, Springfield, MA; Bob Hammel et al., *Glory of Old IU* (Champaign, IL,

2000); Jan Hubbard, ed., *The Official NBA Encyclopedia*, 3rd ed. (New York, 2000); Neil D. Isaacs, *All the Moves: A History of College Basketball* (Philadelphia, PA, 1975); Ronald L. Mendell, *Who's Who in Basketball* (New Rochelle, NY, 1973); *TSN Official NBA Register, 2004–2005* (St. Louis, MO, 2004); Ronald L. Thomas, *Walt Bellamy: The Saturnine Star* (Indianapolis, IN, 1985); Arthur Triche, *From Sweet Lou to 'Nique; Twenty-Five Years with the Atlanta Hawks* (Atlanta, GA, 1992).

Peter C. Bjarkman

BENNETT, T. Wesley "Wes" (b. March 31, 1913, Nashville, TN), college player and coach, starred in the mid-1930s for Westminster College of New Wilmington, Pennsylvania, attracted national attention in the first collegiate basketball doubleheader at Madison Square Garden in New York in 1934 and earned HAF College Player of the Year honors in 1935.

Bennett, the son of Talmadge Bennett and May Bennett, moved at age five with his family to Akron, Ohio, and played on an undefeated football team for Akron Fast High School. Akron East inflicted the last defeat on coach Paul Brown's Massillon High School football team before it embarked on a five-year winning streak. Bennett lettered three years on the Akron East basketball team, which lost a state championship game by only two points.

Authorities considered the Westminster College star the nation's premier pivot man in the years when center jumps followed every score. A two-time All-America, Bennett twice led the nation's scorers. In the opening game of the pioneer Madison Square Garden doubleheader on December 29, 1934, he tallied 22 points to help Westminster upset St. Johns University, 37-33. Bennett was named the outstanding collegiate player to appear at Madison Square Garden for the 1934–1935 campaign. After tallying a then remarkable 1,168 career points over three seasons, he graduated with a Bachelor's degree from Westminster College in 1936. Bennett played one season with Akron Firestone Tire and Rubber Company and two campaigns with Akron Goodyear Company in national industrial AAU competition.

In January 1942, Bennett enlisted in the U.S. Marines Corps and participated in South Pacific assaults at Guadalcanal and Cape Gloucester. In 1945 he became the first basketball coach at the new Camp Lejeune, North Carolina Marine base, guiding his team to 21 victories in 25 games. He completed his World War II service as a captain and worked 32 years through 1978 for a welding equipment supply firm in Santa Ana, California. He resides at Solvang, California, with his wife, Janet, and has one son. The HAF Basketball Hall of Fame enshrined him.

BIBLIOGRAPHY: T. Wesley Bennett, letter to Robert B. Van Atta, November 5, 1989; Dan Irwin, Westminster College, letter to Robert B. Van Atta, October 1989; Neil D. Isaacs, *All the Moves—A History of College Basketball* (New York, 1984); Zander Hollander, ed., *The Modern Encyclopedia of Basketball* (New York, 1973); John D. McCallum, *College Basketball U.S.A.* (Briarcliff Manor, NY, 1978); Frank G. Menke, ed., *The Encyclopedia of Sports*, 5th rev. ed. (Cranbury, NJ, 1975); Westminster College Communications Department, Sports Information files, New Wilmington, PA.

Robert B. Van Atta

BENSON, Michael Kent (b. December 27, 1954, New Castle, IN), college and professional player, starred in basketball at Chrysler High in New Castle, where he was named All-City three years. All-NCC and All-State twice as a center, and Mr. Basketball in 1973. Benson led by example and set school career rebound records on New Castle teams that won three sectional, one regional, and one semistate title. His other activities included being president of the Letterman's Club and participation in the FCA. A pleasant, dedicated player, he paced scorers on the 1973 Junior Olympic Team.

The six-foot ten-inch, 240-pound Benson started a record 102 consecutive games at center for Coach Bob Knight's* Indiana University basketball teams from 1973–1974 through 1976–1977. Indiana won two BTC titles and finished the 1975–1976 undefeated; the Hoosiers captured the NCAA championship that season, as Benson was named MVP of the Final Four and co-MVP of the Mid-East Regional. His honors included being selected All-BTC three times, All-America twice, and 1974 College Commissioners' Tournament MVP. Benson finished his career as the Hoosier's second ranking scorer

(1,740 points) and rebounder (1,031). A wrist injury prevented him from trying out for the 1976 U.S. Olympic basketball squad. With football players Archie Griffin of Ohio State University (BTC) and Steve Davis of the University of Oklahoma (BEC), Benson shared national FCA 1976 Athlete of the Year accolades. Scott May* of Indiana University shared the HAF 1976 Player of the Year Award with Benson, the former being the first junior to earn that honor. Benson also made the All-America Academic Team in 1975–1976 and 1976–1977, and was selected to the All-1970s NCAA Tournament Team.

The Milwaukee Bucks (NBA) selected Benson in the first round of the 1977 draft. Benson was traded to the Detroit Pistons (NBA) in February 1980, the Utah Jazz (NBA) in August 1986, and the Cleveland Cavaliers (NBA) in October 1987 and later played in Europe. He scored 6,168 career points in 680 NBA games, averaged 9.1 points, and made 3,881 rebounds. His honors included the Branch Rickey Award in 1980 and 1981 and the 1982 PBWAA Walter Kennedy Citizenship Award. In 1989 Benson was named to the "Dream Team," comprising the best high school players in Indiana history. He married Monica Sutton on June 24, 1978, and has three daughters.

BIBLIOGRAPHY: Peter C. Bjarkman, *The Biographical History of Basketball* (Chicago, IL, 2000); Morgan G. Brenner, *College Basketball's National Championships* (Lanham, MD, 1999); Mike Douchant, *Encyclopedia of College Basketball* (Detroit, MI, 1995); Joe Gergen, *The Final Four* (St. Louis, MO, 1987); Bob Hammel et al., *Glory of Old IU* (Champaign, IL, 2000); Tim Hosey and Bob Percival, *Bobby Knight: Countdown to Victory* (New York, 1983); Jan Hubbard, ed., *The Official NBA Encyclopedia*, 3rd ed. (New York, 2000); Ray Marquette, *Indiana University Basketball, 1976: The Perfect Season* (Bloomington, IN, 1976); *TSN Official NBA Register, 1986–1987* (St. Louis, MO, 1986).

Thomas P. Wolf

BERENSON, Senda. *See* Abbott, Senda Berenson

BIAS, Leonard Kevin "Len" (b. November 18, 1963, Hyattsville, MD; d. June 19, 1986, Landover, MD), college player, starred in basketball for the University of Maryland Terrapins and saw his professional career cut short by a cocaine-induced heart attack.

Bias, the son of James Bias and Lonice Bias, grew up in the Washington, D.C. area with his younger brother, Jay. Although cut from his junior high school basketball team, he developed a passion for basketball while playing under coach Bob Wagner at Northwestern High School. Wagner admired Bias's work ethic and assisted his high school star in considering over 150 collegiate offers. Bias finally selected the nearby University of Maryland over ACC rival North Carolina State University.

During his four year tenure at Maryland from 1982 to 1986, Bias averaged 16.4 points and 5.7 rebounds. In his senior year, he made consensus All-America, with a scoring average of over 23 points. Although Maryland did not win a national championship, the Terrapins appeared in the NCAA tournament in each of Bias's four seasons there. In nine NCAA tournament games, the six-foot eight-inch, 210-pound forward averaged 18.7 points and 7.4 rebounds.

During the summer of his junior year, Bias worked at a summer camp with Red Auerbach*, the president and general manager of the Boston Celtics (NBA). Auerbach advised the Maryland star to improve his game by completing his four year college eligibility. Bias followed Auerbach's suggestion and stayed in school, but did not complete his Bachelor's degree in general studies.

Auerbach's relationship with Bias culminated in the Boston Celtics making the Maryland player the second overall pick in the 1986 NBA draft. On June 17, 1986, Bias was drafted and introduced to the media in New York City's Felt Forum. The following day, he and his agent negotiated an endorsement package with Reebok. On the evening of June 18, Bias left his parents' home for his dormitory room. At the university, he partied with several friends. When Bias suffered a seizure in the early morning hours of June 19, paramedics were summoned to the university. He was pronounced dead at Leland Memorial Hospital. An autopsy revealed that his death was due to heart failure induced by cocaine usage.

Family and friends insisted that Bias was not a frequent drug user, but the investigation into his death led to coach Lefty Dreisell's* resignation at Maryland and a trial, in which Bias's friend, Brian Tribble, was acquitted for supplying the deadly drugs. As Celtics star Larry Bird* reflected, Bias's premature death was "the cruelest thing ever."

BIBLIOGRAPHY: Lewis Cole, *Never Too Young to Die: The Death of Len Bias* (New York, 1989); Jack McCallum, "The Cruelest Thing Ever," *SI* 65 (June 30, 1986), pp. 20–24; Ira Berkow, "Death of a Young Star," *NYT*, June 21, 1986, pp. 47–48; Mike Douchant, *Encyclopedia of College Basketball* (Detroit, MI, 1995); Paul McMullen, *Maryland Basketball* (Baltimore, MD, 2002).

Ron Briley

BIASONE, Daniel "Danny" (b. February 22, 1909, Miglianico of Abruzzoi, Italy; d. May 5, 1992, Syracuse, NY), professional owner, was the son of Leo Biasone and Bambina Biasone and immigrated to the United States with his mother and brothers in 1920 to reunite with his father, who had arrived several years earlier. He graduated from Blodgett Vocational High School in Syracuse, New York in 1928. Biasone owned and operated a bowling alley, the Eastwood Recreation Center in Syracuse, beginning in 1941. Following World War II, he established a semipro basketball team. His team joined the NBL as the Syracuse Nationals for the $1,000 entry fee and began NBL play for the 1946–1947 season.

In 1949 the NBL merged with the BAA to form the NBA. Biasone's Nationals were the top draw in the NBA in the early years, averaging over 5,000 fans per game. Syracuse fielded a terrific team, led by Dolph Schayes*, Paul Seymour*, and Johnny Kerr*, and played in the NBA Finals in 1950 and 1954, losing to the Minneapolis Lakers on both occasions. The Nationals later added George Yardley* to their talented roster.

Following the 1954 season, Biasone pushed through a rule change that created the 24-second shot clock. This revolutionary change speeded up play and perhaps saved the NBA. He settled on 24 seconds, dividing the number of seconds in a 48 minute game (2,880) by the average number of shots taken in a game by both teams (around 120). In 1955, NBA teams averaged 14 more points than the previous year. Syracuse also won its only NBA championship that year, defeating the Fort Wayne Pistons in seven games. The 1955 Nationals were also the first NBA champions to feature black players: Earl Lloyd* and Jim Tucker. In 1963 Biasone sold the Nationals to a group that moved the franchise to Philadelphia as the 76ers.

Biasone and his wife, Rachel, were married for nearly 50 years and had no children. A true NBA pioneer, he was given the Naismith Memorial Basketball Hall of Fame's John Bunn Award in 1982 and was enshrined into the Naismith Memorial Basketball Hall of Fame as a contributor posthumously in 2000.

BIBLIOGRAPHY: Peter C. Bjarkman, *The Biographical History of Basketball* (Chicago, IL, 2000); Gene Brown, ed., *The Complete Book of Basketball* (New York, 1980); Zander Hollander, ed., *The Pro Basketball Encyclopedia* (Los Angeles, CA, 1977); Nell D. Isaacs, *Vintage NBA* (Silver Spring, MD, 1996); Terry Pluto, *Tall Tales* (New York, 1992); Ken Shouler et al., *Total Basketball* (Wilmington, DE, 2003); *Syracuse Post-Standard*, May 19, 1992; *Syracuse Post Standard*, March 14, 1996.

Curtice R. Mang

BING, David "Dave" (b. November 24, 1943, Washington, DC), college and professional player, starred in the NBA for 12 seasons (1967–1978) and led the NBA in 1968 in scoring with 2,142 points (27.1 points average) for the Detroit Pistons. He starred nine seasons with Detroit, where he was a four-time team scoring leader. Bing, a 1966 first-round draft choice, easily won the 1967 NBA Rookie of the Year Award by scoring 1,600 points for a 20.0 points-per-game average. Bing was named in 1968 and 1971 to the All-NBA First Team and in 1974 to the All-NBA Second Team. Between 1968 and 1976, he participated in seven NBA All-Star Games and in 1976 was named MVP of the annual spectacle. Bing's 54 points against the Chicago Bulls paced the NBA in scoring in 1971 for a single game. Besides ranking consistently among NBA assist leaders, he amassed 18,327 career points, averaged 20.3 points, and tallied an additional 477 points in 31 playoff games over five years. In 1977, he won the J. Walter Kennedy Citizenship Award.

Bing is the son of Hasker Bing, a brick layer, and Juanita Bing. As a child Bing suffered a severe eye injury that required surgery. It originally was feared that he would lose the use of the eye, but he fully recovered. He starred in basketball and baseball at Spingarn High School in Washington, D.C., where he graduated in 1962. The six-foot three-inch, 185-pound Bing was recruited for basketball by Syracuse University and set several Orangemen records during his three-year (1964–1966) varsity career. He broke the sophomore scoring record with 556 points and the single-season scoring record as a senior with 794 points (28.4 points average). He compiled 1,883 career points to exceed the existing school record by over 400 points. A skilled playmaker, Bing led 17-8 Syracuse to the 1964 NIT. The Orangemen suffered a 77-68 first-round NIT loss to New York University. The season performance marked a dramatic turnaround, however, as Syracuse had dropped 27 consecutive games two years earlier. Bing averaged 23.2 points as a junior and received some All-America mention, including a First Team pick by *TSN*. He finished the 1966 senior season as the fifth-leading scorer in the nation and a consensus All-America. Bing led the 22-6 Syracuse team to the NCAA East Regional Tournament finals, where the Orangemen lost 91-81 to Duke University.

Bing married his high school sweetheart, Avis, at age 19, while at Syracuse, and worked as a part-time custodian to support the family. They had three daughters, but later divorced. He took great interest in developing the basketball skills of young boys and held a basketball clinic in Syracuse. After turning pro, Bing observed: "The pros are much tougher on defense, and it's harder to get around them. Once you do, there is the big man standing there waiting for you. Even the easy shots are much harder." A detached retina in 1972 threatened to end his NBA playing career. The next season, however, he rebounded with 1,840 points and a 22.4 points average. Bing in August 1975 was traded to the Washington Bullets (NBA), garnering 1,326 points and 678 points the next two seasons. He was waived by the Bullets in September 1977 and signed as a free agent with the Boston Celtics (NBA). He retired following the 1978 season after producing 1,088 points in 80 games. Playing with noncontenders most of his career, Bing stated: "I didn't get much fanfare my rookie year, and in most of the other years we didn't win. I felt I did a creditable job and that's enough for me." Bing opened basketball camps for boys in Thomasville, Michigan and the Pocono Mountain area of Pennsylvania. Bing formed Bing Steel Company, finishing steel parts for automobiles and was named National Minority Small Businessman of the Year in 1984. Bing Steel rose to $61 million in sales by 1990. He expanded his empire by 2000 to include nine corporations, netting $7 million in profits with $300 million in sales. He serves on Standard Federal Bank's board of directors. In 1990, he was elected to the Naismith Memorial Basketball Hall of Fame. He in 1996 was named one of the 50 Greatest Players in NBA history.

BIBLIOGRAPHY: Dave Bing file, Naismith Memorial Basketball Hall of Fame, Springfield, MA; Jan Hubbard, ed., *The Official NBA Encyclopedia*, 3rd ed. (New York, 2000); Thomas Kellner, "Rebound Man," *Forbes* (September 18, 2000); *The Lincoln Library of Sports Champions*, vol. 2 (Columbus, OH, 1974); Ronald C. Modra, "Life Lessons from a Man of Steel," *SI* 75 (August 19, 1991); Bob Snyder, ed., *Syracuse Basketball* (Champaign, IL, 2000); *TSN Official NBA Register, 2004–2005* (St. Louis, MO, 2004).

James D. Whalen

BIRD, Larry Joe (b. December 7, 1956, French Lick, IN), college and professional coach, and executive player, is the son of Joe Bird, a furniture finisher, and Georgia Bird, who were divorced when Larry was a child. His mother took care of Larry and his four brothers and sister while working as a restaurant cook and a dietary supervisor for a local nursing home. Bird attended Spring Valley High School, where he played guard as a six-foot sophomore and junior before growing four inches. His senior year he emerged as a forward with a 30.6 points and 20 rebounds average. Bird experienced difficulty adjusting to college at Indiana University for under a month in 1974. He transferred to Northwood Institute, a small junior college in West Baden, Indiana. After only two months, Bird left Northwood to work for the French Lick

City Department as a garbage collector and road and park worker. He married Janet Condra in November 1975, but they divorced. He later married Dinah Mattingly.

Bird accepted a scholarship to Indiana State University, where he sat out the 1975–1976 season in order to regain his eligibility. In his first season at Indiana State, he averaged 32.8 points and led his team to a 25-3 record. In 1977–1978 Bird averaged 30 points, as Indiana State finished at 23-9 and reached the quarterfinals of the NIT. Although drafted by the Boston Celtics (NBA) in the first round in 1978, he decided to finish his education and play his senior year at Indiana State. During his final year, Bird led his team to an undefeated regular-season record and number-one ranking in the polls. He averaged 14.9 rebounds, scored 975 points, and finished second nationally with 28.6 points per game. Besides making All-America for the second consecutive year, Bird was selected College Player of the Year by the AP, UPI, and the NABC. He led Indiana State to the NCAA final game before losing to Michigan State.

On graduation Bird signed a five-year contract with the Boston Celtics (NBA) for a reported $3.25 million, making him the highest-paid rookie in NBA history. His rookie year (1979–1980) performance more than justified his salary, as he averaged 21.3 points and 10.4 rebounds to lead a previously losing Celtics team to a 61-21 record. Bird was selected NBA Rookie of the Year and finished third in the MVP vote. The Celtics lost in the playoffs, but won the NBA championship in 1980–1981 by defeating the Houston Rockets. Bird averaged 21.2 points and 10.9 rebounds and led all forwards with 5.5 assists per game. In 1981–1982 he again helped the Celtics to the playoffs, but was limited by a fractured cheekbone. The Celtics lost that year to the Philadelphia 76ers. During 1983–1984, Bird once more led the Celtics to the NBA championship over the Los Angeles Lakers and was chosen the NBA's MVP.

Bird repeated as NBA MVP in pacing the Celtics to the 1984–1985 Eastern Conference title and scored a career high 2,295 points and 28.7 points per game. The Los Angeles Lakers dethroned the Celtics in the 1985 NBA championship series. Bird averaged 25.8 points in leading the Celtics to the 1985–1986 NBA championship over the Houston Rockets, was selected NBA MVP for the third consecutive time, became the first basketball player awarded *TSN* Man of the Year, and was chosen AP Male Athlete of the Year. In March 1985 Bird set a club record by tallying 60 points in a game against the Atlanta Hawks. In 1986–1987 he averaged 28.1 points in helping the Celtics capture the Eastern Conference title. Boston, however, lost the NBA championship to the Lakers. The following season, he ranked third in scoring and averaged 29.9 points. Bird, who finished second in the MVP voting, enjoyed two outstanding individual performances with 24 points in the first quarter of Game 1 and 20 points in the final quarter of Game 7 of the Eastern Conference semifinals against the Atlanta Hawks. The Detroit Pistons, however, eliminated the Celtics in the Eastern Conference Finals. After missing nearly all of the 1988–1989 season, he averaged 24.3 points in 1989–1990 and retired after the 1991–1992 season. Bird was named to the All-NBA First Team nine consecutive years, from 1980 through 1988, and the All-NBA Second Team in 1990, and was chosen NBA Playoff MVP in 1984 and 1986. He held the NBA playoff record for most points (632) in one year (1984), led the NBA in all-time three-point field goals (455) and dominated the 3-point field goal competition at the annual NBA All-Star games. He led the NBA in free throw percentage in 1983–1984, 1985–1986, and 1986–1987, holds the NBA career playoff record for most defensive rebounds (1,323), leads the Celtics in all-time steals (1,556) and made the All-Star team each of his first nine and his last three NBA seasons. During 13 NBA seasons, Bird tallied 8,591 field goals and 3,960 free throws for 21,791 points (24.3 points average), made 8,974 rebounds, and 5,695 assists in 897 games.

Bird played on the gold medal–winning U.S. Olympic team in 1992 and served as special assistant for the Boston Celtics from 1993 to 1997. He was named one of the 50 Greatest Players in NBA history in 1996 and was elected to the Naismith Memorial Basketball Hall of Fame in 1998. Bird coached the Indiana Pacers (NBA) from 1997 to 2000, being named NBA

Coach of the Year in 1998. Indiana finished in second place in the Central Division with a 58-24 record in 1997–1998 and reached the Eastern Conference Finals before losing to the Chicago Bulls. The Pacers won the Central Division with a 33-17 mark in 1998–1999 and again made the Eastern Conference Finals, being eliminated by the New York Knicks. Indiana repeated as Central Division Champions with a 56-26 mark in 1999–2000 and lost to the Los Angeles Lakers, 4 games to 2, in the NBA Finals. In three NBA seasons as head coach before resigning, Bird compiled a 147-67 regular-season record and 32-20 playoff record. He has served as president of Basketball Operations for Indiana since July 2003. The Pacers reached the Eastern Conference Finals in 2004 and the second round of the NBA playoffs in 2005.

BIBLIOGRAPHY: Larry Bird with Bob Ryan, *Drive: The Story of My Life* (New York, 1989); Larry Bird file, Naismith Memorial Basketball Hall of Fame, Springfield, MA; Peter C. Bjarkman, *The Boston Celtics Encyclopedia* (Champaign, IL, 1998); Frederick L. Corn, *Basketball's Magnificent Bird: The Larry Bird Story* (New York, 1982); "Larry Bird," *CB* (1982), pp. 34–37; Zander Hollander, ed., *The Modern Encyclopedia of Basketball* (Garden City, NY, 1979); Jan Hubbard, ed., *The Official NBA Encyclopedia* (New York, 2000); Roland Lazenby, *The NBA Finals* (Indianapolis, IN, 1996); Lee Daniel Levine, *The Making of an American Sports Legend* (New York, 1988); *TSN Official NBA Register, 2004–2005* (St. Louis, MO, 2004); Bruce Weber, *Magic Johnson Larry Bird* (New York, 1986).

Stephen D. Bodayla

BIRD, Suzanne Brigit "Sue" (b. October 16, 1980, Syosset, NY), college and professional player, is the daughter of Herschel Bird, a retired doctor, and Nancy Bird, a high school nurse. A natural athlete the charming, charismatic Bird excelled at soccer, tennis, track and field, and especially basketball. After her youth team played during half-time of a St. John's University women's game, a stunned security guard asked Bird to sign her first autograph. Although Bird was just 11 years old, the guard was convinced she was headed for fame.

At Christ the King High School in Queens from 1994 through 1998, Bird continued to shine both on and off the court. She made the honor roll, belonged to the National Honor Society, and lettered in soccer, track and field, and basketball. As point guard, Bird helped lead her high school team to two New York state championships. She also earned various individual awards, including being 1997–1998 New York State Tournament MVP, 1997 AAU All-America, and 1998 Player of the Year.

The heavily recruited five-foot nine-inch, 150 pound Bird signed with the University of Connecticut's Huskies, coached by Geno Auriemma*, and played basketball there from 1998–1999 through 2001–2002. After only playing eight games in her freshman campaign, she tore her ACL in practice and was benched for the rest of the season. Upon fully recovering Bird returned to the game with a renewed intensity. She became Connecticut's three point (45.9 percent) and free throw leader (89.2 percent). By graduation, Bird ranked eighteenth on the Huskies' all-time scoring list with 1,378 career points, second in assists (585), and seventh in steals (243). Diana Taurasi* was the only other Connecticut player who generated over 1,000 points, 500 assists, and 200 steals in a career. Bird proved instrumental in the Huskies national championships in 2000 and 2002. In recognition of her skill and character, Bird received numerous awards, including All-America honors twice, the 2002 Wade Trophy, the 2002 AP and Naismith Player of the Year, the 2002 Honda Award, and the Conseco/Nancy Lieberman-Cline Point Guard of the Year Award three times. She also played on the 2004 gold medal U.S. Olympic women's basketball team.

Bird graduated in 2002 with a Bachelor's degree in Communication Science and became the WNBA's number-one overall draft pick. She immediately impacted the Seattle Storm (WNBA), averaging 14.4 points and six assists in 32 games and leading the WNBA with a .911 free throw percentage. Bird, one of two rookies to make the All-WNBA First Team, finished runner-up for the Rookie of the Year award. Bird repeated on the All-WNBA First Team in 2003, averaging 12.4 points and 6.5 assists. She again earned All-WNBA First Team honors in 2004, finishing second in the WNBA with 184 assists (5.4 average) and fourth in three pointers with a .438 percentage and averaging 12.9 points in 34 games. Bird made 42 assists and 12 steals in 8 WNBA playoff games, helping the Storm win their first WNBA title. Seattle defeated the Connecticut Sun, 2-1, in the WNBA Finals. In three WNBA seasons, she has recorded 1,320 points, 596 assists, and 154 steals in 100 regular season games and 96 points, 56 assists, and 17 steals in 10 playoff games.

BIBLIOGRAPHY: Kelli Anderson, "The Sky's the Limit," *SI* 97 (July 1, 2002), pp.48–51; *TSN Official WNBA Guide and Register, 2004* (St. Louis, MO, 2004); University of Connecticut Huskies page, www.uconnhuskies.com; WNBA website, www.wnba.com.

Lisa A. Ennis

BIRDSONG, Otis Lee (b. December 9, 1955, Winter Haven, FL), college and professional player, sports agent, and sportscaster, enjoyed a happy childhood playing family sports and games. He had three brothers and seven sisters and attended Winter Haven High School in Winter Haven, Florida.

The six-foot four-inch, 200-pound guard attended the University of Houston, where his athleticism and scoring ability made him a crowd favorite with Cougar fans. Birdsong, the first University of Houston sophomore to tally 1,000 career points, set a SWC scoring record with a 30.3 points average. During his collegiate career, he amassed 2,832 points to place him twelfth on the NCAA's all-time scoring list. His stellar play earned him recognition as the SWC Player of the Decade for the 1970s. He made consensus All-America in 1977 and helped the United States win a gold medal at the 1975 Pan American Games.

In 1977 Birdsong was drafted in the first round as the second pick by the Kansas City Kings (NBA). Kansas City traded him in June 1981 to the New Jersey Nets (NBA). He was waived by the Nets in August 1988. In March 1989, the Boston Celtics (NBA) signed him to a 10-day contract. Birdsong was re-signed by Boston in April for the rest of the season. He concluded his playing career with the Tulsa Fast Breakers (CBA) in 1988–1989.

In his four years with Kansas City from 1977 to 1981, Birdsong's scoring average steadily improved from 15.8 points his rookie year to 24.6 points in 1980–1981. The 1983–1984, 1984–1985, and 1985–1986 seasons were his best ones with New Jersey, as he scored 1,365, 1,155, and 1,214 points respectively. Birdsong in 1986 suffered a serious leg injury that limited his 1986–1987 season to just seven games. In 696 regular season NBA games, he tallied 12,544 points (18.0 point average), 2,072 rebounds (3.0 average), and 2,260 assists (3.2 average). He averaged 15.6 points in 35 playoff games.

Birdsong participated in four NBA All-Star Games in 1979, 1980, 1981, and 1984. He made *TSN* All-America team in 1977 and the All-NBA Second Team in 1981. The University of Houston honored Birdsong in January 1997 by retiring his number 10 uniform.

Birdsong co-founded Promotions International with Roger Staubach, the celebrated Dallas Cowboys quarterback. PI markets and promotes athletes and celebrities. Birdsong has worked Houston Cougar basketball radio broadcasts and serves as a color announcer for CUSA. In 2000, he and Jo Jo White* sponsored a children's fantasy camp in Philadelphia, Pennsylvania. In association with the Cooper Aerobic Institute in Dallas, Texas, Birdsong has operated basketball camps. He and his wife, Candace, have two sons, Sidney and Sean.

BIBLIOGRAPHY: Bob Rosen, materials supplied by Elias Sports Bureau, New York, NY, May 28, 2003; Rick Poulter, Sports Information, University of Houston, Houston, TX, May 28, 2003; Ken Shouler et al., *Total Basketball* (Wilmington, DE, 2003); *TSN Official Basketball Register, 1988–1989* (St. Louis, MO, 1988).

Scott A.G.M. Crawford

BLACKMAN, Rolando Antonio "Ro" (b. February 26, 1959, Panama City, Panama), college and professional player and executive, acquired a reputation as a consummate, if unflashy, professional for the expansion Dallas Mavericks (NBA). At age eight, Blackman and his sister, Angela, left their native Panama in 1967 to live with their grandmother in East Flatbush, Brooklyn, New York. Their parents, John Blackman, a computer programmer for the U.S. government, and Gloria Blackman, followed three years later, but separated soon thereafter. Blackman, who grew up in Brooklyn, preferred soccer, but switched to basketball at the Ditmas neighborhood playground. The switch proved difficult because he was cut from his seventh-, eighth-, and ninth-grade basketball teams at Meyer Levin Junior High School. Blackman was not deterred, however, spending his summers working out at 6 A.M. with the inspirational playground coach, Teddy Gustus, instead of the ever-present Tomahawks and the Jolly Stompers gangs.

For safety reasons, Blackman enrolled in William E. Grady Vocational School on Coney Island, New York. Under coach Fred Moscowitz, he blossomed and prepared for collegiate basketball. Six times a month, he also watched his idols, Earl Monroe*, Walt Frazier*, and Bill Bradley*, play for the New York Knicks (NBA) at the fabled Madison Square Garden in New York.

The heavily recruited six-foot six-inch, 206-pound Blackman spurned big-name schools for Kansas State University (BEC), where he was coached by Jack Hartman, who served as a second father. Blackman became a team leader as a sophomore, earning First-Team All-BEC honors. Three times, he was selected the BEC Defensive Player of the Year. In 1981, *TSN* named him First Team All-America. For 121 college games, he shot .517 percent, scored 1,844 points, and averaged 15.2 points.

Although still a Panamanian citizen in 1980 (he became a U.S. citizen in 1986), Blackman won a spot on the 1980 U.S. Olympic team. President Jimmy Carter, however, barred American teams from competition in the Moscow, Russia Summer Olympic Games in retaliation for the Soviet invasion of Afghanistan.

Blackman, the ninth player selected in the 1981 NBA draft, joined the Dallas Mavericks (NBA). With volatile forward Mark Aguirre* and steady backcourt mate Derek Harper, he quickly became a mainstay of coach Dick Motta's* team. Blackman was named team captain in 1983 and was voted six times Most Popular Maverick by the Dallas fans. The Mavs reached the playoffs six times from 1984 to 1990, as Blackman improved his performance to 21.6 points a game. He was known for both his uncanny ability to sink the clutch shot at the buzzer to win games and his smothering defense against the NBA's best guards. The four-time NBA All-Star (1985–1987, 1990) scored 17.8 points a game.

The Mavericks' team performance declined disastrously in the wake of poor personnel decisions, causing the front office to rebuild for the future. In June 1992, Dallas traded Blackman to the New York Knicks (NBA), where he joined Patrick Ewing* in contending for the NBA championship. But Blackman did not keep John Starks from the starting guard position. The Knicks reached the NBA playoffs in 1993 and the NBA Finals in 1994, losing to the Houston Rockets in seven games. He retired from the NBA following the 1993–1994 season, but played in Greece in 1994–1995 and in Italy in 1995–1996. Blackman held the Mavericks' career records in game starts (781), minutes played (29,684), points (16,643, a 19.2-point scoring average), field goals made (6,487), and free throws made (3,501). During 13 NBA seasons, he tallied 17,623 points (18.0 point average), grabbed 3,278 rebounds, and dished out 2,981 assists in 980 games.

Others laud Blackman for his straight-arrow lifestyle and tireless charitable actions. He and his wife, Tamara, have four children, Valarie, Brittany, Briana, and Vernell. His community activities include Big Brothers and Big Sisters, the Special Olympics, the Muscular Dystrophy Association, and the American Cancer Society. He has also worked to renovate the Ditmas playground on which he grew up. Blackman aspired to become a television news anchorman like his favorite Peter Jennings of ABC News. Consequently, he has taken classes at Columbia School of Journalism, hosted his own weekly radio program in Dallas, Texas, and interned at several television stations. He has served in player development for the Dallas Mavericks since 2000–2001.

BIBLIOGRAPHY: Dan Baldwin, "Honor Guards," *D Magazine* 18 (October 1991), pp. 27–29; Curtis Bunn, "A Ro Model for Starks," *New York Daily News*, February 4, 1994, p. 73; Dallas Mavericks press release, 1994; Cecil Harris, "Rolando Blackman: Living the Dream," *City Sun*, January 17–23, 1990, pp. 39–40; Rafael Hermoso, "Blackman: Mavs' Loss City's Gain," *New York Newsday*,

June 25, 1992, p. 127; Jan Hubbard, ed., *The Official NBA Encyclopedia*, 3rd ed. (New York, 2000); New York Knicks press release, 1994; Ian O'Connor, "The Real Ro," *New York Daily News*, August 23, 1992, pp. 74–75; Bill Reel, "Rolando, the Man," *Brooklyn Sunday Newsday*, August 30, 1992; Steve Serby, "Roland's Return Great for Apple," New York *Post*, June 25, 1992, pp. 46, 67; *TSN Official NBA Register, 2004–2005* (St. Louis, MO, 2004); Mark Zeske, "The Go-To Guy," *Beckett Basketball Monthly* 2 (November 1991), pp. 41–42.

Bruce J. Dierenfield

BLAZEJOWSKI, Carol Ann "Blaze" (b. September 29, 1956, Elizabeth, NJ), college and professional player and executive, is the daughter of Leon Blazejowski and Grace (John) Blazejowski, of Polish ancestry. She grew up in Cranford, New Jersey, where she developed a natural interest in sports. She tried softball first before playing basketball at age 10, primarily competing with and against boys on playground courts. At Cranford High School, she did not play girls' basketball until her senior year in 1974.

Blazejowski attended Montclair State College in Upper Montclair, New Jersey, (1974–1978) and graduated with a B+ average and a Bachelor's degree in physical education. Known initially for her scoring, she averaged 19.6 and 28.5 points in her first two seasons there. Her textbook-perfect jump shot developed partially from watching pro games on television. During her sophomore season, Montclair State made the AIAW tournament and lost there in the consolation finals. Blazejowski led AIAW tournament scorers, setting a single-game scoring mark with 44 points and was selected to the All-Tournament team. From 1976 to 1978, she was also named an All-America. Although considered one of the nation's best shooters, she was only an alternate on the 1976 women's Olympic basketball team in Montreal, Canada.

During her junior and senior years, Blazejowski became the best known player in women's basketball. She led the nation in scoring with averages of 33.5 in 1977 and 38.6 in 1978, finishing her career with a collegiate record 3,199 points. In a game against Queens College in Madison Square Garden in New York, the intense five-foot ten-inch, 150-pound forward set a court record for both men and women with 52 points before a crowd of 12,000 spectators. In 1977 she led scorers in the World University Games and garnered 38 points in a losing effort against the Soviet Union in the title game. Montclair State made the AIAW tournament again in 1978, finishing third. Blazejowski passed 3,000 career points during the tourney and scored 40 and 41 points in her final two games. After the season, she was honored as the first recipient of the Wade Trophy for being the nation's finest player.

In 1978 Blazejowski was drafted in the first round by the New Jersey Gems of the fledgling WBL, but postponed a pro career to pursue the Olympics. For the next two years, Blazejowski competed for the amateur Allentown (Pennsylvania) Crestettes and represented the U.S. on several international teams. In the 1978 and 1979 AAU tournaments, she frequently scored over 40 points in games and led her team to the semifinals both times and a second place finish once. At the eighth World Basketball Championships for women, she led the U.S. to the title by scoring 25 points in the final against Canada, and was the only American named to the All-Tournament team. Blazejowski was selected for the U.S. Olympic team in 1980. The team captured the pre-Olympic qualifying tournament in Varna, Bulgaria, but the U.S. boycott prevented them from competing in Moscow, which greatly disappointed her.

In the fall of 1980, Blazejowski signed a three-year contract with the New Jersey Gems (WBL) for $150,000 and became the WBL's highest-paid player. She averaged 30 points a game in leading her team to the championship playoffs and was named First Team All-Pro. After the WBL subsequently folded, Blazejowski sued the club for $110,000 in backpay and bonuses. She participated in ABC's *Women Superstars* in 1981 and 1982, finishing second once and setting two bowling records. Blazejowski served as a promotional representative for Adidas for ten years. She joined the NBA as Director of Licensing from 1990 to 1995.

When the WNBA was formed in 1996, Blazejowski became Director of Basketball Development. Since 1997, she has served as general manager and vice-president for the New York Liberty (WNBA). The Liberty won Eastern Conference Championships in 1997, 1999, and 2000, but lost three WNBA Finals to the Houston Comets. She was named to the Naismith Memorial Basketball Hall of Fame in 1994 and the Women's Basketball Hall of Fame in 1999 as a charter member. She lives with her partner, Joyce, and their two children.

BIBLIOGRAPHY: Carol Blazejowski file, Naismith Memorial Basketball Hall of Fame, Springfield, MA; Carol Blazejowski, "The Olympic Promise . . ." *Converse Yearbook,* 1980, p. 22; Mike Douchant, *Encyclopedia of College Basketball* (Detroit, MI, 1995); D. D. Eisenberg, "Carol Blazejowski: Pro in an Amateur World," *womenSports* 1 (January 1979), pp. 10–13; Kent Hannon, "No One Is Hotter Than the Blaze," *SI* 46 (January 2, 1977), pp. 35–36; *New York Liberty Media Guide, 2004* (New York, 2004). Maureen Wendelken, "Profile" Carol Blazejowski *Coaching Women's Athletics* (January–February 1979).

Dennis S. Clark

BLOOD, Ernest Artel "Prof" (b. October 4, 1872, Manchester, NH; d. February 5, 1955, New Smyrna Beach, FL), high school and college coach, led YMCA, high school, prep, and college teams to a phenomenal 1,268-165 win-loss record throughout his 51-year career. Blood began playing basketball the year it was invented in 1891, and, from 1895 to 1906, he served as instructor and coached the game at YMCAs in Nashua, New Hampshire, Rutland, Vermont, Somerville, Massachusetts, and Brooklyn, New York. From 1906 to 1915, Blood coached Potsdam State Normal and Training High School (now Potsdam State University) to 72 wins in 74 games. He started the accomplished basketball program that exists there today.

Blood's greatest achievement came during his nine-year tenure, from 1915 to 1924, at Passaic (New Jersey) High School, where he coached the "Wonder Teams" to a 200-1 record and compiled a 159-game winning streak over five and one-half seasons. The victory string, believed the longest in basketball history, began December 17, 1919 and ended February 6, 1925, with Hackensack's 39-35 defeat of Passaic. Nicknamed "Prof," Blood led Passaic through all but the last 12 games of the incredible streak. His Passaic teams won seven State Championships against high school, college, and community opponents. Blood rated the 1921–1922 team, which won 33 consecutive victories and outscored the opposition 2,293-612, as his best squad. Blood, who theorized that the best defense was a powerful or "superlative" offense, allowed his Passaic players (including his sons, Ben and Paul) to use any type of shot with natural body movement. His players used the hook and one-handed shots before other teams attempted these now basic skills.

In 1925 and 1926, Blood coached the basketball squad at the U.S. Military Academy at West Point to an 11-6 record. He joined St. Benedict's Prep School in Newark, New Jersey, as mentor in 1926 and remained there until his retirement in 1949. At St. Benedict's, he compiled an impressive 421-128 mark and produced five state prep school championship teams. Blood also coached the Clarkson College of Technology in Potsdam to a 40-5 record. He was married to Margaret Thomas of England until her death in 1948 and then wed Myrtle Dilley of Michigan. He had three children, Ben, Paul, and Ernestine. On April 26, 1960, he was enshrined into the Naismith Memorial Basketball Hall of Fame as an outstanding coach. Blood was elected in July 1981 to the Potsdam State University Sports Hall of Fame.

BIBLIOGRAPHY: Peter C. Bjarkman, *The Biographical History of Basketball* (Chicago, IL, 2000); Ernest A. Blood file, Naismith Memorial Basketball Hall of Fame, Springfield, MA.

Catherine M. Derrick

BOEHEIM, James Arthur, Jr. (b. November 17, 1944, Lyons, NY), college player and coach, is the son of James Boeheim Sr., a mortician, and Janet Boeheim, and grew up in Lyons, New York, near Syracuse. The six-foot four-inch, 135-pound Boeheim starred at guard on his high school basketball team and declined partial scholarships from Colgate University and Cornell University (IvL) to attend Syracuse University. Although not receiving an athletic scholarship, he played varsity basketball for three years and roomed with star David Bing*. After receiving his Bachelor's degree in history and social science from Syracuse in 1966, Boeheim remained there as a graduate assistant basketball coach and varsity golf coach. He became a full-time assistant basketball coach in 1972 and moved up to head coach in 1976.

Syracuse was not considered a major basketball power, but Boeheim brought it to national prominence. By 2005 he ranked second among active NCAA Division I coaches in winning percentage and twenty-second in all-time Division I wins. Only the legendary Everett Case* of North Carolina State University (ACC) and Dennis Crum* of the University of Louisville (MC) reached 300 wins at an earlier age than Boeheim. Through the 2004–2005 season, Boeheim's perennial NCAA tournament Syracuse teams compiled a 703-win, 241-loss record. In the 1987 NCAA championship game, Syracuse lost by one point to Indiana University. Syracuse defeated the University of Kansas, 81-78, in the 2003 National Championship Game, finishing with a 30-5 record. Syracuse has ranked in the top twenty 17 times under Boeheim.

An aggressive BEaC recruiter, Boeheim has brought Sherman Douglas, Derrick Coleman*, Billy Owens, Earl Washington, Greece's Ronnie Seikaly, Carmelo Anthony* and other recognized stars to Syracuse. Syracuse won Big East Conference titles in 1980 and 1991, and shared titles in 1986, 1987, 1990, 1998, 2000, and 2003. Boeheim's up-tempo, high-scoring basketball style has placed Syracuse near the top in team points scored annually and also has attracted record crowds to the University's Carrier Dome. Syracuse led the NCAA in on-campus basketball attendance from 1985 to 1988, averaging almost 29,000 spectators per game in 1988 and setting a single-game record of 32,602 in a game against Georgetown University in 1987.

Boeheim, who is animated on the sideline during a game, has allegedly been distant and aloof with his players. His friends, however, consider him a mild-mannered, straightforward coach with great pride. The Naismith Memorial Basketball Hall of Fame enshrined him in 2005. He and his wife, Elaine, have one daughter, Elizabeth.

BIBLIOGRAPHY: Jim Boeheim, interview with Daniel R. Gilbert, May 29, 1990; Mike Douchant, *Encyclopedia of College Basketball* (Detroit, MI, 1995); *NCAA Men's Basketball Records, 2004* (Indianapolis, IN, 2003); Roy S. Johnson, "Final 4 Coaches Clash in Style," *NYT*, March 27, 1987, p. D23; William F. Reed, "Winning Numbers," *SI* 70 (January 9, 1989), p. 107; William C. Rhoden, "His Record of Success Is Sure, But Boeheim Is Still a Mystery," *NYT*, March 7, 1988, pp. C1, C6; Bob Snyder, ed., *Syracuse Basketball* (Champaign, IL, 1999); George Vecsey, "Let's Change the Subject," *NYT*, April 1, 1987, p. A28.

Daniel R. Gilbert

BOONE, Ronald Bruce "Ron" (b. September 6, 1946, Oklahoma City, OK), college and professional player and sportscaster, is the son of Herman Boone and Olivia (Wilson) Boone. After starring in several sports at Omaha Tech, Boone played basketball one year at Iowa Western CC before transferring to Idaho State University (BSkC), where he averaged 20 points and was twice named All-BSkC. Drafted in 1968 by the Phoenix Suns (NBA) in the eleventh round (one hundred and forty-seventh pick overall) and the Dallas Chaparrals (ABA) in the eighth round, Boone progressed from a long shot to an All-Star during eight ABA and five NBA seasons.

The six-foot two-inch, 200-pound guard, named to the 1969 ABA All-Rookie Team after averaging 18.9 points with the Chaparrals, was traded in January 1971 to the Utah Stars (ABA). Boone enjoyed his finest professional seasons with the Stars, sparking Utah to an ABA championship in 1971 and four consecutive Western Division titles from 1971 to 1974. Besides being elected to the ABA All-Star team four times (1971, 1974–1976), he was named All-ABA Second Team in 1974 and All-ABA First Team in 1975. When Utah folded in December 1975, Boone was sold to the St. Louis Spirits (ABA). Kansas City (NBA) selected him in the August 1976 dispersal draft following the demise of the ABA. Boone promptly led the Kings in scoring with a 22.2-point average. After playing in 1978–1979 with the Los Angeles Lakers (NBA), he was traded to the Utah Jazz (NBA) in October 1979 and ended his career there in 1981.

Boone, an unselfish, all-around player, ranked either first or second on his team nine times in assists and six times in scoring during his first 10 seasons and led Kansas City in both categories in 1977–1978. Over a 13-year career, he averaged 3.7 assists and 4.2 rebounds and scored in double figures in 11 seasons. Boone finished with 17,437 points for a 16.8 average (18.4 in the ABA and 13.9 in the NBA). A career .837 free throw shooter, the remarkably durable performer never missed a game in 13 seasons and held the professional basketball record for the most consecutive games played with 1,041 (662, ABA; 379, NBA).

Boone, who serves as the color commentator for Utah Jazz radio and television broadcasts and cohost of a radio sports talk show in Salt Lake City, Utah, married Jacqueline Cotton in 1971 and has two children. His son, Jaron, entered the University of Nebraska (BEC) on a basketball scholarship.

BIBLIOGRAPHY: Ronald Boone, interview with Larry R. Gerlach, December 7, 1993; Jan Hubbard, ed., *The Official NBA Encyclopedia*, 3rd ed. (New York, 2000); David S. Neft and Richard M. Cohen, *The Sports Encyclopedia: Pro Basketball*, 5th ed. (New York, 1992); Martin Taragano, *Basketball Biographies: . . . 1891–1990* (Jefferson, NC, 1991); *TSN Official NBA Register, 2004–2005* (St. Louis, MO, 2004).

Larry R. Gerlach

BORGMANN, Bernard "Benny" (b. November 21, 1899, Haledon, NJ; d. November 11, 1978, Hawthorne, NJ), professional basketball and baseball player, coach, and manager, is best known as one of the Original Celtics and as a member of the Naismith Memorial Basketball Hall of Fame. Ironically he spent more time in baseball as a player, coach, scout and manager. Borgmann lived in New Jersey his entire life. He graduated from Clifton High School (New Jersey) in 1917 and immediately excelled as a shooting forward for several local basketball clubs. In 1921 he joined the Kingston Colonels (NYSL) and averaged 10.8 points at a time when most clubs scored only 20 to 25 points a game. In 1922–1923 the five-foot eight-inch, 170-pound star led the NYSL in field goals, free throws, total points, and scoring average (nearly 12 points per game).

Borgmann also signed a baseball contract in 1923 and performed in the Boston Red Sox (AL) organization's farm system until 1931, with the understanding that he would not have to report for spring training until the basketball season had concluded. His dual career undoubtedly cost the smooth shortstop a chance at playing in the majors. During those early days of pro basketball, players often performed for more than one team. Accordingly, Borgmann appeared with Kingston and the Paterson Legionnaires of the MeL in 1923–1924. In 1924 his Kingston team won the world title from the Original Celtics. His final season with Kingston and the Legionnaires came in 1925–1926. The next season, he joined the Fort Wayne Hoosiers of the ABL. Borgmann led the league in points average with 11.2 and finished second in total points. The next year, he paced the Hoosiers to first place in their division and ranked third in scoring. In 1928–1929 he led the ABL in free throws, total points, and scoring average. Borgmann played with Paterson in 1929–1930, leading the league in scoring. When Paterson disbanded in midseason, he signed with the Chicago Bruins. The Bruins were owned by George Halas, better known for his pioneering work in pro football.

Borgmann played basketball well into his thirties with the Brooklyn Americans and the Newark Mules, and closed his pro career with New Britain, Connecticut, in 1936–1937. At age 38, he led the ABL in scoring. His baseball career continued as well. He joined the St. Louis Cardinals (NL) organization in 1932 as a player and remained in management until 1964 with that club. Borgmann took a defense related job with an aircraft firm during World War II and coached another Paterson team from 1945–1946 through 1947. He coached at St. Michael's College in Winooski, Vermont (1948–1949) and at Muhlenberg College in Allentown, Pennsylvania (1950–1956).

Although he is remembered as a member of the Original Celtics, Borgmann spent a limited career with them. Rules governing pro basketball were lax in those days, with Borgmann actually playing only for part of one season (1926–1927). Still, when he was named to the Naismith Memorial Hall of Fame, it was both as a member of that team and on his own as a player (1961).

Borgmann estimated that he had played 3,000 basketball games and 2,000 baseball games. He did not retire from baseball until 1974 as a regional scout for the Oakland A's (AL). He had spent more than 50 years in pro sports. His wife, Lillian Stockinger, married Borgmann in 1920. Borgmann spent his retirement years with the New Jersey's Old Timers Athletic Association, which organizes youth programs in baseball, football, soccer, and basketball.

BIBLIOGRAPHY: Bernard Borgmann file, Naismith Memorial Basketball Hall of Fame, Springfield, MA; Zander Hollander, ed., *NBA Official Encyclopedia of Pro Basketball* (New York, 1981); Murry R. Nelson, *The Originals: The New York Celtics Invent Modern Basketball* (Bowling Green, OH, 1999); Sandy Padwe, *Basketball's Hall of Fame* (New York, 1970); Robert W. Peterson, *Cages to Jump Shots in Basketball's Early Years* (New York, 1990).

Jay Berman and Wayne Patterson

BORYLA, Vincent Joseph "Vince" (b. March 11, 1927, Hammond, IN), college and professional player, coach, scout, and executive, is the son of Vincent Stanley Boryla and Phyllis (Tiliczuk) Boryla and possessed one of the greatest hook shots in basketball history. Boryla, a six-foot five-inch, 200-pound forward, played for several colleges, but his career was interrupted by military service during World War II. After graduating from East Chicago (Indiana) High School, he began his college basketball career at the University of Notre Dame in the summer of 1944. As a freshman, Boryla broke Notre Dame records for most points scored in one season (322) and one game (31, against the University of Detroit). After one season there, he transferred to the U.S. Naval Academy. Boryla already had spent a few months in the U.S. Navy at the Great Lakes Naval Training Station. He re-enrolled at Notre Dame after spending some time at Annapolis, but left the South Bend, Indiana School in 1946 to enlist in the U.S. Army. The U.S. Army assigned Boryla to Denver, Colorado, where he played for two seasons with the Denver Nuggets (AAU) and twice was named AAU All-America. In 1948, he made the U.S. Olympic team and helped the United States to win a gold medal in basketball at the London, England Games.

After the Olympics, the peripatetic Boryla was discharged from the U.S. Army and enrolled at the University of Denver. He made First-Team All-America in his only season (1948–1949) at Denver and then turned professional. After leaving college, Boryla played in the NBA from 1949 to 1954 with the New York Knicks (NBA); he tallied 3,187 career points with an 11.2 points average and primarily used the hook shot. The Knicks won regular-season Eastern Division titles in 1952–1953 and 1953–1954; the team also lost in the NBA Finals to the Rochester Royals in 1951 and the Minneapolis Lakers in the next two seasons. Boryla played in the NBA's first All-Star Game in 1951 in Boston. He coached the Knicks from the middle of the 1955–1956 season through the 1957–1958 season, ending with a career NBA coaching record of 80 wins and 85 losses. Boryla served as the Knicks general manager for five years following his coaching career. He scouted for the Knicks, but continued to pursue business and real estate interests in the Denver area. In 1970, Boryla helped negotiate the purchase of the Los Angeles Stars (ABA) and moved the franchise to Salt Lake City, Utah. The club became the Utah Stars and in 1971 won its only ABA championship. From 1984 through October 1987, he served as president of the Denver Nuggets (NBA). Boryla, in 1948, wed Catherine Brogan of Denver, by whom he had one daughter and four sons.

BIBLIOGRAPHY: Vincent Boryla, telephone interviews with Bill Mallon, May 9, 1993, June 1, 1993; Vincent Boryla file, University of Notre Dame Sports Information, Notre Dame, IN; Mike Douchant, *Encyclopedia of College Basketball* (Detroit, MI, 1995); Jan Hubbard, ed., *The Official NBA Basketball Encyclopedia*, 3rd ed. (New York, 2000); Neil D. Isaacs, *Vintage NBA* (Silver Spring, MD, 1996); Bill Mallon and Ian Buchanan, *Quest for Gold: The Encyclopedia of American Olympians* (New York, 1983); Martin Taragano, *Basketball Biographies 1891–1990* (Jefferson, NC, 1991).

Bill Mallon

BOUSHKA, Richard J. "Dick" (b. July 29, 1934, St. Louis, MO), college and amateur player, is the son of Richard Boushka and Mildred (Eberle) Boushka and graduated from

Champion Jesuit High School in Prairie du Chain, Wisconsin. During his senior year, Boushka set the single-game scoring record for the Wisconsin High School basketball tournament with 42 points and made the All-State basketball team. He played basketball at St. Louis University, where he made the All-MVC team for three consecutive years and the 1954–1955 All-America squad in his senior year. His 1,440 points and 20.1-point average established a St. Louis University scoring mark.

In 1955–1956, Boushka joined the Wichita (Kansas) Vickers (NIBL) and made the All-Star basketball team his rookie year. The Seattle (Washington) Buchan Bakers, the 1956 National AAU tournament champion, added Boushka for the U.S. Olympic tournament at Kansas City, Missouri. After this tournament, the USOC selected him to join the 1956 U.S. Olympic team. The U.S. basketball squad won the gold medal at the Melbourne, Australia Summer Games. In the 1956–1957 season, Boushka played for Kirkland (Washington) Air Force Base. Kirkland won the National Air Force basketball championship, as he was named the tournament MVP. Boushka then joined an Air Force All-Star team, which breezed to the 1957 National AAU basketball tournament title. He was named to the AAU All-America basketball squad and was selected the tournament's MVP.

Boushka returned to the Wichita Vickers in 1957 for three more seasons and led the Vickers to a share of the NIBL 1957–1958 title. In the 1958–1959 campaign, he led the NIBL in scoring with a 25.2-point average and directed the Vickers to their only AAU basketball championship. The Vickers pummeled the Phillips 66ers, 105–83. For a second time, Boushka was named to the AAU All-America basketball team and the tournament's MVP. In 1959, he also played on the successful U.S. team at the Pan-American games in Chicago, Illinois. Boushka once again made the NIBL All-Star basketball team in 1959–1960, as he led the NIBL in scoring with a 27.7-point scoring average, the highest in NIBL history. Although the Vickers fell in the quarterfinal round of the 1960 National AAU basketball tournament, he joined the Akron Goodyears for the Olympic tournament in Denver, Colorado, and was named an alternate member of the U.S. Olympic team.

After the 1959–1960 season, Boushka retired from AAU basketball. He was a member of the HAF Hall of Fame, St. Louis University Sports Hall of Fame, and Missouri Sports Hall of Fame and presided over the Naismith Memorial Basketball Hall of Fame. Boushka served as an executive in the oil business until 1980 and now presides over Boushka Properties. He and his wife, Joan, live in Wichita and have five children, Richard, Michael, James, Patrick, and John.

BIBLIOGRAPHY: Dick Boushka scrapbooks, in possession of Dick Boushka, Wichita, KS; Bill Mallon and Ian Buchanan, *Quest for Gold: The Encyclopedia of American Olympians* (New York, 1984); Alexander Weyand, *The Cavalcade of Basketball* (New York, 1960).

Adolph H. Grundman

BRADDS, Gary Lee "Tex" (b. July 26, 1942, Jamestown, OH; d. July 15, 1983, Greenview, OH), college and professional player, was the son of Donald Bradds, and Helen Bradds. His father served as a Greene County, Ohio official and County Council member. Bradds, a six-foot eight-inch, 220-pound forward-center enjoyed a phenomenal basketball career at Greenview (Ohio) High School and graduated in 1961. He was widely recruited and originally enrolled at the University of Kentucky. After spending only two days there, he returned to his home state to attend Ohio State University. Bradds spent his sophomore season as a reserve center behind All-America Jerry Lucas* during the regular season. When Lucas was injured and could not start during the NCAA tournament, Bradds was rushed into action as his replacement. He played in four tournament games and performed exceptionally well, but could not halt state rival the University of Cincinnati from capturing its second consecutive National Championship.

In the following two seasons, Bradds exploded on the college basketball scene in a fashion seldom equalled. As a junior, he averaged 28.0 points and 13.0 rebounds and made the All-America Second Team. In his senior season, 1963–1964, Bradds enjoyed a career year, averaging 30.6 points and 13.4 rebounds. He was unanimously chosen First Team All-America and was named Player of the Year by the AP and the UPI. Bradds netted 735 points his final season and ranks second on the Buckeyes all time list in points and points average. He ranks twelfth in career scoring with 1,530 points and scored at least 40 points in six consecutive games during his final season. Bradds set school records when he posted 49 points and 20 field goals against the University of Illinois on February 10, 1964. He participated on two BTC championship teams.

Following graduation from Ohio State in 1964, Bradds was selected by the Baltimore Bullets (NBA) as the third choice in the first round of the 1964 NBA draft. He joined the Bullets in 1964–1965, but was used sparingly over two seasons due to multiple injuries. After sitting out the full 1966–1967 season and part of the 1967–1968 campaign, Bradds tried to rehabilitate by playing in the NABL. Bradds joined the Oakland Oaks (ABA) during the 1967–1968 season and played two seasons there. His second season easily marked his most productive year as a professional. He registered 1,399 points and 577 rebounds in 75 games, averaging 18.7 points and 7.7 rebounds. Bradds split the 1969–1970 season between the Washington Capitols (ABA) and the Carolina Cougars (ABA), compiling a 13.4 point average in 60 games. He joined the Texas Chaparrals (ABA) in 1970–1971 and ended his professional career after appearing in 26 games.

In five full NBA-ABA seasons, Bradds scored 3,106 points and cleared 1,398 rebounds in 254 regular season games. He also recorded 391 points and 181 rebounds in 22 playoff games.

Bradds played on the U.S. men's basketball team that captured the gold medal in the 1963 Pan American Games. On January 27, 2001, his jersey number 35 was retired by the Ohio State University Athletic Department.

Bradds later served as principal of the elementary school in Bowersville, Ohio, and of his alma mater, Greenview High School. He died at age 40 from cancer, survived by a son and daughter.

BIBLIOGRAPHY: Peter J. Bjarkman, *The Biographical History of Basketball* (Chicago, IL, 2000); "Gary Bradds," *Biography and Statistics*, http://www.hickok sports.com (2004); "Gary Bradds," *Retired Jersey #35*, http://www.ohiostatebuckeyes.ocsn.com (2001); "Gary Bradds, *Scoring Streak*, http://www.ohiostatebuckeyes.ocsn.com (2003); "Gary Bradds," *Statistics*, http://www.basketball reference.com. (2004); Gary K. Johnson, ed., *NCAA Men's Basketball's Finest* (Overland Park, KS, 1991); David S. Neft et al., *The Sports Encyclopedia: Pro Basketball*, 5th ed. (New York, 1992); "OSU," *Record Book*, http://www.ohiostate.theinsiders.com (2004).

John L. Evers

BRADLEY, William Warren "Bill" (b. July 28, 1943, Crystal City, MO), college and professional player, ranks among the greatest figures in IvL sports history and rose to prominence in national politics. The only child of banker Warren Bradley and Susan (Crowe) Bradley, he grew up in affluence and divided his youth between Missouri and West Palm Beach, Florida. He was encouraged in both music and athletics, becoming an outstanding basketball player at Crystal City High School. Although not naturally fast or a good jumper, he practiced incessantly with weighted shoes. On graduation he was recruited by over 70 colleges and universities, including Coach Adolph Rupp's* University of Kentucky.

Bradley chose Princeton University for its educational advantages and continued the honors-level work he had begun in high school. As a freshman, he set a basketball record with 57 consecutive free throws. The next season he averaged 27.3 points, 90 percent free throw shooting, and over 12 rebounds. During Bradley's varsity career, the Tigers won three IvL titles. Altogether, he scored 2,503 points (the then fourth highest total in college basketball history), averaged 30.1 points, and was named All-America three times. His greatest games were his 41-point effort in an 80-78 loss to heavily favored University of Michigan in the 1964 Holiday Festival (Princeton led 75-63 when Bradley fouled out after dominating his college rival Cazzie Russell*) and a 58-point mark against Wichita State University in the 1965 NCAA tournament, a single-game record. After captaining the triumphant U.S. Olympic team in 1964 in Tokyo, Japan, Bradley graduated with honors in 1965 and was awarded a Rhodes Scholarship to Oxford.

Drafted by the New York Knickerbockers (NBA), the six-foot five-inch, 210-pound Bradley completed his Oxford studies and a term in the U.S. Air Force Reserve before returning to basketball in 1967. Although not an instant NBA success, he developed into one of the Knicks' most solid players at forward and helped them win NBA titles in 1970 and 1973. His 12.4 points career average for a team with stars Willis Reed*, Walt Frazier*, and Dave DeBusschere* failed to indicate his overall value. During 10 NBA seasons, he scored 9,217 points and compiled an 84 percent free throw mark and 2,354 rebounds. The Knicks retired his uniform number 24.

On retirement from play after the 1976–1977 season, Bradley began his political career. He was elected as U.S. Senator (Democrat) from New Jersey, replacing Clifford Case in 1979. In the Senate, he gained an enviable reputation for committee work in energy, conservation, finance, and tax policy. Re-elected in 1984, he supported the Equal Rights Amendment and Federal Communications Commission help for his adopted state of New Jersey. He was re-elected in 1990 and gave a keynote address at the 1992 Democratic National Convention. Bradley did not seek re-election in 1996 and unsuccessfully sought the Democratic party nomination for president in 2000. Bradley married Ernestine Schlant, a Comparative Literature professor at Montclair State College, in 1974, has one daughter, Theresa, and lives in Union, New Jersey. In addition to numerous civic honors and several honorary degrees, he was elected to the Naismith Memorial Basketball Hall of Fame in 1983, and has been active in Presbyterian Church work.

BIBLIOGRAPHY: Bill Bradley file, Naismith Memorial Basketball Hall of Fame, Springfield, MA; William Bradley, *Life on the Run* (New York, 1976); "Bill Bradley," Lewis Cole, *Dream Team—The Candid Story of the Champion 1969–1970 Knicks* (New York, 1981); *CB* (1982), pp.44–47; Zander Hollander, ed., *The Modern Encyclopedia of Basketball* (Garden City, NY, 1979); Jan Hubbard, ed., *The Official NBA Encyclopedia*, 3rd ed. (New York, 2000); George Kalinsky, *The New York Knicks: The Official 50th Anniversary Celebration* (New York, 1996); *The Lincoln Library of Sports Champions*, vol. 3 (Columbus, OH, 1974); John McPhee, *A Sense of Where You Are* (New York, 1978); *Who's Who in Politics* (New York, 1995).

Leonard H. Frey

BRAND, Elton Tyron (b. March 11, 1979, Cortland, NY), college and professional player, was reared in Peekskill, New York by his mother, Daisy Brand. The six-foot eight-inch, 260-pounder, starred in basketball for four seasons at Peekskill High School and was named to the 1997 *Parade* and McDonald's All-America teams.

Brand attended Duke University from 1997 to 1999, majoring in sociology. He averaged 13.4 points and 7.3 rebounds in basketball as a freshman in 1998, but missed 15 games in midseason because of a broken left foot. Brand made a full recovery and emerged as the nation's dominant college player in 1998–1999. The powerful, low-post player exhibited unusual quickness for a player with his bulk. He averaged 17.7 points and 9.8 rebounds in 1999, leading Duke to a 37-2 record. Duke, however, was upset in the 1999 NCAA Finals by the University of Connecticut.

Brand was chosen to every 1999 All-America team and was selected AP Player of the Year. He also won the Wooden and Naismith awards and was voted ACC Player of the Year. Brand declared for the NBA draft after the 1999 season, ending his Duke career with 972 points, 536 rebounds, a 61.2 percent field goal percentage, and 16.2 points and 8.9 rebounds averages.

The Chicago Bulls (NBA) selected Brand as the first pick of the 1999 NBA draft. He justified their faith by averaging 20.1 points and 10 rebounds and was named NBA Co-Rookie of the Year in 1999–2000.

Following a comparable 2000–2001 season, Brand was traded to the Los Angeles Clippers (NBA) in June 2001 and continued to be among the NBA's most productive power forwards. He was named to the 2002 NBA All-Star Game and played that summer for the United States national team in the World Championships. Brand led the NBA in offensive rebounding in 2002 with 5.0 per game. He led the Clippers in rebounding and finished second on the team in scoring in 2003–2004 and 2004–2005, averaging 20.0 points and 10.3 rebounds in 69 games in the former and 20.0 points and 9.5 rebounds in 81 games in the latter. Through the 2004–2005 season, Brand has compiled NBA averages of 19.5 points, 10.4 rebounds, and 2.0 blocked shots in 447 games. The PBWAA named him the 2002 recipient of the Magic Johnson Award, presented to the NBA player who best combines performance and media awareness.

BIBLIOGRAPHY: *Duke University Basketball Media Guide 1998, 1999* (Durham, NC, 1998, 1999); Barry Jacobs, "Brand Recognition," *Sport* 90 (January 1999), pp. 84–85; Jack McCallum, "Clippers Hip," *SI* 96 (January 7, 2002), pp. 62–65; Ken Shouler et al., *Total Basketball* (Wilmington, DE, 2003); *TSN Official NBA Register 2004–2005* (St. Louis, MO, 2004); Ian Thomsen, "Passing Marks," *SI* 95 (March 12, 2001), pp. 76–77.

Jim L. Sumner

BRAUN, Carl August (b. September 25, 1927, Brooklyn, NY), college and professional athlete and coach, pursued a professional baseball career as a pitcher before a torn muscle forced him to concentrate fully on basketball. A versatile athlete, Braun starred as a basketball player at Colgate University and signed a minor league baseball contract with the New York Yankees (AL). An injury ended Braun's pitching career, but he defeated future baseball Hall-of-Famer Robin Roberts three times in minor league games.

The six-foot five-inch, 180-pound guard began his professional basketball career with the New York Knickerbockers (BAA) in 1947 as a 20-year-old. With the exception of spending the 1950–1951 and 1951–1952 seasons in the U.S. Army, Braun played with the Knicks (NBA) through the 1960–1961 campaign. His playing career concluded the next season with the Boston Celtics (NBA). In each of his first seven BAA/NBA seasons, he led the Knicks in scoring. Although never averaging over 15.4 points in the low-scoring era through 1956, Braun finished four times among the BAA/NBA's top ten. He enjoyed his most productive professional season in 1957–1958, registering career highs in field goals (426), free-throw percentage (.849), assists (393), total points (1,173), and points per game (16.5).

A mediocre free throw shooter before his U.S. Army service, Braun ranked among NBA's top 10 foul shooters from 1952 to 1959. During the late 1950s Braun's focus shifted from scorer to playmaker. From the 1955–1956 through 1958–1959 seasons, he ranked among the NBA's top 10 in assists per game.

A back injury limited Braun to 54 games in 1959–1960 and to only 15 games in 1960–1961. In mid-December 1959, he replaced Andrew "Fuzzy" Levane as Knickerbockers coach. Under Braun, the Knicks compiled a 19-29 win-loss record over the remainder of the 1959–1960 season and a 21-58 mark for the NBA's worst record by far in 1960–1961. The Knicks fired Braun at season's end. Braun was selected to play in five straight NBA All-Star Games from 1953 through 1957 but missed the 1956 game with an injury.

BIBLIOGRAPHY: Carl Braun file, Naismith Memorial Basketball Hall of Fame, Springfield, MA; Zander Hollander, ed., *The Modern Encyclopedia of Basketball*, rev. ed. (New York, 1973); Jan Hubbard ed., *The Official NBA Basketball Encyclopedia*, 3rd ed. (New York, 2000); Neil D. Isaacs, *Vintage NBA* (Silver Spring, MD, 1996); Ronald L. Mendell, *Who's Who in Basketball* (New Rochelle, NY, 1973); *NYT*, December 19, 1959; May 9, 1961; "One of the Pros," *Newsweek* 52 (December 29, 1958), p. 42; Ken Shouler et al., *Total Basketball* (Wilmington, DE, 2003).

Frederick Ivor-Campbell and Wayne Patterson

BRAXTON, Janice Lawrence (b. June 7, 1962, Lucedale, MS), college and professional player and coach, made all-state in basketball at Lucedale High School and helped the Louisiana Technical University Lady Bulldogs win national basketball championships in 1981 and 1982. As a sophomore in 1981–1982, she was chosen MVP of the NCAA women's championship tournament and led all players with a 22.8 point per game average. Braxton was named a Kodak All-America in 1983 and 1984. She scored 2,403 points and made 1,097 rebounds during her college career. Braxton averaged 9.5 points and 6 rebounds on the United States women's gold-medal Olympic basketball team in 1984, before joining the New York entry in the short-lived WABA the same year.

Braxton played professionally 13 seasons in the ItL with Vicenza and Messina, averaging almost 23 points and nearly 11 rebounds. The six-foot three-inch, 175-pound forward helped Vicenza capture four ItL championships and made the 1997 ItL All-Star team.

Braxton signed with the Cleveland Rockers (WNBA) in 1997, joining two of the league's best players, Eva Nemcova and Suzie McConnell Serio. As a forward and center, she averaged 11.5 points and 7.6 rebounds. In 1998, Braxton averaged 9.8 points and 5.6 rebounds for the Rockers. The following season, she slipped to 5.8 points and 4.3 rebounds per game. Her WNBA career totals included 733 points, 468 rebounds, 156 assists, 106 steals, and 56 blocked shots in 81 games.

Braxton retired from the hardwood after the 1999 WNBA campaign to assist her husband, Steve, with their jewelry store in Oakwood, Ohio. In 2003, she returned to professional basketball as assistant coach to Dan Hughes with the Cleveland Rockers. She resides with her husband in Twinsburg, Ohio.

BIBLIOGRAPHY: Jack O'Breza Jr. "Braxton hopes to lift Rockers to top of WNBA," *Sun Newspapers* (June 26, 1997), web archives, pp. 1–2; Hickok Sports, *Sports Biographies Janice Lawrence* (www.hickoksports.com, June 26, 2003), pp. 1–2; CNN Sports Illustrated, *WNBA Basketball* (www.cnnsi.com October 14, 1999), pp. 1–2; USA Today, *WNBA Statistics 1997, 1998, 1999* (www.usatoday.com, June 15, 1999).

Frank J. Olmsted

BRENNAN, Joseph R. (b. November 15, 1900, Brooklyn, NY; d. May 10, 1989, New York, NY), professional player and college coach, attended St. Augustine Academy and played basketball there for four years. After his high school graduation in 1919, Brennan immediately began playing pro basketball for the all-Irish Brooklyn Visitation team. This team ranked second only to the Original Celtics. In the early years of pro basketball, players performed for several teams in different leagues during the same season. During a 19-year career, Brennan played for Troy, New York of the NYSL, Holyoke, Massachusetts in the ML, and Wilkes-Barre and Philadelphia, Pennsylvania of the EL. His other teams included the Brooklyn (New York) Jewels, Whirlwinds, and Dodgers. In addition, he played many exhibition games with the Union City, New Jersey Reds.

In 1922 Brennan led the Reds to a memorable 26-24 triumph over the Celtics in a contest marked by one of his many personal duels with Nat Holman*. Brennan scored three of his team's five field goals, including the winning basket with 20 seconds left in the game. His Brooklyn Visitation Triangles in 1922 won the Metropolitan title for the second consecutive year, as he scored 19 points in the closing win over Trenton. The victory gave Brooklyn the championship and Brennan the scoring title over perennial scoring leader Benny Borgmann*, 190 points to 184.

Although drafted by Fort Wayne, Indiana of the new ABL in 1925, Brennan was reluctant to leave New York because he held a job with the Emigrant Savings Bank in Manhattan. Fort Wayne traded him back to the Visitations for Rusty Saunders just one day before he led the Brooklyn squad to a 28-24 victory over the Celtics in Madison Square Garden in New York. Brennan scored the winning basket and drew the fifth foul on the legendary Dutch Dehnert*. Brennan continued playing for the local team in the MeL, but his Brooklyn team in January 1928 entered the ABL. The next year he led the club in scoring and ranked second in the ABL in points per game behind Borgmann, despite missing all the road games because of his banking job. Before temporarily retiring after the winter season, Brennan led the Visitations to the ABL title, widely held to be the world championship. In 1931 his Visitations again won. The Depression caused the leagues to fold, but the ABL was revived in 1933. Brennan helped the Visitations capture the ABL title once more in 1935.

In four separate leagues during the 1920s, Brennan averaged an extraordinary 7.3 points. During that era, center jumps followed every score. Brennan's best scoring year came in 1923–1924, as he made 370 points and averaged 9.5 points. During his playing career, Brennan captained nine of his 10 teams. In an era of few regular coaches, captains assumed their functions and even arranged schedules. When Brennan retired from active playing in 1936, he became freshman basketball coach at Manhattan College and won 80 of 87 games in three years at the helm there. In 1941 Brennan became head coach at St. Francis College, where his teams won 96 games and lost 46 and captured the Sergeant Edmund Buckley Trophy in Brennan's last year (1948) of coaching. He never played on or coached a team that had a losing season.

Brennan stayed with the Emigrant Savings Bank until 1961, leaving as a vice president. He became president of the Atlantic Savings and Loan Association of Brooklyn until his 1968 retirement. Six years later Brennan was elected to the Naismith Memorial Basketball of Fame. In 1950 the Basketball Old Timers of New York voted him second only to Johnny Beckman* of the Original Celtics as his era's greatest pro player. Newsmen had debated in 1936 whether he or Holman deserved the title of "Babe Ruth of Basketball." The 5-foot 11½-inch, 160-pound Brennan lived in New York City with his wife, Irene. They had three sons, Joseph, Thomas, and Gregory.

BIBLIOGRAPHY: Bernie Beglane, "Joe Brennan Enters Hall," *Long Island Press*, April 27, 1975; Joseph R. Brennan file, Naismith Memorial Basketball Hall of Fame, Springfield, MA; Zander Hollander, ed., *The NBA's Official Encyclopedia of Professional Basketball* (New York, 1981); David Neft et al., *The Pro Sports Encyclopedia: Pro Basketball*, 5th ed. (New York, 1992); Murry R. Nelson, *The Originals: The New York Celtics Invent Modern Basketball* (Bowling Green, OH, 1999).

John D. Windhausen

BRIAN, Frank Sands "Flash" "Frankie" (b. May 1, 1923, Zachary, LA), college and professional player, graduated from Zachary, Louisiana High School and played basketball at guard for Louisiana State University (SEC) in 1942–1943 and 1945–1947, serving from 1943 to 1945 in the armed forces. During his sophomore year, LSU compiled an 18-4 record under coach Dale Morey in 1942–1943. The popular Brian helped coach Harry Rabenhorst's Tigers to an 18-3 mark and second-place SEC finish in 1945–1946, and a 17-4 slate in 1946–1947.

In 1947, the Anderson (Indiana) Duffy Packers (NBL) drafted the six-foot one-inch, 180-pound Brian. As a rookie starting guard, Brian led the 42-18 Packers in scoring with 651 points (11-point average) in 1947–1948 and made the All-NBL Second Team. Anderson finished second in the Eastern Division and reached the NBL semifinals. Brian attained All-NBL First Team honors in 1948–1949, helping the 49-15 Packers dominate the NBL. He paced Anderson in scoring with 633 points (9.9-point average) and the NBL in foul shooting percentage (78.5 percent). The Packers defeated the Oshkosh (Wisconsin) All-Stars to take the NBL championship, with Brian scoring 79 points (11.3-point average). Anderson joined the NBA in 1949–1950, finishing second in the Western Division. Brian, a Second Team All-NBA selection, ranked third among NBA scorers with 1,138 points for a career-best 17.8-point average and fifth with an 82.4 foul shooting percentage. He tallied nearly 12 points a game during the playoffs, but the Minneapolis Lakers eliminated Anderson in the semifinals. When the Packers' franchise folded, the Chicago Stags (NBA) assumed Brian's contract and sent him to the Tri-Cities Blackhawks (NBA) for rookie guard Bob Cousy*. During the 1950–1951 season for the struggling Blackhawks, Brian attained career highs in points (1,144), rebounds (244), and assists (266). Besides repeating as an All-NBA Second Team member, he scored 14 points in the first NBA All-Star Game. Tri-Cities traded Brian to the Fort Wayne Pistons (NBA) before the 1951–1952 campaign.

Brian completed his NBA career with the Pistons, retiring after the 1955–1956 season. Although Fort Wayne struggled in 1951–1952, he ranked sixth in NBA scoring with 1,051 points (15.9-point average) and fourth in foul shooting (84.8 percentage) and appeared in his second consecutive All-Star Game. Subsequent acquisitions of veteran guards Andy Phillip*, Fred Scolari*, and Max Zaslofsky* gradually diminished Brian's playing time. Nevertheless, he ranked second in NBA foul shooting in 1954–1955 with a career-high 85.1 percentage. Fort Wayne won Western Division titles in 1954–1955 and 1955–1956 and lost the seven-game 1955 NBA Finals to the Syracuse Nationals, as Brian averaged nearly 10 points. During his NBL-NBA career, the Hanna, Louisiana resident scored 6,663 points (11.9-point average), converted 81.2 percent of his foul shots, grabbed 903 rebounds, and dished out 1,138 assists in 561 games. In 56 NBL-NBA playoff games, he scored 520 points (9.3-point average), converted 81.2 percent of his foul shots, and made 93 assists.

BIBLIOGRAPHY: Jan Hubbard, ed., *The Official NBA Encyclopedia*, 3rd ed. (New York, 2000); Neil D. Isaacs, *Vintage NBA* (Silver Spring, MD, 1996); David S. Neft and Richard M. Cohen, eds., *The Sports Encyclopedia: Pro Basketball*, 5th ed. (New York, 1992); Ken Shouler et al., *Total Basketball* (Wilmington, DE, 2003); *TSN NBA Register, 2004–2005* (St. Louis, MO, 2004).

David L. Porter

BRIDGES, William C. "Bill" (b. April 4, 1939, Hobbs, NM), college and professional player, played basketball well enough at Hobbs (New Mexico) High School to win a scholarship to the University of Kansas in 1957. At Kansas, he averaged 16.1 points and 14 rebounds his senior year (1960–1961) and scored 1,028 points (13.2 points per game) and made 1,081 rebounds in three seasons there. The six-foot six-inch, 235-pound Bridges was drafted in the third round by the Chicago Packers (NBA) franchise. After he signed in 1961 with the Kansas City Steers of Abe Saperstein's* new ABL, Chicago traded Bridges' rights to the St. Louis Hawks (NBA) in June 1962. On December 9, 1962, he set the ABL single-game scoring record with 55 points against Oakland. The same year, he made the ABL All-Star team and led the ABL in rebounding.

When the ABL folded in midseason of 1962–1963, Bridges was leading the league in both scoring (29.8 points per game) and rebounding (15 rebounds per game). The Hawks consequently were excited to get him. Although his statistics may have been less impressive, he made a significant contribution there and participated in the 1967, 1968, and 1970 All-Star Games. In his best year (1966–1967), Bridges averaged 17.4 points and 15 rebounds. He was selected to the Second Team All-NBA Defensive Team in 1969 and 1970. He was traded to the hapless Philadelphia 76ers (NBA) in 1971 and, much to his delight, to the winning Los Angeles Lakers (NBA) in 1972.

After being cut by the Lakers in December 1974, Bridges signed with the Golden State Warriors (NBA) in March 1975. With the Warriors, he played a reserve role for Coach Al Attles'* NBA championship team that year. He retired after the 1974–1975 season, having enjoyed a long and accomplished career culminating as a member of a championship team.

Bridges' modest estimate of his own career was not shared by anyone else who saw him perform. He intimidated players with the physique of a defensive end in football and was one of the smartest players of his time. Bridges, one of the foremost examples of a power forward able to compete against taller players, averaged 11.9 rebounds and 11.9 points. Altogether, he scored 11,012 points and made 11,054 rebounds in 926 games.

BIBLIOGRAPHY: Bill Beck, "ABL Folds; Hawks May Get Bridges," *St. Louis Post Dispatch*, December 31, 1962; "Bridges, Counts Traded to Lakers for Ellis," Los Angeles *Times*, November 3, 1972; George Cunningham, "Hawks Defense Is Strength," *Atlanta Constitution*, September 28, 1968; Jan Hubbard, ed., *The Official NBA Encyclopedia*, 3rd ed. (New York, 2000); Terry Pluto, *Loose Balls* (New York, 1990); *TSN Official NBA Register, 2004–2005* (St. Louis, MO, 2004); Arthur Triche, ed., *From Sweet Lou to 'Nique: Twenty-Five Years with the Atlanta Hawks* (Atlanta, GA, 1992).

Joel Westerholm

BROBERG, Gustave, Jr. "Gus" (b. June 16, 1920, Torrington, CT), college athlete, is the son of Gustave Broberg Sr., and ranks among the greatest IvL athletes and as Dartmouth College's finest basketball player. Broberg starred in basketball, baseball, and football at Torrington High School, being honored by the state of Connecticut for his accomplishments. At Dartmouth, he played forward for coach Osborne Cowles's perennial IvL Championship basketball teams, led the IvL in basketball scoring for three consecutive seasons from 1939 through 1941, and also excelled as a centerfielder for Jeff Tesreau's baseball team. The era normally produced low-scoring basketball games, but

Broberg scored at least 20 points 12 times and tallied a career-high 29 points against the University of Pennsylvania in 1940. He set a New England record for consecutive free throw conversions (56) in 1939 and 1940 and averaged 14.4 points in three varsity seasons; 52-16 Dartmouth captured three IvL titles in that span. His best season on the baseball diamond came in 1939, when he batted .308 and led the team in several categories.

The Rochester-Cincinnati Royals (NBL) basketball team and the New York Yankees (AL) baseball team drafted Broberg in 1941, but he joined the military service as a U.S. Marines pilot. In 1945 he lost his right arm above the elbow when his plane crash-landed at Okinawa. Broberg graduated from the University of Virginia Law School in 1948 and commenced a highly successful career as an attorney and municipal court judge, serving for many years in Palm Beach, Florida. He married Stewart Colwell in 1946 and has two children, Kristin and Peter. The latter starred as a pitcher at Dartmouth and performed in the major leagues for several seasons.

Broberg's numerous honors have included consensus All-IvL selection in basketball for three seasons, an HAF All-America designation, and election to the HAF Basketball Hall of Fame (1955) and (with his son) the Palm Beach County Hall of Fame (1984). The six-foot, 190-pound Palm Beach–area resident has practiced law with the prestigious Coe and Broberg firm. Broberg, who was named by high school mentor Connie Donahue and college coach Cowles as their greatest player ever, possessed a lethal hook shot and wide-ranging court skills. Broberg's greatest sports memories include his 25-point effort in a triumph over powerful Stanford University during the 1938–1939 season and a 51-50 loss to the University of Wisconsin, the eventual titlist, in the 1941 NCAA Tournament.

BIBLIOGRAPHY: Gus Broberg, telephone interview with Leonard Frey, 1990; Gus Broberg file, Broberg residence, Palm Beach, FL; Dartmouth College Sports Information and Alumni Records Offices, Hanover, NH; Mike Douchant, *Encyclopedia of College Basketball* (Detroit, MI, 1995) Neil Isaacs, *All the Moves: A History of College Basketball* (Philadelphia, PA, 1975); Alexander Weyand, *The Cavalcade of Basketball* (New York, 1960).

Leonard H. Frey

BROWN, Cynthia Louise "Cindy" (b. March 16, 1965, Portland, OR), college and professional player, graduated from Ulysses S. Grant High School in Portland and starred in basketball at Long Beach State University from 1983 to 1987. The six-foot one-inch, 183-pound small forward set two NCAA records in 1987, including a single-season points record (974) and a single-game points record (60). She amassed 2,669 points in 128 games over four years, with her combined points plus rebounds (3,880) being the sixth highest ever. These accomplishments are remarkable considering that the three-point shot did not exist at that time. Brown was named to the All-Tournament Team at the 1987 NCAA Women's Final Four and first-team All-America in 1986 and 1987. She played on the gold medal–winning U.S. Olympic Basketball Team in 1988.

In the late 1980s, no opportunities existed in the U.S. for women to play professionally. Brown, one of the first players to score more than 2,000 points and tally more than 1,000 rebounds in a college career, began her professional career in Europe. She played for Sidis Ancona in Italy in 1987–1988; Toshiba Yana Gi Cho in Japan from 1988 to 1992; Faenza Errieti Club in Italy from 1992 to 1994; Elitzur Holon in Israel from 1994 to 1996; and briefly for US Valenciennes Orchies in France. In 1996, Brown became the second "premier" player drafted by the Seattle Reign of the newly formed ABL. She took a $50,000 pay cut to come home, but deemed it worthwhile just for the chance to hear "go team" in English and to be part of ABL history. The popularity and following of Brown and other ABL players proved that women could indeed earn a living as basketball players without having to go overseas. She was named to the All-ABL Second Team in 1997, having averaged 17.5 points and 8.3 rebounds in 38 games. In 1998, Brown was assigned to the Detroit Shock, a WNBA expansion team. She averaged 11.8 points and 10 rebounds in 1998, making the All-WNBA Second Team and setting a WNBA single season record with

301 rebounds. Detroit traded her to the Utah Starzz (WNBA) in July 1999. She retired from WNBA play after the 1999 season, having scored 532 points (8.9-point average) and made 447 rebounds (7.5 rebound average) in 60 games.

BIBLIOGRAPHY: Peter C. Bjarkman, *The Biographical History of Basketball* (Chicago, IL, 2000); *Houston Chronicle*, January 28, 1998, p. 10; *NYT*, November 14, 1997, p. C7; *Seattle Post-Intelligencer*, August 10, 1996, p. D2; *Seattle Times*, June 25, 1996, p. C6; *StarzzFan/Cindy Brown* at http://www.starzzfan.com/FPCindy.htm; *TSN Official WNBA Guide and Register, 2000* (St. Louis, MO, 2000); *Who's Who Among African Americans*, 16th ed. (Detroit, MI, 2003).

Jeannie P. Miller

BROWN, Lawrence Harvey "Larry" (b. September 14, 1940, Brooklyn, NY), college and professional player and coach, is the son of Robert C. Brown and Alice (Haas) Brown. He grew up on Long Island, not far from his birthplace, and starred in several sports at Long Beach High School. Brown enrolled at the University of North Carolina in 1959 and played basketball for the Tar Heels for three years. He started in his final two seasons, averaging 16.5 points to lead the Tar Heels as a junior. He was named team captain as a senior. He made All-ACC and All-America teams as a senior. After graduating with a Bachelor's degree in American History in 1963, Brown participated on the U.S. Olympic Basketball Team, which won the Gold Medal in Tokyo, Japan in 1964.

Brown played two years as a guard with the Akron (Ohio) Goodyears. The five-foot nine-inch, 160-pound Brown then spent two years as an assistant coach at his alma mater before joining the ABA's New Orleans Bucs in the 1967–1968 season. He became a regular his rookie year, appearing in 78 games and averaging 13.4 points. He averaged 81.3 percent from the free throw line that year. Always a fine foul shooter, Brown compiled an identical 81.3 percent figure for his five-year pro career and made 1,413 of 1,737 free throws. Brown also was known for his passing and frequent assists, leading the ABA three times. Subsequently he started for the Oakland Oaks (ABA) in the 1968–1969 season and then moved to the Washington Capitals (ABA) in 1969–1970, and to the Virginia Squires (ABA) in 1970–1971. During that season, he was traded to the Denver Rockets (ABA).

Brown retired as a player after the 1971–1972 season to coach the Carolina Cougars (ABA). In his first year, Carolina finished first in its division with a 57-27 record. It marked the first of nine division titles in Brown's pro coaching career. His Carolina team slipped to third in 1973–1974 but still made the ABA playoffs. Brown was hired to coach the Denver Rockets before the 1974 season and led them to a 65-19 finish in his first year. The ABA named him Coach of the Year three times. After the 1975–1976 season, the Rockets (renamed the Nuggets) were absorbed by the NBA. From 1974–1975 through 1977–1978, Brown won four consecutive divisional titles.

Brown resigned from the Nuggets on February 1, 1979. Two months later, he became head coach at UCLA in taking one of the most prestigious positions in college basketball. He stayed at UCLA for two years with a 42-17 mark, but left after the 1980–1981 season to return to the NBA. Brown spent nearly two years with the New Jersey Nets before becoming head coach of the University of Kansas Jayhawks in 1983. As he had done everywhere, Brown continued to win. Kansas finished 135-44 in Brown's five years there, making the Jayhawks a consistent BEC power. After the 1986–1987 season, Brown was given a four-year contract extension. His 1987–1988 squad, paced by Danny Manning, finished the regular season unranked with a 27-11 mark before upsetting the University of Oklahoma 83-79, to win the NCAA championship. Manning, named All-America and College Player of the Year, paced the Jayhawks with 31 points in the championship game. Brown won the Naismith Coach of the Year Award for guiding Kansas to the NCAA championship. His record as a college coach through 1987–1988 was 177-61, a 74 percent success rate. Brown and his wife, Barbara, a University of Kansas graduate and a marketing executive, had three children, Kristen, Melissa, and Alli, before their 1988 divorce. He coached San Antonio (NBA) from 1988 until January 1992, guiding the Spurs to Midwest Division titles in 1989–1990 and 1990–1991. Brown served from February 1992 through the 1992–1993 season as head coach of the Los Angeles Clippers (NBA). He coached the Indiana Pacers (NBA) from 1993–1994 through 1996–1997, finishing first in the Central Division in 1994–1995 and reaching the Eastern Conference finals in 1994 and 1995. Brown served as head coach of the Philadelphia 76ers (NBA) from 1997–1998 through 2002–2003, winning the Atlantic Division in 2000–2001 with a 56-26 record. Philadelphia, led by Allen Iverson*, defeated the Milwaukee Bucks four games to three, in the Eastern Conference finals and lost to the Los Angeles Lakers four to one in the NBA Finals. Brown, who earned NBA Coach of the Year honors in 2001, resigned as 76ers head coach after the 2002–2003 season and replaced Rick Carlisle as head coach of the Detroit Pistons (NBA). He guided Detroit to a 54-28 record, second best in the Eastern Conference in 2003–2004, drawing upon Richard Hamilton, Rasheed Wallace, and Ben Wallace*. Detroit defeated the Milwaukee Bucks (4-1), New Jersey Nets (4-3), and Indiana Pacers (4-2), in the playoffs and upset the heavily-favored Los Angeles Lakers (4-1) in the NBA Finals, making Brown the first coach to win both NCAA and NBA titles. Brown also coached the 2004 U.S. Olympic team to a bronze medal and earned an ESPY Award as best coach/manager. Detroit again placed second in the Eastern Division with a 54–28 record in 2004–2005, reaching the NBA finals against the San Antonio Spurs. In 21 NBA seasons, he has compiled a 939-703 win-loss mark (.572 winning percentage) in regular-season play and an 92-79 mark in NBA playoffs through the 2005 Eastern Conference Finals. Brown was elected to the Naismith Memorial Basketball Hall of Fame in 2002.

BIBLIOGRAPHY: Jay Berman, interviews with University of Kansas Sports Information Director, June 1987; Larry Brown file, Naismith Memorial Basketball Hall of Fame, Springfield, MA; *Philadelphia 76ers Media Guide*, 2002–2003 (Philadelphia, PA, 2002); *Detroit Pistons Media Guide, 2004–2005* (Detroit, MI, 2004); Mike Douchant, *Encyclopedia of College Basketball* (Detroit, MI, 1995); Ken Shouler et al., *Total Basketball* (Wilmington, DE, 2003); *TSN NBA Register, 2004–2005* (St. Louis, MO, 2004); *UCLA Basketball Media Guide, 1979* (Los Angeles, CA, 1979), pp. 22–24.

Jay Berman

BROWN, Roger A. "The Rajah" (b. May 22, 1942, New York, NY; d. March 4, 1997, Indianapolis, IN), professional player, starred in basketball on New York City playgrounds and at Wingate High School in Brooklyn. On March 15, 1960, Brown scored 39 points in a 62-59 loss to Boys High School in the PSAL high school semifinal game at Madison Square Garden in New York. Boys High School featured his friend Connie Hawkins*. After breaking Tony Jackson's city career scoring record, the six-foot four-inch, 205-pound Brown was named *Parade* Third Team High School All-America and was recruited by the University of Dayton.

Brown and Hawkins were later tainted by their relationship with former NBA star Jack Molinas. Molinas asked them for the telephone numbers of other former New York schoolboy stars. The duo did not know Molinas was contacting their friends to ask them to shave points in a college basketball gambling scheme. Because Brown and Hawkins had accepted money, the use of a car, and dinners from attorney Molinas, the district attorney subpoenaed them. Consequently Brown never played a basketball game at Dayton.

Brown performed amateur basketball for the Firestone Company and worked the midnight shift in a General Motors plant. In 1967, the Indiana Pacers of the new ABA signed him after a tryout. Oscar Robertson* had suggested his hometown franchise take a look at Brown, whom he called the best player not playing in the NBA. The 25-year-old Brown was the first player ever signed by the Pacers and averaged 17.4 points and 6.5 rebounds during his eight year ABA career. Brown helped his club to three ABA championships, often saving his best performances for the playoffs. He was named ABA playoff MVP in 1970. His lifetime ABA playoff scoring average was 18.7 points. The four-time ABA All-Star set a record by making 21 consecutive field goals. His 10,058 points still rank him as the third leading scorer in Pacers' history and as only the second ABA player to score 10,000 points.

In 1996, Brown became the first player ever to perform exclusively in the ABA and first ever nominated to the Naismith Memorial Basketball Hall of Fame. He was selected unanimously to the ABA's All-Time 30 Greatest Team. Brown, Mel Daniels*, and George McGinnis* remain the only three Pacers whose jersey numerals have been retired. Because Brown had no available insurance funds when diagnosed with terminal liver cancer, the Pacers established the Roger Brown Legacy Fund to help defray his medical expenses before his death at age 54.

BIBLIOGRAPHY: Hal Bock, "Remembering a Rivalry," undated AP sports article; Ted Gould, *Pioneers at the Hardwood* (Bloomington, IN, 1998); Jan Hubbard, *The Official NBA Encyclopedia*, 3rd ed. (New York, 2000); Terry Pluto, *Loose Balls* (New York, 1990); "Remember the ABA" website; David Wolf, *Foul!—The Connie Hawkins Story* (New York, 1972).

Bijan C. Bayne

BROWN, Walter A. (b. February 10, 1905, Hopkinton, MA; d. September 7, 1964, Hyannis, MA), sports promoter, was the son of George Brown and Elizabeth (Gallagher) Brown of Hopkinton, Massachusetts. His father served as general manager of the Boston Arena and president of the Boston Garden-Arena Corporation. After attending Boston Latin School, Hopkinton High School, and Exeter Academy, he apprenticed in sports promotion under his father. In 1931 Brown began a brief term as secretary of the Boston Tigers in the CAHL. In 1933 he coached the first American team to win a world amateur hockey title, defeating Toronto 2-1 at Prague, Czechoslovakia. Shortly after his father's death in 1937, Walter was named President of the Boston Garden-Arena Corporation and held that position until 1964. From 1942 to 1945, Brown served in the U.S. Army as lieutenant colonel attached to the General Staff Corps.

In 1946 Brown helped to found the NBA. He was co-owner and president of the Boston Celtics, a team he named and later helped to guide to seven world championships in eight years. Brown consistently maintained a high payroll in order to retain Bob Cousy*, Bill Russell*, and other stars. In 1950 Brown enjoyed a personal highlight by picking Cousy's name out of a hat in a dispersal draft. Brown also remained heavily involved in hockey as president of the Boston Bruins (NHL) and treasurer of the Ice Capades. In 1947 he was named President of the IHF. Brown served as a vice president of the AHAUS and chaired the U.S. Olympic Ice Hockey Commission for the 1964 games. Perhaps the most widely known international sports figure outside of active competition, Brown exhibited down-to-earth characteristics and liked to do business with a handshake. A shrewd and imaginative showman, he initiated the Ice Follies, helped to organize the Ice Capades, directed the Boston Marathon, staged an indoor ski-jumping contest, and promoted boxing matches.

Brown received numerous acclamations, including being made a Knight of Malta, the highest Catholic honor. From 1961 to 1964, he served as chairman of the Naismith Memorial Basketball Hall of Fame board of directors. The NBA honored Brown by naming its championship bowl after him. The oldest son of seven children, Brown and his wife, Marjorie, and had one daughter, Marjorie. He was president of the Boston Bruins (NHL), Boston Celtics (NBA), Boston Garden-Arena Corporation, and the Boston AA. Besides being on the NBA and NHL board of governors, Brown was elected to both the Hockey and Naismith Memorial Basketball halls of fame.

BIBLIOGRAPHY: Peter C. Bjarkman, *The Boston Celtics Encyclopedia* (Champaign, IL, 1998); *Boston Globe*, September 8–10, 1964; Walter Brown file, Naismith Memorial Basketball Hall of Fame, Springfield, MA; Jack Clary, *Basketball's Great Dynasties: The Celtics* (New York, 1992); Jeff Greenfield, *World's Greatest Team* (New York, 1976); Tom Henshaw, *Boston Celtics, A Championship Tradition* (Englewood Cliffs, NJ, 1974); Leonard Koppett, *24 Seconds to Shoot: An Informal History of the NBA* (New York, 1968); Ronald L. Mendell, *Who's Who in Basketball* (New Rochelle, NY, 1973); Jerry Nason, "Boston's Last Sportsman," *Sportscape*, December 1982, pp. 21–23; Bob Ryan, *The Boston Celtics—The History, Legends and Images of America's Most Celebrated Team* (Reading, MA, 1989); Dan Shaughnessy, *Ever Green: The Boston Celtics* (New York,

1990); George Sullivan, *The Picture History of the Boston Celtics* (New York, 1982).

Daniel Frio

BRYANT, Kobe B. (b. August 23, 1978, Philadelphia, PA), high school and professional player, is the son of Joe "Jelly Bean" Bryant, who played for the Philadelphia 76ers among other NBA teams, and Pamela Bryant, a homemaker. The six-foot seven-inch, 210-pound guard graduated from Lower Merion High School in Ardmore, Pennsylvania in 1996. During his senior year, he led the team to the state championship and became the leading scorer in Pennsylvania high school history. Bryant was also named the National High School Player of the Year by *USA Today* and *Parade* magazine and entered the NBA draft in May 1996. He was chosen in the first round by the Charlotte Hornets (NBA) as the 13th overall choice in the draft and was traded to the Los Angeles Lakers (NBA) on July 11, 1996 for Vlade Divac. He became the sixth high school player in history to go directly to the NBA.

On November 3, 1996, 18-year-old Bryant became the second youngest player ever to play in an NBA game against the Minnesota Timberwolves. His first career start took place on January 28, 1997, against the Dallas Mavericks. In his first year with the Lakers, Bryant was named to the NBA All-Rookie Second Team, playing in 71 games and averaging 7.6 points on 15.5 minutes per game. During the 1997–1998 season, he doubled his scoring, averaging 15.4 points per game, 3.1 rebounds, and 2.5 assists in 26 minutes per game. Bryant was the highest scoring non-starter in the NBA, and the highest scoring reserve in Los Angeles Laker history. In the playoffs, he appeared in 11 of the 13 games, averaging 8.7 points and 1.9 rebounds.

In 1998–1999, Bryant started every game of a lockout-shortened season, averaging 19.9 points, 5.3 rebounds, and 3.8 assists. In the playoffs, he ranked second in team scoring, averaging 19.8 points. Bryant also was named to the All-NBA Third Team. In 1999–2000, he increased his scoring average to 22.5 points and made 6.3 rebounds and 4.9 assists in 38.2 minutes, despite missing the first 15 games of the season because of a broken right hand. In the playoffs he led the team in scoring six times and helped the Lakers win the title over the Indiana Pacers, playing alongside Shaquille O'Neal*.

In 2000–2001, Bryant averaged a career-high 28.5 points in 40.9 minutes of play. He was named the NBA Player of the Month for December. Bryant appeared in 16 games and averaged 29.4 points in the playoffs, helping the Lakers win a second consecutive championship. In 2001–2002, he was named to First Team All-NBA honors and averaged 25.2 points in 80 games. The Lakers won a third consecutive title, as Bryant scored 26.6 points per game, and led the team in scoring in 10 playoff games.

Bryant repeated on the All-NBA First Team and made the All-NBA Defensive First Team in 2002–2003, ranking second in the NBA in scoring with 2,461 points (30.0 points average) and sixth in steal with 181 (2.2 steal average). The Lakers finished fifth in the Western Conference and were eliminated by the San Antonio Spurs in the conference semifinals. Bryant started that season in the All-Star Game, scored 40 or more points in nine straight games, and made 12 three-pointers in a 45-point performance against the Seattle SuperSonics.

Bryant was arrested in July 2003 after a 19-year-old hotel worker accused him of sexual assault at the Lodge and Spa at Cordillera, Colorado. He maintained his innocence, but Eagle County district attorney Mark Hulbert charged him in July 2003 with alleged sexual assault. The accuser filed a civil lawsuit against Bryant in August 2004, seeking unspecified damages. Prosecutors dropped the rape charges against Bryant in September 2004 because the accuser did not want to pursue the case. The civil suit, however, was settled out of court. The incident tarnished Bryant's reputation as a product endorser.

Bryant again made the All-NBA First Team and the All-NBA Defensive First Team in 2003–2004, finishing fourth in scoring with 1,557 points (24.0 point average) in 65 games. He averaged 27.0 points, 6.6 rebounds, and 6.1 assists after the All-Star break, helping the Lakers to the best NBA record (25–7) over that span. He scored 45 and 37 points in his final two games to give the Lakers the Pacific Division title and made two critical three-pointers to detest the Portland Trail Blazers in overtime, giving his team second seed in the playoffs. He garnered All-NBA Third Team honors in 2005. He led the Lakers in points (24.5 points average) and assists (5.5 assist average) in the playoffs, but the Detroit Pistons upset Los Angeles, four games to one, in the NBA Finals. Bryant ranked second in scoring with a 27.6 point average and again made the All-Star team in 2004–2005, but the Lakers missed the playoffs. In nine seasons through 2004–2005, Bryant has compiled 14,034 points in 627 games for a 22.4 point average. He has snagged 3,209 rebounds (5.1 rebound average), dished out 2,788 assists, and had 912 steals. He owns three NBA championship rings and has played in seven All-Star Games. In 119 playoff games, he has scored 2,694 points for a 22.6-point average. Bryant has posted 577 rebounds, 528 assists, and 161 steals. He signed a seven-year $136.4 million contract in July 2004.

Bryant is married to Vanessa Bryant and has a daughter, Natalia Diamante.

BIBLIOGRAPHY: *TSN Official NBA Register, 2004–2005* (St. Louis, MO, 2004); *Los Angeles Lakers 2004–2005 Media Guide* (Los Angeles, CA, 2004); *Great Athletes*, Vol. 1 (Pasadena, CA, 2002); David L. Porter, ed., *Latino and African American Athletes Today* (Westport, CT, 2004).

Robert L. Cannon

BUBAS, Victor Albert "Vic" (b. January 28, 1927, Gary, IN), college player and coach, was the third child of Joseph Bubas and Katharine Bubas. His father owned and operated a Gary, Indiana hardware store. Bubas graduated from Gary's Lew Wallace High School in 1944 and served in the U.S. Army after graduation. Following his discharge, he was discovered playing AAU basketball by North Carolina State University (SC/ACC) coach Everett Case*. Bubas attended North Carolina State from 1947 until his graduation in 1951. A defensive-oriented, playmaking guard, he averaged 6.3 points and played on four SC championship teams. His senior year saw him named one of 12 members of Golden Chain, a leadership and scholarship fraternity.

Bubas remained at North Carolina State as freshman coach from 1952 through 1955, compiling a 64-10 record. From the 1956 through 1959 seasons, he served as varsity assistant to Case. In May 1959, Bubas was named head basketball coach at nearby Duke University (ACC). He enjoyed immediate success, coaching a mediocre Blue Devil club to an ACC championship in the 1960 postseason tournament and Duke's first two victories in the NCAA tournament. The Blue Devils also won the ACC title in 1963, 1964, and 1966 and finished first during the regular season in 1963, 1964, 1965, and 1966. Duke advanced to the NCAA Final Four in 1963, 1964, and 1966, coming in second in 1964 and third the other two seasons. The Blue Devils were invited to the NIT in 1967 and 1968 and finished in the final AP top 10 from 1961 to 1966 and in 1968. Bubas's five All-Americas included Art Heyman* (consensus National Player of the Year in 1963), Jeff Mullins*, Jack Marin, Bob Verga, and Mike Lewis. His 10-year 213-67 mark at Duke included a 22-6 record in the ACC tournament and an 11-4 slate in the NCAA tournament. The ACC named Bubas Coach of the Year in 1963, 1964, and 1966. Bubas, who resigned from coaching after the 1969 season to become director of public relations at Duke, was vice president of community relations at the school from 1974 until 1976. In 1976 he became the first SBC commissioner, a position he held until his retirement in 1990. During his tenure, the SBC obtained an automatic berth in the NCAA basketball tournament.

The soft-spoken Bubas proved a highly organized recruiter and an astute judge of talent. His assistant coaches at Duke included future NBA coaches Chuck Daly* and Hubie Brown. Bubas married Tootie Boldt in 1949 and has three daughters, Sandy, Vikki, and Karen. He is a member of the North Carolina and Duke University Sports halls of fame.

BIBLIOGRAPHY: Smith Barrier, *On Tobacco Road: Basketball in North Carolina* (New York, 1983); Peter C. Bjarkman, *ACC—Atlantic Coast Conference Basketball* (Indianapolis, IN, 1996); Peter C. Bjarkman, *The Biographical History of Basketball* (Chicago, IL, 2000); Bill Brill, *Duke Basketball: An Illustrated History* (Dallas, TX, 1986); Vic Bubas file, Sports Information Department, Duke University, Durham, NC; Mike Douchant, *Encyclopedia of College Basketball* (Detroit, MI, 1995); Ron Morris, *ACC*

Basketball: An Illustrated History (Chapel Hill, NC, 1988).

Jim L. Sumner

BUNN, John William (b. September 26, 1898, Wellston, OH; d. August 13, 1979, Newbury Park, CA), college coach and administrator, was the son of Peter H. Bunn and Lena M. (Janke) Bunn. He graduated from Humboldt (Kansas) High School in 1916 as a 12-letter man and class valedictorian. He then attended the University of Kansas, where he became the only Jayhawk to earn 10 varsity letters in football, basketball, and baseball. A Mechanical Engineering major, he became fascinated with basketball through his association with the game's inventor, James Naismith*, and the legendary coach, Forrest C. "Phog" Allen*. After graduation in 1921, Bunn remained at Kansas for nine years as assistant coach, assistant athletic director (1926–1930), and professor of Industrial Engineering.

In 1930 Bunn became head basketball coach and professor of Physical Education at Stanford University. By featuring the spectacular play of three-time All-American Angelo "Hank" Luisetti* and establishing an unprecedented coast-to-coast schedule, Bunn brought Stanford basketball to national prominence. From 1936 to 1938, the Indians won three consecutive PCC championships. The 1937 squad finished 25-2 and was named HAF national champions. Bunn left coaching in 1939 to become Dean of Men at Stanford but soon tired of the administrative life, and in 1945 was named an athletic consultant for the U.S. War Department. During the next six years, he traveled often to Europe to supervise the establishment of athletic facilities and programs for U.S. military personnel. He returned to athletics as head basketball coach and director of athletics both at Springfield College in Massachusetts (1947–1956) and at Colorado State College in Greeley (1957–1963).

Despite a modest 321-306 career win-loss record, Bunn was an internationally recognized coach. A defensive specialist who developed the popular situation zone defense, he was a masterful teacher of the game and authored six influential books on coaching, officiating, and team play. His most famous book, *The Scientific Principles of Coaching*, a pioneering work applying the principles of mechanical engineering to athletic performance, was translated into several foreign languages. Dubbed "America's Ambassador of Basketball," Bunn traveled frequently to Europe and, under the auspices of the AIA Foundation, to Japan, Korea, and Australia to conduct basketball clinics and lecture on the mechanical analysis approach to physical education.

Widely acclaimed by his peers, Bunn held every office in the NABC (including president, 1949–1950) and served on every NABC committee save high school and press. A member for 30 years of the important rules committee, Bunn from 1959 to 1967 was editor of the official NCAA *Basketball Guide* and interpreter of the *Official Rules*. He personally initiated many rule changes, including the elimination of the center jump after a field goal. At Springfield College, he was elected secretary-treasurer and then president of the NEBCA. In 1961 he received the coveted NABC Metropolitan Award and was named to the HAF Hall of Fame. In 1965 he became the first executive director of the NBF.

While at Springfield College, Bunn was named chairman of the Naismith Memorial Basketball Hall of Fame Committee. Largely through his efforts from 1949 to 1963, the Basketball Hall of Fame became a reality on that campus. Fittingly, Bunn was elected to the Naismith Memorial Basketball Hall of Fame in 1964 and awarded an honorary Doctor of Humanities degree from Springfield College in 1975. He and his wife, Bonnie, had no children.

BIBLIOGRAPHY: Peter C. Bjarkman, *Hoopla: A Century of College Basketball, 1896–1996* (Indianapolis, IN, 1996); John W. Bunn, *The Art of Basketball Officiating* (New York, 1948); John W. Bunn, *The Art of Officiating Sports* (New York, 1950); John W. Bunn, *Basketball Methods* (New York, 1939); John W. Bunn, *Basketball Techniques and Team Play* (Englewood Cliffs, NJ, 1964); John W. Bunn, *The Philosophy of Coaching* (New York, 1960); John W. Bunn, *The Scientific Principles of Coaching* (New York, 1955); John W. Bunn file, Naismith Memorial Basketball Hall of Fame, Springfield, MA; Blair Kerkhoff, *Phog Allen—The Father of Basketball Coaching* (Indianapolis, IN, 1996); Don E. Liebendorfer, *The Color of Life Is Red: A History of Stanford Athletics,*

1892–1972 (Palo Alto, CA, 1972); Ronald L. Mendell, *Who's Who in Basketball* (New Rochelle, NY, 1973); *NCAA Men's Basketball Records, 2004* (Indianapolis, IN, 2003); *News Chronicle* (Thousand Oaks, CA), August 15, 1979; Sandy Padwe, *Basketball's Hall of Fame* (Englewood Cliffs, NJ, 1970); *Springfield* (MA) *Daily News*, August 14, 1979; *Springfield* (MA) *Morning Union*, August 15, 1979.

Larry R. Gerlach

BUSS, Jerry H. (b. January 27, 1933, Salt Lake City, UT), executive, is the son of Lydus Buss and Jessie Buss. He graduated from the University of Wyoming with a Bachelor's degree in chemistry, and earned a Masters degree and a Ph.D. in physical chemistry in 1959 from the University of Southern California (USC). He was employed as a chemist in the Bureau of Mines, taught chemistry at USC, worked in the missile division of McDonnell Douglas in Los Angeles, and served as a partner in Marizmi-Buss Associates. Buss purchased the Los Angeles Strings (WTTL) in 1974 and incorporated certain promotional ideas that soon helped the team lead the league in attendance. In 1978, the Strings won the world team tennis championship. He also owned the Los Angeles Kings (NHL) until 1988.

In 1979 Buss bought the Los Angeles Lakers (NBA) and their home court, the Forum, from Jack Kent Cooke in reportedly the largest sports transaction up to that time. When the Staples Center was built in downtown Los Angeles, he moved the Lakers there from suburban Inglewood.

Many of Buss's basketball contributions concern marketing and promotion. He made an agreement with Great Western Bank in 1988 that allowed the bank to transform the Forum into the Great Western Forum in exchange for a large amount of cash. Buss helped start the Prime Ticket Network in 1985, which became the FOX Sports Net West and Net West 2 and eventually became one of the nation's largest regional sports cable networks.

During Buss's ownership, the Lakers enjoyed great success. From the 1979–1980 season to the start of the 2004–2005 campaign, the Lakers boasted the NBA's highest winning percentage (.684, 1363-629), and won eight NBA championships. Much of that success came from astute player decisions made by former Lakers Vice President and General Manager Jerry West*. Kareem Abdul-Jabbar* and Magic Johnson* represented one championship era. Under coach Phil Jackson*, the Lakers won three consecutive championships from 2000 through 2002 with Shaquille O'Neal* and Kobe Bryant*. The Detroit Pistons upset the heavily-favored Lakers four games to one in the 2004 NBA Finals. Buss also served two terms as president of the NBA Board of Governors.

He was formerly married to JoAnn Buss, and has four children, John, Jim, Jeanie, and Jane, some of whom are actively involved with his teams.

BIBLIOGRAPHY: Roland Lazenby, *The Lakers: A Basketball Journey* (New York, 1993); Franz Lidz, "She's Got Balls," *SI* (November 2, 1998), pp. 100–110; *Los Angeles Lakers Media Guide, 1979–1980* (Los Angeles, CA, 1979); *Los Angeles Lakers Media Guide, 2004–2005* (Los Angeles, CA, 2004); *Who's Who In America*, 47th ed. (1992–1993).

Robert L. Cannon

C

CALHOUN, James "Jim" (b. August 24, 1942, Braintree, MA), college player and coach, is the eldest of six children of James Calhoun Sr., a merchant seaman, and Kathleen Calhoun. After graduating from Braintree High School as a three-sport letter winner, Calhoun attended American International College (AIC) in 1962 and played on the basketball team as a forward. The six-foot five-inch, 220-pound Calhoun led AIC in scoring as a junior and senior and served as captain. He graduated with a Bachelor of Arts degree in sociology in 1966.

Calhoun served as an assistant basketball coach at AIC from 1966 to 1968. After several years coaching at high school basketball, he served as head basketball coach at Northeastern University in Boston from 1972 to 1986. He became the winningest coach in school history with a 248-137 record and was inducted into the Northeastern University Sports Hall of Fame.

In 1986, Calhoun became the head basketball coach of the University of Connecticut (U. Conn). He steadily transformed Connecticut basketball from a regional program into one of the best in the nation. Connecticut had won only four NCAA tournament games before Calhoun's arrival. The Huskies won the 1988 NIT Championship and reached the Elite Eight round of the NCAA Tournament in 1989–1990. Calhoun was named the 1989–1990 College Basketball National Coach of the Year and BEaC Coach of the Year. On March 29, 1999, Connecticut defeated top ranked Duke University 77-74 in the title game for the NCAA National Championship. Calhoun received the 1999 Winged Foot Award as National Coach of the Year, earned the Victor Award as 1998–1999 College Basketball National Coach of the Year, and was named the NABC District I Coach of the Year. In 2002, he was selected as a charter member of the New England Basketball Hall of Fame. The Naismith Memorial Basketball Hall of Fame enshrined him in 2005.

In January 2003, Calhoun was diagnosed with an early stage of prostate cancer. He underwent successful surgery in February 2003 and returned to the sidelines just 15 days later. He guided Connecticut to a 27-6 regular season record and his second NCAA Championship in 2004, as the Huskies edged Duke 79-78 in the NCAA semifinals, and defeated Georgia Tech 82-73 in the NCAA title game. Calhoun has compiled a 455-173 record in his 19 seasons at Connecticut, and a 703-310 career coaching mark in 33 seasons. His star players have included Reggie Lewis, Clifford Robinson, Ray Allen*, Donyell Marshall, Richard Hamilton, Emeka Okafor*, and Ben Gordon. In April 2003, Calhoun received the Metropolitan Award from the NABC.

Calhoun, a member of the AIC Board of Trustees, married Patricia McDevitt in 1967 and has two sons, James, 3rd and Jeffrey. He and his wife reside in Mansfield, Connecticut and founded the Calhoun Cardiology Research Fund at the UConn Health Center. Calhoun is Honorary Chairman of the Connecticut Children's Medical Center and Children's Miracle Network.

BIBLIOGRAPHY: Jim Calhoun and Leigh Montville, *Dare to Dream: Connecticut Basketball's Remarkable March to the National Championship* (New York, 1999); Jack Carey, "UConn Wrecks Tech,"

USA Today, April 6, 2004, p. 1C; Chris Lawlor, "Jim Dandy: Interview with J. Calhoun," *Coach and Athletic Director* 69 (April 2000), pp. 48–60; Malcolm Moran, "UConn Meets Own Expectations," *USA Today*, April 7, 2004 p. 6C; *NCAA Men's Basketball Records, 2004* (Indianapolis, IN, 2003); David Scott, "Beauty in the East," *Sport* 90 (February 1999), pp. 64–67.

Di Su

CALVERLEY, Ernest A., Sr. (b. January 30, 1924, Pawtucket, RI; d. October 20, 2003, Providence, RI), college and professional player, college coach, and administrator, spent nearly all of his life associated with sports. He attended East High School in Pawtucket, Rhode Island, where he excelled in basketball and earned three consecutive First Team All-State selections in 1940, 1941, and 1942.

Following graduation from high school in 1942, Calverley starred as a basketball player for Rhode Island State College (now the University of Rhode Island) between 1942 and 1946. The five-foot ten-inch, 155-pound All-America excelled as a playmaker and "pure shooter" from anywhere on the court. Calverley led the nation in scoring in 1943–1944, averaging 26.7 points as Rhode Island led the nation with 78.8 points per game. He was named the MVP of the 1946 NIT and was selected to the NIT'S 50-Year Team. Calverley also became the first collegian to record at least 45 points twice in one season, tallying 48 points against Northwestern University and netting 45 against the University of Maine.

Calverley remains best known and earned legendary status because of his sensational last second game-winning shot against Bowling Green University in the 1946 NIT. Fans still talk about this spectacular "shot heard around the world." His "buzzer-beater" heave from beyond midcourt at Madison Square Garden in New York has been estimated between 55 feet and 62 feet. The successful field goal forced the game into overtime, which Rhode Island won. The Rams eventually lost to the University of Kentucky 46-45 in the championship game, when Calverley fouled the Wildcats freshman guard Ralph Beard*, Beard sank the game-deciding free throw to give Kentucky the NIT championship. Coach Adolph Rupp's* Wildcats featured the "Fabulous Five" of Beard, Alex Groza*, Ken Rollins, Cliff Barker, and "Wah Wah" Jones*.

Following his graduation from Rhode Island State in 1946, Calverley played professional basketball with the Providence Steamrollers (BAA) between 1946–1947 and 1948–1949. His best season came his rookie year, when he dished out 202 assists to lead the BAA and averaged 14.3 points. During his professional career, Calverley averaged 11.9 points and 3.5 assists in 165 regular season games. He was the first player to sign a BAA contract.

Calverley was named head basketball coach at the University of Rhode Island in 1957 and continued the "fast break" attack or the "run and shoot" offense made famous by his legendary coach Frank Keaney*. He coached the Rams for 11 seasons, compiling a 139-114 win-loss record. Calverley took Rhode Island to the 1961 and 1966 NCAA Tournament, losing both times in the first round. From 1968 to 1985, he served as associate athletic director at his alma mater.

Calverley was inducted into the University of Rhode Island, Rhode Island, and New England Sports halls of fame. His death in 2003 was due to complications from diabetes. He was survived by his wife and a son, Ernest A. Jr., the athletic director at Greater Lawrence Tech High School in West Andover, Massachusetts.

BIBLIOGRAPHY: Peter J. Bjarkman, *The Biographical History of Basketball* (Chicago, IL, 2000); "Ernie Calverley," *Abstract*, http://www.cnnsi.com (2003); "Ernie Calverley," *Blog of Death*, http://www.blogofdeath.com (2004); "Ernie Calverley," *Obituary*, http://www.twoolympion.com (2004); Jan Hubbard, ed., *The Official NBA Encyclopedia*, 3rd ed. (New York, 2000); David S. Neft et al., *The Sports Encyclopedia: Pro Basketball*, 5th ed. (New York, 1992).

John L. Evers

CALVIN, Mack "The Bug" (b. July 27, 1947, Fort Worth, TX), college and professional player, coach, and sportscaster, became a basketball legend in the Long Beach, California area as a six-foot, 165-pound point guard. Calvin graduated from Long Beach Polytech High School in 1965, attended Long Beach City College for two years, and enrolled at the University of Southern California (USC). His major college basketball career began in 1967 with the Trojans under head coach Bob Boyd. He captained USC in 1969, won the Ernie Holbrook Most Inspirational Trojan Player Award in 1968 and 1969, and was named to the All-PEC First Team in 1969. Following his graduation from USC, Calvin was drafted by both the NBA and ABA and signed with the Los Angeles Stars (ABA). He played for the Stars in 1969–1970 and the Miami Floridians (ABA) the next two seasons. Calvin performed with the Carolina Cougars (ABA) in 1972–1973 and 1973–1974 and moved to the Denver Nuggets (ABA) for one season. Calvin spent 1975–1976 with the Virginia Squires (ABA), the last season before the ABA-NBA merger. He split 1976–1977 among the Los Angeles Lakers (NBA), San Antonio Spurs (NBA), and Denver Nuggets (NBA), spent 1977–1978 with Denver, and 1979–1980 with the Utah Jazz (NBA), and completed his NBA playing career in 1980–1981 with the Cleveland Cavaliers (NBA). He played 222 regular-season games in four NBA seasons.

Calvin, known for his defensive skills, ball handling, and free throw shooting, was named to the Top 30 ABA Players of All-Time. He played for nine different franchises in his professional career and ranks eighth on the ABA career scoring list with 10,620 points. Calvin made the 1969–1970 ABA All-Rookie Team, three ABA First Teams and one All-NBA Second Team, and played in five ABA All-Star Games. Calvin led the ABA in free throw percentage (.896 percent) and assists (570) in 1974–1975 and paced the ABA career in career free throws made (3,554) and attempted (4,105). He set ABA single-season records with 696 free throws made and 804 free throws attempted in 1970–1971 and led the ABA in career free throw percentage (.866 percent) and for a single season (89.6 percent), in 1974–1975. In 1977 Calvin was inducted into the Long Beach City College Alumni Hall of Fame. During his 11 year ABA-NBA career, he recorded 11,172 points, posted 86.3 percent free throw shooting, handed out 3,617 assists, and made 485 steals in 755 games.

Calvin held numerous basketball coaching positions at the high school, college and professional levels. He served as an assistant basketball coach for the Milwaukee Bucks (NBA) from 1987–1998 through 1991–1992 and Los Angeles Clippers (NBA) in 1992–1993 and as head coach for the Mexico City Aztecs (CBA). He also was head basketball coach in 1996–1997 at California State University–Dominguez Hills and completed his coaching career at Dominguez High School (Compton, California) in 2002.

Calvin handles color commentating for basketball games on Fox Sports West. He and his wife, who has undergone a kidney transplant, have separated. He takes care of two elderly friends and hopes to re-enter coaching.

BIBLIOGRAPHY: "Mack Calvin," *ABA*, http://www.remembertheaba.com (2003); "Mack Calvin," *Career Laker Stats*, http://www.lakerstats.com (2004); "Mack Calvin," *Coaching News*, http://www.socalhoops.com (2003); "Mack Calvin," *Stats, History and Awards*, http://www.basketballreference.com (2003); Jan Hubbard, ed., *The Official NBA Encyclopedia*, 3rd ed. (New York, 2000); Terry Pluto, *Loose Balls* (New York, 1990).

John L. Evers

CAMBY, Marcus D. (b. March 24, 1974, Hartford, CT), college and professional player, is the son of Ames Mandeville, who was mainly absent from Camby's life, and Janice Camby, a social worker, who brought up Marcus and his two younger sisters, Monica and Mia. Camby began playing basketball at the age of five and played forward and center for the Hartford Public High School basketball team. He led Hartford to two state championship titles and an undefeated season in his senior year.

Camby entered the University of Massachusetts at Amherst in 1993, majoring in education. The six-foot eleven-inch, 225-pounder led the Minutemen to three consecutive ATC championships, the Sweet-Sixteen round in 1994–1995, and their first ever NCAA Final Four appearance in 1995–1996. Camby's last season at Massachusetts featured 20.5 points, 8.2 rebounds, and 3.9 blocks per game. He was named ATC Player of the Year and National Player of the Year and won the James A. Naismith Award, John R. Wooden Award, and the Adolph Rupp Trophy.

In 1996, Camby was selected by the Toronto

Raptors (NBA) as the second overall pick in the NBA draft. In his rookie season, he averaged 14.8 points, 6.3 rebounds, and 2.06 blocks, was selected to the Schick All-Rookie First Team, and was named Rookie of the Month in March 1997. In 1997–1998, Camby led the NBA in blocked shots with 3.65 per game. In June 1998, the Raptors traded Camby to the New York Knicks (NBA). The Knicks barely made a playoff spot in the Eastern Conference in 1998–1999, but, with Camby's help, won the Eastern Conference championship. Although losing to the San Antonio Spurs in the championship series, the Knicks became the first eighth-seeded team in playoffs history to reach the NBA Finals. Camby was traded to the Denver Nuggets (NBA) in June 2002 and averaged 7.6 points, 7.2 rebounds, and 1.38 blocks per game in his first season there. He helped Denver make the playoffs in 2003–2004, ranking seventh in blocked shots (2.59 average), sharing ninth in rebounds (10.1 average), and tallying 8.6 points per game. Camby tallied 12 points and 16 rebounds in the Game 3 victory, 14 rebounds in Game 4, and 41 points total in the first four games of the first round of the playoffs, but the Minnesota Timberwolves eliminated Denver in five games. He led the NBA with 199 blocked shots (3.0 average) and averaged 10.3 points and 10.0 rebounds in 2004–2005, helping the Nuggets reach the playoffs. He averaged 10.2 points and 11.2 rebounds in five games in the first round playoff loss to the San Antonio Spurs. Camby made the All-Defensive Second Team in 2005. His NBA career totals include 5,237 points and 4,215 rebounds in 490 regular season games and 423 points and 410 rebounds in 50 playoff games.

Camby founded the CambyLand Youth Foundation in 1996 to help children in his hometown. He also established a scholarship for senior student athletes at Hartford Public High School to further their education.

BIBLIOGRAPHY: Rick Hornung, "Hoop Schemes" *SN* 113 (February 1998), pp. 69–72+; Yongsoo Park, "Marcus Camby," *CB* 61 (January 2000), pp. 26–31; Selena Roberts, "Troubling Ties that Bind," *NYT* (November 2, 1998), p. D1; *TSN Official NBA Register, 2004–2005* (St. Louis, MO, 2004); Ken Shouler et al., *Total Basketball* (Wilmington, DE, 2003).

Di Su

CANN, Howard Goodsell (b. October 11, 1895, Bridgeport, CT; d. December 18, 1992, Dobbs Ferry, NY), college player and coach, was the son of Professor Frank H. Cann. The Canns moved in 1899 to New York City, where Frank became professor at New York University (NYU). Howard attended New York City's Commerce High School from 1909 to 1913, starring in basketball. After graduating in 1913, he attended NYU from 1914 to 1920 and excelled as an all-around athlete there. Cann led the basketball team in scoring as a freshman in 1914 and was the triple threat (punter, lineman, halfback) captain of the 1917 football team. After serving in the U.S. Navy in World War I, he returned to NYU in 1919. He was named HAF Player of the Year in 1920 and was judged as NYU's greatest athlete. Cann won a shotput track and field championship and played at tackle and fullback in football. Cann, an All-America forward in basketball for NYU's Violets, led his team to the AAU championship in 1920 with a 49-24 victory over Rutgers. He made the U.S. Olympic track team in 1920, the year he received his Bachelor of Science degree in Industrial Engineering.

As NYU basketball coach from 1922 to 1958, Cann compiled a 429-235 record for a .639 winning average. Cann, who also coached the NYU football team in 1932 and 1933, guided the Violets to the HAF National Basketball Championship for the 1935 season. The Violets that season finished 19-1 and outscored their opponents 740-489. His 1933–1934 team, led by Jim Lancaster, finished 16-0 for NYU's only undefeated team. The Coach of the Year in 1947, Cann in 1967 won the New York Writers Distinguished Service Award and the NABC Merit Award and was elected in 1967 as coach to the Naismith Memorial Basketball Hall of Fame. He died after a long illness.

BIBLIOGRAPHY: Peter C. Bjarkman, *Hoopla: A Century of College Basketball, 1896–1996* (Indianapolis, IN, 1946); Howard Cann file, Naismith Memorial Basketball Hall of Fame, Springfield, MA; Mike Douchant, *Encyclopedia of College Basketball* (Detroit, MI, 1995); Ronald L. Mendell, *Who's Who in Basketball* (New Rochelle, NY, 1973); *NCAA Men's Basketball Records, 2004* (Indianapolis, IN, 2003); Sandy Padwe, *Basketball's Hall of Fame* (Englewood Cliffs, NJ, 1970); Paul Soderberg, and Helen Washington, *The Big Book of Halls of Fame in the United States and Canada* (New York, 1977).

Frederick J. Augustyn Jr.

CARLSON, Henry Clifford (b. July 4, 1894, Murray City, OH; d. November 1, 1964, Ligonier, PA), college player and coach, was the son and stepson of miners who died in mining accidents. His family could not afford to send him to college after he graduated from high school in 1912, but he attended Bellefonte Academy in Fayette, Pennsylvania. At the Academy, Carlson starred in three sports for two years before entering the University of Pittsburgh on an athletic scholarship. He earned nine varsity letters in football, basketball, and baseball, and starred in football. During his gridiron career, the Pittsburgh Panthers lost only one game. Carlson captained the 1917 undefeated team and was named an All-America end. After his college graduation, he played professional football for the Cleveland Indians in 1919 to help finance his medical training. He completed his M.D. degree in 1920, and practiced medicine for 11 years at Carnegie Steel and U.S. Steel Corporations.

Beginning in 1922, Carlson also coached men's basketball at the University of Pittsburgh. During Carlson's 31-year career, his teams compiled 369 wins and 247 losses. Carlson's coaching success largely can be traced to his development of the first patterned offense, called the "figure-8" or "continuity." This style, quickly copied and expanded by other schools, consisted of three players moving in a figure-eight shape, while the other two players remained stationary. In Carlson's sixth year, he led the Panthers to a perfect 21-victory campaign to make them unofficial national champions. His undefeated team included captain Sykes Reed, Jerry Wunderlick, Lester Cohen, Stanley Wrobleski, Paul Fisher, Red McMahon, Carl Sandberg, and, especially, Charley Hyatt*.

Besides his novel offense, Carlson pioneered other aspects of the game. He promoted national competition and in 1931–1932 became the first eastern coach to take a team westward. Pittsburgh faced "Phog" Allen's* University of Kansas team before competing against the University of Colorado, Stanford University, and the University of Southern California. His victories over powerful western teams helped to restore prestige to eastern basketball. Carlson also established the first basketball clinics at his alma mater.

Carlson gained renown for his showmanship and the response he provoked from fans on the road. With Pittsburgh leading just 3-2 away from home, Carlson instructed his players to hold the ball for the rest of the first half. The hometown fans verbally abused Carlson, prompting him to yawn and toss peanuts into the crowd. At West Virginia University in Morgantown, West Virginia, Carlson shouted repeatedly "this burns me up" in obvious reference to what he regarded as partisan officiating. One spectator decided to cool Carlson down with a bucket of water. When Pittsburgh defeated Washington and Jefferson, a matronly lady belted him on the head with an umbrella.

For his athletic achievements, Carlson was elected in 1937 as president of the NABC, and in 1959 to the Naismith Memorial Basketball Hall of Fame as a charter inductee. The University of Pittsburgh chose him for the Dapper Dan Hall of Fame. Carlson also was named to the Coaches' Hall of Fame. After retiring as coach in 1953, Carlson directed the student health services at Pittsburgh until reaching 70 years of age. He then left the university permanently with his second wife, Alice. His first wife, Mary, had died in 1946.

BIBLIOGRAPHY: Henry Clifford Carlson, *Basketball: The American Game* (New York, 1938); Henry Carlson file, Naismith Memorial Basketball Hall of Fame, Springfield, MA; Zander Hollander, ed., *The Modern Encyclopedia of Basketball* (Garden City, NY, 1979); Neil D. Isaacs, *All the Moves: A History of College Basketball* (Philadelphia, PA, 1975); *NCAA Men's Basketball Records, 2004* (Indianapolis, IN, 2003); Jim O'Brien, ed., *Hall to Pitt: A Sports History of the University of Pittsburgh* (Pittsburgh, PA, 1982); *Pitt News*, November 1964; *Pittsburgh Press*, November 26, 1964; *Pittsburgh Sun-Telegraph*, March 4, 1956.

Bruce J. Dierenfield

CARNESECCA, Luigi "Lou" "Louie" (b. January 5, 1925, New York, NY), college and professional coach, led St. John's University of

New York (BEaC) to a postseason national tournament in each of his 24 seasons as head coach. The only child of Italian immigrants Alfredo Carnesecca, a stonecutter and a grocery store proprietor, and Adele Carnesecca, the five-foot seven-inch Lou lacked the height to play basketball effectively and decided to coach the game. His first experience coaching came in a CYO league while he attended St. Ann's Academy in Manhattan. After graduating from St. Ann's in 1943, Carnesecca joined the U.S. Coast Guard and served on a troop transport in the Pacific theater during World War II. He briefly pursued premedical studies at Fordham University before transferring to St. John's, where he played baseball and assisted basketball coach Frank McGuire*. Upon earning a Bachelor's degree from St. John's in 1950, Carnesecca taught health and civics and coached basketball at St. Ann's. He married childhood sweetheart Mary Chiesa in 1951 and had one daughter, Enes. Carnesecca's seven seasons saw the school move to Queens to become Archbishop Molloy High School and his team take three National Catholic High School Championships. He meanwhile, earned a Master's degree in educational guidance from St. John's.

Carnesecca returned to St. John's as assistant basketball coach for Joe Lapchick* in 1957, succeeding Lapchick as head coach in 1965. St. John's reached the NIT finals in 1970, after which Carnesecca accepted an offer as coach and general manager of the professional New York Nets (ABA). Despite having losing seasons in 1970–1971 and 1972–1973 and an overall 114-138 win-loss mark in three seasons, Carnesecca's Nets reached the ABA playoffs each time. The 44-40 Nets squad reached the ABA Finals in 1971–1972, but after three years, Carnesecca recognized that his strength and passion rested in the teaching role of college coaching and returned in 1973 to St. John's, where he worked until 1991.

Under Carnesecca, St. John's competed in 18 NCAA tournaments and in six postseason NITs. The Redmen appeared in the NCAA's Final Four in 1985, captured the NIT Championship in 1989, and reached the NCAA Final Eight in 1991. Although initially opposing St. John's entry into the newly formed BEaC in 1979, Carnesecca became a strong proponent of conference play. In 13 BEaC seasons, St. John's shared the regular-season title three times (1980, 1983, 1986), won the crown outright in 1985, and captured the BEaC postseason tournament in 1983 and 1986. In 1983, 1985, and 1986, Carnesecca was selected BEaC Coach of the Year. He was named national Coach of the Year in 1983 and 1985. In 24 seasons, he compiled a 526-200 mark at St. John's. In 1992 he joined the Naismith Memorial Basketball Hall of Fame.

Ever the teacher, Carnesecca operated a summer basketball camp with Bernie "Red" Sarachek for over three decades in upstate New York and conducted basketball clinics in six European countries and around the world.

BIBLIOGRAPHY: Peter C. Bjarkman, *The Biographical History of Basketball* (Chicago, IL, 2000); Lou Carnesecca, with Phil Pepe, *Louie: In Season* (New York, 1988); Lou Carnesecca file, Naismith Memorial Basketball Hall of Fame, Springfield, MA; Mike Douchant, *Encyclopedia of College Basketball* (Detroit, MI, 1995); *NCAA Men's Basketball Records, 2004* (Indianapolis, IN, 2003); *1989–1990 Redmen Basketball Media Guide* (Brooklyn, NY, 1989); William C. Rhoden, "Hometown Talent Creates a Charisma," *NYT*, January 13, 1985, p. S9, George Vecsey "Looie Makes the Four," *NYT*, March 25, 1985, pp. C1, C6; Vic Ziegel, "The Gospel According to Lou," *New York* 16 (February 7, 1983), pp. 78–79.

Frederick Ivor-Campbell

CARNEVALE, Bernard L. "Ben" (b. October 30, 1915, Raritan, NJ), college and professional player, coach, and administrator, excelled in basketball at Somerville (New Jersey) High School and New York University (NYU). Under coach Howard Cann*, Carnevale played on the 1934 national championship NYU team and in 1938 captained the Violets, won All-District honors, and was chosen MVP. After graduation, he played two seasons (1938–1940) for the Jersey City Reds in the early professional leagues. Carnevale's basketball coaching career began with Cranford (New Jersey) High School, compiling 75 victories (1939–1942) and guiding his team to three consecutive state championship tournaments.

After serving in the U.S. Navy (1942–1945), Carnevale embarked on a 22-year college basketball coaching career. In Carnevale's two campaigns as University of North Carolina coach, the Tar Heels captured 51 of 62 games and two SC titles. The 1946 Tar Heels made the NCAA Finals before losing the National Championship to Oklahoma Agricultural and Mechanical (A&M) University 43-40. As head basketball coach at the U.S. Naval Academy for 20 years (1947–1966), Carnevale led his teams to 257 victories and only 158 losses. A master coach of average material, Carnevale saw his Navy teams qualify for five NCAA tournaments and two NITs. He was named College Coach of the Year in 1947 and coached the Eastern team in the annual All-Star Game in 1947 and 1967.

Equally renowned for his success as an administrator, Carnevale served as athletic director at NYU (1967–1972) and the College of William and Mary (1973–1981) until his retirement. For 20 years, Carnevale served on the Olympic basketball committee and chaired the group from 1964 to 1968. He served as president of the NABC and as a member of the NCAA Basketball Tournament Committee. He was elected president of the NACDA, IBB, and NIT, and chaired the ECAC basketball tournament committee. Carnevale was inducted into the HAF Basketball Hall of Fame (1966), Naismith Memorial Basketball Hall of Fame (1969), and NYU Hall of Fame (1976).

BIBLIOGRAPHY: Ben Carnevale file, Naismith Memorial Basketball Hall of Fame, Springfield, MA; *Converse Basketball Yearbook, 1970*; *Naismith Memorial Basketball Hall of Fame Official Souvenir Book, 1974* (Springfield, MA, 1974); *NCAA Men's Basketball Records, 2004* (Indianapolis, IN, 2003); *William and Mary Football Yearbook* (Williamsburg, VA, 1979).

John L. Evers

CARPENTER, Gordon "Shorty" (b. September 24, 1919, Ash Flat, AR; d. March 8, 1988, Denver, CO), college and amateur player, coach, and official, was the son of Odus Carpenter, and Virgie (Wadley) Carpenter, and ranked among the finest basketball players in Arkansas history. Carpenter's basketball career began in Ash Flat, a tiny hamlet of 300 people in the Ozarks. Nicknamed "Shorty," he perfected his game on outdoor courts and a gymnasium built by the Works Progress Administration during the Great Depression. In 1939, his senior year, Carpenter led Ash Flat to victories over Little Rock and Pine Bluff, Arkansas, to win the state championship. The six-foot six-inch 200-pounder possessed excellent speed and a fierce competitive attitude. Upon graduation, Carpenter played basketball at the University of Arkansas (SWC) for two years under Glen Rose and his senior year under Eugene Lambert. He started as a sophomore for the Razorbacks, who performed a perfect 12-0 slate in SWC play and lost in the championship game of the NCAA regional at Kansas City, Missouri, to Washington State University. Arkansas shared the SWC title in Carpenter's junior year. As a senior, he made the All-SWC squad.

After completing his 1943 season at Arkansas, Carpenter joined the powerful Phillips 66 basketball team of Bartlesville, Oklahoma, in time to enter his first AAU tournament in March. Several businesses employed basketball players, who performed a regular schedule and participated in a weeklong national tournament at Denver, Colorado. This tournament featured some of the nation's best players and teams. Between 1943 and 1948, Phillips 66 won the national championship a record six consecutive times. Carpenter made the AAU All-America team each year from 1943 to 1947. He scored 2,366 points, ranking as the fifth leading scorer in Phillips history. The 66ers, coached by Bud Browning, featured Bob Kurland*, Jesse "Cab" Renick, and Carpenter. In March 1948, Phillips 66 defeated Adolph Rupp's* University of Kentucky Wildcats 53-49 in the finals of the Olympic tournament at Madison Square Garden in New York. The starting five for Phillips 66 consequently made up part of the 1948 U.S. Olympic team, coached by Browning and Rupp. The United States won the gold medal at London, England in 1948, barely defeating a scrappy Argentine team 59-47. With four minutes left in the game and the United States trailing by six points, Browning inserted Carpenter into the game. Carpenter responded by scoring 10 points in two minutes to help secure the victory.

After 1948, Carpenter moved to Denver, Colorado, with his wife, Mildred, and played and coached three years for the Denver Chevrolets (AAU). In 1950, he made the AAU All-America team for the sixth and last time. Carpenter, who left basketball from 1951 until 1954, returned as an official and eventually worked games in the BSC and BEC. He and his wife had four children, David, Mark, Craig, and Carol. Carpenter, inducted into the HAF Hall of Fame in 1960 and the Arkansas Sports Hall of Fame in 1965, worked for Chevrolet until retiring in 1987.

BIBLIOGRAPHY: Gordon Carpenter scrapbooks, in possession of Mildred Carpenter, Denver, CO; Alexander M. Weyand, *The Cavalcade of Basketball* (New York, 1960).

Adolph H. Grundman

CARR, Austin George (b. March 10, 1948, Washington, DC), college and professional player, enjoyed the most prolific career in the University of Notre Dame basketball history. Carr starred in basketball, baseball, and cross country at Mackin High School in Washington, D.C., captaining his prep school basketball and baseball squads. After enrolling at Notre Dame, the six-foot four-inch, 200-pound Carr enjoyed one of the most sensational scoring careers in the history of college basketball. He averaged 38 points both his junior and senior seasons and amassed over 2,200 points in those two campaigns alone. His individual scoring records set at Notre Dame include most points in a single game (61), most points in a single home game (55), most points in a half (38), most field goals attempted in a game (44), most field goals made in a game (25), most field goals consecutively made in a game (14), most points in a season (1,106), highest points per game season average (38.1), most field goals attempted and made in a season (832 and 444), most career points (2,560), highest career scoring average (34.6), most career field goals attempted and made (1,923 and 1,107), and highest career free throw percentage (.814).

During his final two Notre Dame seasons, Carr finished as the nation's second leading scorer with 38.1 and 37.9 point averages, winning All-America honors both years and leading his Irish teams to 21-8 and 20-9 records. A disappointing senior season saw the highly touted Irish eliminated in the semifinal round of the Mid-West Regional of the NCAA tournament and the postseason resignation of Coach Johnny Dee.* Nevertheless, Carr became one of the most decorated players in NCAA history. He was voted Player of the Year by wide margins in both the AP and UPI final-season polls, and chosen a First Team All-America by every known survey in the nation. Carr closed his college career as the second player in history to score over 1,000 points in two seasons (Pete Maravich* of Louisiana State University was the first). Carr remains among career NCAA leaders in total points and scoring average. This latter accomplishment is all the more remarkable because Carr's career occurred before the reinstitution of freshman eligibility, and thus spanned only three seasons. In the summer of 1971 Carr reached the pinnacle of his basketball career when the Cleveland Cavaliers (NBA) selected him as the first player chosen in that year's NBA draft.

Carr's pro basketball career never quite measured up to his promise as a collegian, although he averaged slightly over 20 points each of his first three NBA campaigns. He enjoyed nine full NBA seasons for Cleveland before being claimed by the Dallas Mavericks (NBA) in the NBA expansion draft of 1980, a selection that effectively marked the end of Carr's pro career. Carr appeared only briefly in eight games with Dallas in the fall of 1980 before retiring. During nearly a decade in Cleveland, he had amassed over 10,000 NBA points. He never again approached a 20 points average during his final six seasons as a Cavalier, departing the NBA with a 16.2 point career scoring average. This decline in offensive productivity may have been partly due to a painful knee injury in December 1974. On retirement in 1980, however, Carr still ranked among Cleveland's all-time career leaders in several categories: games played (635), minutes played (19,003), field goals attempted (9,480), free throws made (1,719), free throws attempted (2,127), and assists (1,820). He was also the first Cleveland Cavaliers player ever selected to the NBA All-Rookie Team (1972) and represented the Cavaliers in the 1974 NBA All-Star Game in Seattle, Washington. In

1977 Carr was the media's selection as Cleveland's MVP. The popular Carr also remained active in community affairs throughout his pro playing career. A 1980 winner of the prestigious Walter Kennedy NBA Citizenship Award, he also was a 1977 Kennedy Award finalist. Subsequently Carr enjoyed careers as a successful Indianapolis, Indiana businessman and a popular Cleveland sports broadcaster. Since 1991, he has served as Director of Community and Business Development for the Cavaliers and as a television commentator for Cleveland games.

BIBLIOGRAPHY: Peter C. Bjarkman, *Hoopla: A Century of College Basketball, 1896–1996* (Indianapolis, IN, 1996); Zander Hollander, ed., *The NBA's Official Encyclopedia of Pro Basketball*, 35th Anniv. Ed. (New York, 1981); Jan Hubbard, ed., *The Official NBA Encyclopedia*, 3rd ed. (New York, 2000); Tim Neely, *Hooping It Up: The Complete History of Notre Dame Basketball* (Notre Dame, IN, 1985).

Peter C. Bjarkman

CARRIL, Peter Joseph (b. July 10, 1930, Bethlehem, PA), college player and coach, graduated from Liberty High School in Bethlehem, Pennsylvania in 1948 and lettered in basketball from 1948 to 1952 at Lafayette College in Easton, Pennsylvania under coach Butch Van Breda Kolff*. After coaching at Easton High School and Reading High School, Carril coached basketball in 1966–1967 at Lehigh University in Bethlehem. His tenure as basketball coach at Princeton University (IvL) began in 1967.

Carril's father, a native of Spain who worked for 39 years with Bethlehem Steel Company, had a colossal influence on Carril, urging his son to use his head and think clearly. Carril's credo consequently stressed teaching rather than winning and recruiting. John Wooden* may have been the most successful coach in college basketball and Bobby Knight* may have been the game's most tempestuous coach, but Carril may have been college basketball's finest teacher. Although the game has seen many terrific motivators, Carril proved a brilliant teacher of students recruited for academic strengths rather than great athleticism, amazing size, and awesome power. At Princeton University, he could not recruit the sky-walkers, stellar high school sensations, and "long range bombers" that fired up basketball programs at UCLA, the University of Kentucky, or the University of Michigan.

Carril stuck to practice, hard work, and determination. He demanded that his players be disciplined and schooled in the fundamentals. The highlight of Carril's career came in March 1996. In front of a vast national television audience, his Tigers defeated the UCLA Bruins 43–41 in the first round of the NCAA tournament. The Bruins were heavily favored as the defending national champions. This defining moment came after Carril had taught and coached 29 years in an IvL more known for its distinguished academic alumnae rather than its basketball teams. Carril's impeccable Princeton record included 525 victories, 273 losses, and 13 IvL Championships.

Following his upset victory over the Bruins in 1996, Carril became an assistant basketball coach with the Sacramento Kings (NBA). He married Dolores Halteman and has two grown children, Peter and Lisa.

Carril's biographical coaching manifesto, *The Smart Take From the Strong* (1997) remains a delightful, whimsical teaching manual. Carril plays down the cult of personality and wonders why a prestigious university employed a little man with balding hair who smoked cigars. Princeton simply recognized Carril as an exemplary teacher, whose impact on players seemed to make them better people. John McPhee likens Carril to Civil War icon Stonewall Jackson, both being unforgettable in defeat and unbelievable in victory. He was inducted into the Naismith Memorial Basketball Hall of Fame in 1997.

BIBLIOGRAPHY: Pete Carril with Don White, *The Smart Take From the Strong* (New York, 1997); Pete Carril file, Naismith Memorial Basketball Hall of Fame, Springfield, MA; Mike Douchant, *Encyclopedia of College Basketball* (Detroit, MI, 1995); *NCAA Men's Basketball Records, 2004* (Indianapolis, IN, 2003). www.princeton.edu/~paw/archiveold/hoops/carril.html

Scott A.G.M. Crawford

CARTER, Vincent Lamar, Jr. "Vince" (b. January 26, 1977, Daytona Beach, FL), college and professional player, is the son of Vincent Carter Sr. and Michelle Carter, a teacher. His parents divorced when Vince was seven. Michelle remarried Harry Robinson, also a teacher. In seventh grade, Carter started dunking the ball. He led Mainland High School to the Florida Class 6A basketball championship in his senior year and was selected to the 1995 USA Junior National Team. The talented Carter also played saxophone and drum. In 1995 he entered the University of North Carolina at Chapel Hill, majoring in African American Studies.

In his freshman year, the six-foot six-inch, 225-pound guard-forward averaged 7.5 points in 31 games. He helped the Tar Heels win the ACC title in 1996–1997 and reach the NCAA Final Four twice in 1997 and 1998. In 1997–1998, Carter was named First Team All-ACC and Second Team All-America. He was selected fifth overall by the Golden State Warriors (NBA) in the June 1998 NBA draft and was immediately traded to the Toronto Raptors (NBA).

During his rookie season, Carter led all rookies in scoring (18.3 points average) and blocked shots (1.54 average). He was named NBA Rookie of the Month in March and April and eventually earned Schick Rookie of the Year honors. In 1999–2000, Carter averaged 25.7 points and 5.8 rebounds and led the Raptors to their first winning season and playoff berth. He was voted to the NBA All-Star Team as a starter and won the 2000 NBA.com Slam Dunk Contest. Carter joined the 2000 U.S.A. Olympic team, which won the Gold Medal at the Olympic Games in Sydney, Australia. In 2000–2001, he led the Raptors to the Eastern Conference Semifinals, averaged 27.6 points and 5.5 rebounds, and was selected to the All-NBA Second Team. In August 2001, Carter signed a six-year $94 million contract extension with the Raptors. He averaged 24.7 points and 5.2 rebounds in 2001–2002, 20.6 points and 4.4 rebounds in 2002–2003, 22.5 points and 4.8 rebounds in 2003–2004, and 24.5 points and 5.2 rebounds in 2004–2005. He averaged 26.8 points in four games in the first round playoff sweep by the Miami Heat. His NBA career totals include 10,989 points and 2,426 rebounds in 460 regular-season games and 492 points and 130 rebounds in 19 playoff games. He also made the Eastern Conference All-Star Team in 2000, 2001, 2002, 2003, 2004, and 2005. In December 2004, the New Jersey Nets (NBA) acquired him for Alonzo Mourning, Eric Williams, Aaron Williams, and two first round draft picks.

Carter, nicknamed "Air Canada," founded the Embassy of Hope Foundation and serves as President of Visions In Flight, Inc. He was named a "Goodwill Ambassador" by Big Brothers/Big Sisters of America in 1998. Carter earned his Bachelor's degree from North Carolina in May 2001 and has a younger brother, Chris.

BIBLIOGRAPHY: Peter G. Herman, "Vince Carter," *CB* 63 (April 2002), pp. 16–20; David G. Oblender ed., *Contemporary Black Biography* 26 (2000); Phil Taylor and David Sabino, "Fresh Vince," *SI* 92 (February 28, 2000), pp. 36–41; Ken Shouler et al., *Total Basketball* (Wilmington, DE, 2003); *TSN Official NBA Register, 2004–2005* (St. Louis, MO, 2004); Chris Young, *Drive: How Vince Carter Conquered the NBA* (Toronto, Canada, 2001).

Di Su

CASE, Everett Norris (b. June 21, 1900, Anderson, IN; d. April 30, 1966, Raleigh, NC), college coach, guided North Carolina State University to 10 SC and ACC titles and to five NCAA and three NIT appearances in 18 years. After assuming the head coaching position at North Carolina State for the 1946–1947 season, Case led the Wolfpack to seven consecutive SC regular-season titles and six postseason tournament championships during his era before falling to Wake Forest University 71–70 in the Wolfpack's final SC tournament. In 1954 North Carolina State became a member of the new ACC, finishing fourth in the final standings and taking the ACC postseason tournament by defeating the Demon Deacons 82–80. The Wolfpack posted three more ACC titles (1955, 1956, 1959), and averaged a remarkable 25 victories in each of Case's first 13 seasons. Case in 1982 was named to the Naismith Memorial Basketball Hall of Fame.

Case never played high school or college basketball, but was influenced by the Indiana hardcourt tradition and became thoroughly familiar with the game. At age 18, he coached his first winning basketball team at Connersville (IN) High School. Case emphasized pattern basketball but occasionally used the fast break. The silver-haired "old gray fox" was known for inspiring his players with emotional exhortations.

North Carolina State University under Case was only mildly successful in national postseason tournament play. The Wolfpack placed third in the 1947 NIT after losing 60-42 to the University of Kentucky's "Fabulous Five" in the semifinals and defeating West Virginia University 64–52 in the consolation game. Similarly, North Carolina State took third in the 1950 NCAA Tournament when dropping a close 78–73 semifinal decision to ultimate champion CCNY and defeating Baylor University 53–41 in the consolation contest. The eight-team field included Holy Cross College, which lost 87-74 to the Wolfpack in the first round, marking the Crusaders' Bob Cousy's* final appearance as a collegian. North Carolina State was led by Vic Bubas*, All-Americans Dick Dickey, and Sam Ranzino. The Wolfpack suffered first-round losses in the 1948 NIT (75-64 to DePaul University), 1952 NCAA (60–49 to St. John's University), and 1956 NCAA (79-78 to Canisius College in four overtimes) tournament. North Carolina State was eliminated in the second round of the 1951 NIT (71–59 to Seton Hall University with Walter Dukes*), 1951 NCAA (84-70 to the University of Illinois), and 1954 NCAA (88–81 to eventual national champion LaSalle University with Tom Gola*) tournaments.

North Carolina State University in 1951 led the nation in scoring, averaging 77.9 points. Ranzino, Bubas, and center Paul Horvath, all four-year veterans, were permitted to play in the NIT, but were declared ineligible for the NCAA tourney. In subsequent seasons, Case developed All-Americans Bob Speight (1953), Ron Shavlik* (1955–1956), guard Vic Molodet (1956), and John Richter (1959). Celebrated "Hot Rod" Hundley* sought to enroll at North Carolina State in 1954, the same year the ACC and NCAA announced sanctions against the Wolfpack for recruiting violations. Case, however, advised Hundley to enroll at West Virginia University.

North Carolina State University's fortunes under Case took a downturn his final five seasons when his teams averaged only 11 victories annually and produced only one winning record. Case suffered from an ulcer and quit coaching after the second game of the 1965 season, an 86–80 loss to Wake Forest University, stating that the "emotion of the game is too great." Press Maravich succeeded Case as head coach and guided the Wolfpack to the 1965 NCAA tournament. Case finished with a 379–134 (.738 percent) career record in 18-plus seasons at North Carolina State. Case, who never married, suffered for three years from a bone disease (myeloma) and spent his final year in a wheel chair after spinal cord surgery. He succumbed to complications from an operation for a bleeding ulcer.

BIBLIOGRAPHY: Peter C. Bjarkman, *ACC-Atlantic Coast Conference Basketball* (Indianapolis, IN, 1996); Everett Case file, Naismith Memorial Basketball Hall of Fame, Springfield, MA; Neil D. Isaacs, *All The Moves: A History of College Basketball* (Philadelphia, PA, 1975); William G. Mokray, ed., *Ronald Encyclopedia of Basketball* (New York, 1963); Ron Morris, ed., *ACC Basketball: An Illustrated History* (Chapel Hill, NC, 1986); *NCAA Official Collegiate Basketball Guides, 1951–1966* (New York, 1951–1966); *NIT Quarter-Final Program*, New York, March 13, 1951; *NYT*, May 1, 1966; Ken Rappoport, *The Classic: History of the NCAA Championship* (Mission, KS, 1979); Alexander M. Weyand, *The Cavalcade of Basketball* (New York, 1960).

James D. Whalen and Wayne Patterson

CATCHINGS, Tamika Devonne (b. July 21, 1979, Stratford, NJ), college and professional player, is the daughter of Harvey Catchings, who played in the NBA from 1974 until 1986 and often took her to pick-up games, and Wanda Catchings. Throughout her childhood, Catchings showed a special interest and ability in basketball. At Stevenson High School in Lincolnshire, IL, she and her older sister, Tauja, both excelled in the sport. Tamika played basketball there from 1993 to 1995 and became the first underclassman to win Illinois' Miss Basketball honors as a sophomore. When her parents divorced in 1995, she moved back to Duncanville, Texas with her mother, Wanda. Tauja stayed with Harvey in Illinois. Tamika played at Duncanville High School from 1995 to 1997 helping lead them to a state title and being named the Naismith National Schoolgirl Player of the Year (1997). She also maintained a B average despite a severe hearing loss, participated in volleyball and track and field, and recorded a quintuple-double with 25 points, 18 rebounds, 11 assists, 10 steals, and 10 blocked shots in a basketball game.

The highly recruited six-foot, 160-pound Catchings, known for her work ethic and winning personality, chose to attend the University of Tennessee (SEC) and starred for the Volunteers from 1997–2001. At Tennessee, she earned All-America honors all four years and amassed a freshman record of 18.2 points per game. Catchings ranked third in Tennessee's all-time scoring (2,113) and rebounds (1,004), and recorded 33 double-doubles. She proved instrumental in the Lady Vols' 1998 NCAA championship and 39-0 undefeated season. In 2000 Catchings won Naismith National and College Player of the Year honors. She also received the Reynolds Society Achievement Award, given by the Massachusetts Eye and Ear Infirmary to an individual who has overcome a hearing, vision, or voice loss and shown exemplary character. During her senior year, she tore the anterior cruciate ligament on her right knee and was forced to watch from the bench.

Despite her injury, Catchings was selected third in the 2001 WNBA draft by the Indiana Fever. During practice, she tore cartilage in the same knee and sat out the entire 2001 season. In 2002, she led the WNBA in points (594), three point shots (76), and steals (94), and finished second in rebounding (296), sixth in blocked shots (43), and tenth in assists (118) in 32 games. She scored 12 points in the WNBA All-Star Game and averaged 20.3 points and 32 rebounds in three playoff games, earning WNBA Rookie of the Year honors. In 2003, Catchings led the WNBA in minutes played (1,210), finished second in scoring (671 points), and steals (72) and fifth in rebounds (272) in 34 games. The following season, she ranked third in the WNBA in rebounds (249) and fourth in scoring (568 points) and steals (67) in 34 games. In 100 WNBA games, Catchings has tallied 1,833 points, 797 rebounds, and 233 steals. She was named to the All-WNBA First Team in 2002 and 2003. She played on the 2004 U.S. Olympic women's basketball team, which won the gold medal.

BIBLIOGRAPHY: Kelli Anderson, "Now Hear This," *SI* 89 (November 23, 1998); Dan Fleser, "The Next Big Thing," *TSN* 48 (November 30, 1998), pp. 90–91; Chamique Holdsclaw, *Chamique* (New York, 2000); Pat Summitt, *Raise the Roof* (New York, 1998); WNBA website, www.wnba.com.; *WNBA Official Guide and Register, 2004* (St. Louis, MO, 2003).

Lisa A. Ennis

CERVI, Alfred Nicholas "Al" "Digger" (b. February 12, 1917, Buffalo, NY), college and professional player and coach, is the son of Faust Cervi, a building contractor, and Assunta (Malone) Cervi. He played basketball and football at East High School in Buffalo before leaving school his junior year to help in the family business. Cervi, who never attended college, married Ruth Marion Smith of Buffalo in 1941 and has three children, Allen, Kathleen, and Marcia. The five-foot eleven-inch 185-pounder joined the Buffalo Bisons of the newly formed NBL in the 1937–1938 season, scoring 44 points in nine games. Cervi served in the U.S. Army-Air Force from 1940 through 1945 and made the NCAA Tournament All-Star Team in 1942.

Cervi joined the new Rochester Royals (NBL) franchise as team captain in 1945 and made the All-NBL First Team from the 1945–1946 through 1948–1949 seasons and the All-NBA Second Team during the 1949–1950 campaign. His outstanding accolades included being the NBL's best defensive player, one of the leading NBL scorers, and a great clutch performer. In 1945–1946 the veteran guard teamed with former collegians Bob Davies*, Red Holzman*, George Glamack*, and Fuzzy Levane to help Rochester win the NBL championship. The Royals lost the NBL championship to the Chicago Gears in 1946–1947, but Cervi led the NBL in scoring with 632 points, averaged 14.4 points, and was selected NBL MVP. In 1947–1948 the Minneapolis Lakers defeated the injury-riddled Royals in the NBL Finals. The Syracuse Nationals (NBL) hired Cervi as player-coach in 1948. Cervi scored a career-high 695 points in 1948–1949, averaging 12.2 points in 57 contests. *The Coach Sports Extra* chose him to the All-U.S. team during the 1948–1949 and 1949–1950 seasons. Cervi played through the 1952–1953 season, tallying 3,917 career points and averaging 10.1 points in 389 NBL-NBA games.

Cervi enjoyed considerable success as Syracuse coach from the 1948–1949 through the 1955–1956 seasons. During his initial season, he guided Syracuse to a 40-23 mark and second place finish in the Eastern Division to garner Coach of the Year honors. Syracuse enjoyed its best regular season under Cervi in 1949–1950, placing first in the Eastern Division with a 51-13 record. Cervi and forward Dolph Schayes* paced the Nationals to the Eastern Division championship over the New York Knickerbockers, but the Nationals lost the NBA Finals in six games to the Minneapolis Lakers. In 1951–1952 the Nationals compiled a 40-26 mark for a first place regular-season finish before falling to the Knicks in the Eastern Division finals. Cervi coached the Eastern All-Stars to victories over the Western All-Stars in 1952 at Boston, Massachusetts and 1955 at New York. Syracuse recorded successive second-place regular-season performances in 1952–1953 and 1953–1954. In 1954 Cervi steered Syracuse to the Eastern Division title over the Boston Celtics to earn Coach of the Year honors. Minneapolis, however, defeated Syracuse in seven contests to capture the NBA championship. NBA Coach of the Year honors also were bestowed on Cervi in 1949–1950, 1951–1952, and 1954–1955.

Cervi's 43-29 1954–1955 squad earned first place in the Eastern Division regular season and captured the Eastern Division playoff crown over Boston. Schayes, an excellent rebounder, and Paul Seymour*, an outstanding passer, paced the Nationals to their first NBA championship in seven games over the Fort Wayne Pistons. Valuable supportive roles were played by Red Rocha, Earl Lloyd*, and George King*. The tempestuous Cervi left the Nationals after a disappointing performance in 1955–1956 and coached the Philadelphia Warriors (NBA) to fourth place in 1958–1959 before retiring. As an NBA coach for nine seasons, he compiled a 366–264 mark, three Eastern Division titles, and one NBA championship. Cervi's 266–127 record as a player-coach may be the best in pro basketball history.

Cervi subsequently worked as sales manager for Eastern Freightways and Berman's Motor Express, both trucking firms, and directed the Al Cervi Boys' and Girls' Basketball Camps for 28 years at Hobart and William Smith Colleges in Geneva, New York. He was named to the Rochester Hall of Fame in 1942 and the Naismith Memorial Basketball Hall of Fame in 1985. His other honors include being selected to the All-Time Rochester Pro Five by the Rochester Press Radio Club in 1948 and winning the Lawrence Skiddy Award as Syracuse Athlete of the Year in 1950. He also was chosen one of the All-Time Greats of the Pro Game by the Stadium Club of Rochester in 1970 and as the best guard from 1946 through 1956 by *All/Sports Pro Magazine* in 1971. In 1982 the *Rochester Democrat and Chronicle* Press Club gave Cervi the first Golden Glow Award for his contributions to basketball and the city.

BIBLIOGRAPHY: Peter C. Bjarkman, *The Encyclopedia of Pro Basketball Team Histories* (New York, 1994); Alfred N. Cervi to David L. Porter, January 10, 1988; Alfred N. Cervi file, Naismith Memorial Basketball Hall of Fame, Springfield, MA; Jan Hubbard, ed., *The Official NBA Encyclopedia*, 3rd ed. (New York, 2000); Neil D. Isaacs, *Vintage NBA* (Silver Spring, MD, 1996); Ed Linn, "Coach with the Terrible Temper," *SEP* 228 (February 18, 1956), pp. 25ff; Charles Salzberg, *From Set Shot to Slam Dunk—The Glory Days of Basketball in the Words of Those Who Played It* (New York, 1987).

David L. Porter and Wayne Patterson

CHAMBERLAIN, Wilton Norman "Wilt" "Wilt the Stilt" "The Big Dipper" (b. August 21, 1936, Philadelphia, PA; d. October 12, 1999, Bel Air, CA), college athlete and professional player and coach, is one of nine children (two died in infancy) born to William and Olivia Chamberlain. His father was employed as a welder, custodian, and handyman, while his mother worked as a part-time domestic to provide a comfortable lifestyle for the large family. A gifted athlete, Wilt excelled at track and basketball in junior and senior high school. At Overbrook High School in Philadelphia, he competed in the 440- and 880-yard dashes and won the city championship in the shotput and high jump as a senior. As the nation's premier prep basketball player, he scored 2,252 points in three years (90 points in one game) and led

Overbrook to a 58-3 record and two city championships. After his senior season, the Philadelphia Warriors (NBA) claimed future territorial draft rights to him, and Forrest C. "Phog" Allen*, of the University of Kansas, won the fierce recruiting battle for his college services.

Chamberlain was the most heralded player in college history. To counter his awesome ability, numerous rule changes were made, including widening the lane, instituting offensive goaltending, and revising rules governing inbounding the ball and shooting free throws. Nonetheless, he scored 52 points in his varsity debut as a sophomore and led the Jayhawks to the NCAA Finals, where Kansas lost in triple overtime to top-ranked University of North Carolina, 54-53. Although twice named All-America, he was frustrated by the gang-guarding and stalling tactics of opponents and left Kansas after his junior year to tour with the Harlem Globetrotters. At Kansas, he lettered in track and field three years, running the 100-yard dash in 10.9 seconds and the 440-yard dash in 48.9 seconds. He also exceeded 50 feet in the triple jump, threw the shot put 56 feet, and leaped nearly 6-feet 7-inches in winning the BEC high jump title three years.

Chamberlain joined the Philadelphia Warriors (NBA) for the 1959–1960 NBA season and immediately became a superstar. An All-Star and All-NBA First Team selection, he was named MVP and Rookie of the Year after setting eight NBA season records, including total points (2,707), scoring average (37.6), and rebounds (1,941). During 14 NBA seasons with the Philadelphia Warriors (1959–1961), Golden State Warriors (1962–1965), Philadelphia 76ers (1965–1968), and Los Angeles Lakers (1968–1973), he was named MVP four times (1960, 1966–1968) and All-NBA First Team seven times (1960–1962, 1964, 1966–1968) and All-NBA Second Team three times (1963, 1965, 1972). Selected to 13 All-Star Games (every year except 1970), Chamberlain set career records for most minutes played (388) and rebounds (197) and in 1960 was named MVP. In 1962 he set single All-Star Game highs for points scored (42), field goals made (17), and free throws attempted (18).

The seven-foot one-inch, 275-pound Chamberlain was a prodigious scorer. Relying on a fade-away jump shot early in his career and then utilizing unstoppable fingertip rolls and dunks, he posted a career record 30.1 points per game average and became the first player to exceed 30,000 points (31,419). He led the NBA in scoring seven consecutive years (1959–1965) and enjoyed his greatest offensive season in 1961–1962, when he established the astounding records of 4,029 total points, 50.4 points per game, and 100 points in a single game on March 2, 1962 against the New York Knickerbockers in Hershey, Pennsylvania. Although leading the NBA in field goal percentage nine times (1960–1961, 1962–1963, 1964–1965 to 1968–1969, 1971–1972 to 1972–1973), he shot free throws poorly, with a career average of slightly over 50 percent. He often was deliberately fouled while shooting field goals.

A peerless rebounder, Chamberlain led the NBA in rebounding 11 times (1959–1960 to 1962–1963, 1965–1966 to 1967–1968, and 1970–1971 to 1972–1973), set career records for total rebounds (23,924) and per game average (22.9), and in 1960–1961 grabbed a record 55 caroms in a single game.

Chamberlain emphasized scoring and rebounding early in his career, but later stressed playmaking and defense with great success. He paced the NBA in assists in 1967–1968 (702) and was named to the All-Defensive team in 1971–1972 and 1972–1973. The only player ever to lead the NBA in field goal percentage, rebounding, and assists in the same season (1967–1968), Chamberlain proved a remarkably durable and determined player. He led the NBA eight times in the most minutes played and set records for average minutes per game for career (45.8) and season (48.5), most minutes played in a season (3,806 in 1962–1963), most complete games played (79), and most consecutive complete games (47). He never fouled out in 1,045 games over 14 seasons.

After the 1972–1973 season, Chamberlain signed a three-year contract as player-coach with the San Diego Conquistadors (ABA). But the Lakers secured a court injunction to prevent him from playing during his "option" year, forcing him to spend the season as an unenthusiastic and unsuccessful coach. The Conquistadors tied for last in the Western Division, made the playoffs by means of a tie-breaker game, and finished the season with a mediocre 38-47 record (.447). Weary of the game and with no goals unreached, he obtained his release from San Diego in 1974 and retired. He subsequently rejected several offers to return to the NBA.

When Chamberlain left the NBA in 1973, he had led the 76ers (1967) and Lakers (1972) to championships and held or shared 43 NBA records. He was the most dominant player in basketball history and perhaps the most dominant athlete in any sport. He revolutionized the game by ushering in the era of the prevalent center. Statistically and physically, he dwarfed the competition and still dominates the record book many years after retirement. The game's most prolific scorer, he held the top four, 15 of the top 18, and 49 of the top 60 marks for points scored in a single game; the four highest season scoring totals; and the five highest season per-game averages. He recorded the top seven season rebound totals and five of the top eight, and 24 of the top 40 single-game rebound marks. He also held the top five season minutes-played tallies and the top seven marks for average minutes per game.

The moody, outspoken, egotistical, and independent Chamberlain was a controversial player who, despite his achievements and notoriety, generally was underestimated and misunderstood. He clashed with coaches and teammates over practice habits and demanded preferential treatment, but also possessed a fierce desire to excel and repeatedly changed his game to meet the demands of the coach and the composition of the team. His feats often were attributed simply to his prodigious size, but he was a superb all-around athlete who possessed exceptional speed, strength, and stamina and received serious offers to become a pro boxer and football player. He was labeled a "loser" because Kansas failed to win the NCAA title and his NBA teams finished second so often to the Boston Celtics, but each team he played for performed much better after he joined the squad and his teams alone regularly challenged basketball's greatest dynasty. The press and fans gave him second billing to Bill Russell*, but he consistently outperformed the Celtics' center in direct competition and posted superior season and career marks. He despised the nickname "Wilt the Stilt," preferring "The Big Dipper" instead, and perceptively explained his lack of recognition and appreciation by noting, "Nobody roots for Goliath."

In retirement, Chamberlain cultivated his all-around athletic interests and abilities. He sponsored several track and field clubs in the Los Angeles area, played professional volleyball, and helped to found the IVA. While continuing to receive inquiries about returning to pro basketball, he excelled in various sports, ranging from volleyball to waterskiing and polo. He appeared in numerous commercials and played a supporting role in the movie *Conan the Destroyer* (1984). A confirmed bachelor, he lived in the huge, luxurious house he designed in Bel Air, CA, overlooking Los Angeles. Chamberlain, elected to the Naismith Memorial Basketball Hall of Fame in 1978, was a great athlete whose prodigious individual basketball feats will probably never be equaled.

Chamberlain, who authored the wildly-publicized, *A View from Above* (1991), was named to the NBA's 50th Anniversary All-Time Team in 1996. He owned Wilt Chamberlain Restaurants, Inc. from 1992 until his death.

BIBLIOGRAPHY: Peter Carry, "High but No Longer Mighty," *SI* 39 (October 29, 1973), pp. 44–53; Wilt Chamberlain, "Why I Am Quitting College," *Look* 22 (June 10, 1958), pp. 91–94ff.; Wilt Chamberlain, as told to Tim Cohane, "Pro Basketball Has Ganged Up on Me," *Look* 24 (March 1, 1960), pp. 51–55ff.; Wilt Chamberlain, *A View from Above* (New York, 1991); Wilt Chamberlain with Roy Blount Jr., "My Impact Will Be Everlasting," *SI* 41 (October 7, 1974), pp. 36–37ff.; Wilt Chamberlain and David Shaw, *Wilt: Just Like Any Other.7-Foot Black Millionaire Who Lives Next Door* (New York, 1973); Wilt Chamberlain file, Naismith Memorial Basketball Hall of Fame, Springfield, MA; *CB* (1960), pp. 85–86; Frank Deford, "On Top—But in Trouble," *SI* 30 (January 27, 1969), pp. 10–13; Glenn Dickey, *The History of Professional Basketball Since 1896* (Briarcliff Manor, NY, 1982); Jan Hubbard, ed., *The Official NBA Encyclopedia*, 3rd ed. (New York, 2000), Bill Libby, *Goliath: The Wilt Chamberlain Story* (New York, 1977), Wayne Lynch, *Season of the 76ers* (New York, 2002); Ralph Novak, "Wilt Chamberlain," *People* 22 (July 30, 1984), pp. 43–47; *NYT*, September 27, 1973, October 2 and 11, 1973, March 30, 1974, October 1, 1974, February 4, 1979; October 13, 1999; Billy Packer and Roland Lazenby, *College Basketball's 25 Greatest Teams* (St. Louis, MO, 1989); Louie Robinson, "The High Price of Being Wilt Chamberlain," *Ebony* 29 (January 1974), pp. 94–101; George Sullivan, *Wilt Chamberlain* rev. ed., (New York, 1971); *TSN Official NBA Guide, 2004–2005* (St. Louis, MO, 2004); *TSN*, February 6, 1982, April 16 and May 28, 1984; A. S. Young, "The Track Team That Wilt Built," *Ebony* 37 (October 1982), pp. 68–72.

Larry R. Gerlach

CHAMBERS, Thomas Doane "Tom" (b. June 21, 1959, Ogden, UT), college and professional player and executive, spent his formative years in Boulder, Colorado, and played basketball at Fairview High School, where he earned All-America honors while averaging 27.6 points and 17.3 rebounds as a senior. Chambers attended the University of Utah (WAC), where he made the All-WAC Second Team as a sophomore and junior. During his senior season, he led Utah to a 25-5 record and paced the Redskins in scoring with 18.6 points per game. His honors included making the All-WAC First Team and earning Honorable Mention All-America. He completed his collegiate career as Utah's sixth all-time leading scorer and second all-time leading rebounder.

The San Diego Clippers (NBA) selected the 6-foot 10-inch, 230-pound Chambers in the first round in 1981. As a rookie, Chambers led the Clippers in scoring with a 17.2 point average and pulled down 6.9 rebounds per game. He provided one of the few bright spots in an otherwise dismal season for San Diego. His second pro season also proved solid, as he scored 17.6 points per game.

In August 1983, San Diego traded Chambers to the Seattle SuperSonics (NBA). He averaged 18.1 points in his first year with Seattle and saw his first playoff action. He played five seasons with the SuperSonics and enjoyed his best season in 1986–1987, averaging 23.3 points. Chambers also appeared in his first All-Star Game, replacing the injured Ralph Sampson. Before his hometown Seattle crowd, he scored 34 points and was named the game's MVP.

In July 1988, Chambers signed with the Phoenix Suns (NBA) as the first unrestricted free agent in NBA history. In his first year with Phoenix, he set career highs in nearly all offensive statistical categories. His season featured a 25.7 point scoring average and a team-leading 8.4 rebounds per game. Chambers and Kevin Johnson* helped the Suns improve by 27 wins to 55 victories and a trip to the Western Conference finals. The 1989–1990 season saw Chambers fare even better, as he finished fourth in the NBA in scoring with 27.2 points per game and attained a career-high and team-record 60 points in a March game against Seattle.

A painful back limited Chambers the following two seasons, as his scoring average declined to 19.9 points per game in 1990–1991 and 16.6 points per game in 1991–1992. In June 1992, Phoenix traded for All-Star forward Charles Barkley* and moved Chambers to the bench. Although no longer the primary focus of the Phoenix offense, Chambers adapted well to his new reserve role. He recorded career lows in minutes played and scoring, but his valuable experience and clutch substitute play helped the Suns post a 62-20 record. In August 1993, the Utah Jazz (NBA) signed Chambers as a free agent. His point production declined further, but he played a valuable supportive role. He played with Utah through 1994–1995, spent 1995–1996 with Maccabo Tel-Aviv (Israeli League) and finished his NBA career with Charlotte (NBA) in 1996–1997 and briefly with the Philadelphia 76ers (NBA) in 1997–1998.

One of the most fluid, versatile players to play in the NBA, Chambers excelled at both the forward and center positions. He used his quickness against centers or strong forwards and his size to his advantage against small forwards. He played in 16 NBA seasons through 1997–1998, scored 20,049 points for a 18.1 points average, and grabbed 6,703 rebounds (6.1 average). A four-time All-Star Game performer (1987, 1989, 1990, 1991), he compiled an impressive 19.3 scoring average in those contests. Chambers, who made Second Team All-NBA as a forward in 1989 and 1990, has two daughters, Erika and

Megen, and one son, Skyler. Since December 1997 he has served as community relations representative for the Phoenix Suns.

BIBLIOGRAPHY: *Fast Break 3* (December 1991); Jan Hubbard, ed., *The Official NBA Encyclopedia*, 3rd ed. (New York, 2000); *Phoenix Suns Media Guide, 1992–1993* (Phoenix, AZ, 1992); Salt Lake City Tribune Staff, ed., *Runnin' Utes Basketball* (Champaign, IL, 1998); Ken Shouler et al., *Total Basketball* (Wilmington, DE, 2003); Martin Taragano, *Basketball Biographies 1891–1990* (Jefferson, NC, 1991); *TSN Official NBA Guide*, 1996–1997 (St. Louis, MO, 1996); *TSN Official NBA Register, 2004–2005* (St. Louis, MO, 2004).

Curtice R. Mang

CHANEY, John (b. January 21, 1932, Jacksonville, FL), college and professional player and coach, was named 1987 USBWA Coach of the Year and consensus 1988 Coach of the Year. Chaney, who served as basketball coach at Cheyney State University (1973–1982) and Temple University (ATC, 1983–present), has compiled a 708-283 win–loss career record and ranks percentage wise (.714) among the ten winningest active NCAA Division I coaches. His teams have averaged 22 wins per season, posting at least 20 triumphs in 23 of 32 campaigns.

Chaney's father, Sylvester, worked as a carpenter, while his mother, Earley, was employed as a seamstress. The Chaneys settled in Philadelphia, Pennsylvania, where John attended Benjamin Franklin High School and was selected the PPL's basketball MVP in 1950. Chaney garnered more basketball honors at Bethune-Cookman College in Florida, making All-SIAA, NAIA All-America, and 1953 MVP at the NAIA Championships. He graduated from Bethune-Cookman with a Bachelor's degree in 1953 and later earned a Master's degree there.

Chaney played for 10 EPBL seasons, making All-EPBL seven times and being named the EPBL's MVP twice. Cheyney State appointed him as head basketball coach in 1972. Chaney guided the Wolves to five NCAA Division II Regional titles and compiled a 10-year composite 225-59 win–loss record. Cheyney State captured the 1978 Division II national championship, logging a superlative 27-2 school record. Chaney, an instructor in the university's Department of HPER, received the State of Pennsylvania Distinguished Faculty Award in 1979.

Temple University had not produced consecutive 25-win seasons or participated in consecutive NCAA Tournaments before Chaney became the Owls' head basketball coach in 1982. He piloted Temple to 18 consecutive postseason tournaments, including 14 NCAA and four NIT competitions. A four-time ATC Coach of the Year, Chaney was named Kodak District Coach of the Year each year from 1984 through 1988. He guided the Owls to ATC titles in 1985, 1987, 1988, 1990, 1998, 1999, 2000, and 2002 and coached talented performers including Terence Stansbury, Ramon Rivas, Nate Blackwell, Tim Perry, Duane Causwell, and All-America Mark Macon. The 1986–1987 Temple squad ranked eighth in the final AP and UPI polls with a 32-4 mark. The following season, the 32-2 Owls were rated regular-season national champions by both wire services and advanced to the NCAA Final Eight. Temple also reached the NCAA Final Eight in 1992–1993 and 1998–1999. Chaney's record at Temple through 2004–2005 remains 496 wins and only 236 losses (.678 percent). Chaney was suspended in February 2005 for three weeks for ordering rough play by one of his players, who broke the arm of a St. Joseph's University player. He married Jeanne Dixon of Philadelphia in 1953 and has two sons, Darryl and John, and one daughter, Pamela. In 2001, he was inducted into the Naismith Memorial Basketball Hall of Fame.

BIBLIOGRAPHY: John Chaney file, Naismith Memorial Basketball Hall of Fame, Springfield MA; Reíd Cherner, "Chaney Builds Winners Even When He's Losing," *USA Today*, January 14, 2004, pp. 1c–2c; Mike Douchant, *Encyclopedia of College Basketball* (Detroit, MI, 1995); *NCAA Men's Basketball Records, 2004* (Indianapolis, 2003); Sports Information Office, Temple University, Philadelphia, PA, September 1990; *TSN 2004–2005 College Basketball Yearbook* (St. Louis, MO, 2004).

James D. Whalen

CHAPPELL, Leonard Roy "Lenny" (b. January 31, 1941, Portage, PA), college and professional player, is the son of John Chappell, a coal miner, and Helen Chappell. Chappell grew up in Portage, Pennsylvania, and starred in basketball at Portage Area High School.

The six-foot eight-inch, 240-pound Chappell attended Wake Forest University (ACC) from 1958 to 1962. Blessed with strength, agility, and shooting ability, he keyed Wake Forest to the 1961 and 1962 ACC basketball championships and the 1962 NCAA Final Four, the Demon Deacons only appearance in that event. Chappell led the ACC in scoring in 1961 with 26.6 points per game and the following season with 30.1 points per contest. He also paced the ACC in rebounding those two seasons. Chappell was selected ACC Player of the Year in 1961 and 1962 and First-Team All-ACC in 1960, 1961, and 1962. AP named him First-Team All-America in 1962. He finished his varsity career at Wake Forest with 2,165 points (24.0 point average) and 1,213 rebounds (13.9 average) in 87 games.

The Syracuse Nationals (NBA) selected Chappell in the first round of the 1962 draft. Chappell played for eight NBA teams through 1971. His best season came in 1964, when he averaged 17.1 points for the Philadelphia 76ers (NBA) and New York Knicks (NBA). Chappell finished his pro career in 1972 with the Dallas Chaparrals (ABA), where he averaged 7.7 points and 4.0 rebounds. He scored 5,621 career points and made 3,113 rebounds in the NBA, averaging 9.5 points and 5.3 rebounds in 591 regular-season games.

Subsequently, Chappell has engaged in the sporting goods business in Milwaukee. He married Ellen Brager in 1964 and had a daughter, Kirsten. He married Joanna Totushek in 1978. Their sons John and Jason play basketball at the University of South Carolina and the University of Wisconsin, respectively.

BIBLIOGRAPHY: Peter C. Bjarkman, *ACC-Atlantic Coast Conference Basketball* (Indianapolis, IN, 1996); Mike Douchant, *Encyclopedia of College Basketball* (Detroit, MI, 1995); Jan Hubbard, ed., *The Official NBA Encyclopedia*, 3rd ed. (New York, 2000); Horace "Bones" McKinney, *Honk Your Horn if You Love Basketball* (Gastonia, NC, 1988); Ron Morris, *ACC Basketball: An Illustrated History* (Chapel Hill, NC 1988).

Jim L. Sumner

CHEANEY, Calbert Nathaniel (b. July 17, 1971, Evansville, IN), college and professional player, is a six-foot seven-inch, 217-pound, left handed guard-forward who is a high percentage shooter from anywhere on the floor. He was brought up by his mother, Gwendolyn (Gwen) Cheaney, who saw her son play in nearly all his high school and college games. Cheaney, who is married and has a son and daughter, graduated from Harrison High School in Evansville, Indiana in 1989. He performed as an All-Stater in basketball for the Warriors and was selected the top high school player in the nation his senior year. He also excelled in track and field, winning the Indiana State Track and Field Championship in the 300 and 110 meter hurdles.

A recruiting war developed between Purdue University and Indiana University for Cheaney's services. Cheaney joined Coach Bob Knight* and Indiana University, graduating in 1993 with a Bachelor's degree in criminal justice. In four seasons at Indiana, he scored 2,613 career points in 132 regular season games and averaged 19.9 points with an excellent .599 shooting percentage from the field. During this span, Indiana compiled a 105-27 won loss record and one BTC Championship. Cheaney also played in 18 NCAA tournament playoff games and averaged 21.5 points. His 26.5 point average in 1993 topped all NCAA tournament players. Cheaney's final season at Indiana was capped with numerous accolades and awards. He was named Player of the Year by the AP, UPI, the USBWA and the NABC. Cheaney won both the Wooden and Naismith awards and was selected First Team All-America. He was selected to the All-BTC First Team three consecutive seasons and earned the MVP honors in 1993.

The Washington Bullets (NBA) selected Cheaney in the first round as the sixth pick overall, of the 1993 NBA draft. He spent six seasons with the Washington franchise (the team changed its nickname to "Wizards" in 1997. His scoring average reached double figures in his first five seasons, with his most productive season coming in 1994–1995, when he averaged 16.6 points. In those six NBA seasons, Cheaney scored 5,404 points and averaged 12.7 points in 424 games.

Cheaney became a free agent and signed with the Boston Celtics (NBA) in August 1999 as a reserve. Boston traded him to the Denver Nuggets (NBA) in October 2000. Several injuries over the next two seasons limited his playing time with Denver. The Utah Jazz (NBA) signed him as a free agent in July 2002. Cheaney averaged 8.6 points in 81 games for the Jazz and experienced the NBA playoffs for the second time, averaging 8.4 points in eight career playoff appearances. The Golden State Warriors (NBA) signed him as a free agent in August 2003. He tallied 7.6 points per game in 79 games in 2003–2004 and averaged 4.5 points in 55 games in 2004–2005. In 12 NBA seasons, Cheaney scored 8,034 points, and averaged 10.3 points in 783 games.

BIBLIOGRAPHY: "Calbert Cheaney," *Background*, http://www.nba.com (2003); "Calbert Cheaney," *Career Statistics*, http://www.nba.com (2003); "Calbert Cheaney," *His Ten Years in the NBA*, http://www.nba.com (2003); "Calbert Cheaney," *Player Bio*, http://www.nba.com (2003); "Calbert Cheaney," *Player Profile*, http://www.nba.com (2003); Mike Douchant, *Encyclopedia of College Basketball* (Detroit, MI, 1995); Ken Shouler et al., *Total Basketball* (Wilmington, DE, 2003); *TSN Official NBA Register, 2004–2005* (St. Louis, MO, 2004).

John L. Evers

CHEEKS, Maurice Edward "Mo" (b. September 8, 1956, Chicago, IL), college and professional player and coach, is one of four sons of Moses Cheeks and Marjorie Cheeks, grew up in Chicago's South Side Robert Taylor Homes, and starred in basketball at DuSable High School. West Texas State University (MVC) recruited Cheeks and a teammate. His friend subsequently attended another college, while the homesick Cheeks almost abandoned his basketball career as a freshman. However, Cheeks's mother persuaded him to stay at West Texas, where he joined Oscar Robertson* as the only players to be selected All-MVC for three years.

Cheeks remained relatively unknown as a senior on an eight win, 19 loss team, employing a slow, half-court offense. The Dallas Cowboys (NFL) briefly considered him as a possible defensive back although he had never played football, but the Philadelphia 76ers' (NBA) wily assistant coach-scout Jack McMahon, as well as the Los Angeles Lakers (NBA) liked him as a potential basketball point guard. After Creeks starred in a Pizza Hut College All-Star Game, the 76ers invited him to a tryout camp and ultimately selected him in the second round of the 1978 NBA draft.

Surprisingly, Cheeks started at point guard and played over 3,200 minutes in 82 games in his rookie season. By the mid-1980s, he led the Philadelphia fast break and made pinpoint passes to taller players inside. Although trained as a defensive specialist, Cheeks scored frequently off steals and developed an outstanding jump shot. Defenses overplayed the inside on the 76ers' big men, enabling him to win several games with jump shots from beyond the perimeter. Cheeks performed with the better known superstars, Julius "Dr. J." Erving*, Moses Malone*, Andrew Toney, and Bobby Jones*, helping the 76ers make nine consecutive playoffs and reach the 1980 and 1982 NBA Finals. Philadelphia captured the 1983 NBA Championship, winning 12 of 13 playoff games and sweeping the Los Angeles Lakers. Cheeks started in the 1983 NBA All-Star Game and also made the 1986, 1987, and 1988 squads.

The durable six-foot one-inch, 180-pound Cheeks always ranked near the top of the NBA in minutes played even though often suffering from nagging injuries. He also needed to adjust to new 76ers personnel because of Malone's trade to the Washington Bullets in June 1986, and the retirements of Erving in 1987 and shooting guard Toney in 1988. Cheeks readily adapted to the play of new stars, including flamboyant Charles Barkley*, and the gradual development of a new squad. In August 1989, the rebuilding 76ers traded Cheeks to the San Antonio Spurs (NBA) for younger players. The New York Knicks (NBA) acquired him in February 1990 and signed him to a contract through the 1990–1991 season. In October 1991 New York traded Cheeks to the Atlanta Hawks (NBA). Cheeks finished his NBA playing career with the New Jersey Nets (NBA) in 1992–1993.

During 15 NBA seasons, Cheeks scored 12,195 career points, made 2,310 steals (third all-time), made 7,392 assists, and played 31.6 minutes per game. From 1982–1983 through 1985–1986, he made the NBA All-Defensive Team. He averaged over 12 points and seven steals per game with Philadelphia and improved in all categories during the playoffs.

Cheeks always avoided the attention given to his era's ranking stars, but the media knew him as self-effacing yet friendly. Contemporaries admired him for his intensity, enthusiasm for the game, and ultimate team play on both offense and defense. He served as assistant basketball coach for the Quad City Thunder (CBA) in 1993–1994 and the Philadelphia 76ers from 1994–1995 to 2000–2001 and has served as head coach of Portland (NBA) since then, guiding the Trail Blazers to a 49-33 mark in 2001–2002 and 50-32 mark in 2002–2003. Portland lost in the first round of the Western Conference Playoffs both seasons, being eliminated in seven games by Dallas in 2002. The Trail Blazers slipped to a 41-41 mark in 2003–2004 and missed the playoffs. Portland fired Cheeks in March 2005. Two months later, the Philadelphia 76ers named him head coach. With portland, he compiled a 162-139 regular season record and a 3-7 playoff mark. He is married and has two children.

BIBLIOGRAPHY: Peter C. Bjarkman, *The Encyclopedia of Pro Basketball Team Histories* (New York, 1994) *Chicago Tribune*, February 10, 1986, January 18, 1987, February 7, 1988, December 30, 1988; Jack Hayes, "Hoop and Glory," *Chicago* (March 1989), pp. 113–115, 142–144; Jan Hubbard, ed., *The Official NBA Basketball Encyclopedia*, 3rd ed. (New York, 2000); *Philadelphia Inquirer*, February 27, 1983, April 10, 1984, April 21, 1985, April 8, 1986, August 16, 1986, August 24, 1986, October 4, 1986, December 9, 1986, August 29, 1989, October 29, 1989, November 16, 1989; Ken Shouler et al., *Total Basketball* (Wilmington, DE, 2003); *USA Today*, April 23, 1991; *Who's Who Among Black Americans*, 5th ed. (1988), p. 129.

Daniel R. Gilbert

CHUCKOVITS, Charles H. "Chuck" (b. July 10, 1912, Akron, OH), college and professional player and referee, was a six-foot one-inch, 175-pound forward who set college and NBL scoring records in the late 1930s and early 1940s. Chuckovits, one of the first one-hand shooters, single-handedly put the University of Toledo (OC) on the basketball map with his scoring feats from 1936 through 1938. In three varsity seasons under coach William Anderson*, he tallied 17.4 points per game to eclipse Hank Luisetti's* 16.2 points scoring average. Luisetti scored more career points, however, because he played 43 more varsity games. Chuckovits, who earned All-America honors in 1938, graduated with a Bachelor's degree from Toledo in 1939.

Chuckovits experienced a disappointing rookie season with the Hammond (Indiana) Ciesar All-Americans (NBL) in 1939–1940 and starred for the nonleague Toledo White Huts the next season. The 1941 World Professional Tournament at Chicago saw him score a record 82 points for Toledo in four games. For the 1941–1942 season, Chuckovits joined the Toledo Jim White Chevrolets (NBL). Toledo struggled in the NBL cellar with a 3-21 win-loss mark, but Chuckovits broke the NBL's scoring record with 406 points and an 18.5 point average; runner-up Bobby McDermott* of the Fort Wayne Zollner Pistons (NBL) tallied 13.2 points per contest. Statisticians have calculated that Chuckovits's 1941–1942 figures were equivalent to 46.3 points per game today. The Toledo club disbanded in December 1942. Chuckovits joined the U.S. Army in June 1943 and led several service teams in scoring.

Following his December 1945 discharge, Chuckovits worked 31 years as an executive for Owen-Illinois Corporation, retiring as the company's senior labor contract negotiator. The Toledo resident refereed in the NBL, NBA, and BTC, and officiated NCAA tournaments.

BIBLIOGRAPHY: Charles H. Chuckovits, interview with Robert W. Peterson, June 7, 1987; Chuck Chuckovits file, Naismith Memorial Basketball Hall of Fame, Springfield, MA; William F. Himmelman, unpublished research, Norwood, NJ; Robert W. Peterson, *Cages to Jump Shots: Pro Basketball's Early Years* (New York, 1990); *Toledo Blade*, 1936–1943; Ken Shouler et al., *Total Basketball* (Wilmington, DE, 2003); Alexander Weyand, *The Cavalcade of Basketball* (New York, 1960).

Robert W. Peterson

COBB, John Blackwell "Jack" "Spratt" "Mr. Basketball" (b. August 4, 1904, Durham, NC; d. September 9, 1966, Greenville, NC), college player, was the youngest of four children of James S. Cobb, an American Tobacco Company employee, and Nannie (Orr) Cobb. Cobb, who grew up in Durham, North Carolina began playing basketball at the local YMCA and graduated from Woodberry (Virginia) Forest High School.

Cobb earned a Bachelor's degree from the University of North Carolina at Chapel Hill in 1927, being selected a basketball All-America from 1924 through 1926. North Carolina employed the excellent six-foot two-inch, 175-pound forward as a quick, good ball handler and a fine defensive player who could score either inside or outside. As a sophomore in 1924, he led the Tar Heels to a 26-0 record and the mythical HAF national championship. In 1926, the HAF named him Player of the Year. Cobb led North Carolina to a three-year 64-10 win-loss record and the 1924, 1925, and 1926 SC Championships in the postseason tournament. Cobb, who averaged around 15 points overall, was nicknamed "Spratt" by teammates and also was known around campus as "Mr. Basketball."

A serious automobile accident in April 1929 resulted in the amputation of Cobb's right leg just above the ankle. Consequently, Cobb abandoned his major coaching ambitions and sold insurance in Durham. The Ligget and Myers Tobacco Company hired him for their Washington, North Carolina office. Cobb later served as a branch manager for that firm in Greenville, North Carolina. Despite his disability, he played golf and coached local Little League baseball teams. Cobb married Rebecca Govaerts in 1936 and had two children, Annie and John Jr. His honors included the North Carolina Sports Hall of Fame and the HAF College Basketball Hall of Fame.

BIBLIOGRAPHY: Smith Barrier, *On Tobacco Road: Basketball in North Carolina* (New York, 1983); John Cobb file, Alummi Office, University of North Carolina, Chapel Hill, NC; David Glenn et al., *Carolina Court* (Chapel Hill, NC, 1992); Bob Quincy, *They Made the Bell Tower Chime* (Chapel Hill, NC, 1973); Ken Rappoport, *Tales from the Tar Heel Locker Room* (Champaign, IL, 2002); Ken Rappoport, *Tar Heel: North Carolina Basketball* (Huntsville, IL, 1976).

Jim L. Sumner

COLEMAN, Derrick D. (b. June 21, 1967, Mobile, AL), college and professional player, played basketball four years at Syracuse University. The six-foot ten-inch, 270-pound Coleman, who grew up in Detroit, Michigan, participated basketball at Northern High School in Detroit and has spent his NBA career as a power forward and center.

Coleman enjoyed a successful basketball career at Syracuse University as a four-year starter, being named BEaC Freshman of the Year in 1987. In 1990, as a senior, he was selected BEaC Player of the Year and College Player of the Year and made *TSN* All-America First Team. Coleman became the first player in NCAA basketball history to score 2,000 points, haul down 1,500 rebounds, and block 300 shots. He left Syracuse as the all-time Orangeman leading scorer with 2,143 points and the NCAA leader in rebounds with 1,537 in 143 games.

The New Jersey (NBA) selected Coleman in the first round as the first pick in the 1990 NBA draft. He led all rookies in scoring and rebounds, was voted 1990–1991 NBA Rookie of the Year, and was named to the NBA All-Rookie First Team. Coleman started for the East Team at the 1994 NBA All-Star Game, and played that summer for the United States on the gold medal team at the World Championships of Basketball. Coleman, one of 160 NBA players to score 12,000 points, has played for four teams during his NBA career, namely the New Jersey Nets from 1990 until 1995, the Philadelphia 76ers (NBA) between 1995 and 1998, the Charlotte Hornets (NBA) between 1998 and 2001, the 76ers from October 2001 through August 2004, and the Detroit Pistons (NBA) from August 2004 to January 2005. Commissioner David Stern suspended him for one game for his role in a melee that occurred on and off the court in a game with the Indiana Pacers on November 19, 2004 at the Palace in Auburn Hills, Michigan. He has totalled 12,886 points, 7,232 rebounds, and 1,985 assists in 781 regular-season games over his career. His teams made the playoffs during seven seasons, with Coleman averaging 16.8 points and 9.9 rebounds in 39 games. He and his wife, Gina, and have one son, Derrick Jr.

BIBLIOGRAPHY: Mike Douchant, *Encyclopedia of College Basketball* (Detroit, MI, 1995); http://www.gast-gazette.com/portal/sports/Hornets/Players/44coleman.htm; http//www.hoopshype.com/players/derrick_coleman.htm?nav=page; http://www.nba.com/playerfile/derrick_coleman/?nav=page; Ken Shouler et al., *Total Basketball* (Wilmington, DE, 2003); *TSN Official NBA Register, 2004–2005* (St. Louis, MO, 2004).

Maureen M. Smith

COLLINS, Paul Douglas, "Doug," "The Lone Ranger" (b. July 28, 1951, Christopher, IL), college and professional player, coach and sportscaster, is the son of Paul Collins, former Franklin County (Illinois) sheriff, and Geraldine Collins. Collins graduated in 1969 from Benton (Illinois) High School, where he averaged 26 points in basketball his senior season. Collins graduated with a Bachelor's degree from Illinois State University in 1973. In three basketball seasons with the Redbirds, he scored 2,240 points in 77 games and averaged 29.1 points. Collins played on the 1972 United States Olympic Team that lost the gold medal to the Russian team. He was also selected First Team All-America and Academic All-America in 1973.

The Philadelphia 76ers (NBA) selected Collins in the first round (first pick overall) of the 1973 NBA draft. The six-foot six-inch, 180-pound guard played eight years with the 76ers. Considered a "pure shooter," he recorded a .501 career field goal shooting percentage while scoring 7,427 career points in 415 regular-season and averaging 17.9 points. Collins, selected to play in four NBA All-Star Games from 1976 to 1979, scored 687 points and averaged 21.5 points in 32 NBA playoff games. He averaged 22.4 points in the 1976–1977 NBA playoffs, but the 76ers lost to the Portland Trail Blazers in six games in the NBA Finals.

Collins began his basketball coaching career in 1981 as an assistant at the University of Pennsylvania and the following two seasons assisted at Arizona State University. After one year as an NBA broadcaster-analyst with CBS Sports, he joined the Chicago Bulls (NBA) organization in May 1986 as their head basketball coach and maintained that position until being dismissed in 1989. Collins returned as an analyst for Turner Sports television between 1989 and 1995, when the Detroit Pistons (NBA) selected him as their head coach. The Detroit management became dissatisfied with the team's progress and dismissed Collins in February 1998. From 1998 through 2001, he served as an analyst on NBC Sports.

When the Washington (NBA) franchise became the Wizards in 2001 and Michael Jordan* was named team president and decided to make a comeback, Collins was chosen as the club's head coach. He served as their head coach two seasons, finishing with identical 37-45 win-loss records both campaigns. In May 2003, Collins was released by the organization.

In eight years as an NBA coach, Collins won 332 regular-season games while losing 287 times. His squads have appeared in the NBA playoffs five times, recording a 15-23 win-loss record. In 1997 he was selected as one of the All-Star Game coaches.

Collins and his wife, Kathy, have two children: Chris, an assistant basketball coach at Duke University, and a daughter, Kelly.

BIBLIOGRAPHY: Michael O. Chapman, *The Doug Collins Story* (Dubuque, IA, 1996); "Doug Collins," *Coaches Bio*, http://www.hoopshype.com (2003); "Doug Collins," *Coaches*, http://www.nba.com (2003); Gary K. Johnson, *NCAA Men's Basketball's Finest* (Overland Park, KS, 1998); Ken Shouler et al., *Total Basketball* (Wilmington, DE, 2003); *TSN Official NBA Register, 2002–2003* (St. Louis, MO, 2002).

John L. Evers

CONRADT, Jody (b. May 13, 1941, Goldthwaite, TX), college player, coach, and athletic administrator, grew up in a small farming and ranching community about 100 miles northwest of Austin, the daughter of an athletic-minded family. In Texas, six-player girls' basketball provided the best opportunity for females to compete athletically at that time. Conradt averaged 40 points in high school and played basketball at Baylor University (SWC), where she obtained a Bachelor's degree in physical education in 1963. She accepted a teaching job at Waco

Midway High School, but coaching became the focus of her life. Conradt never married.

After developing some coaching ideas at the high school level, Conradt in 1969 was appointed women's coach for basketball, volleyball, and track and field at Sam Houston State University with only a $600 annual budget. Four years later, she became coordinator of women's athletics at the University of Texas at Arlington, in suburban Dallas. Conradt created a women's basketball program that attracted the attention of other schools when her teams upset more powerful opponents. Her teams used a tough man-to-man defense, developed from reading an outline of coach Dean Smith's* run and jump defense. In 1976, the University of Texas at Austin (SWC) hired Conradt to build its program to national prominence; her first team finished 36-10. The Lady Longhorns, the dominant women's basketball team of the 1980s, ranked in the AP top ten 11 of 12 years between the 1979 and 1990 seasons and returned to the top ten in 2003 with a fifth-place ranking, followed by a fourth-place ranking in 2004. Texas won the national championship in 1986 and was ranked number one nationally for four consecutive years from 1984 to 1988. The 34-0 championship Longhorn team, sparked by Clarissa Davis*, Andrea Lloyd, and Kamie Ethridge*, defeated the Cheryl Miller*-led University of Southern California squad 97-81 for the 1986 NCCA title in Lexington, Kentucky. Conradt in 1993 became the first women's coach to record 600 wins, having recorded over 500 victories at the University of Texas. She has compiled a 869-278 record for a .758 winning percentage, in 36 years of college coaching. One of her biggest accomplishments—a SWC record 183 consecutive game victory streak—lasted from January 1978 to January 1990. Another accomplishment of lasting satisfaction involved attracting new fans. Texas led the nation in women's home basketball attendance from 1986 to 1991, including an NCCA record average of 8,481 spectators for one season. "We proved to a skeptical audience," Conradt stated, "that women's basketball was appealing. It was fun. We did our part to legitimize the sport and change the face of women's basketball." In 1992, Texas appointed Conradt women's athletic director, reducing the opportunities for her favorite hobby of playing golf.

Conradt, named national Coach of the Year three times (1980, 1984, 1986) and SWC Coach of the Year five times, received the WBCA Carol Eckman Award in 1987 and was inducted into the Texas Women's Hall of Fame in 1986. In 1998, she was inducted into the Naismith Memorial Basketball Hall of Fame. Many of her former Longhorn players coach sports throughout the southwest.

BIBLIOGRAPHY: Peter C. Bjarkman, *The Biographical History of Basketball* (Chicago, IL, 2000); Rick Cantu, "Conradt Refused to Let Ego Get Inflated," *Austin* (TX) *American Statesman*, December 13, 1992, pp. C1+; Jody Conradt file, Naismith Memorial Basketball Hall of Fame, Springfield, MA; Mike Douchant, *Encyclopedia of College Basketball* (Detroit, MI, 1995); Nena Ray Hawkes and John F. Suggar, *Celebrating Women Coaches: A Biographical Dictionary* (Westport, CT, 2000); Skip Hollandsworth, "She's Stealing the Heart of Texas," *WSFi* 9 (February 1987), pp. 49–51, 72; Anne Janette Johnson, *Great Women in Sports* (Detroit, MI, 1996), Ivy McLemore, "600: Conradt Charters Club," *Houston Post*, December 12, 1992, pp. C1, C8; Steve Richardson, "599 and Counting: UT's Jody Conradt on Verge of Another Milestone," *Dallas Morning News*, December 13, 1992, pp. C1–C3; Victoria Sherrow, *Encyclopedia of Women and Sports* (Santa Barbara, CA, 1996); Rosemarie Skaine, *Women College Basketball Coaches* (Jefferson, NC, 2001).

Dennis S. Clark

COOPER, Charles Theodore "Tarzan" (b. August 30, 1907, Newark, DE; d. December 19, 1980, Philadelphia, PA), professional player, performed 11 years (1929–1939) with the legendary New York Renaissance team. The Rens amassed a 1,303–203 record during that period as the top pro team of the 1930s and were elected as a team in 1963 to the Naismith Memorial Basketball Hall of Fame. Four years later, Cooper was honored individually when inducted into the same Hall of Fame as a player. He was the MVP and leader of the Rens' 1939 World Champions, which captured the title by defeating the Harlem Globetrotters in Chicago. The African-American, six-foot four-inch Cooper was tall for that era of under-six-footers and excelled at the center position. The son of Theodore Cooper and Evelyn Cooper, he starred on the Philadelphia Central High School basketball team before graduating in 1925. Cooper played with the pro Philadelphia Panthers in 1925 and for the Philadelphia Giants the next three years.

Rens' owner Robert Douglas* observed the skills of the talented Cooper and signed him for the 1929 season. The Rens borrowed their name from the Harlem Renaissance Casino ballroom, where they played their home games. The shorter players, including Clarence "Fats" Jenkins*, Eyre "Bruiser" Saitch*, and Bill Yancey*, scored well from outside, while the muscular Cooper put in whatever they missed. The Rens gained parity with the Original Celtics as the nation's leading pro basketball team. The two clubs met several times each year, with mutual respect developing between them. Immortal Celtics center Joe Lapchick* often called Cooper the finest center he had ever seen.

Because of racial discrimination in the 1920s and 1930s, the Rens were barred from most hotels and restaurants, often ate cold sandwiches, and slept on the team bus. The Renaissance Casino closed during the Depression, forcing the Rens to play road games for entire seasons. They faced any opponent anywhere and usually won before capacity crowds. Douglas signed "Wee Willie" Smith* in 1932 to complete the Rens' heralded "Magnificent Seven" that included James "Pappy" Ricks and John "Casey" Holt. The Rens in 1933 defeated the Original Celtics in seven of eight games and won 88 consecutive contests a year later during a 127-7 season. Smith explained the Rens' strategy. "If you dribble the ball and the ball is on the floor and a man went to cut, you couldn't get it to him, so that was our theory of not dribbling. To get the ball to the backboard sometimes, you had to dribble. But most of the time we would come up with the ball off the backboard and pass it to an outlet man . . . keep it moving all the time." Cooper in 1940 joined the Washington Bears and led them to the 1943 "World's Pro Title."

BIBLIOGRAPHY: Charles Cooper file, Naismith Memorial Basketball Hall of Fame, Springfield, MA; Jan Hubbard, ed., *The Official NBA Encyclopedia*, 3rd ed. (New York, 2000); Neil D. Isaacs, *All the Moves: A History of College Basketball* (Philadelphia, PA, 1975); Murray A. Nelson, *The Originals—The New York Celtics Invent Modern Basketball* (Bowling Green, OH, 1999); *NYT*, December 24, 1980, p. A14; Robert W. Peterson, *Cages to Jumpshots: Pro Basketball Early Years* (New York, 1990); Susan J. Rayl, *The New York Renaissance Professional Black Basketball Team, 1923–1950* (Syracuse, NY, 2001); Bijan C. Rayne, *"Sky Kings": Black Pioneers of Professional Basketball* (New York, 1997).

James D. Whalen and Wayne Patterson

COOPER, Cynthia Lynne "Coop" (b. April 14, 1963, Chicago, IL), college and professional player and coach, is the daughter of Kenny Cooper and Mary Cobbs. Cooper's father moved out of their lives when she was only six years old and left her mother to support eight children. She grew up in the Watts area of central Los Angeles and learned basketball fundamentals from her brothers and her mother on the outdoor courts.

Cooper graduated in 1981 from Alan Locke High School in Los Angeles, where she excelled in basketball and track and field. She led the Saints to the 1981 California 4A State Basketball Championship, averaging 31 points, tallying a career-high and school record 45 points in one game, and being named the Los Angeles Player of the Year.

Cooper, highly recruited by numerous universities, signed to play basketball for the University of Southern California. During her four seasons (1982–1984, 1986), USC compiled a 114-15 win-loss record and appeared in the NCAA Division I Tournament four years and the NCAA Final Four three of the four years. The Lady Trojans won National Championships in 1983 and 1984. Cooper was named to the 1986 NCAA Final Four All-Tournament Team and was selected All Pac-West Conference First Team in 1985–1986. She completed her collegiate career with 1,559 points, 1,381 assists, and 256 steals in 121 games.

In 1986, Cooper began her professional basketball career in the European professional leagues. She played for Segovia, Spain in 1986–1987; Parma, Italy between 1987 and 1994; and Alcamo, Italy between 1994 and 1996. In 10 professional seasons in the Spanish and

Italian Leagues, Cooper led in scoring eight times and finished second twice. She earned MVP honors in the 1987 European All-Star Game, led scorers with 37.5 points per game in the 1996 European Cup, and was named to the 1996–1997 Italian League All-Star Team. Cooper played on the USA Women's Olympic basketball team that captured the gold medal in 1988 and the bronze medal in 1992. She also earned a gold medal in the 1986 and 1990 Goodwill Games, gold medals in the 1986 and 1990 World Championships, and a gold medal in the 1987 Pan American Games.

The five-foot ten-inch, 150-pound guard returned to the United States and was assigned to the Houston Comets (WNBA) in January 1997. In her first four seasons with Houston, Cooper led the Comets to four consecutive WNBA Championships and was selected the MVP in 1997 and 1998. She was named to the All-WNBA First Team all four years and led the WNBA in scoring in 1997 with 22.2 points per game, 1998 with 22.7 points per game, and 1999 with 22.1 points per game.

Cooper retired following the 2000 season and was named head coach of the Phoenix Mercury (WNBA) in January 2001. The Mercury posted a 13-19 win-loss record in her first season and a 6-4 record in 2002 before Cooper resigned on June 26. The 40-year-old became the oldest player to take part in an WNBA game when she signed to play with Houston again in 2003. After appearing in only four games in 2003, Cooper was sidelined for the season with a shoulder injury and again retired. Cooper scored 2,601 career points in 120 games, averaging 21.0 points. In 19 career WNBA playoff games, she averaged 23.3 points and was named WNBA Finals MVP four consecutive years. She played in the 1999 WNBA All-Star Game and scored seven points.

Her autobiography, entitled *She Got Game*, was released in 1999. She resides in Sugar Land, Texas with her husband, Brian Dyke, sons Tyquon, Anthony, and Tyrone, and twins Brian Jr. and Cyan.

BIBLIOGRAPHY: "Cynthia Cooper," *Basketball*, http://www.sportsillustrated.cnn.com (2003); "Cynthia Cooper," *Bio*, http://www.wnba.com (2003); "Cynthia Cooper," *Biography*, http://www.angelfire.com (2003); "Cynthia Cooper," *Player Info*, http://www.wnba.com (2003); Cynthia Cooper, *She Got Game* (New York, 1999); "Cynthia Cooper," *Speakers*, http://www.all-americanspeakers.com (2003); James Ponti, *WNBA* (New York, 1999); *TSN Official WNBA Guide and Register, 2003* (St. Louis, MO, 2003).

John L. Evers

COSTELLO, Lawrence Ronald "Larry" (b. July 2, 1931, Minoa, NY; d. December 11, 2001, Ft. Myers, FL), college and professional player and coach, compiled one of the highest winning percentages among NBA coaches after an accomplished career as a player with Niagara University and three NBA teams. The son of Charles H. Costello and Ethel M. (Greiner) Costello, he began his basketball career in junior high school with the St. Mary's Church team at Minoa, New York, and competed in high school as a 98 pound football player. After leaving Minoa High, Costello matriculated at Niagara University and played baseball there. He graduated from Niagara with a Bachelor of Science degree in 1954 and did postgraduate work at Syracuse University. Costello sparked his freshman basketball team at Niagara to a 23-0 record and then averaged 15 points for the Purple Eagle varsity under coach John "Taps" Gallagher. One of his most memorable games with Niagara came in a six-overtime contest in the NIT in 1953. The Eagles won 88-81 as Costello played over 69 minutes before fouling out in the last seconds of play. An All-America in 1953–1954, he won the Niagara Medal in 1954 and was named to Niagara's Sports Hall of Fame in 1964.

A second-round draft choice of the Philadelphia Warriors (NBA) in 1954, Costello spent the next campaign in the U.S. Army overseas in Germany in 1955 and played for the Army European Championship 86th Regiment team. He returned to the Warriors for the 1956–1957 season before being sold to the Syracuse Nationals (NBA). Costello played with Syracuse for the next six seasons and two more when the team was moved to Philadelphia before a ripped thigh muscle forced his retirement. In 1965 and 1966 he coached East Syracuse-Minoa High School to the conference title before the 76ers, with heavy losses at guard, coaxed him out of retirement.

Costello played two more seasons with Philadelphia until an Achilles tendon injury forced his retirement. His comeback enabled him to be a part of the 1966–1967 championship 76ers team. The last of the two-handed NBA set shot artists, he set several NBA free throw records and scored 8,622 points in 12 regular seasons and 592 points in the playoffs. His career free throw percentage of .841 ranked among the NBA's all-time best foul shooters. Costello made 2,432 of 2,891 attempts in regular-season play and had an even better .852 in playoffs. In 1963 and 1965, he led the NBA in free throw accuracy. He was selected for six NBA All-Star Games.

The six-foot one-inch, 188-pound Costello then switched to coaching and assisted Alex Hannum* in 1967–1968 at Philadelphia. He was slated to remain there as player personnel director, but accepted the head coaching position with the Milwaukee Bucks (NBA) in April 1968. In just over eight seasons with the Bucks and part of another with the Chicago Bulls (NBA), Costello compiled a 430-300 record in regular-season play and went 37-23 in playoffs. He coached one NBA championship team, the 1970–1971 Bucks, and four division titlists. For the 1979–1980 season, Costello coached the Milwaukee Does of the pro WBL and then became head coach at Utica College in New York. There, he had a 77-106 record in seven years for the team that tried to jump from Division III to Division I competition, and then retired in June 1987 when the experiment was abandoned. Costello, who resided in New Hartford, New York, married Barbara C. Brown on May 4, 1963, and had four daughters: Lesley Sue, Pamela Lynn, Coleen, and Amy. Barbara, originally from Homer, New York, and her daughter Amy were also outstanding basketball players. Among other honors, "Larry" Costello was named the 1960 Athlete of the Year in Syracuse.

BIBLIOGRAPHY: Peter C. Bjarkman, *The Encyclopedia of Pro Basketball Team Histories* (New York, 1994); Glenn Dickey, *The History of Professional Basketball Since 1896* (Briarcliff Manor, NY, 1982); Jan Hubbard, ed., *The Official NBA Encyclopedia*, 3rd ed. (New York, 2000); Neil D. Isaacs, *All the Moves: A History of College Basketball* (New York, 1975); Wayne Lynch, *Season of the 76ers* (New York, 2002); Milwaukee Bucks Basketball Club files, Milwaukee, WI; Niagara University Sports Information files, Niagara, NY; *TSN Official NBA Guides, 1956–1979* (St. Louis, MO, 1956–1977; *TSN Official Register, 2004–2005* (St. Louis, MO, 2004); *Utica College 1986–87 Men's Basketball Prospectus* (Utica, NY, 1986); *WWA*, 37th ed. (1972–1973), p. 663.

Robert B. Van Atta

COUSY, Robert Joseph "Bob" (b. August 9, 1928, New York, NY), college and professional player, coach, executive, and sportscaster, is the son of taxi driver-airline worker Joseph Cousy and secretary-language teacher Julliette (Corlet) Cousy. His parents arrived in the United States on a ship from France a few months before Cousy was born. He graduated from Andrew Jackson High School in St. Albans, New York, where he lettered in basketball and won the New York City scoring title as a senior. He then graduated in 1950 from Holy Cross College, where he was chosen a basketball All-America and co-captain in his senior year. He married Marie "Missie" Ritterbusch on December 9, 1950, and has two daughters.

During Cousy's tenure, Holy Cross won 18 straight games in 1947–1948 before losing to the University of Kentucky in the NCAA regional playoffs, and 26 consecutive contests in 1949–1950 before an NCAA playoff loss to North Carolina State University. The Crusaders' NCAA championship was gained in 1946–1947, when Cousy substituted and averaged 7.5 points. At Holy Cross, he pleased crowds with his ball handling and trick passing. The Boston Celtics (NBA) did not draft Cousy, but acquired him through a three-team drawing when the Chicago Stags (NBA), who owned his rights, disbanded. The NBA ordered Chicago's three best players—Max Zaslofsky*, Andy Phillip*, and Cousy—to be selected by Boston, New York, and Philadelphia. None wanted Cousy, the untested rookie.

Cousy's arrival in Boston coincided with that of head coach Arnold "Red" Auerbach*, whose fast-break philosophy ideally suited Cousy's remarkable talents. From 1951 to 1963, Cousy became a perennial NBA All-Star. He did not make the All-NBA Team in his rookie year, but was a First Team All-NBA until the 1961–1962 season, when he made the All-NBA Second Team, a spot he held until his retirement. Cousy captained the squad seven of those campaigns. Although scoring prolifically, he proved even more valuable as Boston's floor general and led the NBA in assists eight straight seasons. Sports authority Herbert Warren Wind described the "razzle-dazzle improvisation" as Cousy's trademark. Sportswriter Jack Kelly wrote, "I saw him put salt and pepper on the ball, chew it up, then spit it into the basket," while sports editor Stanley Frank named Cousy the "Houdini of the Hardwood."

Cousy was named the NBA's Rookie of the Year, finishing ninth in the NBA scoring race. He did not achieve his full potential until midway through his second season, when his teammates adapted to his unique style of play. The NBA's third highest scorer, Cousy possessed court magic that packed arenas everywhere and boosted interest in pro ball when it needed it the most. Despite its scoring powerhouse, however, Boston won no championships until Bill Russell* arrived in 1956–1957. Russell and Cousy spearheaded the Celtics to championships in six of the latter's remaining seven years. Cousy also spearheaded the organization of the NBA Players' Union in 1955. Noted for his courage and frank honesty, he remained a force in the union's leadership. As an active player, he conducted basketball clinics for the U.S. State Department in Europe, Africa, and the Middle East. Cousy, whose popularity led to numerous commercial endorsements, became the part-owner of a boys' camp and opened an insurance agency.

The extremely articulate, intelligent Cousy emphasized that his exceptional peripheral vision, large hands, sloping shoulders, long arms, and extremely sturdy legs were ideally suited to basketball. Although only six-feet one-inch, 175-pounds, he nevertheless, proved an exceptional rebounder and averaged 5.2 rebounds over his career. Cousy's most notable career marks included his 16,960 points (18.4 per game average), 6,959 assists (7.5 per game), and .803 foul shooting percentage. In 109 playoff games, he performed comparably with 18.5 points per game, 8.6 assists per game, and an .801 foul shooting percentage. Despite his aggressive, "killer instinct" playing style, Cousy fouled out only 20 times in his career. His career .375 field goal percentage with a .397 single-season peak ranked high during his period of play. Cousy particularly played effectively in All-Star Games, winning MVP awards in 1954 and 1957. The Celtics retired his uniform number 14.

Cousy coached basketball at Boston College from 1963 to 1969, taking them to five NCAA tournaments. He coached the Cincinnati Royals (NBA) from 1969 to 1974 and reactivated himself as a 41-year-old player, thus becoming the then oldest performer in NBA history. He later served as commissioner of the ASL and as the Massachusetts honorary chairman of the Cystic Fibrosis Foundation. Cousy, actively interested in golf and tennis, was elected to the Naismith Memorial Basketball Hall of Fame in 1970 and the All-NBA Silver Anniversary Team in 1971. He also made the 35th Anniversary All-Time Team in 1980 and was named one of the 50 Greatest Players in NBA history in 1996. Cousy served as a television analyst for Boston Celtics games and serves as marketing consultant for the Celtics.

BIBLIOGRAPHY: Dave Anderson, "Final Whistle," *SEP* 236 (March 16, 1963), pp. 34–35; Peter C. Bjarkman, *The Boston Celtics Encyclopedia* (Champaign, IL, 1998); Bob Cousy with John Devaney, *The Killer Instinct* (New York, 1975); Bob Cousy as told to Al Hirshberg, *Basketball Is My Life* (Englewood Cliffs, NJ, 1958); Bob Cousy with Edward Linn, *The Last Loud Roar* (Englewood Cliffs, NJ, 1964); Bob Cousy and Bob Ryan, *Cousy on the Celtic Mystique* (New York, 1988); Bob Cousy file, Naismith Memorial Basketball Hall of Fame, Springfield, MA; Stanley Frank, "Basketball's Amazing Showboat," *SEP* 227 (December 18, 1954), pp. 25ff.; Al Hirshberg, "A Visit with Bob Cousy," *SEP* 232 (December 12, 1959), pp. 30ff.; Neil D. Isaacs, *Vintage NBA* (Silver Spring, MD, 1996); Robert Rice, "A Victim of Noblesse Oblige," *New Yorker* 36 (February 4, 1961), pp. 38–40ff.; Bob Ryan, *The Boston Celtics—The History, Legends, and Images of America's Most Celebrated Team* (Reading, MA, 1989), Don Shaughnessy, *Ever Green: The Boston Celtics—A History in the Words of their Players, Coaches, Fans, and Foes, from 1946 to the Present* (New York, 1990); Herbert

Warren Wind, "Farewell to Cousy," *New Yorker* 39 (March 23, 1963), pp. 146ff.

John E. DiMeglio

COWAN, Catherine Ann. *See* Rush, Catherine Cowan "Cathy"

COWENS, David Williams "Dave" (b. October 25, 1948, Covington, KY), college and professional basketball player and coach, is the son of John Cowens and Ruth Cowens. His father's occupations included insurance sales, barber, and retail store manager. Cowens married his wife, DeBorah Ann, on April 15, 1978 and has two children, Meghan Laurel and Samantha Rose. The "big redhead" started out as a swimmer at the Newport Catholic High School in Newport, Kentucky, which he attended from 1962 to 1966. He began playing basketball his junior year and helped his high school team make the state tournament. Legendary coach Adolph Rupp* of the University of Kentucky showed little interest in recruiting him. Cowens attended Florida State University in Tallahassee, Florida, where he played center from 1966 to 1970. Over his collegiate career, he averaged 19 points and 17 rebounds and shot 51 percent from the field.

Arnold "Red" Auerbach* of the Boston Celtics (NBA) drafted Cowens in the first round as the fourth overall pick in the 1970 NBA draft on the recommendation of the former great Celtics center and player-coach Bill Russell*. At six-feet nine-inches and 230 pounds, Cowens was considered too small to play center. Many critics did not think that Cowens could fill Russell's shoes or help the Celtics return to past glory days. The Celtics had plummeted from world championship stature in the 1968–1969 season under player-coach Russell to sixth place in the Eastern Division in 1969–1970. Cowens quickly silenced the critics. During the preseason annual Maurice Stokes Benefit Game in August 1970, Cowens scored 32 points, grabbed 12 rebounds, and was named the game's MVP. During his rookie year (1970–1971), he averaged 17 points and 15 rebounds, shared Rookie of the Year Award with Portland's Geoff Petrie, and finished seventh in the NBA in rebounding.

Cowens established a precedent for future centers. He played with intensity, aggressiveness, recklessness, and great hustle, showed unusual quickness for a center, and proved offensive minded. Rather than following the traditional notion of basketball center as back-to-the-basket pivot man, Cowens roamed the outside shooting soft jumpers or driving to the basket. His playing credo was to go all out all the time at both ends of the court. He played pro basketball with the Boston Celtics from 1970 to 1980 and served as player-coach of the Celtics for the 1978–1979 season, compiling 24 wins, 41 losses, and a .397 winning percentage. Because the coaching role did not quite fit Cowens, he returned in the 1979–1980 season just as a player. During the 1980–1981 and 1981–1982 seasons, he voluntarily retired from basketball. He returned to pro basketball with the Milwaukee Bucks (NBA) for the 1982–1983 season and coached the Bay State Bombardiers (CBA) to a 20-28 mark in the 1984–1985 season. The Celtics retired his uniform number 18.

During his pro career, Cowens averaged 17.6 points and 13.6 rebounds and shot 46 percent from the field and 78 percent from the free throw line in 766 NBA regular-season games. He appeared in 89 NBA playoff games, averaging 18.9 points and 14.4 rebounds and shooting 45 percent from the field. He also was selected for seven NBA All-Star games from 1972 to 1978, but did not play in the 1977 contest because of an injury. Besides being named to the NBA All-Rookie team in 1971, Cowens was named the NBA All-Star Game MVP and NBA MVP in 1973. He made the NBA All-Defensive Second Team in 1975 and 1980 and the All-NBA Second Team in 1973, 1975, and 1976, and played for the Celtics' 1974 and 1976 NBA championship teams. He was named to the Naismith Memorial Basketball Hall of Fame in 1990 and one of the 50 Greatest Players in NBA History in 1996.

Cowens served as assistant coach of the San Antonio Spurs (NBA) 1994–1996 and as head coach of the Charlotte Hornets (NBA) from 1996–1997 until March 1999, guiding Charlotte to a 54-28 mark in 1996–1997 and a 51-31 slate in 1997–1998. After being assistant coach of the Golden State Warriors in 2000, he took over the head-coaching reins there in 2000–2001 and compiled a 25–80 overall record. Brian Winters replaced him as head coach in December 2001. In six seasons, Cowens finished 161-191 with a .457 winning percentage. In May, Chicago's expansion WNBA franchise named Cowens as its first head coach and general manager.

During most of his pro career, Cowens was considered eccentric, short-tempered, emotional, intense, and a supreme individualist. His counterculture lifestyle consisted of ignoring the limelight and superstar status. Cowens did not desire prestige or fame from basketball and enjoyed eclectic activities, including music appreciation, auto repair, and self home construction.

BIBLIOGRAPHY: Peter C. Bjarkman, *The Boston Celtics Encyclopedia* (Champaign, IL, 1998); Peter Carry, "Boston's Perpetual Motion Machine," *SI* 38 (April 2, 1973), pp. 34–45; Peter Carry, "It Was a Brief Time-Out," *SI* 34 (January 11, 1971), pp. 22–23; Anthony Cotton, "Taking a Shot at the Bucks," *SI* 57 (October 11, 1982), pp. 68–70; Dave Cowens file, Naismith Memorial Basketball Hall of Fame, Springfield, MA; Merv Harris, *The Lonely Heroes: Professional Basketball's Great Centers* (New York, 1975); Zander Hollander, ed., *The NBA's Official Encyclopedia of Pro Basketball* (New York, 1981); John Papanek, "Back in Business in Boston," *SI* 46 (January 24, 1977), pp. 22–29; John Papanek, "Call It the Red-headed League," *SI* 49 (November 27, 1978), pp. 24–27; Bob Ryan, *The Boston Celtics—The History Legends, and Images of America's Most Celebrated Team* (Reading, MA, 1989); Dan Shaughnessy, *Ever Green: The Boston Celtics—A History in the Words of Their Players, Coaches, Fans, and Foes, from 1946 to the Present* (New York, 1990); *TSN Official NBA Register, 2004–2005* (St. Louis, MO, 2004).

Kant Patel

CRAWFORD, Joan Audrey "Jodie" (b. August 22, 1937, Fort Smith, AR), college player and coach, is the daughter of Monroe Crawford and Iris (Blan) Crawford. The second oldest of five children, she had two brothers, Robert and Barry, and two sisters, Judy and Ella. In the fifth grade, Crawford became interested in basketball and joined the school team. After reaching junior high school, she learned fundamentals from her brother Robert. He showed her how to pivot, shoot from different angles, and make hook and jump shots. This backyard practice improved her skills so much that she was invited to play on the senior team as a high school freshman. During Crawford's four years of competition, Van Buren (Arkansas) High lost only one game. Athletics helped Crawford to overcome shyness caused by a congenital speech defect.

After graduating from high school in 1955, Crawford received a scholarship to Clarendon JC in Texas and graduated from there two years later. Clarendon advanced to the quarterfinals of the national AAU tournament in 1957 before losing to the eventual champions. For her scoring and leadership, Crawford was selected to the All-America team. She was offered a further scholarship to Wayland Baptist College, but instead joined women's amateur basketball power Nashville BC in Tennessee. Although dropping a business program after a short time, she continued working for Nashville BC as a supervisor of the mailroom and played on the company basketball team. Over 12 seasons, Nashville BC won 10 AAU national championships and Crawford was named an All-America each year. From 1962 through 1964, she was selected the MVP of the national tournament. In the 1964 AAU title contest, she scored 23 points in Nashville BC's 58–46 victory over Wayland Baptist. Playing a roving position, she excelled at rebounding and shooting a devastating hook shot from short or long range.

Nashville BC, created by H. O. Balls and coached by John Head*, dominated women's basketball from the early 1950s until disbanding after the 1969 season. It attracted some of the nation's finest women players and became a consistent champion after Crawford joined the squad. Crawford played on several U.S. international teams, including those defeating the Russians for the 1957 world championship and winning the Pan American Games of 1963. In the Pan American final against Brazil, she scored a game high 27 points. During her basketball career, Crawford led scorers in over one-half of the contests.

For two years Crawford coached a women's AAU team, but the squad never advanced past the regional tournament level. Crawford worked as assistant supervisor of the data center at Northwestern University and was elected to the AAU (1961), HAF (1966), and Arkansas Sports (1978) halls of fame. In 1997, Crawford was inducted into the Naismith Memorial Basketball Hall of Fame.

BIBLIOGRAPHY: Joan Crawford file, Naismith Memorial Basketball Hall of Fame, Springfield, MA; Joan S. Hult and Marianna Trickell, *A Century of Women's Basketball: From Frailty to Final Four* (Reston, VA, 1991); "Miss Joan Crawford, Basketball Hall of Fame," *Women's Sports Reporter* (January/February 1970), pp. 4, 30; Victoria Sherrow, *Encyclopedia of Women and Sports* (Santa Barbara, CA, 1996).

Dennis S. Clark

CRAWFORD, Marianne. *See* Stanley, Marianne Crawford

CRIBBS, Claire Linton (b. August 13, 1912, Irwin, PA; d. September 14, 1985, Bellaire, OH), college athlete, was the son of Wade L. Cribbs, burgess (mayor) of Irwin and a strong sports booster, and Pearl (Wolff) Cribbs, and starred in basketball at Jeannette (Pennsylvania) High School. He worked in a foundry and played basketball for a town team. University of Pittsburgh coach Henry C. Carlson* saw one of Cribbs's games at nearby Pittsburgh and persuaded him to matriculate at the school.

The slightly over six-feet-tall Cribbs recalled that he "wore corduroy pants with shiny knees, an old slouch hat, and ate a lot of beans" when he entered Pittsburgh. On the basketball court, he played forward, center, and occasionally some guard as one of Pittsburgh's all-time premier players. Cribbs, an All-East Conference selection three years and All-America choice twice, led Pittsburgh to a 53-15 win-loss record from 1931–1932 through 1933–1934 and to three conference championships. In direct confrontations, he outperformed "Moose" Krause* of the University of Notre Dame and John Wooden* of Purdue University. He broke Pittsburgh's career scoring mark and finished among the national point leaders.

After briefly pitching for the Baltimore Orioles baseball club (IL), Cribbs joined Warren Consolidated High School at Tiltonsville, Ohio, as a teacher and coach in 1936 and coached baseball star Bill Mazeroski. World War II saw him serve as a U.S. Navy gunnery officer on convoy duty to England and Russia and in the Pacific theater at Okinawa. In 1949 he joined Bellaire (Ohio) High School as a history teacher and basketball coach. At times, he also coached track and field and assisted in football. Under Cribbs, Bellaire basketball teams won over 400 games and won 57 consecutive home games. Cribbs, who retired in 1977, belonged to the OBCA and to the University of Pittsburgh, Westmoreland County (Pennsylvania) and Ohio Valley Dapper Dan Halls of Fame. He and his wife, Betty (Briggs) Cribbs, had two children, Clair Linton (Lin) and Judy.

BIBLIOGRAPHY: *Bellaire* (OH) *Times-Leader*, 1949–1977; Mike Douchant, *Encyclopedia of College Basketball* (Detroit, MI, 1995); Don Hall, *A History of Jeannette* (Jeannette, PA, 1976); *Irwin* (PA) *Standard-Observer*, n.d.; Jim O'Brien, ed., *Hail to Pitt, A Sports History of the University of Pittsburgh* (Pittsburgh, PA, 1982); *University of Pittsburgh Basketball Media Guide, 1989* (Pittsburgh, PA, 1989); Westmoreland County Sports Hall of Fame files; *Wheeling* (WV) *News-Register*, n.d.

Robert B. Van Atta

CRUM, Denzil Edwin "Denny" "Cool Hand Luke" (b. March 2, 1937, San Fernando, CA), college player and coach, is the son of Alwin Denzil Crum, an aircraft mechanic and sheet-metal worker, and June (Turner) Crum. The Crums settled in the San Fernando Valley during the 1930s. Crum grew up in a predominantly rural periphery of Los Angeles, where he engaged in hunting, fishing, baseball, and basketball. His basketball career began at San Fernando High School, where he had attained All-League status by his senior year in 1955. At nearby Pierce JC, he averaged 27.1 points the next year and was named Southern California JC Player of the Year in 1956–1957. During the 1957–1958 and 1958–1959 seasons, he played guard for John Wooden's* UCLA Bruins and achieved PCC Honorable Mention as a starter his senior year.

During the 1959–1960 and 1960–1961 seasons, Crum served as a graduate assistant basketball coach for Wooden at UCLA. From 1961–1962 through 1967–1968, he was head basketball coach at his alma mater, Pierce JC, and compiled 84 wins and only 40 losses there. Crum returned to UCLA as Wooden's top assistant coach during the 1968–1969, 1969–1970, and 1970–1971 National Championship seasons, when the Bruins recorded a composite 86-4 win-loss mark. His strong personality made it difficult for him to serve as an assistant coach for someone else. He revered Coach Wooden and got along well with him, but some reported differences occurred. In 1971 Crum accepted the head coaching position at the University of Louisville, replacing John Dromo. From 1972 to 2001, Crum's Louisville Cardinals won 675 games and lost only 295 for a .696 winning percentage. More remarkably, he became the youngest and least experienced coach to have won 300 games, having accomplished that feat early in the 1983–1984 season. In February 1988 he tied Jerry Tarkanian* for reaching the 400-victory plateau, the second earliest of any major college coach. Crum's teams at Louisville won 20 or more games in all but nine seasons that he coached. Crum's Cardinals made 23 trips to the NCAA Tournament and three to the NIT. Louisville won 12 MC regular-season titles and 11 MC Tournament titles from 1975–1976 through 1994–1995. Louisville did not win any title under Crum after shifting to Conference USA. Crum took Louisville to the NCAA Final Four on five occasions, losing to Wooden's UCLA team in both the 1972 and 1975 semifinals, defeating Larry Brown's* UCLA team for the national championship in 1980, losing to Georgetown University in the 1982 semifinals, and triumphing over Duke University for the national championship in 1986. In 1983 and 1986, he was named *TSN* College Basketball Coach of the Year. Crum coached the U.S. squad, who were upset by Brazil in the 1987 Pan American Games at Indianapolis, Indiana.

Crum's coaching style won respect from players, coaches, and the press. Nicknamed "Cool Hand Luke" by television commentator and esteemed former coach Al McGuire*, Crum utilized a mellower version of Wooden's coaching style. His fast-break offense and pressing defense resembled Wooden's format adapted to the more individualized players he recruited to Louisville. A formidable recruiter, Crum brought in Bill Walton*, Jamaal Wilkes*, Larry Farmer, and others to UCLA, and a parade of All-Americas and ultimate NBA professionals to Louisville. Crum was considered the "Ultimate Savior" of the UCLA basketball program. He might have been tempted to succeed Wooden in 1975 but was not offered the job then. By the time UCLA approached him to succeed Gary Cunningham in 1979, he had lost interest. Crum enjoys being a horse-raising gentleman farmer in Jeffersonville, Kentucky, where he resides with his wife, Joyce, and their son, Robert Scott. He retired following the 2000–2001 season. In 1994, he was inducted into the Naismith Memorial Basketball Hall of Fame.

BIBLIOGRAPHY: Dwight Chapin and Jeff Prugh, *The Wizard of Westwood: Coach John Wooden and His UCLA Bruins* (Boston, MA, 1973); Denny Crum file, Naismith Memorial Basketball Hall of Fame, Springfield, MA; Denzil Edwin Crum, questionnaire to Barry M. Schutz, August 1984; Mike Douchant, *Encyclopedia of College Basketball* (Detroit, MI, 1995); Scott Howard Cooper, *The Bruins 100* (Lenexa, KS, 1999); *NCAA Men's Basketball Records, 2004* (Indianapolis, IN, 2003); *University of Louisville Basketball Press Guide, 2000–2001* (Louisville, KY, 2000).

Barry M. Schutz

CRUTCHER, Hazel Leona Walker (b. August 8, 1914, Ashdown, AR), college and professional player, is the daughter of Herbert Walker, a farmer, and Minnie (Chauncey) Walker. After graduating from Ashdown (Arkansas) High School in 1932, she attended Tulsa (Oklahoma) BC from 1932 through 1934. In 1934 she married train brakeman Gene Crutcher, who was killed in a railroad accident in 1940, and had no children. Hazel started playing organized basketball in 1928 at Ashdown High School and made All-District and All-State as a forward there. Hazel received a basketball scholarship from Tulsa BC, where she played for two years and helped the Stenos win the 1932–1933 and 1933–1934 National AAU championships. During the next 12 years, she played with Lion Oil Company of El Dorado, Arkansas and Lewis and Norwood Flyers Insurance, Arkansas Motor Coaches, and Dr. Pepper Bottling Company, all of Little Rock, Arkansas. In 1936–1937, 1939–1940, and 1940–1941, she helped the Norwood Flyers win the National AAU championships. Hazel was named an All-America 11 times (1934–1938, 1940–1945). The holder of the national free throw record with 49 out of 50, she won the national free throw title six years and the international free throw title twice.

After playing three seasons (1946–1947 to 1948–1949) professionally with Olsen's All-American Red Heads, Crutcher organized her own team, the Arkansas Travelers. Between October and May of each year, this seven-woman team played seven nights a week, up to 11 games a week, and over 200 games a season throughout the U.S. against men's teams with men's rules. During her regular half-time free throw shoot-out, she always defeated the local champion with her famed two-handed shot. Hazel arranged the team's schedule, handled its finances, and directed all the publicity. The Arkansas Travelers, although primarily entertainment oriented, still won about 80 percent of their games. After 37 basketball seasons, five-foot nine-inch, 140-pound Hazel retired from competition in 1966. She spent the next 16 years in Little Rock caring for her parents. She also gave basketball clinics in schools and colleges, helped with the Special Olympics, and currently enjoys golf and fishing. In 1940 Hazel was elected into the HAF Hall of Fame and was named by the AP as the nation's top female athlete. After being inducted in 1959 into the Arkansas Sports Hall of Fame, she was selected in 1976 to the Four States Area Hall of Fame and the Texarkana Bi-Centennial Hall of Fame.

BIBLIOGRAPHY: Robert Carey, "Hazel Walker and the Arkansas Travelers," *SI* 41 (November 11, 1974), pp. 11, 12, 14, 16; Hazel Walker Crutcher to Angela Lumpkin, June 1, 1984; September 1984; Carolina F. Magruder to Angela Lumpkin, September 1983; Arthur Seesholtz to Angela Lumpkin, September 1984.

Angela Lumpkin

CUMMINGS, Robert Terrell "Terry" (b. March 15, 1961, Hammond, IN), college and professional player, is the son of John L. Cummings and Verda (White) Cummings. He grew up in the inner city streets of Chicago, Illinois and graduated in 1979 from Carver High School in Chicago, where he excelled in basketball for the Challengers. Cummings enrolled at DePaul University to play basketball under the legendary Coach Ray Meyer*. He led the Blue Demons to a 79-6 win-loss record in three seasons and three NCAA tournament appearances, being upset in the first round each time. Cummings scored 1,398 career points and pulled down 857 rebounds in 85 games, earning unanimous First Team All-America honors in 1982.

Cummings and his wife, Vonnie, are divorced and have three sons, Tony, Sean, and T. J. He was selected following his junior year by the San Diego Clippers (NBA) in the first round as the second pick overall of the 1982 NBA draft. A six-foot nine-inch, 250-pound forward, Cummings remains one of just eight players in NBA history to perform at least 18 years. He played for seven different NBA clubs: the San Diego Clippers 1982–1984, Milwaukee Bucks 1984–1989 and 1995–1996, San Antonio Spurs 1989–1995, Seattle SuperSonics 1996–1997, New York Knicks and Philadelphia 76ers 1997–1998, and the Golden State Warriors 1998–2000. An ordained Pentecostal Minister, he retired from NBA basketball following the 2000 season.

In 18 NBA seasons, Cummings played in 1,183 regular-season games to rank 17th in NBA history. He compiled 19,460 career points (29th best all-time) and made 8,045 field goals (22nd). Cummings averaged 23.7 points and 10.6 rebounds per game during his first year in the NBA, making the NBA All-Rookie First Team in 1983 and earning Rookie of the Year honors. He was selected to the All-NBA Second Team in 1985, the All-NBA Third Team in 1989, and made the Eastern Conference All-Star Team the same two seasons. From 1982–1983 through 1991–1992, Cummings averaged from 17.3 points to 23.7 points. In seven of his first 10 NBA seasons, he averaged at least 20 points. He completed his NBA career with averages of 16.4 points and 7.3 rebounds per game. Cummings appeared in the NBA playoffs in 13 of his 18 NBA seasons, helping his team capture the division championship six times. He appeared in 110 NBA playoff games, scoring 1,664 points for an average of 15.1 points and grabbing 742 rebounds for an average of 6.7 boards.

BIBLIOGRAPHY: "Terry Cummings," *Biography, Career Highlights, Career Statistics, DePaul, Ministries*, http://www.terrycummings.com (2003); Gary K. Johnson, *NCAA Men's Basketball's Finest* (Overland Park, KS, 1998); Ray Meyer and Ray Sons, *Coach* (Chicago, IL, 1987); Ken Shouler et al., *Total*

Basketball (Wilmington, DE, 2003); *TSN Official NBA Register, 2004–2005* (St. Louis, MO, 2004).

John L. Evers

CUNNINGHAM, William John "Billy" "Kangaroo Kid" (b. June 3, 1943, Brooklyn, NY), college and professional player, coach, and sportscaster, is the son of a fire chief and a prep All-America. He learned his basketball skills on the playgrounds of Manhattan Beach and the courts of Erasmus Hall High School, where he led an undefeated team to the New York City title in 1961. Although recruited by the University of North Carolina's Frank McGuire*, Cunningham played for Dean Smith* because McGuire joined the pro ranks. At North Carolina, the six-foot seven-inch, 210-pound Cunningham earned the nickname "Kangaroo Kid" for his unusual leaping ability. The Tar Heels' MVP from 1963 through 1965, Cunningham made the All-ACC team three times and the 1965 All-America team. Cunningham, who earned a Bachelor's degree in History at North Carolina, scored 1,709 career points and established career and seasonal rebound records with 1,062 and 379, respectively.

After being selected by the Philadelphia 76ers (NBA) in the first round of the 1965 NBA draft, Cunningham made the All-NBA Rookie team in 1966. He spent seven seasons (1966–1972) with the 76ers, establishing himself as one of the NBA's top players in 1966–1967 by helping the 76ers take the NBA championship. Cunningham teamed with Hal Greer*, Wilt Chamberlain*, and Chet Walker*, as Philadelphia defeated the San Francisco Warriors, four games to two. On becoming a free agent after the 1972 season, Cunningham signed with the Carolina Cougars (ABA). He captured the MVP award and made the ABA All-Star First Team his first season there, leading his team to the best ABA regular-season record. After two ABA seasons, Cunningham returned to the 76ers, albeit with a kidney ailment. Later he sustained a serious knee injury and retired before the 1976–1977 season.

During his (NBA and ABA) pro career, Cunningham played in 770 regular-season games, recorded 7,981 rebounds, and scored 16,310 points for a 21.2 point average. He played in 54 playoff games, recorded 514 rebounds, and scored 1,061 points for a 19.6 point average. Cunningham led Philadelphia in scoring and rebounding (1969–1972) and in assists (1972, 1975). In 1973 he paced Carolina in scoring, rebounds, assists, and steals. Besides starting for the NBA All-Stars from 1969 through 1971, Cunningham participated on the 1973 ABA All-Star team and made the All-NBA First Team in 1969, 1970, and 1971 and All-NBA Second Team in 1972.

Named head coach of the Philadelphia 76ers in 1977, Cunningham guided his NBA team to 454 wins in 650 regular-season games until retiring after the 1984–1985 season. The 76ers finished first or second in the Atlantic Division of the NBA for eight consecutive seasons. Cunningham's teams won 66 of 95 NBA playoff games, captured the NBA title in four games over the Los Angeles Lakers in 1983, and finished runner-up to the Lakers in 1980 and 1982. Although displaying a carefree attitude, Cunningham never failed to give 100 percent. The very intense player and coach (whose jersey number 32 has been retired by the Philadelphia 76ers) was often temperamental and angry with officials. Married in 1966, Cunningham and his wife, Sondra, have one daughter, Stephanie. Cunningham, a former CBS television pro basketball analyst, was elected to the Naismith Memorial Basketball Hall of Fame in 1986 and was part owner of the Miami Heat (NBA), an expansion team, from 1987 to 1995. He was named one of the 50 Greatest Players in NBA History in 1996.

BIBLIOGRAPHY: Smith Barrier, *On Tobacco Road, Basketball in North Carolina* (New York, 1983); Peter C. Bjarkman, *The History of the NBA* (New York, 1992); Billy Cunningham file, Naismith Memorial Basketball Hall of Fame, Springfield, MA; David Glenn et al., *Carolina Report* (Chapel Hill, NC, 1992); Zander Hollander, ed., *The Pro Basketball Encyclopedia* (Los Angeles, CA, 1977); Wayne Lynch, *Season of the 76ers* (New York, 2002); *The Carolina Bluebook, 1975–1976* (Greensboro, NC, 1975); Claudia Mitrol, *Philadelphia's Greatest Sports Moments* (Champaign, IL, 2000); Terry Pluto, *Loose Balls* (New York, 1990); Ken Rappoport, *Tales from the Tar Heel Locker Room* (Champaign, IL, 2002); Ken Rappoport, *Tar Heel: North Carolina*

Basketball (New York, 1976); Lenox Rawlings, "Cunningham Picks Off MVP in ABA," *TSN*, March 31, 1973, p. 5; *TSN Official NBA Register, 2004–2005* (St. Louis, MO, 2004).

John L. Evers

CURRY, Denise Marie (b. August 22, 1959, Davis, CA), college player, enjoyed an incredible basketball career at UCLA from 1978 to 1981 and gained recognition as the greatest offensive forward—among men or women—in Bruins history. When people consider the great basketball players from UCLA, they often think of Lew Alcindor (Kareem Abdul-Jabbar*) and Bill Walton*. Curry, however, actually ranks as the most consistent basketball player ever to perform at UCLA. Curry set 14 Bruins records during her four-year career. Curry's 3,171 career points made her the leading scorer in UCLA history, considerably above Alcindor's 2,325-point output. In single-season scoring, Curry's name appears in the first four spots. She scored 930 points her senior year after recording 855-, 803-, and 610-point seasons previously and averaged 24.6 points. Curry scored double figures in 94 straight games and tallied 20 or more points 65 times. She scored a Bruins and personal high 65 points in a game against the University of Oregon. In the free throw department, Curry converted 426 attempts during her career, 150 in a season, and 12 straight in a single game. All these marks stand as school highs. Curry made 11 for 11 from the charity stripe against California State University Long Beach and left UCLA with a record .818 career free throw percentage. Along with Curry's high-scoring records goes her Bruins record .607 career field goal percentage. Curry also dominated in the rebounding department. She set a record with 1,310 rebounds, averaging a record 10.1 points. Curry stands second in career blocked shots at UCLA with 77 and fifth in assists with 353. She also ranks fourth in single-season assists at 133. Curry was selected both All-America and WCAA Conference Player of the Year on three occasions. She helped lead the U.S. to a Silver Medal in 1979 at the Pan American Games and a World Championship Gold Medal. Besides pacing scorers three years on the U.S. National Team, Curry was the only U.S. 1980 team member to be chosen to the World All-Tournament team at the Olympic Pre-Qualifying Tournament. She was elected to the Naismith Memorial Basketball Hall of Fame in 1997.

BIBLIOGRAPHY: Peter C. Bjarkman, *The Biographical History of Basketball* (Chicago, IL, 2000); Denise Curry file, Naismith Memorial Basketball Hall of Fame, Springfield, MA; Joan S. Hult and Marianna Trekell, *A Century of Women's Basketball: From Frailty to Final Four* (Reston, VA, 1991); Victoria Sherrow, *Encyclopedia of Women and Sports* (Santa Barbara, CA, 1996); Sports Information, UCLA, Los Angeles, CA to Jeff Sanderson, September 1987.

Jeff Sanderson

D

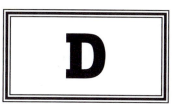

DALLMAR, Howard "Howie" (b. May 24, 1922, San Francisco, CA; d. December 19, 1991, Menlo Park, CA), college and professional player and coach, starred in basketball at the high school, college, and professional levels and coached the University of Pennsylvania from 1948 to 1953 and Stanford University from 1954 to 1975. After winning All-City honors at San Francisco's Lowell High School in 1939 and 1940, Dallmar played basketball one year at Menlo JC and transferred to Stanford University. In the 1941–1942 season, the six-foot four-inch, 200-pound Dallmar started for Everett Dean's* team that won the NCAA championship by defeating Dartmouth College 53-38. Dean's top eight players came from the Bay Area and included Jim Pollard*, a future NBA star. In the championship game, Pollard, the team's high scorer, was sidelined with the flu. Dallmar tallied 15 points, leading all scorers and winning MVP honors.

After the 1943 season, Dallmar's collegiate career was interrupted. Stanford dropped intercollegiate sports for the duration of the Second World War, and Dallmar entered the U.S. Navy. During the 1944–1945 season, the Navy stationed Dallmar in Philadelphia, Pennsylvania, to attend pre-flight training school and allowed him to enroll at the University of Pennsylvania. With Dallmar, Penn won the Ivy League title and ended Dartmouth College's string of seven consecutive league titles.

In 1946 Dallmar signed with the Philadelphia Warriors (BAA), leading the team in assists (104) as a rookie and scoring the winning basket in the final game of the BAA Championship series against the Chicago Stags. He paced the BAA in assists (120) and made the All-BAA team in 1947–1948, but the Warriors lost the championship series to the Baltimore Bullets.

In 1948–1949, Dallmar played his last year with the Warriors while beginning his coaching career at the University of Pennsylvania. In three years, he scored 1,408 points (9.6 point average) in 146 games for the Warriors. During six seasons, Dallmar compiled a 105-51 record at Pennsylvania. The Quakers won an IvL championship in 1953 with a perfect 14-0 record, earning their first NCAA appearance.

Dallmar returned to Stanford in the fall of 1954 and guided its basketball program for 21 seasons, the longest tenure of any Cardinal basketball coach. He coached until 1975, leaving Stanford with 256 wins and 264 losses. For his NCAA career, Dallmar's teams registered 361 wins and 316 losses. Dallmar later sold real estate and participated in various civic projects in Menlo Park, California. He and his wife, Helen, had two daughters, Elsa and Suzanne, and a son, Howie Jr.

BIBLIOGRAPHY: Mike Douchant, *Encyclopedia of College Basketball* (Detroit, MI, 1995); Joe Gergen, *The Final Four: An Illustrated History of College Basketball's Showcase Event* (St. Louis, MO, 1987); Jan Hubbard, ed., *The Official NBA Encyclopedia*, 3rd ed. (New York, 2000); Neil D. Isaacs, *Vintage NBA* (Silver Spring, MD, 1996); Don E. Liebendorfer, *The Color of Life is Red: A History of Stanford Athletics 1892–1972* (Palo Alto, CA, 1972); Robert W. Peterson, *Cages to Jump Shots: Pro Basketball's Early Years* (New York, 1990).

Adolph H. Grundman

DALY, Charles Joseph "Chuck" (b. July 20, 1930, Kane, PA), college and professional player, coach, and sportscaster, has enjoyed a basketball career characterized by his hard drive and skillful use of people. Daly, born to traveling salesman Earl Daly and Geraldine Daly in a western Pennsylvania coal mining town during the Great Depression, captured the sports fever of that region. He soon developed an aggressive defensive style, the eventual hallmark of all his teams.

Daly's scrappy high school hoop performance won a basketball scholarship to St. Bonaventure University in New York. The six-foot two-inch, 180-pounder, however, left that powerhouse program after one year, realizing that he stood little chance of playing regularly. In 1949, Daly transferred to Bloomsburg State College in Pennsylvania. During his two collegiate basketball seasons as a forward, he scored 418 points in 32 games for a 13.1-point average in the 1950–1951 and 1951–1952 campaigns.

Despite his undistinguished playing career, Daly made basketball coaching his life's work. Like most ambitious, successful coaches, he continually sought better positions. After a two-year military hitch, Daly began his coaching career at Punxsutawney (Pennsylvania) High School in 1955. After becoming frustrated at his low pay and anonymity, he wrote a letter to Duke University basketball coach Vic Bubas* asking for a job. Daly surprisingly was offered a spot as an assistant basketball coach at Duke University (ACC) from 1963 to 1969 before advancing to the head coaching job at Boston College from 1969 to 1971. His teams, laboring in the shadow of the previous coach, NBA legend Bob Cousy*, finished 26-24 over two seasons. When the University of Pennsylvania (IvL) head coaching job became available, he accepted that assignment. From 1971 to 1977, Daly led the Quakers to a .767 winning percentage and four IvL titles and NCAA berths, more than any other coach in the Quakers' history. His star performers included Kevin McDonald, Bob Morse, Corky Calhoun, Phil Hankinson, Ron Haigler, and Edward Stefanski. He also earned a Master's degree in educational administration at Pennsylvania State University in 1958.

Daly, who chafed under IvL recruiting restrictions, jumped from the collegiate ranks in 1978 to become an assistant coach of the Philadelphia 76ers (NBA). Working under Billy Cunningham*, he helped the 76ers win two Atlantic Division titles and place second twice during his four-year-tenure there. Philadelphia made the playoffs each of his seasons there.

Daly, nonetheless, yearned for an NBA head coaching job and earned a chance in 1981 with the lowly Cleveland Cavaliers (NBA). Unfortunately, his team won only nine of its first 41 games, resulting in his midyear dismissal. Daly finally got his break, when he moved to the equally inept Detroit Pistons (NBA) the next season. The Pistons featured a talented backcourt in Isiah Thomas* and Joe Dumars* and an aggressive frontcourt of "Bad Boys" including Bill Laimbeer*, Dennis Rodman*, and Rick Mahorn. Daly never experienced a losing record in the Motor City and was known as a "players' coach." His Pistons won three Central Division titles and three Eastern Conference titles, registered five consecutive 50-plus win seasons, and garnered NBA championships in 1989 and 1990, only the third time in NBA history that the same team won consecutive titles. Red Auerbach's* Boston Celtics and Pat Riley's* Los Angeles Lakers also accomplished the feat. Daly's winning percentage with the Pistons reached .633, as the Pistons made the playoffs all his nine years there.

Having conquered the NBA and grown weary of team infighting, Daly resigned from the Pistons in 1992. He then assumed the challenge of coaching the U.S. Olympic basketball team in the 1992 Barcelona, Spain Summer Olympic Games. With NBA players being permitted for the first time, his team marked perhaps the greatest ever assembled in any venue. Michael Jordan*, Magic Johnson*, Larry Bird*, and their teammates predictably decimated their international competition by the greatest margins in Olympic basketball history, capturing a gold medal for the United States.

Daly's desire to continue NBA coaching led him to decline a lucrative television analyst's position and accept the helm of the New Jersey Nets (NBA). In 1992–1993, the Nets, led by Derrick Coleman*, Drazen Petrovic, and Kenny

Anderson, compiled a 43-39 record for third place in the Atlantic Division. Despite the tragic death of Petrovic, New Jersey repeated in third place in 1993–1994 with a 45-37 mark; Daly resigned after the season. In 1994, he was elected to the Naismith Memorial Basketball Hall of Fame. He worked for the Turner Network as a basketball analyst from 1994 through the 1996–1997 season. Daly was named one of the Top Ten Coaches in NBA History in 1996. He coached the Orlando Magic (NBA) in 1997–1998 and 1998–1999, garnering a 33-17 mark the latter lockout-shortened campaign. He achieved an overall NBA coaching record of 638-437 for a .593 winning percentage and a 75–51 playoff mark.

Daly joined the Vancouver Grizzlies (NBA) as a special consultant to the president in May 2000. The Grizzlies moved to Memphis for the 2001–2002 season. Daly, an avid golfer, enjoys fine clothes, crooners Frank Sinatra and Bobby Short, and mystery novels. He and his wife, Terry, have one daughter, Cydney.

BIBLIOGRAPHY: Chuck Daly, letter to Bruce Dierenfield, March 1994; "Chuck Daly," *CB* (1991), pp. 172–175; Chuck Daly file, Naismith Memorial Basketball Hall of Fame, Springfield, MA; Jerry Green, *The Detroit Pistons* (Chicago, IL, 1991); Jack McCallum, "A Perfect Fit," *SI* 71 (December 18, 1989), pp. 52–58; New Jersey Nets press release, 1994; Cameron Stauth, *The Franchise* (New York, 1990); *TSN Official NBA Register, 2004–2005* (St. Louis, MO, 2004).

Bruce J. Dierenfield

DAMPIER, Louie "Lou" "Little Louie" (b. November 20, 1944, Indianapolis, IN), college and professional player and coach, averaged 24.0 points in basketball for the Southport (Indiana) High School Cardinals in 1963. He participated on the 1963 Indiana All Stars and was inducted in the Indiana Basketball Hall of Fame in 1993.

Dampier played basketball for Adolph Rupp* and baseball at the University of Kentucky. In three varsity basketball seasons between 1964–1965 and 1966–1967, the six-foot, 175-pound guard compiled 1,575 points, grabbed 409 rebounds, handed out 134 assists, and recorded 50.8 field goal shooting and a 83.4 free throw shooting percentages. He performed on the 1965–1966 team nicknamed "Rupp's Runts" that lost the championship game of the NCAA tournament to Texas Western University. Dampier averaged 22.8 points and 6.3 rebounds in four NCAA tournament games.

One of the most popular players in Wildcats history, Dampier ranks among the Top 10 in several school career categories. He shared team MVP honors with Pat Riley* in 1966 and 1967 and saw his jersey number 10 retired. His other honors included All-SEC First Team three times, Second Team All-America, Academic All-SEC, and Academic All-America twice, and All-NCAA Regional and Final Four Teams once.

The Kentucky Colonels (ABA) selected Dampier in the first round of the 1968 ABA draft. Dampier also was chosen 38th overall by the Cincinnati Royals (NBA) in the 1968 NBA draft. He joined Kentucky in 1968, combining with Byron Beck of the Denver Nuggets as the only ABA players to perform all nine seasons with the same franchise.

The most productive shooter in the ABA, Dampier holds several ABA career and season records and played in 728 regular season ABA games. He remains the ABA all-time leader in scoring with 13,726 points and assists with 4,084. Dampier played 27,770 minutes, made 5,290 field goals, and 794 three-point field goals, all ABA records. He set ABA records with 199 three point field goals during the 1968–1969 season and 94 career ABA playoff games appearances.

After earning All-Rookie Team honors, Dampier was named to the All-ABA Second Team four times, helped lead the Colonels to the ABA playoffs nine consecutive times, and reached the ABA Finals three times. He appeared in seven ABA All-Star Games, and in 1975 helped Kentucky win the ABA title, defeating the Indiana Pacers in five games.

When the ABA and NBA merged following the 1975–1976 season, Dampier was selected by the San Antonio Spurs (NBA) and played three seasons for the Spurs before retiring as a professional basketball player. He was later named to a 30 man All-ABA Team.

Between 1983 and 1998, Dampier owned an

audio-visual distributing company in Kentucky. He served as an assistant coach with the Denver Nuggets (NBA) from 1998 to 2002. He and his wife, Judy, have four children, Danielle, Nick, Rob, and Jay.

BIBLIOGRAPHY: Peter C. Bjarkman, *The Biographical History of Basketball* (Chicago, IL, 2000); "Louie Dampier," *Assistant Coach*, http://www.nba.com (2004); "Louie Dampier," *Career Statistics*, http://www.ukfans.net (2004); "Louie Dampier," *Indiana Basketball Hall of Fame*, http://www.hoopshall.com (2004); "Louie Dampier," *Statistics*, http://www.basket ball reference.com (2004); Jan Hubbard, ed., *The Official NBA Encyclopedia*, 3rd ed. (New York, 2000); Gary K. Johnson, *NCAA Men's Basketball's Finest* (Overland Park, KS, 1998); David S. Neft et al., *The Encyclopedia of Sports: Pro Basketball*, 5th ed. (New York, 1992).

John L. Evers

DANDRIDGE, Robert L., Jr. "Bobby" "Pick" "Greyhound" (b. November 15, 1947, Richmond, VA), college and professional player, is the son of Robert Dandridge Sr., and developed his basketball skills on Richmond playgrounds. He earned All-State basketball honors, leading Maggie Walker (Richmond, Virginia) High School to the city championship during his senior year in 1965. Although talented, the slender, six-foot six-inch, 179-pounder attracted few major college basketball recruiters. Norfolk State University showed the greatest interest. Norfolk State's program, its run-and-shoot style of play, and its close proximity to his home appealed to Dandridge, who accepted the school's scholarship offer. Dandridge embarked on an outstanding college career in 1966 and set several Norfolk State records, scoring 53 points in a single game as a senior. He averaged 25.5 points over three seasons and 32.8 points in his senior year. During the late 1960s, Norfolk State finished among the top 10 college basketball teams in scoring.

Dandridge's scoring ability, speed, and excellent defensive play impressed NBA scouts. His suspect physique, however, contributed to a fourth-round draft selection by the Milwaukee Bucks (NBA) in 1969. An impressive rookie camp performance earned him a starting role. Dandridge made the All-Rookie Team with teammate Lew Alcindor (Kareem Abdul-Jabbar*). Many knowledgeable observers speculated that Dandridge would have been named NBA Rookie of the Year if Alcindor had not been on the ballot. During nine seasons with the Bucks, Dandridge averaged 19.2 points, made three NBA All-Star teams (1973, 1975–1976), and helped bring the 1971 NBA Championship to Milwaukee. During his tenure with the Bucks, he was nicknamed "Greyhound" because he loved to run. In August 1977 the Washington Bullets (NBA) signed him as a free agent. Dandridge played four seasons with the Bullets, averaging 18 points. In 1978 he was selected to his fourth All-Star team and led the Bullets to the NBA Championship. Few players have won NBA Championships with two different teams.

Nagging injuries slowed the "Greyhound" and forced his retirement after the 1981–1982 season. During his 13-year NBA career, Dandridge scored 10,511 points and averaged 18.5 points during the regular season and averaged 20.1 points in 93 playoff contests. He resides with his wife, Barbara, and daughters, Shana and Amid, in Richmond, Virginia, and directs several small business interests.

BIBLIOGRAPHY: Larry Fox, *Illustrated History of Basketball* (New York, 1974); *Milwaukee Bucks Media Guides*, 1970, 1975, 1977 (Milwaukee, WI, 1970, 1975, 1977); *Norfolk State University Basketball Guide, 1968–1969* (Norfolk, VA, 1968); Wayne Patterson and Lisa Fisher, *100 Greatest Basketball Players* (New York, 1989); Ken Shouler et al., *Total Basketball* (Wilmington, DE, 2003); *Washington Bullets Media Guide, 1978* (Washington DC, 1978).

Jerry Jaye Wright

DANIELS, Melvin Joe "Mel" (b. July 20, 1944, North Brook Township, NC), college and professional athlete, coach, and scout, is the son of Maceo Daniels and Bernice Daniels and graduated from Pershing High School in Detroit, Michigan in 1963. Although Daniels did not grow up on the inner city playgrounds, his six-foot three-inch height as a sophomore prompted basketball coach Will Robinson to recruit him. That event marked a turning point in his life. By his senior year, Daniels had grown four more inches and become one of the top centers in Detroit's scholastic leagues.

Daniels spent two years at Burlington (Iowa) JC, where he quickly became a formidable junior college basketball center, averaged 25.2 points and 10 rebounds, and made JC All-America in 1964. He transferred to the University of New Mexico (WAC) in September 1964, and played center for coach Bob King for the next three seasons. Daniels, a dominant WAC player at six-feet nine-inches and 228-pounds, averaged almost 20 points and 11 rebounds. The Lobos compiled a 19-8 win-loss season mark in 1966–1967, as Daniels established new school season records for points per game (21.5), total points (581), and rebounds per game (11.9) and set new Lobo career marks of total points (1,537) and career field goals (594). His honors included making the All-WAC team at center for two consecutive years and being named a 1967 HAF All-America.

In 1967 Daniels left New Mexico for the professional basketball ranks without receiving a Bachelor's degree. The Minnesota Muskies (ABA) signed him to a three-year, no-cut contract of $24,500 per year while the Cincinnati Royals (NBA) only made him a token offer. "Money was the No. 1 reason I signed with the ABA, and No. 2 the league was new," remarked the 225 pound Daniels. He enjoyed a sensational rookie season in 1967–1968, averaging 22.2 points and making 1,213 rebounds in 78 games at center. The ABA's Rookie of the Year and MVP made the All-ABA First Team at center and started in the All-Star Game.

The Indiana Pacers (ABA) secured Daniels's contract for what he referred to as a "cup of coffee," in one of the great coups among professional basketball trades. In 1968–1969, Daniels tallied 24.0 points per game and 1,256 total rebounds. His ABA honors included appearing in the All-Star Game, leading the ABA in rebounds, and making the All-ABA Team. He performed well with the Pacers through the 1973 season, helping Indiana capture ABA Championships in 1970 and 1972. Daniels, who averaged 18.7 points and 17.6 rebounds in 1969–1970 and 19.2 points and 16.4 rebounds in 1971–1972, made ABA MVP (1971), the All-ABA Team (1969–1970 through 1971–1972), the All-Star Team (1970 through 1972), All-Star Game MVP (1971), and *TSN* ABA Player of the Year (1971).

Daniels' last two Pacers seasons saw him average 18.5 points and 15.4 rebounds in 1972–1973, and 15.4 points and 11.6 rebounds in 1973–1974. During the 1972–1973 season, he became the first ABA player to score 10,000 career points. Daniels completed his ABA career as a reserve with the Memphis Sounds (ABA) in 1974–1975 and briefly appeared with the New York Nets (NBA) in 1976–1977. During his ABA career, he scored 11,739 points (18.9 points average), made 9,494 rebounds, and appeared in seven ABA All-Star games. In 109 ABA playoff games, he tallied 1,901 points and averaged 17.4 points.

In September 1977, Daniels helped Bob King at Indiana State University (MVC) as a volunteer assistant basketball coach. Because Daniels had not earned his Bachelor's degree, he could not be hired as a regular assistant coach. He worked for the 1977–1978 and 1978–1979 seasons specifically with the Sycamores "big men," including Larry Bird*. Indiana State reached the 1979 NCAA Championship game against Michigan State University. Bird attributed much of his collegiate success and smooth transition to the NBA to Daniel's coaching and their one-on-one sessions.

Daniels scouted for the Indiana Pacers (NBA) organization from 1984–1985 to 1995–1996 and has served as their director of player personnel since 1996. He and his wife, Cecilia Josephine, whom he married in 1967, reside on his Circle M Ranch in Sheridan, Indiana, where he raises quarter horses.

BIBLIOGRAPHY: "Daniels Scores 10,000," *NYT*, November 10, 1972, p. 29; Dick Denny, "Daniels Itching for Shot at NBA Stars," *TSN*, March 27, 1971, p. 5; Tim Edwards, interview with Robert Saunders, March 29, 1990; "Exhibition All-Star Game," *NYT*, May 25, 1972, p. 62; Todd Gould, *Pioneers of the Hardwood* (Bloomington, IN, 1998); Jan Hubbard, ed., *The Official NBA Basketball Encyclopedia*, 3rd ed. (New York, 2000); Tom James, interview with Robert Saunders, March 28, 1990; "NBA Defeats ABA," *NYT*, May 1972, p. 23; Terry Pluto, *Loose Balls: The Short, Wild Life of the American Basketball Association* (New York, 1990); *TSN Official NBA Register, 2004–2005* (St. Louis, MO, 2004); *University of New Mexico All-Time Records Basketball Guide, 1988* (Albuquerque, NM, 1988),

p. 126; *University of New Mexico Basketball Media Guide, 1966–1967* (Albuquerque, NM, 1966).

Robert C. Saunders

DANTLEY, Adrian Delano (b. February 28, 1956, Washington, DC), college and professional basketball player, is one of many Washington, D.C., metropolitan area stars to achieve All-America and All-Pro honors in the roundball sport. A standout scholastic player at basketball-rich DeMatha Prep School of Hyattsville, Maryland, Dantley enjoyed three spectacular years at University of Notre Dame with averages of 18.3, 30.3, and 28.6 points. He became the ninth player in NCAA history chosen for two consecutive years as consensus All-America, the only forward besides David Thompson* of North Carolina State University to achieve such distinction to that time. His career 25.8 point college scoring average ranks him second behind only Austin Carr* in scoring in Notre Dame history with 2,223 career points. As a sophomore, Dantley finished second nationally in scoring average and first in total points. He then briefly entered his name in the NBA hardship draft before withdrawing at the last moment to return to Notre Dame for his junior season. An Irish co-captain during his junior year, Dantley was the leading scorer in 27 of the team's 29 games and also averaged over 10 rebounds.

Passing up his final college season, Dantley was the sixth player overall named in the 1976 NBA draft. He was chosen by the Buffalo Braves (NBA), with whom he began his spectacular pro career. Before entering the pro ranks, however, Dantley excelled as the leading scorer and dominant player on the 1976 U.S. Olympic basketball squad. The U.S. team recorded a perfect 6-0 record to win the gold medal at the XXI Olympiad in Montreal, Canada. The ex-Irish star led the Olympians with 116 points and a 19.3 point average, recording 30 points in the final winning effort over Yugoslavia, in spite of a painful gash over his right eye that required eight stitches. A durable player, he missed only one game during his three varsity seasons at Notre Dame and averaged better than 34 minutes of playing time. His greatest asset as a collegian, however, may have been shooting accuracy. Dantley converted on a spectacular 58.9 percent of his field goal attempts during his final season and averaged a remarkable 56.2 percent from the field over a three-year span. Individual Notre Dame basketball records held by Dantley include most free throws attempted and made in a single season (314, 253) and in a career (769, 615), respectively.

Dantley's rookie NBA season fulfilled every expectation, as he averaged 20.3 points for the Buffalo Braves to become the first rookie in five seasons to top the 20 points-per-game plateau. He also shot 52 percent from the floor and set a Buffalo rookie record for points scored with 1,564, surpassing the mark of teammate Bob McAdoo*. Dantley further foreshadowed what was to become the trademark of his NBA career by drawing fouls, as he made 582 trips to the charity stripe to rank fifth in the NBA in that department. He easily won 1976 NBA Rookie of the Year honors. Despite a brilliant rookie season, Dantley was traded at the beginning of the next campaign to the Indiana Pacers (NBA), where he was a leading scorer until being exchanged again in December to the Los Angeles Lakers (NBA). In September 1979 Dantley was acquired by the Utah Jazz (NBA), with whom he finally found a more permanent home for his consistent offensive talents. With the Jazz, Dantley consistently ranked near the top of NBA individual scoring lists. He compiled a 28.0-point average his first season with Utah for fourth best overall in the NBA. From 1980 to 1984, Dantley was the NBA's premier scorer with consistent averages of 30.7, 30.3, 30.7, and 30.6. In 1981 and 1984, he led the NBA in scoring and made the All-NBA Second Team. A severe injury to his shooting wrist limited him to 22 games during the 1982–1983 season. On January 4, 1984, Dantley tied an NBA record by making 28 free throws in one game against the Houston Rockets. In 1984–1985 he was hampered by an early season contract dispute and a hamstring injury, which caused him to miss playing time. Consequently he slumped to 26.6 points-per-game, seventh among NBA scorers. He regained earlier form for the 1985–1986 season, tying for second place among NBA scores with a 29.8 point average. The six-foot five-inch, 210-pound Dantley was traded to the Detroit

Pistons (NBA) in August 1986. In 1986–1987 the 210-pounder averaged 21.5 points in helping Detroit to the NBA Eastern Conference finals against the Boston Celtics. In December 1987, against the Portland Trail Blazers, Dantley became the thirteenth NBA player to score 20,000 career points. He led Detroit in scoring with a 20.0 points average during the regular season (1987–1988) and helped the 54-28 Pistons to the Central Division crown. Detroit upset the Boston Celtics in the Eastern Conference finals before losing to the Los Angeles Lakers four games to three in the NBA Finals. Dantley paced the Pistons with a 21.3 points-per-game average in the NBA Championship series. He was traded to the Dallas Mavericks (NBA) for Mark Aguirre* in February 1989 and finished his NBA career with the Milwaukee Bucks (NBA) in 1990–1991. Dantley played with Breeze Milan (ItL) in 1991–1992. During 15 NBA seasons, he scored 23,177 points (24.3 point average) and made 5,455 rebounds (5.7 rebound average). He averaged 21.3 points and 5.4 rebounds in 73 playoff games.

BIBLIOGRAPHY: Peter C. Bjarkman, *The Biographical History of Basketball* (Chicago, IL, 2000); Mike Douchant, *Encyclopedia of College Basketball* (Detroit, MI, 1995); Tim Neely, *Hooping It Up: The Complete History of Notre Dame Basketball* (Notre Dame, 1985); Ken Shouler et al., *Total Basketball* (Wilmington, DE, 2003); *TSN Official NBA Register, 2004–2005* (St. Louis, MO, 2004).

Peter C. Bjarkman

DAUGHERTY, Bradley Lee "Brad" (b. October 19, 1965, Asheville, NC), college and professional player and sportscaster, is the son of Roy Daugherty and Dorothy Daugherty. His father served in the United States Army before becoming a clerk for a manufacturing firm, Kearfaut. Daugherty grew up in Black Mountain, North Carolina and attended Owen High School in nearby Swannanoa, North Carolina, where he was named a *Parade* and McDonald's All-America in basketball.

Daugherty attended the University of North Carolina from 1982 to 1986, where he developed into an unusually efficient low-post scorer. The seven-foot, 250-pound center made 62 percent of his field goals for the Tar Heels. Daugherty scored 1,912 points in 133 games at North Carolina, averaging 14.2 points and 7.4 rebounds. He led the ACC in rebounding in 1985 and paced the NCAA in field goal percentage in 1986. Daugherty was voted First-Team All-ACC in 1985 and 1986 and Second-Team All-America by AP in 1986. He graduated with a Bachelor's degree in Radio, Television, and Motion Pictures.

The Philadelphia 76ers (NBA) made Daugherty the top pick in the 1986 NBA draft, but immediately traded him to the Cleveland Cavaliers (NBA). Daugherty became a mainstay for Cleveland, starting at center from his rookie season through the 1994 campaign, when a bad back forced his retirement. He averaged 19 points and 9.5 rebounds in 548 NBA career games and appeared in five All-Star games. As a professional, Daugherty scored 10,938 points, pulled down 5,227 rebounds, and made 53.2 percent of his field goals. Cleveland retired his uniform number 43.

Daugherty later became a television analyst for college basketball. He and his wife, Heidi Rost Daugherty, have two children, Colton and Brianna.

BIBLIOGRAPHY: Art Chansky, *The Dean's List: A Celebration of Tar Heel Basketball and Dean Smith* (New York, 1996); David Daly, *One to Remember* (Ashboro, NC, 1991); Hank Hersch, "A Down-Home Hoedown," *SI* 76 (January 20, 1992), pp. 26–29; Jan Hubbard, ed., *The Official NBA Encyclopedia*, 3rd ed. (New York, 2000); Ron Morris, *ACC Basketball: An Illustrated History* (Chapel Hill, NC, 1988); Ken Rappoport, *Tales from the Tar Heel Locker Room* (Champaign, IL, 2002); Dean Smith, *A Coach's Life: My Forty Years in Basketball* (New York, 1999).

Jim L. Sumner

DAVIES, Charles Robinson "Chick" (b. 1900, New Castle, PA; d. April 15, 1985, Pittsburgh, PA), college player and coach, was the son of a steel worker and grew up in Homestead, Pennsylvania. Davies quit public school at age 14 to work in the steel mills and enlisted in the U.S. Navy in 1910. After becoming head basketball coach at Duquesne in 1924, he earned his high school diploma, B.A., and Master's degrees from Duquesne. Davies coached both intercollegiate and interscholastic basketball in the Pittsburgh area for 31 years, with a combined record of 505 victories against 143 defeats. He served as head basketball coach at Duquesne University until 1948, compiling a 314-106 record and ranking eleventh on the NCAA all-time list at the time of his death.

Under Davies, the Iron Dukes gained national prominence by the late 1930s. His most famous teams, the 1939–1940 and 1940–1941 squads, used only six players in most games. His 1939–1940 team played in both the NCAA and the then–more prestigious NIT postseason tournaments, ending with a 20-3 record. The following season, Duquesne lost to the University of Colorado in the NIT championship game and posted a 17-3 record. Davies coached All-Americas Paul Birch in 1935, Herb Bonn in 1936, and Moe Becker in 1941. Dudey Moore, one of his former players, succeeded Davies as head coach and maintained the Iron Dukes' winning tradition.

After leaving Duquesne, Davies coached at Homestead High School, near Pittsburgh, for 10 years. He enjoyed seven winning seasons there, guiding Homestead to the 1950 Pennsylvania State scholastic championship.

His coaching emphasized a disciplined control game and adept ball handling, out-finessing the opposition, working for high-percentage open shots, and a strong defense. His salary as head coach at Duquesne University started at only $300 yearly and reached $3,500 his final year there. Survivors included one son, Charles Jr., and one daughter, Elizabeth Ann.

BIBLIOGRAPHY: Paul Demilio, Archives, Duquesne University Library, Pittsburgh, PA, fax letter to David L. Porter, September 8, 1994; Mike Douchant, *Encyclopedia of College Basketball* (Detroit, MI, 1995); *Duquesne University Basketball Media Guides*; Lou Kasperik (1939–1941 player) interview with Robert Van Atta; Derry, PA, 1993; *NCAA Men's Basketball Records, 2004* (Indianapolis, IN, 2003); Chet Smith and Marty Wolfson, *Greater Pittsburgh History of Sports* (Pittsburgh, PA, 1969); *TSN*, April 29, 1985, p. 48.

Robert B. Van Atta

DAVIES, Robert Edris "Bob" "The Harrisburg Houdini" (b. January 15, 1920, Harrisburg, PA; d. April 22, 1990, Hilton Head, SC), college and professional player and coach, is the son of sales manager Edris C. Davies and Esther M. Davies. A 1937 graduate of John Harris High School in Harrisburg, Pennsylvania, Davies excelled in football, baseball, basketball, and track and field. The second four-sport letterman in the school's history, Davies attended Franklin and Marshall College. He enrolled at Seton Hall University on a baseball scholarship arranged by the Boston Red Sox (AL). Davies, however, chose to concentrate on basketball. Before his graduation in 1942, Davies twice made All-America, captained the team for two years, and was awarded MVP for three years. Davies led the Pirates to 43 consecutive victories from 1939 to 1941, a 55-5 overall record, a NIT bid, and was named the MVP in the 1942 College All-Star Game in Chicago. Considered a complete player, Davies earned the nickname "The Harrisburg Houdini" for his excellent dribbling ability, ball control, and behind-the-back maneuvers.

As a U.S. Navy member (1942–1945), the six-foot one-inch, 175-pound Davies directed the Great Lakes Naval Training Station to the service title in 1943. He played briefly with the Brooklyn Indians (NBL) in 1943–1944 and New York Gothams (NBL) in 1944–1945. Davies joined the Rochester Royals (NBL) in 1945 and starred for the next 10 seasons, sparking them to world titles in 1946 and 1951. Rochester transferred to the BAA in 1948 and NBA in 1949. He led the NBA in playmaking in 1949 with 321 assists and paced his club in that category for seven seasons, including an NBA record 20 in one game. Davies was named to the All-NBL-BAA Team twice and won the NBL's MVP award in 1947. Besides receiving All-NBA honors four times (1950–1953), Davies played in the first four All-Star Games (1951–1954).

During his pro career, Davies scored 7,770 points and recorded 2,250 assists in 569 games. Although playing for the Royals, Davies in 1947 coached Seton Hall to a 24-3 record. After retiring from pro basketball, he coached Gettysburg College in six sports for two seasons and in 1957 joined the Converse Rubber Company in sales and promotions. By 1984 he represented their company in 11 states. Married to

Mary Helfrich in 1942, Davies had four children, James, Robert, Richard, and Carole. He was named to the NBA Twenty-Fifth Anniversary All-Time Team in 1970 as the "Sixth Greatest Player of the First Half-Century." A member of the Seton Hall and Pennsylvania Sports halls of fame, he was elected to the Naismith Memorial Basketball Hall of Fame in 1969. The Sacramento Kings (formerly Rochester Royals) retired his uniform number 11 in 1990. He died after battling cancer.

BIBLIOGRAPHY: Peter C. Bjarkman, *The History of the NBA* (New York, 1992); Bob Davies file, Naismith Memorial Basketball Hall of Fame, Springfield, MA; Jan Hubbard, ed., *The Official NBA Encyclopedia*, 3rd ed. (New York, 2000); Leonard Koppett, *24 Seconds to Shoot* (New York, 1990); Ken Shouler et al., *Total Basketball* (Wilmington, DE, 2003); Neil D. Isaacs, *Vintage NBA* (Silver Spring, MD, 1996); *TSN Official NBA Register, 2004–2005* (St. Louis, MO, 2004).

John L. Evers

DAVIS, Walter Paul "Sweet D" (b. September 9, 1956, Pineville, NC), college and professional player, is one of thirteen children of Edward Davis, and led South Mecklenburg High School in suburban Charlotte, North Carolina to the 1970, 1971, and 1972 state high school championships.

Davis earned a Bachelor's degree in recreation administration from the University of North Carolina in 1977, and played basketball under coach Dean Smith*. The six-foot six-inch, 185-pounder, who was an unusually smooth player, started four years at forward and soon acquired the nickname "Sweet D." The consistent scorer compiled respective single-season scoring averages of 14.3, 16.1, 16.6, and 15.5, and finished his college career with 1,863 points. His honors included making the 1976 U.S. Men's Olympic basketball team, and being named Second Team All-ACC in 1976 and First Team All-ACC in 1977. North Carolina finished second in the 1977 NCAA tournament.

The Phoenix Suns selected Davis fifth in the first round of the 1977 NBA draft. Davis, utilizing his quickness and shooting ability, averaged 24.2 points as a rookie, was named NBA Rookie of the Year, and made the All-NBA Second Team. Phoenix moved him from forward to guard in the 1979–1980 season. Davis continued prolific scoring and participated in the NBA All-Star Game from 1978 through 1981, in 1984, and in 1987. A severe knee injury limited him to only 23 games in the 1984–1985 season.

Davis underwent treatment for alcohol and cocaine abuse during the 1985–1986 season and in the spring of 1987. In July 1988 the Denver Nuggets (NBA) signed him as a free agent. In January 1991, Denver traded Davis to the Portland Trail Blazers (NBA). Portland compiled the NBA's best record in 1990–1991, as Davis averaged 13.0 points, but the Trail Blazers lost to the Los Angeles Lakers in the Western Conference Finals. In October 1991, Denver signed him again. Davis ended his NBA playing career with Denver in 1991–1992. During 15 NBA seasons, he had played in 1,033 games, scored 19,521 points, averaged 18.9 points, made 3,053 rebounds, and recorded 3,878 assists. His career .511 field goal percentage and .851 free throw percentage verify his considerable shooting skills. Davis and his wife, Susan, have two children.

BIBLIOGRAPHY: Peter C. Bjarkman, *ACC—Atlantic Coast Conference Basketball* (Indianapolis, IN, 1996); Art Chansky, *The Dean's List* (New York, 1996); Smith Barrier, *On Tobacco Road, Basketball in North Carolina* (New York, 1983); Jan Hubbard, ed., *The Official NBA Encyclopedia*, 3rd ed. (New York, 2000); Ron Morris, *ACC Basketball: An Illustrated History* (Chapel Hill, NC, 1988); Ken Rappoport, *Tales from the Tar Heel Locker Room* (Champaign, IL, 2002); Dean Smith, *A Coach's Life: My Forty Years in Basketball* (New York, 1999); Curry Kirkpatrick, "It's Whoosh! Boom! Whoop! Time," *SI* 48 (February 20, 1978), pp. 14–17; *TSN*, February 18, 1978, p. 3, January 20, 1979, p. 3; *TSN Official 2004–2005 NBA Register* (St. Louis, MO, 2004); *USA Today*, April 23, 1991; Bob Wischnia, "Loneliness of the Suns' Good Humor Man," *Sport* 68 (January 1979), pp. 82–86.

Jim L. Sumner

DAVIS-WRIGHTSIL, Clarissa Glennet (b. June 4, 1967, San Antonio, TX), college and professional player and executive, graduated from John Jay High School in San Antonio, Texas, where she established numerous school records in women's basketball. As a freshman, Davis-Wrightsil proved a major component in the University of Texas Longhorns 34-0 season and 1986 NCAA Championship. The three-time NCAA All-America twice captured the Naismith Player of the Year Award and was named SWC Player-of-the-Decade for the 1980s. She graduated in 1989 with a Bachelors degree in speech communication. Davis-Wrightsil played professionally in Italy in 1990–1991 before joining the 1992 United States Olympic squad in Barcelona, Spain, where she averaged 13 points for the bronze medal U.S. team. She played professional basketball in Japan for the 1992–1993 season and Turkey from 1994 to 1996. From 1996 to 1998, Davis-Wrightsil performed in the ABL with the New England Blizzard, Long Beach (California) Stingrays and San Jose (California) Lasers, averaging 12 points and 5.5 rebounds with the Lasers in the 1998–1999 season. The six-foot one-inch, 163-pound forward returned to Turkey to play for the Fenerbahce team (TWBL) in 1998–1999. Davis-Wrightsil signed with the Phoenix (Arizona) Mercury (WNBA) and averaged 9.3 points and 2.7 rebounds for 1999, her last season as a player.

Davis-Wrightsil's proudest moment came with bringing a WNBA team to her hometown. She led a successful campaign by selling 6,300 season-ticket deposits to insure the Utah Starzz WNBA franchise would be transferred to San Antonio for the 2003 season. Davis-Wrightsil serves as the chief operating officer for the San Antonio Silver Stars (WNBA) and as Director of the Coalition for Women's Basketball. The Silver Stars struggled with a 12-22 mark in 2003 and 9-25 mark in 2004.

Davis-Wrightsil, who is married, was elected to the Texas Basketball Hall of Fame, the San Antonio Sports Hall of Fame, and the University of Texas Hall of Honors. She established the TEAMXPRESS Foundation, which offers outreach and summer programs for young women to encourage reading, leadership, community volunteerism, self-esteem, and a healthy lifestyle. She considers this a way to give thanks to God for the talents she has been given.

BIBLIOGRAPHY: W. Scott Bailey, "San Antonio's new WNBA team is shooting for the stars," *San Antonio Business Journal* (February 3, 2003), archives; Jennifer Bellis, "WNBA gives S.A. court date," *San Antonio Express-News* (web posting November 14, 2002), pp. 1–3; NBA Media Ventures, "WNBA in San Antonio 2003," *Spurs.com* (2003), pp. 1–4; San Jose Lasers, "Clarissa Davis-Wrightsil," *San Jose Lasers Observer 1998–1999*; TEAM XPRESS Foundation, "Empowering girls through sports," teamxpress.org (March 25, 2003), p. 1; *TSN Official WNBA Guide and Register, 2004* (St. Louis, MO, 2004).

Frank J. Olmsted

DAWKINS, Johnny Earl, Jr. (b. September 29, 1963, Washington, D.C.), college and professional player and college coach, is the son of Johnny Dawkins Sr., a bus operator, and Peggy Dawkins, a social worker. Dawkins graduated from Mackin Catholic High School in Washington, D.C., where he was named a *Parade* and McDonald's All-America.

Dawkins attended Duke University from 1982 to 1986 and is widely credited as being the key recruit in Mike Krzyzewski's* revival of that ACC program. The six-foot two-inch, 160-pounder combined exceptional quickness and leaping ability with intelligence and ball skills to become one of the nation's top guards. He remains the only player to lead Duke in scoring four seasons. Dawkins scored 2,556 career points in 133 games, ranking first in Duke history and second in ACC history. He averaged 19.2 points and scored in double figures in 129 games, an NCAA record. Dawkins made 50.8 percent of his field goals and 79.0 percent of his free throws and compiled 555 assists.

Dawkins was selected Second-Team All-ACC in 1983 and 1984 and First-Team All-ACC in 1985 and 1986. He was named First-Team AP All-America in 1985 and First-Team UPI All-America in 1985 and 1986. Dawkins won the 1986 Naismith Award, leading Duke to an NCAA-record 37 wins and second place in the NCAA Tournament. He was named to the 1986 All Final-Four team, played on the 1983 United States World University team, and was an alternate on the 1984 United States Olympic team. Duke retired his uniform number 24. Dawkins received his Bachelor's degree in Political Science in 1986.

The San Antonio Spurs (NBA) selected Dawkins in the first round of the 1986 NBA draft. Despite suffering a serious knee injury in 1990, he played with San Antonio from 1986 to 1989, the Philadelphia 76ers (NBA) from 1990 to 1994, and Detroit Pistons (NBA) in 1994 and 1995. Dawkins averaged 11.1 points and 5.5 assists in 541 NBA games and made 85.7 percent of his free throws. He became an assistant basketball coach at Duke in 1998–1999. Dawkins married Tracy Warren in 1988, and has four children, Aubrey, Jillian, Blair, and Sean.

BIBLIOGRAPHY: Bill Brill, *Duke Basketball: An Illustrated History* (Dallas, TX, 1986); Richard Demak, "All Work and No Play," *SI* 67 (April 29, 1991), p. 56; Mike Douchant, *Encyclopedia of College Basketball* (Detroit, MI, 1995); *Duke Basketball Yearbook*, 2002–2003 (Durham, NC, 2002); Jan Hubbard, ed., *The Official NBA Encyclopedia*, 3rd ed. (New York, 2000); Curry Kirkpatrick, "One Devil of a Team," *SI* 64 (March 17, 1986), pp. 20–24.

Jim L. Sumner

DEAN, Everett S. (b. March 18, 1898, Livonia, IN; d. October 26, 1993, Caldwell, ID), college basketball and baseball player and coach, was born on a farm and played basketball at the Hardinsburg Indiana grade school playground in 1912. He starred in football, basketball, and baseball at Salem (Indiana) High School, playing in the State basketball tournament in 1917. After enrolling at Indiana University in 1917, he won letters in football, basketball, and baseball as a freshman. In basketball, he made the All BTC and All-America squads at center. Dean worked his way through Indiana University on a pick and shovel crew and as a clothing and jewelry salesman and swimming pool lifeguard. One of the nation's leading college baseball players, he rejected several major league offers to enter coaching. He captained the Hoosier basketball squad as a senior and received the BTC medal for proficiency in scholarship and athletics.

Dean married Lena Graves in 1922 and had two daughters. After graduating from Indiana University in 1922, he coached at Carleton College (Minnesota) for three years, won three conference championships in basketball, and captured one baseball title. His cage teams won 48 of 52 games and were declared Middle Western champions. In the summer of 1924, Dean taught baseball and basketball in a coaching school at Indiana University. At the school's end, he joined Indiana University as basketball and baseball coach. The only BTC mentor to coach two sports, he directed the Hoosier teams for 14 years. His baseball squads won three BTC titles and finished runners-up four times, while his basketball aggregates captured BTC titles in 1926, 1928, and 1936. His cage teams recorded 96 BTC wins, and 162 overall victories to only 93 total losses.

Dean moved to Stanford University in 1938 and coached the Indians basketball squad to 166 victories and 120 defeats in 11 seasons. His 1942 Stanford team, led by All-American Jim Pollard*, finished 28-4 and captured the NCAA title with a 53-38 triumph over Dartmouth College. His Stanford baseball squads also won three PCC titles. After coaching both sports for 11 years, he dropped the taxing two-sport routine and handled baseball his last seasons there until retirement in 1955. Dean was elected to the Naismith Memorial Basketball Hall of Fame as a coach in 1966 and to the Baseball Coaches Hall of Fame. In 1960 he won Indiana University's Distinguished Alumni Award. The author of two important basketball books, Dean resided in Orleans, Indiana, and served in 1984 as honorary coach for Bobby Knight's* Olympic basketball team.

BIBLIOGRAPHY: Gary Cavalli, *Stanford Sports* (Palo Alto, CA, 1982); Everett S. Dean file, Naismith Memorial Basketball Hall of Fame, Springfield, MA; Mike Douchant, *Encyclopedia of College Basketball* (Detroit, MI, 1995); George Gardner, "Hoosier Hero," Indiana University Sports Release, February 28, 1938; Bob Hammel et al., *Glory of Old IU* (Champaign, IL, 2000); Zander Hollander, ed., *The Modern Encyclopedia of Basketball* (Garden City, NY, 1969), *Indiana Basketball Coaches Record, 1984*; Indiana University Basketball Program, February 28, 1961; Don E. Liebendorfer, *The Color of Life is Red: A History of Stanford Athletics 1892–1972* (Palo Alto, CA, 1972); Bob Menke, "The Dean Team," *Indiana Alumni*, April 1982, pp. 9–11.

Stan W. Carlson

DeBERNARDI, Forrest Sale "Red" "De" (b. February 3, 1899, Nevada, MO; d. April 29,

1970, Dallas, TX), college player, began his successful basketball career at Iola, Kansas, where he won recognition for his all-around ability in basketball. After three seasons at Iola, DeBernardi transferred to Northeast High School in Kansas City (Missouri) and was selected All-City and to the All-Star team. In 1920 he continued his education and basketball career at Westminster College in Fulton, Missouri. During his Westminster years, DeBernardi lettered in basketball, track and field, tennis, and baseball. Basketball was his greatest love and brought him the greatest success. The faculty at Westminster agreed to let him join the Kansas City AC in quest of a national basketball title. Although his team finished third in the tournament, he was selected an All-America center. He again was granted permission to play for the Kansas City AC the next season, leading the team to a national title and being selected All-America a second straight year. DeBernardi transferred to the University of Kansas while continuing to play for the Kansas City AC, where once again he made All-America. In 1923 he joined the Hillyard Chemical Company in St. Joseph, Missouri, where part of his job was to organize a basketball team able to compete with the best in amateur basketball. In their first season, the Hillyard club managed a second-place finish and DeBernardi another All-America selection. He guided Hillyard for five seasons, including championship seasons in 1926 and 1927. De Bernardi left Hillyard and accepted a position at Cook Paint Company in Kansas City directing a new team for this organization to consecutive championships in 1928 and 1929. DeBernardi won great recognition for his four straight national championships involving two teams. Altogether, he competed in 11 national tournaments and received First-Team All-America Honors seven times. In 1938 the AP of New York, in collaboration with a number of the nation's leading coaches and officials, picked an All-Time, All-America College Basketball squad, with DeBernardi as All-Time center. He in 1952 was presented with the HAF Award, which today sits in a trophy case at Westminster College. DeBernardi was inducted into the Naismith Memorial Basketball Hall of Fame in 1961.

BIBLIOGRAPHY: Forrest DeBernardi file, Naismith Memorial Basketball Hall of Fame, Springfield, MA; Sandy Padwe, *Basketball's Hall of Fame* (Englewood Cliffs, NJ, 1970); Wayne Patterson, Naismith Memorial Basketball Hall of Fame, to Jeff Sanderson, August 1987.

Jeff Sanderson and Wayne Patterson

DeBUSSCHERE, David Albert "Dave" (b. October 16, 1940, Detroit, MI; d. June 11, 2003, New York, NY), college and professional basketball and baseball player, coach, and sports administrator, was the son of Marcel and Dorothy DeBusschere and grew up in Detroit, Michigan, where he was a sensational multitalented athlete starring in basketball and baseball. He led Austin High School in Detroit to the state basketball championship his senior year and was the best amateur pitching prospect in the Detroit area. The highly recruited star attended the University of Detroit and helped the Titans achieve national recognition. During his career, he became the leading basketball scorer in University of Detroit history and led an amateur baseball team to a national sandlot title. On graduation from Detroit in 1962, DeBusschere was sought by both pro basketball and baseball teams. He signed with the Detroit Pistons (NBA) as a "territorial pick," and as a pitcher with the Chicago White Sox (AL).

The six-foot six-inch, 225-pound DeBusschere played both sports until 1964, when he was named player-coach of the Detroit Pistons (NBA). The additional coaching responsibilities forced DeBusschere to give up baseball. With the Chicago White Sox in 1962 and 1963, the right-hander appeared in 36 games, struck out 61 batters in 102.1 innings, and compiled a 3-4 record (.429) and a 2.90 earned run average. He coached the Pistons for almost three seasons (1964–1965 through 1966–1967) and resigned as coach with a 79-143 record. As a player, however, he continued being successful and was named an All-Star member in the 1965–1966 season. DeBusschere's game included being a good rebounder, an excellent defensive player, a good offensive player, and a hard worker on the court. He starred for the Pistons until December 19, 1968, when he was traded to the New York Knickerbockers (NBA) in exchange for center Walt Bellamy*. This trade, according to most critics, led to the Knicks' world championship in 1969–1970. With the acquisition of DeBusschere, Willis Reed* became a center and Bill Bradley* became a starting forward. DeBusschere made the All-NBA Second Team in 1969. He played key roles not only in the 1969–1970 and 1972–1973 Knicks' championship seasons, but also was named to the NBA All-Defensive team each of his seasons there. DeBusschere retired as a player after the 1973–1974 season with a career average of 16.1 points and 11 rebounds. His career totals included 15,053 points scored and 9,618 rebounds.

After his playing career, DeBusschere served one year as vice president and general manager of the New York Nets (ABA) and as ABA commissioner its final season in 1975–1976. After this experience, he became involved with sports promotions and communications for several years. He returned to the New York Knicks in 1982, where he served as vice president and director of operations until his dismissal in January 1986. In 1982 he was elected to the Naismith Memorial Basketball Hall of Fame. He was named one of the 50 Greatest Players in NBA History in 1996.

BIBLIOGRAPHY: Bill Bradley, *Life on the Run* (New York, 1976); Lewis Cole, *Dream Team* (New York, 1981); David DeBusschere, *The Open Man: A Championship Diary* (New York, 1990); David DeBusschere file, Naismith Memorial Basketball Hall of Fame, Springfield, MA; Jan Hubbard, ed., *The Official NBA Encyclopedia*, 3rd ed. (New York, 2000); Phil Jackson and Charles Rosen, *Maverick: More Than a Game* (Chicago, IL, 1975); *The Lincoln Library of Sports Champions*, vol. 4 (Columbus, OH, 1974); New York Knickerbockers, Department of Public Relations, New York, NY; Phil Pepe, *The Incredible Knicks* (New York, 1970); Ken Shouler et al., *Total Basketball* (Wilmington, DE, 2003).

William A. Sutton

DEE, John F. "Johnny" (b. September 12, 1923, Cedar Rapids, IA), college player and amateur coach, is the son of John F. Dee and Melinda (Dieterlie) Dee, and began his athletic career at Loyola Academy in Chicago where he competed in basketball, football, and track and field. Dee, however, learned basketball from coach Leonard Sachs*, who produced some outstanding teams at Loyola University. As a youngster, he served as a waterboy and scoreboard keeper for Sachs. Although Dee expected to play for Sachs at Loyola, World War II and the latter's untimely death from a heart attack in 1942 sidetracked Dee's plans. After spending a semester at Loyola, Dee joined the U.S. Coast Guard for two years. He was discharged in 1944 and enrolled at the University of Notre Dame, where he played for two seasons. Although only five feet eight inches, the very strong, extremely aggressive Dee possessed a deadly two-handed set shot. In 41 games with the Irish, he averaged 10 points. During his first season, he tied the existing Chicago Stadium scoring record with 27 points. After two successful years at Notre Dame, Dee returned to Loyola University in 1946 for his senior year. When Dee scored 23 points in a 60-53 Loyola victory over Indiana University, Branch McCracken*, the Hoosiers coach, described the shooting exhibition as the best he had seen in a college or professional game.

Dee launched his coaching career in 1947 at St. Mel's High School in the CCL. For the 1951–1952 season, he returned to Notre Dame as assistant basketball coach under John Jordan. The University of Alabama (SEC) in 1952 made him head basketball and assistant football coach. In four years at Alabama, Dee's basketball squads compiled a 68-25 record. His 1955–1956 Crimson Tide finished a perfect 14-0 to become the first basketball team outside of Adolph Rupp's* University of Kentucky Wildcats to enjoy a perfect SEC season record. Because the SEC had allowed freshmen to play varsity basketball, Dee's starting five was ineligible for the NCAA tournament. The NCAA tournament limited competition to players with no more than three years of eligibility. Dee, shut out of the NCAA tournament, took his seniors to the 1956 AAU tournament in Denver, Colorado, where they played as the ADA Oilers. Bud Adams, later the owner of the Houston Oilers (NFL), sponsored the ADA Oilers. In the AAU semifinals, the powerful Phillips 66ers defeated Dee's team 71-69. A victory would have given Dee's club an opportunity to participate in the Olympic tournament.

The 1956 AAU tournament altered the direction of Dee's career. George Kolowich, president of the Denver-Chicago Trucking Company, offered him the head coaching position of Denver's D-C Truckers and entry in the powerful NIBL. In five seasons, Dee guided the D-C Truckers to one NIBL title and two AAU finals. More important, he revived basketball enthusiasm in Denver, pouring his enormous energy into ticket sales and promotions. As the NIBL faded, Dee joined the ABL for the 1962–1963 season with the Kansas City Steers. The Steers compiled a 25-9 record before the ABL collapsed. In 1964, Notre Dame hired him as head coach to revive its basketball program. In seven years, Dee's Notre Dame teams won 116 against 80 losses. His Irish squad compiled four consecutive 20-win seasons, made four NCAA tournament appearances, and participated in one NIT tournament. His best player, Austin Carr*, was selected first in the 1971 NBA draft. Dee's most memorable victory came in 1971, when the Irish triumphed 89-82 over coach John Wooden's* undefeated UCLA Bruins.

Dee never coached again after the 1970–1971 season, despite his impressive 346-191 overall coaching record. He returned to Denver and pursued a career in law and politics, serving between 1975 and 1979 as Denver's city auditor. He and his wife, Katherine, have three children, Melinda, Dennis, and John III.

BIBLIOGRAPHY: John Dee scrapbooks, in possession of John Dee, Denver, CO; Chris Dortch, *String Music: Inside the Rise of SEC Basketball* (Dulles, VA, 2002); *NCAA Men's Basketball Records, 2004* (Indianapolis, IN, 2003); Tim Neely, *Hooping It Up: The Complete History of Notre Dame Basketball* (Notre Dame, IN, 1985); Alexander Weyand, *The Cavalcade of Basketball* (New York, 1960).

Adolph H. Grundman

DEHNERT, Henry "Dutch" (b. April 5, 1898, New York, NY; d. April 20, 1979, Far Rockaway, NY), professional player and coach, did not play basketball in either high school or college. He gained his early experience as a professional player with up to five teams in a single season and played in the NYSL, PSL, ISL, and NEL. His success in these leagues interested Jim Furey*, owner of the New York Original Celtics.

In 1922 Furey signed Dehnert and all other Original Celtics to exclusive contracts, an unheard of concept at the time in pro basketball. The team enjoyed immediate success by winning the EL title the same year. The Celtics won 13 straight games in the MeL the next year before withdrawing to concentrate on more lucrative barnstorming junkets and quickly became the era's most famous team. Dehnert proved a key ingredient on the team, featuring stars Joe Lapchick*, Nat Holman*, Johnny Beckman*, and Davey Banks*. From 1922 until 1930, Dehnert enjoyed his peak years as a player. At six-feet one-inch and a rock-hard 210 pounds, he combined speed, skilled ball handling, and adapt passing, and played strong defense.

The Original Celtics, an inventive and creative team, devised the give-and-go play, the switching man-to-man defense, and the pivot play, Dehnert's personal invention. The play was conceived in Chattanooga, Tennessee, where the Celtics battled a strong local club. As the game started, the Celtics were troubled by the locals' "standing guard." Dehnert suggested that he could stand in front of the player, blocking him out of the Celtics' passing lanes. He would back in against the player, take a pass from Holman or Beckman, and pass off to one or the other as they cut past, picking off the defender. If the player guarding him committed too much to one side, Dehnert would turn the opposite way into the basket for an easy lay-up. This simple, revolutionary maneuver became the mainstay of the Celtics' attack over the next decade and largely contributed to their dominance of the game during the era. Dehnert became one of basketball's best known and highest paid performers because of his skilled execution of the pivot play.

In 1926 the Celtics joined the ABL. The Celtics dominated the ABL, winning consecutive championships during the 1926–1927 and 1927–1928 seasons. When the ABL forced the team to dissolve, Dehnert joined the Cleveland Rosenblums with teammates Lapchick and Pete Barry, and helped Cleveland capture championships in 1928–1929 and 1929–1930. After the ABL's collapse in 1931, Dehnert and the Celtics resumed their barnstorming trips. On his retirement, Dehnert had participated in over 1,900 Celtics' victories.

Dehnert coached in the 1940s. He was mentor of the Detroit Eagles for the 1940–1941 and 1941–1942 campaigns, winning the World Professional Tournament in Chicago in 1941. He piloted Harrisburg, Pennsylvania (ABL) for the 1942–1943 season. Dehnert coached the Sheboygan, Wisconsin Redskins (NBL), winning the Western Division title during the 1944–1945 and 1945–1946 seasons. He then coached the Cleveland Rebels of the newly formed BAA in 1946–1947, but was fired at midseason. Dehnert won 73 games and lost 64 for a .533 record during five years of major league coaching. He finished his coaching career with minor-league assignments at Chattanooga and Saratoga Springs, New York.

Dehnert worked as a mutual clerk at New York state racetracks during his later years and in 1968 was elected to the Naismith Memorial Basketball Hall of Fame. Dehnert's invention of the pivot play revolutionized basketball, became the basic offensive implement of every team, and remains a staple of modern basketball.

BIBLIOGRAPHY: Peter C. Bjarkman, *The Biographical History of Basketball* (Chicago, IL, 2000); Stanley Cohen, *The Game They Played* (New York, 1977); Dutch Dehnert file, Naismith Memorial Basketball Hall of Fame, Springfield, MA; Larry Fox, *Illustrated History of Basketball* (New York, 1974); Zander Hollander, ed., *Pro Basketball Encyclopedia* (Los Angeles, CA, 1977); Neil D. Isaacs, *All the Moves* (Philadelphia, PA, 1975); Joe Lapchick, *My Life In Basketball* (New York, 1965); Murry R. Nelson, *The Originals: the New York Celtics Invent Modern Basketball* (Bowling Green, OH, 1999); *NYT*, 1923–1941, April 16, 1979; Robert W. Peterson, *Cages to Jumpshots: Pro Basketball's Early Years* (New York, 1990); Ken Shouler et al., *Total Basketball* (Wilmington, DE, 2003).

Karel de Veer

DIDDLE, Edgar Allen, Sr. "Uncle Ed" (b. March 12, 1895, Gradyville, KY; d. January 2, 1970, Bowling Green, KY), college player, coach, and administrator, guided Western Kentucky University (1923–1964) to 759 basketball triumphs in 1,061 games for a .715 winning percentage. Diddle amassed the ninth highest number of victories of any college coach in history and became the only one to coach 1,000 games at one school. His teams won or shared 32 conference titles in three leagues (capturing 10 OVC titles his last 16 years) and competed in three NCAA postseason tourneys and eight NITs. Diddle suffered only five losing seasons in 42 years, two coming in his last two campaigns at Western Kentucky University. From 1934 to 1943 and 1947 to 1954, the Hilltoppers produced 20-victory seasons all but one year while averaging 25 victories each year. Diddle in 1971 was named to the coaches' category of the Naismith Memorial Basketball Hall of Fame.

Diddle starred on the football and basketball teams at Centre College of Kentucky between 1915 and 1920. A left halfback and basketball guard, Diddle played in both sports with All-Americas "Bo" McMillin, "Red" Roberts, and James Weaver, and noted college football coach "Matty" Bell. Centre lost only one of 17 football games in Diddle's last two seasons and finished 11-0 in basketball his final year. Diddle graduated with a Bachelor's degree in 1920 from Centre College and served in the U.S. Navy the next year when his former football teammates defeated Harvard University in the "upset of the century." Western Kentucky University hired Diddle in the fall of 1922, when the school was known as Western Kentucky Teachers College with few athletic facilities and no tradition. Basketball was played on tobacco warehouse floors against minor Kentucky and Tennessee colleges and major colleges' junior varsities. A campus gymnasium ultimately was constructed and schedules became increasingly rigorous to include several SC and SEC foes and regular-season engagements at New York's Madison Square Garden.

The colorful Diddle waved, tossed, and chewed a red towel along the sidelines during games to the delight of spectators. Occasionally he draped it over his face in response to a sudden reversal in game action. Diddle was homespun, easygoing, sad-eyed, dead-panned, and a leading proponent of the fast break, raising the Hilltoppers to a national power and one of the nation's most consistent teams. In 1940 Diddle's 24-6 netters lost by one point to Duquesne

University in the first round of the eight-team NCAA Tournament. Western Kentucky University advanced to the finals of the 1942 NIT (a field that included Long Island University, CCNY, and Rhode Island State University) before falling to West Virginia University 47-45. The 29-5 Hilltoppers led for 35 minutes, but two Mountaineers each converted a free throw with 20 seconds remaining to snatch the victory. First- or second-round losses in subsequent NITs were suffered in 1943 (60-58 to Fordham University), 1948 (60-53 to St. Louis University with Western Kentucky taking third place), 1949 (95-86 to Bradley University), 1950 (69-60 to St. John's University), 1952 (70-69 to St. Bonaventure University), 1953 (69-61 to Du-quesne), and 1954 (75-69 to Holy Cross College). Twice Ohio State University's three-year veterans Jerry Lucas*, John Havlicek*, and Mel Nowell overwhelmed Western Kentucky University in the second round of the NCAA tournament, winning 98-79 in 1960 and 93-73 in 1962.

Diddle developed several stars of All-America caliber, including Will McCrocklin, Carlisle Towery, Oran McKinney, Marion Spears, Don Ray, Johnny Oldham (who replaced Diddle in 1965 as head coach), Bob Lavoy, Art Spoelstra, Tom Marshall, and Robert Rascoe. The $3 million, 13,800-seat E. A. Diddle Arena was constructed in 1963 as a lasting memorial to the departing coach-athletic director. Diddle, who married Margaret Louise Monin and had two children, suffered a heart attack, his thirteenth since the early 1950s, and died at Bowling Green Hospital.

BIBLIOGRAPHY: Edgar Diddle file, Naismith Memorial Basketball Hall of Fame, Springfield, MA; Mike Douchant, *Encyclopedia of College Basketball* (Detroit, MI, 1995); Zander Hollander, ed., *The NBA's Official Encyclopedia of Pro Basketball,* 35th Anniv. Ed. (New York, 1981); Neil D. Isaacs, *All the Moves: A History of College Basketball* (Philadelphia, PA, 1975); William G. Mokray, ed., *Ronald Encyclopedia of Basketball* (New York, 1963); *NIT First Round Program,* New York, March 8, 1952; *NYT,* January 3, 1970; *Official Collegiate Basketball Guides, 1951–1965* (New York, 1951–1965); Alexander M. Weyand, *The Cavalcade of Basketball* (New York, 1960).

James D. Whalen and Wayne Patterson

DISCHINGER, Terry Gilbert (b. November 21, 1940, Terre Haute, IN), college and professional player, is the son of Donas "Don" Dischinger, a teacher and coach, and Clara (Wood) Dischinger, a hospital lab technician and teacher. A heart murmur, attributed to his rapid growth, and a knee problem restricted his pre–high school athletic career. Subsequently, Dischinger excelled in several sports. His team won the Babe Ruth League World Series. As the first baseman Dischinger led the squad in hitting. At Garfield High School in Terre Haute Indiana, he lettered in baseball, placed among the top three in both hurdling events at the state track and field finals, and made All-State in basketball as a center and in football as an end. The National Honor Society member finished as valedictorian, played trombone in the school band, and served as president of the Methodist Youth Foundation. In 1989, he was voted to the second squad of Indiana's high school all-time "Dream Team."

At Purdue University (BTC), this six-foot seven-inch, 190-pound center-forward earned a Bachelor's degree in chemical engineering in 1963. His honors included making All-BTC and All-America from 1960 through 1962 and being the youngest member of the victorious 1960 U.S. Olympic basketball team. Terre Haute declared September 26, 1960 to be "Terry Dischinger Day." He was inducted into the U.S. Olympic Hall of Fame in 1984 and to the HAF Hall of Fame. Dischinger averaged 28.5 points at Purdue, converting 55.3 percent of his field goals and 81.9 percent of his free throws. He also exceeded 50 points in two games and scored 1,979 career points.

Although Dischinger frequently denied professional aspirations, the Chicago Zephyrs (NBA) drafted him in the second round. In 1963 the NBA Rookie of the Year recorded a career high 25.5 points per game. He was selected an All-Star for three consecutive seasons, two with the Zephyrs, who moved to Baltimore, and one with the Detroit Pistons (NBA). (The Baltimore Bullets had traded Dischinger in June 1964 to Detroit.) Army service from 1965 to 1967 saw him captain a chemical warfare unit. He returned to the Pistons in 1967 and remained there until traded in July 1972 to the Portland Trail

Blazers (NBA). Dischinger completed his NBA career in 1973, having played in three NBA All-Star Games, and shot 50.6 percent from the field during his NBA career. In nine NBA seasons, Dischinger scored 9,012 points and averaged 13.8 points.

Dischinger completed his dental degree in 1974 at the University of Tennessee-Memphis and was awarded the certificate of orthodonture in 1977 from the University of Oregon. He married Mary Dunn, a Purdue student, in June 1962 and has two sons, Terry Jr., and Bill, and a daughter, Kelly. The Dischingers reside in Lake Oswego, Oregon.

BIBLIOGRAPHY: Peter C. Bjarkman, *The Biographical History of Basketball* (Chicago, IL, 2000); Jan Hubbard, ed., *The Official NBA Basketball Encyclopedia*, 3rd ed. (New York, 2000); Mike Douchant, *Encyclopedia of College Basketball* (Detroit, MI, 1995); Neil Isaacs, *All the Moves: A History of College Basketball* (Philadelphia, PA, 1975); Lafayette Journal and Courier Staff, ed., *Most Memorable Moments in Purdue Basketball History* (Champaign, IL, 1998); William G. Mokray, *Basketball Stars of 1961* (New York, 1961); *TSN Official NBA Guide 1973–1974* (St. Louis, MO, 1973).

Thomas P. Wolf

DONOVAN, Anne Theresa (b. November 1, 1961, Ridgewood, NJ), college and professional player and coach, grew up playing basketball in her driveway with her close-knit Irish-American family of eight. Although known for her kind and relaxed nature, the already six-foot one-inch Donovan led Paramus High School to two consecutive undefeated seasons and two state championships. As a senior, she averaged 35 points and 17 rebounds.

With over 2,583 career scholastic points, the now six-foot eight-inch Donovan was the most recruited female player in the nation. She signed with the Old Dominion University Lady Monarchs, tallying a school-record 2,719 points, 1,976 rebounds, and 801 blocked shots in 136 games from 1979 to 1983. Donovan led the Lady Monarchs to a 37-1 record and the AIAW national title as a freshman. She held 25 Old Dominion records upon graduation and was selected an All-America and the 1983 Naismith and Champion Player of the Year.

Named to three Olympic teams, Donovan won gold medals in 1984 and 1988; The United States boycotted the 1980 Olympics. Donovan played on a total of 12 U.S. national basketball teams. With no American women's professional league, she spent five seasons with Shizuoka, Japan from 1984 to 1988 and one with Modena, Italy in 1989.

Donovan returned to Old Dominion in 1990 as the Lady Monarchs' assistant basketball coach. From 1990 until 1995, the Lady Monarchs won four conference titles and made five NCAA tournament appearances. In 1995, Donovan moved to Greenville, North Carolina to become head coach of the East Carolina Lady Pirates. She coached there from 1995 to 1997, compiling 33-51 overall record and moving the team from last place to a conference championship appearance. She also served as assistant coach to the 1997 U.S. Women's World Championship qualifying team.

In 1998 Donovan became the head coach for the Philadelphia Rage in the newly formed American Basketball League (ABL). The Rage performed 9-5 under Donovan, but the ABL folded in 1998. In October 1999, Donovan accepted a temporary head coach position with the Indiana Fever (WNBA) and compiled a 9-23 record in 2000. This led to a permanent position as the head coach of the Charlotte Sting (WNBA) in March 2001; she attained identical 18-14 records in 2001 and 2002. In 2002, Donovan again was named as assistant coach to the USA Women's Basketball Team and signed on with the Seattle Storm as head coach; Seattle finished 18-16 in 2003 and fared second best in the WBA with a 20-14 mark in 2004. In five WNBA seasons, Donovan has boasted a 83-81 regular season record and 10-8 playoff mark, and she took a last place team to the WNBA Finals in 2001 and guided the Seattle Storm to the 2004 WNBA championship, edging the Connecticut Sun 2-1 in the WNBA Finals. Donovan was inducted into the Naismith Basketball Hall of Fame in 1995, the Women's Basketball Hall of Fame in 1991, and the New Jersey Sportswriters Association Hall of Fame in 2000.

BIBLIOGRAPHY: Mike Douchant, *Encyclopedia of College Basketball* (Detroit, MI, 1995); Thomas E.

Macklin, "A League of Her Own," *World of Hibernia* 6 (Autumn 2000), pp. 119–121; Chuck O'Donnell, "Anne Donovan," *BskD* 28 (March 2001), pp. 82–86; William C. Rhoden, "Donovan Having Fun Shooting for the Gold," *NYT Biographical Service* (August 1987), pp. 832–33; *TSN Official WNBA Guide and Register, 2004* (St. Louis, MO, 2004); WNBA website, www.wnba.com.

Lisa A. Ennis

DOUGLAS, Robert L. "Bob" (b. November 4, 1884, St. Kitts, British West Indies; d. July 16, 1979, New York, NY), professional player and owner, founded the New York Renaissance pro basketball team in 1922. The Rens compiled 2,318 victories over the next 22 years, averaging 105 triumphs annually, and were elected as a team in 1963 to the Naismith Memorial Basketball Hall of Fame. In 1971 Douglas was named to the same Hall of Fame for his contributions to the game. The Rens captured the 1931 World Professional Championship by defeating the Harlem Globetrotters in Chicago and were acclaimed the top basketball team of the decade.

Douglas came to the United States at age four in 1888 and exhibited early interest in the budding indoor sport. He played with the New York Spartans at the Harlem Commonwealth Arena before founding the Rens. Douglas rented the Renaissance Casino ballroom in Harlem, adopted the name "Rens" for his team, and shared the facility during the big band era with the Count Basie and Jimmy Lunsford bands. In the mid-1920s Douglas signed Clarence "Fats" Jenkins*, James "Pappy" Ricks, and Eyre "Bruiser" Saitch*, all of whom later formed part of the Rens' celebrated "Magnificent Seven."

Most of the Rens' games were played on the road, as they barnstormed from Boston, Massachusetts to Kansas City, Missouri, playing any team, black or white, that would schedule them. Barred from most hotels and restaurants because of racial discrimination, Douglas established temporary Rens headquarters in Chicago, Indianapolis, Indiana, or other large-city hotels that catered to blacks. The Rens traveled up to 200 miles distance by bus to towns for games, sometimes playing twice on Sunday, before returning to home base. Often the Rens slept on the bus and ate cold sandwiches en route. Douglas also signed John "Casey" Holt and Bill Yancey* to player contracts. By the time Abe Saperstein* organized the Harlem Globetrotters in 1926, the Rens already had become one of the nation's leading pro basketball teams. In 1927 the Rens split a six-game series with the legendary New York Original Celtics, a long-time, mutually respected rival.

Douglas added height to his squad by signing 6-foot 4-inch Charles "Tarzan" Cooper* in 1929 and 6-foot 5-inch "Wee" Willie Smith* in 1932, thus completing the "Magnificent Seven." The Rens and Original Celtics drew sellout crowds, attracting 15,000 fans in Cleveland, OH, and Kansas City, Missouri. The Celtics in 1933 were past their prime when they lost to the younger Rens in seven of eight encounters. The Rens had become nearly unbeatable by 1934, posting 88 consecutive triumphs while finishing with a 127-7 record. Douglas, who married Cora Dismond and had no children, served as the first president of the New York Pioneer AC and managed the Renaissance Ballroom until 1973. New York's summer pro league, the Robert L. Douglas Basketball League, is named in his honor.

BIBLIOGRAPHY: Robert L. Douglas file, Naismith Memorial Basketball Hall of Fame, Springfield, MA; Jan Hubbard, ed., *The Official NBA Encyclopedia*, 3rd ed. (New York, 1981); Neil D. Issacs, *All the Moves: A History of College Basketball* (Philadelphia, PA, 1975); Murry R. Nelson, *The Originals: The New York Celtics Invent Modern Basketball* (Bowling Green, OH, 1999); *NYT*, July 17, 1979; Susan J. Rayl, *The New York Renaissance Professional Black Basketball Team, 1923–1950* (Syracuse, NY, 2001); Ken Shouler et al., *Total Basketball* (Wilmington, DE, 2003); Kenneth Shropshire and Todd Boyd, eds., *Basketball Stories* (New York, 2000).

James D. Whalen and Wayne Patterson

DRAKE, Bruce (b. December 5, 1905, Gentry, TX; d. December 2, 1983, Norman, OK), college athlete and basketball coach, was the son of contractor Walter Drake and Erma Drake and moved to Oklahoma as a child. Drake played year-round backyard basketball and attended Oklahoma City High School, where he participated in all major sports except football. His basketball skills blossomed under coach Roy Bennett. After matriculating at the University of Oklahoma in 1925, he remained an all-around athlete. A championship pole-vaulter clearing 13 feet, he captained the track and field squad his senior year and won both the Rice University and University of Kansas relays. He twice lettered at quarterback for the Sooners in 1927 and 1928, becoming the only football letterman in University of Oklahoma history never to have played high school football. Basketball was his forte, as he played forward for Hugh McDermott's 18-0 1928 Sooners that captured the MVC Championship. In 1929 the Sooners switched to the BSC. Team captain Drake changed to the guard position, as Oklahoma recorded another undefeated season (10-0) and the BSC title. He received the Letzeiser Award as the outstanding senior man in 1929.

In 1930 Drake joined the University of Oklahoma's Physical Education faculty and served as assistant basketball coach. He married Myrtle Tosh of Oklahoma City, and had two daughters, Donna and Deonne. He in 1938 succeeded McDermott as Sooners basketball coach, a position he held until 1955. His chief coaching rivals included "Phog" Allen* of the University of Kansas and Henry Iba* of Oklahoma Agricultural and Mechanical (A&M). Drake's frequently outmanned Sooners relied on clever passing and ball control to win or tie for six BSC championships and earn three second places. Only four Drake teams finished below .500 percent in BSC play during his 17 years. His Sooners squads won 200 games while losing 191. His three NCAA tournament teams lost to eventual champions University of Oregon (1939), University of Wyoming (1943), and Holy Cross College (1947 finals).

Drake's Sooners faced several dominating centers, including Slim Wintermute of Oregon, Harry Boykoff of St. John's University, Milo Komenich of Wyoming, and homestate rival Bob Kurland* of the Oklahoma A&M University Aggies, during the 1940s. When Kurland snared 22 shots in the 1943 59-40 Aggie romp over the Sooners, Drake began his one-man campaign to outlaw goaltending. He invited James St. Clair, chairman of the NCAA Rules Committee, to attend the next Sooners-Aggies contest. He posted St. Clair on a platform above the north goal to look down on Kurland's goaltending and observe what retaliation it might provoke. St. Clair instead observed a Sooners' stall, a 14-11 Aggies victory, and a very dull game. In future contests, Drake had Harold Hines literally sit on the ball at halfcourt and also arranged for the 5-foot 5-inch Hines to jump center against the 7-foot Kurland. Finally the NCAA Rules Committee outlawed goaltending. Later Drake chaired the NCAA Rules Committee for five years.

During Drake's last years at the University of Oklahoma, he developed the "shuffle" or continuity offense to enable his small, clever ball handlers to weave around and screen the larger opponents. The Sooners upset the Aggies several times with the aid of the "shuffle." Besides serving as basketball coach, Drake founded golf at the University of Oklahoma. His golfers once swept 33 consecutive dual meets. In 1933 the Sooners' Walter Emery won the NCAA golf championship. Although the Sooners had no pool, Drake established swimming at Norman. His swimming squads broke several BSC records and twice placed in the NCAA meet. Pressured into resigning in 1955, Drake directed the U.S. Air Force Armed Services team to a championship. This feat enabled him to assist Gerald Tucker* as coach of the U.S. Olympic team, which annihilated the Soviet Union at Melbourne, Australia, in 1956. The next year he led the Wichita Vickers to a tie for the National Industrial Basketball League championship. Drake's teams won or tied for nine championships in twenty years. Until his death, he conducted basketball clinics around the world.

His honors included HAF All-America, 1992; president of the NBA, 1951; Oklahoma Athletic Hall of Fame; HAF Coaching Hall of Fame, 1961; and Naismith Memorial Basketball Hall of Fame, 1973. He coached champions at the college, AAU, Armed Forces, and Olympic levels and produced three All-Americas and five Olympians. He also initiated the use of the timer's gun to signal halftime and the game's end, and championed the widening of the 6-foot lane. Drake always was known as a true sportsman. Oklahoma twice won the BSC sportsmanship trophy for the school whose players, coach, and spectators demonstrated the best courtside manners. His "Roundball Runts" competed evenly with the taller goliaths who began to dominate the game. Drake's innovations in rules and coaching philosophy enabled underdogs to compete with heavily favored foes.

BIBLIOGRAPHY: Mike Douchant, *Encyclopedia of College Basketball* (Detroit, MI, 1995); Bruce Drake file, Naismith Memorial Basketball Hall of Fame, Springfield, MA; Bill Gutman, *The History of NCAA Basketball* (New York, 1993); Bruce Drake as told to Harold Keith, "Seven Foot Trouble," *SEP* 216 (Feburary 19, 1944), pp. 16–17, 88; Harold Keith, "Bruce Drake and the Goal Tending War," *Sooner Magazine* 4 (Winter 1984), pp. 13–19.

Gregory S. Sojka

DREXLER, Clyde Austin (b. June 22, 1962, New Orleans, LA), college and professional player coach, and executive, is one of five siblings and the son of James Drexler Sr. and Eunice (Scott) Drexler, a supermarket cashier who stressed education as the first priority to her children. Drexler's family moved to Houston, Texas, when he was four years old. He did not begin playing basketball until his junior year in high school, but started two years at Sterling High School. His honors included being named Sterling's MVP and an All-Houston Independent School District selection as a senior.

Drexler, recruited by only three colleges, attended the local University of Houston (SWC). The Cougars, led by Drexler and Hakeem Olajuwon*, became known as "Phi Slama Jama" for their above-the-rim acrobatics. Houston made two consecutive trips to the NCAA Final Four, including reaching the championship game against North Carolina State University in 1983. Drexler, a tremendous leaper, scored and rebounded in double figures in 45 games during his college career and became the first Houston player to score more than 1,000 points, grab over 900 rebounds, and earn 300 assists in a career. As a junior, he was named the SWC Player of the Year.

The six-foot seven-inch, 222-pound Drexler skipped his senior season, becoming eligible for the 1983 NBA draft. The Portland Trail Blazers (NBA) chose Drexler in the first round. In his rookie season with Portland, he averaged 7.7 points and joined two other Trail Blazers appearing in all 82 games. The next season, Portland moved him into the starting lineup. Drexler responded with a 17.2-point scoring average and finished second on the Trail Blazers in assists. His offensive production steadily increased each season. In 1985–1986, he scored 18.5 points per game and appeared in his first All-Star Game, tallying 10 points in 15 minutes. Drexler averaged 27.0 points in 1987–1988 and a career-high 27.2 points in 1988–1989. Although he had become one of the NBA premier players, the Trail Blazers encountered trouble advancing beyond the first round of the playoffs. In June 1989, Portland obtained power forward Buck Williams from the New Jersey Nets (NBA) to help solidify the Trail Blazers. Although Drexler's scoring average dipped to 23.4 points, Portland won 20 more games than the previous season and reached the NBA Finals before falling to the Detroit Pistons.

Portland posted the best NBA record with 63-19 in 1990–1991, but the Los Angeles Lakers (NBA) upset them in the Western Conference finals. Drexler's scoring average fell for the second consecutive season, as he averaged 21.5 points. The Trail Blazers returned to the NBA Finals in the 1991–1992 season, losing 4-2 to the Chicago Bulls (NBA). Drexler started for the Western Conference All-Stars, garnering 22 points, nine rebounds, and six assists. He recorded a 25.0-point scoring average, was named to the All-NBA First Team, and played on the U.S. "Dream Team" that won the Olympic gold medal at the 1992 Barcelona, Spain Summer Olympic Games. Knee and hamstring injuries limited Drexler to just 49 games during the 1992–1993 season and kept his season average below 20 points per game for the first time in seven seasons. He started his second consecutive All-Star Game, but Portland was eliminated in the first round of the playoffs. The following season, Drexler placed second on the Trail Blazers in scoring and helped Portland again reach the playoffs. In February 1995, Portland traded him to the Houston Rockets (NBA) for Otis Thorpe. Houston won the NBA Championship in 1995, as Drexler averaged 20.5 points and 7 rebounds in 22 playoff games.

He spent the rest of his NBA career with Houston, retiring after the 1997–1998 season.

Drexler compiled 22,195 points (20.4-point average) and 2,207 steals in 1,088 regular season games, finishing among the top 10 in steals several seasons. He ranked fifth on the all-time steals list and remains Portland's all-time leader in games played (867), points scored (18,040), rebounds (5,339) and steals (1,795). He averaged 20.4 points, 6.9 assists, 6.1 assists, and nearly 2 steals in 45 playoff games. His size, quickness, and agility enabled him to play effectively at both forward and guard throughout his career. He appeared in nine All-Star Games, and in 1996 he was selected one of the 50 Greatest Players in NBA History. Drexler coached the University of Houston from 1998 to 2000, compiling a 19-39 record. He served as special assistant to the general manager of the Denver Nuggets (NBA) in 2001 and assistant coach in 2002. In 2004, he was elected to the Naismith Memorial Basketball Hall of Fame. Drexler and his wife, Gaynell, a lawyer, have two sons, Austin and Adam, and two daughters, Elise and Enka.

BIBLIOGRAPHY: Peter C. Bjarkman, *The Biographical History of Basketball* (Chicago, IL, 2000); Mike Douchant, *Encyclopedia of College Basketball* (Detroit, MI, 1995); Clyde Drexler file, Naismith Memorial Basketball Hall of Fame, Springfield, MA; *Great Athletes—The Twentieth Century*, vol. 5 (Pasadena, CA, 1992); *Portland Trail Blazers Media Guide*, 1993–1994 (Portland, OR, 1993); Ken Shouler et al., *Total Basketball* (Wilmington, DE, 2003); *TSN Official NBA Guide, 1994–1995* (St Louis, MO, 1994); *TSN Official NBA Register, 2004–2005* (St. Louis, MO, 2004).

Curtice R. Mang

DRIESELL, Charles G. "Lefty" (b. December 25, 1931, Norfolk, VA), college player, coach, and sportscaster, made All-State in basketball at Granby High School in Norfolk, Virginia and graduated from there in 1950. Driesell attended Duke University, where he enjoyed more success as a student than as a basketball player. He graduated with a Bachelor's degree from Duke in 1954 and immediately became junior varsity basketball coach at Granby High School. In 1957, Driesell became head basketball coach at Newport News (Virginia) High School. Newport News High School compiled a 57-game winning streak under his direction and won a state championship. In 1960 he became head basketball coach at Davidson College in North Carolina. The first season marked the first losing campaign of his career. Subsequent seasons saw impressive records for Driesell's squads, including a third place finish in the AP polls for the 1968–1969 season. He quit Davidson that year, which never before or since fielded such a successful basketball program.

In 1968–1969, Driesell took a previously losing University of Maryland team to a .500 record. Three years later, the Terrapins won the ACC playoffs and the NIT. Maryland's 23 victories marked his personal high there. In 1973–1974 Maryland ranked fifth in the AP polls, won the ACC regular-season title, and reached the final eight of the NCAA Championships behind pro-bound Leonard Elmore and Tom McMillen. The 1980–1981 Maryland squad finished eighteenth in the national polls, after which Earnest Graham, Greg Manning, Albert King, and Buck Williams were all drafted by the NBA from Driesell's squad. During 1983–1984, Driesell finally won his first full-fledged ACC championship. The next season, he joined only four other active coaches in achieving 500 lifetime victories by defeating Towson State University at home on February 21, 1985.

In 1985, the University of Maryland reached the second round of the NCAA tournament behind the phenomenal play of Leonard Bias*, who had a season record of 743 points, 23.2 points per game, and a .544 shooting percentage. A repeat All-America his senior year, Bias seemingly had the world at his feet when the NBA champion Boston Celtics selected him as their very first choice in the 1986 draft. The night of his selection, Bias flew back from Boston, Massachusetts to College Park, Maryland, and fell seriously ill at a party in one of the university dormitories. He had fallen victim to a fatal drug overdose. Eventually some University of Maryland players were indicted for their involvement in the incident but later were cleared. Driesell resigned after Bias' death and became assistant athletic director. He served as sports information director at the University of

Maryland and a television analyst for college basketball games.

Driesell coached at James Madison from 1988–1989 through 1996–1997, compiling a 115-73 record. James Madison enjoyed a 73-27 mark, five SC titles, four NIT appearances, and one NCAA post season appearance his first six seasons, but Driesell met less success thereafter. He coached at Georgia State University from 1997 to 2003, compiling a 103-69 mark in six seasons.

Driesell compiled a lifetime college coaching record of 786 wins and 394 losses through 2002–2003, putting him fifth on the all-time college coaches' victory list. In 1973 Driesell won the NCAA Award of Valor for saving 10 children and several adults from a fire at a seashore resort. He and his wife, Joyce, have three children. Chuck played with his father's basketball team. Driesell was a fine coach, whose somewhat disappointing record in postseason play is probably more a reflection of the highly competitive ACC than of Driesell or his teams. Unfortunately, Driesell may never escape the shadow of the Bias tragedy.

BIBLIOGRAPHY: Peter C. Bjarkman, *ACC-Atlantic Coast Conference Basketball* (Indianapolis, IN, 1996); Peter C. Bjarkman, *The Biographical History of Basketball* (Chicago, IL, 2000); Mike Douchant, *Encyclopedia of College Basketball* (Detroit, MI, 1995); *Georgia State University Basketball Media Guide, 2003–2004* (Atlanta, GA, 2003); Paul McMullen, *Maryland Basketball* (Baltimore, MD, 2002); *Maryland Basketball* (College Park, MD, 1985); *NCAA Men's Basketball Records 2004* (Indianapolis, IN, 2003).

John David Healy

DRYSDALE, Ann Elizabeth Meyers (b. March 26, 1955, San Diego, CA), college player and announcer, is the daughter of Bob and Patricia Meyers and is the sixth of 11 children in an athletic family. Her father played basketball at guard for Marquette University and with the Milwaukee (Wisconsin) Shooting Stars, while her brother Dave was a basketball All-America at UCLA and a starting forward in the NBA. As a youngster, Ann was dedicated to sports and entertained dreams of Olympic competition in track and field. At age 15, she placed third in the high jump at the State Junior Olympics meet. She lettered in seven sports at Sonora High School in La Habra, California, but basketball became her focus. As a senior in 1974, she became the first high school player to make a U.S. national team that toured the U.S. and played against the Soviet Union.

The next fall, Meyers entered UCLA as the first woman on a full athletic scholarship. An immediate star, she led the Bruins to postseason tournament appearances every season and to a national championship in 1978. Ann was named an All-America four times, the first in the modern era. She was considered her era's most complete all-around woman player, with her greatest skill being the ability to inspire her teammates. In 1978 she was chosen UCLA Athlete of the Year and Broderick Award and Cup winner for college athletics.

Meyers played on many U.S. national teams, including those that won a gold medal in the Pan American Games in 1975, earned a silver medal in the Montreal, Canada Olympics in 1976 (the first in which a women's basketball competition was held), and finished second in the World University Games in 1977. In 1979 she captained U.S. teams that won two gold medals and one silver medal in international competition, and carried the flag in opening ceremonies at the Pan American Games in Puerto Rico.

After college, Meyers initially passed up a chance to sign with the WPBL to train for the 1980 Olympics. But the Indiana Pacers of the men's NBA offered her a $50,000 no-cut contract. Her tryout was a national media event, and although Meyers did not make the team, she became a color analyst for the Pacers' broadcasts. Ann played for the New Jersey Gems (WPBL) in 1979–1980. She averaged 22.2 points, led the WPBL in steals at 4.9 per game, and was named co-MVP for the season. Ann finished fourth in the 1979 Superstars competition on television. Seeing the money-making potential of the athletic show, she began training for the all-around event. She won the women's Superstars each of the next three years, before being retired from competition.

During a contract dispute with the New Jersey

Gems in 1980–1981, Meyers attended a broadcasting school and made this her new career. She provided color commentary for women's basketball at the 1984 Los Angeles Olympic Games and in 1987 did BTC games for a cable company in Chicago. Meyers serves as a women's basketball analyst for ESPN, and currently lives in Palm Springs, California. She married baseball player–sportscaster Don Drysdale in 1986. They had three children Don, Jr., Darren, and Drew Ann. Ann was elected to the Naismith Memorial Basketball Hall of Fame in 1993 and is a member of the Orange County Hall of Fame. Her college jersey was retired in the Naismith Memorial Basketball Hall of Fame in 1978.

BIBLIOGRAPHY: Ann Drysdale file, Naismith Memorial Basketball Hall of Fame, Springfield, MA; Arnold Hano, "An All American in the Family," *Air California Magazine* (February 1976), pp. 14–17; Michelle Himmelberg, "Learning to Speak Out," *Orange County Register*, February 13, 1987, pp. D1, 9; Joan S. Hult and Marianna Trekell, *A Century of Women's Basketball: From Frailty to Final Four* (Reston, VA, 1991); Anne Johnson, *Great Women in Sports* (Detroit, MI, 1996).

Dennis S. Clark

DUER, Alva Owen "Mr. NAIA" (b. November 18, 1904, Sylvia, KS; d. November 18, 1987, Porterfield, CA), college player and coach, was the son of Kansas dirt farmers Harry and Sarah Duer. One of 11 children, he early on experienced the value of hard work and determination. Duer graduated from Stafford (Kansas) High School in 1923 and entered Kansas State Teachers College at Emporia the next year. There he played basketball and football and held two part-time jobs. Both jobs proved influential in the balance of his life. As a table waiter at Cole's Cafe in Emporia, he met Juanita Reed and married her on December 24, 1927. His job as janitor at the Stafford Bank won him a favor with bank president C. O. White, who loaned him $750 for the venture to Columbia University in New York City.

Duer graduated from Columbia in 1929 with a Bachelor's degree in physical education and returned to Sylvia, Kansas to teach and coach for the next three years. He served as superintendent at Rolla, Kansas from 1932 to 1934 and at Buffalo-Little River Kansas from 1934 to 1938. During those summers, he worked on his Master's degree at the University of Southern California. In California he attended church with Hugh Tiner, president of the newly founded Pepperdine College. During the 1939–1940 season, Duer accepted Tiner's invitation to coach basketball and serve as athletic director at Pepperdine College. His coaching record over the next nine seasons grew to 176-95. His 1942–1946 teams advanced to the NAIA Basketball Championship Tournament, which Duer had advocated. The 1944–1945 team finished runner-up to Loyola University of New Orleans in the NAIA Championship after losing 49-36. In 1945–1946 Duer's team again advanced to NAIA semifinals and defeated Loyola to capture third place. Duer's coaching success included his postseason accomplishments and significant performances by his teams, which in five separate seasons won 22 or more games.

In 1940 Duer served the NAIA as district chairman of the current District 3 covering California. Duer was elected to the NAIA Executive Committee in 1943, became president of the NAIA in the 1946–1947 season, and then resigned as Pepperdine's coach in 1948. Duer became executive director of the NAIA in 1949 when organization founder Emil Liston* died. Duer's multiple responsibilities expanded, serving as Pepperdine's dean of students and athletic director on the U.S. Olympic Basketball Committee until 1952. His involvement in the 1938 First National Championship Tournament earned him the nickname "Mr. NAIA."

Duer's foresight expanded the NAIA to include other national championships. In 1952 the 225-member organization added national championships in outdoor track and field, golf, and tennis, and officially became the NAIA. Duer worked diligently to assure the NAIA representation on the U.S. Olympic Board of Directors, Executive Committee, and Games Committee. He also obtained direct qualifications for NAIA athletes in Pan American and Olympic Trials based on NAIA national championships. His superior leadership and strong moral attitude strengthened the NAIA, as it expanded to 558-member colleges and universities with national championships in sixteen sports by 1971. Duer and the NAIA were challenged in 1955 on a decision that he and NAIA founder Liston had made in 1947, when they began admitting teams with black players. McNeese State University in Louisiana notified the NAIA that it would withdraw from the NAIA tournament if it had to play integrated teams. Because Duer held to his convictions, McNeese State played in the tournament against black players and won the 1955 NAIA championship.

When the NAIA headquarters were moved in 1957 to Kansas City, Missouri, Duer resigned his duties at Pepperdine and moved with the NAIA. He served on the President's Council on Physical Fitness and received an Honorary Doctor of Laws degree from Westminster College (Pennsylvania) in 1959. During the early 1960s, he was the AAU representative to IBFUS. In 1960 Duer was elected to the USBA Ethics Committee and participated on the AAU board of directors. In 1961 the NAIA honored him with election to its Hall of Fame as a general contributor.

Throughout the 1960s, Duer's organizational abilities involved him with the USOC. He was appointed in 1963 to the USOC board of directors and chaired the Olympic Supplies and Equipment Committee from 1964 to 1968. Subsequently he was elected to the USOC executive board of directors, Executive Committee, Legislative Committee, and Eligibility Committee. In 1965 Duer began a lengthy appointment to the U.S. Department of State Sports Advisory Committee. Duer's continuous involvement in Kansas City Rotary as chairman of the Youth Committee helped to spark formation of the Kansas City Amateur Sports Hall of Fame. Findlay College in Ohio presented Duer with an Honorary Doctor of Education degree in 1969. Duer also won the Olympic Torch Award and served capably as the third vice president of the USOC in 1972. Duer, who retired from the NAIA in 1975, was inducted in 1976 into the HAF Hall of Fame and later as a charter member of the Pepperdine Athletic Hall of Fame.

Duer served on the board of directors of the Naismith Memorial Basketball Hall of Fame and as an honorary member of the Athletic Institute Board of Directors. Duer became one of few non-Jews to receive the Kansas City Jewish Community Center Award for Outstanding Service. Besides being named to the Kansas City Hall of Champions, he was elected as a contributor to the Naismith Basketball Hall of Fame in 1982. Duer in May 1983 was selected as a Paul Harris Fellow by the Rotary International. In April 1985 Pepperdine College fondly presented Duer with an honorary Doctorate of Laws degree. Throughout his lifetime, Duer championed the small college. He advocated that an athletic program is part of the total educational program, not a commercial venture dependent on gate receipts. Duer's life emulated the standards his early religious training provided. This background enhanced his belief in the NAIA slogan: "Athletics—Education for Leadership, Character, Citizenship." Duer and his wife, Juanita, resided in Kansas City, Missouri, and had two children, Beth and Larry.

BIBLIOGRAPHY: Alva O. Duer to Sara-Jane Griffin, January 30, 1985; Alva O. Duer file, Naismith Memorial Basketball Hall of Fame, Springfield, MA; Alva O. Duer file, NAIA, Kansas City, MO; Alva O. Duer file, Pepperdine University, Malibu, CA; William Richardson, "Al Duer Symbolic of NAIA," *Kansas City Star*, March 4, 1971; William Sharp, "Duer to Be Honored by NAIA," *Kansas City Star*, January 31, 1971; Gib Twyman, "It's Harvest Time for Duer and He's Reaping Big Reward," *Kansas City Star*, March 7, 1982.

Sara-Jane Griffin

DUKES, Walter F. (b. June 23, 1930, Youngstown, OH; d. March 13, 2001, Detroit, MI), college and professional player, was the son of a factory operator and a tailor and moved to Rochester, New York, at age 10. Dukes starred at Rochester East High School in basketball, football, baseball, and track and field and graduated in 1949 from Seton Hall Prep School, where he participated in cross country and track and field. In 1949, his team won the mile relay at the Penn Relay Carnival in Philadelphia.

Dukes, who planned to become a lawyer, enrolled in 1949 at Seton Hall University and earned a "B" academic average in economics.

The coordinated, mobile, seven-foot 220-pounder impressed classmates as good-natured, friendly, conscientious, and modest. John "Honey" Russell* lauded Dukes, who performed four varsity basketball seasons, as the best player he had ever coached. The agile and graceful Dukes shot equally well with both hands, converting nearly 50 percent of his baskets and over 70 percent of his foul shots. Defensively, his height and cat-quick reflexes enabled him to seize rebounds and start the fast break.

During 89 career basketball games for the Pirates, Dukes scored 1,779 points (20-point average) and converted an NCAA record 611 foul shots. A broken leg sidelined him most of his freshman basketball season, but he competed that spring in the 440-yard run and the 880-yard run. As a sophomore in 1950–1951, Dukes scored 404 points and guided 24-7 Seton Hall to the NIT semifinals. (Seton Hall lost the semifinals to Brigham Young University.) Dukes earned Second Team All-America honors in 1951–1952 for 25-2 Seton Hall and scored a school record 524 points (20.2-point average). His 19.7 rebounds per game ranked second nationally. Three-point losses to Siena University and Loyola University marred a perfect regular season. LaSalle University eliminated the Pirates in the NIT first round.

In 1952–1953, Dukes enjoyed one of the best seasons in NCAA history. Dukes, a First Team All-America, combined with guard Richie Regan to lead 31-2 Seton Hall. Besides scoring 861 points (26.1-point average), he snared 734 rebounds. The Pirates won 27 consecutive games and averaged around 80 points. At the NIT, Seton Hall conquered St. John's University 58-46 in the finals before a record Madison Square Garden crowd of 18,496. Dukes, a superlative defender, scored 21 points against St. John's and tallied 70 points in three NIT games to earn MVP honors. Seton Hall ranked second to Indiana University in the final AP poll.

After spending two seasons with the Harlem Globetrotters, Dukes performed in the NBA for losing teams from 1955–1956 through 1962–1963. His NBA career included stints with the New York Knickerbockers in 1955–1956, Minneapolis Lakers in 1956–1957, and Detroit Pistons from 1957–1958 through 1962–1963. Dukes's best offensive production came in 1959–1960, when he scored 1,004 points (15.2-point average). Dukes ranked among NBA leaders five seasons in personal fouls and rebounds, grabbing a career-high 1,028 rebounds in 1960–1961. During eight NBA seasons, he tallied 5,765 points (10.4-point average), made 6,223 rebounds (11.3 rebound average), and committed 2,260 personal fouls in 553 games. His 121 game disqualifications rank second in NBA history. Dukes appeared in 35 playoff games, scoring 447 points (12.8-point average) and making 432 rebounds (12.3 rebound average). He started at center for the West All-Stars in 1960 and appeared as a reserve the following year.

BIBLIOGRAPHY: Peter C. Bjarkman, *The Biographical History of Basketball* (Chicago, IL, 2000); Mike Douchant, *Encyclopedia of College Basketball* (Detroit, MI, 1995); Zander Hollander, "The Pros Can't Wait for Dukes," *Sport* 14 (April 1953), pp. 46–47, 77–78; Jan Hubbard, ed., *The Official NBA Encyclopedia*, 3rd ed. (New York, 2000); Neil D. Isaacs, *All the Moves: A History of College Basketball* (Philadelphia, PA, 1975); John D. McCallum, *College Basketball U.S.A. Since 1892* (New York, 1978); *NCAA Official Collegiate Basketball Record Book*, 1955 (New York, 1955); David S. Neft and Richard M. Cohen, eds., *The Sports Encyclopedia: Pro Basketball*, 5th ed. (New York, 1992); "Reluctant Hero," *Newsweek* 41 (January 26, 1953), pp. 96–97; "Taskmaster & Pupil," *Time* 61 (February 15, 1953), pp. 76–78; Alexander Weyand, *The Cavalcade of Basketball* (New York, 1960).

David L. Porter

DUMARS, Joe, III (b. May 24, 1963, Shreveport, LA), college and professional player and executive, is the son of Joe Dumars II, a truck driver, and Ophelia Dumars. Dumars, one of six children, graduated from Natchitoches Central High School in Natchitoches, Louisiana. In 1985 he graduated with a Bachelor's degree in business management from McNeese State University, where he was the all-time leading basketball scorer. The four times All-SoC selection averaged more than 22.3 points over four-years and ranked sixth best in scoring in the nation in 1984.

Dumars, drafted 18th in the first round by the

Detroit Pistons (NBA), became the nicest, most scholarly member of the famed Detroit "Bad Boys." As the six-foot three-inch, 190-pound shooting guard for the team, Dumars led Detroit in scoring for four years and helped the Pistons win consecutive NBA championships in 1989 and 1990. He was named to the NBA All-Rookie team in 1986 and the NBA First Team All-Defense in 1989 and 1990. In 1989, Dumars was selected NBA Finals MVP after averaging 27.3 points for the series. Dumars co-captained the U.S. Olympic basketball team in 1996 and received the NBA's inaugural Sportsmanship Award. Thereafter, the award was named for him. He won the IBM Award in 1989 and the J. Walter Kennedy NBA Citizenship Award for community service in 1994. Dumars retired as a player in 1999, having scored 16,401 points in 1,018 games and averaging 16.1 points. He made 84.3 percent of his of free throws, and 46 percent of field goals over 14 years. He averaged 15.6 points in 112 NBA playoff games and appeared in six All-Star Games, the last in 1997. The Pistons retired his jersey on June 6, 2000.

Prior to being named President of Detroit Pistons Basketball Operations in June 2000, Dumars served as the Club Director of Player Personnel in 1999 and 2000. He strengthened the Pistons by acquiring Ben Wallace* from the Orlando Magic in August 2000, free agent Chauncey Billups in July 2002, Richard Hamilton from the Washington Wizards in September 2002, and Rasheed Wallace from the Portland Trail Blazers in 2004, drafting Tayshaun Prince in June 2002, and hiring Larry Brown* as coach in 2003. Detroit finished 54-28, second best in the Eastern Conference, in 2003–2004, defeated the Milwaukee Bucks (four games to one), New Jersey Nets (4-3), and Indiana Pacers (4-2), in the playoffs, then upset the Los Angeles Lakers (4-1) in the NBA Finals. Detroit again placed second in the Eastern Conference in 2004–2005 with a 54-28 mark, reaching the NBA Finals against the San Antonio Spurs. In 2002, Dumars built a fieldhouse in Sterling Heights, Michigan with professional hardwood floors, basketball leagues, and facilities for various participator sports. A generous, caring individual, Dumars sponsors a celebrity tennis classic benefiting children's services for the needy at three Detroit area hospitals and supports various other charitable causes. He was selected the Sales and Marketing Executives of Detroit Communicator of the Year in 1996.

Dumars and his wife, Debbie, have one son, Jordan, and one daughter, Aren.

BIBLIOGRAPHY: *Detroit News*, January 10, 1990, pp. E1–3; *Detroit News*, April 11, 1990, p. F7; *Detroit News*, June 17, 1990, p. A12; *Detroit News*, January 3, 1996, p. D4; *Mike Douchant, Encyclopedia of College Basketball* (Detroit, MI, 1995); Jerry Green, *The Detroit Pistons: Capturing a Remarkable Era* (Chicago, IL, 1991); Jan Hubbard, ed., *The Official NBA Encyclopedia*, 3rd ed. (New York, 2000); Armen Keteyian et al., *Money Players: Days and Nights Inside the New NBA* (New York, 1997); *Macomb Daily*, December 1, 2002; John McCallum, "Nicely Done, Joe," *SI* 100 (June 28, 2004), pp. 64–66; NBA.com; *TSN Official NBA Guide, 2000–2001* (St. Louis, MO, 2000).

Keith McClellan

DUNCAN, Timothy Theodore "Tim" (b. April 25, 1976, St. Croix, Virgin Islands), college and professional player, is the son of William and Ione Duncan. Duncan graduated from St. Duncan's Episcopal High School in the Virgin Islands and with a Bachelor's degree in psychology from Wake Forest University. The seven-foot, 260-pound center starred in basketball for Wake Forest coach Dave Odom from 1993–1994 through 1996–1997, helping lead the Demon Deacons to ACC Championships in 1995 and 1996. During Duncan's final year, the squad was ranked second nationally for 10 weeks, the school's highest poll standing ever. Wake Forest finished in the top 10 in 1995, 1996, and 1997, establishing the schools' best single-season records (26-6) in 1995 and 1996. Duncan earned consensus All-America honors in 1996 and 1997 and won the Naismith and Wooden awards. In 128 games, he scored 2,117 points (16.5 point average) and made 1,570 rebounds (12.3 rebound average). He holds the NCAA records for most career rebounds and led the NCAA Division I with 14.7 rebounds per game in 1997.

The San Antonio Spurs (NBA) selected Duncan with the first overall pick of the 1997 NBA draft. Duncan helped revive the struggling franchise, which had finished 20-62 in 1996–1997, and has established himself as a force at forward. He started 82 games and averaged 21.1 point, 11.9 rebounds, and 2.5 blocked shots. More impressively, the Spurs finished 56-26. Duncan was named Rookie of the Year and to the All-NBA First Team and All-NBA Defensive First Team. He has earned both honors each of his first six seasons. Additionally, Duncan helped San Antonio to the NBA Championship (earning Finals MVP) during the 1998–1999 season, capping the Spurs' run with a five-game series victory over the New York Knicks. He has continued to post impressive numbers in both the regular season and playoffs. His individual averages include 22.5 points, 12.2 rebounds, and 2.5 blocks in 586 regular-season games and 24.1 points and 12.9 rebounds in 98 playoff games over eight seasons through the 2005 Western Conference Finals. His highest scoring average (25.5 points) came in 2001–2002, when he earned his first NBA MVP Award. His scoring dipped slightly in 2002–2003 to 23.3 points, but he posted career highs in blocks (2.9) and rebounds (12.9) en route to another MVP trophy. He led the Spurs to another NBA Championship and was again named NBA Finals MVP in 2003. San Antonio defeated the New Jersey Nets 4-2 in the NBA Finals, as Duncan set NBA Finals records for the most blocked shots in a single game (8) and series (32). Duncan led the Spurs to the second best Western Conference record (57–25) in 2003–2004, becoming just the sixth player to be named to the All-NBA First Team in each of his initial seven seasons. He was the only NBA player to rank among the top ten in points (22.3), rebounds (12.4), blocks (2.68), and field goal percentage (.501). Duncan also was named to the NBA All-Star team for the sixth time. The Los Angeles Lakers eliminated the Spurs in the second round of the playoffs, but Duncan tallied 30 points in Game 1 and 21 rebounds in Game 5. Duncan played on the bronze-medal winning 2004 U.S. Olympic Team. Although limited to 66 games in 2004–2005, he led San Antonio in scoring (20.3 point average), rebounds, and blocked shots and helped the Spurs to the second best Western Conference mark. Duncan made the All-Star team for the seventh time and the All-NBA First Team and the Defensive First Team for the eighth consecutive time. He led the Spurs to the NBA finals against the Detroit Pistons, averaging 24.9 points and 11.7 assists in 16 games through the Western Conference Finals.

Duncan also is very active in the community. He and his wife, Amy, who Duncan married in the summer of 2001, support the Children's Bereavement Center, the Children's Center of San Antonio, and the Cancer Therapy and Research Center. His Tim Duncan Foundation, established in November 2001, helps fund nonprofit groups in health awareness, education, and youth sports, and helped pay for the installation of a wooden basketball court at Central High School in St. Croix. Duncan purchases a block of 40 tickets for each Spurs' home game for participants in the Tim Duncan Character Champions Program. *TSN* gave him the "Good Guys" Award in both 2001 and 2002.

BIBLIOGRAPHY: Jan Hubbard, ed., *The Official NBA Encyclopedia*, 3rd. ed. (New York, 2000); Ken Shouler et al., *Total Basketball* (Wilmington, DE, 2003); *TSN Official NBA Guide, 2004–2005* (St. Louis, MO, 2004); *TSN Official NBA Register, 2003–2004* (St. Louis, MO, 2004); *Wake Forest University Basketball Media Guide, 1996–1997, 1997–1998* (Winston-Salem, NC, 1996, 1997).

Jorge Iber

DURHAM, Hugh N. (b. October 26, 1937, Louisville, KY), college player, coach, and executive, excelled in four sports at Eastern High School in Louisville, where he graduated in 1955.

Durham starred in basketball between 1957 and 1959 at Florida State University, where he earned a Bachelor's degree in business administration in 1959 and a Master's degree in the same field in 1961. An outstanding guard in basketball for the Seminoles, the five-foot eleven-inch, 160-pound Durham set several school records. He scored 1,381 points in three seasons for an 18.9 point average, ranking him ninth on the all-time list. Durham's 21.9 point average his senior season ranks him second, while his .777 career free throw shooting percentage places him fourth. He tallied 43 points against Stetson University as a junior, ranking second for a single game.

Durham was elected to the Florida State University, the Kentucky High School, and the

Florida Sports halls of fame. The Seminoles MVP Award has been named in his honor. He and his wife, Malinda, have three sons, David, Doug, and Jim.

Durham began his coaching career in 1959 as an assistant basketball coach at Florida State, and replaced Bud Kennedy as head coach in 1966. From 1967 through 1978, Durham compiled a 230-95 win-loss record for a .708 winning percentage to top all Seminole coaches. His 1968 and 1972 teams qualified for the NCAA tournament, with his 27-6 1972 squad advancing to the NCAA Finals before losing 81-76 to UCLA. In 1978, Durham's final season at Florida State, the Seminoles won the MC, and he was named MC Coach of the Year.

Durham accepted the University of Georgia head basketball coaching position before the 1978–1979 season. In 17 seasons there, he compiled a 297-215 win-loss record, led the Bulldogs to five NCAA tournament appearances, seven NIT appearances, one SEC Championship, and one SEC tournament title, and was selected SEC Coach of the Year five times. The 1983 squad advanced to the NCAA Final Four before losing 67-60 to the eventual champion, North Carolina State University. At the conclusion of the 1995 season, Durham was fired at Georgia because the administration wanted to change the direction of the program. After being out of coaching for two seasons, he was named head basketball coach and assistant athletic director at Jacksonville University in March 1997. In March 2001, he was appointed athletic director. Through the 2005 season, he led the Dolphins to a 106-119 win-loss record. In 37 years as a head coach, Durham's teams posted 633 victories and lost 429 times. He became just the 17th coach to lead a team into 1,000 Division I basketball games and ranked ninth among active coaches with 617 triumphs upon his retirement in March 2005. Durham, only one of 11 coaches to take two different schools to the NCAA Final Four, remains the winningest coach at both Florida State and Georgia. He is one of only three coaches to win 200 games at two different Division I schools and ranks fifth among Division I coaches with 35 seasons coached. Durham has coached some of the game's best players including Dave Cowens*, Vern Fleming, and Dominique Wilkins*.

BIBLIOGRAPHY: Mike Douchant, *Encyclopedia of College Basketball* (Detroit, MI, 1995); Chris Dortch, *String Music: Inside the Rise of SEC Basketball* (Dulles, VA, 2002); "Hugh Durham," *Athletic Director*, http://www.fansonly.com (2003); "Hugh Durham," *Florida State Hall of Fame*, http://www.seminoles.com (2003); "Hugh Durham," *1,000th Game*, http://www.sportingnews.com (2003); "Hugh Durham," *Profile*, http://www.judolphins.ocsn.com (2003); Gary K. Johnson, ed., *NCAA Men's Basketball's Finest* (Overland Park, KS, 1998); *NCAA Men's Basketball Records, 2004* (Indianapolis, IN, 2003).

John L. Evers

E

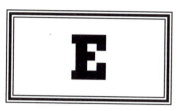

EDDLEMAN, Thomas Dwight "Dike" (b. December 27, 1922, Centralia, IL; d. August 1, 2001, Champaign, IL), college and professional player, was the son of Thomas Edward Eddleman, railroad conductor, and Alma Marie (Snider) Eddleman. "Dike" married Teddy Townsley, his high school sweetheart, on December 25, 1945 and had four children: Tom, Diana, Nancy, and Kristy. He graduated in 1946 from Centralia High School, where he starred in three sports under the famed coach A. L. Trout. Eddleman made All-State in football as a senior, led the Orphans to the 1942 state basketball championship while scoring 2,702 career points, and won the state championship as a high jumper in 1940, 1941 and 1942.

Eddleman attended the University of Illinois between 1942 and 1949 with a three year military interruption, competing in track and field, basketball, and football, and earning 11 varsity letters. He competed in major events, including the Rose Bowl in football, the NCAA Final Four in basketball, and the Olympics in track and field.

Eddleman set BTC football records in punting and kick returns, including highest season punting average (43 yards), best season punt return average (32.8), and longest punt return (92 yards). His 88 yard punt against the University of Iowa Hawkeyes remains a record. He won five BTC individual titles in track and field, captured the NCAA championship in the high jump in 1948 and finished fourth in the high jump during the 1948 Summer Olympic Games in London, England. In basketball, the six-foot three-inch, 189-pound guard-forward topped the famed "Whiz Kids" in scoring in two of his three seasons with a 13.9 point average in 1947–1948 and a 13.1 point average in 1948–1949 and made All-BTC as a junior. The following year, he led Illinois to the NCAA Final Four, was selected Second Team All-America, and earned team MVP honors as the Orange and Blue captain.

After graduating from Illinois in 1949, Eddleman played basketball professionally in the NBL and NBA. During his four-year professional career between 1949 and 1953, he played with the Tri-Cities Black Hawks (NBL), the Milwaukee Hawks (NBA), and the Fort Wayne Zollner Pistons (NBA). Eddleman appeared in 266 regular season games, averaging 12.1 points. In 12 playoff games, he averaged 7.5 points. On December 18, 1952, the two-time NBA All-Star registered the best NBA single-game scoring mark for the season with 48 points.

After retiring from professional basketball in 1953, Eddleman worked 18 years as an executive with Central Soya in Gibson City, Illinois. He returned to Champaign, Illinois in 1969 to join the University of Illinois Athletic Association, a fundraising organization for the athletic program. Largely through Eddleman's efforts, over $4.5 million has been raised. He retired in 1992, but served as Director Emeritus of the "Fighting Illini" Scholarship Fund.

BIBLIOGRAPHY: Mike Douchant, *Encyclopedia of College Basketball* (Detroit, MI, 1995); "Dwight "Dike" Eddleman," *Illini Sports Legend*, http://www.dailyillini.com (2001); "Dwight "Dike" Eddleman," *Tribute to "Dike,"* http://www.fansonly.com (2001);

Diana Lenzi, *"Dike" Eddleman: Illinois' Greatest Athlete* (Champaign, IL, 1997).

John L. Evers

EDMUNDSON, Clarence Sinclair "Hec" (b. August 3, 1887, Moscow, ID; d. August 6, 1964, Seattle, WA), Olympic track and field figure and college basketball player and coach, excelled as a track and field and basketball coach at the University of Washington. As a boy in the Palouse region of western Idaho, he acquired his unusual nickname. Dashing down dirt roads, he frequently uttered "Aw, heck!" in self-criticism of his efforts and became known as "Hec." Edmundson, an outstanding, versatile runner at the University Prep High School and the University of Idaho, sometimes ran the quarter-mile, half-mile, and one-mile runs, and one-mile relay in a single meet. He captained his college track team, won a national half-mile championship in 1909, and played basketball. In 1910 he graduated from Idaho with a Bachelor's degree in agriculture.

Edmundson represented the U.S. in the 1912 Olympics, held in Stockholm, Sweden. After just missing the finals at 400 meters, he finished seventh in the 800-meter race. Subsequently Edmundson directed the University of Idaho track and field (1913–1917) and basketball teams. His 1918 cagers won 12 of 13 games and outscored their opponents 507-343. In 1919 he and his wife, Mary (Zona), moved to Seattle, where he was hired as head track and field coach and trainer for the University of Washington. During the next 35 seasons, his track squads dominated Northern Division competition by winning three PCC meets and finishing five times among the top five schools at the NCAA Championships. His teams placed second nationally in 1929 and 1930. Seven of his track and field pupils were individual collegiate titlists.

Edmundson encountered even greater success as the Huskies' basketball coach. In 27 seasons between 1920 and 1947, Edmundson's teams won 473 games and lost 193 for a 71 percent winning rate. The Huskies garnered 10 Northern Division championships, including five straight from 1928 to 1932. Basketball historian Alexander Weyand rated Edmundson's 22-3 squad of 1931 as the second best team in the nation. His 1936 team won four of five games at the Olympic Trials, while his 1943 Huskies participated in the NCAA postseason tournament. Individual cagers under his direction were named All-PCC 23 times and All-America six times. All-Americans included Ralph Cairney and Ralph Bishop, the only college player selected for the 1936 Olympic Team. When Edmundson retired in 1947 as basketball coach, the university fieldhouse was renamed in his honor.

Edmundson died from a stroke and was survived by his wife, brother Clifford, sister Winfred, and only son, James. Edmundson popularized the "race-horse" or fast-break style of basketball. In his 1931 book, he stressed the importance of passing, shooting, and offensive play. He and Tubby Graves co-founded the Washington State High School Tournament and introduced the five-man handshake used by basketball teams as they take the floor. A member of the HAF Hall of Fame for both basketball and track and field, he was one of the first college coaches to compile over 500 career basketball victories.

BIBLIOGRAPHY: *Converse Yearbook* (Malden, MA, 1964), p. 49; Mike Douchant, *Encyclopedia of College Basketball* (Detroit, MI, 1995); Clarence Edmundson and Robert Morris, *Basketball for Players, Officials, and Spectators* (Seattle, WA, 1931); Ronald L. Mendell, *Who's Who in Basketball* (New Rochelle, NY, 1973); *NYT*, August 8, 1964, p. 19; John Thompson, "Uncle 'Hec' Edmundson," *Washington Coach* (1954), p. 7; "Tribute to a Gallant Coach," *Seattle Times*, August 7, 1964, p. 13.

Dennis S. Clark

EDWARDS, Leroy "Cowboy" (b. April 11, 1914, Indianapolis, IN; d. August 25, 1971), college and professional player, was named HAF 1935 Player of the Year as a star University of Kentucky (SEC) basketball center. The six-foot four-inch, 200-pounder made consensus All-America in 1935, scoring 343 points and averaging 16.3 points for the Wildcats. Kentucky tied Louisiana State University (LSU) for the SEC Championship, triumphing in all 11 SEC games and finishing with a 19-2 win-loss overall record. Edwards, who exhibited a deadly hook shot with either hand, tallied 34 points in Kentucky's 63-42 triumph over Creighton University and outscored the entire University of Chicago squad with 26 points in a 42-16 Wildcats victory. He and forward David Lawrence shared First Team All-SEC honors under legendary coach Adolph Rupp*. The HAF Basketball Hall of Fame enshrined him.

Edwards graduated in 1933 from Arsenal Technical School in Indianapolis, where he starred as a cager. Edwards left the University of Kentucky after one varsity season and performed from 1935 through 1937 with the Indianapolis Kautskys professional club. In 1937 the Oshkosh (Wisconsin) All-Stars (NBL) signed him. Edwards, a five-time All-NBL center, led the NBL in scoring from 1937–1938 to 1939–1940 with averages of 16.2, 11.9, and 12.9 points, respectively. He produced 3,221 career points in 12 regular seasons with Oshkosh, averaging 10.0 points. In NBL playoffs, he tallied 548 points for a 9.6 points per game average.

During Edwards's first three seasons with Oshkosh, the All-Stars lost NBL Finals twice to Akron (Ohio) Firestone and once to Akron Goodyear. Oshkosh entered the first annual WBT in 1939 at Chicago, losing the finals to the New York Renaissance. Edwards led all scorers and was named All-WBT center. Oshkosh coach George Hotchkiss unveiled a new offensive weapon in 1940 that helped the All-Stars capture the 1941 and 1942 NBL titles. Edwards teamed with six-foot five-inch Bob Carpenter in double pivot, as the All-Stars finished with 18-6 and 20-4 regular-season marks in 1940–1941 and 1941–1942; Oshkosh humbled Sheboygan (Wisconsin) and Fort Wayne (Indiana) in the NBL Finals.

Other Oshkosh players included guards Herm Witasek and Charley Shipp in the 1940s. Oshkosh eliminated the Chicago American Gears at the 1946 WBT semifinals. Edwards tallied 24 points, giving "the Gears' George Mikan* a lesson in center play." Fort Wayne, however, downed Oshkosh in the WBT Finals. Edwards's NBL career ended in 1949.

BIBLIOGRAPHY: Peter C. Bjarkman, *The Biographical History of Basketball* (Chicago, IL, 2000); Leroy Edwards file, Naismith Memorial Basketball Hall of Fame, Springfield, MA; Jan Hubbard, ed., *The Official NBA Basketball Encyclopedia*, 3rd ed. (New York, 2000); Frank G. Menke, ed., *The All-Sports Record Book* (New York, 1950); William G. Mokray, ed., *Ronald Encyclopedia of Basketball* (New York, 1963); Bert Nelli, *The Winning Tradition: A History of Kentucky Wildcat Basketball* (Lexington, KY, 1984); Robert W. Peterson, *Cages to Jump Shots: Pro Basketball's Early Years* (New York, 1990); Russell Rice, *Kentucky Basketball's Big Blue Machine* (Huntsville, AL, 1976); Ken Shouler et al., *Total Basketball* (Wilmington, DE, 2003); *Kentucky Basketball Encyclopedia* (Champaign, IL, 2000); Gregory Kent Stanley, *Before Big Blue* (Lexington, KY, 1996); Alan Ross, *Wildcat Wisdom* (Nashville, TN, 1999).

James D. Whalen and Wayne Patterson

EDWARDS, Teresa (b. July 19, 1964, Cairo, GA), college and professional player and coach, is the daughter of Leroy Copeland and Mildred Edwards, who worked for Roddenbury Pickles. Copeland provided some financial help, but Edwards brought up Teresa and her siblings alone. Edwards learned basketball in the backyard with her four younger brothers, using garbage cans for hoops. She started four years in basketball at Cairo (Georgia) High School, leading the Syrupmaids to 58 victories in 61 games during her junior and senior years. Edwards scored 1,982 career points at Cairo High, being named the 1982 Georgia High School Player of the Year. She earned a Bachelor's degree in leisure studies from the University of Georgia in Athens, starting four years at point guard. Edwards scored 1,989 career points, establishing school records of 653 assists and 324 steals. She enabled the Lady Bulldogs to gain national prominence in women's basketball, recording 116 victories against just 17 defeats in her four years on the hardwood there. She was selected All-SEC First Team from 1984 to 1986, and All-America in 1985 and 1986, and remains one of only three Georgia women basketball players to have her number (5) retired.

Edwards played basketball professionally from 1987 to 1995 in Italy, Japan, Spain, and France. She always returned home, however, to perform for U.S. national teams, being the youngest member of the 1984 U.S. Olympic basketball squad and the oldest player on the 2000 U.S. team. At the 1996 Olympics in Atlanta, Georgia, Edwards recited the Olympic athlete's oath on behalf of all Olympic athletes.

She remains the only American basketball player, male or female, to play in five different Olympic competitions, claiming four gold medals and one bronze medal. Edwards also won eleven gold medals on U.S. teams in the Goodwill Games, U.S. Olympic Cup, World Championships, Pan American Games, and U.S. Olympic Festival games. She played on the 1995–1996 U.S. Women's National team, which finished undefeated in 60 contests.

Edwards was a founding player of the ABL, as well as the only player elected to its governing board. She starred for the Atlanta Glory (ABL) from 1995 to 1998, and recorded 15 victories and 29 defeats as player and head coach during the 1997–1998 campaign. Edwards made All-ABL First Team in 1997 and 1998 and led the ABL in assists (293) in 1998. When the ABL folded in December 1998, the five-foot eleven-inch point guard and forward, then a member of the Philadelphia Rage, held the ABL single-game records of 46 points and 14 assists and also ranked first with a 21-points-per-game career scoring average. During three ABL seasons, Edwards averaged 20.8 points, 6.4 assists, and 6.0 rebounds in 98 games. She declined an offer to play in the upstart WNBA, instead training for the 2000 Olympics. Edwards played in France in 2002 before becoming the 14th overall pick in the 2003 WNBA draft by the Minnesota Lynx despite being 38 years old. She averaged 7.7 points and 3.3 assists for the 2003 season and 5.7 points and 2.3 assists in 2004. The Lynx reached the WNBA playoffs both times, but were eliminated in the first round. She retired following the 2004 season.

Edwards, who is single, lives in Atlanta and frequently serves as a motivational speaker in Finding Leaders Among Minorities Everywhere (FLAME), encouraging young women to set high goals in education, careers, and sports no matter what their social or economic background. Cairo, also the birthplace of Jackie Robinson, named a street for Edwards.

BIBLIOGRAPHY: Geoff Calkins, "Teresa Edwards Caps a Distinguished Career with Gold," *Sydney Olympic Commentary: Nando Media*, October 1, 2000, archive pp. 1–3; Sara Corbett, *Venus to the Hoop* (New York, 1997); Nicole Ellis, "Teresa Edwards: Rookie in Name Only," WNBA.com (2003); FLAME profiles, "Teresa Edwards," *Finding Leaders Among Minorities Everywhere* (2003); Anne Janette Johnson, *Great Women In Sports* (Detroit, MI, 1991); Marc Lancaster, "Teresa Edwards," *Online Athens Dogbites* (Athens, GA, 2003), pp. 1–6; Robert Markel et al., *The Women's Sports Encyclopedia* (New York, 1997); James Ponti, *WNBA Stars of Women's Basketball* (New York, 1999); *TSN Official WNBA Guide and Register, 2004* (St. Louis, MO, 2004).

Frank J. Olmsted

ELLIOTT, Sean Michael (b. February 2, 1968, Tucson, AZ), college and professional player, is one of two sons of Robert Elliott, a medical technologist, and Odiemae Elliott, a nurse, and attended Cholla High School in Tucson, where he earned three letters in basketball for coach Mel Karrie. As a senior, he averaged 33.4 points and 14.1 rebounds while frequently being triple-teamed and led Cholla to a 24-3 win-loss record. In 1985 he earned the Arizona Player of the Year award and made four different high school All-America teams.

Coach Lute Olson* recruited Elliott to play basketball at the nearby University of Arizona (PTC). Elliott enjoyed instant success as a freshman, averaging 15.6 points and sharing 1986 PTC Co-Rookie of the Year honors with UCLA's Pooh Richardson. His scoring average improved to 19.3 points, as he led the Wildcats in assists as a sophomore and earned All-PTC honors. No sophomore in PTC history had scored 1,000 total points in two seasons. Elliott led the 35-3 Wildcats to the NCAA Final Four the following season, but the University of Oklahoma defeated Arizona 86-78. In 1987–1988, he became the first Arizona player to score over 700 season points (743), averaged 19.6 points, and was chosen consensus All-America and PTC Player of the Year. Elliott's scoring average increased to 22.3 points his senior year, as he scored 735 total points. PTC Player of the Year and consensus All-America honors again followed. Elliott also won the John Wooden Award as the nation's top collegiate basketball player.

Elliott became the PTC all-time scoring leader with 2,555 career points, surpassing Kareem Abdul-Jabbar* (then Lew Alcindor). He scored in double figures in 128 of 133 games, including a career-high 36 points against the University of Pittsburgh. During Elliott's Arizona career, the 108-28 Wildcats appeared in the NCAA Tournament for all four years. He was also named Arizona's MVP in each of his four seasons.

The San Antonio Spurs selected the six-foot eight-inch, 205-pound Elliott as the third player chosen in the 1989 NBA draft. He, 1990 NBA Rookie of the Year David Robinson*, and newly acquired Terry Cummings* helped transform San Antonio from a 21-61 team in 1988–1989 into a solid 56-26 playoff contender. Elliott played with San Antonio through the 2000–2001 season except for spending 1993–1994 with Detroit. In 1990–1991, he tallied 15.9 points per contest for the 55-27 Spurs. San Antonio lost to the Portland Trail Blazers in the 1990 Western Conference semifinals and to the Golden State Warriors in the first round of the 1991 NBA playoffs. His best season came in 1995–1996, when he averaged 20.0 points and 5.1 rebounds a game. Elliott performed in the 1993 and 1996 All-Star Games and for the 1999 NBA championship team. Health problems forced him to retire following the 2000–2001 season. Elliott averaged 10.0 points and grabbed 3.7 rebounds in his initial NBA season, making the NBA All-Rookie Second Team. During 12 NBA seasons, he scored 10,544 points and made 3,204 rebounds in 742 games regular season and averaged 13.2 points in 85 playoff games. The NBA All-Rookie Second Team included Elliott in 1990.

BIBLIOGRAPHY: *Arizona Daily Star*, January 31, 1985, April 6, 1989, June 28, 1989; Mike Douchant, *Encyclopedia of College Basketball* (Detroit, MI, 1995); Ken Shouler et al., *Total Basketball* (Wilmington, DE, 2003); *TSN Official NBA Register, 2001–2002* (St. Louis, MO, 2001); *University of Arizona Media Guide, 1988–1989* (Tucson, AZ, 1988); *USA Today*, April 23, 1991.

Curtice R. Mang

ELLIS, Clifford "Cliff" (b. December 5, 1945, Chipley, FL), college coach and executive, attended Chipley High School and graduated with a Bachelor's degree from Florida State University in 1968.

Ellis followed a career path typical of a coach on the move even if it meant adopting a peripatetic lifestyle. He began his basketball coaching career at Niceville High School in Ocala, Florida, compiling a 20-5 record in 1971–1972. From 1972 to 1975, Ellis coached basketball and served as athletic director at Cumberland College in Lebanon, Tennessee.

Ellis next coached basketball at the University of South Alabama, guiding the Jaguars to a 171-84 win-loss record from 1975 to 1984. During his first year, the South Alabama athletic department strongly considered a drop to NCAA Division II. Ellis contested this move successfully and, in the early 1980s, helped the Jaguars attain basketball ranking in the nation's Top 20.

From 1985 to 1994, Ellis served as head basketball coach at Clemson University. His presence energized the Clemson basketball program to such an extent that the Tigers recorded 19 wins and a NIT Final Eight berth in the 1985–1986 season. In 1986–1987, Clemson became the most successful team in Tiger history with a 25-6 record and number 13 national ranking. Ellis was selected as ACC Coach of the Year. During his decade at Clemson, he took the Tigers to three NCAA and five NIT postseason appearances.

Ellis came to Auburn University as head basketball coach in 1995 and averaged 18 wins a season there until being fired in March 2004. Auburn had struggled to a disappointing 14-14 season after reaching the Sweet 16 in 2003. Men's basketball has always taken a backseat to Auburn's storied football program, but Ellis rewrote that script. During his last three seasons, the Auburn Tigers sold 10,500 season tickets. In the 1998–1999 season, the Tigers were ranked as high as number two nationally with a 29-4 season record and won the SEC Championship.

The Tigers 24 wins in 1999–2000 marked the second highest in school history. Auburn played in the SEC tournament championship game, with Mamadou N'daiye and Chris Porter being taken in the NBA draft.

Ellis compiled a NCAA Division I head coaching record of 500-309 in 27 seasons and garnered the 1999 John and Nellie Wooden National Coach of the Year honors. Other groups recognizing him as Coach of the Year were the

AP, *SI*, *TSN*, and *Basketball News*. He ranked second among active SEC coaches in total victories when fired.

Ellis married Carolyn Ratzlaff and has three children, Chryssa, Clay, and Anna Catherine. His hobbies and interests include music, writing, and ostrich farming. He released a 1991 record entitled "Loveland" and has authored three basketball books, most notably *Cliff Ellis: The Winning Edge* (2000).

BIBLIOGRAPHY: Lauren Rippy, Eastern Illinois University research graduate student, materials collected June 12, 2003; http://www.newsobserver.com/sports/college/wfu/story/236657/p-2207l696.html; *NCAA Men's Basketball Records, 2004* (Indianapolis, IN, 2003); http://www.auburntigers.com/mensbasketball/page.cfm?docid=2570; Chris Dorten, *String Music: Inside the Rise of SEC Basketball* (Dulles, VA, 2002).

Scott A.G.M. Crawford

EMBRY, Wayne Richard (b. March 26, 1937, Springfield, OH), college and professional player and executive, is the son of Floyd Embry and Anna Elizabeth (Gardner) Embry and graduated with a B.S. degree from Miami University of Ohio in 1958. The six-foot eight-inch, 255-pound center starred for coach Bill Rohr, helping Miami (MAC) to a 14-9 record as a sophomore in 1955–1956. Embry paced the 1956–1957 Indians to a 12-8 mark, MAC title, and a first-round NCAA Mideast Regional tournament appearance. His scoring and rebounding helped Miami repeat as MAC champion in 1957–1958 and reach the semifinal round of the NCAA Mideast Regional tournament.

The Cincinnati Royals (NBA) chose Embry in the 1958 draft. Embry starred with Cincinnati from the 1958–1959 through 1965–1966 seasons, being selected for the 1961 through 1965 All-Star Games. He started at center as a rookie, averaging 11.4 points Cincinnati struggled Embry's first three seasons but recorded winning marks and made the NBA playoffs the next five seasons. In 1961–1962, Embry recorded career highs in points scored (1,484), scoring average (19.8), field goal percentage (69), rebounds (977), and rebound average (13). NBA statistics listed him seventh in rebounds and ninth in field goal percentage. He enjoyed his second-best season in 1962–1963, scoring 1,411 points, averaging 18.6 points, and ranking sixth among NBA rebounders with 936. Cincinnati, led by brilliant guard Oscar Robertson* set a franchise record with 55 victories in 1963–1964. Embry averaged 17.8 points, placed tenth among NBA rebounders with 925, and led the NBA in personal fouls. His offensive production declined the next two seasons. The Royals traded Embry in September 1966 to the Boston Celtics (NBA), where he played a reserve role for two campaigns. In May 1968, the Milwaukee Bucks (NBA) selected him in the expansion draft. Embry ended his NBA playing career in 1968–1969, tallying over 13 points per game for the struggling franchise.

During 11 NBA seasons, Embry scored 10,380 points (12.5-point average) and made 7,544 rebounds in 831 games. He appeared in 56 NBA playoff games from 1961–1962 through 1967–1968, scoring 566 points (10.1-point average) and grabbing 448 rebounds. Cincinnati reached the NBA semifinals in 1963 and 1964, while Boston followed suit in 1967. His lone NBA championship came as a reserve with the 1967–1968 Celtics, who defeated the Los Angeles Lakers in a six-game NBA Finals. Embry scored 32 points in four All-Star Games, missing the 1963 contest with an injury.

Embry, a trustee of the Naismith Memorial Basketball Hall of Fame, married Theresa Jackson on June 6, 1959, and has three children, Deborah, Jill, and Wayne. After serving as director of recreation for Boston, Massachusetts, in 1969–1970, he rejoined the Milwaukee Bucks as general manager from 1972 to 1977 and vice president and consultant from 1977 to 1985. Milwaukee made the NBA Finals in 1974 and the Eastern Conference Finals in 1982–1983 and 1983–1984. Embry served as vice president and consultant for the Indiana Pacers (NBA) in 1985–1986 and as vice president and general manager of the Cleveland Cavaliers (NBA) from 1986 to 1994. He served as president and chief operating officer of the Cavaliers from 1994 to 2000 and as a consultant for them from 2000 to 2002. Cleveland made six playoff appearances in his first eight years. Embry was named *TSN* 1991–1992 NBA Executive of the Year and was elected to the Naismith Memorial Basketball Hall of Fame in 1999. He has been senior adviser to the general manager of the Toronto Raptors (NBA) since 2004. He serves as CEO of three banks and a member of the board of the Cleveland Federal Reserve Board.

BIBLIOGRAPHY: Wayne Embry file, Naismith Memorial Basketball Hall of Fame, Springfield, MA; Zander Hollander, ed., *The Modern Encyclopedia of Basketball*, rev. ed. (New York, 1973); Jan Hubbard, ed., *The Official NBA Basketball Encyclopedia*, 3rd ed. (New York, 2000); David S. Neft and Richard M. Cohen, eds., *The Sports Encyclopedia: Pro Basketball*, 5th ed. (New York, 1992); *TSN Official NBA Guide, 1969–1970, 2001–2002* (St. Louis, MO, 1969, 2001); *WWA*, 47th ed. (1992–1993), p. 992.

David L. Porter

ENDACOTT, Paul (b. July 13, 1902, Lawrence, KS; d. 1997), college player, was the son of Frank Endacott and Rebecca (Herning) Endacott, owners of a horse collar manufacturing company. He was one of five brothers, including J. Earl, George, Norman, and Arthur, and also had a sister, Grace. After graduating from Lawrence High School, the bright student earned a Bachelor's degree in civil engineering from the University of Kansas in 1923. He worked for Phillips Petroleum Company in Bartlesville, Oklahoma, serving as its president from 1951 to 1967. He married Lucille Easter on October 4, 1930 and had two sons, Donald and Richard.

Endacott was introduced to basketball one Saturday morning at the Lawrence YMCA when James Naismith* was refining his rules during church league games. He developed into an All-State basketball guard his senior year in high school and played his freshman year at the University of Kansas under first-year coach Forrest "Phog" Allen*. Endacott earned All-MVC Second-Team honors once and first-team honors twice. He led the Jayhawks to the mythical national title in 1923 and the first ever undefeated MVC record. Although rarely scoring in double figures in games whose tallies seldom exceeded the twenties, the five-foot ten-inch guard excelled defensively. In the MVC championship game, he controlled the center jump consistently against a much taller Missouri opponent. Endacott's outstanding play kept substitute Adolph Rupp* of Halstead, Kansas on the bench for most of his playing career. As a senior, Endacott earned HAF Player of the Year honors.

Besides being selected to the HAF All-Time All-America Second Team and Phog Allen's National All-Time College Team, Endacott was elected to the Naismith Memorial Basketball Hall of Fame in 1971 and received the Sportsmen's World Award in 1969. Endacott was honored many times by his alma mater for his service to its Alumni and Endowment Associations. Endacott, called by Allen the "greatest guard" he ever coached, played for the AAU powerhouse Phillips 66ers when he first began working for the company. His successful business career testified to the discipline and intelligence he exhibited as an athlete.

BIBLIOGRAPHY: Tom Boyd and Daniel B. Droege, *Phillips: The First 66 Years* (Bartlesville, OK, 1983); Paul Endacott file, Naismith Memorial Basketball Hall of Fame, Springfield, MA; Blair Kerkhoff, *Phog Allen: The Father of Basketball Coaching* (Indianapolis, IN, 1996); Norman M. Lobsenz, *The Boots Adams Story* (Bartlesville, OK, 1965); University Archives, Spencer Research Library, University of Kansas, Lawrence, KS.

Gregory S. Sojka

ENGLISH, Alexander "Alex" (b. January 5, 1954, Columbia, SC), college and professional player and coach, coach, and executive, developed as one of the most potent offensive stars in the NBA during the first half of the 1980s. A star player and all-time career scoring record-holder at the University of South Carolina with 1,972 points, English was chosen on the second round of the annual NBA player draft in 1976 by the Milwaukee Bucks (NBA). After completing two seasons with the Milwaukee club, English signed with the Indiana Pacers (NBA) as a free agent in June 1978, and subsequently was traded, along with a first-round draft choice, to the Denver Nuggets (NBA) for veteran star George McGinnis*. This trade quickly proved one of the most lopsided in NBA history. The veteran McGinnis, a superstar with Indiana during the earlier ABA period of that franchise, was considerably beyond his career prime and saw little further productive playing time before his 1983 retirement. English, however, enjoyed immediate success at Denver, averaging 23.8 points there during his first full season in 1981–1982 and being selected for the All-NBA Second Team.

English, one of 12 children raised by grandparents, launched his basketball career at Dreher High School in Columbia, SC. He stayed close to home for a brilliant college career under Coach Frank McGuire*, scoring a record 1,972 points as a four-year starter for the Gamecocks between 1972 and 1976. The first black sports star at South Carolina started every game of his four-year college career. The six-foot seven-inch, 190-pound forward became only the third player in school history to record over 1,000 rebounds, connected on better than 50 percent of his field goal attempts over a four-year period, and was named to two independent All-America teams during the 1975 and 1976 seasons. A soft-spoken individual off the basketball court, English was a gifted student in undergraduate days and developed interests that he still maintains in art, sculpture, literature, and, especially poetry. He graduated with a Bachelor's degree in English in 1976. English privately has published a 54-page collected volume of his own verse and was known around the pro basketball world as the poet laureate of the NBA. He and his wife, Vanessa, have one daughter, Jad-Li, and two sons, Alex Jr., and William.

Although English's pro basketball career began somewhat quietly at Milwaukee (1976–1978) and Indiana (1978–1980), his first three seasons indicated promise of greatness. In his second NBA year, he averaged just under 10 points for a full 82-game schedule and ranked fifth in the NBA with an outstanding .542 shooting percentage. His first year with the Indiana club and only third in the NBA saw English finish second on the team in rebounding (8.1 per game) and in field goal percentage (.511), third in assists (271), and fourth in scoring (16.0 per game). After the 1980 trade to Denver, English fully established himself among the NBA's premier offensive players. He appeared in 8 consecutive NBA All-Star games between 1982 and 1989 scoring 13 points in 19 minutes during the 1984 game played on his home court in Denver's McNichols Sports Arena. A career peak was reached in 1982–1983, when he became the NBA scoring champion with a 28.4 points average. In 1983–1984 English's scoring average dropped to 26.4, fourth in the NBA. During the 1985–1986 season, he finished in a second-place tie with Adrian Dantley* behind Dominique Wilkins in the scoring race with an outstanding 29.8 average. In 1984–1985 English led his Denver team in minutes played, offensive rebounds, and blocked shots, proving his overall value as an outstanding offensive and defensive performer and one of the NBA's most talented athletes. In November 1985 English scored a career-high 54 points against the Houston Rockets. He finished third in 1986–1987 in NBA scoring with a 28.6 points average. His point production dropped to 25.0 points per game in 1987–1988, but English helped the 54-28 Nuggets take the Central Division title. In 1982, 1983, and 1986, he made the All-NBA Second Team. In 1988, he won the J Walter Kennedy Citizenship Award. In August 1990, the Dallas Mavericks (NBA) signed English as a free agent. He retired from the NBA following the 1990–1991 season with 25,613 points (21.5 point average) and 6,538 rebounds. English briefly played for Depi Napoli (Italian League) in 1991–1992. He was elected to the Naismith Memorial Basketball Hall of Fame in 1997. English served as head coach of the North Charleston Lowgaters (NBDL) in 2001–2002, finishing first with a 36-20 record. He joined the Atlanta Hawks (NBA) as Director of Player Development in 2002 and served as assistant coach in 2003–2004. The Toronto Raptors (NBA) appointed him as director of player development and assistant coach in 2004. The Denver Nuggets retired his uniform number two.

BIBLIOGRAPHY: Peter C. Bjarkman, *The Encyclopedia of Pro Basketball Team Histories* (New York, 1994); Alex English file, Naismith Memorial Basketball Hall of Fame, Springfield, MA; Alex English and Gary Diesohn, *The English Language* (Chicago, IL, 1986); "English Speaks Consistency," *TSN* 3 (March 25, 1983), p.5; Ken Shouler et al., *Total*

Basketball (Wilmington, DE, 2003); Kevin Simpson, "Alex English; The Most Underrated Player in the NBA," *Basketball Digest* 9 (May 1982), pp. 18–22; *TSN Official NBA Register, 2004–2005* (St. Louis, MO, 2004).

Peter C. Bjarkman

ENKE, Fred A. (b. July 12, 1897, Rochester, MN; d. November 2, 1985), college sports player and coach, excelled especially at the University of Arizona. He grew up in southeastern Minnesota and attended the University of Minnesota, where he started on the varsity basketball team and lettered twice in football. Enke played on the 13-0 Golden Gophers' 1918–1919 basketball team, which claimed the BTC title and HAF National Championship Award. He graduated in 1921 with a Bachelor's degree in civil engineering. His coaching career began the next fall at South Dakota State University, where he served as assistant football and basketball coach. Two years later, he moved to the University of Louisville and became the school's first athletic director. At Louisville, he coached football, basketball (13-20 record), baseball, and track and field for two seasons. On June 16, 1923, he married his wife, Charline, who died in 1974. They had one son, Fred W.

In 1925 Enke traveled to Tucson, Arizona, and joined the expanding staff of J. F. "Pop" McKale as assistant football and head basketball coach at the University of Arizona. He coached basketball for 36 years, served as head football coach for one season (1931), and assisted as football line coach and scout through 1946. He started the varsity golf program there, with his golfers compiling a 209-101-13 meet record from 1935 to 1966. They won eleven BoC titles and finished seventh twice at the NCAA golf championships.

Enke enjoyed his greatest success in basketball. Although never blessed with exceptional players, he schooled his squads well in fundamentals and produced consistent winners. They won 11 BoC titles and recorded seven consecutive championships between 1943 and 1951. This period, the most productive of his coaching career, included several top 20 rankings and four postseason tournament appearances: the NIT in 1946 and 1950 and a dual appearance in the NCAA and NIT in 1951. Enke's cagers won 81 straight home games from 1945 until 1951 in the old Bear Down Gymnasium and then the second longest, and now tied for the fifth longest, home winning streak in college basketball history. His best players were brothers Stewart and Morris Udall (who gained fame in politics), son Fred (an All-America football halfback, who played seven years in the NFL), Link Richmond, Leon Blevins, and Roger Johnson.

Enke retired as basketball coach in 1961 with a 510-326 record at the University of Arizona. His 523 career victories were the fifth highest then and still rank high in college history. He became the first Arizona coach elected by the HAF Hall of Fame (1951) and the initial basketball coach inducted into the Arizona Sports Hall of Fame in 1969. Enke, along with his son, were charter members of the University of Arizona Sports Hall of Fame (1976).

BIBLIOGRAPHY: Peter C. Bjarkman, *Hoopla: A Century of College Basketball* (Indianapolis, IN, 1996); Ronald L. Mendell, *Who's Who in Basketball* (New Rochelle, NY, 1973); *Minnesota Alumni News* 77 (October, 1977), p. 15.

Dennis S. Clark

ENRIGHT, James Edward "Jim" (b. April 3, 1910, Sodus, MI; d. December 20, 1981, Chicago, IL), basketball official and sports journalist, grew up in Eau Claire, Michigan and graduated in 1928 from Eau Claire High School. As a high school athlete, the five-foot nine-inch, 175-pound Enright twice captained the reserve basketball team and co-captained the varsity squad as a non-starter his senior year. He also played third base and outfield on the high school baseball team. Enright's experience as high school yearbook editor helped launch his sports journalism career. In 1928 he became a sportswriter for the *News-Palladium* of Benton Harbor, Michigan.

In 1930 Enright was "drafted" to officiate a grade school basketball game for Benton Harbor Elementary School. From the grade school game, he embarked on a 30-year basketball officiating career that included championship high school,

AAU, college, and professional contests. From 1930 to 1937, Enright officiated high school football, baseball, and basketball, and college basketball in Michigan. Simultaneously Enright pursued his journalism career by becoming sports editor of the *News-Palladium* in 1934.

Enright in 1937 married Hellen Linderman of Benton Harbor and had one daughter, Lenna. That same year the Enrights moved to Chicago where Jim became a sportswriter for the *Chicago Evening American* (later *Chicago Today* and Chicago's *American*). Enright officiated industrial AAU basketball in the Chicago area from 1937 to 1943 and NBA games during its formative years. In 1944 Enright began officiating BTC college games. His rapport with players, coaches, and fans earned him popularity, respect, and additional officiating assignments with the BEC and MVC. For the next 24 seasons, Enright regularly officiated for the three conferences and handled key games and tournaments. Enright, who was assigned two NCAA regional tournaments (1952 and 1953) and the NCAA Final Four in 1954, was named Referee of the Year in 1956 by the Rockne Club of Kansas City, Missouri. In 1958 and 1968, Enright conducted officiating clinics in Europe.

Enright retired from officiating in 1960 but remained active in basketball and sportswriting. A USBWA member, he served as president of the Chicago chapter three times and of the national organization in 1967. Additionally, Enright was year-to-year member of the AP's Ratings and All-America Selection Committee. In 1968 Enright was presented the Old Timers Official Associated Award for dedication and loyal service to basketball officiating. He was elected in 1978 to the Naismith Memorial Basketball Hall of Fame as a referee.

BIBLIOGRAPHY: James Enright file, Naismith Memorial Basketball Hall of Fame, Springfield, MA; Zander Hollander, ed., *The Modern Encyclopedia of Basketball* (Garden City, NY, 1979); Jan Hubbard, ed., *The Official NBA Encyclopedia*, 3rd ed. (New York, 2000).

Jerry Jaye Wright

ERVING, Julius Winfield, II "Dr. J" (b. February 22, 1950, Hempstead, NY), college and professional player and executive, is the son of Julius Erving and Callie (Erving) Lindsey and grew up in Hempstead, New York. His parents separated when he was three. His mother worked as a domestic. Erving played basketball at Roosevelt High School and on the playground courts in and around New York City. He led Roosevelt in scoring and rebounding, making All-Conference as a junior and senior. Erving, a highly recruited athlete, received over 100 basketball scholarship offers before deciding to attend the University of Massachusetts. Erving starred at Massachusetts for a little-publicized team, averaging 26 points and 20 rebounds as a sophomore and 27 points and 19 rebounds as a junior. After his junior year, Erving turned pro to capitalize on the competition between the NBA and the ABA. The Virginia Squires (ABA) signed Erving to a four-year contract for $500,000. Erving proved well worth the investment by averaging 27 points and 16 rebounds and leading the Squires to a playoff berth during his 1971–1972 rookie season. The press and fans began calling him "Dr. J" or "Doctor," nicknames bestowed on him by a high school teammate during their playing days.

During his second season (1972–1973) with the Squires, the six-foot seven-inch, 210-pound Erving steadily became the dominant ABA player in averaging 32 points and 22 rebounds. He also led the Squires to the ABA playoffs, made First Team All-ABA for the first of four consecutive times, and was an ABA All-Star for each of his five ABA seasons. Erving's game combined grace and power. He made flashy passes to teammates, displayed exciting drives to the hoop usually culminating in a swooping lay-up or dunk, and proved a powerful rebounder, often snatching rebounds one-handed. This talent made Erving a fans' player and gate attraction, leading to his unsuccessful attempt to sign with the Atlanta Hawks (NBA). Erving's maneuvers caused a rift in his relationship with the Squires, who soon traded him to the New York Nets (ABA).

New York played in the Nassau Coliseum, near where Erving grew up. The Nets, who competed for fans with the NBA world champion New York Knickerbockers, needed a drawing card and received much more with Erving. In his first season, Erving led the Nets to the

ABA championship, paced the ABA in scoring, and became ABA and playoff MVP. He was named co-MVP in 1974–1975 with George McGinnis and won the MVP award for the regular season and the playoffs for the second time in 1975–1976, once again leading the Nets to the ABA championship.

After the 1975–1976 season, the ABA and NBA merged as the NBA. After a series of contract manipulations, Erving in 1976 became a member of the Philadelphia 76ers. The 76ers qualified for the playoffs every year after he joined. Every pro team Erving played for made the playoffs while he was a member. During his career with the 76ers through 1986–1987, Erving was selected NBA MVP in 1981, an NBA All-Star 11 seasons, and an All-Star MVP in 1977 and 1983. He also helped to lead the 76ers to the NBA championship in 1982–1983. He was named to the 35th Anniversary NBA All-Time Team in 1980 and one of the 50 Greatest Players in NBA History in 1996. His combined ABA and NBA regular season career totals until his retirement after the 1986–1987 season included 1,243 games played, 11,818 field goals, 30,026 total points, and 24.2 points per game average. Erving ranks fifteenth in career scoring and was the ninth player to tally 25,000 points. Upon his retirement, he led the 76ers in all-time blocked shots with 1,293. Erving was named to the All-NBA First Team in 1978 and from 1980 through 1983 and the All-NBA Second Team in 1977 and 1984. He served as an NBC-Sports analyst for NBA Showtime and as executive vice president of the Orlando Magic (NBA) from 1997 to 2003. He also has co-owned Coca-Cola Bottling Company of Philadelphia since 1987, is president of JDREG a management-marketing firm, and serves on the board of directors of Meridan Bancorp. The 76ers retired his uniform number 6. He was elected to the Naismith Memorial Basketball Hall of Fame in 1993. Off the court, Temple University conferred a Doctor of Arts degree on him in 1983. Erving participated in many worthwhile causes and received the Father Flanagan Award for service to young people. He married Turquoise Brown in February 1974 and had four children, Cheo, Julius III, Jazmin, and Cory, before their divorce in 2003.

BIBLIOGRAPHY: Marty Bell, *The Legend of Dr. J* (New York, 1981); Julius Erving file, Naismith Memorial Basketball Hall of Fame, Springfield, MA; James Haskins, *Dr. J: Biography of Julius Erving* (New York, 1975); Tony Kornheiser, "Exit Dunking," *Sport* 78 (June 1987), pp. 56–57; *The Lincoln Library of Sports Champions*, Vol. 4 (Columbus, OH, 1974); *Philadelphia 76ers Media Guide*, 1986–1987 (Philadelphia, PA, 1986); Claudia Mitroi, *Philadelphia's Greatest Sports Moments* (Champaign, IL, 2000); Jim O'Brien, *NBA All-Stars* (New York, 1972); Jim O'Brien, "Dr. J's Magic Puts Nets Fans on Their Feet," *TSN*, January 12, 1974 (St. Louis, MO, 1974); Terry Pluto, *Loose Balls* (New York 1990); Ken Shouler et al., *Total Basketball* (Wilmington, DE, 2003); *TSN Official NBA Register, 2004–2005* (St. Louis, MO, 2004); Josh Wilker, *Julius Erving* (New York, 1995).

William A. Sutton

ETHRIDGE, Kamie (b. April 21, 1964, Lubbock, TX), college player and coach, is the daughter of Mitzi Ethridge. The five-foot five-inch point guard starred in basketball at Lubbock Monterey High School and led them to the class 5A title in 1981. In 1982, she joined the University of Texas basketball program under coach Jody Conradt*. Ethridge started and directed the Lady Longhorns from 1983–1984 through 1985–1986. During these seasons, Texas compiled an 124-9 win-loss record. Ethridge capped her college career by leading the Lady Longhorns to the national title in 1986. Texas finished the season 34-0, becoming the first undefeated women's team ever. She won the Broderick Award as College Woman Athlete of the Year and the Wade Trophy for player performance, academics, and community service. Her final career statistics at Texas included 6.3 points and 2.7 rebounds per game, while her 776 assists remain the program's highest total ever. She also played on the USA's 1985 silver medal winners at the World University Games and gold medal winners at the 1986 Goodwill Games, the 1987 Pan American Games, and the 1988 Olympics at Seoul, South Korea.

Ethridge played basketball briefly in Italy before taking an assistant basketball coach position at Illinois State University in 1990. She moved to Vanderbilt University, where she helped lead the Lady Commodores to an NCAA Final Four appearance in 1993. In 1996–1997, Ethridge became an assistant basketball coach at Kansas State University. The Lady Wildcats struggled in Ethridge's first year, but the program became competitive again during the 1998–1999 season, advancing to the second round of the Women's NIT. In 2002–2003, Kansas State finished 29-5 and defeated Harvard University, 79-69, in the first round of the NCAA tournament. The University of Notre Dame ousted Kansas State 59-53 in the second round. The Lady Wildcats fared 24-5 in 2003–2004 and 24-8 in 2004–2005 and were eliminated in the second round of the NCAA tournament both seasons. In February 2000, the University of Texas inducted her in the inaugural class into the school's Women's Athletic Hall of Honor.

BIBLIOGRAPHY: *Kansas State University Women's Basketball Media Guide*, 2003–2004 (Manhattan, KS, 2003); *University of Texas Women's Basketball Media Guide*, 1985–1986, 1986–1987 (Austin, TX, 1985, 1986); *Vanderbilt University Women's Basketball Media Guide*, 1995–1996 (Nashville, TN, 1995).

Jorge Iber

EWING, Patrick Aloysius (b. August 5, 1962, Kingston, Jamaica), college and professional player and coach, is the son of Carl Ewing and Dorothy Ewing. Ewing arrived in the United States in 1975 without ever having played a basketball game. He graduated in 1980 from the Cambridge Latin School, home of several famous alumni, including conductor Leonard Bernstein. Georgetown University's head coach, John Thompson*, persuaded Ewing's mother, who worked in the kitchen of Massachusetts General Hospital, to send him to the District of Columbia school. By the end of his sophomore season (1982–1983), Ewing made the coaches First Team All-America list. In his junior year, the center enjoyed his most productive season as a collegian with 37 games and 1,179 minutes played, shooting .658 percent from the field, .656 percent from the line, and recording 371 rebounds, 608 points, and a 16.4 points average. Ewing led the Hoyas to the 1984 NCAA championship over the University of Houston with his aggressive style of play.

Although Georgetown suffered the loss of most of their regulars during the summer, Hoya rooters expected a repeat of the championship because playmaker Ewing was still there. The seven-foot, 240-pounder preferred to avoid publicity, a trait variously interpreted as arrogance or shyness. Ewing seemed perfectly at home in the art studio where he studied his academic major. His senior season did not entirely fulfill its promise. Ewing's statistics declined, at least marginally, although Georgetown made it to the NCAA Finals. Hoya fans were astonished, however, when BEaC rival Villanova University defeated them for the NCAA championship. Ewing, nevertheless, proved a superior college basketball player. His full career Georgetown statistics included 143 games, 1,382 field goal attempts, 857 field goals made (.620), 740 free throws attempted, 470 free throws made (.635), 1,316 rebounds, 2,184 points, and a 15.3 points average. The 2,184 points ranked him second behind one-time teammate Eric "Sleepy" Floyd on the all-time Georgetown list. A great play maker, Ewing refused to monopolize the ball.

Ewing was considered the clear first choice in the 1985 NBA professional draft. The NBA adopted a lottery-style draft, giving the bottom five teams from the previous season an opportunity at having the best player available. When the New York Knicks won the draft lottery, NBA analysts predicted that the long dormant team would have a great resurgence. Ewing enjoyed a fine initial season by scoring 998 points and averaging 20.4 points despite injuries. He got the benefit of the doubt in being named NBA Rookie of the Year, and made the NBA All-Rookie Team. Nevertheless, the Knicks finished in last place in the Atlantic Division of the Eastern Conference in Ewing's first and second seasons. Ewing developed into one of the NBA's greatest centers, helping the Knicks make the playoffs 13 consecutive seasons and the NBA Finals in 1994 and 1999. In March 1999, he became just the twelfth NBA player to record 20,000 career points and 10,000 career rebounds, Ewing made the All-NBA First Team in

1990, the All-NBA Second Team in 1988, 1989, 1991, 1992, 1993, and 1997, the All-NBA Defensive Team in 1988, 1989, and 1991, and the NBA All-Star Team 11 times. Ewing played on the gold medal–winning 1984 and 1992 Olympic teams and leads the Knicks in career scoring (23,665 points), rebounds (10,759), steals (1,061), and blocked shots (2,758). He finished his career with the Seattle SuperSonics (NBA) in 2000–2001 and Orlando Magic (NBA) in 2001–2002. Ewing was named to the NBA's 50th Anniversary All-Star team in 1996 and has served as an assistant coach for the Washington Wizards (NBA) in 2002–2003 and the Houston Rockets (NBA) since July 2003. During 17 NBA seasons, he recorded 9,702 field goals, (.504 shooting percentage), 5,392 free throws made (.740 percent), 11,607 rebounds, 2,215 assists, 1,136 steals, and 24,815 points for a 21.0 lifetime points-average.

BIBLIOGRAPHY: Peter C. Bjarkman, *The Biographical History of Basketball* (Chicago, IL, 2000); *Current Biography Yearbook* (1989), pp. 576–580; Mike Douchant, *Encyclopedia of College Basketball* (Detroit, MI, 1995); Jan Hubbard, ed., *The Official NBA Encyclopedia*, 3rd ed. (New York, 2000); *NYT*, May 13, 1985; Leonard Shapiro, *Big Man on Campus: John Thompson and the Georgetown Hoyas* (New York, 1991); Ken Shouler, et al., *Total Basketball* (Wilmington, DE, 2000); *TSN Official NBA Register, 2004–2005* (St. Louis, MO, 2004).

John David Healy

F

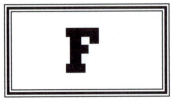

FAGAN, Clifford B. (b. March 3, 1911, Mankato, MN; d. 1996), college player and high school coach, official, and executive, was elected to the Naismith Memorial Basketball Hall of Fame in 1983. Fagan graduated in 1928 from Medina Township High School in Marshall, Wisconsin, where he played basketball and baseball, and earned a Bachelor's degree in 1932 from LaCrosse (Wisconsin) State Teachers College. At LaCrosse, he participated in basketball for three years and garnered All-WSC honors. Fagan's coaching career encompassed five sports at three Wisconsin high schools. He coached football at Fairchild High School from 1932 to 1935; football, basketball, wrestling and baseball at Sturgeon Bay High School from 1935 to 1941; and basketball, football, and boxing at Green Bay East High School in the 1941–1942 academic year. Fagan compiled a 39-14-4 win-loss-tie football coaching record, resulting in five conference titles and five undefeated seasons. Others regarded Fagan, who was an interscholastic official from 1930 to 1946, as a foremost rules authority.

Fagan served as WIAA executive secretary from 1947 to 1957 and as NFSHSAA assistant executive secretary in 1958 and 1959. The NFSHSAA appointed him executive secretary in 1959, a position he held until his 1977 retirement. Fagan's other responsibilities included NBRC secretary from 1958 to 1976; a member of the USOC board of directors from 1964 to 1979; Naismith Memorial Basketball Hall of Fame president from 1966–1972; BFUSA president from 1967 to 1973; ABAUSA president in 1975 and 1976; PAFB treasurer from 1975 to 1980; and FIBA Central Committee service from 1976 to 1980.

Fagan's accomplishments as NFSHSAA executive secretary involved the development of national athletic programs benefiting over 20,000 high schools; construction of the NFSHSAA's first headquarters building in Elgin, Illinois; enrollment of all state associations as national members; establishment of associate membership for Canadian Associations; formalization of a working relationship with the NCAA; organization of an NAAD; securing the rights to the "Illustrated Rules" publications and distributing the publications nationally; and establishment of the national rules film program. Significant honors include membership in the Wisconsin High School Football Coaches Hall of Fame; an honorary doctoral degree from Springfield (Massachusetts) College in 1968; election to the USTFF Hall of Fame in 1971; the IAABO citation for special services to basketball in 1972; the John Bunn Award from the Naismith Memorial Basketball Hall of Fame in 1973; the Bud Wilkinson Award for service to football 1976; the Award of Merit from the NFSHSAA in 1977 and the NIAAA in 1978, and an NABC appreciation award in 1978. Fagan married Kathryn Vera Bailey and had three children, Kathryn, Patrick, and Dennis.

BIBLIOGRAPHY: Walter Byers, "A Tribute to Clifford B. Fagan," July 8, 1977, Clifford B. Fagan file, Naismith Memorial Basketball Hall of Fame, Springfield, MA; *NFSHSAA News*, 1983, p. 26.

John L. Evers and Wayne Patterson

FEERICK, Robert Joseph "Bob" (b. January 2, 1920, San Francisco, CA; d. June 8, 1976, Oakland, CA), college and professional player and coach, graduated from Santa Clara (California) University. At Santa Clara from 1937 to 1941, the six-foot three-inch, 190-pound Feerick was selected an All-Coast performer in basketball in 1940 and 1941 and belonged to the Magicians of Maplewood. He was elected to the Santa Clara Hall of Fame.

Upon returning from the military service, Feerick scored 198 points in 21 games with Oshkosh (Wisconsin) of the NBL during the 1945–1946 season. He joined the Washington Capitols (BAA) in 1946 and starred there four seasons, tallying 2,936 in 221 games for a 13.3-point average. Feerick, who ranked among the top BAA scorers in 1946–1947 and 1947–1948, led the BAA in field goal percentage (.401) in 1946–1947, paced the BAA in free throw percentage (.859) in 1948–1949, and appeared in nine playoff games, averaging 11.2 points. In the 1949–1950 season, he served as player-coach for the 32-36 Capitols.

In 1950, Feerick returned to Santa Clara University CaBA (California Basketball Association) as basketball coach and athletic director. In his 12 seasons as basketball coach, Santa Clara compiled a 193-118 record, won four CABA titles, and made four trips to the NCAA West Regionals. His 1951–1952 quintet advanced to the NCAA Final Four.

In 1962 the San Francisco Warriors (NBA) appointed Feerick as head coach. He coached the Warriors in 1962–1963 to a 31-49 mark and served as the club's general manager from 1963 through 1974. Prior to his death, Feerick was director of player personnel for the Warriors. He married Eleanor Rogus on September 5, 1941, and had four children: Robert Jr., Richard, Dee (deceased), and Charles.

BIBLIOGRAPHY: Peter C. Bjarkman, *The Biographical History of Basketball* (Chicago, IL, 2000); Jan Hubbard, ed., *The Official NBA Basketball Encyclopedia*, 3rd ed. (New York, 2000); Neil D. Isaacs, *Vintage NBA* (Silver Spring, MD, 1996); David Neft and Richard M. Cohen, eds. *The Sports Encyclopedia: Pro Basketball*, 5th ed. (New York, 1992); *NYT*, June 8, 1976; Santa Clara University Sports Information Department, Santa Clara, CA.

Allan Hall

FERRIN, C. Arnold, Jr. "Arnie" (b. July 29, 1925, Ogden, UT), college and professional player and executive, is the great-grandson of a Mormon pioneer who settled the Utah Territory with Brigham Young in 1847, and the son of C. Arnold Ferrin. In the fall of 1943, the six-foot four-inch, 165-pound Ferrin walked-on at the University of Utah to play basketball for veteran coach Vadal Peterson. With upper classmen in military service, five of Peterson's top six players were freshmen. Utah posted a 17-3 record and accepted a bid to play in the NIT, suffering an opening round loss to the University of Kentucky Wildcats. Before the Utes returned to Salt Lake City, Utah, the NCAA Tournament Committee asked them to replace the University of Arkansas. Arkansas had lost two star players in an automobile accident and had pulled out of the tournament. Utah agreed and become the first school to play in both the NCAA and NIT tournaments in the same year. After topping the University of Missouri and Iowa State University in Kansas City, Utah returned to New York's Madison Square Garden and edged Dartmouth College 42-40 in overtime in the NCAA Final. Ferrin led all scorers with 22 points to earn tournament MVP honors, the first freshman to win that recognition. The feat was not duplicated until Pervis Ellison in 1986 with the University of Louisville and Carmelo Anthony* in 2003 with Syracuse University. The "Cinderella Kids" ended their season two nights later with a 43-36 win over NIT champion St. John's University in the Red Cross Game.

Ferrin enlisted in the U.S. Army in the midst of the 1944–1945 season and did not return to the University of Utah until the 1946–1947 season, which ended with a 64-62 victory over the University of Kentucky in the NIT championship game. He completed his college career in 1947–1948, earned All-America honors for the fourth time, and played in two College All-Star Games.

In 1948, the Minneapolis Lakers (NBA) made Ferrin their first round draft choice. He played in the NBA three years, scored 1,037 points in 178 regular season games, and earned two NBA championship rings.

After leaving the NBA, Ferrin worked in private business. The Utah Stars (ABA) made Ferrin their general manager from 1971 until 1974. He served as the athletic director at the University of Utah from 1976 through 1985. In 1988, Ferrin chaired the NCAA Basketball Committee. In 2001, the NACDA and the NIT named him the twentieth person to receive the NACDA/NIT Athletic Directors Award.

Ferrin married RoLayne Rasmussen. They have four children, Arnie III, Bard, Louanne, and Shawn.

BIBLIOGRAPHY: Joe Gergen, *The Final Four: An Illustrated History of College Basketball's Showcase Event* (St. Louis, MO, 1987); Mike Douchant, *Encyclopedia of College Basketball* (Detroit, MI, 1995); Jan Hubbard, ed., *The Official NBA Basketball Encyclopedia*, 3rd ed. (New York, 2000); *Salt Lake City Tribune* Staff, ed., *Runnin' Utes Basketball* (Champaign, IL, 1998).

Adolph H. Grundman

FERRY, Daniel John Willard "Danny" "Beans" "King Footer" (b. October 17, 1966, Bowie, MD), college and professional player and executive, grew up performing basketball. His father, Robert Dean "Bob" Ferry, played center for the St. Louis Hawks (NBA), Detroit Pistons (NBA), and Baltimore Bullets (NBA) from 1959 to 1969 and subsequently became vice president and a recruiter for the Washington Bullets. From 1973 to 1990, the elder Ferry served as the Bullets general manager. Ferry's older brother, Bob Jr., played basketball in high school and for Harvard University (IvL). His mother, Rita (Brooks) Ferry, chauffered her sons from suburban Maryland to Washington, D.C.'s DeMatha High School and Boys' Club teams so that they could learn the intensive urban version of the game. The Bullets, whom Ferry had watched since age six, served as his babysitters.

Ferry had grown to 6 feet 10 inches, 235 pounds by the time he reached high school. DeMatha High School, under legendary coach Morgan Wootten*, won three city basketball championships during Ferry's first three years there and finished second to Spingarn High School in his fourth year. Ferry, known for his intensity and sense of humor, made the All-Met team twice in high school. In 1985 *Parade* voted him the nation's top high school player his senior year. In scholastic competition, he averaged 7 points as a freshman, 10.4 as a sophomore, 16.3 as a junior, and 20 as a senior.

Numerous college teams recruited Ferry, who selected Duke University (ACC) over the University of North Carolina (ACC) because he wanted to start right away. Coach Mike Kryzewski* started him as a freshman. The high expectations of the political science major were exceeded, as he played in an NCAA game in his freshman year, was named ACC Player of the Year twice, and won the 1989 Naismith Award as a senior. Ferry helped the Duke Blue Devils win two consecutive ACC titles in his sophomore and junior years and make the NCAA Final Four. Duke advanced to second place in Ferry's senior year. His points average as a collegian were 5.9 his freshman year, 14.0 his sophomore year, 19.1 his junior year, and 22.7 his senior year.

An injured knee in July 1988 prompted Ferry's release from the U.S. Olympic Basketball team. The Los Angeles Clippers (NBA) selected him second overall in the 1989 NBA draft, but he declined their offer. Ferry followed Tom McMillen's and Bill Bradley's* precedent by playing basketball in the ItL. He joined the new, corporate-sponsored II Messaggero team in Rome, reportedly signing a $2 million, multiyear contract. In 1989–1990, he scored 878 points and averaged 29.3 points for II Messaggero. The contract let him decide annually whether to stay in Italy or move to the NBA. The Cleveland Cavaliers (NBA) acquired Ferry in a November 1989 trade. Ferry played mostly reserve roles with Cleveland from 1990–1991 through 1999–2000 and with the San Antonio Spurs (NBA) from 2000–2001 through 2002–2003. The Indiana Pacers (NBA) acquired him in a three-team July 2003 transaction, but released him before the 2003–2004 season. During 13 NBA seasons through 2002–2003, he tallied 6,439 points (7.0 average) and made 2,550 rebounds (2.8 average) in 917 regular season games. Ferry averaged 3.7 points in 67 playoff games and played on the 2003 NBA championship team. Since 2004, he has served as director of basketball operations for the San Antonio Spurs (NBA). San Antonio reached the 2005 NBA finals against the Detroit Pistons.

BIBLIOGRAPHY: Mike Douchant, *Encyclopedia of College Basketball* (Detroit, MI, 1995); *NCAA Men's Basketball Records, 2004* (Indianapolis, IN, 2003); Curry Kirkpatrick, "He Does the Devil's Work," *SI* 68 (February 15, 1988), pp. 68–70, 73–74; *NYT*, July 21, 1988; Ken Shouler et al., *Total Basketball* (Wilmington, DE, 2003); *TSN Official NBA Register, 2003–2004* (St. Louis, MO, 2004); Washington *Post*, March 6, 1985 March 11, 1985 April 3, 1985, April 14, 1985, February 10, 1988, March 30, 1988, November 1, 1988, January 30, 1989, March 15, 1989, April 12, 1989, June 28, 1989, August 2, 1989, August 3, 1989, August 6, 1989, August 12, 1989, August 17, 1989, August 20, 1989.

Frederick J. Augustyn Jr.

FINLEY, Michael Howard (b. March 6, 1973, Melrose Park, IL), college and professional player, is the son of Bertha Finley, graduated from Proviso East High School in Maywood, Illinois, and studied agricultural economics at the University of Wisconsin. The six-foot seven-inch, 225-pound small forward-guard starred for coach Steve Yoder from 1991–1992 through 1994–1995 and rewrote most of the Badgers' offensive records. Finley's final career averages at Wisconsin included 2,147 points scored (18.7 point average), 739 field goals scored, 1,681 field goals attempted, and 456 free throws made in 115 games, school best in all of these categories. His talents earned him three AP honorable mention All America, two First Team All BTC, and one Second All-BTC selections.

The Phoenix Suns (NBA) selected Finley with the 21st pick of the first round in the 1995 NBA draft. He was named to the NBA All-Rookie Team and finished fourth in the balloting for NBA Rookie of the Year. Finley averaged 15.0 points, 4.6 rebounds, 3.5 assists, and 1.0 steals during the 1995–1996 campaign. He was traded to the Dallas Mavericks (NBA) for Jason Kidd* in December 1996. His scoring increased steadily with a career high 22.6 points per game during 1999–2000. In 2002–2003, Finley helped lead the Mavericks to the team's best record ever (60-22) and the Midwest Division crown. Dallas eliminated the Utah Jazz and Sacramento Kings in the first two rounds of the playoffs, but lost a tough seven-game series to the San Antonio Spurs in the Western Conference finals. Finley ranked second for the Mavericks in scoring with an 18.6 point average in 2003–2004, helping Dallas finish fifth in the Western Conference with 52 victories. He tallied 18 points in victorious Game 3 and averaged 13 points in the first round of the playoffs, but the Sacramento Kings eliminated Dallas in five games. Finley averaged 15.7 points in 2004–2005, helping Dallas win 58 games and make the playoffs. He averaged 13.1 points and 4.3 rebounds in 13 playoff games, with the Phoenix Suns eliminating the Mavericks in the second round. In his 10 NBA seasons, he has averaged 19.0 points, 5.1 rebounds, and 3.7 assists in 735 regular season games. Finley was named to the NBA All Star Game during the 1999–2000 and 2000–2001 seasons and the Team USA squad at the 2002 World Championships.

Finley, who is single, in 2001 signed a seven-year, $102 million contract extension with the Mavericks. He participates with several charitable organizations, including Buckets for Hunger in Madison, Wisconsin, and has purchased a block of tickets for distribution among Dallas area non-profit organizations since 1998–1999.

BIBLIOGRAPHY: Geoffery C. Arnold, "Summer in the NBA is Market Driven," *The Oregonian,* July 14, 2001, p. E01; Lacy J. Banks, "Finley Gets Reward for Paying the Price," *Chicago Sun-Times*, August 10, 2001, p. 150; Lacy J. Banks, "Jordan's Workout Partners Working Towards Goals," *Chicago Sun-Times*, August 26, 2001, p. 125; "Finley Doesn't Forget Madison Commitment," *Dubuque Telegraph Herald*, July 29, 2001, p. C2; Joe Hart, "Mavericks' Finley Soars to New Heights as a Pro," *Madison Capital Times*, February 18, 2003, p. 1C, Jon Masson, "Still Cool After Cashing In," *Wisconsin State Journal*, July 28, 2001, p. E1; Adam Mertz, "Finley Keeping Eye on Badgers," *Madison Capital Times*, March 27, 2002, p. 2C; NBA.com, "Player Profile: Michael Finley,"; Dwain Price, "Finley's Patience Rewarded," *Milwaukee Journal Sentinel*, April 26, 2002, p. 03C; Eddie Sefko, "Finley Puts Mavs on Edge of History," *Seattle Times*, November 28, 2002, p. D8; Ken Shouler et al., *Total Basketball* (Wilmington, DE, 2003); *University of Wisconsin Men's Basketball Media Guides*, 1994–1995, 1996–1997 (Madison, WI, 1994, 1996).

Jorge Iber

FISHER, Harry A. (b. February 6, 1882, New York, NY; d. December 29, 1967, New York, NY), college player and coach and contributor, grew up playing basketball and baseball. He excelled in basketball at City College High School, from which he graduated in 1901. Fisher attained his greatest acclaim as a basketball player at Columbia University in New York City, graduating in 1905 with a Bachelor's degree in chemical engineering. From 1902 to 1905, the five-foot nine-inch, 150-pound Fisher was an outstanding scorer. He led the Lions to undefeated seasons and the EIL (Eastern Intercollegiate League) title in 1904 and 1905. As team captain in 1904 and 1905, Fisher was awarded All-EIL and All-America honors. In 1905 Fisher set a single-game record with 13 field goals, a mark not broken for 48 years. Fisher also played baseball and managed the football team at Columbia University.

Fisher returned to his alma mater in 1906 as the school's first paid full-time basketball coach. From 1906 to 1916, Fisher guided the Lions to 105 victories against 39 defeats and EIL titles in 1911, 1912, and 1914. Fisher was appointed in 1905 to the first committee rewriting regulations for college athletics and served in this capacity and as the first editor of the *Collegiate Guide* until 1915. Fisher, who retired as coach in 1916, was Columbia's graduate manager of athletics (athletic director) from 1911 to 1917. Fisher married Christine Stundt of New York City while coaching at Columbia and had no children.

After the U.S. intervened in World War I, Fisher served in the U.S. Army from 1917 to 1920 and volunteered for chemical warfare. Fisher then officiated basketball until General Douglas MacArthur recruited him in 1921 to coach the U.S. Military Academy at West Point. Fisher guided the basketball cadets from 1921 to 1925, compiling a 46-5 win-loss record. His 1922–1923 undefeated team denied opponents a field goal in its first two games. The winning streak ended at 33 straight triumphs in the 1923–1924 season.

Fisher retired from coaching after the 1925 season with a career record of 151 wins and 44 losses. He continued as a life member on the basketball and football advisory board of the EIL. In 1945 Fisher received the Alumni Athletic Award for his contributions to Columbia University athletics and was elected to the HAF Hall of Fame. In 1973 Fisher was inducted into the Naismith Memorial Basketball Hall of Fame as a contributor. The forceful, demanding, gentlemanly Fisher, a member of Theta Delta Chi fraternity and the New York AC, devoted his entire life in the interest of basketball.

BIBLIOGRAPHY: Harry Fisher file, Naismith Memorial Basketball Hall of Fame, Springfield, MA; Zander Hollander, ed., *The NBA's Official Encyclopedia of Pro Basketball* (New York, 1981); Ronald L. Mendell, *Who's Who in Basketball* (New York, 1973).

Jerry Jaye Wright

FITCH, William Charles "Bill" (b. May 19, 1934, Davenport, IA), college and professional player and coach, coached over 30 seasons and ranks seventh among NBA mentors in career wins. Fitch graduated from a Cedar Rapids (Iowa) High School and in 1954 from Coe College, where he played basketball three seasons and averaged 15.4 points as a senior. He coached basketball at Coe College with indifferent results from 1958–1959 through 1961–1962. Coaching assignments followed at the University of North Dakota (NCC, 1962–1963 through 1966–1967), Bowling Green University (MAC, 1967–1968), and the University of Minnesota (BTC, 1968–1969 through 1969–1970). Fitch gave those basketball programs respectability, coaching with intensity and skill and recruiting with zeal and flair. During Fitch's 12 collegiate seasons, his squads won 181 games and lost 115 decisions.

The newly created Cleveland Cavaliers (NBA) named the six-foot two-inch, 205-pound Fitch coach in 1970 and added general manager duties later. His decisions steadily improved the Cavaliers' professional operations and on-court performance. Fitch oversaw the club's move in 1974 from the old Cleveland Arena to the modern Richfield Coliseum. In 1976 the Cavaliers won the Central Division title and lost in the Eastern Conference finals to the Boston Celtics, the eventual champions. Although making the NBA playoffs the next two seasons, the Cavaliers slumped to a 30-52 win-loss mark in 1978–1979 and saw attendance decline. Fitch's personality conflicts and demanding, paternal style contributed to his resignation. Fitch, an excellent tactician, good judge of talent, and meticulous preparer, proved a tough taskmaster and stern disciplinarian and lacked subtleness in human relations.

The struggling Boston Celtics (NBA) needed a coach with Fitch's qualifications in 1979. Red Auerbach*, a longtime acquaintance, hired Fitch as coach. Fitch's techniques, coupled with the arrival of Larry Bird* and other premier players, helped the Celtics rejoin the NBA's elite. During Fitch's four seasons in Boston, the Celtics won 242 of 328 regular season games, made the NBA playoffs every season, and won the 1981 NBA Championship. Boston lost all four games to the Milwaukee Bucks in the 1983 Eastern Conference semifinals. Growing player dissatisfaction and problems with assistant coach K. C. Jones* caused Fitch to leave Boston to coach the Houston Rockets (NBA). Jones, a Celtics star and extremely likeable person, followed Fitch as Boston coach. Fitch had helped engineer a magnificent Celtics revival, using the very tactics that subsequently led to his termination there.

At Houston, Fitch overcame another tough challenge: the Rockets had won only 14 games in the 1982–1983 campaign, but quickly improved under Fitch. Houston reached the NBA playoffs in four of his five seasons, losing to the Celtics in the 1986 NBA Championship Series. Fitch left Houston following the 1987–1988 season and joined the beleaguered New Jersey Nets (NBA) as head coach in 1989. The Nets managed only 17 victories in Fitch's initial season, only 26 triumphs in 1990–1991, and 40 in 1991–1992, his final campaign there. He coached the Los Angeles Clippers (NBA) from 1994–1995 through 1997–1998, never recording more than 36 victories. Fitch's regular season 944–1,106 career regular-season win-loss record and 55-54 playoff mark through the 1997–1998 campaign did not fully reflect his commitment and resourcefulness, because the two-time NBA Coach of the Year (1976, 1980) often coached troubled franchises and poor teams. Larry Bird called Fitch "the best coach I have worked under," a glowing tribute to his values, convictions, and work ethic.

BIBLIOGRAPHY: Peter C. Bjarkman, *Boston Celtics Encyclopedia* (Champaign, IL, 1998); Jan Hubbard, ed., *The Official NBA Basketball Encyclopedia*, 3rd ed. (New York, 2000); Bob Schron and Kevin Stevens, *The Bird Era: A History of the Boston Celtics, 1978–1988* (Boston, MA, 1988); George Sullivan, *The Picture History of the Boston Celtics* (New York, 1981); *TSN Official NBA Guide, 1997–1998* (St. Louis, MO, 1997); *TSN Official NBA Register, 2004–2005* (St. Louis, MO, 2004); *USA Today*, April 23, 1991.

Gustavo N. Agrait

FITZSIMMONS, Lowell Cotton (b. October 7, 1931, Hannibal, MO); d. July 24, 2004, Phoenix, AZ, college and professional player and coach, executive, and sportscaster, was the son of Clancy Fitzsimmons and Zelda Curry (Gibbs) Fitzsimmons and attended Bowling Green High School in Missouri. Fitzsimmons matriculated at Hannibal-LaGrange College (Missouri) as a freshman before transferring to Midwestern State University in Wichita Falls, Texas. His collegiate varsity basketball scoring average came to 13.3 points.

His basketball coaching career began at Moberly JC in 1958. In nine years there, the five-foot seven-inch, 160-pound Fitzsimmons compiled a 223-59 win-loss record and guided his teams to at least 24 victories in each of his final seven seasons. In 1966 and 1967, Moberly won the National JC basketball title. He was named JC Coach of the Year both seasons. Kansas State University (BEC) named him basketball coach in 1968. Fitzsimmons compiled a 34-20 record in his two seasons there, being selected as the BEC Coach of the Year in 1970.

Fitzsimmons experienced a well-traveled career as an NBA coach. In 1970, he began his NBA career as head coach of the Phoenix Suns. In his first season, the Suns finished with a 48-34 record; Phoenix produced a 49-33 record the next year. Although amassing among the top NBA records both seasons, Phoenix finished third in the Midwest Division behind strong Milwaukee Bucks and Chicago Bulls teams.

For the 1972–1973 season, Fitzsimmons moved to the Atlanta Hawks (NBA) as head basketball coach and guided the Hawks to a 46-36 regular season record and playoff berth. The Hawks did not finish above the .500 mark in any of the next three seasons, however, and failed to make the playoffs. Atlanta fired him near the end of the 1975–1976 season. After serving one year as director of play personnel for the Golden State Warriors (NBA), Fitzsimmons joined the Buffalo Braves (NBA) as head coach. The Braves lacked talent, finishing with a 27-55 record.

The next season, Fitzsimmons guided the Kansas City Kings (NBA) to a 48-34 record and first-place finish in the Midwest Division. He earned his first NBA Coach of the Year Award. Although unable to match his first-year record, Fitzsimmons led the Kings five more seasons and performed one of his best coaching jobs in the 1980–1981 season. The Kings struggled to a 40-42 record through the regular season, but placed second in their division and earned a playoff berth. Kansas City upset the Portland Trail Blazers in the first playoff round and used a slowed-down offensive scheme to defeat the heavily favored Phoenix Suns in the next round. The Houston Rockets ousted Kansas City in the Western Conference Finals.

Fitzsimmons coached the San Antonio Spurs (NBA) from 1984 through 1986, compiling a 76-88 record and two more playoff appearances. In 1987, Phoenix named him the Suns' director of player personnel. He largely engineered a blockbuster multiplayer trade, sending Larry Nance to the Cleveland Cavaliers (NBA) for Kevin Johnson*.

The following year, Fitzsimmons began his second stint as head coach of the Suns. With Johnson and newly acquired Tom Chambers* leading the way, Phoenix compiled a 55-27 record for a 27-victory improvement over the previous season. The Suns appeared in the Western Conference Finals for the first time since 1984, with Fitzsimmons being selected as the NBA Coach of the Year a second time. Fitzsimmons coached the Suns to three more 50-win seasons and one more trip to the Western Conference finals before retiring as coach in 1992. He again coached Phoenix to a 27-22 mark in 1995–1996 and an 0-8 mark in 1996–1997. He served as senior executive vice president and television commentator for the Suns until his death.

During his 21-year NBA coaching career, Fitzsimmons amassed an 832-775 record to rank as the eleventh all-time winningest coach in NBA history. His best seasons as an NBA mentor came in Phoenix, where he compiled a very impressive 341-208 record over eight seasons. The Missouri Basketball Hall of Fame enshrined him in 1988, while the National JC Hall of Fame inducted him in 1985. He married JoAnn D'Andrea in 1978. His son, Gary, served as the assistant general manager of basketball operations for the Golden State Warriors (NBA).

BIBLIOGRAPHY: Jan Hubbard, ed., *The Official NBA Encyclopedia*, 3rd ed. (New York, 2000); *Phoenix Suns Media Guide, 1992–1993* (Phoenix, AZ, 1992); Martin Taragano, *Basketball Biographies . . . 1891–1990* (Jefferson, NC, 1991); *TSN Official NBA Guide, 1994–1995* (St. Louis, MO, 1994); *TSN Official NBA Register, 2004–2005* (St. Louis, MO, 2004).

Curtice R. Mang

FLEISHER, Lawrence "Larry" (b. September 26, 1930, Bronx, NY; d. May 4, 1989, New York, NY), executive, graduated in 1946 from DeWitt Clinton High School in the Bronx, NY and with a Bachelor's degree from New York University. He graduated from Harvard University Law School in 1953 and served in the U.S. Army from 1953 through 1955. He worked with an accounting firm, served as a executive vice president of Restaurant Associates, and practiced law.

In 1962, Tom Heinsohn* of the Boston Celtics asked Fleisher to help form a players organization to try to obtain a pension plan for NBA players. Fleisher formed the NBA Players Association that year and served without a salary as its Executive Director and General Counsel from 1962 until his retirement in October 1988. With considerable dedication and a sincere desire to improve basketball for players, he made the NBAPA the most advanced athletic union in the world and gave the players clout that most other athletes could only dream of. Under his innovative leadership, the NBAPA paved the way for a pension program, minimum salaries, severance pay, disability payments, and other player benefits.

Fleisher helped the newly formed ABA survive in the 1960s and flourish in the early 1970s by signing Zelmo Beaty*, Billy Cunningham*, and Joe Caldwell with ABA teams and encouraging other established NBA players to join the ABA.

Fleisher proved instrumental in the establishment of the free agent system in 1976. He and the NBAPA waged a six-year battle in Congress and before the National Labor Relations Board for a free agent system, resulting in the Oscar Robertson* settlement. The settlement brought innovative forms of free agency and allowed the ABA to merge with the NBA. Fleisher represented hundreds of professional basketball players, including Bill Bradley*, Dave DeBusschere*, John Havlicek*, Bob Lanier*, Willis Reed*, Jerry West*, and Lenny Wilkens*.

Fleisher realized the potential for pro basketball to become an international sport and, as a player agent, sent numerous clients to play in Italy and other European countries. He spread the popularity of basketball abroad, taking NBAPA members on summer tours for games in Brazil, Yugoslavia, Italy, Greece, Israel, and the People's Republic of China.

Fleisher, known for his collective bargaining ability, improved the average NBA player's salary from $9,400 in 1961 to over $600,000 in 1988, the highest in professional sports. He also cut the NBA draft to two rounds and negotiated the agreement that established the NBA salary cap system. His 1988 six-year agreement was lauded as the strongest contract ever negotiated by a sports union. The players and owners became virtual partners, with the players guaranteed 53 percent of NBA revenues in salary or benefits. These gains were accomplished without the need of a player's strike. Fleisher earned the respect and admiration of those at the other side of the bargaining table.

Fleisher established an anti-drug agreement for professional sports that provided for counseling and severe penalties for players involved in the use of hard drugs.

Fleisher recognized that the players and owners needed to work together for the NBA to benefit. He was known for his tough-minded negotiations, financial acumen, and many warm friendships made on both side of the labor issue. Fleisher brought the game into the modern era, creating stars and generating fan interest. In October 1988, he became a corporate vice president in charge of basketball operations for the International Management Group, a Cleveland, Ohio-based sports agency. Fleisher resided in Pound Ridge, New York, with his wife, Vasso, and had three sons, Mark, Eric, and David, and one daughter, Nancy. He died of a heart attack after playing squash at the New York Athletic Club and was inducted into the Naismith Memorial Basketball Hall of Fame in 1991 as a contributor.

BIBLIOGRAPHY: Lawrence Fleisher File, Naismith Memorial Basketball Hall of Fame, Springfield, MA; Jan Hubbard, ed., *The Official NBA Encyclopedia*, 3rd ed. (New York, 2000); Mike Meserole, ed., *Information Please Sports Almanac 1990* (Boston, 1990); *New York Times*, May 5, 1989, p. D17; Ken Shouler et al. *Total Basketball* (Wilmington, DE, 2003).

David L. Porter

FORD, Phil Jackson (b. February 9, 1956, Rocky Mount, NC), college and professional player, is the son of Phil Ford and Mabel Ford, both public-school teachers. Ford played basketball at an early age, honing his game at Buck Leonard Park. He made High School All-America as a basketball forward at Rocky Mount (North Carolina) High School, from which he graduated in 1974.

The six-foot two-inch, 185-pound Ford graduated with a Bachelor's degree in business administration from the University of North Carolina in 1978 after starting four years at point guard. As a freshman, he averaged 16.4 points, led the Tar Heels to the 1975 ACC Tournament Championship, and won the ACC Tournament MVP award. Ford made First Team All-ACC from 1975–1976 to 1977–1978, posting respective scoring averages of 18.6, 18.7, and 20.8 points and tallying a Tar Heel record 2,290 career points. Ford, designated Second Team AP All-America in 1976, was selected First Team in 1977 and 1978. His honors included the 1977 and 1978 McKelvin Awards as the ACC's outstanding athlete and the 1978

John Wooden Award as the nation's outstanding basketball player. Ford, the USBWA, *TSN,* and NABC 1978 national Player of the Year, co-captained the 1976 Olympic gold medal men's basketball team. The great ball handler, fierce and enthusiastic competitor, and cool clutch player masterfully directed coach Dean Smith's* four corners offense. North Carolina won 99 games and lost 25 during Ford's career, finishing second in the 1977 NCAA tournament.

The Kansas City Kings (NBA) drafted Ford second in 1978. Ford averaged 15.9 points and 8.6 assists, earning NBA Rookie-of-the-Year honors. His 681 assists ranked second all-time among rookies, surpassed only by Oscar Robertson*. Ford made All-NBA Second Team in 1979–1980, averaging 16.2 points and 7.4 assists. In 1980–1981 he improved his scoring to 17.5 points per game and averaged 8.8 assists, third best in the NBA. Several injuries, coupled with admitted alcohol abuse, diminished his performance. Kansas City traded him to the Milwaukee Bucks (NBA) in June 1982. Ford spent the 1983–1984 and 1984–1985 campaigns with the Houston Rockets (NBA) and unsuccessfully tried out with the Golden State Warriors (NBA) in 1986. His NBA career included 3,083 assists (6.4 average) and 5,594 points (11.6 average) in 482 games.

Subsequently, Ford worked for North Carolina National Bank, broadcast college basketball for Jefferson Productions, and frequently lectured at schools on drug and alcohol abuse. In the summer of 1988, he was named an assistant basketball coach at his alma mater and married Traci Vample. The Tar Heels reached the NCAA Final Four in 1991, 1995, 1997, and 1998 and won the NCAA Championship in 1993 while Ford coached as an assistant. In 2004, he joined the Detroit Pistons (NBA) as assistant coach. The Pistons reached the 2005 NBA finals against the San Antonio Spurs.

BIBLIOGRAPHY: Smith Barrier, *On Tobacco Road: Basketball in North Carolina* (New York, 1983); Peter C. Bjarkman, *ACC-Atlantic Coast Conference Basketball* (Indianapolis, IN, 1996); Art Chansky, *The Dean's List* (New York, 1996); Mike Douchant, *Encyclopedia of College Basketball* (Detroit, MI, 1995); Phil Ford file, Alumni Office, University of North Carolina, Chapel Hill, NC; Ron Morris, *ACC Basketball: An Illustrated History* (Chapel Hill, NC, 1988); Raleigh (NC) *News and Observer*, January 25, 1976, Sec. IV, p. 3; Ken Rappoport, *Tales from the Tar Heel Locker Room* (Champaign, IL, 2002); Ken Rappoport, *Tar Heel: North Carolina Basketball* (Huntsville, AL, 1976); Dean Smith, *A Coach's Life* (New York, 1999); *TSN Official NBA Basketball Register 1985–1986* (St. Louis, MO, 1985).

Jim L. Sumner

FORD, Terrance Jerod "T. J." (b. March 24, 1983, Baytown, TX), college and professional player, completed his sophomore year in 2002–2003 on the University of Texas men's basketball squad and declared himself an early entry candidate for the June 2003 NBA draft. The Milwaukee Bucks (NBA) selected him in the first round as the eighth pick overall and signed him to a four year contract estimated at $7 million.

Basketball became a way of life in the Ford family, as his parents, Leo Ford and Mary Ford made it top priority. Leo, a well known basketball player in the adult recreational leagues in Houston, Texas, taught his son more than anyone else how to play basketball and has influenced his career profoundly.

Ford graduated from Willowridge High School in Sugar Land, Texas in 2001. He ended his high school basketball career with the Eagles owning a 62-game winning streak. In his final two seasons, Ford led Willowridge to a 36-1 win-loss record, a perfect 39-0 record, and consecutive class AAAAA Texas State Championships. He also dominated the McDonald's High School All-America Game in 2001.

Ford enrolled at the University of Texas as a freshman in 2001–2002 and promptly led the Longhorns to an NCAA "Sweet 16" berth. He was voted National Freshman of the Year by the USBWA, made All-BTWC Second Team and became the first freshman to lead the nation with 8.27 assists per game.

In his sophomore year, Ford again guided the Longhorns squad to the NCAA tournament. Texas advanced to the NCAA Final Four for the first time since 1947 and lost to Syracuse University, the eventual national champion, blocking the Longhorns bid for the title. Ford finished third in the nation in assists with 7.7 assists per game and led the Longhorns in scoring, assists, steals, free throw percentage, and minutes per game. Ford recorded 10 or more assists 9 times in 2002–2003 and 24 times in his two year career. His 527 career assists rank him second on the Longhorn's all-time list. In regularly scheduled games over two seasons, he scored 853 points and dished out 527 assists in 66 games. In two seasons, Ford led the Longhorns to a 48-19 win-loss record. Both squads were ranked in the top three teams in the nation. The five-foot ten-inch, 165-pound point guard played in eight NCAA tournament games and averaged 14.0 points and 8.6 assists.

Ford was named NCAA College Basketball Player of the Year in 2003, won the Naismith and Wooden awards, and was selected Player of the Year by *SI, TSN*, ESPN.com and CBS Sports Line. He was named consensus First Team All-America and made the All-BTWC First Team.

The Milwaukee Bucks (NBA) selected Ford in the first round as eighth pick overall in the 2003 NBA draft. He scored 391 points (9.1 point average) and made 356 assists (6.5 assists average) in 55 games, missing one-third of the season and the playoffs with injuries. Injuries sidelined him for the entire 2004–2005 season.

BIBLIOGRAPHY: *TSN Official NBA Register, 2004–2005* (St. Louis, MO, 2004); "T.J.," *Draft*, http://www.nbadraft.net (2003); "T.J.," *Draft Prospects*, http://www.hoopshype.com (2003); "T.J.," *A Family Affair*, http://www.texassports.com (2003); "T.J.," *Prospect Profile*, http://www.nba.com (2003); Kyle Veltrop, *TSN* (March 10, 2003), pp. 18–20; Alexander Wolff, "Toot the 'horn," *SI* 11 (March 17, 2003), pp. 32–37.

John L. Evers

FORTE, Fulvio Chester, Jr. "Chet" "Chet the Jet" (b. August 7, 1935, Hackensack, NJ; d. May 18, 1996, San Diego, CA), college player and television producer-director, was the only son of Fulvio Chester Forte Sr., a pediatrician, and graduated from Hackensack High School, where he starred in basketball. Columbia University (IvL) basketball coach Lou Rossini recruited the five-foot nine-inch, 145-pound setshot artist to play guard. As a sophomore in 1954–1955, Forte became the first Lion hoopster to score over 500 points in a season. He tallied 559 points (22.4-point average) in 25 games and converted 84 percent of his foul shots, fourth best nationally. Forte helped Columbia share the IvL title and led IvL scorers, making the All-IvL and NYBWA All-Metropolitan teams.

Forte played the first half of the 1955–1956 season, scoring 358 points (22.4-point average) in 16 games and battling Johnny Lee of Yale University for the IvL scoring title. The great dribbler and remarkable shooter made 42.4 percent of his field goals as a repeat All-IvL and NYBWA All-Metropolitan team member. Defenders moved in tight, preventing speedy, feisty Forte from setshooting, forcing him to drive to the basket for lay-ups or take jumpshots. Failure in an organic chemistry course made him academically ineligible for second semester.

In 1956–1957, Forte garnered consensus First Team All-America and All-IvL honors and earned UPI and NYBWA Metropolitan College Basketball Player of the Year accolades. He scored 693 points (28.9-point average) for 18-6 Columbia and ranked fifth nationally in scoring. Columbia shared third place in the IvL, as Forte shattered the IvL single-season scoring mark with 403 points (28.8-point average). At Columbia, he scored 1,610 career points (24.8-point average) in 65 games. He still held 11 school records upon his death.

The Cincinnati Royals (NBA) drafted Forte in 1957, but he played basketball weekends for the Williamsport (Pennsylvania) Billies (EL). After graduating with a B.A. degree in premedicine in 1958, Forte barnstormed with the Harlem Globetrotters. He joined CBS-TV Sports in New York City as an associate producer and was promoted to producer. In 1963, ABC Sports President Roone Arledge hired Forte as a producer and director. Arledge, cognizant of the growing American obsession with sports wanted to make ABC Television the major network for sports programming. Forte remained at ABC Sports until 1987, receiving nine Emmys for outstanding sports production and direction. The perfectionist became the best sports television producer-director, helping build ABC into the top sports television network. After handling NBA games and "Wide World of Sports," he produced and directed "Monday Night Football" from 1970 to 1986 and melded field action, technology, and celebrity into a tight, compelling package. Forte supervised placement of cameras and picked his own crews, searching the sidelines and crowds for action shots. His diverse producer-director sports assignments included the Summer Olympic Games from 1960 to 1984; AFL, NCAA, college bowl, and Super Bowl football games; All-Star, League Championship Series, and World Series baseball games; Kentucky Derby, Preakness, and Belmont Stakes horse racing; and Indianapolis 500 Auto Race, Grand Prix, Daytona 500, and NASCAR races. When Capital Cities acquired ABC-TV in 1986, Forte clashed with Dennis Swanson, the new ABC Sports president, and negotiated a buyout of his contract. From 1989 to 1991, he served as an independent producer and director for sports programs on NBC, ESPN, and other networks. Forte married Patricia Ann Richey on January 27, 1977, and had one daughter, Jacqueline.

Forte became a compulsive gambler by the 1980s and owed over $1.5 million to banks, Atlantic City, New Jersey casinos, and personal debtors. He gambled with funds from Starkives, a talent agency, using investor's money to pay gambling debts. In April 1990, a federal grand jury in Camden, New Jersey, indicted him on nine charges of fraud and failure to file income tax returns. After pleading guilty to three counts, Forte was sentenced in March 1992 to five years' probation. From May 1991 until his death, he enjoyed co-hosting a popular afternoon sports talk show on XTRA-Radio.

BIBLIOGRAPHY: *Dell Basketball Annual*, 1956, 1957, 1958 (New York, 1956, 1957, 1958); Mike Douchant, *Encyclopedia of College* Basketball (Detroit, MI, 1995); Chet Forte, Biographical Sheets, 1993; Zander Hollander, ed., *The Modern Encyclopedia of Basketball*, rev. ed. (New York, 1973); Geofrey Norman, "After the Fall," *SI* 74 (May 20, 1991), pp. 72–76+; *NYT*, March 7, 1957, p. 36; *NYT*, March 14, 1957, p. 37; *NYT*, March 18, 1957, p. 24; *NYT*, March 13, 1992, p. B14; *NYT*, March 14, 1992, p. 37; *NYT Biographical Service*, May 1990, pp. 422–424; *WWA*, 41st ed. (1980–1981), p. 1128.

David L. Porter

FOSTER, Harold E. "Bud" (b. May 30, 1906, Newton KS; d. July 19, 1996), college player and coach, was the son of Sam S. Foster and Clara (Moir) Foster. A graduate of Mason City (Iowa) High School in 1924, Foster led his team as a senior to its third state tournament. He also paced Mason City JC to 21 victories in 1925 before entering the University of Wisconsin, where he starred three years and graduated in 1930. Under famed coach Walter E. "Doc" Meanwell*, Foster played in only eight losing games for the Badgers (13-4 in 1928, 15-2 in both 1929 and 1930) and captained the 1930 team. He was named to several All-BTC and All-Western teams in 1929 and 1930 and made All-America in 1930.

Between 1930 and 1934, Foster played basketball for the Oshkosh (Wisconsin) All-Stars, Duffy Florals of Chicago, and Milwaukee in the early midwestern pro circuits. In 1935, he became head basketball coach at the University of Wisconsin. Foster's teams exhibited Meanwell's patterned style concentrating on ball control. As basketball coach for 25 years at the University of Wisconsin (1935–1959), Foster compiled a 270-264 career record. His teams won three BTC titles (1935, 1941, 1947) and the NCAA crown in 1941. Using a balanced fast break and deliberate attack, Wisconsin defeated Dartmouth College 51-50, University of Pittsburgh 36-30, and Washington State University 39-34 in the championship game at Kansas City. Members on the national championship squad included John Kotz (MVP), Gene Englund, Charlie Epperson, Ted Strain, and Fred Rehm. The Badgers returned to the NCAA tournament in 1947 but lost in the first round.

After his coaching career, Foster served 17 years as professor of athletics and director of grants-in-aid at the University of Wisconsin. Foster, later an emeritus professor, served as NABC president in 1955–1956 and won their Metropolitan Award in 1964. Married to Eleanor Schneider in February 1933, Foster had two children, Stephanie and Brian. He is a member of the HAF Hall of Fame and in 1964 was elected as a player to the Naismith Memorial Basketball Hall of Fame.

BIBLIOGRAPHY: Peter C. Bjarkman, *Big Ten Basketball* (Indianapolis, IN, 1994); Don Kopriva et al., *On Wisconsin* (Champaign, IL, 1998); Harold E. Foster file, Naismith Memorial Basketball Hall of Fame, Springfield, MA; Zander Hollander, ed., *The Pro Basketball Encyclopedia* (Los Angeles, CA, 1977); Ronald L. Mendell, *Who's Who in Basketball* (New Rochelle, NY, 1973); *Naismith Memorial Basketball Hall of Fame Official Souvenir Book* (Springfield, MA, 1974); Ken Shouler et al., *Total Basketball* (Wilmington, DE, 2003); University of Wisconsin Athletic Office, Madison, WI.

John L. Evers

FOUST, Lawrence Michael "Larry" (b. June 24, 1928, Painesville, OH; d. October 27, 1984, Pittsburgh, PA), college and professional player, was one of the first examples of a pro basketball big man (six-feet nine-inches, 250 pounds), demonstrating the complete skills of a well-coordinated athlete in his 12-season NBA career. Foust honed his considerable basketball skills in highly competitive basketball at South Catholic High and LaSalle College, both in Philadelphia. At this unusual time, five Philadelphia college teams were phenomenally successful. During his four years at LaSalle (1946–1950), he scored 1,464 points, averaged 14.2 points, played in the 1948 NIT, and received some All-America mention. As a senior, he was named to the *TSN* All-America Fifth Team. His athletic ability for a big man made him a first-round NBA draft choice for the Chicago Stags (NBA) in 1950, but his draft rights were acquired by the Fort Wayne Pistons (NBA) in the dispersal of the Chicago franchise. In one of his first games as a pro, rookie Foust in November hit a field goal with six seconds left to give the Pistons a 19-18 win over the powerful Minneapolis Lakers. The contest produced a record low score for the NBA and ended the Lakers' 29-game home win streak. In April 1957 the Fort Wayne franchise shifted to Detroit (NBA).

After seven seasons with the Pistons, Foust was traded to Minneapolis (NBA) before the 1957–1958 season. He played two full seasons and much of a third there before being traded in February 1960 to the St. Louis Hawks (NBA). Two full seasons at St. Louis completed his NBA career. Foust scored 11,198 points in regular-season NBA play for a 13.7-point average and added another 902 points in playoff games. He was selected for the first East-West NBA All-Star Game in 1951 and made it seven more consecutive years. Foust was named a First Team All-Star after the 1954–1955 season, in which he led the NBA in field goal percentage. An excellent rebounder, Foust led the NBA with 980 in the 1951–1952 season. In November 1957 for the Lakers, he made 22 of 26 free throws in a game against St. Louis.

BIBLIOGRAPHY: Gene Brown, *NYT Encyclopedia of Sports*, Vol. 3 (New York, 1979); Jan Hubbard, ed., *The Official NBA Encyclopedia*, 3rd ed. (New York, 2000); Neil D. Isaacs, *All the Moves: A History of College Basketball* (Philadelphia, PA, 1975); Neil D. Isaacs, *Vintage NBA* (Silver Spring, MD, 1996); *LaSalle College Basketball Media Guides, 1946–1950* (Philadelphia, PA, 1946–1950); *TSN Official NBA Register, 2004–2005* (St. Louis, MO, 2004); *TSN Official NBA Guides, 1951–1961* (St. Louis, MO, 1951–1961); Stew Thornley, *Basketball's Original Dynasty: The History of the Lakers* (Minneapolis, MN, 1989).

Robert B. Van Atta

FRANCIS, Clarence "Bevo" (b. September 5, 1932, Hammondsville, OH), college and professional player, is the son of a clay miner. After missing two years of school because of chronic anemia as a child, Francis played pick-up basketball games on weekends in a barn. He attended Irondale (Ohio) High School in 1948–1949 but played no basketball. His family moved to Wellsville, Ohio in 1949 amid reports that alumni and boosters exerted undue influence. The OSAA declared Francis ineligible for basketball during the 1949–1950 and 1950–1951 seasons. In 1951–1952, he led Ohio in scoring with 776 points (31.0-point average) in 25 games and tallied 57 points against Alliance High School. Francis outscored the entire opposing team six different times, once by 21 points. His honors included making All-Ohio and receiving an HAF citation. After participating in the North-South classic at Murray, Kentucky, Francis garnered Third Team All-America accolades. He secretly married Mary Chrislip of Wellsville his sophomore year and has one son, Frank.

Although not receiving his high school diploma until January 1953, Francis received 63 college basketball scholarship offers and enrolled at tiny Rio Grande College in Ohio in September 1952. Newt Oliver, his fiery high school basketball coach, became Rio Grande hoops mentor in 1952 and made the six-foot nine-inch center the nation's most publicized, prolific scoring collegiate basketball player. The carefree, shy, unassuming Francis led Rio Grande to a 39-0 record. Several teams triple teamed him in 1952–1953, but he still broke all existing college scoring records with 1,954 points (50.1-point average) in 39 games and helped Rio Grande tally over 100 points a game. In a 150-85 victory over Ashland (Kentucky) JC, he shattered all single-game scoring records with 116 points. Fifty-five of those points came in the 10-minute last quarter. His other offensive outbursts included 76 points against Lees JC, 72 against California (Pennsylvania) State Teacher's College, 69 against Wilberforce University, and 68 against Mountain State College. The NCAA did not share the fans' admiration for Francis's fabulous exploits and refused to recognize any of his records set against non-four-year colleges. Rio Grande had drawn numerous spectators against JC and armed forces teams, profiting considerably on its basketball program. Francis probably rescued the 92-student college from closing for financial reasons. Rio Grande was eliminated in the second round of the 1953 NAIA tournament.

In 1953–1954, Oliver's team scheduled only 27 games and played more formidable opponents in larger arenas. Francis even performed before 13,800 fans at Madison Square Garden in New York. Rio Grande earned up to $35,000 a game and compiled a 20-7 mark, averaging 91.3 points. Francis easily led collegiate scorers with 1,255 points, averaging 46.5 points. His 444 field goals made, 510 free throw attempts, 367 free throws converted, 1,255 points, and 46.5-point average all set NCAA official single-season records. Rio Grande scored 2,465 points, making Francis the only NCAA player to record over half of his team's points in a season. He tallied 113 points against Hillsdale College on February 2, establishing official NCAA records for points, field goals (38), free throws (37), and free throw attempts (45). Other scoring outbursts produced 84, 82, 72, 69, and 61 points. Against Alliance College, he made a record 71 field goal attempts. During two seasons, he scored 1,176 field goals, 898 free throws, and 3,250 career points (50.1-point average). Francis, who made Second Team All-America both years, relinquished his final two years of eligibility and joined the Boston Whirlwinds on professional tours against the Harlem Globetrotters. He played minor league basketball until 1962 and later was employed in construction and trucking.

BIBLIOGRAPHY: Peter C. Bjarkman, *The Biographical History of Basketball* (Chicago, IL, 2000); Ken Davis, "Is Bevo Big League?" *Sport* 16 (January 1954), pp. 26–27, 72–74; *The Lincoln Library of Sports Champions*, vol. 5 (Columbus, OH, 1974), pp. 8–11; Bill Mokray, "Bevo of Rio Grande," *SR: B* 14 (1954), pp. 22–24; *NCAA Official Collegiate Basketball Record Book*, 1955 (New York, 1955); Wayne Patterson and Lisa Fisher, *100 Greatest Basketball Players* (New York, 1989); Reference Librarian, J. A. Davis Library, University of Rio Grande, Rio Grande, OH, letter to David L. Porter, April 5, 1994.

David L. Porter

FRANK, Bertha. *See* Teague, Bertha Frank

FRATELLO, Michael Robert "Mike" "The Czar" (b. February 24, 1947, Hackensack, NJ), college and professional coach and sportscaster, is the son of Vincent Fratello, a champion boxer. The diminutive, five-foot seven-inch, 150-pound Fratello participated in football, basketball, and baseball at Hackensack High School and graduated in 1965. He earned a Bachelor's Degree from Montclair (New Jersey) State University in 1969.

Fratello's first coaching experience came in 1969–1970, when he was named head football and basketball coach at his high school alma mater. The following two seasons, he served as an assistant basketball coach while pursuing graduate work at the University of Rhode Island. He spent from 1972–1973 through 1974–1975 as an assistant basketball coach at James Madison University and worked under coach Rollie Massimino at Villanova University for three seasons.

Fratello moved to the professional ranks as an assistant basketball coach with the Atlanta Hawks (NBA) under the tutelage of Hubie

Brown and Kevin Loughery from 1978–1979 through 1981–1982. The following season, he joined Brown with the New York Knicks (NBA) for one campaign.

Fratello served as head coach of the Atlanta Hawks from 1983 to 1990 and assumed vice presidential duties from 1986 to 1990. In seven seasons as head coach, he compiled a 324-250 win-loss record in regular-season games. Atlanta's best season under Fratello came in 1986–1987, when the Hawks won 57 games to capture the Central Division crown. Following this exceptional season, Fratello was named NBA Coach of the Year. Atlanta qualified for the NBA playoffs in five of his seven seasons at the helm. The Hawks posted an 18-23 win-loss record in postseason play.

In 1990, Fratello joined NBC Sports as an NBA analyst for three years. In 1993, he accepted the head coaching position with the Cleveland Cavaliers (NBA). Fratello led the Cavaliers for six seasons, collecting 224 victories and 212 losses. After winning only two of 14 NBA playoff games in four appearances, the Cavaliers dismissed Fratello in June 1999. He became only the 18th NBA coach to win 500 games with a career record of 612 victories and 428 losses, and qualified for the NBA playoffs in 10 of 14 seasons.

Fratello signed with Turner Sports in 1999 as a NBA analyst and was teamed with Marv Albert, who nicknamed him "Czar of the Telestrator." In March 2003, the Miami Heat (NBA) contracted him to join its broadcasting team. He replaced the ailing Hubie Brown as coach of the Memphis Grizzlies (NBA) in December 2004. Memphis finished 40-26 after his arrival and made the playoffs, being swept by the Phoenix Suns in four games.

BIBLIOGRAPHY: "Mike Fratello," *The Czar Is Back*, http://www.armchairqb.com (1999); "Mike Fratello," *Joins Heat*, http://www.heat.com (2003); "Mike Fratello," *Our Chairman*, http://www.blueandgoldscholarship.com (2002); "Mike Fratello," *Speaker*, http://www.allamericanspeakers.com (2002); "Mike Fratello," *Turner Sports*, http://www.tnt.com (2003); Ken Shouler et al., *Total Basketball* (Wilmington, DE, 2003); *TSN Official NBA Register, 2003–2004* (St. Louis, MO, 2003).

John L. Evers

FRAZIER, Walter, II "Clyde" "Walt" (b. March 29, 1945, Atlanta, GA), college and professional player, is the son of Walter I. Frazier, a hustler, and Eula (Wynn) Frazier. He grew up among eight siblings and played basketball on dirt playgrounds with older children. At David T. Howard High School in Atlanta, Georgia, Frazier excelled in basketball and football. The prep quarterback rejected football scholarships to the University of Kansas and Indiana University to attend Southern Illinois University on a basketball scholarship. The six-foot four-inch, 205-pound Frazier starred for the Salukis from 1963–1964 through 1966–1967, but did not play during the 1965–1966 season because of ineligibility. He married his wife, Marsha, in 1965 and had one son, Walter III, before their divorce. He never remarried. During the 1966–1967 season, Frazier led Southern Illinois University to the NIT Championship. He was named MVP in the NIT, Southern Illinois' MVP, Little All-America, and to *TSN* All-America Second Team.

A first-round choice of the New York Knickerbockers (NBA) in the 1967 NBA draft, Frazier made the All-Rookie team in 1967–1968 and starred with the Knicks for 10 seasons. Frazier, one of the NBA's best defensive players, helped lead the Knicks to their only NBA championships in 1969–1970 and 1972–1973. Frazier excelled as a clutch shooter and tough defender, and was named to the NBA's All-Defensive First Team for seven years (1969–1975). Named to the NBA All-Star First Team (1970, 1972, 1974–1975) and the All-NBA Second Team (1971, 1973), he scored 30 points in the 1975 All-Star Game at Phoenix, Arizona, to become the game's MVP. The Knicks retired his uniform number 10.

After playing two years for the Cleveland Cavaliers (NBA), Frazier retired as a player. In 825 regular-season games through 1978–1979, he scored 15,581 points for an 18.9 points-per-game average and made 5,040 assists (6.1 assists per game). He appeared in 93 playoff games, scoring 1,927 points for a 20.7 points average and making 599 assists. He led the Knicks in scoring five consecutive seasons (1970–1971 through 1974–1975) and in assists 10 straight campaigns (1967–1968 through 1976–1977).

He remains the Knicks' all-time assists leader with 4,791.

Off the court, Frazier exhibited a lively lifestyle with his Rolls Royce and expensively decorated bachelor apartment on Manhattan's East Side. Frazier, a flamboyant dresser and co-author of the book *Clyde*, is the center of attention with an extensive wardrobe and has been named among the 10 best-dressed men in sports. His investments include the "Walt Frazier Enterprises," in which he represents other athletes. He was named to the Naismith Memorial Basketball Hall of Fame in 1987 and the Madison Square Garden Hall of Fame in 1984. He has served as analyst for Knicks games on MSG Network Cable Television since 1989, using creative, often rhyming phrases. He worked as a player agent in Atlanta and hosted a sports bar in New York. The NBA named him one of the 50 Greatest Players in NBA history in 1996.

BIBLIOGRAPHY: *Current Biography Yearbook* (1973), pp. 141–143; Walt Frazier, *Walt Frazier: One Magic Season and a Basketball Life* (New York, 1988); Walt Frazier and Ira Burkow, *Rookin' Steady: A Guide to Basketball and Mr. Cool* (Englewood Cliffs, NJ, 1974); Walt Frazier and Joe Jares, *Clyde: The Walt Frazier Story* (New York, 1970); Walt Frazier file, Naismith Memorial Basketball Hall of Fame, Springfield, MA; Jan Hubbard, ed., *The Official NBA Encyclopedia*, 3rd ed. (New York, 2000); Phil Pepe, "Watch Clyde Glide-Court Magician," *TSN*, February 15, 1975, p. 3; *TSN Official NBA Register, 2004–2005* (St. Louis, MO, 2004).

John L. Evers

FREE, Lloyd. *See* Free, World B.

FREE, World B. (b. Lloyd Free, December 9, 1953, Atlanta, GA), college and professional player, coach, and executive, is the son of Charles Free and Earlene Free and grew up in Brooklyn, New York, where his father worked as a longshoreman. Although born Lloyd Free, he changed his name legally to World B. Free.

Free played college basketball at Guilford College (CrC) in Greensboro, North Carolina. As a freshman, the six-foot two-inch, 180-pound guard teamed with M.L. Carr to lead Guilford to the 1973 NAIA championship. Free, who was named MVP of the tournament—the only freshman so honored—was selected First Team All-NAIA All-America in 1974 and 1975. In the summer of 1974, he was chosen MVP of an NAIA team that won a silver medal in the WCN Tournament in Bogotá, Colombia. His honors also included being named in 1987 to the NAIA Golden Anniversary Team. He scored 2,006 points in three seasons at Guilford, averaging 23.3 points per game.

Free turned professional after the 1975 season. The Philadelphia 76ers (NBA) made him a second-round draft pick. He spent three campaigns in Philadelphia before being traded to the San Diego Clippers (NBA), where he played two seasons. Free played with the Golden State Warriors (NBA) until the middle of the 1983 season, when he was traded to the Cleveland Cavaliers (NBA). He returned to Philadelphia in 1987, played with the Miami Tropics (USBL) in 1987, and finished his career the following season with the Houston Rockets (NBA). Free scored 17,955 NBA points, averaging 20.3 points and compiling 3,319 assists. Free averaged 28.8 points in 1979 and 30.2 points in 1980, finishing behind only George Gervin* in the NBA scoring race each of those seasons. Besides placing in the top 10 in scoring in 1981, 1982, 1983, and 1986, he was named All-NBA Second Team in 1979 and scored 14 points in the 1980 NBA All-Star Game.

The well-traveled Free proved an exciting if erratic player, famous for his creative shot selection. Coaches may have held their objections, but fans loved his daring style. Free, who has not married, served as strength and conditioning coach for the Philadelphia 76ers from 1994 to 1996 and as their community relations player representative since 1996.

BIBLIOGRAPHY: Herb Appenzeller, *Pride in the Past: Guilford College Athletics, 1837–1987* (Greensboro, NC, 1987); World Free file, Guilford College Sports Information Department, Greensboro, NC; Jan Hubbard, ed., *The Official NBA Basketball Encyclopedia*, 3rd ed. (New York, 2000); *TSN Official NBA Register, 2004–2005* (St. Louis, MO, 2004).

Jim L. Sumner

FREEMAN, James A. "Buck" (b. 1904, New York, NY; d. February 13, 1974, Columbia, SC), college player and coach, graduated in 1927 from

St. John's University, where he played basketball four seasons under coach John Crenny. He shared the team lead with an 8.2 point average in 1923–1924 and averaged 7.9 points in 1924–1925. Freeman helped St. John's to an 18-7 record his junior year, scoring a team-high 31 points against New York State-Agriculture. In his final season, he paced St. John's with a 6.8 point average. During 94 career games, he recorded 263 baskets and 166 free throws for 692 points and a 7.4 point average.

Freeman became head basketball coach and athletic director at his alma mater in 1927 and brought St. John's to national basketball prominence. He coached St. John's through 1936, winning 177 of 208 games for an .851 winning percentage. From 1927–1928 through 1930–1931, Freeman's "Wonder Five" became the first of many legendary New York City collegiate teams. Six-foot five-inch center Matty Begovich, forwards Mac Kinsbrunner and Max Posnack, and guards Rip Gerson and Allie Schuckman started all four years, lifting St. John's to an incredible 86-8 record. Freeman successfully adapted the monotonous style passing game of the New York Original Celtics. St. John's employed very disciplined ball control, excellent setshot selection, and tenacious switching defense.

Four of the Wonder Five's eight losses came their first season, as St. John's finished 18-4. Besides upsetting City College of New York, the Wonder Five averaged over 36 points and held opponents to under 10 points per contest. St. John's finished 23-2 in 1928–1929, outscoring opponents by 10 points a game when teams scored around 30 points per contest. Freeman's club used patient offense and air-tight defense to post a 23-1 ledger in 1929–1930. The Wonder Five compiled a 21-1 record against more formidable competition in 1930–1931, ranking second nationally and losing only to New York University. Due to the deliberate offense, college rules soon were changed to introduce the mid-court time line and the backcourt ten-second rule.

Freeman coached St. Johns six more seasons, guiding them to 22-4 in 1931–1932, 23-4 in 1932–1933, 16-3 in 1933–1934, and 18-4 in 1935–1936. St. John's drew huge crowds at Madison Square Garden for college games, enhancing the popularity of the sport.

In September 1937, St. Thomas College appointed Freeman head basketball coach. St. Thomas finished with a 12-9 mark in 1937–1938 under Freeman, averaging more than 40 points a game and finishing undefeated at home. Freeman resigned following that season to become athletic director at Iona Prep School in New York. He returned to St. Thomas (renamed the University of Scranton) during the 1946–1947 season after the team had lost eight of its first nine games. The Royals began to turn their season around under Freeman's leadership, winning nine of their last 19 games. Scranton, however, struggled to 7-20 in 1947–1948 and 9-16 in 1948–1949. Freeman in 1949 became head baseball coach at Ithaca College, having compiled a 37-55 record at Scranton. During his 13 seasons as a college basketball coach, he boasted a 214-86 composite record.

Freeman served as an assistant basketball coach under Frank McGuire* at the University of North Carolina from 1952 to 1961 and at the University of South Carolina from 1964 to 1973. He had coached McGuire at St. John's in the mid-1930s. North Carolina won the NCAA tournament in 1957, defeating Michigan State University 74-70 in triple overtime in the semifinals, and the University of Kansas 54-53 in the finals. The Tar Heels also qualified the NCAA tournament in 1959, while South Carolina made the NCAA tournament each of Freeman's last three years. Freeman, whose expertise helped those schools enjoy winning seasons 15 of 18 times, served as a special assistant and adviser to McGuire in 1973–1974.

BIBLIOGRAPHY: Peter C. Bjarkman, *The Biographical History of Basketball* (Chicago, IL, 2000); Mike Douchant, *Encyclopedia of College Basketball* (Detroit, MI, 1995); "Great Names in St. John's Basketball," http://www.redstormsports.com; *New York Times*, February 16, 1974, p. 34; "The Post-Harding Era 1937–1946," http://academic.Scranton.edu; Ken Shouler et al., *Total Basketball* (Wilmington, DE, 2003); "The Tommies Become the Royals 1946–1955," http://academic.Scranton.edu.

David L. Porter

FREEMAN, Robin (b. 1934, Cincinnati, OH), college player, starred in basketball at Hughes High School in Cincinnati. He found it difficult to shoot because of being guarded so closely and learned the techniques of the jumpshot from Paul Arizin*. The flat-footed setshot was the standard shooting method during this era. In developing an innovative jumpshot, Freeman added the "fadeaway" to the jumper. He first used the shot in competition in November 1951 of his senior year. The ball hit nothing but the net and became known as the "shot that was heard around Cincinnati." With the success of this shot and several more, Freeman went from a good to a sensational player overnight and packed the gymnasiums all over the city. Although not the best all-round player from the Cincinnati area, he made the biggest impact on the city. The five-foot eleven-inch guard became the most productive scorer in Cincinnati high school basketball history. During the 1951–1952 season, he averaged 39.5 points to establish a still-standing record. Freeman earned All-State honors, a scholarship to Ohio State University, and induction into the Greater Cincinnati Basketball Hall of Fame. He became the first player named to the All-Century Team by the *Cincinnati Post*.

Although the local universities recruited him, Freeman chose to play collegiate basketball at Ohio State University. He continued to break records and aroused a "basketball mania" among the fans that had never been seen before. In his sophomore year, Freeman scored 465 points and averaged 21.1 points. He played in only 13 games as a junior in 1954–1955 but recorded 409 points for 31.5 points per game. The publicity and attention caused Freeman stress problems and forced him to drop out of school temporarily. A healthy Freeman returned as a senior, scoring 723 points and averaging 32.9 points. He was named the BTC Player of the Year and a consensus All-America. In 1955–1956, he became the school's first repeat All-America and the BTC's first repeat 30-points-per-game player. One sub-20 point game cost him the national scoring title. Furman University's Darrell Floyd finished with a 33.8 points average when he poured in 62 points against the Citadel, beating Freeman's 32.9 point average. Freeman compiled 1,597 career points and averaged 28.0 points, still a Buckeye record.

Following his senior year, Freeman was drafted by the St. Louis Hawks (NBA) in 1956. Scouts predicted that he would have been an outstanding professional, but he severed the tips of two fingers while chopping wood during the off-season. Freeman had already made up his mind to attend law school and did not intend to play in the NBA. He still practices law in Springfield, Ohio.

BIBLIOGRAPHY: Peter J. Bjarkman, *The Biographical History of Basketball* (Chicago, IL 2000); Gary K. Johnson, *NCAA Men's Basketball's Finest* (Overland Park, KS, 1998); "Robin Freeman," *All-Century Team*, http://www.cincypost.com (1999); "Robin Freeman," *Got Jump on Competition*, http://www.enquirer.com (1997); "Robin Freeman," *A Prep Sensation*, http://www.cincypost.com (1999); "Robin Freeman," *Scoring Mark Still Standing*, http://www.cincinnati.com (2000).

John L. Evers

FRIEDMAN, Max "Marty" (b. July 12, 1889, New York, NY; d. January 1, 1986), professional player, was two years older than the game itself and regarded as the "greatest defensive guard in professional basketball." During a 17-year pro career from 1910 to 1927, Friedman played in every league in the East and usually led his teams to championship titles. Friedman, who did not attend college, played for the University Settlement House Metropolitan AAU champions from 1906 to 1908 in roped arenas and used chicken-wire cages. He frequently participated on three teams in the same season and played every night and often twice on Sunday, earning a top salary of $125 a month. Friedman played guard with Bernard Sedran* in 1908 on the Busy Izzies. The five-foot four-inch, 118-pound Sedran and the five-foot seven-inch, 138-pound Friedman were nicknamed "The Heavenly Twins." In 1909 he turned pro with the New York Roosevelts.

Friedman accomplished many achievements throughout his pro basketball career. His 1914 Utica, New York team won the world championship, while his 1915 Carbondale, Pennsylvania team won 35 straight games and captured the PSL championship as "The Wonder Workers." The onset of World War I and U.S. Army duty did not stop Friedman from playing basketball. After his commanding officer asked him if a great basketball player named "Marty" Friedman was related to him, he participated in U.S. Army basketball and organized a tournament in France with teams of American Expeditionary Forces servicemen. This competition, consisting of over 600 teams, started the Inter-Allied Games, the first international tournament that paved the way for world championship and Olympic recognition. Friedman captained The Tours team, which defeated France, 93-8, for the title in 1919. Dr. James Naismith*, the creator of basketball, witnessed the lopsided game.

Although statistics are incomplete, Friedman scored at least 1,323 pro points. Friedman played in 1921 with the New York Whirlwinds, a team he considered the greatest all-time pro squad. His illustrious teammates included Sedran and Nat Holman*. At the championship game, 11,000 spectators watched the Whirlwinds defeat the Original Celtics 40-27, and saw Friedman hold Celtics shooting phenom Johnny Beckman* to only one field goal. The Celtics won the second game 26-24, but the third and deciding game was never played for fear of the crowd excitement becoming unmanageable. From 1923 to 1927, he finished his incredible career as captain and coach of the Cleveland Rosenblums. Friedman was married to Evelyn Fischer and had two daughters, Ellen and Betty. Until his retirement in 1958, he worked in the real estate business. Besides being selected to numerous all-time pro teams, Friedman was enshrined in 1971 in the Naismith Memorial Basketball Hall of Fame as an outstanding player.

BIBLIOGRAPHY: Max Friedman file, Naismith Memorial Basketball Hall of Fame, Springfield, MA; Murry R. Nelson, *The Originals: The New York Celtics Invent Modern Basketball* (Bowling Green, OH, 1999); Robert W. Peterson, *Cages to Jumpshots: Pro Basketball's Early Years* (New York, 1990); Ken Shouler et al., *Total Basketball* (Wilmington, DE, 2003).

Catherine M. Derrick

FULKS, Joseph Franklin "Joe" (b. October 26, 1921, Birmingham, KY; d. March 21, 1976, Eddyville, KY), college and professional player, was born in a farmhouse and played basketball at Marshall County (Kentucky) High School and Kuttawa (Kentucky) High School, graduating from the latter. In 1938, he led Kuttawa to the Kentucky State tournament semifinals, breaking the state scoring record and making All-State. The six-foot four-inch, 190-pound inch Fulks attended Millsaps College in Jackson, Mississippi and Murray (KY) State University, where he played varsity basketball during the 1941–1942 and 1942–1943 seasons. In 47 games, he scored 621 points and averaged 13.2 points. He was named All-America by the NAIA in 1943 and selected an All-KIAC All-Star both seasons. He developed an innovative jumpshot, using a two-hand shot initially and gradually switching to the one-hand type popular today.

After playing service ball with the San Diego Marines, Fulks in 1947 signed with the Philadelphia Warriors (BAA). During his BAA-NBA career from 1947 to 1954, he scored 8,003 points in 489 regular-season games for a 16.4 points average. In 26 playoff contests, the wavy-haired Fulks averaged 19.0 points. His best pro year came in 1948–1949, when he averaged 26.0 points. On February 10, 1949, Fulks scored 63 points against the Indianapolis Jets (BAA). *TSN* termed him the "greatest basketball player in the country." Fulks, who won a scoring title in the 1946–1947 season and finished second in two other scoring races, also was considered a solid rebounder with exceptional leaping abilities.

Called "modern pro-basketball's first scoring sensation" and the "BAA's first superstar," Fulks was selected a member of the NBA's Silver Anniversary All-Star Team in 1970 and belongs to the NAIA (1952), Murray State, and Naismith Memorial Basketball Hall of Fame (1977). After retiring from basketball, Fulks worked as a production foreman at the GAF Corporation in Calvert, Kentucky, and scouted for the Philadelphia 76ers. He and his wife had four children before their separation. Fulks played on one pro championship team (1946–1947) and was All-BAA First team in 1947, 1948, and 1949. In 1946–1947 he unanimously was selected All-Pro. Fulks developed and popularized jump-shooting and was a pioneer of modern high-scoring basketball. He made the NBA's Silver Anniversary Team in 1970. Shortly after being hired as athletic director at Kentucky State Penitentiary, he was murdered in an argument over a gun with the son of a woman he was dating.

BIBLIOGRAPHY: Peter C. Bjarkman, *The History of the NBA* (New York, 1992); Joe Fulks file, Naismith Memorial Basketball Hall of Fame, Springfield, MA; Neil D. Isaacs, *Vintage NBA* (Silver Spring, MD, 1996); Ronald L. Mendell, *Who's Who in Basketball* (New Rochelle, NY, 1973); Murray State College, *Alumnus Magazine*, 1971, p.5; David S. Neft, *The Sports Encyclopedia: Pro Basketball* (New York, 1975); *Newsweek* 87 (April 5, 1976), p.59; *New York Times*, March 22, 1976; Robert W. Peterson, *Cages to Jumpshots: Pro Basketball's Early Years* (New York, 1990); Ken Shouler et al., *Total Basketball* (Wilmington, DE, 2003).

William A. Gudelunas

FUREY, James A. "Jim" (b. n.a.; d. n.a.), promoter, in November 1918 joined his brother, Tom, in reorganizing the New York Celtics professional basketball team. The Celtics had organized in 1914 as a settlement house team on Manhattan's West Side and had competed for three seasons before disbanding. Furey changed the team name to the Original Celtics and booked games with metropolitan teams. The Celtics, which included Pete Barry and John Whitty, won 65 of 69 games in 1918–1919. Furey the next season added forward Johnny Beckman* and guard Henry "Dutch" Dehnert*. The Celtics and formidable New York Whirlwinds split a two-game series in the spring of 1921 to share the unofficial championship of the metropolitan region.

Furey signed Whirlwinds stars Nat Holman* and Chris Leonard* for the 1921–1922 season and continued to add premier players, including Joe Lapchick*, Davey Banks*, George "Horse" Haggerty*, and Nat Hickey. The Celtics played weaker opponents as an independent because the Eastern League and New York State League refused to let their teams play the Celtics. Furey's efforts to buy the New York Giants (EL) and the Albany Senators (NYSL) failed. Furey took over the struggling Giants, which featured Barney Sedran* and Marty Friedman*, and won the Eastern League crown.

The Celtics briefly participated in the teetering Metropolitan League in 1922–1923 and then embarked on a barnstorming tour from September to April, recording 193 victories, 11 defeats, one tie, and losing three out of five games to the powerful Kingston Colonels. The Celtics featured Holman and Beckman at forwards, Dehnert and Leonard at guards, and Lapchick at center. Furey kept the Celtics intact, signing them to full-season contracts with generous salaries ranging up to $10,000 a year. Teams usually paid players on a nightly cash basis. Half a million spectators saw the Celtics tour 13 northeastern and midwestern states.

Furey's Celtics barnstormed the next three seasons, becoming the most famous team in the first half of the twentieth century. They played 102 to 140 games annually in the northeast, midwest, and south, with 134 wins, 6 losses, and 1 tie against largely amateur teams in 1923–1924, and 90 wins and 12 losses in 1925–1926, splitting six games with the all-black New York Renaissance.

The Celtics experienced management problems and joined the new American Basketball League in 1926–1927. Furey, who worked as head cashier of the Arnold, Constable department store in New York City, was accused in June 1926 of embezzling $187,000 from the store and was sentenced to Sing Sing prison for three years. The Celtics still featured Holman, Lapchick, Dehnert, Leonard, Beckman, and Barry and won consecutive ABL titles in 1926–1927 and 1927–1928.

The ABL dissolved the Celtics because of declining fan attendance and assigned its players to other teams. Lapchick, Holman, and Barry joined the Cleveland Rosenblums, which so dominated the ABL that the league dissolved in 1929, the year Furey was released from prison.

BIBLIOGRAPHY: Peter C. Bjarkman, *The Biographical History of Basketball* (Chicago, IL, 2000); Murry Nelson, *The Originals: The New York Celtics Invent Modern Basketball* (Bowling Green, OH, 1999); Robert W. Peterson, *Cages to Jumpshots: Pro Basketball's Early Years* (New York, 1990); Ken Shouler, et al., *Total Basketball* (Wilmington, DE, 2003).

David L. Porter

G

GAINES, Clarence Edward "Bighouse" (b. May 21, 1923, Paducah, KY; d. April 18, 2005, Winston-Salem, NC), college player, coach, and administrator, guided Winston-Salem (North Carolina) State University to the 1967 NCAA College Division II National Championship, making it the first predominantly black school to achieve an NCAA basketball title. Gaines was named 1967 College Division II Basketball Coach of the Year after guiding the Rams to a 31-1 season. As the coach of Winston-Salem basketball teams for 41 years (1947–1993), he amassed a composite 828-447 (.649 percent) record and remains the fifth winningest coach in NCAA men's basketball history. Gaines was named in 1982 to the Naismith Memorial Basketball Hall of Fame, the first inducted coach to spend an entire career at a black college.

Gaines, the son of Lester Gaines and Olivia (Bolen) Gaines, graduated from Lincoln High School in Paducah, Kentucky in 1941. He was class salutatorian, made All-State in football, and played trumpet in the band. Gaines attended Morgan State University (Maryland), where he starred in football. He played basketball merely to remain in good physical condition between grid seasons. After graduating with a B.S. degree in chemistry from Morgan State in 1945, Gaines earned a Master of Arts degree from Columbia University in New York City. He began coaching basketball as a temporary assignment that developed into a lifelong vocation. The six-foot four-inch, 300-pound Gaines coached fast-break, race-horse basketball, utilizing speed to overwhelm the opposition. Winston-Salem State University belonged to the strong CIAA, which once had 18 member schools and in the early 1970s split into Northern and Southern Divisions. Gaines' early duties included not only coaching and scheduling, but also serving as publicity director for an institution emerging from athletic obscurity.

Gaines led Winston-Salem State University to 17 20-victory seasons, including seven in succession between 1961 and 1967 when the Rams reached the pinnacle of success. The Scarlet and White achieved three consecutive CIAA championships (1961–1963) with 26-5, 24-5, and 23-7 finishes. The Rams' Cleo Hill in 1961 became the greatest scorer in CIAA history (778 points, 27.8 points average, and tenth national ranking) and completed an outstanding four years with 2,352 career points to rank eighth in NCAA College Division history. All-CIAA Ted Blunt and Richard Glover returned the next two seasons to lead the Rams to additional titles.

Winston-Salem State University finished 22-4 in 1964 for the best record in the CIAA, but lost the championship to North Carolina Agricultural and Technical (A&T) State University by a vote of league members. The Rams finished 25-8 in 1965 and 21-5 in 1966 when six-foot four-inch guard Earl "The Pearl" Monroe* sparked them to the CIAA postseason tournament title. Monroe finished the season with 746 points (29.8 points average) and a twelfth-place ranking nationally. Winston-Salem's only loss in 1967 (a second defeat was reversed by forfeit) occurred when North Carolina A&T, whom the Rams had bested twice earlier, defeated them in the CIAA tourney. The Rams entered the NCAA tournament boasting a 101.9 points scoring average.

They triumphed over Baldwin-Wallace College (Ohio) 91-76 and the University of Akron (Ohio) 88-80 in the Mideast Regional to qualify for the quarterfinals at Evansville, Indiana. Winston-Salem State University captured the national championship by defeating Long Island University (New York) 62-54, defending champion Kentucky Wesleyan College 82-73, and Southwest Missouri State University 77-74. The Rams surprised their last three opponents with a deliberate style of play on offense and tenacious defense. Winston-Salem's excellent shooting (over .500 percent team average) enabled them to overcome size and rebounding deficiencies. Monroe took the tournament by storm, averaging over 35 points per game and feeding teammates Gene Smiley and Bill English for easy baskets. Monroe finished the season with 1,329 points (41.5 points average) to lead the nation in scoring with the highest single-season total in NCAA history. He was Division II AP and UPI All-America and 1967 Player of the Year, and was drafted by the Baltimore Bullets (NBA).

Winston-Salem State University captured several CIAA Southern Division titles, including a group of freshmen who produced a 23-7 record in 1975. Three years later, six-foot seven-inch Reginald Gaines led the Rams to the division title with a 28-4 finish. Coach Gaines insisted that his players study, attend classes, and refrain from seeking special privileges. Encouraged by Gaines to graduate, many of his former players are lawyers, physicians, and educators, hold political offices, and own businesses. He retired in 1993 after 47 seasons. Gaines credits his mother, Olivia, and aunt, Nancy Strickland, for character building and instilling in him a fine sense of values. He married Clara Lucille Berry, a Latin teacher, in 1950 and had two children, Clarence Jr. and Lisa, and resided in Winston-Salem. Gaines served as president of the NABC in 1989, president of the CIAA from 1970 to 1974, and on the USOC.

BIBLIOGRAPHY: Peter C. Bjarkman, *A Century of College Basketball, 1896–1996* (Indianapolis, IN, 1996); Clarence Gaines file, Naismith Memorial Basketball Hall of Fame, Springfield, MA; Clarence Gaines file, Winston-Salem State University, Winston-Salem, NC; Nelson George, *Elevating the Game: Black Men in Basketball* (New York, 1992); Neil D. Isaacs, *All the Moves: A History of College Basketball* (Philadelphia, PA, 1975); *NCAA Men's Basketball Records, 2004* (Indianapolis, IN, 2003); *Official Collegiate Basketball Guides, 1951–1981* (New York, 1951–1988); *TCSM,* May 10, 1982, p. 11; Billy Packer with Roland Lazenby *The Golden Game* (Dallas, TX, 1991); Ralph Wiley, "College Basketball Preview 1990–1991: Bighouse," *SI* (November 19, 1990).

James D. Whalen and Wayne Patterson

GALE, Lauren Henry "Laddie" (b. April 19, 1916, Gold Beach, OR; d. July 29, 1996), college player, was the son of Lauren A. Gale and Charlotte (Smith) Gale. After his parents separated, Gale lived with his mother and attended grade school in Portland, Oregon. He moved to Oakridge, Oregon, where his father worked as an engineer on the Southern Pacific Railroad. A natural athlete, Gale started four years on the Oakridge High School basketball team and won All-State honors his senior year in 1935. As a freshman at the University of Oregon, he teamed with Slim Wintermute, Bobby Anet, and Wally Johansen. These four, later nicknamed the "Tall Firs," formed the University of Oregon's nucleus for the next three seasons. The six-foot four-inch Gale and Wintermute, the tallest team members, led Oregon to records of 20-9 in 1936–1937, 25-8 in 1937–1938, and 29-5 in 1938–1939. Oregon tied for the Northern Division title in 1936–1937, but lost in divisional playoffs. Gale missed much of the season because of a broken finger. Although winning the Northern Division Championship in 1937–1938, Oregon lost to Stanford University in the PCC Finals. The next season, they took a second straight Northern Division crown and defeated the University of California-Berkeley for the PCC title. Gale, All-PCC in 1938 and 1939, led the Northern Division in scoring both seasons by averaging 12.5 and 11.6 points. He made some All-America teams in 1938 and was a consensus pick in 1939.

Coach Howard Hobson's* team participated in the initial NCAA tournament in 1939 and defeated the Universities of Texas and Oklahoma and Ohio State University to become the NCAA's first national champion. Because the University of Oregon was a balanced team, the superb-shooting Gale might have scored even more points with another school. Nevertheless, he finished his career at Oregon with 889 points and made the All-Northern Division Commemorative Team for its first 50 years.

Although not initially interested in pro basketball, Gale joined the Detroit Eagles in January 1940 at Wintermute's request and earned $7,500 for three months of play. He entered military service but still played basketball for his camp teams. After World War II, Gale served as player-coach of the Salt Lake City-*Deseret Times* team for two years and of the Oakland Bittners for two seasons. In 1948 he directed the Bittners to the quarterfinals of the Olympic Trials. After working in Salem, Eugene, and Florence, Oregon, Gale settled in Gold Beach with his own real estate business. Married twice, he had three children and two stepchildren. Gale, who helped bring national recognition to Pacific Northwest basketball, is a member of the Oregon Sports Hall of Fame and the Naismith Memorial Basketball Hall of Fame (1976).

BIBLIOGRAPHY: Lauren Gale file, Naismith Memorial Basketball Hall of Fame, Springfield, MA; Howard Hobson, *Shooting Ducks: A History of University of Oregon Basketball* (Portland, OR, 1984); Ronald L. Mendell, *Who's Who in Basketball* (New Rochelle, NY, 1973); *NCAA Men's Basketball Records, 2004* (Indianapolis, IN, 2003); Ken Rappoport, *The Classic: History of the NCAA Championship* (Mission, KS, 1979); Thomas W. Ricker, ed., "Lauren 'Laddie' Gale," *Converse Basketball Yearbook* (Wilmington, MA, 1977), p. 21; Jim Savage, ed., *The Encyclopedia of the NCAA Basketball Tournament* (New York, 1990).

Dennis S. Clark

GALLATIN, Harry "The Horse" (b. April 26, 1926, Roxana, IL), college and professional player and coach, is the son of Henry Gallatin and Cecile Gallatin, and grew up in little Roxana. Gallatin's height of six feet six inches guaranteed him a career in the growing sport of basketball. After graduating from high school in his hometown, Gallatin entered Northeast Missouri State Teachers College. His stay there was interrupted by a hitch in the U.S. Navy (1945–1946). On his return, he joined Northeast Missouri's basketball team, made All-MIAC for two seasons, and averaged 13.2 points per game. That record earned him election to the NAIA Hall of Fame in 1957 and made him the first-round draft pick of the New York Knickerbockers (NBA) in 1948.

Gallatin scored an instant success in New York by using his quickness in the pivot to outrebound bigger, slower men like the Minneapolis Lakers' George Mikan*. From the 1950–1951 season until his retirement after the 1957–1958 season, Gallatin pulled down at least 660 rebounds in a season and averaged well over 10 a game. He also scored in double figures all but his rookie year and played in the All-Star Game seven consecutive years from 1951 to 1957. Gallatin also set a consecutive game streak of 682 regular-season contests. With the Knicks for all but his final season with the Detroit Pistons (1957–1958), he finished his playing career with a scoring average of 13.0 points.

Gallatin then took the head basketball coach's position at Southern Illinois University-Carbondale and enjoyed four winning seasons there with a 79-35 record before joining the St. Louis Hawks (NBA) as coach. Shaping the Hawks squad around a controlled fast break and pattern play, Gallatin led St. Louis to consecutive second-place finishes in 1962–1963 and 1963–1964 and was named Coach of the Year in 1963. The next year, Gallatin was named head coach of his hapless former team, the New York Knicks. Gallatin was replaced by former teammate Dick McGuire* after one and one-half seasons. He compiled a 136-120 record (.531 winning percentage) as a NBA coach.

Gallatin returned to his native state once more, settling in at Southern Illinois University-Edwardsville, and put his 1954 Master of Arts degree from the University of Iowa to good use. After brief stints as athletic director, dean of students, and basketball coach with a 19-31 (.380 winning percentage) record, Gallatin found his niche as an associate professor of physical education and coach of the golf team. An all-around athlete who had even spent two years in 1948–1949 in the Chicago Cubs (NL) minor league baseball system, Gallatin long had harbored an affection for golf and initiated the program at Southern Illinois. He enjoyed considerable success in his first 18 years as its coach, winning 13

NCAA tourney berths in a 15-year period. He currently resides in Edwardsville with his wife, Beverly, and their three sons. Gallatin is best remembered as a tough, physical forward and pivot man who rebounded beyond his size in what the *NYT*'s George Vecsey called "the milk-wagon era" of the NBA. He was elected to the Naismith Memorial Basketball Hall of Fame in 1991.

BIBLIOGRAPHY: Glenn Dickey, *The History of Professional Basketball* (Briarcliff Manor, NY, 1982); Harry Gallatin file, Naismith Memorial Basketball Hall of Fame, Springfield MA; Neil D. Isaacs, *Vintage NBA* (Silver Spring, MD, 1996); *TSN Official NBA Register, 2004–2005* (St. Louis, MO, 2004); Leonard Koppett, *24 Seconds to Shoot: An Informal History of the NBA* (New York, 1968); Ronald L. Mendell, *Who's Who in Basketball* (New Rochelle, NY, 1973); Charles Salzberg, *From Set Shot to Slam Dunk—The Glory Days of Basketball in the Words of Those Who Played It* (New York, 1987); Ken Shouler et al., *Total Basketball* (Wilmington, DE, 2003); George Vecsey, "The Oldest of the Old-Timers," *NYT*, February 7, 1987, p.47.

George Robinson

GARDNER, James Hamlin "The Fox" (b. March 29, 1910, Texico, NM; d. April 9, 2000, Salt Lake City, UT), college player and coach, was the youngest of four children of George M. Gardner and Lilly (Kemp) Gardner and moved to Southern California as a youth. He graduated from Redlands (California) High School as a 16-letter winner in four sports and from the University of Southern California in 1932. At Southern California, Gardner in 1931–1932 captained the basketball squad, led the Trojans in scoring, made the All-PCC team, and won the MVP award. Gardner and his wife, Marion, whom he married on August 29, 1935, had one son, James. Gardner coached an AAU team to a 20-3 mark in 1933–1934 while attending graduate school at the University of Southern California. His Alhambra (California) High School basketball units compiled a 29-11 overall mark in 1934–1935 and 1935–1936, taking two conference titles. Gardner spent four seasons (1936–1937 through 1939–1940) at Modesto (California) Junior College, where his basketball squads won 83 games, lost 27 contests, and took three state titles.

Gardner enjoyed a successful tenure as head basketball coach at Kansas State University (1940–1953) that was interrupted by military service from 1942 to 1946. In 1943 he coached the Olathe (Kansas) Naval Base basketball team to a 31-2 mark. From 1940 to 1943 and 1946 to 1953, Kansas State finished 147-81 overall and 66-46 in the BSC under Gardner's tutelage. The Wildcats won three BSC crowns and made Final Four appearances at the 1948 (fourth place) and 1951 (second place) NCAA tournaments. The formidable University of Kentucky defeated Kansas State, 68-58, in the 1951 NCAA Championship Game at Minneapolis, Minnesota. Howard Shannon, Clarence Brannum, Rick Harmon, Lew Hitch, Ernie Barrett, and Dick Knostman made All-America during Gardner's Kansas State stint. All except Harmon later played professionally in the NBA. In 1950 Kansas State constructed a new basketball arena.

Gardner then coached basketball at the University of Utah from 1953 to 1971, during which time the Utes boasted a 339-154 composite mark and 154-70 SKC and WAC record. The Utah basketball program was rebuilding on Gardner's arrival and won 12 of 26 games his initial season there. From 1954–1955 to 1961–1962, the "Runnin' Redskins" combined fast breaks and high scoring to take five SKC Championships, share another SKC, title, and place second twice. Gardner led his squad to a 51-5 performance in SKC games from 1958–1959 through 1961–1962. The 1960–1961 and 1965–1966 Utes, the latter being the only WAC team to take the Far West regionals, finished fourth in the NCAA championships. Gardner remains the only coach to direct two schools to the NCAA Final Four at least twice. Only Adolph Rupp*, Dean Smith*, Mike Krzyzewski*, Denny Crum*, Bob Knight*, Lute Olson*, Guy Lewis*, and John Wooden*, guided more teams to the Final Four. Utah qualified for either the NCAA or NIT tournaments 10 of Gardner's 18 seasons and experienced only two losing campaigns. All-Americas Art Bunte, Bill McGill, Jerry Chambers, Merv Jackson, and Mike Newlin played under Gardner at Utah, with all except Bunte playing in the NBA.

A proponent of executing fundamentals, Gardner made a considerable impact on college basketball by developing record-keeping and using the fast break. *Championship Basketball with Jack Gardner* described his running, high-scoring basketball style. The Coach of the Year several times, Gardner was elected to the HAF Hall of Fame (1971), Naismith Memorial Basketball Hall of Fame (1984), and Utah Sports Hall of Fame. His other honors included the Dole Rex Award (1955) and the NABC Merit and Honor Award (1969) for his contributions to basketball in the Rocky Mountain area. Gardner also coached the West squad in the 1953 and 1960 College All-Star Games at Kansas City, Missouri, and the East team in the 1964 College All-Star Game at Lexington, Kentucky. In 1964 he coached the tryout camp for the undefeated U.S. Summer Olympic Team.

During 28 years of intercollegiate coaching, Gardner produced 486 victories and only 235 losses for a .674 percentage. He ranked third among active coaches in career victories upon his retirement in 1971. Numerous head coaches, including Ladell Anderson, Tex Winter, Morris Buckwalter, Howard Shannon, Fordy Anderson, and Bob Johnson, either played under or assisted Gardner. Gardner conducted basketball clinics in 39 European, Oriental, and Latin American nations and was National Coordinator in the 1970s for PASE, a program organizing basketball clinics and exchanging coaches with Latin America. During the 1970s, Gardner also coached golf at the University of Utah. He retired as golf coach in 1978 and served as a consultant with the Utah Jazz (NBA) basketball team.

BIBLIOGRAPHY: Mike Douchant, *Encyclopedia of College Basketball* (Detroit, MI, 1995); Jack Gardner to David L. Porter, April 17, 1988; James Gardner file, Naismith Memorial Basketball Hall of Fame, Springfield, MA; *NCAA Men's Basketball Records, 2004* (St. Louis, MO, 2003); Wayne Patterson to David L. Porter, February 29, 1988; Salt Lake City Tribune Staff, ed., *Runnin' Utes Basketball* (Champaign, IL, 1998).

David L. Porter

GARMAKER, Richard Eugene "Dick" (b. October 29, 1932, Hibbing, MN), college and professional player, excelled in basketball at Hibbing (Minnesota) High School and for two years at Hibbing JC. He played basketball during the 1950–1951 and 1951–1952 seasons for the Cardinals before transferring to the University of Minnesota (BTC); because of the transfer rule, Garmaker was not eligible to play during the 1952–1953 season. During this era, the BTC had not used many JC players. Garmaker's scored 37 points in his first conference game for the Gophers in 1954, and became an NCAA consensus All-America the following season. In his junior and senior seasons, he registered 1,008 points, averaged 22.9 points and cleared 340 rebounds for an average of 7.7 boards. The six-foot three-inch, 200-pound Garmaker posted a 40 percent field goal shooting percentage, connecting on 333 field goals in 834 attempts. From the free throw line, he netted 342 free throws in 400 attempts for a 74.3 shooting percentage. In his two seasons at Minnesota, the Gophers triumphed 32 times in 44 games. Garmaker made the All-BTC First Team in 1954 and 1955, with his 1,008 career points ranking him 23rd on the school's all-time scoring list. In 1953–1954, he became the first Gopher to score 500 plus points in a season. He ranks first for average points in a career (22.9) and in the BTC (24.8). Garmaker ranked first in free throws made and attempted in both the BTC and all games in a single season. He netted 181 free throws and 137 in the BTC in one season.

Garmaker was drafted in the first round as the sixth choice overall by the Minneapolis Lakers (NBA) in both the 1954 and 1955 NBA drafts and their territorial pick in 1955. He signed with Minneapolis in 1955 and played four seasons and an additional 44 games with the Lakers in 1959–1960 before being traded to the New York Knicks (NBA) in 1960. He completed his NBA career with the Knicks playing in 26 games in 1960 and 70 games in 1960–1961. Garmaker was involved in a very anxious incident prior to being traded to the Knicks. On January 18, 1960, the Los Angeles Lakers team plane was reported missing. The team plane was enroute from St. Louis to Minneapolis and was forced to crash land in a field near Carroll, Iowa. It was described as a "corn field landing" with no player injuries or major plane damage. Garmaker was one of the Lakers who survived the ordeal.

In six NBA seasons, Garmaker recorded 5,597 career points and averaged 13.3 points in

421 regular season games. He recorded a 40.4 field goal shooting percentage, grabbed 1,748 rebounds, and netted 1,553 of 1,974 free throw attempts. In 1956–1957, Garmaker ranked 10th in scoring in the NBA with 1,117 points and a 16.3 points average and placed third in the NBA in free throw percentage when he sank 365 of 435 free throws for an 83.9 shooting percentage.

Garmaker helped lead the Lakers to the NBA Championship Series in 1958–1959, but Minneapolis lost in four games to the Boston Celtics. He recorded 284 points in 21 NBA playoff games and averaged 13.5 points. Garmaker also played in four NBA All-Star Games, scoring 31 points for a 7.8 points average. Following the 1960–1961 season, he retired from NBA basketball.

BIBLIOGRAPHY: "Dick Garmaker," *National "M" Club*, http://www.gopherm.club.com (2004); "Dick Garmaker," *Statistics*, http://www.basketball reference.com (2004); Jan Hubbard, ed., *The Official NBA Encyclopedia*, 3rd ed. (New York, 2000); Gary K. Johnson, *NCAA Men's Basketball's Finest* (Overland Park, KS, 1998); David S. Neft et al., *The Sports Encyclopedia: Pro Basketball*, 5th ed. (New York, 1993).

John L. Evers

GARNETT, Kevin Maurice (b. May 19, 1976, Mauldin, SC), professional player, is the son of O'Lewis McCullough and Shirley Garnett, a hair stylist. His parents never married each other, and his mother married Ernest Irby when Garnett was five. Garnett joined the Mauldin (South Carolina) High School basketball team in his freshman year. By his junior year, he averaged 27 points, 17 rebounds, and 7 blocks and was named Mr. Basketball in South Carolina. In 1994 Garnett transferred to Farragut Academy in Chicago for his senior year and led the Admirals to the Class AA state quarterfinals with 25.2 points, 17.9 rebounds, 6.7 assists, and 6.5 blocks per game. He was named Mr. Basketball in Illinois National High School Player of the Year by *USA Today*; All-America First Team by *Parade* magazine; and the Most Outstanding Player of the 1995 McDonald's All-America Game.

Garnett declared himself eligible for the 1995 NBA Draft and became the first player in over 20 years to attempt to enter the NBA directly from high school. In June 1995, Garnett was drafted fifth overall by the Minnesota Timberwolves (NBA) and signed a three-year, $5.6 million contract, the maximum allowed to a rookie NBA player.

In his rookie season, the six-foot eleven-inch, 220-pound forward averaged 10.4 points, 6.3 rebounds, and 1.64 blocks and was named the 1995–1996 All-Rookie Second Team. Garnett averaged 17 points, 8 rebounds, and 2.12 blocks in 1996–1997, leading the Timberwolves to their first-ever playoff berth. He was elected to the NBA Western Conference All-Star Team, becoming the youngest player ever named to an All-Star team. Following that season, Garnett accepted a six-year, $125 million contract extension with the Timberwolves. In 1997–1998, he averaged 18.5 points and 9.6 rebounds and was voted to the All-Star team again. Garnett's statistics went up to 20.8 points and 10.4 rebounds per game in 1998–1999, as he was named All-NBA Third Team. His ability to score remained high, as he averaged 22.9 points in 1999–2000, 22.0 in 2000–2001, 21.2 in 2001–2002, 23.0 in 2002–2003, 24.2 in 2003–2004, and 22.2 in 2004–2005. He scored 24 points and grabbed 10 rebounds in the 2000 NBA All-Star Game as a starter, and was named All-NBA First Team and the NBA All-Defensive First Team. He made the All-NBA Second Team in 2001, 2002, and 2005 and the All-NBA First Team in 2003 and 2004, being named NBA MVP the latter season. He also made the All-NBA Defensive First Team for the eighth consecutive time. In 2003–2004, Garnett set career highs with 24.2 points, 13.9 rebounds, and 5.0 assists per game and helped the Timberwolves to the Western Conference's best regular-season record—a franchise best 58-24. He became just the fifth player to lead the NBA in total points (1,987) and rebounds (1,139) and made the NBA All-Defensive First Team. Garnett led Minnesota past the first round of the NBA playoffs for the first time in 2004, but the Los Angeles Lakers ousted the Timberwolves in the Western Conference Finals. He enjoyed an outstanding playoff, combining 430 points with 263 rebounds in 18 games and tallying at least 30 points four times. He led the NBA with 1,108 (13.5) average in 2004–2005, but Minnesota missed the playoffs. Garnett was voted to the

NBA All-Star Team every year since 2000 and in 2003 was named the MVP of the 52nd NBA Annual All-Star Game. His NBA career totals include 15,681 points and 8,601 rebounds in 775 regular games season and 1,041 points and 628 rebounds in 47 playoff games.

Garnett, a Nike spokesperson, has two sisters, Sonya and Ashley. Nicknamed "Da Kid," he made his acting debut when he played basketball legend Wilt Chamberlain* in the movie *Rebound*.

BIBLIOGRAPHY: Steve Aschburner, *NBA All-Star Kevin Garnett* (New York, 2001); Ross Bernstein, *Kevin Garnett: Star Forward* (Berkeley Heights, NJ, 2002); Paul J. Deegan, *Kevin Garnett* (Philadelphia, PA, 1999); Terri Dougherty, *Kevin Garnett* (Edina, MN, 1999); "Garnett, Kevin," *CB* 59 (September 1998), 22–25; Glen Macnow, *Sports Great Kevin Garnett* (Berkeley Heights, NJ, 2000); Arlene Bourgeois Molzhan, *Kevin Garnett* (Mankato, MN, 2001); Ken Shouler et al., *Total Basketball* (Wilmington, DE, 2003); *TSN Official NBA Register, 2004–2005* (St. Louis, MO, 2004); Mark Stewart, *Kevin Garnett: Shake up the Game* (Brookfield, CT, 2002); Stew Thornley, *Super Sports Star Kevin Garnett* (Berkeley Heights, NJ, 2002); John Albert Torres, *Kevin Garnett: "Da Kid"* (Minneapolis, MN, 2000).

Di Su

GATES, William "Pop" (b. August 30, 1917, Decatur, AL; d. December 2, 1999, New York, NY), professional player and coach, starred in basketball for the New York Renaissance, an all-black barnstorming team. The Rens finished with a 111-22 win-loss record in Gates's rookie 1938–1939 season and won the first World Professional Tournament at Chicago, Illinois, in March 1939. The six-foot three-inch, 196-pound Gates led the Rens scoring in the title game against the Oshkosh All-Stars.

Gates moved with his family at age three to Cleveland, Ohio, and at age five to New York City, learning to play basketball in the Harlem YMCA. His integrated Benjamin Franklin High School basketball team won the city championship, as Gates earned All-City honors. After graduating in 1938, he attended Clark University in Atlanta, Georgia. Gates played for the semiprofessional Harlem Yankees. The Renaissance, that era's best team, signed him in late 1938 for $125 a month. He remained with the Rens until 1942. During World War II, he worked as a preflight mechanic at Grumman Aircraft in Bethpage, New York, and played basketball with the Grumman Flyers. The weekends saw him perform with the Washington Bears, which were composed largely of former Rens players. The Bears won the 1943 World Professional Tournament, as Gates finished as runner-up for the MVP trophy.

Gates and Dolly King integrated the NBL in 1946, being signed by Lester Harrison* of the Rochester Royals. Rochester sold Gates to the Buffalo Bisons (NBL) before the 1946 season began. The Buffalo franchise subsequently moved to Moline, Illinois, as the Tri-Cities Blackhawks. He served in 1947–1948 as player-coach of the Dayton Rens (NBL), the first all-black team ever to play in a professional league. From 1948 to 1950, Gates starred for the champion Scranton Miners (ABL). He joined the touring Harlem Globetrotters in 1950 as player-coach and ended his career there in 1955.

During the off-season, Gates worked as a lifeguard, housing guard, and corrections officer in New York City. The New York City resident was elected to the Naismith Memorial Basketball Hall of Fame in 1989 and to the New York City Basketball Hall of Fame in 1994.

BIBLIOGRAPHY: William Gates file, Naismith Memorial Basketball Hall of Fame, Springfield, MA; William Gates, interview with Robert W. Peterson, March 4, 1988; Robert W. Peterson, *Cages to Jump Shots: Pro Basketball's Early Years* (New York, 1990); Susan J. Ray, *The New York Renaissance Professional Black Basketball Team, 1923–1950* (Syracuse, NY, 2001); Josh Wilker, *The Harlem Globetrotters* (New York, 1997); Dave Zinkoff, with Edgar Williams, *Around the World with the Harlem Globetrotters* (Philadelphia, PA, 1953).

Robert W. Peterson

GATHERS, Eric "Hank" (b. February 2, 1967, Philadelphia, PA; d. March 3, 1990, Los Angeles, CA), college player, was the son of Eric Gathers and Lucille Gathers. Gathers exhibited early athletic ability and attended Dobbins Technical High School in Philadelphia, Pennsylvania, with his life-long friend Bo Kimble, future first-round draft choice of the Los Angeles Clippers

(NBA). They played in the Sonny Hill League, one of the inter-city summer basketball leagues that also featured future NBA players Pooh Richardson and Lionel Simmons*. In Gathers' senior year in 1984/1985, he led Dobbins to the Philadelphia Public League Championship, and made the Pennsylvania All-State team.

Gathers played basketball at the University of Southern California in 1985–1986, but became unhappy with the school when the coach resigned. After sitting out the 1986–1987 season, he transferred to Loyola Marymount College in Los Angeles, California. The six-foot seven-inch, 210-pound Gathers enjoyed a strong junior year, averaging 22.5 points and 8.7 rebounds on 60.1 percent shooting. In 1988–1989, his senior year, he proved even more spectacular. Gathers averaged 32.7 points, and 13.7 rebounds to pace the all NCAA Division I players in both categories, becoming only the second Division I player to lead in both areas in the same year. He was named consensus Second-Team All-America in 1990. Gathers averaged 21.3 points and 13.7 rebounds in three NCAA tournament games in 1988 and 1989. During his college career, he scored 2,723 points (23.3 point average) and made 1,128 rebounds (9.6 average) in 117 games.

On December 9, 1989, Gathers fainted at the free-throw line after missing an attempt against the University of California-Santa Barbara. Doctors discovered that he had an irregular heart beat and thought that the condition could be stabilized with medication. A subsequent report listed the cause of Gather's heart problem as myocarditis, an inflammation of the heart. The side effects of the medicine included sluggishness and depression. Gathers was concerned that his playing caliber and his chances of becoming a first-round NBA draft would suffer and convinced his doctors to lower the dosage of the medicine.

On March 3, 1990, in a WCC post-season tournament game against Portland University, Gathers converted a dunk shot and started back upcourt. He collapsed seconds later and died of a heart attack that night. He and his girlfriend, Marva Crump, had a son, Aaron Crump.

BIBLIOGRAPHY: "A Bitter Legacy," *SI* 74 (March 4, 1991), pp. 62–67, 68, 70, 72, 74, 76; "Death on the Court," *SI* 72 (March 12, 1990), pp. 24–25; Mike Douchant, *Encyclopedia of College Basketball* (Detroit, MI, 1995); Bo Kimble, *For You, Hank* (New York, 1992); *Newsmakers 1990*, Issue 3, Gale Research, 1990, http://galenet.galegroup.com.

Robert L. Cannon

GERVIN, George "Iceman" (b. April 27, 1952, Detroit, MI), college and professional player, coach, and executive, starred in both the ABA and NBA. Gervin is a product of schoolyard basketball in one of the worst slum areas of inner-city Detroit. His early life is a remarkable story of timely opportunity and extraordinary career breaks set against the specter of ruthless poverty. These breaks allowed him to escape from a malnourished childhood, a checkered high school career, and an unfortunate college suspension to become one of the most productive scorers in pro basketball history.

Gervin attended Detroit's Martin Luther King High School, where he might have been cut from the varsity team as a skinny five-foot eight-inch sophomore but for the special interest taken by his junior varsity coach, Willie Meriweather. Meriweather had become both a personal tutor on the basketball court and a desperately needed father figure, as Gervin's own father left the family before he was age two. His mother struggled bravely, performing menial labor to hold together her family of six children. Gervin has credited his own survival as a ghetto youth to his fanatic early love for basketball, the sport that occupied his every waking hour during teenage years. He learned schoolyard "moves" on neighborhood courts strewn with trash and rubble. He then honed his skills in private by practicing up to 1,000 shots a night in the local high school gym, where he gained admission from an understanding janitor by first sweeping the gymnasium floor. Gervin improved so markedly by his senior season that, in spite of his unimpressive scholastic record, he earned a basketball scholarship to California State University at Long Beach. Unable to adjust to life away from the inner city, Gervin left that school after one semester and enrolled at Eastern Michigan University. His second opportunity at a promising basketball career also was cut short by an event that almost permanently marred Gervin's life and his budding athletic career. After striking down a Roanoke College player during a heated fracas in an NCAA small-college tournament game, Gervin was suspended from the Eastern Michigan University team. As a follow-up to this bizarre incident, Eastern Michigan coach Jim Dutcher resigned. Gervin was dropped from school, ostensibly for low scores on an NCAA entrance examination taken over a full year earlier.

The suspension might well have been a death knell for Gervin's brief career. His fortunes changed drastically, however, after he was spotted by ABA superscout Johnny Kerr* while playing in a CBL game. Gervin scored 50 points that night for the Pontiac (Michigan) Chaparrals, a semipro team that had signed him for $500 a month. Gervin was offered a pro contract by the Virginia Squires of the fledgling ABA. He then enjoyed the good fortune of rooming with Virginia's Julius Erving*, a contemporary hero on whom he began to pattern his own offensive game. Gervin became an instant scoring star with Virginia and later the San Antonio (ABA) club, which purchased his contract in 1974. When the San Antonio Spurs joined the NBA in 1976, the six-foot seven-inch, 185-pound Gervin became one of the greatest scorers in NBA history and remained a "franchise" player until traded to the Chicago Bulls (NBA) in October 1985. Gervin, the leading vote-getter for both the 1979 and 1980 NBA All-Star Games, was MVP in the 1980 classic. He remains one of only three players to win at least four NBA scoring titles, Michael Jordan* and Wilt Chamberlain* having won 10 and seven, respectively. His numerous scoring achievements include holding the NBA record for most points in a single quarter (33 against New Orleans in 1978) and winning the closest individual scoring race in NBA history, scoring 63 points in the concluding game to edge out David Thompson* of Denver in 1978 by just .06 points. Gervin possessed the eighth-highest career scoring average (26.2 for 791 games) in NBA history. Through the 1985–1986 season, Gervin accumulated 26,595 total points and averaged 25.1 points in his combined ABA and NBA tenure. Gervin played with Banco Roma in the Italian pro basketball league in 1986–1987 and with the Quad City Thunder (CBA) in 1989–1990. Gervin was named to the All-NBA First Team from 1978 through 1982 and the All-NBA Second Team in 1977 and 1983.

Gervin served as assistant coach of the San Antonio Spurs (NBA) in 1992–1993 and 1993–1994 and community relations representative for the Spurs from 1993–1994 through 1999–2000. He compiled a 21-20 record as head coach of the Detroit Dogs (ABA) in 2000–2001, defeating Chicago in the ABA Finals. Since 2001, Gervin has served as vice president of basketball operations for the Detroit Dogs. In 1996, he was elected to the Naismith Memorial Basketball Hall of Fame and was named one of 50 Greatest Players in NBA History. His brother, Derrick, played guard with the New Jersey Nets (NBA) from 1989 through 1991.

BIBLIOGRAPHY: George Gervin file, Naismith Memorial Basketball Hall of Fame, Springfield, MA, "Gervin, Mitchell, Gilmore Spur the Spurs," *NBA Today* 3 (April 29, 1983), pp. 10–11; Jan Hubbard, ed., *The Official NBA Encyclopedia*, 3rd ed. (New York, 2000); Terry Pluto, *Loose Balls* (New York, 1990); Ken Shouler et al., *Total Basketball* (Wilmington, DE, 2003); Kevin Simpson, "When Ice Catches Fire—Watch Out," *Basketball Digest* 11 (December 1983), pp. 52–57; *TSN Official NBA Register, 2004–2005* (St. Louis, MO, 2004); George White, "Ice Man George Gervin's Climb from the Slums to 4 NBA Scoring Titles," *Basketball Digest* 10 (January 1983), pp. 38–43.

Peter C. Bjarkman

GILL, Armony T. "Slats" (b. May 1, 1901, Salem, OR; d. April 5, 1966, Corvallis, OR), college player and coach, played baseball and basketball at Salem High School from 1917 to 1920. He captained the basketball squad and made High School All-State in 1919 and 1920. At Oregon State University, Gill played basketball from 1921 to 1924 and was selected All-America and All-Conference in 1924. He coached for two years at an Oakland, California high school and served as basketball coach from 1929 to 1964 at Oregon State. Gill compiled a 599-392 record and won four PCC titles (1933, 1947, 1949, 1955), tying the University of California-Berkeley in 1958. His teams won eight Northern Division titles (1933, 1935, 1940, 1942, 1947, 1949, 1954, and 1955) and tied for the 1948 Northern Division title, but never captured a national championship. Gill's teams came tantalizingly close to national titles in 1947 and 1955 and finished fourth in the 1949 and 1963 NCAA playoffs.

In 1956 Gill received the Hayward Award as Oregon's top sports figure from the OSWSA. Besides being coach, Gill was director of the Board of Education for School District No. 9 in Corvallis from 1951 to 1955. In 1964 he served as Olympic Trials coach and as NABC West coach. He directed the NCAA Championship Tournament in 1965 and was elected as a coach to the Naismith Memorial Basketball Hall of Fame in 1967. Named as Oregon State University's athletic director in 1964, Gill served in that post until his death after a stroke. Survivors included his wife, Helen, one son, John, and one daughter, Mrs. Jack Stephenson.

The always gracious, gentlemanly Gill demanded perfection of his players. He coached two of college basketball's tallest players, seven-foot three-inch Swede Holbrook and seven-foot one-inch Mel Counts. Gill's 11 All-American players were Mark Grayson, Ed Lewis, Wally Palmberg, John Mandic, Lew Beck, Red Rocha, Cliff Crandall, Holbrook, Dave Gambee, Lee Herman, and Counts. Gill, a community activist and advocate of physical fitness for the average person, participated in the annual "Hearts for Husbands" conventions in Portland. He unfortunately suffered a heart attack in 1960 in Seattle with his basketball team but subsequently recovered and returned as coach. The Coliseum on Oregon State University's campus, built in 1949, was named after Gill following his death.

BIBLIOGRAPHY: Mike Douchant, *Encyclopedia of College Basketball* (Detroit, MI, 1995); Armony Gill file, Naismith Memorial Basketball Hall of Fame, Springfield, MA; Ronald L. Mendell, *Who's Who in Basketball* (New Rochelle, NY, 1973); *NCAA Men's Basketball Records, 2004* (Indianapolis, IN, 2003); *The Oregon Journal* (Portland, OR), April 6, 1966; *The Oregon Statesman* (Salem, OR), April 6, 1966; Sandy Padwe, *Basketball's Hall of Fame* (Englewood Cliffs, NJ, 1970); Paul Soderberg and Helen Washington, eds., *The Big Book of Halls of Fame in the United States and Canada* (New York, 1977).

Frederick J. Augustyn Jr.

GILMORE, Artis (b. September 21, 1949, Chipley, FL), college and professional player, participated in basketball at Chipley (Florida) and Roulhac (Alabama) High Schools and first achieved national recognition by averaging 39 points as a high school senior in Dothan, Alabama. He played two years of basketball at Gardner-Webb JC in Boiling Springs, North Carolina, averaging 22.5 points. In 1969 he enrolled at Jacksonville University. In his first season at Jacksonville, Gilmore led the Dolphins to a 27-2 record. Jacksonville lost to UCLA, 80-69, in the NCAA championship game. As a junior that year, he scored 742 points (26.5 per game average) and made 621 rebounds. The next year, he tallied 570 points (21.9 per game average), made 603 rebounds, and was named First Team All-America. The Dolphins compiled a 22-4 record, but lost in NCAA regional play to Western Kentucky University. In 54 games at Jacksonville, he scored 1,312 points (24.3 per game average) and made 1,224 rebounds for a career-leading 22.7 per game average. Gilmore remains one of few players to average over 20 points and 20 rebounds per game during an NCAA career.

After completion of his college eligibility, the seven-foot two-inch, 255-pound Gilmore was drafted in the first round by the Chicago Bulls (NBA) and Kentucky Colonels (ABA). He signed with the Colonels and immediately became their starting center. He was named ABA Rookie of the Year and Player of the Year as the fourth ABA rookie to score 2,000 points. Gilmore averaged 23.8 points and 17.8 rebounds and led the ABA with 1,471 rebounds, 422 blocked shots, and a .598 field goal percentage. The next season, he also paced the ABA in rebound average per game (17.6), shooting percentage (56), and blocked shots (259). The durable Gilmore was named to the ABA All-Star First Team in each of his five seasons with the Colonels, never missed a regular-season game, and averaged over 20 points. His best ABA season came in 1974–1975, when he led the Colonels to their first and only ABA championship and was named MVP of the championship series. During his ABA career, he scored 9,362 points (22.3 per game average), made 7,169 rebounds, and compiled a .558

shooting percentage. He played in five ABA All-Star Games, being MVP in 1974.

When the ABA folded in 1976, Gilmore was drafted by the Chicago Bulls (NBA). He quickly became the Bulls' starting center and continued his consistent high level of performance. He averaged over 20 points during his first five NBA seasons, and did not miss a game until 1979–1980, when an injury sidelined him for 34 games. The next year, he played in all 82 games and averaged 17.9 points. The Bulls traded him to the San Antonio Spurs (NBA) for Dave Corzine, Mark Olberding, and cash in July 1982.

Gilmore led the Bulls in career blocked shots with 1,017. In June 1987 he was traded back to Chicago for a 1988 second-round draft choice. The Boston Celtics (NBA) signed him as a free agent in January 1988. Gilmore played a reserve role on the Celtics squad that won the Atlantic Division regular season title but was eliminated by the Detroit Pistons in the Eastern Conference finals. Gilmore, who led the NBA in field goal percentage from 1981 through 1984, remains the NBA all-time field goal percentage leader at .599. He retired following the 1987–1988 season with 15,579 points (17.1 points average), blocked 1,747 shots, and snared 9,161 rebounds. His career ended in 1988–1989 with Bologna Arimo (Italian League).

BIBLIOGRAPHY: John Y. Hamilton, "With Ferocious Talent," *Black Sports* 14 (1977), pp. 46–54; Terry Pluto, *Loose Balls* (New York, 1990); Ken Shouler et al., *Total Basketball* (Wilmington, DE, 2003); *TSN Official NBA Guide, 2004–2005* (St. Louis, MO, 2004); *TSN Official NBA Register, 2004–2005* (St. Louis, MO, 2004).

Fred M. Shelley

GLAMACK, George Gregory "Blind Bomber" (b. Gjuro Gregorvitch Glamocli, June 7, 1919, Johnstown, PA; d. March 10, 1987, Rochester, NY), college and professional player and executive, parlayed his size and an ambidextrous hook shot into two College Player of the Year awards and a pro career, despite poor vision. His parents had emigrated to the United States from Belgrade, Yugoslavia. Glamack's father worked as a mechanic at a Johnstown steel mill. A scholastic football and basketball star, Glamack developed a right-handed hook shot in basketball at Allentown (Pennsylvania) Prep School. Glamack used black floor markings for guidance, because he had trouble seeing both teammates and a distant hoop. In his early days at the University of North Carolina, he added a matching left-handed hook shot.

The first basketball All-America at the University of North Carolina, Glamack saw his uniform number 20 retired by the school in 1986. The Tar Heels also retired the uniforms of five others who achieved National Player of the Year distinction for the school. During his college playing days through 1941, Glamack amassed 1,336 career points. This exceptional achievement was bettered by only three college players (William Anderson of Lafayette College, Hank Luisetti* of Stanford University, and Chet Jaworski of the University of Rhode Island) up until that time. As a junior, Glamack averaged the then-almost-unheard-of 20 points to help coach Bill Lange's North Carolina five win the 1939–1940 SC title and compile an 18-3 record. In 1940–1941 Glamack averaged 20.6 points, as his team had the best SC record and was one of eight teams selected for the NCAA Tournament. After North Carolina lost to the University of Pittsburgh 26-20, Glamack scored 31 in his final college game against Dartmouth College. He was named HAF Collegiate Basketball Player of the Year in both his junior and senior seasons. As a senior, he set a long-standing SC one-game record of 45 points against Clemson University. Glamack's total fell only five short of the national record, held then by Luisetti, despite his fouling out with three minutes to play.

The six-foot seven-inch, 230-pound Glamack turned pro for the 1941–1942 season with the Akron, Ohio (NBL) team before obtaining waivers on his bad eyesight to join the U.S. Navy in World War II. There, he played basketball for the Great Lakes Naval Training Center team. When the war ended, he persistently was sought by the Rochester Royals (NBL) and averaged 12.3 points during the 1945–1946 season on the NBL's championship team. He played another year for Rochester, one season and part of another at Indianapolis (NBL), and ended his NBL career with the Hammond Buccaneers in 1949. Glamack scored 2,240 points during his 213-game NBL career for a 10.5

points-per-game average. Glamack became part owner of the short-lived Grand Rapids Hornets pro basketball team and then worked as a beer company executive and real estate broker before health problems beset him. In 1971 a veterans' hospital at Buffalo told him he would never walk again because of crippling arthritis in his legs. With determination, he briefly overcame that handicap before being forced back into a wheelchair for his later years. Basketball promoter Ned Irish*, after traveling to North Carolina to watch Glamack as a collegian, said "that boy did things with a basketball I've never seen before."

BIBLIOGRAPHY: Peter C. Bjarkman, *Hoopla: A Century of College Basketball, 1896–1996* (New York, 1996); *Chapel Hill* (NC) *News*, September 13, 1978, March 15, 1987; Mike Douchant, *Encyclopedia of College Basketball* (Detroit, MI, 1995); Zander Hollander, ed., *The Modern Encyclopedia of Basketball* (Garden City, NY, 1979); Jan Hubbard, ed., *The Official NBA Encyclopedia*, 3rd ed. (New York, 2000); Joe Jares, *Basketball, The American Game* (Chicago, IL, 1971); *NCAA College Basketball All-Time Record Book* (New York, 1970); *Official NCAA Basketball Guide*, 1946–1947 (New York, 1946); Ken Rappoport, *Tales from the Tar Heel Laker Room* (Champaign, IL, 2002); University of North Carolina Sports Information Department, News Release, Chapel Hill, NC, September 6, 1986.

Robert B. Van Atta

GLAMOCLI, Gjuro Gregorvitch. *See* Glamack, George Gregory "Blind Bomber"

GOLA, Thomas Joseph "Mr. All Around" "Tom" (b. January 13, 1933, Philadelphia, PA), college and professional player, is the son of a Philadelphia policeman. He and his wife, Caroline, have one son, Thomas C. Gola. Of Polish descent, Gola began his legendary basketball career in the CYO leagues of Philadelphia. At Philadelphia's LaSalle High School, the sensational six-foot six-inch Gola tallied 2,222 career points. He rejected numerous out-of-town offers to play his intercollegiate ball at LaSalle College. During Gola's college career from 1952 to 1955, LaSalle won 101 of 118 games. A three-time All-America, Gola averaged 20.9 points with the Explorers and handled 2,201 rebounds, or 18.7 per game. When LaSalle won the NIT in his freshman year, Gola shared the MVP award with Norm Grekin. In 1954 Gola led LaSalle to the NCAA championship and won MVP honors in the tournament. The angular Gola, nicknamed "Mr. All Around" by his coach Ken Loeffler*, played guard, forward, and center and also excelled as a defensive player.

After Gola's senior year, the Philadelphia Warriors (NBA) drafted him in the first round as a territorial choice. Gola played in the NBA from 1955 through 1966 except for military service in 1956–1957, enjoying his greatest years with the Warriors. He accompanied the Warriors to San Francisco in 1963 and ended his career with the New York Knickerbockers (NBA) in 1965–1966. Although having a less spectacular pro career, Gola achieved All-Star status in several seasons. Philadelphia relied on Wilt Chamberlain* and Paul Arizin* rather than Gola for scoring. Gola excelled with his defensive skills, strong rebounding, and ability to play both the front and backcourt. In Gola's rookie season (1955–1956), the Warriors won the NBA title. During his NBA career, Gola scored 7,871 points and averaged 11.3 points. He also grabbed 5,617 rebounds and averaged 8.0 per game. Primarily used as a passing guard, he handed out 2,962 career assists for an average of 4.2 per game.

Gola later achieved great notoriety as a Republican politician in a heavily Democratic area. He was elected to the Pennsylvania State Legislature in 1966 and 1968 and as Philadelphia's comptroller in 1970. He became a successful businessman in the Philadelphia area.

Gola played on numerous championship teams. As an eighth-grader, Gola led his squad to the Philadelphia CYO title. The LaSalle High School quintet won the city title in Gola's senior year. Gola then played on NIT and NCAA title-winners as a collegian. He also was a member of one All-Military Service championship team and the title-winning NBA squad of 1955–1956. A true basketball legend in the Philadelphia area, Gola became one of the first tall NBA guards to play regularly and was one of the last players to be drafted on a territorial rights basis. Gola was elected to the Naismith Memorial (1975) and HAF Basketball halls of fame.

BIBLIOGRAPHY: Peter C. Bjarkman, *The Encyclopedia of Pro Basketball From Histories* (New York, 1994); Morgan G. Brenner, *College Basketball's National Championships* (Lanham, MD, 1999); Mike Douchant, *Encyclopedia of College Basketball* (Detroit, MI, 1995); Tom Gola file, Naismith Memorial Basketball Hall of Fame, Springfield, MA; Ronald L. Mendell, *Who's Who in Basketball* (New Rochelle, NY, 1973); Claudia Mitrol, ed., *Philadelphia's Greatest Sports Moments* (Champaign, IL, 2000); David S. Neft et al., *The Sports Encyclopedia: Pro Basketball*, 5th ed. (New York, 1992); *TSN Official NBA Register, 1987–1988* (Philadelphia, PA, 1987).

William A. Gudelunas

GOODRICH, Gail Charles, Jr. (b. April 23, 1943, Los Angeles, CA), college and professional player, learned the sport from his father, Gail Sr., an All-PCC guard at the University of Southern California. Although only six feet one inch and 175 pounds, the left-handed Goodrich loved to drive to the basket and either shoot or pass off. After graduating from Polytechnic High School in Sun Valley, California, Goodrich attended UCLA. Because the Bruins already had Walt Hazzard, coach John Wooden* asked Goodrich to handle the ball less than he did in high school. As a junior, Goodrich led a team of overachievers to the NCAA Finals against Duke University. Although lacking anyone over 6 feet 5 inches tall, the Bruins possessed great quickness and pressed full court from the outset. Goodrich scored 27 points, as UCLA defeated the much bigger Duke University team 98-83 to complete a perfect 30-0 season. In 1964–1965 Goodrich inherited the playmaking duties from the recently graduated Hazzard. He again led UCLA to a second consecutive NCAA title. UCLA defeated the University of Michigan 91-80 in the final game, as Goodrich scored 42 points. As a senior, Goodrich averaged 24.8 points and was named a consensus All-America.

In 1965 the Los Angeles Lakers (NBA) drafted Goodrich in the first round. In three seasons with the Lakers, Goodrich steadily improved. Goodrich was selected by the Phoenix Suns (NBA) in the May 1968 expansion draft and began to flourish there. Although Phoenix won only 16 games in its first season, Goodrich played outstanding. He averaged 23.8 points and handed out 6.4 assists, seventh in the NBA. The Suns improved greatly during the 1969–1970 season with the addition of scorers Connie Hawkins* and Paul Silas*. Goodrich's scoring average dropped, but he finished fifth in the NBA in assists with a 7.5 points average. In May 1970 Goodrich was traded back to the Lakers for Mel Counts. The Lakers already fielded a powerful team that featured Jerry West*, Wilt Chamberlain*, Happy Hairston, and former UCLA teammate Keith Erickson. Goodrich averaged 17.5 points to begin his second stint with the Lakers. In 1971–1972 everything came together for both Goodrich and the Lakers. The Lakers started off with a 39-3 mark, including an incredible 33-game winning streak. The Lakers won a then NBA record 69 games and captured the NBA title. Goodrich led the Lakers in scoring with a 25.9 points average.

Goodrich continued to play and score well for the Lakers the next four seasons. In July 1976, he signed with the New Orleans Jazz (NBA) as a free agent. He played three more seasons there before retiring. Altogether, Goodrich played 14 seasons in the NBA and scored 19,181 points for an 18.6 career scoring average. He played in five All-Star Games (1969, 1972–1975) and was named to the 1974 All-NBA First Team. He was elected to the Naismith Memorial Basketball Hall of Fame in 1996. The Lakers retired his uniform number 25.

BIBLIOGRAPHY: Scott Howard Cooper, *The Bruins 100* (Lenexa, KS, 1999); Gail Goodrich with Rich Levin, *Gail Goodrich's Winning Basketball* (Chicago, IL, 1976); Gail Goodrich file, Naismith Memorial Basketball Hall of Fame, Springfield, MA; Jan Hubbard, ed., *The Official NBA Encyclopedia*, 3rd ed. (New York, 2000); Joe Jares, *Basketball: The American Game* (Chicago, IL, 1971); Roland Lazenby, *The Lakers: A Basketball Journey* (New York, 1993); John D. McCallum, *College Basketball, U.S.A. Since 1892* (Briarcliff Manor, NY, 1978); Billy Packer and Roland Lozenby, *College Basketball's 25 Greatest Teams* (St. Louis, MO, 1989); Ken Rappoport, *The Classic: History of the NCAA Championship*

(Mission, KS, 1979); *TSN Official NBA Guide, 1987–1988* (St. Louis, MO, 1987); *TSN Official NBA Register, 2004–2005* (St. Louis, MO, 2004).

Curtice R. Mang

GOTTLIEB, Edward "The Mogul" "Eddie" "Mr. Basketball" (b. September 15, 1898, Kiev, Russia; d. December 7, 1979, Philadelphia, PA), professional basketball and baseball promoter coach, owner, innovator, and developer, was the son of Russian immigrants Morris Gottlieb and Leah Gottlieb. Gottlieb grew up in the Jewish section of South Philadelphia, attended public schools there, and graduated from Philadelphia's School of Pedagogy. A bachelor, he taught school for a brief period in the Philadelphia area. In 1918 Gottlieb helped organize and promote the Philadelphia SPHAS basketball team. Four years later, the SPHAS defeated the Original New York Celtics. Gottlieb booked the SPHAS in many cities, making it among the nation's most famous barnstorming quintets. Eventually the SPHAS won 11 championships, mainly in the EL and ABL.

Gottlieb also promoted semipro black baseball teams during the major leagues' segregated era. "The Mogul" promoted an all-black game in 1929 in Yankee Stadium in New York, perhaps the first such contest played in a major league park. In view of his deep connections with the Negro Leagues, the National Baseball Hall of Fame designated him an adviser on the induction of Negro League players. Gottlieb also promoted pro wrestling in the Philadelphia area and was a business adviser to the Harlem Globetrotters, with whom he frequently toured. Gottlieb's greatest fame came as a driving force in the early days of the NBA. As coach and part-owner of the Philadelphia Warriors (BAA), Gottlieb in 1946 helped merge the BAA with smaller groups to form the NBA. Sparked by "Jumping Joe" Fulks,* Gottlieb's Warriors in 1947 won the BAA title and probably the NBA's first true championships. Although compiling a lackluster 263-318 pro coaching record, Gottlieb guided the Warriors to two more Eastern Division titles. Overall he coached in the new league between 1947 and 1955.

During the early 1950s, Gottlieb paid approximately $25,000 to become principal owner of the Warriors. In 1963 he sold the team to a San Francisco group for a reported $875,000. Gottlieb built his Philadelphia franchise around local stars Paul Arizin*, Tom Gola*, and Guy Rodgers*. As Warriors owner, he convinced fellow NBA owners to allow him to draft Wilt Chamberlain* of Philadelphia's Overbrook High School as a future territorial draft choice. During the 1955–1956 season, the Warriors won the NBA Championship for Gottlieb. The innovative Gottlieb constantly attempted to enliven NBA games. Besides proposing the 24-second clock, he supported the move to outlaw zone defenses. He backed the idea of the bonus penalty foul shot concept. Until shortly before his death, Gottlieb worked 8 to 12 hours a day for months to arrange the NBA's official schedule. After selling the Warriors, he also served as a special consultant to the NBA.

NBA commissioner Larry O'Brien* termed Gottlieb "Mr. Basketball." The title was well deserved. Gottlieb helped oversee the growth of pro basketball from poorly lighted dance halls to edifices fit for royalty. As a powerful force on the NBA Rules Committee, he rarely resisted any idea that popularized the game. "The Mogul" in the 1950s promoted NBA doubleheaders, giving fans a chance to see four teams in one night and widening the NBA appeal. For his yeoman efforts in promoting pro basketball, Gottlieb was in 1971 elected to the Naismith Memorial Basketball Hall of Fame as a contributor.

BIBLIOGRAPHY: Peter C. Bjarkman, *Encyclopedia of Pro Basketball Team Histories* (New York, 1994); Edward Gottlieb file, Naismith Memorial Basketball Hall of Fame, Springfield, MA; Jan Hubbard, ed., *The Official NBA Encyclopedia*, 3rd ed. (New York, 2000); Neil D. Isaacs, *Vintage NBA* (Silver Spring, MD, 1996); Ralph Hickok, *New Encyclopedia of Sports* (New York, 1977); Ronald L. Mendell, *Who's Who in Basketball* (New Rochelle, NY, 1973); Philadelphia *Inquirer*, December 8, 1979, pp. C1, C4.

William A. Gudelunas

GRANT, Travis, "Machine Gun" (b. January 1, 1950, Clayton, AL), college and professional player, graduated from Barbour County Training School in Clayton and played basketball for coach Lucius Mitchell at Kentucky State College. The six-foot seven-inch, 215-pound forward averaged 27.4 points (on 75 percent shooting) for the 21-2 Thorobreds in 1969–1970, when he was named Third Team (NABC) College Division All-America. The Thorobreds averaged 107 points that season. In a game against Northwood (Illinois) College, Grant tallied 75 points. On February 23, 1970, Kentucky State, ranked sixth nationally in the NAIA, faced 18th ranked Eastern Michigan, starring six-foot eight-inch Earle Higgins and six-foot seven-inch Kennedy Mcintosh. Before 6,500 spectators at Michigan's Bowen Field House in Ypsilanti, Eastern Michigan won the storied contest, 116-98, as Grant netted a customary 36 points.

In 1970–1971, Grant was selected First Team All-America. Led by Grant and Elmore Smith, Kentucky State won three straight NAIA national championships from 1970 to 1972. Grant and Smith formed among the most outstanding player tandems in NAIA history. Grant set the NAIA tournament single-game record with 60 points against Minot State University (North Dakota) in 1972. An uncanny shooter, he averaged 33.4 points during his college career, boasted a .638 field goal percentage for a long-range shooter, and recorded 9.4 rebounds a game. His 4,045 career points set a national record for all college players, surpassing the 3,667 scored by Pete Maravich* of LSU. Grant's 1,760 field goals remain the most in NCAA college basketball history.

The Los Angeles Lakers (NBA) chose Grant as their first pick in the 1972 NBA draft, the 13th player selected overall. After averaging 3.8 points in limited playing time with the Lakers, Grant joined the San Diego Conquistadors (ABA). The Conquistadors were coached by his former teammate Wilt Chamberlain*. Grant averaged 25.2 points for San Diego in 1974–1975. In 1975–1976, he played for both the Kentucky Colonels (ABA) and Indiana Pacers (ABA). In an exhibition game between the Colonels and the Detroit Pistons (NBA) in October 1975, Grant scored 17 points and a game-winning jumpshot with four seconds to play. He shot .529 from field goal range in his three ABA campaigns. During his three ABA seasons, he scored 2,639 points (16.0 average) and averaged 4.6 rebounds. Grant was named to the Kentucky State College Athletic Hall of Fame in 1979 at age 29.

BIBLIOGRAPHY: www.remembertheaba.com; Huron Hardwood, Eastern Michigan basketball history, www.geocities.com; Jan Hubbard, ed., *The Official NBA Encyclopedia*, 3rd ed. (New York, 2000); Kentucky State University athletic web page, www.kysu.edy/athletics; National Association of Intercollegiate Athletics website, www.naia.org/basketball.

Bijan C. Bayne

GREEN, John M. "Jumpin' Johnny" (b. December 8, 1933, Dayton, OH), college and professional player, is the younger of two sons of Katherine Perry and graduated from Dayton (Ohio) Dunbar High School in 1951. Green's rise to basketball stardom took a strange route, for he never played the sport in high school. His play was limited to church league and community center basketball. After holding several odd jobs following graduation, he joined the U.S. Marines in 1952. At the Atsugi Air Base in Japan, he led the basketball team to the All-Central Command and All-Navy Far East titles.

After his discharge in 1955, Green enrolled at Michigan State University (BTC) and reported for freshman basketball practice as a walk-on. Although a raw talent, he exhibited amazing jumping ability. A surprised coach Forddy Anderson* immediately saw Green's great potential. Although playing in only 18 of 26 games as a sophomore, the six-foot five-inch, 200-pound Green scored 238 points (13.2-point average) and grabbed 260 rebounds (14.6 per game). The 16-10 Spartans captured a share of the 1956–1957 BTC crown with Indiana University before suffering an NCAA tournament 74-70 triple-overtime loss to the eventual champion University of North Carolina. Green, a center, made the NCAA tournament All-Star Team, AP Third Team All-America, and First Team BTC. In Green's 1957–1958 junior year, Michigan State improved with a 16-6 record, but finished second to Indiana for the BTC title. Green topped the Spartans with 397 points (18.0 point average) and 392 rebounds (17.8 per game) and set a BTC record with a .538 field goal shooting percentage. His honors included selection to the AP and UP First Team BTC, INS and UP

Second Team All-America, and AP Third Team All-America. Green, elected co-captain of the Spartans his senior year, led the team to a 19-4 mark and their first undisputed BTC crown, scoring 427 points (18.5 point average) and seizing 382 rebounds (16.6 per game). The Spartans were upset by the University of Louisville 88-81 in the NCAA Midwest Region final, despite a 29-point, 23-rebound game by Green, who was named the regional tournament MVP. The 1959 physical education graduate also earned First Team All-America and First Team and MVP BTC honors. Green was elected a charter member of MSU's Athletic Hall of Fame in 1992, had his number 24 retired in 1995, and was presented a Distinguished Alumni award in 2001.

The New York Knickerbockers (NBA) made Green the sixth pick in the 1959 NBA draft. Switched to forward, he scored over 6,000 points and played in three All-Star Games with the Knicks. From 1961 through 1964, he averaged over 15 points and almost 12 rebounds a contest. After spending six years with New York, Green was traded with Johnny Egan and Jim Barnes and $200,000 to the Baltimore Bullets (NBA) for Walt Bellamy* in November 1965 and finished second in the NBA in field goal percentage (.536). Following nearly two years with Baltimore as a reserve, he was selected in the 1967 expansion draft by the San Diego Rockets (NBA). San Diego sent him to the Philadelphia 76ers (NBA) in January 1968. In September 1969, the 36-year-old fringe player became a free agent and signed with the Cincinnati Royals (NBA). Surprisingly, the 1969–1970 and 1970–1971 seasons were among the best of Green's NBA career. He scored a combined 2,468 points (16.1 point average), twice led the NBA in field goal percentage, and appeared in his fourth All-Star Game. After the Royals franchise moved west in 1972, Green played one additional season with the renamed Kansas City-Omaha Kings (NBA) and retired in 1973. Except for his 1967–1968 season with Philadelphia, he never played on a winning team in 14 NBA campaigns. In 1,057 regular-season games, he scored 12,281 points (11.6 point average) and made 9,083 rebounds (8.6 per game). He appeared in 20 NBA playoff games, scoring 160 points (8.0 point average) and grabbing 107 rebounds (5.4 per game).

Green and his wife, Esther (Dorsey), have three children, twin sons, Jeffrey and Johnny, and a daughter, Karen. He owns a McDonald's franchise and resides on Long Island in Dix Hills, New York.

BIBLIOGRAPHY: Jack Ebling and John Farina, *Magic Moments: A Century of Spartan Basketball* (Chelsea, MI, 1998); Johnny Green file, Naismith Memorial Basketball Hall of Fame, Springfield, MA; Johnny Green file, Sports Information Office, Michigan State University, East Lansing, MI; Jan Hubbard, ed., The *Official NBA Encyclopedia*, 3rd ed. (New York, 2000); Martin Taragano, *Basketball Biographies* (Jefferson, NC, 1991); *TSN Official NBA Guide, 2002–2003* (St. Louis, MO, 2002).

Jack C. Braun

GREEN, Sihugo "Si" (b. August 20, 1934, Brooklyn, NY; d. October 4, 1980, Pittsburgh, PA), college and professional player, starred at Duquesne University as a basketball forward-guard from 1954 through 1956 and led the Iron Dukes to the 1955 NIT title, bringing Pittsburgh its only collegiate basketball championship. Green, a six-foot two-inch, 185-pound product of Brooklyn's Boys High School, performed at guard and forward for coach Donald Moore's Iron Dukes. Green's slashing, driving style prompted Nellie King, Duquesne's former sports information director, to call him "the Julius Erving* of his time."

Green possessed great quickness and exceptional jumping ability. During his tenure at Duquesne, the Iron Dukes won 65 and lost only 17 contests. Green teamed with fellow All-America Dick Ricketts to lead Duquesne to the 1955 NIT Championship, scoring 33 points in the 70-58 title game against the University of Dayton. Duquesne's victory avenged a 1954 defeat in the NIT finale to a College of the Holy Cross team paced by Tom Heinsohn*. Green remains Duquesne's only two-time All-America (UP, 1955; UP, AP, 1956), and holds the Iron Dukes' season scoring record with 662 points in 1956. Although playing before freshmen could compete, Green scored 1,605 career points to rank fourth best on Duquesne's all-time scoring list. The 1956 season witnessed him average 24.5 points and 13.2 rebounds.

Subsequently, Green played 10 NBA seasons. The Rochester Royals (NBA) selected him in the first round of the 1956 draft, but the lack of an outside shot limited his professional success. Green played in the NBA for Rochester (1956–1957), the Cincinnati Royals (1957–1959), St. Louis Hawks (1959–1962), Chicago Zephyrs (1962–1963), Baltimore Bullets (1963–1965), and Boston Celtics (1965–1966). Green averaged 9.2 points during his NBA career and enjoyed his most productive season in 1961–1962, averaging 12.7 points per game.

The quiet, dignified Green served as personnel manager and later vice president of operations for Associated Textile Systems, a Pittsburgh rental laundry company. He and his wife, June, had one son, Erich. Duquesne gives an award annually in his name to the top varsity basketball player.

BIBLIOGRAPHY: Peter C. Bjarkman, *The Biographical History of Basketball* (Chicago, IL, 2000); Mike Douchant, *Encyclopedia of College Basketball* (Detroit, MI, 1995); Zander Hollander, ed., *The Modern Encyclopedia of Basketball*, rev. ed. (New York, 1973); Jan Hubbard, ed., *The NBA Basketball Encyclopedia*, 3rd ed. (New York, 2000); Ronald L. Mendell, *Who's Who in Basketball* (New Rochelle, NY, 1973); *Pittsburgh* (PA) *Post-Gazette*, October 6, 1980; *Pittsburgh* (PA) *Press*, October 6, 1980.

Frank W. Thackeray

GREENWOOD, David Kasim (b. May 27, 1957, Lynwood, CA), college and professional player, came from a football-oriented family. His brother, Joe, and several cousins, including Pittsburgh Steeler (NFL) L. C. Greenwood*, excelled in football. The tall, slender Greenwood learned basketball on the schoolyards of south central Los Angeles and starred in basketball at Verbum Dei High School, earning All-America honors his junior and senior seasons. Greenwood, who admired Sidney Wicks*, attended UCLA and started the final 15 basketball games at center his freshman year, as the Bruins (PTC) reached the NCAA Final Four in 1976. UCLA shifted him in 1976–1977 to the forward position, where he averaged 16.7 points. Greenwood attained consensus All-America as a junior and senior, averaging 17.5 and 19.9 points respectively. During his career, UCLA won four consecutive PTC titles.

The Chicago Bulls (NBA) selected Greenwood in the first round of the 1979 draft, the second player chosen overall. He made the NBA All-Rookie Team in 1980, averaging 16.3 points and 9.5 rebounds. The next four seasons saw the six-foot nine-inch, 225-pound forward consistently score in double figures, grab over nine rebounds, and miss only five games. Nagging Achilles tendon injuries, however, limited him to only 61 games in the 1984–1985 season, when his scoring average dipped to 6.1 points per game. Chicago traded Greenwood to the San Antonio Spurs (NBA) in October 1985. Greenwood regained some of his previous form, averaging 11.6 points for the 1986–1987 campaign, and led the Spurs in rebounding. Repeated surgery to repair his Achilles tendon limited his ability and availability. Greenwood was traded to the Denver Nuggets (NBA) in January 1989 and joined the Detroit Pistons (NBA) in October 1989 as a free agent. Detroit used Greenwood sparingly, as he averaged only 1.6 points for the 1989–1990 campaign. He joined the San Antonio Spurs in 1990–1991, tallying 3.8 points in 63 contests in his final NBA season. During 12 NBA seasons, he scored 8,428 points (10.2 points per game) and collected 6,537 rebounds.

BIBLIOGRAPHY: Mike Douchant, *Encyclopedia of College Basketball* (Detroit, MI, 1995); Scott Howard-Cooper, *The Bruins 100* (Lenexa, KS, 1999); *Long Beach* (CA) *Independent*, March 7, 1979; *Los Angeles* (CA) *Herald Examiner*, February 21, 1978; *Official NCAA 1981 Basketball Guide* (Shawnee Mission, KS, 1981); Ken Shouler et al., *Total Basketball* (Wilmington, DE, 2003); *TSN Official NBA Register, 1990–1991* (St. Louis, MO, 1990); *UCLA Basketball Media Guide, 1978* (Los Angeles, CA, 1978); *USA Today*, April 23, 1991.

Curtice R. Mang

GREER, Harold Everett "Hal" (b. June 26, 1936, Huntington, WV), college and professional player, is the son of railroad engineer

William G. Greer and the youngest of nine children. Influenced by his older brother, Greer became a star basketball player and led Douglas High School in Huntington to the Negro State Championship. Greer, whose stepmother strongly influenced his decision to attend Marshall University, became the first black to play for a major college team in West Virginia. During three varsity seasons at Marshall (1955–1956 to 1957–1958), Greer scored 1,377 points and averaged 19.4 points (23.6 points his senior year) and a .545 shooting percentage. After an outstanding college career, Greer was selected in the second round by the Syracuse Nationals in the 1958 NBA draft.

In 15 seasons with Syracuse and the Philadelphia 76ers (the franchise was transferred to Philadelphia in 1963), the six-foot two-inch, 175-pound Greer utilized his speed and athletic ability in quickly adjusting to pro basketball. As a rookie, he started and exhibited phenomenal shooting against the Boston Celtics on February 14, 1959. Greer scored 39 points, including 18 field goals in the first half, and finished the game with 45 points. Greer averaged 20 points by his fourth season and ranked among the NBA's top guards in 1962–1963. After that season, he made the All-NBA Second Team seven consecutive seasons (1962–1963 to 1968–1969). Greer appeared in 10 All-Star Games (1961–1970) and was named the MVP in the 1968 game, scoring 21 points (including 19 in one quarter for an NBA All-Star Game record) and making all eight shots from the floor.

With great speed, shooting touch, and fast-break ability, Greer joined Wilt Chamberlain*, Luke Jackson, Chet Walker*, Larry Costello*, and Billy Cunningham* in leading Philadelphia to the NBA championship in 1967 and ended Boston's long string of titles. Greer led Syracuse and Philadelphia in scoring (1961–1962 to 1964–1965), assists (1963–1964 to 1964–1965, 1968–1969 to 1969–1970), free throw percentage (1963–1964, 1965–1966, 1969–1970, 1970–1971), and field goal percentage (1958–1959, 1959–1960, 1961–1962). Closing his distinguished career in 1973, Greer rank among the greatest NBA guards. Greer established a NBA record for games played (1,122) and still stands high on the all-time list. He ranks on the all-time list in points scored (21,586), field goals attempted (18,811), field goals made (8,504); minutes played (39,788), and personal fouls (3,855). Greer, who led the 76ers in career scoring, averaged 19.2 points and recorded 4,540 career assists. In 92 playoff games, Greer made 303 assists, scored 1,876 points, and averaged 20.4 points. Greer, whose uniform number (15) has been retired and now hangs in the Spectrum in Philadelphia, was elected to the Naismith Memorial Basketball Hall of Fame in 1981. "Hal Greer Boulevard" in Huntington is named in his honor. In 1996, he was named one of the 50 Greatest Players in NBA History.

BIBLIOGRAPHY: Hal Greer file, Naismith Memorial Basketball Hall of Fame, Springfield, MA; Wayne Lynch, *Season of the 76ers* (New York, 2002); Claudia Mitrol, ed., *Philadelphia's Greatest Sports Moments* (Champaign, IL, 2000), Zander Hollander, ed., *The Modern Encyclopedia of Basketball* (Garden City, NY, 1979); Jan Hubbard, ed., *The Official NBA Encyclopedia*, 3rd ed. (New York, 2000); Ken Shouler et al., *Total Basketball* (Wilmington DE, 2003) *TSN NBA Register, 2004–2005* (St. Louis, MO, 2004).

John L. Evers

GREER, Lurlyne Ann. *See* Rogers, Lurlyne Ann Greer

GRENTZ, Theresa Marie Shank (b. March 24, 1952, Spangler, PA), college player and coach, is the daughter of a selector for an Atlantic and Pacific (A&P) warehouse and a nurse. She grew up in Glenolden, Pennsylvania and starred in basketball for Cardinal O'Hara High School in Springfield, Pennsylvania.

The 5-foot 11-inch Grentz played for coach Cathy Rush at Immaculata College in the early 1970s. She proved a dominating presence and star basketball player for the Mighty Macs, as she led Immaculata to three AIAW national championships from 1972 through 1974. Her Immaculata team totaled 74 wins, as she amassed over 1,000 points for the Mighty Macs and earned First Team All-America status three times. Her number 12 jersey was retired by Immaculata, and in 1974 she was named the AMF Collegiate Player of the Year. Grentz, who married in 1974, helped pioneer American women's basketball. On March 23, 1974, she led Immaculata to its third AIAW title in the first ever televised live coverage of a women's college basketball game in the United States. In 59 games, she tallied, 191 points (20.2 point average) and made 965 rebounds.

Upon graduation with a Bachelor's degree in 1974, Grentz taught sixth grade and almost immediately worked as an assistant basketball coach at St. Joseph's College. As head coach at St. Joseph's from 1974 to 1976, she compiled 27 wins with only 5 losses. Grentz moved to Rutgers University as coach from 1976 until 1995, recording 434 wins and 155 defeats. Her Rutgers teams made it into the NCAA championship tournament on nine occasions. Her most successful season came in 1986–1987 with a 30–3 record and a fifth place final NCAA ranking, culminating in Converse National Coach of the Year honors.

Grentz possesses considerable international coaching experience, including coaching the United States teams at the Goodwill Games and the World Championships in 1990 to gold medal triumphs and the 1992 Barcelona, Spain Olympics team to a bronze medal.

In May, 1995, Grentz was named the sixth head women's basketball coach at the University of Illinois. In February 1997, Illinois won its first ever BTC title in women's basketball. Grentz, whose record at Illinois is 175-128 in 10 seasons, compiled career winning percentages at St. Joseph's of .844, at Rutgers of .737, and at Illinois of .578.

Grentz, an avid golfer, lives with her husband, Karl, in Champaign, Illinois and has two sons, Karl and Kevin. In June 2001, she was inducted into the Women's Basketball Hall of Fame. Grentz was named BTC Coach of the Year from 1996 to 1998 and has made nearly 1,000 public appearances in her tenure at Illinois. Her Theresa Grentz Show on WCIA Channel 3 is a remarkable educational vehicle built around her "Pillars of Character" paradigm. This show discusses how she and her players visit with local elementary school children and explore topics such as persistence, service, self-esteem and courage. Her most remarkable feat has been the increased fan support at Illinois, growing from 7,700 fans in 1994 to over 104,000 in 2001. In 31 seasons, she has compiled 636 wins and 283 losses for a .692 winning percentage.

BIBLIOGRAPHY: Mike Douchant, *Encyclopedia on College Basketball* (Detroit, MI, 1995); Mike Koon, "The Theresa Grentz Show," www.fightilliani.com; University of Illinois Sports Information office, assorted promotional materials and press releases, Champaign, IL, May 12, 2003.

Scott A.G.M. Crawford

GRIFFITH, Darrell Steven "Griff" "Golden Griff" "Dr. Dunkenstein" (b. June 16, 1958, Louisville, KY), college and professional player, is the son of Monroe Griffith Sr., a welder and steelworker, and Maxine Griffith. One of five children, the six-foot four-inch, 190-pound Griffith led Male High School of Louisville to the Kentucky State basketball championship in 1975.

Griffith enrolled at the University of Louisville (MC). During his four-year career there from 1977 to 1980, he sparked the Cardinals to a composite record of 101 wins and 25 losses and their first NCAA national championship in 1980. Griffith, who played guard for Louisville and recorded a 48-inch vertical leap, led Louisville to regular-season MC titles in 1977, 1978, and 1980, MC tournament championships in 1978 and 1980, and four straight NCAA tournament appearances.

In 1980, Griffith paced the Denny Crum*–coached Cardinals to a season record of 33 wins and three losses. In the NCAA tournament semifinal against the University of Iowa, he scored 34 points. During the championship game versus UCLA, Griffith tallied a game-high 23 points. UCLA coach Larry Brown* called Griffith, named the tournament's MVP, "the greatest player in the country."

Griffith, who received a Bachelor's degree in mass communications, closed his career at Louisville as the Cardinals' all-time basketball scorer with 2,333 points and the single-season scoring leader with 825 points in 1980. In 1980, *TSN* named him its Player of the Year, while *TSN*, the AP, and UPI placed him on their First-Team All-America teams. His other honors also included the John Wooden Award as college basketball's Player of the Year and the MC Player of the Year. The University of

Louisville retired his jersey at the end of the 1980 season.

The Utah Jazz (NBA) drafted Griffith in the first round as the second pick overall in 1980. Griffith was named 1981 NBA Rookie of the Year, compiling a 20.6 points scoring average. During the 1984–1985 season, he set the NBA single-season mark for three-pointers made with 92 and also averaged a career-high 22.6 points. Griffith spent his entire NBA career from 1980 to 1991 with the Jazz, finishing with 12,391 points for a 16.2 points average. Griffith, the Jazz all-time leader in three-point goals (530), ranks second among Jazz leaders in games played (802) and third in points scored and steals. When the Jazz retired his number in December 1993, Frank Layden, the team's president, commented, "Griff is the guy who changed the way people thought about basketball in Salt Lake City. . . . He is the guy who taught us about winning."

Griffith returned to Louisville after his career with the Jazz and resides there with his wife Kathy and their children. The popular, articulate Griffith has invested in several Louisville business ventures and does promotional and advertising work.

BIBLIOGRAPHY: Morgan G. Brenner, *College Basketball's National Championships* (Lanham, MD, 1999); *Desert News*, October 25, 1993, October 26, 1993; Mike Douchant, *Encyclopedia of College Basketball* (Detroit, MI, 1995); Darrell Griffith file, University of Louisville, Louisville, KY; Jan Hubbard, eds., *The Official NBA Encyclopedia*, 3rd ed. (New York, 2000); Curry Kirkpatrick, "A Big Hand for the Cards," *SI 52* (March 30, 1980), pp. 10–13; *Louisville* (KY) *Courier Journal*, December 4, 1993; *TSN*, March 22, 1980; *University of Louisville 1993–1994 Basketball Information Guide* (Louisville, KY, 1993); *Utah-Jazz Media Guide, 1987–1988* (Salt Lake City, UT, 1987).

Frank W. Thackeray

GRIFFITH, Yolanda Evette (b. March 1, 1970, Chicago, IL), college and professional player, is the youngest of five children and was selected *Parade* magazine All-America in basketball for the 1988–1989 season and first team All-America in softball as a senior at George Washington Carver High School in Chicago, Illinois. Griffith starred in basketball at Palm Beach Junior College (Florida) before transferring to Florida Atlantic University, where she was named 1992–1993 Kodak Division II Player of the Year and averaged over 28 points and 16 rebounds during the 1993–1994 season. As a 19-year-old single mother, she supported both herself and daughter, Candace, by repossessing cars while in college. Griffith played basketball professionally in Germany from 1993 to 1997 and led the European League in 1996–1997 averaging 24.7 points and 16 rebounds. She won a gold medal with the U.S. Olympic team in the 2000 Sidney, Australia games and played for the UMMC Ekaterinburg Russian team in the 2002–2003 off-season.

Griffith was chosen first overall in the 1997 ABL draft by the Long Beach Stingrays. During her rookie campaign, she finished first in steals per game (3.1), second in rebounds per game (11.2), and third in field goal percentage (.541). Griffith earned a starting position in the ABL All Star Game and helped Long Beach to reach the 1997–1998 ABL Finals in their first season. She was named the 1998 ABL Defensive Player of the Year.

Griffith was drafted by the Sacramento Monarchs (WNBA) after the ABL folded in December 1998. She scored career highs of 31 points against Phoenix on June 12, 1999 and eight steals against Washington on July 29, 1999. Griffith led the WNBA in 1999 with 11.3 rebounds and 2.5 steals per game, played in the All Star Game, and was named WNBA 1999 Newcomer of the Year, Defensive Player of the Year, and MVP. She was selected an All Star in 2000 and tied a franchise record with 19 rebounds against Houston on August 6. Griffith paced the WNBA in double-doubles with 17 in 1999 and 18 in 2001. The six-foot four-inch, 174-pound forward led the WNBA with 11.2 rebounds per game in 2001. Although limited to 17 games due to a bulging cervical disc in 2002, Griffith returned to capture WNBA Player of the Week honors between July 29 and August 4 and started every game for Sacramento during the 2003 campaign. In 2004, she led the WNBA with a .519 field goal percentage and shared first with 75 steals. Her WNBA career totals through the 2004 season include 2,837 points scored, 1,659 rebounds, and 357 steals, and a 15.9 points average in 178 games. Griffith has averaged 16.8 points, 8.9 rebounds, and 1.5 steals in 19 WNBA playoff games. She played on the gold medal winning U.S. Olympic team and was named to the All-WNBA Second team in 2000 and 2001.

Griffith who is single, resides with her daughter in Berkeley, California and plans to enter law enforcement after her basketball career is over.

BIBLIOGRAPHY: Nutricise, "Q and A: Yolanda Griffith, professional basketball player," *Womenshealth* (nutricise.com, 2003–2004), pp. 1–3; Sharon Robb, "Yolanda Griffith Hot-Wires the Hoops," *South Florida Sun-Sentinel* (Sept. 15, 2000, archives); *TSN Official WNBA Guide and Register, 2004* (St. Louis MO, 2004); USA Basketball, *Bio: Yolanda Griffith* (USAbasket ball.com, December 26, 2003), pp. 1–4; WNBA, *Yolanda Griffith Player Info* (WNBA.com, October 26, 2003), pp. 1–2.

Frank J. Olmsted

GROAT, Richard Morrow "Dick" (b. November 4, 1930, Swissvale, PA), college and professional basketball and baseball player, was one of the greatest two-sport athletes in American sports history. The son of successful realtor Martin B. Groat, he was one of Pennsylvania's outstanding basketball and baseball stars at Swissvale (Pennsylvania) High School. Groat compiled a 25 points average as a basketball guard and represented the Pittsburgh area on the Hearst Newspapers' All-Star Baseball Team as shortstop. At Duke University from 1948 to 1952, he performed in dazzling fashion in both sports. With 1,886 career points, he ranked as third leading basketball scorer in Duke history. In the 1950–1951 season, he set a then-NCAA record with 831 points and was selected as an All-America guard. Repeating as All-America in 1951–1952, he added 780 points and captained the Blue Devils. During those two seasons, he gained nearly 20 regional and national awards for his basketball prowess and won the acclaim of numerous opponents, coaches, and players alike. As a baseball star at Duke, he batted .386 in 39 games (1951) and .370 in 38 games (1952), and won All-America recognition twice as well as many awards.

One of the relatively few players to move successfully from college to major league baseball without minor league experience, Groat joined the Pittsburgh Pirates (NL) after graduation in 1952. Groat played regular shortstop the next 11 years, missing the 1953 and 1954 seasons to military service. He recorded a career .286 batting average, with a .315 mark in 1957, .300 in 1958, and career-high .325 in 1960. The Pirates won the world championship in 1960, when he was named the NL's MVP. Groat also was selected to the NL All-Star team in 1959–1960 and 1962–1964. Traded to the St. Louis Cardinals (NL) in November 1962, he posted a .319 batting mark in 1963 and received the J. G. Taylor Spink Award as St. Louis Baseball Man of the Year. He batted .292 in 1964, again starring for a world championship team. After moving to the Philadelphia Phillies (NL) in October 1965, Groat finished his major league career with the San Francisco Giants (NL) in 1967. His major league career statistics included 1,929 games, 2,138 hits, 352 doubles, 67 triples, 39 home runs, 829 runs scored, and 707 runs batted in spanning 14 seasons. At six feet and 182 pounds, he was never a power hitter and lack outstanding speed. He proved a superior shortstop like Lou Boudreau, whom he also resembled in his basketball-baseball versatility.

In 1952–1953, Groat played pro basketball with the Fort Wayne Pistons (NBA). Groat made 100 field goals and 109 free throws for 309 points and an 11.9 points average in 26 games. Groat married Barbara Womble in November 1955 and has two daughters, Tracey and Carol. The Pittsburgh area resident has been associated with steel sales and promotion work, remains active in charity fund drives, and is an avid and outstanding amateur golfer.

BIBLIOGRAPHY: Duke University Sports Publicity Department, Durham, NC; Jan Hubbard, ed., *The Official NBA Basketball Encyclopedia*, 3rd ed. (New York, 2000); John Thorn et al., eds., *Total Baseball V* (New York, 1997).

Leonard H. Frey

GROZA, Alex John (b. October 7, 1926, Martins Ferry, OH; d. January 21, 1995, San Diego, CA), college and professional player, coach, executive, and sportscaster, was one of four brothers and the son of a coal miner and mill worker of Hungarian descent. The athletic exploits of Alex, John, Frank, and Lou remained a constant source of conversation in their father's pool room and tavern. Alex, the leading basketball scorer during his last two years at Martins Ferry (Ohio) High School, twice attained All-State honors and set a state record with 628 points as a senior.

After lettering at the University of Kentucky (SEC) in 1944–1945, Groza played basketball in the U.S. Army in 1945–1946 and was voted the nation's outstanding service player. On returning to Kentucky, the six-foot seven-inch, 220-pound center led the Wildcats in scoring and rebounding. Ralph Beard*, Wallace Jones, Kenny Rollins, and Cliff Barker also started on the "Fabulous Five." The Wildcats, under coach Adolph Rupp*, captured successive NCAA titles in 1948 and 1949, as Groza paced scorers and made NCAA Tournament MVP both years. Groza's other honors included being a two-time All-SEC (1948, 1949) and a three-time All-America (1947, 1948, 1949). His Kentucky season scoring record of 698 points in 1948–1949 stood until 1969 when it was broken by Dan Issel*, while his 1,744 career points remained a Wildcat standard until Cotton Nash tallied 1,770 points (1962–1964). Groza led the 1948 U.S. Olympic team in scoring, teaming with his four starting Kentucky teammates to earn gold medals at the 1948 London, England Summer Olympic Games.

In 1949 Groza, Beard, Jones, and Barker joined Joe Holland to form the Indianapolis Olympians (NBA). In two seasons, Groza attained All-NBA First Team both years and led the Olympians to the 1949–1950 Western Division title. His 23.4 points average ranked second only to George Mikan* of the Minneapolis Lakers. Groza led the NBA for both seasons in field goal percentage and scored 18 points in the 1951 All-Star Game. He scored 2,925 points in 130 regular-season NBA games, and averaged 26.0 points in nine playoff contests.

In October 1951, Groza and Beard were indicted for their roles in a collegiate gambling scandal. They were found guilty of controlling the margin of victory, "shaving points" in numerous games. The court indefinitely suspended them, but NBA Commissioner Maurice Podo-loff* then banned them for life.

Groza served as head basketball coach at Bellarmine College in Louisville, Kentucky, for seven seasons and as interim head coach (2-0) with the Kentucky Colonels (ABA) in 1970–1971. His other assignments with the Colonels included being business manager and handling commentary for their television broadcasts. Groza later became general manager of the San Diego Conquistadors (ABA) and compiled a 15-23 win-loss record for part of the 1974–1975 season.

BIBLIOGRAPHY: Mike Douchant, *Encyclopedia of College Basketball* (Detroit, MI, 1995); V. A. Jackson, *Beyond the Baron* (Kuttawah, KY, 1998); *Kentucky Basketball Encyclopedia* (Champaign, IL, 2000); Ronald L. Mendell, *Who's Who in Basketball* (New Rochelle, NY, 1973); David S. Neft, and Richard N. Cohen, eds., *The Sports Encyclopedia: Pro Basketball*, 5th ed. (New York, 1992); Bert Nelli, *The Winning Tradition: A History of Kentucky Wildcat Basketball* (Lexington, KY, 1984); Russell Rice, *Kentucky Basketball's Big Blue Machine* (Huntsville, AL, 1976); Alan Ross, *Wildcat Wisdom* (Nashville, TN, 1999); Ken Shouler et al., *Total Basketball* (Wilmington, DE, 2003); Frank Waldman, ed., *Famous Athletes of Today*, 11th series (Boston, MA, 1949), pp. 19–40.

John L. Evers

GRUENIG, Robert F. "Bob" (b. December 3, 1913, Chicago, IL; d. November 8, 1958, Del Norte, CO), amateur player, began his basketball career at Crane Tech High School as a three-year starter. As the team's center, he led his prep league in scoring all three seasons and set a scoring record of 35 points in one game. After graduation, Gruenig joined the Chicago Rosenburg-Avery team (AAU) and began his long, storied AAU basketball career. At six feet eight inches, 230 pounds, the devastating hook-shooter was one of basketball's first truly big men. Gruenig soon moved from Chicago to Denver, Colorado, which became the center of AAU basketball. At Denver, he performed with and against some of the era's best players and began a business career in the petroleum industry.

In 1937 Gruenig played with the Denver Safeway Store team (AAU), coached by Ev Shelton*. Denver Safeway defeated the Phillips 66 Oilers 43-38 to win the AAU championship. Gruenig was selected an All-America with teammates Jack McCracken* and Jack Colvin. The next season, the Denver Safeway team lost the AAU championship to Kansas City Healy Motors 40-38 on Fred Pralle's basket in the last 40 seconds as Gruenig again made All-America. For the 1939 campaign, Gruenig played for the Denver Nuggets (AAU) under teammate-coach McCracken. The Nuggets won the AAU championship by defeating the Phillips Oilers 25-22. Three years later, Gruenig led the Denver American Legion AAU to the championship by defeating Phillips team again 45-32. In 1943, the Phillips Oilers began a six-year reign as AAU champions. Although unable to capture the championship, Gruenig led the Denver Ambrose team (AAU) to second place finishes in 1944 and 1945. Gruenig remained an annual All-America selection. In 1948 he played with the Denver Murphy-Mahoney team (AAU) and, at age 34, scored 104 points in five tournament games. For his career, Gruenig was selected First Team AAU All-America 10 times. Before his death, Gruenig worked as a lab technician for Empire Petroleum of Denver. He is a member of the Amateur Basketball Hall of Fame and HAF Hall of Fame and in 1963 was elected to the Naismith Memorial Basketball Hall of Fame.

BIBLIOGRAPHY: Robert Gruenig File, Naismith Memorial Basketball Hall of Fame, Springfield, MA; Ronald L. Mendell, *Who's Who in Basketball* (New Rochelle, NY, 1973); Paul Soderberg and Helen Washington, *The Big Book of Halls of Fame in the United States and Canada* (New York, 1977); Alexander M. Weyand, *The Cavalcade of Basketball* (New York, 1960).

George P. Mang

GUERIN, Richard V. "Richie" (b. May 2, 1932, New York, NY), college and professional player and coach, graduated from Iona College in New Rochelle, New York, in 1956. For the basketball squad, he scored 464 points (17.2 points average) in 1951–1952, 392 points (18.7 points average) in 1952–1953, and 519 points (24.7 points average) in the 1953–1954 season. At Iona, he scored 1,375 career points for a 19.9 points average. He served in the U.S. Marines from 1954 to 1956, playing basketball for the Quantico, Virginia Marines and Marine All-star teams. A territorial draft pick of the New York Knickerbockers (NBA), the six-foot four-inch, 210-pound Guerin became an immediate favorite of Knicks fans. He played in his native city from 1956–1957 through 1963–1964, making the All-NBA Second Team each season from 1957–1958 to 1962–1963. Guerin excelled as a defensive player with considerable ball-handling skills and, along with Willie Naulls*, was the only significant bright spot on a cellar-dwelling team. During three New York seasons, he finished among the top five NBA players in assists. Guerin in 1960–1961 finished sixth in overall scoring with a 29.5 point average.

In 1963–1964 Guerin experienced a rough transition after being traded in October to the St. Louis Hawks (NBA) and recorded his first sub-15-points-per-game season since his rookie year. The next season, Guerin became the player-coach of the Hawks, replacing Harry Gallatin*. He remained two more seasons as a regular player while coaching a mediocre team. The 1969–1968 Hawks, led by Lenny Wilkens*, surprisingly surged to a 56-26 record and Western Division championship, with Guerin being named Coach of the Year. In 1968–1969 the Hawks abandoned their small 9,000-seat arena in St. Louis for Atlanta, Georgia. After the 1969–1970 season, Guerin retired as a player. Atlanta suffered losing seasons in 1970–1971 and 1972–1973. Guerin was replaced at the end of the latter season by Lowell Fitzsimmons*. During his playing career, Guerin appeared in 847 games, scoring 5,174 field goals and 4,328 free throws. His 14,676 points amounted to 17.3 points per game. As a coach, he recorded 327 wins and 291 losses for a .529 average in regular-season play and 26-34 in playoffs. Guerin, a fine player and fairly successful coach, lacked the great natural ability of the era's premier guard Bob Cousy*. Guerin's years of playing with such a weak Knicks team probably hurt his career statistics, but perhaps not his assessment relative overall to other players of his era.

BIBLIOGRAPHY: Jan Hubbard, ed., *The Official NBA Encyclopedia*, 3rd ed. (New York, 2000); Joe Jares, *Basketball, The American Game* (Chicago, IL, 1971); *TSN NBA Register, 2004–2005* (St. Louis, MO, 2004); Arthur Triche, ed., *From Sweet Lou to 'Nique: Twenty-Five Years with the Atlanta Hawks* (Atlanta, GA, 1992).

John David Healy

GULICK, Luther Halsey (b. December 4, 1865, Honolulu, HI; d. August 13, 1918, South Casco, ME), sports administrator and basketball pioneer, persuaded Dr. James Naismith* in 1891 to initiate an "indoor game" in the off-season for training at the School for Christian Workers in Springfield, Massachusetts. A YMCA pioneer, Gulick suggested that the organization's leader be educated both physically and scientifically. Gulick consequently developed the triangle symbol, signifying the physical, emotional, and intellectual that is still used by YMCA as the emblem of manhood and service.

The son of missionaries Luther Halsey Gulick and Louisa (Lewis) Gulick, Gulick attended Oberlin Prep School in Ohio (1880–1882, 1883–1886), Sargent Normal School of Physical Education in Cambridge, Massachusetts, and NYU's Medical College (1889). He served as medical examiner of New York City's YMCA, taught at a Harlem girls' school, and served as physical director of a YMCA gymnasium in Jackson, Michigan. Gulick married Charlotte Vetter of South Casco, Maine, on August 13, 1887, and had six children, Louise, Frances, Charlotte, Katherine, Luther, and John Halsey.

At the School for Christian Workers, Gulick guided and promoted basketball during its first years to national and international recognition through YMCA and AAU organizations and by chairing the basketball rules organization (1895). As head of Physical Education for Public Schools in New York City (1903), Gulick promoted his triangle development ideal with younger children and founded the PSAL. He also initiated the nation's first two-minute exercise program in the public schools.

Gulick, a proficient writer and public speaker, became internationally known after presenting several physical training lectures at the 1904 St. Louis, Missouri Exposition. He participated in the national recreation movement and was joint founder and president in 1906 of the PRAA and the NRA. He served on the Olympic Committee for the Athens, Greece Games in 1906 and London, England Games in 1908. Gulick, a delegate to the Second International Congress on School Hygiene in London in 1907, became director of the U.S. Department of Child Hygiene in 1909, and traveled to major cities promoting the value and need of recreation and play in childhood. Besides helping start the Boy Scouts, he and his wife introduced Camp Fire Girls in 1911 to educate women on changing roles outside the home. Gulick began the Sebago Wohelo Camps in South Casco, Maine, where he died of heart failure. Before his death, Gulick traveled to France to study how the YMCA could fulfill the physical, moral, and recreational needs of American soldiers. He led a successful campaign for recruiting physical education and recreation directors for soldiers in the U.S. and overseas.

Gulick edited many publications, including *Physical Education* (1891–1896), *Association Outlook* (1897–1900), *American Physical Education Review* (1901–1903), and the *Gulick Hygiene Series* of lectures. His books and articles include *Physical Measurements and How They Are Used* (1889), *Physical Education for Muscular Exercise* (1904), *The Efficient Life* (1907), *Mind and Work* (1908), *The Healthful Art of Dancing* (1910), *Proposed Changes in Basket Ball Rules* (1909), and *What the Triangle Means*. In 1959, Gulick was enshrined in the Naismith Memorial Basketball Hall of Fame as a contributor.

BIBLIOGRAPHY: Luther Halsey Gulick file, Naismith Memorial Basketball Hall of Fame, Springfield, MA; Joseph F. Kett, *Rites of Passage: Adolescence in America, 1790 to the Present* (New York, 1979); Bernice Larson Webb, *The Basketball Man: James Naismith* (Lawrence, KS, 1973).

Catherine M. Derrick

GUNTER, Sue (b. May 22, 1941, Walnut Grove, MS), player, coach, and executive, excelled as an Olympic player and enjoyed incredible success as a coach. Gunter began her basketball career as a guard at Walnut Grove

(Mississippi) High School and at East Central Community College in Decatur, Mississippi. As a student in the Nashville BC from 1958 to 1962, she played guard for the (AAU) and earned All-America honors in 1960. Gunter also performed on the U.S. National Team from 1960 to 1962. She earned a Masters degree from Peabody College in 1962 and took her first basketball coaching job at Middle Tennessee State University from 1962 to 1964, guiding the Lady Blue Raiders in two undefeated seasons.

Gunter then coached basketball from 1964–1980 at Stephen F. Austin State University in Texas, leading the Ladyjacks to a 266-87 record, four top 10 national rankings, four state titles, and five AIAW tournaments. She also coached softball, tennis, and track and field. In 1980, Gunter left coaching to serve as Stephen F. Austin's Director of Women's Athletics. She then served as head coach for the Louisiana State University Lady Tigers from 1982 through April 2004, when acute bronchitis forced her to retire. The bronchitis sidelined her from game coaching after February 2004, but she advised acting coach Dana "Pokey" Chatman. In 22 seasons at LSU, Gunter led the Lady Tigers to 13 NCAA tournaments, three Elite Eight appearances, an SEC title, an NCAA Final Four appearance, and a 442-220 win-loss record at LSU. Gunter compiled an overall 708-307 career win-loss record. She coached a wealth of talented players including Pokey Chatman, Ke-Ke Tardy, and Seimone Augustus.

In the international arena, Gunter served as the head basketball coach for the U.S. National Team in 1976, 1978, and 1980, assistant coach for the 1976 silver medal Olympic team, and head coach for the 1980 Olympic team. She has won numerous honors, including the 1983 Louisiana Coach of the Year Award, 1994 Carol Eckman Award, 1997 SEC Coach of the Year, 1999 SEC and Louisiana Coach of the Year awards, and the 2002 Louisiana Coach of the Year. Gunter belongs to several halls of fame, including being an inaugural inductee into the Women's Basketball Hall of Fame. The Naismith Memorial Basketball Hall of Fame enshrined her in 2005. Among NCAA women coaches, she ranks third in victories, third in games coached, second in most seasons coached, and fourth in most 20-win seasons. Gunter, who never married, promotes community activism in organizations such as the Baton Rouge Lupus Foundation and the Walk for Alzheimer's.

BIBLIOGRAPHY: Mike Douchant, *Encyclopedia of College Basketball* (Detroit, MI, 1995); Carl DuBois, "Milestone—Coach Gunter seeking 600th Career Win Tonight," *Sunday Advocate* (January 13, 2000); Lee Feinswog, "Coach Enjoys Final Four Ride from Distance," *USA Today*, March 31, 2004, p. 3c; Sam King, "Gunter Earns Praise, Success with Hard Work," *Sunday Advocate* (March 30, 2003); *LSU Women's Basketball Media Guide, 2003–2004* (Baton Rouge, LA, 2003); "Sue Gunter," www.lsusports.net.

Lisa A. Ennis

H

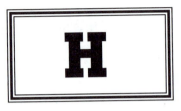

HAGAN, Clifford Oldham "Cliff" (b. December 9, 1931, Owensboro, KY), college and professional player, coach, and administrator, was elected in 1978 to the Naismith Memorial Basketball Hall of Fame. A 1952 and 1954 University of Kentucky consensus All-America forward, he played on the 1951 32-2 Wildcat NCAA tournament champions and the undefeated 25-0 1954 Kentucky five. Hagan, a star performer with the NBA 1958 champion St. Louis Hawks, scored 14,870 points in 13 pro basketball seasons and averaged 17.7 points. He was named to the 1958 and 1959 All-NBA Second Teams and performed in six All-Star games.

Hagan led Owensboro High School in 1949 to the Kentucky State Basketball Championship. He starred three seasons (1950–1951, 1951–1952, 1953–1954) at the University of Kentucky under legendary coach Adolph Rupp*. Kentucky was top-rated each year in the AP and UP polls, finishing with a combined 86-5 record. Kentucky in 1951 defeated the University of Louisville, St. John's University, and the University of Illinois in the NCAA tournament and posted a 68-58 triumph over Kansas State University in the finals for the title. Hagan scored 10 points, second only to Wildcats center Bill Spivey*, in the championship game. In the 1952 NCAA regional finals, St. John's upset Kentucky 64-57. The Wildcats had defeated St. John's earlier in the season by 41 points.

NCAA and SEC investigators in 1953 found recruiting and subsidizing irregularities at the University of Kentucky after a point-shaving scandal and suspended the Wildcats from competition for the entire season. Rupp drilled the squad, however, and had them play intrasquad games before hundreds of loyal fans. In 1954 Kentucky triumphed 73-60 over eventual NCAA tournament champion LaSalle University to win the first midseason University of Kentucky Invitational Tournament championship. The undefeated Wildcats overwhelmed every team except one on their schedule by at least 12 points. The SEC permitted Hagan, Frank Ramsey*, and Lou Tsioropoulos one year of eligibility, even though they had sufficient credits to graduate. The NCAA ruled them ineligible for postseason tournament play, however, considering them graduate students. Kentucky, minus its three top players, declined the NCAA tournament invitation, but savored the undefeated record and wire service top ratings. Hagan averaged 21.6 and 24.0 points his last two seasons with the Wildcats. He earned a Bachelor of Science degree in Education in 1953 at Kentucky and a Master of Science degree in Education in 1958 at Washington University of St. Louis (Missouri).

Hagan served from 1954 to 1956 as an officer in the U.S. Air Force and performed with the Andrews Air Force Base five. In April 1956, the Boston Celtics (NBA) traded Hagan and Ed Macauley to the St. Louis Hawks (NBA) for draft rights to Bill Russell*. He joined the St. Louis Hawks (NBA) in 1956 and helped key the Hawks' five consecutive (1957–1961) Western Division regular-season titles. St. Louis qualified for the playoff championship series each of those years except 1959, when they lost to the Minneapolis Lakers in the Western Division final series. The Hawks met the Boston Celtics the other four years, winning the 1958 NBA championship over the Celtics, four games to two. Hagan in 11 playoff games that year scored 305 points for a 27.7 points average. From 1959 to 1962, his seasonal averages ranged between 21.9 and 24.8 points to rank in the NBA's top ten. In 1960 Hagan (24.8 points average), Bob Pettit* (26.1), and Clyde Lovellette* (20.8) formed one of the best-balanced, highest-scoring (71.7 composite) front lines in NBA history.

The six-foot four-inch, 215-pound Hagan ranked among the all-time great hookshooters. A small forward, he possessed quickness and strength and operated well near the basket. During Hagan's last five seasons (1962–1966) with St. Louis, the Hawks finished second in the Western Division three times and reached the playoff Western Division final series three times. Hagan from 1968 to 1970 served as player-coach of the Dallas Chapparals of the newly organized ABA, guiding them to a composite 109-90 record. After being University of Kentucky assistant athletic director from 1972 to 1975, he succeeded Harry Lancaster in 1975 as athletic director. Hagan oversaw a $7 million annual athletic budget. Under his guidance until 1988, Kentucky constructed a $5 million natatorium, instituted a computerized athletic ticket sales program, and expanded facilities for women at Shively Sports Center and lounge and storage areas at the 57,600-seat Commonwealth Stadium. Rupp Arena hosted NCAA regional basketball and volleyball tournaments and the 1985 basketball Final Four. From 1976 to 1988, the Wildcats won two of three postseason football bowl engagements. Hagan married Martha Milton and has four children, Lisa, Laurie, Amy, and Clifford Jr.

BIBLIOGRAPHY: Peter C. Bjarkman, *The Biographical History of Basketball* (Chicago, IL, 2000); Mike Douchant, *Encyclopedia of College Basketball* (Detroit, MI, 1995); Clifford Hagan file, Naismith Memorial Basketball Hall of Fame, Springfield, MA; Jan Hubbard, ed., *The Official NBA Encyclopedia*, 3rd ed. (New York, 2000); Neil Isaacs, *All the Moves: A History of College Basketball* (Philadelphia, PA, 1975); V. A. Jackson, *Beyond the Baron* (Kuttawah, KY, 1998); *Kentucky Encyclopedia* (Champaign, IL, 2000); William G. Mokray, ed., *Ronald Encyclopedia of Basketball* (New York, 1963); Bert Nelli, *The Winning Tradition: A History of Kentucky Wildcat Basketball* (Lexington, KY, 1984); Russell Rice, *Kentucky Basketball's Big Blue Machine* (Huntsville, AL, 1976); Alan Ross, *Wildcat Wisdom* (Nashville, TN, 1999); *TSN Official NBA Register, 2004–2005* (St. Louis, MO, 2004); *WWA*, 41st ed, (1980–1981), p. 1,394.

James D. Whalen

HAGGERTY, George W. "Hot" "The Horse" (b. July 4, 1891, Springfield, MA; d. June 8, 1961, Reading, PA), professional player, coach, and referee, was the son of Daniel Haggerty, a bricklayer, and Ellen (Shugrue) Haggerty and demonstrated considerable athletic ability at Central High School in Springfield, Massachusetts. After playing semiprofessional basketball with Springfield, Illinois, Haggerty moved to Reading, Pennsylvania, in 1913 and enjoyed immediate stardom with the Bears (EL). In his first season, the Bears won the EL basketball title and defeated Troy, New York, the NYSL champion, for the world crown. In 1920 Haggerty joined the Original Celtics, a New York barnstorming professional quintet that became the most famous team in basketball history. Haggerty, the most publicized performer, teamed with Nat Holman*, Johnny Beckman*, Ernie Reich*, Pete Barry Johnny Whitty, Chris Leonard*, Mike Smolnik, and Dutch Dehnert* to form the legendary Original Celtics. The 1922–1923 Celtics won over 100 games, playing two contests on some days. The Naismith Memorial Basketball Hall of Fame inducted the Original Celtics as a team in 1959. In 1923 the Fort Wayne (Indiana) Knights of Columbus team designated Haggerty as player-coach. Two years later, Haggerty moved to Washington, D.C., as coach of George P. Marshall's Palace team (ABL). He later participated in semiprofessional basketball, performing with 100 different squads in his career. An ankle injury sidelined Haggerty in 1929, when he refereed numerous championship games. Haggerty, a bricklayer, married Marian K. Rhoades, but had no children.

The six-foot four-inch, 230-pound Haggerty, an exceptional defensive player and the sport's first good mobile big center, was considered a giant in his era. His assets included timing rebounds well and being a superb shot blocker. Haggerty often clashed with opposing players, spectators, and referees. A protector of his teammates, he once knocked out a spectator who had insulted a teammate and another time floored a referee who had thought was favoring the opponent. Haggerty, the first player to palm a basketball in one hand, attracted a wide spectator following. The personal foul rule was often waived so audiences could see him in full-time action.

BIBLIOGRAPHY: Peter C. Bjarkman, *The Biographical History of Basketball* (Chicago, IL, 2000); George W. Haggerty file, Naismith Memorial Basketball Hall of Fame, Springfield, MA; Zander Hollander, ed., *The Modern Encyclopedia of Basketball* (New York, 1969); Jan Hubbard, ed., *The Official NBA Basketball Encyclopedia*, 3rd ed. (New York, 2000); Murry R. Nelson, *The Originals: The New York Celtics Invent Modern Basketball* (Bowling Green, OH, 1999); Robert W. Peterson, *Cages to Jump Shots: Pro Basketball's Early Years* (New York, 1990); *Springfield* (MA) *Union News*, 1960; Alexander Weyand, *The Cavalcade of Basketball* (New York, 1960).

John L. Evers and Wayne Patterson

HALDORSON, Burdette Eliele "Burdie" (b. January 12, 1934, Freeborn County, MN), college and amateur player, is the son of Dorothy Haldorson, a public school teacher, and began his basketball career in Austin, Minnesota, where he made the All-State High School basketball team in 1951. Haldorson enrolled at the University of Colorado (BSC) in 1951 and played four varsity basketball seasons for coach Bebe Lee. In 1953–1954 and 1954–1955, he led the Buffaloes to BSC titles and NCAA basketball tournament appearances. Colorado reached the 1954–1955 NCAA Final Four, losing to the University of San Francisco Dons 75-54 in the semifinal round. In Haldorson's junior and senior years at Colorado, he won the BSC basketball scoring championship.

One week after the Final Four tournament, Haldorson embarked upon a remarkable AAU basketball career. In March 1955, he and six Colorado Buffalo teammates entered the National AAU basketball tournament as the Luckett-Nix Clippers. The Clippers, a Boulder, Colorado team, were sponsored by Phillips 66 Petroleum Company jobber Hap Luckett and University of Colorado barber Ed Nix. The Denver fans immediately rallied behind the Clippers, the tournament's Cinderella team and a local favorite, who did not disappoint them. After recording two relatively easy victories, Luckett-Nix stunned the Peoria (Illinois) Caterpillars, winners of the three previous AAU tournaments, 70-67. Haldorson scored 33 points, prompting a *Denver* (Colorado) *Post* writer to describe him as "a high-flying Eagle, soaring all alone above the rest of the flock." The following night, the Clippers defeated the Quantico (Virginia) Marines, led by future NBA star Richie Guerin*, in overtime 63-56. Haldorson scored 24 points in the AAU championship game, but the Phillips 66ers captured the national title 66-64 on a last-second shot.

In 1955, Haldorson joined the Phillips 66ers primarily because he wanted an opportunity to play on the U.S. 1956 Olympic basketball team. His 21.5 point scoring average his first season led all NIBL scorers, helping Phillips 66 win the NIBL crown. Phillips 66 lost the AAU championship game to the Seattle (Washington) Buchan Bakers 59-57, but the second-place finish earned Haldorson an invitation to the U.S. Olympic tournament in Kansas City, Missouri, Phillips won this tournament, as five 66ers, including Haldorson, made the 1956 U.S. Olympic team. The U.S. squad won the gold medal at the Melbourne, Australia Summer Games.

In his next four seasons with the 66ers, Haldorson led Phillips to two NIBL titles and one shared crown. He won the NIBL scoring title in 1957–1958 with a 26.7-point scoring average. During that season and the 1958–1959 campaign, his opponents selected him the NIBL's MVP. In 1958, Haldorson performed on the first U.S. athletic team to play in the Soviet Union. He played on the triumphant U.S. basketball team at the 1959 Pan-American Games in Chicago. Haldorson's final season, the 1959–1960 campaign, also marked an Olympic year. By taking the NIBL title, Phillips earned a place in the Olympic tournament held at Denver. After the tournament, the USOC placed him on the U.S. Olympic basketball team for the second time.

After winning his second Olympic gold medal in basketball at the Rome, Italy Summer Games, Haldorson retired. During his amateur basketball career, he won AAU All-America honors four times and was voted to five consecutive NIBL All-Star teams. He holds almost every Phillips scoring record, including most career points (4,472), highest career point scoring average (19.5), and most points in a game (53). Haldorson, a member of the Colorado, Minnesota, and Olympic halls of fame, worked for the Phillips 66 Oil Company for 10 years and then started his own business, Bonded Petroleum Company, in Colorado Springs, Colorado. He and his wife, Kaye, have three children, Linda, Brian, and Kari.

BIBLIOGRAPHY: Tom Boyd and Daniel B. Droege, *Phillips: The First 66 Years* (Bartlesville, OK, 1983); George Durham, "He's a High Flying Burd!" *SR: B* (1959), pp. 70–72; Bill Mallon and Ian Buchanan, *Quest for Gold: The Encyclopedia of American Olympians* (New York, 1984); *Philnews*, a Phillips 66 monthly magazine, Phillips 66 Archives, Bartlesville, OK; Alexander Weyand, *The Cavalcade of Basketball* (New York, 1960).

Adolph H. Grundman

HANNUM, Alexander Murray "Alex" (b. July 19, 1923, Los Angeles, CA; d. January 18, 2002, San Diego, CA), college and professional player and coach, was the only coach in pro basketball history to win both NBA and ABA championships. Hannum, the son of Edward Hannum and Agnes Hannum, grew up in Los Angeles, where his father owned and operated an oriental rug cleaning business. At Alexander Hamilton High School in Los Angeles, Hannum played center and was named to the All-Western League basketball team as a junior and All-City team as a senior. He entered the University of Southern California on a basketball scholarship in 1941. Hannum served in the U.S. Army as a medical reconditioning instructor from 1943 to 1946, and rose to the rank of sergeant. He returned to Southern California for his junior year in 1946. During his last two years at Southern California, he teamed with Bill Sharman*. In his senior year, he led the Trojans in scoring with an 11.4 points average. After graduating from Southern California in 1948 with a Bachelor's degree in business, Hannum took his six-foot seven-inch, 225-pound frame into the NBL with the Oshkosh (Wisconsin) All-Stars. The next year witnessed the birth of the NBA, where Hannum played for eight years (1948–1949 to 1956–1957) with the Syracuse Nationals, Baltimore Bullets, Rochester Royals, Milwaukee Hawks, Fort Wayne Pistons, and St. Louis Hawks. Hannum, the journeyman forward, ended his pro career averaging 6 points.

Hannum, a superb pro mentor, began his coaching career with the St. Louis Hawks during the 1956–1957 season. Ben Kerner, the Hawks' owner, fired coach Red Holzman* in midseason and named Slater Martin*, Hannum's roommate, as player-coach. Because Martin played regularly and exhibited little interest in coaching and Hannum played infrequently, Hannum began to handle the team from the bench. At Martin's urging, Kerner named Hannum player-coach. The Hawks made the 1957 NBA Finals against the heavily favored Boston Celtics, who were led by Bob Cousy* and rookie Bill Russell*. Although the Celtics won the decisive seventh game by two points in double overtime, the nationally televised championship series helped bring prestige to the young NBA. With Hannum coaching full time and Bob Pettit* starring, the Hawks won the 1958 NBA championship by defeating the Celtics in an exciting seven-game series. Hannum left the NBA after that season to concentrate on his contracting business in California and coach an AAU team.

Hannum returned to pro coaching in 1960 and stayed in it for the next 14 seasons. His coaching career had two distinct trends. He came to a team, invariably improved its record, and always coached for teams with unstable ownership and management, never coaching for long in one place. Hannum coached the Syracuse Nationals (NBA) from 1960 to 1963, finishing his last season there with an excellent 48-32 record. He left Syracuse to coach the San Francisco Warriors (NBA), enabling him to return to California where he continued to operate his own contracting business throughout his entire coaching career. Hannum guided the Warriors, which had finished fourth the previous season, to a first place finish in the Western Division and the NBA Finals before losing to the Celtics. Hannum earned Coach of the Year honors. Wilt Chamberlain*, playing for Hannum in San Francisco, changed his game from offensive oriented to defensive and team oriented. Both player and coach soon tangled with Warriors management. Chamberlain was traded to Philadelphia, and Hannum was fired after the 1965–1966 season.

Hannum began coaching the Philadelphia 76ers (NBA) during the 1966–1967 season and was reunited there with Chamberlain and several former players from the Syracuse Nationals franchise, which had moved to Philadelphia in 1964. Many observers have called the 1966–1967 76ers the greatest team in NBA history. The 76ers set a record with its .840 winning percentage during the regular season, before defeating the Celtics in five games in the Eastern finals and the Warriors in six games for the NBA championship. Hannum had won NBA championships in 1958 with the St. Louis Hawks and in 1967 with the Philadelphia 76ers. During the intervening years (1959 through 1966), the Celtics had won eight straight NBA championships. For those 10 seasons, the only NBA champions were the Boston Celtics and Hannum's teams.

Hannum coached Philadelphia one more year before returning to California as coach of the Oakland Oaks (ABA). The Oaks, a last place team the previous year, won the ABA championship in 1968–1969 with the addition of Hannum and star forward Rick Barry*. When the Oaks folded after that season, Hannum's coaching odyssey took him to San Diego (NBA) and Denver (ABA). At Denver, he was president, general manager, and coach. He ended his pro coaching career after the 1973–1974 season, when the Denver franchise was sold and the new owner did not offer to renew Hannum's contract. Hannum's coaching record was 471-412 (.533) in the NBA and 178-152 (.539) in the ABA.

Hannum lived in Santa Monica, California, with his wife, Marcia, and his daughter, Margaret, after leaving basketball. He owned and operated Alex Hannum General Construction, Incorporated and also had one daughter, Susan, from a previous marriage. Hannum described himself as "an itinerant blue-collar player and coach." Itinerant, yes, but a winner everywhere, as Hannum's 518 NBA wins place him twenty-third on the all-time list as of 2004. Blue collar, yes, as he worked hard and inspired his players to follow suit. Hannum influenced many of his players, such as Larry Brown*, Doug Moe*, Larry Costello*, Billy Cunningham*, and Matt Guokas Jr., to become coaches in the pro ranks. Former player Nate Thurmond* said, "Alex Hannum was a builder of men." Chamberlain asserted simply, "Alex Hannum was the greatest coach I ever had." In 1998, he was elected to the Naismith Memorial Basketball Hall of Fame.

BIBLIOGRAPHY: Peter C. Bjarkman, *The Biographical History of Basketball* (Chicago, IL, 2000); Frank Deford, "Sarge Takes Philly to the Top," *SI* 26 (January 2, 1967), pp. 10–13; Frank Deford, "The Waiting Made It Sweeter," *SI* 26 (May 8, 1967), pp. 54–56; Glenn Dickey, *The History of Professional Basketball Since 1896* (Briarcliff Manor, NY, 1982); Alex Hannum, telephone interview with Mark Altschuler, April 16, 1987; Alexander Hannum file, Naismith Memorial Basketball Hall of Fame, Springfield, MA; Marcia Hannum, telephone interview with Mark Altschuler, April 16, 1987; Zander Hollander, ed., *The Modern Encyclopedia of Basketball* (Garden City, NY, 1979); Jan Hubbard, ed., *The Official NBA Basketball Encyclopedia*, 3rd ed. (New York, 2000); Neil D. Isaacs, *Vintage NBA* (Silver Spring, MD, 1996); Bill Libby, *Goliath: The Wilt Chamberlain Story* (New York, 1977); Wayne Lynch, *Season of the 76ers* (New York, 2002); Ronald L. Mendell, *Who's Who in Basketball* (New Rochelle, NY, 1973); Claudia Mitrol, ed., *Philadelphia's Greatest Sports Moments* (Champaign, IL, 2000); "NBA Coaches Victories," Albuquerque *Tribune* (January 14, 1987), p. B2.

Mark Altschuler

HANSON, Victor Arthur "Vic" (b. July 30, 1903, Watertown, NY; d. April 10, 1982, Syracuse, NY), college athlete and professional basketball player, remains one of the few people enshrined in two sports halls of fame. He was the son of Cornelius Hanson and Catherine Hanson. The Hansons moved to Syracuse, New York, where Victor attended Central High School from 1919 to 1922 and Manlius Military Academy in 1922 and 1923. There, he participated football, baseball, basketball, and track and field. Undefeated in the 100- and 200-yard dashes, he twice led his high school to State Championships. At Manlius Military Academy, he refined his football skills under coach Dr. Harry Kolen.

In the fall of 1923, Hanson enrolled at Syracuse University after screening numerous college scholarship offers. A versatile athlete, he captained Syracuse varsity teams in football, basketball, and baseball in 1926–1927. He earned only nine varsity letters—three in each sport—during his career there because freshmen could not compete on varsity teams. According to sportswriter Grantland Rice, Hanson's football prowess as an end was attributed to "his great speed, exceptional ability at handling a pass, hard, sure tackling and blocking, plus the instinctive knack of diagnosing the play." Hanson, a remarkable athlete for his size, weighed only 160 pounds and stood five-feet ten-inches tall. Hanson, who gained All-Eastern honors in 1925 and AP All-America end accolades in 1926, was inducted into the NFF College Football Hall of Fame in 1973.

During the 1926–1927 basketball season, Hanson made All-America forward and captained the Syracuse University national championship team under Coach Lew Andreas. He also was named All-America in 1925 and again in 1927. He set the single-season Syracuse scoring record with 280 points in 1925–1926 and held it for 20 years. Besides being Player of the Year in 1927, he was named All-Time All-America in 1952 with George Mikan*, Bob Kurland*, Hank Luisetti*, and John Wooden* by Grantland Rice. His college basketball teams established a 48-7 record during three seasons.

Hanson played professionally with the Cleveland Rosenblums and organized the All-American pro basketball team, which defeated most great pro teams of the time. In 1952, he was picked for the HAF Basketball Hall of Fame. A year later, the HAF of Los Angeles named him as the greatest amateur athlete of New York State. Hanson was inducted into the Naismith Memorial Basketball Hall of Fame in 1960. In late 1981 Syracuse University retired his number eight jersey, an honor then shared only by Dave Bing*. The Syracuse Hardwood Club annually presents the Victor Hanson Medal of Excellence to continue his legacy of athletic glory.

In 1954 Hercules Productions Incorporated of Burbank, California asked him to appear in several parts of a film about his athletic career and to serve as its technical adviser. The film was one of a series depicting the lives of All-Americas selected to the HAF Hall of Fame. In 1954–1955, Hanson coached the basketball College All-Americas in a game with the Syracuse Nationals (NBA). Hanson's squad included Larry Costello*, Niagara University; Gene Shue*, University of Maryland; Cliff Hagan* and Frank Ramsey*, University of Kentucky; Bob Pettit*, LSU; Frank Selvy*, Furman University; Bob Leonard*, Indiana University, and Johnny Kerr*, University of Illinois; and other outstanding players.

Although less is written about his baseball achievements, Hanson earned three varsity letters at Syracuse University. A hitter of considerable talent, he batted .400 according to his freshman coach T. Walker "Lefty" Coughlin. His desire for excellence and self-improvement continued throughout his short career in the New York Yankees (AL) farm system and his coaching days. In 1928, he returned to Syracuse as assistant football coach. In 1930, Hanson was appointed head football coach at Syracuse University at age 27. Hanson typically performed well throughout his seven years as head coach, compiling 33 wins, 21 losses, and 5 ties. The 1931 and 1935 teams posted only one loss each, both times to Colgate University. After leaving Syracuse University, he pursued the insurance business and later returned to coaching and teaching at Freeport (New York) High School.

In his later years, Hanson lost the use of his once powerful legs and eventually became bedridden. His mind remained alert, while his undying interest in sports kept him glued to the radio and telephone at his home in Minoa, New York. He was survived by his wife, Dorothy (Burns) Hanson, and two sons, Dr. Victor Jr. and John.

BIBLIOGRAPHY: Peter C. Bjarkman, *The Biographical History of Basketball* (Chicago, IL, 2000); Mike Douchant, *Encyclopedia of College Basketball* (Detroit, MI, 1995); Victor Hansen file, Naismith Memorial Basketball Hall of Fame, Springfield, MA;

Bob Snyder, ed., *Syracuse Basketball* (Champaign, IL, 1999); Zander Hollander, ed., *The Modern Encyclopedia of Basketball* (Garden City, NY, 1979); Ronald L. Mendell, *Who's Who in Basketball* (New Rochelle, NY, 1973); *Syracuse Herald-American*, October 6, 1954; *Syracuse Herald-Journal*, April 10, 1982; *Syracuse Post Standard*, November 24, 1936; February 1, 1939; August 21, 1939; June 6, 1954; August 28, 1954; January 12, 1960; *Syracuse Record*, April 15, 1982; "Vic Hanson and 1923," *Syracuse Alumni News* (October 1953); *Watertown Daily Times*, April 12, 1982.

Sara-Jane Griffin

HARDAWAY, Anfernee Deon "Penny" (b. July 18, 1971, Memphis, TN), college and professional player, was nicknamed "Penny" as a child. The nickname is now routinely used as his Christian name. An only child, Hardaway is the son of Eddie Golden and Fae Hardaway and was brought up by his grandmother, Louise, in an economically depressed down-town Memphis location. In a 1993 *Newsweek* interview, he spoke about one of his lifetime goals. Hardaway wanted to parlay his considerable basketball talents so that his grandmother and mother, Fae Patterson, would have, "the finer things in life. They did so much for me and I want to repay them." He graduated from Thadwell High School in Memphis, and entered Memphis State University.

Nolan Richardson*, the then Arkansas coach, regarded Hardaway as Larry Bird*, Magic Johnson*, and Michael Jordan* all rolled into one. In a March 1993 outing, Hardaway scored 31 points on only 12 shots in a 75-72 win over St. Louis University. The then Memphis State University junior made All-America. In three seasons, he averaged 20.0 points, 7.7 rebounds, and 5.9 assists in 66 games.

His basketball career has been frequently upset by all manner of outside distractions. As a Memphis State student, he was robbed at gunpoint and shot in the leg. In his freshman year, he had to sit out after being unable to meet minimum entrance test standards.

The six-foot seven-inch, 215-pound player passed up his senior year and signed with the Orlando Magic (NBA). His first games were frequently met by boos from fans who believed that Orlando should have selected Chris Webber* rather than Hardaway as their top draft pick. Hardaway found such responses difficult to handle. In a February 1994 interview, he said, "I've been loved everywhere I've ever played." At Memphis, he was perceived as an icon and folk hero after November 23, 1994, when Hardaway took on Webber's Golden State Warriors and steered Orlando to a 120-107 win. Hardaway netted 23 points, 10 more than Webber.

In 1995, Hardaway made the cover of the February 13 *SI* issue. His soaring photograph saw him subtitled as, "out of this world." He started for the Eastern Conference in the NBA All-Star Game in February 1995, only months after signing a nine-year, $70 million contract. His stellar play saw him average 20.7 points and 6.6 assists for Orlando, which finished first with a 36-10 record. He made the All-NBA First Team in 1995 and 1996 and the All-NBA Third Team in 1997.

In 1997 *SI* published a piece headed, "A Penny Saved," describing consecutive games between Orlando and the Miami Heat in which Hardaway poured in 33 and 42 points, respectively. His performances were described as "Jordanesque in their brilliance and courage."

In August 1999, Hardaway was traded to the Phoenix Suns (NBA). A Charles P. Pierce 2000 *Esquire* essay spoke of Hardaway as bigger than Mickey Mouse in Orlando, but was just one of a crowd of tall players in Phoenix. Although repeated injuries in the late 1990s played havoc with his career, Hardaway still negotiated a long term $86 million contract with the Suns in the summer of 1999.

In 2001, Hardaway experienced an athletic renaissance. Despite having four operations on his left knee in four years, the 30-year-old was averaging 18.6 points, 5.2 rebounds and 4.8 assists by mid-December.

In January 2004, the New York Knicks (NBA) acquired Hardaway and Stephan Marbury. The Knicks were rejuvinated after the trade and finished seventh in the Eastern Conference in 2003–2004. The New Jersey Nets swept New York in the first round of the playoffs, with Hardaway tallying 66 points (16.5 point average). Injuries limited him to 37 games in 2004–2005. During 12 NBA seasons through 2004–2005, he has averaged 15.5 points, 5.1

assists, and 4.5 rebounds in 684 regular season games and 20.4 points and 6.2 assists in 64 playoff games. He appeared in the All-Star Games from 1995 through 1998 and played in the gold-medal-winning U.S. Olympic team in 1996.

BIBLIOGRAPHY: Mike Douchant, *Encyclopedia of College Basketball* (Detroit, MI, 1995); J. MacMullan, "Inside the NBA," *SI* 86 (May 12, 1997), pp. 97–99; "Phoenix Suns," *SI* 99 (October 27, 2003), p. 106; C. P. Pierce, "The Disappearance of Anfernee Hardaway," *Esquire* 133 (February 2000), pp. 56–61; Ken Shouler et al., *Total Basketball* (Wilmington, DE, 2003); *TSN Official NBA Register, 2004–2005* (St. Louis, MO, 2004); M. Starr with V. E. Smith, "This Penny is Worth Millions," *Newsweek* 121 (March 15, 1993), p. 70; P. Taylor, "Together Forever," *SI* 80 (February 7, 1994), pp. 50–55; P. Taylor, "A Touch of Magic," *SI* 82 (February 13, 1995), pp. 37–42.

Scott A.G.M. Crawford

HARDAWAY, Timothy Duane "Tim" (b. September 1, 1966, Chicago, IL), college and professional player and sportscaster, excelled as a point guard collegiately at the University of Texas at El Paso (UTEP) and professionally with the Golden State Warriors (NBA) and Miami Heat (NBA). He grew up on the South Side of Chicago. His father, Donald Hardaway, a fabled Chicago playground basketball player who drove a Coca-Cola truck, and mother Gwendolyn Hardaway, a postal worker, divorced in 1978 due to the former's problems with alcohol.

An outstanding basketball player at Carver High School in Chicago, Hardaway played collegiately for coach Don Haskins* at UTEP. At El Paso from 1985–1986 to 1988–1989, he averaged 12.8 points, 2.6 rebounds, and 4.5 assists. The Golden State Warriors selected Hardaway with the fourteenth pick of the 1989 NBA draft. The six-foot, 195-pound guard, nicknamed "Bug" for his relative small size to other basketball players, enjoyed immediate success with the Warriors in 1989–1990, averaging 14.7 points and 8.7 assists and making the 1990 NBA All-Rookie First Team. Using his signature move of the cross over dribble, Hardaway averaged over 20 points and 10 assists for the 1991–1992 and 1992–1993 seasons and was selected for the NBA All-Star Game both years. Due to a knee injury, he missed the 1993–1994 season. Upon returning for the 1995 campaign, he struggled to regain his game and quarreled with coach Rick Adelman*.

In February 1996, the Warriors traded Hardaway to the Miami Heat. Hardaway regained his form under the direction of Pat Riley*, leading the Heat to a 61-21 regular-season record and the Atlantic Division title in 1996–1997. Miami bowed to Michael Jordan* and the Chicago Bulls in the 1997 Eastern Conference Finals. In 2000, he performed for the gold medal–winning Olympic team.

After six successful seasons with the Heat, Hardaway was traded in August 2001 to the Dallas Mavericks (NBA) because Miami attempted to rebuild their team with younger players. He performed with Dallas and the Denver Nuggets (NBA) during the 2001–2002 season, before being waived. Hardaway retired and pursued a broadcasting career with ESPN until being lured back to the sport by the Indiana Pacers (NBA), who hoped to bolster their bench for a playoff run in March 2003. The signing of Hardaway, however, failed to prevent a Pacer exit in the first round of the 2003 playoffs. In 14 NBA seasons, Hardaway averaged 17.7 points, 3.3 rebounds, and 8.2 assists. Hardaway was selected to the All-NBA First Team in 1997, the All-NBA Second Team in 1992, 1998, and 1999, and the All-NBA Third Team in 1993. A five time NBA All-Star, he and his wife, Yolanda, have two children.

BIBLIOGRAPHY: Eddie Mullens, ed., *The Man They Call the Bear* (El Paso, TX, 1990); Bruce Newman, "To the Point," *SI* 74 (February 11, 1991), pp. 52–54; S. L. Price, "Hot Hand," *SI* 86 (May 5, 1997), pp. 28–31; Ken Shouler et al., *Total Basketball* (Wilmington, DE, 2003); *TSN Official NBA Register, 2004–2005* (St. Louis, MO, 2004).

Ron Briley

HARRICK, James R., Sr. "Jim" (b. July 25, 1938, Charleston, WV), college player and coach, is the son of Major Harrick, a hustler and hotel owner, and Helen Harrick. He graduated in 1956 from Stonewall Jackson High School in Charleston, West Virginia, where he played basketball and football. Harrick attended Marshall University for two years and transferred to

Morris Harvey College. He played basketball two years for the Golden Eagles and earned Bachelor's degrees in speech and physical education in 1960.

Harrick married Sally Marple on August 20, 1960 and moved to California, where he was employed as a classroom teacher and earned his Master's degree from the University of Southern California. They have three children, Monte, James Jr., and Glenn.

After serving as assistant basketball coach at Morningside High School in Inglewood, California from 1964 to 1969, Harrick gained his first experience as head basketball coach when he led the Morningside Monarchs to a 103-16 win-loss record from 1970 to 1973. He spent four years as an assistant basketball coach at Utah State University and served in 1977 and 1978 as an assistant coach at UCLA, before being named to his first collegiate head coaching position at Pepperdine University in Malibu, California.

Between 1979–1980 and 1988–1989, Harrick guided the Waves to a 167-97 win-loss record and four of his squads produced 20 or more victories. Six of his teams qualified for postseason play, while his 1981, 1982, 1983, 1985, and 1986 teams captured the WCAC title. He was chosen WCAC Coach of the Year in 1982, 1983, 1985, and 1986.

Harrick was named head basketball coach at UCLA prior to the 1988–1989 season and led the Bruins to an overall 191-63 win-loss record in his eight seasons. All eight of his squads won at least 20 games and qualified for the NCAA tournament. His 1994–1995 Bruins posted a 31-2 overall record and captured the national championship by defeating the University of Arkansas in the NCAA Finals. The 1995–1996 campaign marked his final season as the Bruins head coach. An investigation by the university disclosed that he had misused school funds during a recruiting contact and had given a false account of the incident. Harrick was fired in November 1996 one season after being named National Coach of the Year. Under the tutelage of Harrick, the Bruins won three Pac-10 titles, and averaged over 23 triumphs.

Harrick spent the 1996–1997 season out of coaching before accepting the head basketball coaching position at the University of Rhode Island. He led the Rams to two consecutive NCAA appearances, an ATC title, a trip to the "Elite Eight," and a 45-22 overall record in two seasons.

Harrick was hired in 1999 by the University of Georgia to serve as head coach and resigned his position in March 2003 when he and his son, an assistant coach, were charged with academic fraud and other NCAA violations. In four seasons, Harrick led the Bulldogs to an overall 67-53 record and two appearances in the NCAA tournament. Georgia halted another appearance when it withdrew the top-rated Bulldogs from competition in both the SEC and NCAA tournaments.

The Vancouver expansion team (ABA) hired Harrick as head coach in June 2004. During 23 years as a head coach, Harrick compiled a 470-235 win-loss record and qualified 18 of his squads for postseason play. He remains one of only three coaches in basketball history to lead four different schools to the NCAA tournament. Notable players during Harrick's coaching career include Ed O'Bannon of UCLA, Tyson Wheeler of Rhode Island, and Lance Odom of Georgia.

In 1994, Harrick received an honorary doctorate degree from Morris Harvey College and was inducted into their Sports Hall of Fame.

BIBLIOGRAPHY: Mike Douchant, *Encyclopedia of College Basketball* (Detroit, MI, 1995); "Jim Harrick," *Coaching Career*, http://www.espn.go.com (2003); "Jim Harrick," *Profile*, http://www.georgiadogs.com (2003); "Jim Harrick," *Resigns*, http://www.collegesports.com (2003); "Jim Harrick," *Rhode Island*, http://www.reviewjournal.com (1997); "Jim Harrick," *Suspended*, http://www.ourgeogiahistory.com (2003); Jim Harrick, *Embracing The Legend* (Chicago, IL, 1995); Scott Howard-Cooper, *The Bruins 100* (Lenexa, KS, 1999); Gary K. Johnson, *NCAA Men's Basketball's Finest* (Overland Park, KS, 1998); *NCAA Men's Basketball Records, 2004* (Indianapolis, IN, 2003).

John L. Evers

HARRIS, Lusia. *See* Stewart, Lucia Harris "Lucy"

HARRISON, Lester "Les" (b. August 20, 1904, Rochester, NY; d. December 23, 1997, Rochester, NY), professional basketball player and coach, was the son of Abraham Harrison and Sarah Harrison and had one brother, Jack, and one sister, Evelyn. After participating in playground basketball, he enjoyed a fine high school career as a guard and a semipro and pro basketball career as a coach, owner, and organizer. From 1919 to 1923, he also starred as first baseman for East High School in Rochester, New York. His best basketball game at East High School came when he scored 16 points in his team's 20-16 victory. After graduating from East High School in 1923, Harrison assumed his father's produce business to help put younger brother, Jack, through the University of Rochester.

Between 1923 and 1930, Harrison organized basketball teams and games and played semiprofessional for the Eber Brothers and Seagrams teams. From 1930 to 1943, he coached both organizations. In 1945, Harrison became co-owner with his brother, Jack, and coached the Rochester Pros (NBL). The next year, he changed the team name to the Rochester Royals (NBL). The 1946 Royals won the NBL Championship by defeating the New York Knickerbockers in a seven-game series. The Royals, featuring Bob Davies*, Bob Wanzer*, Joe Coleman, Arnie Risen*, and Arnie Johnson, finished as NBL playoff runners-up in 1947 and 1948 and as BAA runners-up in 1949. Before the 1949–1950 season, Rochester joined the new NBA. Under Harrison's leadership, the Royals won the 1951 NBA title and had posted 394 wins and 220 losses by 1955 when he became owner only. Before the 1957–1958 season, the Royals relocated to Cincinnati. In 1958 Harrison sold the team.

In one of his most notable moves, Harrison in 1946 signed Dolly King of Long Island University as the first black pro basketball player in the NBL. The Royals, the only Eastern NBL team, consequently experienced discriminatory treatment throughout their travels. In 1944 Mayor Fiorello LaGuardia of New York City enlisted Harrison, who possessed great organizational skills, to form the PSAL. During Harrison's tenure as membership chairman, the PSAL provided summer programs for over 800,000 Rochester school age children. Harrison applied his positive thinking and innovative spirit to direct the well-known PSAL programs.

Harrison's enthusiasm and vivacious personality also brought him success in the business world, as he founded his own sports promotion agency, Lester Harrison, Incorporated. Harrison organized the Kodak Classic Collegiate Tournament in 1963, served as tournament director for the University of Rochester Basketball Classic, and belonged to the Board of Directors for three basketball leagues. Originally a proponent of the 30-second clock rule, he served on the Rules Committee when the 24-second clock rule was adopted for the NBA. Harrison strongly favored the new rule to maintain interest in the game both for players and spectators.

A bachelor, Harrison continued actively to promote sports and basketball. The Naismith Memorial Basketball Hall of Fame elected him to membership in 1979 as a contributor. He demonstrated a zealous approach to life, reflected in his major contribution to basketball. In responding to a query about his favorite all-time player, he remarked, "I have no favorites, they are all my favorites." Harrison simply loved basketball and all its trappings.

BIBLIOGRAPHY: Peter C. Bjarkman, *The History of the NBA* (New York, 1992); Lester Harrison to Sara-Jane Griffin, May 18, 1984; Lester Harrison, telephone conversation with Sara-Jane Griffin, May 31, 1984; July 19, 1984; Lester Harrison file, Naismith Memorial Basketball Hall of Fame, Springfield, MA; Jan Hubbard, ed., *The Official NBA Encyclopedia*, 3rd ed. (New York, 2000); Neil D. Isaacs, *Vintage NBA* (Silver Spring, MD, 1996); "Lester Harrison on Plans; Commissioner Kent on Program," *NYT*, May 25, 1944, p. 23.

Sara-Jane Griffin

HARSHMAN, Marvin "Marv" (b. October 4, 1917, Eau Claire, WI), college athlete and basketball coach, probably remains best known for his success as basketball coach at the University of Washington and as the twentieth most successful basketball mentor in college history. He was, however, much more than that. Harshman coached the Huskies for 14 years from the start of the 1972–1973 season through an NCAA appearance in 1984–1985. Thirteen of those seasons produced winning records. The Huskies appeared in the NCAA tournament three times (1976, 1984, and 1985) and in the NIT twice

(1980 and 1982) under Harshman. But that marked only one-third of his career. He also spent 13 years each as head coach of the Huskies' chief rival, Washington State University, and earlier at his alma mater, Pacific Lutheran University, in Tacoma, Washington. In 40 years as a head coach in the state of Washington, Harshman enjoyed a win-loss record of 642-448. The only coaches with more wins, as of his retirement, were Adolph Rupp* (University of Kentucky), "Phog" Allen* (University of Kansas), Henry Iba* (Oklahoma State University), Ed Diddle* (Western Kentucky University), Ray Meyer* (DePaul University), and John Wooden* (UCLA). All seven are members of the Naismith Memorial Basketball Hall of Fame. In 1984, Harshman was elected as a coach to the Naismith Memorial Basketball Hall of Fame.

Harshman started his athletic career as a four-sport star at Lake Stevens (Washington) High School, where his family had moved when he was a child. He graduated from Lake Stevens High School and entered Pacific Lutheran University, starring as a football fullback, a basketball guard, a baseball third baseman, and high jumper and shotputter on the track and field squad. The *New York Sun* named him an All-America in football and basketball. He won 13 letters in four years, including four in football and baseball and two in basketball. After graduating in 1942 with a Bachelor's degree in biological science, Harshman joined the U.S. Navy, and remained in the service until his discharge with the rank of chief petty officer in 1946. In the Navy, he began his coaching career. He was stationed in the Aleutian Islands, where he organized and coached a basketball team.

Harshman began his collegiate coaching career at Pacific Lutheran University in 1946. For several years, he coached the football, track and field, and basketball teams. He coached four NAIA District I basketball champions at Pacific Lutheran and guided his club to the national tournament four times. His 1957 club finished third nationally in District I with a 28-1 record. In 13 years at Washington State University, Harshman produced three second place basketball teams. He recorded winning teams at Washington State, traditionally not a basketball stronghold before his arrival, in five of his last six years. At the University of Washington, Harshman was selected NCAA Division I Coach of the Year in 1984 and was chosen PTC Coach of the Year in 1982 and 1984. He was named Seattle's Man of the Year in Sports in 1975 and won the *Seattle Post-Intelligencer's* Golden Anniversary Coaching Award in 1985. Harshman also coached the U.S. to the 1975 Pan American Games Gold Medal in basketball. His last two teams at Washington (1983–1985) finished 24-7 and 22-10, winning consecutive PTC championships and appearing in the NCAA tournament both times. Those teams were led by All-Americas Detlef Schrempf and Christian Welp.

Shortly before his retirement, Harshman told the AP: "My players don't have to like me, but I do require their respect. I hope I taught them some good values in my career, and I hope they could build on those." Four of Harshman's University of Washington teams won at least 20 games, with 11 of the 14 squads taking at least 16. He also served as president of the NABC and as a member of the board of directors of the Naismith Memorial Basketball Hall of Fame. He and his wife, Dorothy, have three sons, David, Richard, and Brian. David served as an assistant basketball coach at Washington State University.

BIBLIOGRAPHY: Mike Douchant, *Encyclopedia of College Basketball* (Detroit, MI, 1995); Marv Harshman file, Naismith Memorial Basketball Hall of Fame, Springfield, MA; *Los Angeles Times*, 1982–1985; *NCAA Men's Basketball Records, 2004* (Indianapolis, IN, 2003); Terry Mosher, *Harsh* (Silverdale, WA, 1994); Pacific Lutheran University Athletic Department, Tacoma, WA; University of Washington Office of Sports Information, Seattle, WA.

Jay Berman

HASKINS, Donald Lee "Don" "The Bear" "H" (b. March 31, 1930, Enid, OK), college player and coach, is the son of Paul Haskins, a truck driver, and Opal (Richey) Haskins and was nicknamed "H" at Enid High School, where he pitched and played third base on the baseball team and gained All-State honors as a baseball pitcher and basketball player in 1948. Haskins attended Oklahoma Agricultural and Mechanical

(A&M) (renamed Oklahoma State) University (MVC) and played guard and forward for the fabled Hank Iba* on basketball teams that twice won MVC titles and NCAA tournament trips. He was named Second Team All-MVC as a senior, helped Oklahoma A&M to a 23-7 record in 1952–1953, and played for the Artesia REA Travelers (NIBL) from 1953 to 1955.

Haskins in 1955 became basketball coach at Benjamin (Texas) High School, drove a school bus, and coached six-man football and girls basketball. His boys basketball team compiled a 21-10 record. He spent the next four years at Hedley, (Texas) High School, guiding his teams to three district titles, a regional crown, and the school's first trip to the state tournament while achieving an overall 114-24 mark. In 1960–1961 his 25-7 Dumas (Texas) High School squad won the district and regional championships and a state tournament bid. Haskins's six-year 160-41 record and postseason success led to his only college coaching job.

In his first year at Texas Western College (renamed the University of Texas at El Paso), Haskins's 18-6 squad recorded the most victories in the Miners' history. The Miners steadily improved the next two years. After boasting a 16-9 mark in his fourth year, Texas Western enjoyed a brilliant 28-1 campaign in 1965–1966. The season produced an NCAA championship, as the Miners upset the University of Kentucky 72-65 in the title game. This game marked the first national crown of any kind for a Miners team. Even more notable, no team with an all-black starting lineup previously had taken the national basketball crown. Texas-El Paso joined the WAC in 1970 and won or shared the WAC title seven times. Haskins's only assistant coaching job came in the 1972 Munich, Germany Summer Olympic Games, when he helped Iba for the U.S. team. Their players included All-Americas Jim Barnes, Bobby Joe Hill, and Nate Archibald* and highly successful college coach Nolan Richardson*. Haskins was inducted into the Texas Sports Hall of Fame in 1987, and the Naismith Memorial Basketball Hall of Fame in 1997.

In 38 years at Texas-El Paso through 1998–1999, Haskins compiled a 719-353 win-loss mark. Only nine NCAA Division I coaches compiled more career games, and only 13 more career victories. From the outset, "The Bear" stressed defense and rebounding. Nationally, his 1963–1964 Miners team ranked third for fewest points allowed per game and first for highest rebound average. Subsequent teams consistently finished among the national leaders in these statistics. Haskins married Mary Gorman on March 14, 1951, and has four sons, Mark, Brent, Steve, and David. His hobbies are fishing and hunting.

BIBLIOGRAPHY: Frank Deford, "The Champions Get After It," *SI* 25 (December 12, 1966), pp. 26–28, 31; Frank Deford, "Go-Go with Bobby Joe," *SI* 24 (March 28, 1966), pp. 26–29, 60–61; Frank Deford, "Now There Are Four," *SI* 24 (March 21, 1966), pp. 22–24; Mike Douchant, *Encyclopedia of College Basketball* (Detroit, MI, 1995); *ESPN Sports Almmac, 2005* (New York, 2004); Joe Gergen, *The Final Four* (St. Louis, MO, 1987); Don Haskins file, Naismith Memorial Basketball Hall of Fame, Springfield, MA; Eddie Mullens, ed., *The Man They Call the Bear* (El Paso, TX, 1990); *NCAA Men's Basketball Records, 2004* (Indianapolis, IN, 2003); Ray Sanchez, *Basketball's Biggest Upset* (El Paso, TX, 1991).

Thomas P. Wolf

HATCHELL, Sylvia Rhyne (b. February 28, 1952, Gastonia, NC), coach, ranks among the most respected, successful women's basketball coaches in the nation and has one brother and one sister. She received her B.S. degree in physical education (cum laude) from Carson-Newman College in 1974 and M.S. degree in science from the University of Tennessee in 1975. Hatchell, who has loved sports since childhood, participated in multiple sports in college, but found her calling when she was asked to coach a seventh- and eighth-grade girls' basketball team in 1974. After serving as junior varsity women's basketball coach at the University of Tennessee, she coached women's basketball at Francis Marion College to a 272-80 record over 11 years. She became head coach of women's basketball at the University of North Carolina, Chapel Hill in 1986 and has recorded 409 wins and 186 losses through the 2004–2005 season. After 30 years as a head coach, Hatchell has compiled a career record of 658 wins and

266 losses. She coached the University of North Carolina to 13 NCAA tournament appearances and the 1994 NCAA national championship, becoming the first female ACC basketball coach to win a national championship. The Tar Heels finished the 1994 season with the best record (33-2) in women's college basketball and ranked number one in the final *USA Today* coaches' poll. Hatchell has claimed five ACC crowns and coached 14 professional players, four All-Americas, three ACC Rookies of the Year, and four ACC tournament MVPs. The Tar Heels reached the NCAA Sweet Sixteen nine times in 12 years and averaged 27.5 wins during her tenure.

Hatchell also served as assistant coach of the U.S. team at the World University Games in 1983 and 1985; as assistant coach of the U.S. team at the Olympic Games in 1988, Goodwill Games and World Championships, led the U.S. team to the 1994 R. William Jones Cup, and coached the USA team at the World University Games in Fukuoka, Japan to a silver medal in 1995. She was named National Coach of the Year in 1994 by both *USA Today* and *College Sports Magazine*, and Converse NAIA Regular Coach of the Year in 1986. She also was selected as AMF Voit Championship Coach in 1986, Collegiate Basketball Coach of the Year by Athletes International Ministries in 1995, Carson-Newman Distinguished Alumnus of the Year in 1994, an inductee into the Francis Marion University Athletic Hall of Fame, 1993, and USA Women's World University Games All-Time assistant Coach in 1985. Hatchell, who has been instrumental in shaping modern women's basketball, is one of just 11 active Division I coaches to record 600 victories and the only women's basketball coach to have won titles on the AIAW, NAIA, and NCAA levels. She is married to Sammy Hatchell, women's basketball and softball coach at Meredith College in Raleigh, North Carolina, and has one son, Van.

BIBLIOGRAPHY: "Hatchell Staying Through 2008," *GAA Online* (February 18, 2003) http://alumni.unc.edu/car/weekly/story.asp?sid=328; Rosemarie Skaine, *Women College Basketball Coaches* (Jefferson, NC, 2001); "Sylvia Hatchell: Profile," *CAROLINA: The Official Site of Tar Heel Athletics* (June 5, 2003) http://www.TarHeelBlue.com; Bob Turpin, "Nothing Could be Finer than Coaching Basketball at North Carolina: Interview with S. Hatchell," *Coach and Athletic Director* (March 2000), pp. 60–66.

Jeannie P. Miller

HAVLICEK, John J. (b. April 8, 1940, Lansing, OH), college and professional player, is the third child of Frank Havlicek and Amanda (Turkal) Havlicek. His father, a Czechoslovakian immigrant, and his mother, the daughter of a Yugoslavian coal miner, owned a grocery store in Lansing, Ohio. Havlicek earned "B" grades at Bridgeport (Ohio) High School, where he made All-State in both basketball and football. During his senior year, Havlicek received nearly 70 intercollegiate offers to play both sports and chose Ohio State University. The roommate of Jerry Lucas* at Ohio State from 1958 to 1962, Havlicek achieved All-BTC and All-America honors and in 1959–1960 led his school to an NCAA championship. In 1962 Havlicek was drafted by the Cleveland Browns (NFL), the Boston Celtics (NBA) and the Cleveland Pipers of the short-lived ABL. After being cut by the Browns, Havlicek reported to the rookie camp of the Boston Celtics.

At six-feet five-inches, and 205-pounds Havlicek was considered too big for a guard and too small for a forward. In the 1962 NBA draft, Havlicek was a surprise first-round pick. During his 16-year NBA career, the soft-spoken, modest Havlicek attained superstar status and was an NBA All-Star 13 times. Havlicek spent his early years with the Boston Celtics as a successful sixth man, popularizing that role before becoming a starting forward in 1966. Havlicek's constant running and court awareness enabled him to outmaneuver the NBA's larger forwards and pioneer the role of the small NBA forward. Throughout his career, Havlicek exhibited great physical stamina, versatility, discipline, and craftsmanship. By the 1968–1969 season, he was the acknowledged Celtics leader, averaged 21.6 points per game and led his club to a world championship. Havlicek in 1967 married Elizabeth Evans from Painesville, Ohio and has two children, Chris and Jill.

Although offered a $2 million package to play for the Carolina Cougars (ABA), the friendly, loyal Havlicek accepted substantially less from the Boston Celtics. In the 1969–1970 season, Havlicek achieved his highest scoring average with 28.9 points. Havlicek, member of six championship teams his first seven NBA seasons, was named the MVP of the 1974 championship series. On February 2, 1975, he played in his one thousandth NBA game. In 1977 Havlicek chronicled his life in *Hondo: Celtic Man in Motion.* Besides being the first player to score 1,000 or more points 16 consecutive seasons, Havlicek held all-time career records for field goals attempted (23,930) and most playoff games played (172). Havlicek ranks high on the all-time career list for games played (1,270). As an NBA All-Star, Havlicek was tied for most games (13) and ranks third in field goals (74) and fifth in points (179). Havlicek held numerous Celtics team records, including most points (26,395), most field goals made (10,513), most free throws attempted (6,589), and personal fouls (3,281). On April 10, 1978, Havlicek's number 17 was retired at the Boston Garden. He was named to the NBA's Thirty-fifth Anniversary Team in 1980 and was elected to the Naismith Memorial Basketball Hall of Fame in 1984 and to the National High School Sports Hall of Fame in 1987. In 1996, he was selected one of the 50 Greatest Players in NBA History. Red Auerbach* summed up Havlicek's outstanding contributions to the great Celtics' teams by calling him "the guts of the team." He is a franchisee for Wendy's fast food chain and has done promotional work for RJR Nabisco and the Gary Corp Company.

BIBLIOGRAPHY: Arnold Auerbach and Joe Fitzgerald, *Red Auerbach* (New York, 1977); Peter C. Bjarkman, *The Boston Celtics Encyclopedia* (Champaign, IL, 1998); Jack T. Clary, *Basketball's Great Dynasties: The Celtics* (New York, 1992); Ray Fitzgerald, *Champions Remembered* (Brattleboro, VT, 1982); Curry Fitzpatrick, "It's the End of a Long, Long Run," *SI* 48 (April 10, 1978), pp. 28–30; Mark Goodman, "Fond Farewell to Hondo Havlicek," *Sport 66* (May 1978), pp. 53ff.; Jeff Greenfield, *The World's Greatest Team* (New York, 1996); John Havlicek and Bob Ryan, *Hondo: Celtic Man in Motion* (Englewood Cliffs, NJ, 1977); John Havlicek file, Naismith Memorial Basketball Hall of Fame, Springfield, MA; Tom Henshaw, *Boston Celtics: A Championship Tradition* (Englewood Cliffs, NJ, 1974); Leonard Koppett, *24 Seconds to Shoot: An Informal History of the NBA* (New York, 1968); Roland Lazenby, *The NBA Finals* (Indianapolis, IN, 1996); Herman L. Masin, "Here Comes Hondo!" *Senior Scholastic* 94 (March 14, 1969), p. 19; John Powers, *The Short Season* (New York, 1979); Bob Ryan, *The Boston Celtics* (New York, 1989); Dan Shaughnessy, *Ever Green: The Boston Celtics* (New York, 1990); George Sullivan, *The Picture History of the Boston Celtics* (New York, 1982).

Daniel Frio

HAWKINS, Cornelius L. "Connie" "The Hawk" (b. July 17, 1942, Brooklyn, NY), professional player, grew up in the Bedford-Stuyvesant (New York City) slums and participated in basketball to escape his desperate circumstances. At age 10, Hawkins witnessed his mother, Dorothy, go blind and his father, Iziah, desert the family of six children. The legendary Hawkins's astonishing ability to rebound, dribble, and float toward the basket helped Brooklyn Boys High School capture two consecutive city championships. The University of Iowa (BTC) offered him a basketball scholarship in 1960. Before playing a single collegiate game, however, he was wrongly implicated in a basketball gambling scandal, lost his scholarship, and entered early into the ABL.

In 1961, the creation of the ABL enabled Hawkins to show off his exceptional talents. He averaged 27.5 points for the champion Pittsburgh Rens to earn the ABL's MVP honors. The ABL, however, folded midway through its second season, leaving Hawkins unable to support his new family. The Harlem Globetrotters enlisted Hawkins for the next four years for just $125 weekly. With the clowning Globetrotters, Hawkins learned "a lot about ball-handling" including how to palm the basketball with one hand before passing or dribbling it. This colorful, deceptive move became his basketball trademark.

Hawkins left the Globetrotters to join the Pittsburgh Pipers of the newly created ABA in 1967. His $15,000 contract paid dividends, as he averaged 26.8 points and led the Pittsburgh Pipers to the 1968 ABA Championship. The six-foot eight-inch, 205-pound Hawkins earned a second MVP award. A serious knee injury and a franchise shift to Minnesota did not prevent him from scoring a career-high 30.2 points a game and earning All-ABA First Team honors for the second consecutive year.

The door to the NBA opened belatedly in 1969, after Hawkins filed a multimillion dollar lawsuit to gain admittance. The 28-year-old NBA rookie drew glowing praise from his peers for his offensive prowess, feathery grace, and showman's flair. In 1969–1970, he averaged 24.6 points, sixth best in the NBA, for the expansion Phoenix Suns (NBA). Hawkins's flashy moves and unstoppable hesitation hook, however, proved insufficient to lift the Suns into the NBA playoffs in his first season. His scoring average steadily declined in the mid-1970s, causing him to be traded in October 1973 to the Los Angeles Lakers (NBA) and then in 1975 to the lowly Atlanta Hawks (NBA). For his NBA career, Hawkins converted on 46.7 percent of his shots and averaged 16.5 points in 499 games. He played in four All-Star Games and was elected in 1992 to the Naismith Memorial Basketball Hall of Fame.

Hawkins resides in Phoenix, Arizona, where he works in community relations for the Phoenix Suns. He is separated from his wife, Nancy, and has three children.

BIBLIOGRAPHY: Peter C. Bjarkman, *The Biographical History of Basketball* (Chicago, IL, 2000); Peter Bonventre, "Foul!" *Newsweek* 79 (March 6, 1976), p. 65; Peter Carry, "Shining Star under a Cloud," *SI* 29 (December 16, 1968), pp. 51–52; Richard B. Davies, *America's Obsession Sports and Society Since 1945* (Ft. Worth, TX, 1994); Jim Goodrich, "Sun Finally Rises for Connie Hawkins," *Ebony 25* (February 1970), pp. 36–38; Connie Hawkins file, Naismith Memorial Basketball Hall of Fame, Springfield, MA; Jan Hubbard, ed., *The Official NBA Basketball Encyclopedia*, 3rd ed. (New York, 2000); Tex Maule, "A Coming Out Party for Lew and Connie," *SI* 31 (October 6, 1969), pp. 26–27; Jim O'Brien, "The Hawk-Twenty Years Later," *fast-BREAK* 2 (November 1989), pp. 4–6; Terry Pluto, *Loose Balls The Short, Wild Life of the American Basketball Association* (New York, 1990); Lou Sabin and Dave Sendler, *Stars of Pro Basketball* (New York, 1970), pp. 67–81; "Two Big Men," *Newsweek* 74 (November 3, 1969), p. 108; Dave Wolf, *Foul!* (New York, 1972).

Bruce J. Dierenfield

HAWKINS, Hersey R., Jr. (b. September 29, 1966, Chicago, IL), college and professional player, starred four years in basketball at Bradley University in Peoria, Illinois. As a freshman at Westinghouse (Illinois) High School Vocational in Chicago, Illinois, he quit the basketball team after having trouble getting up for the 6 a.m. practices. With encouragement from his mother, Hawkins rejoined the basketball team. He played center for Westinghouse, averaging 36 points as a senior.

Hawkins enjoyed a successful four years in basketball at Bradley University, averaging 24 points. As a senior, he tallied 36 points per game and won the national scoring championship. Hawkins finished his career as the all time leading scorer in Bradley and MVC history with 3,008 points, ranking number six on the NCAA all time scoring list. Twice he earned MVC Player of the Year honors. In 1988, Hawkins was named National College Player of the Year and was selected a consensus All-America. Later that summer, he played on the United States bronze medal team at the Summer Olympic Games in Seoul, South Korea.

The Los Angeles Clippers (NBA) selected six-foot three-inch, 190-pound Hawkins as the sixth pick in the 1988 NBA draft and traded him later that day to the Philadelphia 76ers (NBA). He was voted to the NBA All-Rookie First Team in 1988–1989 and was named an All-Star in 1991. In 1995, Hawkins became the 196th NBA player to score 10,000 points. During his first 10 seasons, he missed only seven games due to injuries. His 527 consecutive game streak was snapped in December 1999. He also played for the Charlotte Hornets (NBA) in 1993–1994 and 1994–1995, Seattle SuperSonics (NBA) from 1995–1996 through 1998–1999, Chicago Bulls (NBA) in 1999–2000, and New Orleans Hornets (NBA) in 2000–2001, winning the NBA's Sportsmanship Award in 1999. Hawkins played 13 NBA seasons and retired in 2001. He finished as one of the NBA's most prolific three point shooters, ranking tenth on the all time three point field goals made with 1,226. Over his career, Hawkins tallied 14,470 points, 1,622 steals, and 3,554 rebounds in 983 regular-season games.

Hawkins, among the first members of the

MVC Hall of Fame, currently serves on the broadcasting staff for the Memphis Grizzlies (NBA). He and his wife, Jennifer, have three sons, Brandon, Corey, and Devon Christopher.

BIBLIOGRAPHY: Mike Douchant, *Encyclopedia of College Basketball* (Detroit, MI, 1995); http://www.christiansportsminute.com/hersey_hawkins.htm; http://www.gast-gazette.com/portal/sports/Hornets/Players/33hawkins.htm; http://www.mvcsports.com/genrel/ hofhawkins.html; http://www.peoplejustlikeus.org/Sports/Hersey_Hawkins.html; Ken Shouler et al., *Total Basketball* (Wilmington, DE, 2003).

Maureen M. Smith

HAYES, Elvin Ernest (b. November 17, 1945, Rayville, LA), college and professional player, is the youngest of six children of Christopher Hayes and Savannah Hayes, cotton mill workers in the small poverty stricken town. The honor student starred in basketball at Eula D. Britton High School in Rayville, Louisiana, where he averaged 35 points and led his team to a 54-game winning streak. After graduation from high school, he accepted a basketball scholarship to the University of Houston (Texas). He joined teammate Don Chaney, who later played and coached in the NBA, as the first black athletes to play for Houston. In his three varsity seasons, Hayes led Houston to an 81-12 record and was named First Team All-America his junior and senior years. His most memorable moment as a college player came on January 20, 1968, when Hayes outdueled fellow All-America Lew Alcindor (Kareem Abdul-Jabbar*) at the Houston Astrodome by scoring 39 points and led Houston to victory over UCLA. The Cougars, however, were eliminated by Alcindor's Bruins in the NCAA semifinals in both 1967 and 1968. During 93 college games, he scored 2,884 points (31.0 points average) and made 1,602 rebounds. He and his wife, Erna, have have four children.

The six-foot nine-inch, 235-pounds Hayes began his NBA career in 1968–1969 with the San Diego Rockets (NBA), averaging 28.4 points to pace the NBA as a rookie and made the All-NBA Rookie team. After the Rockets moved to Houston in 1971, Hayes in June 1972 was traded to the Baltimore Bullets (NBA) for Jack Marin. Hayes remained with the Bullets for the rest of the 1970s, following their move to Washington, D.C. in 1973. During his tenure in Washington, he led the Bullets to three appearances in the NBA Finals and a world championship victory over the Seattle SuperSonics in 1978. The Bullets' victory enabled Hayes to shed his reputation of being unable to win the important games, as Elvin was named the MVP of the championship series. On retiring as an active player, Hayes ranked as the fifth-leading scorer in NBA history. During his 16 NBA seasons, he scored 27,313 points (21.0 points average), made 16,279 rebounds, and blocked 1,771 shots. The much honored Hayes made the All-NBA First Team in 1975, 1977, and 1979 and the All-NBA Second Team in 1973, 1974, and 1976. Hayes, who led the NBA in rebounding in 1969–1970 and 1973–1974, held the all-time NBA regular-season records for games played (1,303), minutes played (50,000), and personal fouls (4,193). He holds Washington franchise records for career scoring (15,551 points) and blocked shots (1,588). Hayes also played in the NBA All-Star Game 12 consecutive seasons (1969–1980), scoring 126 points. He graduated from the University of Houston in 1986 with a B.A. degree in recreation and speech. He was elected to the Naismith Memorial Basketball Hall of Fame in 1990 and was named one of the 50 Greatest Players in NBA History in 1996. The Bullets retired his uniform number 11. Hayes participated in numerous charitable organizations, including the United Way and the Special Olympics. The Houston resident has pursued various business opportunities, including a cattle ranch near Brenham, Texas and a car dealership in Houston.

BIBLIOGRAPHY: S.H. Borchard, *Sports Star Elvin Hayes* (New York, 1980); Elvin Hayes with Bill Gilbert, *They Call Me the 'Big E'* (New York, 1978); Elvin Hayes file, Naismith Memorial Basketball Hall of Fame, Springfield, MA; David Loves, "No Back Seat for Elvin," *Ebony* (March 1968); Billy Packer and Roland Lazenby, *College Basketball's 25 Greatest Teams* (St. Louis, MO, 1989); John Papanek, "The Big E Wants an MVP," *SI* 49 (October 16, 1978), pp. 46–50ff.; *TSN Official NBA Guide, 1979–1980* (St. Louis, MO, 1979); *TSN Official NBA Register, 2004–2005* (St. Louis, MO, 2004).

Fred M. Shelley

HAYNES, Marques Oreole (b. October 3, 1926, Sand Springs, OK), college and professional player and executive, is the youngest of four children born to Matthew Haynes and Hattie Haynes in a weatherbeaten shack near Tulsa, Oklahoma. His father, a domestic, abandoned the family when Marques was age four. Marques developed an interest in basketball naturally, as his sister, Cecil, and brothers, Joe and Wendell, all played the sport in high school. The brothers also played at Langston University (Oklahoma). Marques developed his dribbling skills under the supervision of Wendell Haynes, his junior high school coach. After leading Booker T. Washington High School to the state championship as a senior in 1942, he attended all-black Langston University and received a Bachelor's degree in industrial education in 1946. At Langston, the six-foot, 160-pound guard led the team to a 112-3 record, two conference titles (1944–1945), and a victory over the touring Harlem Globetrotters. In the fall of 1946, Haynes signed with the barnstorming Kansas City Stars, an affiliate of the Globetrotters. In January 1947, he was promoted to the Harlem Globetrotters. From 1947 to 1953, Haynes and Reece "Goose" Tatum* were the team's top stars. Haynes performed dribbling exhibitions, while Tatum entertained with his comic capers. In 1953 Haynes left the Globetrotters over a financial disagreement and formed his own all-black touring team, the Fabulous Magicians. He returned to the Globetrotters in 1972, but joined ex-Globetrotter Meadowlark Lemon's* Bucketeers in 1979. He rejoined the Globetrotters in 1981, before ending his career in 1983 with his own Harlem Magicians.

In 40 seasons as a barnstorming basketball player through 1988, Haynes played more games (over 12,000), traveled more miles (over 4 million), and performed in more locales (every state and in ninety-seven countries on all six continents) than anyone else in history. He entertained and amazed two generations of basketball fans with his dribbling artistry. Possessing fantastic fingertip control of the ball, Haynes, acclaimed "The World's Greatest Dribbler," bounced a basketball three times per second, maintained a dribble one inch off the floor, and performed his dribbling wizardry from virtually any position, including lying on his side, back, or stomach. Although known as an expert dribbler and showman, he was a complete player in his prime and rejected offers by the Philadelphia Warriors (1953) and Minneapolis Lakers (1955) to play in the NBA.

His commitment to barnstorming basketball represented the perpetuation of a black sporting tradition more than the addiction of a basketball junkie to the lifestyle of a roving entertainer. Haynes, who has amassed wealth through real estate and various business ventures and basketball, personifies a commitment to racial solidarity and pride. Born, brought up, and educated in all-black environments, he has engaged in basketball and business ventures that have been black-owned and operated. Although living in a predominantly white society, Haynes has never forgotten his roots and heritage. An intensely private person like many entertainers, Haynes has two daughters, Marsha Kaye and Marquetta. His wife, Joan, a professional model, operates their company, Hayneco, Incorporated, which manufactures air-filtration bags. They live in Dallas, Texas. He was elected to the Naismith Memorial Basketball Hall of Fame in 1998, the NBA Hall of Fame in 1985, Oklahoma Hall of Fame in 1990, the Jim Thorpe Memorial Hall of Fame in 1993, and the Langston University Hall of Fame in 1998. The Globetrotters retired his jersey.

BIBLIOGRAPHY: Frank Deford, "The Bouncing Ball," *SI* 39 (December 3, 1973), pp. 108ff.; Marques Haynes file, Naismith Memorial Basketball Hall of Fame, Springfield, MA; Frank Litsky, *Superstars* (Secaucus, NJ, 1975); Ronald L. Mendell, *Who's Who in Basketball* (New Rochelle, NY, 1973); William Nack, "On the Road Again and Again and . . . ," *SI* 62 (April 22, 1985), pp. 78–92; *NYT*, April 11, 1973; George Vecsey, *Harlem Globetrotters* (New York, 1993); Josh Wilker, *The Harlem Globetrotters* (New York, 1992); Dave Zinkoff with Edgar Williams, *Around the World with the Harlem Globetrotters* (Philadelphia, PA, 1953).

Larry R. Gerlach

HAYWOOD, Spencer (b. April 22, 1949, Silver City, MS), college and professional player, excelled on every level of basketball competition in which he played during a controversial career. Haywood, the eighth of 10 children, grew up in rural Mississippi. His father, a carpenter, died before Spencer was born; his mother worked as a domestic. At age 15, he moved to Detroit, Michigan and starred as a center in basketball at Pershing High School there. His coach, Will Robinson, became his legal guardian. Haywood signed a letter of intent with the University of Tennessee, where he would have become that school's first black basketball player. Unable to pass Tennessee's entrance exam, however, the six-foot nine-inch, 225-pound Haywood instead enrolled at Trinidad State JC in Trinidad, Colorado. Haywood, playing center with the benefit of his four-jointed fingers, led his team in scoring and rebounding during the 1967–1968 season.

Although a planned boycott of the 1968 Olympic Games in Mexico City, Mexico by black athletes did not materialize, many blacks chose not to participate. The best American big men, Kareem Abdul-Jabbar* (Lew Alcindor), Elvin Hayes*, and Wes Unseld*, passed up the Olympics. Coach Hank Iba* consequently chose the 19-year-old Haywood as his starting center. Charlie Scott*, Jo Jo White*, and other players made significant contributions, as the U.S. team surprisingly won the Gold Medal. Young Haywood led the squad in rebounding and scoring with 145 points in nine games. The U.S. defeated Yugoslavia 65-50 in the finals, continuing its undefeated streak in Olympic competition. Iba called Haywood "potentially the best basketball player ever." With the Olympic exposure and academic success in JC, Haywood was recruited by major colleges and played for the University of Detroit, a Jesuit school, in 1968–1969. Detroit, in part, induced Haywood to enroll by naming Will Robinson an assistant coach. In Haywood's first game for Detroit, he shattered a fiberglass backboard with a dunk shot. Haywood led the nation in scoring and rebounding (21.5 rebounds per game) for the 1968–1969 season.

Haywood signed a controversial contract for the 1969–1970 season with the Denver Rockets of the fledgling ABA. The Rockets argued that Haywood was a special hardship case and needed to turn pro to support his mother and siblings. The courts agreed with the Rockets, making Haywood the first player to turn pro less than four years after entering college. He won Rookie of the Year and MVP honors while leading the ABA in scoring (30 points per game) and rebounding (19.5 rebounds per game). He holds the ABA single-season records for most minutes played (3,808), field goals made (986), rebounds (1,637), and rebound average (19.5), all set in 1969–1970. Denver won the Western Division crown, but lost in the semifinals of the ABA playoffs. The next season, Haywood jumped to the Seattle SuperSonics (NBA), causing, as one reporter described it, "a flurry of lawsuits, restraining orders, injunctions, and protests that shook the structure of basketball." The courts again supported Haywood, ruling that he had been coerced into signing a contract with Denver (ABA) and that the four-year rule, which prohibited underclassmen from turning pro, violated free trade. The SuperSonics paid Haywood $1.5 million over five years. He played well for mediocre Seattle teams, consistently ranking among the NBA leaders in points and rebounds and appeared in the 1972–1975 All-Star games.

In October 1975, Bill Russell*, Seattle general manager and coach, honored Haywood's request by trading him to the New York Knickerbockers (NBA). Haywood was hailed as a savior for a declining team, which had lost Willis Reed* and Dave DeBusschere* to retirement. Haywood, no savior to the impatient Knicks fans, drifted to the New Orleans Jazz (NBA, 1979), Los Angeles Lakers (NBA, 1979–1980), and Washington Bullets (NBA, 1981–1983), where he finished his career in 1983. After leaving Seattle, he never attained the same level of excellence in the NBA. He played in Italy during the 1980–1981 and 1981–1982 seasons, where he dominated the league during its initial campaign. Haywood's NBA career included 760 games played, 7,038 rebounds, and 14,592 points (19.2 points per game). He made the ABA All-Star First Team and ABA All-Rookie Team in 1970, the All-NBA First Team in 1972 and 1973, and the All-NBA Second Team in 1974 and 1975.

Controversy clouded Haywood's declining level of play. During his only season with the

Lakers in 1979–1980, Haywood suffered from cocaine addiction and was suspended twice for "activities disruptive to the team." The last suspension came during the NBA championship series against Philadelphia and ended Haywood's tenure with Los Angeles.

Haywood, divorced from African-born model Iman, lives in Detroit and has two daughters. He owns a real estate company and established the Spencer Haywood Foundation, which sponsors basketball and educational summer camps for inner-city youth. Haywood, who conquered his drug addiction problem with a trip in 1984 to a California rehabilitation center, has a collection of over 10,000 jazz albums. Haywood never fulfilled his promise of being "the best basketball player ever," but left his legacy on the game by being instrumental in the ABA-NBA merger and pioneering the now commonplace practice of drafting underclassmen into pro basketball.

BIBLIOGRAPHY: Neil Amdur, "A Man Grown Wise," *NYT*, June 22, 1971, p. 23; Thomas Barry, "Titan from Olympus," *Look* 33 (March 4, 1969), pp. 86–91; Sharon Begley and Lester Sloan, "The Rebel Finds a New Cause," *Newsweek 96* (December 29, 1980), p. 6; Pete Carry, "Anybody Else Care to Bid for Spencer Haywood?" *SI* 34 (January 25, 1971), pp. 52–53; Sam Goldaper, "Haywood's Attempts to Rejoin Lakers Fail," *NYT*, May 13, 1980, p. B19; Sam Goldaper, "Knicks Get Haywood," *NYT*, October 24, 1975, pp. 45–46; "Golden Boy," *Newsweek* 75 (January 6, 1969), p. 59; Jan Hubbard, ed., *The Official NBA Encyclopedia*, 3rd ed. (New York, 2000); Neil D. Isaacs, *All the Moves: A History of College Basketball* (New York, 1975); Curry Kirkpatrick, "The Team That Went Over the Hill," *SI* 28 (April 15, 1968), pp. 91–93; Ronald L. Mendell, *Who's Who in Basketball* (New Rochelle, NY, 1973); William F. Reed, "A Would-be Dunker with Soul," *SI* 30 (January 6, 1969), pp. 40–41; Sue Reilly, "Couples," *People* 13 (April 22, 1980), pp. 53–57; Seattle SuperSonics Public Relations Office, telephone interview with Mark Altschuler, November 10, 1986; Carrie Seidman, "Haywood of Lakers Suspended by Coach," *NYT*, May 9, 1980, p. D18; *TSN Official NBA Register, 2004–2005* (St. Louis, MO, 2004); "Who Owns Haywood?" *Newsweek* 77 (February 15, 1971), p. 79.

Mark Altschuler

HAZZARD, Walter R., Jr. *See* Abdul-Rahmad, Mahdi.

HEAD, John L. (b. July 22, 1915, Springfield, TN; d. May 8, 1980, Henderson, TN), college player and coach, was the son of Robertson County farmers Jesse J. Head and Lula (Lee) Head. He grew up on a farm and graduated from Coopertown (Tennessee) High School in 1934, where he excelled in basketball and baseball. He studied at Lambuth College and Union University in Jackson, Tennessee, where he played football and basketball and served as school photographer. Head also officiated high school basketball games, including tournaments. His introduction to coaching women's basketball came in 1936, when he was asked to direct a sorority team in the campus intramural league. Head taught high school in Robertson County for 12 years and coached football, baseball, and boys' and girls' basketball. He married Verna Covington on September 20, 1938 and had two sons, Ronald and Gerald. Mrs. Head worked closely with his women's teams during his career.

In 1948, Nashville millionaire H. O. Balls hired Head to coach Nashville BC and be the school's field representative. Nashville BC had fielded an amateur women's team for over two decades, but had never produced a national champion. Head's second squad defeated the two-time defending champion Nashville-Goldblumes for the 1950 AAU title. Over 21 seasons, Head's teams recorded a 689-94 slate and won a record 11 AAU national championships. Head's clubs captured eight consecutive titles from 1962 through 1969 and finished second on four other occasions. Before the 1970 basketball season, Balls withdrew sponsorship of the team and Head retired from coaching. During his career there, 20 Nashville BC women made the AAU All-America team 54 times. His best players included Alline Banks Sprouse*, Doris Weems, Katherine Washington, Nera White*, Joan Crawford*, Jill Upton, Rita Horky, Doris Rogers, and Marie Rogers. Many Nashville BC players are in the HAF and AAU halls of fame, with several athletes later becoming coaches.

Head also directed the U.S. women's teams

to championships in the first World Tournament (1953), second World Tournament (1957), and Pan American Games (1963). Many international team players came from Nashville BC. He coached American women in several tours of Europe and Russia between 1958 and 1965, compiling a 40-15 record against foreign teams.

In 1970 Head was inducted into the HAF Hall of Fame, which lauded him as the "Dean of Women's Basketball Coaches" for his 32 years of service. The AAU saluted his retirement with a special night at the national tournament that year in Gallup, New Mexico. He continued as field representative for Nashville Automobile Diesel College until his death.

BIBLIOGRAPHY: John Head, "U.S. Girls 'Hit' in U.S.S.R.," *Converse Yearbook* (1958), p. 23; Wallace R. Lord, ed., "End of an Era," *Converse Yearbook* (1970), p. 53.

Dennis S. Clark

HEAD, Patricia Sue. *See* Summitt, Patricia Sue Head "Pat"

HEARN, Francis Dale "Chick" (b. November 27, 1916, Buda, IL; d. August 5, 2002, Los Angeles, CA), sportscaster and executive, was one of two sons born to a railroad worker. When Hearn was nine, his family moved to East Aurora, Illinois. He starred in basketball at East Aurora High School, but, after his father was seriously injured in an automobile accident, worked to support the family. Hearn gained his nickname of "Chick" in 1938 while playing for an AAU basketball team in Aurora and was known as a practical joker. He married his wife, Marge, on August 13, 1938, a union which lasted 64 years.

Hearn began his broadcasting career for Armed Services Radio during the Second World War. Following his discharge, he worked for a radio station in Aurora. By 1951, Hearn announced Bradley University basketball games for a radio station in Peoria, Illinois. He was hired by NBC the following year and moved to Los Angeles, where he announced USC football games until 1963. Hearn also handled play by play for the Los Angeles Lakers (NBA) beginning in 1961, following the team's move from Minnesota in 1960.

Hearn announced for the Los Angeles Lakers through the 2002 season and began covering a record 3,338 consecutive Laker games on November 21, 1965. The popular announcer introduced numerous phrases which are now common in the basketball lexicon. He is credited with originating such terms as "air ball," "slam dunk," "no harm, no foul," and, for a Laker victory, "put the game in the refrigerator." As a Laker announcer, Hearn was teamed with Al Michaels, "Hot Rod" Hundley*, Lynn Schakleford, Keith Erickson, Pat Riley*, and Stu Lantz.

Hearn continued to provide football commentary and hosted the popular Los Angeles television show "Bowling for Dollars." In the mid 1970s, Laker owner Jack Kent Cooke made him assistant general manager. He relinquished that post under the ownership of Jerry Buss* during the 1980s.

Hearn's consecutive game streak, which he had maintained even through the death of his two children, Gary and Samantha, ended on December 20, 2001, when he underwent heart valve replacement surgery followed by a broken hip. On April 9, 2002, Hearn resumed broadcasting with the Lakers and witnessed the team attain their third straight NBA title. His voice was stilled forever when the 85-year-old Hearn slipped and struck his head at his Encino, California home and never regained consciousness. Hearn was elected to the Naismith Memorial Basketball Hall of Fame in 2003 and American Sportswriters Hall of Fame in 1997.

BIBLIOGRAPHY: Mike Penner and Larry Stewart, "The Lakers' Legendary Voice," *Los Angeles Times*, August 6, 2002; "Lakers Broadcaster Chick Hearn Dies at 85," ESPN Classic, http://espn.go.com/classic.obit/s/2002/0805/1414492.html (June 19, 2003).

Ron Briley

HEERDT, Alfred A. "Allie" (b. August 9, 1881, Buffalo, NY; d. February 4, 1958, Buffalo, NY), professional player and executive, served as player-manager of the Buffalo (New York) Germans, the most famous early-twentieth-century professional basketball team. Heerdt attended Buffalo's public schools and in 1895 organized the Germans basketball team for players 14 years and younger at Buffalo's

German YMCA. His young Germans swept the 1901 AAU Championship at the Pan-American Exposition in Buffalo without losing a game. Three years later, Heerdt starred on the floor and piloted the undefeated Germans to the AAU title in the first truly national basketball tournament at the St. Louis World's Fair.

The Germans turned professional after their St. Louis triumph and made their only extensive barnstorming tour, traveling from Portsmouth, New Hampshire to Kansas City, Kansas, and compiling a 69-19 win-loss record. For the next 20 years, the Germans, alternately called the German Ramblers and Buffalo Orioles, played college and independent teams mostly in New York, Pennsylvania, Ohio, and New England. They did not join a professional league for geographical reasons. The Germans won 111 consecutive games from 1908 to 1911 and were named to the Naismith Memorial Basketball Hall of Fame as a team in 1961.

Heerdt, who was under 6 feet tall, played all positions for the Germans and scored prolifically. In 1910–1911 he averaged 21 points, a respectable team total at that time. Heerdt's second generation Germans entered the ABL in 1925 as the Buffalo Bisons. Buffalo finished ninth and sixth in the split season schedule of this first national professional league. In 1938, Heerdt owned and coached the Buffalo Bisons (NBL) franchise for one season. At the height of the Germans' fame, he also coached at the University of Buffalo, Niagara University, and several high schools. He held an executive position in a Buffalo jewelry business until 1936 and worked at the Chevrolet plant in Buffalo until 1954.

BIBLIOGRAPHY: *Buffalo* (NY) *Courier-Express, Buffalo* (NY) *Morning Express, Buffalo* (NY) *Courier*, 1901–1958; Alfred Heerdt file, Naismith Memorial Basketball Hall of Fame, Springfield, MA; Robert W. Peterson, *Cages to Jump Shots: Pro Basketball's Early Years* (New York, 1990); *Reach Official Basket Ball Guides,* numerous years; Ken Shouler et al., *Total Basketball* (Wilmington, DE, 2003); Alexander Weyand, *The Cavalcade of Basketball* (New York, 1960).

Robert W. Peterson

HEINSOHN, Thomas William "Tom" (b. August 26, 1934, Jersey City, NJ), college and professional player, coach, and announcer, is the son of William B. Heinsohn and Bessie (Paul) Heinsohn and was elected in 1986 to the Naismith Memorial Basketball Hall of Fame. Heinsohn starred nine seasons (1956–1957 to 1964–1965) with Boston (NBA) when the Celtics won eight NBA championships and nine Eastern Division titles. Chosen the 1957 NBA Rookie of the Year with 1,163 points scored and 16.2 points average, Heinsohn was named All-NBA Second Team four consecutive years (1961–1964) and participated in six NBA All-Star Games (1957, 1961–1965). He finished with 12,194 career points (18.6 points average) and contributed an additional 2,058 points (19.8 points average) in 104 playoff games. Heinsohn, the 1973 NBA Coach of the Year, guided Boston in 1974 and 1976 to NBA championships.

Heinsohn starred at center for Union City (New Jersey) St. Michael's High School and graduated from there in 1952. The six-foot seven-inch, 218-pound Heinsohn, an outstanding center for three years (1953–1954 to 1955–1956) at Holy Cross College, led the Crusaders in 1954 to Sugar Bowl and NIT championships and into the 1955 NIT and 1956 NCAA tournament. Heinsohn's 444 points in 1954 established a Holy Cross sophomore scoring record. He outplayed LSU's Bob Pettit* in the Crusaders' 66-56 Sugar Bowl triumph and scored 20 points in Holy Cross' 71-62 NIT title victory over Duquesne University. In 1956 Heinsohn made consensus All-America, scored 740 points, and averaged 27.4 points, ranking fourth highest in the nation and high in NCAA history. During Heinsohn's three-year varsity career, the Crusaders amassed a combined 67-14 win-loss record. Heinsohn produced 1,789 points and compiled an outstanding 22.1 career points average.

Heinsohn graduated with a Bachelor of Science degree in business administration from Holy Cross in 1956 and was a territorial choice of Boston in the first round of the NBA pro draft. An excellent rebounder, he moved to forward and was noted for outside shots with a flat trajectory. He joined a veritable "who's who of basketball" under Coach "Red" Auerbach*, a group that included Bob Cousy*, Bill Russell*, Bill Sharman*, Frank Ramsey*, and, later, John

Havlicek*, Sam Jones*, Tom Sanders*, and K.C. Jones*. Despite this, Heinsohn led the Celtics in scoring in 1959–1960, 1960–1961, and 1961–1962. He retired after the 1965 season after playing in only 67 games, his scoring average having fallen that year to 13.6 points. Heinsohn, a successful head coach of Boston for nine seasons (1969–1970 to 1977–1978), compiled a combined 427-263 (.619 percent) coaching record. He guided the Celtics in 1973 to 68 wins (only 14 losses), the most victories in one season in Boston history. Dave Cowens* (NBA MVP), Paul Silas*, and Jo Jo White* joined veterans Havlicek and Don Nelson* to continue the Celtics' success. The Celtics captured the NBA championship over the Milwaukee Bucks in 1974 and over the Phoenix Suns in 1976. The South Natick, Massachusetts, resident married Diane Regenhard on September 2, 1956 and has one daughter, Donna Marie, and two sons, Paul and David. Heinsohn serves as a basketball analyst for Fox Sports Net New England. The Celtics retired his uniform number 15.

BIBLIOGRAPHY: Peter C. Bjarkman, *The Boston Celtics Encyclopedia* (Champaign, IL, 1998); Jack Clary, *Basketball's Great Dynasties: The Celtics* (New York, 1992); Tom Heinsohn, *Give Em' the Hook* (New York, 1988); Tom Heinsohn file, Naismith Memorial Basketball Hall of Fame, Springfield, MA; Clyde Hirt, ed., *Sports Quarterly Pro Basketball Special* (New York, 1973); Roland Lazenby, *The NBA Finals* (Indianapolis, IN, 1996); *18th Annual NIT Program*, New York, March 15, 1955; *19th Annual NIT Program*, New York, March 24, 1956; Dan Shaughnessy, *Ever Green: The Boston Celtics* (New York, 1990); *TSN Official NBA Register, 2004–2005* (St. Louis, MO, 2004); *WWA*, 39th ed. (1976–1977), p. 1397.

James D. Whalen

HEMRIC, Ned Dixon "Dickie" (b. August 29, 1933, Jonesville, NC), college and professional player, is the ninth of ten children of Robert Lee Hemric, a carpenter, and Alda Joyce (Swain) Hemric. Hemric starred in basketball at Jonesville, North Carolina, High School and earned a basketball scholarship to Wake Forest University after being named MVP of the 1951 North Carolina East-West High School All-Star Game.

Hemric played basketball at Wake Forest from 1951 to 1955. Wake Forest participated in the SC until the 1953–1954 season, when it became a charter member of the ACC. The six-foot six-inch, 230-pound Hemric used his strength and accuracy on hook shots with either hand to become a dominant low-post player. He was named First-Team All-SC in 1952 and 1953 and First-Team All-ACC in 1954 and 1955, SC Player of the Year in 1953, and ACC Player of the Year in 1954 and 1955. He led Wake Forest to the 1953 SC championship, ending North Carolina State University's run of five consecutive titles.

A model of consistency, Hemric averaged 22.4, 24.9, 24.3, and 27.6 points in his four varsity basketball seasons. Freshmen were eligible in 1952. His 2,587 career points and 1,802 career rebounds in 104 games are accepted by the ACC as their top career mark. Hemric led the ACC in rebounding in 1954 and 1955, averaging 19.1 in 1955 for the second-highest mark in ACC history. He ranks fifth in NCAA career rebounds. Wake Forest retired his uniform number 24.

The Boston Celtics (NBA) selected Hemric in the 1955 draft. He played two seasons for Boston, averaging 6.3 points and 5.1 rebounds. Hemric worked in sales and marketing for Goodyear Tire Company until his retirement in 1988. He married Janice Saunders in 1955 and has three children: Ned Jr., John, and Cynthia.

BIBLIOGRAPHY: Peter C. Bjarkman, *Atlantic Coast Conference Basketball* (Indianapolis, IN, 1996); Mike Douchant, *Encyclopedia of College Basketball* (Detroit, MI, 1995); Jan Hubbard, ed., *The Official NBA Encyclopedia*, 3rd ed. (New York, 2000); Horace "Bones" McKinney, *Bones: Honk Your Horn if You Love Basketball* (Gastonia, NC, 1988); Ron Morris, *ACC Basketball: An Illustrated History* (Chapel Hill, NC, 1988).

Jim L. Sumner

HENDERSON, Eli Camden "Cam" (b. February 5, 1890, Marion County, WV; d. May 3, 1956, Cedar Hill, KY), college athlete and coach, ranked among the outstanding, innovative college coaches for over four decades. Henderson excelled academically and athletically at Waynesburg Academy in Waynesburg, Pennsylvania, where he played basketball, football, and baseball and graduated third in his class in 1908. He entered Glenville (West Virginia) State College in 1909, pursuing a teaching degree and excelling in basketball, football, and baseball. The shortage of funds forced him to curtail his formal education in 1911.

Henderson taught at Bristol (West Virginia) High School in 1912 and coached all sports there from 1913 to 1916. His 1915 Bristol High School basketball team won 25 consecutive games. He also coached the local town basketball team and invented the zone defense during a game with the Grafton (West Virginia) YMCA team around Christmas 1914. According to Clair Bee*, the gymnasium floor was extremely slippery due to green pine lumber construction and the players encountered difficulty staying with their man defensively. During halftime, Henderson conceived the idea to station his players in certain zones and instructed them not to move until a shot was taken. This defensive concept worked very effectively.

Salem (West Virginia) College appointed Henderson assistant basketball coach in 1916. He completed his Bachelor's degree at Salem College in 1917 and coached basketball at Shinnaton High School in 1917 and 1918. Henderson joined Muskingum College (OC) in Ohio as head coach in 1919 and assumed a three-sport coaching position in 1922 at Davis and Elkins College. His 1926 Davis and Elkins basketball team won a national record 40 consecutive games. Henderson moved in 1935 to Marshall College (BuC), where he made his mark coaching basketball for 20 years and football for 12 years. His football teams won 68, lost 46, tied 5, and enjoyed three undefeated seasons. Henderson's innovative fast-break style enabled his basketball squads to average 71 points per game from 1945 to 1955.

Henderson's basketball teams compiled a 382-177 win-loss mark spanning 42 years. At Marshall, Henderson finished with a 357-158 record, won four BuC championships (1937–1939, 1947), captured the NAIB Championship and College Coach of the Year honors in 1947, and earned numerous invitational tournament titles. Marshall's 1946 basketball team participated in a tournament in Los Angeles, California during the Christmas holidays shortly before his football team appeared in the Tangerine Bowl in Orlando, Florida on New Year's Day. Henderson broke the color line at Marshall and in his state in 1955 by recruiting basketball star Hal Greer*. Greer later excelled with the Philadelphia 76ers (NBA).

Poor health, including diabetes, forced Henderson's retirement from coaching in 1955. He and his wife, Roxie (Bell) Henderson, resided on a farm near Clarksburg, West Virginia, and had one daughter, Camille. Henderson was inducted into the West Virginia Sports Writers Hall of Fame and the HAF College Football Hall of Fame in 1951.

BIBLIOGRAPHY: Mike Douchant, *Encyclopedia of College Basketball* (Detroit, MI, 1995); Eli Camden Henderson file, Naismith Memorial Basketball Hall of Fame, Springfield, MA; Zander Hollander, ed., *The Modern Encyclopedia of Basketball* (Garden City, NY, 1979); Neil Isaacs, *All the Moves: A History of College Basketball* (Philadelphia, PA, 1975); Marshall University Sports Information Office, Huntington, WV; *NYT*, May 4, 1956.

Jerry Jaye Wright

HENSON, Louis Ray "Lou" (b. January 10, 1932, Okay, OK), college player and coach, ranked second among active mentors and sixth among the all-time NCAA Division I coaches with 779 career victories through 2004. The New Mexico State University (SBC) head basketball coach, who formerly coached at Hardin-Simmons University (BoC) in Texas and the University of Illinois, suffered only four losing seasons and lost 412 games in 41 years. Few other coaches guided two different schools to the NCAA Tournament's Final Four.

The son of Joseph Henson, a farmer, and Lora Henson, Henson attended Okay (Oklahoma) High School and Connor (Oklahoma) JC and starred in basketball at New Mexico State University. He earned a Bachelor's degree in 1956 and later a Master's degree from New Mexico State. Henson joined Las Cruces (New Mexico) High School as head basketball coach from 1957 to 1962, directing the prep squad to a composite 145-23 win-loss record and three consecutive state titles. Hardin-Simmons hired Henson in 1963. He amassed a 67-36 mark in four seasons, twice setting the Cowboy's standard for wins (20) and capturing the 1965 Buffalo Classic.

New Mexico State appointed Henson to rebuild the Roadrunners' basketball program, which had struggled to a 4-22 record in 1965–1966. His success came immediately, as New Mexico State reached the NCAA Tournament the next five seasons. New Mexico State attained an NCCA Final Four third-place finish in 1970, losing to UCLA in the semifinals. The Roadrunners under Henson compiled a combined 173-71 record in nine seasons, ranked among the top 20 four times (including fourth in 1970) in AP and UPI polls, and appeared in six NCAA postseason tourneys. His leading players included Sam Lacey, Jimmy Collins, and Charlie Criss.

Henson moved to the University of Illinois in 1976 as head basketball coach. The Illini had finished only 8-18 the previous season. His squads averaged 15 wins in his first four campaigns and at least 20 victories in 12 of the next 13 seasons. The Illini performed in postseason play 11 consecutive seasons (9 NCAA, 2 NIT), advancing to the 1989 NCAA Final Four. Illinois dropped an 83-81 semifinal contest to eventual champion University of Michigan.

Illinois, which ranked 14th in victories in the 1980s and among the top 20 in eight of 11 seasons (including third in 1989) from 1981 to 1991, won the Illinois Classic many times and shared a BTC Championship in 1984. Henson coached 21 seasons at Illinois through 1995–1996, amassing a composite 423-224 record. He carried a less than stellar 12-12 record in 12 NCAA tournament appearances. Eddie Johnson, Derek Harper, Kenny Battle, and All-America Ken Norman played under Henson. Henson returned to New Mexico State as head coach in 1998 and guided the Roadrunners to a 116-82 record from 1998–1999 through 2003–2004. His teams compiled a 19-20 record in NCAA Tournament play. Cancer and viral encephalitis forced him to retire in January 2005. Henson married Mary Brantner of Las Cruces, New Mexico, in 1954 and has four children.

BIBLIOGRAPHY: Mike Douchant, *Encyclopedia of College Basketball* (Detroit, MI, 1995); *NCAA Men's Basketball Records, 2004* (Indianapolis, IN, 2003); *New Mexico State Basketball Media Guide*, 2004 (Las Cruces, NM, 2004); *TSN College Basketball 2004–2005* (St. Louis, MO, 2004); University of Illinois, Sports Information Office, Champaign, IL, September 1990.

James D. Whalen

HEPBRON, George T. (b. August 27, 1869, Still Pond, MD; d. April 30, 1946, Newark, NJ), referee and executive, was named in 1960 to the referees' division of the Naismith Memorial Basketball Hall of Fame. The earliest outstanding basketball official, Hepbron served from 1896 to 1915 as editor and rules interpreter of the Men's and Women's Basketball Guides. He befriended basketball's originator, Dr. James Naismith*, and in 1896 became the first secretary of the AAU Basketball Committee when that organization assumed jurisdiction of the game. In 1904, Hepbron wrote the sport's first book titled *How to Play Basketball*. When the joint NBRC was formed in 1915, Hepbron was elected secretary. The NBRC standardized playing rules for all levels of amateur basketball, including high school, college, AAU, and YMCA, thus making easier the transition from one playing status to another. Hepbron served on the NBRC until 1936 when he was named a life member.

Two years after Naismith invented basketball, some YMCAs in 1893 were forced to ban the sport because of rough play. Because strict rules of conduct had not been introduced, tackling and body-blocking frequently occurred. Enthusiasts sought to play in dance halls with large floors and space for spectators. The first AAU tournament games were held in Brooklyn, New York, under Hepbron's direction. Hepbron officiated all the contests and disqualified so many players in the tournament finals that the game was halted and continued the next night after additional players were summoned. Hepbron in 1903 became secretary of the USOBC. In 1906 he joined the A. G. Spalding and Brothers Sporting Goods firm as a special representative, a position he held until retiring in 1941.

Hepbron served on the NBOC and the AAU James E. Sullivan Memorial Medal Committee. A top YMCA official, he remained prominent in national and international YMCA affairs for over one-half century. Hepbron, a member of the national YMCA Physical Education Committee, served on 42 national and local YMCA committees at the same time. He was the first secretary of the AtL of North American YMCAs and chaired several physical education groups in the East. Hepbron, who married Ida M. Smith and had two children, resided 42 years in East Orange, New Jersey.

BIBLIOGRAPHY: *AAU Basketball Guide, 1942–1943*; George T. Hepbron file, Naismith Memorial Basketball Hall of Fame, Springfield, MA; William G. Mokray, ed., *Ronald Encyclopedia of Basketball* (New York, 1963); *Newark* (NJ) *Evening News*, May 1, 1946; *NYT*, May 1, 1946; Alexander M. Weyand, *The Cavalcade of Basketball* (New York, 1960).

James D. Whalen and Wayne Patterson

HEYMAN, Arthur Bruce "Art" (b. June 24, 1941, Rockville Centre, NY), college and professional player, attended Oceanside (New York) High School, where he made the 1959 high school All-America basketball team and starred as a goalie on his undefeated high school soccer squad. His stepfather, William Heyman, a draftsman, influenced him to attend Duke University (ACC), where he became the then-leading basketball scorer in Blue Devil history, NCAA 1963 Player of the Year, and a three-time All-America. Heyman averaged 25.1 points during his three-year career, the only Duke player achieving MVP three times. Blue Devil records for most points, most free throws, and highest career scoring average were established by Heyman, who still ranks high in Duke career scoring with 1,984 points. The Blue Devils developed as a basketball power in the early 1960s and advanced to the NCAA Final Four in 1963, when Heyman attained MVP.

The New York Knicks selected Heyman first in the 1963 NBA draft. The six-foot five-inch, 205-pound Heyman made the NBA All-Rookie team in his first season, scoring 1,153 points and averaging 15.4 points. An injury hindered his second season performance. During the 1965–1966 season, he played sparingly for the Cincinnati Royals (NBA) and Philadelphia 76ers (NBA). After skipping professional basketball the following year, Heyman in 1967–1968 joined the New Jersey Nets for 19 games and the Pittsburgh Pipers for 54 games in the newly formed ABA. As one of the ABA's top performers, he helped the Pittsburgh Pipers capture the 1968 ABA championship and recorded 1,349 points for an 18.5 points average. Heyman played in 71 games for the Minnesota Muskies (ABA) during the 1968–1969 season and in only 19 contests of the 1969–1970 campaign for the Pittsburgh Condors (ABA) and the Miami Floridians (ABA). A back injury caused Heyman's retirement from professional basketball. Heyman scored 4,030 points in 310 games, averaging 13.0 points. The controversial Heyman, who was involved in numerous altercations during his playing career, belongs to the HAF College Basketball and Duke University halls of fame and became owner and manager of a New York City restaurant.

BIBLIOGRAPHY: Peter C. Bjarkman, *ACC-Atlantic Coast Conference Basketball* (Indianapolis, IN, 1991); Peter C. Bjarkman, *The Biographical History of Basketball* (Chicago, Il, 2000); Bill Brill, *Duke Basketball: An Illustrated History* (Dallas, TX, 1986); Ray Cave, "Duke's Red-Hot and Blue Devil," *SI* 8 (February 27, 1961), pp.41–42; Mike Douchant, *Encyclopedia of College Basketball* (Detroit, MI, 1995); Duke University, Sports Information Release, Durham, NC, April 3, 1978; Jan Hubbard, ed., *The Official NBA Basketball Encyclopedia*, 3rd ed., (New York, 2000); Ronald L. Mendell, *Who's Who in Basketball* (New Rochelle, NY, 1973); Ron Morris, *ACC Basketball: An Illustrated History* (Chapel Hill, NC, 1988); Terry Pluto, *Loose Balls: The Short Wild Life of the American Basketball Association* (New York, 1990).

John L. Evers

HICKEY, Edgar S. "Ed" "The Little General" (b. December 20, 1902, Reynolds, NE; d. December 7, 1980, Mesa, AZ), college player and coach, was the son of real estate and land broker Christopher Hickey and Fern Hickey and had two sisters, Lola, his twin, and Thelma. Hickey, a well-rounded athlete at Trinity College High School in Sioux City, Iowa, participated in football, basketball, baseball, and wrestling. He attended prep school at Spalding Academy in Nebraska before entering Creighton University in Omaha, Nebraska as a law student. At Creighton, Hickey quarterbacked the varsity football squad for three years and played on the Bluejays basketball squad for two years. During his senior year, he became basketball coach at Creighton University (Creighton Prep) High School. Hickey's plan to join his father's real estate firm as its attorney abruptly was altered when, just a few months before graduation, his father was killed in an auto accident. The younger Hickey stayed at Creighton Prep School after receiving his Bachelor of Laws degree cum laude in 1927.

Hickey served as Creighton Prep's full-time head coach in football, basketball, and baseball from 1927 to 1934. He became head basketball coach at Creighton University for the 1935–1936 season and accumulated a 132-72 win-loss record during his nine seasons there. His teams finished MVC co-champions in 1935–1936 and in 1941–1942. In 1940–1941 the Bluejays held the NCAA title. Creighton, in the 1942–1943 season, captured both the MVC title and the NIT. Hickey served in the U.S. Navy during World War II as a lieutenant commander, coaching the cadets in basketball and coaching boxing for one season. Because of his Law degree, he often worked in defense of station personnel. He returned to Creighton University in the 1946–1947 season to guide the Bluejays to a 19-8 season.

The next year, "The Little General" moved to St. Louis (Missouri) University and took them to the NIT championship with a 24-3 season. Hickey and "Easy Ed" Macauley*, his phenomenal big man, were nicknamed "Mutt and Jeff" on the court. They made famous Hickey's three-lane fast-break offense, relieving Macauley of some scoring pressures by using his skills to pass and handle the ball. Hickey called the new series of fingertip passes a "Barrel Roll" with endless options. His briefcase of notes contained diagrams and scouting reports. During breaks, he quickly diagrammed situations on the floor in chalk at the side of the court. At St. Louis, basketball attendance soared. The 1947–1948 matchings with Holy Cross College drew a record crowd of 11,216 to Kiel Auditorium, while an estimated 3,000 fans were turned away. St. Louis spoiled the Holy Cross 29-1 record, as Macauley scored 10 points and delivered to the home crowd a 61-46 victory. Hickey's great success at St. Louis included 11 consecutive winning seasons, as he posted a 212-89 win-loss tally. Macauley and D. C. Wilcutt received honors in the 1948 NIT as MVP and second place MVP, respectively, as the team captured the NIT title. In 1952, Ray Steiner of the Billikens made the All-America team. Hickey's St. Louis teams earned honors, including the MVC titles, one Cotton Bowl crown, two Sugar Bowl titles, six NIT appearances, and two NCAA appearances.

Hickey sought to build character and confidence, giving something in return for his players' efforts. Despite his various honors, he was proudest of the fact that nearly 100 percent of his players received degrees. The strict disciplinarian and perfectionist trained his players for the rigors of life as well as winning basketball games. The well-respected Hickey was elected president of the NABC in 1954 and voted Basketball Coach of the Year four other times, including in 1952 by the Rockne Club of Kansas City, Missouri, in 1952 and 1957 by the MVC, and in 1959 by the BWAA.

When Hickey left St. Louis University for Marquette University in 1958–1959 as athletic director and head coach, he demanded and achieved excellence by taking the team to the NCAA title after a 23-6 season. Again in 1960–1961, he took the Marquette Warriors to NCAA glories and captured the Dixie Bowl title. By the time Hickey left Marquette in 1964, he had compiled a 92-70 record and 570–268 mark over 37 years of prep school and college coaching. Hickey's brilliance and devotion inspired him to write numerous basketball articles. His contribution through research and clinics proved popular in the U.S. and overseas. Subsequently Hickey served as secretary-manager of the Terre Haute (Indiana) AC in 1965 and as branch manager until his retirement in 1976. Twice his excellent leadership received American Automobile Association Achievement Awards.

Hickey was inducted into the Naismith Memorial Basketball Hall of Fame (1978); the NFF College Football Hall of Fame as a charter member; the HAF Hall of Fame; the Greater St. Louis Hall of Fame; St. Louis University Hall of Fame; Creighton Prep Hall of Fame; and Creighton University Hall of Fame, being the first Creighton coach to receive this honor. The Alpha Sigma Nu and Delta Theta Pi member became an honorary citizen of Boystown, Nebraska. The Golden Anniversary Award, sponsored by DuPont and the NABC, was bestowed in 1977, "For distinguished achievement in his chosen profession and significant contribution to the game of basketball and society while exhibiting exemplary character and outstanding leadership qualities." He and his first wife, Harriette Barbara Pinkerton, were married July 2, 1924, and had two sons, Edgar Jr. and Patrick. His widow, Ethel Miller Hickey, whom he married May 5, 1965, lives in Mesa, Arizona.

BIBLIOGRAPHY: Janet Cohen, "Building a Case for Hickey: The Dean of Basketball Coaches" (New York, 1977); "Eddie Hickey Gains Award," *Omaha World Herald,* March 28, 1977; William Fay, "Inside Sports: St. Louis University," *Collier's* 123 (February 5, 1949), p. 40; Edgar S. Hickey file, Naismith Memorial Basketball Hall of Fame, Springfield, MA; Ethel Hickey to Sara-Jane Griffin, March 8, 1985; "Hot Shots from St. Louis," *Time* 51 (January 12, 1948), p. 40; Neil D. Isaacs, *All the Moves: A History of College Basketball* (Philadelphia, PA, 1975); *Marquette Basketball Media Guide, 1963–1964* (Milwaukee, WI, 1963); Ronald L. Mendell, *Who's Who in Basketball* (New Rochelle, NY, 1973); *Prep Alumni News* (Fall 1981), p. 3; "Scouting Reports: The Top 20 Teams," *SI* 17 (December 10, 1962), p. 54; "Stop St. Louis," *Time* 53 (January 24, 1949), p. 64; "St. Louis Blues," *Newsweek* 31 (March 29, 1948), p. 77; Betsy Van Sickle, telephone conversation with Sara-Jane Griffin, Marquette University, Public Relations, Milwaukee, WI, January 1985.

Sara-Jane Griffin

HICKOX, Edward J. (b. April 10, 1878, Cleveland, OH; d. January 28, 1966, Springfield, MA), college football player and basketball coach and administrator, served from 1930 to 1948 on the NBRC and chaired the NBRC in 1946 and 1947. Hickox, a charter member in 1927 of the NABC, served as its president from 1944 to 1946. A recipient of the HAF Achievement Award, he was named NABC Man of the Year in 1949. In 1958, Hickox was inducted into the NAIA Hall of Fame for his "outstanding coaching record and insistence upon high ethical and moral standards in athletics." A year later, he was named to the Naismith Memorial Basketball Hall of Fame as a contributor.

The orphaned Hickox served in 1899 as valedictorian of the graduating class at Western Reserve Seminary in West Farmington, OH. In the fall of 1901, the 23-year-old Hickox enrolled at Ohio Wesleyan University. For the next four years, he starred on the Battling Bishops' football teams that finished with a composite 25-14-0 record. Hickox' participation in basketball at Ohio Wesleyan was limited, since it was not adopted as an official sport until later. He earned school tuition by washing dishes at a boarding house for four years and in 1905 graduated from Ohio Wesleyan University with a Bachelor of Arts degree in Liberal Arts. Hickox pursued his education further, earning a Bachelor's degree in physical education from Springfield (Massachusetts) College in 1914 and a Master of Arts degree in education from Columbia University in New York City in 1921.

Hickox was director of physical education at Colorado College between 1914 and 1917 and served as their first varsity basketball coach. A World War I infantry lieutenant, he was wounded in France in 1917 and recuperated for one year in a military hospital. Hickox was awarded the Purple Heart and received a citation for gallantry in action. In 1922, he joined the faculty at Springfield College as teacher of mathematics and physics, varsity football coach, and freshman basketball mentor. After being appointed head varsity basketball coach at Springfield College in 1926, Hickox relinquished his position as gridiron coach. He guided the Maroons for 16 years to a composite 205-81 (.716 percent) win-loss record. Triumphs were made over the best Eastern teams, including CCNY, Villanova University, Rutgers University, Holy Cross College, the University of Rhode Island, Providence College, Yale University, Harvard University, Dartmouth College, Cornell University, and Columbia University, while LIU and St. John's University inflicted marginal losses. His charges captured New England championships in 1926–1927 (13-1 record), 1927–1928 (18-2), 1935-1936 (17-4), 1936–1937 (18-3), and 1939–1940 (16-3). Springfield College represented New England in the 1936 Olympic Trials and suffered a 1940 NCAA Tournament first-round loss to eventual champion Indiana University. The Maroons finished with under six defeats in nine of Hickox'

16 seasons and suffered only one losing season. In Hickox' final year (1941), Springfield posted only a 9-11 record.

Hickox joined neighboring American International College (Massachusetts) from 1943 to 1948 as head basketball coach, served from 1952 to 1963 as volunteer executive secretary of the Naismith Memorial Basketball Hall of Fame, and worked continuously from 1946 to 1966 as NABC historian. In 1914 he married Iowa schoolteacher Gena B. Groe, who later joined the faculty of Springfield College as professor of English. She served there until her retirement in 1952. Hickox in 1961 received an honorary Doctor of Humanities degree from Springfield College and was cited as "a faithful example to teaching, creating through coaching the means of making men."

BIBLIOGRAPHY: Edward J. Hickox file, Naismith Memorial Basketball Hall of Fame, Springfield, MA; William G. Mokray, ed., *Ronald Encyclopedia of Basketball* (New York, 1963); Ken Rappoport, *The Classic: History of the NCAA Championship* (Mission, KS, 1979).

James D. Whalen and Wayne Patterson

HILL, Grant Henry (b. October 5, 1972, Dallas, TX), college and professional player, is the only child of Calvin Hill and Janet Hill. His father, a Yale University graduate, played professional football and consulted for the Dallas Cowboys (NFL). His mother graduated from Wellesley College, where she roomed with Hillary Rodham Clinton. She is an attorney who served as the Special Assistant to the Secretary of the Army from 1978 to 1981 and is Vice President for Alexander and Associates.

Grant grew up in Reston, Virginia with many rules and few privileges. He was expected to study hard and never attended a dance or a party until age 16. Hill started playing varsity basketball as a freshman at South Lakes High School in Reston and advanced to the state finals twice. He attended Duke University because they treated him with respect. Hill emerged as a team leader, helping the Blue Devils win two NCAA championships. The All-America won the Henry Iba* Award as the nation's best collegiate defensive player in 1992 and the ACC Player of the Year Award in 1994. He converted 53 percent of his shots and 70 percent of his free throws, while averaging 14.9 points and six rebounds. He earned a Bachelor's degree from Duke in 1994.

Hill was selected third in the NBA draft of 1994 by the Detroit Pistons (NBA) and signed an eight-year, $45 million contract. Several commercial endorsements followed. He was named a NBA All-Star in his rookie season and for the next five years. Hill participated in the All-Star Weekend's slam-dunk contest and won a gold medal with the U.S. Olympic team in 1996. With the Pistons, the six-foot eight-inch, 225-pound forward averaged 1,566 points per year, 22 points per game, and eight rebounds per game. He made the NBA All-Rookie Team in 1995, the All-NBA First Team in 1997, and the All-NBA Second Team in 1996, 1998, 1999, and 2000. He also appeared in the 2000, 2001, and 2005 All-Star Games, but was injured in the 2001 contest.

After being traded to the Orlando Magic (NBA) in August 2000, Hill signed a $93 million contract. An ankle injury caused him to miss 281 games over four years. He underwent five operations to realign his left ankle and reshape his heel, his most recent being in March 2003. He missed the entire 2003–2004 season, but returned to his old form by averaging 19.7 points in 67 games in 2004–2005. Hill has scored 11,421 points in 549 NBA games and averaged 20.8 points and 7.5 rebounds. He is married to Tamia Hill, a singer, songwriter, and actress from Windsor, Connecticut; Grant does not smoke, and has never touched alcohol.

BIBLIOGRAPHY: Bill Brill with Mike Krzyzewski, *A Season Is a Lifetime* (New York, 1993); Mike Cragg with Mike Sobb, *Back to Back* (Durham, NC, 1992); *Detroit News*, January 19, 1996, p. F3; *Detroit News*, July 5, 1996; *Detroit News*, March 22, 1999, p. E1–2; *Detroit News*, January 9, 2000, p. C6; *Detroit News*, January 30, 2000, p. D1; *Detroit News*, November 24, 2002, p. C14; *Esquire* 131 (February 1995), p. 60; Mike Douchant, *Encyclopedia of College Basketball* (Detroit, MI, 1995); Roscoe Nance, "After Long Climb, Hill Back on Top," *USA Today*, November 24, 2004, pp. 1C–2C; NBA.com; *NYT*, March 18, 2003, p. C19; *TSN Official Basketball Register, 2004–2005* (St. Louis, MO, 2004); Ken Shouler, *Total Basketball* (Wilmington, DE, 2003); *SI* 88, (February 1, 1993), p. 58; *SI* 91 (January 22, 1996),

p. 59; *Time* 153 (February 13, 1995), p. 78; *USA Today*, December 6, 1994, p. C1; *USA Today*, December 18, 1994, p. 4; *USA Today*, May 18, 1995, p. B5 C3; *USA Today* January 26, 1996, p. C1.

Keith McClellan

HINKLE, Paul D. "Tony" (b. December 19, 1899, Logansport, IN; d. September 21, 1992, Indianapolis, IN), college athlete and basketball and football coach, established his reputation over almost five decades as one of the true giants within the college coaching ranks. This reputation flourished despite Hinkle's personal choice to devote his entire coaching career to a single, small, unheralded Indiana school. Hinkle starred in football, basketball, and baseball throughout his high school and college career in the Chicago metropolitan area, graduating from Chicago Calumet High School in 1916 and from the University of Chicago in 1921. He remains one of only three athletes ever to win three varsity sports letters in a single season (1920–1921) at the University of Chicago Hinkle won three varsity letters in football, basketball, and track and field. He was elected All-WC in basketball and basketball team captain for a two-year period. Hinkle was elected a HAF Basketball All-America for the 1920 college season.

Hinkle's only coaching assignment began at Butler University in Indianapolis, Indiana at the beginning of the 1921 season. He was hired as an assistant by his former Chicago coach Pat Page* and continued for almost five decades until his retirement in 1970. During that one-half century, Hinkle served as basketball, football, and baseball coach and athletic director and became the true dean among Indiana college and scholastic coaches. At one time, over 50 of his former players and assistants were actively employed as coaches within Indiana alone. This role as progenitor of basketball coaching talent was perhaps Hinkle's greatest single contribution to the sport. Coach Marvin Wood, one of his most notable disciples, developed a "cat-and-mouse" offensive style that foreshadowed the later famous North Carolina four-corner offense and propelled tiny Milan High School to a miracle Indiana state championship season in 1954. His own college coaching successes, however, are equally legendary, as Hinkle led his Butler basketball teams to over 600 victories in 44 years of varsity coaching and achieved a national championship in 1929. Hinkle regularly scheduled larger schools and more powerful opponents, and built a national reputation for Butler by continually defeating heavily favored BTC opposition such as Purdue University and Indiana University during his first three decades there. His football and basketball teams won around 400 games.

Further achievements in Hinkle's illustrious career included coaching the Great Lakes Naval Training Station team to 98 victories during the 1942–1944 wartime period and to the National Service title during the 1942–1943 season. Hinkle served on the collegiate NBRC in 1937–1938 and again from 1942 to 1948, chairing that committee between 1948 and 1950. He also was NABC president in 1954–1955 and received the prestigious NABC Metropolitan Award for outstanding service in 1962. Hinkle's stature within the "hotbed" basketball state of Indiana was recognized further when the Indianapolis press community requested him to select his "All-Dream" Indiana High School Squad in March 1972. His mythical All-Star team included such notables as Robert "Fuzzy" Vandiver*, George McGinnis*, Oscar Robertson*, and Homer Stonebraker. The most fitting recognition of his outstanding coaching career, however, came with his election in 1965 to the Naismith Memorial Basketball Hall of Fame. His five decades of contributions to the athletic programs at Butler University are forever commemorated by the Tony Hinkle Memorial Fieldhouse on the Butler campus. This longtime site for state high school championship basketball games was the location for filming of the 1985 movie *Hoosiers*, a nostalgic Hollywood-made portrait of glamorous "Hoosier Hysteria"-style high school basketball in Indiana.

BIBLIOGRAPHY: Peter C. Bjarkman, *The Biographical History of Basketball* (Chicago, IL, 2000); Paul D. Hinkle file, Naismith Memorial Basketball Hall of Fame, Springfield, MA; Zander Hollander, ed., *The Modern Encyclopedia of Basketball* (Garden City, NY, 1979); *Indianapolis Star*, September 22, 1992; Neil D. Isaacs, *All the Moves: A History of College Basketball* (Philadelphia, PA, 1975); Ronald L.

Mendell, *Who's Who in Basketball* (New Rochelle, NY, 1973); Sandy Padwe, *Basketball's Hall of Fame* (Englewood Cliffs, NJ, 1970); Bob Williams, *Hoosier Hysteria: Indiana High School Basketball* (South Bend, IN, 1982).

Peter C. Bjarkman

HOBSON, Howard A. "Hobby" (b. July 4, 1903, Portland, OR; d. June 9, 1991, Portland, OR), college athlete and basketball coach, played basketball from 1919 to 1922 at Franklin High School in Portland, Oregon, where he won 12 athletic letters and made All-State. At the University of Oregon from 1923 to 1926, he captained both the baseball team and the basketball team for two years. Hobson was basketball coach at Kelso (Washington) High School and Benson (Oregon) High School from 1926 to 1928. From 1928 to 1953, he coached basketball at Southern Oregon College, the University of Oregon, and Yale University with a 495-291 composite record.

Hobson excelled at the University of Oregon, where he coached for 12 years with a 241-137 record. His Oregon team won the NCAA title in 1939 and PCC titles from 1937 to 1939. Oregon, nicknamed the "Tall Firs," finished 29-5 in 1939 and defeated Ohio State University 46-33 for the inaugural NCAA title. The Oregon Ducks helped pioneer intersectional play, being the first Western team to travel east for basketball games. Hobson's Yale teams compiled a 121-118 record and from 1947 to 1956 won or tied five Big Three crowns. Hobson, president of the NABC in 1947 and 1948, served on the USOC 12 years and the NBRC four years. He conducted basketball clinics in the U.S. and in 15 foreign countries and was elected as a coach to the Naismith Memorial Basketball Hall of Fame in 1965. Before retirement, he served as vice president and sports editor of Ronald Press. He and his wife, Jennie, had one son, Howard, Jr. Hobson authored *Basketball Illustrated* (1948) and *Scientific Basketball: For Coaches, Players, Officials, Spectators, and Sportswriters* (1949). He made the first proposals for a three-point field goal, shot clock, and wider free throw lanes.

BIBLIOGRAPHY: Peter C. Bjarkman, *The Biographical History of Basketball* (Chicago, IL, 2000); Mike Douchant, *Encyclopedia of College Basketball* (Detroit, MI, 1995); Howard A. Hobson, *Shooting Ducks: A History of University of Oregon Basketball* (Portland, OR, 1984); Howard A. Hobson file, Naismith Memorial Basketball Hall of Fame, Springfield, MA; Ronald L. Mendell, *Who's Who in Basketball* (New Rochelle, NY, 1973); Sandy Padwe, *Basketball's Hall of Fame* (Englewood Cliffs, NJ, 1970); Paul Soderberg and Helen Washington, comps. and eds., *The Big Book of Halls of Fame in the United States and Canada* (New York, 1977).

Frederick J. Augustyn Jr.

HOLDSCLAW, Chamique Shaunta (b. August 9, 1977, Flushing, NY), college and professional player, is the daughter of Willie Johnson Holdsclaw, a car mechanic, and Bonita Holdsclaw, a data entry clerk. When she was 11, her parents separated, her mother entered rehabilitation, and Chamique and her younger brother, Davon, went to live with their grandmother, June Holdsclaw, in the Astoria House Project in Queens. June gave Holdsclaw a stable, secure home life, enrolling her in jazz and ballet and sending her to private schools. Her uncle introduced her to basketball when she was 9. Holdsclaw started playing basketball on the courts at Astoria House regularly after moving in with her grandmother.

Holdsclaw played basketball for Christ the King High School from 1991 to 1995, leading her team to four state titles and an overall record of 106-4. She averaged 24.8 points and 15.9 rebounds, was named New York's Miss Basketball three times, and won the Naismith Award for High School Player of the Year in 1995.

The heavily recruited six-foot two-inch, 170-pound Holdsclaw chose the University of Tennessee, where she played from 1995 to 1999 and amassed an overall win-loss record of 131-17, 3,025 career points, and 1,295 rebounds. As a freshman, she led the Lady Vols in scoring and rebounding and was the only freshman named to the All-America First Team. Holdsclaw paced the Lady Vols to an amazing three consecutive national titles in 1996, 1997, and 1998 with a perfect 39-0 season. Holdsclaw, often credited with revolutionizing the women's game, was the first female player to win the James E. Sullivan Memorial Award for the nation's top amateur athlete. Her many other awards include *SI*

Women's Player of the Year (1999), the ESPY Award for Female Athlete of the Year from ESPN (1999), and the ESPY Award for Women's Basketball Player of the Year in 1998 and 1999. During her career at Tennessee, she was the youngest and only college player on the U.S. National Women's Team. Holdsclaw led the team in scoring and rebounding, winning USAB's Female Athlete of the Year in 1997. Holdsclaw graduated with a Bachelor's degree in political science in 1999.

In 1999 Holdsclaw was drafted by the WNBA's struggling Washington Mystics. She was named the 1999 WNBA Rookie of the Year and received the Naismith Award in 2000 for the Women's Player of the Century. She led the WNBA in scoring (19.9 points average) and rebounding (11.6 average) in 2002 and in rebounding (10.1) in 2003. Injuries and depression caused by the deaths of her grandparents limited her to 23 games in 2004. The Los Angeles Sparks (WNBA) acquired her in a March 2005 trade. During her six years in the WNBA, Holdsclaw has 2,960 career points (18.3 average) and 1,459 rebounds (9.0 average) in 162 games. She appeared in the 1999, 2000, and 2003 WNBA All-Star games and paces her team in scoring and rebounds. She participated in the 2000 and 2003 WNBA playoffs, averaging 17.7 points. Her honors include making the All-WNBA Second Team in 1999, 2001, and 2002. She lives in Alexandria, Virginia, with her boyfriend, Larry Williams.

BIBLIOGRAPHY: "Chamique Holdsclaw," *Biography Today* (September 2000), pp. 64–79; Chamique Holdsclaw, *Chamique* (New York, 2000); Allison Samuels, "She's Got Her Own Game," *Newsweek* 133 (March 15, 1999), pp. 63; Pat Summitt, *Raise the Roof* (New York, 1998); *TSN Official WNBA Guide and Register, 2004* (St. Louis, MO, 2004); WNBA website, www.wnba.com.

Lisa A. Ennis

HOLMAN, Nathan "Nat" (b. October 19, 1896, New York, NY; February 12, 1995, Riverdale, Bronx, NY), college and professional player and coach, is the son of Louis Holman, a grocery store operator, and Mary (Goldman) Holman. Holman became Professor of Physical Education at CCNY in 1917, just before receiving a Bachelor of Science degree in Physical Education from Savage School of Physical Education. He then became head basketball coach at CCNY and simultaneously played professionally for several New York teams, including the Whirlwinds, the Nationals, and the Original Celtics. The Celtics were the era's finest team, featuring Holman, Johnny Beckman*, Dutch Dehnert*, and Joe Lapchick*. Holman, a deft passer and playmaker for this Celtic aggregation, devised the pivot play and man-to-man defensive switch. In 1926–1927 he joined the Brooklyn Visitation (ABL), leading the team with an 8.8 points average. In 1929–1930 Holman played for Syracuse (ABL) and the Chicago Bruins (ABL).

Holman left pro athletics but continued to coach winning CCNY basketball teams. He authored *Scientific Basketball*, a textbook for coaches, in 1927. During the 1930s, He taught basketball for the U.S. State Department in foreign countries such as Japan and Israel. Holman became chairman of Physical Education at CCNY in 1930 and served from 1933 to 1937 as president of the NCBAA. During World War II, he served in the U.S. Navy. Holman returned to civilian life after World War II and coached CCNY in 1950 to NCAA and NIT titles. The 1950 team became the only one ever to win both tournaments. (The NIT then was considered a prestigious tournament featuring many top teams that the NCAA would not take for its championship playoffs.) Key CCNY players included Ed Roman, Irwin Dombrot, Floyd Lane, and Ed Warner.

Jubilation turned to horror the next year, however, when the New York district attorney announced that he was investigating allegations that certain CCNY players had accepted bribes to fix the point spread on games held in Madison Square Garden in New York. Two players subsequently were convicted of criminal involvement in this scheme. No one questioned Holman's integrity or team discipline, but he was coach when the scandal occurred. The incident left a bad impression of Holman, Madison Square Garden leadership, and basketball in general. In 1952 Holman resigned as coach and the school deemphasized basketball. He was suspended by the New York City Board of Higher Education before being vindicated and reinstated two years later. CCNY has not influenced national basketball circles since, although Holman returned to coach them in 1955–1956 and 1959–1960.

Overall, Holman recorded 420 wins and 190 losses for a .689 percentage, among the best all-time coaching marks. His fast-paced collegiate offense became known as "New York style basketball." In 1964 he was elected to the Naismith Memorial Basketball Hall of Fame. He also was inducted into the HAF Hall of Fame, and was named the third greatest player of the half-century. Holman became president of the U.S. Committee for Sports for Israel in 1973 and later resigned. On November 2, 1945, he married Ruth Jackson. He lived in New York City and traditionally attended the CCNY-Fordham University basketball game at Madison Square Garden, where he was still "Mr. Basketball."

BIBLIOGRAPHY: Bill Gutman, *The History of NCAA Basketball* (New York, 1993); Nat Holman, *Championship Basketball* (New York, 1930); Nat Holman, *Holman: Basketball* (New York, 1950); Nat Holman, *Scientific Basketball* (New York, 1922); Nat Holman file, Naismith Memorial Basketball Hall of Fame, Springfield, MA; Murry Nelson, *The Originals: The New York Celtics Invent Modern Basketball* (Bowling Green, OH, 1999); *New York Times*, February 13, 1995; Billy Packer and Roland Lazenby, *College Basketball's 25 Greatest Teams* (St. Louis, MO, 1989); Charles Rosen, *Scandals of '51* (New York, 1979); Robert W. Peterson, *Cages to Jumpshots* (New York, 1998), *Who's Who in American Jewry* (New York, 1980).

John David Healy

HOLZMAN, William "Red" (b. August 10, 1920, Manhattan, NY; d. November 13, 1998, New Hyde Park, NY), college and professional player, coach, and executive, was the son of Abraham Holzman, a tailor, and Sophie (Edglowitz) Holzman. He moved to Brooklyn at age four and graduated in 1938 from Franklin Lane High School in Brooklyn. Holzman attended the University of Baltimore, where he played basketball at guard during the 1938–1939 season. He transferred to CCNY after his freshman year and participated in basketball during the 1941–1942 and 1942–1943 seasons. In 39 games for CCNY, the 5-foot 10-inch, 180-pound redhead made 87 field goals and 88 free throws for 454 points and averaged 11.6 points. The scrappy, aggressive backcourt performer exhibited exceptional defensive play. He spent from 1942 through 1945 in the U.S. Navy as a chief petty officer and played basketball two seasons at the Norfolk, Virginia, Naval Training Station.

In 1945 Holzman joined the new Rochester Royals (NBL) franchise and compiled 365 points (10.7 points per game) his rookie season as a teammate of Bob Davies*, Al Cervi*, George Glamack*, and Fuzzy Levane. Rochester won the NBL championship that year by defeating the Fort Wayne Pistons and Sheboygan Redskins in the playoffs. Holzman performed with Rochester through the 1952–1953 season, helping the Royals make the playoffs each season. The NBL named him to its All-Star First Team in 1945–1946 and 1947–1948 and its All-Star Second Team in 1946–1947. Holzman attained career highs in total points (609) in 1947–1948 and scoring average (12.0) in 1946–1947. Rochester switched to the newly formed NBA for the 1949–1950 season and finished second during the 1949–1950 and 1950–1951 regular seasons. The Royals won the 1950–1951 NBA championship by defeating Fort Wayne, the Minneapolis Lakers, and the New York Knickerbockers. Holzman's final NBA season came with the 1953–1954 Milwaukee Hawks. During his NBA career, Holzman made 1,447 field goals and 774 free throws for 3,668 points (7.4 points average) in 496 games. In 56 NBA playoff games, he tallied 410 points (7.3 points per game).

Holzman began his coaching career with Milwaukee (NBA) in 1953–1954 and experienced two losing seasons there before the franchise moved to St. Louis. The 33-39 Hawks made the playoffs in 1955–1956, as Holzman nurtured center Bob Pettit* into one of the greatest players in pro basketball history. Holzman left St. Louis after the club's 14-19 start in January 1957 and joined the New York Knickerbockers (NBA) as an assistant coach and head scout in 1958. He became the Knicks head coach in 1967–1968 and guided them to their best performance since the 1958–1959 campaign, combining a pressing defense with an all-out running offense. New York enjoyed winning seasons in Holzman's first seven campaigns there and made the playoffs his initial eight years. The 60-22 Knicks won the Eastern Division in 1969–1970 and took the NBA championship in seven games over the Los Angeles Lakers. The Knicks' 60 regular-season victories established a club record. Center Willis Reed* led a balanced squad that included Walt Frazier*, Cazzie Russell*, Bill Bradley*, Dave DeBusschere*, and Dick Barnett*.

Holzman steered New York to first place in the Atlantic Division during the regular season in 1970–1971 and second place finishes the next three seasons. The 57-25 1972–1973 New York squad took the NBA championship with a five-game triumph over Los Angeles. Holzman coached the Knicks through the 1976–1977 season when Reed assumed the reins. From the spring of 1970 through the 1975–1976 season, he also served as club general manager. Holzman replaced Reed as head coach just 14 games into the 1978–1979 campaign. His only winning season after the 1973–1974 campaign came in 1980–1981 when New York enjoyed a 50-32 regular-season mark before being eliminated in the playoffs. Holzman retired after the 1981–1982 season and remained with the Knicks as a consultant. During his 18-year NBA coaching career, he compiled an impressive 696-604 (.535) regular-season record and 58-47 playoff mark. Five Holzman clubs attained at least 50 victories. At his retirement, he held the best win-loss record of active coaches and ranked second behind Red Auerbach* in career victories. His honors included being named NBA Coach of the Year in 1970 and being elected to the Naismith Memorial Basketball Hall of Fame in 1985 and the Madison Square Garden Hall of Fame in 1984. He was selected one of the Top Ten Coaches in NBA History in 1996. The Cedarhurst, New York resident lived with his wife, Selma, whom he married in 1942, and had one daughter, Gail Bonnie.

BIBLIOGRAPHY: Phil Berger, *Miracle of 33rd Street* (New York, 1970); Lewis Cole, *Dream Team* (New York, 1981); Jan Hubbard, ed., *The Official NBA Encyclopedia*, 3rd ed. (New York, 2000); Red Holzman and Harvey Frommer, *Red on Red* (New York, 1987); Red Holzman file, Naismith Memorial Basketball Hall of Fame, Springfield, MA; Neil D. Isaacs, *Vintage NBA* (Silver Spring, MD, 1996); Roland Lazenby, *The NBA Finals* (Indianapolis, IN, 1996); Phil Pepe, *The Incredible Knicks* (New York, 1970); *TSN Official NBA Register, 2004–2005* (St. Louis, MO, 2004); *WWA*, 41st ed. (1980–1981), p. 1600.

David L. Porter

HOSKINS, Patricia (b. February 19, 1967, Greenville, MS), college player, enjoyed a spectacular basketball career with the Mississippi Valley State University Devilettes. In 1985–1986, Hoskins captured the SWAC Freshman of the Year honors. She was named All-Conference all four years at Mississippi Valley State, culminating in Player of the Year accolades in 1988. Hoskins led Mississippi Valley State to the SWAC championship in the 1987–1988 campaign, scoring 55 points while garnering 27 rebounds against Southern University. She later equaled her scoring best with 55 points against Alabama State University. In the 1988–1989, Hoskins became only the second woman in NCAA history to capture the scoring (33.6 points average) and rebounding (16.2 rebounds per game) titles in the same season. Her 33.6 points average set the NCAA single-season scoring record. Hoskin's dominance of Mississippi Valley State women's basketball earned her the nickname, "The Franchise." Hoskins finished her collegiate career with 3,122 points, breaking Lorri Bauman's record of 3,115 points established in 1984 with Drake University. She did not realize she had broken the scoring record until informed after the game by the sports information director. Hoskins averaged an amazing 28.4 points over her four-year career despite confronting defenses that often triple teamed her. Her career scoring record received surprisingly little attention until Southwest Missouri State University's Jackie Stiles* broke it on March 1, 2001 in Springfield, Missouri, with Hoskins and her son in the stands. Hoskins was honored at a postgame ceremony and received a standing ovation when she was introduced. On November 30, 2001, Hoskins was inducted into the SWAC Hall of Fame in Birmingham, Alabama. She resides in Greenville, Mississippi.

BIBLIOGRAPHY: Chuck Schoffner, "NCAA Record-Holder Finally Gets Her Due," *AP* (March 3, 2001), p. 1; Southwest Athletic Conference, "SWAC to Induct Eleven into Hall of Fame," *SWAC News and*

Features (November 2001), pp. 1–4; Michelle Voepel, "Stiles is something special," ESPN.com (March 7, 2001), pp. 1–4.

Frank J. Olmsted

HOUBREGS, Robert J. "Bob" (b. March 12, 1932, Vancouver, British Columbia, Canada), college and professional player and executive, still holds many of the career basketball scoring records at the University of Washington even though he played before freshmen were eligible. Houbregs, a six-foot eight-inch, 225-pound center known for his hookshot, remains Washington's only consensus All-America basketball choice (1953). In 1952–1953, he led the Huskies to third place nationally for their highest finish in the NCAA Tournament and their best record (30-3) in history. Houbregs' family moved from Vancouver, British Columbia to Seattle, Washington, when he was a child. He was chosen All-City in basketball at Queen Anne High School in Seattle in 1949.

In 1950–1951, Houbregs made All-PCC as a sophomore for the 24-6 Washington Huskies. In 16 PCC games, he led Washington in most offensive categories and averaged 12.4 points. As a junior, he again was named All-PCC to help the Huskies finish 14-2 in PCC play and 25-6 overall and led the club with 19.3 points per game. Houbregs enjoyed a great senior campaign, being named to the AP, UP, Converse, HAF, *Collier's*, and all other All-America teams. His coach, Tippy Dye, called him "the greatest pivot man in college basketball," while UCLA's legendary coach John Wooden* claimed that Houbregs possessed a better hookshot than the great George Mikan*. Houbregs scored a still team record 49 points in one game and added 45- and 42-point performances that same season. He finished his college career with 1,774 points, which remained the Huskie record until 1988; Chris Welp needed four seasons to break Houbregs' mark. Among the records Houbregs still holds at Washington include single-game scoring with the 49-point performance, single-season points average (25.6 points in 1953), and career scoring average (19.5 points).

Houbregs was picked in the first round of the 1953 NBA draft by the Milwaukee Hawks (NBA), and played five seasons with the Hawks, Baltimore Bullets (NBA), Boston Celtics (NBA), Fort Wayne Pistons (NBA), and Detroit Pistons (NBA). In the 1955–1956 season with Fort Wayne, Houbregs finished eighth in the NBA in field goal percentage (43 percent) by making 247 of 575 shots. The next year with the same team, he placed fourth in field goal percentage with 253 of 585 shots for a 43.2 percent mark. In 281 career games, he tallied 2,611 points for a 9.3 point average.

Houbregs served as general manager of the Seattle SuperSonics (NBA) from 1970 until 1973. Houbregs was named to the Huskie Sports Hall of Fame in 1979 as the only basketball player so honored in that group's first year. In 1985 he again was honored by his alma mater as part of the outstanding 1952–1953 30-3 team. Two years later, he was elected to the Naismith Memorial Basketball Hall of Fame. Houbregs has been national sales manager for Converse, Incorporated. He is based in Andover, Massachusetts, where he lives with his wife, Ardis A. (Olson) Houbregs. They have four children: Robert Jr., Todd, Jol, and Guy.

BIBLIOGRAPHY: Robert Houbregs file, Naismith Memorial Basketball Hall of Fame, Springfield, MA; Jan Hubbard, ed., *The Official NBA Encyclopedia*, 3rd. ed. (New York, 2000); Neil D. Isaacs, *Vintage NBA* (Silver Spring, MD, 1996); University of Washington Sports Information Office, Seattle, WA.

Jay Berman

HOWELL, Bailey E. (b. January 20, 1937, Middleton, TN), college and professional player and coach, is the son of Walter E. Howell and Martha (Pirtle) Howell and excelled as an athlete and student at Middleton High School. Howell graduated in 1955, holding the Middleton and Tennessee State records for most points scored in a season by making 1,137 points (33 points average) his senior year. A great rebounder and scorer from inside and outside, he converted Mississippi State University's basketball program into a successful one. As a sophomore in 1955–1956, Howell led the nation in field goal percentage (56.8 percent), ranked in the top 10 in scoring and rebounds, and helped Mississippi State enjoy its winningest season with a 17-8 mark. The 1957–1958 team, sparked by Howell, finished with a 20-5 mark. During his senior year, he was the SEC's premier player and earned consensus All-America honors. Howell finished second nationally in both rebounding (15.1 rebounds average) and scoring (27.5 points average), leading the Bulldogs to a 24-1 season and their first SEC championship. Mississippi State later withdrew from the NCAA tournament because of the presence of black players. Howell joined Tom Gola* and Elgin Baylor* as the only college players to score over 2,000 points and grab over 1,000 rebounds in a three-year career. At Mississippi State, he set school records with 2,030 points and 1,277 rebounds.

From 1959 through 1971, Howell averaged double figures in scoring in the NBA. The Detroit Pistons (NBA) made the blond, crew-cut, six-foot seven-inch, 205-pound Howell their first draft pick in 1959. Howell played his first five seasons with Detroit, leading the Pistons in scoring four times and rebounding three times. With the Baltimore Bullets (NBA) from 1964 through 1966, he finished runner-up in team scoring. After leading the Bullets in rebounding during 1965–1966, he was traded in September 1966 to the Boston Celtics (NBA) for Mel Counts. This marked the first time that Boston coach Red Auerbach* had traded one of his own players to bring an outsider to the champion Celtics. Auerbach's move paid dividends, as Howell became the team's second-leading scorer (behind John Havlicek*) and rebounder (after Bill Russell*) for three straight seasons (1966–1967 through 1968–1969). Howell played all 82 games for the 1969–1970 Celtics and the 1970–1971 Philadelphia 76ers, with whom he finished his career.

A bruising rebounder and physical defensive player, Howell committed 3,498 personal fouls during his 12-year career and retired ranked fifth in that category. He entered the celebrated 10,000 points scoring club during the 1964–1965 season and retired with 17,770 points (18.7 points average) and 9,383 rebounds. Howell made six NBA All-Star teams and was honored on the All-NBA Second Team in 1962–1963, when he averaged 22.7 points per game and registered 910 rebounds. His teams made the playoffs 10 times. He always shot well from both the floor and the foul line and performed consistently both in the playoffs and regular season. Upon his retirement, he ranked in the top 10 in 11 all-time statistical categories and as fourth best in scoring average. He played on the last two championship teams (1967–1968, 1968–1969) in the Celtics dynasty. The Celtics defeated the Los Angeles Lakers in both 1968 and 1969, getting by the Wilt Chamberlain*—led Philadelphia 76ers in the 1968 Eastern Division finals.

After leaving the NBA, Howell pursued graduate work at Mississippi State University and served as an assistant basketball coach there. He and his wife, Mary Lou, have two married daughters, Amy Lee and Mary Beth. The youngest daughter, Anne Martha, lived at home with her parents in Starkville, Mississippi, where Howell is sales representative for Converse Shoes. He was elected to the Naismith Memorial Basketball Hall of Fame in 1997.

BIBLIOGRAPHY: Peter C. Bjarkman, *The Boston Celtics Encyclopedia* (Champaign, IL, 1998); Boston Celtics Public Relations Office, telephone interview with Mark Altschuler, November 7, 1986; "Boston's Old, Old Pros," *Newsweek 73* (May 19, 1969), p. 77; Jack Clary, *Basketball's Great Dynasties: The Celtics* (New York, 1992); Detroit Pistons Public Relations Office, telephone interview with Mark Altschuler, November 10, 1986; Joe Fitzgerald, *That Championship Feeling: The Story of the Boston Celtics* (New York, 1975); Zander Hollander, ed., *The Modern Encyclopedia of Basketball* (Garden City, NY, 1979); Bailey Howell, telephone interview with Mark Altschuler, November 23, 1986; Bailey Howell file, Naismith Memorial Basketball Hall of Fame, Springfield, MA; Mary Lou Howell telephone interview with Mark Altschuler, November 10, 1986; Jan Hubbard, ed., *The Official NBA Encyclopedia*, 3rd ed. (New York, 2000); "Last Drop in the Bucket," *SI* 30 (May 12, 1969), pp. 22–24; Roland Lazenby, *The NBA Finals* (Indianapolis, IN, 1996); Herman L. Masin, "Howell-lujah!" *Senior Scholastic* 74 (February 20, 1959), p. 50; Ronald L. Mendell, *Who's Who in Basketball* (New Rochelle, NY, 1973); Mississippi State University Sports Information Office, telephone interview with Mark Altschuler, November 10, 1986; *NCAA Basketball Guide, 1984* (Shawnee Mission, KS, 1984); Bob Ryan, *The Boston Celtics* (Reading, MA, 1989); Dan Shaughnessy, *Ever*

Green: The Boston Celtics (New York, 1990); *TSN Official NBA Guide, 1983–1984* (St. Louis, MO, 1983); *TSN Official NBA Register, 2004–2005* (St. Louis, MO, 2004); "This One Was Worth Shouting About," *SI* 28 (May 13, 1968), pp. 34–37.

Mark Altschuler and Steve Ollove

HOYT, George Hogsett "Mr. Basketball" (b. August 9, 1883, South Boston, MA; d. November 11, 1962, Dorchester, MA), college referee, was nicknamed "Mr. Basketball" and became New England's top official. Hoyt played in city amateur leagues beginning in 1902 and later coached several American Legion, school, company, and city teams in the Boston area. Although believing that tall players were important, he liked an open style of play and insisted that every successful team needed a "little guy" to set up the big plays.

Hoyt played an instrumental role in developing a uniform set of rules, interpretations, and enforcement procedures. In the *Converse Basketball Yearbook, 1923*, he stated that many rules were unnecessary and first noted the distinctions in officiating style between Eastern and Western referees. These subjects were discussed in his book, *The Theory and Practice of Basketball Officiating*. Hoyt founded an organization and event raising the standards of basketball rules and the referee's role as enforcer. The EMBAO, of which Hoyt served two years as president, sought to provide the sport with more informed, competent officials. He pioneered the NEIBT, hoping to decrease the disparity among the rules and to develop and encourage otherwise difficult interstate competition. As chief of officials for the NEIBT, he directed and instructed referees during the transition.

As a referee, Hoyt often officiated two games a day because high schools and colleges demanded his services. At the time, most amateur games used only one referee. Hoyt, a sporting goods salesman, was enshrined in the Naismith Memorial Basketball Hall of Fame in 1961 as a referee. "Basketball," he once said, "is a game of science, not brute strength."

BIBLIOGRAPHY: George H. Hoyt file, Naismith Memorial Basketball Hall of Fame, Springfield, MA.

Catherine M. Derrick

HUDSON, Louis Clyde "Sweet Lou" (b. July 11, 1944, Greensboro, NC), college and professional player, is the son of Vernon Harold Hudson and Cleola Lee (Allison) Hudson and starred on the Dudley High School basketball team in Greensboro, North Carolina. Hudson earned a basketball scholarship to the University of Minnesota, graduating with a Bachelor's degree in 1966. In the 1964–1965 season at Minnesota, he averaged 23.3 points and was named an HAF First Team All-America. His production as a senior was limited by a broken wrist, but he still averaged 19.8 points in 17 games. Princeton University star Bill Bradley* called him "the best college player I've seen in the past season." At Minnesota three seasons, he scored 1,329 points (20.4 points average) and made 576 rebounds in 65 career games.

The St. Louis Hawks (NBA) made Hudson their first pick in the draft and the fifth overall choice. Hudson proved a wise choice, making the NBA All-Rookie team that year. After the Hawks moved to Atlanta, he became one of the city's most popular athletes. The six-foot five-inch, 210-pound Hudson played in every All-Star Game between 1969 and 1974 and was named to the All-NBA Second Team in 1970. In 1971 he was named the Hawks MVP and Most Popular Player and one of the 10 Outstanding Young People in Atlanta. His best season came in 1972–1973, when he averaged 27.1 points for the fourth best in the NBA. Because his Atlanta teams did not fare well in the playoffs, Hudson was delighted to be traded to the Los Angeles Lakers (NBA) on September 30, 1977, for Ollie Johnson. As a reserve, he averaged over 13 points for the Lakers his first year there. The Lakers, however, never won the NBA championship he coveted in his two seasons before retirement.

During his 13-year career, Hudson scored 17,940 points, averaged 20.2 points and made 3,926 rebounds. He played well at both the small forward and big guard positions and ranked among the era's finest pure shooters. One writer called Hudson "basketball's greatest shooter" because he could score consistently from any distance. Hudson, one of the smoothest players during his NBA career, was nicknamed "Sweet Lou." He certainly was a treat to watch, provided you were not guarding him.

BIBLIOGRAPHY: George Cunningham, " 'I'm at 5 or 6 Now, Pistol,' " *Atlanta Constitution*, October 10, 1970; "Hawks Draft Lou Hudson," *St. Louis Post-Dispatch,* May 11, 1966; Jan Hubbard, ed., *The Official NBA Encyclopedia*, 3rd ed. (New York, 2000); "Hudson Traded," *Atlanta Constitution*, October 1, 1977; "Lakers Obtain Lou Hudson," *Los Angeles Times*, October 1, 1977; *TSN Official NBA Register, 2004–2005* (St. Louis, MO, 2004); Arthur Triche, ed., *From Sweet Lou to 'Nique: Twenty-Five Years with the Atlanta Hawks* (Atlanta, GA, 1992); *WWA*, 38th ed. (1974–1975), p. 1512.

Joel Westerholm

HUGGINS, Robert Edward "Bob" (b. September 21, 1953, Morgantown, WV), college player and coach, is the son of Charles Huggins, a basketball coach, and Norma Mae Huggins, who worked at a basketball camp that her husband developed over 30 years ago. Huggins played basketball under his father, who coached at Indian Valley South High School in Gnadenhutten, Ohio. He led the 26-0 Rebels to the state championship and was named Ohio Player of the Year as a senior. A three-time All-Ohio selection, the six-foot, four-inch Huggins scored 2,438 career points to rank seventh on the state's all-time scoring list.

A 1972 high school graduate, Huggins attended Ohio University as a freshman and transferred to West Virginia University. He averaged 13.2 points in basketball and was the named the Mountaineer's MVP as a senior. A two-time academic All-America, Huggins graduated magna cum laude from West Virginia in 1977 with a Bachelor's degree. He married June Ann Fillman on August 19, 1977 and has two children, Jenna and Jacque.

His first basketball coaching experience came when he served as a graduate assistant in the West Virginia Mountaineer program while earning a Master's degree in health administration in 1978. Huggins assisted Eldon Miller at Ohio State University the next two seasons. His first basketball head-coaching experience came in 1980 at Walsh College in Canton, Ohio. He posted a 71-26 win-loss record in three seasons at Walsh and twice was named District Coach of the Year. His 1982–1983 squad compiled a 34-1 win-loss record, his highest victory total in his career. Huggins served one year as an assistant basketball coach at the University of Central Florida before being named head coach at the University of Akron. He compiled a 97-46 win-loss record in five seasons, guided the Zips to postseason play in three campaigns, and was named Ohio Valley Coach of the Year twice.

In March 1989, Huggins was appointed head basketball coach at the University of Cincinnati. From 1989–1990 through 2004–2005, he has compiled a 399-127 win-loss record and a .759 winning percentage in 16 seasons. During his 24-year head-coaching career, his teams have won 567 games and lost 199 times for a .740 winning percentage. Huggins has steered the Bobcats to ten conference championships and eight league tournament crowns. His squads have qualified for postseason play all 16 years, advancing to the NCAA Elite Eight in the NCAA tournament three times and advancing to the Final Four in 1992. The Bearcats have appeared in 14 consecutive NCAA tournaments and have posted a 20-14 win-loss record. At Cincinnati, his squads have won 20 or more games 14 times. He was named GMC Coach of the Year in 1992 and 1993 and CUSA Coach of the Year by ESPN in 2002, co-national Coach of the Year by *TSN* in 2000, and National Coach of the Year in 1998 by *BT*. He received National Coach of the Year honors from *Hoop Scoop* in 1992 and from *Playboy* in 1993 and also served on the coaching staff for the 1993 U.S. World University Games gold medal–winning team. Outstanding Bearcat performers under his guidance have included Danny Fortson, Nick Van Exel, and Kenyon Martin*.

In September 2002, Huggins suffered a serious heart attack at a Pittsburgh, Pennsylvania airport. Corrective surgery allowed him to return to his coaching duties for the 2002–2003 season. Cincinnati suspended him for 77 days in the summer 2004 after he was arrested for drunken driving.

BIBLIOGRAPHY: "Bob Huggins," *From My Seat*, http://www.bearcatnews.com (2003); "Bob Huggins," *Mother Dies*, http://www.canoe.ca/Slam (2003); Bob Huggins, *Press for Success* (Chicago, IL, 1995); "Bob Huggins," *Time Line*, http://www.enquirer.com (2003); "Bob Huggins," *You Name It*, http://ucbearcats.com (2003); "Cincinnati Basketball," *102 Seasons*, http://www.ucbearcats.com (2003); *NCAA Men's Basketball Records 2004* (Indianapolis, IN, 2003); "University of Cincinnati," *In The NCAA*, http://www.ucbearcats.com (2003); Tom Weir, "Huggins has Heart for Work," *USA Today*, November, 11, 2004, pp. 1C–2C.

John L. Evers

HUNDLEY, Rodney Clark "Hot Rod" (b. October 26, 1934, Charleston, WV), college and professional player and sportscaster, is the son of a meat-cutter, pool-shark, gambling father, and a mother who reportedly worked as a madam at a brothel. His parents divorced and left West Virginia when he was very young. Hundley was brought up by several different people around the Charleston area and found a home on the playgrounds, developing the skills that would make him the first real basketball hero from West Virginia.

Over 100 schools tried to recruit Hundley, with Everett Case*, head coach at North Carolina State University (ACC), displaying particular persistence. Hundley had planned on enrolling at North Carolina State in 1954, but that same year the ACC and NCAA announced sanctions against the Wolfpack for recruiting violations. Case advised him to attend West Virginia University (SC) instead. Red Brown, the new athletic director at West Virginia, signed Hundley and even became his legal guardian.

Hundley's freshman year did little to sharpen his basketball skills, as the Mountaineers played against weak competition. He spiced up blowout games by taking shots from his knees and behind his back and spinning the ball on his fingertips. Hundley averaged 35 points for the freshman team, even though not shooting in six games. As a sophomore, he helped lead West Virginia to 19 wins and their first SC title. He paced the Mountaineers in scoring with 711 points, establishing a new national scoring record for sophomores and being named the MVP of the SC tournament.

Hundley improved his junior year, scoring 798 points. West Virginia won the SC title for the second consecutive year, as he again was named the SC tournament MVP. Hundley's final collegiate season saw him score less but enjoy it more. West Virginia finished with a 25-5 record and clinched the SC title for the third straight year, as Hundley finally won All-America honors. Many scouts and sportswriters considered him the best college player ever.

The six-foot four-inch, 185-pound Hundley was selected in the first round of the 1957 NBA draft by the Minneapolis Lakers. His NBA career, however, never matched his college accomplishments. In six seasons with the Minneapolis-Los Angeles Lakers (NBA), he averaged only 8.4 points. His best year came during the 1959–1960 campaign, when he averaged 12.8 points and finished eighth in the NBA in assists with a 4.6 assists average.

Hundley retired from the Lakers in 1964 and moved to the broadcast booth. He broadcast Los Angeles Lakers (NBA) games for two years before joining the Phoenix Suns (NBA) announcing team in 1969. In 1974, Hundley became the announcer for the expansion New Orleans Jazz (NBA). He moved with the Jazz when it relocated to Utah and has remained its play-by-play broadcaster ever since. He also spent five years broadcasting the CBS NBA "Game of the Week."

As his nickname denotes, "Hot Rod" was known more as an entertainer than as a player. Hundley, who appeared in NBA All-Star Games in 1960 and 1961, was named to the NCAA Silver Anniversary All-America team in 1982 and was selected to the West Virginia Sports Hall of Fame. He was inducted into the West Virginia University Hall of Fame. Hundley has three daughters, Kimberly, Jackie, and Jennifer, and resides in Salt Lake City, Utah. He authored, *You Gotta Love It, Baby* (1998).

BIBLIOGRAPHY: Peter C. Bjarkman, *The Biographical History of Basketball* (Chicago, IL, 2000); Mike Douchant, *Encyclopedia of College Basketball* (Detroit, MI, 1995); Hot Rod Hundley with Tom McEachin, *You Gotta Love It, Baby* (Champaign, IL, 1998); Neil D. Isaacs, *All the Moves* (Philadelphia, PA, 1975); Bruce Nash and Allan Zullo, *Basketball Hall of Shame* (New York, 1991); Terry Pluto, *Tall Tales* (New York, 1992); Ken Shouler, et al., *Total Basketball* (Wilmington, DE, 2003); *TSN Official NBA Guide, 1961–1962* (St. Louis, MO, 1961); *Utah Jazz Media Guide 2003–2004* (Salt Lake City, UT, 2003); Alexander M. Weyand, *Cavalcade of Basketball* (New York, 1960).

Curtice R. Mang

HUTCHINS, Melvin R. "Mel" "Hutch" (b. November 22, 1928, Sacramento, CA), college and professional player, is the son of native Utahans who moved to California in 1924. His sister, Colleen Kay Hutchins, was named Miss Utah and Miss America in 1952 and married Ernie Vandeweghe, former UCLA and New York Knicks (NBA) star. Vandeweghe later became a successful doctor in the Los Angeles, California area.

Hutchins, a six-foot six-inch, 200-pound forward, enrolled at Brigham Young University (BYU) in 1947 and lettered four years as a skillful basketball player. Between 1948 and 1951, he led the Cougars to an 88-45 win-loss record. After future Hall-of-Famer Stan Watts* became basketball head coach in 1949, BYU posted a two year 50-21 win-loss record. The Cougars advanced to the NCAA tournament both seasons and captured the 1951 NIT with a 62-43 triumph over the University of Dayton in the championship game. BYU won conference championships in three of Hutchins four years. The HAF, *Look* magazine, and Converse Basketball Shoes named him to the All-America collegiate basketball team in 1951. A 1951 graduate of BYU, he was named to the 1971 Silver Anniversary All-America Team.

Hutchins, a first round draft choice in 1951, signed with the Milwaukee Hawks (NBA). In his first season, he posted 607 points, grabbed 880 rebounds to share first place in the NBA, averaged 13.3 rebounds to share second place in the NBA, and was named NBA Rookie of the Year. After his second season with Milwaukee, Hutchins was traded to the Fort Wayne Zollner Pistons (NBA) and played there four seasons. He helped lead the Pistons to Western Division championships in 1955 and 1956, but lost in the 1955 NBA Finals to the Syracuse Nationals and the 1956 NBA Finals to the Philadelphia Warriors.

In four seasons with Fort Wayne, Hutchins posted 3,287 points, grabbed 2,427 rebounds, and handed out 847 assists in 282 regularly scheduled games. He performed in 27 NBA playoff games and averaged 11.7 points. Hutchins was chosen to play in six NBA All-Star Games, but appeared in only four of those classics and recorded 26 points. Hutchins completed his NBA career in 1957–1958, performing 18 games with the New York Knicks (NBA). In seven NBA seasons, he compiled 4,851 points, 4,196 rebounds, and 1,298 assists in 437 regularly scheduled games.

Hutchins later gained recognition as an amateur golfer in northern California and participated in water ski meets.

BIBLIOGRAPHY: Kenneth N. Carlson, *College Basketball Scores* (Lynnwood, WA, 1990); "Mel Hutchins," *BYU Club*, http://www.cougarclub.com (2004); "Mel Hutchins," *History*, http://byucougars.com (2001); "Mel Hutchins," *Statistics*, http://www.basketballreference.com (2004); Jan Hubbard, ed., *The Official NBA Encyclopedia*, 3rd ed. (New York, 2000); David S. Neft et al., *The Sports Encyclopedia: Pro Basketball*, 5th ed. (New York, 1992).

John L. Evers

HYATT, Charles "Chuck" (b. February 28, 1908, Syracuse, NY; d. May 8, 1978, St. Petersburg, FL), college player and coach, was chosen First Team All-America for 10 years in scholastic, collegiate, and AAU ranks. At high school, he led his Uniontown, Pennsylvania team as a junior to its first state championship in 1925 and the next year to the final state playoffs. Hyatt, a First Team All-State two years, made national Scholastic All-America his senior year.

At the University of Pittsburgh, Hyatt scored an exceptional 880 points from 1928 through 1930 and made First Team All-America all three years. In 1928 and 1930, he led Pittsburgh to national HAF collegiate championships. The Panthers finished 21-0 his sophomore year, defeating five BTC teams and two top eastern powers. Pittsburgh nipped the University of Notre Dame 24-22 on Hyatt's last-second shot. He considered a 37-35 win over Montana State University his most memorable game that season. Hyatt scored 28 of Pittsburgh's points, including the winning field goal in the last 10 seconds. He led the nation in scoring with 266 points his sophomore year. As a junior, Hyatt scored 300 points for a 16-5 Pittsburgh team. The Panthers regained the national championship with a 23-2 record the next year, as he again led the nation with 314 points. The HAF named the six-foot, 170-pound forward the Collegiate Player of the Year.

Hyatt joined the Phillips 66 Oilers in national AAU competition, then the nation's top basketball. He played for six years and then as player-coach and was named AAU All-America six times. The Oilers lost the national championship game to the Denver Safeways in 1937 and to the Denver Nuggets in 1939. With the addition of Stanford University's Hank Luisetti*, Coach Hyatt's team won the AAU title in 1940.

After 20 years as a basketball player, Hyatt retired at age 37 in 1945. He was a sales field representative for Spalding Sporting Goods Company and in 1959 was named with the first-year Naismith Memorial Basketball Hall of Fame selections. His son, Charley, died at sea in 1973 after service in the Vietnam War.

BIBLIOGRAPHY: Bill Gutman, *The History of NCAA Basketball* (New York, 1993); Zander Hollander, ed., *The Modern Encyclopedia of Basketball* (Garden City, NY, 1979); Jan Hubbard, ed., *The Official NBA Encyclopedia*, 3rd ed. (New York, 2000); Charles Hyatt file, Naismith Memorial Basketball Hall of Fame Springfield, MA; Joe Jares, *Basketball, the American Game* (Chicago, IL, 1971); John D. McCallum, *College Basketball U.S.A. Since 1892* (Briarcliff Manor, NY, 1978); Jim O'Brien, *Hail to Pitt, A Sports History of the University of Pittsburgh* (Pittsburgh, PA, 1982); *Pittsburgh Post-Gazette*, May 10, 1978; E. Trasel Rowland, *Pennsylvania Basketball Record Book* (Bryn Mawr, PA, 1954); *Uniontown* (PA) *Herald-Standard*, 1924–1926; University of Pittsburgh, Alumni Association and Sports Information files, Pittsburgh, PA.

Robert B. Van Atta

I

IBA, Henry Payne "Hank" (b. April 6, 1904, Easton, MO; d. January 15, 1993, Stillwater, OK), college coach and athletic director, was born into a family of basketball players. His father, salesman Henry Burkey Iba, and his mother, Zylfa (Payne) Iba, a homemaker, had an active family. His sister, Lucille, kept score, while Hank and his brothers, Earl, Clarence, Howard, played for Easton High School. The Iba brothers all played college basketball and pursued coaching careers, most notably Clarence at University of Tulsa. Henry attended Westminster College and received his Bachelor's degree from Maryville College in the summer of 1929 after coaching basketball at Classen High School in Oklahoma City, Oklahoma. At Westminister College, Iba earned four varsity letters and made All-Conference honors in 1927 and 1928. He closed out his playing career in AAU basketball with Sterling Milk of Oklahoma City and Hillyards of St. Joseph, Missouri.

During three years at Classen High School, Iba produced a 51-5 record. He coached his alma mater, Maryville College, to a 101-14 record from 1929 to 1933 and piloted his club to conference runner-up in 1932. After coaching at the University of Colorado in 1933–1934, Iba moved to Oklahoma State (then Oklahoma Agricultural and Mechanical, or A&M) University. Until retiring in 1970, he spent the rest of his career at Oklahoma A&M as both head basketball coach and athletic director and spent several years as head baseball coach. At the Stillwater institution, he compiled the majority of his 767 victories. Iba ranks eighth in collegiate victories among NCAA Division I college coaches. His Aggies captured 14 MVC titles and the BEC Championship in 1964–1965, secured two consecutive NCAA titles in 1945 and 1946, and finished runner-up in the 1949 NCAA competition. In 1946, his squad comprised the entire All-MVC All-Star Team. Iba is the only coach to guide two U.S. Olympic basketball teams to gold medals, accomplishing the feat at the 1964 Tokyo, Japan Olympic Games and the 1968 Mexico City, Mexico Olympic Games. Unfortunately his coaching career concluded with the controversial loss to the USSR in the 1972 Munich, Germany Olympic Games. Before that time, the U.S. had won the gold medal every time since the inception of basketball as an Olympic sport in 1936.

In recognition of his outstanding coaching career, Iba received two Coach of the Year Awards and the NABC Metropolitan Award in 1948 and was elected president of the NBCA in 1968. The Missouri, Oklahoma, Westminister College, Olympic and HAF Halls of Fame all inducted Iba. The Naismith Memorial Basketball Hall of Fame made him a member in 1968. During Iba's time as Athletic Director, Oklahoma State University won 24 of its 30 NCAA titles and received three football bowl bids. This record ranks second only to the University of Southern California. He also coached numerous players, including Jack Hartman, who became mentors. Iba married Doyne Williams on August 25, 1930. Their only son, Moe, former University of Nebraska head basketball coach, played for his father from 1959 to 1962.

Under the steady patience and tutelage of

Coach Iba, Bob Kurland* developed from raw talent into one of the first two dominant seven-foot centers who could score, rebound, and defend. Oklahoma State University fans frequently complained about Iba's ball control, offensive weaving patterns that produced low scoring totals. But they cheered his "swinging gate" defense (a man-to-man with team flow), which discouraged the toughest of opponents and set a BEC playing style that still survives.

BIBLIOGRAPHY: Morgan G. Brenner, *College Basketball's National Champions* (Lanham, MD, 1999); John Paul Bischoff, *Mr. Iba: Basketball's Aggie Iron Duke* (1980); Tom C. Brody, "The Man Who Said Control the Ball," *SI* 27 (December 4, 1967), pp. 36–43; Tom C. Brody, "Who Says You Can't Win 'em All?" *SI* 20 (April 13, 1964), pp. 104–105; Doris Dellinger, *A History of the Oklahoma State University Intercollegiate Athletics* (Stillwater, OK, 1987); Bruce Drake, "Seven-Foot Trouble," *SEP* 216 (February 19, 1944), pp. 16–17, 88; Stanley Frank, "High Guy," *Collier's* 115 (March 17, 1945), pp. 32, 84; Bill Gutman, *The History of NCAA Basketball* (New York, 1993); Zander Hollander, ed., *Modern Encyclopedia of Basketball* (Garden City, NY, 1979); Henry Iba file, Naismith Memorial Basketball Hall of Fame, Springfield, MA; Henry P. Iba, "1947 Basketball Forecast," *Collier's* 118 (December 21, 1946), pp. 16, 38; Neil D. Isaacs; *All the Moves: A History of College Basketball* (Philadelphia, PA, 1975); Frank Litsky, *Superstars* (New York, 1975); John D. McCallum, *College Basketball, U.S.A.* (Briarcliff Manor, NY, 1978); Herman L. Masin, "Winter Wonders," *Scholastic* 50 (February 3, 1947), p. 34; *NYT*, January 16, 1993; Michael Mckenzie *Oklahoma State University: History-Making Basketball* (1992); Sandy Padwe, *Basketball's Hall of Fame* (Englewood, Cliffs, NJ, 1970); Billy Packer, et al., *College Basketball's 25 Greatest Teams* (St. Louis, MO, 1989).

Gregory S. Sojka

IRISH, Edward Simmons "Ned" (b. May 6, 1905, Lake George, NY; d. January 21, 1982, New York, NY), sports journalist and college and professional basketball promoter, was the son of Clifford Irish and Madeleine (Lancaster) Irish. Irish was left fatherless at age three and grew up with his mother. His mother worked as a dermatologist at Erasmus Hall High School in Brooklyn, New York, from which Irish graduated in 1924. His father's untimely death necessitated that Irish assist with the family income. As a high school student, Irish worked at a soda fountain and covered schoolboy sports for local newspapers. The business-minded Irish in 1924 attended the University of Pennsylvania because no New York newspaper had a student correspondent there. From his freshman year through graduation in 1928, he covered University of Pennsylvania sports for six New York and four Philadelphia papers and made the school's athletic teams one of the best covered in the eastern U.S. In 1928 he began working full-time as a sportswriter for the *New York World-Telegram*.

Irish covered many sports, but especially liked college basketball and its future as a spectator sport. The inspiration for college basketball doubleheaders in Madison Square Garden in New York City supposedly came to Irish in 1933, when assigned to cover a game at Manhattan College. In 1931, Irish had helped New York City mayor James J. "Jimmy" Walker promote benefit basketball games at Madison Square Garden to help the mayor's Unemployment Relief Fund for Depression victims. Walker's successful program convinced Irish that New Yorkers loved basketball. Irish believed that top teams across the nation could oppose local schools in Madison Square Garden, enabling more fans to enjoy basketball.

In 1933, Irish approached General John Reed Kilpatrick, president of Madison Square Garden, with his idea. After an agreement was made, 16,188 spectators witnessed Irish's first intersectional college basketball doubleheader on December 29, 1934. NYU defeated the University of Notre Dame 25-18, while Westminster College (Pennsylvania) edged St. John's University in the nightcap. Irish booked eight doubleheaders into Madison Square Garden during the 1934–1935 season, drawing some 99,528 fans. The venture's early success prompted Irish to leave the *New York World-Telegram* in 1934 and become basketball director of Madison Square Garden. From 1935 to 1949, he brought top college teams with name coaches and players to compete against New York schools. Coach Hank Iba's* Oklahoma Agricultural and Mechanical University teams and Stanford University's Hank Luisetti* were among those who saw action in Madison Square Garden. In 1937 Irish and the MBWANY initiated the first major postseason tournament, the NIT.

Under Irish's direction, basketball doubleheaders in Madison Square Garden drew over 500,000 spectators per season from 1942 to 1949. Irish received the NABC Metropolitan Award in 1946 for his contribution to the game. The same year, he expanded his basketball interest by helping form the NBA and founding the New York Knickerbockers (NBA) pro team. His basketball doubleheaders ended abruptly in 1951 with news of a point-shaving scandal. Within a decade, only small crowds attended doubleheaders involving only local teams. By 1967 Irish concentrated on the NBA Knickerbockers.

Through his love and dedication, Irish made basketball truly national in scope with intersectional play, helped standardize rules and coaching techniques, and created greater spectator interest. For his contributions, Irish was elected to the Naismith Memorial Basketball Hall of Fame in 1964.

BIBLIOGRAPHY: Joseph J. Cook and Joseph J. Cook II, *Famous Firsts in Basketball* (New York, 1978); Bill Gutman, *The History of NCAA Basketball* (New York, 1993); Zander Hollander, ed., *The Modern Encyclopedia of Basketball* (Garden City, NY, 1979); Jan Hubbard, ed. *The Official NBA Encyclopedia*, 3rd ed. (New York, 2000); Ned Irish file, Naismith Memorial Basketball Hall of Fame, Springfield, MA; Neil D. Isaacs, *Vintage NBA* (Silver Spring, MD, 1996); John D. McCallum, *College Basketball USA Since 1892* (Briarcliff Manor, NY, 1978); Ronald L. Mendell, *Who's Who in Basketball* (New Rochelle, NY, 1973); Billy Packer and Roland Lazenby, *College Basketball's 25 Greatest Teams* (St. Louis, MO, 1989); Bernice L. Webb, *The Basketball Man James Naismith* (Lawrence, KS, 1973).

Jerry Jaye Wright

ISSEL, Daniel Paul "Dan" (b. October 25, 1948, Batavia, IL), college and professional player, starred for his Batavia Bulldogs High School basketball team. Issel led his squad to two consecutive conference championships and set numerous individual records. His tremendous high school career naturally impressed college recruiters across the nation, giving him his pick of fine schools. He chose the University of Kentucky, which fielded one of the nation's best college basketball teams, and played under the recognized dean of college coaches, Adolph Rupp*. Rupp molded Issel into a solid, mature, and consistent player. Issel gave his coach four excellent seasons, scoring 2,138 total points, averaging 25.8 points and pulling down 1,078 rebounds. He also made All-America both his junior and senior years (1968–1969 and 1969–1970) at Kentucky.

In 1970, the six-foot nine-inch, 235-pound Issel was selected by the Kentucky Colonels (ABA) in the first round of the ABA's college draft and the Detroit Pistons (NBA) in the eighth round of the NBA's draft. He never seriously considered the Pistons, preferring to play in his adopted state of Kentucky. With the Colonels for five seasons (1970–1971 to 1974–1975), Issel established an impressive set of statistics, records, and honors. He led the ABA in scoring in 1970–1971 with 2,480 points, was named to the ABA's All-Star First Team, and was proclaimed Rookie of the Year. During the next season (1971–1972), Issel set the ABA scoring record with 2,538 points and was voted MVP in that year's All-Star Game. He never again matched his first two spectacular years with the Colonels, but compiled a respectable 25.6 points average during his seasons in the ABA and played in every All-Star Game during this period. He made the ABA All-Star Second Team in 1971, 1973, 1974, and 1976.

Kentucky traded Issel in September 1975 to the Baltimore Claws (ABA) for Tom Owens and cash. Baltimore then immediately sent Issel to the Denver Nuggets (ABA) for Dave Robisch and cash. Issel played the rest of his career with Denver from October 1975 through the Nuggets' entry into the NBA in 1976 to their defeat by the Los Angeles Lakers in the NBA Western Division playoffs in April 1985. Although his scoring-record days were over, he consistently averaged over 20 points in seven of 10 seasons with the Nuggets. In 1982 Issel combined with Alex English* and Kiki Vandeweghe* to give Denver the first frontcourt since 1961 to have each player average over 20 points. He played in one NBA All-Star Game (1977) during this period. Issel retired at the end of the 1985 season after a 15-year pro career that included 1,218 games, 10,421 field goals, 6,571 free throws, and a scoring average of 18.3 points. He holds the Nuggets franchise record for most rebounds (6,630) and held Nuggets team records for points scored, field goals made and attempted, free throws made and attempted, assists, steals, games, and minutes played. In 1985, he won the J. Walter Kennedy Citizenship Award. He was elected to the Naismith Memorial Basketball Hall of Fame in 1993 and coached the Denver Nuggets from 1992–1993 to January 1995 and 1999–2000 to December 2002, compiling a 180-208 record and .464 winning percentage. He also served as vice president of the Nuggets from March 1998 to August 2001. Issel moved back to Kentucky on retirement and resides on an 160-acre farm in Versailles, where he raises horses. He and his wife, Cherie, have on daughter, Sheridan, and one son, Scott.

BIBLIOGRAPHY: Dan Issel and Buddy Martin, *Parting Shots* (Chicago, IL, 1985); Dan Issel file, Naismith Memorial Basketball Hall of Fame, Springfield, MA; V.A. Jackson, *Beyond the Baron* (Kuttawah, KY, 1998); *Kentucky Basketball Encyclopedia* (Champaign, IL, 2000); Bert Nell, *The Winning Tradition: A History of Kentucky Wildcat Basketball* (Lexington, KY, 1984); *News from NBA*, April 15, 1985; *NYT*, April 7, 1979; *NYT*, February 26, 1981; *NYT*, January 23, 1985; Terry Pluto, *Loose Balls* (New York, 1990); Russel Rice, *Kentucky Basketball Big Blue Machine* (Huntsville, AL, 1976); *Alan Ross, Wildcat Wisdom* (Nashville, TN, 1999); Ken Shouler et al., *Total Basketball* (Wilmington, DE, 2000); *TSN Official NBA Register, 2004–2005* (St. Louis, MO, 2004).

Christopher E. Guthrie

IVERSON, Allen Ezail (b. June 7, 1975, Hampton, VA), college and professional player, has spent his entire NBA career with the Philadelphia 76ers. Iverson's upbringing and subsequent life has often been convoluted, confused, and fraught with tension. His mother, Ann Iverson, gave birth to her son when she was just 16. Allen Brougton, his father, abandoned the family before Iverson was born. His later, de facto father, Michael Freeman, was arrested in 1991 and 1994 and found guilty of distributing drugs. Iverson, dirt poor, lived a peripatetic existence in apartments that sometimes lacked hot water or electricity.

Iverson's mother introduced him to basketball, but his predilection was for football. In his junior year at Bethel High School, his team won the Virginia State Class AAA football championship. In 1992, Iverson was selected as Virginia High School Player of the Year in basketball and football.

In February 1993, Iverson got involved in, according to Di Su, a "maiming by mob" gang-related incident. A five-year prison sentence, however, eventually was commuted to a four-month detention period. His later life has been dogged with controversy. Iverson was placed on two years probation following a 1997 high-speed car chase, which revealed that he possessed marijuana and a gun. In July 2002 another headline incident reported Iverson with a handgun and charging wildly through a community in Philadelphia.

Iverson completed his high school education at Richard M. Millburn in Virginia Beach in 1994 and enrolled at Georgetown University in Washington, D.C. In two short years at Georgetown, he excelled in basketball. He averaged 23 points and won numerous honors, including a gold medal with the USA team at the 1995 World University Games.

In June 1996, Iverson was drafted by the Philadelphia 76ers as the first overall pick. The six-foot 165-pounder quickly set records. His 1,787 points set a 76er all-time rookie record. In 1997, he was named Schick NBA Rookie of the Year, the first 76er to ever win the award. Iverson led the NBA in scoring with 26.8 points per game in 1998–1999, was named the NBA MVP with 31.1 points and 2.51 steals per game in 2000–2001, and finished second in the NBA in scoring with a 26.4 point average in 2003–2004. He paced the NBA in scoring with 2,302 points (30.7 point average) in 2004–2005, helping the 76ers reach the playoffs. He averaged 31.2 points and 10.0 assists in five games in the first round playoff loss to the Detroit Pistons. He was chosen the MVP of the 2001 All-Star Game and the 2005 All-Star Game.

He was named All-NBA First Team in 1999, 2001, and 2005 and All-NBA Second Team in 2000, 2002, and 2003 and played on the U.S. Olympic team in 2004. In nine NBA seasons from 1996–1997 through 2004–2005, Iverson compiled 16,738 career points for an average of 27.4 points, 6.0 assists, and 2.4 steals in 610 regular-season games. In 62 NBA playoff games, he has scored 1,899 points and has averaged 30.6 points, 6.1 assists, and 2.19 steals.

Iverson married Tawanna Turner on August 23, 2001 and has two children, Tiaura and Allen Jr. He is known for his various braided hairstyles and more than 20 tattoos, and has attempted to promote positive public relations, initiating a charity foundation called Crossover Productions to produce wholesome entertainment for youth. His embrace of in-your-face rap music and concerns with his personal retinue/entourage known as "Iverson's Posse" position him as the *infant terrible* of modern basketball. This "posse" has even become grist for cultural commentators, who question Iverson's resistance to structures of authority.

Iverson's favorite book is *The Color Purple*, while his favorite actors are Al Pacino and Halle Berry. *SI*'s "101 Most Influential Minorities" ranks Iverson in 48th place, based on his lifetime Reebok contract with Iverson's special shoes, "Answer 6," which generates more than $7 million annually. He is midway through a lucrative $70 million, six-year contract with Philadelphia.

BIBLIOGRAPHY: Di Su, "Allen Iverson," *Scribner Encyclopedia of American Lives* (New York, 2002), Vol. 1, pp. 448–450; "101 Most Influential Minorities in Sport," *SI* 98 (May 5, 2003), p. 42; Nikki Giovanni, "Iverson's Posse," in D. K. Wiggins and P. B. Miller, eds., *A Documentary History of the African American Experience in Sports* (Urbana, IL, 2003), pp. 411–413; http://home.c2i,net/espurkel/totusn.htm; Lauren Rippy, Eastern Illinois University research graduate student, materials collected June 9–10, 2003; Ken Shouler et al., *Total Basketball* (Wilmington, DE, 2003); *TSN Official NBA Register, 2004–2005* (St. Louis, MO, 2004).

Scott A.G.M. Crawford

IZZO, Thomas "Tom" (b. January 30, 1955, Iron Mountain, MI), college player and coach, Izzo is the son of Carl Izzo and Dorothy Izzo and graduated from Iron Mountain High School in 1973 and Northern Michigan University in 1977. At Northern Michigan, he set a school basketball record for minutes played in a season, was selected the team's MVP, and was named a NCAA Division II Third Team All-America at guard. Izzo was inducted into the Northern Michigan University Hall of Fame in 1990 and the Michigan Upper Peninsula Hall of Fame in 1998. He has honorary degrees from Michigan State University and Northern Michigan. He and his wife, Lupe, have two children, Raquel and Steven. His best friend, Steve Mariucci, coaches the Detroit Lions NFL team and was a high school classmate and college roommate.

Izzo began his basketball coaching career at Ishpeming (Michigan) High School in 1977–1978, and served as assistant basketball coach at Northern Michigan, the University of Tulsa (Oklahoma), and Michigan State University before succeeding Jud Heathcote as head coach at Michigan State in 1995. His teams are noted for defenses that "peel the paint off the floor," rebound with ferocity, and typically are aggressive, disciplined, and confident. Michigan State has been established an elite program since Izzo became their head coach. His overall record as Michigan State head coach through the 2004–2005 season is 233-94, while his winning percentage in the NCAA Tournament is .767. His teams won the NCAA championship in 2000 and BTC Championships in 1998, 1999, 2000, and, 2001. Izzo has won numerous coaching honors including head coach of the 1997 BTC All-Star team, AP National Coach of the Year, *BN* National Coach of the Year, USBWA National Coach of the Year, BTC Coach of the Year, assistant coach of the 2001 Goodwill Games, and head coach of the 2002 NABC All-Star Game. He also coached the U.S. National team in the Pan-American games in 2003. Izzo, whose salary was raised to $1.3 million in 2001, serves on the John R. Wooden* Award Board of Governors, and on the Board of Sparrow Hospital in Lansing, Michigan. His former assistant coaches are now head coaches at Marquette University (Wisconsin), University of Arkansas, University of Toledo (Ohio), and University of

Dayton (Ohio); seven of his former players perform in the NBA. His players rank above average among BTC teams in graduation rates. In March 2003, he served as a color commentator for CBS.

BIBLIOGRAPHY: *Detroit News*, February 11, 1996, p. E11; *Detroit News*, February 23, 2001, p. H4; *Detroit News*, November 8, 2001, p. E1; *Detroit Free Press*, March 18, 2003, pp. E1, E4; *Detroit Free Press*, March 30, 2003, pp. F1, F5; *Detroit Free Press*, April 4, 2003, p. D2; *Detroit Free Press*, April 10, 2003, p. D2; Jack Ebling et al., *Magic Moments* (Chelsea, MI, 1998); Michigan State University, Sports Information, East Lansing, MI, April 15, 2003; *NCAA Men's Basketball Records, 2004* (Indianapolis, IN, 2003); *NYT*, March 30, 2003, pp. D1, D3; *NYT*, April 7, 2003, p. D1.

Keith McClellan

J

JACKSON, Phillip D. "Phil" "The Mop" (b. September 17, 1945, Deer Lodge, MT), college and professional basketball player, coach, and sportscaster, is the son of Charles Jackson and Elizabeth Jackson, both Evangelical ministers. He graduated from Williston (North Dakota) High School in 1963, where he participated in several sports and led the basketball team to the state championship and MVP honors.

A 1967 graduate of the University of North Dakota, Jackson made the NCAA Division II All-America basketball team twice and played in 86 Fighting Sioux games for future NBA coach Bill Fitch*. He scored 1,708 career points and averaged 27.4 points as a senior.

The New York Knicks (NBA) selected Jackson in the second round (17th pick overall) of the 1967 NBA draft. Jackson, a six-foot eight-inch, 230-pound forward-center, played 11 seasons with the Knicks and proved a key sixth-man reserve on the 1973 NBA championship team. He finished his playing career as a player-assistant coach with the New Jersey Nets (NBA) in 1979–1980. Jackson appeared in 807 NBA regular-season games, scoring 5,428 points, averaging 6.7 points, clearing 3,454 rebounds, and averaging 4.3 boards. After serving as a full-time assistant for the Nets in 1980–1981, he spent the following year as a broadcaster for the Nets.

Jackson began his coaching career in 1982–1983 with the Albany (New York) Patroons (CBA). He guided the Patroons for five seasons, winning the CBA championship in 1983 and Coach of the Year honors in 1985.

After returning to the NBA in 1987–1988 as an assistant coach with the Chicago Bulls (NBA), Jackson was named head coach when Doug Collins* was fired in 1989. After a successful first NBA season, Jackson, along with premier players Michael Jordan* and Scottie Pippen*, led the Bulls to three consecutive NBA championships in 1991–1993. Following the 1993 championship season, Jordan retired to pursue a professional baseball career. In Jordan's nearly two years absence, the Bulls did not retain their championships. Upon Jordan's return to the NBA, the Bulls captured the NBA championship in 1996 and set an NBA record with 72 wins and only 10 losses. Chicago repeated as NBA champions in 1997 and 1998. Following their sixth NBA championship, Jackson retired from coaching, Jordan retired as a player, and Pippen was later traded.

After a one year absence from coaching, Jackson in 1999 was named head coach of the Los Angeles Lakers (NBA). Blessed with talented players Shaquille O'Neal* and Kobe Bryant*, he led the Lakers to the NBA title in his first season as their coach. Under Jackson, the Lakers won three consecutive NBA Championships (2000–2002) and recorded 13 consecutive NBA playoff series triumphs before losing to the San Antonio Spurs in 2003. The Lakers won the Pacific Division crown with 56 victories in 2003–2004, but were upset by the Detroit Pistons 4-1 in the NBA Finals. Following the playoffs, Jackson resigned as Lakers Coach.

Through 2004, Jackson compiled a career 832-316 win-loss record in regular-season games and a 175-69 career playoff record. He holds the NBA record for highest winning percentage in both the regular season and playoffs, and for career playoff victories and shares the NBA record for most NBA championships with Red Auerbach*. In 14 NBA seasons, his teams have appeared in the playoffs each year and have won 10 division titles, nine conference crowns, and nine NBA Championships. He remains the only person to both play and coach teams to titles for the NBA and CBA. Jackson also was named NBA Coach of the Year in 1996.

Jackson and his first wife, Maxine, were married in 1967 and had a daughter, Elizabeth, before their 1972 divorce. Jackson and his second wife, June, were married in 1974 and had four children, Chelsea, Brooke, and twins, Ben and Charlie, before their divorce. He dated Jeannie Buss, daughter of Lakers owner Jerry Buss*.

Jackson authored or co-authored several books including *Maverick* (1995), *Sacred Hoops* (1995), *More Than A Game* (2001), and *Last Season: A Team in Search of its Soul* (2004).

BIBLIOGRAPHY: "Phil Jackson," *Coaches*, http://www.hoopshype.com (2003); "Phil Jackson," *Coaches Bio*, http://www.nba.com (2003); Phil Jackson, *Last Season: A Team in Search of its Soul* (New York, 2004); Phil Jackson with Charley Rosen, *More Than A Game* (New York, 2001); Phil Jackson and Hugh Delehenty, *Sacred Hoops* (New York, 1995); Roland Lazenby, *Mind Games* (New York, 2001); Ken Shouler et al., *Total Basketball* (Wilmington, DE, 2003); *TSN Official NBA Register, 2004–2005* (St. Louis, MO, 2004).

John L. Evers

JAMES, LeBron (b. December 30, 1984, Akron, OH), professional player, is the son of Gloria James and her "significant other," Eddie Jackson; LeBron addresses Jackson as "Dad."

At the end of his junior year at St. Vincent-St. Mary High School in Akron, Ohio, rumors spread that James wanted to enter the NBA draft. This, of course, was impossible because he legally was not allowed to give up his amateur status until he finished high school. In his senior year, his mother negotiated the purchase of a $50,000 Hummer recreational vehicle that caused colossal negative feedback. People questioned the nature of the loan collateral. James later admitted accepting limited edition designer leisure jackets worth $845. The OHSAA suspended him for the rest of the season due to the violation. Although eventually reinstated, he missed some critical end-of-season games.

Prior to the June 2003 NBA draft lottery, James found himself perhaps the most highly touted, publicized player in high school basketball history. The six-foot eight-inch, 240-pound 18-year-old possessed superior skills. At St. Vincent-St. Mary High School, James was selected three times as Ohio State Mr. Basketball. In his senior year, he averaged 32 points, 10 rebounds, five assists, and four steals for his state-championship winning team in 2003. James led his team to three state championships in four years. An unnamed NBA scout, in a *SI* piece on May 2, 2003, stated James possessed the whole package and the potential to become the next Michael Jordan*. James possesses rare athleticism as a swingman, who can shoot superbly from the outside and aggressively dominate on the inside. He and five other high school seniors applied for early entry to the NBA draft. On May 22, BBC and major U.S. television networks announced that James had agreed to a $90 million deal with Nike. The May 5, 2003 issue of *SI* listed the most influential minorities in sports, ranking James in the final position at number 101. James wears number 23 as a tribute to Michael Jordan.

The Cleveland Cavaliers (NBA) selected James first in the June 2003 NBA draft. James lived up to expectations, becoming just the second player (joining Phoenix Suns forward Amare Stoudemire) to come into the league directly from high school and earn NBA Rookie of the Year honors. He averaged 20.9 points (second to Carmelo Anthony* among rookies), 5.9 assists, and 5.5 rebounds and helped the Cavaliers improve from 17 wins to 35 victories. He also became the youngest NBA player to tally at least 40 points in a single game, recording 41 points and 13 assists in a March 2004 107-104 victory over the New Jersey Nets. Sixteen of those points, including the Cavaliers' final 10, came in the fourth quarter. James made the All-NBA Rookie Team and played on the 2004 U.S. Olympic team. James ranked third in the NBA in scoring with 2,175 points (27.2 point average) and averaged 7.4 rebounds and 7.2 assists in 80 games in 2004–2005, but the Cavaliers barely missed the playoffs. He became the youngest player to score 50 points in 24 NBA games, tallying a franchise record 56 points in a 105-98 loss to the Toronto Raptors on March 21, and appeared in the All-Star Game. He garnered All-NBA Second Team honors in 2005.

BIBLIOGRAPHY: Israel Gutierrez, "Jordan: James will start at the bottom," *St. Louis Post Dispatch*, April 6, 2003; "LeBron James Back in the Game," Channelonenews.com/articles/2003/02/06/ap_James/; "LeBron James Is Ready for the NBA," *AP*, April 8 2003; "101 Most Influential Minorities in Sports," *SI* 98 (May 2, 2003); Lauren Rippy, Eastern Illinois University research graduate student, materials collected June 11-12, 2003; *TSN Official NBA Register, 2004–2005* (St. Louis, MO, 2004).

Scott A.G.M. Crawford

JAMISON, Antawn Cortez (b. June 12, 1976, Shreveport, LA), college and professional player, is the son of Albert Jamison and Kathy Jamison, and has a brother, Albert Jr., a sister, Latasha, and one daughter, Alexis. Jamison's parents were very strict and insisted that he attend church and complete his education. He graduated from Providence High School in Charlotte, North Carolina in 1995. An outstanding athlete, Jamison excelled in basketball and quarterbacked the football team. He was recruited by the legendary University of North Carolina head basketball coach, Dean Smith* and played for the Tar Heels for three seasons from 1995–1996 through 1997–1998 before declaring entry into the NBA draft.

In his first season as a Tar Heel, six-foot nine-inch, 223-pound Jamison averaged 15.1 points and 9.7 rebounds and was named First Team All-ACC as a freshman. The following year, he led North Carolina with 19.1 points and 9.4 rebounds per game, earned All-America honors, and was selected again to the All-ACC First Team. As a junior, Jamison paced the Tar Heels in scoring (22.2 points per game) and rebounding (10.5 per game). He earned All-America honors for the second consecutive time and All-ACC accolades a third time. Following his junior season, Jamison garnered the National Player of the Year honors with both the John Wooden* and James A. Naismith* awards. In his three seasons, he became the Tar Heels fourth all-time rebounder with 1,027 and seventh leading scorer with 1,974 points. Promising to complete his education, he returned to North Carolina and earned a Bachelor's degree in African Studies on December 18, 1999.

After his junior season, Jamison was selected by the Toronto Raptors (NBA) in the first round as the fourth pick overall in the 1998 NBA draft. The Raptors traded his draft rights to the Golden State Warriors (NBA) for the draft rights to North Carolina teammate Vince Carter* and cash. In his first NBA year in 1998–1999, Jamison led all rookies in double-doubles and rebounds per game. He averaged 9.6 points and was named to the 1998–1999 Schick All-Rookie Second Team. Jamison missed the second half of the 1999–2000 season due to a knee injury and subsequent surgery. In the 2000–2001 season, he established career highs in nearly every offensive category. Jamison averaged 24.9 points and 8.7 rebounds and enjoyed consecutive contests with 50 or more points. The following season, he led the Warriors in scoring, field goals, and free throws made. In 2002–2003, Jamison completed his fourth consecutive season of averaging 19.0 or more points. He won the NBA's Sixth Man award in 2004, playing a reserve role for the first time in his NBA career with the Dallas Mavericks. Jamison averaged 14.8 points and 6.3 rebounds and played all 82 games, upping his then league-best streak to 328 consecutive games. He appeared in his first NBA playoffs, scoring 20 points in Game 3 and 65 points total in the first-round loss in five games to the Sacramento Kings. The Washington Wizards (NBA) acquired him in a June 2004 trade. His consecutive game streak ended in 2004–2005, when he appeared in 68 games. Jamison averaged 19.6 points and 7.6 rebounds, helping the Wizards to the playoffs and appeared in the All-Star Game. He averaged 18.5 points and 6.3 rebounds in 10 playoff games with the Miami Heat, eliminating Washington in the second round. He has played in eight NBA seasons, scoring 9,321 points for a 19.2 point average and pulling down 3,548 rebounds or 7.3 rebounds per game in 486 regularly scheduled games. In 15 NBA playoff games, he has scored 250 points and has averaged 16.7 points and 5.9 rebounds.

BIBLIOGRAPHY: "Antawn Jamison," *Bio*, http://www.nba.com (2003); "Antawn Jamison," *Growing*

Up, http://www.antawnjamison.net (2003); "Antawn Jamison," *Statistics-Averages-Totals*, http://www.nba.com (2003); "Antawn Jamison," *UNC*, http://www.antawnjamison.net (2003); Ken Shouler et al., *Total Basketball* (Wilmington, DE, 2003); Dean Smith, *A Coach's Life: My Forty Years in Basketball* (New York, 1999); *TSN Official NBA Register, 2004–2005* (St. Louis, MO, 2004).

John L. Evers

JEANNETTE, Harry Edward "Buddy" (b. September 15, 1917, New Kensington, PA; d. March 11, 1998, Nashua, NH), college and professional player, coach, and executive, starred in professional basketball during the 1940s and later coached in the BAA, NBA, and ABA. He played high school basketball in New Kensington, Pennsylvania, and starred at Washington and Jefferson College (Pennsylvania) from 1934 to 1938.

After graduation from Washington and Jefferson, Jeannette expected to become a high school coach and teacher. No job materialized, causing him to join the Warren (Pennsylvania) Penns (NBL). His other NBL clubs included the Cleveland White Horses in 1938–1939 and Detroit Eagles from 1939 to 1941. He also played with Elmira, New York (NYPL) in 1939 and Saratoga, New York (NYSL) in 1942. The aggressive 5-foot 11-inch, 175-pound forward-guard made the all-tourney team in the 1941 and 1942 World Professional Tournaments in Chicago; his Detroit Eagles won the 1941 tournament.

Jeannette performed for the Sheboygan (Wisconsin) Redskins (NBL) in 1942–1943 and then joined the Fort Wayne (Indiana) Zollner Pistons, (NBL), winners of the 1943–1944 NBL championships and three consecutive World Professional Tournaments (1944–1946). His next assignment came as player-coach of the Baltimore Bullets, ABL champions in 1946–1947. Jeannette's $15,000 salary was believed to be the highest in professional basketball. He guided the Bullets as player-coach to the BAA's second title in 1947–1948. In 300 NBL-ABL games, he scored 2,317 points and averaged 7.7 points.

Jeannette left the Bullets in 1950 after compiling a 96-117 win-loss record as coach. After coaching Georgetown University to a 49-49 mark from 1953 to 1957, he left basketball to engage in the produce and liquor businesses. Jeannette served as coach and general manager of the Baltimore Bullets (NBA), compiling a 37-43 mark in 1964–1965 and 3-13 mark in 1966-1967. His last association with basketball came as front office man and coach of the Pittsburgh Pipers (ABA) from 1969 through 1972, garnering a 15-30 mark in 1969–1970. Jeannette worked in sales until 1984 for Penn Athletic Sporting Goods, a subsidiary of General Tire Company, and resided in Nashua, New Hampshire. He was elected to the Naismith Memorial Basketball Hall of Fame in 1994.

BIBLIOGRAPHY: "Basketball's Biggest Little Man," *Argosy* (February 1949); Peter C. Bjarkman, *The Biographical History of Basketball* (Chicago, IL, 2000); Jan Hubbard, ed., *The Official NBA Basketball Encyclopedia*, 3rd ed. (New York, 2000); Neil D. Issacs, *Vintage NBA* (Silver Spring, MD, 1996); Harry Jeannette, interview with Robert W. Peterson, March 20, 1987; Harry Jeannette file, Naismith Memorial Basketball Hall of Fame, Springfield, MA; Robert W. Peterson, *Cages to Jump Shots: Pro Basketball's Early Years* (New York, 1990); *TSN Official NBA Register, 2004–2005* (St. Louis, MO, 2004).

Robert W. Peterson

JENKINS, Clarence R. "Fats" (b. January 10, 1898, New York, NY; d. December 6, 1968, Philadelphia, PA), professional baseball and basketball player, was the elder of two sons of Charles B. Jenkins and Nellie Jenkins. The Harlem-born Jenkins attended Commerce High School in Manhattan and played his first competitive sport at age 14, with a youth basketball team sponsored by St. Phillip's Episcopal Church. He turned pro as a baseball outfielder in 1920, and spent the best seasons of his 20-year career with the New York Black Yankees (NNL) and Harrisburg Giants (ECL). He also played for the New York Lincoln Giants (ANL), Atlantic City Bacharach Giants (ECL), Baltimore Black Sox (ANL), Philadelphia Stars (ANL), Brooklyn Eagles (ANL), and Brooklyn Royal Giants (NNL) whom he managed in 1940. Although not considered a strong hitter by contemporaries, Jenkins batted .417 in three games against major league pitching in 1931 and is credited with a .331 career batting average in Negro baseball. As a New York Black

Yankee in 1933 and a Brooklyn Eagle (NNL) in 1935, he played for the East in All-Star Negro League games against the West. Nicknamed "Fats" after a more deserving brother, the five-foot seven-inch, 180-pound Jenkins was fast afield and on the bases. He proved an ideal lead-off batter, equally skillful at dragging bunts or belting line drives. He fielded well, possessed a good arm, and was an acknowledged team leader.

Despite these varied abilities, Jenkins never ranked among the topmost Negro League stars. In basketball, however, he was unqualifiedly among the best. He joined the New York Renaissance in 1924 and captained them for many years. Founded in 1922, the Rens were named after the Renaissance Casino, whose ballroom was their home court. Barnstorming the East and South, they played up to 200 games a year and scored numerous notable triumphs over the famous Original Celtics. They played serious, classic basketball without clowning. Offensively, they stressed movement without the ball, minimum dribbles, short passes, and cuts and pickoffs, while defensively they favored tight man-to-man coverage.

Jenkins and his baseball colleague Bill Yancey* were included among the Rens' now-legendary "Magnificent Seven," a squad that played together for many years. Between 1932 and 1936, the Seven won 473 games, including 88 consecutively, and lost only 49 contests. Fats, billed as the "fastest man in basketball," excelled as an offensive leader. He used his speed to launch the Rens' fast break and shot with accuracy from as far as 15 feet out. Despite being the Rens' shortest man, Jenkins usually guarded the opponent's top scorer. He opened a package store in New York and became a boxing referee in New York City. He was elected to the Naismith Memorial Basketball Hall of Fame with his fellow Rens in 1963.

BIBLIOGRAPHY: *Afro-American*, Philadelphia, December 21, 1968; *Amsterdam News*, New York, December 14, 1968; Leon Day, telephone interviews with A. D. Suehsdorf, May 10, 1984; Edwin Bancroft Henderson, *The Negro in Sports*, rev. ed. (Washington, DC, 1949); Zander Hollander, ed., *The Pro Basketball Encyclopedia* (Los Angeles, CA, 1977); John Holway, *Voices from the Great Black Baseball Leagues* (New York, 1975); Clarence Jenkins file, Naismith Memorial Basketball Hall of Fame, Springfield, MA; Robert W. Peterson, *Only the Ball Was White* (Englewood Cliffs, NJ, 1970); Susan J. Rayl, *The New York Renaissance Professional Black Basketball Team, 1923–1950* (Syracuse, NY, 2001); James A. Riley, *The All-Time All-Stars of Black Baseball* (Cocoa, FL, 1983); Ken Shouler et al., *Total Basketball* (Wilmington, DE, 2003); Monte Irvin, August 29, September 20, 1983; William "Judy" Johnson, September 21, 1983; Walter "Buck" Leonard, September 21, 1983; Ted Page, October 3, 1983; Eyre Saitch, April 17 and 23, May 10, 1984; Normal C. Webb, December 18, 28, 1983.

A. D. Suehsdorf

JOHNSON, Dennis Wayne "DJ" (b. September 18, 1954, San Pedro, CA), college and professional player and coach, was a six-foot four-inch, 200-pound guard. A model team player during an outstanding NBA career, he excelled as one of the premier defensive specialists. Johnson attended Harbor JC in Wilmington, California and transferred two years later to Pepperdine University (California), where he occasionally even played center for the basketball team. The junior, eligible in 1976, was selected by the Seattle SuperSonics (NBA) in the second round as the twenty-ninth pick overall in the NBA draft. A resourceful, consistent, and tenacious all-court performer, he provided a stabilizing influence and leadership. The NBA teams Johnson performed for during his 11 year career won over two-thirds of their regular-season games, seven division titles, and three NBA championships. Although his main responsibility was guarding some of the toughest offensive NBA players, Johnson also polished his own offensive skills to become a credible performer from the perimeter and from close range with his strong drives and moves.

Johnson's four seasons with the SuperSonics peaked in 1978–1979, when he led Seattle to the NBA championship and was selected the MVP of the playoffs. In June 1980 and already established as one of the top NBA guards, he was traded to the Phoenix Suns (NBA) for Paul Westphal*. Johnson's three years with Phoenix were productive ones on the court, but unhappy ones personally because "DJ" and his coach, John MacLeod*, slowly grew apart. On June 27, 1983, he was traded to the Boston Celtics (NBA) with one first-round and one third-round draft choice for center Rick Robey and two second-round draft picks.

During his tenure with the Celtics, Johnson unquestionably proved his worth as an unselfish, team-oriented player. Johnson fit perfectly into the Celtics' cohesive style and became, in his own low-key way, a fundamental part of Boston's strong 1980s teams. Boston and the Los Angeles Lakers dominated the NBA over that period. During Johnson's seven years as a Celtic, Boston reached the playoff finals four times and won two NBA championships. Although Johnson's contributions to his teams went far beyond numbers, his statistics were impressive. In 14 NBA seasons through 1989–1990, he recorded 1,100 games played, 5,832 fields goals (44.5 percent), 79.7 percent of his free throws, 5.0 assists per game, and 15,535 points (14.1 points per game).

His varied awards included All-NBA First Team (1981), All-NBA Second Team (1980), and 10 consecutive years on the NBA's All-Defensive Teams. He made the NBA All-Defensive First Team in 1979–1983 and 1987 and NBA All-Defensive Second Team from 1984 to 1986 and was selected five times to play in the All-Star Game. Johnson's achievements, along with the wide respect he commanded from his peers, was further proof that pro basketball is the quintessential team game and a game in which poise is more important than flash. To reach the pinnacle, a player has to become multidimensional. Johnson was such a player, combining ability and attitude, hustle and thinking, and seriousness as a person with a zest for the joy of the game. He served as assistant coach of the Boston Celtics from 1993–1994 through 1996–1997 and as head coach of the Lacrosse (Wisconsin) Catbirds (CBA) in 1999–2000, compiling a 14-22 mark and .389 winning percentage. He was appointed assistant coach of the Los Angeles Clippers (NBA) in February 2000 and became their interim head coach during the 2002–2003 season. He compiled an 8-16 record. In August 2004, he was named head coach of the Florida Flame (WBDL).

BIBLIOGRAPHY: Peter C. Bjarkman, *The Boston Celtics Encyclopedia* (Champaign, IL, 1998); *Boston Celtics Media Guide, 1987–1988* (Boston, MA, 1987); *Boston Celtics Pride 2* (February 2, 1987); *Hoop Magazine*, NBA Today Edition, 13 (Summer 1987); Dennis Johnson file, Naismith Memorial Basketball Hall of Fame, Springfield, MA; Roland Lazenby, *The NBA Finals* (Indianapolis, IN, 1996); *TSN Official NBA Guide, 1987–1988* (St. Louis, MO, 1987); *TSN Official NBA Register, 2004–2005* (St. Louis, MO, 2004).

Gustavo N. Agrait

JOHNSON, Earvin, Jr. "Magic" (b. August 14, 1959, Lansing, MI), college and professional player, coach, and executive, is the second son of Earvin Johnson and Christine Johnson. His father had migrated from Brookhaven, Mississippi to work in the Oldsmobile plants at Lansing, Michigan. Johnson learned basketball fundamentals from his father, who often watched college and pro games. He developed his "hoopsy doopsy style," emphasizing passing and the inside game, because of his desire to remain on the often crowded courts of Main Street School and the local Boys' Club.

At Lansing's Everett High School, Johnson was coached by George Fox and surrounded by talented teammates. During his sophomore and junior years, he led Everett High School to the State Class A quarterfinals and semifinals, was named UPI Prep Player of the Year in Michigan, and was selected to the All-State teams. Johnson led his team as a senior to a 27-1 record and helped defeat Birmingham Brother Rice 62-56 for the Class A State Championship. In the title game, he scored 34 points and made 14 rebounds and four assists. For the season, the six-foot eight-inch, 200-pound guard scored 805 points for a 28.8 points average, made 16.8 rebounds per game, dished out 208 assists, and recorded 99 steals. Besides repeating as an All-State selection, he was named UPI Prep Player of the Year.

Johnson enrolled in 1977 at Michigan State

University, where he helped the Spartans make a 25-5 record and secure a BTC title. In the finals of the NCAA Mideast Regionals, the University of Kentucky defeated Michigan State 52-49. Johnson made the All-BTC Team and was selected Third Team All-America. The 1978–1979 Michigan State squad completed a 13-5 BTC record to share the title with Purdue University and the University of Iowa. The Johnson-led Spartans demolished their opposition in the NCAA Playoffs and played Indiana State University and its star, Larry Bird* in the NCAA finals. The Spartans forced Bird into shooting .333, while Johnson scored 24 points to give Michigan State a 75-64 victory. Johnson again made All-BTC and All-America and set a team assists record. His coach, Jud Heathcote, remembers Johnson "as the player who put the effectiveness of the pass back in the game." Johnson's infectious smile and enthusiasm for the game created a charisma that few athletes have achieved.

After the 1978–1979 season, Johnson signed a $600,000 contract with the Los Angeles Lakers (NBA). During his rookie year, he led the Lakers to a 60-22 regular-season record and averaged 18 points, over seven rebounds, and seven assists. Johnson led the Lakers to the NBA title, playing every position in the final game. He scored 42 points, including making all 14 foul shots that game, and was named playoff MVP. The next season, he averaged 18.8 points, 7.7 rebounds, 7.3 assists, and 3.4 steals. During the 1980–1981 season, Johnson suffered a knee injury and still increased his average to 21.6 points, 8.6 rebounds, 8.5 assists, and 3.4 steals. Although his individual statistics improved, the Lakers were defeated by the Houston Rockets in the opening round of the NBA playoffs.

In 1981–1982, Johnson made the All-NBA Second Team, averaged 18.6 points, led the NBA for the second consecutive year with a career-high 208 steals, and recorded 743 assists. Los Angeles won the 1982 NBA championship by defeating the Philadelphia 76ers in the NBA Finals, as he was named playoff MVP. His scoring average dropped the next year, but he made a career-high 751 rebounds, led the NBA in assists (829), and was selected to the All-NBA First Team. The Lakers, however, lost to Philadelphia in the NBA Finals. In 1983–1984 Johnson repeated as All-NBA First Team selected and assists leader (875). The Celtics defeated Los Angeles in the NBA Finals. During 1984–1985, he tallied 18.3 points per game, increased his assists to 968, and repeated on the All-NBA First Team; The Lakers dethroned Boston as NBA champions. Johnson raised his scoring average to 18.8 points and again dished out over 900 assists to lead the NBA in 1985–1986, but the Houston Rockets eliminated his club in the Western Conference Finals.

The 1987 NBA MVP and the *TSN* NBA Player of the Year, Johnson was selected to the All-NBA First Team for the fifth consecutive time. His best NBA season included a career-high 23.9 points per game and an NBA-leading and career-high 977 assists (12.3 assists per game). He earned the NBA playoff MVP for the third time, as Los Angeles dethroned the Celtics in the NBA Championship series. In the 1987–1988 season, Johnson paced the 62-20 Lakers to another Western Conference title and again made the All-NBA First Team. He averaged 19.6 points and ranked second in assists with 858 (11.9 assists per game). He helped the Lakers capture their second consecutive NBA championship, scoring 21.2 points per game and recording 91 assists in the final seven-game series against the Detroit Pistons. Johnson holds the all-time NBA playoff record for most assists 2,346 and the single-game playoff record for most assists (24) against the Phoenix Suns on May 15, 1984. Johnson also has the NBA championship game mark for most assists (21) against Boston on June 3, 1984. The 12-time NBA All-Star (1980, 1982–1992) holds the NBA All-Star Game record for career assists (127) and single-game assists (22). In 1987 Johnson broke Jerry West's* club record for assists, accomplishing the feat in five fewer seasons. During 13 NBA seasons, Johnson scored 17,707 points (19.5 points average), made 10,141 assists, and recorded 1,724 steals in 906 NBA games. He played in 190 playoff games, serving 3,701 points (19.5 point average), and posting 1,465 rebounds, 2,346 assists, and 358 steals. Johnson made the All-NBA First Team in 1989, 1990, and 1991, was named NBA MVP in 1989 and 1990, and was selected NBA All-Star

Game MVP in 1990 and 1992. The Lakers boasted the best regular-season record in their division in 1989–1990, but lost in the playoffs to the Phoenix Suns. Los Angeles returned to the NBA finals in 1991 for the ninth time in 12 years, but the Chicago Bulls prevailed in five games.

In November 1991, Johnson startled the sports world announcing that he had tested positive for HIV during a routine physical examination and was retiring from the NBA on the advice of his physician. He received medical clearance to play in the 1992 All-Star Game, tallying 25 points. Johnson played on the U.S. Olympic Dream Team that won the gold medal at the 1992 Olympic Games. He served as broadcaster for NBC Sports from 1992–1994 and briefly coached the Los Angeles Lakers to a 5-11 record in 1993–1994. Since 1994–1995, he has served as Vice President of the Los Angeles Lakers. Johnson co-authored *Magic* (1983) and *My Life* (1992). The recipient of the J. Walter Kennedy Citizenship Award in 1992, he was named to the NBA 50th Anniversary All-Time Team in 1996 and to the Naismith Memorial Basketball Hall of Fame in 2002. Johnson directs and overseas numerous business interests. Magic owns 70 Starbucks stores in 38 cities, concentrated in inner city and other diverse neighborhoods. Johnson has made similar efforts with restaurants and movie theaters. NASCAR in May 2004 named him an adviser and spokesman to diversify its fan base. He married Erletha "Cookie" Kelly in September 1991 and has three children, Earvin III, Andre (from a previous relationship), and Elisa (adopted).

BIBLIOGRAPHY: Jack Ebling, et al., *Magic Moments* (Chelsea, MI, 1998); Randy Harvey, "Magic," *Sport* 73 (February 1982), pp. 20–27; Earle Eldridge, "Rebounding from Basketball Court to Boardroom," *USA Today*, November 8, 2004, p. 5B; James Haskins, *"Magic": A Biography of Earvin Johnson* (Hillside, NJ, 1982); Joe Jares, "Just Another Guy Named Earvin," *SI* 48 (January 23, 1978), pp. 48–52; Earvin Johnson and Richard Levin, *Magic* (New York, 1983); Earvin Johnson and William Novak, *My Life* (New York 1992); Magic Johnson file, Naismith Memorial Basketball Hall of Fame, Springfield, MA; Larry Keith, "He's Gone to the Head of the Class," *SI* 49 (November 27, 1978), pp. 48–53; Roland Lazenby, *The Lakers* (New York, 1993); Roland Lazenby, *The NBA Finals* (Indianapolis, IN, 1996); Lazenby, *College Basketball U.S.A. Since 1892* (Briarcliff Manor, NY, 1978); Bruce Newman, "'Magic' Scoring as Well as Passing," *SI* 51 (November 19, 1979), pp. 34–35; Scott Ostler and Steve Springer, *Winnin' Times: The Rise and Rise of the Los Angeles Lakers* (New York, 1986); John Papanek, "And Now for My Reappearing Act," *SI* 54 (March 9, 1981), pp. 14–17; Pat Riley, *Showtime* (New York, 1988); Robert Stern, *They Were Number One: History of the NCAA Basketball Tournament* (New York, 1983); *TSN Official NBA Register, 2004–2005* (St. Louis, MO, 2004).

John D. McCallum and Lawrence E. Ziewacz

JOHNSON, Gus, Jr. "Honeycomb" (b. December 13, 1938, Akron, OH; d. April 28, 1987, Akron, OH), college and professional player, was the son of Gus Johnson Sr., and one of six children. Johnson played on the same Akron (Ohio) Central High School team as Nate Thurmond*, later with the San Francisco Warriors (NBA). He entered University of Akron in 1959, but dropped out and worked briefly for the Cuyahoga County, Ohio treasurer's office. Johnson then attended Boise (Idaho) JC and the University of Idaho. He was the second-round draft choice of the Baltimore Bullets (NBA) in 1963 and made the Bullets a perennial title contender. Johnson scored 1,352 points in his first year and made the All-Star team his second season, scoring 25 points in 25 minutes of playing time. In 1966–1967 he enjoyed his best statistical year, scoring 1,511 points and averaging 20.7 points. Johnson appeared in the All-Star Game again from 1968 through 1971.

During 1969–1970, Johnson led what was probably the best Bullets team to that point in the franchise's history. Baltimore lost in the playoffs to the NBA championship-bound New York Knickerbockers. He was bothered by an injury in the 1971–1972 season and was traded to the Phoenix Suns (NBA) in April 1972. His last season (1972–1973) came with the Indiana Pacers (ABA), winners of the ABA title. The six-foot six-inch, 235-pound Johnson was a devastating corner man and the prototype of the NBA power forwards, later represented fully in

Julius Erving*. He became one of the first to use the slam dunk. Twice named to the All-NBA Defensive Team (1970, 1971), "Honeycomb" engaged in some classic match-ups with the New York Knicks' Dave DeBusschere*. Johnson's pro career included 631 games played, 4,254 field goals, 1,723 free throws, 10,243 points, and a 16.2 points average. He also averaged 12.7 rebounds and placed fifth in rebounding during the 1969–1970 season. He made the All-NBA Second Team in 1968, 1966, 1970, and 1971 and the NBA All-Rookie Team in 1964. In 1986 Johnson was diagnosed as having an inoperable brain tumor. The Bullets retired his uniform number. He was survived by four daughters.

BIBLIOGRAPHY: Peter C. Bjarkman, *The History of the NBA* (New York, 1992); Jan Hubbard, ed., *The Official NBA Encyclopedia*, 3rd ed. (New York, 2000); *NYT*, April 30, 1987; Ken Shouler et al., *Total Basketball* (Wilmington, DE, 2003); *TSN Official NBA Register, 2004–2005* (St. Louis, MO, 2004).

John David Healy

JOHNSON, Kevin Maurice (b. March 4, 1966, Sacramento, CA), college and professional player, grew up with his mother, Georgia West, and grandparents, George Peat and Georgia Peat, and attended Sacramento (California) High School, where he led the state in basketball scoring as a senior with a 32.5 point average. His final season included a game in which he scored 56 points.

Johnson stayed close to home, attending the University of California at Berkeley (PTC). The lightning-quick basketball guard became California's all-time leader in scoring with 1,655 points, assists with 521, and steals with 155. He posted the first recorded triple-double in PTC history, making 22 points, 10 rebounds, and 12 assists against the University of Arizona. His junior and senior seasons saw him named to the All-PTC First Team. The Oakland Athletics (AL) selected Johnson, an excellent baseball player, in the 1986 draft, but basketball remained his primary focus.

The six-foot one-inch, 190-pound Johnson was chosen seventh in 1987 by the Cleveland Cavaliers (NBA). Johnson remained with Cleveland for only part of his rookie season before being sent in a February 1988 multiplayer trade to the Phoenix Suns (NBA). He started 25 of 28 games after the trade and finished his first NBA season with a 9.2 point scoring average. Both Johnson and the Suns flourished in his first full season in Phoenix. Johnson averaged 20.4 points and set a Suns record with 991 assists, as he and Tom Chambers* led Phoenix to a 55-27 mark. He became only the fifth player in NBA history to average over 20 points and 10 assists, being selected as the NBA's Most Improved Player.

Johnson, the prototypical point guard, not only directed the offense, but also provided a major scoring threat. He continued scoring over 20 points per game and dishing out over 10 assists per game for the 1989–1990 and 1990–1991 seasons. The following season saw Johnson's scoring average fall below 20 points per game for the first time since his rookie season, but he finished second in the NBA in assists with a 10.7 average.

Injuries limited Johnson's 1992–1993 season to only 49 games. Both his scoring and assist averages dropped, while his role changed. Johnson no longer served as the focal point of the Phoenix offense because the Suns acquired Charles Barkley* in June 1992. With Johnson concentrating more on defense, the Suns finished the season with the best NBA record at 62-20. Johnson averaged 20.0 points and ranked fifth among NBA leaders with 637 assists (9.5 average) in 1993–1994, helping 56-26 Phoenix compile the third-best Western Conference record. During 12 NBA seasons, Johnson scored 13,127 points (17.9 point average), recorded 6,711 assists (9.1 average), and made 1,082 steals. He played 62 minutes in a triple-overtime, June 1993 game against Chicago, setting an NBA Finals record. He remains the Sun's all-time assists leader with 6,518.

One of his dreams came true in 1992, when his St. Hope Academy officially opened in Sacramento. This organization, founded by Johnson, targeted inner-city youth at risk by providing them opportunities for educational, spiritual, and social edification. The unmarried Johnson devotes most of his time to this organization.

Johnson spent the rest of his NBA playing career with Phoenix, retiring initially in October 1999 and permanently in August 2000. Johnson appeared in three All-Star Games, starting for the West in 1991. An All-NBA Second Team selection in 1989, 1990, 1991, and 1994 and a Third Team selection in 1992, he received the J. Walter Kennedy Citizenship Award in 1991. Johnson played on Dream Team II, which won the gold medal in the 1994 World Championship of Basketball in Toronto, Canada.

BIBLIOGRAPHY: Jan Hubbard, ed., *The Official NBA Encyclopedia*, 3rd ed. (New York, 2000); *Fast Break* 3 (November 1991); *Phoenix Suns Media Guide, 1999–2000* (Phoenix, AZ, 1999); Ken Shouler et al., *Total Basketball* (Wilmington, DE, 2003); *TSN Official NBA Guide, 1999–2000* (St. Louis, MO, 1999); *TSN Official NBA Register, 2004–2005* (St. Louis, MO, 2004).

Curtice R. Mang

JOHNSON, Larry Demetric (b. March 14, 1969, Tyler, TX), college and professional player, was brought up by his mother, Dortha Johnson, in Dixon Circle, South Dallas, Texas. Johnson graduated from Skyline High School in 1987 after being the National High School Player of the Year in basketball. He attended Odessa JC in Texas, where he averaged 20.6 points in 1988 and 1989. Johnson transferred to the University of Nevada, Las Vegas and graduated with a Bachelor's degree in 1991. He led the Rebels to the NCAA championship in 1991, being named an All-America and winning the Naismith* and Wooden* awards. With Nevada Las Vegas, he averaged 21.6 points and 11.2 rebounds in 75 games.

Nicknamed "King of the Court," Johnson was selected first by the Charlotte Hornets (NBA) in the 1991 draft. In 1992, he averaged 19.2 points and was named NBA Rookie of the Year. The six-foot seven-inch, 250-pound forward in 1993 led Charlotte to the NBA playoffs, was named to All-NBA Second Team, and was selected an All-Star starter. In the summer 1993, the Hornets signed Johnson to a contract extension worth $84 million for 12 years. During his third season, he suffered a back injury and missed 31 games. After competing on the gold medal–winning World Championship team in 1996, Johnson tallied a career-high 44 points against the Boston Celtics.

After Johnson was traded to the New York Knicks (NBA) in July 1996, his career went downhill. He averaged a career-low 12.0 points in his first season with New York (1996–1997), but posted four double-doubles later that season. Johnson reached a career highlight in 1999, making a four-point play against Indiana to lead the Knicks into the NBA Finals. "The King of the Court" played his 600th career game in January 2000 and scored his 10,000th career point. He ended his NBA playing career in 2001–2002 as a two-time All-Star, whose career did not reach full potential because of a recurring back problem. In 10 NBA seasons, he scored 11,450 points (16.2 points average) and made 5,300 rebounds (7.5 average).

Johnson married Celeste Wingfield in 1994, and has three children, Larry Jr., Lance, and Lasani. He planned to spend more time with his family and may become a high school basketball coach. Johnson, who is involved with the United Way, donated $1 million to build a recreation center in his hometown.

BIBLIOGRAPHY: Bill Gutman, *Larry Johnson, King of the Court* (Brookfield, CT, 1995); Darryl Howerton, "The Sport Q&A: Larry Johnson Interview," *Sport* 86 (April 1995), pp. 86–89; "Larry Johnson," *Contemporary Black Biography* 28 (2003), http://www.galenet.com/servlet/bioRC); Glen Macnow, "Professional Basketball Player," *Newsmakers* 3 (1993), pp. 63–66; Leigh Montville, "Out of the Hood," *SI* 76 (April 1992), pp. 48–53; Michael A. Parae, *Sports Stars* (Detroit, MI, 1994) pp. 247–252; Ken Shouler et al., *Total Basketball* (Wilmington, DE, 2003).

Njoki-Wa-Kinyatti

JOHNSON, Marques Kevin (b. February 8, 1956, Natchitoches, LA), college and professional player, is one of four children and was named after former Harlem Globetrotters great, Marques Haynes*. His parents, Jeff Johnson, an industrial arts teacher, and Baasha Johnson, a librarian, moved to Los Angeles when Marques was five years old. Johnson attended Dorsey High School, but transferred to Crenshaw High School after his sophomore season because his father liked the latter's style of basketball play.

Johnson made the All-City team as a junior, as Crenshaw finished undefeated. His 36 points and 29 points in the final two games of the Los Angeles High School Tournament brought Crenshaw the 1973 city basketball title.

Over 200 scholarship offers came from colleges nationwide, but Johnson attended nearby UCLA from 1973 to 1977. Johnson substituted as a freshman, averaging 7.2 points. As a starting forward, he tallied 11.6 points per game his second season and helped the Bruins capture the 1975 national title. UCLA relied on Johnson as a primary offensive weapon in 1975–1976, as he scored 17.3 points per game. His senior season saw him average 21.4 points record over 10 rebounds per game, make consensus All-America, and be named *TSN* 1977 Player of the Year. He also captured the Wooden* and Naismith* award.

The Milwaukee Bucks chose the six-foot seven-inch, 225-pound Johnson third in the 1977 NBA draft. Johnson instantly starred at forward with the Bucks tallying 19.5 points per game and making the NBA All-Rookie team. He scored a career-high 25.6 points per game and led Milwaukee in points his second season, tallying 10 points in his first All-Star appearance that season. Johnson led the Bucks in scoring the following two seasons, averaging 21.7 and 20.3 points. From the 1979–1980 campaign to the 1983–1984 season, he helped the Bucks win five consecutive Midwest Division titles.

In September 1984, Milwaukee traded Johnson, Junior Bridgeman, and Harvey Catchings to the Los Angeles Clippers (NBA). Injuries and the adjustment to new teammates affected Johnson's play, as his scoring average dipped to 16.4 points. The 1985–1986 season witnessed Johnson's resurgence with 20.3 points per game, as he was named the NBA Comeback Player of the Year. A back injury limited him to only 10 games in 1986–1987 and sidelined him the next two seasons. In October 1989 Johnson attempted a comeback with the Golden State Warriors (NBA), coached by his former Milwaukee coach, Don Nelson*. The Warriors released Johnson in November 1989 after he averaged only 4.0 points in 10 contests, ending his NBA career.

Johnson's 11 NBA seasons produced 20.1 points regular-season scoring average for 13,892 career points, and a 21.5 point per game playoff scoring average. The five-time All-Star made the All-NBA First Team in 1979 and the All-NBA Second Team in 1980 and 1981.

BIBLIOGRAPHY: Phil Berger, "High Marques for UCLA," *Sport* 53 (February 1977), pp. 42–49; Morgan G. Brenner, *College Basketball's National Championships* (Lanham, MD, 1999); Mike Douchant, *Encyclopedia of College Basketball* (Detroit, MI, 1995); Jan Hubbard, ed., *The Official NBA Encyclopedia*, 3rd ed. (New York, 2000); Scott Howard-Cooper, *The Bruins 100* (Lenexa, KS, 1999); *Los Angeles Times*, March 5, 1975; *TSN Official 1987–1988 NBA Guide* (St. Louis, MO, 1987); *TSN Official 1990–1991 NBA Register* (St. Louis, MO, 1990).

Curtice R. Mang

JOHNSON, William Claude "Bill" "Skinny" (b. August 16, 1911, Oklahoma City, OK; d. February 5, 1980, place unknown), college player and coach, graduated from Central High School in Oklahoma City, Oklahoma in 1929. Johnson was coached by George Rody at Central High School, where he played three years of varsity basketball from 1927 to 1929 and received All-Conference honors twice and All-America recognition in 1929. He led his conference in scoring in 1929, along with being selected team captain. Johnson also enjoyed tennis, reigning as conference singles champion in 1928. He attended the University of Kansas from 1930 to 1933, participating in basketball three years under head coach Forrest "Phog" Allen*. Johnson's team won the BSC championship, as he was chosen a Second Team BSC All-Star in 1930–1931. During his 1931–1932 season, his team again won the BSC championship. This time he made First Team BSC and was named to the All-Star Phi Delta Theta National Team. In 1932–1933, Johnson was chosen First Team All-America.

Johnson continued his basketball career for Southern Kansas in the Missouri Valley AAU League. His Southern Kansas team won three AAU championships from 1934 to 1936. Over that stretch, he annually was selected an All-America. Johnson served in the U.S. National Reserve from 1943 to 1946 and later became basketball coach at Cleveland Chiropractor College (Ohio), managing a record of 16 wins and a mere two losses. He directed his team to both the Naismith Industrial League and Kansas City Independent Tournament championships. Johnson was named in 1973 to the Phi Delta Theta Half Decade All-Star Team and in 1975 was chosen All-Time Great in Oklahoma. He was selected to the Naismith Memorial Basketball Hall of Fame in 1976.

BIBLIOGRAPHY: Forrest C. Allen, *Coach Phog Allen's Sports Stories* (Lawrence, KS, 1947); John Hendel, *Kansas Jayhawks* (Coal Valley, IL, 1991); William Johnson file, Naismith Memorial Basketball Hall of Fame, Springfield, MA; Blair Kerkhoff, *Phog Allen: The Father of Basketball Coaching* (Indianapolis, IN, 1996); Sandy Padwe, *Basketball's Hall of Fame* (Englewood Cliffs, NJ, 1970).

Jeff Sanderson and Wayne Patterson

JOHNSTON, Donald Neil "Gabby" (b. February 4, 1929, Chillicothe, OH; d. September 27, 1978, Bedford, TX), college and professional player and coach, appeared in both the NBA and pro baseball. A high school athlete in Chillicothe, Ohio, he matriculated at Ohio State University and played basketball for two years (1946–1947, 1947–1948) without great distinction. Johnson opted to play pro baseball, losing the balance of his eligibility. In the Philadelphia Phillies (NL) minor league system with Terre Haute (Indiana) of the Class B 3IL, the right-handed Johnston compiled a 10-12 (3.14 ERA) pitching record in 1949 and an 11-12 (2.89 ERA) season in 1950. He led the 3IL in shutouts with five in 1949 and finished third in the 3IL in ERA the next year.

After a slow start with the Philadelphia Warriors (NBA) his first season (1951–1952), the six-foot eight-inch, 200-pound Johnston became a standout the next campaign. He was named to the All-NBA First Team the next four years from 1953 to 1956, and made the All-NBA Second Team in 1956–1957. Johnston led NBA scorers for three seasons (1952–1953, 1953–1954, 1954–1955), in rebounding once (1954–1955), and in field goal percentage three times (1952–1953, 1955–1956, 1956–1957). He played in six NBA All-Star Games from 1953 through 1958 and helped the Warriors win the 1956 NBA championship. During the 1953–1954 season, Johnston enjoyed five of the six top individual NBA game highs and led the NBA with a 50-point effort against Syracuse. The next season, his 45-point total against Rochester and his 39 rebounds against Syracuse marked the top NBA single-game performances. He appeared 23 playoff games, averaging 15 points.

Johnston surpassed the 10,000-point milestone by 23 points before concluding his NBA playing career during the 1958–1959 season. The next two seasons, he coached the Warriors to second place Eastern Division finishes and a 95-59 (.617) overall mark. Johnston then signed with the Pittsburgh Rens (ABL) as player-coach for the 1961–1962 campaign. He played only five games before settling in as a bench coach and leading the team to second place in its division. Johnston coached for the first 22 games of the next season, compiling a 53-50 overall record. He coached Wilmington, Delaware (EBL) to a 12-16 mark (.429) in 1964–1965 and a 20-8 (.714) record and a first place Eastern Division finish in 1965–1966. Wilmington won the 1966 EBL playoffs, four games to two. In 1990, he was elected to the Naismith Memorial Basketball Hall of Fame.

BIBLIOGRAPHY: Peter C. Bjarkman, *The Encyclopedia of Basketball Team Histories* (New York, 1994); Zander Hollander, ed., *The Modern Encyclopedia of Basketball*, rev. ed. (Garden City, NY, 1979); Jan Hubbard, ed., *The Official NBA Encyclopedia*, 3rd ed. (New York, 2000); Nell D. Isaacs, *Vintage NBA* (Silver Spring, MD, 1996); Neil Johnston file, Naismith Memorial Basketball Hall of Fame, Springfield, MA; Ken Shouler et al., *Total Basketball* (Wilmington, DE, 2003); *TSN NBA Register, 2004–2005* (St. Louis, MO, 2004); *TSN Official NBA Guide, 1959–1960* (St. Louis, MO, 1959); *TSN Official Baseball Guides, 1950, 1951* (St. Louis, MO, 1950, 1951).

Robert B. Van Atta

JONES, Eddie Charles (b. October 20, 1971, Toledo, OH), college and professional player, grew up in Pompano Beach, Florida. Jones, whose parents divorced when he was 16 years old, graduated from Ely High School, where he starred in basketball. He enrolled at Temple

University and played basketball as a forward from 1991–1992 through 1993–1994. He led the Owls to the NCAA tournament Elite Eight and competed at the World Championships. The ATC Player of the Year in 1994, Jones was named an honorable mention All-America. With Temple, he averaged 16.0 points and 6.1 rebounds in 92 games. He earned a Bachelor of Science degree in sports management in 1994.

The six-foot six-inch, 200-pound Jones was drafted in 1994 by the Los Angeles Lakers (NBA) as the tenth overall pick. Jones, who made the NBA All-Rookie First Team in 1994–1995, helped the Lakers reach the Western Conference semifinals in 1995. During his second season, he enjoyed a career-high 3.5 assists and a team-high 1.84 steals while averaging 31.2 minutes in 70 games. He was selected for the NBA All-Star Game in 1997 and 1998, made the NBA All-Defensive Second Team in 1997–1998, and was selected the Player of the Month for November 1997.

The four-year shooting guard was traded to Charlotte Hornets (NBA) in March 1999. His arrival turned the Hornets around, as Jones led Charlotte in scoring with 17.0 points per game in 1999. He made the All-NBA Third Team in 2000 and NBA All-Defensive Second Team in 1998, 1999, and 2000. As a starter in the NBA All-Star Game in 2000, Jones scored 10 points. He recorded a game-high 32 points in a 103-95 win over the Cleveland Cavaliers in 1999. He scored a season-high 34 points against the New York Knicks and led the NBA with 2.7 steals per game in 2000.

The Miami Heat (NBA) acquired Jones in an August 2000 trade. Jones led the Heat in steals a team-high 29 times and in blocked shots 24 times. The three-time All-Star was selected the Player of the Week in December 2001 and January 2002. In 2002–2003 Jones missed 35 games due to injuries, but still led the Heat with an 18.5 scoring average. He tallied 17.3 points per game in 2003–2004 and 12.7 points in 2004–2005, helping the Heat finish first in the Eastern Conference. He averaged 13.7 points and 5.8 rebounds in 15 playoff games in 2005, with the Detroit Pistons eliminating the Heat in the Eastern Conference Finals. In 10 NBA seasons, he has scored 12,601 points (16.4 average) and recorded 1,395 steals in 768 games. He has averaged 13.8 points and 4.3 rebounds in 71 playoff games.

Jones, who has a foundation for underprivileged children, works with Nike and American Express. He and his wife, Trina, have two daughters, Alexis and Chloe.

BIBLIOGRAPHY: Delong, "Loss of Jones Stings Hornets," *TSN* 224 (January 2000, online version); Eddie Jones Biography, http://www.geocities.com/Colosseum/Stands/8670/EddieJBio.html; *TSN Official NBA Register, 2004–2005* (St. Louis, MO, 2004); Ken Shouler et al., *Total Basketball* (Wilmington, DE, 2003); Phil Taylor, "Basketball Jones," *SI* 87 (December 1997), pp. 52–60.

Njoki-Wa-Kinyatti

JONES, James "Jimmy" (b. January 1, 1945, Tallulah, LA), player, graduated in 1963 from Tallulah (Louisiana) High School and in 1967 with a Bachelor's degree from Grambling College. He starred in basketball at both schools and was the first player ever drafted and signed by the New Orleans Buccaneers (ABA) franchise in 1967. The Baltimore Bullets (NBA) also selected him in the second round of the 1967 NBA draft, but Jones figured that Earl Monroe*, their top pick, would get more playing time. Baltimore coach Gene Shue* planned to use Jones to run the Bullets offense and later tried unsuccessfully to get Jones to switch leagues.

The six-foot four-inch, 190-pound Jones instead played with New Orleans from 1967–1968 through 1969–1970 and the Memphis Pros (ABA) in 1970–1971. He made the All-ABA Rookie Team in 1967–1968, averaging 18.8 points and 5.7 rebounds and leading the ABA in minutes played with 3,255. New Orleans reached the ABA Finals before losing four games to three to the Pittsburgh Condors, as Jones averaged 22.1 points in 17 playoff games. His best NBA season came in 1968–1969, when he averaged career highs of 26.6 points and 5.7 rebounds and became just the second ABA player to score over 2,000 points in one season. Jones tallied a career-best 30.2 points in 11 playoff games. In 1969–1970, he averaged 20.7 points, but New Orleans missed the playoffs. His point production dropped slightly to 19.6 points in 1970–1971 after the New Orleans franchise moved to Memphis.

In October 1971, Jones signed a lucrative,

multi-year contract with the Utah Stars (ABA) as a free agent; he had found a contract loophole with the mismanaged Memphis team. Commissioner Jack Dolph ordered Utah to give up a first-round draft choice to Memphis as compensation. Jones spent the next three seasons with Utah, averaging between 15.5 points and 16.7 points. He recorded a career-high 6.2 assists per game in 1971–1972 and led the ABA in free throw percentage (.884) in 1973–1974. Utah reached the 1974 ABA Finals before losing to New York, as Jones averaged 20.8 points in 18 playoff games.

Jones ranked among ABA career leaders in nearly every category, finishing fifth in career assists with 2,786 (5.1 average), seventh in minutes played with 20,873, ninth in field goal percentage with .510, and eleventh in career-scoring with 10,465 points (19.2 average) in 546 games. He made the All-ABA First Team in 1969, 1973, and 1974 and appeared in six ABA All-Star Games, averaging 10.3 points. In the ABA, Jones excelled as a one-on-one player, demonstrated excellent speed and quickness, and proved a fine shooter and excellent passer.

Jones spent his final three seasons from 1974–1975 through 1976–1977 with the Washington Bullets (NBA) as a reserve. He tallied 909 points (6.4 point average) in 140 regular-season games and 130 points (7.2 point average) in 18 playoff games.

BIBLIOGRAPHY: Jan Hubbard, ed., *The Official NBA Encyclopedia*, 3rd ed. (New York, 2000); "Jimmy Jones," http:/www.remembertheaba.com/Tribute Material/Jimmy Jones.html; Terry Pluto, *Loose Balls: The Short, Wild Life of the American Basketball Association* (New York, 1990); Ken Shouler et al., *Total Basketball* (Wilmington, DE, 2003).

David L. Porter

JONES, K. C. (b. May 25, 1932, Tyler, TX), college and professional player and coach, is the son of oilfield worker K.C. Jones and Eula Jones. After moving to San Francisco, California, at age nine, Jones excelled in football and basketball at Commerce High School there. At the University of San Francisco, he did not play during his junior season (1953–1954) because of surgery. Over the next two seasons, Jones and Bill Russell* led the way for the virtually unstoppable Dons. With a 28-1 record as national defensive leaders, San Francisco captured the 1955 NCAA championship by defeating LaSalle College. The Dons stretched their victory string to 55 games in 1955–1956 by winning 29 consecutive games, successfully defended their NCAA crown with a victory over the University of Iowa, and became the first undefeated team to win the NCAA championship. A Second Team All-America selection, Jones was ruled ineligible for the NCAA tournament because he had performed in his fifth season. He participated on the 1956 gold medal U.S. Olympic basketball team and was named to the AAU All-America team while serving in the U.S. Army from 1956 to 1958.

After being drafted by the Los Angeles Rams (NFL) and Boston Celtics (NBA), Jones joined the latter. The six-foot one-inch, 200-pound ball-hawking, playmaking guard excelled on defense and teamed with Bob Cousy* and Russell to lead the Celtics to eight NBA championships from 1958–1959 to 1965–1966. In nine seasons with Boston, he led the Celtics in assists (1963–1964 to 1965–1966), played in 675 regular-season and 105 playoff games, and scored 5,667 total points.

Jones served as head basketball coach at Brandeis University (Massachusetts) (1968–1970), assistant coach for the Los Angeles Lakers (NBA) in 1971, and head coach of the San Diego Conquistadors (ABA) in 1972 and Capital (Washington) Bullets (NBA) from 1973–1974 to 1975–1976. His records were 35-32 with Brandeis and 30-54 with the Conquistadors. He guided the Bullets to the NBA championship series in 1975 before losing the title to the Golden State Warriors. After being an assistant coach with the Boston Celtics (1976–1977 to 1982–1983), Jones was named their head coach and led them to the 1984 NBA title over the Los Angeles Lakers. Although the Atlantic Division champion in 1985, the Celtics relinquished the NBA crown to the Lakers. The Celtics regained the NBA championship by defeating the Houston Rockets in 1986, lost to the Los Angeles Lakers in the 1987 NBA Finals, and were eliminated in seven games by the Detroit Pistons in the 1988 Eastern Conference finals. Boston took the Atlantic Division each of Jones' five seasons at the helm there before his retirement at the end of the 1987–1988 season. He served as vice president of basketball operations for the Celtics in 1988–1989 and as assistant coach of the Seattle SuperSonics (NBA) in 1989–1990. Jones coached Seattle to a 41-41 record in 1990–1991 and 18-18 record in 1991–1992. He returned to the NBA as assistant coach of the Detroit Pistons (NBA) in 1994–1995 and Boston Celtics in 1996–1997. Jones coached New England (ABL) to a 24-20 mark in 1997–1998 and 3-10 slate in 1998–1999. In 10 NBA seasons, his clubs compiled 522 victories and 252 losses (.674 winning percentage).

Jones, who coached the NBA All-Star Game in 1975 and 1984 through 1987, used an easy-going style and relied considerably on player input. Uncomfortable in the NBA limelight, Jones is a family man. He and his wife, Ellen, have one son, Kent. Jones has five other children, Leslie, K.C., Kelley, Brynna, and Holly, from a previous marriage. He was elected to the Naismith Memorial Basketball Hall of Fame in 1989.

BIBLIOGRAPHY: Peter C. Bjarkman, *The Boston Celtics Encyclopedia* (Champaign, IL, 1998); Morgan G. Brenner, *College Basketball's National Championships* (Lanham, MD, 1999); David DuPree, "K.C. Jones," *USA Today*, May 9, 1985, p. 12C; Jeff Greenfield, *The World's Greatest Team* (New York, 1979); Zander Hollander, ed., *The Modern Encyclopedia of Basketball* (Garden City, NY, 1979); Jan Hubbard, ed., *The Official NBA Encyclopedia*, 3rd ed. (New York, 2000); K.C. Jones file, Naismith Memorial Basketball Hall of Fame, Springfield, MA; *TSN Official NBA Register, 2004–2005* (St. Louis, MO, 2004); Billy Packer and Roland Lazenby, *College Basketball's 25 Greatest Teams* (St Louis, MO, 1989); K.C. Jones and Jack Warner, *Rebound: The Autobiography of K.C. Jones and an Inside look at the Champion Boston Celtics* (Boston, MA, 1986).

John L. Evers

JONES, Robert Clyde "Bobby" (b. December 18, 1951, Akron, OH) college and professional player, is the son of James Robert Jones and Hazel Fletcher Jones. His father worked for Goodyear Tires and moved the family frequently. The Jones family moved in 1963 to Charlotte, North Carolina, where Bobby lived through high school. His father played for the University of Oklahoma's 1947 NCAA Finals runner-up basketball team, while his mother excelled for the AAU Nashville BC. His older brother, Kirby, also played basketball for Oklahoma. Jones attended South Mecklenburg High School, which captured the 1970 North Carolina 4-A (large school) state basketball championship. Jones, also a standout high jumper, won North Carolina state high school titles in 1968 and 1970.

Jones attended the University of North Carolina from 1970 to 1974. He played on the Tar Heels 1972 NCAA Final Four team and the 1972 United States Men's Olympic basketball team, which won a silver medal. Jones scored 1,264 points and grabbed 817 rebounds in 108 games spanning three varsity seasons, averaging 13.7 points and 8.9 rebounds and making 60.8 percent of his field goals. Jones was named Second-Team AP and UPI All-America in 1974, Second-Team All-ACC in 1973, and First-Team All-ACC the following season. He graduated with a Bachelor's degree in psychology.

Jones played the 1975 and 1976 seasons with the Denver Nuggets (ABA) and remained with that team when they joined the NBA for the 1976–1977 season. He was traded to the Philadelphia 76ers (NBA) in August 1978 and stayed there until his retirement in 1986, playing on the 1983 title team.

Jones averaged 11.5 points in the NBA and 14.9 points in the ABA, leading the ABA in field goal percentage in 1975 and 1976 and the NBA in the same category in 1978. His forte, however, was defense. At six-feet nine-inches and 210 pounds, he used his quickness, leaping ability, and intelligence to become one of the best defensive players in NBA history. Jones was named to the NBA All-Defensive Team every year from 1977 through 1984 and made the second-team in 1985. He played in four NBA All-Star Games and one ABA All-Star Game and recorded 1,387 steals and 1,319 blocked shots in his combined NBA-ABA career.

Jones suffered from epilepsy and an irregular heart-beat. A deeply religious man, he participates in the Fellowship of Christian Athletes and frequently speaks to youth groups. Jones has served as a coach, teacher, and administrator at Charlotte Christian School since 1988. He and his wife, Tess (West) Jones, were married in 1974 and have three children.

BIBLIOGRAPHY: Art Chansky, *The Dean's List: A Celebration of Tar Heel Basketball and Dean Smith* (New York, 1996); Jan Hubbard, ed., *The Official NBA Encyclopedia*, 3rd ed. (New York, 2000); Ron Morris, *ACC Basketball: An Illustrated History* (Chapel Hill, NC, 1988); Woodrow Paige, "Mr. Clean Does Denver's Dirty Work," *Sport* 66 (June 1978), pp. 34–35; Terry Pluto, *Loose Balls* (New York, 1990); Ken Rappoport, *Tales from the Tar Heel Locker Room* (Champaign, IL, 2002); Ken Shouler et al., *Total Basketball* (Wilmington, DE, 2003); Dean Smith with John Kilgo and Sally Jenkins, *A Coach's Life: My 40 Years in College Basketball* (New York, 1999); Pat Williams with Bill Lyons, *We Owed You One: The Uphill Struggle of the Philadelphia 76ers* (Wilmington, DE, 1983).

Jim L. Sumner

JONES, Samuel "Sam" (b. June 24, 1933, Wilmington, NC), college and professional player and coach, was born to a desperately poor family. The only child of Mrs. Louise K. Davis, Jones worked as a room-service waiter in Atlantic City, New Jersey and as a steelworker in Gary, Indiana and prepped five years at Laurinburg Institute in North Carolina. He rejected a scholarship from the University of Notre Dame to attend all-black North Carolina College, where he averaged 18.6 points his senior year. Jones interrupted his studies with a two-year U.S. Army stint and in 1956 left the military service to finish his degree. In 1957, he was picked in the first round by the NBA champion Boston Celtics. Coach Red Auerbach* had selected an "unknown," who had not earned All-America or sectional honors. After spending three years on the Celtics' bench, Jones teamed with K. C. Jones* in the Celtics' backcourt. One of the "Jones Boys," the slim, rangy guard became an offensive powerhouse. The six-foot four-inch, 205-pounder, a prototype of the tall guard, played 12 years in Boston and finished with a career average of 17.6 points. Considered one of the fastest NBA guards, he popularized his unorthodox "bankshot" in leading the Celtics in scoring for three seasons.

Jones amassed numerous NBA accolades and records in his career. A five-time All-Star player, he averaged 8.2 points per game. Besides making the All-NBA Second Team three times (1965 to 1967), Jones played on 10 Celtics championship teams (including eight consecutive from 1958–1959 to 1965–1966). He ranked second in NBA playoff games (154) and fourth in playoff points (2,909). Third on the Celtics' career points list (15,344), Jones set a then–club record of 51 points against the Detroit Pistons in 1965. From 1959–1960 to 1965–1966, he led the Celtics in shooting percentage. In 1964 Jones enjoyed his best season in averaging 26 points.

On March 9, 1969, the Celtics retired his uniform number 24 at Boston Garden in front of his wife, Gladys, and their five children. Jones coached at Federal City College (Washington, D.C.) from 1969 to 1973 and North Carolina Agricultural and Technical University in 1973–1974 compiling a 44-55 (.444) record. Jones, elected to the NBA's Silver Anniversary Team in 1962 and the NAIA Hall of Fame, served as assistant coach for New Orleans Jazz (NBA) in 1974–1975, became the first black ever accorded entry into the North Carolina Hall of Fame, and was named in 1984 to the Naismith Memorial Basketball Hall of Fame. He was chosen one of the 50 Greatest Players in NBA History in 1996. The clutch-shooter with a wonderful eye came from an obscure sports background to the zenith of pro basketball. Jones scouts for the Boston Celtics and is a spokesman for the Thurgood Marshall Black Education Fund.

BIBLIOGRAPHY: Arnold Auerbach and Joe Fitzgerald, *Red Auerbach* (New York, 1977); Peter C. Bjarkman, *The Boston Celtics Encyclopedia* (Champaign, IL, 1998); *Boston Globe*, March 10, 1969; *Boston Herald*, March 10, 1969; Jeff Greenfield, *World's Greatest Team* (New York, 1976); Edwin Henderson, *International Library of Afro-American Life and History: The Black Athlete* (Cornwells Heights, PA, 1976); Samuel Jones file, Naismith Memorial Basketball Hall of Fame, Springfield, MA; Roland Lazenby, *The NBA Finals* (Indianapolis, IN, 1996); Bob Ryan, *Celtics Pride* (Boston, MA, 1975); Ken Shouler et al., *Total Basketball* (Wilmington, DE, 2003); George Sullivan, *The Picture History of the Boston Celtics* (New York, 1982); *TSN Official NBA Register 2004–2005* (St. Louis, MO, 2004); George Walsh, "Jones and Jones at Court," *SI* 14 (March 20, 1961), pp. 49–52.

Daniel Frio

JONES, Walter "Larry" (b. September 22, 1942, Columbus, OH), college and professional player, graduated from high school in Columbus, Ohio and graduated with a Bachelor's degree in 1964 from the University of Toledo, where he led the MAC three consecutive years in scoring from 1961–1962 through 1963–1964 and made All-America in 1964. He once scored 35 points with a broken wrist for the Rockets.

The Philadelphia 76ers (NBA) drafted the six-foot two-inch, 180-pound guard in 1964. Jones averaged just 5.7 points in 23 games as a reserve in 1964–1965 and played in the Eastern League in 1964–1965 and 1965–1966. He did not participate in basketball in 1966–1967 and may never have had a chance for professional stardom without the advent of the ABA.

The Denver Rockets (ABA) drafted Jones for the inaugural 1967–1968 ABA campaign. Jones spent his first three ABA seasons with Denver, making the All-ABA First Team each season. In 1967–1968, he averaged 22.9 points and a career-high 7.9 rebounds. He became the first ABA player to score 50 points in a game with 52 points against the Oakland Oaks. Jones also tallied 29 points in one playoff game against New Orleans. His best season came in 1968–1969, when he led the ABA in scoring with a career-best 2,133 points (28.4 point average), in free throws attempted (760), and free throws made (591). Jones set an ABA record by scoring 30 or more points in 23 straight regular-season games and averaged 22.0 points in seven playoff games. In 1969–1970, he averaged 24.9 points and career-best 5.7 assists during the regular season and 26.6 points and 6.3 rebounds in 12 playoff games. The Los Angeles Stars defeated Denver four games to one in the ABA Finals.

In 1970, Denver sent Jones, Greg Wittman, and a number two draft choice to the Floridians (ABA) for Larry Cannon, Don Sidle, and a number-one draft choice. Jones was unhappy with the money the Rockets were paying teammate Spencer Haywood* and asked to be traded. Until Haywood's arrival, Jones was the ABA's highest paid player at $23,000 a year. In 1970–1971, Jones teamed with Mack Calvin* to form the highest scoring backcourt combination in pro basketball history. The pair averaged over 51 points per game, with Jones ranking seventh in scoring with a 24.3 points average. He also averaged 5.4 rebounds and 4.6 assists during the regular season and 17.2 points and 6.2 rebounds in eight playoff games. Jones remained in professional basketball three more seasons, spending 1971–1972 with Florida, 1973–1973 with the Utah Stars and Dallas Chaparrals (ABA), and 1973–1974 with the Philadelphia 76ers (NBA).

During his NBA-ABA career, Jones scored 10,505 points (19.1 point average) with 2,725 rebounds (4.9 average), and 2,030 assists (3.7 average) in 551 games. As an ABA star, he tallied 9,651 points (21.2 point average) with 2,484 rebounds (5.4 average), and 1,760 assists (3.9 average) in 456 games. Jones, one of the most prolific scorers in ABA history, recorded 662 points (18.9 points average) with 164 rebounds (4.7 average), and 160 assists (4.6 average) in 35 playoff games. He made the ABA All-Star team his first four years, averaging 16.0 points, 6.5 rebounds, and 4.3 assists. He made 30 points in the 1970 All-Star Game, as the West routed the East, 128-98.

Jones won acclaim as a long-range jump-shooter and did not crash the boards very often. He was founder and first president of the ABA Players' Association and became the first ABA player to score over 2,000 points in a season, a feat he accomplished twice.

BIBLIOGRAPHY: Jan Hubbard, ed., *The Offcial NBA Encyclopedia*, 3rd ed. (New York, 2000); "Larry Jones," http://www.remembertheaba.com/TributeMaterial/L.Jones.html; Terry Pluto, *Loose Balls: The Short Wild Life of the American Basketball Association* (New York, 1990); Ken Shouler et al., *Total Basketball* (Wilmington, DE, 2003); *TSN Official ABA Guide, 1970–1971* (St. Louis, MO, 1970).

David L. Porter

JORDAN, Michael Jeffery (b. February 17, 1963, Brooklyn, NY), college and professional player and executive, is the son of James Jordan, an electrical engineer for General Electric Company, and Deloris Jordan, an employee at United Carolina Bank. Jordan claims the one event in his life that led to his success as a basketball player was not being promoted to the varsity team at Laney High School in Wilmington,

North Carolina, after his junior varsity team had completed its season. This event, which occurred during his sophomore year at Laney, led to his taking the game more seriously. A superb athlete, he played football and was the MVP on a state basketball championship team. Jordan was not heavily recruited even though he averaged over 20 points. He wanted to attend UCLA and liked the University of Virginia, but neither school recruited him. He attended the University of North Carolina because he liked the atmosphere and academics there.

Jordan became a starting guard at the University of North Carolina as a freshman in 1981–1982 and enjoyed a sensational season. He scored a career-high 39 points against Georgia Institute of Technology, averaged 13.5 points and was named ACC Rookie of the Year. His most memorable event of that season was making a shot in the closing seconds of the NCAA Finals to give North Carolina the national championship with a 63-62 victory over Georgetown (Washington D.C.) University. During his sophomore and junior seasons at the University of North Carolina, the six-foot six-inch, 226-pound Jordan averaged 20.0 and 19.6 points, respectively. He helped lead the Tar Heels into the NCAA tournament after the 1982–1983 and 1983–1984 seasons, but North Carolina was unable to reach the Final Four again. After the 1982–1983 season, Jordan was the leading scorer and led the U.S. team to the gold medal in the Pan American Games held in Caracas, Venezuela. He received All-America honors after both the 1982–1983 and the 1983–1984 seasons and was named National Player of the Year after his sophomore year by *TSN*. Jordan scored 1,754 points (17.4 point average) in 101 games, helping North Carolina finish 88-13.

Jordan was signed by the Chicago Bulls (NBA) in 1984 after being the third overall player selected in the NBA draft. He won NBA Rookie of the Year honors in 1985, averaging 28.2 points. A broken bone in his foot limited him to 18 regular-season games in 1985–1986, but he starred in the three-game, first-round playoff series against the Boston Celtics. Jordan averaged 43.7 points in that series and set a single-game playoff scoring record on April 20, 1986, by tallying 63 points in an overtime loss at the Boston Garden. Jordan enjoyed perhaps his best statistical season in 1986–1987, leading the NBA in scoring with 3,041 points and a 37.1 points average. His honors that season included being named to the NBA All-Star East squad and being selected on the All-NBA First Team. Jordan broke Chet Walker's* regular-season club record in late February 1987 by scoring 58 points against the New Jersey Nets. This record lasted only six days, as he scored 61 points in a 125-120 overtime victory against the Detroit Pistons and tallied 26 of the Bulls' 33 fourth-quarter points. In April 1987, Jordan scored 61 points against the Atlanta Hawks to become the second player in NBA history to tally 3,000 points in a season and set an NBA mark with 23 consecutive points. His regular-season all-around performance earned him the Seagram Sports Award as the NBA's best player. Jordan won the NBA All-Star Game MVP award in 1988 by tallying 40 points for the East squad and edged Dominique Wilkins* in the slam dunk competition. During the 1987–1988 season, the Bulls enjoyed their first 50 victory campaign in 14 seasons, but were eliminated by the Detroit Pistons in the NBA playoffs. Jordan was named the NBA MVP, NBA Defensive Player of the Year, and *TSN* Player of the Year; made the All-NBA First Team; and repeated as NBA scoring champion with 2,868 points (35.0 points average). Jordan also paced the NBA with 259 steals (3.16 steals average). No NBA player previously had won the scoring title and defensive award in the same season. Jordan also became the only NBA player to record 200 steals and 100 blocked shots in a season, accomplishing that feat in the 1986–1987 and 1987–1988 seasons.

Jordan helped the Chicago Bulls win six NBA Championships (1991–1993, 1996–1998). He was named the MVP of all six NBA Finals, averaging a record 41.0 points in the 1993 NBA Finals against the Phoenix Suns. Jordan was selected to the All-NBA First Team 10 times (1987–1993, 1996–1998) the All-Defensive First Team nine times (1988–1993, 1996–1998), and the All-NBA Second Team (1985); he started at guard in 12 NBA All-Star Games (1985, 1987–1993, 1996–1998), being the first player ever to receive over two million votes in fan-balloting. He was chosen MVP of the All-Star classic in 1988, 1996, and 1998. Jordan set NBA regular-season records for the most seasons leading the NBA in scoring (10, 1986–1987 through 1992–1993, 1995–1996 through 1997–1998 and the most consecutive seasons leading the NBA in scoring (7, 1986–1987 through 1992–1993). He was selected NBA MVP five times (1988, 1991, 1992, 1996, 1998), NBA Defensive Player of the Year in 1988, and won the IBM Award for all-around contributions to his team's success in 1985 and 1989. He scored a career-high 69 points against the Cleveland Cavaliers on March 28, 1990.

Following the 1993 NBA championship, Jordan's father was murdered in a robbery by two teenagers. Jordan lost his will to play pro basketball and played professional baseball with the Birmingham, Alabama, Barons (Southern League) and the Scottsdale, Arizona, Scorpions (Arizona Fall League) in the Chicago White Sox (AL) organization. He rejoined the Chicago Bulls for the final 17 games of the 1994–1995 season and led the Bulls to three straight NBA titles, pacing the NBA in scoring each season. Chicago won 72 games in 1995–1996, becoming the first NBA team to win 70 games in a season. Jordan was selected one of the 50 Greatest Players in NBA History in 1996 and temporarily retired in January 1999. Jordan served from January 2001 to September 2001 as president of the Washington Wizards (WBA), handling the basketball operations. In September 2001, he returned to the NBA as an active player with the Wizards. Jordan played two seasons and, in January 2003, passed Wilt Chamberlain* as the third leading scorer in NBA history. He was selected to play in his fourteenth All-Star Game in 15 seasons and retired following the 2002–2003 season.

During 15 NBA seasons, Jordan compiled 32,292 points (30.1 point average), collected 6,672 rebounds, dished out 5,633 assists, recorded 2,514 steals, and blocked 893 shots in 1,072 regular season games. He averaged 30 or more points eight seasons, and leads the Bulls in career scoring (29,277 points), assists (5,012), and steals (2,306). In 179 NBA playoff games, Jordan compiled 5,987 points and averaged 33.4 points, both postseason records. He also posted playoff totals of 1,152 rebounds, 1,022 assists, 158 blocked shots, record 376 steals, and 1,463 free throws made. Jordan scored 262 points in 14 All-Star Games, holds career records for highest point-average (18.7) and most steals (37), and recorded the only triple-double in All-Star Game history in 1997.

Jordan married Juanita Vanoy in September 1989. They reside in Highland Park, Illinois with their three children, Jessica, Jasmine, and Marcus. He has made numerous endorsements and commercials. The Bulls retired his jersey number 23 in 1994 and built a life-size statue of him in front of the United Center.

BIBLIOGRAPHY: "Bulls Announce Signing of Michael Jordan," Chicago Bulls press release, September 12, 1984; Frank Deford, "One of a Kind," *SI* 25 (June 22, 1992), pp. 48–50; Jordan Deutsch, *Avon Superstars: Kevin McHale, Michael Jordan* (New York, 1987); Bob Greene, *Hang Time* (New York, 1992); Bill Gutman, *Michael Jordan* (New York, 1991); Margaret S. Howell, "Family Priorities: Kids and Sports," *Cape Fear Tidewater*, August 1984; Michael Jordan, *For the Love of the Game* (New York, 1998); Michael Jordan, *Rare Air* (New York, 1993); Walter La Feber, *Michael Jordan and the New Global Capitalism* (New York, 2000); Roland Lazenby, *The NBA Finals* (Indianapolis, IN, 1996); Sam Smith, *The Jordan Rules* (New York, 1992); Sam Smith, "Setback as a Prep Inspired Jordan," *Chicago Tribune*, December 25, 1984, pp. 1–9; *TSN Official NBA Register, 2004–2005* (St. Louis, MO, 2004); *University of North Carolina Basketball Guide, 1983* (Chapel Hill, NC, 1983); Peter Vecsey, "Air Jordan Chartering New Course," *New York Post*, October 20, 1984, p. 40.

William A. Sutton

JULIAN, Alvin F. "Doggie" (b. April 5, 1901, Reading, PA; d. July 28, 1967, Hanover, NH), college athlete and coach, was a leader in the basketball community and a versatile participant in other athletic activities for over 30 years. Julian starred in baseball, football, and basketball at Bucknell University (Pennsylvania) before graduation in 1923 and played baseball as a catcher with Reading, Pennsylvania (IL) before pursuing a coaching career.

After several years of high school football and basketball coaching, Julian in 1936 moved to Muhlenberg College (Pennsylvania) in a similar capacity. There he compiled a 129-71 basketball record in nine seasons, twice taking his teams to the NIT. Julian went to the College of Holy Cross (Massachusetts) in 1945 and enjoyed his greatest success, winning the NCAA title in 1946–1947. His Crusaders squad that year finished 23-3 and featured outstanding players like George Kaftan*, Frank Oftring, Joe Mullaney, and freshman Bob Cousy*, his greatest protégé. Julian's 1947–1948 team nearly repeated as national champions, losing to the University of Kentucky 60-52 in the NCAA semifinals. At Holy Cross, he compiled a fine 65-10 basketball record and coached the football backfield; he also was backfield coach for the Boston Yanks (NFL). From 1948–1949 to 1949–1950, he coached the Boston Celtics (NBA) to a 47-81 record in their formative NBA years.

Julian returned to college coaching with Dartmouth College (New Hampshire) in 1950–1951 and spent the remainder of his life there. After a 3-23 start, he gradually improved the Big Green's fortunes. By the late 1950s, Julian won three IvL championships (1956, 1958, 1959) and defeated powers like West Virginia University in NCAA tournament play. His outstanding players included Dave Gavitt (later Dartmouth's basketball coach) and Rudy LaRusso*, longtime NBA standout with the Los Angeles Lakers. After several lean years in the early 1960s, Julian in 1966 had the makings of another strong team. Dartmouth recorded an opening-round victory over the University of Rochester in the Kodak City Classic in December, when Julian suffered a serious stroke. He was returned to Hanover, New Hampshire, where he died six months later. Survivors included his wife, Lee, two sons, and a daughter.

Julian initiated the expanded participation format of recent NCAA tournament play and served as president of the NABC group. He authored *Bread and Butter Basketball*, a popular text, and was elected to the Naismith Memorial Basketball Hall of Fame in 1968 as a coach. During his college coaching career, he compiled 386 victories to rank among the leaders in this category.

BIBLIOGRAPHY: Peter C. Bjarkman, *The Boston Celtics Encyclopedia* (Champaign, IL, 1998); Dartmouth College, Bureau of Athletic Information, Hanover, NH; Mike Douchant, *Encyclopedia of College Basketball* (Detroit, MI, 1995); Zander Hollander, ed., *The Modern Encyclopedia of Basketball* (Garden City, NY, 1973); Alvin Julian file, Naismith Memorial Basketball Hall of Fame, Springfield, MA; *NCAA Men's Basketball Records, 2004* (Indianapolis, IN, 2003).

Leonard H. Frey

K

KAFTAN, George A. "The Golden Greek" (b. February 22, 1928, New York, NY), college and professional player and coach, led the College of the Holy Cross to the 1947 NCAA basketball title, garnering All-America and NCAA tournament MVP honors. His parents were Greek immigrants Angelo Kaftan, a restaurateur, and Esther Kaftan. Born premature, Kaftan was given little chance of surviving and did not begin playing basketball until his sophomore year at Xavier High School in Manhattan. As a senior, he led Xavier to a 25-4 record and captured the New York City scoring title with 435 points.

Kaftan attended Holy Cross, where he played for Alvin "Doggie" Julian*. The six-foot three-inch, 200-pounder made his mark quickly, setting the single-season scoring record as a freshman with 237 points. Kaftan's sophomore season in 1946–1947, however, marked his most memorable. He broke his season scoring record with 468 points, lifting the Crusaders to a 27-3 record. In the 1947 NCAA tournament, Holy Cross defeated the U.S. Naval Academy and CCNY en route to the championship game and triumphed 58-47 over the University of Oklahoma for the title. The 19-year-old Kaftan was named NCAA tournament MVP, leading in nearly all offensive categories. He scored 63 points in three games, including 30 points against CCNY, and fell one point shy of the NCAA record. Kaftan scored 41 points in three games against the University of Michigan, University of Kentucky, and Kansas State University, leading the Crusaders to a third-place finish in the 1948 NCAA tournament.

From 1946 to 1949, Kaftan totaled 1,177 career points and was twice named an HAF and Converse All-America. He broke nearly every individual record at Holy Cross, while Julian's squads shattered every team record. By his junior year, Kaftan was considered the college's greatest basketball player. Many of his accomplishments, however, soon were surpassed by teammate Bob Cousy*. Kaftan was named to the NCAA Final Four All-1940s Team.

Kaftan graduated in February 1949 after playing only 14 games that season for the Crusaders. He promptly signed with the struggling Boston Celtics (NBA) and averaged 14.5 points in 21 games his rookie 1948–1949 season, the most prolific of his NBA career. Kaftan spent another year with Boston and two seasons with the New York Knicks (NBA) as a low-scoring role-player. The Knicks, however, finished runner-up for the NBA crown both seasons Kaftan played there. He completed his basketball career with the Baltimore Bullets (NBA), contributing nearly six points per game in 1952–1953. For his NBA career, Kaftan scored 1,594 points in 212 games and averaged 7.5 points.

After retiring from professional basketball, Kaftan practiced dentistry on Long Island and taught biology and coached men's basketball at C. W. Post College. He coached 15 years there from 1958 through 1972, compiling a 188-101 record and .651 winning percentage, and served on the NIT Selection Committee. Kaftan and his wife reside in Long Island, New York, and have three daughters.

BIBLIOGRAPHY: Morgan G. Brenner, *College Basketball's National Championships* (Lanham, MD,

1999); Mike Douchant, *Encyclopedia of College Basketball* (Detroit, MI, 1995); *Holy Cross Basketball Media Guide, 1947–1948, 1948–1949, 1949–1950* (Worcester, MA, 1947, 1948, 1949); Jan Hubbard, ed., *The Official NBA Basketball Encyclopedia*, 3rd ed. (New York, 2000); George Kaftan clipping file, College of Holy Cross Archives, Worcester, MA; Ronald L. Mendell, *Who's Who in Basketball* (New Rochelle, NY, 1973).

Brian L. Laughlin

KARL, George Matthew (b. May 12, 1951, Penn Hills, PA), college and professional player and coach, is the son of Joseph Karl, who worked until his death at age 95 as a service representative for Bell and Howell Company, and Edith Karl. Karl graduated from Penn (Pennsylvania) High School and majored in political science at the University of North Carolina, where, as a junior, he helped lead the Tar Heels basketball team to the 1972 NCAA Final Four. During his sophomore year in 1970–1971, he helped North Carolina to win the NIT. His college career included 1,293 points (13.8 points per game), 394 assists (4.2 per game) and 279 rebounds (3.0 per game) in 94 games.

Six-foot two-inch, 190-pound Karl divided five professional seasons between the ABA and the NBA, averaging 6.5 points and 3.0 assists over 264 games as a solid journeyman player with a good work ethic. These qualities have marked his subsequent role as basketball coach. Although selected by the New York Knicks (NBA) in the fourth round of the 1973 draft, Karl played with the San Antonio Spurs (ABA, NBA) from 1973 through 1978. He served as an assistant coach with the Spurs from 1978 to 1980.

Karl's first head coaching basketball position came from 1980 to 1983 with the Montana Golden Nuggets (CBA) as he compiled a 90-42 record and was named CBA Coach of the Year in 1981 and 1983. Karl joined the Cleveland Cavaliers (NBA) as director of player acquisition and was made head coach within a year. His NBA career has been marked by successes and a "rolling stone" credo. Karl served as head coach with Cleveland in 1984–1985 and 1985–1986, the Golden State Warriors (NBA) in 1986–1987 and 1987–1988, and Seattle SuperSonics (NBA) from 1991–1992 to 1997–1998. He joined the Milwaukee Bucks (NBA) in 1998–1999 and left after the 2002–2003 season. In January 2005, Karl became head coach of the Denver Nuggets (NBA). He also squeezed in head coaching positions with the Albany Patroons (CBA) in 1988–1989 and 1990–1991 and Real Madrid of the Spanish League in 1989–1990 and 1991–1992.

On January 19, 2001 at Charlotte, North Carolina, Karl became only the twentieth NBA coach to take part in 1,000 NBA games. Eleven days later, he became the seventeenth NBA coach to win 600 games and accomplished the feat quicker than all but five coaches in NBA history. In his six seasons with Seattle, his team averaged 59 wins per season. Over his last decade, he did not post a losing season. Karl became head coach of the struggling Denver Nuggets in January 2005, guiding them to a 32-8 record and seventh place Western Conference finish. The San Antonio Spurs eliminated Denver in five games in the first round of the playoffs. During 17 NBA seasons, he has compiled a 740-507 regular-season record and 60-72 playoff record.

Karl and his wife, Cathy, have a daughter, Kelci and a son, Coby. Nicknamed "Drumstick" and "Stumpy," Karl enjoys jet skiing, golf, tennis, and watching sporting events. His favorite author is Herman Hesse, while his top movies are "Paper Chase" and "Butch Cassidy and the Sundance Kid." His "Friends of Hoop" Foundation helps high school student athletes in Milwaukee, Wisconsin and Seattle, Washington to acquire skills and education to compete for college scholarships. He operates an annual George Karl Basketball Camp each summer at Whitefish Bay High School in Wisconsin.

Karl experienced misfortune in 2002 as coach of the USA team at the World Championships, culminating in no medals and losing to Argentina, Yugoslavia, and Spain.

BIBLIOGRAPHY: Lauren Rippy, Eastern Illinois University research graduate student, materials collected May 28, 2003; http://www.nba.com/coachfile/georgeKarl; Chris Ballard, "Can the Remade Bucks Hold onto a Berth and End George Karl's Agony?" *SI* 98 (March 31, 2003), pp. 34–41. *TSN Official NBA Register, 2004–2005* (St. Louis, MO, 2004); Ken

Shouler et al., *Total Basketball* (Wilmington, DE, 2003); George M. Karl, *The Game's The Best* (New York, 1997).

Scott A.G.M. Crawford

KEADY, Gene (b. May 21, 1936, Larned, KS), college athlete and basketball coach, is the son of Lloyd Keady and Mary Helen (Montgomery) Keady. Lloyd, an amateur boxer, worked in and owned a greenhouse. Gene starred in four sports at Larned High School in Kansas and continued his athletic endeavors at Garden City (KS) Junior College. A three-sport star at Kansas State University, he earned a Bachelor's degree in biological science and physical education. After being a college quarterback, Keady played briefly with the Pittsburgh Steelers (NFL) in 1958. He began his basketball coaching career at Beloit (Kansas) High School from 1959 to 1965 and compiled a 102-47 win-loss record. Keady was named head basketball coach at Hutchinson (Kansas) Junior College in 1966, compiling an eight-year 187-48 win-loss record and six league championships. He moved to the University of Arkansas as assistant basketball coach to Eddie Sutton* from 1975 to 1978. Keady served two years as head basketball coach at Western Kentucky University, leading the Hilltoppers to a 38-19 win-loss record and one NCAA national tournament appearance.

In April 1982, Purdue University selected Keady as head basketball coach. Keady completed his 25th season in 2004–2005 with the Purdue basketball program, retiring in March 2005. He remains the all time winning coach in Boilermaker history, passing Ward Lambert* in 1997. Keady enjoyed a career coaching record of 512 victories and 270 losses. In the BTC, his clubs won 275 times and lost just 182. Under his leadership, Purdue suffered only three losing seasons and has won at least 20 games 15 times. Keady's squads fared 20-19 in 18 NCAA tournament appearances, reaching the NCAA Elite Eight twice and the NCAA Sweet Sixteen five times, and making three trips to the NIT. He led the Boilermakers to seven BTC titles and was named BTC Coach of the Year a record seven times. Keady was selected National Coach of the Year six times and to the National Junior College Basketball Hall of Fame as a player and a coach. Numerous outstanding players contributed to his coaching success. Glenn Robinson* was named a two-time All-America, led the nation in scoring average in 1993–1994, and was selected the 1993–1994 National Player of the Year. Keith Edmonson was chosen All-America in 1982, while Robinson, Stephen Scheffler, and Jim Rowinski were BTC MVPs in 1994, 1990, and 1984, respectively.

Keady, former President of the NABC, led in handling issues confronting college basketball. Internationally, he served on the coaching staff for the 2000 Olympic Games in Sydney, Australia, helping Team USA to a gold medal. Keady coached Team USA in the 1989 World University Games, capturing the gold medal, while his Team USA earned a bronze medal in the 1991 Pan American Games. He also served on the coaching staff and assisted with the selection of the 1984 and 1988 Team USA Olympic squads.

Keady and his wife, Patricia, were married in 1980. They reside in Lafayette, Indiana and have three children: Lisa, Beverly and Dan. He was married previously to the Kansas State University homecoming queen.

BIBLIOGRAPHY: Peter C. Bjarkman, *Big Ten Basketball* (Indianapolis, IN, 1994); Mike Douchant, *Encyclopedia of College Basketball* (Detroit, MI, 1995); "Gene Keady," *Bio*, http://www.usabasketball.com (2003); "Gene Keady," *Career Records*, http://www.cbssportsline.com (2000); "Gene Keady," *Coaching Records*, http://www.mrhoops.com (2003); "Gene Keady," *Profile*, http://www.purduesports.ocsa.com (2003); Lafayette Journal and Courier Staff, ed., *Most Memorable Moments in Purdue Basketball History* (Champaign, IL, 1998); Mark Montieth, *Passion Play* (Chicago, IL, 1988).

John L. Evers

KEANEY, Frank W. (b. June 5, 1886, Boston, MA; d. October 10, 1967, Wakefield, RI), college athlete and coach, graduated from Boston's Cambridge Latin High School in 1906 and Bates College in 1911. Keaney earned Phi Beta Kappa honors while working his way through Bates College. A four-sport star at Bates, he set school baseball records by batting .410 and stealing 38 bases. His coaching career began at high schools in Putnam, Connecticut, Woonsocket, Rhode Island, and Everett, Massachusetts. He then became director of athletics at the University of Rhode Island. The versatile Keaney coached all sports at Rhode Island and taught chemistry. With his wife, Winifred, a Bates classmate, they formed the Physical Education Department at Rhode Island. For 13 years, his wife coached all women's sports teams. The imaginative Keaney changed basketball's slow offensive pattern to the fast-break, high-scoring style. He became the first college coach to use the fast break almost exclusively, to use smaller hoops in practice to improve marksmanship, and to introduce the full-court press from the beginning of the game, defeating more talented opponents strictly on superior conditioning.

The architect of modern "run-and-shoot" basketball, Keaney guided his Rhode Island team to 87 points in his coaching debut (1920), one of the highest totals scored by a college team to that time. In 1927 Rhode Island began moving toward point-a-minute production by averaging 40.5 points. After averaging 48.2 points in 1935, the Rams in 1936 became the first college team to score better than 50 points per game. Keaney's 1939 team averaged 70.7 points and featured Chester Jaworski, Rhode Island's first All-America. The 1941 squad ranked among Keaney's best with stars Stan Stutz* and Warner "Flip" Keaney, his son. In 1943, the Rams became the first college team in history to average over two points a minute by scoring 80.7 points per game. Keaney's highest-scoring five, the 1947 squad, averaged 82.4 points and became one of his four teams to play in the NIT. Although Ernie Calverley* was named the NIT's MVP, Rhode Island lost a narrow 46-45 decision to the University of Kentucky in the title game.

Keaney retired from coaching after the 1948 season with 403 victories and 124 losses (.765 winning percentage) in 28 seasons. Although primarily known as a basketball coach, he guided the Rams football teams to a 70-84-13 record (1920–1940) and baseball squads to a 197-97-1 composite mark (1920–1948). Keaney continued as athletic director until 1957 and received the NABC Metropolitan Award. A member of the AABC and HAF halls of fame, he was elected in 1960 as a coach to the Naismith Memorial Basketball Hall of Fame.

BIBLIOGRAPHY: Peter C. Bjarkman, *The Biographical History of Basketball* (Chicago, IL, 2000); *Converse Basketball Yearbook, 1968; Converse Basketball Yearbook, 1975*; Mike Douchant, *Encyclopedia of College Basketball* (Detroit, MI, 1995); Bill Gutman, *The History of NCAA Basketball* (New York, 1993); Neil D. Isaacs, *All the Moves: A History of College Basketball* (New York, 1975); Frank Keaney file, Naismith Memorial Basketball Hall of Fame, Springfield, MA.

John L. Evers

KELLY, Pamela R. (b. March 17, 1960, Columbia, LA), college player, was known for her speed and grace as a post player under the basket in high school and college. As a high school student at Caldwell Parish (Louisiana), Kelly led her basketball team to a 110-12 win-loss record during four years from 1974–1975 through 1977–1978. Kelly's college career proved even more impressive. During her freshman season at Louisiana Tech University, the Lady Techsters advanced to the team's first AIAW Final Four and lost to Old Dominion University, Kelly averaged 19 points and 9.8 rebounds in 38 games.

Kelly continued to improve. During her sophomore season, she averaged 20.7 points and 10.9 rebounds and became the first Lady Techster to earn Kodak All-America honors. Kelly scored 932 points and made 491 rebounds, setting a single-season school records. During her junior year, she helped lead Louisiana Tech to an undefeated 34-0 season and the team's first national AIAW championship title. Kelly posted 17.5 points and 9.5 rebounds per game, clinching Kodak All-America honors a second time. At the end of the 1980–1981 season, she was named Louisiana's Top College Athlete of the Year.

Kelly ended her college career, averaging 20.3 points and 9.1 rebounds tallying 2,979 career points, and making 1,511 career rebounds in 153 games. She again was named a Kodak All-America in 1982–1983, helping lead the Lady Techsters to second consecutive national and first NCAA title and becoming the first Lady Techster to win the Wade Trophy. The Lady Techsters further honored Kelly by retiring her jersey number 41 and inducting her into the Louisiana Tech Hall of Fame in 1984. Kelly graduated in 1983 with a Bachelor's degree in health and physical education. She lives in Waldolf, Maryland with her husband and two sons and teaches health and physical education.

BIBLIOGRAPHY: Mike Douchant, *Encyclopedia of College Basketball* (Detroit, MI, 1995); Jim McLain, "Ex-La. Tech star Flowers Tops the Team," *Sports News* (July 8, 2000); "Pam Kelly," Louisiana Sports Hall of Fame, www.lasportshof.com; *25th Anniversary Media Guide* (Ruston, LA, 1985).

Lisa A. Ennis

KEMP, Shawn T. (b. November 26, 1969, Elkhart, IN), professional player, graduated in 1987 from Concord High School in Elkhart, Indiana, where he starred in basketball. The six-foot seven-inch, 280-pound forward was brought up by Barbara Kemp, a retired hospital employee. Kemp enrolled at University of Kentucky in 1988, but did not play basketball there and left to attend Trinity JC in Texas in 1989.

Kemp was selected by the Seattle SuperSonics (NBA) as the 17th overall pick in the NBA draft in 1989 and averaged 6.5 points as a rookie. He became the Sonics' all-time blocked shots leader with 959 from 1989–1990 through 1996–1997. Nicknamed "Reign Man," Kemp led Seattle in the playoffs with 13.4 point and 7.2 rebound averages. Kemp, who suffered an injury in 1992–1993, recorded a team-high 30 points and 14 rebounds in games after the injury. He led the Sonics with 5,978 rebounds, 10,148 points, and 775 steals from 1989–1990 through 1996–1997. Kemp was named to the NBA All-Star team from 1993 through 1998, made the All-NBA Second Team from 1994 to 1996, and was a member of the gold medal–winning Dream Team II in the 1994 World Championship in Toronto, Canada. He was selected to the all-tournament team, averaging 9.4 points and 6.8 rebounds. He recorded a 19.6 points average and a career-best 11.4 rebounds average, leading Seattle to the 1996 playoffs.

Kemp was acquired by the Cleveland Cavaliers (NBA) in September 1997. The Cavalier forward averaged 18.0 points and 9.3 rebounds in 1997–1998, leading Cleveland to the playoffs. The first All-Star Game starter for the Cavaliers in 1998, he posted 12 points and game-highs of 11 rebounds and four steals. In 1999, Kemp ranked twelfth in the NBA in scoring with a career-high 20.5 points average and averaged 9.2 rebounds. He led the Cavaliers in scoring in 31 games, recorded double-doubles in 42 contests, and tallied his 12,000th career-point in 1998–1999.

In August 2000, Kemp was traded to the Portland Trail Blazers (NBA) and averaged 6.5 points and 3.8 rebounds in 68 games. His career took a downhill spiral after he was acquired by Portland. Kemp missed several games during drug rehabilitation. He averaged 6.1 points and 3.8 rebounds in 75 games during his last season there in 2001–2002.

The six-time All-Star was signed by the Orlando Magic (NBA) in September 2002. Kemp, whose career has been ruined by weight problems and drug abuse problems, averaged 6.8 points and 5.7 rebounds in 79 games in 2002–2003. The talented forward was suspended several times for violating the NBA's drug policy and is struggling to rejuvenate his career. Orlando released him following the 2002–2003 season. Through 2002–2003, he scored 15,347 points (14.6 average), made 8,834 rebounds (8.4 average), and blocked 1,229 shots (1.2 average) in 1,051 games. He partly owns the Oklahoma Storm (USBL) and signed to play with them in April 2004.

Kemp, who is single, has seven children by six women. He dresses as "Santa Kemp" every Christmas, helping distribute toys to underprivileged children, and works with charities to help buy wheelchairs.

BIBLIOGRAPHY: Tim Keown, "Reign Man," *SI* 84 (February 19, 1996), pp. 70–76; Edward, Kiersh, "Sonic Boom," *Sport* 85 (June 1994), pp. 48–50; Jackie MacMullan, "Turning the Page," *SI* 88 (April 20, 1998), pp. 86–87; Ken Shouler et al., *Total Basketball* (Wilmington, DE, 2003); Stew Thornley, *Shawn Kemp: Star Forward* (Springfield, NJ, 1998); Rick Weinberg, "Q&A: Shawn Kemp and Gary Payton," "Interview," *Sport* 88 (June 1997), pp. 34–36.

Njoki-Wa-Kinyatti

KENNEDY, James Walter (b. June 8, 1912, Stamford, CT; d. June 26, 1977, Stamford, CT), sports coach, journalist, and professional basketball executive, was the son of Michael James Kennedy and Lottie (Hofman) Kennedy. Kennedy wanted to be an athlete, but a bout with polio as a youngster ended that dream. After graduating from high school in his native Stamford, he enrolled at the University of Notre Dame and worked part time for the *South Bend Tribune*. Kennedy graduated with a Bachelor's degree in journalism and business administration in 1934. He returned to his alma mater as sports information director during World War II and did graduate work at the University of Notre Dame (Indiana), Yale University (Connecticut), and NYU.

Kennedy, a multitalented individual, worked as a high school coach, public relations man, politician, and director of many projects. In the late 1930s, he coached highly successful teams and was athletic director at St. Basil's Preparatory School in Stamford, Connecticut. Kennedy was a *TSN* correspondent covering the old baseball Class B CL and assisted broadcaster Ted Husing. After being public relations director of the old BAA from 1946 to 1949, he operated his own public relations and business management office and represented the Harlem Globetrotters as press chief. Kennedy was elected mayor of Stamford in 1959 and was serving his second term when the NBA owners in 1963 voted him into the commissioner's office. In 1962, he was campaign manager for Democrat Abraham Ribicoff, who was elected as U.S. Senator. Kennedy inaugurated Aggravation Day in Stamford, opening his door to citizens having complaints against the city government; the situation remained similar in the NBA.

Succeeding first NBA commissioner Maurice Podoloff*, the likable, approachable Kennedy became an iron-handed executive and let everyone know precisely where he stood on issues. He quickly exerted his authority, slapping Arnold "Red" Auerbach* with a $500 fine for rowdy conduct during a preseason 1963 game. His major challenges included implementing an expansion program and developing a television contract so that the NBA could become a national sport available to fans everywhere. By his 1975 retirement, Kennedy primarily arranged NBA expansion from nine to 18 teams and a national television contract. Kennedy, succeeded by Lawrence F. O'Brien* as NBA commissioner in 1975, received the Gold Key Award in 1971, and was named Knight of St. Gregory (1966), the highest honor given to Catholic laymen for contribution to state and church. In 1980, he was elected as a contributor to the Naismith Memorial Basketball Hall of Fame. He married Marion McRedmond in 1940 and had six children, David, Michael, Robert, Francis, Kathleen, and Marie.

BIBLIOGRAPHY: Peter C. Bjarkman, *The History of the NBA* (New York, 1992); Jan Hubbard, ed., *The Official NBA Encyclopedia*, 3rd ed. (New York, 2000); J. Walter Kennedy file, Naismith Memorial Basketball Hall of Fame, Springfield, MA; Ronald L. Mendell, *Who's Who in Basketball* (New Rochelle, NY, 1973); *NYT*, June 27, 1977, pp. 1, 30; "Obituaries," *TSN*, July 9, 1977, p. 54; Ken Shouler et al., *Total Basketball* (Wilmington, DE, 2003); *TSN Official NBA Guide, 1970–1971* (St. Louis, MO, 1970).

John L. Evers

KENNEDY, Matthew Patrick "Pat" (b. January 28, 1908, Hoboken, NJ; d. June 16, 1957, Mineola, NY), college and professional referee, officiated high school, college, and professional games from 1928 to 1956 as one of basketball's most colorful referees. Named in 1959 to the Naismith Memorial Basketball Hall of Fame, Kennedy often officiated 10 games a week and over 150 games a season. He began refereeing in the professional ABL at age 20 and refereed his first college contest when CCNY's Nat Holman* hired him for a home game with Rutgers College. Soon Kennedy officiated top intersectional college attractions in New York's Madison Square Garden. He exhibited fairness, honesty, and intense showmanship that startled players and entertained spectators.

Kennedy graduated in 1926 from Hoboken, New Jersey's Demarest High School, where he participated in several varsity sports. A 1928 graduate of Montclair State College in Upper Montclair, New Jersey, he became a physical education instructor in Hoboken and officiated basketball games at night and on weekends. When calling a foul or other rules infraction, Kennedy bellowed, "No! No! No! *NO*! You can't do that!" and exhibited a red face, swollen neck veins, prancing legs, and flailing arms. The slender, muscular referee remained one of the few sports officials regarded as a gate attraction. He lost 5 to 10 pounds during a game, but then replaced it with beer and midnight sandwiches. Some coaches called him a showman and believed that they could do without his theatrics. After Kennedy went into his act while calling a traveling violation on all-time Stanford University immortal Hank Luisetti*, the latter said quietly, "You know, Pat, I heard you were crazy, but no one told me you were that crazy!"

During a benefit game in 1934 before a sellout crowd in Brooklyn between the pro New York Celtics and Brooklyn Visitations, Kennedy called a foul on a player. The player protested by ripping off the referee's shirt. Kennedy retaliated by calling three fouls on the perpetrator, but finished the game topless. In 1943 St. John's University (New York) and the University of Wyoming were engaged in a tense struggle at Madison Square Garden before 18,000 spectators when one of the Redmen sank a half-court shot to tie the game with 10 seconds remaining. Kennedy alone heard over the din that the St. John's captain called for time out. Wyoming's Kenny Sailors* dribbled the length of the floor to score what appeared to be the winning basket. After pandemonium ceased, the referee made it quite clear that the basket did not count. Wyoming coach Everett Shelton* graciously supported his decision, after which the Cowboys won in overtime. Kennedy's game control averted many troublesome situations. He halted a rough game at Madison Square Garden between St. John's and a southern team after the visitors hurled several profanities at him and the opposition. The crowd became silent, as Kennedy bellowed that technical fouls would be called with the next swear word and players would be ejected if it occurred too often.

Kennedy married Frances Russo and had two daughters, Patricia and Janet. Besides officiating basketball games, he umpired baseball games in the ISL and IL. Between 1946 and 1950, Kennedy served as NBA supervisor of referees. Kennedy left the NBA to tour the world with the Harlem Globetrotters as referee. He died after being ill for over one year.

BIBLIOGRAPHY: Jan Hubbard, ed., *The Official NBA Encyclopedia*, 3rd ed. (New York, 2000); Matthew Kennedy file, Naismith Memorial Basketball Hall of Fame, Springfield, MA; William G. Mokray, ed., *Ronald Encyclopedia of Basketball* (New York, 1963); *NYT*, June 17, 1957; Bill Stern, "Lay That Whistle Down!" *Liberty* (February 16, 1944), pp. 26–27, 66.

James D. Whalen and Wayne Patterson

KEOGAN, George E. (b. March 8, 1890, Detroit Lakes, MN, d. February 17, 1943, South Bend, IN), college coach, graduated from Detroit Lakes (Minnesota) High School in 1909. Keogan attended the University of Minnesota, graduating from the School of Dentistry. He planned to pursue a dentistry career and use coaching as a preliminary means of financing, but abandoned those plans after early coaching success. Keogan began an illustrious basketball coaching career in high schools at Lockport, Illinois and Riverside, Illinois and later coached the sport at Superior State College (Wisconsin), St. Louis University (Missouri), St. Thomas College (Minnesota), Allegheny College (Pennsylvania), and Valparaiso University (Indiana).

Keogan joined the University of Notre Dame as basketball coach in 1923. Fighting Irish basketball squads rivaled the achievements and performance of the Fighting Irish football teams. Although college basketball had not achieved the national popularity of college football, he considerably enhanced spectator acceptance of the cage game. Keogan guided Notre Dame for 20 years to 327 victories and only 96 defeats for a formidable .773 winning percentage. An astute student of basketball, he created the shifting man-to-man defense. Keogan followed pro basketball in its early stages, learning much from the Original New York Celtics and their great pivotman Dutch Dehnert*. He adapted the successful use of pivots and cuts from Dehnert's example.

In Keogan's early years at Notre Dame, the Fighting Irish cage teams enjoyed phenomenal success. From 1925 through 1928, his teams won 56 games and lost only five contests. His 1935–1936 and 1936–1937 teams posted a composite 42-5 mark and made strong claims to the national college basketball championship. From 1938 through 1943, Notre Dame never lost more than six games in a season. His 1937–1938 squad compiled a 20-3 slate, while his 1938–1939 and 1939–1940 teams each enjoyed 15-6 records. The 1940–1941 squad finished 17-5 and the 1941–1942 team won 16 and lost 6. The 1942–1943 squad, which began with Keogan coaching and ended with Ed Krause* at the helm, recorded 18 victories against only two defeats. Keogan's brilliant coaching record suddenly was terminated with his death during that season. Keogan, who helped develop college basketball as an innovator and visionary, was enshrined in the Naismith Memorial Basketball Hall of Fame as a coach in 1961.

BIBLIOGRAPHY: Peter C. Bjarkman, *Hoopla: A Century of College Basketball, 1896–1996* (Indianapolis, IN, 1996); "The Career of George E. Keogan," University of Notre Dame sports release, undated, South Bend, IN; Mike Douchant, *Encyclopedia of College Basketball* (Detroit, MI, 1995); Bill Gutman, *The History of NCAA Basketball* (New York, 1993); Zander Hollander, ed., *The Modern Encyclopedia of Basketball* (Garden City, NY, 1969); George Keogan file, Naismith Memorial Basketball Hall of Fame, Springfield, MA; Tim Neely, *Hooping It Up: The Complete History of Notre Dame Basketball* (South Bend, IN, 1985); *Notre Dame Basketball Guide, 1983* (South Bend, IN, 1983); *South Bend Mirror*, February 19, 1943; *South Bend Tribune*, March 20 and April 16, 1961.

Stan W. Carlson

KERR, John G. "Red" (b. August 17, 1932, Chicago, IL), college and professional player, coach, and announcer, is the son of a soccer player from Glasgow, Scotland. Kerr played soccer through his junior year at Tilden Technical High School in Chicago. Upon growing eight inches between his junior and senior years, he inevitably was discovered by Tilden's basketball coach and pressed into service on the hardwood. At nearly his adult height of six-feet nine-inches, Kerr starred for Tilden and attracted recruiters from some 45 colleges. He chose the University of Illinois and enjoyed great success there under basketball coach Harry Coombes. During his senior year in 1953–1954, Kerr captained the basketball team, was the second-leading scorer in the BTC with 25.3 points per game, and was selected BTC Player of the Year by the *Chicago Tribune*.

Not surprisingly the 230-pound Kerr was selected in the first round of the 1954 draft by the NBA Syracuse Nationals (later the Philadelphia 76ers). At Syracuse, he teamed effectively with Dolph Schayes* and Red Rocha to give the Nationals a potent front line and in 1955 an NBA championship. Kerr played 11 seasons with the Syracuse-Philadelphia franchise, anchoring the pivot with his effective passing, rebounding, and scoring. He played his final NBA season (1965–1966) with the Baltimore Bullets. Kerr set a consecutive-game streak record of 844 regular-season games, which stood until the 1982–1983 season. With a career scoring average of 13.8 points, he is one of the few players to accumulate over 10,000 points and 10,000 rebounds in the NBA. Tom Heinsohn*, a longtime opponent, called Kerr "the first real excellent passing big center. He was the first guy that really went outside and turned around to look at the basket. Most guys were low-post players and [Bill] Russell* drove a lot of those guys out, but Kerr adapted and adapted nicely." He appeared in three All-Star Games.

In 1966–1967, Kerr assumed the head coach position with the new Chicago Bulls (NBA) franchise. Returning to his hometown, he became the first and only coach to lead an expansion team to the playoffs in their first year. Kerr earned 1967 NBA Coach of the Year honors. The Bulls repeated the playoff appearance the next year (1967–1968), with a dismal 29-53 record. Kerr moved to another expansion NBA franchise the next season, coaching the Phoenix Suns (NBA). He remains the only man ever to coach two NBA expansion franchises in their inaugural seasons. Regrettably, the Phoenix club proved unsalvageable, causing Kerr's departure midway into its second season.

After holding administrative posts with several ABA and NBA franchises, Kerr returned to Chicago and participated on the Bulls' television and radio broadcasting team for over two decades. Kerr, who also owns his own insurance investment consulting firm, lives in suburban Riverside, Illinois with his wife, Betsy, and their five children.

BIBLIOGRAPHY: Peter C. Bjarkman, *The History of the NBA* (New York, 1992); *Chicago Bulls Media Guide, 2002–2003* (Chicago, IL, 2002); Glenn Dickey, *The History of Professional Basketball* (Briarcliff Manor, NY, 1982); Jan Hubbard, ed., *The Official NBA*

Encyclopedia, 3rd ed. (New York, 2000); Leonard Koppett, *24 Seconds to Shoot: An Informal History of the NBA* (New York, 1968); Ronald L. Mendell, *Who's Who in Basketball* (New Rochelle, NY, 1973); Charles Salzberg, *From Set Shot to Slam Dunk* (New York, 1987); *TSN Official NBA Register, 2004–2005* (St. Louis, MO, 2004).

George Robinson

KIDD, Jason Frederick (b. March 23, 1973, San Francisco, CA), college and professional player, led the New Jersey Nets (NBA) to the NBA Finals in 2002 and 2003. He and his two younger sisters were brought up on a small ranch outside Oakland, California by Steve Kidd, a Trans World Airlines employee, and Anne Kidd, a computer analyst. With a white mother and black father, Kidd asserts that the racial diversity of his family broadened his cultural horizons.

Kidd emerged as a prep basketball star with St. Joseph of Notre Dame, a small Roman Catholic high school in Alameda, California. During his junior and senior seasons, St. Joseph won state championships. He twice was named California Player of the Year and received the 1992 Naismith* Award as the nation's finest high school basketball player.

Despite struggling with college entrance examinations, the highly recruited Kidd was selected by the nearby University of California at Berkeley. With aggressive defense, timely scoring, and outstanding ball handling, the six-foot four-inch, 212-pound guard helped revive the California basketball program. Some observers, however, blamed Kidd for the ouster of coach Lou Campanelli. During his sophomore year, he averaged 16.7 points, 9.3 rebounds, and 9.1 assists and earned First Team All-America honors. The Californian then decided to enter the NBA draft.

Kidd received unfavorable publicity for a paternity suit (his son, Jason, was born in November 1993), allegations of abuse toward a girlfriend, and pleading no contest to leaving the scene of an automobile accident. Nevertheless, he was selected by the Dallas Mavericks (NBA) with the second pick in the 1994 draft. During his rookie season with the Mavericks, Kidd averaged 11.7 points and 7.7 assists and shared the NBA Rookie of the Year title with Grant Hill*. During his second season, he increased his production to 16.6 points and 9.7 assists per game and was selected for the All-Star Game. His confrontations with management and teammates, however, led to his being traded to Phoenix Suns (NBA) in December 1996.

Kidd continued his outstanding play with Phoenix ranking among the NBA's leaders, being a perennial All-Star, and leading the Suns to the playoffs from 1996–1997 through 2000–2001. His arrest in January 2001 for spousal abuse led Phoenix to trade him to the New Jersey Nets in July of that year.

Kidd maintains that his arrest and subsequent counseling made him a better person and forced him to readjust his priorities. After arriving in New Jersey, he was named co-captain. Under his leadership and superlative play, the Nets reached the NBA Finals in both 2002 and 2003. Kidd helped New Jersey reach the second round of the playoffs in 2003–2004, but was held scoreless in the decisive seventh-game loss to the Detroit Pistons. He led the Nets in assists, rebounds, and steals in 2004–2005, helping New Jersey to the playoffs. He averaged 17.3 points and 7.3 assists in four games in the first round playoff sweep by the Miami Heat. He was named to the All-NBA First Team in 1999, 2000, 2001, 2002, and 2004. Kidd also made the All-NBA Second Team in 2003 and led the NBA in assists in 2003–2004. He made the All-NBA Defensive First Team in 1999, 2001, and 2002 and the All-NBA Defensive Second Team in 2000, 2003, 2004, and 2005. The eight time All-Star has averaged 6.4 rebounds, 14.8 points, and 9.3 assists in 786 regular season games through the 2004–2005 season and averaged 16.6 points and 9.1 assists in 77 playoff games. He and his wife, Joumana (Samaha), have three children.

BIBLIOGRAPHY: Johnette Howard, "The Ball's in His Hands," *SI* 85 (November 11, 1996), pp. 94–96; Don Howesteen, "Dream On," *Sport* 91 (February 2000), pp. 24–27; Phil Taylor, "Breathtaking," *SI* 92 (December 4, 2000), pp. 62–64; *TSN Official NBA Register, 2004–2005* (St. Louis, MO, 2004).

Ron Briley

KING, Bernard (b. December 4, 1956, Brooklyn, NY), college and professional player, is the brother of Albert King, who starred in basketball at the University of Maryland and later played in the NBA from 1981 to 1992. A basketball forward, Bernard graduated from Brooklyn, New York's Fort Hamilton High School. In 1973 King entered the University of Tennessee, where he scored 1,962 points and made 1,004 rebounds in three seasons. He scored on 59 percent of his 1,374 field goal attempts, leading all major college players in field goal percentage during his 1974–1975 sophomore year. After his final collegiate season, King was named to *TSN* All-America Second Team. The seventh pick of the New Jersey Nets (NBA) in the first round of the 1977 NBA draft, he made the All-Rookie Team in the 1977–1978 season, scored over 1,900 points, and made 751 rebounds. After falling to 1,769 points the next campaign, he was traded to the Utah Jazz (NBA) for Rich Kelly on October 2, 1979. The injured King played in only 19 games.

Utah traded King to the Golden State Warriors (NBA) at the start of the 1980–1981 season for Wayne Cooper and a second-round draft choice. He responded by being named Comeback Player of the Year and by returning to his rookie form with a .588 field goal percentage. In 1982, King scored six points in his first of four NBA All-Star Game appearances. He finished the 1981–1982 season with 1,832 points and 469 rebounds. A free agent, King was signed by the New York Knickerbockers (NBA) in September 1982. When Golden State matched New York's contract terms, New York was forced to trade Michael Ray Richardson for the rights to King. The Knicks acquisition promptly scored 1,486 points and helped lead the 1982–1983 Knicks to the playoffs, during which he enjoyed a .577 field goal percentage in six games. In February 1984, King became the first NBA player to score at least 50 points on consecutive nights since Wilt Chamberlain* accomplished that feat in January 1962. He won the 1984–1985 NBA scoring championship with 809 points (32.9 points per game). In December 1984, King set a Knicks record by scoring 60 points against the New Jersey Nets.

On March 23, 1985, however, King injured his right knee and missed every Knicks game for two years until returning to the team briefly in the spring of 1987. New York missed the playoffs in both those King-less seasons, showing how much the Knicks really missed him. In October 1987, King joined the Washington Bullets (NBA) as a free agent and enjoyed a resurgence in helping his club make the NBA playoffs. In 69 games, he scored 1,188 points (17.0 points average) and made one-half of his field goal attempts. He starred for Washington the next three seasons, finishing third in scoring in 1990–1991 with a 28.4 point average. After missing the 1990–1991 season with injuries, he finished his NBA career with the New Jersey Nets (NBA) in 1991–1992. King appeared in 874 games, scored 19,655 points (22.5 point average), grabbed 5,060 rebounds, and made 2,863 assists. He made the All-NBA First Team in 1984 and 1985, All-NBA Second Team in 1982 and All-NBA Third Team in 1991. A great percentage shooter, the six-foot seven-inch, 205-pounder lives with his wife, Colette, in Franklin Lakes, New Jersey.

BIBLIOGRAPHY: Peter C. Bjarkman, *The Encyclopedia of Pro Basketball Team Histories* (New York, 1994); Jan Hubbard, ed., *The Official NBA Encyclopedia*, 3rd ed. (New York, 2000); Ken Shouler et al., *Total Basketball* (Wilmington, DE, 2003); *TSN Official NBA Register, 2004–2005* (St. Louis, MO, 2004).

John David Healy

KING, George Smith, Jr. (b. August 16, 1928, Charleston, WV), college and professional player, coach, and administrator, is the son of George S. King Sr. He excelled in basketball at Stonewall Jackson High School in Charleston, West Virginia before graduating in 1946.

King enrolled at Morris Harvey College (West Virginia) and became the school's leading basketball scorer. In 1948–1949, he scored 757 points and paced the nation's small college scorers with a 29.1 point average in 26 games. King registered 967 points in 31 games and averaged 31.2 points the following year, becoming the first player at any level to average 30 or more points in one season.

The Chicago Stags (NBA) selected King as their eighth-round draft choice in 1950, but did not sign him. The Syracuse Nationals (NBA) signed the six-foot, 185-pound guard in 1951. He played five years for the Nationals before taking voluntary retirement. King returned to the NBA to play the 1957–1958 season with the

Cincinnati Royals (NBA) before officially retiring. He enjoyed two exceptional seasons with Syracuse. The Nationals reached the NBA Finals in 1954, but lost in seven games to George Mikan* and the Minneapolis Lakers (NBA). The following year, Syracuse captured its only NBA title by defeating the Fort Wayne Zollner Pistons in seven games. In the championship game, King netted a free throw in the final seconds and stole the ball to preserve a 92-91 decision.

In six NBA seasons, King scored 4,219 points, handed out 1,958 assists, and made 1,606 rebounds in 411 regularly scheduled games. In 39 NBA playoff games, King recorded 420 points, 149 rebounds, and 180 assists.

In 1958, King was named assistant basketball coach at West Virginia University. He worked under Fred Schaus and helped Jerry West* and the Mountaineers reach the 1959 NCAA championship game, before losing 71-70 to the University of California at Berkeley. King coached the West Virginia basketball program between 1960 and 1965 to a 102-43 win-loss record and took the Mountaineers to the NCAA tournament three times.

King was named head basketball coach at Purdue University following the 1965 season and served as the Boilermakers mentor through the 1971–1972 season. He compiled a 109-64 win-loss record and captured one BTC championship, two second places, and one third place. With Rick Mount* as leading scorer and King at the helm, Purdue advanced to the NCAA tournament for the first time in school history in 1969. The Boilermakers upset the University of North Carolina in the third round before losing to Lew Alcindor (Kareem Abdul-Jabbar*) and the UCLA Bruins in the championship game.

King served as Athletic Director at Purdue between 1971 and 1992. He chaired the NACDA, received the James J. Corbett Award for his devotion and work for the betterment of athletics, and was inducted into the Purdue Intercollegiate Athletic Hall of Fame in November 2001.

BIBLIOGRAPHY: Peter C. Bjarkman, *The Biographical History of Basketball* (Chicago, IL, 2000); Gary T. Brown, ed., *The Official NCAA Men's College Basketball Record Book* (Overland Park, KS, 1997); "George King," *Purdue Coach*, http://www.purdueexponent.com (2004); "George King," *Special Feature*, http://www.*msnsportsnet*.com (2004); "George King," *Statistics*, http://www.basketball reference.com (2004); Jan Hubbard, ed., *The Official NBA Encyclopedia*, 3rd ed. (New York, 2000); David S. Neft et al., *The Sports Encyclopedia: Pro Basketball*, 5th ed. (New York, 1992); Mark Rudner, Director, *Big 10 Men's Record Book* (1987–1988).

John L. Evers

KNIGHT, Robert Montgomery "Bobby" (b. October 25, 1940, Massillon, OH), college athlete and basketball coach, is the only child of Carroll "Pat" Knight, a railroad worker, and Hazel Knight. An excellent basketball player for the Orrville (Ohio) High School Red Raiders, Knight in his senior season was the third-leading scorer in the Central Buckeye Scholastic League with 18.0 points per game and was named to the All-League First Team. He earned 10 varsity letters in basketball, football, and baseball at Ohio State University and starred as sixth man on the Buckeyes' 1960 national championship basketball team, featuring Jerry Lucas*, Larry Siegfried, and John Havlicek*. During his three years as a varsity player at Columbus under coach Fred Taylor*, Ohio State won three consecutive BTCs titles. The six-foot two-inch Knight started occasionally on the 1961 and 1962 teams, which both finished second in the NCAA tournament.

On leaving Ohio State University, Knight served one season as an assistant basketball coach at Cuyahoga Falls (Ohio) High School. He volunteered for military induction with the understanding that he would be assigned to a $99-a-month position as assistant basketball coach under Taylor "Tates" Locke at the U.S. Military Academy. On Locke's resignation two years later, West Point officials surprised the basketball world by naming Knight the Academy's new head varsity basketball mentor. At age 24, Knight became not only the youngest West Point coach ever, but the youngest varsity coach in major college basketball history. In five years under his tutelage, Army teams finished 102-50, led the nation three consecutive times in team defense, twice finished second in that statistical category, and appeared in four NIT tournaments. Only Hank Iba* of Oklahoma State University had coached teams to three consecutive rankings as the nation's best defensive unit. In the tradition of Taylor and Locke, Knight built West Point teams that stressed well-disciplined, tightly controlled styles of play. On leaving West Point in 1971, he called the decision "the toughest in my life." Knight had dreamed of coaching in the BTC and an offer from Indiana University made that dream a reality. Mike Krzyzewski*, his best West Point player, became a successful coach at Duke University.

In 30 years as head coach of the Indiana University Hoosiers from 1972 to 2000, Knight became one of the most highly successful and controversial coaches in college basketball history. Yardsticks of his success include an undefeated (32-0) national championship team in 1976; a second national title in 1981; a third national crown in 1987; third-place NCAA tournament finishes in 1973 and 1992, Regional runner-up finishes in 1975, 1984, and 1993, numerous All-Americas and professional stars developed under his mentorship, such as Steve Alford*, Isiah Thomas*, Kent Benson*, Scotty May*, Bobby Wilkerson, Quinn Buckner, Mike Woodson, Calbert Cheaney*, and A. J. Guyton; selection as Pan American team coach (1979) and U.S. Olympic coach (1984); NIT and NCAA postseason national tournament titles; and BTC championships in 1973–1974, 1976, 1981, 1983, 1987, 1989, and 1993. Knight was selected as head coach at Indiana because of his strict defensive philosophy. During his first decade in the BTC, average scores dropped from 74.0 to 68.9 points and Knight revolutionized BTC play with his ball-control strategies.

With Knight's coaching successes also came controversy. Mild storms have surrounded an enigmatic coach, who has been labeled variously as an egomaniac, tunnel-visioned and self-centered, a superb disciplinarian, a leader and teacher of young men, and the greatest college coach in history. Knight has insisted on total dedication to a team concept from his players, a demand to which many pampered athletes of the modern era have not been able to adjust. His behavior on the sidelines often has been outrageous. Well-publicized incidents include his making an analogy between stress and rape in an NBC television interview in May 1988, taking Indiana players off the court after he had drawn a third technical foul and automatic ejection from an exhibition game with the Soviet Union in 1987, throwing a chair onto the playing floor in a 1985 contest against Purdue University, pulling Hoosier player Jim Wiseman off the court by his jersey before a full house in Assembly Hall in Bloomington, Indiana in 1976, and allegedly striking a Puerto Rican security guard during a 1979 Pan American team practice. Yet amid this controversy, Knight continued to produce championship teams. When Knight achieved his 300th college victory at age 39, he became the youngest college coach to accomplish that feat. In 2000, a three-year-old video was discovered showing him choking Neil Reed, a player, for over two seconds. Indiana University trustees suspended him and warned him that no further outbursts would be tolerated. He was fired on September 10, 2000 after roughly grabbing a student by the arm; Indiana president Myles Brand dismissed Knight for his "pattern of unacceptable behavior." Knight had compiled a career 661-240 record at the BTC school. In March 2001, Texas Technological University in Lubbock hired him to coach. Knight guided Texas Tech to a 23-9 mark in 2001–2002, a 22-13 mark in 2002–2003, a 23-17 mark in 2003–2004, and a 22-11 March in 2004–2005. In 39 seasons, he has compiled 854 wins, 333 losses, and a .719 winning percentage and ranks third in career victories. Sixteen of his assistant coaches became head college coaches. Knight produced an enviable win-loss record, but exhibited lack of self-control. In February 2004, Texas Tech reprimanded him for a verbal confrontation with chancellor David Smith. He was elected to the Naismith Memorial Basketball Hall of Fame in 1991. Knight and his former wife, Nancy, have two sons. Knight married Karen Veith Edgar on May 23, 1988.

BIBLIOGRAPHY: Steve Alford with John Garrity, *Playing for Knight: My Six Seasons with Coach Knight* (New York, 1989); Phil Berger, *Knight Fall* (New York, NY, 2000); Peter C. Bjarkman, *Big Ten Basketball* (Indianapolis, IN, 1994); Peter C. Bjarkman, *The Biographical History of Basketball* (Chicago, IL, 2000); Mike Douchant, *Encyclopedia of College Basketball* (Detroit, MI, 1995); John Feinstein,

A Season Inside (New York, 1988); John Feinstein, *A Season on the Brink: A Year with Bob Knight and the Indiana Hoosiers* (New York, 1986); Bob Hammel, et al., *Glory of Old IU* (Champaign, IL, 2000); Time Hosey and Bob Perceival, *Bobby Knight: Countdown to Perfection* (New York, 1983); Joan Mellen, *Bob Knight: His Own Man* (New York, 1988); Ronald L. Mendell, *Who's Who in Basketball* (New Rochelle, NY, 1973).

Peter C. Bjarkman

KRAUSE, Edward Walter "Moose" (b. February 2, 1913, Chicago, IL; December 10, 1992, South Bend, IN), college athlete, basketball coach, and administrator, was the son of Walter Krause and Theresa (Krauklis) Krause and began his varied athletic career as a three-sport star at Chicago's De La Salle High School. Krause moved on to the University of Notre Dame (Indiana), where he became a three-time college HAF All-American in both football (1931–1933) and basketball (1932–1934) and established one of the truly legendary athletic careers on the storied South Bend, Indiana campus. Although a starting tackle on the Fighting Irish football teams of 1931–1933, he competed in the first college All-Star Game against the Chicago Bears in 1934. Krause excelled even more in basketball. The Fighting Irish teams of Hall of Fame coach George Keogan* posted a three-season 54-12 record and brought a marked resurgence of Notre Dame basketball from the doldrums of the late 1920s. Krause, the most prolific Notre Dame scorer since the days of dirt floors, became the first player to average over 10 points since the early free throw shooting specialists. His dominance as a player was partly revealed by the establishment of the three-second offensive zone rule, which was conceived mainly to stop the bulky Notre Dame star. The true giant in his era stood six feet three inches and weighed 215 pounds. The consensus All-America center from 1932 to 1934 led the Irish to a 54-12 record. He also lettered in varsity track and field and played one year of varsity baseball at Notre Dame. Krause's personal popularity with classmates grew so much that he became the only Notre Dame student or athlete to be awarded a trophy spontaneously by his fellow undergraduates.

Krause's reputation as a college player ultimately was based on his amazing offensive performances in an era of low-scoring and ball-control play. He established the then single-game, season (10.1 points per game in 1933), and career scoring marks, amassing 547 points for a 8.8 points average in three seasons. Krause was selected team captain for the 1934 season, the year of his graduation. He became coach and athletic director at St. Mary's of Minnesota from 1934 to 1939 and rebuilt the sagging College of Holy Cross (Massachusetts) basketball program in the early 1940s. On returning to his alma mater, Krause served as head basketball coach in the post–World War II era (1946–1951) and then as athletic director for the next three decades. His basketball coaching record of 98 wins and 48 losses (.671 percentage) was impressive enough, but his coaching tenure was marked by tragedy, disappointment, and strange twists of fate. Krause probably would never have coached at Notre Dame except for some bizarre events. When ill health restricted the schedule of Keogan in 1942, his young assistant, Ray Meyer*, took over most of the coaching duties and was groomed as Keogan's heir apparent. But Meyer accepted an attractive coaching offer at DePaul University, where he built his own coaching legend during four subsequent decades. Keogan's untimely death in 1943 resulted in new assistant Krause taking the basketball helm as interim coach and being elevated to the permanent post three years later. Although Krause's early years as head basketball coach were sucessful enough when judged by his winning records alone, he devoted increasingly less time to the sport. Krause served as assistant football coach in 1946 and 1947, assistant athletic director in 1948, and as full-time athletic director beginning in 1949. In the late 1940s, Irish basketball fortunes continued to slide and the records leveled off to 15-9 and 13-11 in his final two years. He announced his retirement as active coach at the outset of his farewell season in 1950. Ironically, Krause's final dissension-filled year as Irish mentor came in the very season that an entire college basketball world was rocked to its very foundations by the now-infamous college betting scandals. If Krause enjoyed a somewhat less than spectacular college coaching career, his legend as player remained unblemished. Krause remained as athletic director until his retirement in 1980. He was elected to the Naismith Memorial Basketball Hall of Fame in 1975 as one of the game's first true offensive stars. Krause married Elizabeth Linden on August 27, 1938, and had three children, Edward, Mary, and Philip.

BIBLIOGRAPHY: Peter C. Bjarkman, *The Biographical History of Basketball* (Chicago, IL, 2000); Peter C. Bjarkman, *Hoopla: A Century of College Basketball, 1891–1996* (Indianapolis, IN, 1996); Mike Douchant, *Encyclopedia of College Basketball* (Detroit, MI, 1995); Zander Hollander, ed., *The Pro Basketball Encyclopedia* (Los Angeles, CA, 1977); Edward Krause file, Naismith Memorial Basketball Hall of Fame, Springfield, MA; Ronald L. Mendell, *Who's Who in Basketball* (New Rochelle, NY, 1973); Tim Neely, *Hooping It Up: The Complete History of Notre Dame Basketball* (Notre Dame, IN, 1985).

Peter C. Bjarkman

KRZYZEWSKI, Michael William "Mike" (b. February 13, 1947, Chicago, IL), college player and coach, attended Weber High School in Chicago, where he participated in basketball. His father, William Krzyzewski, worked as an elevator operator, while his mother, Emily Krzyzewski, cleaned offices at night to pay her son's tuition to Catholic schools. Krzyzewski earned a Bachelor's degree from the U.S. Military Academy and lettered from 1966–1967 through 1968–1969 in basketball. Under coach Bob Knight*, the Cadets advanced to the NIT semifinals Krzyzewski's senior season.

After being head basketball coach for service teams from 1969 to 1972, Krzyzewski served as head basketball coach at the U.S. Military Academy Prep School in Belvoir, Virginia from 1972 to 1974 and graduate assistant basketball coach in 1975–1976 under Knight at Indiana University (BTC). The U.S. Military Academy at West Point named him head basketball coach in 1976. Krzyzewski spent five years building the basketball program at his alma mater, directing the Cadets to a 73-59 win-loss record and two NIT berths. In 1977, he was selected NABC District II and NYBWA Coach of the Year.

Duke University (ACC) named Krzyzewski head basketball coach in 1981. He has led the Blue Devils to a 648-187 win-loss record in 25 seasons. His 648 triumphs set a record for coaching victories at Duke, ranking him ahead of Eddie Cameron (226) and Vic Bubas* (213). He has enjoyed twenty 20-win seasons since 1984, 13 consecutive NCAA Tournament appearances, 10 NCAA Final Four berths since 1986, and nine ACC Championships (1986, 1988, 1992, 1999–2004). Duke finished second in the 1986 and 1990 NCAA Championship Games, losing 72-69 to the University of Louisville and 103-73 to the University of Nevada at Las Vegas, respectively. Krzyzewski's 1986 Duke squad established an NCAA record by winning 37 games, and claimed titles in the Big Apple NIT, the ACC regular season, the ACC Tournament, and the NCAA East Regional. In 1991, 32-7 Duke captured its first NCAA title, upsetting Nevada–Las Vegas 79-77 in the semifinals and defeating the University of Kansas 72-65 in the finals. The Blue Devils retained the NCAA title in 1992 by defeating the University of Michigan 71-51 and lost to the University of Arkansas 76-72 in the 1994 NCAA championship game. Duke finished first in the final AP poll from 1999 through 2003, losing to the University of Connecticut 77-74, in the 1999 NCAA championship game and winning the NCAA title in 2001 with an 82-72 triumph over the University of Arizona. The Blue Devils reached the NCAA semifinals in 2004 before being edged 79-78, by the University of Connecticut. National Player of the Year awards went to Duke's Johnny Dawkins* in 1986, Danny Ferry* in 1989, Christian Laettner* in 1992, Elton Brand* in 1999, Shane Battier* in 2001, and Jason Williams* in 2002. In 1987, Tommy Amaker received national Defensive Player of the Year honors. Christian Laetner was named NCAA tournament MVP in 1991. Bobby Hurley and Shane Battier followed suit in 1992 and 2001, respectively. Krzyzewski's accolades include NABC District V Coach of the Year in 1984; ACC Coach of the Year in 1984, 1986, and 1987; UPI National Coach of the Year in 1986; Naismith* National Coach of the Year in 1989, 1992, and 1999; and NABC Co-coach of the Year in 1999. His career record includes 721 wins and 247 losses in 30 seasons. He has compiled a 66-18 record in NCAA tournaments, three NCAA titles, and most victories in tournament history, being renowned for his success in recruiting, teaching, and training future pro stars.

Krzyzewski, who has been involved with basketball on the international level, served as assistant coach for the U.S. team during the 1979 Pan American Games, the 1984 U.S. Olympic Trials, and the 1984 Los Angeles Summer Olympic Games. Head coaching assignments have included the 1983 National Sports Festival, the 1987 World University Games, the 1990 Goodwill Games, and the 1990 World Championships. He served as assistant coach of the U.S. Olympic team in 1992, and was selected to the Naismith Memorial Basketball Hall of Fame in 2003. He was also inducted into the Polish-American Hall of Fame. In July 2004, he declined a $40 million, five-year offer to coach the Los Angeles Lakers (NBA). He married Carol Mickie Marsh in 1969 and has three daughters, Debbie, Lindy, and Jamie.

BIBLIOGRAPHY: Bill Brill, *Duke Basketball: An Illustrated History* (Dallas, TX, 1986); Bill Brill with Mike Krzyzewski, *A Season Is a Lifetime* (New York, 1993); Mike Cragg with Mike Sobb, *Back to Back* (Durham, NC, 1992); Mike Cragg with Mike Sobb, *Crowning Glory* (Durham, NC, 1991); Gregg Doyel, *Building the Duke Dynasty* (Addax Publishing Group, 1999); *Duke 2004–2005 Basketball Media Guide* (Durham, NC, 2004); Mike Krzyzewski with Donald T. Phillips, *Five Point Play* (New York, 2001); Mike Krzyzewski with Donald T. Phillips, *Leading with the Heart* (New York, 2000); *NCAA Official 1991 Basketball Records* (Overland Park, KS, 1991); *TSN 2004–2005 College Basketball Yearbook* (St. Louis, MO, 2004).

John L. Evers

KUNDLA, John Albert "Johnny" "Ace of the Thirties" (b. July 3, 1916, Star Junction, PA), college and professional player and coach, moved to Minneapolis, Minnesota at an early age and played basketball on neighborhood teams. At Minneapolis Central High School, he starred in baseball and basketball. In 1935, the senior forward was named an All-City cager. The six-foot two-inch, 180-pound Kundla attended the University of Minnesota from 1935 to 1939, graduating with a Bachelor of Science degree in education. He played three seasons as a Gophers forward and started in 55 out of 60 games, averaging 9.4 points. Kundla also led the Gophers to the 1937 BTC Championship and captained the squad in 1939. Known for his two-handed underhand shot, he was awarded the BTC medal for combined scholastic and athletic efficiency. At the University of Minnesota, Kundla also played first base for the Gophers baseball team. He spent one year after graduation playing pro baseball for Paducah, Kentucky (KL), a Brooklyn Dodgers (NL) farm club.

Kundla returned to Minnesota in 1940 to serve as basketball coach for Ascension Grade School in Minneapolis and as assistant coach for the Gophers basketball team. He married Marie Fritz in 1941 and has six children, Kathy, Karen, David, Jim, Tom, and Jack. In 1943 Kundla became basketball, football, and baseball coach for De La Salle High School in Minneapolis. After a brief tour in the U.S. Navy at the end of World War II, he became basketball coach for the College of St. Thomas in St. Paul, Minnesota and resumed his assistant coaching duties at the University of Minnesota. In 1946, he received a Master's degree in education from the University of Minnesota.

Kundla won greatest acclaim as coach of the Minneapolis Lakers (NBL, 1947–1949 and NBA, 1949–1959). The Lakers captured five world championships (1949–1950, 1952–1954) and six Western Division championships (1948, 1950, 1951, 1953–1954, 1957), compiling a win-loss record of 423-302 in the regular season and 60-35 in playoffs. Often described as scholarly and reserved, he stressed defense and discipline. His star players included George Mikan*, Jim Pollard*, Vern Mikkelsen*, Slater Martin*, and Herm Schaffer.

In 1959, Kundla became head basketball coach for the University of Minnesota after the Lakers' NBA franchise was moved to Los Angeles. His coaching record there stood at 121 wins and 116 losses. Kundla coached the U.S. basketball team to the championship of the World University Games in 1965 and also was assistant coach for the U.S. basketball squad in the 1967 Pan American Games. In 1968, Kundla joined the University of Minnesota's athletic department to teach basketball, tennis, and racquetball. He also occasionally scouted for the Philadelphia 76ers (NBA). Kundla retired from

Minnesota in 1981 to write a book for coaches on basketball fundamentals. He was elected to the Naismith Memorial Basketball Hall of Fame in 1995 and selected one of the Top Ten Coaches in NBA History in 1996.

BIBLIOGRAPHY: Jack Clary, *Basketball's Greatest Dynasties: The Lakers* (New York, 1992); Dick Gordon, "John Kundla Grew Up to His Feet," *Minneapolis Tribune*, December 30, 1962, p. 1; Jan Hubbard, ed., *The Official NBA Encyclopedia*, 3rd ed. (New York, 2000); Gary Johnston, "Johnny Kundla: He'll Retire with Memories of Coaching Lakers and U of M Gophers in Basketball Glory Days," *Brooklyn Center Post*, July 2, 1981, p. 1; Neil D. Isaacs, *Vintage NBA* (Silver Spring, MD, 1996); John Kundla file, Naismith Memorial Basketball Hall of Fame, Springfield, MA; "Kundla Out as Coach: No Cage Successor Yet," *Minnesota Daily*, April 10, 1968, p. 1; Ronald L. Mendell, *Who's Who in Basketball* (New Rochelle, NY, 1973); "Pillsbury House Gave Kundla His Start," *Minneapolis Star*, October 4, 1957, p. 14; Don Riley, "The Coach: When You Think of John Kundla, You Think of a Winner," *St. Paul Pioneer Press*, August 23, 1981, p. 1; Don Riley, "Kundla Named University Coach on Four-Year Contract," *St. Paul Pioneer Press*, April 10, 1959, p. 30; Jim Ryan, "Ex-Gopher Coach Enjoys Teaching," *Minnesota Daily*, August 11, 1980, p. 8; Ken Shouler et al., *Total Basketball* (Wilmington, DE, 2003); Stew Thornley, *Basketball's Original Dynasty: The History of the Lakers* (Minneapolis, MN, 1989); *TSN Official NBA Register, 2004–2005* (St. Louis, MO, 2004); Jay Weiner, "That Last Championship Season," *Minneapolis Tribune*, June 1, 1986, p. 4C.

Mary Lou Gust

KURLAND, Robert Albert "Foothills" "Bob" (b. December 23, 1924, St. Louis, MO), college player, sprouted to six-feet six-inches tall by age 13. He attended Jennings High School in metropolitan St. Louis, Missouri earning three letters in basketball and two in track and field. After graduating from Oklahoma Agricultural and Mechanical (A&M) University with a Bachelor of Science degree in secondary education and as a three-time All-America, Kurland played six years of AAU basketball for the Phillips 66ers and developed into a top-flight executive. He and his wife, Barbara, have four children, R. Alexander, Ross Alan, Dana Marie, and Barbara Ann.

Kurland did not participate in organized sports until high school because his parents feared that their oversized, uncoordinated son would injure the other boys. Consequently the redhead spent his spare time fishing on the banks of the Mississippi River and hunting game in the countryside. Although winning the State "B" Class high jump championship in 1942 and leading his basketball team to two state tournaments, the gangly youth still lacked complete coordination. Walter Rulon, his coach, persuaded Oklahoma A&M University coach Henry Iba* of Kurland's vast potential. Iba worked patiently with Kurland, whose size prohibited him from serving in the armed forces, as the big redhead missed the rim and backboard with his first 200 hook shots. As a freshman, "Foothills" played sparingly and perfected goaltending in practice by batting the ball off the rim and away from the basket.

With increased playing time his sophomore year, Kurland provoked controversy by goaltending. Bruce Drake*, coach of archrival University of Oklahoma, stationed an NCAA official on a platform over the basket during the 1944 Aggies-Sooners game in Norman, Oklahoma. Drake's team lost the game, but influenced a rule change to prevent Kurland's favorite defensive play. The rule change forced Kurland to develop more mobility and skill as an all-around player, helping the Aggies win consecutive NCAA championships in 1946 and 1947. Although normally a defensive player within Iba's deliberate style of play, he concluded his college career by scoring 58 points. St. Louis University All-American "Easy" Ed Macauley* guarded him in that game.

Rejecting lucrative offers of as much as $15,000 to play in the relatively new NBL, Kurland chose the unique executive training program for former athletes at a growing company in nearby Bartlesville, Oklahoma. During six seasons for the Phillips 66ers, he led his "Oilers" to three AAU championships and an incredible 369-26 overall record. Kurland in 1948 and 1952 became the first American to play on two Olympic basketball championship teams. His awards included a national scoring championship, a HAF MVP award in 1946, a Naismith Memorial Basketball Hall of Fame induction in

1961, and All-America AAU selection six times. His AAU career featured a 12-point average during the nearly 60-game seasons. One highlight occurred in the 1948 Olympic playoff finale when Phillips defeated NCAA champion University of Kentucky. Kurland paced the 53-49 victory with 20 points while holding Wildcats All-American Alex Groza* to four points. Kurland managed special product sales in the marketing division of Phillips Petroleum products group.

BIBLIOGRAPHY: John Paul Bischoff, *Mr. Iba: Basketball's Aggie Iron Duke* (Oklahoma Heritage Association, 1980); Peter C. Bjarkman, *Hoopla: A Century of College Basketball, 1896–1996* (Indianapolis, IN, 1996); "Bob Kurland," *Sports Review* (1953); Morgan C. Brenner, *College Basketball's National Championships* (Lanham, MD, 1999); Doris Dellinger, *A History of the Oklahoma State University Athletics* (Stillwater, OK, 1987); Mike Douchant, *Encyclopedia of College Basketball* (Detroit, MI, 1995); Bruce Drake, "Seven-Foot Trouble: Should the Rules Be Changed to Give the Small Man a Chance," *SEP* 216 (February 19, 1944), pp. 16–17ff.; Zander Hollander, ed., *The Modern Encyclopedia of Basketball* (Garden City, NY, 1979); Harold Keith, "Bruce Drake and the Goal-Tending War," *Sooner Magazine* (Winter 1984), pp. 13–19; Bob Kurland file, Naismith Memorial Basketball Hall of Fame, Springfield, MA; Michael McKenzie, *Oklahoma State University: History Making Basketball* (Wadsworth Publishing Company, 1992); Billy Packer and Roland Lazenby, *College Basketball's 25 Greatest Teams* (St. Louis, MO, 1989); Sandy Padwe, *Basketball's Hall of Fame* (Englewood Cliffs, NJ, 1970).

Gregory S. Sojka

L

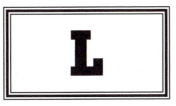

LAETTNER, Christian Donald (b. August 17, 1969, Buffalo, NY), college and professional player, is the son of George Laettner, a newspaper printer, and Bonnie Laettner, a schoolteacher, and was selected a High School All-America at Nichols Academy in Buffalo, New York, from where he graduated in 1988.

Laettner matriculated at Duke University (North Carolina, ACC), leading the Blue Devils to the 1991 and 1992 NCAA Championships and becoming one of the most celebrated college players ever. Under the tutelage of head coach Mike Krzyzewski*, the six-foot eleven-inch, 230-pound forward-center was named Second Team All-ACC in 1990 and First-Team All-ACC in 1991 and 1992. His honors included being voted ACC Player of the Year in 1992 and winning the McKelvin Award as the ACC's top athlete in 1991 and 1992. Laettner, named Second Team AP All-America in 1991, made every All-America First Team in 1992 and captured every major Player of the Year honor, including the Wooden* Award, Naismith* Award, Eastman Award, and Rupp* Award. He led Duke in rebounding in 1990, 1991, and 1992 and in scoring in 1991 and 1992. Laettner ended his college career with 2,460 points, 1,149 rebounds, a .574 field goal percentage, and an .806 free throw percentage. Duke retired his number 32. Laettner, who played on both the 1990 U.S. National Team and the 1991 U.S. Pan-American team, was the only collegian selected to participate on the gold medal–winning 1992 U.S. Olympic team at the Barcelona, Spain Summer Games.

Laettner enjoyed exceptional success in the NCAA tournament and started in every Final Four from 1989 through 1992, becoming the first player to start in four Final Fours. His 407 points set an NCAA tournament career scoring record. He was named to the All-Eastern Regional team in 1989, 1990, and 1992 and the All-Midwest Regional squad in 1991. His last-second baskets gave Duke one-point victories in the 1990 and 1992 Eastern Regional finals, with Laettner being voted Eastern Regional MVP in both of those seasons. He was selected to the NCAA All-Final Four team in 1990, 1991, and 1992, earning Final Four MVP honors in 1991. Laettner's two free throws gave Duke a 79-77 victory over defending national champion University of Nevada at Las Vegas in the 1991 Final Four. He led all scorers in the 1991 and 1992 national title games.

Laettner's aggressiveness made him a controversial player. Some applauded his intensity and desire to win, while others criticized him as immature. The matinee idol received attention from various non-sports media outlets.

The Minnesota Timberwolves (NBA) made Laettner the number-three pick in the 1992 NBA draft. Laettner immediately starred in Minnesota, scoring 1,472 points for an average of 18.2 points, snaring 708 rebounds for an average of 8.7 rebounds, and making the NBA All-Rookie First Team in 1992–1993. In 1993–1994, he led the Timberwolves in scoring with 1,173 points (16.8 points average) and 602 rebounds. He played with Minnesota until traded to the Atlanta Hawks (NBA) in February 1996. Laettner performed with the Atlanta Hawks in 1996–1997 and 1997–1998, the Detroit Pistons

(NBA) in 1998–1999 and 1999–2000, and split the 2000–2001 season between the Dallas Mavericks (NBA) and Washington Wizards (NBA). He played for the Washington Wizards from February 2001 through June 2004, when the Dallas Mavericks (NBA) reacquired him in a trade. The Golden State Warriors (NBA) secured Laettner in an August 2004 trade but waived him the next month. In September 2004 the Miami Heat (NBA) signed him to a one-year contract. Altogether, he has tallied 11,121 points (12.8 average) and grabbed 5,805 rebounds (6.7 average) in 868 regular season games and 10.5 points and 4.7 rebounds in 45 playoff games. He played in the 1997 All-Star Game and also continued to generate as much publicity for his personality as for his basketball abilities. The Ponte Vedra Beach, Florida resident has experienced back problems and violated the NBA's substance abuse policy.

BIBLIOGRAPHY: Peter C. Bjarkman, *ACC-Atlantic Coast Conference Basketball* (Indianapolis, IN, 1996); Bill Brill with Mike Krzyzewski, *A Season Is a Lifetime* (New York, 1993); Mike Cragg and Mike Sobb, *Back to Back: The Story of Duke's 1992 NCAA Basketball Championship* (Durham, NC, 1992); Mike Cragg and Mike Sobb, *Crowning Glory: The Story of Duke's 1991 Championship Season* (Durham, NC, 1991); Mike Douchant, *Encyclopedia of College Basketball* (Detroit, MI, 1995); Curry Kirkpatrick, "Devilishly Different," *SI* 75 (November 25, 1991), pp. 62–73; Christian Laettner files, Duke Sports Information Department, Duke University, Durham, NC; Ken Shouler et al., *Total Basketball* (Wilmington, DE, 2003); *TSN Official Basketball Register, 2004–2005* (St. Louis, MO, 2004); Alexander Wolff, "The Man Couldn't Miss," *SI* 76 (April 6, 1992), pp. 16–17; Alexander Wolff, "The Shot Heard Round the World," *SI* 77 (December 28, 1992), pp. 32–42.

Jim L. Sumner

LAIMBEER, William J., Jr. "Bill" (b. May 19, 1957, Boston, MA), college and professional player, sportscaster, and coach, is the son of William Laimbeer Sr., a technical writer, and graduated from high school in Palos Verdes, California and in 1979 from the University of Notre Dame (Indiana) with a Bachelor's degree in economics. Laimbeer also attended Owens Technical JC in Ohio in 1976–1977 and played basketball three years at Notre Dame, averaging 7.4 points and 6.3 rebounds. He married his wife, Chris, in 1979 and has two children, Eric William and Keriann.

Laimbeer played for Brescia (ItL) in 1979–1980 and was drafted in the third round as the 65th pick overall by the Cleveland Cavaliers (NBA) in 1979. Cleveland traded him to the Detroit Pistons (NBA) in February 1982. Laimbeer, a center, could not jump and was not as athletic as opposing players, but was willing to do whatever it took to win and had "court savvy." An iron man, he engaged in bumping, grinding, screening, preening, fouling, and brawling, "I was the enforcement section," Laimbeer observed. He made most of his points on soft push shots from the perimeter. His rough, aggressive play made him one of the most reviled players in the NBA and the poster boy for the legendary Piston "Bad Boys." Players fouled him flagrantly, costing him a fractured cheekbone in October 1990. Laimbeer returned within days and played with a plastic mask. He missed only eight NBA games, including two for fighting, in 14 years. He came through when he was needed most. His can-do spirit proved instrumental in bringing Detroit its first two NBA titles in franchise history in 1989 and 1990. He retired in December 1993. During his 14-year NBA career, the six-foot eleven-inch, 245-pound Laimbeer tallied 13,790 points, averaged 12.9 points, made 83.7 percent of his free throws, and gathered a franchise record 9,430 rebounds in 1,068 games. He led the NBA in rebounds (1,075) in 1985–1986 and made the NBA All-Star team four times.

Laimbeer became President and CEO of Laimbeer Packaging, a corrugated box company. In 2002 he was hired as a WKBD television color commentator for the Detroit Pistons games and became consultant and head coach of the Detroit Shock (WNBA), compiling a 9-13 record in 2002 and a 25-9 record in 2003. Detroit won the WNBA championship in 2003, defeating the Los Angeles Sparks, two games to one in the WNBA Finals. Detroit finished 17-17 in 2004 and was eliminated by New York in the first round of the WNBA playoffs. His jersey was retired by the Pistons.

BIBLIOGRAPHY: *Detroit Free Press*, April 6, 2003, p. 12D; *Detroit News*, April 29, 1990, p. E4;

Detroit News, May 2, 1990, p. C4; *Detroit News*, May 25, 1990, p. D1; *Detroit News*, June 8, 1990, p. D7; *Detroit News*, October 30, 1990, p. D2; *Detroit News*, December 24, 1990, p. D3; Jerry Green, *The Detroit Pistons: Capturing a Remarkable Era* (Chicago, IL, 1991); Armen Keteyian et al., *Money Players: Days and Nights Inside the New NBA* (New York, 1997); Roland Lazenby, *The Detroit Pistons 1988–89* (Dallas, TX, 1988); Ken Shouler et al., *Total Basketball* (Wilmington, DE, 2003), *TSN Official NBA Register, 2004–2005* (St. Louis, MO, 2004); *TSN Official WNBA Guide and Register, 2004* (St. Louis, MO, 2004).

Keith McClellan

LAMAR, Dwight "Bo" (b. April 7, 1951, Columbus, OH), college and professional player, was brought up by his mother, Lucy Lamar, and learned his hoop fundamentals at the 11th Avenue Recreation Center in Columbus, Ohio. Lamar's father died when Dwight was only five years old. Lamar led the Columbus North High School basketball squad in scoring as a sophomore and the city in total points as a junior. The Lamars moved the following year, when he averaged 18 points for Columbus East High School. Lamar teamed with Ed Ratleff and Nick Conner, leading Columbus East to the 1969 state championship with a 25-0 win-loss record. Ratleff later was selected a two-time All-America at Long Beach (California) State University, while Conner started at center for the University of Illinois.

At Southwestern Louisiana University, Lamar became the first basketball player to win both the NCAA Division II and Division I scoring crowns. Southwestern Louisiana performed at the NCAA Division II level in 1969–1970 and 1970–1971, as Lamar recorded 1,044 points in 29 games and averaged 36.0 points in his second season. In 1971–1972, the Ragin' Cajuns joined the Division I ranks. Lamar scored a school record 1,054 points in 29 games and averaged 36.3 points that season. Under coach Beryl Shipley, the six-foot one-inch, 180-pound guard scored a career high and school record 62 points in 1971 against Northeast Louisiana University. Lamar tallied 3,493 career points in 112 games and averaged 31.2 points—both school marks. Lamar and Ratleff made consensus All-America in 1972 and 1973. The Ragin' Cajuns placed third in the NCAA Division II National Tournament in 1971 and appeared in the NCAA Division I Tournament in 1972 and 1973, although the NCAA voided their participation on both levels.

Lamar performed with the 1973–1974 San Diego Sails (ABA), scoring 1,713 points, averaging 20.4 points, and making the ABA All-Rookie Team. The following season saw him finish ninth in ABA scoring (1,606) and sixth in assists (427). A hand injury limited him to only 41 appearances in 1975–1976, as he split the season with the Sails and Indiana Pacers (ABA). Lamar tallied 3,976 points and averaged 19.9 points in 202 regular-season ABA games and recorded 165 points in six playoff games. His professional career ended the following season with the Los Angeles Lakers (NBA). Lamar scored 502 points in 71 regular season games and 33 points in 10 playoff contests. Lamar aspired to coach junior high school basketball and develop a summer club for boys. He and his wife, Peggy, have two children, Stephanie and Starr.

BIBLIOGRAPHY: Mike Douchant, *Encyclopedia of College Basketball* (Detroit, MI, 1995); Dwight Lamar file, Naismith Memorial Basketball Hall of Fame, Springfield, MA; Ronald L. Mendell, *Who's Who in Basketball* (New Rochelle, NY, 1973); *Official NCAA 1995 Basketball Records* (Overland Park, KS, 1995); Jan Hubbard, ed., *The Official NBA Encyclopedia*, 3rd ed. (New York, 2000); Terry Pluto, *Loose Balls: The Short, Wild Life of the American Basketball Association* (New York, 1990); William F. Reed, "Good Times Come to Cajun Country," *SI* 25 (December 20, 1971), pp. 20–21; *Southwestern Louisiana University Basketball Media Guide 1980–1981* (Lafayette, LA, 1980).

John L. Evers and Wayne Patterson

LAMBERT, Ward Lewis "Piggy" (b. May 28, 1888, Deadwood, SD; d. January 20, 1958, Lafayette, IN), college athlete and coach and professional basketball executive, was the son of Clay Lambert and grew up in Crawfordsville, Indiana. Lambert, whose nickname came from the pigtails that hung down from his sock cap, attended his town's Wabash College. Despite his five-foot six-inch, 114-pound frame, he led the Wabash basketball team in scoring as a sophomore forward. The next year, Lambert continued intercollegiate basketball competition and coached the Wabash High School team. In his senior year, he coached his own team. Lambert also played football and baseball at Wabash. After graduation in 1911, he secured a scholarship and entered the graduate school chemistry program at the University of Minnesota. Within one year, however, Lambert abandoned plans for a science career and accepted a basketball coaching position at Lebanon (Indiana) High School. After four years of producing excellent basketball squads there, he was hired in 1916 to coach Purdue University's (Indiana) basketball and baseball teams and serve as backfield coach in football. During World War I, Lambert enlisted in the U.S. Army and reached the rank of lieutenant in Field Artillery.

Lambert resumed his basketball coaching duties at Purdue University in 1919 and retained them until early 1946. During his career, he compiled an unparalleled WC-BTC record of 228 wins and only 105 losses and captured 11 outright or shared WC-BTC titles. Lambert's total victories surpassed his leading rival, Walter "Doc" Meanwell* of the University of Wisconsin. Overall, his Boilermakers teams won 371 times and suffered just 152 defeats, a remarkable .710 winning percentage. His 1932 Purdue basketball team won the national championship. Only three of his Purdue squads experienced losing seasons. Lambert possessed the extraordinary ability to take players with average ability and transform them into fundamentally sound performers. Lafayette Jefferson, for example, was not recruited by any other college, but Lambert helped him to set a WC scoring record and become an All-American. Lambert ultimately directed nine All-Americas, including Don White, Candy Miller, Norm Cotton, Bob Kessler, George Spradling, Jewell Young*, and Fred Beretta, and 19 All-WC players.

Lambert played a major role in reviving Purdue University basketball fortunes and in boosting the WC-BTC to a high level of respectability. Much of Lambert's success can be traced to his innovative style of play and his ability to recruit suitable players to execute his strategy. Although most teams used pattern offenses such as Doc Carlson's* figure-8, he initiated the fast break when the ball changed hands. This system depended on three essential elements, which took years to develop. Lambert required a tall center who could rebound the missed shots of opponents and fire the ball to streaking teammates; the guards or forwards, who received the ball, needed to be adept ball-handlers; and the perimeter players had to play aggressive, ball-hawking defense that would deny their opponents unguarded shots at the basket. Lambert found the right players in six-foot seven-inch Charles "Stretch" Murphy* and John Wooden*, who was described by his coach as a "physical marvel." But size alone did not constitute the basis for his brand of basketball. His 1934 team contained no starter over six feet tall, but became the highest-scoring squad in WC history and won the WC championship. Lambert looked for an agile mind that would react quickly to the situation. "Basketball is a mental game," he often said. "Since only 30 percent of all situations can be anticipated in basketball, you have to be mentally ready for nearly anything." Besides mental alertness, he valued aggressiveness.

As a bench coach, Lambert nervously paced the sidelines. He shouted, clapped his hands, jumped up and down, and followed the play by racing down the floor. Occasionally Lambert rushed over to the referee to inform him of what he saw as an erroneous call, which prompted one official to remark that "the little guy over there has never been wrong on a basketball floor in his life." He influenced college basketball in other ways besides his team's "run-run-run" offense. Lambert wrote a popular textbook, *Practical Basketball*, one of the early "Bibles" of the sport, and contributed articles to leading magazines, such as *Time*, *Basketball Illustrated*, *Collier's*, and *Esquire*. In addition, he conducted coaching clinics throughout the nation. Many of his players became high school and college coaches.

In 1946, Lambert ended his head coaching career because of ill health and became commissioner of the pro NBL. He was succeeded as coach by former player Mel Taube. Three years later, Lambert returned to Purdue University with his wife, Grayce, and coached freshman basketball and baseball. Lambert, who had no children, was elected to the Naismith Memorial Basketball Hall of Fame in 1960.

BIBLIOGRAPHY: Peter C. Bjarkman, *Big Ten Basketball* (Indianapolis, IN, 1994); Mike Douchant, *Encyclopedia of College Basketball* (Detroit, MI, 1995); Zander Hollander, ed., *The Modern Encyclopedia of Basketball* (Garden City, NY, 1979); *Indianapolis News*, January 20, 1958; *Indianapolis Star*, January 21, 1958; Neil D. Isaacs, *All the Moves: A History of College Basketball* (Philadelphia, PA, 1975); *Lafayette Journal and Courier*, January 20, 1958; *Lafayette Journal and Courier* Staff, ed., *Most Memorable Moments in Purdue Basketball History* (Champaign, IL, 1998); Ward L. Lambert, *Practical Basketball* (Chicago, IL, 1932); Ward Lambert file, Naismith Memorial Basketball Hall of Fame, Springfield, MA; Purdue University news releases, West Lafayette, IN, 1946, January 1958; *Sport Scene Magazine* (February 1983), pp. 6–8; Alexander M. Weyand, *The Cavalcade of Basketball* (Garden City, NY, 1979).

Bruce J. Dierenfield

LANDERS, Andrew "Andy" (b. October 8, 1952, Maryville, TN), college coach, attended Friendsville High School in Tennessee and enjoyed playing all team sports as a teenager. Home was constant physical activity, as Landers had five brothers and sisters. He studied at Tennessee Tech University as both undergraduate and graduate, earning Bachelors and Masters degrees in physical education in 1974 and 1975.

Landers began his basketball coaching career at Roane (Tennessee) from 1975 to 1979, but his stellar coaching reputation was built around his extraordinary tenure at the University of Georgia since 1979. In 2004, completed a quarter century of coaching the Lady Bulldogs and has produced premier teams throughout his career with a 634-199 record.

Landers was named National Coach of the Year in 1986, 1987, 1996, and 2000 and SEC Coach of the Year in 1984, 1991, and 1996, making consistency among his hallmarks. He compiled twenty 20-win seasons, fourteen 25-victory seasons, and three 30-win seasons at Georgia, qualifying for 21 NCAA tournaments and reaching the NCAA Final Four in 1983, 1985, 1995, 1996, and 1999. Landers coached the Bulldogs to SEC titles in 1983, 1984, 1986, 1991, 1996, 1997, and 2000 and SEC tournament titles in 1983, 1984, 1986, and 2001.

As head coach, Landers has taken special pride in developing talent. The Bulldogs have produced 11 Kodak All-Americas and two U.S. Olympians, who have earned a combined six gold medals. His most notable feat may have been grooming college stars for professional basketball. During 2002, 10 former University of Georgia players appeared on WNBA rosters. Landers' 24.4 wins average during his 26 seasons with the Bulldogs rank him second among active coaches with comparable service.

Two former-Bulldog WNBA players have commented on Landers' rare ability as a life educator rather than just being a college coach. Lady Hardmon, formerly of the Sacramento Monarchs (WNBA), has said, "Coach Landers taught me to relate life to basketball. When Coach Landers compared life to basketball, it always made me stop and think. It still does." Former Monarchs teammate La'Keshia Frett observed, "He [Landers] taught me the importance of wanting to do everything the right way—both on and off the basketball court. I rely on that every day."

When the Lady Bulldogs dedicated a new expensive locker room in October 2001, Landers' imprimatur was unmistakable. The facility was filled with alumnae photographs showing the Lady Bulldogs and their family entourages.

Landers married Pam McClellan on June 20, 1981 and has two sons, Andrew Lauren and Andrew Joseph. He was named Naismith Coach of the Year in 1996 and has contributed to manuals, including *Defensive Basketball Drills*.

BIBLIOGRAPHY: Lauren Rippy, Eastern Illinois University, research graduate student, material collected June 12, 2003; http://georgiadogs.oscn.com/sports/w-baskbl/mtt/landersandyyoo.html.

Scott A.G.M. Crawford

LANIER, Robert Jerry, Jr. "Bob" (b. September 10, 1948, Buffalo, NY), college and professional player, coach, and executive, is the son of Robert Jerry Lanier and Nannette (Naarford) Lanier and lived in one of Buffalo, New York's poorest neighborhood. Lanier made All-America twice at St. Bonaventure University (New York) and starred 14 seasons in the NBA. Although not making his Bennett High School basketball team until his junior year, he led the

St. Bonaventure University basketball team to the NCAA semifinals in 1970. During his three-year college career, Lanier set St. Bonaventure's single-game scoring records with 51- and 50-point games, made 2,067 career points for a 27.5 points average, and grabbed 1,180 rebounds for a 15.7 rebounds average.

The six-foot eleven-inch, 265-pound Lanier, who wore size 19 sneakers, led the Bonnies his senior year to a 25-1 record. His club lost only a two-point squeaker to Villanova University (Pennsylvania) and captured the Holiday Festival Tournament in New York City by whipping Purdue University (Indiana) in the championship finale. He outscored Purdue marksman Rick Mount* by making 50 points and hitting an incredible 18 of 22 shots. In the NCAA regionals, the Bonnies defeated Davidson University (North Carolina) 80-72, behind his 28 points. Lanier scored 18 points to help the Bonnies triumph over Villanova University 97-74 in the regional final to avenge their only loss, but tore ligaments in his knee when Villanova's Chris Ford fell across his leg. St. Bonaventure did not fare well without Lanier in the NCAA semifinal round. Despite a game and gritty performance, the underdog Bonnies bowed 91-83, to the tall, talented Jacksonville University (Florida) Dolphins. He earned a Bachelor of Arts degree in business administration in 1970.

The Detroit Pistons (NBA) drafted Lanier first in 1970. Lanier promptly made the NBA All-Rookie team, which featured luminaries Dave Cowens*, Pete Maravich*, and Calvin Murphy*. He played for Detroit until February 4, 1980, when the Milwaukee Bucks (NBA) acquired him in a trade for Kent Benson*. In 13 seasons, Lanier made the NBA All-Star team eight times. He edged Spencer Haywood* for the game MVP in 1974, scoring 12 of his 24 points in the final quarter to lead the West to a 134-123 victory over the East. The Pistons retired his uniform number 16.

Despite seven knee operations, Lanier completed 14 years in the NBA before retiring after the 1983–1984 season. In 959 games, he scored 19,248 points (20.1 points average) to rank thirty-fourth on the all-time NBA list, made 9,698 rebounds, and played over 32,000 career minutes. Lanier was the Detroit Pistons' all-time leading scorer; ranked second in club assists, steals, and free throws; and held career, season, and game club rebounding records. He was given the Walter Kennedy Citizenship Award in 1978 by the PBWAA. Lanier chaired the NBA Stay in School Program from 1989 to 1994 and joined the Golden State Warriors (NBA) as assistant coach in 1994. He replaced Don Nelson* as head coach in February 1995, guiding Golden State to a 12-25 record. Since 1996, Lanier has served as Special Assistant to the NBA Commissioner and chaired the NBA Team-Up Program. He was elected to the Naismith Memorial Basketball Hall of Fame in 1992. He also founded Bob Lanier Enterprises in 1996 and serves as its president. Lanier lived with his wife, Shirley, and their four children, in Mequon, Wisconsin before their divorce in the 1980s. He resides in Scottsdale, Arizona, with his wife, Rose, and their four children.

BIBLIOGRAPHY: *Detroit Free Press*, 1973–1983; Jan Hubbard, ed., *The Official NBA Encyclopedia*, 3rd ed. (New York, 2000); Robert Lanier file, Naismith Memorial Basketball Hall of Fame, Springfield, MA; Ronald L. Mendell, *Who's Who in Basketball* (New Rochelle, NY, 1973); *Milwaukee Bucks, 1983–1984 Media Guide* (Milwaukee, WI, 1983); *St. Bonaventure University Basketball, 1982–1983* (St. Bonaventure, NY, 1982); Ken Shouler et al., *Total Basketball* (Wilmington, DE, 2003); Robert Stern, *They Were Number One: A History of the NCAA Basketball Tournament* (New York, 1983); *TSN Official NBA Register, 2004–2005* (St. Louis, MO, 2004).

Lawrence E. Ziewacz

LAPCHICK, Joseph Bohomiel "Joe" (b. April 12, 1900, Yonkers, NY; d. August 10, 1970, New York, NY), professional player and college and pro basketball coach, was born of immigrant parents, Joseph Lapchick and Frances (Kassik) Lapchick. Lapchick, whose father was a policeman, resided most of his life in the New York City area. At age 12, he began playing basketball for the Trinity Church Midgets. A high school education was not possible because Lapchick needed to contribute to his family's income. He worked as an apprentice machinist earning $15 per week in 1915 when he first played professionally with the Yonkers Bantams for $5 per game. Lapchick had grown to six feet five inches, 185 pounds by 1917 and could command $7 per game from the Whirlwinds, one of the many New York pro teams. Through 1919, he played for up to four teams at one time. His rate of pay climbed to $10 per game and eventually up to $75 per game, although his standard fee was $1 per minute. From 1919 to 1923, Lapchick played for Troy (New York) in the semipro NYSL as a six foot six inch center.

For the 1923–1924 season, Lapchick joined the New York Original Celtics, the city's top pro team. The Celtics' center teamed with Dutch Dehnert*, Johnny Beckman*, Pete Barry, Davey Banks*, Nat Holman*, and George "Horse" Haggerty*. The Celtics revolutionized the game, developing switching defenses and the "give and go" offense. Lapchick, probably the game's first coordinated big man, was a great leaper, possessed a fine shot, and controlled the center taps that followed each made basket in the early days. The Celtics' joined the ABL in its second season (1926–1927) after playing independently for more money previously. They dominated the ABL the first two years, representing Brooklyn and then New York City. In 1927–1928, the Celtics boasted a combined record of 80-20, including playoffs, and won the playoffs each year.

The ABL dissolved the Celtics because of the competitive imbalance. Lapchick joined teammates Barry, Dehnert, and Beckman on the Cleveland (Ohio) Rosenblums (ABL). The Rosenblums, led by Lapchick, won the ABL Championships in 1928–1929 and 1929–1930. Their 72-33 record was by far the best in pro basketball. Owner Max Rosenblum dissolved the team for the Depression years of 1930–1931. As a free agent, Lapchick signed with the second-year Toledo (Ohio) ABL franchise. Surrounded with aging teammates, however, he could not help the team to a winning record. The same year marked the demise of the ABL. For the next six years, Lapchick played for Kate Smith's Celtics on the exhibition circuit. During his 19 year playing career, he had been the best pro center.

Holman, former teammate and head coach at CCNY, recommended Lapchick to the administration at St. John's University (New York). Although having no formal high school and college education, Lapchick was named head basketball coach at St. John's in 1937. From 1937 until his resignation in 1947, Lapchick coached the Redmen to 181 victories and won NIT Championships in 1943 and 1944. President Ned Irish* of the New York Knickerbockers (BAA) asked him to replace Neil Cohalen as coach of his pro New York Knicks team, causing Lapchick to decline a $12,000-a-year salary offer from St. John's. He said, "I'm just an old pro at heart." For the next 12 years, Lapchick coached the Knicks to a 326-247 record. The Knicks appeared in the NBA Finals in 1951, 1952, and 1953, but lost all three playoffs. The pro game was rough on the intense Lapchick. He left the pros after the 1956 season because of "poor health and too many sleepless nights."

His retirement lasted one month, as Lapchick returned in 1957 to St. John's University to coach the Redmen basketball squad again. He remained at St. John's until retiring in 1965 because of several minor heart attacks. His second stint at St. John's produced two more NIT Championships in 1959 and 1965. Lapchick left college basketball coaching with a remarkable 334-130 record. (.720), among the 40 best winning percentages for college coaches having at least 10 years' experience. Writer Arthur Daley wrote of Lapchick "defense was his specialty. He has the uncanny knack of being able to watch an enemy team in action and instantly being able to detect flaws in the action which can be exploited by adequate counter measures. That was an art he carried with him from his old Celtic days." Lapchick spent his retirement as sports coordinator for Kutshers CC in Monticello, New York until his death. Truly he bridged the gap between the early days of basketball and its modern era. In 1966 he was elected to the Naismith Memorial Basketball Hall of Fame.

BIBLIOGRAPHY: Peter C. Bjarkman, *The Biographical History of Basketball* (Chicago, IL, 2000); Al Hirshberg, *Basketball's Greatest Teams* (New York, 1966); Jan Hubbard, ed., *The Official NBA Encyclopedia*, 3rd ed. (New York, 2000); Neil D. Isaacs, *Vintage NBA* (Silver Spring, MD, 1996); Joe Lapchick, *Fifty Years of Basketball* (New York, 1968); Joseph Lapchick file, Naismith Memorial Basketball Hall of Fame, Springfield, MA; *The Lincoln Library of*

Sports Champions, vol. 7 (Columbus, OH, 1974); John D. McCallum, *College Basketball, USA Since 1892* (Briarcliff Manor, NY, 1978); Ronald L. Mendell, *Who's Who in Basketball* (New Rochelle, NY, 1973); Murry R. Nelson, *The Originals: The New York Celtics Invent Modern Basketball* (Bowling Green, OH, 1999); Robert W. Peterson, *Cages to Jump Shots: Pro Basketball's Early Years* (New York, 1990); Paul Soderberg and Helen Washington, *The Big Book of Halls of Fame in the U.S. and Canada* (New York, 1977).

George P. Mang

LaRUSSO, Rudolph Anton "Rudy" (b. November 11, 1937, Brooklyn, NY; d. July 9, 2004, Los Angeles, CA), college and professional player, graduated from James Madison High School in Brooklyn, New York where he led the basketball team to the Brooklyn championship and second in the All-City championships in 1954–1955. He was named to the All-City Second Team in 1954–1955.

Although accepted at Harvard University (Massachusetts), LaRusso matriculated at Dartmouth College (New Hampshire). He played center in basketball his freshman year in 1955–1956, but coach "Doggie" Julian* switched him to forward to take advantage of his outside shot. LaRusso scored 1,167 points in 80 games from 1955–1956 through 1958–1959 for 15th all-time best in Dartmouth history. He tallied 529 points his senior year, eighth-best for a single season at Dartmouth. His best single-game performance was 30 points against Butler College (Indiana) on December 18, 1958. LaRusso holds all major Dartmouth rebounding records, including best single-game (32), season (503, 1957–1958); and career (1,239, from 1955–1956 through 1958–1959). LaRusso led Dartmouth to the Eastern championship finals, losing to Temple University (Pennsylvania). He made First Team All-IvL in 1957–1958 and 1958–1959.

The six-foot eight-inch, 220-pound LaRusso was drafted in 1959 by the Minneapolis Lakers (NBA). At the forward position opposite Elgin Baylor* in his first year with the Lakers, he averaged 13.7 points and collected 679 rebounds in 71 games. LaRusso averaged in double-figures in scoring in each of his eight seasons with the Minneapolis and Los Angeles Lakers. His top mark of 17.1 points per game came in 1961–1962, when Baylor was in the military service. He helped the Lakers reach the NBA Finals in 1962, 1963, 1965, and 1966, but the Boston Celtics won the NBA championship each time. His rebound totals ranged from 647 to 828 over his 10-year NBA career. In January 1967, the Lakers traded LaRusso to the Detroit Pistons (NBA) in a three-way deal involving Ray Scott and Mel Counts. LaRusso, however, refused to report to the Pistons. In August 1967, Detroit sold him to the San Francisco Warriors (NBA). LaRusso's last two years were spent with the Warriors, where he averaged over 20 points and over eight rebounds. During 10 NBA seasons, he scored 11,507 points (15.6 point average) in 737 games and averaged 14.5 points in 93 playoff games. LaRusso appeared in four All-Star games, averaging 7.3 points and 4.2 rebounds. He was named to the Second Team NBA All-Defensive Team in 1968–1969.

In 1982, LaRusso was voted to the All-IvL Silver Anniversary Basketball Team. He has been nominated to the New England Basketball Hall of Fame and resided in Los Angeles. He died after a long battle with Parkinson's disease.

BIBLIOGRAPHY: Dartmouth College Sports Information Department letter and media release, Hanover, NH, June 16, 2003; Jan Hubbard, ed., *The Official NBA Encyclopedia*, 3rd ed. (New York, 2000); *Los Angeles Lakers Media Guide, 1966–1967* (Los Angeles, CA, 1966); *San Francisco Warriors Media Guide, 1968–1969* (San Francisco, CA, 1968); *TSN Official NBA Guide 1969–1970* (St. Louis, MO, 1969).

Robert L. Cannon

LAVELLI, Anthony, Jr. "Tony" (b. July 11, 1926, Somerville, MA; d. January 8, 1998, Laconia, NH), college and professional player, made the All-America basketball squad three times at Yale University (Connecticut; IvL) and set a career NCAA scoring record with 1,964 points from 1946 to 1949. The first freshman selected to the HAF All-America First Team, Lavelli averaged 20.2 points in 97 career contests with the Elis. The six-foot three-inch, 185-pound center-forward led the nation with a 22.4 point scoring average in 1949. His 215 free throws in 1949 established an all-time foul conversion mark.

Lavelli graduated from Somerville High School in 1944, having starred in basketball. At Williston Academy Preparatory School for one year, he led the netters to an undefeated season. Williston coach Dale Lash declared, "He's the best basketball player I've ever seen—and the hardest worker." Lavelli practiced many hours developing his sweeping, ambidextrous, extended-arm hookshot, which caromed off the backboard. He pioneered one-handed free throws, with his big hands and excellent touch enabling high accuracy.

Lavelli, the son of Anthony Lavelli Sr. and Ida (Christopher) Lavelli, attempted to enlist in the U.S. military service, but was rejected because of weak arches. Robert "Red" Rolfe a Yale basketball coach and former New York Yankees (AL) baseball star, guided Lavelli during his freshman season. The 14-1 Elis compiled their best win-loss basketball record in 51 years. Lavelli, the two-time Bulldog captain, set a Yale single-game scoring record in 1946 with 39 points against the U.S. Military Academy. In 1949 he tallied 40 points against Princeton (New Jersey) University and 52 points against Williams College (Massachusetts). Coach Howard Hobson* guided the 22-8 Elis to the 1949 IvL Championship and a 71-67 loss to University of Illinois in the first round of the NCAA Tournament. Lavelli tallied 27 points against the Illini and participated in the East-West All-Star Game at Madison Square Garden. The HAF Basketball Hall of Fame enshrined him.

The talented musician majored in the theory and composition of music and participated in Beta Theta Pi, Torch Honor Society, and Skull and Bones before his 1949 graduation from Yale. He attended the Juilliard School of Music and founded Bella Music and Theatre Associates in New York City. His NBA career included stints with the Boston Celtics in 1949–1950 and the New York Knicks in 1950–1951. In two NBA seasons, he tallied 591 points and averaged 6.9 points.

BIBLIOGRAPHY: Peter C. Bjarkman, *Biographical History of Basketball* (Chicago, IL, 2000); Mike Douchant, *Encyclopedia of College Basketball* (Detroit, MI, 1995); Jan Hubbard, ed., *The Official NBA Encyclopedia*, 3rd ed. (New York, 2000); Diane E. Kaplan, Yale University Library Archivist, letter to James D. Whalen, January 1991; Anthony Lavelli, Jr., file, Naismith Memorial Basketball Hall of Fame, Springfield, MA; Frank G. Menke, ed., *The All-Sports Record Book* (New York, 1950); William G. Mokray, ed., *Ronald Encyclopedia of Basketball* (New York, 1963); *NCAA Basketball Guide, 1951* (New York, 1951); *NCAA Basketball Guide, 1995* (Overland Park, KS, 1995); Ken Rappoport, *The Classic* (Mission, KS, 1979).

James D. Whalen and Wayne Patterson

LAWRENCE, Janice. *See* Braxton, Janice Lawrence

LEITH, Lloyd Raymond "Mr. Basketball" (b. December 7, 1902, San Francisco, CA; d. October 1, 1979, San Francisco, CA), college referee and professional scout, graduated from Polytechnic High School in San Francisco in 1921 and earned a Bachelor's degree from the University of California-Berkeley in 1927. Leith captained his high school and college basketball squads before beginning a successful coaching and officiating career in 1927. From the 1931–1932 through 1939–1940 seasons, he coached the Balboa Mission High School basketball squad in Washington State to 207 victories and an average of 23 triumphs per season. The poor quality of officiating at Pacific Coast high school basketball games prompted him to take ameliorative steps. The truly dedicated, hardworking Leith organized basketball officials in the San Francisco Bay area and began to train them, assign them to games, and grade their game performance.

For 25 years, Leith refereed PCC college basketball games involving the University of Southern California, UCLA, University of California-Berkeley, Stanford University (California), the University of Oregon, Oregon State University, the University of Washington, and Washington State University. His other assignments included handling National AAU Tournament basketball games at Denver, Colorado that featured the Phillips 66ers, Oakland (California) Bittners, Peoria (Illinois) Caterpillar Diesels, and other powerful amateur teams. Leith also refereed NCAA basketball tournaments, including many regional contests, for 16 years. The classic 1957 NCAA championship game, in which the University of North Carolina edged Wilt Chamberlain's* University of Kansas 54-53 in triple overtime, was officiated by him. Leith, who played active roles in the CBOA and the IAABO, supervised PCC basketball referees for seven years and spent eight years as an NBA observer-scout. He became the first great Pacific Coast referee in an era noted for distinguished East Coast officials. Under Leith's guidance, Pacific Coast officiating improved considerably in quality and won greater respect from both PCC players and coaches. Westerners deservedly recognized him as "Mr. Basketball." In 1982, Leith became the tenth referee elected to the Naismith Memorial Basketball Hall of Fame.

BIBLIOGRAPHY: Jan Hubbard, ed., *The Official NBA Encyclopedia*, 3rd ed. (New York, 2000); Lloyd R. Leith file, Naismith Memorial Basketball Hall of Fame, Springfield, MA; Wayne Patterson to David L. Porter, February 29, 1988; Frank V. Phelps to David L. Porter, March 29, 1988; *TSN*, October 27, 1979.

David L. Porter

LEMON, Meadow George, III "Meadowlark" "The Clown Prince of Basketball" (b. April 25, 1933, Lexington, SC), professional player, performed with the Harlem (New York) Globetrotters and was among the most popular players in the long history of the organization. Lemon, the son of Meadow Lemon and Maime (Nesbitts) Lemon, grew up in Wilmington, North Carolina, where he graduated from Williston High School in 1952 and was an All-State football and basketball player. He witnessed the film *The Harlem Globetrotter Story* and was intrigued by the team's tricky ball-handling and humorous stunts. His high school basketball co-coach, E. A. "Spike" Corbin, drove him to nearby towns to watch the Globetrotters play. One night in Raleigh, North Carolina, Lemon asked Globetrotters star Marques Haynes* to let him try on a team uniform. His wish was granted, fortifying his intense desire to join the organization in the future. Corbin encouraged Lemon to write Globetrotters coach Abe Saperstein* for a tryout. Saperstein instructed him to continue practicing.

The six-foot two-inch, 180-pound Lemon enrolled at Florida Agricultural and Mechanical University in 1952. After spending only two weeks there, he was drafted into the U.S. Army and served two years in West Germany. Noting that a Globetrotters European engagement was scheduled in a nearby city, Lemon secured a pass to contact Saperstein personally. Saperstein permitted him to work out with the team and was astonished at the latter's ball-handling and shooting ability. Saperstein assured Lemon that he had a job with the organization as soon as he was discharged from the U.S. Army.

Lemon joined the Globetrotters in the fall of 1954 and soon added the colorful "lark" to his first name. He capitalized on an opportunity for immediate stardom when the veteran "Goose" Tatum* left the team, "Showboat" Hall contracted pneumonia, and Sam Wheeler broke his knee. The center of team high jinks, Lemon led teammates in comical football and baseball formations, the medicine ball–basketball switch, the rubber-banded foul shot, and the wild heave into the audience of a supposed bucket of water (actually filled with confetti). "I've always wanted to be a comedian and a basketball player," he said, "and being a Globetrotter combines both." The Globetrotters played 275 games each year, 175 in North America and 100 on other continents. Lemon performed in over 5,000 games, often joining the halftime entertainers with wisecracks and singing songs. Gifted with a pleasant voice, he sang professionally and appeared with teammates on network television. Asked if he ever grew weary of hearing the Globetrotters' warmup song, "Sweet Georgia Brown," Lemon replied, "You can't ever get tired of something that's been such an important part of your life." He was inducted into the Naismith Memorial Basketball Hall of Fame in 2003. Lemon, who married Willie Maultsby, has five children—George, Beverly, Donna, Robin, and Jonathan—and resides in surburban Fairfield, Connecticut.

BIBLIOGRAPHY: Peter C. Bjarkman, *The Biographical History of Basketball* (Chicago, IL, 2000); Meadowlark Lemon and Jerry B. Jenkins, *Meadowlark* (Nashville, TN, 1987); Meadowlark Lemon file, Naismith Memorial Basketball Hall of Fame, Springfield, MA; *The Lincoln Library of Sports Champions*, vol. 7 (Columbus, OH, 1974); George Vecsey, *The Harlem Globetrotters* (New

York, 1973); Josh Wilker, *The Harlem Globetrotters* (New York, 1997).

James D. Whalen

LEMONS, A.E., Jr. "Abe" (b. November 21, 1922, Walters, OK), college player, coach, and administrator, coached Oklahoma City (Oklahoma) University, Pan-American University of Texas, and the University of Texas basketball teams to a 597-344 composite record over 34 years. His teams made eight NCAA tournament trips and earned two NIT berths.

Lemons's parents did not name him, giving him the initials A.E. after his father. Lemons failed eighth grade and subsequently spent an extra year in public school. At age 19, he began playing high school basketball. The season's performance earned him a scholarship at Southwestern Oklahoma University, where he stayed one year. Since he needed a full first name to enlist with the armed forces, Lemons placed a "B" between the "A" and "E" on his birth certificate and joined the U.S. Merchant Marine in 1942 for World War II service. After World War II, the 24-year-old entered Oklahoma City University and became the school's career leading scorer with a 7.1 points average. Upon graduation in 1949, he was named assistant basketball coach under Doyle Parrack.

Parrack led Oklahoma City to four straight NCAA tournaments from 1952 to 1955. Lemons kept up the winning tradition upon being named head coach in 1956. His 1956 and 1957 teams finished Regional runner-up, the first two of his seven tournament entries at Oklahoma City. Between 1956 and 1973, Oklahoma City won 308 games, lost 179 contests, led the nation in scoring three times, played twice in the NIT, and produced seven All-America players.

Lemons moved to Pan-American University as head basketball coach and athletic director in 1974, doubling his earlier $14,000 salary. He coached only three years at Pan-American, producing a 55-16 record. In 1976, Pan-American boasted the nation's leading scorer in Marshall Rogers.

University of Texas (SWC) athletic director and former football coach Darrell Royal, who hoped to raise Longhorn basketball to the level of its football and baseball programs, hired Lemons as head basketball coach in 1977. In six years, Lemons produced a 110-63 record at Texas. His Longhorns won the NIT title in 1978, when he was named NABC Coach of the Year. His 1979 squad reached the NCAA tournament. In 1982, however, new Texas athletic director Delodd Doss wanted different leadership and fired him as coach. Lemons continued to serve as assistant athletic director until Oklahoma City rehired him for the 1984 season. Lemons produced a 123-84 record in seven more years at Oklahoma City. Oklahoma City switched from the NCAA to the NAIA in 1986. In 1987, his team finished 34-1 and was seeded first in the NAIA tournament. He retired after the 1990 season, having compiled a 597-344 record for 34 seasons.

Lemons, often called the funniest man in basketball, became widely known for his exciting, high-scoring teams and colorful players. He and his wife, Betty Jo, have two daughters.

BIBLIOGRAPHY: Frank Deford, "Abe Lemons and His Poor Ol' Hongry Farm Boys," *SI* 22 (January 4, 1965), pp. 46–47; Mike Douchant, *Encyclopedia of College Basketball* (Detroit, MI, 1995); *NCAA Men's Basketball Records, 2004* (Indianapolis, IN, 2004); *NCAA Basketball's Finest* (Overland Park, KS, 1991); *NYT*, March 11, 1982, sec. 2, p. 17; *NYT*, April 10, 1983, sec. 5, p. 5; Edwin Shrake, "A Shot of Lemons to Cure the Blues," *SI* 46 (January 17, 1977), pp. 32–39.

Brian L. Laughlin

LEONARD, Christopher Michael "Archie" "Chick" "The Dog" "Chris" (b. 1891, New York, NY; d. May 11, 1957, Manhasset, NY), college and professional player, was the son of Michael Leonard, manager of a piano-moving company in New York. Leonard, who married Agatha Taylor and had one sister, attended Manhattan College and played basketball there from 1909 to 1912.

Leonard began his professional basketball career in 1912 and performed for several teams, including the Philadelphia, Pennsylvania Jasper Jewels (EL), Bridgeport, Connecticut Blue Ribbons (ISL), Paterson, New Jersey Crescents (ISL), Newark, New Jersey Turners (ISL), Hazelton, Pennsylvania Mountaineers (PSL), and Glens Falls, New York (NYSL). After serving as an infantryman in World War I, he resumed his professional basketball career. He starred for the Germantown, Pennsylvania Hessians (PSL), Albany, New York Senators (NYSL) and the New York Whirlwinds, a team organized by promoter Tex Rickard. Jim Furey* spotted Leonard and teammate Nat Holman* in a 1921 New York Celtic-Whirlwind matchup and signed them to contracts with the Original Celtics in 1922. Furey and his brother, Tom, had organized and Original Celtics in 1918.

Leonard, one of the best-known Celtic players, ranked among the best shooters and team players of the 1920s. The Celtics originally used the six-foot 190-pounder at center but shifted him to guard in 1923, when Joe Lapchick* joined the team as a center. Leonard's teammates referred to him as "The Dog" because of his tenacious play on the court but also nicknamed him "Archie," "Chick," and "Chris."

The Original Celtics dominated professional basketball in the 1920s, averaging wins in five of every six games. Most of their games took place on the road in old barns, armories, and dance halls. The Celtics, who made famous the pivot play, the switching defense, and the give-and-go offense, joined the ABL in 1927 and easily won the ABL Championship in 1927 and 1928.

Leonard retired from professional basketball in 1927 when the Original Celtics disbanded for the first time. He owned the Leonard Delivery and Warehouse Corporation in the Bronx, New York from 1933 until his death and also served until about 1952 as an assistant coach for high school basketball teams in Great Neck, New York and Manhasset, New York.

BIBLIOGRAPHY: Glenn Dickey, *The History of Professional Basketball Since 1896* (New York, 1982); Bill Himmelman, telephone conversation with Susan J. Rayl, Norwood, NJ, October 1993; Zander Hollander, ed., *The Modern Encyclopedia of Basketball* (New York, 1973); Christopher Leonard file, Manhattan College Sports Information Department, New York, NY; Murry R. Nelson, *The Originals: The New York Celtics Invent Modern Basketball* (Bowling Green, OH, 1999); *NYT*, May 13, 1957, p. 31; Robert W. Peterson, *From Cages to Jump Shots* (New York, 1990); Ken Shouler et al., *Total Basketball* (Wilmington, DE, 2003).

Susan J. Rayl

LEONARD, William Robert "Bob" "Slick" (b. July 17, 1932, Terre Haute, IN), college and professional player, coach, and sportscaster, resides in Carmel, Indiana with Nancy, his wife of 45 years, and has five children: Terryl, Bob, Bill, Tom, and Tim. Nancy is a licensed real estate broker.

Leonard graduated in 1950 from Terre Haute Gerstmeyer (Indiana) High School, where he excelled as an all round athlete between 1946 and 1950. He was selected as an alternate to the 1950 Indiana All-Star basketball team and won the state championship in tennis his senior year. Leonard was named to the Indiana All-Star Team for the 1941–1950 decade.

A three-year letterman in basketball at Indiana University from 1952 to 1954, Leonard captained the Hoosiers his senior year. He was selected MVP as a sophomore of the East-West College All-Star Game and was chosen the Hoosiers MVP in 1952. Leonard played on BTC championship teams in 1953 and 1954 and made All-BTC and All-America both seasons. In a dramatic finish at the 1953 NCAA Finals, he netted a free throw in the closing seconds to defeat the University of Kansas 69-68 for the title. He joined the Hoosier 1,000 point club, scoring 1,098 career points (319 in 1951–1952, 424 in 1952–1953, 355 in 1953–1954) and averaged 15.3 points. He became the first person inducted into the Indiana University Sports Hall of Fame.

Leonard, a six-foot three-inch, 185-pound guard, was selected as a first round draft choice by the Minneapolis Lakers (NBA) and played for Minneapolis from 1956–1957 to 1959–1960 and with the Los Angeles Lakers (NBA) in 1960–1961. He was selected in the expansion draft by the Chicago Packers (NBA) in 1961 and played 32 games for the Chicago Zephyrs (NBA) in 1962–1963 before being named head coach. In seven NBA seasons, Leonard compiled 4,204 points, 1,217 rebounds, and 1,427 assists in 426 regular season games. In 34 NBA playoff games, he tallied 334 points and averaged 9.8 points.

Leonard began his professional basketball coaching career during the 1962–1963 season, guiding the Zephyrs to a 13-29 win-loss record. The following year, he fared 31-49 as head coach of the Baltimore Bullets (NBA). Leonard was named assistant coach of the newly formed Indiana Pacers (ABA) in 1967–1968. He became the head coach of the Pacers in the ABA's second season and held that position through the 1975–1976 season when the NBA and ABA merged. Leonard's teams won an unprecedented three ABA championships and made the ABA Finals five times. His 387 wins made him the Pacers' all time winningest coach. When the franchise joined the NBA after the merger, Leonard remained the head coach for four seasons and recorded 142 triumphs before retiring as a coach.

Leonard's professional coaching career spanned 14 years. In eight years of ABA coaching, his teams won 387 contests and lost 270 times. In six NBA seasons, he recorded 186 triumphs and 264 losses. Leonard has achieved great success in coaching with 573 career victories and three ABA championships.

Between 1980 and 1990, Leonard served as director of intramural and club sports at Stanford University (California). Since 1990, he has become quite popular as an analyst, sportscaster, and crowd motivator for the Pacers on their radio and television networks. He was named one of the 50 Greatest Players in Indiana History.

BIBLIOGRAPHY: Peter C. Bjarkman, *The Biographical History of Basketball* (Chicago, IL, 2000); "Bob Leonard," *History*, http://www.iuhoosiers.com (2004); "Bob Leonard," *Stastistics*, http://www.basketballreference.com (2004); "Bobby Leonard," *Hall of Fame*, http://www.hoopshall.com (2004); "Bobby Leonard," *Profile*, http://www.nba.com (2004); Jan Hubbard, *The Official NBA Encyclopedia*, 3rd ed. (New York, 2000); "Nancy Leonard," *Family*, http://www.nba.com (2004); David S. Neft et al., *The Sports Encyclopedia: Pro Basketball*, 5th ed. (New York, 1992); Herb Schwomeyer, *Hoosier Hysteria* (Greenfield, IN, 1970).

John L. Evers

LESLIE, Lisa DeShaun (b. July 7, 1972, Compton, CA), college and professional player, is the daughter of Walter Leslie, a semiprofessional basketball player who left the family when Lisa was four, and Christine Leslie-Espinoza. Leslie-Espinoza supported three daughters as an over-the-road truck driver.

Leslie averaged 27 points and 15 rebounds in basketball for Morningside High School in Inglewood, California. Every major college recruited the six-foot five-inch, 170-pound center and A student. In the final contest of the 1989–1990 season against South Torrance (California) High School, she recorded a staggering 101 points by halftime, giving Morningside the lead, 102-24. The South Torrance players voted at halftime to forfeit the lopsided game.

Leslie accepted a basketball scholarship to University of Southern California and led all U.S. freshmen women in basketball scoring and rebounding. She played the center position on the U.S. women's team at the World University Games in Great Britain and awed fans with powerful slam dunks, leading the U.S. to a gold medal over Spain. At USC, Leslie won All America honors in 1992, 1993, and 1994 and unanimously was selected 1994 National Player of the Year. With Leslie, USC made the NCAA tournament four times and advanced to the NCAA Elite Eight in 1992 and 1994. She played professional basketball for Alcamo, Italy during the 1994–1995 season.

Leslie made the U.S. women's basketball team for the 1996 Atlanta, Georgia Olympics. Coach Tara VanDerveer* took the team on a year-long tour in 1995–1996 and won 52 consecutive games against the best teams in the world. At the 1996 Olympics, Leslie set an American women's Olympic record with 35 points against Japan in the semifinals and poured in 29 points in the finals against Brazil to capture the gold medal.

In 1997, Leslie signed with the Los Angeles Sparks of the new eight-team WNBA. She averaged 15.9 points and 9.5 rebounds her rookie season. Leslie was named WNBA MVP in 2001, averaging 19.5 points and 9.6 rebounds in 31 games. The Houston Comets' four year reign as WNBA champions ended on August 20, 2001, when Leslie scored 28 points and recorded 18 rebounds, leading Los Angeles to a 70-58 victory and eliminating Houston from the playoffs. The Los Angeles Sparks swept the Charlotte Sting three games to none to win the 2001 WNBA title, with Leslie being named series MVP. She recorded the first dunk in WNBA history on July 22, 2002. Leslie averaged

16.2 points and 10.2 rebounds during the 2002 regular season and 19.3 points and 7.8 rebounds in the 2002 WNBA playoffs. Los Angeles swept the New York Liberty in the WNBA Finals, with Leslie repeating as MVP. Leslie earned her second WNBA regular season MVP Award in 2004, leading the WNBA in rebounds with 9.9 points per game and the Sparks to the best WNBA record with a 25-9 mark. She led the WNBA with 98 blocked shots, being named WNBA Defensive Player of the Year. Leslie ranked second in the WNBA in points (598) and field goal percentage (.494). She played in six WNBA All-Star Games, sustaining a knee injury in the 2003 midseason classic and being named three time All-Star Game MVP. Through the 2004 WNBA season, Leslie's career totals include 4,215 points scored, 2,292 rebounds, and 309 steals, with a 17.6 point average, in 239 games. Leslie tallied 644 points and 314 rebounds in 33 WNBA playoff games. She performed on the 2004 U.S. Olympic women's basketball team, which won the gold medal. She made the All-WNBA First Team in 1997, 2000, 2001, 2002, 2003, and 2004 and the All-WNBA Second Team in 1998 and 1999.

Leslie enjoyed a successful modeling career with the Wilhelmina Modeling Agency of New York and has been featured in *Vogue*, *Newsweek*, and numerous sports publications. In October 1998, she dedicated the Lisa Leslie Sports Complex at Morningside High School. Leslie received the 1999 Young Heroes Award for work with Los Angeles area foster children through the Big Sisters Guild. She also served as spokesperson for the WNBA Breast Health Awareness campaign and as an ESPN analyst.

BIBLIOGRAPHY: AP, "Leslie, Sparks End Houston's Four-Year Reign as Champions," *St. Louis Post-Dispatch*, August 21, 2001, p. E7; Oscar Dixon, "Goal Sparks Leslie's Mission," *USA Today*, August 21, 2001, p. 3C; Robyn Norwood, "Sparks Win Another Title for LA in Series Sweep," *St. Louis Post-Dispatch*, September 2, 2001, p. D7; James Ponti, *WNBA Stars of Women's Basketball* (New York, 1999); Mark Stewart, *Lisa Leslie: Queen of the Court* (New York, 1998); *TSN Official WNBA Guide and Register 2004* (St. Louis, MO, 2004); USA Basketball, *1998 USA Basketball Women's World Championship Media Guide* (1998); WNBA, *WNBA Player Directory*, "Profiles: Lisa Leslie Player File" (2003).

Frank J. Olmsted

LEWIS, Guy Vernon (b. March 19, 1922, Arp, TX), college player and coach, coached 30 seasons at the University of Houston. Lewis grew up in the famed East Texas oilfields and married Dena Nelson of nearby Troup, Texas in 1942. They have three children, Sherry, Vern, and Terry. The six-foot three-inch Lewis gained as much fame through his sideline habits and style of dress as he did for being the thirty-first all-time winningest college basketball coach with 592 wins. His trademarks included a red and white-polka-dot towel that was tossed high into the air at the end of each game in which his team was victorious, brightly hued sports coats and suits, two dozen cups of water he drank each game, and high-scoring teams.

A U.S. Army Air Force veteran and former standout basketball and football athlete at Arp (Texas) High School, Lewis became a two-time All-LSC basketball star on the first University of Houston (Texas) intercollegiate athletic teams. With Lewis as leading scorer, the 1945–1946 Cougars captured the LSC Championship. He was the first Houston player to top 30 points when he made 34 against Southwest Texas State University. In 1946–1947, Lewis paced the Cougars to another LSC title and scored a record 38 points in one game. He averaged 20.3 points by scoring 729 points in 36 games during his two-year career.

Lewis rejoined the University of Houston in 1953 as assistant basketball coach. He became head coach in 1956–1957 and weathered three straight losing seasons before turning the Cougars into long-term winners. Upon retiring at the end of the 1985–1986 campaign, Lewis had guided Houston to 27 consecutive non-losing records. In posting a career 592-279 record, he coached 14 teams to 20 or more wins. The Cougars won 31 games in 1967–1968 and 1982–1983 and 32 games in 1983–1984. Lewis was selected National Coach of the Year in 1968 and the AP Coach of the Year in 1983. He guided 14 Cougar teams to the NCAA playoffs and five teams to the Final Four. The Cougars lost in the 1983 final game 54-52 to North Carolina

State University on a last-second shot, and bowed 84-75 Georgetown (Washington, D.C.) University in the 1984 championship game. Houston also lost the 1977 NIT Championship game 94-91 to St. Bonaventure University. An independent team until joining the SWC in 1975, the Cougars captured regular-season championships in 1982–1983 and 1983–1984.

Lewis popularized basketball in Texas in the mid-1960s by featuring fast-break offenses and pressing defenses, causing his teams to be known as Phi Slamma Jamma. He traveled worldwide to spread the word of basketball and teach it. Lewis recruited and coached such great players as Elvin Hayes*, Don Chaney, Hakeem Olajuwon*, Clyde Drexler*, Dwight Jones, Ted Luckenbill, Louis Dunbar, Ollie Taylor, and Otis Birdsong*.

BIBLIOGRAPHY: Peter C. Bjarkman, *Hoopla: A Century of College Basketball, 1896–1996* (Indianapolis, IN, 1996); Peter C. Bjarkman, *The Biographical History of Basketball* (Chicago, IL, 2000); Morgan G. Brenner, *College Basketball's National Championships* (Lanham, MD, 1999); Mike Douchant, *Encyclopedia of College Basketball* (Detroit, MI, 1995); Houston *Chronicle*, January 22, 1986; Billy Packer and Roland Lazenby, *College Basketball's 25 Greatest Teams* (St. Louis, MO, 1989); *University of Houston Basketball Media Guide, 1982, 1984* (Houston, TX, 1982, 1984).

Joe Lee Smith

LIEBERMAN-CLINE, Nancy "Fire" "Lady Magic" (b. July 1, 1958, Brooklyn, NY), college and professional player, coach, executive, and sportscaster, is the daughter of Jerome Lieberman and Renee Lieberman. Along with older brother, Clifford, the family moved to Far Rockaway, New York when she was a baby. Her parents separated and later divorced, with the two children being brought up by their mother. Lieberman-Cline put her energy and free time into sports. After initially playing football with boys and then baseball and softball, she finally settled on basketball. Her skills were formed on the playgrounds of Long Island and New York City with and against males. Lieberman-Cline did not compete on a girls' team until her sophomore year of high school, when Far Rockaway High School lost in the city championships by one point. Two years later, her high school reached the quarterfinals of the city championships. During her prep years, Lieberman-Cline also played for the New York Chuckles in AAU competition and De Salle of the CYO and continued her local schoolyard games. She made the U.S. Pan American squad in 1975, and a year later became the youngest member of the U.S. Olympic team, being a playmaker and the top reserve on the silver medal–winning U.S. squad at Montreal, Canada.

Lieberman-Cline was recruited by most of the major women's basketball powers after graduation from high school in 1976, but chose Old Dominion University in Norfolk, Virginia. During her freshman year, she averaged 20.9 points in leading her school to a berth in the NWIT in Texas. Lieberman-Cline also paced the U.S. junior team to an undefeated summer and two tournament titles. Marianne Stanley* became Old Dominion's coach for the 1977–1978 season, as the Lady Monarchs won the NWIT and finished with a 30-4 record. Lieberman-Cline was named an All-America, the first of three such awards. In 1978–1979 and 1979–1980, Old Dominion won consecutive AIAW national collegiate tournaments with 35-1 and 37-1 slates. She moderated her scoring to become the team's playmaker, spiritual leader, and top defender. During her 134-game college career, Lieberman-Cline averaged 18.1 points and 9.0 rebounds. Her 561 steals and 961 assists were believed to be records at least for modern collegiate times. Lieberman-Cline claimed many honors, including the Wade Trophy in both 1979 and 1980 as the best player in the nation. She competed for the U.S. national team, which won the eighth World Women's Basketball Championship in Seoul, Korea. She also was selected for the 1980 Olympic team, but quit because of the U.S. boycott of the Moscow, Russia Games.

Lieberman-Cline was the first draft choice of Dallas (WPBL) and signed with the Diamonds for over $100,000. Under her leadership, Dallas improved from 7-28 in 1979–1980 to 27-9 in 1980–1981 and won the Coastal Division. She scored 26.3 points per game for the second-highest average, finished fourth in rebounding and third in free throw percentage, and led the

WPBL in steals. Lieberman-Cline was named All-Pro and Rookie of the Year. In the playoffs, Dallas eliminated New Jersey and then lost to Nebraska in the championship series. The WPBL folded after her first season. For the next three years, Lieberman-Cline became a roving promoter of women's basketball and engaged in other sports activities. She acted as trainer and motivator for Martina Navratilova during the period when the latter became the dominant women's tennis player in the world. Lieberman-Cline competed in ABC Television's *Superstars* four straight winters, winning the all-around event in 1984. She also authored an autobiography, *Lady Magic*, and co-authored a book on women's basketball, giving practical advice on basic techniques and skills.

The WABA was formed in 1984 with Lieberman-Cline being the first draft pick of the Dallas franchise. She signed a three-year contract for $250,000. The Diamonds won their first 10 games and easily took the WABA championship with a 21-2 record. The WABA failed because of financial problems without any playoffs being held. In 1986, she became the first woman to play in a men's professional basketball league when she joined the Springfield (Massachusetts) Flame of the summer USBL. The 1987–1988 campaign saw her on a European tour with the Washington Generals against the Harlem Globetrotters. Lieberman-Cline played with the U.S. Women's basketball team through 1991, but was passed over for the 1992 Olympic team. She retired from basketball in 1992, the first American woman ever to make a million dollars as a basketball star. Lieberman-Cline saw her dream realized for a legitimate women's pro circuit with the June 1997 debut of the summer-season WBNA and played guard for the Phoenix Mercury (WNBA). She coached the Detroit Shock (WNBA) to marks of 17-13 in 1998, 15-17 in 1999, and 14-18 in 2000, serving also as general manager. In 1980, Lieberman-Cline was named Jewish Athlete of the Year and Broderick Cup recipient as the top female college athlete. She is a member of the New York City PSAL Hall of Fame (1979). Her college uniform jersey—number 10—hangs in the Naismith Memorial Basketball Hall of Fame, which she was elected to in 1996. She married Tim Cline of the New Haven Skyhawks (USBL) on May 18, 1988 and served as a commentator for NBC at the 1988 Seoul, South Korea Summer Olympic Games.

BIBLIOGRAPHY: Peter C. Bjarkman, *The Biographical History of Basketball* (Chicago, IL, 2000); Lee Green, "Queen of Diamonds," *Women's Sports* 3 (March 1981), pp. 22–27; Anne Janette Johnson, *Great Women in Sports* (Detroit, MI, 1991); Roy S. Johnson, "Nancy's Back in Business," *Women's Sports* 6 (October 1984), pp. 24–26; Nancy Lieberman-Cline, with Debbie Jennings, *Lady Magic* (Champaign, IL, 1992); Nancy Lieberman, with Myra and Harvey Frommer, *Basketball My Way* (New York, 1982); Nancy Lieberman-Cline file, Naismith Memorial Basketball Hall of Fame, Springfield, MA; Jim O'Brien, "My Daughter the Doctor (J)," *Street and Smith's Basketball Yearbook 1977–1978*, pp. 42–43; Richard Sowers, "Lieberman's Stage Inappropriate for Leading Lady," *TSN* (April 18, 1988), pp. 31, 44; *TSN Official WNBA Guide and Register, 2002* (St. Louis, MO, 2002).

Dennis S. Clark

LISTON, Emil Sycamore (b. August 21, 1890, Stockton, MO; d. October 26, 1949, Baldwin City, KS), college athlete, coach, and administrator, graduated from Baker Academy in Baldwin City, Kansas in 1909 and earned a Bachelor of Arts degree from hometown Baker University in 1913. After winning 11 letters in basketball, football, baseball, and soccer at Baker University, he played pro baseball for five years. Liston, who received a Master of Education degree in physical education from Harvard University (Massachusetts) in 1930, married Marie Thogmartin and had no children.

Liston's initial basketball coaching assignment came from 1911 to 1913 at Baldwin City High School, with his 1912 squad taking the Kansas state championship. Liston from 1913 to 1915 was director of Physical Education and coached several athletic teams at Fort Scott (Kansas) High School. Under his leadership, Fort Scott reestablished the basketball program and won the District and Southeast Kansas Tournament championships. He the next year served as head basketball and baseball coach and assistant football coach at Kemper Military School in Boonville, Missouri, guiding his basketball team to the military school championship.

Michigan College of Mines in Houghton hired Liston as director of athletics in 1916. During the next two years, he restored the school's basketball program and founded an Upper Peninsula basketball tournament for high schools. Liston joined Wesleyan University in Middletown, Connecticut as instructor of physical education and as head football (10-3-0), basketball, and baseball coach from 1918 to 1920. His Cardinals baseball team captured a LTC title with victories over Williams College and Amherst College.

From 1920 to 1945, Liston returned to his alma mater at Baker University as athletic director and head basketball and baseball coach. He also coached football there until 1937. His Wildcats won KC football championships in 1922, 1927–1928, and 1934, and finished second in 1923, 1931, and 1935 while compiling a 79-59 overall mark under Liston. Baker University appeared in 21 consecutive football games without defeat from the 1926 through 1928 seasons. His basketball teams garnered KC titles in 1934–1935 and 1936–1937 and placed second in 1927–1928 and third in 1925–1926, 1933–1934, and 1934–1935. Baker University's baseball squads consistently produced winning records under Liston's direction. As Baker University athletic director, he established intramural athletics, instituted a Department of Physical Education with a coaching major, and raised funds for the construction of a football stadium and modern cinder track. The Wildcats took eight KC track and field titles in nine years (1928–1936) and started the annual Baker University Relays.

Liston, who usually spent summers in the Baker University Public Relations Office contacting prospective students and raising money from alumnae, organized the KCCA and served three years as its president. Besides representing the KC at four AFCA and NCAA national meetings, he helped form the AFCA National Membership Committee in 1931 and was an AFCA District Representative in 1934. Liston chaired the Missouri Valley AAU Records Committee (1935–1937) and participated on the National AAU Records Committee (1936–1937). His other activities included teaching football at Harvard University in the summers of 1928 and 1929, directing the coaching school at Baker University in 1933, and teaching baseball at the KSHSACSA in Topeka in 1934.

Liston resigned his Baker University position in 1945 to work full time for the NAIB. In 1937, he had gained national prominence by establishing the NAIB. The NAIB had started after Liston attended a national AAU meeting at Denver, Colorado in December 1936 as a Missouri Valley District representative. Liston in 1940 became the first NAIB executive secretary-treasurer and served in that capacity at a Kansas City, Missouri hotel office until his death. The NAIB organized and administered small-college basketball at the national level, drawing up rules and standards for district and national competition. Liston's group also sought to provide uniformity and equity in policies and practices and conducted workshops and clinics for basketball coaches. The annual NAIB basketball tournament began at Kansas City, Missouri in 1937 and expanded from an eight-team field to a 32-team field the next year. The NAIB basketball tournament rapidly became one of Kansas City's biggest sports attractions.

Liston suffered a severe broken knee when refereeing a high school football game in October 1943 and a heart attack in Colorado the next year. He died of a heart attack at his home and was elected to the Naismith Memorial Basketball Hall of Fame as a contributor in 1974.

BIBLIOGRAPHY: John Forbes to David L. Porter, March 9, 1988; *Kansas City Times*, October 27, 1949; Emil Liston file, Naismith Memorial Basketball Hall of Fame, Springfield, MA; *NYT*, October 27, 1949; Wayne Patterson to David L. Porter, February 29, 1988.

David L. Porter

LITWACK, Harry (b. September 20, 1907, Galicia, Austria; d. August 9, 1999, Huntingdon Valley, PA), college and professional player and coach, was the son of shoe repairman Jacob Litwack and Rachel (Rech) Litwack. Litwack attended South Philadelphia (Pennsylvania) High School (1921–1925), where he played guard on the basketball team and made the All-Scholastic team as a member of the PHSL Champions his senior year. He captained Temple

University's basketball team for two years and helped it win a significant victory over major power Princeton University. After graduating in 1930, Litwack played six seasons (1930–1931 to 1935–1936) "always as a leader" with the Philadelphia SPHAS and helped them capture championships in both the EBL and ABL. He laid the foundation for his later career by coaching the basketball team of Simon Gratz High School in Philadelphia to a 15-2 record in 1930, guiding the Temple University (Pennsylvania) freshmen to a 181-32 mark from 1931 to 1951, and serving as an assistant coach of the Philadelphia Warriors (NBA) in 1950–1951 under Edward Gottlieb*. Litwack, who resided in Miami Beach, Florida, married Estelle Cabot on June 7, 1943 and had two daughters, Lois and Rochelle.

As head coach at Temple University between 1952–1953 and 1972–1973, Litwack posted 373 wins and 193 losses. Temple appeared in 13 postseason tournaments, including six NCAA playoffs, and experienced just one losing season. He often developed his players, including Guy Rodgers*, to achieve their greatest potential. Litwack recognized the latent talent of the underrated, diminutive Rodgers and entrusted him with the floor leadership of the Owls as a sophomore. Rodgers responded by leading Temple to a 67-16 record over three years, highlighted by third-place finishes in the 1956 and 1958 NCAA championships. Coach Litwack's ability to do "more with less" was also demonstrated by his NIT Championship club in 1969. Rival St. Joseph's College (Pennsylvania) coach Jack McKinney claimed that the Temple team "doesn't appear to have much talent, but they get the most out of what they have." Litwack's achievements have been recognized by his selection to the South Philadelphia High School, Temple University, Pennsylvania State, and Naismith Memorial Basketball (1975) Halls of Fame. Litwack co-owned with Bill Foster, head basketball coach at the University of Miami in Florida, the Pocono All-Star Sports Resort in East Stroudsburg, Pennsylvania.

BIBLIOGRAPHY: Peter C. Bjarkman, *Hoopla: A Century of College Basketball, 1896–1996* (Indianapolis, IN, 1996); Mike Douchant, *Encyclopedia of College Basketball* (Detroit, MI, 1995); Bill Gutman, *The History of NCAA Basketball* (New York 1993); Zander Hollander, ed., *The Modern Encyclopedia of Basketball* (Garden City, NY, 1979); Harry Litwack, telephone interview with John G. Muncie, 1985; Harry Litwack file, Naismith Memorial Basketball Hall of Fame, Springfield, MA; *Philadelphia Inquirer*, 1921–1925, 1952–1973.

John G. Muncie

LLOYD, Earl Francis (b. April 3, 1928, Alexandria, VA), college and professional player, coach, and scout, is the son of Theodore Lloyd and Daisy Lloyd. Lloyd played basketball at segregated Parker-Gray High School in Alexandria, Virginia and at West Virginia State College, then an all black college in Institute, West Virginia, near Charleston. He starred for the Yellow Jackets in 1948 and 1949, helping them win successive CIAA championships.

In April 1950, the Washington Capitols (NBA) selected the six-foot six-inch, 225-pound Lloyd in the ninth round of the NBA draft as the second African-American player chosen by an NBA team. Chuck Cooper* was chosen in the second round on the same day by the Boston Celtics (NBA). With Cooper and Nat "Sweetwater" Clifton, who was sold to the New York Knicks by the Harlem Globetrotters, Lloyd became one of the first three African-Americans to integrate the NBA in the 1950–1951 season. Because of the NBA schedule, he became the first AfricanAmerican to play in an NBA game. The Capitols lost to the Rochester Royals on October 31, 1950, as Lloyd scored six points and grabbed 10 rebounds. After Lloyd played just seven games, the United States Army interrupted his NBA career. He joined the Syracuse Nationals (NBA) in 1952. Syracuse had picked him in the 1951 dispersal draft following the dissolution of the Washington Capitols.

Lloyd played six seasons with the Syracuse Nationals as a tough defender and rebounder who could run the court. He helped the Nationals win the 1955 NBA championship. Syracuse squeaked by the Ft. Wayne Pistons 92-91 in the seventh game of the NBA Finals. In 1958, the Nationals traded Lloyd to the Detroit Pistons (NBA). Lloyd retired in 1960, having scored

4,682 points in 560 games in nine NBA seasons for an 8.4 point average.

Lloyd served the Pistons as an assistant coach between 1960 and 1968 and then as head scout. He became the NBA's second black head coach, compiling a 22-55 record in 1971–1972. Lloyd subsequently worked for Chrysler, the Detroit Board of Education for 10 years, and in the community relations department of Dave Bing, Incorporated. In 1993, the Virginia Sports Hall of Fame inducted him. In 2003, Lloyd was elected to the Naismith Memorial Basketball Hall of Fame. He and his wife, Charlita, have three sons, Kenneth, Kevin, and David.

BIBLIOGRAPHY: Bijan C. Bayne, *Sky Kings* (New York, 1997); Peter C. Bjarkman, *The Biographical History of Basketball* (Chicago, IL, 2000); Earl Lloyd, phone interview with Adolph Grundman, July 9, 2003; Earl Lloyd file, Naismith Memorial Basketball Hall of Fame, Springfield, MA; Ken Shouler et al., *Total Basketball* (Wilmington, DE, 2003); George Sipple, "Earl Lloyd Chosen for Basketball Hall," freep.com; Ron Thomas, *They Cleared the Lane: The NBA's Black Pioneers* (Lincoln, NE, 2002).

Adolph H. Grundman

LOBO, Rebecca Rose "Lobocop" (b. October 6, 1973, Hartford, CT), college and professional player and sportscaster, is the daughter of Dennis Lobo and RuthAnn (McLaughlin) Lobo, both teachers. Her father, who is a basketball coach, honed her skills. Lobo, who graduated from Southwick–Tolland (Massachusetts) Regional High School in 1992, became the all-time leading scorer in Massachusetts state history with 2,740 career points. In her first high school game, Lobo scored 32 points.

The six-foot four-inch, 185-pound Lobo was recruited by more than 100 colleges and universities. She chose the University of Connecticut because it was closer to home and emphasized academic excellence. Her first three seasons at Connecticut prepared her for an NCAA national championship her senior season. In 1993–1994, the Huskies finished with a 30-5 record, but were defeated early in the NCAA tournament. In her senior year, Connecticut went undefeated. Lobo captained the 1994–1995 National championship team, leading the Huskies to a perfect 35-0 record.

Numerous awards followed the championship season. Lobo won the 1995 ESPY Award for the Outstanding Female Athlete from ESPN, Female Athlete of the Year Award by the AP, Women's Basketball Player of the Year Award by the NCAA, Woman of the Year Award by the Woman's Sports Foundation, the Wade Trophy for the best female basketball player in NCAA Division I, and Kodak First Team All-America in 1994 and 1995. She graduated from Connecticut in 1995 with a Bachelor's degree in political science. Lobo averaged 17.0 points, 10 rebounds, and three blocked shots for Connecticut. Following graduation, she participated on the 1996 U.S. Women's basketball team at the Olympic Games in Atlanta, Georgia and helped them capture the gold medal.

Lobo signed with the New York Liberty (WNBA) in January 1997. She entered the professional ranks among the biggest stars in a new league. Her celebrity satus helped the WNBA get off to a good start. Lobo is credited with improving the profile of the WNBA and women's professional sports. She was often criticized as a player who earned more media attention than deserved.

Lobo enjoyed two solid years with the Liberty, averaging 12.4 points in 1997 and 11.7 points the following season. She made the All-WNBA Second Team in 1997 and was selected for the Eastern All-Star team. Injuries began to plague her in 1999, when she hurt her left knee requiring corrective surgery to the anterior cruciate ligament. Lobo reinjured her knee, was sidelined for the 1999 and 2000 seasons, and played in only 16 games in 2001 before being traded in April 2002 to the Houston Comets (WNBA). Her comeback with the Comets saw her appear in 21 games in 2002 before being released. She signed with the Connecticut Sun (WNBA) and appeared in 25 games in 2003. In six WNBA seasons, Lobo scored 808 points in 121 games for an 8.7 points average, pulled down 500 rebounds, handed out 115 assists, made 62 steals, and blocked 104 shots.

On April 12, 2003, Lobo and *Sports Illustrated* writer, Steve Rushin, were married before she reported to the Connecticut Sun training camp. She serves as an analyst for college basketball games.

BIBLIOGRAPHY: Peter C. Bjarkman, *The Biographical History of Basketball* (Chicago, IL, 2000); "Rebecca Lobo," *Background*, http://www.wnba.com (2003); "Rebecca Lobo," *Biographical Essay*, http://www.galegroup.com (2003); "Rebecca Lobo," *Celebrity*, http://www.usaweekend.com (2003); "Rebecca Lobo," *Savors Perfect Season*, http://www.geocities.com (2003); "Rebecca Lobo," *Statistics*, http://www.wnba.com (2003); *TSN Official WNBA Guide and Register, 2004*.

John L. Evers

LOEFFLER, Kenneth D. "Ken" (b. April 14, 1902, Beaver Falls, PA; d. January 1, 1975, Rumson, NJ), college and professional player and coach, led LaSalle College to the 1952 NIT and 1954 NCAA Championships. As head coach of the Explorers from 1950 to 1955, Loeffler took LaSalle to two NCAA tournaments and four NITs. LaSalle reached the NCAA Finals again in 1955. He led the St. Louis Bombers (BAA) to the 1947–1948 Western Division championship after a second place finish in 1946–1947. In 1964, Loeffler was elected as a coach to the Naismith Memorial Basketball Hall of Fame. He amassed a 323-217 (.598 winning percentage) composite record in 23 years at five colleges and a 79-90 mark during three years in the pro ranks.

Loeffler graduated from Penn State University (Pennsylvania) in 1924 after starring three years at forward on outstanding Nittany Lions basketball teams with a composite 35-8 record. After serving from 1924 to 1928 as a Pittsburgh, Pennsylvania newspaper columnist, he became head basketball coach in 1929 at Geneva College in his hometown of Beaver Falls, Pennsylvania and led them in seven seasons to 95 wins against 55 losses. Geneva finished the 1935 season by upsetting CCNY 50-27, and ending Long Island University's (New York) home winning streak with a 43-42 triumph. Loeffler earned a Bachelor of Laws degree in 1934 from the University of Pittsburgh. He was head basketball coach from 1936 to 1942 at Yale University (Connecticut), compiling a mediocre 61-82 composite record. Loeffler served as a major in the U.S. Army Air Force between 1942 and 1945 and then coached University of Denver's five to a 9-15 finish in 1945–1946.

In the fall of 1946, the St. Louis Bombers of the newly formed BAA signed Loeffler as their first head coach. He led the Bombers for two seasons to 38-23 and 29-19 finishes for second and first places in the BAA Western Division and semifinal playoff losses to the Philadelphia Warriors both years. In 1949 Loeffler coached the last place Providence Steamrollers (BAA) to a 12-48 finish in the Eastern Division. The colorful raconteur, poet, and scholar stressed defense and became an early proponent of the motion offense that used all five men in a figure-eight pattern.

Loeffler's finest coaching years came at LaSalle College in Philadelphia, where he guided the Explorers to six consecutive 20-victory campaigns and a composite 145-30 record. LaSalle's 1950 squad, led by Larry Foust* and Jim Phelan*, lost to Duquesne University (Pennsylvania) 49-47 in the NIT quarterfinals at New York's Madison Square Garden. In 1951, St. Louis University (Missouri), coached by Ed Hickey*, convincingly defeated the Explorers 73-61 in the NIT. The unseeded 1952 LaSalle squad triumphed over Seton Hall University (New Jersey) with Walter Dukes*; St. John's University (New York), the NCAA tournament runner-up with Bob "Zeke" Zawoluk; and Duquesne with Dick Ricketts and Jim Tucker to reach the NIT Finals. The Explorers upset a veteran University of Dayton team, the defending NIT finalists, 75-64 before 18,485 spectators at Madison Square Garden to capture the 1952 NIT title. Sensational LaSalle freshman Tom Gola and Norm Grekin were named NIT MVPs. LaSalle lost 70-65 to NCAA champion University of Kansas (with Clyde Lovellette*) in the 1952 Olympic playoffs after leading for 33 minutes and then were defeated by to the AAU's Phillips Oilers. In 1953, LaSalle dropped a 75-74 heartbreaker to St. John's University in the NIT quarterfinals to finish the season with an outstanding 25-3 record.

LaSalle faced its strongest test in the opening round of the 1954 NCAA tournament at Kansas City, Missouri, where the Explorers triumphed 76-74 over Fordham University (New

York). Loeffler's squad defeated North Carolina State University, Navy, and Penn State University and played Bradley University (Illinois) in the finals before a sellout crowd of 10,550 spectators. When Gola picked up four personal fouls in the first half against the Bradley Braves, Loeffler switched to a 2-3 zone defense. The maneuver kept Gola in the game as LaSalle triumphed 92-76, to take the NCAA title in its first attempt. LaSalle's 92 points broke the old NCAA tournament scoring record by 12 points. Gola, who scored 114 points in five NCAA games and was voted MVP, received help from teammates Frank O'Hara and Charles Singley.

"Three times a bridesmaid, but never a bride" described LaSalle's fate in 1955. The Explorers lost to the host team 63-54 in the finals of the University of Kentucky Invitational Tournament; 67-65 to Duquesne University in the New York Holiday Festival; and 77-63 to the University of San Francisco in the NCAA tournament at Kansas City, Missouri. The San Francisco Dons, led by legendary center Bill Russell* and guard K.C. Jones*, proved too much for LaSalle and held Gola to 16 points. Gola, a four-year All-America, scored 750 points for the season and finished with 2,462 career points. He and Loeffler made an eight-week U.S. State Department basketball tour of Latin America in 1955.

Loeffler coached Texas Agricultural and Mechanical University the next two seasons, inheriting a basketball team that was short on height and talent and that had finished with a combined 6-40 record the two previous years. The Aggies struggled to a 13-35 composite mark under Loeffler, who resigned after being accused of recruiting violations. He taught Business Law at Monmouth (Illinois) College and the University of Nevada-Reno until retirement in 1972. Loeffler, who was married and had one son, Kenneth II, died of a heart attack.

BIBLIOGRAPHY: *Albany* (NY) *Times-Union*, January 4, 1975; Morgan G. Brenner, *College Basketball's National Championships* (Lanham, MD, 1999); Peter C. Bjarkman, *Hoopla: A Century of College Basketball, 1896–1996* (Indianapolis, IN, 1996); Mike Douchant, *Encyclopedia of College Basketball* (Detroit, MI, 1995); Jan Hubbard, ed., *The Official NBA Encyclopedia*, 3rd ed. (New York, 2000); Neil D. Isaacs, *All the Moves: A History of College Basketball* (Philadelphia, PA, 1975); Neil D. Isaacs, *Vintage NBA* (Silver Spring, MD, 1996); Leonard Koppett, *24 Seconds to Shoot: An Informal History of the NBA* (New York, 1968); Ken Loeffler file, Naismith Memorial Basketball Hall of Fame Springfield, MA; Claudia Mitroi, ed., *Philadelphia's Greatest Sports Moments* (Champaign, IL, 2000); William G. Mokray, ed., *Ronald Encyclopedia of Basketball* (New York, 1963); *NCAA Men's Basketball Records, 2004* (Indianapolis, IN, 2004); NIT Finals Program, New York, March 15, 1952; *NYT*, January 3, 1975.

James D. Whalen

LONBORG, Arthur C. "Dutch" (b. March 16, 1898, Gardner, IL; d. January 31, 1985, Lawrence, KS), college athlete, basketball coach, and administrator, moved as a youth to northeastern Kansas, where his father, Carl, worked for the Atchison, Topeka, and Santa Fe Railroad. His mother, Nellie, operated a boarding house and brought up their five sons, Louis, William, John, Arthur, and Adolph. Arthur played basketball at Horton (Kansas) High School from 1912 to 1916 and starred for coach "Phog" Allen* at the University of Kansas. Lonborg earned nine letters in three sports for the Jayhawks. He was selected All-MVC as a football quarterback (1920) and end (1917, 1919). He missed the 1918 season while in military service and started at third base on the Jayhawks baseball squad.

Basketball remained Lonborg's forte, as he made All-MVC for two years at the guard position. During the 1918–1919 season, he gained Second Team All-America honors and captained the basketball season during his senior year in 1919–1920. Before graduating in 1921 with a Bachelor of Laws degree, Lonborg played AAU basketball for the Kansas City AC and gained All-America honors. He initially postponed practicing law for one year to try coaching. An illustrious coaching career sidetracked the promising barrister from ever establishing a legal career. At McPherson (Kansas) College, Lonborg coached all team sports from 1921 through 1923 and saw his basketball teams post a 23-4 record. He coached basketball at Washburn University of Topeka (Kansas) from 1923 to 1927. His 1925 Ichabods defeated the Hillyard

Chemical Company of St. Joseph, Missouri 42-30 to win the AAU championship. Center Gerald Spohn scored 62 points in four games, while Arthur Brewster earned All-America honors at guard to make Washburn the last University team to win an AAU championship. Lonborg married Edna Stansberger in 1924 and had one son, Arthur. He posted 63 wins and 15 defeats during four seasons at Washburn.

This success propelled Lonborg in 1927 to the head basketball coaching position at Northwestern University, where he stayed 23 years. His initial Northwestern team became the Wildcats' first basketball squad to win at least 10 games. During this period, he brought the Wildcats their first WC-BTC championship in 1931 and WC-BTC co-title in 1933. His 1931 champions personified the large, fast players, who later characterized WC-BTC basketball. His 1931 team, featuring Captain Bert Riel, Joseph Reiff*, and Robert McCarnes, posted a 16-1 record and captured the WC-BTC title. Reiff, a six-foot three-inch sophomore center, led the WC-BTC in scoring and passed the ball flawlessly from the pivot in Lonborg's set-play offense. During the 1940s, Lonborg coached College All-Star teams to six victories in nine games against the pro champions in Chicago.

After winning 237 games at Northwestern University (Illinois), Lonborg became athletic director at the University of Kansas in 1950. During 14 years there, he led his alma mater into national prominence. No Kansas team had won a national title before Lonborg's reign, but the Jayhawks captured four under his leadership including basketball (1952), cross-country (1953), and track and field (1959, 1960). The Jayhawks also garnered 38 BEC titles, averaging almost three per year. Kansas' athletic facilities and performances greatly improved during his reign. Lonborg added to Memorial Football Stadium, built the first BEC enclosed baseball park, and oversaw the construction of Allen Fieldhouse, the nation's second largest on-campus basketball arena at the time. He officially retired in 1964, but continued as "director of events" until 1973.

Lonborg's impact on basketball extended into the executive and administrative areas, as he chaired the NCAA Tournament Committee (1947–1960) and the USOBC (1957–1960). He served as the president of the NABC in 1935 and the IBFUS in 1962. In addition, Lonborg managed the 1960 U.S. Olympic Basketball Team and directed the U.S. Basketball Committee for the 1959 Pan American Games. His five Hall-of-Fame memberships include the HAF Hall of Fame (twice; as coach and as athletic director), Kansas Sports Hall of Fame, Washburn Hall of Fame, and the Naismith Memorial Basketball Hall of Fame (1973). He achieved basketball success as an athlete, coach, and administrator. Lonborg's burgeoning career indicates well how basketball grew from a regional, amateur activity into the national and international arenas during the middle of the twentieth century.

BIBLIOGRAPHY: Forrest C. Allen, *Better Basketball* (New York, 1952); Forrest C. Allen, *Coach Phog Allen's Sports Stories* (Lawrence, KS, 1947); Peter C. Bjarkman, *Big Ten Basketball* (Indianapolis, IN, 1994); Mike Douchant, *Encyclopedia of College Basketball* (Detroit, MI, 1995); Blair Kerkhoff, *Phog Allen: The Father of Basketball Coaching* (Indianapolis, IN, 1996); Arthur Lonborg file, Naismith Memorial Basketball Hall of Fame, Springfield, MA; John D. McCallum; *College Basketball, U.S.A. Since 1892* (Briarcliff Manor, NY, 1978); John Mendel, *Kansas Jayhawks* (Coal Valley, IL, 1991); *NCAA Men's Basketball Records, 2003* (Indianapolis, 2003); Alexander M. Weyand, *The Cavalcade of Basketball* (New York, 1960).

Gregory S. Sojka

LONG, Denise. *See* Andre, Denise Long Sturdy

LORENZEN, Lynne Frances (b. November 9, 1968, Waterloo, IA), high school and college player, is the daughter of Russell Lorenzen, a farmer, and Frances (Billerbeck) Lorenzen and has three older brothers and two older sisters. Her mother played forward for the 1952 Iowa state championship Reinbeck High School basketball squad, and her sisters, Lori and Jill, also participated in high school basketball. Lorenzen grew up on farms near Dysart and then Ventura and graduated fourth in her class from Ventura High School in 1987. Her high school activities included playing the trumpet and French horn in the band, dancing, and winning the state track and field high jump championship twice and the long jump title once.

The six-foot two-inch Lorenzen broke the all-time national high school basketball scoring record held by Denise Long Sturdy Andre*. Altogether, she tallied 6,496 regular-season points, 240 playoff points and averaged over 60 points. Lorenzen had learned to play basketball and develop a superb jumpshot by aiming at a metal backboard in her family's barn. Besides being selected to the All-State basketball team three consecutive years, she led Ventura High School to the state tournament as a freshman, sophomore, and senior. Her four seasons of the six-player-halfcourt game came under coach Chuck Bredlow in a gymnasium seating only 450 spectators. As a ninth-grader, Lorenzen scored 44 points in her first game, broke the state freshman record with 1,173 season points, and made the All-State Basketball Third Team. Her career low-point game also came that year when Klemme High School held her to 24 points. In 1985, she shattered the state sophomore record with 1,858 season points. The next year saw her tally a game-high 100 points, 11 short of the all-time state record, and become only the third high schooler to surpass 5,000 career points. Riceville High School, however, eliminated Ventura 86-84 in overtime in the Sectional finals. Two or three defenders frequently guarded Lorenzen, who capitalized on excellent shot selection and displayed 76 percent field goal accuracy from within ten feet of the basket.

As a senior, Lorenzen averaged 65 points in leading Ventura High School to the state six-player championship with a 27-0 regular-season and 31-0 overall mark. In February 1987, she broke the national high school scoring mark with a 54-point performance in Ventura's 87-51 defeat of Meservey-Thornton High School in the first round of the Class 1-A sectional tournament. The national news media and over 4,000 spectators witnessed Lorenzen shatter the record in her 104th game, 11 fewer than Long played to set the record. At the state tournament, she scored 62 points in a 106-51 rout over Lone Tree High School. No team had tallied that many points in a tournament game since 1968. Lorenzen garnered 61 points in the 90-69 defeat of Dike High School and 31 points in the 86-76 victory over Denison High School. Ventura took the state championship by defeating Southeast Polk High School 90-69, as Lorenzen scored 59 points. She converted 28 of 32 shot attempts and assisted on practically every other score. Ventura became the first high school to win 30 games since Des Moines East High School in 1979 and the first Class 1-A institution to win a state championship since Lakeview-Auburn High School in 1976.

In 1987, Lorenzen was named High School Female Athlete of the Year in Iowa, made the *Parade* Second Team All-America Squad, and earned the Naismith Award as National Female Player of the Year. The heavily recruited Lorenzen ultimately chose Iowa State University over Ohio State University, Penn State University, the University of Iowa, and the University of Arizona. She spent her freshman year adjusting to the five-player, full-court college game under coach Pam Wettig. Lorenzen played basketball four years at Iowa State, and earned a Bachelor's degree in elementary education with an emphasis on Spanish in 1992. In 1993, she was inducted into the Iowa High School Athletic Union Basketball Hall of Fame. Lorenzen serves as an instructor in adult basic education at Shutter Creek Correctional Institution in North Bend, Oregon and resides in Coos Bay, Oregon. She is married and has one child. Lorenzen has retained humility, generously credited teammates for her success, and viewed basketball as fun. Her summer recreational activities include water skiing, bicycling, and golf.

BIBLIOGRAPHY: *Des Moines Register*, February 15–16, 1987; *Des Moines Register*, March 11–15, 1987; *Des Moines Register*, April 14, 1987; *Des Moines Register*, March 4, 2001; Janice A. Beran, *From Six-on-Six to Full Court* (Ames, IA, 1993); Frances Lorenzen to David L. Porter, January 6, 1988.

David L. Porter

LOVE, Robert Earl "Butterbean" (b. December 8, 1942, Delhi, LA), college and professional player and executive, grew up in poverty as one of 14 children in rural Louisiana and was nicknamed "Butterbean" after his favorite food. Because his family could not afford to buy a basketball net, he nailed a coat hanger he had pulled into the shape of a hoop to the side of his grandmother's house to practice his shooting. Love grew to six feet eight inches and starred in basketball as a high school senior at Moorehouse High School in Bastrop, Louisiana and earned a basketball scholarship to Southern University in Baton Rouge, Louisiana, in 1961.

Love was named All-SWC three consecutive seasons and became the first player from Southern ever named NAIA All-America. He earned his Bachelor's degree from Southern in food and nutrition in 1965. Love was selected by the Cincinnati Royals (NBA) in the 1966 draft. After playing two seasons as a reserve on a Royals team that starred Oscar Robertson* and Jerry Lucas*, he was selected by the then-expansion Milwaukee Bucks (NBA) in May 1968. The Bucks dealt Love to the Chicago Bulls (NBA) in November 1968. During his eight seasons with Chicago, Love led the Bulls in scoring seven times. A deadly jumpshooter, he averaged 21.0 points in 1969–1970, 25.2 points in 1970–1971, a team record 25.8 points in 1971–1972, 23.1 points in 1972–1973, 21.8 points in 1973–1974, and 22.0 points in 1974–1975. Love, a three-time NBA All-Star, retired as the Bulls all-time scoring leader with 12,623 points and was one of the NBA's premier defensive forwards. With Love, Chet Walker*, Jerry Sloan*, and Norm Van Lier*, Chicago proved a formidable team. Love's NBA career ended with the Seattle SuperSonics (NBA) in 1976–1977 because of a back injury. During 11 NBA seasons, he scored 13,895 points, average 117.6 points, and made 4,653 rebounds (5.9 average) in 789 regular season games; he averaged 22.9 points and 7.5 rebounds in 47 playoff games. Love ranks as the second all-time leading scorer in Chicago Bulls history.

In 1984, his first wife left him because she did not want to be married to a stutterer. Stuttering had plagued Love since childhood. When Love was a busboy and dishwasher for $4.45 an hour at Nordstrom's Department Store in Seattle, basketball fans often recognized him and said, "Hey, that's Bob Love, he used to be a great basketball player. What's he doing in here busing tables?" In 1988, one of Nordstrom's owners took an interest in 45-year old Love. A speech therapist worked with him on his speech impediment.

In 1992, Steve Schanwald, the Chicago Bulls vice president of marketing and broadcasting, named Love the team's director of community affairs. Love still holds that position, making over 300 public appearances a year. A motivational speaker, he was inducted into the Louisiana Sports Hall of Fame and has won the NBA's Oscar Robertson Leadership Award. On January 19, 1994, the Bulls retired Love's number 10 jersey. On his 53rd birthday, December 8, 1995, he married Rachel Dixon during halftime of a Bulls–San Antonio Spurs game.

BIBLIOGRAPHY: Rick Davis, *Butterbean: When Glory Is Just a Whisper* (Chicago, IL, 1994); history-makers.com; Jan Hubbard, ed., *The Official NBA Encyclopedia*, 3rd ed. (New York, 2000); Bob Love with Mel Watkins, *The Bob Love Story: If It's Gonna Be, It's Up to Me* (New York, 1999); nba.com; sterlingspeakers.com.

Bijan C. Bayne

LOVELLETTE, Clyde Edward (b. September 7, 1929, Terre Haute, IN), college and professional player, is the son of locomotive engineer John Lovellette and Myrtle Lovellette and attended Terre Haute (Indiana) Garfield High School. The two-year All-State performer led Garfield to the 1947 state tournament championship game before losing 68-58 to Shelbyville High School. At the University of Kansas from 1949 to 1952, Lovellette played under legendary Forrest "Phog" Allen* and helped foster the trend of tall, high-scoring centers. The six-foot nine-inch, 240-pounder won the BEC scoring title as a sophomore with a 21.8 points average; as a junior, Lovellette again paced the BEC in scoring with 22.8 points per game. In his final season (1952), Kansas won the NCAA championship. Lovellette scored 141 points in four games for an NCAA tournament record and was named the MVP. He tallied 44 points against St. Louis University for a new single-game NCAA tournament mark. Lovellette made 315 field goals and scored 795 points for a 28.4 points average that season to lead the nation in each category. A two-time All-America, Lovellette scored a then college record 1,888 career points (24.5 points average). He participated on the U.S. Olympic team that won the gold medal at the 1952 Games in Helsinki, Finland, and played AAU basketball for one season after graduation.

Lovellette began his pro career with the Minneapolis (now Los Angeles) Lakers (NBA) and helped them win the 1953–1954 NBA championship. He became the first hoopster to play on an NCAA, Olympic, and NBA championship squad. (Others include Bill Russell*, K.C. Jones*, and Jerry Lucas*.) Lovellette later played for the NBA's Cincinnati Royals (1957–1958), St. Louis Hawks (1958–1959 to 1961–1962), and Boston Celtics (1962–1963 to 1963–1964), twice winning NBA championships with the latter. He appeared in the NBA championship series in 1960 and 1961 with the Hawks, which lost both times to Boston. With Minneapolis, Lovellette led the Lakers four times in field goal percentage, three times in rebounds, and twice in scoring. In 1955–1956, he scored 1,526 points (fourth best in the NBA) and made 992 rebounds (NBA third best). His best season came in 1957–1958, when he paced Cincinnati in scoring with 1,659 points and compiled a 23.4 point average, ranking fourth in the NBA. He led St. Louis in field goal and free throw percentage in the 1959–1960 and 1960–1961 seasons.

One of the most physical centers in NBA history, Lovellette played in 773 regular-season and playoff games, scored 12,910 points (16.7 points average), and grabbed 7,220 rebounds (9.3 rebounds average) in 11 seasons. He played in three NBA All-Star Games (1956, 1960–1961) and in 1956 was named to the All-NBA Second Team. A member of HAF Hall of Fame, Lovellette in 1952 was selected as their Player of the Year. After leaving basketball, he served as a television sports director and as a sheriff in Terre Haute. Lovellette also directed a nursing home in Illinois, owned an antique shop in Massachusetts, and coached at St. Anthony's School in New Bedford, Massachusetts. He lives in Wabash, Indiana and is the director of the Vocational Education program at White's Institute, the largest residential childcare facility in the state. Lovellette's first wife, Sally, whom he married in 1952, is deceased. He married Judy Jean Wray in 1970 and has five children, Cynthia, Linda, Cherie, Barry, and Robb. In 1988, he was elected as a player to the Naismith Memorial Basketball Hall of Fame.

BIBLIOGRAPHY: Morgan G. Brenner, *College Basketball's National Championships* (Lanham, MD, 1999); John Devaney, *Where Are They Today?* (New York, 1985); John Hendel, *Kansas Jayhawks* (Coal Valley, IL, 1991); Zander Hollander, ed., *The Modern Encyclopedia of Basketball* (Garden City, NY, 1979); Jan Hubbard, ed., *The Official NBA Encyclopedia*, 3rd ed. (New York, 2000); Blair Kerkhoff, *Phog Allen: The Father of Basketball Coaching* (Indianapolis, IN, 1996); Donald Lazenby, *The NBA Finals* (Indianapolis, IN, 1996); Clyde Lovellette file, Naismith Memorial Basketball Hall of Fame Springfield, MA; Ken Shouler et al., *Total Basketball* (Wilmington, DE, 2003); Stew Thornley, *Basketball's Original Dynasty: The History of the Minneapolis Lakers* (Minneapolis, MN, 1989).

John L. Evers

LUBIN, Frank John (b. January 7, 1910, East Los Angeles, CA), college and amateur player and coach, is the son of Konstantin Lubin and Antoinina (Vausokaite) Lubin and participated in three sports at Lincoln High School in Los Angeles, California. After high school graduation, Lubin enrolled at UCLA in 1927 and started three years on the basketball team. Upon graduation in 1931, he abandoned dreams of law school and worked as a laborer with Universal Studios because the United States had sunk into the Great Depression. This job enabled him to play on Universal's AAU basketball team. Lubin's first distinction in AAU basketball came in 1936, when his Universal team played in the Olympic basketball tournament in New York. Universal had finished in second place at the national AAU tournament in Denver, Colorado, and won the Olympic tournament by edging the AAU champions, the McPherson Globe Oilers, 44-43.

The victory secured a place for Lubin on the first U.S. Olympic basketball team. He captained the 1936 Olympic squad. After winning a gold medal in the Berlin, Germany Summer Olympic Games, Lubin, whose parents were Lithuanian, received an invitation from the Lithuanian government to visit that nation. This marked the beginning of a three-year odyssey in which he became a Lithuanian citizen and played on and coached Lithuania's national team. Lubin played under his Lithuanian name, Pranas Lubinas, becoming "The Godfather of Lithuanian Basketball." He scored the winning basket against Latvia, enabling Lithuania to win the 1939 European championship 36-35. Lubin also coached Lithuania's women's team, which included his wife, Mary Agnes, whom he met in Wichita, Kansas.

Upon returning to the United States in 1939, Lubin moved over to Twentieth Century Fox to work as a stagehand and continued his basketball career. Before playing in Lithuania, he had been named an AAU All-America. Besides exhibiting excellent basketball skills, Lubin also proved a popular showman. One of his favorite routines involved dressing up as Frankenstein and mingling with the crowd. Lubin, who made the AAU All-America team in 1941, 1942, and 1945, played in his last AAU tournament in 1951 and scored 37 points in a tournament game at age 41.

In 1981, the LABC chose Lubin as one of the 20 best basketball players from Southern California. When the Soviet Union's basketball team defeated the United States and won the gold medal at the 1988 Seoul, South Korea Summer Olympics, four of its players came from Lithuania. The Soviet team was coached by Lubin's students. In 1988, Lithuania invited him to celebrate the fiftieth anniversary of its European Cup. After retiring from Twentieth Century Fox, Lubin joined the Spirit Team, a group of past Olympians working with young people. He and his wife live in Glendale, California, and have two children, Joan and John.

BIBLIOGRAPHY: Bill Mallon and Ian Buchanan, *Quest for Gold: The Encyclopedia of American Olympians* (New York, 1984); Alfred Erich Senn, "American Lithuanians and the Politics of Basketball in Lithuania, 1935–1939," *JBS* (Summer 1988), pp. 146–156; Ken Shouler et al., *Total Basketball* (Wilmington, DE, 2003); Andy Wodka, "The Godfather," *OL* (February 1990), pp. 28–30.

Adolph H. Grundman

LUCAS, Jerry Ray (b. March 30, 1940, Middletown, OH), college and professional player, was one of the most dominant players in the history of the collegiate roundball sport. As a standout player from a town known as the "high school basketball capital of Ohio," Lucas led basketball-rich Middletown High School to 76 consecutive victories and two straight state championships. His teams rarely knew defeat while led by the incomparable six-foot seven-inch schoolboy center. By the conclusion of his sophomore year, Lucas already was being touted as the greatest Ohio schoolboy player ever. In the final two games of the state tournament that season, he led his team to victory by shooting only when necessary and still averaged 48.5 points. Despite his own self-doubts about his basketball abilities and his early claims that he was not interested in a pro sports life, Lucas finished his prep career as the nation's greatest high school scorer (2,466 points) of his time. He actively was recruited by over 150 colleges, including every important basketball school in the nation. As a straight-A student, Lucas elected to enroll at nearby Ohio State University on a full academic scholarship.

The Ohio State basketball team for which Lucas performed in the early 1960s was one of the greatest college units of all time with players like John Havlicek*, Larry Siegfried, and Bobby Knight*. The Fred Taylor*–coached teams of those years amassed an overall winning record of 78-6, appeared in three consecutive NCAA tournament final games, won three-straight BTC titles, and captured the national championship in Lucas' sophomore year. His greatest single-season performance came that sophomore national championship campaign, as Lucas averaged 26.3 points and 16.4 rebounds, shot a stunning .637 percent from the floor, and was chosen unanimous First Team All-America. During all three seasons at Ohio State, Lucas led the nation in field goal shooting accuracy. In his junior year, the Buckeyes won 27 consecutive regular-season games before bowing in the national finals. Lucas was chosen National College Player of the Year for the second consecutive season.

Drafted by the Cincinnati Royals (NBA) as a territorial choice in 1962, Lucas again indicated his unwillingness to pursue a full-time pro basketball lifestyle and expressed preference for a business career. He signed a combined business-basketball contract instead with the newly formed Cleveland Pipers (ABL) and was forced to sit out the 1962–1963 season because the Cleveland club folded before playing its first ABL game. Lucas finally succumbed to offers from Cincinnati (NBA), however, and enjoyed a highly successful six-year career in the Queen City before being traded to San Francisco (NBA) in October 1969. As a first-year performer with the Royals in 1963, he continued his brilliant play by shooting .527 percent from the floor with a 17.7 points average and taking NBA Rookie of the Year honors as anticipated. During his tenure at Cincinnati, he became only the third player in NBA history to average 20 points and 20 rebounds for a season and made the NBA All-Star team nearly every year.

But by 1970, Lucas suffered a mid-career slump and seemed to have lost his interest in the game. When traded to the New York Knickerbockers (NBA) for Cazzie Russell*, however in May 1971 he suddenly found himself with a running team that suited his open offensive style and played the game "the way it was meant to be played." In his two seasons with New York, Lucas enjoyed two trips to the title series against Los Angeles and won his first NBA crown in 1973 before willingly retiring from the game. He ranked among the top 20 all-time NBA rebounders (12,942). In 829 career games, Lucas scored 14,053 points (17.0 points average) and made around 50 percent of his field goal attempts. But perhaps he will be best remembered for his dazzling play on a 1960 U.S. Gold Medal Olympic team that many consider to be the finest amateur basketball squad ever assembled. At the conclusion of his playing career, Lucas achieved an additional notoriety as co-author with Harry Lorayne of a best-selling book titled *The Memory Book* about self-discipline and memory control. He was elected to the Naismith Memorial Basketball Hall of Fame in 1979, and named one of the 50 Greatest Players in NBA History in 1996.

BIBLIOGRAPHY: Peter C. Bjarkman, *Big Ten Basketball* (Indianapolis, IN, 1994); Morgan G. Brenner, *College Basketball's National Championships* (Lanham, MD, 1999); Mike Douchant, *Encyclopedia of College Basketball* (Detroit, MI, 1995); Jan Hubbard, ed., *The Official NBA Encyclopedia*, 3rd ed. (New York, 2000); George Kalinsky, *The New York Knicks: The Official 50th Anniversary Celebration* (New York, 1996); *The Lincoln Library of Sports Champions*, vol. 7 (Columbus, OH, 1974); Harry Lorayne and Jerry Lucas, *The Memory Book* (New York, 1974); Jerry Lucas file, Naismith Memorial Basketball Hall of Fame, Springfield, MA; Ken Shouler et al., *Total Basketball* (Wilmington, DE, 2003).

Peter C. Bjarkman

LUCAS, John Harding, Jr. "Luke" (b. October 31, 1953, Durham, NC), college and professional athlete, is the son of John H. Lucas Sr. and Blondola Lucas, both high school principals. Lucas enjoyed a storied basketball and tennis career at Hillside High School, breaking Pete Maravich's* North Carolina State scholastic basketball scoring record and playing on the U.S. Junior Davis Cup tennis team. Over 400 colleges tendered scholarship offers, with Lucas choosing the University of Maryland (ACC) because he could pursue his twin athletic loves there.

Authorities regarded Lucas as the greatest guard in Maryland's history. Freshman eligibility enabled Lucas to become the Terrapins' third all-time basketball scorer with 2,015 points and an 18.3 point average. He holds second-place on the career assists list. Under coach "Lefty" Driesell*, Lucas, Tom McMillen, and Len Elmore helped the Terrapins to register a 92-23 win-loss record between 1972 and 1976 and win the 1975 regular-season ACC Championship. Lucas, who also captured two ACC tennis singles titles and an ACC doubles title, became Maryland's only three-time All-ACC First-Team basketball player and earned consensus All-America as a junior and senior in both sports.

The Houston Rockets (NBA) drafted the six-foot three-inch, 185-pound Lucas first in the 1976 draft, making him the first guard selected number one since Maravich. His consistent guard play, effervescent personality, and "Boy Scout" character quickly made him a valuable, attractive basketball player. He made the NBA All-Rookie team, averaging 11.1 points and 5.6 assists. The Golden Gaters and New Orleans Nets (WTTL) enlisted Lucas in 1977 and 1978, making him the first person to play both basketball and tennis professionally. As the only black in the WTTL, Lucas made an odd couple with 43-year-old white transsexual Renee Richards.

Lucas battled cocaine dependency for several years, jeopardizing his professional basketball career. He admitted to wanting "to do anything once in life just to try it" and to "getting in with some wrong people." Unsurprisingly, NBA teams waived or traded him eight times. His NBA stops included the Houston Rockets three times (1976–1978, 1984–1986, 1989–1991), and the Golden State Warriors (1978–1981), Washington Bullets (1981–1983), San Antonio Spurs (1983–1984), and Milwaukee Bucks (1986–1988) once each. Since no NBA team would risk signing him, Lucas played briefly in 1983 for the Lancaster Lightning (CBA). In December 1984, the 31-year-old tested positive for cocaine a third time. The Rockets consequently placed him on leave of absence, causing him temporarily to retire from professional basketball, explaining, "I can't take it anymore. It's the travel, the road and the life style." He underwent drug rehabilitation, returned to the NBA, and kept off cocaine after 1986. He retired following the 1990–1991 season.

Lucas started antidrug programs to assist others, currently heading the NBAPA Drug Program and Students Taking Action Not Drugs (STAND). The highly honored John Lucas Fitness System, a training regimen for recovering drug addicts, the chronically depressed, and the elderly, cooperates with Houston, Texas hospitals.

In 14 NBA seasons, Lucas scored 9,951 points (10.7 point average) and assisted on 6,454 baskets (7.0 per game average) in 928 games. His assist total ranked among all-time leaders. He holds the NBA record for most assists in one quarter, recording 14 against the Denver Nuggets on April 15, 1984. Lucas coached the San Antonio Spurs (NBA) to marks of 39-22 in 1992–1993 and 55-27 in 1993–1994. He piloted the Philadelphia 76ers (NBA) to losing records in 1994–1995 and 1995–1996 and the Cleveland Cavaliers (NBA) to losing marks in 2001–2002 and 2002–2003. His teams finished 173-258 in the regular season and 6-8 in NBA playoffs. Lucas, who married Debbie Fozard and has three children, Tarvia, John, and Jai, earned a Master's degree in secondary education from the University of San Francisco in 1980. His son John played basketball for Baylor University (Texas) and Oklahoma State University.

BIBLIOGRAPHY: Peter C. Bjarkman, *ACC: Atlantic Coast Conference Basketball* (Indianapolis, IN, 1996); Peter C. Bjarkman, *The Biographical History of Basketball* (Chicago, IL, 2000); Mike Douchant, *Encyclopedia of College Basketball* (Detroit, MI, 1995); Zander Hollander, ed., *The Complete Handbook of Pro Basketball—1990* (New York, 1989); Jan Hubbard, ed., *The Official NBA Encyclopedia*, 3rd ed. (New York, 2000); "Lucas Retires, Cites Pressure," *NYT*, December 11, 1984, p. B17; Jack McCallum, "John Lucas: Picking Up the Pieces," *SI* 54 (June 8, 1981), pp. 34–36, 39–40; Paul McMullen, *Maryland Basketball* (Baltimore, MD, 2002); *Houston Rockets Media Guide, 1989–1990* (Houston, TX, 1989), pp. 30–31; Ken Shouler et al., *Total Basketball* (Wilmington, DE, 2003); *TSN Official NBA Register, 1990–1991* (St. Louis, MO, 1990); University of Maryland Sports Information Office, letter to Bruce J. Dierenfield, July 11, 1990.

Bruce J. Dierenfield

LUISETTI, Angelo Joseph "Hank" (b. June 16, 1916, San Francisco, CA; d. December 17, 2002, San Mateo, CA), college player, was the son of Steven Luisetti, a restaurant owner, and Amalia (Grossi) Luisetti and wore painful braces as a child to straighten out his bowed legs. He started playing basketball at a playground near his home, often competing against taller youngsters. Consequently Luisetti shot the ball from a distance, usually with one hand rather than the two-hand set-shot style of that era. He continued to develop his unusual shooting style at San Francisco's Galileo High School and received a basketball scholarship to Stanford University (California).

After entering Stanford University in the fall of 1934, Luisetti developed his skills over four years in becoming the game's first modern player. Besides using his running one-handed shots, he was the first player to dribble and pass behind his back and switch positions on the court to meet changing game situations. His main attributes included perfect coordination, tremendous spring in his legs, excellent speed, and quick reactions. A fierce competitor, Luisetti also possessed great powers of relaxation and a keen eye. Although weighing just 165 pounds as a freshman, the six-foot two and a half-inch Luisetti reached 184 pounds by his senior year. After starring on an undefeated Stanford University freshman team, he led the Indians varsity to three consecutive PCC championships and to Team of the Year honors for the 1936–1937 season. As a sophomore, Luisetti scored 416 points and received All-America honors. After that season, he participated briefly on the Stanford track and field team as a high jumper and tied for first place in his only meet.

During his junior season, Luisetti played one of the finest all-around games ever seen in Madison Square Garden in New York. On December 30, 1936, he scored 15 points, as Stanford University ended Long Island University's (New York) 43-game winning streak 45-31. When Luisetti walked off the floor, he received a standing ovation from the crowd. Long Island University coach Clair Bee* boasted, "I can't remember anybody who could do more things." During 1936–1937, Luisetti tallied 410 points and was named Collegiate Player of the Year. Elected team captain as a senior, he became the first collegian to score 50 points in a game. On January 1, 1938, Luisetti made 23 field goals and four free throws as Stanford defeated Duquesne University (Pennsylvania) 92-27, and finished with a 21-3 record. Named Collegiate Player of the Year once again, he scored 465 points to set a new four-year college scoring mark of 1,596 points and averaged 16.5 points.

After his college career, Luisetti played AAU basketball. In 1938, Hollywood capitalized on his fame and paid him $10,000 to appear in *Campus Confessions* with Betty Grable. The AAU suspended Luisetti for a year because he had acted as a professional while making the movie. He returned to AAU competition in 1939–1940 and was named the outstanding player in the AAU national tournament, setting a tournament scoring record. Luisetti joined the Phillips 66 Oilers in 1941, but played little after injuring his knee. He married Jane Rossiter on April 18, 1941, and had one daughter, Nancy, and one son, Steven; he remarried after Jane's death. After enlisting in the U.S. Navy during World War II, Luisetti was assigned to St. Mary's Preflight School and averaged 30 points. Before sea duty in 1944, he was hospitalized with spinal meningitis and lost 40 pounds during his many months in the hospital. Although Luisetti recovered, doctors advised him that playing basketball again would endanger his health.

Luisetti worked for John Hancock Life Insurance, joined Stewart Chevrolet Company in San Francisco, California, and coached their team several seasons, winning the AAU crown in 1950–1951. He left coaching after that season and conducted basketball clinics in the San Francisco Bay Area. After serving as sales manager of Stewart Chevrolet for several years, he joined E.F. McDonald Travel Company and served as president of their West Coast region before retiring. After his college career, Luisetti continued to accumulate honors and finished second to George Mikan* in an AP poll to select the best basketball player of the first half of the twentieth century. Besides being elected to the Naismith Memorial Basketball Hall of Fame in 1959 as a charter member, he also was selected to the HAF All-Time All-America team and the Stanford Hall of Fame.

BIBLIOGRAPHY: Peter C. Bjarkman, *The Biographical History of Basketball* (Chicago, IL, 2000); Gary Cavalli, *Stanford Sports* (Palo Alto, CA, 1982); Mike Douchant, *Encyclopedia of College Basketball* (Detroit, MI, 1995); Don E. Liebendorfer, *The Color of Life Is Red* (Palo Alto, CA, 1972); Hank Luisetti file, Naismith Memorial Basketball Hall of Fame, Springfield, MA; Ronald L. Mendell, *Who's Who in Basketball* (New York, 1973); Sandy Padwe, *Basketball's Hall of Fame* (Englewood Cliffs, NJ, 1970); Ken Shouler et al., *Total Basketball* (Wilmington, DE, 2003).

Jay Langhammer

M

MACAULEY, Charles Edward, Jr. "Easy Ed" (b. March 22, 1928, St. Louis, MO), college and professional player, is the son of Charles Edward Macauley Sr., attended University High School in St. Louis, Missouri and averaged only 6.8 points over 81 games in three years. In 1945, he enrolled at St. Louis University and emerged as a star there. Macauley led the nation with a .524 field goal percentage in 1946–1947. During his junior and senior years, he was selected an All-America. In 1948, Macauley was chosen MVP in the NIT. The AP selected him Player of the Year in 1949.

On graduation, Macauley signed a two-year, $30,000 contract with the St. Louis Bombers (NBA). He averaged an impressive 16.1 points his rookie season to finish fifth highest in the NBA, but the St. Louis franchise folded at the end of the 1949–1950 season. The New York Knicks (NBA) reportedly offered to purchase the defunct St. Louis franchise solely to obtain Macauley, but the NBA refused to sanction the deal and he signed with the Boston Celtics (NBA) instead. Throughout his career, Macauley was nicknamed "Easy Ed." Although some suggest that this nickname originated with his easy-going personality, it is more likely a reflection of his style of play. At six feet eight inches and under 200 pounds, Macauley could not battle under the basket with the era's beefier big men. A finesse player, he smoothly and gracefully outmaneuvered his defenders for easy lay-ups and gentle, accurate hookshots.

Macauley enjoyed immediate success in Boston, where he joined Bob Cousy* and Bill Sharman* to give the Celtics one of the greatest scoring combinations in pro basketball history. An All-NBA First Team player from 1950–1951 through 1952–1953 and All-NBA Second Team player in 1953–1954, he was named the outstanding player in the NBA's first All-Star Game in 1951. Macauley played in eight NBA All-Star Games and was the only unanimous selection for the 1954 game. During six years with Boston, he always ranked among the NBA leaders in both points per game and field goal accuracy. Macauley average over 17 points each season. In perhaps his greatest pro game on March 6, 1953, he scored 46 points against the George Mikan*–led Minneapolis Lakers.

Macauley figured in perhaps the most important and controversial trade in pro basketball history. In April 1956, the Celtics traded him to the St. Louis Hawks (NBA) for draft rights to Bill Russell*, who had made All-America at the University of San Francisco and played on the 1956 U.S. Olympic basketball team. The unsuccessful St. Louis franchise possessed draft rights to Russell, but suspected that he would sign with the Harlem Globetrotters and thus traded those rights for longtime hometown hero Macauley. The Celtics later signed Russell. Macauley combined with Bob Pettit* to bring St. Louis two Western Division titles, capped off by a defeat of the Celtics for the 1958 NBA championship. Macauley, who retired after the 1958–1959 season and became coach and general manager of the team, had scored 11,234 points (17.5 points average) in under nine NBA seasons.

During Macauley's two seasons as coach, the Hawks won two Western Division titles with a

43–19 mark in 1958–1959 and 46–29 mark in 1959–1960. He resigned as general manager in 1962 to engage in various business enterprises and later was a sports announcer in St. Louis. In 1960, he became the youngest person elected to the Naismith Memorial Basketball Hall of Fame.

BIBLIOGRAPHY: Peter C. Bjarkman, *The Boston Celtics Encyclopedia* (Champaign, IL, 1998); Zander Hollander, ed., *The Modern Encyclopedia of Basketball* (Garden City, NY, 1979); Jan Hubbard, ed., *The Official NBA Encyclopedia*, 3rd ed. (New York, 2000); Neil D. Isaacs, *Vintage NBA* (Silver Spring, MD, 1996); Ed Macauley file, Naismith Memorial Basketball Hall of Fame, Springfield, MA; Charles Salzberg, *From Set Shot to Slam Dunk* (New York, 1987); Ken Shouler et al., *Total Basketball* (Wilmington, DE, 2003); Paul Soderberg and Helen Washington, comp. and ed., *The Big Book of Halls of Fame in the United States and Canada* (New York, 1977); *TSN Official NBA Register, 2004–2005* (St. Louis, MO, 2004).

Stephen D. Bodayla

MacLEOD, John Matthew (b. October 3, 1937, New Albany, IN), college and professional athlete, coach, and sportscaster, is the son of Dan J. MacLeod, a government employee, and Elizabeth (Welsh) MacLeod, and began playing basketball in grade school. MacLeod also entered the sprints and short-distance events in track and field, caught and played outfield for high school, college and LABF teams, and boxed occasionally as an amateur. He graduated in 1955 from Our Lady of Providence High School in Clarksville, Indiana, where he substituted at forward on the basketball squad. At Bellarmine College (Kentucky), the six-foot, 170-pound MacLeod earned a Bachelor's degree in history in 1959 and performed guard in basketball. In 1965, he received a Master's degree in history and physical education from Indiana State University.

Assistant basketball coaching assignments followed at DeSales High School in Louisville, Kentucky in 1962–1963 and at Cathedral High School in Indianapolis, Indiana in 1965–1966. His first head basketball coaching job came from 1963 through 1965 at Smithville (Indiana) High School, where his record included 16 wins and 26 losses. He served as freshman basketball coach in 1966–1967 and head coach from 1967 to 1973 at the University of Oklahoma (BEC). His varsity squads compiled a 90-67 record.

In the NBA, MacLeod coached the Phoenix Suns from 1973 to 1987 to a 579-543 regular-season record and 37-44 playoff mark, and the Dallas Mavericks from 1987 to 1989 to a 96-79 regular-season record and a 10-7 playoff slate. The Los Angeles Lakers defeated Dallas in the seventh game of the 1988 Western Conference Finals. This loss to the eventual NBA champions marked the highest finish for the Mavericks. His November 1989 dismissal was attributed to the recurrent drug problems of forward Roy Tarpley and the team's lack of motivation. After leaving the Dallas team ranking eighth among coaches in NBA career victories with 675 regular-season wins, the South Bend, Indiana resident handled color commentary for the television broadcasts of the Detroit Pistons (NBA) games.

During the 1990–1991 season, MacLeod replaced Stu Jackson as head coach of the New York Knickerbockers (NBA) and compiled a disappointing 32-35 mark. After the Chicago Bulls swept the Knickerbockers in the first round of the NBA playoffs, he resigned. Altogether, his NBA clubs recorded 707 career victories and 657 losses.

In May 1991, the University of Notre Dame (Indiana) named MacLeod head coach. He coached at Notre Dame from 1991–1992 through 1998–1999, recording a 106-124 mark. His best season came in 1994–1995, when the Fighting Irish finished 15-12 in their last year before joining the Big East Conference. Notre Dame lost to the University of Virginia in the NIT Finals in 1992 and to the University of Michigan 67-66 in the NIT quarterfinals in 1997. During 14 intercollegiate seasons, his clubs finished 196-193 for a .504 winning percentage. He served as associate head coach of the Denver Nuggets (NBA) from 2002 to 2004.

MacLeod married Carol Ann McGroder on January 18, 1974, and has two children, Kathleen and Matthew. He participated in the Society for the Blind in 1959–1960, when he served in the U.S. Army Reserve. His other positions include Treasurer of the NBA and honorary (active) coach for the Arizona Special Olympics.

BIBLIOGRAPHY: Jan Hubbard, ed., *The Official NBA Encyclopedia*, 3rd ed. (New York, 2000); Jim Moore, *The Phoenix Suns* (Mankato, MN, 1984); Steve Pate, *The Dallas Mavericks '87–88* (Dallas, TX, 1987); Ken Shouler et al., *Total Basketball* (Wilmington, DE, 2003); *TSN Official 2004–2005 NBA Register* (St. Louis, MO, 2004).

Thomas P. Wolf

McADOO, Robert Allen "Bob" (b. September 25, 1951, Greensboro, NC), college and professional player and coach, was named All-NBA First Team and voted the NBA's MVP in 1975. The 1973 NBA Rookie of the Year, McAdoo led the NBA in scoring for three consecutive years (1973–1974 through 1975–1976) with point averages of 30.6, 34.5, and 31.1, respectively. In 1973–1974, he shot 54.7 percent from the floor to top the NBA, was named All-NBA Second Team, and finished runner-up to Kareem Abdul-Jabbar* for MVP. Between 1974 and 1978, McAdoo played in five NBA All-Star Games and averaged 17.6 points. He was chosen 1971–1972 consensus All-America center for the University of North Carolina.

The six-foot nine-inch, 225-pound McAdoo starred as a basketball center and won the track and field high jump championship at Greensboro High School, where he graduated in 1969. He enrolled at Vincennes JC in Indiana and led the basketball squad in 1969–1970 and 1970–1971, averaging 19.3 and 25.0 points. University of North Carolina coach Dean Smith* recruited the talented McAdoo, who in 1971–1972 led the Tar Heels to the ACC championship and a 26-5 finish. North Carolina scored easy triumphs over the University of South Carolina and University of Pennsylvania to capture the 1971–1972 NCAA East Regional title, but suffered a four-point setback to Florida State University in the NCAA semifinals at Los Angeles. The Tar Heels rebounded with a 105-91 triumph over the University of Louisville to take third place. McAdoo led all players in the final two contests, averaging 27 points and 17 rebounds. He was named to the NCAA All-Tournament team with UCLA's Bill Walton* and Keith Wilkes and finished the season with 604 points for a 19.5 points average.

Despite having one more year of college eligibility, McAdoo in 1972 declared himself a hardship case and was drafted as the second pick in the first round by the Buffalo Braves (NBA). McAdoo, who performed at forward his first year, achieved a swift rise to stardom. He was switched in 1974 to a more natural center position and became one of the best outside shooters from the pivot in the NBA. In December 1976, Buffalo traded McAdoo to the New York Knickerbockers (NBA). Between 1976–1977 and 1979–1980, McAdoo played with New York, the Boston Celtics (NBA), and the Detroit Pistons (NBA) while achieving excellent scoring averages between 21.1 and 26.5 points. He was waived by Detroit in March 1981 and was signed by the New Jersey Nets (NBA) as a free agent. McAdoo was traded the next December to Los Angeles, where he helped the Lakers to NBA championships in 1981–1982 and 1984–1985. He was signed in January 1986 by the Philadelphia 76ers (NBA) as a free agent, but appeared in only 29 games and averaged 10.1 points. McAdoo played in Italy with Tracer Milan (1986–1988), Philips Milano (1988–1990), Filanto Forli (1990–1992), and Teamsystem Fabraano (*1992–1993*). In 852 career NBA games, he scored 18,787 points (22.1 points average) and made 8,048 rebounds. He has served as assistant coach of the Miami Heat (NBA) since September 1995 and was elected to the Naismith Memorial Basketball Hall of Fame in 2000. The Heat reached the 2005 Eastern Conference finals against the Detroit Pistons.

BIBLIOGRAPHY: Peter C. Bjarkman, *ACC: Atlantic Coast Conference Basketball* (Indianapolis, IN, 1996); Art Chansky, *The Dean's List* (New York, 1996); Jan Hubbard, ed., *The Official NBA Encyclopedia*, 3rd ed. (New York, 2000); Neil D. Isaacs, *All the Moves: A History of College Basketball* (Philadel-phia, PA, 1975); *The Lincoln Library of Today's Champions*, vol. 8 (Columbus, OH, 1974); Bob McAdoo file, Naismith Memorial Basketball Hall of Fame, Springfield, MA; *NCAA Official College Basketball Guide, 1973* (Phoenix, AZ, 1973); Ken Rappoport, *Tales from the Tar Heel Locker Room* (Champaign, IL, 2002); Ken Shouler, et al., *Total Basketball* (Wilmington, DE, 2003); Dean Smith, *A Coach's Life: My Forty Years in*

Basketball (New York, 1999); *TSN Official NBA Register, 2004–2005* (St. Louis, MO, 2004).

James D. Whalen

McCARTY, Stephanie White. *See* White, Stephanie

McCLAIN, Katrina (b. September 19, 1965, Charleston, SC), college and professional player, has two brothers and three sisters. She began playing basketball as a child and displayed superior athletic skills at St. Andrews High School in Charleston, South Carolina. The six-foot two-inch forward played basketball at the University of Georgia from 1983–1984 to 1986–1987, helping the Bulldogs compile a 116-15 record, four NCAA tournament appearances, and SEC titles in 1984 and 1986. She saw her jersey retired, marking only the third time for a Georgia woman basketball player, and still ranks as the Bulldogs' second highest scorer.

At the 1985 World University Games, McClain was the leading scorer and rebounder, averaging 17.3 points and 7.7 rebounds. She played on the gold medal–winning teams at the 1986 and 1990 USA World Championships, at the 1986 and 1990 Goodwill Games, and at the 1987 USA Pan American Games, averaging 17.8 points and 10.0 rebounds. McClain was named consensus All-America in 1986 and 1987, National Player of the Year in 1987, and USA Basketball Female Athlete of the Year in 1988 and 1992. She performed on the 1988 and 1992 USA Olympic teams that won the bronze medal in the former and the gold in the latter, being the leading scorer (17.6 point average) and rebounder (10.4 rebound average). She was also on the bronze medal–winning 1994 World Championship team, making the five-member World Championship All-Tournament Team, and the 1995–1996 USA Basketball Women's National Team.

McClain played professionally in Japan for Kyoto Petroleum from 1989 to 1991, in Italy with Sidis Ancona in 1992, and in Spain with Valencia in 1993–1994. She played on the team that defeated Brazil to win the gold medal at the 1996 Olympic Games in Atlanta, Georgia, making her one of only three, three-time U.S. Olympic basketball players. McClain joined the Atlanta Glory (ABL) as a forward in 1997, was honored as an ABL All-Star in 1998, and was inducted into Georgia's Athletic Association Circle of Honor in 1998. Although idle for nearly a year after having a baby, she still was named an alternate on the 2000 Olympic team. McClain was recognized as the top post player in Olympic history and holds the Olympic records for points and rebounds. She lives in Atlanta and has two children.

BIBLIOGRAPHY: *Atlanta* (Georgia) *Journal Constitution*, August 10, 2000, p. F3; Sara Corbet, *Venus at the Hoop: A Gold Medal Year for Women's Basketball* (New York, 1997); Mike Douchant, *Encyclopedia of College Basketball* (Detroit, MI, 1995); Georgia Bulldogs: The Official Site of the University of Georgia Bulldogs, http://georgiadogs.ocsn.com/traditions/olympians/mcclain_katrina.shtml (June, 2003); "Katrina McClain," http://washingtonpost.com:Katrina McClain (June, 2003); *Post and Courier* (Charleston, SC), June 14, 2001, p. 6; *Who's Who Among African Americans*, 16th ed. (Detroit, MI, 2003).

Jeannie P. Miller

McCRACKEN, Emmett Branch "Big Bear" "Mac" (b. June 9, 1908, Monrovia, IN; d. June 4, 1970, Bloomington, IN), college player and coach, grew up on a farm in Monrovia, Indiana 40 miles from Bloomington. McCracken first practiced basketball by using an inflated pig's bladder and a peach basket. At Indiana University, he allegedly came to basketball tryouts without his shoes "because that's the way he'd always played." McCracken played basketball at Monrovia High School from 1923 to 1926, leading his teams to Tri-State titles the final two years. He never played football until seeing his first game as a college freshman. At Indiana University from 1926 to 1930, McCracken earned three varsity letters as an end in football. He played forward, center, and guard in basketball, pacing the Hoosiers in scoring for three years. As a senior, McCracken set a WC record with 147 points and was selected consensus All-America. He made the All-WC team three times, was voted WC MVP in 1928, and scored 525 career points at Indiana University.

From 1930 to 1937, McCracken coached basketball at Ball State University (Indiana), where he married Mary Jo Pittenger, the president's daughter. They had one son, David, who coached a high school basketball team in Greencastle, Indiana. During World War II, he served in the U.S. Navy and became a commander. From 1938 to 1965, except for military service, McCracken coached basketball at Indiana University. He initially succeeded his former coach, Naismith Memorial Basketball Hall of Fame member Everett Dean*. Although coaching in probably the nation's toughest league, McCracken directed his Hoosiers to national titles in 1940 and 1953, successive BTC Championships in 1953 and 1954, a BTC title in 1958, and a co-championship in 1957. Under his tutelage, Indiana ranked among the most important teams with its "run-run-run" or fast-break style and a hawking defense. The Indiana cagers, during McCracken's tenure, were nicknamed the "Hurrying Hoosiers." In the Hoosiers' 1939–1940 and 1952–1953 NCAA title seasons, McCracken was chosen Coach of the Year. McCracken, elected in 1960 as a player to the Naismith Memorial Basketball Hall of Fame and in 1957 as a coach to the HAF Hall of Fame, became one of the first members elected to the Indiana High School Hall of Fame.

McCracken conducted basketball clinics in Japan and elsewhere in the Far East in 1951 and in Europe in 1953 at the request of the U.S. State Department. At Indiana University, he coached stars Bob Leonard*, brothers Dick* and Tom Van Arsdale*, Don Schlundt*, Bill Garrett, Jay McCreary, Jimmie Rayl, Hallie Bryant, and Jon McGlocklin. Former player Lou Watson replaced him in 1965 as coach at Indiana University. McCracken, nicknamed "Big Bear" because of his six-foot four-inch size and his tendency to scowl on the bench, paced nervously during games. The workaholic coach sometimes consumed 30 cups of coffee a day and instilled much team and school spirit in his players. "Big Bear" wrote one book, *Indiana Basketball*, describing the team he loved so much. As a college basketball coach, McCracken compiled a 457-215 lifetime win-loss record that included 364-174 at Indiana University and 93-41 at Ball State. He served in an administrative capacity at Indiana University from 1965 until his death as a result of a heart ailment.

BIBLIOGRAPHY: Peter C. Bjarkman, *Biographical History of Basketball* (Chicago, IL, 2000); Peter C. Bjarkman, *Big Ten Basketball* (Indianapolis, IN, 1996); Morgan G. Brenner, *College Basketball's National Championships* (Lanham, MD, 1999); Mike Douchant, *Encyclopedia of College Basketball* (Detroit, MI, 1995); Joe Gergen, *The Final Four—An Illustrated History of Basketball's Showcase Event* (St. Louis, MO, 1987); Bob Hammel et al., *Glory of Old IU* (Champaign, IL, 2000); Ralph Hickok, *Who Was Who in American Sports* (New York, 1971); Indianapolis *News*, June 4, 1970; *Indianapolis Star*, June 5, 1970; *NYT*, June 5, 1970; Branch McCracken File, Naismith Memorial Basketball Hall of Fame, Springfield, MA; Billy Packer and Roland Lazenby, *College Basketball's 25 Greatest Teams* (St. Louis, MO, 1989); Sandy Padwe, *Basketball's Hall of Fame* (Englewood Cliffs, NJ, 1970); Paul Soderberg and Helen Washington, comp. and ed., *The Big Book of Halls of Fame in the United States and Canada* (New York, 1977); Donald E. Thompson, comp., *Indiana Authors and Their Books* (Crawfordsville, IN, 1974).

Frederick J. Augustyn Jr.

McCRACKEN, John "Jumpin Jack" (b. June 11, 1911, Chickasha, OK; d. January 5, 1958, Denver, CO), college player and coach, moved with his family to Oklahoma City, Oklahoma, where he became a three-year basketball standout at Classen High School. At Classen High School, the six-foot two-inch McCracken played center and was named to the All-State team in 1928–1929. His team placed second in the national tournament played in Chicago, Illinois, and he earned High School All-America honors. McCracken followed his high school coach, Hank Iba*, to Northwest Missouri State Teachers College in Maryville, Missouri. Under Iba's tutelage, he played both center and forward. The Bobcats won 43 consecutive games with McCracken and recorded a perfect 31-0 season in 1930–1931. For the 1931–1932 season, McCracken was named a college All-America. Northwest Missouri State was invited to the National AAU tournament in 1932 and advanced to the finals before losing to the Henry Clothiers of Wichita, Kansas 15–14. McCracken was named to the All-America team.

In 1933 McCracken embarked on a lengthy, successful career in AAU basketball. The

Denver, Colorado, resident played for various AAU teams and starred on the 1937 Denver Safeway team, which defeated the Phillips 66 Oilers of Bartlesville, Oklahoma 43-38, for the AAU championship. McCracken, a forward, joined two other members of the Safeway Club on the AAU All-America team that year. In 1938 Safeway lost in the finals of the AAU tournament to Healy Motors of Kansas City, Missouri 40-38 on a last-second basket. McCracken was again named AAU All-America, this time at guard. He moved to the Denver Nuggets in 1939 as player-coach, repeating as an AAU All-America guard and leading the Nuggets to the AAU championship over the Phillips 66 Oilers 25-22. After the 1939 season, he was named the greatest player of all time by the AAU. McCracken continued to play and coach in the AAU tournament until 1945 and led two more teams, including the Phillips 66 Oilers, to AAU championships. He was named an AAU All-America eight times during his career. McCracken, considered by Iba among the best players he ever coached, was named to the NAIA Hall of Fame, Amateur Basketball Hall of Fame, and the HAF Hall of Fame. In 1962, he was elected to the Naismith Memorial Basketball Hall of Fame.

BIBLIOGRAPHY: John McCracken file, Naismith Memorial Basketball Hall of Fame, Springfield, MA; Ronald L. Mendell, *Who's Who in Basketball* (New York, 1973); Paul Soderberg and Helen Washington, Comp. and ed. *The Big Book of Halls of Fame in the United States and Canada* (New York, 1977); Alexander M. Weyand, *The Cavalcade of Basketball* (New York, 1960).

George P. Mang

McCRAY, Nikki Kensengane (b. December 17, 1971, Colliersville, TN), college and professional player, is the oldest of four children of Bobby Albright and Sallie Coleman, assembly line workers. McCray's favorite sport was track and field, as she competed in the 100 meters and long jump at Colliersville High School from 1986 to 1990. A natural athlete, McCray began to play basketball in her grandparents' backyard with her male cousins at only nine years old. In high school, she started for the varsity team. Her speed and jumping ability made her a standout guard, helping her team reach to the Tennessee state tournament junior and senior years. McCray also earned All America honors from both *Parade* magazine and *USA Today*, averaging 27 points and 10 rebounds per game her senior year.

The heavily recruited five-foot eleven-inch, 158-pound McCray enrolled at the University of Tennessee in 1990 to play for the Lady Vols. She tore her anterior cruciate ligament, forcing her to sit out her freshman year. During the four years from 1991–1992 to 1994–1995 that McCray started for the Lady Vols, Tennessee compiled a 122-11 record, won three SEC regular-season titles from 1993 to 1995 and two SEC Tournament titles in 1992 and 1994, and made four trips to the NCAA tournament. She was named SEC Player of the Year in 1994 and 1995 and set career records with 292 steals and 1,566 points. McCray graduated in 1995 with a Bachelor's degree in sports marketing and education.

In 1995, McCray was invited to play on the U.S. Women's National Team. International play proved challenging for McCray, but she soon established herself as a defensive force helping the team win gold medals during the 1996 and 2000 Olympics and the 1998 World Championship. After the 1996 Olympics, McCray signed with Columbus Quest of the newly formed (ABL). She helped lead the Quest to a 31-9 season in 1996–1997, averaging 19.9 points per game. The Quest won the ABL championship, with McCray earning the first ABL MVP award. In September 1997, McCray left the ABL for the WNBA. She played for the Washington Mystics (WNBA) from 1997 through 2001, the Indiana Fever (WNBA) in 2002 and 2003, the Phoenix Mercury (WNBA) in 2004, and the San Antonio Silver Stars (WNBA) since 2005. Through 2004, she has tallied 2,490 points (11.4 average) and 432 assists (1.98 average) in 218 games and played in the WNBA All-Star Game from 1999 to 2001. Her teams were eliminated in the first rounds of the WNBA playoffs in 2000 and 2002. McCray married her college sweetheart, Thomas Penson, in 1999 and serves as a spokesperson for Fila athletic shoes.

BIBLIOGRAPHY: "Nikki McCray," *Athletes and Coaches of Summer* (Detroit, MI, 2000), Athelia

Knight, "Starring Role," *Washington Post* (June 18, 1998); Jeff Pearlman, "Big Time, Big Bucks," *SI* 89 (July 27, 1998), pp.36–37; *TSN Official WNBA Guide and Register, 2004* (St. Louis, MO, 2004); *WNBA* website www.wnba.com.

Lisa A. Ennis

McCUTCHAN, Arad (b. July 4, 1912, Evansville, IN; d. June 16, 1993, Jasper, IN), college player and coach, ranked as perhaps the most successful college-division coach in college basketball history. McCutchan, who earned a Bachelor's degree from Evansville (Indiana) College and a Master's degree from Columbia Teachers College, starred for four years in basketball as an undergraduate and led his team in scoring in all but his freshman season. He returned to Evansville College as the most successful coach in the colorful history of the Purple Aces' basketball program. His many storied achievements included five national titles, two National Coach of the Year selections, and several All-America players, among them Jerry Sloan*, Ed Smallwood, and Larry Humes. In his best single campaign, he guided the 1965 Purple Aces to a glowing 29-0 mark and defeated such national powers as the University of Notre Dame (Indiana), Louisiana State University, Northwestern University (Illinois), and the University of Iowa. From 1947 through 1977, McCutchan compiled a 514-314 career record to become the winningest college-division coach ever to that time. He also coached the 1971 victorious U.S. Pan American Games basketball team.

The Evansville basketball program under McCutchan provided a model of small-college success. As annual host school for the NCAA college-division tournament, Evansville won titles five times during the first 16 seasons of play. The peak years under McCutchan featured Sloan, among the finest all-around small-college players of all time. The scrappy six-foot six-inch Evansville College star later recorded notable successes of his own as an NBA player and coach. The undefeated 1965 national championship team marked McCutchan's finest achievement by defeating Southern Illinois University in an overtime thriller for the title. Sloan outdueled All-America Walt Frazier* for tournament MVP honors. In December 1977, successor coach Bobby Watson and the Evansville team were killed in a plane crash. In 1980, McCutchan was elected to the Naismith Memorial Basketball Hall of Fame.

BIBLIOGRAPHY: Peter C. Bjarkman, *The Biographical History of Basketball* (Chicago, IL, 2000); Neil D. Isaacs, *All the Moves: A History of College Basketball* (Philadelphia, PA, 1975); Arad McCutchan file, Naismith Memorial Basketball Hall of Fame, Springfield, MA; Ronald L. Mendell, *Who's Who in Basketball* (New Rochelle, NY, 1973).

Peter C. Bjarkman

McDERMOTT, Robert "Mr. Basketball" (b. January 7, 1914, Whitestone, Queens, NY; d. October 4, 1963, Yonkers, NY), professional player and coach, attended Flushing (New York) High School one year and played pro basketball without having any college experience. He and his wife, Virginia, had five children. The five-foot eleven-inch guard possessed basketball's best two-handed setshot and scored from anywhere inside half-court. McDermott finished second in ABL scoring in 1934–1935 and led the Brooklyn Visitations to the ABL championship. The next year, he paced Tunkhannock, Pennsylvania to the NYPL title. His 32-point performance that season broke Johnny Beckman's* playoff single-game scoring record. From 1936 to 1939, McDermott starred for the Original Celtics and quickly became the sport's best player and biggest box office attraction. He led the ABL in scoring in 1939–1940 and rejoined the Original Celtics in 1940–1941.

McDermott from 1941–1942 through 1945–1946 was named the NBL's MVP as a member of the Fort Wayne Zollner Pistons (NBL) and made the NBL All-Star team. Subsequent honors included his being on the NBL All-Star First Team in 1946–1947 and the NBL All-Star Second Team the next season. In 1941–1942, he placed second in NBL scoring and led Fort Wayne to the NBL Finals. The next season, McDermott paced both NBL scorers and field goal shooters in helping the Pistons to the NBL Finals and topped the Pro World Tournament in total points. Fort Wayne took the 1943–1944 NBL championship, as McDermott finished second among NBL scorers. The Pistons also won an unprecedented three consecutive World Pro Tournaments from 1944 to 1946. McDermott, MVP of the 1944 tournament, was selected to the NBL All-Star First Team at those three tournaments. In 1944–1945, he broke the NBL season field goals record (258) in directing Fort Wayne to another NBL title and became one of the first two pro players to average over 20 points per game, featuring an NBL single-game record of 36 points against Cleveland. McDermott, named Fort Wayne player-coach before the 1946–1947 campaign, repeated as second highest NBL scorer and helped the Pistons defeat the College All-Stars before a then-record 23,912 spectators. In 1946–1947, the Chicago Gears (NBL) hired him as player-coach. McDermott combined with George Mikan* in directing Chicago to the NBL championship. He led the Tri-Cities Blackhawks to the NBL Western Division Finals in 1947–1948 and completed his NBL playing career with the Hammond, Indiana Buccaneers (NBL) in 1948–1949. McDermott scored 48 points in an exhibition game for the Wilkes-Barre, Pennsylvania Barons against the New York Knickerbockers (NBA) and averaged 17 points in 1949–1950 until a back injury ended his career. He later worked as a security guard at Yonkers Raceway and died two weeks after being injured in a traffic accident there.

McDermott, the only basketball player to lead three leagues (ABL, NYSL, NBL) in scoring and the only pro basketball player-coach to guide two teams to titles, ranked first in NBL career scoring and second in NBL playoff scoring, 54 points behind Leroy Edwards*. He often scored over 20 points in a game when contests lasted only 40 minutes and when teams played more deliberate styles. Besides leading the NBL in scoring three times and finishing second five times, McDermott made 10 All-Star teams. He paced Fort Wayne in scoring all six seasons there and helped them capture four NBL first place regular-season finishes and three NBL playoff titles. In 1946, NBL coaches and players joined sports editors in voting him "the Greatest Player of All-Time." McDermott's other awards included being selected to the All-Time team with Dutch Dehnert*, Nat Holman*, Beckman, and Edwards by ex-pro players and reporters in 1946, being chosen to the "All-World Team" by *Collier's* in 1950, and being voted the "Greatest Fort Wayne Player of All Time" in 1954. In 1988, he was named to the Naismith Memorial Basketball Hall of Fame.

BIBLIOGRAPHY: Zander Hollander, ed., *The NBA's Official Encyclopedia of Pro Basketball* (New York, 1981); Neil D. Isaacs, *Vintage NBA* (Silver Spring, MD, 1996); Robert McDermott file, Naismith Memorial Basketball Hall of Fame, Springfield, MA; Murry R. Nelson, *The Originals—The New York Celtics Invent Modern Basketball* (Bowling Green, OH, 1999); *NYT*, October 5, 1963; Wayne Patterson to David L. Porter, February 15, 1988; Robert W. Peterson, *Cages to Jump Shots: Pro Basketball's Early Years* (New York, 1990); Ken Shouler et al., *Total Basketball* (Wilmington, DE, 2003); Richard F. Triptow, *The Dynasty That Never Was* (Chicago, IL, 1997).

David L. Porter

McGINNIS, George F. (b. August 12, 1950, Indianapolis, IN), college and professional player, is the youngest of two children born to Burnie McGinnis and Willie McGinnis. At Indianapolis Washington High School, McGinnis was named as an end to the consensus 1968 and 1969 High School All-America football teams. In 1968–1969, as a senior forward, he led Washington's basketball team to a 31-0 record and state championship. McGinnis averaged 32.5 points that season, breaking Oscar Robertson's* Indianapolis high school season and career records, and was named "Mr. Basketball" in Indiana. In the annual two-game series between Indiana and Kentucky High School All-Stars, he scored 76 composite points and pulled down 30 rebounds in the two Indiana victories. In 1970, McGinnis played on the U.S. basketball team in the World University Games in Turin, Italy. McGinnis received more than 350 scholarship offers from various colleges and universities before choosing to attend Indiana University. In his only season at Indiana, he in 1970–1971 was the nation's fourth best scorer (29.9 points per game) and the twelfth best rebounder (14.5 rebounds per game), and received All-America recognition. His amateur career was once characterized as "like a man among boys."

In 1971 the six-foot eight-inch, 235-pound McGinnis signed as an undergraduate free agent with the Indiana Pacers (ABA). The Philadelphia 76ers (NBA), in order to secure the NBA rights, selected him in the second round (twenty-second overall selection) of the 1973 draft. During 11 pro seasons with the Indiana Pacers (ABA, 1971–1975), Philadelphia 76ers (NBA, 1975–1978), Denver Nuggets (NBA, 1978–1980), and Indiana Pacers (NBA, 1980–1982), he played on two ABA championship teams (1971–1972, 1972–1973), in three consecutive ABA All-Star Games (1972–1974) and in three NBA All-Star Games (1976, 1977, 1979). McGinnis, who was selected to the 1972 ABA All-Rookie team, was named 1973 ABA playoff MVP with 431 points, 222 rebounds, and 39 assists. He led the ABA in scoring in 1974–1975 with 2,353 points and was named the 1975 Co-MVP with Julius Erving* of the New Jersey Nets. He made the ABA All-Star First Team in 1974 and 1975 and the ABA All-Star Second Team in 1973. On October 27, 1982, McGinnis was waived by the Indiana Pacers. Six days later, the Pacers retired the number 30 jersey worn by McGinnis in recognition of his being the team's third leading scorer (11,213 points) and its top scorer for average (19.9 points). Once among the greatest forwards in basketball history and one of the best players produced in basketball-rich Indiana, McGinnis resides in Indianapolis.

BIBLIOGRAPHY: Mike Chappell, "McGinnis Honored to Have Pacer Jersey Retired," Indianapolis *Star*, November 2, 1985; Bob Gould, *Pioneers of the Hardwood* (Bloomington, IN, 1998); Bob Hammel et al., *Glory of Old IU* (Champaign, IL, 2000); Mark Heisler, "George McGinnis: He's Come a Long Way from Haulsville," Philadelphia *Evening Bulletin*, September 24, 1975; Jan Hubbard, ed., *The Official NBA Encyclopedia*, 3rd ed. (New York, 2000); Jerry Kirschenbaum, "Big City Country Boy," *SI* 43 (October 27, 1975), pp. 38ff; Bill Livingston, "76ers' McGinnis: A Little Ham, a Lot of Talent," *TSN*, February 28, 1976; *NYT*, April 8, 1975; Jim O'Brien, "Muscles McGinnis a Deal," *TSN*, February 24, 1973; Woodrow Paige, Jr., "George McGinnis: The Shots Stopped Dropping," Denver *Post*, November 8, 1982; Terry Pluto, *Loose Balls* (New York, 1990); Ken Shouler, et al., *Total Basketball* (Wilmington, DE, 2003); *TSN Official NBA Register, 2004–2005* (St. Louis, MO, 2004).

James E. Welch

McGRADY, Tracy Lamar, Jr. (b. May 24, 1979, Bartow, FL), player, is the son of Tracy McGrady Sr. and Melanise (Williford) McGrady, and was brought up by his mother and maternal grandmother, Roberta Williford. McGrady attended Auburndale (Florida) High School, where he averaged 23 points and 12 rebounds in basketball as a junior in 1995–1996. His name did not appear on any recruiting service lists of Division I prospects because he was never recruited to summer camps and Auburndale never appeared in high-profile tournaments.

In May 1996, Mount Zion Christian Academy in Durham, North Carolina gave McGrady a basketball scholarship. Under coach Joe Hopkins, McGrady averaged 28 points, nine rebounds, and eight assists in 1996–1997 and led Mount Zion to a second place national ranking in *USA Today*. In one game, he recorded 36 points, 11 rebounds, seven assists, three blocks, four steals, and eight dunks.

McGrady skipped college to play professional basketball. The Toronto Raptors (NBA) selected the six-foot nine-inch, 210-pound shooting guard in the first round as the ninth pick overall of the 1997 NBA draft. McGrady signed a lucrative contract with Nike shoes and donated $300,000 to Mount Zion. He played reserve roles in his first two seasons with Toronto and started at guard in 1999–2000, averaging 16 points and helping the Raptors make the NBA playoffs.

Toronto traded McGrady to the Orlando Magic (NBA) for a future first-round draft pick in August 2000. McGrady averaged nearly 27 points in 2000–2001, being voted the NBA's Most Improved Player and making the All-NBA Second Team. In the first round of the NBA playoffs, McGrady averaged nearly 34 points against the Milwaukee Bucks.

With the absence of Grant Hill* in 2001–2002, McGrady was forced to carry much of the offensive load and was often assigned to defend the other teams' best offensive player. He demonstrated versatility and flair, averaging nearly 26 points and defending well. McGrady led the Magic in rebounding (nearly eight a game) as a backcourt player and made 103 three-pointers. He again led the Magic to the NBA playoffs, averaging over 30 points against the Charlotte Hornets in the first round.

McGrady took his game to an even higher level in 2002–2003, leading the NBA in scoring with 2,407 points (32.1 point average) and averaging 5.5 assists and 1.7 steals. An All-NBA First Team selection, he broke a Magic record with over 50 points in one game and tallied over 40 points in consecutive November games. The Detroit Pistons, however, ousted the Magic in the first round of the 2003 NBA playoffs.

McGrady repeated as NBA scoring titlist in 2003–2004, tallying 1,878 points (28.0 point average) and again averaging 5.5 assists and 1.7 steals in 67 games. He converted his first eight three pointers while scoring 36 first half points against the Cleveland Cavaliers and in February became the second youngest player to reach 10,000 career points. McGrady tallied a team-record and NBA-season best 62 points against the Washington Bullets in March, becoming just the third NBA player in 12 years to score that many points. He made the All–NBA Second Team, but Orlando recorded an NBA–low 21 victories and missed the NBA playoffs. The Houston Rockets (NBA) acquired McGrady in a seven-player blockbuster trade in June 2004. McGrady averaged 25.7 points in 2004–2005, helping Houston make the playoffs with 51 wins. He averaged 30.7 points, 7.4 rebounds, and 6.7 assists in seven games in the first playoff loss to the Dallas Mavericks. He earned All-NBA Third Team honors in 2005.

Through the 2004–2005 season, McGrady has tallied 13,702 points (22.3 average), 3,911 rebounds (6.4 average), and 2,753 assists (4.5 average) in 615 games. In 18 NBA playoff games, he has averaged 29.8 points, 6.8 rebounds, and 5.8 assists. McGrady has played in five consecutive NBA All-Star games since 2001, scoring 24 points in 2002 and 29 points in 2003. He resides in Isleworth, Florida, with his fiance and daughter, Layla.

BIBLIOGRAPHY: Greg Boeck, "McGrady finds footing after falling into funk," *USAT*, November 20, 2003, p. 3C; Tim Carothers, "A Tough Question," *SI* 87 (December 29, 1997–January 5, 1998), pp. 55–59; Tim Carothers, "Onward Christian Soldier," *SI* 86 (February 10, 1997), pp. 40–44; *Orlando Magic Media Guide*, 2003–2004; Ken Shouler et al., *Total Basketball* (Wilmington, DE, 2003); *TSN Official NBA Register, 2004–2005* (St. Louis, MO, 2004); L. Jon Wertheim, "Rare Pro," *SI* 91 (November 1, 1998), pp. 72–74.

David L. Porter

McGUIRE, Alfred James "Al" (b. September 7, 1931, New York, NY; d. January 26, 2001, Milwaukee, WI), college and professional player, coach, administrator, and broadcaster, grew up in the Irish section of Rockaway Beach in Brooklyn, New York, where his parents, John McGuire and Winifred (Sullivan) McGuire, owned a tavern. He graduated from St. John's Prep School and from St. John's University with a Bachelor of Arts degree in 1952. A six-foot two-inch guard, McGuire captained the 1950–1951 St. John's Redmen squad that finished third in the NIT. He briefly played professionally in the NBA, averaging four points for four seasons with the New York Knicks (1950–1951–1952–1953) and the Baltimore Bullets (1953–1954). McGuire played one year at St. John's (1948–1949) and three years for the Knicks with his brother, Richard "Tricky Dick" McGuire*, an All-Star player and future NBA coach.

McGuire began his basketball coaching career in 1955 as an assistant at Dartmouth College and in 1957 was named head coach at Belmont Abbey College (North Carolina). In seven seasons (1957–1964), he led the Crusaders to a 109-64 record and five post-season tournaments. In 1964 McGuire became the head basketball coach and athletic director at Marquette University. During 13 seasons, he compiled a 295-80 mark (.787 winning percentage) and guided his 1970–1971 team to a 39-game winning streak. His Warriors made 11 post-season appearances, winning the NIT title in 1970 and the NCAA championship in 1977. The quintessential New York City Irishman, his coaching style reflected his flamboyant, street-smart personality. At Marquette, he was known for improvisational sideline coaching during games, loosely structured practice sessions, fiery battles with referees, a tenacious defensive style, a star system that featured the dominant senior player, and extraordinary rapport and recruiting success with black athletes. Although his wisecracks, clever wit, and street-corner aphorisms made him a rare media celebrity coach, McGuire also exhibited substance. In 20 seasons, he posted a career record of 404 victories against 144 defeats for a lifetime .737 winning percentage (18th all-time among division I coaches, and was voted national Coach of the Year in 1971 and 1974).

McGuire retired from coaching in 1977 to serve as vice-chairman of the board of Medalist Industries, a sporting goods conglomerate, and joined NBC-TV in 1978 as a color man for college basketball broadcasts. From 1978 to 1981, the emotional McGuire teamed with the clinical Billy Packer and play-by-play announcer Dick Enberg to form an extraordinarily popular broadcast team. When Packer left the network, McGuire became an even greater media star. Critics complained that his cuteness, catchy phrases, and volatile personality detracted from the contest, but his popularity grew as his infectious charm and fast-paced, free-spirited, spontaneous, humorous, and irreverent commentary matched the tempo of the game itself. He spent 23 years as a broadcaster, announcing for CBS from 1992 until his retirement in March 2000 because of a blood disorder. McGuire married Patricia Sharkey in 1953 and had three children, Al Jr. (whom he coached at Marquette University), Noreen, and Robert. In 1992, he was elected to the Naismith Memorial Basketball Hall of Fame.

BIBLIOGRAPHY: Morgan G. Brenner, *College Basketball's National Championships* (Lanham, MD, 1999); Mike Douchant, *Encyclopedia of College Basketball* (Detroit, MI, 1995); Joe Gergen, *The Final Four—An Illustrated History of College Basketball's Showcase Event* (St. Louis, MO, 1987); Paul Good, "Al McGuire," *Sport* 68 (March 1979), pp. 25–28; Larry Keith, "A Conversation with Chairman Al," *SI* 47 (November 28, 1977), pp. 34–37; Curry Kirkpatrick, "Get Da Shoodah, Said Faddah," *SI* 36 (February 21, 1972), pp. 14–15; Curry Kirkpatrick, "You Know Me, Al," *SI* 36 (January 17, 1972), pp. 15–17; Barry McDermott, "Al, You Went Out in Style," *SI* 46 (April 4, 1977), pp. 20–23; "Al Mc-Guire: Interview," *Sport* 75 (March 1984), pp. 39ff.; Al McGuire file, Naismith Memorial Basketball Hall of Fame, Springfield, MA; Ronald L. Mendell, *Who's Who in Basketball* (New Rochelle, NY, 1973); *NCAA Men's Basketball Records, 2004* (Indianapolis, IN, 2003); *NYT*, April 12, 1964; *NYT*, March 22, 1970; *NYT*, March 23, 1971; *NYT*, March 26, 1974; *NYT*, March 29, 1977; Billy Packer with Roland Lazenby, *Hoops! Confessions of a College Basketball Analyst* (Chicago, IL, 1985); S. D. Solomon, "Coach of the Year Becomes a Rookie," *Fortune* 97 (January 30, 1978), pp. 111–112; *TSN*, February 28, 1983; *TSN*, April 11, 1983; *TSN*, March 25, 1985; *WWA*, 43rd ed. (1984–1985), p. 2193.

Larry R. Gerlach

McGUIRE, Frank Joseph (b. November 8, 1916, New York, NY; d. October 11, 1994, Columbia, SC), college athlete and professional basketball player, coach, referee, and administrator, was the first coach to win 100 games at three colleges and take two schools to the NCAA Finals. McGuire served as head coach five years (1948–1949 to 1952–1953) at St. John's University (New York; 103-35 record), nine years (1953–1954 to 1961–1962) at the University of North Carolina (164-58), and 16 years (1965–1966 to 1980–1981) at the University of South Carolina (283-142), amassing a composite 550-235 (.701 percent) record. In 1976, he was elected to the Naismith Memorial Basketball Hall of Fame. Besides being named 1952 Metropolitan New York College Coach of the Year by the NYWA, McGuire was selected 1957 National College Coach of the Year by the NBCA and both wire services. His undefeated (32-0) North Carolina Tar Heels defeated Kansas 54-53 to win the 1957 NCAA championship, the first titlist to represent the ACC. He guided the Philadelphia Warriors (NBA) in 1962 to second place in the Eastern Division with a 49-31 record.

McGuire, the son of New York City policeman Robert McGuire and Anne (Lynch) McGuire, was the youngest of 13 children. McGuire was only two years old when his father died. The Greenwich Village product was a New York City All-Star in football, basketball, and baseball at Xavier High School before graduating in 1932. A baseball pitcher, he captained the 1936 St. John's University baseball and basketball teams. His Redmen basketball squads finished 47-15 over three years. McGuire played physical basketball, being tough on defense and a good rebounder. He earned a Bachelor of Science degree from St. John's in 1936 and returned to Xavier High School as a teacher, head baseball coach, and assistant football coach. Simultaneously, McGuire played basketball with the pro New York Visitations (ABL) and refereed high school and college basketball games. He served in the U.S. Navy from 1943 to 1946 and returned to Xavier High School for six months before assuming the head basketball coaching position at St. John's.

McGuire, whose first season at St. John's was devoted to rebuilding, guided the Redmen the next four years to two NCAA tournaments, four NITs, and three 20-plus-victory seasons. Al McGuire* (no relation), All-America center Bob "Zeke" Zawoluk, Jack McMahon, and Ronnie MacGilvary led St. John's to the 1950 and 1951 NIT semifinals before Bradley University (Illinois) and the University of Dayton (Ohio) upset the Redmen. In 1952 St. John's defeated North Carolina State University 60-49 and top-ranked University of Kentucky 64-57 in the NCAA Eastern Regional Tournament. The Redmen frequently drew fouls on the aggressive Wildcats and shutdown Kentucky's fast break. Zawoluk set an NCAA tournament scoring record against Kentucky with 32 points, while McMahon finished with 18. St. John's outrebounded taller University of Illinois with Johnny Kerr* in the NCAA semifinals in triumphing 61-59. University of Kansas All-America center Clyde Lovellette* scored 33 points against St. John's in the title game before 11,302 spectators at Kansas City's Edmundson Pavilion to help Kansas triumph 80-63. The Jayhawks led the entire game, holding Zawoluk to six points in the first half.

McGuire, whose five-year St. John's contract expired in 1952, became head coach at the University of North Carolina. He inherited a squad with two consecutive losing seasons, but reversed the trend with a first-year 17-10 finish. McGuire attracted New York and New Jersey talent, referred to as "Yankee Rebels" by sportswriters. In 1957 North Carolina won the ACC tournament and defeated Yale University (Connecticut), Canisius University (New York), and Syracuse (New York) University in early rounds of the NCAA tournament. The lead changed 22 times in the semifinals against Michigan State University before North Carolina triumphed 74-70 in triple overtime. The undefeated Tar Heels and Kansas, rated one and two in the national polls, faced each other in the NCAA title game before 10,500 spectators at Kansas City. The Jayhawks shot a poor 27 percent from the floor compared with North Carolina's 65 percent in the first half, but stayed with the Tar Heels throughout regulation time. With six seconds remaining in the third overtime, North Carolina's center Joe Quigg sank two free throws to win the game 54-53, and the NCAA championship for the Tar Heels. Kansas All-America center Wilt Chamberlain* outscored North Carolina's All-America forward Lenny Rosenbluth*, 23 to 20, but the latter received fine support from Quigg, Pete Brennan, Tom Kearns, and Bob Cunningham. McGuire guided North Carolina to the 1959 NCAA tournament, where the Tar Heels lost to Navy in the first round.

McGuire in 1962 coached Philadelphia (NBA) and guided the Warriors past Syracuse in the Eastern Division semifinal playoff series. He had joined forces with Chamberlain, Philadelphia's league-leading scorer and rebounder, Tom Gola*, Guy Rodgers Jr.*, and Paul Arizin*. The Boston Celtics nipped the Warriors 109-107, in the seventh game of the Eastern Division finals when Sam Jones* sank the winning basket with two seconds remaining. McGuire in 1964 became associate athletic director and head basketball coach of the South Carolina Gamecocks. The smiling, dimple-checked Irishman, who emphasized tough defense, won many games with bench strategy. In 31 years of coaching, McGuire experienced only three losing seasons. He directed South Carolina to four consecutive NCAA tournaments (1971–1974) with All-Americas John Roche, Tom Riker, and Kevin Joyce. The Gamecocks finished the 1970 ACC regular season in first place and won the ACC 1971 postseason tournament, but left the ACC in 1972 to become independent. McGuire retired after the 1980 season.

McGuire married Patricia Johnson in 1941 and had three children: Frank Jr., Patricia Jeanne, and Carol Anne. He earned a Master of Science degree in Physical Education from NYU in 1949, and in 1961 a Doctor of Humane Letters degree from Belmont Abbey College (North Carolina). McGuire wrote two books, *Offensive Basketball* (1958) and *Defensive Basketball* (1959). A basketball clinic lecturer, he served as president of the Cerebral Palsy Foundation and chaired Heart Fund and Multiple Sclerosis campaigns.

BIBLIOGRAPHY: Peter C. Bjarkman, *ACC: Atlantic Coast Conference Basketball* (Indianapolis, IN, 1996); Morgan G. Brenner, *College Basketball's National Championships* (Lanham, MD, 1994); Mike Douchant, *Encyclopedia of College Basketball* (Detroit, MI, 1995); Milton Gross, "McGuire, McGuire and McGuire," *Sport* 7 (February 1949), pp. 40–42, 82–83; Jan Hubbard, ed., *The Official NBA Encyclopedia*, 3rd ed. (New York, 2000); Frank McGuire file, Naismith Memorial Basketball Hall of Fame, Springfield, MA; William G. Mokray, ed., *Ronald Encyclopedia of Basketball* (New York, 1963); Billy Packer and Roland Lazenby, *College Basketball's 25 Greatest Teams* (St. Louis, MO, 1989); Ken Rappoport, *The Classic: A History of the NCAA Championship* (Mission, KS, 1979); Ken Rappoport, *Tales from the Tar Heel Locker Room* (Champaign, IL, 2002); Ken Rappoport, *Tar Heel: North Carolina Basketball* (New York, 1976); Alexander M. Weyand, *The Cavalcade of Basketball* (New York, 1960); *WWA*, 39th ed. 1981 (1976–1977), p. 2111.

James D. Whalen

McGUIRE, Richard "Dick" (b. January 25, 1926, Huntington, NY), college and professional player, coach, and scout, is the son of John McGuire and Winifred McGuire. His father, who was born in Ireland and came to the United States in 1916, owned a hotel and tavern in Queens, New York. His mother won amateur swimming titles in her hometown in England. Richard was the second of four children. His younger brother Al* coached Marquette University to an NCAA basketball championship in 1977 and broadcast for NBC and CBS television. Dick remains one of the NBA's hometown boys who made good. Although born on Long Island, McGuire began his basketball career at LaSalle Academy in Manhattan. He played most of his college ball at St. John's University (New York) except for spending one year at Dartmouth College (New Hampshire) during World War II as part of a U.S. Navy program. At St. John's, McGuire starred as a basketball guard with surprising cleverness and flashy ball-handling and passing and was selected four times All-Metropolitan. In 1944 at Dartmouth, he made All-America Second Team.

After graduating from St. John's University in 1949, McGuire was drafted in the first round by the New York Knickerbockers (NBA). He justified that choice by making a then–NBA rookie record 286 assists in 68 games. McGuire played eight seasons with the Knicks, leading New York in assists six consecutive seasons from 1949–1950 through 1955–1956. He ranked second on the all-time Knicks career assists list with 2,950. McGuire led the NBA in assists in 1949–1950 and was named to the All-NBA Second Team in 1951. A poor shooter, the six-foot, 180-pounder was never a formidable scorer. In his career he scored 5,921 points, averaging 8.0 points per game. His average points figures with the Knicks hovered near double figures, ranging from a high of 9.2 points (1951–1952) to a low of 5.13 points in 1956–1957. The last mark may have convinced Knicks management to trade him to the Detroit Pistons (NBA) for a first-round draft pick in September 1957. McGuire played three more seasons with the Pistons, scoring 8.1, 9.2, and 7.1 points per game, and recording 454, 443, and 358 assists, respectively. In December 1959, he was named playing coach of the Pistons and led Detroit to a second-place finish in the Western Division. McGuire retired as an active player at the end of the 1959–1960 season and remained as head coach of Detroit for three more years, directing the Pistons to three consecutive third place finishes. In 1965 he took the Knicks' head coaching job, replacing former teammate Harry Gallatin*. After two consecutive fourth-place finishes and a 15-22 start in 1967–1968, McGuire was replaced by Red Holzman*. McGuire stayed on as chief scout until 2004 and now serves as senior basketball consultant. He currently resides in Dix Hills, New York, not far from his birthplace, with his wife, Teri, and their four children.

McGuire was elected to the Naismith Memorial Basketball Hall of Fame in 1993. One of McGuire's former nemeses, Tommy Heinsohn*, remarked, "I think Dick never got the accolades that he deserved. The best passing guards in the entire league in the years that I played were Bob Cousy* and Dick McGuire. He was a premier fast-break player. When the Knicks won, it was because McGuire was passing the ball the way he did."

BIBLIOGRAPHY: Glenn Dickey, *The History of Professional Basketball* (Briarcliff Manor, NY, 1982);

Milton Gross, "McGuire, McGuire and McGuire," *Sport* 6 (February 1949), pp. 40–42, 82–83; Jan Hubbard, ed., *The Official NBA Encyclopedia*, 3rd ed., (New York, 2000); Neil D. Isaacs, *Vintage NBA* (Silver Spring, MD, 1996); Leonard Koppett, *24 Seconds to Shoot: An Informal History of the NBA* (New York, 1968); Richard McGuire file, Naismith Memorial Basketball Hall of Fame, Springfield, MA; Ronald L. Mendell, *Who's Who in Basketball* (New Rochelle, NY, 1973); *New York Knickerbockers, Media Guide, 1986–1987* (New York, 1986); Ken Shouler et al., *Total Basketball* (Wilmington, DE, 2003); *TSN Official NBA Register, 2004–2005* (St. Louis, MO, 2004).

George Robinson

McHALE, Kevin Edward (b. December 19, 1957, Hibbing, MN), college and professional player and coach, attended Hibbing (Minnesota) High School and the University of Minnesota (BTC), where he starred in basketball, was named team MVP in 1979 and 1980, and made all-BTC his senior year. His 281 rebounds ranked eighth in Minnesota history. The Boston Celtics (NBA) selected McHale third in the 1980 NBA draft. In his rookie season, he scored 818 points in 82 contests and averaged 10 points. The six-foot ten-inch, 225-pound forward's performance earned him selection on the NBA All-Rookie Team.

From 1981 to 1984, McHale appeared in 82 games annually. His scoring output increased each year from 13.6 points per game in 1981–1982 to 18.4 points in 1983–1984. He played in 413 consecutive NBA games. The 1984 and 1985 campaigns saw him selected the NBA best sixth man, as he continually came off the bench to spark the Celtics. McHale tallied 1,565 points for a 19.8 per game average in 1984–1985 and averaged 21.3 points in 1985–1986. His most productive season came in 1986–1987 with 2,008 points and 26.1 point average. The following season, his scoring average dropped to 22.6.

McHale, who made the NBA All-Defensive First Team from 1986 through 1988 and All-NBA First Team in 1987, in 1987–1988 led the NBA in field goal percentage with .604 and averaged 8.4 rebounds. He missed the first 14 games that season while recovering from off-season surgery on a broken foot, which had plagued him in the 1987 playoffs. Additional acclaim came to him as a quality shot-blocker and a good rebounder. In the 1989–1990 season, McHale joined Larry Bird* and Magic Johnson* as the only NBA players shooting over 50 percent from the floor and 90 percent from the free throw line. McHale participated in the 1984 and 1986–1991 NBA All-Star Games. Boston won the NBA championship in 1981, 1984, and 1986 during McHale's tenure. The Celtics won the Eastern Division in the 1980–1981 campaign and from 1983 through 1987. He retired following the 1992–1993 season. During 13 NBA seasons, he scored 17,335 points (17.9 point average) and 7,122 rebounds (7.3 rebound average) in 971 games. McHale appeared in 169 NBA playoff games, scoring 3,182 points for a 18.8 average. McHale, considered both a "super guy" and a super talent, became almost unstoppable as a low-post player. He served as assistant general manager of the Minnesota Timberwolves (NBA) in 1994–1995 and as their vice president of basketball operations since May 1995. He replaced Flip Saunders as head coach of the struggling Timberwolves in February 2005 and guided them to a 19-12 record, but Minnesota missed the playoffs. McHale was named among the 50 greatest players in NBA history in 1996 and was selected to the Naismith Memorial Basketball Hall of Fame in 1999. Off the court, he follows ice hockey and displays dry, rapid-fire wit. McHale, whose salary now exceeds $1.3 million annually, fishes avidly.

BIBLIOGRAPHY: Peter C. Bjarkman, *The Boston Celtics Encyclopedia* (Champaign, IL, 1998); Jordan Deutsch, *Avon Superstars: Kevin McHale, Michael Jordan* (New York, 1987); Zander Hollander, ed., *Complete Handbook of Pro Basketball 1990* (New York, 1989); Roland Lazenby, *The NBA Finals* (Indianapolis, IN, 1996); Kevin McHale, letter to Stan W. Carlson, March 1990; Kevin McHale file, Naismith Memorial Basketball Hall of Fame, Springfield, MA; *Minnesota Timberwolves Media Guide, 2004–2005* (Minneapolis, MN, 2004); Bob Schron and Kevin Stevens, *The Bird Era: A History of the Boston Celtics, 1978–1988* (Boston, MA, 1988); Don Shaughnessy, *Ever Green* (New York, 1990); *TSN Official NBA Register, 2004–2005* (St. Louis, MO, 2004); Ken Shouler et al., *Total Basketball* (Wilmington, DE, 2003); *University of Minnesota Basketball Media Guide, 1988* (Minneapolis, MN, 1988).

Stan W. Carlson

McKINNEY, Horace Albert "Bones" (b. January 1, 1919, Lowland, NC; d. May 16, 1997, Raleigh, NC), college and professional player, coach, and sportscaster, was the youngest of four children of Martin Van Buren McKinney and Julia B. McKinney. His father, a farmer, died when McKinney was two. In 1924, his mother moved to Durham, North Carolina, to work in a mill.

The restless McKinney dropped out of Durham High School for two years, but returned to lead that school to 69 consecutive basketball wins and three consecutive state championships. He graduated in 1940 and subsequently entered North Carolina State College (SC), leading the SC in scoring in 1941–1942. The U.S. Army drafted him in 1942. After his discharge, McKinney enrolled at the University of North Carolina (SC). A six-foot six-inch, 187-pound stringbean, McKinney sparked the Tar Heels to a 29-5 win-loss mark and a second-place finish in the 1946 NCAA tournament.

McKinney dropped out of North Carolina after the 1946 season to support his family. He played for the Washington Capitals (BAA, NBA) from 1946 until that club folded in January 1951. McKinney completed that season and the 1951–1952 campaign with the Boston Celtics (NBA). His honors included being named First Team All-BAA in 1947 and Second Team All-NBA in 1949. He tallied 2,994 points and averaged 9.4 points per game in his six pro seasons, and served as a player-coach for Washington in 1950–1951, when they compiled a 10-25 mark.

In 1952 McKinney entered Southeastern Baptist Seminary in Wake Forest, North Carolina, where he became an ordained Baptist minister and preached part-time in a Raleigh, North Carolina church. He served as an assistant basketball coach at Wake Forest University (ACC) until March 1957, when he became head coach. Wake Forest enjoyed among its greatest successes under McKinney, recording a third-place finish in the 1962 NCAA tournament and ACC titles in 1961 and 1962. He compiled a 122-94 mark in eight seasons at Wake Forest.

McKinney left Wake Forest after the 1965 season, but returned to the sidelines to coach the Carolina Cougars (ABA) to a 42-42 mark in 1969–1970. His retirement came in the middle of the following season with a 17-25 mark. After leaving coaching, he broadcast basketball games and engaged in business in Hickory, North Carolina.

McKinney, a colorful and highly animated player and coach, once wore a seatbelt on the bench in an unsuccessful attempt to stay seated. He married Edna Ruth Stell in 1941, had six children, and is a member of the North Carolina Sports Hall of Fame.

BIBLIOGRAPHY: Smith Barrier, *On Tobacco Road: Basketball in North Carolina* (New York, 1983); Peter C. Bjarkman, *ACC: Atlantic Coast Conference Basketball* (Indianapolis, IN, 1996); Neil D. Isaacs, *Vintage NBA* (Silver Spring, MD, 1996); Bones McKinney with Garland Atkins, *Bones: Honk Your Horn If You Love Basketball* (Gastonia, NC, 1988); Horace McKinney file, Wake Forest University Sports Information Department, Winston-Salem, NC; Ron Morris, *ACC Basketball: An Illustrated History* (Chapel Hill, NC, 1988); Ken Shouler, et al., *Total Basketball* (Wilmington, DE, 2003).

Jim L. Sumner

McLENDON, John B. (b. April 5, 1915, Hiawatha, KS; d. October 8, 1999, Cleveland Heights, OH), college and professional coach, was one of the nation's first black basketball mentors. McLendon graduated from Summer (Kansas) High School in 1932, attended Kansas City (Missouri) JC, and earned a Bachelor of Science degree in Education from the University of Kansas in 1936. Although physically athletic, he was prevented from playing competitively at both the high school and college levels because he was black. At the University of Kansas, McLendon learned about basketball from its inventor, Dr. James Naismith*. During this time, he also coached nearby Lawrence Memorial High School to the Kansas-Missouri Athletic Conference Championship in 1936. McLendon continued his education at the University of Iowa, earning a Master of Arts degree there in 1937. He married Joanna L. Owens and had four children, Querida, John III, Herbert, and Nannette.

As a college basketball coach, McLendon saw his teams win 523 of 685 games (76 percent) over a 25-year career. He directed North Carolina College from 1940 to 1952, winning four CIAA championships. His players included

Rudolph Roberson, the first black to establish a national college scoring record with 58 points, and Harold Hunter, one of the first blacks to play in the NBA. After a two-year stint at Hampton Institute in Virginia, McLendon assumed the coaching reins at Tennessee Agricultural and Industrial State University in Nashville. In five seasons, the Tigers, led by Richard Barnett* and John Barnhill, won four MAA championships and three consecutive national NAIA titles from the 1956–1957 through 1958–1959 seasons. No other college coach had accomplished that feat. In the mid-1960s McLendon coached briefly at Kentucky State University and Cleveland State University, making one additional trip to the NAIA national tournament.

McLendon coached at the amateur and professional levels with the Cleveland Pipers (ABL) between the 1959–1960 and 1961–1962 campaigns. His squad in August 1960 became the only amateur team ever to defeat a U.S. Olympic team. In 1961, the Pipers took the NIBL and AAU national championships. The next season, the Pipers turned pro and won the Eastern Division of the short-lived ABL. McLendon also directed the Denver Rockets (ABA) to a 9-19 slate in 1969–1970. McLendon received many honors and served on many committees. He was selected CIAA Coach of the Year (1948), Coach of the Decade (1946–1955), and NAIA Coach of the Year in 1958, and was elected to the HAF Hall of Fame (1962), NAIA Hall of Fame, and Naismith Memorial Basketball Hall of Fame (1978). He wrote two books, *Fast Break Basketball* and *The Fast Break Game*. He later served as national promotional representative for Converse Rubber Company and lived in Elk Grove Village, Illinois.

BIBLIOGRAPHY: John McLendon file, Naismith Memorial Basketball Hall of Fame, Springfield, MA; Ronald L. Mendell, *Who's Who in Basketball* (New Rochelle, NY, 1973); *Who's Who Among Black Americans* (Lake Forest, IL, 1985).

Dennis S. Clark and Wayne Patterson

MAJERLE, Daniel Lewis "Thunder Dan" (b. September 9, 1965, Traverse City, MI), college and professional player and sportscaster, is one of three sons of Frank Majerle, a barber, and Sally Majerle, a secretary. Majerle graduated in 1983 from Traverse City (Michigan) High School, where he averaged 37.5 points and 16 rebounds as a senior and gained unanimous Class A All-State honors. Nicknamed "Thunder Dan" for his rugged inside play and rousing dunks, he starred in basketball at Central Michigan University (MAC) from 1984–1985 to 1987–1988. The six-foot six-inch, 222-pound forward was selected a three-time First Team All-MAC. As a junior in 1986–1987, he led the Chippawas to the MAC crown and an NCAA tournament bid. He scored 759 points (23.7 points average) and grabbed 346 rebounds (10.8 per game) in 1987–1988 and finished his Central Michigan career ranked second in points scored (2,055), steals (171), and field goal percentage (.536). Central Michigan retired the 1988 graduate's number 44 jersey in 1995.

The Phoenix Suns (NBA) made Majerle their number-one pick in the 1988 NBA draft. Due to his competitive fire and versatility as a guard-forward, the rookie immediately became one of the NBA's best sixth men and proved crucial to the Suns reaching the Western Conference Finals in 1989 and 1990 and the NBA Finals in 1993. Majerle evolved from a player who thrived on drives to the basket into a long distance threat, tying for the NBA lead with Reggie Miller* in three-pointers made (167) in 1992–1993 and leading the NBA in three-pointers with an NBA single-season record (192) in 1993–1994. In his best NBA campaigns from 1991–1992 to 1994–1995, he scored 5,407 points and averaged 16.5 points. He was named to the NBA's All-Defensive Second Team in 1990–1991 and 1992–1993, and appeared in the 1992, 1993 and 1995 NBA All-Star Games, averaging 10.7 points.

In October 1995, Phoenix traded Majerle, Antonio Long, and a first round draft pick to the Cleveland Cavaliers (NBA) for John Williams. After a season with the Cavs, Majerle became a free agent and signed with the Miami Heat (NBA) in 1996. Miami won four consecutive Atlantic Division titles from the 1996–1997 through the 1999–2000 seasons, but never advanced beyond the Eastern Conference Finals. Majerle played five seasons with the Heat, but injuries and limited play hurt his offensive production. The free agent returned to Phoenix in July 2001. After the Suns' 36-48 record in 2001–2002 and failure to make the playoffs, the popular Majerle retired. He was inducted into the franchise's "Ring of Honor" in 2003.

During 14 NBA seasons, Majerle tallied 10,925 points (11.4 points average), seized 4,265 rebounds (4.5 per game), and tallied 2,755 assists (2.9 per game) in 955 regular season games. He recorded 1,441 points (11.7 points average), made 609 rebounds (5.0 per game), and totaled 304 assists (2.5 per game) in 123 playoff games. Majerle shares the NBA Finals single-series record for most three-point field goals made with 17 against Chicago in 1993, and the single-game NBA Finals and playoff records for most minutes played with no personal fouls (659) and most minutes played with no turnovers (59) on June 13, 1993 in three overtimes at Chicago. Among all-time career NBA leaders, he ranks fifth in three-point field goals made and sixth in three-point field goals attempted.

Majerle led scorers for the bronze medal–winning USA basketball team at the 1988 Olympic Games in Seoul, South Korea. He also played on "Dream Team II," which won the gold medal in the 1994 World Championship of Basketball in Toronto, Canada. Majerle and his wife, Tina, have four children. Majerle is an avid golfer who plays on the Celebrity Golf Association tour and owns Majerle's Sports Grill in Phoenix, AZ. He has served as television analyst for Phoenix games since 2004.

BIBLIOGRAPHY: Jan Hubbard, ed., *The Official NBA Encyclopedia*, 3rd ed. (New York, 2000); Dan Majerle file, Naismith Memorial Basketball Hall of Fame, Springfield, MA; Dan Majerle file, Sports Information Office, Central Michigan University, Mount Pleasant, MI; *TSN Official NBA Guide, 2002–2003* (St. Louis, MO, 2002); *TSN Official NBA Register, 2002–2003* (St. Louis, MO, 2002).

Jack C. Braun

MAJERUS, Rick (b. February 17, 1948, Sheboygan, WI), college player and coach and sportscaster, is the son of Raymond Majerus, a union organizer and representative, and Alyce Majerus. The family moved to Milwaukee, Wisconsin, where Rick graduated from Marquette University High School in 1966. He did not make the high school basketball team and learned his basketball playing on the outdoor courts and in the CYO leagues.

Majerus attended Marquette University and earned a place on the freshman team as a walk-on. Unable to make the team the following season, he served as an assistant basketball coach at St. Sebastian Junior High School until earning a Bachelor's degree in history from Marquette in 1970. Al McGuire*, head basketball coach at Marquette, hired Majerus as one of his assistants in 1971. For the next 12 years McGuire, Majerus and Hank Raymonds compiled a 277-76 win-loss record, two NCAA Final Four appearances, and one NCAA championship. Raymonds was promoted to head basketball coach in 1978. Majerus served as Marquette's head coach between 1983–1984 and 1985–1986, posting a 56-35 win-loss record. After being as an assistant coach with the Milwaukee Bucks (NBA) in 1986–1987, he was named head basketball coach at Ball State University (Indiana) in 1987. In 1987–1988 and 1988–1989, he led the Cardinals to a 43-17 win-loss record.

In 1989, Majerus was named head basketball coach at the University of Utah. For 15 seasons from 1989–1990 through 2003–2004, he led the Utes to a 326-95 win-loss record and nine WAC Championships. Under Majerus, Utah never experienced a losing season and his teams averaged 21 victories each year. The "Runnin' Utes" played in the NCAA tournament 10 times with Majerus at the helm. Utah's highest finish came in 1998, when they lost in the championship game to the University of Kentucky.

In January 2004, Majerus resigned as Utah coach because of heart problems and joined ESPN as a college basketball analyst. Majerus was selected National Coach of the Year five times, District Coach of the Year seven times, WAC Coach of the Year five times, and Utah Sports Person of the Year twice. As a head coach and assistant coach for 33 years, he was involved in 752 victories, 27 postseason appearances, an NIT Final Four, three NCAA Final Fours, and one NCAA national championship. Outstanding players who contributed to his coaching success included Dean Meminger, Jim Chones, and Butch Lee from Marquette and

Mike Doleac, Andre Miller, and Keith Van Horn from Utah. The University of Southern California appointed Majerus head coach in December 2004, but he backed out of the deal a few days later.

On the international scene, Majerus served as head coach for the U.S. Basketball Team in the 1997 World Championships and served as assistant coach for "Dream Team II" in 1994 and the 1993 U.S. team that toured Europe.

Majerus, along with Gene Wojciechowski, co-authored a 1998 book entitled *My Life On A Napkin*. He was married to Cloe in 1987, but they were divorced two years later and he has been a bachelor since.

BIBLIOGRAPHY: Gary K. Johnson, *NCAA Men's Basketball's Finest* (Overland Park, KS, 1998); Rick Majerus with Gene Wojciechowski, *My Life On A Napkin* (New York, 1998); *NCAA Men's Basketball Records, 2004* (Indianapolis, IN, 2003); "Rick Majerus," *Profile*, http://www.utahutes.com (2003); Salt Lake City Tribune staff, ed., *Runnin' Utes Basketball* (Champaign, IL, 1998).

John L. Evers

MALONE, Karl Anthony "The Mailman" (b. July 24, 1963, Summerfield, LA), player, is the son of P.J. Malone and Shirley Ann Jackson. His father committed suicide when Karl was three, and his mother five years later married Ed Turner. Malone graduated from Summerfield (Louisiana) High School in 1981 and was named three-time All-SoC First Teamer at Louisiana Tech University, where he earned the nickname "The Mailman" because he always delivered in the clutch. He tallied 1,716 points and grabbed 859 rebounds in his Louisiana Tech career and in 1985 led all NCAA tournament players with a 12.4 rebounding average. The Utah Jazz (NBA) chose Malone as the thirteenth pick in the first round of the 1985 NBA draft. The six-foot nine-inch, 256-pound was named to the 1986 All-Rookie Team and quickly developed into one of the NBA's premier power forwards.

Malone's development from raw rookie to superstar reflected his dedication to improving his skills and commitment to weightlifting to increase his strength and endurance. Malone, considered the NBA's strongest player, possesses unusual speed and agility for his size. One of the most durable players in NBA history, he missed only eight games in his first 18 seasons and was the only player to have logged over 3,000 minutes for nine consecutive seasons from 1987–1988 to 1995–1996.

The leading rebounder in Jazz history, Malone paced Utah in career rebounding with 19,601 and career scoring with 34,707 points. However, he was best known as a multidimensional offensive force. With outside jump shots, powerful low-post moves, and thunderous dunks at the end of fast breaks, the consistent and profilic scorer averaged between 20 and 31 points from 1986–1987 to 2002–2003. He led the Jazz in scoring and rebounding each season from 1986–1987 to 2002–2003 and ranked among the top NBA scorers, finishing second four straight years from 1989 to 1992 and in 1997; third in 1993, 1998, and 1999; fourth in 1995 and 1996; and fifth in 1994 and 2000. During 19 NBA seasons, Malone tallied 36,928 points and ranked fourth in NBA history with a career-season scoring average of 25.0 points. He recorded 14,968 rebounds in 1,476 games, averaging over 10 per contest.

After being selected All-NBA Second-Team in 1988, Malone made the All-NBA First Team selection the next 11 years from 1989 to 1999. He made the All-NBA Second Team in 2000 and the All-NBA Third Team in 2001. Malone also made the NBA All-Defensive First Team in 1997, 1998, and 1999. He was elected to the All-Star team 11 consecutive years from 1988 to 1998 and three other times, being named the MVP of the 1989 game and Co-MVP in 1993 with Jazz teammate John Stockton*. His 12.1 point scoring average ranks high in All-Star history. A member of the "Dream Team" that captured the gold medal in basketball for the United States in the 1992 Summer Olympics at Barcelona, Spain, Malone tied for team honors in rebounding. He also played on the gold medal–winning team at the 1996 Atlanta, Georgia Olympic Games and was named to the NBA 50th Anniversary All-time team in 1996. In July 2003, Malone signed with the Los Angeles Lakers (NBA) as a free agent. He retired following the 2003–2004 season.

Malone appeared in 193 playoff games, tallying 4,761 points (24.7 average) and making 2,062 rebounds (10.7 average). He led Utah to the NBA Finals against the Chicago Bulls in 1997 and 1998 and played with the Lakers in the NBA Finals against the Detroit Pistons in 2004. Malone appeared in the most NBA playoff games without winning a championship. Injuries sidelined him for the last game of the 2004 NBA Finals. He set a single-game playoff record for most free throws made without missing (18) in May 1997 against the Los Angeles Lakers and shares the single-game playoff record for most free throws made in one half (19) in May 1991 against the Portland Trail Blazers.

With business interests extending beyond the basketball court, Malone has fulfilled his childhood dreams of being a cowboy and truck driver as the owner of several cattle ranches and a long-haul trucking company. He married Kay Ann Kinsey, former Miss Idaho USA, in 1990 and has two children.

BIBLIOGRAPHY: Peter C. Bjarkman, *The Biographical History of Basketball* (Chicago, IL, 2000); *CB* (New York, 1993), pp. 37–41; Chuck Daly with Alex Sachare, *America's Dream Team: The Quest for Olympic Gold* (Atlanta, GA, 1992); Phil Elderkin, "Karl Malone Makes Hard Work Pay Off," *BskD* 16 (June–July 1989), pp. 72–74; Jan Hubbard, ed., *The Official NBA Encyclopedia*, 3rd ed. (New York, 2000); Kurt Kragthorpe, "Karl Malone: Utah's Jazzy Young Leader," *BskD* 15 (January 1988), pp. 16–22; Clay Latimer, *Special Delivery: The Amazing Basketball Career of* Karl Malone (Lenexa, KS, 1999); Clay Latimer, "This Mailman Only Rings Once," *BskD* 18 (April 1991), pp. 38–41; Roland Lazenby, *Stockton to Malone: The Rise of the Utah Jazz* (Lenexa, KS, 1998); Karl Malone, interview with Larry R. Gerlach, December 7, 1993; Jack McCallum, "Big Wheel," *SI* 76 (April 27, 1992), pp. 62–74; Craig Neff, "The Mailman Does Deliver," *SI* 62 (January 14, 1985), pp. 88, 90, 94; *Salt Lake* (UT) *Tribune*, January 31, 1993; *Salt Lake Tribune*, February 20, 1993; *Salt Lake Tribune*, October 17, 1993; Robert E. Schnakenberg, *Teammates: Karl Malone and John Stockton* (Brookfield, CT, 1998); Ken Shouler et al., *Total Basketball* (Wilmington, DE, 2003); *TSN*, November 8, 1993; *TSN Official NBA Guide, 2004–2005* (St. Louis, MO, 2004); *TSN Official NBA Register, 2004–2005* (St. Louis, MO, 2004); *Utah Jazz 2003–2004 Media Guide* (Salt Lake City, UT, 2003); Ralph Wiley, "Does He Ever Deliver!" *SI* 69 (November 7, 1988), pp. 72–77.

Larry R. Gerlach

MALONE, Moses Eugene (b. March 23, 1955, Petersburg, VA), professional player, is the son of Mary Malone; His father left home when Moses was two. Malone grew up with his mother, a nurse's aide and supermarket meatpacker. At Petersburg (Virginia) High School, he established new standards for Virginia high school basketball in leading his team to 50 straight victories and two consecutive state championships. During his senior year, Malone averaged 36 points, 26 rebounds, and 12 blocked shots. He consequently was chosen the second time as a High School All-America and became the most highly recruited high school basketball player in history, with over 300 colleges offering him scholarships. Although Malone selected the University of Maryland, he was drafted by the Utah Stars (ABA) after enrolling for the fall 1974 semester and signed a $3 million, five-year contract.

Malone's signing raised cries of outrage from within and outside the sport because a high school player had never gone directly to the pros. Many doubted the 19-year-old could play at that level, but Malone proved them wrong immediately. Despite the pressure, he averaged 18.8 points and led the Utah Stars in rebounds his rookie year. After Utah went bankrupt the next year, Malone played for the St. Louis Spirits (ABA) and missed half the season because of a fractured foot. The 1976–1977 season was divided among the Portland Trail Blazers (NBA), Buffalo Braves (NBA), and Houston Rockets (NBA). He signed a three-year, $3 million contract with the Houston Rockets and remained there through the 1980–1981 season. In 1979 he set the single-season NBA record for most offensive rebounds (587). During that span, Malone averaged over 20 points and emerged as the NBA's leading rebounder. In 1979 he was selected the NBA's MVP, making 17.6 rebounds and 24.8 points.

As a free agent, Malone, in 1982, signed a six-year pact with the Philadelphia 76ers (NBA) for an annual salary of $2.2 million. Besides leading the 76ers to the NBA championship in

1983, he averaged 24.5 points and led the NBA in rebounding (1,194) for the third consecutive season. In both the 1981–1982 and the 1982–1983 seasons, he was selected the NBA's MVP. He made a record 21 offensive rebounds against Seattle on February 11, 1982. Malone led the NBA in rebounding in 1983–1984 (950) and 1984–1985 (1,031), as Philadelphia made the NBA playoffs both seasons. In June 1986, the 76ers traded him to the Washington Bullets (NBA). He tallied 24.1 points-per-game and made 824 rebounds in 1986–1987 in helping the Bullets to the NBA playoffs. His point production dropped to 20.4 points-per-game the next year, but he ranked eighth in rebounding (884), as the Bullets made the playoffs again.

In August 1988, the Atlanta Hawks (NBA) signed Malone a three-year, $1.5 million contract. Malone spent three seasons with Atlanta averaging, around 20 points and 11 rebounds and helping Atlanta make the playoffs twice. He played with the Milwaukee Bucks (NBA) in 1991–1992 and 1992–1993 and the Philadelphia 76ers in 1993–1994 and ended his NBA career with the San Antonio Spurs (NBA) in 1994–1995. He was inducted into the Naismith Memorial Basketball Hall of Fame in 2001.

Malone was selected All-NBA First Team in 1979, 1982, 1983, and 1986 and made the Second Team in 1980, 1981, 1984, and 1987. An All-Star Game choice every season from 1978 through 1989, he was named to the NBA All-Defensive First Team in 1983 and Second Team in 1979. His combined ABA-NBA career statistics in 19 seasons include 27,409 points (20.6 points per game average), 16,212 rebounds, and 1,733 blocked shots in 1,329 games. He holds NBA career records for most consecutive games without disqualification (1,212) from 1978 through 1995 and for most offensive rebounds (6,731).

Although not tall for an NBA center at six feet ten inches, the muscular 250-pound Malone played very well with his taller opponents. Many consider him to have been the dominant pro center.

BIBLIOGRAPHY: Peter C. Bjarkman, *The Biographical History of Basketball* (Chicago, IL, 2000); Jan Hubbard, ed., *The Official NBA Encyclopedia*, 3rd ed. (New York, 2000); Moses Malone file, Naismith Memorial Basketball Hall of Fame, Springfield, MA; Jack McCallum, "Back to Haunt the 76ers," *SI* (March 15, 1987); Claudia Mitroi, ed., *Philadelphia's Greatest Sports Moments* (Champaign, IL, 2000); *NYT Biographical Service*, vol. 5; "Playboy Interview: Moses Malone," *Playboy* 31 (March 1984), pp. 53–68; John O'Keefe, "Catching Up with Moses Malone, NBA All-Star Center," *SI* 90 (April 12, 1999); Ken Shouler et al., *Total Basketball* (Wilmington, DE, 2002); *TSN Official Register, 2004–2005* (St. Louis, MO, 2004).

Stephen D. Bodayla

MANNING, Daniel Ricardo "Danny" "D" "EZD" (b. May 17, 1966, Hattiesburg, MS), college athlete, and executive, enjoyed a brilliant four-year basketball career at the University of Kansas (BEC) and led the Jayhawks to the NCAA championship in 1988. The son of Ed Manning and Darnelle Manning, he starred athletically at Page High School in Greensboro, North Carolina as a sophomore and junior, and at Lawrence (Kansas) High School as a senior. Page High School won the 1983 North Carolina state championship with a 26-0 record. As a sophomore, his 23-5 team placed third in the state tourney. Manning transferred to Lawrence when his father became assistant coach to Larry Brown* at the University of Kansas. The 22-2 Lawrence High School basketball squad finished second in the state in 1983–1984, as he averaged 22.7 points and 4.2 blocked shots as a senior. Delray Brooks of Providence, Rhode Island and Manning were the only high school athletes invited to the 1984 Olympic basketball trials.

Manning elected to attend the University of Kansas, and was selected NBC-TV Freshman of the Year and BEC Newcomer of the Year in 1984–1985. In a game against Oklahoma State University, Manning set a BEC record for highest field-goal percentage (.937) when he converted 15 of 16 shots from the field. As a sophomore, he was selected 1986 BEC Player of the Year and reached the finals for the Naismith and Wooden awards. The consensus Second-Team All-America was chosen most outstanding performer in the NCAA Midwest Regional, as Kansas advanced to the NCAA Final Four. He set a BEC record for most shots made in one half without a miss, making all eight shots against Oklahoma State.

As a junior, Manning became the Jayhawks' 39th All-America and joined Fred Pralle (1938), Howard Engleman (1941), Charlie Black (1943), Clyde Lovellette* (1951, 1952), and Wilt Chamberlain* (1957, 1958) as the only Kansas consensus All-Americas. BEC Player of the Year honors again were accorded Manning, who tallied 860 points.

In August 1987, the six-foot ten-inch, 230 pound Manning competed for the United States at the Pan-American games at Indianapolis, Indiana, leading his team in scoring. As a senior, he scored 942 points and directed the Jayhawks to the 1988 NCAA championship. The title marked the perfect ending for the most spectacular four-year career in Kansas basketball history. His 31-point, 18-rebound, five-steal, dominating performance in the 83-79 upset of powerful University of Oklahoma was second only by Bill Walton's* 44-point effort in 1973 for the most outstanding individual effort at a national championship game. Manning, who earned All-America honors and made tournament MVP, received the John R. Wooden Award as the nation's top college basketball player. His 2,951 career points set a BEC all-time career scoring mark.

After competing on the U.S. Olympic basketball team in Seoul, South Korea 1988 Summer Olympic Games, Manning signed a five-year, $10.5 million NBA contract with the Los Angeles Clippers and became the then-third-highest-paid rookie in NBA history. He played with the Los Angeles Clippers from 1988 through February 1994, the Atlanta Hawks (NBA) in 1994, the Phoenix Suns (NBA) from September 1994 to 1999, the Milwaukee Bucks (NBA) in 1999–2000, the Utah Jazz (NBA) in 2000–2001, the Dallas Mavericks (NBA) in 2001–2002, and Detroit Pistons (NBA) in 2002–2003, winning the NBA Sixth Man Award in 1998. In 2003, he returned to the University of Kansas as director of student athlete development and basketball team manager. During 15 NBA seasons, he scored 12,367 points in 883 games and averaged 14.0 points per game. He averaged 14.6 points and 4.7 rebounds in 43 NBA playoff games and played in the 1993 and 1994 All-Star Games.

BIBLIOGRAPHY: Peter C. Bjarkman, *The Biographical History of Basketball* (Chicago, IL, 2000); Morgan G. Brenner, *College Basketball's National Championships* (Lanham, MD, 1999); Clipping file, University Archives, University of Kansas, Lawrence, KS; Mike Douchant, *Encyclopedia of College Basketball* (Detroit, MI, 1995); John Hendel, *Kansas Jayhawks* (Coal Valley, IL, 1991); Ken Shouler et al., *Total Basketball* (Wilmington, DE, 2003); *TSN Official Basketball Register, 2003–2004* (St. Louis, MO, 2003); *University of Kansas National Championship, 1988* (Charlotte, NC, 1988); *USA Today*, April 23, 1991; Chuck Woodling, *Against All Odds: How Kansas Won the 1988 NCAA Championship* (Lawrence, KS, 1989).

Arthur F. McClure

MARAVICH, Peter Press "Pistol Pete" (b. June 22, 1947, Aliquippa, PA; d. January 5, 1988, Pasadena, CA), college and professional player, was a high-scoring guard and great showman during a spectacular career. The son of Press Maravich, former NBL and BAA guard and college basketball coach, and Helen (Gravor) Maravich, he was nicknamed "Pistol Pete" early in his youth by his father. Maravich starred in basketball at Needham-Broughton High School in Raleigh, North Carolina. At LSU (SEC), he played basketball under his father, made All-America three times, and set 11 NCAA, 26 SEC, and 22 school records. The six-foot five-inch, 200-pound Maravich averaged 44.2 points in 83 contests, led the NCAA in scoring three times, and became college basketball's all-time leading scorer with 3,667 points. He scored 1,138 points in 1967–1968, 1,148 tallies in 1968–1969, and 1,381 markers in 1969–1970, while averaging 43.8, 44.2, and 44.5 points, respectively. Maravich scored 69 points against the University of Alabama in 1970, 66 points against Tulane University (Louisiana), 64 points against the University of Kentucky, and 61 points against Vanderbilt University (Tennessee). Noted for his mop of brown hair and floppy socks, Maravich pleased crowds with his exceptional ball-handling and shooting skills. He earned a Bachelor's degree in Business Administration from LSU.

The Atlanta Hawks (NBA), selecting third, made Maravich its top choice in the 1970 NBA draft. The Hawks gained draft rights to Maravich by trading Zelmo Beaty* to San Francisco for the Warriors' first-round pick. After ranking eighth in NBA scoring his rookie (1970–1971) season, Maravich was plagued by injuries the next campaign. He posted a 26.1 points scoring average in 1972–1973 and finished second with a 27.7 points scoring average in 1973–1974 behind Bob McAdoo*. During the off-season, Maravich was traded to a new expansion team, the New Orleans Jazz (NBA). As the Jazz struggled to be competitive, Maravich peaked as an NBA star. He made the All-NBA First Team in 1976 and 1977 and the All-NBA Second Team in 1973 and 1978. Maravich led the NBA in scoring in 1976–1977 with a career high 31.1 points average after finishing third the previous season with a 25.9 average. He enjoyed his last great season in 1977–1978 with 27.0 points per game. He slipped to a 22.6 points average a year later and retired following the 1979–1980 campaign, after the move of the Jazz from New Orleans to Utah and a subpar 17.1 points-average. In 10 NBA seasons, Maravich scored 15,948 points in 658 games for a 24.2 points career average. His one-game high, a 68-point explosion, came on February 25, 1977 against the New York Knickerbockers. He tied the NBA record for most free throws made in one quarter by making 14 in the third period against the Buffalo Braves on November 28, 1973.

A born-again Christian, Maravich lived in rural Louisiana, conducted basketball clinics, gave television commentaries, and filmed instructional videos. Maravich, elected to the Naismith Memorial Basketball Hall of Fame in 1987, died of a heart attack shortly after a pick-up basketball game. He was survived by his wife, Jackie Elliser, whom he married in January 1976, and two sons, Jason and Joshua. He was named one of the 50 Greatest Players in NBA History in 1996.

BIBLIOGRAPHY: *Atlanta Hawks Press Guide, 1970* (Atlanta, GA, 1970); Phil Berger, *Forever Showtime: The Checkered Life of Pete Maravich* (New York, 1999); Chris Dortch, *String Music* (Dulles, VA, 2002); Mike Douchant, *The Encyclopedia of College Basketball* (Detroit, MI, 1995); Zander Hollander, ed., *The Modern Encyclopedia of Basketball* (Garden City, NY, 1973); Jan Hubbard, ed., *The Official NBA Encyclopedia*, 3rd ed. (New York, 2000); *LSU Basketball Guide, 1969* (Baton Rouge, LA, 1969); Pete Maravich with Daniel Campbell, *Heir to a Dream* (New York, 1987); Pete Maravich file, Naismith Memorial Basketball Hall of Fame, Springfield, MA; Ronald L. Mendell, *Who's Who in Basketball* (New Rochelle, NY, 1973); Paul Soderberg and Helen Washington, *The Big Book of Halls of Fame in the United States and Canada* (New York, 1977); *TSN Official NBA Register, 2004–2005* (St. Louis, MO, 2004).

Joe Lee Smith

MARTIN, Kenyon Lee (b. December 30, 1977, Saginaw, MI), college and professional player, is the son of Paul Roby and Lydia Martin. He was brought up in Oak Cliff, Dallas, Texas by his mother, Lydia, and his older sister, Tamara, and graduated from Bryan Adams High School in Dallas. Martin graduated with a B.S. degree from the University of Cincinnati in 2000. The six-foot nine-inch, 234-pounder led CUSA players in scoring (13.9 points average) and in rebounds (6.3 average). He was named First Team All-America and CUSA Player of the Year in 2000 and CUSA Defensive Player of the Year in 1998, 1999, and 2000. Martin started 31 games as senior, averaging 18.9 points, 9.7 rebounds, and 3.45 blocked shots. He earned Naismith, Wooden, Robertson, and AP National Player of the Year awards. During his four seasons, he averaged 11.0 points and 7.5 rebounds in 116 games.

The first pick of the New Jersey Nets (NBA) in the 2000 NBA draft, Martin averaged 12.0 points and recorded team-highs with 7.4 rebounds and 1.66 blocked shots per game in 2000–2001. He was named NBA All-Rookie First Team in 2000–2001, NBA Rookie of the Month in November 2000, and NBA Co-Rookie in March 2001. Martin enjoyed three straight games of 20-plus points in 2000–2001, including a career-high 31 points. He recorded his first career double-double with 15 points and 13 rebounds against the Indiana Pacers, and made career-high tying five blocks in 2000–2001. In 2000–2001, Martin also recorded his first career triple-double with 18 points and career game-highs of 15 rebounds and 11 assists. He finished first on the Nets in blocks (113) and third in steals (78), but missed 12 games with injury.

In 2001–2002, Martin averaged 14.9 points and 5.3 rebounds to help New Jersey win the Eastern Conference. An outstanding scorer, Martin led the Nets in scoring 15 times, in rebound seven times, and in steals 13 times. Martin averaged a team-high 16 points and 5.8 boards per game during the 2001–2002 NBA playoffs and played in the NBA Finals against the Los Angeles Lakers. In 2002–2003, he averaged a career-high 16.7 points and made 8.3 rebounds per game to help the Nets reach the NBA Finals against the San Antonio Spurs. He tied his career best 16.7 points average and averaged a career high 9.5 rebounds in 2003–2004, as New Jersey won the Atlantic Division. Martin scored 36 points and made 13 rebounds in Game 4 to help New Jersey sweep the New York Knicks in the first round, but the Detroit Pistons eliminated the Nets in seven games in the second round. In July 2004, the Denver Nuggets (NBA) acquired Martin from the Nets for three future first round draft picks. He averaged 15.5 points and 7.3 rebounds in 2004–2005, helping Denver reach the playoffs. He averaged 12.4 points and 5.6 rebounds in five games in the first round playoff loss to the San Antonio Spurs.

Martin, one of the top defensive forwards, committed six flagrant fouls in 2002–2003 and was suspended seven times. He remains a thunderous dunker with superb shot-blocking ability. In five NBA seasons, Martin has scored 5,356 points (15.2 average) and made 2,658 rebounds (7.5 average) in 353 regular-season games. He made the All-NBA Rookie First Team in 2001 and appeared in the 2004 and 2005 All-Star Games. He has averaged 17.6 points and 8.0 rebounds in 56 playoff games.

Martin married Fatimah Conley right before his rookie season. They have a son, and appeared in the 2004 and 2005 All-Star Games. Kenyon Jr., but are divorced. On August 16, 2003, he married Heather Thompson in Las Vagas, Nevada.

BIBLIOGRAPHY: Chris Ballard, "New Jersey Nets," *SI* 93 (October 2000), pp. 168–169; Sachin Shenolikar, "How K-Mart Gives the Nets Their Rugged Edge," *SI for Kids* 15 (June 2003), pp. 52–54; Ken Shouler et al., *Total Basketball* (Wilmington, DE, 2003); *TSN Official NBA Register, 2004–2005* (St. Louis, MO, 2004); Grant Wahl, "Grand Kenyon: High-Flying, Shot-Defying Cincinnati Center Kenyon Martin Is Taking His Game and the Bearcats To New Heights," *SI* 92 (February 2000), pp. 56–59.

Njoki-Wa-Kinyatti

MARTIN, Slater Nelson, Jr. "Dugie" (b. October 22, 1925, El Mina, TX), college and professional player, is the son of Slater Martin Sr., of Scotch-Irish and American Indian descent, and graduated from Jefferson Davis High School in Houston, Texas. Martin and neighbor Jamie Owens led the school to Texas state titles in basketball in 1942 and 1943. During World War II, Martin served with the U.S. Navy for 33 months. Of diminutive size, the five-foot ten-inch, 155-pounder graduated from the University of Texas with a Bachelor's degree in physical education in 1949. Martin, whose wife's name is Faye, held down a guard position and was selected on the HAF mythical basketball team in 1949. In his senior year at Texas, he averaged 16 points and led the Longhorns in scoring. His stellar all-around playing performances caused Texas coach Jack Gray to rate him as the outstanding SWC player. In 1947 and 1948, he played for Texas in the NCAA basketball tournaments. His top college performance came with a 49-point game against TCU.

The colorful Martin joined the Minneapolis Lakers (NBA) for the 1949–1950 season. A speed merchant with good outside shots, he was rated the best small defensive NBA player. The excellent playmaker, a forerunner of the modern point guard, helped the Lakers capture NBA championships in the 1949–1950, 1951–1952, 1952–1953, and 1953–1954 campaigns. In 67 games his rookie season, Martin scored 106 field goals and 59 free throws for 271 points and averaged four points. Although assists were not recorded then, he set up many baskets for George Mikan* and Jim Pollard*. During the 1954–1955 season, he ranked among NBA leaders with 427 assists and averaged almost six assists per game. In 1955 and 1956, Martin was selected at guard on the All-NBA Second Team. He was named on the All-NBA Second Team with the St. Louis Hawks (NBA) from 1957 through 1959 and helped them with the NBA title in the 1957–1958 campaign.

During 10 NBA seasons, Martin performed for the Minneapolis Lakers (1949–1956), New York Knickerbockers (1956–1957), and St. Louis Hawks (1957–1959). He played in 681 career games, scoring 2,225 field goals and 2,490 free throws for 6,940 points for a 10.2 points average. Martin also played semipro baseball during summers and participates in recreational golf. He was elected to the Texas Sports Hall of Fame and in 1981 to the Naismith Memorial Basketball Hall of Fame. Martin resides in the Houston area, where he has worked in the building construction business and owns a restaurant.

BIBLIOGRAPHY: Stan W. Carlson, *World Champions, Laker Basketball* (Minneapolis, MN, 1951); Zander Hollander, ed., *The Modern Encyclopedia of Basketball* (Garden City, NY, 1969); Jan Hubbard, ed., *The Official NBA Encyclopedia*, 3rd ed. (New York, 2000); Neil D. Isaacs, *Vintage NBA* (Silver Spring, MD, 1996); Roland Lazenby, *NBA Finals* (Indianapolis, IN, 1996); Slater Martin file, Naismith Memorial Basketball Hall of Fame, Springfield, MA; George Mikan with Joseph Oberle, *Unstoppable: the Story of George Mikan* (Indianapolis, IN, 1997); Minneapolis Lakers game programs and publicity releases, 1947, 1955; *Minneapolis* (MN) *Star-Journal*, 1949–1956; Minneapolis (MN) *Tribune*, 1949–1956; Stew Thornley, *Basketball's Original Dynasty: The History of the Lakers* (Minneapolis, MN, 1989); *TSN Official Basketball Register, 2004–2005* (St. Louis, MO, 2004).

Stan W. Carlson

MAY, Scott Glenn (b. March 19, 1954, Waynesboro, MS), college and professional player, is the son of Charles May and Ruby May and grew up in Sandusky, Ohio, where his father worked in a steel foundry. At Sandusky High School, May was chosen an All-Ohio end in football and ranked among the nation's 10 best in the discus throw. During his senior year, Sandusky switched him in basketball from center to forward. He averaged 28.8 points and made the All-Ohio and All-America high school basketball teams. His 1,022 career points remains a school record.

Low test scores forced the six-foot seven-inch, 210-pound May to sit out his freshman year at Indiana University (BTC), where new coach Bob Knight* was creating a basketball dynasty. During 1973–1974, May's performance helped Indiana achieve a 23-3 win-loss mark. The Hoosiers shared the BTC championship but lost the playoff game 75-67 to the University of Michigan. The following year, May tallied 16.3 points and led the Hoosiers to an undefeated regular season. His awards included being chosen All-America and All-BTC and winning the Silver Basketball as the Outstanding BTC Player, honors he repeated the next year. In the BTC Finals against Purdue University, May broke his left arm near the wrist. He saw very limited action as the Hoosiers won their first two 1975 NCAA tournament games over the University of Texas at El Paso 78-63 and Oregon State University 81-71. The regional finals saw May limited to only a few minutes of action. Indiana lost 92-90, to the University of Kentucky, a team the Hoosiers had defeated 98-74 earlier on his 25 points.

After the removal of a 13 inch pin, May spent the 1975 summer at Indiana working with weights to restore his arm's strength. The 1975–1976 Indiana team became the only aggregate since the fabled UCLA squads of John Wooden* to complete an undefeated season. In the 1976 NCAA title game, the Hoosiers faced the University of Michigan. The Wolverines already had lost to the Hoosiers 80-74 and 72-67. A 1975 rule permitted more than one team from a conference to participate in the NCAA playoffs. Despite an injury to guard Bobby Wilkerson, co-captains Quinn Buckner and May led Indiana to a 86-68 win.

May established an Indiana season scoring record with 752 points and averaged 23.3 points in 1975–1976. His 1,953 career points ranked second to Don Schlundt* in the Hoosier record book. His honors included being named AP, NABC, and *TSN* Player of the Year; UPI gave him the Naismith Award. He was named Co-MVP in the Mid-East Regional and selected for the 1976 U.S. Olympic basketball team, winners of the gold medal at the Montreal, Canada Summer Olympics. In 1986, the Indiana University Sports Hall of Fame inducted him.

The Chicago Bulls (NBA) selected May as the second player chosen in the NBA draft. May helped the Bulls reach the 1977 playoffs, but Chicago lost to the eventual champions, the Portland Trail Blazers. May received honorable mention for NBA Rookie of the Year. After performing for five seasons with Chicago, he spent the 1981–1982 campaign with the Milwaukee Bucks (NBA) and one month in 1982 with the Detroit Pistons (NBA). May scored 690 NBA points and averaged 10.4 points before playing professionally in Italy from 1983 to 1989. May, who married Debbie Lowery on February 11, 1985, and has two sons, Scott and Sean, resides in Bloomington, Indiana, operates an apartment rental business, and coaches All-Star teams of Indiana high school players. Sean stars in basketball at the University of North Carolina.

BIBLIOGRAPHY: Peter C. Bjarkman, *Big Ten Basketball* (Indianapolis, IN, 1994); Peter C. Bjarkman, *The Biographical History of Basketball* (Chicago, IL, 2000); Morgan G. Brenner *College Basketball's National Championships* (Lanham, MD, 1999); Edward F. Dolan Jr., and Richard B. Lyttle, *Scott May: Basketball Champion* (Garden City, NY, 1978); Mike Douchant, *Encyclopedia of College Basketball* (Detroit, MI, 1995); Joe Gergen, *The Final Four* (St. Louis, MO, 1987); Bob Hammel et al., *Glory of IU* (Champaign, IL, 2000); Tim Hosey and Bob Percival, *Bobby Knight: Countdown to Perfection* (New York, 1983); Jan Hubbard, ed., *The Official NBA Encyclopedia*, 3rd ed. (New York, 2000); *TSN Official NBA Register*, 1990–1991 (St. Louis, MO, 1990).

Thomas P. Wolf

MEANWELL, Walter Earnest "Doc" "Little Doctor" "Napoleon of Basketball" "the Little Giant" "the Wizard" (b. January 26, 1884, Leeds, England; d. December 2, 1953, Madison, WI), college coach and author, was the son of a lineman and shoemaker who immigrated with his family in 1887 to Rochester, New York. A major basketball figure, Meanwell incorporated patterns and tactical maneuvers into what had been a helter-skelter game. His system featured the short pass, crisscross, dribble, and block.

Meanwell graduated from Rochester High School and won the amateur lightweight wrestling championship of the Dominion of Canada as an entrant for the Rochester AC. He captained the AC's baseball and basketball teams, but did not compete in college sports. After graduating from the University of Maryland Medical School in Baltimore in 1909, Meanwell interned at Maryland General Hospital and in 1911 was named athletic director of Clifton Park in Baltimore. He served as supervisor of recreation for the city of Baltimore and as athletic director at Baltimore's Loyola University. Meanwell developed the short pass because his team in the BPAL could use only a small amount of space in a settlement house.

After joining the University of Wisconsin as coach in 1912, Meanwell began using these new tactics in college basketball. Although some players on his initial team sought to have him fired because of his unorthodox methods, they relented when the Badgers finished the season undefeated. During Meanwell's first three seasons at Wisconsin, the Badgers won 35 of 36 games. They set a record in 1912 and 1913 by winning 23 straight WC games and tied another mark by triumphing in 29 consecutive games. Meanwell coached at the University of Wisconsin until 1917 and received his Doctor of Public Health degree in 1915. He captained a medical corps in World War I and later earned a certificate of merit for his services during World War II.

From 1918 to 1920, Meanwell coached at the University of Missouri and fielded MVC title winners in both football and basketball. His cagers won two MVC titles. Meanwell coached basketball at the University of Wisconsin from 1921 to 1933 and served as athletic director there from 1933 to 1935. Wisconsin dominated Midwestern teams with the tightly disciplined Meanwell system of scientific basketball, largely developed in the 1912 season. Meanwell trained many future coaches, enabling other teams to develop appropriate methods of defense. He developed coaches including Harold "Bud" Foster*, who succeeded him at Wisconsin, Rollie Williams, Bill Chandler, Harold Olsen*, and Gus Tebell. A flamboyant, controversial coach, the short Meanwell almost never admitted defeat and often possessed a short temper. Subject to outbursts during games, the perfectionist uttered obscenities on the court and required his players to follow his dictates.

During 20 seasons under "Old Doc," University of Wisconsin teams won over 70 percent of their games. Meanwell compiled a 246-99 record at Wisconsin and a career 290-101 intercollegiate mark, including the University of Missouri years. The Badgers won four WC championships (1911–1912, 1912–1913, 1913–1914, and 1915–1916) and finished second four times (1920–1921, 1922–1923, 1923–1924, and 1928–1929). Meanwell's 1922–1923 team ranked as the best defensive team to that time in the WC. It kept opposing teams to 161 points in 12 WC games and only 199 points in 15 games. He ended his coaching career by leading Wisconsin during the 1933–1934 season to a second place WC finish.

During his coaching career, Meanwell served on the NBRC and USOBC, and held charter member ship in the NABC. Elected as coach to both the Naismith Memorial Basketball Hall of Fame (1959) and the HAF Hall of Fame, he pioneered in giving basketball clinics and developed both the valve for the laceless basketball and the basketball shoe that bore his name. His publications include *Basket Ball for Men* (1922); *The Science of Basket Ball for Men* (1924); and *Training, Conditioning, and the Care of Injuries* (1931), a book he co-authored with Knute Rockne.

Meanwell practiced medicine in Madison, Wisconsin after his active retirement from athletics, but always remained a coach at heart. "Old Doc" invited boys from his suburban village of Shorewood Hills, Wisconsin on Sundays to teach them the basketball rules that he helped formulate. Youngsters practiced on a court he and his son, Walter, built near their home. Meanwell died after surgery, being survived his wife, Helen (Grath) Meanwell, his son, Walter, and two daughters, Margaret and Helen. In May 1953, a few months before his death, the "Napoleon of Basketball" received a cup from the IBA for outstanding contributions to the game.

BIBLIOGRAPHY: Peter C. Bjarkman, *Big Ten Basketball* (Indianapolis, IN, 1994); Mike Douchant, *Encyclopedia of College Basketball* (Detroit, MI, 1995); Ralph Hickok, *Who Was Who in American Sports* (New York, 1971); Don Kopriva et al., *On Wisconsin* (Champaign, IL, 1998); Walter Meanwell file, Naismith Memorial Basketball Hall of Fame, Springfield, MA; Ronald L. Mendell, *Who's Who in Basketball* (New Rochelle, NY, 1973); *Milwaukee Journal*, December 3, 1953; *Milwaukee Sentinel*, December 3, 1953; *NYT*, December 3, 1953; Sandy Padwe, *Basketball's Hall of Fame* (Englewood Cliffs, NJ, 1970); Paul Soderberg and Helen Washington, comp. and ed., *The Big Book of Halls of Fame in the United States and Canada* (New York, 1977); *Wisconsin State Journal*, December 3, 1953.

Frederick J. Augustyn Jr.

MEARS, Ramon B. "Ray" (b. November 8, 1926, Dover, OH), college player, coach, and administrator, is the son of a working-class family in a northwestern Ohio steel town. He aspired to be a great athlete, but tested positive for tuberculosis in eleventh grade and was encouraged to quit sports. In order to keep close to basketball, Mears directed a sixth-grade team to a league championship as his first coaching experience. He worked in local steel mills to save money to attend Miami University of Ohio, where he also played basketball in the late 1940s. Mears, who earned a Master's degree from Kent State University (Ohio), married Dana Davis, and has three sons, Steven, Michael, and Matthew.

Mears coached high school basketball at Cadiz, Ohio, and Cleveland's West Tech before becoming head coach of Wittenberg University, a small Lutheran school in Springfield, Ohio. In six seasons from 1957 to 1962, the Wittenberg Tigers won 121 games and lost only 23 contests. Wittenberg led the nation in scoring defense his last three years, holding opponents to 46.8, 43.8, and 41.9 points per game, and won an NCAA College Division tournament championship in 1961. His coaching philosophy was strongly influenced by acquaintance with Clair Bee*, who advocated playing zone defenses, taking the high percentage shot, and keeping errors to a minimum.

The University of Tennessee in 1963 hired Mears to build a winning tradition in the University of Kentucky–dominated SEC. Mears compiled a 278-112 win-loss mark in 15 years, recording seven 20-win seasons, winning the 1967 SEC championship, sharing the 1972 and 1977 titles, and making six postseason tournament appearances. Tennessee also rejected another NIT bid. His last three squads featured future NBA players Ernie Grunfeld and Bernard King*, who combined to average 50 points and brought Tennessee much national attention. Mears's coaching career was terminated in 1978 by a "nervous problem," later identified as bipolar disorder (manic depression). Mears never experienced a losing season, compiling a 399-135 career coaching record. His .747 winning percentage ranks fourteenth best in college basketball history. He served as athletic director at the University of Tennessee-Martin from 1980 to 1989.

Mears, selected SEC Coach of the Year in 1967 and 1977, was elected to the Miami of Ohio and Tennessee Sports halls of fame and the Wittenberg University Athletic Hall of Honor. Although a premier coach, he may be remembered longer for masterful promotion of basketball at both Wittenberg and Tennessee. His promotions included having players introduced by spotlights or crashing through a paper tiger's head, using special uniforms and player chairs, employing orange and white basketballs, conducting spectacular pregame ball-handling drills, using basketball-juggling unicycle riders, adopting catchy program slogans ("TNT-Tennessee's Nuclear Tempered Offense," "Big Orange Country"), engaging in pregame walks that incited opponents, wearing Laurel and Hardy ties, and creating special big-game strategies. Mears orchestrated exciting basketball events.

BIBLIOGRAPHY: Ben Byrd, *The Basketball Vols: University of Tennessee Basketball* (Huntsville, AL, 1974); Chris Dortch, *String Music* (Dulles, VA, 2002); Mike Douchant, *Encyclopedia of College Basketball* (Detroit, MI, 1995); Barry McDermott, "It's the Bernie and Ernie Show," *SI* 44 (February 9, 1976), pp. 18–25; Ronald L. Mendell, *Who's Who in Basketball* (New Rochelle, NY, 1973); *NCAA Men's Basketball Records, 2004* (Indianapolis IN, 2003); Jim Steele, "Ray Mears: The Master Promoter Who Made Tennessee Big Orange Country," *Rocky Top Views*, October 16, 1991, pp. 8–9; Martin West, "Ray Mears Era (1962–78) Ends at Tennessee," Knoxville (TN) *News-Sentinel,* March 7, 1978, pp. 12–13.

Dennis S. Clark

MEYER, Raymond Joseph "Ray" (b. December 18, 1913, Chicago, IL), college player and coach, is the youngest in a family of three daughters and six sons. His father, Joseph, a wholesale candy salesman, died when he was very young. Meyer's mother, Barbara, and his older brothers proved very influential in his development. During his youth, he participated in basketball, football, baseball, and softball. After injuring a knee, Meyer gave up football and later baseball to concentrate on basketball. On graduation from St. Agatha's Elementary School in Chicago, he considered becoming a priest and enrolled at the Quigley Preparatory Seminary in Chicago. After two and one half years, Meyer decided against the priesthood and enrolled at St. Patrick's Academy in Chicago. At St. Patrick's Academy, his basketball abilities and future success began to emerge. In 1932 he helped lead his squad to a berth in the National Catholic High School Tournament.

On graduation, Meyer enrolled at Northwestern University (Illinois) and planned to play both basketball and football. His enrollment at Northwestern lasted only one day because a longtime friend, Edward "Moose" Krause*, convinced him to enroll at the University of Notre Dame. At Notre Dame, he was told by legendary Irish coach George Keogan* that he should play only basketball. Meyer spent his freshman year on the bench, but made some important contributions his sophomore season (1935–1936) until he suffered a knee injury. During that season, he played in a rare 20-20 tie game; no overtime period was played between Notre Dame and Northwestern on December 31, 1935. After recovering from the injury, Meyer played his final two seasons at Notre Dame and was elected team captain both seasons. He graduated from Notre Dame in 1938 with a Bachelor's degree in social work and received the Byron V. Kanaley Award for academic and athletic excellence.

After graduation, Meyer joined the Chicago Relief Association and coached and played for the LaSalle Hotel Cavaliers in national AAU competition. On June 22, 1938, he married Mary Margaret Delaney, whom he had met while helping coach St. Agatha's girls teams some years earlier. At this time, Meyer decided he wanted to be a full-time basketball coach. After declining a high school coaching job, he returned to the University of Notre Dame to become an assistant coach for the 1940–1941 and 1941–1942 seasons. Because of Keogan's poor health, Meyer assumed a major role in coaching and directing the Notre Dame squad to a 33-11 record. His next position, secured with the backing and support of Keogan, came as head coach of DePaul University in Chicago. Meyer remained at DePaul for the next 42 years and compiled a career record of 724 wins and 354 losses, for a .671 winning percentage. He ranks thirteenth on the all-time victory list for Division I coaches, enjoyed an astounding 37 winning seasons, and recorded 20 20-win seasons, including seven consecutive. His teams made 13 NCAA playoff appearances, including one Final Four appearance and seven NIT appearances, winning the NIT Championship in 1945 over Bowling Green (Ohio) University 71-54.

In 1978, Meyer was elected as a coach to the Naismith Memorial Basketball Hall of Fame. He had previously been elected to the Illinois and Oklahoma Athletic halls of fame and was named the USBWA Coach of the Year in 1978. Meyer was selected Coach of the Year again in 1979 by the NABC and in 1984 by UPI. His other coaching highlights included being the first and only coach of the College All-Stars, a team assembled annually for 11 years to play a coast-to-coast series with the Harlem Globetrotters. He also served as an advisory coach for the Chicago American Gears (NBL) and the Minneapolis Lakers (NBA). Some noteworthy players who played for Meyer include George Mikan*, Mark Aguirre*, and Terry Cummings*. On his retirement as DePaul University coach after the 1983–1984 season, Meyer was succeeded by his son, Joey, who had served as his assistant for 11 years. Meyer and his wife, Marge, have six children and 15 grandchildren. He remained active in broadcasting and maintains an office in the DePaul Athletic Department.

BIBLIOGRAPHY: Department of Sports Information, DePaul University, Chicago, IL; Mike Douchant, *The Encyclopedia of College Basketball* (Detroit, MI, 1995); James Enright, *Ray Meyer, America's #1 Basketball Coach* (Chicago, IL, 1980); Ray Meyer file, Naismith Memorial Basketball Hall of Fame, Springfield, MA; Ray Meyer and Ray Sons, *Coach* (Chicago, IL, 1987); *NCAA Men's Basketball Records, 2004* (Indianapolis, IN, 2003).

William A. Sutton

MEYERS, Ann Elizabeth. *See* Drysdale, Ann Elizabeth Meyers

MIHALIK, Zigmund John "Red" (b. September 22, 1916, Ford City, PA; d. October 25, 1996, Ford City, PA), college and professional referee, officiated six NCAA Basketball Finals, the 1964 Tokyo, Japan and 1968 Mexico City, Mexico Olympic Games, 12 Dixie and Poinsettia Classics; and seven Kentucky Invitational Tournaments in a career spanning more than 40 years. Mihalik was named in 1985 to the Naismith Memorial Basketball Hall of Fame's referee category and was voted by Dell Publications in 1951 as the best U.S. referee. Dell stated: "Fairness is a fetish with Red, as it is with most officials. He's not whistle-happy and he has the guts to make the big call without hesitation. His mental alertness and physical condition enable him to be in good position 99 percent of the time." A popular referee, he officiated BTC, ACC, NBA, and AAU games and NIT and early-round NCAA basketball tournaments.

Mihalik played three years of varsity basketball at Ford City High School before graduating in 1935. He worked his first contest when he was drafted to officiate a high school basketball game on a snowy 1935 night when the regular referees failed to appear. The experience spurred Mihalik to continue to referee high school junior-varsity and varsity contests played around Ford City. While serving three years in the U.S. Air Force during World War II, he officiated or played in hundreds of basketball games. After military discharge, Mihalik in February 1946 refereed his first college basketball game when the University of Pittsburgh met Pennsylvania State University's Nittany Lions' coach Johnny Lawther was pleased with Mihalik's work and recommended "Red" to the ECAC. Soon Mihalik officiated college basketball games extensively in the East, South, and Midwest. During the late 1940s and early 1950s, he refereed basketball games in Europe, Southeast Asia, and South America for the U.S. State Department. He worked Denver Nuggets and Peoria Caterpillars AAU League games plus a few contests in the fledgling NBA, but concentrated on intercollegiate competition.

Between 1956 and 1965, Mihalik officiated six NCAA basketball tournament finals. His first came when the University of San Francisco, led by Bill Russell* and K.C. Jones*, triumphed over the University of Iowa. His final two were UCLA's consecutive victories over Duke University and the University of Michigan when Walt Hazzard and Gail Goodrich* starred for the Bruins. Mihalik competed against other referees during the Olympic Trials before the final selection of basketball officials was made. He declined an invitation to officiate at the 1972 Munich, West Germany Olympic Games, stating that "it's time for someone else to go."

Mihalik's major college officiating career ended abruptly in 1972 while he was refereeing a game in Athens, Georgia between Auburn (Alabama) University and the University of Georgia. His knee was severely damaged by a Georgia player, who had intercepted a pass, instantly changed direction, and trampled Mihalik trailing the action. He later refereed junior varsity, girls', and junior high contests at nearby Worthington and Kittanning (Pennsylvania) High Schools and occasionally women's varsity games at Indiana (Pennsylvania) University. Mihalik, who married Helen Morgenstern, once observed: "The nicest thing about this game that you can do is get wrapped up in kids. I enjoy it so much to work with them, to help them feel loose. . . . This is still what is important to me."

BIBLIOGRAPHY: Zigmund Mihalik file, Naismith Memorial Basketball Hall of Fame, Springfield, MA; *Pittsburgh Press*, March 31, 1985.

James D. Whalen and Wayne Patterson

MIKAN, George Lawrence, Jr. (b. July 18, 1924, Joliet, IL; d. June 1, 2005, Scottsdale, AZ), college and professional player, coach, and executive, excelled as pro basketball's first superstar. His father, restauranteur George Sr., worked with him many hours a day; his mother, Minnie (Blinstrup) Mikan co-owned the restaurant. George suffered a broken leg when attending Joliet (Illinois) Catholic High School and was bedridden for 18 months, never playing basketball in high school. During that period, he grew from five feet eleven inches to six feet seven inches. In 1942, Mikan chose to attend DePaul University and enrolled on his own. That same year, Ray Meyer* took the basketball head-coaching position at DePaul.

Meyer developed a workout schedule for Mikan that consisted of skipping rope, shadowboxing, using a punching bag, modern and ballet dancing, and 200 hook shots with each hand every day. The regimen paid off, as Meyer transformed Mikan into an aggressive, dominating basketball center. Mikan was chosen All-America the next three years, scoring 1,970 points in his college career. During his junior and senior years, he led the nation in scoring and averaged 23.9 and 23.1 points, respectively. Mikan's greatest individual achievement of 120 points in three games enabled DePaul to win the 1945 NIT championship. He also was selected HAF College Player of the Year during his last two DePaul years. On May 1947, Mikan married Patricia Lu DeVaney. They had six children.

After completing a stellar college career, Mikan signed a $60,000, five-year contract with the Chicago Gears (NBL) in 1946. The next year (1947–1948), the Chicago franchise folded and the players were dispersed throughout the NBL. Mikan joined the Minneapolis Lakers (NBL), where he led the NBL in scoring with a 21.3 points average, was unanimous choice as NBL MVP, and led the Lakers to a NBL title and the World Tournament championship. After the 1947–1948 season, the NBL merged with the BAA to form the NBA. With Mikan as the dominant center and outstanding scorer, the Lakers became a dynasty and won the NBA championship five of the next six years. Mikan led the NBA in scoring three straight years (1948–1949 to 1950–1951) and averaged over 27 points, when few players were scoring over 20 points per game. In response to his scoring, the NBA widened the foul lanes from six to 12 feet and developed the three-second lane violation rule. The new rule caused his scoring production to drop. At the end of the 1953–1954 season, Mikan retired at age 30 except for a short stint in the 1955–1956 campaign. He made the All-NBL First Team in 1947 and 1948, All-BAA First Team in 1949, and All-NBA First Team from 1950 through 1954.

Mikan, who had spent his off-seasons studying law at DePaul University and passed the bar, agreed to become Lakers general manager and opened a law practice. At the time of his retirement, he held numerous NBA records, including most points in a career (11,764) and season (1,932) and NBA career scoring average (23.1) and highest season scoring average (28.4). Mikan was selected to the NBA All-Star team six consecutive years. He briefly returned to pro basketball as coach of the 9-30 Lakers during the 1957–1958 season and as ABA commissioner from 1967 to 1969. His honors included being named by the AP as the greatest basketball player of the first half of the twentieth century; being inducted into the Naismith Memorial Basketball Hall of Fame in 1960; being selected to the NBA Silver Anniversary Team, 35th Anniversary Team, and one of the 50 Greatest Players in NBA History; and being chosen for the All-Time All-America Team by HAF. He suffered from diabetes and kidney problems and pressed the NBA and the players union to boost the pensions for those who played in the league before 1965.

BIBLIOGRAPHY: Zander Hollander, ed., *The Modern Encyclopedia of Basketball* (Garden City, NY, 1979); Zander Hollander, ed., *The Pro Basketball Encyclopedia* (Los Angeles, CA, 1977); Jan Hubbard, ed., *The Official NBA Encyclopedia*, 3rd. ed. (New York, 2000); Neil D. Isaacs, *Vintage NBA* (Silver Spring, MD, 1996); Roland Lazenby, *The NBA Finals* (Indianapolis, IN, 1996); Ronald L. Mendell, *Who's Who in Basketball* (New Rochelle, NY, 1973); Ray Meyer and Ray Sons, *Coach* (Chicago, IL, 1987); George Mikan, *Mr. Basketball*, (New York, 1951); George Mikan and Joseph Oberle, *Unstoppable: The Story of George Mikan* (Indianapolis, IN, 1997); George Mikan file, Naismith Memorial Basketball Hall of Fame, Springfield, MA; David S. Neft et al., *The Sports Encyclopedia: Basketball*, 5th ed. (New York, 1992); *NYT*, February 23, 1949; *NYT*, February 17, 1950; *NYT*, September 25, 1954; *NYT*, October 6, 1954; Sandy Padwe, *Basketball's Hall of Fame* (Englewood Cliffs, NJ, 1970); Phil Pepe, *Greatest Stars of the NBA* (Englewood Cliffs, NJ, 1970); Ken Shouler et al., *Total Basketball* (Wilmington, DE, 2003); *TSN* Official *Basketball Register, 2004–2005* (St. Louis, MO, 2004); Stew Thornley, *Basketball's Original Dynasty: The History of the Lakers* (Minneapolis, MN, 1989); Richard Triptow, *The Dynasty That Never Was* (Chicago, IL, 1996).

Tony Ladd

MIKKELSEN, Arild Verner Agerskov "Vern" (b. October 21, 1928, Fresno, CA), college and professional player and coach, was perhaps the first authentic power forward in the NBA, a league he starred in for 10 years in the early post-war years when it was becoming truly national. Mikkelsen, whose Minneapolis Lakers (NBA) have been called one of the era's two great teams, came from tiny Hamline University in nearby St. Paul, Minnesota. Although born in central California, he moved with his Danish-born parents to Minnesota to be closer to relatives when he was a child. He attended high school in Askov, Minnesota and then entered Hamline University (Minnesota) in 1945. Mikkelsen scored 123 points in 17 games his freshman basketball season; freshmen were eligible to compete for Division II schools at the time. In 1946–1947 as a sometime starter, Mikkelsen made 102 field goals and 52 free throws for 256 points and averaged 9.8 points.

The next year, Mikkelsen became a star. Starting virtually every game, he nearly doubled his field goal production with 199 and more than doubled his free throws with 119 for 517 points and 16.7 points per game. As a senior in 1949, Mikkelsen drew everyone's attention. He was named the Second Team center on the Converse All-America squad, joining stars Ed Macauley*, Ernie Vandeweghe, and Alex Groza*. Mikkelsen also was selected Second Team All-America by the HAF and Fourth Team All-America by *TSN*. He sank 203 of 377 shots from the field that year for 54 percent (first among all Division II schools) and made 64 percent from the free throw line. Mikkelsen's 17.3 points per game ranked him fourteenth nationally in scoring. As a fitting end to his college career, he led all scorers in the East-West All-Star Game with 17 points for the West team; the West team, however, suffered a one-point loss. He graduated from Hamline University with Bachelor's and Master's degrees in 1949 before joining the Minneapolis Lakers (NBA), who made him a first-round draft choice.

Mikkelsen enjoyed instant success in the NBA. As a rookie, he played in an impressive 68 games and made 288 field goals, 215 free throws, and 791 points. His scoring average was 11.6 points. In the 1950–1951 season, his 359 field goals and 186 free throws produced 904 points, gave him 14.1 points per game, and put him on the All-NBA Second Team. Mikkelsen also was named to the All-NBA Second Team in 1952, 1953, and 1955, but never earned All-NBA First Team honors. His Minneapolis Lakers team won NBA championships in 1950, 1952, 1953, and 1954. Mikkelsen was a consistent player rather than a great point producer. In 1954–1955, he averaged 18.7 points. George Mikan* was hurt that year, causing Mikkelsen to spend more time in the post than in other years. Many clubs followed the plan of just getting the ball into the "big man." That meant Mikan in Minneapolis' case.

At six feet eight inches and 230 pounds, Mikkelsen was one of the NBA's first big men. He was not big enough to move Mikan from the post and consequently became a power forward. The plan worked, as Minneapolis consistently won during his decade as a player there. Mikkelsen compiled points-per-game averages in his ten years with the Lakers of 11.6, 14.1, 15.3, 15.0, 11.1, 18.7, 13.4, 13.7, 17.3, and 13.8. During one six-year span, the dependable player missed only one game. Lakers' teammates rewarded Mikkelsen for his leadership by naming him team captain for six consecutive seasons. He also appeared in the NBA playoffs nine times, played in six All-Star Games, and holds the NBA career record with 127 disqualifications.

Mikkelsen retired with 10,063 career points, one of the first NBA players to reach the 10,000 plateau. Many experts think the Lakers dominated the game in the early 1950s because they were the first team to initiate playing with three big men—Mikan, Mikkelsen, and Jim Pollard*—and two smaller guards. After his playing days, Mikkelsen taught school for a time and traveled to Scandinavia for the U.S. State Department. He briefly returned to basketball as head coach and general manager of the Minnesota Pipers (ABA) entry in 1968. After compiling a 6-7 record, Mikkelsen left pro coaching. He was inducted into the NAIA Basketball Hall of Fame and was elected to the Naismith Memorial Basketball Hall of Fame in 1995.

BIBLIOGRAPHY: Zander Hollander, ed., *Modern Encyclopedia of Basketball* (Garden City, NY, 1979); Jan Hubbard, ed., *The Official NBA Encyclopedia*, 3rd ed, (New York, 2000); Neil D. Isaacs, *Vintage NBA* (Silver Spring, MD, 1996); Roland Lazenby, *The NBA Finals* (Indianapolis, IN, 1996); Vern Mikkelsen file, Naismith Memorial Basketball Hall of Fame, Springfield, MA; William G. Mokray, ed., *Encyclopedia of Basketball*, 2nd ed. (New York, 1963); Ken Shouler et al., *Total Basketball* (Wilmington, DE, 2003); *TSN Official NBA Register, 2004–2005* (St. Louis, MO, 2004); Stew Thornley, *Basketball's Original Dynasty: The History of the Lakers* (Minneapolis, MN, 1989).

Jay Berman

MILLER, Cheryl DeAnne "Silk" (b. January 3, 1964, Riverside, CA), college player and professional coach and sportscaster, holds many records. On January 27, 1983, became the first woman to dunk a basketball in regulation play. Miller accomplished that feat for Riverside (California) Polytechnic High School while scoring 105 points to defeat Norte Vista (California) High School 179-15. The third of Saul and Carrie Miller's five children, Cheryl credits her father with developing the athletic talents of his children. Her father, a high school All-State basketball forward in Memphis, Tennessee, played three years at LeMoyne-Owen College (Tennessee) before enlisting in the U.S. Air Force in 1951. Her brother, Saul Jr., participated in basketball at Ramona High School and played saxophone with the 15th Air Force Band. Darrell, the second child, played outfield for the California Angels (AL) baseball club. Younger brother, Reggie*, excelled at forward for the UCLA basketball team and plays guard with the Indiana Pacers (NBA), while sister, Tammy, was a high school volleyball player. Cheryl, nicknamed "Silk" because of her playing style, achieved superstar status in the 1980s.

At Riverside Poly High School, Miller played 90 games, scored 3,026 points, and averaged 32.8 points. She made 1,105 of 1,621 field goal attempts, 286 of 422 free throws, 1,353 rebounds, and 368 assists. From 1979 through 1982, she led Riverside Poly to an incredible 132-4 record. Miller holds the CIF records for most career points (3,405), most season points (1,156), and most game points (105). As a junior, she averaged a record 37.5 points per game. Miller was the first person, male or female, ever selected four consecutive seasons to the *Parade* All-America Team. She made consensus All-America (1979–1982); AAU All-America (1979–1982); All-CIF (1979–1982) MVP winning honors; All-USA Development League (1978–1980); and *Street and Smith's* top high school basketball player (1981–1982). Besides being the only prep athlete named to the U.S. national team, Miller was named Riverside (CA) County Player of the Year (1980–1982). At Riverside Poly, she maintained a "B" academic average, finished first runner-up for Homecoming Queen, belonged to the Black Student Union, and played varsity softball.

At the University of Southern California, Miller's honors included Eastman Kodak All-America (1983–1986); ABAUSA All-America (1983–1984); Naismith All-America (1983–1986); Fast Break All-America (1983); WCAC All-Conference Team (1983–1985); NCAA West Regional All-Tournament Team (1983–1986); and NCAA Tournament MVP (1983–1984). Under Coach Linda Sharp, she combined with twins Paula and Pam McGee, Kathy Doyle, Tracy Longo, Rhonda Windham, and Cynthia Cooper* to produce the Trojans' first NCAA championship in 1983. As a freshman that year, Miller made 268 of 486 attempted field goals and 137 of 186 free throws attempted in 33 games; 320 rebounds for a 9.7 rebounds average; and 115 assists. She scored 673 season points, averaged 20.4 points, and made a game-high 39 points. Miller also was named the Winston Holiday Classic MVP and helped the U.S. women's team take the gold medal at the 1983 Pan-American Games.

By the 1983–1984 season, Miller had grown another inch taller to her full status of six feet three inches. She led the Southern California team to a 24-4 regular-season record, averaging over 20 points and 10 rebounds. Along with the McGee twins, Miller sparked the Trojans to a second consecutive NCAA women's basketball championship with a 72-61 victory over Louisiana Tech University. She scored 16 points in the final game and was selected NCAA tournament MVP. Miller won the Naismith Trophy and Broderick Award as Female Basketball Player of the Year, was selected WCAA MVP, and was chosen co-winner of the Broderick Cup as Female Athlete of the Year. Her "Silken"-style pre-game dances and superior skills thrilled audiences and transformed women's basketball into a dynamic spectator sport. She led the U.S. gold medal women's basketball team in scoring at the 1984 Los Angeles Summer Olympic Games.

Miller's best college season came in 1984–1985. Her school records set that campaign included highest scoring average (26.8 points), most rebounds (474), highest rebounds average (15.8), and most free throws (201). Miller also established Southern California individual game highs for most points (45) and free throws made (21) against the University of Arizona on February 28, 1985, most rebounds (24, against the University of Iowa on December 12, 1984), and most field goals (17, against Louisiana Tech University on January 26, 1985). Besides repeating as Naismith Trophy Player of the Year, she was named ESPN Woman Athlete of the Year, Champion Player of the Year, WCAA Conference MVP, and All-WCAA First Team member.

During her senior year, Miller won the Naismith Trophy for the third consecutive year and the Broderick Award as the Female College Basketball Player of the Year. She finished fourth nationally in scoring average (25.4 points) and set school season records for most points (814) and steals (127) in 32 games. Miller paced the Trojans to a 31-5 record and the NCAA championship game, which the University of Texas won 97-81. Her other honors that year included being the first female basketball player nominated for the Sullivan Memorial Trophy, making the NCAA Final Four All-Tournament Team, and being selected West NCAA Regional MVP, Pac-West MVP, Champion and USBWA Player of the Year, and U.S. Sports Academy Athlete of the Year. Miller made the Northern Lights All-Tournament Team at Anchorage, Alaska and was chosen MVP of the Transamerica USC Basketball Classic and the Maryland Thanksgiving Tournament. She broke several Southern California career records, including scoring (3,018 points in 128 games), rebounding (1,534), field goals made (1,159), free throws made (700), and steals (462). The Trojans in March 1986 retired her uniform jersey, making Miller the first Southern California basketball player so honored. In 1986, she earned a Bachelor's degree in sports information.

The California Stars (NWBA) drafted Miller in the first round in 1986, but the NWBA dissolved that year. Miller helped the United States defeat the Soviet Union for the gold medal at the Goodwill Games in Moscow, U.S.S.R. in July 1986 and at the World Basketball Championships in Moscow in August 1986. Extensive knee surgery caused her to miss the 1987 Pan-American Games. Miller joined ABC Sports in January 1988, doing halftime features for men's college basketball games and conducting interviews at the 1988 Calgary, Canada Winter Olympic Games. Miller's knee injury prevented her from making the 1988 U.S. Olympic basketball team.

Miller coached Southern California to a 26-4 record and PTC title in 1993–1994 and an 18-10 record in 1994–1995. She was inducted into the International Women's Sports Hall of Fame in 1991, the Naismith Memorial Basketball Hall of Fame in 1995, and the Women's Basketball Hall of Fame in 1999. *Sport* named her Female Athlete of the Decade in 1999. Miller coached the Phoenix Mercury (WNBA) to records of 16-12 in 1997, 19-11 in 1998, 15-17 in 1999, and 20-12 in 2000, finishing first in the Western Conference in 1997. She compiled a 70-52 regular season record and 3-6 playoff mark. She also serves as an NBA analyst for TNT telecasts.

BIBLIOGRAPHY: "Best Bets from the U.S.," *Women's Sports* 5 (November 1983), pp. 36–37; Mike Douchant, *Encyclopedia of College Basketball* (Detroit, MI, 1995); Carol Edwards, "Hail Miller and Women of Troy! NCAA Champs," *TSN*, April 11, 1983, p. 39; Elise Frantom, sports release, University of Southern California, Los Angeles, 1983; "The Heroines," *Newsweek* 10 (February 21, 1983), pp. 82–83; Roger Jackson, "She May Well Be the Best Ever," *SI* 57 (November 29, 1982), pp. 90–91; Anne Jannette Johnson, *Great Women in Sports* (Detroit, MI, 1996); Curry Kirkpatrick, "Lights! Camera! Cheryl," *SI* 63 (November 20, 1985); Michele Kort, "A Tale of Two Cities," *Women's Sports* 6 (March 1984), pp. 18–21; Jill Lieber, "Stars of Stage, Screen, and Court," *SI* 60 (April 9, 1984), pp. 46, 48; Cheryl Miller file, Naismith Memorial Basketball Hall of Fame, Springfield, MA; Knolly Moses, "Playing Your Way Through College," *Essence* 14 (August 1983), p. 52; Craig Neff, "Welcome to Miller Time," *SI* 58 (April 11, 1983), pp. 24–25; Lisa Schmidt, "AKA the Cheryl Miller Show," *Women's Sports* 5 (March 1983), pp. 13–14; "Shooting for the NBA," *Ebony* 37 (May 1982), pp. 67–68, 70; Rosemarie Skaine, *Women College Basketball Coaches* (Jefferson, NC, 2001); *TSN Official WNBA Guide and Register, 2001* (St. Louis, MO, 2001); University of Southern California Sports Information Office, Los Angeles, to David L. Porter, March 22, 1988; Kelly Whiteside, *WNBA: A Celebration: Commemorating the Birth of a League* (New York, 1998).

Sara-Jane Griffin

MILLER, Lawrence James "Larry" (b. April 4, 1946, Allentown, PA), college and professional player, grew up in Catasauqua, Pennsylvania, where he starred in prep school basketball. Miller attended the University of North Carolina from 1964 to 1968. After a season on the freshman basketball team, he averaged 20.9, 21.9, and 22.4 points in three varsity seasons for the Tar Heels. Miller scored 1,982 career points at North Carolina, averaging 21.8 points. The powerfully built six-foot four-inch, 215-pound forward also averaged 9.2 rebounds during his varsity career.

Miller, a crucial component in Dean Smith's* first North Carolina powerhouses, was selected Second Team All-ACC in 1966 and First Team All-ACC in 1967 and 1968. He led the Tar Heels to the NCAA Final Four in 1967 and 1968, being named ACC Player of the Year both seasons. Miller remains the only North Carolina player to win this award twice. He received the McKelvin Award, presented to the ACC's top athlete in 1967 and 1968. Miller was named Second Team All-America by AP and Third Team All-America by UPI in 1967. The following season, he was selected First Team All-America by AP and Second Team by UPI.

Miller played with the Los Angeles Stars (ABA) from 1968 through 1970, Carolina Cougars (ABA) from 1970 to 1972, San Diego Conquistadors (ABA) from 1972 to 1974, Virginia Squires (ABA) in 1974, and Utah Stars (ABA) in 1974–1975, averaging 13.6 points and 5.0 rebounds in 486 ABA games. His best season came in 1971–1972, when he averaged 18.4 points for Carolina. On March 18, 1972, Miller set an ABA record by scoring 67 points against the Memphis Tams. He was named to the 1969 ABA All-Rookie team and was selected one of the ACC's top 50 basketball players.

BIBLIOGRAPHY: Art Chansky, *Dean' Domain* (Marietta, GA, 1999); Ron Morris, *ACC Basketball: An Illustrated History* (Chapel Hill, NC, 1988); Ken Rappoport, *Tar Heel: North Carolina Basketball* (Huntsville, AL, 1976); Ken Shouler et al., *Total Basketball* (Wilmington, DE, 2003); *University of North Carolina Men's Basketball Media Guide 2004* (Chapel Hill, NC, 2004).

Jim L. Sumner

MILLER, Ralph Howard (b. March 9, 1919, Chanute, KS; d. May 15, 2001, Black Butte, OR), college athlete and basketball coach, was the son of Harold C. Miller, a schoolteacher, and Ruth L. Miller. Miller, a versatile athlete, attended Chanute (Kansas) High School, where he earned 13 varsity letters in five sports. At the University of Kansas, he earned his Bachelor's degree in education in 1942. Miller married Emily Jean Milam and served three years in the U.S. Air Force, being discharged as a first lieutenant. They had four children, Susan Langer, Ralph Jr., Paul, and Shannon.

At Chanute High School, Miller received All-League honors in football three times and All-State basketball laurels. On graduation, he held the state prep track and field low-hurdles record. At the University of Kansas, Miller earned three varsity letters in both football and basketball. Several of his passing records remain intact from his days as Jayhawks' quarterback. An All-BSC basketball performer for two years, Miller learned fundamentals and strategy from masterful coach "Phog" Allen*. He began his coaching career at Wichita East High School, where his teams won 63 of 80 games and captured a state title in 1951.

Perennial second-division finisher Wichita (Kansas) State University hired the successful 31-year-old high school coach to reinvigorate its basketball program. Wichita State competed in the so-called "Valley of Death" and scheduled such national powers as the University of Cincinnati (Ohio), Ohio State University, and the University of San Francisco (California). Despite such competition, the Shockers won 220 games from 1950 to 1964 and one MVC title and received three NIT bids (1954, 1962, 1963) and one NCAA bid (1964). At the University of Iowa from 1964–1965 to 1969–1970, Miller compiled 95 basketball victories and two BTC titles. In his final season (1969–1970), Iowa won the BTC crown with a perfect 14-0 record and earned an NCAA bid. Miller coached basketball at Oregon State University from 1970–1971 to 1988–1989 and improved his winning percentage over the first decade. From 1980–1981 to 1983–1984, his Beavers captured four consecutive PTC titles, won 99 of 106 games, and compiled a 64-8 PTC record. Miller's team played in the NCAA tournament each of these four seasons and four additional years. His 1980–1981 squad was ranked number one for nine straight weeks. Miller's 38-year record of 657-382 made him the twenty-second winningest all-time coach in NCAA Division I college basketball. He suffered just three losing seasons.

Miller was one of few coaches who have been honored twice as Coach of the Year in three major basketball conferences. At Wichita State University, he was named the MVC's top mentor in 1954 and 1964. Miller won similar honors at the University of Iowa in the BTC in 1968 and 1970 and at Oregon State University in the PTC in 1981. At Oregon State, he added citations from NBC-TV and ESPN. In 1982, the AP and other wire services named Miller National Coach of the Year. Miller repeated in 1983 as AP National Coach of the Year. He was inducted into the Kansas and University of Kansas Sports halls of fame. Miller, who never coached a team to the NCAA Final Four, was elected in 1988 to the Naismith Memorial Basketball Hall of Fame and received the NIT Man of the Year Award. Miller's teaching skills developed and produced nearly 20 NBA players. His coaching philosophy featured "pressure basketball" developed at Wichita's East High School, using full-court pressing defense ("automatic pick-up rule") and a fast-break attack with little dribbling and sharp passing. His teams frequently limited opponents to under 60 points per game, attesting to the wisdom of his reliable system developed in a coaching career spanning four decades. Miller retired following the 1988–1989 season. The court at Oregon State is named after him.

BIBLIOGRAPHY: Mike Douchant, *Encyclopedia of College Basketball* (Detroit, MI, 1995); Mike Finn et al., *Hawkeye Legends, Lists and Lore* (Champaign, IL, 1998); Joe Jares, "The Dealers Roll to a Title," *SI* 32 (March 3, 1970), pp. 47–48; Blair Kerkhoff, *Phog Allen—The Father of Basketball Coaching* (Indianapolis, IN, 1996); Curry Kirkpatrick and Ken Wheeler, "Bunch of Eager Beavers," *SI* 52 (February 18, 1980), pp. 18–20; Ralph Miller file, Naismith Memorial Basketball Hall of Fame, Springfield, MA; *NCAA Men's Basketball Records, 2004* (Indianapolis, IN, 2003); B.J. Phillips, "Pass Masters of the Game," *Time* 117 (March 2, 1981), p. 80.

Gregory S. Sojka

MILLER, Reginald Wayne "Reggie" (b. August 24, 1965, Riverside, CA), college and professional player, is one of five children born to Saul Miller, a chief master sergeant in the U.S. Air Force, and Carrie Miller, a nurse. He suffered from a congenital deformity of his hips and wore steel braces until he was age four.

Making up for lost time, Miller developed a passion for athletics. Initially, he hoped to emulate his bother, Darrell, who played major league baseball for the California Angels (AL). Finding baseball too slow, Miller turned to basketball. He often played in the shadow of his older sister, Cheryl*, who once scored over 100 points in a high school game and in 1984 led the U.S. to its first Olympic gold medal in women's basketball. The shot-blocking ability of his sister led Miller to develop his trademark high-arching three-point shot. Miller, however, soon emerged as a star in his own right, leading Riverside (California) Polytechnic High School to state championships during his junior and senior years, averaging over 30 points in his final season.

Following high school graduation in 1983, Miller accepted a basketball scholarship to UCLA. During the 1984–1985 season, he led the Bruins to the NIT championship. His senior season saw him average 22.3 points. The six-foot seven-inch, 190-pound guard was selected by the Indiana Pacers (NBA) with the eleventh pick of the NBA draft.

During his rookie NBA campaign, Miller averaged only 10 points. In the 1988–1989 season, he emerged as one of the top NBA three-point shooters, averaging a career-best 24.6 points. The next season, he led the NBA with 167 three-point field goals.

Miller also developed a reputation for "trash talking" on the court. This side of his personality was exhibited when the Pacer star verbally jousted with New York celebrity fan filmmaker Spike Lee during the 1994 Eastern Conference Finals with the New York Knicks. Although the Knicks prevailed in seven games, Miller taunted Lee and the New York crowd by scoring 25 points in the final quarter of Game Five. The following season, the Pacers triumphed over the Knicks in a hotly contested series, only to be eliminated by the Orlando Magic in the Eastern Conference Finals.

Miller starred for the gold medal–winning U.S. Olympic team in 1996, but has never been able to achieve a NBA championship with the Pacers. Slowing somewhat with age, he averaged only 12.6 points and 2.5 rebounds during the 2002–2003 campaign, 10.0 points and 2.4 rebounds in 2003–2004, and 14.8 points and 2.4 rebounds in 2004–2005. Commissioner David Stern* suspended him for one game for his role in a melee that occurred on and off the court in a game with the Detroit Pistons on November 19, 2004 at The Palace in Auburn Hills, Michigan. The five-time All-Star remains the all-time NBA three-point shooter with 2,560 goals. Miller ranks twelfth on the all-time scoring list with 25,279 points in 1,389 regular season games through the 2004 season and has tallied 2,779 points in 131 playoff games. He remains the all-time playoff leader in three-point field goals made (299) and attempted (754) and fourth among active leaders in points scored. Miller has made several game-winning shots in the playoffs. He was selected to the All-NBA Third Team in 1995, 1996, and 1998. Miller married model Marita Stavrou on August 29, 1992, but the couple separated in August 2000 and later divorced. He remains active in Indianapolis, Indiana civic affairs and hopes to gain a championship ring with the Pacers.

BIBLIOGRAPHY: Ted Cox, *Reggie Miller: Basketball Sharp-Shooter* (New York, 1995); Jack McCallum, "Heroic Measures," *SI* 92 (May 22, 2000), pp. 64–71; Reggie Miller, *I Love Being the Enemy: A Season on the Court with the NBA's Best Shooter and Sharpest Tongue* (New York, 1995); Roscoe Nance, "Pacers No Longer Miller's Team, But He's the Big Shot," *USA Today*, May 24, 2004, p. 3C; Ken Shouler et al., *Total Basketball* (Wilmington, DE, 2003); *TSN Official NBA Register, 2004–2005* (St. Louis, MO, 2004); Barry Wilner, *Reggie Miller* (New York, 1997).

Ron Briley

MODZELEWSKI, Stanley J. *See* Stutz, Stanley J.

MOE, Douglas Edwin "Doug" (b. September 21, 1938, Brooklyn, NY), college and professional player and coach, is the son of Gunar Moe and Dolores Moe and did not become a basketball starter at Erasmus Hall High School in Brooklyn, New York until his senior year. After graduating from Erasmus Hall, Moe attended Bullis Prep School in Washington, D.C. for one year. He joined other New York city area stars in playing college basketball at the University of North Carolina (ACC) under Frank McGuire* and Dean Smith*. North Carolina employed the six-foot six-inch, 220-pound Moe, a hard-nosed forward, for his defensive skills. Moe made All-ACC in 1958–1959 and 1960–1961, but missed the first half of the 1959–1960 campaign for academic reasons. He enjoyed a superb senior season on the court, averaging 20.4 points and 14.0 rebounds. Moe, who attained Second Team AP All-America and First Team USBWA All-America, finished his Tar Heel career with 987 points and 635 rebounds in 60 games.

After the 1961 season, the media reported that Moe had been contacted that season by gamblers. Although refusing to shave points, Moe had accepted $75 for expenses and not disclosed these bribe attempts to authorities. North Carolina consequently suspended him in the spring of 1961. Although Moe never was charged with a crime, the NBA blacklisted him. Moe briefly sold insurance before enrolling in 1963 at Elon (North Carolina) College (NSIC), where he served as an assistant basketball coach and received his Bachelor's degree in physical education in 1965. He played basketball in Italy in 1965–1966 and 1966–1967 for Petrarca of Padua and led the ItL in scoring in both seasons.

The New Orleans Buccaneers (ABA) signed Moe when it entered the ABA in 1967. In the 1967–1968 season, he finished second in the ABA in scoring with 24.2 points per game and made All-ABA First Team. In June 1968 New Orleans traded Moe to the Oakland Oaks (ABA), where he made All-ABA Second Team and helped that franchise win the ABA title. Moe was dealt to the Carolina Cougars (ABA) in June 1969 and to the Virginia Squires (ABA) in July 1970. A bad knee forced his retirement following the 1971–1972 campaign. He finished his ABA career with 6,161 points, a 16.3 point average, 2,560 rebounds, and a 6.8 rebounds average.

Assistant coaching assignments followed with Carolina in 1972–1973 and 1973–1974 and the Denver Rockets (ABA) in 1974–1975 and 1975–1976. The San Antonio Spurs, by then merged into the NBA, appointed Moe head coach in 1976. Moe guided the Spurs to Central Division titles in 1977–1978 and 1978–1979, but was fired in 1980. In December 1980, he replaced Don Walsh, ironically a former Tar Heel teammate, as head coach of the Denver Nuggets (NBA). At Denver, the irreverent iconoclast disdained set offenses, lengthy practices, and even neckties. His fast-paced Denver offense broke NBA scoring records, tallying 126.5 points average in 1981–1982. Moe gradually gained respect as an innovative, successful coach, and won the 1987–1988 NBA Coach of the Year Award. Under Moe, Denver captured Midwest Division titles in 1984–1985 and 1987–1988. Paul Westhead replaced Moe as Denver head coach following the 1989–1990 season. He then coached the Philadelphia 76ers (NBA) to a 19-37 mark in 1992–1993 and served as coaching consultant for the Denver Nuggets from 2002 to February 2005, when he became assistant coach there. In 15 NBA seasons, Moe record stood at 628-529 in regular contests and 33-50 in the playoffs. He married North Carolina graduate Louise Jane Twisdale in 1961 and has two sons, Doug and David. A third son died in infancy.

BIBLIOGRAPHY: Peter C. Bjarkman, *ACC: Atlantic Coast Conference* (Indianapolis, IN, 1996);

Bob Diddlebock, "Beers With Doug Moe," *Sport* 80 (February 1989), pp. 21–22; Bruce Newman, "This Joker is Wild," *SI* 69 (November 7, 1988), pp. 102–106; *NYT*, December 5, 1984, p. 29; Terry Pluto, *Loose Balls: The Short, Wild Life of the American Basketball Association* (New York, 1990); Ken Rappoport, *Tales from the Tar Heel Locker Room* (Champaign, IL, 2002); Ken Rappoport, *Tar Heel: North Carolina Basketball* (Huntsville, AL, 1976); Ken Shouler et al., *Total Basketball* Wilmington, DE, 2003); *TSN*, January 10, 1970, p. 13; *TSN*, November 25, 1985, p. 39; *TSN*, April 14, 1986, p. 31; *TSN Official NBA Register, 2004–2005* (St. Louis, MO, 2004); *University of North Carolina Basketball Guide, 1961* (Chapel Hill, NC, 1961).

Jim L. Sumner

MOIR, John (b. May 22, 1917, Rutherglen, Scotland; d. November 15, 1975, Carlisle, PA), college and professional player, was selected a three-time All-America and HAF Player of the Year in 1936 under coach George Keogan* at the University of Notre Dame (Indiana). The son of John Moir, a carpenter, and Elizabeth Moir, he was one of three children and immigrated with his family to Niagara Falls, New York, in 1923. Moir stood only five feet two inches when he entered Niagara Falls High School and did not play basketball. Upon graduation, Moir enrolled in Trott Vocational School. He enjoyed his first chance to play organized basketball and grew to six feet two inches and 184 pounds. After finishing his vocational education, Moir worked as a bookkeeper for American Sales Book Company and performed on the company's industrial league team. His job performance garnered him offers to attend college, something he had not previously considered.

Moir chose Notre Dame and played basketball there under Keogan. In his first season of eligibility as a sophomore, he paced the 22-2-1 Fighting Irish to the 1936 HAF national championship and was named HAF Player of the Year. Moir led Notre Dame in scoring during each of his three seasons, averaging 11.3, 13.2, and 10.5 points. He also broke all Notre Dame scoring records of Ed "Moose" Krause*, a three-time All-America. Teammate Paul Nowak* joined Moir as three-time HAF and Consensus All-Americas, two of only 18 consensus All-Americas in college basketball history. His outstanding teammates also included Naismith Memorial Basketball Hall of Fame coach Ray Meyer* of DePaul University and George Ireland, longtime mentor of Loyola (Illinois) University.

Moir and Nowak both played with the Akron (Ohio) Firestone Non-Skids (NBL) upon graduation and helped the Firestones garner NBL championships in 1938–1939 and 1939–1940. Moir averaged seven points over the two seasons and led the 1940 playoffs in scoring with an 11-point average. He spent the 1940–1941 campaign with Akron and joined the independent Rochester (New York) Seagrams in 1941, the predecessor of the NBA's Rochester Royals. The Seagrams disbanded during World War II. After World War II, Moir ended his basketball career with the Cleveland (Ohio) Allmen Transfers (NBL) in 1945–1946. In four NBL seasons, he scored 562 points in 89 games and averaged 6.5 points. Moir, who subsequently worked for the Carlisle Tire and Rubber Company, and his wife, Marjorie, had two daughters and one son.

BIBLIOGRAPHY: Mike Douchant, *Encyclopedia of College Basketball* (Detroit, MI, 1995); Ronald L. Mendell, *Who's Who in Basketball* (New Rochelle, NY, 1973); Tim Neely, *Hooping It Up: The Complete History of Notre Dame Basketball* (Notre Dame, IN, 1985); David S. Neft and Richard M. Cohen, eds., *The Sports Encyclopedia: Pro Basketball,* 5th ed. (New York, 1992); *Notre Dame Basketball Guide 1991–1992* (Notre Dame, IN, 1991); Ken Shouler et al., *Total Basketball* (Wilmington, DE, 2003); *South Bend* (IN) *Tribune,* November 18, 1975; C. H. Welsh scrapbook, Archives of the University of Notre Dame, Notre Dame, IN.

Brian L. Laughlin

MOKRAY, William George "Bill" (b. June 6, 1907, Passaic, NJ; d. March 22, 1974, Revere, MA), sports executive and basketball historian, was the son of George Mokray, a banker, and Anna (Yusoff) Mokray. Mokray became interested in sports, especially basketball while attending Passaic (New Jersey) High School. He watched the school's "Wonder Teams" of the early 1920s, winners of 159 games in a row. Mokray developed statistics and records for these teams and wrote about their exploits throughout his life. After graduation, he attended Rhode Island State College and earned a Bachelor of Science degree in 1929. Mokray participated in cross-country at Rhode Island State, but did not try out for basketball because of weak eyesight. Simultaneously he worked as a sports correspondent for the *Providence Journal-Bulletin.* Immediately after graduation, Mokray was hired by his alma mater as its first sports publicity director. He held this post until 1942 and helped to publicize the Rams fast-breaking style of basketball. On May 31, 1941, Mokray married Margaret Ellen MacNulty. They had two sons, William and Walter.

In 1944, Mokray became the first director of college basketball at the Boston Garden in Boston, Massachusetts. On the establishment of the Boston Celtics (BAA) franchise in 1946, he also became the team's public relations director. Mokray continued in both these positions until 1957, working closely with Walter Brown*. He was promoted to vice president and director of promotions for the Celtics and continued in these positions until his retirement in 1969. Concurrently Mokray worked on the staff of Converse Rubber Company from 1946 to 1973, collecting statistics and writing basketball articles for its unique annual *Basketball Yearbook.* He pioneered as a pro basketball statistician and founded the *Official NBA Guide*, serving as its editor for nine years. In 1957, Mokray authored the history of basketball for the *Encyclopedia Britannica.* Six years later, he wrote the 900-page *Ronald Basketball Encyclopedia.* The encyclopedia was selected as one of the best reference books of 1963.

Mokray chaired the Naismith Memorial Basketball Hall of Fame Honors Committee from its establishment in 1959 to 1964 and led the effort to secure a basketball postage stamp, which was issued in 1961. His extensive personal sports library was donated to the Hickcox Library at the Naismith Memorial Basketball Hall of Fame. He held honorary membership on the NCBAA and IAABO, although never coaching or refereeing. Mokary was selected to the Naismith Memorial Basketball Hall of Fame (1965), NAIA Hall of Fame (1967), and HAF Hall of Fame (1972) for his extensive contributions to sports.

BIBLIOGRAPHY: Ronald L. Mendell, *Who's Who in Basketball* (New Rochelle, NY, 1973); William Mokray file, Naismith Memorial Basketball Hall of Fame, Springfield, MA; *NCAB* (New York, 1979), pp. 298–299; Thomas W. Ricker, ed., "William G. 'Bill' Mokray," *Converse 1974 Basketball Yearbook* (1974), pp. 33ff.

Dennis S. Clark

MONCRIEF, Sidney A. "The Squid" (b. September 21, 1957, Little Rock, AR), college and professional player and coach, is the son of Orel Moncrief and Bernice (Perkins) Moncrief and ranked among the all-around great basketball players. He was overshadowed by Earvin "Magic" Johnson* and Larry Bird* with their championships. Moncrief consistently played on winning college and pro teams, but had no championships to his credit. The second youngest of seven children, he grew up in the East Little Rock, Arkansas government projects. Sidney's parents divorced when he was very young. From then on, Sidney had little contact with his father. His mother taught her children discipline. Moncrief, who does not view himself as a victim of racism, says, "I learned to take all the abuse and adversity. I like to think I'm a nice person but deep down I'm hard. If the situation requires it, I can be aggressive. I have been before." Indeed, fighting was one of Moncrief's main activities as a youth. An indifferent student, he blossomed as both student and athlete in his senior year at Little Rock (Arkansas) Hall High School and led them in basketball rebounding and scoring that year.

In 1975 Moncrief arrived at the University of Arkansas as a six-foot four-inch, 183-pound forward with great leaping ability and underdeveloped ball-handling skills. In 1975–1976, he led the nation in field goal percentage with .665, still an all-time record for a freshman. Arkansas, although traditionally a football school, emerged as a basketball power during the Moncrief years. The next year, the Razorbacks finished 26-2 under Coach Eddie Sutton*. As a junior in 1977–1978, Moncrief teamed with six-foot four-inch seniors Ron Brewer and Marvin Delph to lead Arkansas to a 32-4 record and the NCAA semifinals. In 1978–1979 without Brewer and Delph, the Razorbacks made the

Midwest Finals before losing to Larry Bird's Indiana State University 73-71. Moncrief, known for his defensive ability, guarded Bird and held him to six points in the final 10 minutes of the game.

Moncrief graduated in 1979 with a Bachelor of Science degree in physical education after gaining All-America honors and leading the Razorbacks in scoring and rebounding as a senior. He married his longtime sweetheart, Debra Bunting, just before his senior year. With his new wife, degree, and well-rounded skills as a basketball player, Moncrief joined the Milwaukee Bucks (NBA) to begin his pro career. The Bucks had made him the fifth overall pick in the NBA draft. In Moncrief's first seven years with Milwaukee, the Bucks won the Midwest Division title each year and usually lost to the Philadelphia 76ers in the playoffs. He remained the only constant during those seven years, while other important players (such as Brian Winters, Bob Lanier*, and Marques Johnson*) came and went.

After making the starting lineup in his second year with the Bucks, Moncrief compiled consistent, quietly spectacular statistics. In 1983–1984, a typical year, he led the Bucks in scoring (20.9 points per game), rebounding (6.7 rebounds per game), and assists (4.5 assists per game). Moncrief also set an NBA record for free throws made (528) on nearly 85 percent shooting while playing about the best defense at the guard position in the NBA. He was named NBA Defensive Player of the Year in 1982 and 1983. Moncrief became the team leader by always playing hard, even in practice, and helping younger players. He generally did not participate in locker room banter, but led by example. Despite chronically aching knees, he missed few NBA games. In May 1986, however, Moncrief suffered from plantar fascitis ("jogger's heel") of his left foot during the playoff round with Philadelphia. Filled with pain, he played in only three of the seven playoff games and helped the Bucks win all three games in which he played. In Game 7, the Bucks defeated the Sixers, as a hobbled Moncrief scored 23 points. The Bucks, with Moncrief still hobbling, lost to the Boston Celtics in the Eastern Conference Finals. He remained with the Bucks through 1988–1989. After briefly retiring, Moncrief finished his NBA career with the Atlanta Hawks (NBA) in 1990–1991. In 11 NBA seasons, Moncrief's career totals were 11,931 points (15.6 points average) 3,575 rebounds, and 2,793 assists in 767 regular season games. He appeared in five All-Star Games, made the All-NBA First Team in 1983, and made the All-NBA Second Team in 1982, 1984, 1985, and 1986. Moncrief was head coach of the University of Arkansas-Little Rock in 1999–2000 and assistant coach of the Dallas Mavericks (NBA) from 2000 to 2003.

Moncrief lives in Little Rock, Arkansas, with his wife, Debra, a registered nurse. They have no children. Moncrief remains a folk hero in Arkansas. He serves on two corporate boards and donates his time to various civic and charitable organizations, aimed mostly toward helping poor youngsters in his home state. Observers say that Moncrief "has done more than anyone to help race relations in Arkansas," and "he could be elected governor if he'd be willing to take the cut in salary."

BIBLIOGRAPHY: Jaime Diaz, "He's Good All Over," *SI* 63 (October 28, 1985), pp. 68–73; Jan Hubbard, ed., *The Official NBA Encyclopedia*, 3rd ed. (New York, 2000); Neil D. Isaacs, *All the Moves: A History of College Basketball* (New York, 1975); Larry Keith, "Now the Razors Have the Edge," *SI* 48 (February 13, 1978), pp. 20–21; Jack McCallum, "Getting a Monkey Off Their Bucks," *SI* 64 (May 19, 1986), pp. 42–45; Milwaukee Bucks Public Relations Office, Milwaukee, WI, telephone interview with Mark Altschuler, November 7, 1986; Sidney Moncrief to Mark Altschuler, November 30, 1986; Bruce Newman, "The Green Monsters," *SI* 56 (April 19, 1982), pp. 33–34; Ken Shouler et al., *Total Basketball* (Wilmington, DE, 2003); *TSN Official NBA Register, 2004–2005* (St. Louis, MO, 2004); University of Arkansas Sports Information Office, Fayetteville, AR, telephone interview with Mark Altschuler, November 6, 1986; *WWA*, 44th ed. (1986–1987), p. 1969.

Mark Altschuler

MONROE, Vernon Earl "The Pearl" (b. November 21, 1944, Philadelphia, PA), college and professional player, is the only son of Vernon Monroe and Rose Monroe and attended John Bartram High School in South Philadelphia. At six feet two inches, he played center on the varsity basketball team and averaged 21.7 points his senior year. After graduation, Monroe worked in a factory for one year and attended Winston-Salem (North Carolina) College, majoring in elementary education. He played guard four years for the Winston-Salem Rams, averaging seven points his freshman year, 23 points his sophomore year, 30 points his junior year, and 44.5 points his senior year. During his spectacular 1966–1967 senior year, Monroe set the small-college record for total points in one season (1,329), was named NCAA College Division Player of the Year, and led the Rams to the NCAA College Division championship.

The Baltimore Bullets (NBA) selected Monroe during the first round of the 1967 NBA college draft to enliven a virtually dormant offense. He did not let them down, being named NBA Rookie of the Year in 1967–1968 and to the All-NBA First Team in 1969. Backed up by Wes Unseld* and Gus Johnson*, Monroe led a razzle-dazzle Baltimore offense that featured one of the most spectacular fast breaks in the NBA and propelled "The Pearl" into basketball superstardom. He averaged 23.7 points with the Bullets and led them into the playoffs every one of his four years there. Monroe claimed to be bored in Baltimore and asked to be traded in 1971. In November 1971, he was traded to the New York Knickerbockers (NBA) for Mike Riordan, Dave Stallworth, and some cash. New York already possessed much offensive talent, including Willis Reed*, Walt Frazier*, Bill Bradley*, Dave DeBusschere*, and Jerry Lucas*, and concentrated on defense, working for the open shot, and teamwork. Monroe encountered some initial difficulty adapting to this new environment and spent much of his first season with the Knicks on the bench. By the end of the 1971–1972 season, however, he successfully had made the transition. Although averaging only 11.9 points, he had become a regular and important part of New York's team-oriented offense.

Monroe's career with the Knicks throughout the rest of the 1970s continued to be productive. His annual points average was never spectacular (15.5 points in 1972–1973, 14.0 points in 1973–1974, 20.9 points in 1974–1975, 20.7 points in 1975–1976, 19.9 points in 1976–1977, 17.8 points in 1977–1978, 12.3 points in 1978–1979, and 7.4 points in 1979–1980 for a 13.5 points average with New York), but his flamboyant style of play and fierce intensity ignited both his teammates and New York fans for nearly a decade. The Knicks elected him captain in 1976 in recognition of these talents. Monroe also played in four All-Star Games, scoring 40 total points, and in 82 playoff games, averaging 17.9 points. He helped the Knicks win the 1973 NBA championship.

Monroe retired after the 1979–1980 season, after increased knee problems and reduced playing time. He had played 926 career games and made 6,906 field goals and 3,642 free throws for 17,454 total points and an 18.8 points-average. Subsequently he managed his New York City entertainment enterprises, Tiffany Entertainment Corporation, and Pretty Pearl Records. Outside of an occasional old-timers basketball game for the Washington Wizards or the New York Knicks, Monroe associates little with pro basketball. Yet the memory of the "Pearl" twisting, spinning, and faking his way through taller, stronger defenders toward the basket will live on for all those who appreciate real basketball talent. He was selected to the NAIA Basketball Hall of Fame in 1975 and the Naismith Memorial Basketball Hall of Fame in 1990. In 1996, he was named one of the 50 Greatest Players in NBA History.

BIBLIOGRAPHY: Frank Deford, "Doctor Works His Magic," *SI* 29 (November 4, 1968), pp. 30–33; Donald Gaines, *Street Players* (New York, 2000); Merv Harris, *On the Court with Superstars of the NBA* (New York, 1973); Robert Blake Jackson, *Earl the Pearl: The Story of Earl Monroe* (New York, 1974); George Kalinsky, *The New York Knicks: The Official 50th Anniversary Celebration* (New York, 1996); Roland Lazenby, *The NBA Finals* (Indianapolis, IN, 1996); Earl Monroe file, Naismith Memorial Basketball Hall of Fame, Springfield, MA; *NYT*, January 20, 1979; *NYT*, April 30, 1980; *NYT*, April 23, 1983; Ken Shouler et al., *Total Basketball* (Wilmington, DE, 2003); *TSN Official NBA Register, 2004–2005* (St. Louis, MO, 2004).

Christopher E. Guthrie

MONTGOMERY, Michael (b. February 27, 1947, Long Beach, CA), college and professional coach, received his Bachelor of Arts degree in physical education from California State

University Long Beach in 1969 and earned a Master of Arts degree in physical education from Colorado. State University in 1976. Montgomery served as an assistant basketball coach at the U.S. Coast Guard Academy (*Connecticut*), Colorado State University, The Citadel (South Carolina), the University of Florida, and the University of Montana before becoming head basketball coach at the University of Montana in 1978. In eight seasons at Montana, Montgomery won 154 contests and lost 77. In his last four years, his teams won at least 21 games each campaign. His .667 winning percentage at Montana ranks fifth best in BSkC history. Four of his players were drafted by the NBA.

In 1986, Montgomery was named head coach of the Stanford University basketball team. The Cardinal had not appeared in a NCAA tournament since 1942. He piloted the Cardinal to a 21-12 record and NIT berth in 1987–1988, Stanford's first postseason appearance in 46 seasons. Stanford also played in the NIT in 1990, 1991, and 1994. Montgomery guided his teams to 12 NCAA postseason tournaments in 1988–1989, 1991–1992, and every season from 1994–1995 to 2003–2004. He directed the Cardinal to the NCAA Final Four in 1997–1998. Montgomery led Stanford to its first ever number one national ranking in 1999–2000, earning him Naismith College Basketball Coach of the Year and *BT* 2000 Coach of the Year honors. In 2000–2001, he established a Stanford school record with 31 victories. Montgomery's 2003–2004 squad won 30 contests, its fourth PTC championship in six years, and a number-one national ranking. He in 2004 won the Wooden "Legends of Coaching" Lifetime Achievement Award and *BT* Coach of the Year Award.

In May 2004, the Golden State Warriors (NBA) named Montgomery head coach. Golden State finished 34-48 in Montgomery's initial season. His college coaching career includes a 393-168 record at Stanford and an overall 547-244 record through the 2003–2004 campaign. Seven of Montgomery's Stanford players have performed in the NBA. Montgomery and his wife, Sarah, have two children and reside in Menlo Park, California.

BIBLIOGRAPHY: Tim Korte, "Stanford Comes Up Short Against Alabama in NCAA Tournament," AP (March 20, 2004), pp. 1–3; SportsLine.com wire reports, "Montgomery Agrees to Extension through the 2007–2008 season," AP (July 24, 2003), p. 1; Stanford Cardinal Official Athetic Website, "Mike Montgomery, Josh Childress Honored by *Basketball Times*," *College Sports Online, Inc.* (March 24, 2004), pp. 1–2; Stanford University, "Mike Montgomery; Profile," *Student Advantage* (February 13, 2004), pp. 1–5.

Frank J. Olmsted

MOORE, Billie (b. May 5, 1943, Humansville, MO), college player, coach, and executive, is one of three children of Billie Moore, educator and coach, and Glestner (Robinson) Moore, a homemaker, and also had two step siblings from her widowed father's first marriage.

When Moore was age three, the family moved to the small farming community of Westmoreland, Kansas. Her father taught and served as principal in the local schools there. Throughout her grade school days, Moore proved an accomplished basketball and baseball player on local teams coached by her father. Due to its small size, the Westmoreland High School did not sponsor any athletic teams. An official from Ohse Meats Company recruited Moore to play softball and basketball during her sophomore year in high school. The company also offered her father a position as personnel director. He resigned his principalship in Westmoreland and moved the family to Topeka, Kansas, where he continued to coach his daughter.

Following high school graduation in 1961, Moore attended Washburn University in Topeka. After graduating with a Bachelor's degree in physical education in 1966, she taught two years at Boswell Junior High School and coached all the school's teams. Moore was invited to participate at the National Institute of Basketball and met Charlotte West there. West invited Moore to become her assistant basketball coach at Southern Illinois University and pursue a Master's degree, which she earned in 1968.

Moore also began to play softball for the Raybestos Brakettes and performed alongside Lou Albrecht, women's basketball coach at California State University at Fullerton. When Albrecht left California State for a business opportunity, she recommended that the school interview Moore. Moore was hired as the women's basketball coach and athletic director. In eight seasons at California Fullerton, Moore compiled 140 wins with just 15 defeats and attained a national championship in 1970. She was appointed to coach the first U.S. Olympic women's basketball team, which earned a silver medal at the 1976 games in Montreal, Canada.

In 1977, Moore was lured to UCLA as women's head basketball coach. During her initial season, UCLA finished 27-3 and won a national AIAW championship. She continued to coach at UCLA until retirement in 1993. During her tenure, Moore's UCLA teams fared 296-181 with nine PAC-10 Conference championships and eight finishes among the nation's top ten. She also influenced women's basketball through her tutelage of Ann Meyers Drysdale*, Denise Curry*, Pat Summitt*, and other players.

Moore, who devotes considerable time to golf, was selected to the Naismith Memorial Basketball Hall of Fame in 2000. She received the Naismith's Women's Outstanding Contribution to Basketball Award in 2003.

BIBLIOGRAPHY: Mike Douchant, *Encyclopedia of College Basketball* (Detroit, MI, 1995); Billie Moore file, Naismith Memorial Basketball Hall of Fame, Springfield, MA; Billie Moore, *Basketball Theory and Practice* (New York, 1980); Nena Rey Hawkes and John F. Seggar, *Celebrating Women Coaches: A Biographical Dictionary* (Westport, CT, 2000); Rosemarie Skaine, *Women College Basketball Coaches* (Jefferson, NC, 2001).

Ron Briley

MORGAN, Ralph (b. March 9, 1884, Philadelphia, PA; d. January 5, 1965, Wyncote, PA), college innovator, played a leading role in early-twentieth-century basketball rules and conference formation. For his lifetime contributions to the sport, he was elected to the Naismith Memorial Hall of Fame as a charter member in 1959 and to the HAF Hall of Fame in 1943. The son of George Morgan and Mary Frances Reed (Churchman) Morgan, he graduated from Germantown Friends School at Philadelphia, Pennsylvania in 1902 and the University of Pennsylvania in 1906. Morgan played basketball and football at Friends School and became basketball student manager as a Pennsylvania freshman. He founded the CBRC in 1905 and NBRC later remaining a member for 26 years. In 1905 the CBRC drafted rules more adaptable to the college game than the AAU rules then in use.

The University of Pennsylvania joined the InL in 1904, but the InL foundered after the 1908 season. After a two-year lapse, Morgan called the teams together and formed the EIBL (later IvL) in 1910. He served as the EIBL secretary-treasurer from 1911 to 1920 and as statistician-recorder from 1911 to 1960. The EIBL started in 1911 with Columbia (New York), Cornell (New York), Pennsylvania, Princeton (New Jersey), and Yale universities (Connecticut) and added Dartmouth College (New Hampshire) the next season and Harvard University (Massachusetts) later. Morgan also was appointed to the central committee on officials. He was named an honorary member of the NBCUS, which included the NCAA, NFSHSAA, and YMCA, as one of few accorded this honor. Morgan also wrote the EIBL season previews for the *NCAA Annual Basketball Guides* from 1905 until his death.

After serving as a corporate officer and executive, Morgan joined the Chain Store Fund, a New York investment trust, in 1929. He in 1933 became president of his own firm of investment counselors—Morgan, Rogers, and Roberts, Incorporated—with offices on Wall Street in New York City. On December 11, 1911, he married Josephine Dando Sill. They had two children, Maryallis (Mrs. Henry S. Hamilton) and James. After his first wife died in 1940, he married Mrs. Eleanor J. Mathieu on February 24, 1951. Morgan served as president of the University of Pennsylvania Alumni Society from 1938 until 1941, was a University trustee, and resided in Wyncote, Pennsylvania, outside Philadelphia.

BIBLIOGRAPHY: Gene Brown, ed., *NYT Encyclopedia of Sports: Basketball*, vol. 3 (New York, 1979); Mike Douchant, *Encyclopedia of College Basketball* (Detroit, MI, 1995); Zander Hollander, ed., *The NBA's Official Encyclopedia of Pro Basketball* (New York, 1981); John McCallum, *College Bas-*

ketball, U.S.A. Since 1892 (Briarcliff Manor, NY, 1978); Ralph Morgan file, Naismith Memorial Basketball Hall of Fame, Springfield, MA; *NCAA Official Basketball Guide, 1947* (New York, 1947); *Who Was Who in America*, vol. 4 (1961–1968), p. 678.

Robert B. Van Atta

MORGENWECK, Frank "Pop" (b. July 15, 1875, Egg Harbor, NJ; d. December 8, 1941, place unknown), professional owner, manager, and promoter, operated clubs in more than 14 Eastern and Midwestern U.S. cities from 1901 to 1932. He was named to the Naismith Memorial Basketball Hall of Fame as a contributor in 1962, having guided Kingston, New York (1912, 1925), Paterson, New Jersey (1917), and the Rochester, New York Centrals (1930) to pro basketball league championships, and Kingston (1916), Paterson (1920), Fort Wayne, Indiana (1928), and the Chicago Bruins (1931) to second place finishes. A pro basketball pioneer, Morgenweck discovered or developed future pro stars George Henschel, Carl Husta, Mickey Husta, Lloyd Kinzig, Jimmy Clinton, and Maurice Tome.

After helping his brother, William, develop a franchise in the NPBL, Morgenweck in 1901 bought the Penn Bicycle Club (NPBL) and managed the organization for three years. Between 1904 and 1910, he transferred his club to Camden, New Jersey, Springfield, Massachusetts, and South Framingham, Massachusetts. In 1911 Morgenweck moved the team to Kingston, which finished third in the HRL. Kingston annexed the HRL title in 1912 before the HRL disbanded. Morgenweck in 1914 owned franchises in Poughkeepsie, New York and Kingston in the fledgling NYSL and discovered future Original Celtic Johnny Beckman*. He had a disagreement over finances in Kingston and transferred the club to Cohoes, New York for one year, guiding the team to a fourth-place finish. Kingston, a member of the ISL in 1916, won the first-half season title under Morgenweck, but lost to Paterson in the season-ending playoff.

Maintaining ISL and franchise solvency during the development era of pro basketball was difficult at best and resembled the growing pains experienced in pro football. Armories were no longer available during World War I and travel restrictions and expenses mounted, forcing some teams to relocate. Morgenweck moved his team in 1917 to Paterson, where it defeated the Newark (New Jersey) Turners in a playoff for the ISL title. Over the next eight years, he developed future pro greats Benny Borgmann*, George Artus, Rusty Saunders, and Ed "Stretch" Miller. Back in Kingston in 1925, his squad captured the MeL championship by defeating the Original Celtics in a title playoff series. The powerful ABL in 1927 competed against the MeL for top players by paying higher salaries, causing the latter league to fold. Morgenweck declined pro football magnate George Preston Marshall's offer of $5,000 to move his team to Washington, D.C. He instead shifted the club to Fort Wayne, where in 1928 his netters won the second-half season ABL title. Fort Wayne dropped the playoff series to the Original Celtics four games to one. Morgenweck's Rochester Centrals produced their first championship in 29 years by capturing the 1930 ABL title with star six-foot nine-inch center William "Tiny" Hearn from Georgia Tech University. The Centrals lost to the Cleveland Rosenblums, however, in a postseason contest to decide the national pro basketball champion. Legendary pro football owner-coach George Halas hired Morgenweck the next year to coach the Chicago Bruins basketball team that finished a close second to Fort Wayne for the ABL championship. Morgenweck, who married Ida Brill and had two children, was elected president of the prestigious Old Timers pro basketball organization. This group included many star players and coaches from past decades.

BIBLIOGRAPHY: William G. Mokray, ed., *Ronald Encyclopedia of Basketball* (New York, 1963); Frank Morgenweck file, Naismith Memorial Basketball Hall of Fame, Springfield, MA; Robert W. Peterson, *Cages to Jump Shots: Pro Basketball's Early Years* (New York, 1990); Ken Shouler et al., *Total Basketball* (Wilmington, DE, 2003).

James D. Whalen and Wayne Patterson

MOTTA, John Richard "Dick" (b. September 3, 1931, Union, UT), college and professional coach, is the son of Ambrose Motta and Zelda Motta and grew up on his Italian immigrant father's 15-acre truck farm. Motta attended Jordan

(Utah) High School (1946–1949), where he was cut from the basketball team, and Utah State University (1949–1953). On graduation, he taught in a junior high school. He on June 4, 1954 married Janice Fraser, who accompanied him when he served two years in the U.S. Air Force. The Mottas have three children. Motta coached from 1956 to 1959 at the high school in Grace, Utah, where he won the state basketball championship. He in 1960 was hired as basketball coach at Weber State JC (Utah), which expanded two years later to a four-year school. His 156-43 record at Weber State included three BSkC championships.

In 1968, the five-foot ten-inch, 170-pound Motta began coaching the Chicago Bulls (NBA). Bringing his own style of discipline to the Bulls' practices, he used a rugged defense and patterned offense to qualify Chicago for the playoffs during six of his eight seasons from 1968–1969 to 1975–1976 there. In 1971, Motta was voted Coach of the Year after leading Chicago to a 51-31 record and a second-place finish in the Midwest Division. Chicago in 1975 won the Midwest Division, but lost the Western championship to the Golden State Warriors, the eventual playoff winner.

Several disputes between Motta and the Chicago players and management led him to become coach of the Washington Bullets (NBA) in 1976. Although possessing several top-flight players such as Elvin Hayes*, Wes Unseld*, and Phil Chenier, the Bullets continually had lacked success in the playoffs. Motta was asked to bring discipline to a franchise. In his second year with the team, the Bullets in 1977–1978 finished 44-38 for second place in the Central Division. Washington prevailed in the playoffs, eliminating the Central Division champion San Antonio Spurs and defeating the Philadelphia 76ers in the Eastern Conference final series. Motta, when asked about his team's chances, added a phrase to sports vocabulary by replying that the "opera is not over until the fat lady sings." The fat lady finally sang in the seventh and final playoff game on Wednesday, June 7, when Motta's Bullets defeated the Seattle SuperSonics 105-99 on the latter's home floor to win the NBA championship. During the next season, the Bullets finished with the best record in the NBA and again advanced to the championship series against Seattle. Seattle, however, won four of the five games this time.

In 1980, Motta was hired to organize the new Dallas Mavericks NBA team. Beginning with only 15 wins in the first season, the team improved each year and finished second in the Midwest Division in 1983–1984 and third in 1984–1985 and 1985–1986. Dallas won the Midwest Division with Motta's career best 55-27 mark, after which John MacLeod* replaced him as head coach. Motta broadcast for the Detroit Pistons (NBA) from 1988 through January 1990 and worked as a consultant for the Mavericks in 1990. He coached the Sacramento Kings (NBA) to losing records from January 1990 to December 1991 and the Dallas Mavericks to fifth place finishes from 1994 to 1996. Motta joined the Denver Nuggets (NBA) as assistant coach in July 1996. After taking over as head coach that November, he guided the struggling club to a 17-52 record. As of 2005, the disciplined, hard-nosed, five-foot ten-inch Motta, ranked ninth in career NBA wins (991) and had 1,087 career NBA losses for a .477 winning percentage.

BIBLIOGRAPHY: Frank Deford, "Beware, Little Big Man Is Here," Chicago *Tribune*, October 8, 1975; Brian Doyle, "Forget the Fat Lady: For the NBA Champ Bullets, the Game Is Over When Coach Dick Motta Smiles," *People Weekly* 11 (April 16, 1979), pp. 109–110; Jan Hubbard, ed., *The Official NBA Encyclopedia*, 3rd ed. (New York, 2000); Curry Kirkpatrick, "Choice Seats at the Bull Ring," *SI* 44 (February 2, 1976), pp. 21–22, 27; "He Rocks the Boat with the Old College Try," *SI* 29 (November 11, 1968), pp. 54–55; Bob Logan, *The Bulls and Chicago: A Stormy Affair* (Chicago, IL, 1975); John Papanek, "So What's the Motta" *SI* 48 (May 29, 1978), pp. 100, 102; *TSN Official NBA Register, 2004–2005* (St. Louis, MO, 2004); *Washington* (D.C.) *Post*, June 8, 1978; *Washington Post*, June 9, 1978.

Jon S. Moran

MOUNT, Richard C. Rick "The Rocket" (b. January 5, 1947, Lebanon, IN), college and professional player, is the son of Pete Mount and was perhaps the best pure shooter in the game's history, enjoying one of its most spectacular if short-lived and ill-fated careers. At Lebanon High School on the outskirts of Indianapolis, Indiana, in the mid-1960s, Mount rewrote most state and national prep scoring standards in averaging 27.3 points and making 2,595 points over a 94-game career. He was honored as Indiana State Mr. Basketball at the conclusion of his 1966 senior season. But perhaps the most noteworthy distinction of his phenomenal prep school career occurred when Mount became the first high schooler ever featured on a cover of *SI*. His father starred at the same Lebanon High School during their 1943 state runner-up season. The Mount tradition was carried on at Lebanon High in the mid-1980s by his son, Rick Jr., a standout player when only a freshman. The senior Mount became the most sensational roundball talent ever to emerge from the heartlands of Indiana before Larry Bird*. His talents triggered a huge recruiting war, as thousands of local Lebanon boosters pressured the youngster to play at Purdue University rather than the University of Kentucky, Duke University (North Carolina), or University of Miami (Florida). He ultimately joined the Purdue Boilermakers and promptly became the most glamorous offensive player in BTC history.

In Mount's first varsity college game, the Purdue University Boilermakers dedicated a new 14,000-seat Mackey Arena home floor against Lew Alcindor's* UCLA Bruins. Mount scored 28 points in a heart-stopping loss to the defending national champions. During his remaining three varsity seasons, the six-foot four-inch jump-shooting guard, known as "The Rocket," established 10 BTC scoring marks and paced the BTC in scoring each season. Mount's finest year came in 1969, when the junior sharpshooter led Purdue to a BTC title and NCAA championship game against Alcindor's UCLA. His career 2,323 total points ranked second all-time in the BTC and seventh all-time nationally. Mount averaged 39.4 points in BTC games in 1970 for a BTC record and 35.4 points for the entire season, very high in NCAA history. He holds the BTC career scoring mark at 34.8 points per game, the single-game mark of 61 points against the University of Iowa in February 1970, and made consensus All-America his final two seasons at Purdue.

Mount's pro fortunes proved disappointing. Although playing for five seasons in the ABA (he rejected NBA offers in 1970 to remain close to home with the Indiana Pacers), he became a journeyman ABA pro player and marginal shooting guard. Mount spent two years with the Pacers (ABA), two with the Kentucky Colonels (ABA), and one final season with the Memphis Pros and Utah Stars (ABA), averaging only 11.2 points over his five-year tenure. He enjoyed his career-best 14.9 points average with Kentucky in 1973. Mount never seemed happy with the pro lifestyle or the grind of the pro schedule, as basketball was no longer fun for the rural boy from Lebanon. He later complained that "they tried to make a ball-handling guard out of me when I went to the pros." The magic was gone, causing one of the greatest shooters of all-time to fade as rapidly as he had appeared. Ill fortune continued to plague Mount after his playing days. A business venture in hometown Lebanon ended in bankruptcy. A possible prep school coaching position was lost through failure to complete his undergraduate degree. Controversy surrounded the high school "redshirting" of his athletically promising but less phenomenally talented son. But for a few short years, Rick Mount's career had shone as brightly as any ever spawned by the basketball-rich tradition of the Indiana heartlands.

BIBLIOGRAPHY: Peter C. Bjarkman, *Big Ten Basketball* (Indianapolis, IN, 1994); Todd Gould, *Pioneers of the Hardwood* (Bloomington, IN, 1998); Jan Hubbard, ed., *The Official NBA Encyclopedia*, 3rd ed. (New York, 2000); Neil D. Isaacs, *All the Moves: A History of College Basketball* (Philadelphia, PA, 1975); *Lafayette Journal and Courier* Staff, ed., *Most Memorable Moments in Purdue Basketball History* (Champaign, IL, 1998); Ronald L. Mendell, *Who's Who in Basketball* (New Rochelle, NY, 1973); Terry Pluto, *Loose Balls* (New York, 1990); Bob Williams, *Hoosier Hysteria: Indiana High School Basketball* (South Bend, IN, 1982).

Peter C. Bjarkman

MOURNING, Alonzo Harding, Jr. "Zo" (b. February 8, 1970, Chesapeake, VA), college and professional player, is the son of Alonzo Mourning Sr., a machinist in the Portsmouth, Virginia shipyards, and Julia Mourning, and grew up in unsettled circumstances. His parents separated in 1980 and eventually divorced in 1983. Mourning lived in a foster home run by the Threet family, who cared for 49 children.

At Indian River High School, the six-foot three-inch Mourning proved a dominating basketball presence. In 1987, his undefeated team won the Virginia State Class AAA Championship. A year later, Mourning was rated the nation's premier high school basketball player. Gatorade and *USA Today* categorized him as National High School Player of the Year.

As a Georgetown University (Washington, D.C., BEaC) freshman in 1988–1989, Mourning averaged 13.2 points, 7.3 rebounds, and 4.9 blocks. The 1989–1990 and 1990–1991 seasons were less successful, but he earned recognition as BEaC Co-Defensive Player of the Year and First Team All-BEaC in 1990.

In his banner 1991–1992 senior year, everything came together for Mourning. He averaged 21.7 points, 10.7 rebounds, and 5 blocks. By the season's end, he had amassed 2,000 career points, the MVP Award of the BEaC Tournament, and a Bachelor's degree in sociology.

From 1992–1993 through 1994–1995, Mourning starred with the Charlotte Hornets, an NBA expansion team. His major accomplishments included transforming the Hornets into a playoff contender, playing for the successful U.S. squad at the 1994 World Championships, and being selected as an NBA All-Star team member in 1995.

From 1995 to 2003, Mourning performed for the Miami Heat (NBA). Although his 1997–1998 season was plagued with injuries, he returned to top form by decade's end. In the 1999–2000 season, Mourning averaged 21.7 points, 9.5 rebounds and 3.7 blocks. The athletic high point of his life may have been a gold medal with the U.S. team at the 2000 Olympics in Sydney, Australia.

From 1995 to 2003, Mourning battled with the life threatening kidney disease known as focal glomerulosclerosis. This illness meant that a kidney transplant hung over him. Nevertheless, Mourning established an enviable reputation as an industrious player with a feisty persona. He was nominated to the Eastern Conference team for the 2001 NBA All-Star Game and has appeared in 55-career NBA playoff games, averaging 19.9 points and 9.5 rebounds. Mourning sat out the 2002–2003 season because of his health problems, the final year of a seven-year, $105 million deal with the Heat. He signed as a free agent with the New Jersey Nets (NBA) in July 2003, but the seven-time All-Star only played in 12 games in 2003–2004 because his kidney disease had worsened and required a transplant. In December 2004, the Toronto Raptors (NBA) acquired Mourning and four other players for Vince Carter*. Mourning never reported to Toronto and rejoined the Miami Heat in March 2005 as a backup to Shaquille O'Neal*. During his NBA career, he has tallied 12,992 points (19.4 average) and made 6,335 rebounds (9.4 average) in 671 regular-season games. He has averaged 16.9 points, 8.5 rebounds, and 2.7 blocked shots in 70 playoff games.

Mourning married Tracy Wilson on August 30, 1997 in the Caribbean; they have two children. He maintains broad interests in philanthropy and social betterment. He represents the NBA as their mouthpiece on prevention of child abuse and promoted a charity occasion called "Zo's Summer Grove," which supports volunteer groups in South Florida. In 2001, Mourning was honored by *USA Weekend Magazine* with their annual Most Caring Athlete Award. He received the J. Walter Kennedy Citizenship Award in 2002.

BIBLIOGRAPHY: Di Su, "Alonzo Mourning," *Scribner's Encyclopedia of American Lives*, vol. 2 (New York, 2002), pp. 163–165; Roscoe Nance, "Illness Ends Mourning's Career," *USA Today*, November 25, 2003, p.lc; Leonard Shapiro, *Big Man on Campus: John Thompson and the Georgetown Hoyas* (1991); *TSN Official NBA Register, 2004–2005* (St. Louis, MO, 2004); *Who's Who Among African Americans* (New York, 1997); Ken Shouler et al., *Total Basketball* (Wilmington, DE, 2003); http://www.basketball.com/biosmen/alonzomourning.bio.html.

Scott A.G.M. Crawford

MULLIN, Christopher Paul "Chris" (b. July 30, 1963, New York, NY), college and professional player and executive, is the son of Rod Mullin and Eileen Mullin. Mullin transferred at age 17 from Power Memorial Academy in Manhattan to Xaverian High School in Brooklyn, New York, where he led his team to the state basketball title. The six-foot seven-inch, 220-pounder played basketball from 1981–1982 through 1984–1985 at St. John's University (BEaC), leading the Redmen to the NCAA Final Four in 1985 and pacing tourney scorers. His 2,440 career points set all-time BEaC and St.

John's scoring marks. Mullin led the Redmen in career games (125), steals (211), and free throw percentage (.848). He attained double figures in scoring in his final 100 games and participated on the gold medalist U.S. basketball team at the 1984 Los Angeles and 1992 Barcelona, Spain Summer Olympic Games. A two-time All-America, Mullin in 1985 won the John Wooden Award as the nation's top college player.

The Golden State Warriors chose Mullin in the first round of the 1985 NBA draft. He made 896 free throws in 1985–1986, the second-best rookie mark in NBA history. During the 1988–1989 season, Mullin became one of the sport's best all-around players, making the All-NBA Second Team and averaging 26.5 points, 5.9 rebounds, and 5.1 assists. He joined Wilt Chamberlain* and Rick Barry* as the only Warriors to tally 2,000 points, 400 rebounds, and 400 assists in a season, and scored a career-high 47 points on April 13, 1989 in an overtime game against the Los Angeles Clippers. He made the All-NBA Third Team in 1989–1990, averaging 25.1 points and 5.9 rebounds. In 1990–1991, Mullin paced the Warriors in scoring, averaged 25.7 points. He played 16 seasons, scoring 17,911 points in 986 regular-season contests and averaging 18.2 points and made the All-NBA Second Team. His best season came in 1991–1992, when he led the NBA in minutes played (3,346), averaged 25.6 points, and made the All-NBA First Team. Mullin remained with Golden State until traded to the Indiana Pacers (NBA) in August 1997. He spent the 1997–1998 through 1999–2000 seasons with Indiana and rejoined the Golden State Warriors for his final season in 2000–2001. Mullin remains the Warriors career leader in steals with 1,376, and, along with Chamberlain, was the only Warrior to average 25 points five straight seasons. Mullin also tallied 982 points in 71 playoff games. His best overall playoff performance came in 1989, when he averaged 29.4 points in eight appearances. He scored 41 points in Game two of the Western Conference semifinals, but the Los Angeles Lakers eliminated the Warriors. Mullin missed a month of the 1987–1988 season undergoing alcohol rehabilitation and later suffered hand, finger, and leg injuries. Mullin, a bachelor, resides in Alameda, California, and played in the NBA All-Star Games from 1989 through 1992. He has served as a special assistant for the Warriors since 2002.

BIBLIOGRAPHY: Peter C. Bjarkman, *The Biographical History of Basketball* (Chicago, IL, 2000); Mike Douchant, *Encyclopedia of College Basketball* (Detroit, MI, 1995); *Golden State Warriors Media Guide, 2000–2001* (San Francisco, CA, 2000); Curry Kirkpatrick, "Just a Guy from Da Naybuhhood," *SI* 24 (November 26, 1984), pp. 42–44, 49–50, 52, 57; *NCAA Men's Basketball Record, 2003* (Indianapolis, IN, 2004); *Redmen Basketball Guide, 1984–1985* (Brooklyn, NY, 1984); Ken Shouler et al., *Total Basketball* (Wilmington, DE, 2003); *TSN Official NBA Register, 2004–2005* (St. Louis, MO, 2004); *USA Today*, April 23, 1991.

John L. Evers

MULLINS, Jeffrey Vincent "Jeff" (b. March 18, 1942, Astoria, NY), college and professional player and college coach, is the son of Vincent Mullins and Mary (Eustace) Mullins. Mullins grew up in Staatsburg, New York and attended Lafayette High School in Lexington, Kentucky, after his father, who worked for IBM, was transferred to that city in 1956.

Mullins attended Duke University (North Carolina) from 1960 to 1964. The smooth, six-foot four-inch, 190-pound forward was named First-Team All-ACC in basketball in 1962, 1963, and 1964 and teamed with Art Heyman* to lead Duke to the 1963 NCAA Final Four. The following year he led Duke to the NCAA title game against UCLA, was named ACC Player of the Year in 1964, and was selected Second-Team All-America by AP and UPI All-America. He averaged 21.9 points and 9.0 rebounds at Duke. Mullins played for the 1964 United States Olympic basketball team, which captured the gold medal. He graduated from Duke with Bachelor's degree in business administration.

The Atlanta Hawks (NBA) made Mullins the fifth pick of the 1964 draft. Mullins played sparingly for the Hawks for two seasons before being selected by the Chicago Bulls (NBA) in the 1966 expansion draft. Chicago quickly traded him to the San Francisco Warriors (NBA). Mullins became a mainstay in San Francisco, averaging over 20 points on four occasions and playing in the 1969, 1970, and 1971

NBA All-Star Games. He also earned a Master's degree in business administration from Golden Gate University.

Mullins retired following an injury-plagued 1976 season, having scored 13,017 points and averaged 16.2 points in 802 NBA games. He was assistant athletic director at Duke in 1976–1977, a television commentator, and a businessman. Mullins served as head basketball coach at UNC-Charlotte from 1985 to 1996, compiling a 182-142 record and coaching that team to three NCAA tournament appearances. He married Candy Johnson in 1966 and has two daughters, Kelly and Kristine.

BIBLIOGRAPHY: Peter C. Bjarkman, *ACC: Atlantic Coast Conference Basketball* (Indianapolis, IN, 1996); Bill Brill, *Duke Basketball: An Illustrated History* (Dallas, TX, 1986); Jan Hubbard, ed., *The Official NBA Encyclopedia*, 3rd ed. (New York, 2000); Ron Morris, *ACC Basketball: An Illustrated History* (Chapel Hill, NC, 1988).

Jim L. Sumner

MURPHY, Calvin Jerome (b. May 9, 1948, Norwalk, CT), college and professional player, executive, and sportcaster, gained fame as a young baton twirler and then as a basketball player at Norwalk (Connecticut) High School. He was named a High School Basketball All-America, although standing only five feet nine inches, and accepted a basketball scholarship to Niagara (New York) University. In his three varsity basketball seasons at Niagara, Murphy was selected All-America each year. After Niagara compiled mediocre records during his first two years, he led the Eagles to a 22-7 record in 1969–1970. The Eagles advanced to the NCAA Eastern semifinals before losing to North Carolina State University. He completed his college career with 2,548 points in 77 games and a 33.1 career point average, ranking fourth on the all-time list behind Pete Maravich*, Austin Carr*, and Oscar Robertson*.

Although some scouts had misgivings about his stature, the 165-pound Murphy was drafted by the San Diego Rockets (NBA) in the second round. He averaged 15.8 points his first season in 1970–1971 and was named to the NBA All-Rookie team. Murphy spent his entire pro career with the Rockets in San Diego and Houston and appeared in the 1979 All-Star Game. On his retirement in 1983, he ranked nineteenth on the all-time NBA scoring list with 1,165 steals in 13 seasons. Murphy especially was renowned for his free throw shooting ability. He holds the NBA record for highest free throw percentage in a season (.958) and held the mark for making 78 straight free throws in 1980–1981. His lifetime free throw percentage of .892 (3,445 of 3,864) ranks fourth in NBA history behind Mark Price*, Rick Barry* and Steve Nash. He led the NBA in free throw percentage in 1980–1981 (.958) and 1982–1983 (.920). Murphy retired from the Rockets as the team's all-time leader in points scored (17,949), assists (4,402), steals (1,165), games played (1,002), and minutes played (30,607). He scored nearly 18 points per game and enjoyed his best season in 1977–1978, when he averaged 25.6 points. Murphy universally was regarded as one of the best small guards ever to play basketball. He has 14 children and worked until 2004 as community services advisor for the Houston Rockets, doubling as a television analyst. The Naismith Memorial Basketball Hall of Fame inducted him in 1993. He also belongs to the City of Houston Hall of Fame and the Connecticut High School Coaches Association Hall of Fame. In December 2004, he was acquitted of charges he sexually abused five of his 10 daughters more than a decade ago.

BIBLIOGRAPHY: Fiftieth Anniversary Program, All-College Tournament, Oklahoma City, OK, 1985; Mickey Herskiwitz, "'Pocket Rocket' Still Flying High," *Houston* (Texas) *Post*, February 20, 1986; Jan Hubbard, ed., *The Official NBA Encyclopedia*, 3rd ed. (New York, 2000); Calvin Murphy file, Naismith Memorial Basketball Hall of Fame, Springfield, MA; "Pro Basketball's Tiny Giant," *Ebony* 26 (February 1971), pp. 38–42; Ken Shouler et al., *Total Basketball* (Wilmington, DE, 2003); *TSN Official NBA Guide, 2002–2003* (St. Louis, MO 2002); *TSN Official NBA Register, 2004–2005* (St. Louis, MO 2004).

Fred M. Shelley

MURPHY, Charles "Stretch" (b. April 10, 1907, Marion, IN; d. August 24, 1992, Tampa, FL), college player, was one of the first true physical giants and dominant offensive forces of the college roundball game. Murphy stood an exceptional six feet six inches and rated among the best defensive ballplayers of the two decades between America's world wars. He ranked among WC leading scorers during the Ward "Piggy" Lambert* and Johnny Wooden* "Golden Era" of Purdue University (Indiana) basketball. Murphy established one of the earliest legends in Indiana high school basketball annals. He teamed with Bob Chapman to lead his Marion High School team to a 1926 Indiana State Championship, achieved with a 30-23 victory in the finals over highly touted Martinsville. Martinsville featured Wooden and Les Reynolds, long considered two of the finest Hoosier players before the modern era.

Murphy and Wooden, stars of the 1926 Indiana high school championship game, reunited to team for several glorious seasons at Purdue University under Coach Lambert. Murphy and Wooden became the first two three-time All-Americas in Purdue basketball history, directing the Boilermakers during that period to two successive WC crowns and a much-cherished national championship. "Stretch," mammoth for players of his day, set a WC individual game and season scoring record with 26 and 143 points, respectively, during the 1928–1929 season, and also was named to the HAF All-America teams of 1928, 1929, and 1930. Wooden, two years his junior, duplicated this feat in 1930, 1931, and 1932. This period clearly marked Purdue's emergence as a national basketball power. For the final two years of Murphy's college career, long lines of Purdue students waited hours outside the Memorial Gymnasium attempting to buy scarce tickets for the limited schedule of home games.

It is hard to grasp the full impact of Murphy on the Purdue University basketball fortunes of the late 1920s—and on the college game in general—without first appreciating the innovative nature of the Lambert system. Lambert abandoned long prevailing WC styles of play and pioneered a revolutionary running game. This was predicated on a quick-breaking offense and a dominant big man to control defensive rebounding and initiate a transition-style game plan. Murphy controlled the boards and Lloyd Kemmer and later Wooden led the offensive down-court charges. Purdue consistently averaged nearly 40 points and outscored all WC rivals by over 100 points during the 1928–1929 campaign. During Murphy's senior season, Purdue became the first undefeated WC team in 11 seasons of WC competition. In the five years of the Murphy-Wooden era at Purdue, Lambert's teams posted a 70-14 record and recorded such lopsided victories as 64-16 against powerhouse University of Chicago, and 60-14 over archrival Ohio State University. While Murphy's basketball playing career ended with his 1930 graduation from Purdue, teammate Wooden became the most successful basketball coach in collegiate history at UCLA during the 1960s and 1970s. The two always will be linked together in the minds of Boilermakers alumni as the dominant stars of the pre–World War II formative years in Purdue University basketball. Murphy was elected to the Naismith Memorial Basketball Hall of Fame in 1960, one of the rare unmatched big men of the first four decades of the game.

BIBLIOGRAPHY: Peter C. Bjarkman, *Big Ten Basketball* (Indianapolis, IN, 1994); Zander Hollander, ed., *The Pro Basketball Encyclopedia* (Los Angeles, CA, 1977); Neil D. Isaacs, *All the Moves: A History of College Basketball* (Philadelphia, PA, 1975); *Lafayette Journal and Courier* Staff, eds., *Most Memorable Moments in Purdue Basketball History* (Champaign, IL, 1998); Charles Murphy file, Naismith Memorial Basketball Hall of Fame, Springfield, MA; Bob Williams, *Hoosier Hysteria: Indiana High School Basketball* (South Bend, IN, 1982).

Peter C. Bjarkman

MUTH, Renie. *See* Portland, Renie Muth

MUTOMBO, Dikembe (b. June 25, 1966, Kinshasa, Zaire), college and professional player, developed as a center with superior defensive skills. Mutombo, whose full name is Dikembe Mutombo Mpolondo Mukamba Jean Jacque Wamutombo, is one of nine children of Mukamba Mutombo, a school administrator, and Biamba Dikembe Mutombo. Mutombo preferred soccer to basketball while growing up in Kinshasa, Zaire. His interest changed when he played basketball for his high schools, the Institute Kasai and Institute Boboto, and later for the national team of Zaire.

Mutombo attended Georgetown University (Washington, D.C., BEaC) to play basketball for coach John Thompson*. He played basketball for three seasons with the Hoyas, becoming the school's all-time leader in field goal percentage (64.4 percent) and ranking second in blocked shots. Mutombo averaged 9.9 points and 8.6 rebounds in 96 collegiate games, was named BEaC Co-Defensive Player of the Year as a junior, and was selected BEaC Defensive Player of the Year, All-BEaC First Team, and *TSN* All-America Third Team in his final season. He graduated from Georgetown in 1991 with Bachelor degrees in linguistics and diplomacy.

In the 1991 NBA draft, the seven-foot, two-inch, 261-pound Mutombo was selected by the Denver Nuggets (NBA) in the first round as the fourth pick overall. He has played professionally 14 years, beginning in 1991 with the Nuggets. Mutombo was signed as a free agent in 1996 by the Atlanta Hawks (NBA) and remained there until traded to the Philadelphia 76ers (NBA) in February 2001. He proved instrumental in leading the 76ers to the NBA Finals, playing in all 23 playoff games before losing to the Los Angeles Lakers in the championship series.

Mutombo, who was often called "Drac" and "The Sultan of Swat," was traded to New Jersey Nets (NBA) in August 2002. He was used in a reserve role in the Nets drive to the NBA Finals against the San Antonio Spurs. Mutombo spent the 2003–2004 season with the New York Knicks (NBA) and was traded to the Chicago Bulls (NBA) in August 2004. The following month, the Houston Rockets (NBA) acquired him for three players.

In 14 NBA seasons, Mutombo has tallied 11,196 points, pulled down 11,333 rebounds, and blocked 3,097 shots in 1,009 regular-season games. In 86 playoff games, he has averaged 10.3 points, 2.7 blocks, and 10.5 rebounds. In eight NBA All-Star Game appearances, Mutombo has started three times, scored 50 points, snagged 74 rebounds, and blocked 10 shots.

Mutombo, the Denver Nuggets all-time leader in blocked shots with 1,486, led the NBA in blocked shots per game in 1993–1994, 1994–1995, and 1995–1996, and in total rebounds in 1994–1995, 1996–1997, 1998–1999, and 1999–2000. Besides being named the NBA Defensive Player of the Year in 1995, 1997, 1998, and 2001, he was also selected on the NBA All-Defensive First Team in 1997, 1998, and 2001 and the NBA All-Defensive Second Team in 1995, 1999, and 2002. A member of the NBA All-Rookie First Team in 1992, he was chosen to the All-NBA Second Team in 2001 and the All-NBA Third Team in 1998 and 2002.

Mutombo and his wife, Rose, have a daughter, Carrie Biambi, a son, Dikembe Mutombo Jr. and four adopted children. Mutombo, who speaks four languages and five African dialects, has established a foundation to provide humanitarian assistance. In his homeland, he has helped in developing a telephone system, transportation system, a hospital, and medical care for his people and still hopes to build a basketball arena.

BIBLIOGRAPHY: "Dikembe Mutombo," *Bio*, http://www.nba.com (2003); "Dikembe Mutombo," *The Man*, http://www.maykuth.com (2003); "Dikembe Mutombo," *Player Info*, http://www.nba.com (2003); "Dikembe Mutombo," *Shot Blocker, Family Man, Humanitarian*, http://www.canoe.ca (2003); "Dikembe Mutombo," *Stats*, http://www.nba.com (2003); Leonard Shapiro, *Big Man on Campus: John Thompson and the Georgetown Hoyas* (1991); Ken Shouler et al., *Total Basketball* (Wilmington, DE, 2003); *TSN Official NBA Register, 2004–2005* (St. Louis, MO, 2004).

John L. Evers

N

NAISMITH, James "Jim" (b. November 6, 1861, Almonte, Ontario, Canada; d. November 28, 1939, Lawrence, KS), inventor, coach, and administrator, was one of three children born on a farm to John Naismith and Margaret (Young) Naismith. Orphaned when their parents died in 1870 of typhoid fever, the Naismith children grew up with their maternal grandmother and then-bachelor uncle Peter Young. A high school drop-out at age 15, James lived the rough, raucous life of a lumberjack for five years before resuming his education in 1881. He received a high school diploma in 1883 and graduated with honors from McGill University in Montreal, Canada with a Bachelor's degree in Philosophy in 1887. Intent on becoming a clergyman, he developed a love for rugby football, gymnastics, and other sports at McGill. Naismith combined vocational ambition and avocational interest by working as a Physical Education instructor at McGill and studying Theology at the Presbyterian Theological College in Montreal. Even before completing studies and being licensed for the ministry in 1890, he embraced the precepts of Muscular Christianity and combined a career in religion with athletics by becoming an instructor in the YMCA.

In 1891 Naismith enrolled in the International YMCA Training School in Springfield, Massachusetts, where he invented basketball. Basketball developed from a class assignment to devise an indoor game to be played in gymnasiums during the winter. Naismith was determined to develop a team game to be played in gymnasiums by using a ball, but avoiding the violence associated with running and tackling, hitting, or kicking. He created a game featuring tossing or bouncing a soccer ball into a peach basket suspended from the balcony railing at either end of the gym. First played in December 1891, basketball proved an instant success and spread rapidly across the nation and abroad partly because of YMCA sponsorship.

After completing the two-year training program, Naismith remained on the school's staff as a full-time teacher. In 1895, he moved to Colorado to become the director and instructor of the Denver YMCA. With his interest in physical education sparking an interest in health science, Naismith received the Doctor of Medicine degree from the Gross Medical School in Denver in 1898. Upon graduation, he became director of chapel and director (and sole instructor) of Physical Education at the University of Kansas. Regular religious exercises soon were discontinued, but Naismith remained professor of Physical Education until retiring in 1937. He introduced basketball to Kansas and coached the varsity team from 1899 to 1909, compiling an undistinguished record of 53 wins and 55 losses. At Kansas, Naismith also initiated fencing and an intramural sports program. Ordained as a minister in 1916, he served as chaplain to the Kansas National Guard stationed on the Texas-Mexico border in 1916 and with the YMCA in France from 1917 to 1919 during World War I.

The vigorously intellectual Naismith earned four degrees in the disparate fields of Philosophy, Religion, Physical Education, and Medicine. He also received an honorary Master's degree in Physical Education from the YMCA School in Springfield in 1911 and an honorary

Doctor of Divinity degree from the Presbyterian Theological College in Montreal in 1939. Naismith became a naturalized U.S. citizen on May 4, 1925 and married Maude Evelyn Sherman in 1894. They had five children, Margaret, Hellen, John, Maude, and James. After his wife died in 1937, he married Florence Mary (Kinsley) Kincaid in June 1939.

During his lifetime, Naismith received little recognition or remuneration as the "father of basketball." A reserved man who neither sought publicity nor engaged in self-promotion, he was a physical educator who embraced recreational sport but shunned the ethos of competitive athletics. Moreover, his only contribution to basketball remained the initial, critical act of creating the game. Naismith played no role in refining the primitive game through rule revisions, advancing techniques of coaching, or promoting the game through publications. He regularly attended University of Kansas games, but was not an avid fan or serious student of basketball and preferred other sports to his own invention. Naismith was overshadowed on campus and in basketball circles by his protégé, Forrest C. "Phog" Allen*. His lifelong association with basketball remained largely honorific or ceremonial, such as being made a life member of committees and being present at the introduction of basketball as an Olympic sport in Berlin, Germany in 1936. The embodiment of his Scottish Presbyterian heritage, the reserved, idealistic, gentle, self-effacing Naismith taught physical fitness and right conduct to youth through sport. His posthumously published *Basketball: Its Origin and Development* (1941) revealed more about the game than the man. Characteristically, he inconspicuously belonged to numerous church, lodge, medical, and physical education associations.

Naismith, who liked to be called "Jim," became famous because of an act from which he never sought fame or fortune and to which he attached no special personal, social, or athletic significance. Nonetheless, for his historic act of creation, he richly deserves having the Naismith Memorial Basketball Hall of Fame in Springfield, Massachusetts named in his honor and having the distinction of being among the charter enshrinees in 1959.

BIBLIOGRAPHY: John Dewar, "The Life and Professional Contributions of James Naismith," Ed. D. dissertation, Florida State University, 1965; Mike Douchant, *Encyclopedia of College Basketball* (Detroit, MI, 1995); Bill Gutman, *The History of NCAA Basketball* (New York, 1993); Ronald L. Mendell, *Who's Who in Basketball* (New Rochelle, NY, 1973); Grace Naismith, "Father Basketball," *SI* 2 (January 31, 1955), pp. 64–65; James Naismith, "Basket Ball," *American Physical Education Review* 19 (May 1914), pp. 339–351; James Naismith, *Basketball: Its Origin and Development* (New York, 1941); James Naismith file, Naismith Memorial Basketball Hall of Fame, Springfield, MA; *NYT*, November 28, 1939; Sandy Padwe, *Basketball's Hall of Fame* (Englewood Cliffs, NJ, 1970); *Springfield* (MA) *Sunday Republican*, April 14, 1968; Ken Shouler et al., *Total Basketball* (Wilmington, DE, 2003); Bernice Larson Webb, *The Basketball Man: James Naismith* (Lawrence, KS, 1973).

Larry R. Gerlach

NAULLS, William Dean "Willie" "The Whale" (b. October 7, 1934, Dallas, TX), college and professional player, attended the University of California at Los Angeles (UCLA), and played professionally basketball for the St. Louis Hawks (NBA), New York Knicks (NBA), San Francisco Warriors (NBA), and Boston Celtics (NBA).

Naulls grew up in Southern California, where he excelled in basketball and graduated from San Pedro High School in 1952. He attended UCLA between 1952 and 1956 and earned a Bachelor of Arts degree in sociology. Naulls broke most of the UCLA scoring and rebounding records and became coach John Wooden's* first consensus All-America. In three varsity seasons, the six-foot seven-inch, 225-pound forward scored 1,225 points and averaged 15.5 points in 79 games. He recorded a school record 28 rebounds against Arizona State University and averaged 23.6 points as a senior. Naulls was named to the Class of 1956 Silver Anniversary All-America Team and was ranked by coach Wooden among the Top 10 players in UCLA basketball history. In 1986, he was inducted into the UCLA Athletic Hall of Fame.

Naulls, drafted by the St. Louis Hawks (NBA) in 1956, was traded to New York in December

1956. He played six years for the Knicks and averaged 19.3 points and 10.7 rebounds. He captained the team four seasons, was selected the team MVP three times, led the team in rebounds four years, and played in four NBA All-Star Games.

New York traded Naulls to San Francisco in December 1962. Naulls played one season for the Warriors before being sold in September 1963 to the Boston Celtics. He played three seasons under coach "Red" Auerbach*, completing his professional playing career on three World Championship Boston Celtic teams. His Boston teammates included John Havlicek*, Bill Russell*, Sam Jones*, K. C. Jones*, Don Nelson*, Tommy Heinsohn*, and "Satch" Sanders. In 10 NBA seasons, Naulls scored 11,305 points in 716 regular-season games and averaged 15.8 points. His most productive season came in 1961–1962, when he averaged 25.0 points. Naulls collected 6,508 career rebounds for 9.1 boards per game and handed out 1,114 assists. In 35 NBA playoff games, he scored 248 points for a 7.1 point average and pulled down 134 rebounds.

Upon retirement from professional basketball in 1966, Naulls founded Willie Naulls Enterprises, the business undertakings of which were established in minority communities and offered job opportunities to local residents. In 1987, he received the call to ministry. After completing six years of advanced education, Naulls earned a Master's degree in theology from Fuller Theological Seminary in Pasadena, California and founded Willie Naulls Ministries in 1993. He moved to Gainesville, Florida in 1998 to begin a new ministry partnership at the Creekside Community Church. He oversees the Gainesville Academy for Training of Rising Stars (G.A.T.O.R.S.), which attempts to identify and prepare young deprived people to compete in today's world.

Naulls and his wife, Ann, have four children, Lisa, Shannon, Jonah, and Malaika. Ann, a medical doctor with speciality in gynecology, oversees communications and accounting for their various efforts.

BIBLIOGRAPHY: Dwight Chapin and Jeff Prugh, *The Wizard of Westwood: Coach John Wooden and His UCLA Bruins* (Boston, MA, 1973); Jan Hubbard, ed., *The Official NBA Encyclopedia*, 3rd ed. (New York, 2000); David F. Neft et al., *The Sports Encyclopedia: Pro Basketball*, 5th ed. (New York, 1992); "Willie Naulls," *New Ministry Partnership*, http://www.creeksidecc.org (2002); "Willie Naulls," *New York Knicks*, http://www.sportingnews.com (2000); "Willie Naulls," *Stats, History and Awards*, http://www.basketballreference.com (2003); John Wooden, *They Call Me Coach* (Waco, TX, 1972).

John L. Evers

NELSON, Donald Arvid "Don" "Nellie" (b. May 15, 1940, Muskegon, MI), college and professional player, coach, and executive, comprised an unlikely candidate for a professional basketball career. The youngest of three children, he is the son of Arvid Nelson and Agnes Nelson. His parents moved several times around the Midwest for financial reasons and settled on his grandfather's isolated farm, where he attended a one-room schoolhouse. The Nelsons later moved to Rock Island, Illinois, to find more lucrative work and enable their strapping son to play basketball.

Basketball gave Nelson a ticket from Rock Island to professional competition. Only three colleges recruited him, but he rewrote the offensive record book for the University of Iowa (BTC) from 1959 to 1962 and averaged 23.8 points during his last two seasons. Nelson was named First-Team All-BTC and Second-Team All-America after the 1960–1961 and 1961–1962 campaigns. He graduated from Iowa as the Hawkeyes' all-time leading scorer with 1,522 points, a mark that stood until 1980. The Chicago Zephyrs (NBA) selected Nelson in the third round in 1962, but sold him to the Los Angeles Lakers (NBA) in September 1963. The Lakers waived the mediocre forward in October 1965. Nelson's sporting fortunes changed when the Boston Celtics (NBA) signed him the same month. He admitted that the Celtics "were more my kind of team—more team-oriented, more physical."

Nelson helped the Celtics capture five NBA championships between 1966 and his 1976 retirement. The team's seventh man, he exhibited plodding physical play at six feet six inches and 210 pounds, unartistic but accurate jumpshots, and one-handed free throws. Nelson remained the consummate team player, accepting without complaint his reserve role and consistently scoring in double figures. His coaches, the legendary Arnold "Red" Auerbach*, Bill Russell*, and Tom Heinsohn*, utilized him in nearly every game. Nelson's most dramatic play came against the Lakers with the score tied very late in the seventh game of the 1969 NBA World Championship Series. He grabbed a loose ball and sank a desperation shot that bounced high off the rim, giving the Celtics consecutive titles. This feat remained unmatched by any NBA team until 1988. For the Celtics, the blond, stoic Nelson scored 9,968 points (11.4 average) and collected 4,517 rebounds (5.2 average) in 872 regular-season games. He led the NBA in field goal percentage in 1975, converting 53.9 percent of his attempts. The Celtics reached the playoffs nine times, with Nelson averaging 11.1 points and 4.8 rebounds. During his 14-year career, including playoffs, Nelson scored 10,898 points (10.3 average) and corralled 5,192 rebounds (4.9 average) in 1,053 games.

Nelson, an important cog in the Celtics basketball dynasty, joined the basketball elite as a coach. In 1976, the Milwaukee Bucks (NBA) appointed him assistant coach to Larry Costello*. Costello resigned 18 games into the season, making an amazed Nelson head coach. Nelson led the Bucks to seven consecutive division (one Midwest and six Central) titles in 11 years and a .611 winning percentage. Only the Celtics have captured more consecutive division crowns, with nine. Nelson was named NBA Coach of the Year three times (1983, 1985, 1992) and reached the 500-win plateau faster than any previous NBA mentor. Despite this stellar record, he left the Bucks in 1987. According to Nelson, new owner Herb Kohl made life so "uncomfortable for me that he drove me out of a state and city that I love."

Nelson resurfaced as coach and general manager of the Golden State Warriors (NBA) when George Karl* resigned in 1988. The Warriors' win-loss record under Nelson improved by 23 games over the previous year to 43-39, the fifth-best climb in NBA history. Nelson joined Auerbach and Joe Lapchick* as the only NBA coaches to achieve eight consecutive winning seasons. He coached Golden State through the 1994–1995 season, compiling a 277-260 mark. His best record there came in 1991–1992, when Golden State finished 55-27 and second in the Pacific Division. The Warriors fared only 9-15 in four NBA playoff appearances. Nelson coached the New York Knicks (NBA) to a 34-25 slate in 1995–1996. He served as head coach of the Dallas Mavericks (NBA) from December 1997 to March 2004, reviving a struggling franchise. Dallas increased its victory total each of his first six seasons, finished second in the Midwest Division from 2000–2001 through 2002–2003, and made the NBA playoffs from 2000–2001 through 2003–2004, reaching the Western Conference Finals in 2002–2003. In 27 seasons, Nelson's career coaching record boasted 1,190 victories and 880 losses for a .574 regular-season winning percentage. Only one other person had appeared in 1,000 NBA regular-season games as a player and coach. He also holds the record for participating in 305 NBA playoff games, 150 as a player. His clubs finished 70-85 in NBA playoffs. He was named one of the Top Ten Coaches in NBA History in 1996 and coached Team USA to a gold medal in the 1994 World Championships. Nelson, whose trademarks on the sidelines have been his muskie ties and his athletic shoes, is divorced and has four children, Julie, Donn, Chris, and Katie.

BIBLIOGRAPHY: Peter C. Bjarkman, *The Boston Celtics Encyclopedia* (Champaign, IL, 1998); *Boston Celtics Media Guide, 1989–1990* (Boston, MA, 1989); Jeff Chapman, "Nelson Gunning to Join 1,000/600 Club Tonight," *Oakland Tribune*, January 15, 1990; Jeff Chapman, "Warriors' 'Big Whistle,' " *Oakland Tribune,* July 22, 1988; *Golden State Warriors Media Guide, 1989–1990* (San Francisco, CA, 1989); Mike Lageschulte, letter to Bruce J. Dierenfield, July 12, 1990; "Dave Newhouse, 'A Man Named Nellie,' " *Oakland Tribune,* June 14, 1987; Dave Newhouse, "Nellie's Folks," *Oakland Tribune*, May 8, 1989, pp. D1, D7; Dave Newhouse, "The Nelson Look," *Oakland Tribune*, June 28, 1988; Dave Newhouse, "Warrior Pride," *Oakland Tribune*, February 5, 1989; Wayne Patterson telephone interview with Bruce J. Dierenfield, July 16, 1990; Ken Shouler et al., *Total Basketball* (Wilmington, DE, 2003); *TSN Official NBA Register, 2003–2004* (St. Louis, MO, 2004); "A Stunned Nelson Assumes Post as Bucks' Head Coach," *NYT*, November 24, 1976, p. L30; *USA Today,* March 21, 2005.

Bruce J. Dierenfield

NELSON, Jameer (b. February 9, 1982, Chester, PA), college and professional player, is the son of Floyd Nelson and Linda Billings, and graduated in 2000 from Chester (Pennsylvania) High School. The 5-foot 11-inch, 190-pound point guard earned First Team All-State accolades in basketball in 1999–2000, leading Chester to the state championship. He averaged 21 points, seven assists, and six rebounds and was named Schoolsports.com State Player of the Year.

Nelson graduated from St. Joseph's University (Pennsylvania) in 2004 with a Bachelor's degree in sociology, and starred in basketball for four years under coach Phil Martelli, becoming the Hawks' career leader in points (2,094), assists (713), and steals (256). He ranks third in assists, ninth in points, and tenth in steals among ATC career leaders, having helped the Hawks compile a 98-28 record and make four postseason appearances. St. Joseph's retired his uniform number 14.

Nelson was named *SI* National Freshman of the Year in 2001, making the ATC Second Team and earning ATC and All-Big 5 Rookie of the Year honors. He demolished the school record with an ATC-best 213 assists (6.4 average), led St. Joseph's with 55 steals (1.67 average), and averaged 12.5 points, as St. Joseph's reached the Sweet 16 of the NCAA tournament. In 2001–2002, Nelson averaged 14.4 points and 6.3 assists and made the All-ATC and All-Big 5 First Teams. St. Joseph's made the NCAA tournament the following season, when he paced the Hawks with 19.1 points and 4.7 assists per game while averaging 5.1 rebounds. His honors included AP Honorable Mention All-America, All-ATC First Team, Big 5 MVP, and NABC and USBWA All-District First Team.

During his senior season, Nelson led St. Joseph's in points (20.6 average), rebounds (4.7 average), assists (5.3 average), and steals (2.9 average). The Hawks finished with a perfect 27-0 regular-season record and a school-best 30-2 final record, and reached the Elite Eight of the NCAA tournament. Nelson owned a double-figure scoring streak of 41 games and tallied 98 points in four NCAA games, including a season-high 33 points against Liberty University (Virginia). The AP, *TSN, BT,* ESPN.com, FoxSports.com, and Chevrolet named him National Player of the Year. A unanimous AP All-America selection, he received the inaugural Bob Cousy Point Guard Award, and won the Wooden Award, Naismith Award, Rupp Award, Oscar Robertson Trophy, Senior Class Award, and Frances Pomeroy Naismith Award. Nelson, who made the All-Big 5 First Team for the fourth consecutive year and won MVP honors for the second straight year, co-captained the Hawks and combined with Delonte West to give St. Joseph's among the best backcourts in the nation.

The Denver Nuggets (NBA) selected Nelson as the twentieth overall pick in the June 2004 draft and traded him to the Orlando Magic (NBA) for a future first round draft pick. Nelson tallied 689 points (8.7 average) and 237 assists (3.0 average) in 79 games in 2004–2005. Nelson is single and has a son, Jameer Jr. A quiet leader, he has an infectious smile and plays unselfishly.

BIBLIOGRAPHY: Erik Brady, "Nelson Has Infectious Smile, Style," *USA Today*, February 5, 2004, p. 1C–2C; www.sjuhawks.com; www.woodenaward.com; Steve Wieberg, "NCAA Tournament $2 Million: A Star Player's Value," *USA Today*, March 17, 2004, pp. 1A–2A.

David L. Porter

NEUMANN, Carl John "Johnny" (b. September 11, 1951, Cincinnati, OH), college and professional player and coach, is the son of R. H. Neumann, a traveling salesman who pushed his two sons to excel in basketball. When the boys were young, their father moved the family to Memphis, Tennessee. His brother, Bob, played basketball for Memphis State University, while he starred for Overton High School in Memphis. During his senior year in high school, Neumann averaged 35.4 points. An injury to his shooting hand, however, denied Overton a state championship.

Highly recruited by college coaches, Neumann remained near home and played basketball for the University of Mississippi. Expectations were raised that he would be the South's next Pete Maravich*. Neumann did not disappoint, averaging 38.4 points on the freshman team, but struggled with academics and team rules. During the following summer, he eloped with and married high school student Carolyn DeViney.

As a sophomore, the flamboyant Neumann led the nation in scoring with a 40.1 point scoring average and was a consensus second team All-America. The 19-year-old then declared himself a hardship case and left the university for professional basketball.

Taking advantage of the rivalry between the ABA and NBA, Neumann signed a lucrative contract with the Memphis Pros (ABA). The six-foot six-inch, 200-pound guard/forward, however, did not attain the consistent level of his college play. Although averaging 18.3 points and 19.6 points during his first two seasons in Memphis, he quarreled with management and teammates. During the 1974 season, Neumann was traded to the Utah Stars (ABA), and began an ABA odyssey that would take him to the Virginia Squires and Indiana Pacers in 1974, 1975 and back to Virginia and then the Kentucky Colonels in 1975–1976. In 1976–1977, with the merger of the ABA and NBA, he played for the Buffalo Braves (NBA) and Los Angeles Lakers (NBA). Neumann returned to Indiana for the 1977–1978 campaign, averaging 4.2 points in 20 games. In seven ABA-NBA seasons, Neumann averaged a modest 13.2 points in 455 games.

The relatively young 27-year-old Neumann, who had gained the reputation of a malcontent, left the NBA. He still believed that he could play and moved to Italy, earning MVP honors. He moved on to Greece and began his basketball coaching career.

Upon returning to the United States in the early 1980s, Neumann coached in the CBA. In 1982, he finished runner-up to George Karl* for CBA Coach of the Year. In the mid 1980s, the nomadic Neumann resumed his international coaching career with stops in Belgium, Greece, Cyprus, and Lebanon. In the 2002 World Basketball Championship at Indianapolis, Indiana, Lebanon was soundly defeated in three games. After a dispute with the Lebanese Basketball Federation, he was relieved of his coaching duties. The flamboyant coach left Indiana for his home in Greece, asserting that his basketball coaching career was far from over.

BIBLIOGRAPHY: Conrad Brunner, "Where Are They Now?: Johnny Neumann," Indiana Pacers, http://www.nba.com/pacers/news/johnny_neumann.html (June 19, 2003); Chris Dortch, *String of Music* (Dulles, VA, 2002); Joaquin M. Henson, "World Basketball: Johnny B. Gone," Newsflash, http://www.newsflash.org/2002/09/sp/spoo2177.htm (June 19, 2003); Jan Hubbard, ed., *The Official NBA Encyclopedia*, 3rd ed. (New York, 2000); Curry Kirkpatrick, "Red-Hot New Pistol in Rebel Land," *SI* 34 (February 8, 1971), pp. 42–45; Terry Pluto, *Loose Balls* (New York, 1991).

Ron Briley

NEWELL, Peter "Pete" (b. August 31, 1915, Vancouver, British Columbia, Canada), college and professional coach, sportscaster, and athletic administrator, is the youngest of eight children of Peter Newell, a Knights of Columbus worker, and Alice (Heffron) Newell and was one of the best strategists and innovative college basketball tacticians during the immediate post–World War II era. Newell mentored basketball at the University of San Francisco (California), Michigan State University, and the University of California-Berkeley between 1947 and 1960, establishing an overall win-loss record of 234-123 and capturing both the NIT and NCAA college hoop crowns. Newell, who also had served as athletic director for eight years at California-Berkeley, joined the NBA professional ranks as general manager with the San Diego Rockets (1969–1971) and later the Los Angeles Lakers (1972–1976). When the San Diego Rockets franchise was relocated in Houston in 1971, Newell remained in an administrative capacity. He scouted and urged drafting such later NBA stars as Rudy Tomjanovich*, Don Adams, Chris Meely, Calvin Murphy*, and Curtis Perry.

Newell's remarkable coaching career was launched in spectacular fashion in just four short seasons (1946–1947 to 1949–1950) with the University of San Francisco Dons. By establishing a pioneer system of tight, aggressive defense and disciplined, patterned offense, Newell constructed a highly competitive basketball program. San Francisco enjoyed immediate success with an NIT title in 1949 and set the stage for those later fabled NCAA championship teams with Bill Russell* and K.C. Jones*. The Dons' 1949 NIT squad also featured John Benington, Rene Herrerias, and Ross Giudice. These three subsequently skillful coaches stand as testimonies to the effectiveness of Newell's teachings and the success of his West Coast–style of play. Newell's style was acquired from his playing days at Loyola Los Angeles College under James Needles. Needles' Loyola team also provided two of Newell's best coaching rivals, Scotty McDonald and Phil Woolpert*. Wool-pert, his immediate successor at San Francisco, inherited the championship Dons teams of the Bill Russell–era.

The pinnacle of Newell's coaching success came during the 1958–1959 and 1959–1960 seasons when his University of California-Berkeley Golden Bears achieved two consecutive appearances in the NCAA championship game. His tension-packed victory in 1959 for the school's first title was followed by a disappointing 20-point loss to the Ohio State University Buckeyes of Jerry Lucas* and John Havlicek* the next season. Newell's finest accomplishments of those two glory seasons for the Golden Bears included victories over the University of Cincinnati Bearcats, led by the incomparable Oscar Robertson*, in two successive seasons of Final Four play. He coached the U.S. Olympic basketball team to a six-game sweep and gold medal at the 1960 Olympic Games in Rome, Italy. That blue chip squad boasted stars Oscar Robertson, Jerry West*, Jerry Lucas, Bob Boozer, Terry Dischinger*, Darrall Imhoff, Adrian Smith, and Walt Bellamy*, and provided Americans with one of their most glorious moments in the international basketball arena. In fitting tribute to his long tenure as an outstanding coach and inventive strategist of the game, Newell has been enshrined in the HAF Basketball Hall of Fame and was elected as a contributor to the Naismith Memorial Basketball Hall of Fame in 1978. Newell's coaching style epitomized the controlled and aggressively patterned play of the Needles-MacDonald basketball tradition, which dominated California for almost two decades before John Wooden* brought his loose, fast-breaking style to UCLA from the heartland of Indiana. From 1977 until September 1986, Newell served as a talent consultant for the Golden State Warriors (NBA). Newell broadcast University of Southern California games and in 1976 developed his Big Man's Camp. He became director of player personnel for the Warriors in 1984 and scouted for the Cleveland Cavaliers (NBA) from 1991 to 2000. He married Florence J. O'Connor and has four children. California-Berkeley named its basketball court after him.

BIBLIOGRAPHY: Robert H. Boyle, "We Don't Concede Anything," *SI* 12 (January 18, 1960); Mike Douchant, *Encyclopedia of College Basketball* (Detroit, MI, 1995); Jack Ebling et al., *Magic Moments* (Chelsea, MI, 1998); Neil D. Isaacs, *All the Moves: A History of College Basketball* (Philadelphia, PA, 1975); Bruce Jenkins, *A Good Man: The Peter Newell Story* (New York, 1999); Ronald L. Mendell, *Who's Who in Basketball* (New Rochelle, NY, 1973); *NCAA Men's Basketball Records, 2004* (Indianapolis, IN, 2003); Pete Newell file, Naismith Memorial Basketball Hall of Fame, Springfield, MA.

Peter C. Bjarkman

NEWTON, Charles Martin "C. M." (b. February 2, 1930, Rockwood, TN), player, coach, and executive, graduated in 1948 from Ft. Lauderdale, FL High School, where he made All-State as a football quarterback, basketball guard-forward, and baseball pitcher. He accepted a basketball scholarship to play under Adolph Rupp* at the University of Kentucky, graduating with a Bachelor's degree in 1952. The six-foot two-inch, 190-pound Newton lettered on Kentucky's 1950–1951 NCAA championship team, scoring 23 points in 18 games as a reserve. He also pitched on the Wildcats baseball team that appeared in the NCAA tournament.

Newton signed with the New York Yankees (AL) and pitched in the minor leagues from 1952 to 1955. During the off-season, he helped coach basketball and baseball at Transylvania College in Lexington, Kentucky and officiated basketball games. He also served as a lieutenant in the U.S. Air Force, being head athletic officer at Andrews Air Force Base in Washington, D.C.

In 1956, Newton became head basketball coach and chairman of the physical education department at Transylvania College. He guided Transylvania to a 169-137 record in 12 seasons and to the NAIA Tournament in 1963, and integrated the team in 1965 with the school's first African-American player.

In 1968, Paul Bear Bryant hired Newton to revive the downtrodden basketball program at the University of Alabama (SEC). After Alabama struggled with a 4-20 mark in 1968–1969,

Newton integrated the Alabama program by signing Wendell Hudson, an African American forward. Newton orchestrated a complete turnaround in the Crimson's Tide's fortunes, compiling a sparkling 211-123 record in 12 years through 1980. Alabama won three consecutive SEC championships from 1974 to 1976 and played in four NIT and two NCAA tournaments. Newton was named AP SEC Coach of the Year in 1972 and 1976 and UPI Coach of the Year in 1972 and 1978.

Newton served as assistant commissioner of the SEC in 1980–1981, but missed coaching and in 1981 became head basketball coach at Vanderbilt University (Tennessee). He gradually rebuilt the Vanderbilt program, compiling a 129-115 record from 1981–1982 to 1988–1989. His best seasons there came in 1987–1988 and 1988–1989, when he was named SEC Coach of the Year and helped Vanderbilt advance to the NCAA tournament. During his 32 year coaching career, Newton compiled a composite 509-375 record.

Newton returned to his alma mater at Kentucky as athletic director from 1989 to 2000. He hired Rick Pitino* as head basketball coach to revive the basketball program wracked by scandal. Pitino returned the Kentucky men's basketball program to national prominence and eventually won a national championship. In 1995 Newton hired Bernadette Mattox as the school's first African American women's basketball coach. In 1997 he appointed Orlando "Tubby" Smith as the first African American head coach of the Kentucky men's basketball team. Smith guided Kentucky to the NCAA basketball title in 1998.

Newton also played key administrative roles in promoting basketball. He served on the NABC Board of Directors for 11 years (1977–1980, 1981–1989) and chaired the NCAA Rules Committee from 1979 to 1985, establishing the 45-second shot clock, the three-point shot, and the coaches box. Newton served as team manager of the 1984 U.S. Olympic team; as president of USA Basketball from 1992 to 1996, changing the Olympic team from college players to NBA players and overseeing the selection of the 1992 Dream Team; and has increased support for the women's Olympic team. He has represented North America on the FIBA Central Board since 1994 and served from 1992 to 1999 on the NCAA Division I Basketball Committee, organizing and overseeing the NCAA tournament. He served as CEO of World Basketball Championships in Indianapolis, Indiana in 2002, and in September 2003 was named a consultant to the SEC Commissioner.

Newton married his high school sweetheart, Evelyn, in 1951 and has three children. He received the John Bunn Award in 1997 for his lifetime service to the sport and was elected to the Naismith Memorial Basketball Hall of Fame as a contributor in 2000.

BIBLIOGRAPHY: "C. M. Newton," http://www.ukfans.net/jps/uk/Statistics/Players/NewtonC.M.htm; "C. M. Newton Named Consultant in Southeastern Conference," http://www.allsports.com; http://www.hoophall.com/halloffamers/Newton.htm; Tony Neely and Brooks Downing, *The Right Stuff* (Naismith Memorial Basketball Hall of Fame, Springfield, MA); C. M. Newton file, Naismith Memorial Basketball Hall of Fame, Springfield, MA.

David L. Porter

NIXON, Norman Ellard "Norm" (b. October 10, 1955, Macon, GA), college and professional player, graduated with honors from Southwest High School in Macon, Georgia, where he served as class president and made All-State in football, basketball, and track and field. The six-foot two-inch, 175-pound over-achiever earned a Bachelor's degree from Duquesne University in Pittsburgh, Pennsylvania, and established several school basketball records. His 1,805 career points in 104 games put him second on the school's all-time career scoring list. Nixon also ranked second in season scoring with 661 points his senior year, and set school marks for career field goals with 753 season field goals with 279 in 1976–1977, and career assists with 557. His scoring ability and assists attracted the attention of professional scouts, although Nixon lacked height. At Duquesne, Nixon's premier scoring effort came in a 38-point performance against Gannon University (Pennsylvania) in 1977. His 29-point effort helped the Dukes defeat the University of Detroit (Michigan) in 1977 to shatter the Titans 21-game victory streak. This performance ranks among the best in Pittsburgh Civic Arena history.

Nixon played professionally in the NBA from 1977 to 1986 and in 1988–1989, missing the 1987–1988 season with an Achilles tendon injury. He performed with the Los Angeles Lakers (NBA) from 1978 through 1983, the San Diego Clippers (NBA) the next season, and the Los Angeles Clippers (NBA) from 1984 to 1986. The Clippers released him in 1989. He played six games with Scavolini Pesaro (ItL) in 1988–1989. Nixon, a two-time NBA All-Star, scored 12,065 career points (15.7 points average), 6,386 assists (tenth best in league history), and 1,187 steals. The Lakers won NBA championships in 1979–1980 and 1981–1982 with Nixon in the backcourt.

BIBLIOGRAPHY: *Duquesne University Basketball Media Guide*, Duquesne University Sports Information files, Pittsburgh, PA; Jan Hubbard, ed., *The Official NBA Basketball Encyclopedia*, 3rd ed. (New York, 2000); Roland Lazenby, *The Lakers: A Basketball Journey* (New York, 1996); Roland Lazenby, *The NBA Finals* (Indianapolis, IN, 1996); Ken Shouler et al., *Total Basketball* (Wilmington, DE, 2003); *TSN Official NBA Register, 2004–2005* (St. Louis, MO, 2004).

Robert B. Van Atta

NOWAK, Paul (b. March 15, 1914, South Bend, IN; d. January 10, 1983, Treasure Island, FL), college and professional player, was selected an All-America basketball center for three years from 1935–1936 to 1937–1938 at the University of Notre Dame, and helped the Akron (Ohio) Firestones win consecutive NBL titles in 1938–1939 and 1939–1940. The six-foot five-inch, 205-pound Nowak, an HAF Basketball Hall of Fame member, starred on Notre Dame's 22-2 1936 national championship team under coach George Keogan*. An adept rebounder and pick-setter, Nowak averaged 7.0, 6.9, and 7.5 points over three varsity campaigns. His teammates included leading scorer John Moir*, George Ireland, and two-time captain Ray Meyer*. The Irish posted consecutive 20-3 win-loss records during Nowak's junior and senior seasons, splitting six games with the prestigious NYU and University of Kentucky quintets, and overwhelming the 1937 BTC co-champion University of Minnesota 44-18.

Nowak starred three years on the hardcourt at South Bend (Indiana) High School and graduated with a Bachelor's degree from the University of Notre Dame (Indiana) in 1938. The Akron (Ohio) Firestone Non-Skids (NBL) signed Nowak, who helped the club finish 24-3 in 1938–1939 and defeat the Oshkosh (Wisconsin) All-Stars in three of five games for the 1939 NBL title. Akron compiled an 18-9 mark in 1939–1940, triumphing over the Detroit (Michigan) Eagles and Oshkosh to achieve the 1940 NBL Championship. Injuries sidelined Nowak part of the 1940–1941 season, as the 13-11 Firestone Non-Skids slipped to third place in the NBL. In 1941–1942, he played one game with the Toledo (Ohio) Jim Whites Chevrolets (NBL). Nowak finished his professional basketball career with the Rochester (New York) Royals (NBL) and Philadelphia (Pennsylvania) Sphas. He owned a retail package store for several years until retiring to Treasure Island, Florida.

BIBLIOGRAPHY: Mike Douchant, *Encyclopedia of College Basketball* (Detroit, MI, 1995); Frank G. Menke, ed., *The All-Sports Record Book* (New York, 1950); William G. Mokray, ed., *Ronald Encyclopedia of Basketball* (New York, 1963); Tim Neely, *Hooping It Up: The Complete History of Notre Dame Basketball* (Notre Dame, IN, 1985); *Notre Dame Basketball Guide, 1982–1983* (Notre Dame, IN, 1982); Paul Nowak file, Naismith Memorial Basketball Hall of Fame, Springfield, MA; Robert W. Peterson, *Cages to Jump Shots: Pro Basketball's Early Years* (New York, 1990); Ken Shouler et al., *Total Basketball* (Wilmington, DE, 2003); Alexander Weyand, *The Cavalcade of Basketball* (New York, 1960).

James D. Whalen and Wayne Patterson

NOWITZKI, Dirk Werner (b. June 19, 1978, Wurzburg, Germany), professional player, is the son of Joerg Nowitzki and Helen Nowitzki and graduated from Rontgen Gymnasium in Wurz-burg, Germany. His older sister, Silke, works for the NBA in International TV. After serving a mandatory stint in the Germany Army from September 1997 to June 1998, Nowitzki was named Germany's 1998 Player of the Year. The seven-foot, 250-pound center was selected ninth in the 1998 NBA draft by the Milwaukee Bucks (NBA) and was immediately traded to the Dallas Mavericks (NBA). He has been identified as the best European import and one of the best players the NBA.

After his rookie season, Nowitzki enjoyed a super sophomore campaign in 1999–2000 and finished second in voting for Most Improved Player. He averaged 17.5 points, 7.5 rebounds, and 2.5 assists in 82 games. Nowitzki was the first Dallas Maverick to be named to an All-NBA Team, making All-NBA Third Team in 2000–2001, and was one of only two Mavericks to start all 82 games that season. He became only the second player in NBA history to make 100 three-point field goals and block 100 shots in a season. Despite his height, Nowitzki has excellent three-point shooting abilities. In 2002–2003, Nowitzki led the Dallas Mavericks to the Western Conference Championships before losing to the eventual champion and cross-state rival San Antonio Spurs (NBA). He was named *Time* magazine's Person of the Week in May 2003 for fulfilling the promise of globalization in the NBA, and was selected to play in the NBA All-Star Game in 2002, 2003, 2004, and 2005. Nowitzki ranked ninth in the NBA with a 21.8 point scoring average in 2003–2004 and fourth in scoring with a 26.1 point average in 2004–2005, helping Dallas reach the playoffs both years. He averaged 23.7 points and 10.1 rebounds in 13 playoff games in 2005, with the San Antonio Spurs eliminating the Mavericks in the second round. He tallied 32 points and 13 rebounds in Game 1 and 31 points and 14 rebounds in Game 5 of the first round of the 2004 Western Conference playoffs, but the Sacramento Kings eliminated Dallas in five games. Through 2004–2005, he has recorded 11,106 points (21.3 average) and 4,421 rebounds (8.5 average) in 522 regular-season games; he has tallied 1,332 points (25.1 average) in 53 playoff games. He was named to the All-NBA Second Team in 2002 and 2003, ranking sixth in the NBA in scoring the latter season, and to the All-NBA Third Team in 2004 and to the All-NBA First Team in 2005.

Nowitzki has accumulated an excellent record of service for the German National Team, being top scorer for his homeland in the 2002 World Championships and the 2001 European Championship. He played on the 1996 German National Junior Team, 1996 European Junior Select Team, 1996 World Junior German Under-22 National Team, and in the 1998–1999 German League All-Star Game.

BIBLIOGRAPHY: http://www.bballone.com/dirkn/dirknowitzki.html; http://www.nba.com/playerfile/dirk_nowitzki/bio.html; Frank Pellegrini, "Person of the Week: Dirk Nowitzki," 03 May 2003, http://www.time.com/pow/article/0,8599,235128,00.html; *TSN Official NBA Register, 2004–2005* (St Louis, MO, 2004); Ken Shouler et al., *Total Basketball* (Wilmington, DE, 2003).

Maureen M. Smith

NUCATOLA, Giovanni John "Johnny" (b. November 17, 1907, New York, NY; d. May 8, 2000, Scotch Plains, NJ), college and professional player and referee, was the son of Stefano Nucatola and Carola Agnes (Parmigiani) Nucatola and called "basketball's greatest official" by Coach Clair Bee*. Nucatola graduated from Newtown High School (New York), where he later coached, in 1926 and Jamaica (New York) Teachers College in 1930 and resided in the New York area his entire life. After playing pro basketball, he worked as an educator and basketball coach and referee. The five-foot ten-inch, 190-pound Nucatola served in the U.S. Air Force during World War II and was Dean of Boys at Bayside High School in New York. He continued to officiate basketball games, including those of the pro BAA, ABL, and NBA and many college conferences. He quit officiating pro basketball games over a dispute with some owners, but handled the NIT and NCAA tournaments for 18 years during his career.

Upon retiring from officiating, Nucatola became the supervisor of officials for the IvL and ECAC. He was vindicated in his dispute with pro basketball when the NBA later named him its supervisor of officials, a job from which he retired in 1977. Nucatola believed that the official's most important duty was to make the right call rather than merely assert authority and urged officials to be willing to reconsider their calls. To that end, he also favored using three-man officiating crews. Whatever his philosophy, he ranked among the era's most respected officials. Coach Pete Newell* said that he knew of "no official more dedicated or conscientious." Norvall Neve, commissioner of the MVC, added, "No one man is more respected as a Basketball Official than John Nucatola." Nucatola was elected to the Naismith Memorial Basketball Hall of Fame as a referee in 1977. He married Philomena DeVito on January 20, 1930.

BIBLIOGRAPHY: Zander Hollander, ed., *The NBA's Official Encyclopedia of Pro Basketball* (New York, 1981); Jan Hubbard, ed., *The Official NBA Encyclopedia of Basketball*, 3rd ed. (New York, 2000); John Nucatola, *Officiating Basketball*, Richard T. Corrado, ed. (Flushing, NY, 1959); John Nucatola file, Naismith Memorial Basketball Hall of Fame, Springfield, MA.

Joel Westerholm

O

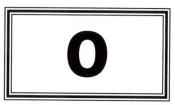

O'BANNON, Edward Charles, Jr. "Ed" (b. August 14, 1972, Los Angeles, CA), college and professional player, is the son of Edward O'Bannon Sr., a former UCLA football player, and Madeline O'Bannon. He has a younger brother, Charles, who also played pro basketball, and two older half brothers. O'Bannon attended Artesia (California) High School and was named to the First-Team All-America squad of *Parade* magazine his junior year, averaging 29.3 points and 14.8 rebounds. In his senior year, he led Artesia to the Southern California CIF 4A title and the California state Division II championship, averaging 24.6 points and 9.7 rebounds. He was selected to the First-Team All-America squads by *Parade* magazine, McDonald's, and Converse and was named the nation's high school Player of the Year of *BT*.

O'Bannon missed the 1990–1991 season because of a torn knee ligament, but played for UCLA in the 1991–1992 season. He started the eleventh game of the year against the University of Oregon, 15 months after surgery to replace the ligament. O'Bannon was UCLA's most honored player in 1992–1993, earning Honorable Mention All-America from UPI. The six-foot eight-inch, 217-pounder averaged 16.7 points and led UCLA in rebounding, averaging 7.0 per game. During the 1993–1994 season, he paced the PTC in rebounding, averaged 18.2 points, and was named UCLA's MVP.

In his senior year, 1994–1995, O'Bannon was selected a Consensus First-Team All-America and averaged 20.4 points, 8.3 rebounds, and 2.5 assists. He won the 1995 John R. Wooden National Player of the Year Award and enjoyed a 30-point, 17-rebound game against the University of Arkansas to spark UCLA's victory in the NCAA championship game.

O'Bannon was drafted in the first round by the New Jersey Nets (NBA) in 1995, but experienced a short professional career. He played one year with New Jersey, averaging 6.2 points in 64 games, and part of the next year with the Dallas Mavericks (NBA), averaging 3.7 points. He later played with several teams in the European pro league. He and his wife, Maria Bravo, have a son, Aaron.

BIBLIOGRAPHY: *The Complete Marquis Who's Who* (Farmington Hills, MI, 2001); Scott Howard-Cooper, *The Bruins 100* (Lenexa, KS, 1999); Jan Hubbard, ed., *The Official NBA Encyclopedia*, 3rd ed. (New York, 2000); *UCLA Basketball Media Guide, 1995–1996* (Los Angeles, CA, 1995).

Robert L. Cannon

O'BRIEN, John Joseph (b. November 4, 1888, Brooklyn, NY; d. December 9, 1967, Oceanside, NY), college and professional referee and executive, was the son of John T. O'Brien and Margaret (Monohan) O'Brien, both of Irish descent. O'Brien graduated from Commercial High School in Brooklyn, New York, 1907 and attended St. John's University in New York. The versatile athlete played basketball, baseball, and football in high school and later participated in pro basketball with city-organized teams and the YMCA. From 1910 to 1930, O'Brien refereed in high school, college, and pro basketball. He refereed for the EIBL from 1915 to 1930 and officiated in the SIBL from 1920 to 1930. An active businessman, O'Brien lent his organizational expertise to his beloved basketball. He worked from 1913 to 1957 for Coverdale and Colpitts, consulting engineers headquartered on Wall Street in New York. He also served as vice president, secretary, and treasurer of the Pierce Oil Corporation (1930–1940); vice president, secretary, and treasurer of the Minneapolis and St. Louis Railway Company (1930–1940), and trustee of the West Caddo Oil Syndicate (1922–1940).

The enormously energetic, six-foot, 210-pound O'Brien, a fashion plate who often changed several times daily, held up to five jobs simultaneously. In basketball, he helped organize the ISL in 1914 and served as its president from 1915 to 1917. Besides refereeing the first Army–Navy basketball contest in 1920, O'Brien organized the MeL in 1921 and served as its president and treasurer from 1922 to 1928. In 1921, he established the Brooklyn Arcadians. Most important, O'Brien presided over the pro ABL, a predecessor of the NBA, from its reorganization in 1928 until its disbandment in 1953. During his tenure, he brought increased dignity and integrity to basketball. Not surprisingly, O'Brien persuaded the ABL to disband rather than sign Ralph Beard*, Alex Groza*, Sherman White, and Bill Spivey*, players implicated in the college point-shaving scandals of the late 1940s. He concluded that the ABL could not survive the factional fighting over whether or not to sign those players.

O'Brien also trained Pat Kennedy*, Matty Begovich, John Stevens, and other well-known officials. He married Florence Gladys Cornerford, was survived by sons John Jr. (captain of the Columbia University basketball team in 1937), and Emmett, and daughters Vecilia, Maureen, and Patricia. A third son, Jeremiah, was killed during World War II as a U.S. Air Force pilot. O'Brien, elected in 1961 to the Naismith Memorial Basketball Hall of Fame as a contributor, died after a stroke at his Rockville Center, New York home.

BIBLIOGRAPHY: George Gipe, *The Great American Sports Book* (Garden City, NY, 1978); Ronald L. Mendell, *Who's Who in Basketball* (New Rochelle, NY, 1973); *Newsday*, December 11, 1967; *NYT*, December 11, 1967; John O'Brien file, Naismith Memorial Basketball Hall of Fame, Springfield, MA; Sandy Padwe, *Basketball Hall of Fame* (Englewood Cliffs, NJ, 1970); Robert W. Peterson, *Cager to Jump shots: Pro Basketball's Early Years* (New York, 1990); Ken Shouler et al., *Total Basketball* (Wilmington, DE, 2003); Paul Soderberg and Helen Washington, comp. and ed., *The Big Book of Halls of Fame in the United States and Canada* (New York, 1977).

Frederick J. Augustyn Jr.

O'BRIEN, John Thomas "Johnny" (b. December 11, 1930, South Amboy, NJ), college athlete and professional baseball player, is the son of Edward J. O'Brien, a marine foreman for the Pennsylvania Railroad, and the twin brother of Edward, a Seattle University basketball player and Pittsburgh Pirates (NL) baseball player. O'Brien graduated in 1948 from St. Mary's High School in South Amboy, New Jersey, where he starred in baseball and made All-State for the state titlist basketball team. He originally planned to play college basketball near home, but major universities considered him too small. O'Brien played shortstop for South Amboy at the 1949 Semi-Pro Baseball Tournament in Wichita, Kansas.

Al Brightman, Seattle (Washington) University head basketball coach, recruited the five-foot nine-inch, 170-pound O'Brien for his relatively small Jesuit school. O'Brien performed B-plus academic work and graduated from Seattle University with a Bachelor's degree in business in 1956. The fearless, friendly, popular, humorous guard made Seattle a nationally known basketball program. His natural instincts, speed, incredible spring, catlike quickness, and accurate hook, jump, and bankshots placed him among the sport's biggest showmen. As a sophomore guard, he scored 766 points for the 32-5 Chieftains in 1950–1951. The NCAA officially credited O'Brien with 248 baskets and 187 free throws for 683 points (20.7 points average) in 33 games. Seattle reached the third round of the 1951 National Catholic tournament and then upset the Harlem Globetrotters 84-81 as O'Brien tallied 43 points. He in February 1952 broke the NCAA season scoring record of 967 points, held by George King* of Morris Harvey College (West Virginia). Altogether, O'Brien scored 1,051 points for the 29-8 Chieftains and set a national season record with 361 free throws. The NCAA officially listed him with 314 baskets and 342 free throws for 970 points (27.7 points average) in 35 games. In the NIT, Seattle lost to powerful College of the Holy Cross (Massachusetts) 77-72. The Second Team All-America made only three baskets, but broke a Madison Square Garden record with 15 foul shots.

O'Brien earned unanimous First Team All-America honors as a senior, leading the nation with 884 points (28.5 points average) on 276 baskets and 332 free throws, and ranking among the top five in field goal accuracy. Seattle showcased his talents in Eastern doubleheaders before enormous crowds. In December 1952, the Chieftains capitalized on 62 points by the O'Brien twins to upset NYU 102-101. A week later, O'Brien shattered a Boston Garden scoring record with 41 points in a 99-86 triumph over Boston College. The 29-4 Seattle quintet reached the second round of the NCAA Far West Regional. According to the NCAA, he established career scoring records with 838 field goals and 861 free throws for 2,537 points (25.6 points average). Nate DeLong of River Falls (Wisconsin) State University held the previous NCAA scoring record with 2,445 career points. O'Brien also played shortstop in baseball for the Chieftains, batting over .430 in 1953.

The Pittsburgh Pirates (NL) signed the O'Brien twins to $40,000 bonus baseball contracts, employing them as a double-play combination in 1953. O'Brien batted .247 in 89 games that season, mostly as a second baseman. The twins were drafted into the U.S. Army in September 1953 and played professional basketball for Lancaster, Pennsylvania (EL). Johnny married Jean Kumhera in the fall of 1954 and returned to Pittsburgh in June 1955, batting .299 in 84 games. Bill Mazeroski replaced O'Brien as regular second baseman in 1956, causing the latter to become a part-time pitcher. O'Brien divided the 1958 campaign between Pittsburgh, the St. Louis Cardinals (NL), and Rochester, New York (IL), split the 1959 season with the Milwaukee Braves (NL) and Rochester, and ended his baseball career in 1960 with Seattle (PCL). In six major league seasons, O'Brien batted .250 with four home runs and 59 RBI and compiled a 1-3 record with a 5.61 ERA. The Seattle, Washington resident served as a King County commissioner and headed security at the Kingdome, home of the Seattle Mariners (AL) and Seahawks (NFL).

BIBLIOGRAPHY: *The Baseball Encyclopedia*, 9th ed. (New York, 1993); Peter C. Bjarkman, *The Biographical History of Basketball* (Chicago, IL, 2000); Mike Douchant, *Encyclopedia of College Basketball* (Detroit, MI, 1995); Larry Fox, *Little Men in Sports* (New York, 1963); Zander Hollander, ed., *The Modern Encyclopedia of Basketball*, rev. ed. (New York, 1973); Rich Marazzi and Len Fiorito, *Aaron to Zuverink* (New York, 1982); Ken Shouler et al., *Total Basketball* (Wilmington, DE, 2003); Boyd Smith, "Deadeye Johnny O'Brien," *Sport* 14 (February 1953), pp. 38–39, 82–83; Emmett Watson, "The Clan O'Brien Sticks Together," *Sport* 21 (February 1956), pp. 30–33, 95.

David L. Porter

O'BRIEN, Lawrence Francis, Jr. "Larry" (b. July 7, 1917, Springfield, MA; d. September 28, 1990, New York, NY), professional executive, was a first-generation, Irish-American basketball fan. O'Brien appropriately was born in Springfield, Massachusetts where the sport was invented and where its Naismith Memorial Basketball Hall of Fame is located. For many years, he forsook his vocation to include his passion for politics and became one of the top political consultants and operatives of his time. O'Brien's rise to the apex of the political process and above the rim in pro basketball as the NBA's commissioner from June 1, 1975 to February 1, 1984 epitomized determination and perseverance.

O'Brien was the son of Lawrence F. O'Brien Sr., and Myra (Sweeney) O'Brien, who were from County Cork, Ireland and had immigrated to the United States, where they married. He received his Bachelor of Law degree in 1942 from Northeastern University (Massachusetts). After serving in the U.S. Army from 1942 to 1945, O'Brien worked as administrative assistant to U.S. Representative (Massachusetts) Foster Furcolo (1948–1950), as campaign director and adviser to U.S. Senator (Massachusetts) John F. Kennedy (1952–1958), as special assistant for congressional relations to Presidents Kennedy and Lyndon B. Johnson (1961–1965), as postmaster general of the United States (1965–1968), and as national chairman of the Democratic party (1968–1969, 1970–1972).

As NBA commissioner, O'Brien added institutional strength to the NBA so that it could react better to a more challenging, complex, and competitive operating environment. His most important achievements were (1) an agreement on a collective bargaining pact with the NBAPA and settlement of the Oscar Robertson* suit (1976); (2) absorption of the four strongest ABA teams (1976); (3) adoption of the three-point field goal (1979); (4) expansion of the NBA to 23 teams with the addition of the Dallas Mavericks (1980); (5) record-breaking television agreements with CBS (1978, 1982) plus the pioneering agreements with the ESPN and USA Cable Networks; and (6) the landmark collective bargaining with the NBAPA and the innovative Anti-Drug Program (1983). His term also saw the NBA climb above the 10-million attendance mark in one season for the first time, record a 300 percent increase in television revenue, and double gate receipts.

O'Brien was named Sportsman of the Year by *TSN* in 1976. The author of an autobiographical book, *No Final Victories*, he married Elva Lena Brassard of Springfield, Massachusetts on May 30, 1944, and had one son, Lawrence Francis III. O'Brien may have recorded his final victory by the time of turning over the NBA reins to his executive vice president David Stern*. Under O'Brien, the NBA had added depth to its quality and significantly expanded its exposure while maintaining stability. The NBA, thus, was poised to reach toward the impressive heights it has achieved ever since. O'Brien was elected to the Naismith Memorial Basketball Hall of Fame in 1991.

BIBLIOGRAPHY: Jan Hubbard, ed., *The Official NBA Encyclopedia*, 3rd ed. (New York, 2000); *NBA Today*, December 12, 1983; *NYT*, September 29, 1990; Lawrence F. O'Brien, *No Final Victories* (New York, 1974); Lawrence O'Brien file, Naismith Memorial Basketball Hall of Fame, Springfield, MA; Lawrence O'Brien Papers, John F. Kennedy Library, Boston, MA; Ken Shouler et al., *Total Basketball* (Wilmington, DE, 2003).

Gustavo N. Agrait

OHL, Donald Jay "Don" "Waxey" (b. April 18, 1936, Murphysboro, IL), college, amateur, and professional player, is the son of Elmer Ohl and Blanche (Brendel) Ohl. As a senior, he led Edwardsville High School to the semifinals of the Illinois High School basketball championship in 1954 and was selected to the All-Tournament team. The six-foot three-inch, 190-pound Ohl enrolled at the University of Illinois (BTC) and played three varsity seasons for coach Harry Combes, graduating in 1959 with a Bachelor's degree in business. The Illini enjoyed less than stellar success during Ohl's junior and senior seasons, but the quick guard and occasional forward averaged 17.6 points, was twice named to the First Team BTC, and made Second Team All-America in 1958.

The Philadelphia Warriors (NBA) made Ohl their fifth pick in the 1958 NBA draft, but showed little interest in signing the Illinois star. Ohl's self doubts about his prospects for a successful NBA career, and the opportunity to play basketball at a high level while simultaneously pursuing business opportunities it afforded, persuaded him to join the Peoria (Illinois) Caterpillars (NIBL). Ohl averaged 18.0 points in 1958–1959 and 15.4 points the following season, being twice named AAU All-America and leading the Cats to the AAU national title in 1960. The Detroit Pistons (NBA) paid Philadelphia little more than the $500 NBA waiver price to acquire Ohl's services in June 1960. In his inaugural 1960–1961 NBA season, the rookie posted a 13.3 point scoring average and quickly became one of the league's premier outside shooters. He averaged 18.1 points the next three seasons with the Pistons. Ohl, acquired by the Baltimore Bullets (NBA) in a seven-player trade in June 1964, continued to record impressive offensive numbers. He averaged 19.7 points with the Bullets until injuries and surgery slowed him in the 1966–1967 season. In January 1968, Ohl was traded to the St. Louis Hawks (NBA) for rookie forward Tom Workman and the Hawks' number-two draft choice. The Hawks won the Western Division that season and again in 1969–1970 after the franchise moved to Atlanta. Ohl was used primarily as a reserve, however, and saw his offensive production decline. After a season low average of 6.2 points in 1969–1970, he retired. Ohl appeared in five consecutive NBA All-Star Games from 1963 through 1967, averaging 9.2 points. During 10 NBA seasons, Ohl scored 11,549 points (15.9 points average) and recorded 2,243 assists (3.1 per game) in 727 games. In 47 NBA playoff games, he averaged 16.9 points. He was elected a player charter member of the IBCA Hall of Fame in 1973.

After owning a stationery store and an office supply company in Edwardsville, Illinois, Ohl became a divisional director of the Individual Assurance Company, with responsibility for coverage of bank related insurance programs in the state of Illinois. Now retired, he and his wife, Judy (Webber) Ohl, reside in Edwardsville and have a son, Donald Jr., and two daughters, Pamela Lee and Tracey Lynn.

BIBLIOGRAPHY: Peter C. Bjarkman, *Big Ten Basketball* (Indianapolis, IN, 1994); Jan Hubbard, ed., *The Official NBA Encyclopedia*, 3rd ed. (New York, 2000); Don Ohl, telephone interview with Jack C. Braun, July 25, 2003; Don Ohl file, Naismith Memorial Basketball Hall of Fame, Springfield, MA; Don Ohl file, Sports Information Office, University of Illinois, Champaign, IL; Martin Taragano, *Basketball Biographies* (Jefferson, NC, 1991); *TSN Official NBA Guide, 2004–2005* (St. Louis, MO, 2004).

Jack C. Braun

OKAFOR, Chukwuemeka Noubuisi "Emeka" (b. September 28, 1982, Houston, TX), college and professional player, is the son of Plus Okafor, a certified public accountant, and Celestina Okafor, a nurse, both Biafran immigrants, and graduated in 2001 from Bellaire High School in Houston, Texas. The six-foot nine-inch, 252-pound center averaged 22 points, 16 rebounds, and six blocked shots in basketball as senior, helping Bellaire finish 26-5. He was named MVP for victorious Team USA at the Pittsburgh Hoops Classic 2001 All-Star Game, posting 26 points, 12 rebounds, and 10 blocked shots.

Coach Jim Calhoun* recruited Okafor to play basketball at the University of Connecticut (BEaC). The extremely intelligent, hard-working, and focused Okafor resembled Bill Russell* with dominant rebounding and shot-blocking. In 2001–2002, he averaged 7.9 points, 9.0 rebounds, and 4.1 blocked shots with a .590 field goal percentage in 34 games. His 138 blocked shots led the BEaC and ranked third in the NCAA, while his rebound average stood second among NCAA freshmen. He averaged 8.8 points and 8.3 rebounds in the NCAA tournament. *TSN*, *BN*, and *BT* named him to the Freshman All-America First Team.

Okafor paced Connecticut to a 23-10 record in 2002–2003, averaging 15.9 points, 11.2 rebounds, and 4.7 blocked shots with a .580 field goal percentage. He ranked first in blocked shots and seventh in rebounding in the NCAA and led the BEaC in blocked shots, rebounds, and double-doubles (22). Okafor drove Connecticut to the Sweet Sixteen of the NCAA tournament, averaging 19.7 points, 13.3 rebounds, and 4.7 blocked shots. He made the Wooden Award All-America and Verizon Academic All-America First Teams, and was named NABC National Defensive and BEaC Defensive Player of the Year. He was selected to the All-BEaC First Team and paced Team USA in the Pan American Games with a 12.0 point average.

Okafor led 33-6 Connecticut to its second national championship in 2003–2004, averaging 17.6 points, 11.5 rebounds, and four blocked shots with a .599 field goal percentage. He ranked first nationally in blocked shots and double-doubles (23) and second in rebounding despite missing three games with back and arm injuries. Two quick fouls sidelined Okafor for the last 16 minutes of the first half of the NCAA semifinals, but he recorded 18 points, six of his seven rebounds, and both blocked shots in the second half to help the Huskies edge Duke University 79-78. He combined 24 points with 15 rebounds, as Connecticut defeated Georgia Institute of Technology 82-75 in the NCAA title game. Besides finishing runner-up to Jameer Nelson* for College Player of the Year, he was named consensus All America and Academic All-America of the Year and won an ESPY Award as the best male college athlete.

Okafor, who is single, tallied over 1,000 career points and rebounds in just three years. He earned a Bachelor's degree in Finance a year early in May 2003, boasting a 3.8 grade point average, and played on the 2004 bronze medal winning U.S. Olympic basketball team. The expansion Charlotte Bobcats (NBA) selected Okafor as the second overall pick in the first round of the June 2004 draft. Okafor led Charlotte in scoring with 1,105 points, rebounds with 795, and blocked shots with 125 in 73 games in 2004–2005. He was named NBA Rookie of the Year and made the All-NBA Rookie Team.

BIBLIOGRAPHY: Jack Carey, "UConn Wrecks Tech," *USA Today*, April 6, 2004, p. 1C; "Emeka Okafor," All Players Search, ESPN.com; Gene Garber, "It's True, Okafor's That Good," http:sports-att.espn.go.com, March 26, 2004; Andy Latack, "Double Major," *ESPN The Magazine* (February 17, 2004); Howard Richman, "UConn Star Emeka, Father Split Paths in KC," *Twin Cities Pioneer Press*, in http://www.twincities.com; http://usocpressbox.org/usoc/pressbox.nsf, April 1, 2004; *TSN Official NBA Register, 2004–2005* (St. Louis, MO, 2004).

David L. Porter

OLAJUWON, Hakeem Abdul "The Dream" (b. January 21, 1963, Lagos, Nigeria), college and professional player, made a most improbable journey to NBA stardom. His parents, Salaam Olajuwon and Abike Olajuwon, operated a profitable cement business in Lagos, Nigeria, and encouraged him to play sports, but basketball was regarded as a minor sport then. Consequently, Hakeem, whose name means "wise one" in Arabic, excelled at soccer, team handball, field hockey, and the high jump at the Moslem Teacher's College in Lagos. His introduction to competitive basketball came in 1978, when his college asked him to play in a basketball tournament.

In 1980, Olajuwon emigrated to Houston, Texas as an imported six-foot ten-inch Goliath from Nigeria. Twice he led coach Guy Lewis's* University of Houston basketball team to SWC championships, as the Cougars compiled an 88-16 record. A panel of media and coaches selected the catlike Olajuwon SWC Player of the Decade for the 1980s. Three times he led his Houston team to the NCAA Final Four as a member of the dunking "Phi Slamma Jamma." In 1983, Olajuwon came within one basket of helping the University of Houston win an NCAA national championship. He watched futilely, however, as North Carolina State University snatched victory on a miraculous, last-second shot.

During his collegiate career, Olajuwon collected 1,067 rebounds and 1,332 points for a 13.3 points average. In 1983–1984, he led the nation with a .675 percent field goal accuracy and a 13.5 rebounding average per game, only the third player in NCAA Division I history to lead the nation in at least two categories.

After Olajuwon completed his collegiate basketball apprenticeship, the Houston Rockets (NBA) bet their franchise on his continued improvement. Although the Rockets often produced disappointing results, Olajuwon performed extraordinarily and quickly won numerous awards. In 1985, he was selected for the NBA Rookie Team and finished runner-up to Michael Jordan* for Rookie of the Year. His other honors included being named NBA Defensive Player of the Year (1993, 1994), making the All-NBA First Team (1987–1989, 1993, 1994, 1997), All-NBA Second Team (1986, 1990, 1991), All-NBA Third Team (1991, 1995, 1999), and All-Defensive First Team (1987–1988, 1990, 1993, 1994), and earning Player of the Month four times and Player of the Week six times. Although given the IBM Award for overall statistical contributions to the Rockets in 1993, Olajuwon finished second that year to Charles Barkley* of the Phoenix Suns in the NBA's MVP voting. Olajuwon, the second center in NBA history with Kareem Abdul-Jabbar* selected All-NBA First Team and All-Defensive Team in the same season, became only the third player in NBA history to have 2,000 points, 1,000 rebounds, and 300 blocked shots in the same campaign, and the first player in NBA history to record at least 26,000 points, 13,000 rebounds, and 9,000 combined steals, assists, and blocks for a career.

During 18 NBA seasons, Olajuwon compiled 26,946 points (21.8 points average), 13,748 rebounds (11.1 average), 3,830 blocks, 3,058 assists, and 2,162 steals. He rewrote the Houston Rockets' record book as the team's career leader in points (26,511) rebounds (13,282), steals (2,088), blocked shots (3,040), and free throw attempts (7,537). Following the 1993–1994 season, Olajuwon was selected NBA MVP for the first time, named NBA Defensive Player of the

Year for the second consecutive year, and made the NBA All-Defensive First Team for the fifth time. No foreign-born player previously had garnered NBA MVP honors. Olajuwon also was named MVP of the 1994 NBA playoffs, helping the Houston Rockets win their first NBA title; the Rockets defeated the New York Knicks in the seven-game NBA Finals.

Olajuwon helped the Rockets win another NBA title in 1995, averaging 33.0 points in 22 playoff games as he again earned NBA Finals MVP honors. Olajuwon remained with Houston through the 2000–2001 season, helping the Rockets reach the Western Conference Finals in 1997. He averaged 25.9 points and 11.2 rebounds in 145 playoff games and scored 117 points and made 94 rebounds in 12 All-Star Games. Olajuwon was named to the NBA's 50th Anniversary All-Time Team in 1996 and played on the gold medal–winning U.S. Olympic team in 1996 (he became an American citizen in 1993). He was traded to the Toronto Raptors (NBA) in August 2001 and retired after the 2002–2003 season. Olajuwon holds the NBA career record for blocked shots (3,830) and led the NBA in rebounds and blocked shots twice. He married Delia Asafi in 2000 and has two children. Olajuwon concentrates on developing his overall condition off the court, especially after enduring problems with phlebitis, a shattered right eye socket, a rapid heartbeat, and a hamstring pull. His regimen includes practicing Islam, a strict diet, and quiet time at home. In his spare time, he operates an export sporting goods business to Nigeria. Olajuwon, who has gradually adjusted to life in the United States, speaks English, French, and four Nigerian dialects. Although he sees his five-year-old daughter, Abby, infrequently because she lives in Los Angeles, California, Olajuwon still finds family in south Texas. Three brothers and a nephew live nearby and join him for family meals, including an appetizing stew called *fufu* that Olajuwon makes himself.

BIBLIOGRAPHY: Morgan G. Brenner, *College Basketball's National Championships* (Lanham, MD, 1999); John Capouya, "Beers with Hakeem Olajuwon," *Sport* 79 (April 1988), pp. 21–23; Robert Falkoff, "MVP Talk Must Include Olajuwon," *Houston* (TX) *Post*, February 21, 1993, pp. B1–B2; Lianne Hart, "With 'Twin Towers' Ralph Sampson and Hakeem Olajuwon, Houston Rockets to the Top of the NBA," *People Weekly* 22 (December 17, 1984), pp. 144–146; Richard Hoffer, " 'H' as in Hot," *SI* 74 (April 8, 1991), pp. 54–59; *Houston Rockets Media Guide, 2000* (Houston, TX, 2000); Charles Leershen, "Rampaging Rookies," *Newsweek* 104 (November 26, 1984), pp. 121–122; Jackie MacMullan, "Dream Season," *Boston* (MA) *Globe*, January 12, 1994, pp. 49, 53; Jack McCallum, "Double Trouble, Houston Style," *SI* 61 (November 5, 1984), pp. 18–21; Jack McCallum, "A Dream Come True," *SI* 76 (March 22, 1993), pp. 16–21; *TSN Official NBA Register, 2004–2005* (St. Louis, MO, 2004); Michael Murphy, "End of Dream? From Raw Talent to Icon, Olajuwon Does It All Here," *Houston Chronicle*, March 14, 2001; Hakeem Olajuwon with Peter Khobler, *Living the Dream* (Boston, MA, 1996); Ken Shouler et al., *Total Basketball* (Wilmington, DE, 2003); Renee D. Turner, "The House Hakeem Olajuwon Helped Design," *Ebony* 47 (March 1991), pp. 46–48, 50.

Bruce J. Dierenfield

OLSEN, Harold G. (b. May 10, 1895, Rice Lake, WI; d. October 29, 1953, Evanston, IL), college and professional player and coach, graduated from Rice Lake (Wisconsin) High School in 1913 and excelled there in three sports. Olsen, a University of Wisconsin (WC) product from 1914 to 1917, played basketball under Walter E. "Doc" Meanwell* and also participated in football and baseball. The calm, mild-mannered athlete won three varsity basketball letters, captained the 1916–1917 Badgers team, and was named to the All-WC team for two years. Besides being WC Champions in two of his four seasons, Wisconsin generally was considered the nation's number one team in 1916. After graduation, Olsen enlisted in the U.S. Army Air Force and was discharged as a second lieutenant. He accepted his first basketball coaching assignment at Bradley University (Illinois) in 1919 and coached at Ripon (Wisconsin) College from 1920 to 1922. Olsen became head basketball coach at Ohio State University in 1923 and held that post through 1946. His 259-197 Ohio State record included five WC championships (1925, 1933, 1939, 1944, 1945). He compiled a 306-234 overall collegiate record.

Olsen, one of basketball's outstanding figures and most progressive leaders, helped initiate the

NCAA postseason national playoffs. Under his guidance, the tournament grew from a small start in 1939 to one of the nation's greatest promotions. Olsen's team participated in the first NCAA Tournament at Evanston, Illinois, losing in the championship game to the University of Oregon. The Buckeyes appeared in the 1944, 1945, and 1946 NCAA Tournaments, losing in the semifinals each time. They defeated the University of California-Berkeley in 1946 for a third place finish. A prominent basketball administrator for nearly 31 years, Olsen served as president of the NABC (1933), chaired the NCAA basketball playoff committee eight years, chaired the CBRC, and participated on the 1948 USOC. He helped initiate the 10-second rule, which forced a team to bring the ball across midcourt within that time. In 1945 NABC awarded him its annual trophy for contributing "the most outstanding service to the game over a period of years."

Olsen resigned the Ohio State University position in 1946 to coach the newly organized Chicago Stags in the pro BAA. During his three-year tenure with the Stags, Chicago compiled a 113-76 record. Chicago won the Western Division of the BAA in 1947, but lost the championship series to the Philadelphia Warriors. When the BAA disbanded, Olsen became head basketball coach at Northwestern University (Illinois). His Wildcats teams won 19 of 44 games between 1950 and 1952 before ill health forced his retirement. He and his wife, who died in 1952, had one daughter. Olsen, a member of the HAF Hall of Fame, was elected as a contributor to the Naismith Memorial Basketball Hall of Fame in 1959.

BIBLIOGRAPHY: Peter C. Bjarkman, *Big Ten Basketball* (Indianapolis, IN, 1994); Peter C. Bjarkman, *Hoopla! A Century of College Basketball* (Indianapolis, IN, 1996); *Chicago Daily Tribune*, October 30, 1953, Part 4, p. 1; Mike Douchant, *Encyclopedia of College Basketball* (Detroit, MI, 1995); Joe Gergen, *The Final Four* (St. Louis, MO, 1987); Neil D. Isaacs, *Vintage NBA* (Silver Spring, MD, 1996); Don Kopriva et al., *On Wisconsin* (Champaign, IL, 2001); Ronald L. Mendell, *Who's Who in Basketball* (New Rochelle, NY, 1973); *NCAA Men's Basketball Records, 2004* (Indianapolis, IN, 2003); Harold Olsen file, Naismith Memorial Basketball Hall of Fame, Springfield, MA; Jim Savage, ed., *The Encyclopedia of the NCAA Basketball Tournament* (New York, 1990); Ken Shouler et al., *Total Basketball* (Wilmington, DE, 2003).

John L. Evers

OLSON, Robert Luther "Lute" (b. September 22, 1934, Mayville, ND), college athlete and coach, is the son of Albert W. Olson, a farmer, and Alinda E. (Halvorson) Olson and spent three years at Mayville (North Dakota) High School, where he participated in football, basketball, baseball, and track and field. Olson graduated from Grand Forks (North Dakota) Central High School, playing football and basketball. Grand Forks did not field a baseball team, but he played American Legion baseball.

At Augsburg College (MCC) in Minneapolis, Minnesota, Olson competed in three major sports and earned four letters each in football and basketball. His honors included being an All-MCC end in football, gridiron co-captain as a senior, and an All-MCC forward in basketball. In baseball, the six-foot two-inch, 200-pound right-hander pitched and played first base. He graduated from Augsburg with a Bachelor's degree in history and physical education in 1956 and later earned a Master's degree from Chapman College in Orange, California.

Olson began coaching basketball at Mahnomen (Minnesota) High School in 1957. His other scholastic head coaching assignments included Two Harbors (Minnesota) High School from 1958 to 1961, Western High School in 1963, and Loara High School in 1964, the latter two located in Anaheim, California. Long Beach (California) City College appointed Olson head basketball coach from 1970 to 1973, as he amassed 104 victories, only 20 losses, and three MC titles. His 1971 team captured the California JC Championship, with Olson earning MC Coach of the Year in three consecutive seasons.

In 1974 Olson moved to Long Beach State College (PCAC), where his team achieved 24 victories in 26 contests. For nine seasons, he coached at the University of Iowa (BTC). The Hawkeyes finished with 19 wins and 10 losses in 1976–1977 and 20 victories and seven setbacks in 1977–1978. His last five Iowa seasons featured five consecutive 20-victory seasons and trips to the NCAA regionals, and an NCAA 1980 Final Four appearance. His nine Iowa seasons produced 167 victories, 91 losses, two BTC Coach of the Year awards, and 1980 National Coach of the Year honors.

Olson has coached the University of Arizona basketball program since 1984, boasting 549 wins and 164 losses in 22 years. The Wildcats had won only one PTC game in 1983. After finishing with 11 victories and 17 losses in Olson's first season, Arizona captured an NCAA title in 1999, reached the NCAA Finals in 2001, lost in the NCAA semifinals in 1988 and 1994, and won 10 PTC Championships. Consecutive PTC titles were won in 1988–1991. In Olson's 22 seasons at Arizona, his teams have averaged around 25 victories per season. Under him, Arizona boasted the nation's longest home-court winning streak. Olson, who has been named PTC Coach of the Year several times, has compiled 741 victories and 256 losses in 32 seasons for a .743 winning percentage through 2004. He has compiled a 45-26 record in NCAA tournament play, and has guided Arizona to the NCAA playoffs since 1988.

Olson married Roberta Rae Russell on November 27, 1953 and has three daughters, Vicki, Jodi, and Christi, and two sons, Greg and Steve. He participates in many civic activities, including the Salvation Army holiday fund drive, United Way, Easter Seals, leukemia fund raising, and Special Olympics, and has raised $340,000 for an arthritis center.

Olson especially treasures coaching the 1986 U.S. basketball team to a World Championship and a victory over the U.S.S.R. Other highlights remain Iowa's 1980 Eastern Regional win over Georgetown University, leading to the NCAA Final Four, Arizona's 1988 triumph over the University of North Carolina, leading to another Final Four appearance, the Wildcats' 84-79 overtime victory over the University of Kentucky for the 1997 NCAA championship, and Arizona reaching the NCAA Finals in 2001. He was elected to the Naismith Memorial Basketball Hall of Fame in 2002.

BIBLIOGRAPHY: Mike Douchant, *Encyclopedia of College Basketball* (Detroit, MI, 1995); Mike Finn et al., *Hawkeye Legends, Lists, and Lore* (Champaign, IL, 1998); *NCAA Men's Basketball Records, 2004* (Indianapolis, IN, 2003); Lute Olson to Stan W. Carlson, February 1990; Lute Olson file, Naismith Memorial Basketball Hall of Fame, Springfield, MA; Ken Shouler et al., *Total Basketball* (Wilmington, DE, 2003); *TSN College Basketball 2004–2005*; *University of Arizona 2004 Basketball Media Guide* (Tucson, AZ, 2003).

Stan W. Carlson

O'NEAL, Jermaine (b. October 13, 1978, Columbia, SC), professional player, was reared, given financial assistance, motivated, and encouraged by his mother, Angela Ocean, and his high school basketball coach, George Glymph. He graduated from Eau Claire High School in Columbia, South Carolina in 1996. O'Neal led the Shamrocks to a four-year, 97-16 win-loss record and to three AAA state championships and runner-up the remaining year. He recorded 1,372 career points and pulled down 833 rebounds. The six-foot eleven-inch, 230-pound O'Neal eclipsed the school records for blocked shots with 16 in one game, 170 in a season, and 397 in his career. Following his senior season, he was named Player of the Year and Mr. Basketball in South Carolina and was selected to *USA Today's* All-USA First Team and to the AP All-State First Team. O'Neal played in the McDonald's All-America Game and the Hoops Summit Game. On February 5, 2003, Eau Claire High School retired his jersey as the first ever by his school.

O'Neal was selected out of high school by the Portland Trail Blazers (NBA) in the first round as the 17th pick overall of the 1996 NBA draft. On December 5 of his rookie season, he became the youngest player to start in a NBA game. O'Neal played for the Trail Blazers from 1996–1997 through 1999–2000 and was traded with Joe Kleine to the Indiana Pacers (NBA) for Dale Davis. He averaged 3.1 points and 3.1 rebounds in 211 games for the Blazers. Since joining the Pacers, nearly all his statistical categories have improved dramatically. From 2000–2001 through 2003–2004, O'Neal has scored at least 1,000 points each season and averaged 193 blocked shots and 781 rebounds per season. In 2002–2003, he scored a career high 1,600 points, averaged 20.8 points, and snagged 21 rebounds against the Washington Wizards and blocked 10 shots against the Toronto Raptors, both career highs. Indiana led the NBA with a 61-21 record in 2003–2004, as O'Neal averaged 20.1 points and 10.0 rebounds. He helped the Pacers reach the Eastern Conference Finals before losing to the Detroit Pistons. Commissioner David Stern* suspended O'Neal 25 games for his involvement in a melee that occurred on and off the court among players and fans during a game between Indiana and the Detroit Pistons on November 19, 2004 at The Palace in Auburn Hills, Michigan. O'Neal averaged 24.3 points, and 8.8 rebounds in 44 games in 2004–2005, helping Indiana to the playoffs.

In seven NBA seasons from 1996–1997 through 2004–2005, O'Neal has averaged 13.3 points, 7.4 rebounds, and 1.79 blocked shots in 563 regular-season games. In 57 postseason games, he recorded 595 points, 365 rebounds, and 81 blocked shots. He has appeared in four NBA All-Star Games and started the 2002–2003 classic.

O'Neal earned the 2002 NBA Most Improved Player Award, made the All NBA Third Team in 2002 and 2003, and All-NBA Second Team in 2004. He was selected for the 2001 Goodwill Games participation, the 2002 U.S. World Championship team, the 2003 U.S. Senior National Team, and the 2004 U.S. Olympic team, which won a bronze medal.

BIBLIOGRAPHY: "Jermaine O'Neal," *Background and Personal*, http://www.nba.com (2003); "Jermaine O'Neal," *Bio*, http://www.usabasketball.com (2003); "Jermaine O'Neal," *Career Highlights*, http://www.nba.com (2003); "Jermaine O'Neal," *Player*, http://www.usbasket.com (2003); "Jermaine O'Neal," *Player Info*, http://www.nba.com (2003); Ken Shouler et al., *Total Basketball* (Wilmington, DE, 2003); *TSN Official NBA Register, 2004–2005* (St. Louis, MO, 2004).

John L. Evers

O'NEAL, Shaquille Rashaun "Shaq" (b. March 6, 1972, Newark, NJ), college and professional player, is the son of Philip Harrison, a U.S. Army sergeant, and Lucille O'Neal, and was born two years before his parents married. O'Neal, whose first name means "little warrior," attended grade schools in Newark, New Jersey, and on military bases in Bayonne, New Jersey, Eatontown, New Jersey, Fort Stewart, Georgia, and Germany. His first exposure to basketball came in Germany. O'Neal graduated in 1989 from Cole High School in San Antonio, Texas, where he averaged 30 points, 22 rebounds, and six assists as a senior. In one game alone, he scored 27 points, grabbed 36 rebounds, and blocked 26 shots.

LSU (SEC) coach Dale Brown won the recruiting battle for the seven-foot one-inch, 301-pound O'Neal's services. In 1989–1990, O'Neal gave the 23-9 Tigers a powerful inside game, while All-America guard Chris Jackson connected well from the outside. As a freshman, O'Neal scored 445 points (13.9 points average), ranked sixth nationally with 115 blocked shots (3.6 average), and placed ninth with 385 rebounds (12.0 rebounds average). LSU shared second place in the SEC and made the second round of the NCAA tournament. In 1990–1991, O'Neal earned AP and UPI Player of the Year honors, made consensus All-America, and gave the Tigers a powerful inside game and share of the SEC title. He led the nation with 411 rebounds (14.7 per game), ranked third with 140 blocked shots (five per game), and placed seventh with 774 points (27.6 average). The 20-10 Tigers lacked an outside game, however, and were eliminated in the first round of the NCAA tournament. In 1991–1992, LSU compiled a 21-10 record, placed second in the SEC, and reached the second round of the NCAA tournament. O'Neal repeated as an All-America, pacing the nation with 157 blocked shots (5.2 per game), ranking second with 421 rebounds (14.0 average), and scoring 722 points (24.1 points average). David Robinson* of the U.S. Naval Academy (Maryland) recorded the only higher season blocked-shot figure in NCAA history. During his three-year LSU career, O'Neal scored 1,941 points (21.6 points average), converted 61 percent of his field goals, made 1,217 rebounds (13.5 average), and blocked 412 shots (4.6 average) in 90 games. He ranks second to Robinson in NCAA career blocked-shots average and fifth in career rebound average. He graduated from LSU in December 2000.

In 1992, the Orlando Magic (NBA) made O'Neal the first player selected in the draft. O'Neal paid immediate dividends for Orlando, garnering NBA Rookie of the Year and NBA All-Rookie First Team honors. In 1992–1993, he ranked eighth in scoring with 1,893 points (23.4 average), fourth in field goal percentage

(56.2 percent), and second in rebounds with 1,122 (13.9 average) and blocked shots with 286 (3.53 per game) in 81 games. Orlando finished with a 41-41 record, fourth in the Atlantic Division. O'Neal scored a season-high 46 points against the Detroit Pistons on February 16 and destroyed the entire hydraulic basket support system in a nationally televised game on February 7 against the Phoenix Suns. He dunked a follow shot with such force that the basket collapsed, delaying the game 35 minutes. David Robinson of the San Antonio Spurs edged O'Neal for the 1993–1994 NBA scoring title by tallying 71 points on the final night. For that season, O'Neal notched 2,377 points (29.3 points average), led the NBA in field goal percentage (59.9 percent), placed second in rebounds with 1,072 (17.3 average), and sixth in blocked shots with 231 (2.9 average). He established NBA season highs with 15 blocked shots against the New Jersey Nets on November 20, and 14 offensive rebounds against the Boston Celtics on February 15. Orlando finished second in the Atlantic Division and made the NBA playoffs for the first time in 1993–1994, boasting a 50-32 record. In 1994–1995, O'Neal led the NBA in scoring with 2,315 points (29.3 point average) to help Orlando capture the Atlantic Division with a 57-25 record and reach the NBA Finals. The Houston Rockets swept the Magic in the NBA Finals. O'Neal left Orlando after the 1995–1996 season, signing with the Los Angeles Lakers (NBA). He still holds the Magic career records for rebounds (3,691) and blocked shots (824). In 1996, O'Neal was named to the NBA 50th Anniversary All-Time Team in 1996.

O'Neal enjoyed phenomenal success with the Lakers from 1996 to 2004. He led the NBA in scoring with 1,289 points (26.3 points average) in 1998–1999 and with 2,344 points (a career high 29.7 points average) in 1999–2000; in free throws made with 432 in 1999–2000; in field goals made with 510 in 1998–1999, 956 in 1999–2000, and 813 in 2000–2001; and field goal percentage with .584 in 1997–1998, .576 in 1998–1999, .574 in 1999–2000, .592 in 2000–2001, .579 in 2001–2002, and .584 in 2003–2004. O'Neal helped the Lakers capture three consecutive championships from 2000 to 2002, being NBA Finals MVP in 2000 against the Indiana Pacers and in 2001 against the Philadelphia 76ers, and setting NBA Finals records for most points (145) and free throws made (45) against the New Jersey Nets in 2002. He led Los Angeles to the NBA Finals in 2004 before the Detroit Pistons upset the Lakers four games to one. He led Los Angeles in rebounds (13.2 average) and blocked shots (2.8 average) in the playoffs, and tallied 36 points and 20 rebounds in the Game 4 loss in the NBA Finals. He holds or shares several NBA single game playoff records.

In July 2004, the Miami Heat (NBA) acquired him in a trade. O'Neal helped Miami win the Eastern Conference in 2004–2005, tallying 1,669 points (22.9 average) and 760 rebounds (10.4 average) in 93 games. He finished second in the NBA MVP balloting. He averaged 19.4 points and 7.8 rebounds in 13 playoff games, with the Detroit Pistons eliminating the Heat in the Eastern Conference Finals.

O'Neal has gathered numerous NBA honors. He was named NBA MVP in 2000, leading the NBA in scoring, field goals made, and free throws made, helping Los Angeles take the Western Division with an NBA-best 67-15 record. O'Neal made the All-NBA First Team in 1998 and 2000–2005; the All-NBA Second Team in 1995 and 1999, and the All-NBA Third Team in 1994, 1996, and 1997. He was selected to the NBA All-Defensive Second Team in 2000, 2001, and 2003 and won the IBM Award in 2000 and 2001. O'Neal has played in nine All-Star Games (1993–1996, 1998, 2000, 2003, 2004, 2005), scoring 158 points, being Co-MVP of the 2000 game and MVP of the 2004 game.

Through the 2004–2005 season, O'Neal has compiled 23,583 points (26.7 points average), 10,541 rebounds (12.0 average), and 2,273 blocked shots (2.6 average) in 882 regular-season contests. He posted a career high 61 points against the Los Angeles Clippers on March 6, 2000 and collected a career best 28 rebounds and 15 blocked shots against the New Jersey Nets on November 20, 1993. In 171 NBA playoff games, he has averaged 26.6 points, 12.6 rebounds, and 2.25 blocked shots. O'Neal starred on Dream Team II, which won the gold medal in the 1994 World Championship of Basketball in Toronto, Canada and the gold medal–winning U.S. Olympic team at the Atlanta, Georgia Games in 1996.

O'Neal, who wears a size 20 shoe, possesses enormous crowd appeal as one the NBA's marquee players since the retirement of Michael Jordan*. He has negotiated millions in endorsement deals, including his own signature ball, a record label, his own line of clothing, a basketball shoe, and a toy action figure. He co-authored *Shaq Attaq!* with Jack McCallum in 1993, and *Shaq Talks Back* in 2001. He starred in the movies *Kaazam* and *Steel*, appeared in *Freddy Got Fingered*, *Good Burger*, and *Blue Chips*. He has released five rap albums: *Shaq Diesel*, *Shaq Fu: Da Return*, *You Can't Stop the Reign*, *Respect*, and a greatest hits album. He married Shaunie Nelson in December 2002. They have three children. O'Neal has another child from a previous marriage.

BIBLIOGRAPHY: *ESPN Sports Almanac 2005* (New York, 2004); Jan Hubbard, ed., *The Official NBA Encyclopedia*, 3rd ed. (New York, 2000); Shaquille O'Neal, "The Real Shaquille," *USA Weekend* (October 1–3, 1993), pp. 6–8; Shaquille O'Neal, *Shaq Talks Back* (New York, 2001); Shaquille O'Neal and Jack McCallum, *Shaq Attaq!* (New York, 1993); Ken Shouler et al., *Total Basketball* (Wilmington, DE, 2003); *TSN College Basketball Yearbook*, 1990–1993; *TSN Official NBA Guide, 2004–2005* (St. Louis, MO, 2004); *TSN Official NBA Register, 2004–2005* (St. Louis, MO, 2004); *Street and Smith College and Prep Basketball Yearbook*, 1989–1993; *USA Today*, February 18, 1993, pp. A1–A2.

David L. Porter

P

PAGE, Harlan Orville "Pat" (b. March 20, 1887, Chicago, IL; d. November 23, 1965, Chicago, IL), college athlete and coach, was one of the most distinguished players and coaches produced by the University of Chicago during the first four decades of the college roundball game. An honors graduate of Chicago's Lewis Institute in 1906 and the University of Chicago in 1910, Page led his high school team to a Midwest school championship season in 1906. The fabulous four-sport star at the University of Chicago excelled as a stellar defensive player and accurate-shooting left-handed guard. Page, particularly adept as a skilled baseball pitcher and talented basketball sharpshooter, performed for football coach Amos Alonzo Stagg as an end and effective southpaw passer.

Page declined a dozen pro baseball offers to sign as a pitching prospect. His Chicago teams subsequently won WC basketball titles in 1907, 1909, and 1910, and a National AAU title in 1907. This four-year glory period in University of Chicago basketball was highlighted, however, by an exciting two-game series sweep over the University of Pennsylvania for the national college championship in 1908 and by an undefeated season in 1908–1909.

The 1907–1910 University of Chicago teams marked the true beginnings of Midwest basketball glory and were the proud forerunners of BTC basketball tradition. Those teams were built by Joseph E. Raycroft, perhaps the most outstanding coach of the pre-war era, and were led on court by powerful John Schommer*, later inventor of the modern basketball backboard, and outstanding shooter Page. In the championship series with the University of Pennsylvania, Chicago eked out an initial 21-18 victory on four field goals by Schommer. Page's final clutch basket actually was shot from under his legs when he was about to be tied up. Schommer's mobility and Page's quickness allowed Raycroft-coached teams to nullify the existing strategies of one basket-hanger and three moving men and to introduce for the first time a five-man running team concept of basketball. In 1910, Page was voted College Player of the Year for his on-court performance. The diminutive five-foot nine-inch, 160-pounder was indisputably the best all-around player in the early decades of Chicago college basketball.

Page's playing skills and achievements, however, were not the full extent of his impact on the growing sport of college basketball. He launched an illustrious coaching career at his alma mater (1911–1920) and later coached at Butler University (Indiana; 1921–1925, 1930–1933), Indiana University (1925–1930), and the College of Idaho (1937–1939). His coaching achievements included a National AAU basketball title in 1924 at Butler and a career record of 200 wins and 127 losses. Ironically, Page's most lasting impact on the basketball and athletic programs at Butler University was his decision to hire former University of Chicago star player Tony Hinkle* as Butler's assistant coach. Hinkle's own coaching career at the small Indianapolis school spanned nearly five full decades (1921–1970) and earned him a Naismith Memorial Basketball Hall of Fame niche in 1965 alongside his famous mentor. After his college basketball coaching career, Page served for several years as a veteran batting practice pitcher with both the Chicago Cubs (NL) and Chicago White Sox (AL). Page ranked among the college roundball game's greatest early shooting guards, a distinction that ultimately earned him a Naismith Memorial Basketball Hall of Fame election as collegiate player in 1962.

BIBLIOGRAPHY: Peter C. Bjarkman, *Big Ten Basketball* (Indianapolis, IN, 1994); Zander Hollander, ed., *The Modern Encyclopedia of Basketball* (Garden City, NY, 1979); Neil D. Isaacs, *All the Moves: A History of College Basketball* (Philadelphia, PA, 1975); Ronald L. Mendell, *Who's Who in Basketball* (New Rochelle, NY, 1973); William G. Mokray, ed., *Ronald Encyclopedia of Basketball* (New York, 1963); Harlan Page file, Naismith Memorial Basketball Hall of Fame, Springfield, MA.

Peter C. Bjarkman

PARISH, Robert Lee "Chief" (b. August 30, 1953, Shreveport, LA), college and professional player and coach, attended Woodlawn High School in Shreveport, Louisiana, where he played four years of prep basketball. Parish enrolled at Centenary College (Louisiana), being named to the *TSN* All-America First Team in 1976 and participating for the gold-medal winners in the 1975 World University games. In four years at Centenary, he averaged 21.6 points in 108 collegiate games. The seven-foot ½-inch, 230-pound hoopster scored 50 points against the University of Southern Mississippi and once grabbed 33 rebounds in a game.

The Golden State Warriors (NBA) selected Parish in the first round of the 1976 draft as the eighth pick overall. He played his first four NBA seasons in Oakland and in June 1980 was involved in a blockbuster trade. Golden State sent him to the Boston Celtics (NBA) along with first-round pick Kevin McHale*. With the sudden retirement of Dave Cowens*, Parish became the Boston starting center. Parish, who appeared in nine All-Star Games (1981–1987, 1990–1991), finished runner-up to Larry Bird* in the 1982 All-Star MVP balloting. The durable Parish produced a streak of 116 straight playoff appearances and played in 99 of 100 games in the 1985–1986 season.

For seven NBA seasons from 1985–1986 through 1991–1992, Parish placed among the NBA's top 10 in field goal accuracy each year. He scored the 10,000th point of his career on February 26, 1984 against the Phoenix Suns and grabbed his 10,000th rebound on February 22, 1989 against the Philadelphia 76ers.

The 1991–1992 season saw Parish setting many NBA milestones. In his sixteenth NBA season, Parish tallied his 20,000th point on January 17, 1992 against Philadelphia. An exceptionally conditioned athlete, he missed few games in his long professional career. Parish played from 1994 to 1996 with Charlotte and ended his NBA career with the Chicago Bulls (NBA) in 1996–1997. The often underrated, very steady performer was overshadowed by teammates Bird and McHale. He remains the Celtics all-time blocked shot leader with 1,703. Upon his retirement the oldest NBA player, notched 23,334 career points (14.5 points average) and 14,715 rebounds (9.1 average) in 21 NBA Seasons. Parish and Kareem Abdul-Jabbar* were the first to compile NBA career marks of 23,000 points, 14,000 rebounds, 2,200 blocks, and 1,500 games.

Parish and his wife, Nancy, have one son, Justin. Parish resides in the Boston, Massachusetts area, where his recreational pleasures include judo, racquetball, backgammon, jazz music, boxing, reading, and horror films. He lists Boston's 1981 NBA championship over the Houston Rockets as his most memorable basketball experience. Parish was named one of the 50 Greatest Players in NBA History in 1996 and coached the Maryland Mustangs (USBL) to a 19-11 record and a first-place finish in 2000–2001, being named USBL Coach of the Year. He was elected to the Naismith Memorial Basketball Hall of Fame in 2003.

BIBLIOGRAPHY: Peter C. Bjarkman, *The Boston Celtics Encyclopedia* (Champaign, IL, 1998); *Boston Celtics Pre-Season Media Guide, 1993* (Boston, MA, 1993); *Complete Handbook of Pro Basketball* (New York, 1993); Jan Hubbard, ed., *Official NBA Basketball Encyclopedia*, 3rd ed. (New York, 2000); Robert Parish file, Naismith Memorial Basketball Hall of Fame, Springfield, MA; Roland Lazenby, *The NBA Finals* (Indianapolis, IN, 1996); Robert Parish, letter to Stan W. Carlson, December 1992; Ken Shouler et al., *Total Basketball* (Wilmington DE, 2003); *TSN Official NBA Register, 2004–2005* (St. Louis, MO, 2004).

Stan W. Carlson

PAYTON, Gary Dwayne "The Glove" (b. July 23, 1968, Oakland, CA), college and professional player, is one of four children born to Al Payton, a restaurant owner, and Annie Payton. Payton grew up in the Oakland, California projects and established an early reputation for "trash talking" on the basketball court. Although starring in basketball at Skyline High School in Oakland, he struggled academically to maintain his eligibility. The stern intervention of his father is credited for getting Payton back on track, and he received a basketball scholarship to Oregon State University.

Payton thrived under coach Ralph Miller*, starting every game during his four-year tenure at Oregon State from 1986 to 1990. During his senior year, he averaged 25.7 points, earned All-America honors, and was selected by *SI* as College Player of the Year. He left Oregon State as the Beavers' all-time leading scorer with 2,972 points in 120 games.

The six-foot four-inch, 180-pound point guard was selected by the Seattle SuperSonics (NBA) with the second pick in the 1990 NBA draft. During the 1990–1991 season, Payton led NBA rookies in steals (165) and assists (528), while averaging 7.2 points. He struggled under the offensive system of Seattle coach K.C. Jones* and welcomed the hiring of George Karl* in January 1992. Under the guidance of Karl and assistant coach Tim Grgurich, Payton became an All-Star during the 1993–1994 season and averaged 16.5 points and 6.0 assists. The SuperSonics carried the best winning percentage in the NBA, but were ousted by the Denver Nuggets in the first round of the playoffs.

After another early playoff exit in 1995, Payton and the SuperSonics enjoyed an outstanding 1995–1996 campaign. Nicknamed "The Glove," he was named the NBA's Defensive Player of the Year, averaging 2.85 steals, 19.3 points, and 7.5 assists. With Payton as their leader, Seattle reached the NBA Finals before bowing to Michael Jordan* and the Chicago Bulls. He finished 1996 by playing for the gold medal–winning U.S. Olympic basketball team.

Payton continued to excel for the SuperSonics, but Seattle failed to reach the NBA Finals again. In January 2003, the nine-time All-Star was reunited with Karl after being traded to the Milwaukee Bucks (NBA) for Ray Allen*. In July 2003, the Los Angeles Lakers (NBA) signed him as a free agent. He helped Los Angeles win the Pacific Division in 2003–2004, but the Detroit Pistons upset the Lakers four games to one in the NBA Finals. The Boston Celtics (NBA) acquired him in August 2004. His veteran leadership helped the Celtics reach the playoffs in 2004–2005. He averaged 10.3 points and 4.6 assists in seven games in the first round playoff loss to the Indiana Pacers. Through the 2004–2005 season, Payton averaged 4.7 rebounds, 7.2 assists, and 17.6 points in 1,186 regular-season games. In 129 playoff games, he has averaged 15.7 points, 6.0 assists, and 1.5 steals. He was selected to the All-NBA First Team in 1998 and 2000, the All-NBA Second Team in 1995–1997, 1999, and 2002; and the All-NBA Third Team in 1994 and 2001.

Known for his civic commitment, Payton established a foundation for underprivileged children in 1996. Payton and his wife, Monique, have three children.

BIBLIOGRAPHY: Howard Blatt, *Gary Payton* (New York, 1998); Dan Dieffenbach, "Pressure Point," *Sport* 86 (January 1995), pp. 94–96; Judith J. Mandell, *Super Sports Star Gary Payton* (New York, 2001); Michael A. Pare, *Sports Stars Series* (Detroit, MI, 1997); Ken Shouler et al., *Total Basketball* (Wilmington, DE, 2003); Phil Taylor, "Talk Show," *SI* 84 (May 13, 1996), pp. 38–40.

Ron Briley

PETTIT, Robert Lee, Jr. "Bob" (b. December 12, 1932, Baton Rouge, LA), college and professional player, was named the 1956 and 1959 NBA MVP as a member of the St. Louis Hawks (NBA). The six-foot nine-inch, 215-pound forward was elected in 1970 to the Naismith Memorial Basketball Hall of Fame and the NBA's 25th Anniversary All-Time Team, and was chosen in 1980 to the NBA's 35th Anniversary Team. He was named one of the 50 Greatest Players in NBA history in 1996. Pettit made All-NBA First Team his first 10 years (1954–1955 to 1963–1964) and All-NBA Second Team his final season (1964–1965). He retired as the then-highest scorer in NBA history with 20,880 points for a 26.4 points average and the third highest rebounder with 12,849 rebounds for

16.2 rebounds per game. Pettit was named NBA Rookie of the Year in 1955 and played on the 1958 St. Louis NBA championship team. He ranked among the NBA's top five scorers and rebounders every year except his final season when, plagued by injuries, he fell to seventh. Pettit led the NBA in scoring in 1955–1956 (25.7 points average) and 1958–1959 (29.2 points average), and in rebounding in 1955–1956 (16.2 rebounds average). He averaged 20.4 points in 11 NBA All-Star Games and was voted the game's MVP in 1956, 1958, 1959, and 1962.

Pettit's six-foot six-inch father, Robert Sr., was employed as a county sheriff in Louisiana. His mother, Margaret worked as realtor. As a freshman at Baton Rouge (Louisiana) High School, Pettit was cut from the basketball and baseball squads, and gave up football after the first scrimmage when a ball carrier ran through his position at right tackle for a 65-yard touchdown. After being cut again from the basketball squad the next year, Pettit was encouraged by his father to practice on the backyard hoop and engage in church-league basketball. He made the high school starting five as a junior, but did not show signs of stardom until his senior year, when he led Baton Rouge High School to its first state championship in over 20 years. Pettit in 1950 was named First Team All-State center and graduated from high school that spring.

Pettit received several college basketball scholarship offers, attending LSU in his home town. In three varsity seasons (1951–1952 to 1953–1954), he made All-SEC center three times and All-America twice and paced Tigers teams to a composite 62-15 record. His 27.4 career point average ranked second among NCAA all-time scorers. LSU won the SEC title in 1952–1953, but lost to ultimate champion Indiana University 80-67 in the NCAA tournament semifinals. The Tigers in 1954 finished undefeated in the SEC and tied with the University of Kentucky before losing 63-56 to the Wildcats in the playoff. After Kentucky declined the automatic NCAA tournament bid, LSU accepted the invitation and lost 78-70 to Pennsylvania State University in the second round. Pettit engaged in two years of postseason play, averaging 30.5 points in six NCAA tournament games. He graduated from LSU in 1954.

Pettit, although regarded too light to succeed in the NBA, was drafted by the Milwaukee Hawks (NBA) in the first round of the 1954 pro draft. The downtrodden Hawks had finished in last place with a 21-51 mark in the Western Division the previous year, and improved little to 29-46 in his initial season. Despite playing much of his third year with a cast protecting a broken wrist, he led the then St. Louis Hawks to their first NBA playoff championship series before losing to the Boston Celtics in seven games. In five seasons (1956–1957 to 1960–1961), St. Louis played in four championship series against Boston and won the NBA title in 1957–1958. Pettit scored 50 points in the sixth and final game of the 1958 series, including the winning basket in the Hawks' 110-109 triumph. St. Louis in 1961–1962 fell to a 29-51 record and fourth-place finish in the Western Division, although Pettit compiled the highest scoring (31.1 points) and second highest rebounding (18.7) averages of his career and earned his last NBA MVP award. The Hawks placed second in the Western Division during his last three seasons. Despite missing 30 games in 1965 because of injuries, he still managed a 22.5 points scoring average and 12.4 rebounds per game.

The superstar Pettit was lean, graceful, superbly conditioned, dedicated, and always a gentleman on and off the court. He adapted quickly his first season in the NBA to playing a forward position, having performed his entire career at center. Pettit possessed an excellent jumpshot and combined toughness with finesse. Former St. Louis teammate and coach Ed Macauley* praised him by stating: "He is a miracle of consistent class. What you notice about him is that he's fast, he makes every move count, he's smart, he has a wonderful touch with the ball." Former NBA superstar and occasional adversary Bill Russell* observed, "Bob made 'second effort' a part of the sports vocabulary. He kept coming at you more than any man in the game. He was always battling for position, fighting you off the boards."

After the 1965 season, Pettit realized that the spring was going from his legs and that his future performances would be downhill and consequently retired while still at the peak of his career. He owns a Prudential Securities insurance business, maintains interests in a home development business, and enjoys water skiing and country music. The New Orleans resident married Carol Crowell in June 1965 and has three children.

BIBLIOGRAPHY: *CB* (1961), pp. 361–362; Jan Hubbard ed., *The Official NBA Encyclopedia,* 3rd ed. (New York, 2000); Neil D. Isaacs, *Vintage NBA* (Silver Spring, MD, 1996); *The Lincoln Library of Sports Champions,* vol. 10 (Columbus, OH, 1974); Sandy Padwe, *Basketball's Hall of Fame* (New York, 1973); Bob Pettit and Bob Wolff, *Bob Pettit: The Drive Within Me* (New York, 1966); Robert Pettit file, Naismith Memorial Basketball Hall of Fame, Springfield, MA; Ken Shouler et al., *Total Basketball* (Wilmington, DE, 2003); *TSN Official NBA Register, 2004–2005* (St. Louis, MO, 2004).

James D. Whalen

PHELAN, James J. "Jim" (b. March 19, 1929, Philadelphia, PA), college and professional player and coach, grew up in Philadelphia, Pennsylvania and ranked among the top basketball players in the city. He graduated in 1947 from LaSalle College High School in Philadelphia, being an All-Catholic performer in basketball in 1946 and 1947 and All-City in 1947. Phelan graduated from LaSalle College in 1951 with a Bachelor's degree in business. He made the All-Philadelphia team in basketball in 1949, 1950, and 1951 and was selected Honorable Mention All-America in 1951. He captained the 1951 Explorer squad that played in the NIT; and was inducted into the LaSalle Hall of Athletes in 1964.

Phelan served in the U.S. Marine Corps from 1951 to 1953, including duty in Korea. He played basketball for the Quantico Marines, being their MVP in 1952 and making the All-Armed Forces team in 1952 and the All-Marine team in 1952 and 1953. He was selected as an eighth round pick in the 1951 NBA draft and played briefly for the Philadelphia Warriors (NBA) and the Pottstown (Pennsylvania) Packers (EL) in 1953–1954.

Phelan began his coaching career as an assistant basketball coach at his alma mater in 1953. He assisted Ken Loeffler* and helped the Explorers capture the NCAA national championship. The following year, Phelan was named head basketball coach at Mount St. Mary's College in Emmitsburg, Maryland. He remained in that position for 49 years until retiring following the 2002–2003 season. Phelan compiled a 830-524 win-loss record and ranks fourth on the NCAA's all-time list of career wins behind only Dean Smith* (879) and Adolph Rupp* (876) and Bob Knight (832). When the Mountaineers played their final game for Phelan on March 1, 2003, it marked the 1,354th game coached by Phelan, an NCAA record for most career games coached. Phelan, the only person to coach 49 years at one school, also set a NCAA record for length of service as a head coach. He led 16 of his Mountaineer teams to the NCAA tournament. Five squads reached the NCAA Division II Final Four, with his 1962 Mountaineer contingent capturing the NCAA College Division National Championship at Roberts Stadium in Evansville, Indiana. Nineteen of his teams won at least 20 games in one season, while his 1981 squad posted a school record winning 28 of 31 games. Phelan's 1995 and 1999 squads captured NEC championships and qualified for the NCAA Division I Tournament, while he was selected the National Coach of the Year in 1962 and 1981.

Outstanding basketball players under the tutelage of Phelan included Fred Carter, former Philadelphia 76ers (NBA) head coach and NBA player with the 76ers, Washington Bullets, and Milwaukee Bucks; Jack Sullivan, the school's all-time leading scorer with 2,672 points; and John O'Reilly, a two-time All-America who led the 1962 championship team.

In March 2003, www.collegeinsider.com renamed the National Coach of the Year Award to honor Phelan. He remains the only college basketball coach ever to win 800 or more games and not be in the Naismith Memorial Basketball Hall of Fame. Phelan and his wife, Dottie, have five children, Jim, Lynne, Carol, Larry, and Bob.

BIBLIOGRAPHY: "Jim Phelan," *Coach of the Year Award, Profile, Final Game*, http://www.mountathletics.ocsn.com (2003); "Jim Phelan," *Profiles*, http://www.emmitsburgdispatch.com (2003); "Jim Phelan," *Retires*, http://www.northeastconference.org (2003); Gary K. Johnson, *NCAA Men's Basketball's Finest* (Overland Park, KS, 1998); *NCAA Men's Basketball Records, 2004* (Indianapolis, IN, 2003).

John L. Evers

PHELPS, Richard Frederick "Digger" (b. July 4, 1941, Beacon, NY), college player, coach, and sportscaster, is the son of Richard Phelps, a mortician, and Margaret Phelps and worked in his father's business on weekends and during summers, acquiring the nickname "Digger" from friends. A 1969 graduate of Beacon (New York) High School, Phelps performed in football, baseball, basketball, and track and field there. Basketball comprised his strongest sport, but he lacked athletic talent.

In 1959, Phelps enrolled at Rider College in Lawrenceville, New Jersey to pursue a business degree and intended to enter business with his father. Phelps exhibited basketball prowess and helped the Broncs reach the 1963 NAIA tournament in Kansas City, Missouri. He accidently became interested in coaching when his former high school coach, Tom Winterbottom, conducted a 1963 summer league in Beacon. Winterbottom convinced the reluctant Phelps to coach. Phelps really enjoyed coaching that summer and decided not to attend embalming school. He returned to Rider for a Master's degree in business education and pursued coaching. As a graduate assistant, Phelps helped the Rider basketball program gain national recognition. He conceived the game plan for the upset of NYU in 1964, ending the Violets' 23-year home-court winning streak. The successful strategy gave Digger his coaching confidence, and he stated, "That's when I knew I could do it . . . how to stop people."

In 1964, Phelps received his Master's degree, married Terry Godwin, and accepted a teaching and coaching position at Junior High School No. 4 in Trenton, New Jersey, where he led the school's basketball team to a 2-6 win-loss record. In 1965, he became head basketball coach at St. Gabriel's High School in Hazelton, Pennsylvania, and led them to the Pennsylvania Class C Scholastic title. Phelps's infatuation with the University of Notre Dame (Indiana) flourished. In October 1965, Phelps wrote Notre Dame's football coach, Ara Parseghian, of his plans to become basketball coach at Notre Dame. In 1966, the 26-year-old moved to the college ranks as a basketball assistant to Dick Harter at the University of Pennsylvania (IvL). His Penn freshmen squads over the next four seasons compiled 65 wins against 20 losses, including an undefeated 21-0 season in 1968. Fordham University (New York) named Phelps head basketball coach in 1970. Under Phelps, Fordham improved from 10–15 to 26 wins, three losses and upset Notre Dame 94–88 in the 1971 NCAA East Regional.

In 1971, Notre Dame appointed Phelps head basketball coach. With only one letterman, Phelps struggled through a disappointing 6-20 initial season. This marked the first of only three losing seasons that Notre Dame basketball experienced during Phelps's tenure. In 1972–1973, the Irish compiled 18 wins and 12 losses and a second place NIT finish. The 1973–1974 season produced a remarkable 24 wins and two losses and third place in the NCCA Mid-East Regional, as Phelps was selected UPI and BWAA Coach of the Year. Phelps resigned as Notre Dame head coach in April 1991 after the Irish struggled to a 12-20 mark. Under Phelps, Notre Dame won 393 of 590 games. No Notre Dame basketball coach compiled more victories or defeats. In 20 seasons as a collegiate coach, Phelps amassed 419 wins and 200 losses and made three NIT appearances and 14 NCAA appearances. His 1977–1978 squad made the NCAA Final Four, suffering a 90-86 loss to Duke University in the semifinals.

Phelps loved to prepare Notre Dame for highly regarded opponents and especially enjoyed ending UCLA's record 88-game winning streak in 1974. His system produced 10 All-Americas, including four Academic All-Americas. Nineteen players entered the NBA, nine as first-round draft choices. However, the flamboyant, sometimes controversial, often candid, outspoken Phelps viewed some things in life as being far more important than basketball. His ability to blend athletic and academic ability enabled all his players to graduate, earning him the respect of educators, administrators, and peers. The NABC member developed key legislation regarding recruiting and academic problems of college athletes.

Phelps has co-authored two books: *A Coach's World* and *Digger Phelps and Notre Dame Basketball.* The longtime stamp collector serves on the Citizen's Stamp Advisory Committee of the U.S. Postal Service, volunteers with Special Olympic programs, and enjoys painting. Phelps serves as a college basketball analyst for ESPN. Phelps and his wife, Terry, who possesses a Ph.D. and teaches in the Notre Dame School of Law, have three children, Karen, Rick, and Jennifer.

BIBLIOGRAPHY: *Des Moines* (IA) *Register*, April 16, 1991, p. 15; *NCAA Official Men's Basketball Records, 2004* (Indianapolis, IN, 2003); Tim Neely, *Hooping It Up: The Complete History of Notre Dame Basketball* (Notre Dame, IN, 1985); *Notre Dame Basketball Media Guide, 1990–91* (Notre Dame, IN, 1990), Richard Phelps and Larry Keith, *A Coach's World* (New York, 1974); Richard Phelps and Pat Scanlon, *Digger Phelps and Notre Dame Basketball* (Englewood Cliffs, NJ, 1981).

Jerry Jaye Wright

PHILLIP, Andrew Michael "Andy" (b. March 7, 1922, Granite City, IL; d. April 28, 2001, Rancho Mirage, CA), college and professional player, starred in baseball and basketball at Granite City (Illinois) High School and the University of Illinois. Phillip served as basketball floor leader of the "Whiz Kids" during the Illini glory years of the early 1940s. As a sophomore in 1941–1942, he led Illinois to the WC title by setting WC scoring records. The next year, Phillip broke his own scoring marks and sparked Illinois to a perfect (12-0) WC record and a 17-1 overall slate. Both years he made consensus First Team All-America. After his junior season, Phillip joined the U.S. Marines and spent the next three years as a lieutenant in the Pacific. On returning to Illinois in 1946–1947 to finish his education, he ranked among the nation's top basketball players and was named to several All-America teams.

A great competitor who always played his best in the big games, Phillip played 11 pro seasons from 1947–1948 to 1957–1958. He was known for his quick hands and passing ability and ranked with Bob Cousy* and Dick McGuire* as the era's best playmakers. A territorial draft choice of the Chicago Stags (BAA), Phillip began his career in the BAA, which later became the NBA. He finished runner-up in assists in the 1948–1949 BAA and 1949–1950 NBA seasons. When the Stags folded in 1950, Phillip was picked by the Philadelphia Warriors (NBA). Teamed with prolific scorers Joe Fulks* and Paul Arizin*, he led the NBA in assists the next two seasons. In 1951–1952, he became the first NBA player to register over 500 assists with 539 and established an NBA mark with 8.2 assists per game.

Phillip was traded to the Fort Wayne Pistons (NBA) during the 1952–1953 season and placed second to Cousy in assists his first two seasons there. In his final two seasons with the Pistons, he finished third and fourth in assists. In 1956, Boston Celtics (NBA) coach "Red" Auerbach* persuaded Phillip not to retire. The old playmaker joined the Celtics and became part of Boston's first NBA championship team in 1956–1957. He retired to enter business in California, but coached the Chicago Majors (ABL) in 1961–1962. Phillip played in five NBA All-Star Games (1951–1955), averaging seven points and six assists. He was All-NBA Second Team in 1952 and 1953. In pro seasons, he averaged 9.1 points, 5.4 assists, and 4.4 rebounds in 701 regular season games and 6.4 points, 3.7 assists, and 3.3 rebounds in 67 playoff games. He was elected to the Naismith Memorial Basketball Hall of Fame in 1961.

BIBLIOGRAPHY: Peter C. Bjarkman, *Big Ten Basketball* (Indianapolis, IN, 1994); Joe Fitzgerald, *That Championship Feeling: The Story of the Boston Celtics* (New York, 1975); Jan Hubbard, ed., *The Official NBA Encyclopedia*, 3rd ed. (New York, 2000); Neil D. Isaacs, *Vintage NBA* (Silver Spring, MD, 1996); Dick Kaegel, ed., *NCAA Basketball* (St. Louis, MO, 1983); Leonard Koppett, *24 Seconds to Shoot: An Informal History of the NBA* (New York, 1968); Andrew Phillip file, Naismith Memorial Basketball Hall of Fame, Springfield, MA; Ken Shouler et al., *Total Basketball* (Wilmington, DE, 2003); *TSN Official NBA Register, 1987–1988* (St. Louis, MO, 1987).

Steve Ollove

PIERCE, Paul Anthony (b. October 13, 1977, Oakland, CA), college and professional player, is the son of Lorraine Hosey and attended the University of Kansas, where he majored in criminology and delinquency studies. In three years of basketball at Kansas, he averaged 16.4 points and 6.3 rebounds in 108 games. Pierce was named BEC Freshman of the Year after starting 33 of Jayhawks 34 games and averaging 11.7 points and 5.3 rebounds. He earned

First Team All-America honors as a junior in 1997–1998.

The six-foot six-inch, 230-pound forward was selected as the tenth overall pick in the 1998 draft by the Boston Celtics (NBA). Pierce was named to the 1999 Schick NBA All-Rookie First Team, leading the Celtics in three-point scoring, three-point percentage, and steals. He was selected to the NBA Rookie All-Star Game in 2000. In September 2000, he underwent surgery after suffering multiple stab wounds at a Boston nightclub. The only Celtic to start all 82 games in the 2000–2001 season, Pierce scored 2,071 points to become the first Celtic to score 2,000 points since Larry Bird* in 1987–1988.

Pierce signed a multi-year contract extension with the Celtics in August 2001 and made his first NBA All-Star appearance in 2002, scoring 19 points and collecting seven rebounds in 23 minutes. For the second straight season, he was the only Celtic to start all 82 games. Pierce ranked third in NBA scoring with 2,144 points and in the top ten in several categories, including free throws made, three-point field goals made and attempted, free throws attempted, field goals made, steals, and minutes played per game. He led the Celtics into the playoffs and the Eastern Conference Finals versus the New Jersey Nets, averaging 30.2 points in the first round of the playoffs and 24.6 points for the postseason. Pierce established an NBA record when he made all 21 free throw attempts in a playoff game against the Indiana Pacers. He again led the Celtics and ranked fifth in the NBA in scoring with 1,836 points (23.0 points average) in 2003–2004, but Boston struggled to make the playoffs. Indiana swept the Celtics in the first round, limiting Pierce to a 20.7 points average. Pierce paced the Celtics in scoring with 1,769 points (21.6 average) and steals with 133 in 2004–2005, helping the Celtics reach the playoffs. He averaged 22.9 points and 7.7 rebounds in seven games in the first round playoff loss to the Indiana Pacers. Through 2004–2005, he has scored 12,086 points (23.0 average) and made 3,432 rebounds (6.5 average) in 526 games and tallied 908 points and 316 rebounds in 37 playoff games.

Pierce made his second, third, and fourth NBA All-Star Game appearances in 2003, 2004, and 2005 and was selected to the All-NBA Third Team in 2002 and 2003. He participated on the U.S. National Team that lost three games in the 2002 World Championships and played for the 1996 USA Basketball 22 and Under World Championship Qualifying Team and the 1995 U.S. Olympic Festival West Team.

BIBLIOGRAPHY: http://www.hoopshype.com/players/paul_pierce.htm; http://www.nba.com/player/file/paul_pierce/bio.html; http://www.usabasketball.com/biosmen/paul_pierce_bio.html; *TSN Official NBA Register, 2004–2005* (St. Louis, MO, 2004); Ken Shouler et al., *Total Basketball* (Wilmington, DE, 2003).

Maureen M. Smith

PIPPEN, Scottie (b. September 25, 1965, Hamburg, AK), college and professional player, is one of 12 children born to Preston Pippen, who worked long hours at a paper mill, and Ethel Pippen, a homemaker. The large family struggled economically after his father suffered a stroke during Scottie's freshman year at Hamburg (Arkansas) High School. Pippen stayed in school, graduating in 1983.

Pippen played high school basketball, but did not participate on a regular basis until his senior year, when a growth spurt brought him to six-foot one-inch. College recruiters were not interested in Pippen, but his high school coach, Donald Wayne, persuaded the University of Central Arkansas, an NAIA school, to give him an opportunity. Pippen attended Central Arkansas on a work-study basis. He continued to grow and started for Central Arkansas as a senior guard in 1986–1987, averaging 23.6 points, 10 rebounds, and 4.3 assists.

After graduating in 1987 with a B.A. degree in industrial education, Pippen was overlooked by many NBA scouts. His outstanding performance at an all-star contest in Virginia, however, attracted the attention of the NBA. The Seattle SuperSonics (NBA) selected Pippen with the fifth pick of the 1987 draft and then traded the prospect to the Chicago Bulls (NBA) for Olden Polynice.

During his first two NBA seasons, Pippen often was used as a reserve player. Pippen's playing time and effectiveness increased when Phil Jackson* assumed the coaching reins of the

Bulls during the 1989–1990 season and installed his triangle offense, taking advantage of Pippen's versatility. Pippen responded by averaging 16.5 points, 6.7 rebounds, and 5.4 assists, earning his first selection to the NBA All-Star Game. In 1991, Pippen and Michael Jordan* led the Bulls to their first NBA championship. Doubts about Pippen were dispelled with his strong defense against Magic Johnson* of the Los Angeles Lakers and his 23 points in the deciding fifth game of the series. Pippen and Jordan keyed the Chicago NBA championships in 1992 and 1993, with the former also contributing to the 1992 Olympic gold medal–winning team.

Just before the 1993–1994 season, Jordan retired to pursue a career in professional baseball; Pippen became the MVP on the Bulls. He enjoyed an outstanding season, averaging 22.0 points, 8.7 rebounds, and 2.93 steals, but the Bulls lost in the Eastern Conference Finals to the New York Knicks. With the return of Jordan, the Bulls again attained NBA championships in 1996, 1997, and 1998. Pippen also played on the 1996 Olympic gold medal-winning team.

After the 1998 season, Jordan retired. Pippen was dealt to the Houston Rockets (NBA) in January 1999, but failed to fit into the Houston offensive scheme. The Rockets traded Pippen in October 1999 to the Portland Trail Blazers (NBA), where the six-foot seven-inch, 228-pound guard-forward again attained the top of his game with 17.6 points and 7.3 rebounds per game. Portland, however, was eliminated by the Los Angeles Lakers in the 2000 Western Conference Finals. In July 2003, Pippen signed as a free agent with the Chicago Bulls. Injuries limited Pippen to 23 games in 2003–2004 and led to his retirement as an active player in March 2004.

During 17 NBA seasons, the seven-time All-Star scored 18,940 points and averaged 16.1 points, 6.4 rebounds, and 5.2 assists in 1,178 regular-season games and averaged 17.5 points and 7.6 assists in 208 playoff games. Pippen was named to the All-NBA First Team in 1994, 1995, and 1996, the All-NBA Second Team in 1992 and 1997, and the All-NBA Third Team in 1993 and 1998. He was also selected to the NBA's Fiftieth Anniversary All-Time Team in 1996. Active in charity work, he has been married to Karen McCullom and Yvette DeLeone and has four children.

BIBLIOGRAPHY: Johnette Howard, "Breakthrough," *Sport* 83 (February 1992), pp. 66–70; Bruce Newman, "Now You See Him," *SI* 67 (November 30, 1987), pp. 67–68; Scottie Pippen with Greg Brown, *Reach Higher* (New York, 1997); Bob Schnakenberg, *Scottie Pippen: Reluctant Superstar* (New York, 1997); Ken Shouler et al., *Total Basketball* (Wilmington, DE, 2003); *TSN Official NBA Register, 2004–2005* (St. Louis, MO, 2004).

Ron Briley

PITINO, Richard "Rick" (b. September 18, 1952, New York, NY), college and professional player and coach, graduated from St. Dominic's High School in Oyster Bay, New York in 1970. The six-foot, 165-pound Pitino attended the University of Massachusetts and played guard between 1970 and 1974. His best season with the Minutemen came as a freshman in 1970–1971, when he scored 306 points (16.1 points average). He saw his scoring production drop to 115 points (4.3 average) in 1972–1973 and rise slightly to 136 points (5.2 average) in 1973–1974. His coaching apprenticeship came as an assistant at the University of Hawaii in 1975–1976 and Syracuse (New York) University from 1976 to 1978. For the next five seasons, Pitino served as head coach at Boston (Massachusetts) University. The Terriers enjoyed winning marks of 17-9 in 1978–1979 and 21-9 in 1979–1980. After struggling to a 13-14 record in 1980–1981, Boston University rebounded with 19-9 in 1981–1982 and 21-10 in 1982–1983.

The New York Knickerbockers (NBA) hired Pitino as an assistant basketball coach from 1983 to 1985. After the Knicks plunged to a last-place Atlantic Division finish in 1984–1985, Pitino returned to the collegiate ranks as head coach at Providence College. The Friars attained a 17-14 mark in 1985–1986 and boasted a stellar 25-8 record in 1986–1987. *TSN* and NABC named him 1987 College Coach of the Year for unexpectedly guiding Providence to the NCAA Final Four, where the Friars lost the semifinals 77-63 to Syracuse University. In 1987, Pitino rejoined the New York Knickerbockers (NBA) as head coach. The Knicks shared second place in the Atlantic Division with a lackluster 38-44 mark in 1987–1988 and lost to the Boston Celtics in the first round of the NBA playoffs. New York won the Atlantic Division with a 52-30 record in 1988–1989. Center Patrick Ewing* ranked among NBA leaders in scoring, field goal percentage, and blocked shots. The Knicks ousted the Philadelphia 76ers in the first playoff round, but the Chicago Bulls eliminated them in the Eastern Conference semifinals.

Pitino landed among the nation's most prestigious collegiate jobs, taking over a beleaguered University of Kentucky program from Eddie Sutton*. He coached the Wildcats from 1989–1990 through 1996–1997, compiling a 219-50 record. Kentucky overachieved Pitino's first year with a 14-14 overall record, winning all nine SEC home games and breaking seven NCAA three-point records. Pitino recruited forward Jamal Mashburn, one of the nation's best and most versatile players. Kentucky improved to a 22-6 mark in 1990–1991, using a full-court press and making three-pointers. During the 1991–1992 season, the Wildcats won the SEC title and ranked second nationally with a 29-7 mark. Mashburn averaged 21.8 points and 7.8 rebounds, led the Wildcats with 65 steals, and shot .567 from the field. Pitino's club came within a miracle shot by Christian Laettner* of Duke University of being the first SEC team since 1986 to reach the Final Four. In 1992–1993, Kentucky ranked second nationally with a 30-4 record and second in the SEC East with a 13-3 mark. Mashburn made First Team All-America and helped Kentucky reach the Final Four, but the Wildcats bowed 81-70 to the University of Michigan. Kentucky recorded a 27-7 mark and shared the SEC title in 1993–1994, but Marquette University (Wisconsin) upset the Wildcats in the second round of the NCAA tournament. Kentucky improved to 28-5 in 1994–1995, winning the SEC title and losing to the University of North Carolina in the regional finals. His best season come in 1995–1996, when the 28-2 Wildcats won the SEC crown and defeated Syracuse University 96-67 in the NCAA championship game. The Wildcats fared 35-5 in 1996–1997 and again reached the NCAA Finals before losing to the University of Arizona 84-79 in overtime.

In May 1997, the Boston Celtics (NBA) named Pitino president and head coach. Under Pitino, Boston struggled to 36-46, 19-31, 35-47, and 12-22 records from 1997–1998 through 2000–2001; never finished higher than fifth place in the Atlantic Division; and did not make the playoffs. In January 2001, Jim O'Brien replaced him as head coach. During six NBA seasons, Pitino compiled a 192-220 regular-season mark and a 6-7 playoff mark.

Pitino has coached the University of Louisville (Kentucky) since 2001, compiling a 67-35 record through 2005. The Cardinals fared 19-13 in 2001–2002 and 25-7 in 2002–2003, finishing second in CUSA and reaching the second round of the NCAA tournament. Louisville was 26-9 in 2003–2004 and lost in the first round of the NCAA tournament. The Cardinals finished 33-5 in 2004–2005 and lost to the University of Illinois in the NCAA semifinals, becoming the first coach to guide three schools to the NCAA Final Four. During 17 collegiate seasons, he has recorded 449 victories and just 159, losses for a .738 winning percentage. He and his wife have four children.

BIBLIOGRAPHY: Peter C. Bjarkman, *The Biographical History of Basketball* (Chicago, IL, 2000); Richard Coren, *Providence College Basketball* (Charleston, SC, 2002); Mike Douchant, *Encyclopedia of College Basketball* (Detroit, MI, 1995); *Kentucky Basketball Encyclopedia* (Champaign, IL, 2000); *NCAA Men's Basketball Records, 2004* (Indianapolis, IN, 2003); Alan Ross, *Wildcat Wisdom* (Nashville, TN, 1999); Ken Shouler et al., *Total Basketball* (Wilmington, DE, 2003); *TSN College Basketball 2003–2004*; *TSN Official NBA Register, 2000–2001* (St. Louis, MO, 2000); Lonnie Wheeler, *Blue Yonder* (Wilmington, OH, 1998); *WWA*, 48th ed. (1994), p. 2728.

David L. Porter

PODOLOFF, Maurice (b. August 18, 1890, Elisabethgrad, Russia; d. November 24, 1985, New Haven, CT), professional basketball and hockey administrator, became instrumental in the development of modern basketball. He graduated from Hillhouse High School in New Haven, Connecticut in 1909, New Haven's Yale University in 1913, and Yale Law School in 1915. After practicing law, Podoloff entered the family real estate business in New Haven. He married Gertrude Perry of New Haven and had three children, William, Richard, and Evelyn. Podoloff purchased the half-completed New Haven Arena, primarily used for ice shows and college hockey games. He built the New Haven franchise (CAHL) and in 1935 became the president of the AHL.

In 1946 Al Sutphin, owner of the Cleveland Arena and prominent member of the AMA, approached Podoloff about forming a pro basketball league to increase revenue for the arena owners. On June 6, 1946, the 11-team BAA was formed with Podoloff as president. This marked the first time that one person led two pro leagues simultaneously. At Toronto, Canada, on November 1, 1946, the New York Knickerbockers defeated the Toronto Huskies 68-66 in the first BAA game. The BAA, however, did not succeed its first season. Podoloff realized that enabling graduated college players to enter the BAA was essential for the game's growth. In 1947 the BAA inaugurated a draft that gave the last place team the top college player. The draft strengthened the weaker teams and stopped interleague bidding.

The NBL, in existence since 1937, was forced to compete in salary wars with the BAA for the best players. After the BAA signed Minneapolis and three other top NBL franchises, the two leagues merged on August 11, 1949, as the current NBA and named Podoloff president. As president for 17 years Podoloff expanded the NBA to 17 teams, formed three divisions, and scheduled 557 games. In 1954, he increased the national recognition of the game significantly by securing its first television contract for $3,000 per game. A lawyer with virtually no previous knowledge of sports, he used great organizational and administrative skills to save the NBA in its often stormy formative years. Podoloff treated all teams and owners fairly regardless of their relative power and placed the welfare of the game, players, and fans above all other interests. He arranged the construction and use of the first 24-second shot clock, introduced in 1954 by Dan Biasone. This time restriction reduced the stalling technique and increased the pace of the game, thus greatly enhancing fan interest.

Podoloff in 1962 received the State of Connecticut's Gold Medal Key Award, and in 1965 was awarded the plaque for meritorious service to the NBA. The Podoloff Cup is presented annually to the NBA MVP. He retired as NBA president in 1963 and was enshrined into the Naismith Memorial Basketball Hall of Fame in 1974 as an outstanding contributor to the game.

BIBLIOGRAPHY: Peter C. Bjarkman, *The History of the NBA* (New York, 1992); Jan Hubbard, ed., *The Official NBA Encyclopedia*, 3rd ed. (New York, 2000); Neil D. Isaacs, *Vintage NBA* (Silver Spring, MD, 1996); Leonard Koppett, *24 Seconds to Shoot* (New York, 1970); Maurice Podoloff file, Naismith Memorial Basketball Hall of Fame, Springfield, MA; Ken Shouler et al., *Total Basketball* (Wilmington, DE, 2003).

Catherine M. Derrick

POLLARD, James Clifford "Jim" "The Kangaroo Kid" (b. July 9, 1922, Oakland, CA; d. January 22, 1993, Stockton, CA), college and professional basketball player coach, and executive, was the youngest of five children of Henry Pollard, a carpenter, and Suzie Elora Pollard, a homemaker. He was of English ancestry and was nicknamed "The Kangaroo Kid" because of his extraordinary leaping ability. The six-foot three and a half-inch, 190-pound Pollard prepped at Oakland (California) Tech High School and made the 1939 All-America high school basketball team. He enrolled at Stanford University (California) and played on the 1941–1942 Indians basketball team that won the NCAA championship by defeating Dartmouth College (New Hampshire) 53-38 at Kansas City, Missouri. Pollard completed his Bachelor degree work at the University of Minnesota while playing for the Minneapolis Lakers (NBA). He was named a college All-America and in 1941–1942, was selected to the Pacific All-Star team in 1943–1944 and 1944–1945; and chosen an All-America and MVP in the 1946 and 1947 AAU tournaments at San Diego, California. Pollard made the AAU All-America team at Denver, Colorado in 1946–1947 and participated on the College All-Star team in 1947, being named MVP in that classic. During World War II military service, he starred on the U.S. Coast Guard basketball team.

With the Minneapolis Lakers (NBA), Pollard consistently was an NBA All-Star selection. He made the All-NBA First Team in 1949 and

1950, and the All-NBA Second Team in the 1952 and 1954 seasons. Pollard starred on the 1949, 1950, and 1952–1954 NBA championship Lakers teams under Coach John Kundla*. Before the Lakers joined the NBA, they played the 1947–1948 season in the NBL. With Pollard and George Mikan*, the Lakers won the NBL championship by defeating the Rochester Royals in three of four games. Before 16,478 at Madison Square Garden in New York, Pollard led the West team with 23 points in an overtime loss in the 1954 East-West All-Star Game. In eight pro basketball seasons (1947–1948 to 1954–1955), he played in 497 games, scored 2,609 field goals and 1,304 free throws for 6,522 points, and averaged 13.1 points. In 1952, players who had performed in the NBA since its inception as the BAA selected Pollard as the best player of the period ahead of Mikan and other superstars in a poll. His jumpshot—his best weapon—was called the best corner shot ever. He did everything on a basketball court with finesse and was considered one of the cleanest basketball players, committing only 194 personal fouls in one three-year period. Pollard started in four NBA All-Star Games and made 1,417 assists and 2,487 rebounds during his NBA career. He was chosen All-Time Pacific Coast forward in 1955 and was elected as a player to the Naismith Memorial Basketball Hall of Fame in 1977. Pollard also was inducted into the HAF Hall of Fame, National AAU Hall of Fame, and Stanford University Hall of Fame.

From 1956 through 1958, Pollard coached basketball at LaSalle College. His squads finished with 15-10 and 17-9 marks in 1956–1957 and 1957–1958 and won 16 games his final season there. For the last part of the 1959–1960 season, he coached the Minneapolis Lakers (NBA) to a 14-25 mark. After that season, the Lakers franchise moved to Los Angeles, California. Pollard coached the Chicago Packers (NBA) to an 18-62 record in 1961–1962 and was selected in 1964 by the Academy of Sports to its All-Time NBA Team. He coached the Minnesota Muskies (ABA) to a 50-28 record in 1967–1968 and the Miami Floridians (ABA) to a 48–50 mark from 1968 to 1970. Pollard served as coach and athletic director at Fort Lauderdale (Florida) University from 1971 through 1973. During his competitive pro career, Pollard worked as an automobile salesman in Minneapolis, Minnesota, and played summer baseball with the Jordan, Minnesota, squad. Later he was affiliated with the food market business. Pollard returned to California in 1979 and served as a teacher, counselor, and coach in the Lodi Unified School District and California Youth Authority. He married Arilee Hansen in June 1944 and had three children.

BIBLIOGRAPHY: George Barton, *My Lifetime in Sports* (Minneapolis, MN, 1954); Stan W. Carlson, *Laker Basketball* (Minneapolis, MN, 1953); Jack Clary, *Basketball's Greatest Dynasty: The Lakers* (New York, 1992); Zander Hollander, ed., *The Modern Encyclopedia of Basketball* (Garden City, NY, 1979); Neil D. Isaacs, *Vintage NBA* (Silver Spring, MD, 1996); Roland Lazenby, *The NBA Finals* (Indianapolis, IN, 1996); Minneapolis Laker Programs and Publicity Releases, 1947, 1955; Jim Pollard file, Naismith Memorial Basketball Hall of Fame, Springfield, MA; Ken Shouler et al., *Total Basketball* (Wilmington, DE, 2003); Stew Thornley, *Basketball's Original Dynasty* (Minneapolis, MN, 1989); *TSN Official NBA Register, 2004–2005* (St. Louis, MO, 2004).

Stan W. Carlson

POPOVICH, Gregg Charles "Pop" (b. January 28, 1949, East Chicago, IN), college and professional player, coach, and executive, is the son of a Gary, Indiana steelworker and a descendant of Slavic ancestry. Popovich attended Merrillville (Indiana) High School and was cut from the basketball team as a sophomore in 1963. He made the team the following year and in 1965 became its best player on the squad.

Following graduation, Popovich earned an appointment to the U.S. Air Force Academy (Colorado). The six-foot two-inch, 195-pound guard-forward played four years of basketball at the Academy, leading the Falcons in scoring with an average of 14.3 points as a senior and served as the team captain. A 1970 graduate from the Academy with a Bachelor's degree in Soviet Studies, Popovich began serving his military commitment and represented the United States on the National AAU team touring the Soviet Union. He returned to the Academy as an assistant basketball coach for six years before being head basketball coach at Pomona-Pitzer College in Claremont, California from 1979–1980 through 1985–1986.

Popovich served as an assistant coach to Larry Brown* at the University of Kansas in 1987–1988, when the Jayhawks won the NCAA championship. When Brown accepted the head coaching position with the San Antonio Spurs (NBA) the following year, Popovich accompanied him. He assisted Don Nelson* of the Golden State Warriors (NBA) in 1992–1993 and 1993–1994.

In May 1994, Popovich returned to San Antonio as the Spurs executive vice president and general manager and maintained that position until July 1, 2002. One of his first transactions involved dismissing Spurs head coach Bob Hill and assuming the coaching duties himself. From 1996–1997 through 2004–2005, Popovich's Spurs recorded a 455-233 regular-season win-loss record for the best mark in franchise history. With the "Twin Towers" David Robinson* and Tim Duncan* spearheading the attack and the coaching prowess of Popovich, the Spurs captured five division titles, two Western Conference titles, and two NBA championships. In the 2002–2003 campaign, San Antonio established a new franchise record with 60 triumphs (41 of the last 50) and only 22 losses. The Spurs won 59 games in 2004–2005 and reached the NBA Finals against the Detroit Pistons. Their first NBA championship came during the 1998–1999 season shortened because of the imposed "lockout" by management. San Antonio recorded a 15-2 playoff record and defeated the New York Knicks in five games to earn the title. The Spurs second NBA championship came in 2003 when they defeated the New Jersey Nets in six games. With Popovich at the helm, San Antonio has produced a 65-38 win-loss record in NBA playoff games over eight seasons through the 2005 Western Conference Finals. For his skill in leading the Spurs, he was voted the 2002–2003 NBA Coach of the Year Award.

Popovich and Erin, his wife of 28 years, have two children, Micky and Jill, and work together offering their time and caring to the members of the organization, their families, and the community.

BIBLIOGRAPHY: Marty Burns, "Pop Culture," *SI* 91 (July 1, 1999), pp. 36–42; "Gregg Popovich," *Background*, http://www.geocities.com (2003); "Gregg Popovich," *Better Believer*, http://www.cnn/si.com (1999); "Gregg Popovich," *Brash, Disciplined And In Control*, http://www.canoe.ca (1999); "Gregg Popovich," *Coach Bio*, http://www.nba.com (2003); *San Antonio Spurs: Game Time Program* (2000–2001), p. 49; Ken Shouler et al., *Total Basketball* (Wilmington, DE, 2003); *TSN Official NBA Register, 2004–2005* (St. Louis, MO, 2004).

John L. Evers

PORTER, Henry Van Arsdale "H.V." (b. October 2, 1891, Spring Lake Township, Tazewell County, IL; d. October 27, 1975, St. Petersburg, FL), equipment inventor, rules-maker, and athletic administrator, was the youngest of five children born to Alfred W. Porter and Sallie B. (Heyers) Porter on a farm near Manito, Illinois. With no secondary school in the community, Porter in 1909 at age 17 entered the Illinois State Normal School in Champaign and received both a high school diploma (1913) and a Bachelor's degree (1918) there. In 1925, he received a Master of Arts degree in education from the University of Illinois. A baseball letterman in college, Porter never played basketball beyond intramurals. Nevertheless, he made an enormous contribution to the game, especially at the high school level.

From 1913 to 1928, Porter served as principal, teacher, and athletic coach at rural Illinois high schools in Mount Zion (1913–1914), Keithsburg (1914–1915), Delevan (1915–1918), and Athens (1918–1928). He then turned to athletic administration. As assistant executive secretary of the IHSAA (1928–1940). Porter published the nation's first state association sports magazine, *The Illinois Athlete*. In 1940, he was appointed the first full-time executive secretary and editor of publications of the NFSHSAA, headquartered in Chicago, and held these posts until retirement in 1958. With Lynn W. St. John*, Porter helped organize the NBCUS. He was the first representative from the high school ranks on the NBRC and served for 30 years, 18 as recording and executive secretary.

In 1929, Porter began work to remedy the defects of cumbersome size, variable circumference, irregular construction, and exorbitant expense of the 32-inch sewn leather basketball. The result, patented in 1935, was the modern

29½-inch molded basketball. Because the original rectangular backboard contained much unused space and sometimes obstructed shot attempts, in 1933 he designed the popular fan-shaped backboard. He later developed the modern high school track and field discus and the 39-inch hurdle.

Throughout the 1930s, Porter and Oswald Tower* reworked the complicated and inconsistent rules governing high school basketball. In 1936, he published the first of the NFSHSAA's official rulebooks, simplifying and standardizing the game across the nation. Porter also made sweeping revisions in high school football rules that sharply distinguished the scholastic game from the college version. His codification of high school rules later extended to baseball, soccer, and track and field. Besides writing numerous handbooks and devising rules tests, Porter worked with Forrest C. "Phog" Allen* in developing illustrated manuals and films to demonstrate rule applications. He also inaugurated the NFSHSAA's training program for officials and nationwide meetings for the purpose of rules experimentation and data gathering.

For his important contributions to the creation of modern equipment, pioneering role in rules development, and administrative service to high school athletics, Porter was elected to the Illinois Basketball Hall of Fame, the HAF Hall of Fame, and in 1960 as a contributor to the Naismith Memorial Basketball Hall of Fame. He married Grace Krumminga in 1924 and had no children.

BIBLIOGRAPHY: Ronald L. Mendell, *Who's Who in Basketball* (New Rochelle, NY, 1973); Sandy Padwe, *Basketball's Hall of Fame* (Englewood Cliffs, NJ, 1970); Henry Van Arsdale Porter file, Naismith Memorial Basketball Hall of Fame, Springfield, MA; *St. Petersburg* (FL) *Times*, October 30, 1975.

Larry R. Gerlach

PORTER, Kevin "K.P." (b. April 17, 1950, Chicago, IL), college and professional player and coach, is the first son of R. L. and Mildred Porter and graduated from Chicago's DuSable High School, earning All-City and All-State basketball honors for three seasons. The Illinois Coaches Hall of Fame inducted Porter, who compiled a career scoring average of 24.5 points. He made basketball All-America at St. Francis College of Pennsylvania, averaging 23.5 points from 1968 to 1972.

Porter also achieved NBA stardom, but personality clashes, differences over team offensive strategy, and injuries marred his professional career. Porter's difficulties partly stemmed from his family background. As the eldest of 10 children in a poor family, he recalled having "the world on my shoulders. . . . I felt I had a lot to prove." Porter often battled himself, as his short, 5-foot 11-inch, 170-pound frame intensified his aggressiveness. The third-round 1972 draft choice lasted 10 years in the NBA before an injury in 1982 ended his playing career. He participated in 659 regular-season NBA games for the Washington Bullets (1972–1975, 1979–1983), Detroit Pistons (1975–1977, 1978–1979), and the New Jersey Nets (1977–1978).

Porter penetrated the heart of the defense with stutter-step dribbles and flashy passes to his team's top scorer. Washington teammate Elvin Hayes* called him "the most exciting playmaking guard in the league." With Wes Unseld* rebounding, Porter streaking down the court, and Hayes scoring, the Bullets finished first in the Central Division three consecutive seasons. The Golden State Warriors swept the Bullets in the 1975 NBA Championship Series and Porter became the scapegoat. Washington shipped Porter to the Detroit Pistons (NBA) in August 1975, but he wrenched his knee early in the 1975–1976 season and nearly experienced a mental breakdown because "basketball was everything" to him. Porter's knee healed, but Detroit traded him to the marginal New Jersey Nets (NBA) in November 1977 when he clashed with Pistons' coach Herb Brown. He returned to the Pistons in September 1978, setting the NBA season record for assists with 1,099 and a 13.4 average.

The Bullets signed Porter as a free agent in July 1979, but he disagreed with new coach Dick Motta*. Motta preferred a patterned offense run by large defensive guards. Porter eventually gained Motta's confidence and led the NBA in assists in 1981 (734) before rupturing his Achilles tendon. During his career, Porter paced the NBA in assists in 1974–1975, 1977–1978, 1978–1979, and 1980–1981 and averaged 11.6 points (7,645 career points) and 8.1 assists (5,314 career assists). Until 1990, he held the NBA record for most assists in a single game with 29 against the Houston Rockets on February 24, 1978.

Subsequently, Porter coached basketball at his alma mater, St. Francis (NEC), compiling a 42-68 win-loss record from 1983–1984 until his dismissal following the 1986–1987 season. He moved to Central State University in Ohio in 1987, amassing a 28-29 coaching mark. He and his wife, Cleota, have three children, Kevin Jr., Kandance, and Kelly.

BIBLIOGRAPHY: David DuPree, "Porter Accepts the Blame; Hayes Defends Play," *Washington* (DC) *Post*, November 7, 1979, pp. D1, D3; David DuPree, "Porter Catalyst in Bullet Streak," *Washington Post*, March 25, 1980, pp. E1, E2; David DuPree, "Porter Earns Pay, Whole Lot More," *Washington Post*, May 14, 1975, pp. F1, F4; Jan Hubbard, eds., *The Official NBA Basketball Encyclopedia*, 3rd ed. (New York, 2000); Jane Leavy, "Little K. P. Grows Up, Finds He's a Big Man," *Washington Post*, February 25, 1981, pp. E1, E2; *1989–1990 Bullets Media Guide* (Washington, DC, 1989); *Saint Francis College of Pennsylvania, Basketball Media Guide,* 1989–1990 (Loretto, PA, 1989).

Bruce J. Dierenfield

PORTLAND, Rene Muth (b. April 1, 1954, Broomall, PA), college player and coach, serves as the head basketball coach of the Lady Lions of Pennsylvania State University. Portland, the daughter of a hardware store owner and Margaret Muth, grew up in suburban Philadelphia, Pennsylvania and graduated in 1971 from Villa Marie Maria Academy in Malvern, Pennsylvania. Her high school basketball coach helped her become a dominant player on the floor. Portland enrolled at Immaculata College (Pennsylvania) and in her first three years led the "Macs" to three consecutive AIAW National Championships and a second place finish in 1975. The Macs recorded an 85-5 four-year win-loss record under Naismith Memorial Basketball Hall of Fame coach Cathy Rush*. Portland won the Outstanding College Athlete of America Award three times and was named All-America by the New York press.

Portland earned a Bachelor's degree in social science in 1975 and remained at her alma mater for one year as an assistant basketball coach. Her first experience as a head coach came in 1976–1977 and 1977–1978, posting an overall 40-20 win-loss record.

Named head basketball coach at Penn State by athletic director Joe Paterno in 1980, Portland completed her 25th year in 2004–2005 as the Lady Lions head coach and has compiled a 581-204 win-loss record there. She has posted a 668-224 overall career coaching record and has never experienced a losing season. The 1999–2000 Lady Lions set an all-time season school high with 30 victories, while the 1998 Penn State unit captured the WNIT with a 59-56 road victory over Baylor University (Texas). The Lady Lions advanced to the NCAA Final Four in 2000 before losing to the eventual champion, the University of Connecticut. Penn State reached the NCAA "Sweet Sixteen" in 2002 and 2003 and the "Elite Eight" in 2004. On December 5, 2002, Portland became only the seventh women's basketball coach to win at least 600 games.

The Lady Lions participated in the ATC for eight years, recording 96 victories, 26 losses, two ATC regular-season crowns, and seven ATC titles. Penn State joined the BTC in 1992, compiling a 172-54 overall record, five BTC regular-season championships, and two BTC tournament titles. Notable players, who came under the tutelage of Portland, include her daughter, Christine, Susan Robinson, Kelly Mazzante, and Tanisha Wright.

Internationally, Portland served on the coaching staff of the 1985 Olympic Festival team, the 1986 and 1996 Junior National team, and the 1999 World University Games team; and as the head coach of the 1997 Junior National team, leading them to their first ever gold medal.

Portland has received numerous coaching awards, including the USBWA National Coach of the Year in 1992; ATC Coach of the Year in 1993; and BTC Coach of the Year in 1994, 2000, 2003, and 2004; and was inducted into the Pennsylvania Sports Hall of Fame in 2001. She and her husband, John, have three children, Christine, John Jr., and Stephen.

BIBLIOGRAPHY: "Rene Portland," *Celebrates 600th Win*, http://www.collegian.psu.edu (2003); "Rene Portland," *Head Coach*, http://www.psu.edu

(2003); "Rene Portland," *Meet the Coach*, http://www.gopsusports.com (2003);"Rene Portland," *Pennsylvania Sports Hall of Fame*, http://www.pasportshalloffamedec.com (2003); "Rene Portland," *Perfect Fit*, http:// www.livesite.pittsburghlive.com (2003); "Rene Portland," *Q and A* http://www.bigten.org (2003); Rosemarie Skaine, *Women College Basketball Coaches* (Jefferson, NC, 2001).

John L. Evers

PRICE, William Mark "Mark" (b. February 15, 1964, Bartlesville, OK), college and professional player and coach, is the son of Denny Price and Ann Price. His father played basketball at the University of Oklahoma and coached basketball from the high school to the professional level. He has two brothers, Matt and Brent, who played college basketball; Brent also performed in the NBA.

Price graduated from Enid (Oklahoma) High School and was named the high school basketball Player of the Year in Oklahoma. He led the state in scoring his junior and senior seasons and in 1982 tied his father's single-game state tournament standard of 42 points.

Price attended Georgia Institute of Technology between 1982–1983 and 1985–1986 and played basketball under coach Bobby Cremins. He paced the ACC in scoring as a freshman and led the "Ramblin Wreck" to its first ACC championship in 1985 and consecutive trips to the NCAA tournament. Price was selected All-ACC four times and scored 2,193 career points, fifth on the school's all time scoring list. He converted 424 of 479, or 85 percent, of his free throws attempted.

Price was selected by the Dallas Mavericks (NBA) in the second round as the 25th pick overall of the 1986 NBA draft. His rights were traded in June 1986 to the Cleveland Cavaliers (NBA). The six-foot, 180-pound guard spent his first nine seasons with the Cavaliers, making the All NBA First Team in 1993 and All-NBA Third Team in 1989, 1992, and 1994. Price holds Cleveland franchise career records for assists (4,206), steals (734), free throw percentage (.904), and three-point field goals made (802) and attempted (1,960). He won the NBA Long-Distance Shootout in 1993 and 1994 played on Dream Team II that captured a gold medal in the 1994 World Championships. Price played in the 1989, 1992, 1993, and 1994 All-Star Games. In September 1995, Cleveland traded him to the Washington Bullets (NBA). Price was signed by the Golden State Warriors (NBA) in July 1996. In October 1997, Golden State traded him to the Orlando Magic (NBA).

Price retired after the 1997–1998 season, having compiled 10,989 points (15.2 points average), handed out 4,863 assists, and made 860 steals in 722 regular-season games. He converted 2,135 of 2,362 free throw attempts for an NBA record .904 free throw percentage. In 47 NBA playoff games, Price netted 818 points and 202 of 214 free throw attempts for an NBA record .944 shooting percentage.

Price returned to his Georgia Tech alma mater as an assistant basketball coach in 1998–1999, coached basketball at Whitefield Academy in Georgia, and currently serves as head coach of a private high school in Metro Atlanta.

Price married Laura (Marbot), a Georgia Tech student. They have four children, Caroline, Brittany, Hudson, and Joshua. Convention Hall in Enid houses the Mark Price Arena, named after its' basketball hero.

BIBLIOGRAPHY: Peter C. Bjarkman, *ACC: Atlantic Coast Conference Basketball* (Indianapolis, IN, 1996); Jan Hubbard, ed., *The Official NBA Encyclopedia*, 3rd ed. (New York, 2000); "Mark Price," *Men's Basketball*, http://www.ramblin_wreck.fansonly.com (1999); "Mark Price," *Oklahoma History*, http://www.ok-history.mus.ok.us/ (2004); "Mark Price," *Retirement*, http://www.ardmorite.com (1999); "Mark Price," *Stats, History and Awards*, http://www.basketballreference.com (2003); "Mark Price," *Vertical Files, Oklahoma Historical Society*, http://www.ok-history.mus.ok.us/ (2004); *TSN Official NBA Register, 2004–2005* (St. Louis, MO, 2004).

John L. Evers

Q

QUIGLEY, Ernest Cosmas "Ernie" (b. March 22, 1880, New Castle, New Brunswick, Canada; d. December 10, 1960, Lawrence, KS), sports official and athletics administrator, was the son of Lawrence B. Quigley and Mary J. (Wier) Quigley. Quigley graduated from Concordia (Kansas) High School in 1900 and entered the University of Kansas, where he quarterbacked the football team, participated in track and field, and played basketball for James Naismith*. Quigley left Kansas in 1902 to become football coach at Central Missouri State University in Warrensburg, Missouri, and moved to St. Mary's College of Kansas, where he served as athletics director and football, basketball, baseball, and track and field coach from 1903 to 1914.

Quigley began officiating sports events to supplement his income, but it soon became a year-round activity. He refereed college football for 40 years from 1904 to 1943, working classics including the Army-Navy and Yale University-Harvard University series, three Rose Bowls, and one Cotton Bowl, then the Dixie Classic. Quigley also officiated college and AAU basketball for 37 years from 1906 to 1942, refereeing NCAA and NIBL tournaments, 19 consecutive AAU national championships, and the U.S. Olympic basketball finals in 1936. Quigley began umpiring baseball in 1910 after breaking his hand playing in the minor leagues, spending two seasons in the WeIL (Western International League) and working the NYSL in 1912. He started the 1913 season in the IL, but advanced to the NL in June. During 24 years, Quigley ranked among the NL's most respected arbiters and umpired six World Series (1916, 1919, 1921, 1924, 1927, and 1935). He served as the NL's supervisor of umpires in 1936 and public relations director from 1937 to 1944.

From 1944 to 1950, Quigley was the athletics director at the University of Kansas (BSC). He quickly retired the department's large debt and reinvigorated the Jayhawks athletics programs, hiring outstanding football, basketball, and track and field coaches. In 1958, Kansas named its baseball facility Quigley Field in his honor.

The greatest all-around sports official in history, Quigley estimated that during 40 years he traveled 100,000 miles a year and officiated some 5,400 baseball games, 1,500 basketball games, and 400 football games. The National Baseball Congress in 1957 established an award in his name to be given annually to the nation's top amateur umpire. Quigley was inducted in 1956 into the NAIA Hall of Fame and in 1961 became the second referee elected to the Naismith Memorial Basketball Hall of Fame. He married Margaret Darlington and had two sons, Ernest Jr., and Henry.

BIBLIOGRAPHY: Mike Fisher, *Deaner: Fifty Years of University of Kansas Athletics* (Kansas City, MO, 1986); Blair Kerkhoff, *Phog Allen: The Father of Basketball* (Indianapolis, IN, 1996); Ronald L. Mendell, *Who's Who in Basketball* (New Rochelle, NY, 1973); Sandy Padwe, *Basketball's Hall of Fame* (Englewood Cliffs, NJ, 1970); Ernest Quigley file, Naismith Memorial Basketball Hall of Fame, Springfield, MA; Ernest Quigley file, National Baseball Hall of Fame, Cooperstown, NY; Ernest Quigley file, University Archives, University of Kansas, Lawrence, KS; *TSN*, December 21, 1960; Bernice Larson Webb, *The Basketball Man, James Naismith* (Lawrence, KS, 1973).

Larry R. Gerlach

R

RAMSAY, John T. "Jack" (b. February 23, 1925, Philadelphia, PA), college and professional player and coach, is the son of John Ramsay and Anne Ramsay. Ramsay, whose father worked in the mortgage and loan business, was married in May 1949. He and his wife, Jean, have five children: John, Christopher, Susan, Sharon, and Carolyn. Ramsay attended Upper Darby High School in Upper Darby, Pennsylvania, where he played on three state championship basketball teams. His high school coach instilled in him a strong belief in organization and discipline. After graduation from high school, he earned an athletic scholarship from St. Joseph's College in Philadelphia, Pennsylvania. After Ramsay spent the 1942–1943 academic year there, World War II interrupted his college career for three years. He returned to St. Joseph's College in 1946 and became the team captain on a moderately successful basketball team before graduating in 1949. From 1949 to 1955, Ramsay played in the EBL with Harrisburg, Pennsylvania and Sunbury, Pennsylvania. He also taught, coached, and took graduate courses and earned a Doctoral degree in education from the University of Pennsylvania in 1963.

A major career break for Ramsay came in 1956, when he took the head basketball coaching job at his alma mater, St. Joseph's College. He quickly became a successful college basketball coach. During 11 seasons from 1955–1956 to 1965–1966, Ramsay's clubs compiled 234 wins, 72 losses and a .765 winning percentage. In his first year, he brought St. Joseph's from a 12-14 record to a 23-6 mark. His teams notched seven 20-game winning seasons and participated in 10 major postseason tournaments.

Ramsay became the general manager of the Philadelphia 76ers (NBA) in the NBA's Eastern Division for the 1967–1968 season, the year the club won the NBA championship with center Wilt Chamberlain*. After the title season, he became the head coach of the 76ers. Unfortunately, that same year Chamberlain was traded to the Los Angeles Lakers. Ramsay coached the 76ers for four seasons from 1968–1972, compiling a 174-154 record. Only during his final year (1971–1972) of coaching did the 76ers have a losing season with a 30-52 record.

In 1972, Ramsay became the head coach of the expansion Buffalo Braves (NBA) of the NBA's then Atlantic Division. After a miserable initial season (1972–1973) with a 21-61 record, he guided Buffalo to the playoffs for the next three consecutive seasons and compiled the fourth best NBA overall record (137-109). In 1976 Ramsay became head coach of the Portland Trail Blazers (NBA) of the NBA's Pacific Division. His crowning glory came during his first season (1976–1977), when the Trail Blazers compiled a 49-33 regular-season record and made the playoffs. With center Bill Walton* and Coach Ramsay's "team concept," the Trail Blazers took the NBA Championship by winning 14 games and losing only five games in the playoffs. Ramsay coached the Portland Trail Blazers from 1976–1977 to 1985–1986 and notched a 453-367 record there. During the 1984–1985 season, Portland recorded a 42-40 mark and finished in second place behind the Pacific Division champion Lakers. From 1976–1977 to 1984–1985, the Trail Blazers experienced a losing season only in 1979–1980. In 1986–1987,

Ramsay coached the Indiana Pacers (NBA) to a 41-41 mark and a fourth-place Central Division finish. The Pacers dropped to a 38-44 record in 1987–1988 and an 0-7 slate in 1988–1989, missing the playoffs. Ramsay's overall NBA coaching career statistics over 20 seasons included 864 wins, 783 losses, and a .525 winning percentage, making him the tenth all-time winningest NBA coach. Ramsay, who resigned in November 1988 as Pacers' coach, strongly emphasized physical conditioning, discipline, mental toughness, hard work, and honesty. He was elected to the Naismith Memorial Basketball Hall of Fame in 1992 and was named one of the top 10 coaches in NBA history in 1996. Ramsay served as a television analyst for the Miami Heat (NBA) from 1992 to 2001 and for ESPN. Ramsay engages in various physical activities, including tennis, bicycling, surfing, jogging, and jumping rope. He was considered one of the most ethical, honorable, responsible, and principled men in pro sports and wrote an excellent book, *The Coach's Art*.

BIBLIOGRAPHY: Frank Coffey and Tom Biracree, *The Pride of Portland* (New York, 1979); David Halberstam, *The Breaks of the Game* (New York, 1981); Jan Hubbard, ed., *The Official NBA Encyclopedia*, 3rd ed. (New York, 2000); Wayne Lynch, *Season of the 76ers* (New York, 2002); Claudia Mitrol, ed., *Philadelphia's Greatest Sports Moments* (Champaign, IL, 2000); John Papanek, "A Man Who Never Lets Down," *SI* 57 (November 1, 1982), pp. 80–94; Jack Ramsay file, Naismith Memorial Basketball Hall of Fame, Springfield, MA; Jack Scott, *Bill Walton: On the Road with the Portland Trail Blazers* (New York, 1978); *TSN Official NBA Guide, 1987–1988* (St. Louis, MO, 1987); *TSN Official NBA Register, 2004–2005* (St. Louis, MO, 2004).

Kant Patel

RAMSEY, Frank Vernon, Jr. "The Kentucky Colonel" (b. July 13, 1931, Madisonville, KY), college and professional player, is a son of Frank Ramsey, Sr., and was a 1948 High School Basketball All-America from Madisonville, Kentucky. Ramsey later starred in basketball at the University of Kentucky. As a sophomore, he quarterbacked Adolph Rupp's* Wildcats cagers to a 32-2 record and the NCAA championship. The next year, Ramsey's team finished 29-3. The 1952–1953 squad was placed on probation for recruiting violations, giving him another year of eligibility. In 1953–1954, he teamed with All-America Cliff Hagan* to lead Kentucky to the Wildcat's first perfect season (25-0) and the SEC title. The Wildcats rejected a bid to the NCAA tournament when their three senior players were declared ineligible for postseason play because of the suspended season.

In a surprise move during the 1953 NBA draft, Coach "Red" Auerbach* selected Ramsey first and Hagan third for the Boston Celtics (NBA). Although both played another year at the University of Kentucky, they were eligible for the draft because their senior class had graduated. Hagan eventually played his NBA career with the St. Louis Hawks while Ramsey became the prototype sixth man for the Celtics. After his rookie season, Ramsey spent a year in the military service. He returned to join Bill Russell* and became an integral part of seven NBA championship teams in the next eight years. Originally a guard, the six-foot three-inch Ramsey was shifted to forward in his sixth-man role and achieved his success by being quicker and smarter than opponents.

Nicknamed "The Kentucky Colonel," Ramsey became a confident, cerebral player excelling in clutch situations. In 1957, he scored the ultimate "dream shot" by making an off-balance 20-footer that defeated the St. Louis Hawks in double overtime of the seventh game in the championship series and brought the Celtics their first NBA title.

In a 1964 *SI* article, Ramsey explained "some of the finer points of basketball strategy" and stressed the ability to draw fouls "by providing good, heartwarming drama" for the fans and referees. A shrewd businessman whose opinions were respected by his teammates, Ramsey conducted unique contract negotiations. Each year, Ramsey signed two copies of a blank contract and told Celtics owner Walter Brown* to fill in the salary he thought he was worth and send him a copy. Ramsey retired in 1964 after six straight Celtics NBA championships to manage his construction business in Madisonville. In nine seasons, he scored 8,378 points and averaged 13.4 points in a reserve role. Ramsey, whose uniform number 23 has been retired by the Celtics, was elected as a player to the Naismith Memorial Basketball Hall of Fame in 1982.

BIBLIOGRAPHY: Peter C. Bjarkman, *The Boston Celtics Encyclopedia* (Champaign, IL, 1998); Jack Clary, *Basketball's Great Dynasties: The Celtics* (New York, 1992); Frank Deford, "Smart Moves by a Master of Deception," *SI* 19 (December 9, 1963), pp. 57–63; Joe Fitzgerald, *That Championship Feeling: The Story of the Boston Celtics* (New York, 1975); Jeff Greenfield, *The World's Greatest Team: A Portrait of the Boston Celtics, 1957–69* (New York, 1976); Zander Hollander, ed., *The Modern Encyclopedia of Basketball* (Garden City, NY, 1979); Jan Hubbard, ed., *The Official NBA Encyclopedia*, 3rd ed. (New York, 2000); *Kentucky Basketball Encyclopedia* (Champaign, IL, 2000); Roland Lazenby, *The NBA Finals* (Indianapolis, IN, 1996); *NCAA Men's Basketball Records 2004* (Indianapolis, IN, 2003); Bert Nelli, *The Winning Tradition: A History of Kentucky Wildcat Basketball* (Lexington, KY, 1984); Frank Ramsey file, Naismith Memorial Basketball Hall of Fame, Springfield, MA: Russell Rice, *Kentucky's Big Blue Machine* (Huntsville, AL, 1976).

Steve Ollove

REDIN, Harley J. (b. August 29, 1919, Silverton, TX), college player and coach, is the son of Alvin Redin and Winnie (Joiner) Redin. Redin's father encouraged his interest in sports and possessed the only two-goal basketball court in town. Redin graduated from Silverton (Texas) High School in 1935 and lettered four times in basketball. He graduated in 1937 from John Tarleton State JC (Texas), where he played on two undefeated basketball squads during the school's collegiate record-setting 86-game winning streak. Although a JC, Tarleton State often played four-year schools. Tarleton's victory string, compiled between 1933 and 1938, was not broken until UCLA won 88 consecutive games in the 1970s. Redin finished his education at North Texas State University, earning a Bachelor of Science degree in 1942 and a Master of Science degree in 1948. He played basketball one season, but dropped out of school to serve in the U.S. Marine Air Corps during World War II. As a bomber pilot, Redin logged 50 combat missions over the South Pacific and attained the rank of captain. On July 2, 1946, he married Winona Tullos and has two sons, Kenny and Van.

In 1946, Redin became men's basketball coach and athletic director at Wayland Baptist JC near Silverton. Two years later, Wayland Baptist became a full four-year institution. During the next nine years, his squads compiled a 171-97 mark and made trips to the NAIA postseason tournament in 1954, 1955, and 1957. His 1953–1954 Pioneers squad still holds the school record for most consecutive wins, fewest defeats, and highest winning percentage. Redin encountered even greater success as the women's basketball coach. He began directing the Wayland Baptist Flying Queens in 1955 and for two seasons served as both men's and women's basketball coach. His first two teams were undefeated and won the national AAU championship tournament. Redin scored victories in his first 76 games as women's coach, helping Wayland Baptist bring its all-time collegiate winning streak to 131 games in 1958. For 18 seasons, the reserved, purposeful coach compiled a remarkable 431-66 record. The Flying Queens won AAU national titles in 1956, 1957, 1959, 1961, 1970, 1971, and finished second six other times. They also recorded five straight NWIT championships between 1969 and his retirement in 1973. He coached 36 players who won All-America honors 65 times.

A longtime member of the AAU Women's Basketball Rules Committee, Redin advocated the unlimited dribble and other progressive rule changes. He served 15 years on the USOC and was international coach for women's teams at the Pan American Games (1959, 1971), the World Tournament (1963), and against the Russian National team on exchange tours between 1959 and 1962. Thirty-two of Redin's Wayland Baptist players participated on U.S. national teams. He wrote two books on women's basketball. *The Queens Fly High* (1958) and *Basketball Guide For Girls* (1970). Both stress the importance of developing solid fundamental skills. Redin, senior vice president at City National Bank in Plainview, Texas, boosts Wayland Baptist athletics and enjoys flying and old cars as hobbies. He has been elected to the Panhandle Sports and HAF halls of fame.

BIBLIOGRAPHY: Harley J. Redin, *Basketball Guide for Girls* (Plainview, TX, 1970); Harley J. Redin, *The Queens Fly High* (Plainview, TX, 1958); "The Unlimited Dribble: An Experiment," *Amateur Athlete* (April 1961), pp. 17ff.; Garet von Netzer,

"After 18 Busy Years, the Man in Women's Basketball Retires," *AAU News*, May 1973, pp. 8–9.

Dennis S. Clark

REED, Willis, Jr. (b. June 25, 1942, Hico, LA), college and professional player and executive, is the son of truck driver Willis Reed Sr., and Inell (Ross) Reed, a domestic worker. He grew up in segregated Bernice, Louisiana, participating in football, baseball, track and field, and basketball at Westside High School. At Grambling (Louisiana) College from 1961 to 1964, Reed played three times in the NAIA basketball tournament and helped his team to the 1961 championship. The six-foot ten-inch, 240-pounder made Little All-America three times, played on the U.S. basketball team in the Pan American Games in Brazil, and was named in 1970 to the NAIA Hall of Fame. He earned a B.A. degree in physical education in 1964.

A second-round choice in the 1964 NBA draft, the left-handed Reed played 10 seasons for the New York Knickerbockers (NBA). He was named NBA Rookie of the Year (1965) and led his squad to the 1970 and 1973 NBA titles, winning the playoff MVP award both times. An All-Star his first seven years before injuries slowed him down, Reed in 1969–1970 became the first player ever named MVP for the All-Star Game, regular season, and playoffs the same season. Although injured in Game 5 of the championship series against the Los Angeles Lakers, he returned in Game 7 to give the Knicks a psychological lift, carrying them to their first title. After suffering another injury-plagued season in 1973–1974, Reed retired as a player at age 31. Besides averaging 18.7 points, he left the Knicks as the club's leading scorer with 12,183 career points and the squad's all-time leading board man with 8,414 rebounds. He made the All-NBA First Team in 1970 and All-NBA Second Team in 1967, 1968, 1969, and 1971. Reed led the Knicks five times in scoring and six times in rebounding. Reed, whose jersey number 19 retired in 1976, was named in 1982 to the Naismith Memorial Basketball Hall of Fame.

In 1977 Reed replaced William "Red" Holzman* as Knicks head coach. He led New York into the NBA playoffs his first season, but was fired the next campaign when he challenged owner Sonny Werblin concerning personnel decisions. Reed compiled a 49-47 mark in his brief tenure with the Knickerbockers. At St. John's University, he worked one season as a voluntary assistant under Lou Carnesecca*. Reed served as head coach at Creighton University (Nebraska) from 1981–1982 through 1984–1985 and compiled a 52-65 overall record there. His 1983–1984 Bluejays finished 17-14 before losing in the first round of the NIT. Reed posted a 20-11 mark his final season at Creighton University and resigned in May 1985, citing pressures of recruiting. An assistant coach for the Atlanta Hawks (NBA) from 1985 to 1987 and the Sacramento Kings (NBA) in 1987–1988, he was named head coach of the struggling 12-42 New Jersey Nets (NBA) in February 1988. The Nets finished the 1987–1988 season with a 7-21 record and 1988–1989 season with a 26-56 mark under Reed. As an NBA coach, Reed notched a 82-124 overall mark for a .398 winning percentage. He served the Nets as general manager–vice president of basketball operations from 1988 to 1996 and as senior vice president from 1996 to 2003. He served as special basketball advisor to the New York Knicks in 2003–2004. In June 2004, the New Orleans Hornets (NBA) named him vice president of basketball operations. He was named one of the 50 Greatest Players in NBA History in 1996.

On the court, Reed's determination and enthusiastic leadership inspired his teammates. He combined a tremendous will to win with hard work, sacrifice, and commitment. An unrelenting will enabled him to overcome the frustration and anguish of continual injuries. Off the court, Reed exhibited unusual warmth, sensitivity, humility, and a happy-go-lucky attitude. He married Geraldine Oliver in February 1963 and divorced in 1969. In August 1983, Reed married Gale Kennedy. They have two children. Karl and Veronica, two children by a previous marriage, attended Creighton University. The Knicks captain wrote two books, *A Will to Win* and *A View from the Rim*, which describe his career.

BIBLIOGRAPHY: Jan Hubbard, ed., *The Official NBA Encyclopedia*, 3rd ed. (New York, CA, 2000); George Kalinsky, *The New York Knicks* (New York,

1996); Roland Lazenby, *The NBA Finals* (Indianapolis, IN, 1996); Willis Reed, with George Kalinsky, *A Will to Win* (New York, 1973); Willis Reed, with Phil Pepe, *A View from the Rim* (Philadelphia, PA, 1971); Willis Reed file, Naismith Memorial Basketball Hall of Fame, Springfield, MA; Ken Shouler et al., *Total Basketball* (Wilmington, DE, 2003); *TSN Official NBA Guide, 1974–1975* (St. Louis, MO, 1974); *TSN Official NBA Register, 2004–2005* (St. Louis, MO, 2004).

John L. Evers

REICH, Ernest B. "Ernie" "Tiger" (b. 1893, New York, NY; d. February 24, 1922, New York, NY), professional player, starred with the Original Celtics, a New York–based, barnstorming, professional basketball team. Reich came from a rough, brawling New York City neighborhood and attended school there. His basketball participation began with St. Gabriel's, an independent city club. Jack Murray, Chris Leonard*, Rudy Gallagher, and Johnny Beckman* teamed with Reich for St. Gabriel's. Reich remained with the Saints from 1905 to 1910, when he joined the White Plains, New York Lambs (HRL) club. He starred for the Sheepshead Bay (New York) Five in 1912, Jersey City Saints (New Jersey, ISL) in 1913, and ended his minor league career with Norwalk, Connecticut (CtL) in 1914. The following season featured Reich's promotion to the De Neri, Pennsylvania Dudes (EL). World War I intervened for two years, but he returned to professional basketball in 1918 for the Reading, Pennsylvania, Bears (EL). Reich captained the Scranton, Pennsylvania Miners 1919 EL titlists and excelled for both Stamford, Connecticut (EL) and Reading Bears (EL) in 1920.

Jim Furey* organized New York's Original Celtics in 1920 and recruited Reich as one of his first players. Reich's career ended as Celtics captain during the 1921–1922 season. The guard-forward's major assets included getting the tap from center and demonstrating unparalleled passing and dribbling skills. He ranked among his era's greatest players and was well liked by eastern audiences. Reich teamed with George "Horse" Haggerty*, Nat Holman*, Beckman, Pete Barry, Johnny Whitly, Leonard, Mike Smolnik, and Dutch Dehnert* on the legendary Celtics quintet. The Original Celtics earned an unprecedented honor in 1959, being inducted as a team into the Naismith Memorial Basketball Hall of Fame.

Reich died of double pneumonia at age 29 while at his playing peak and was survived by his wife, Mary E. (Murphy) Reich, and one daughter, Evelyn. His brother, Al, boxed professionally as a heavyweight.

BIBLIOGRAPHY: Jan Hubbard, ed., *The Official NBA Basketball Encyclopedia*, 3rd ed. (New York, 2000); David S. Neft et al., *The Sports Encyclopedia: Pro Basketball*, 5th ed. (New York, 1992); Murry Nelson, *The Originals: The New York Celtics Invent Modern Basketball* (Bowling Green, OH, 1999); *NYT*, February 25, 1922; Robert W. Peterson, *Cages to Jump Shots: Pro Basketball's Early Years* (New York, 1990); Ernest B. Reich file, Naismith Memorial Basketball Hall of Fame, Springfield, MA; Ken Shouler et al., *Total Basketball* (Wilmington, DE, 2003); *Springfield* (MA) *Union News*, February 24, 1922; Alexander Weyand, *The Cavalcade of Basketball* (New York, 1960).

John L. Evers and Wayne Patterson

REID, William A., Jr. "Bill" (b. September 28, 1893, Adrian, MI; d. October 30, 1955, Hamilton, NY), college player and coach, was the son of William Reid, a family barbershop partner. Reid made All-State as a basketball center at Adrian (Michigan) High School from 1909 to 1912 and captained his Michigan state championship team in 1912. He played basketball at Colgate University (New York) from 1914 to 1917 before graduating in 1918. He participated for the American Expeditionary Force basketball squad in 1918–1919, helping his team win an armed services title in 1919.

After being director of athletics at the University of Detroit (Michigan) for one year, Reid returned to Colgate University to coach baseball and basketball. From 1920 to 1939, he coached the Red Raiders' baseball team to a 236-118 win-loss mark. His 1923 squad won the ECAC baseball championship and compiled 23 straight victories. As Colgate basketball coach from 1920 to 1930, Reid achieved a 151-56 composite record. He became associate professor of physical education in 1928 and served as that school's athletic director from 1936 to 1956. Reid also served as vice president of the NCAA from 1942 to 1946 and as president of the ECAC and of the EIFA from 1944 to 1945. For his contributions, Reid in 1946 received an honorary Doctor of Laws degree from Colgate as a distinguished coach and administrator. In 1963, he was elected as a contributor to the Naismith Memorial Basketball Hall of Fame.

BIBLIOGRAPHY: Ralph Hickok, *Who Was Who in American Sports* (New York, 1971); Ronald L. Mendell, *Who's Who in Basketball* (New Rochelle, NY, 1973); *NYT*, October 31, 1955; Sandy Padwe, *Basketball's Hall of Fame* (Englewood Cliffs, NJ, 1970); William Reid file, Naismith Memorial Basketball Hall of Fame, Springfield, MA; Paul Soderberg and Helen Washington, comp. and ed., *The Big Book of Halls of Fame in the United States and Canada* (New York, 1977).

Frederick J. Augustyn Jr.

REIFF, Joseph "Joe" (b. June 6, 1911, Muskogee, OK), college and amateur player and referee, graduated in 1929 from Crane Technical High School in Chicago, Illinois and with a Bachelor's degree in 1933 from Northwestern University (Illinois; WC), where he starred in basketball three years from 1930–1931 through 1932–1933. Arthur "Dutch" Lonborg* coached Northwestern to its first WC basketball title in 1930–1931 with an 11-1 record. Lonborg employed the sensational six-foot three-inch Reiff at center with forwards Bert Riel and Robert McCarnes and guards Frank Marshall and Arthur Smith. Reiff led the WC in scoring with 123 points (10.0 points average) in 12 games and performed as the center pivot on set plays. Northwestern finished 16-1 overall, losing 34-28 to the University of Illinois. Besides sweeping all other WC rivals, the Wildcats defeated the University of Notre Dame (Indiana) twice and the University of Alabama and Bradley University (Illinois) once each. The HAF named Reiff to its First Team All-America and designated Northwestern as national champions.

The Wildcats shared second place in the WC with the University of Minnesota in 1931–1932, trailing HAF national champion Purdue University (Indiana). Guard John Wooden* of Purdue led the WC in scoring, denying the slender, indefatigable Reiff a second consecutive title. Reiff again paced Northwestern, finishing second in the WC scoring race and making Third Team All-America as a forward. In 1932–1933, the Wildcats tied Ohio State University for the WC title with a 10-2 record. Reiff tallied 168 points (14.0 average) in 12 games to lead the WC in scoring for a second time, followed by teammate Elmer Johnson with 109 points. Don Brewer, Nelson Culver, Al Kawal, and Eggs Manske played valuable supporting roles. Northwestern finished 15-4 overall, splitting series with Purdue, Illinois, Notre Dame, and Marquette University (Wisconsin). Reiff earned First Team All-America honors as a forward.

After the 1933 season, Reiff starred at forward for Rosenberg-Avery of Chicago in the national AAU basketball tournament and made the All-AAU team. Rosenberg-Avery lost the AAU championship game 25-23 to the undefeated Diamond D-X Oilers of Tulsa, Oklahoma. Reiff, who practiced as an attorney, married Clarisse Livingston and has two sons, Joseph and Philip. From 1937 to 1947, he refereed WC basketball games.

BIBLIOGRAPHY: Peter C. Bjarkman, *Big Ten Basketball* (Indianapolis, IN, 1994); Mike Douchant, *Encyclopedia of College Basketball* (Detroit, MI, 1995); *NCAA Official Collegiate Basketball Record Book, 1955* (New York, 1955); Wayne Patterson, Naismith Memorial Basketball Hall of Fame, Springfield, MA, letter to David L. Porter, February 8, 1994; Alexander M. Weyand, *The Cavalcade of Basketball* (New York, 1960); Kenneth Wilson and Jerry Brondfield, *The Big Ten* (Englewood Cliffs, NJ, 1967).

David L. Porter

RICE, Glen Anthony (b. May 28, 1967, Jacksonville, AK), college and professional player, is the son of Thomas Rice and Ernestine Rice. One of four children, he moved at age 10 to Flint, Michigan with his mother when his parents separated.

At Flint Northwestern High School, Rice was named an All-State forward in basketball and led his team to 28 straight victories and the state Class A championship. In 1985, he was selected Michigan high school's Mr. Basketball. Hounded by college recruiters, he signed with the University of Michigan because he felt comfortable with Coach Bill Frieder.

Rice experienced difficulty adjusting to the cultural shock and campus life as a freshman, but was helped by his pastor. He became the all-time BTC leading scorer in basketball, the first Wolverine player to win consecutive BTC scoring titles (22.1 point and 25.6 point averages), and a two-time All-America. In 1989 he won the Silver Basketball as the BTC MVP, making 51 percent of his three-point shots.

In 1988–1989, Rice made 51 of his 82 shots from the floor (62.2 percent), including 20-of-33 three-point shots (60.6 percent), to lead his team to the NCAA national championship. He averaged 31.3 points and 36 minutes, and made the NCAA tournament's "All-Windex" team with nearly six rebounds per game. He averaged only two fouls and broke Bill Bradley*'s NCAA tourney scoring record with 184 points in six games.

Rice was selected fourth overall in the 1989 NBA draft, and signed a five-year $8.5 million contract with the Miami Heat (NBA) on his wife Tracey's 22nd birthday. He made the NBA All-Rookie Second Team and was selected Miami's MVP for two seasons.

Rice played six seasons with Heat, three with the Charlotte Hornets (NBA), two with the Los Angeles Lakers (NBA), one with the New York Knicks (NBA) two with the Houston Rockets (NBA), and one with the Los Angeles Clippers (NBA). Rice, a three-time NBA All-Star, started for the 2000 Lakers' NBA champions. In 1996–1997, he led the NBA's in three-point shooting. During his 15-year, 1,000 game NBA career, Rice shot 45.6 percent, averaged 18.3 points and 4.4 rebounds, and scored more than 40 points 16 times. He is ranked third in three-pointers made (1,554) and ninth among active players in free throw percentage (84.5 percent). Rice, the career Miami scoring leader with 9,248 points, made the All-NBA Second Team in 1997 and the All-NBA Third Team in 1998.

After divorcing Tracey, Rice married Cristina Fernandez in 1997. He has four children.

BIBLIOGRAPHY: *Ann Arbor* (MI) *News*, May 13, 1985, p. E1; *Ann Arbor News*, November 10, 1988; *Ann Arbor News*, March 11, 1989, p. D1; *Ann Arbor News*, June 28, 1989; *Ann Arbor News*, November 12, 1989, p. D13; Peter C. Bjarkman, *Big Ten Basketball* (Indianapolis, IN, 1994); *Chicago Tribune*, May 12, 1989; *Detroit* (MI) *News*, March 19, 1989, p. 1C; *Detroit News*, March 31, 1989, pp. 1E, 5E; *Detroit News*, October 6, 1989; Mike Douchant, *Encyclopedia of College Basketball* (Detroit, MI, 1995); *Houston Rockets Preseason Guide, 2002–2003* (Houston, TX, 2002); NBA Media Ventures, 2003; Ken Shouler et al., *Total Basketball* (Wilmington, DE, 2003); *TSN Official NBA Register, 2004–2005* (St. Louis, MO, 2004); University of Michigan Sports Information, player profile, Ann Arbor, MI.

Keith McClellan

RICHARDSON, Nolan, Jr. (b. December 27, 1941, El Paso, TX), college player and coach, served as University of Arkansas (SWC) head basketball coach from 1986 through 2002 after similar positions at Western Texas JC and the University of Tulsa (MVC). Richardson enjoyed a 17-year combined 609-220 record boasting a national JC championship, an NIT title, and an NCAA crown in 16 tournament trips.

Richardson was brought up from age three by Rose Richardson, his paternal grandmother. His mother died when he was three, while his father, Nolan Sr., died when he reached age 12. Richardson, the first African American to attend El Paso (Texas) Bowie High School in 1955, earned All-District honors in baseball, basketball, and football. He played baseball at Eastern Arizona JC in Thatcher, Arizona, being selected an All-America first baseman. The Houston Astros (NL) drafted him in 1960, but he did not sign. Richardson returned to El Paso and enrolled at Texas Western University, which had no baseball team. He joined its basketball team, one of the first African American to do so. Richardson averaged nearly 20 points as a sophomore, while new coach Don Haskins* transformed him from a scorer to a defensive star in 1962. Haskins greatly influenced Richardson's future coaching style.

After graduating from Texas Western in 1964, Richardson tried out with the San Diego Chargers (NFL) and Dallas Chaparrals (ABA). A recurring hamstring injury, however, kept him off both teams. He returned to Bowie High School in El Paso as the first African American coach at a desegregated Texas high school and was named Coach of the Year three times in 10 seasons. Western Texas JC appointed Richardson head basketball coach in 1978, making him the first African American coach at an integrated Texas JC. In three seasons at Western Texas, Richardson's clubs finished 100-13 and won the 1980 JC national championship with star guard Paul Pressey.

Richardson was hired to head the University of Tulsa basketball program in 1981, becoming the first African American coach at a major Oklahoma university. Tulsa produced a 119–37 record in his five seasons there and earned postseason tournament bids every season. Tulsa played in two NIT tournaments, winning the 1981 title, and participated in the 1982, 1984, and 1985 NCAA tournaments.

In 1986, the University of Arkansas selected Richardson as head basketball coach to replace Eddie Sutton*, making him the first African American head coach in SWC history. Richardson struggled his first two years, beset by team drug problems and his daughter, Yvonne's, fight against and death from leukemia. In his 17 seasons at Arkansas, Richardson produced a 390-170 record during the regular season and 26-12 in 13 NCAA tournament appearances. His 1989–1990 squad shared third in the NCAA tournament, while his 1990–1991 team finished regional runner-up. He guided the 31-3 1993–1994 Razorbacks to the school's first national hoop title, making him the second African American coach with John Thompson* of Georgetown University to garner an NCAA Division I basketball crown. Arkansas started five underclassmen during the 1993–1994 campaign and rallied from a 10 points deficit in the final 17 minutes to defeat Duke University 76-72 in the championship game. Versatile Scotty Thurman arced a dramatic three-point shot with just 50 seconds left to break a 70-70 tie and propel the Razorbacks to victory. Guard Corey Beck and forward Corliss Williamson also sparked Richardson's squad. In 1994–1995, the Razorbacks finished 27-6 and lost to UCLA, 89-70 in the NCAA championship game. Arkansas fared 22-10 in 1999–2000 and reached the second round of the NCAA tournament. He cut ties with Arkansas in an abrupt, controversial departure in 2002.

Richardson serves as chairman of Easter Seals and on the board of directors of the American Red Cross. He has three children, Madalyn, Bradley and Nolan III, from his first marriage. He and his second wife, Rose (Davila) Richardson, had two children, Yvonne and Sylvia.

BIBLIOGRAPHY: Morgan G. Brenner, *College Basketball's National Championships* (Lanham, MD, 1999); Frank Deford, "Got to Do Some Coaching," *SI* 68 (March 7, 1988), pp. 94–106; *Des Moines* (IA) *Register*, April 5, 1994, pp. 15, 35; Mike Douchant, *Encyclopedia of College Basketball* (Detroit, MI, 1995); *NCAA Basketball Finest* (Overland Park, KS, 1991); *NCAA Men's Basketball Records, 2004* (Indianapolis, IN, 2003); *Official NCAA Final Four* (Overland Park, KS, 1993); Gene Wojciechowski, "College Basketball Report," *TSN*, September 21, 1992, p. 55.

Brian L. Laughlin

RICHMOND, Mitchell James "Mitch" (b. June 20, 1965, Fort Lauderdale, FL), college and professional player, is the son of Mitchell James Richmond and graduated from Boyd Anderson High School in Fort Lauderdale, Florida. Richmond attended Moberly (Missouri) Area JC and earned his Bachelor of Arts degree in social sciences from Kansas State University in 1988. He averaged 13.1 points and 5.6 rebounds in 78 games for Moberly in 1984–1985 and 1985–1986 and 20.7 points and 6.0 rebounds in 64 games for Kansas State in 1986–1987 and 1987–1988. Selected as the fifth pick of the 1988 NBA draft by the Golden State Warriors (NBA), he was voted 1989 NBA Rookie of the Year and named to the NBA All-Rookie First Team after averaging 22.0 points and 5.9 rebounds in 79 games. He played for the Warriors until being traded to the Sacramento Kings (NBA) in November 1991.

Richmond enjoyed a successful career with the Sacramento Kings, being named to the All-NBA Second Team in 1994, 1995, and 1997 and to the All-NBA Third Team in 1996. He was selected to the NBA All-Star Game six consecutive years from 1993 to 1998, averaging 9.5 points and 2.2 assists. Richmond was chosen MVP in the 1995 All-Star Game, scoring 23 points in 22 minutes. In 1997–1998, he became only the fourth player in NBA history to average 21 points in each of his first 10 seasons, joining the elite company of Michael Jordan*, Kareem Abdul-Jabbar*, and Oscar Robertson*. That season, Richmond led the Kings in scoring for the seventh straight season and in three-point field goals made and attempted, three-point percentage, free throw percentage, and steals. He ended the season as the Kings' all-time franchise leader in several categories, including three-pointers made (993) and attempted (2,460), and ranks second in steals (670), third in points (12,070) and eighth in assists (2,028). In May 1998, Richmond was traded to the Washington Wizards (NBA) for Chris Webber*. He signed with the Los Angeles Lakers (NBA) in 2001–2002 and retired after the Lakers won the 2002 championship title.

During his NBA career, six-foot five-inch, 215-pound Richmond averaged 21.0 points, 3.9 rebounds, and 3.5 assists, scoring 20,497 points and making 3,801 rebounds and 3,398 assists in 976 games. He appeared in 23 career NBA playoff games, averaging 19.5 points, 5.3 rebounds, and 3.0 assists. Richmond scored his 18,000th point in a victory over Orlando Magic on March 31, 1999 and recorded his 1000th steal versus the Charlotte Hornets on March 12, 1999. He played on the 1996 U.S. Dream Team that won the gold medal at the Atlanta, Georgia Olympics, and participated on the U.S. team that won the bronze medal at the 1988 Seoul, South Korea Olympics. He and his wife, Juli, have two sons, Phillip and Jerin.

BIBLIOGRAPHY: http://www.hoopshype.com/players/mitch_richmond.htm; http://www.nba.com/playerfile/mitch_richmond/bio.html; http://www.washingtonpost.com/wp-srv/sports/olympics/longterm/bball/mens/richmond; *TSN Official NBA Register, 2004–2005* (St. Louis, MO, 2004); Ken Shouler et al., *Total Basketball* (Wilmington, DE, 2003).

Maureen M. Smith

RIEBE, Melvin Russell "Mel" "Mouse" (b. July 12, 1916, Cleveland, OH; d. July 25, 1977, Youngstown, OH), professional player and coach, was one of five children born to Frank Riebe and Elsie Riebe in a working-class family. He had three brothers, Bill, Roland, and Harvey, and one sister, Nadine.

All four Riebe boys starred in athletics at Euclid High School in Ohio and possessed exceptional talent in baseball and basketball. Harvey, the youngest, played organized baseball and caught four years with the Detroit Tigers (AL). A five-year period of military duty interrupted Harvey's professional baseball ambitions. Bill played two seasons of professional basketball with Mel for the Cleveland (Ohio) Allmen Transfer Company (NBL). His father never played professional sports, but showed exceptional talent for statistics.

Mel, the oldest son, graduated from the College of Wooster in Ohio and married Bette (Heeter). He enjoyed six successful years in the NBL and BAA. Often used on the pivot, the five-foot eleven-inch, 180-pound Riebe possessed unequalled talent to operate in and around the basket and developed a hookshot that was difficult to defend because of his quickness and accuracy.

Riebe began his professional basketball career in 1943 with the Cleveland Chase Brass (NBL). He scored 323 points in 18 games, averaged 17.9 points, and was named NBL Rookie of the Year. In his first NBL season, Riebe led all players in field goals made, total points, and points average and was named to the All-NBL Team. By the 1944–1945 season, he had perfected his famous hookshot, again led the NBL in field goals made and points averages, and repeated on the All-NBL Team. Riebe became the first pro player to average 20 points. In 1944–1945, he registered 607 points in 30 NBL games and averaged 20.2 points. His 1945–1946 season was interrupted by a call to serve in the military, but Riebe the following year joined the Cleveland Rebels (BAA) in the first season for the rival BAA. He played for the Boston Celtics (BAA) in 1947–1948 and split the 1948–1949 season between the Celtics and the Providence (Rhode Island) Steamrollers (BAA).

During his professional career, Riebe played in 53 NBL games and ranked second to George Mikan* in scoring with 1,002 points during that period. He participated in 146 BAA games, becoming that league's all-time scoring leader with 1,575 points. In 199 NBL and BAA games between 1943–1944 and 1948–1949, Riebe connected on 1,009 field goals, netted 559 free throws, and compiled 2,577 points. He registered 129 points and averaged of 12.9 points in 10 NBL and BAA playoff games.

In 1954–1955, Riebe served as head baseball coach and swimming coach at the College of Wooster. The Fighting Scots finished with a 6-7 win-loss record in baseball and a 4-7 record in dual swim meets.

BIBLIOGRAPHY: Peter C. Bjarkman, *The Biographical History of Basketball* (Chicago, IL, 2000); "Fritz Riebe", *Local Deaths*, http://www.woosterdaily record.com (2001): "Hank Riebe," *Remembering "Hank" Riebe*, http://www.baseballlibrary.com (2001); Jan Hubbard, ed., *The Official NBA Encyclopedia*, 3rd ed. (New York, 2000); Neil D. Isaacs, *Vintage NBA* (Silver Spring, MD, 1996); "Mel Riebe," *Career Statistics*, http://www.celtination.com (2004); "Mel Riebe," *Stats, History and Awards*, http://www. basketballreference.com (2003); David S. Neft et al., *The Sports Encyclopedia: Pro Basketball*, 5th ed. (New York, 1993); Ken Shouler et al., *Total Basketball* (Wilmington, DE, 2003).

John L. Evers

RILEY, Patrick James "Pat" (b. March 20, 1945, Rome, NY), college and professional player, broadcaster, and coach, is the son of Leon R. Riley, a former major league baseball player and minor league manager, and Chris Riley. His brother, Lee, played defensive back in the NFL. At Linton High School in Schenectady, New York, Riley became an All-Eastern High School basketball All-America and an All-State football quarterback. Although offered a football scholarship from the University of Alabama, he chose to play basketball at the University of Kentucky. The six-foot four-inch, 205-pound guard-forward played for the legendary Adolph Rupp* from 1963–1964 to 1966–1967 and led the number one–ranked Wildcats to the NCAA title game in 1966 before losing 72-65 to Texas Western College. The team's MVP three years and captain as a senior, he paced "Rupp's Runts" in scoring with 541 points and a 21.6 points average in 1966. Riley, who graduated in 1967, scored 1,464 points for an 18.3 points average and collected 672 rebounds in 80 games at Kentucky. An All-SEC selection in 1965–1966, he in 1966 was named All-America, MVP in the NCAA Mideast Regional tournament, and an All-NCAA tournament team member.

Riley was selected seventh in the first round of the 1967 NBA draft by the San Diego Rockets (NBA). He was also chosen by the Dallas Cowboys (NFL) as a cornerback on the eleventh round of the NFL draft. After playing three seasons for the Rockets (1967–1968 to 1969–1970), Riley performed for the Los Angeles Lakers from 1970–1971 to 1974–1975 and participated on the club's record-setting NBA championship team in 1971–1972. His best season came in 1974–1975, when he averaged 11 points and enjoyed a career-high 38-point performance. The Lakers traded Riley to the Phoenix Suns (NBA) early the next season, after which he retired. During his pro career, he scored 3,906 points in 528 regular-season and 251 points 44 playoff games.

Riley served as Chick Hearn's* colorman on Los Angeles Lakers broadcasts and in 1979 was named Lakers assistant coach. In 1981, he replaced Paul Westhead as head coach and led the club to the NBA title, defeating the Philadelphia 76ers in six games. Riley recorded his 400th career victory in March 1988 against the New York Knickerbockers, accomplishing the feat in his 540th game, the quickest in NBA history. Former Philadelphia 76ers coach Billy Cunningham* had held the previous record, having registered his 400th victory in 572 games. Riley coached the Lakers through 1989–1990, compiling a 533-194 win-loss mark and .733 winning percentage. He was named NBA Coach of the Year in 1990. Riley's teams have compiled a 102-47 playoff record and have taken four NBA titles in seven trips to the finals. The Lakers won Pacific Division championships nine consecutive seasons, and defeated the Boston Celtics in six games to capture the 1985 and 1987 NBA crowns and the Detroit Pistons in seven games to take the 1988 NBA title. Riley coached the New York Knicks (NBA) from 1991–1992 through 1994–1995, compiling a 223-97 regular-season record, a 29-23 playoff mark, and three Atlantic Division titles. New York finished 60-22 in 1992–1993 and reached the Eastern Conference Finals before losing to the Chicago Bulls four games to two, with Riley earning Coach of the Year honors. The following year, the Knicks fared 57-25 and lost to the Houston Rockets in seven games in the NBA Finals.

Riley coached the Miami Heat (NBA) from 1995 to 2003, boasting a 354-270 regular-season mark and 18-25 playoff mark through 2002–2003. His best season there come in 1996–1997, when the Heat finished first in the Atlantic Division with a 61-21 record and lost to the Chicago Bulls in five games in the Eastern Conference Finals. Riley was named NBA Coach of the Year for the third time in 1997. Miami enjoyed winning records and made the playoffs the next four seasons and won the Atlantic Division from 1997–1998 through 2000–2001, but struggled in 2001–2002 and 2002–2003. Riley has served as club president since 1995. The Heat reached the 2005 Eastern Conference Finals against the Detroit Pistons.

During 21 NBA seasons, Riley enjoyed 1,110 wins with just 569 losses for a .661 regular-season winning percentage and a 155-100 playoff mark. He was named one of the Top 10 Coaches in NBA History in 1996. An impeccable dresser who designs many of his own clothes, Riley and his wife, Chris, reside in Brentwood, California.

BIBLIOGRAPHY: Mark Heisler, *The Lives of Riley* (New York, 1994); Jan Hubbard, ed., *The Official NBA Encyclopedia*, 3rd ed. (New York, 2000); *Los Angeles Lakers Media Guide, 1987–1988* (Los Angeles, CA, 1987); Bert Nelli, *The Winning Tradition: A History of Kentucky Wildcat Basketball* (Lexington, KY, 1984); Scott Ostler and Steve Springer, *Winnin' Times: The Rise and Rise of the Los Angeles Lakers* (New York, 1986); Russell Rice, *Kentucky Basketball's Big Blue Machine* (Huntsville, AL, 1976); Pat Riley, *Showtime* (New York, 1988); Roland Lazenby, *The Lakers: A Basketball Journey* (Indianapolis, IN, 1996); *The TSN Official NBA Register, 2004–2005* (St. Louis, MO, 2004).

John L. Evers

RILEY, Ruth Ellen (b. August 28, 1979, Macy, IN), college and professional player, is the daughter of Sharon Riley and has an older sister, Rachel, and a younger brother, Jacob. Riley began participating in basketball during the fourth grade. She played basketball four years at North Miami High School in Indiana, scoring 1,372 points with 1,011 rebounds and 427 blocked shots. Riley also earned All-State honors in volleyball and the discus in track and field her senior year. She graduated from the University of Notre Dame with a Bachelor's degree in psychology in 2001. A four year starter in basketball, Riley tallied 2,072 points, 1,007 rebounds, and a school record 370 blocked shots in 131 games. The six-foot five-inch, 194-pound center played all 32 games as a freshman. During her sophomore year, her 41 points against Providence (Rhode Island) College on January 30, 1998 established a Notre Dame school record. She was named 1999 BEaC Defensive Player of the Year and was the only unanimous BEaC first team selection. Riley, the first player in Notre Dame women's basketball history to earn AP First-Team All-America honors, was a finalist for the 2000 Naismith Women's Basketball Player of the Year Award.

Riley dominated women's college basketball her senior year, leading Notre Dame to its first ever NCAA national championship. Her 28 points and 13 rebounds powered Notre Dame to a 68-66 victory over Purdue University (Indiana) in the NCAA championship game. Riley was named Most Outstanding Player of the NCAA Final Four, was the first Notre Dame player to capture the Naismith Women's College Player of the Year Award, was unanimously picked First-Team All-America by the AP, and garnered a second consecutive Verizon Women's Basketball Academic All-America First-Team selection. She was the first player to sweep BEaC honors as Player of the Year, Defensive Player of the Year, and Female Scholar-Athlete of the Year.

Riley was picked first overall in the (WNBA) draft by the Miami Sol on April 20, 2001. In two seasons with Miami, she became a strong post player with excellent movement for her size. She possessed a good jumpshot, but her greatest contributions were in rebounding and blocking opponents' shots.

Riley played with Valencia, Spain in the Spanish Professional League and Euroleague in 2002–2003. She was picked by the Detroit Shock as the first overall selection in the 2003 WNBA dispersal draft after the Miami Sol folded. Riley was chosen a 2003 WNBA All-Star and helped Detroit win the WNBA title that year earning the WNBA Finals MVP Award. In four WNBA seasons, she has made 620 rebounds, blocked 198 shots, scored 1,071 points, and recorded 165 assists in 126 games. She played on the gold–medal winning U.S. Olympic Women's basketball team in 2004 and performed in the WNBA playoffs in 2001 and 2004.

Riley, who is single, participates in community outreach programs in the off-season. She enjoys reading and hopes to pursue a career in psychology after her basketball career. She credits her mother as her greatest inspiration.

BIBLIOGRAPHY: Dick Patrick, "Riley Ends Notre Dame Career with Title," *USA Today* (updated April 2, 2001, usatoday.com), pp. 1–3; *TSN Official WNBA Guide and Register, 2004* (St. Louis, MO, 2004); University of Notre Dame, "Ruth Riley Profile," *Student Advantage* (Notre Dame, IN, 2003), pp. 1–5; WNBA, "Ruth Riley Biography," *WNBA.com* (October 2003), pp. 1–2; WNBA, "Ruth Riley Player Information," *WNBA.com* (October, 2003), pp. 1–2.

Frank J. Olmsted

RIPLEY, Elmer "Rip" (b. July 21, 1891, Staten Island, NY; d. April 29, 1982, Staten Island, NY), college and professional player and coach, was born the same year the game was invented. He entered the pro game directly from high school, joining the Carbondale, Pennsylvania Pioneers team in 1908. The five-foot eight-inch Ripley, who possessed a deadly two-handed set shot, performed for over one dozen teams in every Eastern pro league and performed long service in the PSL and ISL. He toured the 1924–1925 season with the famed Original Celtics and joined the ABL in 1925, appearing with Brooklyn, Washington, and Fort Wayne before retiring in 1930.

When still active as a player, Ripley began his 28-year college coaching career. His first assignment came in 1922 at Wagner College (New York), where he remained for three seasons. He coached the Georgetown (Washington. D.C.) University Hoyas for 10 seasons in three periods (1927–1928 to 1928–1929, 1938–1939 to 1942–1943, and 1946–1947 to 1948–1949), with his 1942–1943 team losing to the University of Wyoming in the NCAA Finals. Ripley piloted Yale University (Connecticut) from the 1929–1930 through 1934–1935 seasons, winning the IvL championship in the 1932–1933 campaign. He also coached at Columbia University (New York; 1943–1944 and 1944–1945), the University of Notre Dame (Indiana; 1945–1946), John Carroll University (Ohio; 1950–1951), and the U.S. Military Academy (New York; 1951–1952 to 1952–1953). Overall, his college teams won 298 games and lost 228. His All-Americas included Vince Boryla*, Leo Klier, Billy Hassett, and John Mahnken. Ripley also coached Don Shula, Miami Dolphins (NFL) coach; John McHale, Montreal Expos (NL) president; and William Shea, the lawyer for whom New York's Shea Stadium was named.

During the 1950s, Ripley toured with the Harlem Globetrotters as coach and traveled throughout the world giving basketball clinics. He piloted the Israeli Olympic Team in 1956 and the Canadian Olympic Team in 1960. His last professional positions included brief stints with the Washington Tapers (ABL) in 1961–1962 and Scranton Miners (EBL) in 1962–1963. Ripley remained active in basketball until 82 years old, coaching the Englewood (New Jersey) School for Boys from 1966 until 1973. In 1972 he was elected to the Naismith Memorial Basketball Hall of Fame as a contributor.

BIBLIOGRAPHY: Zander Hollander, ed., *The Complete History of Basketball* (New York, 1975); William Mokray, ed., *Ronald Encyclopedia of Basketball* (New York, 1963); Murray R. Nelson, *The Originals: The New York Celtics Invent Modern Basketball* (Bowling Green, OH, 1999); *NYT*, 1944–1952; *New York Times*, April 19, 1982; Robert W. Peterson, *Cages to Jump Shots: Pro Basketball's Early Years* (New York, 1990); Elmer Ripley file, Naismith Memorial Basketball Hall of Fame, Springfield, MA; Ken Shouler et al., *Total Basketball* (Wilmington, DE, 2003); *Washington Post*, 1927–1929, 1938–1943, 1946–1949.

Karel de Veer

RISEN, Arnold Denny "Arnie" "Stilts" (b. October 9, 1924, Williamstown, KY), college and professional player, is the eldest of four children of John D. Risen, Sr., a railway mail clerk, and Alvira (Scroggins) Risen, and graduated from Williamstown (Kentucky) High School in 1942. After attending Kentucky State University in 1942–1943, Risen starred in basketball at Ohio State University (BTC) from 1943–1944 to 1945–1946. In 1943–1944 he led the 14-7 Buckeyes to the NCAA tournament semifinals, where Dartmouth College (New Hampshire) ousted Ohio State 60-43. The six-foot nine-inch, 210-pound Risen, among the first outstanding slim, mobile, modern basketball centers, made Third Team All-America in 1944–1945. The 15-5 Buckeyes, coached by Harold Olsen*, won the BTC title and again reached the NCAA semifinals before being eliminated by NYU 70-65. In 1945–1946, Risen paced the 16-5 Buckeyes to a third-place finish at the NCAA tournament. The University of North Carolina defeated Ohio State 60-57 in the NCAA semifinals.

Risen joined the Indianapolis Kautskys (NBL) in 1945–1946 and performed there until January 1948, scoring 1,606 points and averaging 13.1 points in 123 regular-season games. In 1946–1947, he led Indianapolis in scoring with 582 points (13.2 points average). In January 1948, the Rochester Royals (NBL) purchased Risen. In 1948, Risen led the 44-16 Royals to first place in the Eastern Division with a 14.5-point scoring average. A broken jaw sidelined Risen from the NBL Finals against the victorious Minneapolis Lakers. Rochester, featuring fast-breaking guards Bob Davies* and Bobby Wanzer*, jumped to the rival BAA before the 1948–1949 season and edged the Lakers for the Western Division regular-season title. Risen paced the BAA in field goal percentage (42.3 percent) and ranked fourth in scoring with 995 points. Minneapolis eliminated Rochester in the BAA semifinals. The Royals, relying on Risen's mobility and Davies's and Wanzer's ball handling, shared the NBA Central Division crown with 51-17 Minneapolis in 1949–1950.

Risen enjoyed his best NBA season in 1950–1951, ranking fourth among NBA rebounders with 795 (12.0 per game) and ninth in scoring with a career-high 1,077 points (16.3-point average). He also led the NBA playoffs in scoring with 273 points (19.5-point average) and 196 rebounds, helping Rochester defeat the New York Knickerbockers in the seven-game NBA Finals. In 1951–1952, Rochester edged the Lakers for the Western Division title with an NBA-best 41-25 record. Risen again placed fourth in rebounds with a career-high 841 rebounds (12.7 average) and ninth in scoring with 1,032 points (15.6-point average). Rochester lost to Minneapolis in the 1952 NBA semifinals. His offensive production declined steadily the next two seasons.

Risen spent his final three NBA campaigns with the Boston Celtics (NBA), who won the NBA title against the St. Louis Hawks in 1957 and the Eastern Division crown in 1957–1958. During 11 NBA seasons, he tallied 7,633 points (12.0 per game) and grabbed 5,011 rebounds in 637 regular-season games and recorded 790 points (13.0-point average) and made 561 rebounds in 61 playoff games. Risen, who married and had one son, Dennis, and one daughter, Barbara, performed in the 1952–1954 NBA All-Star Games and made the All-BAA Second Team in 1949. He was elected to the Naismith Memorial Basketball Hall of Fame in 1998. The Cleveland Heights, Ohio resident helped build a subdivision in Webster, New York following his NBA career and enjoys bowling, golfing, horse racing, and playing cards.

BIBLIOGRAPHY: Peter C. Bjarkman, *The Biographical History of Basketball* (Chicago, IL, 2000); Zander Hollander, ed., *The Modern Encyclopedia of Basketball* (New York, 1973); Jan Hubbard, ed., *The Official NBA Basketball Encyclopedia*, 3rd ed. (New York, 2000); Neil D. Isaacs, *Vintage NBA* (Silver Spring, MD, 1996); Leonard Koppett, *24 Seconds to Shoot: An Informal History of the National Basketball Association* (New York, 1968); Roland Lazenby, *The NBA Finals* (Indianapolis, IN, 1996); David S. Neft and Richard M. Cohen, eds., *The Sports Encyclopedia: Pro Basketball*, 5th ed. (New York, 1992); Robert W. Peterson, *Cages to Jump Shots: Pro Basketball's Early Years* (New York, 1990); Arnold Risen file, Naismith Memorial Basketball Hall of Fame, Springfield, MA; Elizabeth L. Schneider, Director of Grant County Public Library, Williamstown, KY, letter to David L. Porter, March 16, 1994; Ken Shouler et al., *Total Basketball* (Wilmington, DE, 2003).

David L. Porter

RIZZOTTI, Jennifer Marie (b. May 15, 1974, White Plains, NY), college and professional player and coach, is the daughter of Tom Rizzotti and Carol Rizzotti and has two brothers, Tommy and Greg, and a sister, Candice. Rizzotti, a 1992 graduate of New Fairfield (Connecticut) High School, led the Rebels to consecutive state basketball championships in

1991 and 1992. She was selected state Gatorade Player of the Year as a senior.

Rizzotti attended the University of Connecticut between 1992 and 1996 and helped lead the Huskies to the 1995 national championship. In four seasons, she averaged 11.4 points, 4.7 assists, and 3.4 rebounds in 135 games. She established Connecticut career records with 637 assists and 349 steals and single-season records of 222 assists and 112 steals.

Featured on the *SI* April 10, 1995 cover, Rizzotti, a five-foot six-inch, 145-pound point guard, was named the AP National Player of the Year and won the Wade Trophy for the Outstanding Player in NCAA Division I in 1995–1996. She was selected Academic All-America, the BEaC Player of the Year, and the BEaC Women's Basketball Scholar-Athlete of the Year.

Rizzotti graduated from the University of Connecticut in 1996 with a Bachelor's degree in biological science and played basketball three seasons for New England Blizzard (ABL), handing out 4.9 assists per game in 97 games, and recording 919 points for 9.5-point average.

The Houston Comets selected Rizzotti in the 1999 WNBA draft. She played for the Houston Comets in 1999 and 2000 when they repeated as WNBA champions for the third and fourth consecutive times. In April 2001, Rizzotti was traded to the Detroit Shock (WNBA). The following month, the Cleveland Rockers acquired her. In three seasons with the Rockers (2001–2003), Rizzotti scored 356 points and totaled 201 assists in 91 games. The Detroit Shock selected her in the first round in the Dispersal Draft in January 2004, but she retired from the WNBA. In her five-year WNBA career, she has scored 458 points and handed out 264 assists in 148 games. In nine WNBA playoff games, she recorded 18 points.

Rizzotti was named head basketball coach at the University of Hartford (Connecticut) in September 1999. She has guided the Hawks to a school record 16 victories, a first-ever conference championship, and an NCAA tournament appearance.

Rizzotti married William Sullivan on July 17, 1999 in Connecticut. He assists her at the University of Hartford. She was inducted into the Connecticut Women's Basketball Hall of Fame in 2001.

BIBLIOGRAPHY: "Jennifer Rizzotti," *Background*, http://www.wnba.com (2003); "Jennifer Rizzotti," *Family*, http://www.apsedallasnews.com (1999); "Jennifer Rizzotti," *Head Coach*, http://www.hartfordhawks.com (1999); "Jennifer Rizzotti," *Player Info*, http://www.wnba.com (2003); "Jennifer Rizzotti," *Player Profile*, http://www.wnba.com (2003); *TSN Official WNBA Guide and Register, 2004* (St. Louis, MO, 2004).

John L. Evers

ROBERTSON, Alvin Cyrrale (b. July 22, 1962, Barberton, OH), college and professional player, is the son of Robert Robertson, graduated from Barberton (Ohio) High School, where he played basketball, and studied criminal justice at the University of Arkansas. The six-foot four-inch, 190-pound guard starred for coach Eddie Sutton* in 1982–1983 and 1983–1984 after transferring from Crowder (Missouri) JC. In two years with the Razorbacks, he averaged 10.7 points and 3.6 rebounds. Robertson's defensive prowess attracted the attention of SWC coaches and earned him a spot on the 1984 gold medal–winning U.S. Olympic team. He was selected by the San Antonio Spurs (NBA) as their top draft pick in the 1984 NBA draft.

In 1986 Robertson was named the NBA's Defensive Player of the Year and set San Antonio franchise marks for steals in a season (301) and steals per game (3.67). During his NBA career, he averaged 14.0 points, 5.0 assists, 2.7 steals, and 5.2 rebounds in 779 games. Robertson played with the Spurs through 1988–1989, later performed with the Milwaukee Bucks and Detroit Pistons (NBA), and finished his playing career in 1995–1996 with the Toronto Raptors (NBA). He made the All-NBA Second Team in 1986, NBA All-Defensive First Team in 1987 and 1991, and NBA All-Defensive Second Team in 1986 and 1988–1990.

Robertson has experienced many problems off the court. Early in his career, he began using cocaine and was involved several violent altercations with women. In June 1995, Robertson was arrested on charges of burglary, vandalizing a car, assault, and resisting arrest. In October 1996, he was convicted of these charges and placed on 10 years probation. Robertson began operating a construction company in San Antonio while under state supervision. In July 2001, he tested positive for cocaine and was ordered to enter a residential drug rehabilitation program. Robertson later was convicted of parole violations and sexual assault and sentenced to three years in prison. He became an inmate at the Garza West facility of the Texas Department of Criminal Justice in early 2002. Robertson and his wife, Jackie, have been married for 17 years and have three children. He has another son living in Arkansas.

BIBLIOGRAPHY: "Ex-Spur Fouls Out," *San Antonio Express-News*, January 30, 2002, p. 1A; "Ex-Spur Robertson Sentenced to Prison," *Seattle Post-Intelligencer*, January 31, 2002, p. C4; "Flippant Former Spur Lands in the Right Place," *San Antonio Express-News*, January 31, 2002, p. 6B; "From Court to Court," *San Antonio Express-News*, April 29, 2002, p. 6D; Buck Harvey, "From Spurs Pro to Con: Hard Times of Robertson," *San Antonio Express-News*, April 29, 2002, p. 1D; Jan Hubbard, ed., *The Official NBA Encyclopedia*, 3rd ed. (New York, 2000); Mary Ormsby, "Former Raptor Sentenced to Three Years in Jail," *Toronto Star*, January 31, 2002, p. E04; "Rehab of Robertson: When the Camera Lights Go Off," *San Antonio Express-News*, July 31, 2001, p. 1C; Lisa Sandberg, "Ex-Spur Robertson Faces Sex Abuse Allegations," *San Antonio Express-News*, January 29, 2002, p. 3B; University of Arkansas Men's Basketball Media Guide, 1983–1984 (Fayetteville, AR, 1983).

Jorge Iber

ROBERTSON, Oscar Palmer "The Big O" (b. November 24, 1938, Charlotte, TN), college and professional player and sportscaster, is considered by many among the finest players in the history of the game. The youngest of three boys of Henry Robertson, a sanitation worker, Mazell (Bell) Robertson, he grew up in straitened circumstances in Indianapolis, Indiana and played his first basketball with his brothers at the local YMCA. His oldest brother, Bailey, later played for the Harlem Globetrotters. At Indianapolis' Crispus Attucks High School, the all-around athletic starred as a baseball pitcher and excellent track and field high jumper. Robertson led Crispus Attucks High School to two state basketball titles and a 45-game winning streak, made All-State three times, and was chosen for several All-America high school teams. He graduated sixteenth in a class of 171.

The heavily recruited Robertson picked the University of Cincinnati (Ohio) for its proximity to his home. As the first black to play basketball for the school, he averaged 33.8 points for three seasons, recorded a game high of 62 points against North Texas State University his senior year, and set 14 NCAA University Division records in all categories of scoring. Robertson's 62-point performance remained the single-game MVC scoring record until 1988, when Hersey Hawkins* of Bradley University (Illinois) tallied 63 points against the University of Detroit. He captained the undefeated 1960 U.S. Olympic team that won the gold medal and made All-America in each of his varsity years. Unhappy with racial tension in the area, Robertson dropped in scholastic performance somewhat from high school, but graduated with a Bachelor's degree in business administration in 1960. A territorial draft choice of the Cincinnati Royals (NBA), he excelled from the start of his pro career with a 30.5 points average his first season. Robertson averaged better than 25 points during his 14 season career in the NBA and led the NBA in assists six seasons. At the close of his NBA career, he ranked as the all-time leader in assists with 9,887 and averaged better than nine assists. His greatest single season (1963–1964) saw him average 31.4 points and 11 assists, finish second behind Wilt Chamberlain* in scoring, and win the NBA MVP award. Named to the All-NBA First Team for 10 consecutive years, he trailed only Chamberlain in a 1971 nationwide vote for the All-Time NBA Team.

But in his college and pro careers in Cincinnati, Robertson's teams never enjoyed championship seasons. This came after his trade to the Milwaukee Bucks (NBA) for Charlie Paulk and Flynn Robinson in 1969, Bob Cousy's* first year as Cincinnati coach. Teamed with the youthful Lew Alcindor (Kareem Abdul-Jabbar*), he helped secure a title for Milwaukee in 1970–1971, the third year of the franchise. At six-feet five-inches and 215-pounds, "The Big O" finished his NBA career with 26,710 points and an all-time record 7,694 free throws. Coaches "Phog" Allen* of the University of Kansas and "Red" Auerbach* of the Boston Celtics (NBA) rated him the best, most versatile player they had seen. Robertson married former teacher Yvonne Crittenden in June 1960, has three daughters, Shana, Tia, and Mari and resides in Indianapolis. He donated a kidney to one daughter who was suffering from lupus to save her life. In 1980 he was elected as a player to the Naismith Memorial Basketball Hall of Fame. Robertson worked as an ABC Sports radio analyst for basketball games. He served as president of the retired players association and as national director of the Naismith Memorial Basketball Hall of Fame. Robertson was named to the NBA 35th Anniversary All-Time Team in 1980 and one of the 50 Greatest Players in NBA History in 1996. He wrote *The Art of Basketball* (1998) and operates chemical, packaging, media, and real estate companies. He served as interim coach at the University of Cincinnati in July–August, 2004 while coach Bob Huggins* was suspended for drunken driving.

BIBLIOGRAPHY: Peter C. Bjarkman, *The Biographical History of Basketball* (Chicago, IL, 2000); Zander Hollander, ed., *The Modern Encyclopedia of Basketball* (Garden City, NY, 1979); *The Lincoln Library of Sports Champions*, vol. 15 (Columbus, OH, 1974); Randy Roberts, *But They Can't Beat Us* (Champaign, IL, 1999); Oscar Robertson file, Naismith Memorial Basketball Hall of Fame, Springfield, MA; Art Rust, *Illustrated History of the Black Athlete* (Garden City, NY, 1985); Ken Shouler et al., *Total Basketball* (Wilmington, DE, 2003).

Leonard H. Frey

ROBINSON, David Maurice (b. August 6, 1965, Key West, FL), college and professional player, was a seven-foot one-inch, 235-pound tower of strength and quickness and possessed the talent, resources, and attributes to become a preeminent NBA center of the 1990s. Robinson exhibited speed, size, muscle, leaping ability, excellent rebounding, and accurate shooting and enjoyed the advantage of being left-handed, a condition demanding continuous adjustments by his defenders. He also combined intelligence, maturity seriousness, and responsibility, being a true professional and concerned citizen with a superior work ethic. Knowledgeable observers claimed that Robinson needed to develop a desire, intensity, and focus like a Bill Russell* or Kareem Abdul-Jabbar*.

Robinson is the son of Ambrose Robinson, a career Navy man, and Freida Robinson, a nurse. He played high school basketball in Virginia Beach, Virginia and at Osbourn Park High School in Manassas, Virginia. He graduated from the U.S. Naval Academy (Maryland) in 1987, having been selected *TSN* College Player of the Year in 1987 and a *TSN* All-America in 1986 and 1987. At Navy, he averaged 21.0 points, shot over 61 percent from the floor, and rebounded and blocked shots with skill and tenacity. Robinson also averaged 10.5 rebounds and set NCAA Division I records for most blocked shots in a season (207, 1986) and game (14), and career blocked shot average (5.9). The San Antonio Spurs (NBA), then a hapless, doormat franchise, drafted him as their first overall pick following his graduation in 1987. The Spurs knew that Robinson could not join them until the 1989–1990 season because he was required to serve two years in the U.S. Navy.

The Spurs' patience was rewarded handsomely. Robinson's exceptional initial NBA season saw him named NBA Rookie of the Year and, incredibly, Rookie of the Month every month. Robinson made the All-NBA Third Team and the All-Defensive Second Team, scoring 1,993 points, averaging 24.3 points per game, compiling a .531 shooting percentage, snatching 983 rebounds, and blocking over 300 shots. His all-around team-oriented play earned him the Schick Pivotal Player Award, symbolizing his total contribution to the Spurs' success. The Spurs amazingly converted from a 21-61 win-loss record in 1988–1989 to a 56-26 mark in 1989–1990 under Robinson's leadership, the most impressive single-season improvement in NBA history. San Antonio compiled a 55-27 mark in 1990–1991, as Robinson tallied 25.6 points per game, led the NBA in rebounding with 1,063, and ranked second in blocked shots with 320.

Robinson spent his entire NBA career with San Antonio, compiling 20,790 points (21.6 average), 10,497 rebounds (10.6 average), and 2,954 blocked shots (3.0 average) in 987 games. He holds the all-time Spurs records for most points, rebounds, steals (1,388), and blocked shots. Robinson averaged 18.1 points, 10.6 rebounds, and 2.5 blocked shots in 123 playoff games. He was selected to the NBA All-Star Team 10 times (1990–1996, 1998, 2000–2001), averaging 14.1 points. Robinson was named NBA MVP in 1995, All-NBA First Team in 1991–1992, 1995–1996; All-NBA Second Team (1994, 1998); All-NBA Third Team (1990, 1993, 2000–2001); NBA Defensive Player of the Year (1992); NBA All-Defensive First Team (1991–1992, 1995–1996); NBA All-Defensive Second Team (1990, 1993–1994, 1998); and won the IBM Award five times, the NBA Sportsmanship Award in 2001, and the J. Walter Kennedy Citizenship Award in 2003. He led the NBA in scoring with 2,383 points (29.8 point average) in 1993–1994, tally 71 points the final night to edge Shaquille O'Neil.* He also led the league in blocked shots with 320 in 1990–1991 and 305 in 1991–1992; rebounds with 1,063 in 1990–1991 and 1,000 in 1995–1996; and free throws made with 693 in 1993–1994, 656 in 1994–1995, and 626 in 1995–1996.

Robinson was selected to the NBA 50th Anniversary All-Time Team in 1996 and helped San Antonio capture NBA championships in 1999 and 2003, combining with Tim Duncan*. San Antonio shared the Midwest Division title with an NBA best 37-13 record in 1998–1999 and dominated the New York Knicks four games to one in the NBA Finals. The Spurs shared the Midwestern Division crown with an NBA best 60-22 mark in 2002–2003 and defeated the New Jersey Nets four games to two in the NBA Finals. Robinson retired following the 2002–2003 season. He played for the gold medal–winning U.S. basketball squad at the 1992 Barcelona, Spain, and the 1996 Atlanta, Georgia Summer Olympic Games. Robinson remains a glowing example to young and old alike as a person whose style, image, and substance interact both on and off the court. He married Valerie Hoggart in December 1991 and serves as a minister.

BIBLIOGRAPHY: David Branon, "David Robinson: It All Adds Up To Greatness," *Slam Dunk* (1994), pp. 217–224; Greg Donaldson, "Stand and Deliver," *Sport* 81 (November 1990), pp. 69–72, 74; Mike Douchant, *Encyclopedia of College Basketball* (Detroit, MI, 1995); Jan Hubbard, ed., *The Official NBA Encyclopedia*, 3rd ed. (New York, 2000); Roland Lazenby, "Spurs A Dynasty In the Making," *Spurs* (June 25, 1999), pp. 39–48; *NYT*, October 28, 1990; *NCAA Men's Basketball Records, 2004* (Indianapolis, IN, 2003); Ken Shouler et al., *Total Basketball* (Wilmington, DE, 2003); *TSN Official NBA Register, 2005* (St. Louis MO, 2004), *TSN Official NBA Guide, 2002–2003* (St. Louis, MO, 2002); Phil Taylor, "Here's To You Mr Robinson," *SI* 91 (July 7, 1999), pp. 20, 22–23, 25; *USA Today*, April 23, 1991.

Gustavo N. Agrait

ROBINSON, Glenn Allen, Jr. (b. January 10, 1973, Gary, IN), college and professional player, is the son of Glenn Robinson Sr. and Christine Bridgeman. Robinson averaged 25.6 points and 14.6 rebounds in basketball at Roosevelt High School in Gary, Indiana, and was named High School Player of the Year in 1991. He entered Purdue University (Indiana) in 1991 and averaged 24.1 points and 9.2 rebounds in basketball as a sophomore in 1992–1993. In 1993–1994, Robinson was selected First-Team All-America and won the national scoring championship, averaging 30.3 points. He tallied 1,030 points in 1993–1994, the 13th highest in NCAA history. The National College Basketball Player of the Year, he also won the Naismith and Wooden awards. In two seasons at Purdue, he scored 1,706 points (27.5 average) and made 602 rebounds (9.7 average) in 62 games.

The six-foot seven-inch, 230-pound Robinson was selected first pick overall by the Milwaukee Bucks (NBA) in the 1994 draft. An NBA All-Rookie First Team member, Robinson led NBA rookies in scoring with 21.9 points per game in 1994–1995. The NBA Rookie of the Month in December 1994 and April 1995, he ended the year in style by averaging 21.9 points, 6.7 rebounds, and 2.5 assists. Nicknamed "Big Dog," Robinson started all 82 games in 1995–1996 and averaged 20.2 points. In 1996–1997, he reached career-highs with a team best 21.1 points average, 68 blocked shots, .465 field goal shooting percentage and .350 three-point shooting percentages. He led Milwaukee in scoring 36 times and reached double figures in rebounding eight times that season.

In 2000–2001, Robinson enjoyed a career-high 6.9 rebounds per game and paced the Bucks in field goals made (684) and attempted

(1,460). He was named to the NBA All-Star team in 2000 and 2001, scoring 10 points and making six rebounds in 2000. Robinson, the leading scorer in Milwaukee franchise history, averaged 21.1 points and 6.2 rebounds in eight seasons with Milwaukee.

Robinson, who was acquired by the Atlanta Hawks (NBA) in August 2002, was charged with domestic battery and illegal possession of a firearm in July 2003. He led the Hawks in scoring with a 20.8 points average in 2002–2003 and was traded to Philadelphia 76ers (NBA) July 2003. He finished second on the 76ers in scoring with a 16.6 point average in 2003–2004, but played only 42 games. The New Orleans Hornets (NBA) acquired Robinson in February 2005. Injuries sidelined him for the 2004–2005 season. He joined the San Antonio Spurs (NBA) for nine games at the end of the 2004–2005 season and played a reserve role as the Spurs reached the NBA Finals against the Detroit Pistons. In 11 NBA seasons, he has scored 14,234 points (20.7 point average) and made 4,189 rebounds (6.1 average) in 688 games. He was the 159th player in NBA history to pass the 12,000 career point mark.

Robinson remains single and lives in Gary during the off-season. A hometown hero, he runs community activities including annual an All-Star Game in Gary. He was honored when Gary proclaimed August 4, 1994 as "Glenn Robinson Day."

BIBLIOGRAPHY: Mike Douchant, *Encyclopedia of College Basketball* (Detroit, MI, 1995); Michael Farber, "First, but Not Equals: No 1 draft picks basketball and in hockey," *SI* 81 (July 1994), pp. 46–49; "Glenn Robinson," *Sports Stars*, Series 1–4 (1994–1998), http://galenet.galegroup.com; Bruce Newman, "Top Dog," *SI 80* (March 1994), pp. 42–45; Ken Shouler et al., *Total Basketball* (Wilmington, DE, 2003); Phil Taylor, "Two Bucks Worth," *SI* 85 (December 1996), pp. 54–58; *TSN NBA Register, 2004–2005* (St. Louis, MO, 2004).

Njoki-Wa-Kinyatti

RODGERS, Guy William, Jr. (b. September 1, 1935, Philadelphia, PA; d. February 19, 2001, Los Angeles, CA), college and professional player, was the son of Guy Rodgers Sr., grew up in Philadelphia, Pennsylvania, and graduated from Philadelphia's Northeast High School, where he impressed numerous college basketball scouts. He rejected out of town scholarship offers and entered Temple University (Pennsylvania) in 1955. A guard, Rodgers set the Owls' career basketball scoring record with 1,767 points and also became the school's all time assist leader. By his senior year, he twice made consensus All-America and three times was voted MVP of Philadelphia's prestigious "Big 5." In his three varsity seasons, Temple compiled a 74-16 win-loss record and in 1956 and 1958 finished third in the NCAA tournament. Under coach Harry Litwack*, he teamed with Hal Lear to form one of college basketball's most devastating backcourt combinations. Rodgers also holds the Temple record for most assists in one game (15 against Manhattan (New York) College) and season (185 in 1956–1957). When Temple won the 1957 Holiday Festival, he was named MVP. He was elected to Temple's Hall of Fame in 1971.

The Philadelphia Warriors (NBA) drafted Rodgers in 1958. One of the NBA's all-time playmakers, he compiled more lifetime assists by his retirement than any other players except Oscar Robertson* and Bob Cousy*. The small, six-foot 185-pound Rodgers was considered one of the NBA's greatest ball handlers. In his first pro game, he scored 24 points and handed out nine assists against the Boston Celtics. Warriors owner Eddie Gottlieb* termed Rodgers' performance the "most sensational debut" he had witnessed. During his rookie year, Rodgers set a Warriors game record with 18 assists. He teamed with Philadelphia natives Wilt Chamberlain*, Paul Arizin*, and Tom Gola* to give the Warriors a strong local following. Rodgers, along with Gola and Arizin, also had attended city colleges. Rodgers accompanied the Warriors when the franchise shifted to San Francisco in 1963. He played with the Chicago Bulls (NBA) in 1967–1968 and appeared briefly with the Cincinnati Royals (NBA) and Milwaukee Bucks (NBA), retiring after the 1969–1970 season.

During 12 pro seasons, Rodgers made 6,917 assists (7.8 assists per game) and scored 10,415 NBA points for an 11.7 points average. He competed in 892 regular-season NBA contests and 46 postseason playoff games. Rodgers averaged

11.0 points and 6.2 assists in playoff contests. Rodgers was one of the dominant college and pro playmakers of his time. His Temple varsity seasons are still referred to as the "Rodgers era." As a pro, he was compared with the NBA's greatest guards. Rodgers is a member of the HAF Hall of Fame and worked in personnel labor and industrial relations by the Xerox Corporation in Los Angeles.

BIBLIOGRAPHY: Michael Douchant, ed., *Encyclopedia of College Basketball* (Detroit, MI, 1995); Joe Gergen, *The Final Four* (St. Louis, MO, 1989); Jan Hubbard, ed., *The Official NBA Encyclopedia*, 3rd ed. (New York, 2000); Claudia Mitrol, ed., *Philadelphia's Greatest Sports Moments* (Champaign, IL, 2000); Ronald L. Mendell, *Who's Who in Basketball* (New York, 1973); David S. Neft et al., *The Sports Encyclopedia: Pro Basketball*, 3rd ed. (New York, 1992); *TSN Official NBA Register, 2004–2005* (St. Louis, MO, 2004).

William A. Gudelunas

RODMAN, Dennis Keith (b. May 13, 1961, Trenton, NJ), college and professional player, is one of three children born of Philander Rodman Jr., a career military officer, and Shirley Rodman. A few years after Rodman's birth, his parents' marriage collapsed; his mother moved the children to Dallas, Texas. Rodman struggled in adjusting to his single-parent household, as his mother held multiple jobs as a teacher, factory worker, and school bus driver.

Rodman attempted to play high school basketball, but was overshadowed by his sisters, Kim and Debra, both of whom played college basketball. After graduating from South Oak Cliff High School in Dallas in 1979, he worked odd jobs until his arrest for stealing watches while employed as a custodian at the Dallas-Fort Worth Airport. Rodman avoided jail by returning the stolen property. After sprouting to his full height of six feet eight inches, he devoted much of his spare time to playing basketball.

Rodman's sisters helped him obtain a basketball scholarship at Cooke County JC in Gainesville, Texas. He flunked out of Cooke County JC after one semester and returned to Dallas, where he lived on the streets until 1983, when offered a basketball scholarship at Southeastern Oklahoma State University, an NAIA school. In the summer of 1983, Rodman served as a basketball camp counselor and befriended Byrne Rich, a young white boy who killed his best friend in a hunting accident. Byrne's parents welcomed Rodman into their family. With some stability in his life, Rodman enjoyed a successful basketball tenure at Southeastern Oklahoma State from 1983 to 1986. The three-time NAIA All-America led the NAIA in rebounding in 1985 and 1986.

Although his experience was limited, the Detroit Pistons (NBA) tapped Rodman in the second round of the 1986 NBA draft. As a reserve rookie player, he averaged 4.3 rebounds as the Pistons lost to the Boston Celtics in the Eastern Conference Finals. Rodman, however, stirred controversy when he remarked that the Celtics Larry Bird* was overrated because he was a white player. In 1989, the Pistons won the NBA championship and benefited from Rodman's superlative defensive play. The Pistons repeated as NBA champions in 1990, with Rodman averaging 8.8 points and 9.7 rebounds, and earning his first All-Star selection. The Pistons failed to win a third NBA championship, but Rodman led the NBA in rebounding in 1991–1992 (18.7 per game) and 1992–1993 (18.3 per game). When coach Chuck Daly* stepped down after the 1991–1992 season, Rodman's behavior became erratic and confrontational and his marriage to Annie Banks collapsed.

The Pistons shipped Rodman to the San Antonio Spurs (NBA) in October 1993. The 228-pound power forward responded with a third and fourth rebounding title, leading the Spurs into the playoffs in 1993–1994 and 1994–1995. Rodman's antics, his well publicized affair with pop star Madonna, and rebellious attitude were blamed for San Antonio's failures to advance in the playoffs.

Rodman was traded to the Chicago Bulls (NBA) in October 1995 and teamed with Michael Jordan* and Scottie Pippen* for three NBA championships in 1996, 1997, and 1998. He provided the rebounding for Chicago's success and authored a best selling autobiography *Bad As I Wanna Be* (1996), which proclaimed his cross-dressing and sexual liberation.

After being released by a rebuilding Chicago franchise, Rodman played briefly for the Los Angeles Lakers (NBA) in 1998–1999 and Dallas Mavericks (NBA) in 1999–2000 before retiring. A two-time All-Star, he concluded his 14 year NBA career with 11,954 rebounds in 911 games. He was named to the All-NBA Third Team in 1992 and 1995. He became known for his dyed hair, tattoos, and outrageous behavior, but these antics should not obscure his record as one of the best rebounders in NBA history.

BIBLIOGRAPHY: Jerry Green, *The Detroit Pistons: Capturing a Remarkable Era* (Chicago, IL, 1991); Jan Hubbard, ed., *The Official NBA Encyclopedia*, 3rd ed. (New York, 2000); Pat Rich, Dennis Rodman, and Alan Steinberg, *Rebound: The Dennis Rodman Story* (New York, 1994); Dennis Rodman, *Bad As I Wanna Be* (New York, 1996); Roland Lazenby, *The Detroit Pistons 1988–89* (Dallas, TX, 1989); Dennis Rodman and Dave Whitaker, *Words From the Worm: An Unauthorized Trip Through the Mind of Dennis Rodman* (New York, 1997); Bruce Newman, "Black, White—and Gray," *SI* 68 (May 2, 1988), pp. 62–64; and Michael Silver, "Redmond Unchained," *SI* 82 (May 29, 1995), pp. 20–26; Isaiah Thomas with Matt Orbek, *Bad Boys! An Inside Look at the Detroit Pistons 1988–89 Championship Season* (Indianapolis, IN, 1989).

Ron Briley

ROGERS, Lurlyne Ann Greer (b. December 15, 1928, Des Arc, AR), amateur player, is the daughter of Ralph Greer, rural mail carrier and semipro baseball player, and Dada (McCarty) Greer, a high school teacher and coach. She graduated from Des Arc (Arkansas) High School in 1945 and attended Little Rock (Arkansas) JC in 1946. She married Frank W. Rogers in 1956 and has no children. Rogers, who received her first basketball and hoop as a fifth grader, was encouraged by her parents to participate in sports. Her junior high school games were played outdoors, but World War II prevented her from playing high school games. After playing in the Girls' City League in Little Rock in 1944 and 1945 and on an all-star team in the 1945 National AAU tournament, she was invited to join the Little Rock Dr. Pepper team. From 1947 through 1951, Rogers played on the Cooke's Goldblumes team in Nashville, Tennessee and helped them win three National AAU championships from 1948 to 1950. During three seasons with Winston-Salem's (North Carolina) Hanes Hosiery team, she added two more National AAU titles in 1952 and 1953.

For eight consecutive years (1947–1954), Rogers made All-America. In 1952, she was voted the Outstanding Female Amateur Athlete in the Carolinas and received the Lewis E. Teague Memorial Award. Rogers captained the U.S. women's basketball team at the 1955 Pan American Games in Mexico City, Mexico and was inducted in 1967 into the HAF Hall of Fame. In 1956 the five-foot eleven-inch, 155-pounder left sports participation to enter business. She and her husband own and operate cemeteries, including one in their Heber Springs, Arkansas hometown, and enjoy fishing and duck hunting.

BIBLIOGRAPHY: Lurlyne Greer Rogers to Angela Lumpkin, November 1983, June 4, 1984; Joan S. Hult and Marianna Treskell, eds., *A Century of Women's Basketball* (Reston, VA, 1991).

Angela Lumpkin

ROOSMA, John Seiba (b. September 3, 1900, Passaic, NJ; d. November 13, 1983, Verona, NJ), high school and college athlete and basketball referee, grew up in Passaic, New Jersey. Roosma became a key element of Ernest Blood's* Passaic High School "Wonder Teams," which won 159 straight basketball games between 1919 and 1925. He led Passaic High School to 41 of those victories before graduating in 1921. Roosma was named to the All-State team three times and led the state tournament in scoring three times, as Passaic won two state championships. In his senior year, the six-foot one-inch forward scored 882 points. Coach Blood called him the best shooter he had ever seen. Roosma also participated in track and field and played baseball.

On the urging of General Douglas MacArthur, Roosma entered the U.S. Military Academy at West Point, New York. He earned 10 athletic letters in basketball, baseball, football, and soccer. During his basketball career spanning five seasons, Roosma scored 1,126 points in 74 games. He may have been the second collegian to score over 1,000 career points. Army won 31 straight games between 1921 and 1923, with the 17-0 squad of 1923 being considered by some as the unofficial national champion. He averaged 21.3 points that season, and was an

All-Eastern and three-time All-America selection. During his career, Roosma scored nearly 44 percent of Army's points. In 1926, he was awarded the Army Athletic Sabre for being the outstanding athlete in his graduating class.

Roosma, a career Army officer, was stationed in China and served as provost marshal at West Point and as head of Governors Island, New York, before retiring in 1956 with the rank of colonel. He coached and played for many military teams in the U.S. and overseas. At Fort Benning, Georgia, Roosma reportedly averaged 10 baskets for five years while playing against college, pro, and club teams. He also refereed major college games until the outbreak of World War II. Roosma married Marjorie P. Henion and had three children: John, William, and Garret. Roosma was elected to the Naismith Memorial Basketball Hall of Fame (1961), Passaic High School Hall of Fame (1963), HAF Hall of Fame (1973), and New Jersey Sports Hall of Fame (1973). Known as one of basketball's greatest marksmen, he still went to the YMCA three days a week at age 82 and shot baskets for a half hour.

BIBLIOGRAPHY: Ronald L. Mendell, *Who's Who in Basketball* (New Rochelle, NY, 1973); *NCAA Men's Basketball Records, 2004* (Indianapolis, IN, 2003); *NYT*, November 14, 1983, p. B-8; Sandy Padwe, *Basketball's Hall of Fame* (Englewood Cliffs, NJ, 1970); John Roosma file, Naismith Memorial Basketball Hall of Fame, Springfield, MA; Alexander M. Weyand, *The Cavalcade of Basketball* (New York, 1960).

Dennis S. Clark and Wayne Patterson

ROSENBLUTH, Leonard Robert "Lennie" (b. January 22, 1933, New York, NY), college and professional player, is the son of Jack Rosenbluth and Rose (Kaufman) Rosenbluth. He excelled in basketball, following an unusual path to stardom. His father, a New York City housing inspector, played minor league baseball. At James Monroe High School in New York, Rosenbluth saw his scholastic basketball career ended by a coaches' strike. He honed his basketball skills in the local YMCA and subsequently attracted the attention of college coaches as a forward for the Laurel Country Club team in the Catskills. Study at Staunton (Virginia) Military Academy improved his grades for college.

Rosenbluth graduated with a Bachelor's degree in history from the University of North Carolina (ACC) in 1957, the first of many New York City hoop stars recruited to Chapel Hill by coach Frank McGuire*. The skinny, six-foot five-inch, 175-pounder quickly became the Tar Heels' mainstay, using his quickness and leaping ability to score inside at will. In his sophomore year (1954–1955), he averaged 25.5 points (fourth best in the ACC) and 11.7 rebounds (fifth best in the ACC) for a mediocre 10-11 team. Other stars arrived the following season, as the Tar Heels improved to an 18-5 win-loss mark. Rosenbluth led the ACC with 26.7 points per game and averaged 11.4 rebounds, fourth in the ACC. His honors included being named First Team All-ACC as a sophomore and junior and making AP and UPI Second Team All-America in his junior year.

Rosenbluth and North Carolina enjoyed an extraordinary 1956–1957 season. His numerous outstanding plays in March led the Tar Heels to an undefeated 32-0 record and the NCAA championship. North Carolina's last tournament victories included triple overtime thrillers over Michigan State University and the University of Kansas, the latter for the NCAA title. Rosenbluth ranked second in the ACC with 28.0 points per game and averaged 8.8 rebounds. A third consecutive All-ACC designation, the ACC Player of the Year Award, AP and UPI First Team All-America, and the HAF Player of the Year Award were earned by him. His 2,054 career points remained a Tar Heel record until the advent of freshmen eligibility in the 1970s. He was named to the NCAA Final Four All-1950s team. The HAF College Basketball Hall of Fame enshrined him.

A mediocre NBA career followed Rosenbluth's college years. He lacked the height to rebound inside and sufficient perimeter shooting skills to play outside on offense in the NBA, and played poorly defensively. He spent two seasons with the Philadelphia Warriors (NBA), averaging only 4.4 points in 1957–1958 and 3.7 points in 1958–1959. In 82 NBA career games, he scored 342 points and tallied 4.2 points per contest. Rosenbluth barnstormed with a team of former University of North Carolina All-Stars and coached high school basketball in Wilson, North

Carolina. He became a successful high school basketball coach at Coral Gables (Florida) High School in 1965, winning one state championship, seven district championships, and six regional titles. Rosenbluth, who also taught several subjects, married North Carolina graduate Helen Oliver in 1957 and has two children, Elizabeth and Steven.

BIBLIOGRAPHY: Smith Barrier, *On Tobacco Road: Basketball in North Carolina* (New York, 1983); Peter C. Bjarkman, *ACC: Atlantic Coast Conference Basketball* (Indianapolis, IN, 1996); Frank Deford, "The Team That Was Blessed," *SI* 56 (March 29, 1982), pp. 58–62; Mike Douchant, *Encyclopedia of College Basketball* (Detroit, MI, 1995); Jan Hubbard, ed., *The Official NBA Encyclopedia*, 3rd ed. (New York, 2000); Ron Morris, *ACC Basketball: An Illustrated History* (Chapel Hill, NC, 1988); Bob Quincy, *They Made the Bell Tower Chime* (Chapel Hill, NC, 1973); Ken Rappoport, *Tar Heel: North Carolina Basketball* (Huntsville, AL, 1976); Ken Rappoport, *Tales from the Tar Heel Locker Room* (Champaign, IL, 2002); Leonard Rosenbluth file, Alumni Office, University of North Carolina, Chapel Hill, NC.

Jim L. Sumner

ROUNDFIELD, Danny Thomas "Dan" "Rounds" (b. May 26, 1953, Detroit, MI), college and professional player, is the son of James Roundfield and Louise (Patterson) Roundfield and graduated from Detroit (Michigan) Chadsey High School in 1971. Roundfield enrolled at Central Michigan University (MAC), where he starred in basketball from 1972–1973 through 1974–1975 and graduated with a Bachelor's degree in finance in 1975. He made the Second Team All-MAC in 1973 and First Team All-MAC in 1974 and 1975. In the MAC, Roundfield finished second in rebounds each of the three years. In his senior season, he placed third in scoring with a 19.0 points average and first in field goal percentage, setting season (.612) and career (.542) records. The Chippewas compiled a 22-6 record, captured the 1975–1976 MAC title, and received an NCAA tournament bid. Roundfield won the MAC Player-of-the-Year Award and earned co-MVP honors and selec-tion to the NCAA Mid-East Regional All-Tournament team. He ended his college career with 1,318 points (16.7 points average) and 1,031 rebounds (13.0 per game).

After being drafted in 1975 by the Cleveland Cavaliers (NBA) in the second round and the Indiana Pacers (ABA) in the first round (seventh pick overall), the six-foot eight-inch, 315-pound forward signed with the Pacers. He began his professional career in 1975–1976, the last season of the ABA's existence. As a rookie, Roundfield saw little action, averaging only 5.0 points. In 1976–1977, after Indiana joined the NBA, he quickly established himself as a versatile player, averaging 13.9 points and 8.5 rebounds and ranking eighth in the NBA in blocked shots with 131 (2.5 per game). In June 1978, Roundfield signed with the Atlanta Hawks (NBA) as a free agent. He enjoyed his best NBA seasons with Atlanta from 1978–1979 through 1983–1984, scoring 7,644 points (17.6 per game), grabbing 4,658 rebounds (10.7 per game) and blocking 716 shots (1.6 per game). In 1979–1980 Atlanta won the Central Division title, but lost to the Philadelphia 76ers (NBA) in the Eastern Conference Finals four games to one. Roundfield led the Hawks with 837 rebounds (10.3 per game), 1,334 points (16.5 per game) and 139 blocked shots. He enjoyed his best season in 1982–1983, scoring 1,464 points (19.0 average), seizing 880 rebounds (11.4 per game), and blocking 115 shots. Roundfield was selected to the All-NBA Second Team in 1980, the NBA All-Defensive First Team in 1980, 1982, and 1983, and the NBA All-Defensive Second Team in 1981 and 1984. He appeared in his first All-Star Game in 1980, tallying 18 points and seizing 13 rebounds. His nine offensive rebounds established an NBA All-Star record. He was named to the All-Star team in 1981 and 1982, but injuries sidelined him.

In June 1984, Roundfield was traded to the Detroit Pistons (NBA). After one season, he was sent to the Washington Bullets (NBA) for Rick Mahorn and the rights to Mike Gibson. Roundfield completed his NBA career as a reserve with the Bullets in 1987, but played an additional year overseas in the ITL. He in 1994 played on a team representing the National Basketball Retired Players Association, which toured the world to raise funds for NBA old-timers.

In 746 regular-season games over 12 NBA and ABA seasons, Roundfield tallied 11,657 points (14.3 points average), grabbed 7,502 rebounds (9.2 per game), and blocked 1,117 shots. He appeared in 40 playoff games, scoring 599 points (15.0 points average), making 388 rebounds (9.7 per game), and blocking 60 shots.

Roundfield and his wife, Bernadine, have two sons, Corey and Christopher. He works as a senior market development professional with Weston Solutions, an environmental engineering firm in Atlanta, Georgia, and resides in Roswell, Georgia.

BIBLIOGRAPHY: Dan Roundfield, telephone interview with Jack C. Braun, July 3, 2003; Jan Hubbard, ed., *The Official NBA Encyclopedia*, 3rd ed. (New York, 2000); Dan Roundfield file, Naismith Memorial Basketball Hall of Fame, Springfield, MA; Dan Roundfield file, Sports Information Office, Central Michigan University, Mount Pleasant, MI; *TSN Official NBA Guide, 2002–2003* (St. Louis, MO, 2002); Martin Taragano, *Basketball Biographies* (Jefferson, NC, 1991).

Jack C. Braun

ROUNDTREE, Saudia (b. 1976, Anderson, SC), college and professional player and coach, began playing basketball on neighborhood playgrounds and in boys' community recreation leagues. By the eighth grade, Roundtree earned a spot on the Westside High School varsity basketball squad. She played basketball from 1987–1988 to 1991–1992, helping Westside win three South Carolina state championships; the school retired her jersey. After graduation, Roundtree played basketball two years in 1992–1993 and 1993–1994 at Kilgore JC in Texas. She missed the University of Georgia admissions requirement on her ACT score by one point. She earned National JC Player of the Year honors at Kilgore, averaging 26.2 points and graduated with an Associates degree in criminal justice in 1994.

Roundtree entered the University of Georgia in 1994 and made an immediate impact on the Lady Bulldogs basketball program during the 1994–1995 and 1995–1996 seasons. She was named the 1996 National Collegiate Player of the Year, selected SEC Player of the Year, and earned Kodak Award, Naismith Award, and AP All-America honors. During her two seasons at Georgia, Roundtree scored 1,038 points and averaged 15.7 points. She helped Georgia reach the 1996 NCAA Final Four, but the team fell to the University of Tennessee Lady Vols in the championship game. She graduated in 1996 with a B.A. degree in sociology.

Roundtree was drafted in the first round and performed two seasons in the newly formed ABL. She played for the Atlanta Glory (ABL) in 1996–1997 and the Nashville Noise (ABL) in 1997–1998. A consistent leading ABL scorer, Roundtree was selected for the 1997 ABL All-Star team. She also served as a commentator for Media One Communications and as spokesperson for Reebok.

Roundtree left the court in 1998 to work for Suwanee Sports Academy in Georgia, where she ran AAU tournaments and basketball camps. Just a year later, she joined Morris Brown College as assistant basketball coach for the 1999–2000 season. Roundtree also served as interim head coach for the 2000–2001 season and helped basketball program move up to NCAA Division I. In July 2002, she signed a five-year head coaching contract with North Carolina Agricultural and Technical State University. In her first season, she led the Lady Aggies to a 7-21 record, the team's best record in five years.

BIBLIOGRAPHY: "Saudia Roundtree," North Carolina A&T State University website, www.ncat.edu; Alexander Wolff, "Major League," *SI* 84 (February 26, 1996), pp. 44–47.

Lisa A. Ennis

RUBLE, Olan Guy (b. February 17, 1906, Chariton, IA; d. November 11, 1982, Wheaton, IL), college coach and administrator, pioneered in developing women's collegiate and international basketball competition. The son of Lon Ruble and Gertrude (Curtis) Ruble, he grew up and spent most of his life in rural southeastern Iowa. Ruble graduated from Simpson (Iowa) College in 1928 and served 10 years as an instructor and coach in Iowa high schools. His 1930 Mingo team finished second in the state basketball tournament. He married Marguerite Oneall on June 21, 1930 and had one daughter, Linda (Taylor). In 1937, he earned a Master's degree from the University of Iowa.

Between 1938 and 1942, Ruble served as the program director for the Sioux City, Iowa YMCA. He became Director of Athletics and

Physical Education at Iowa Wesleyan College, a small, liberal arts, Methodist-affiliated institution, in 1943. Initially a one-man Athletic Department, Ruble coached football, basketball, track and field, and baseball until 1949. In his first season he started the women's basketball program to provide an outlet for the numerous fine Iowa high school players. At that time, no other Iowa college and few institutions across the nation offered an organized women's intercollegiate program. In 21 seasons with the Tigerettes, Ruble compiled a 626-127 win-loss record. Iowa Wesleyan appeared in the AAU Tournament 20 times and reached the Final Four 10 times, including nine straight between 1956 and 1964. Although never winning the national tournament, Iowa Wesleyan several times ranked as the best college team among the competitors.

Twenty-five times Ruble's players were named All-Americas. His star performers included Janet Thompson, Barbara Johnson, Barbara Sipes, Sandra Fiete, Glenda Nicholson, Rita Horky, Judy Hudson, Lori Williams, and Diane Frieden. He retired from coaching in 1964, but continued as athletic director at Iowa Wesleyan College 10 more years. During his 46-year career, he reportedly never missed a day because of illness. Ruble, a strong advocate of international competition for women, served as head or assistant coach for several U.S. national teams. His most notable were those exchanging tours with the Russians in the early 1960s. He served on the Women's Basketball Committee for two decades and helped secure the inclusion of women's basketball in the Olympic program. In 1967, Ruble was elected to the HAF Hall of Fame, the first women's basketball coach so honored. During his career, he wrote articles on the technical aspects of both football and basketball.

BIBLIOGRAPHY: Olan G. Ruble, *Fundamentals of Football; Kinesology Worksheets* (Mount Pleasant, IA, 1952); Olan G. Ruble, "Rebounding," in *DGWS Selected Basketball Articles* (Flushing, NY, 1964), pp. 49–53; Olan G. Ruble, "Russians Blank U.S. Girls," *Amateur Athlete* (June 1966), pp. 8–9; *TSN*, November 29, 1982, p. 70; Buck Turnbull, "Ruble's Cagers Are Now Grandmothers," *Des Moines Register*, 1974; *Who's Who in the Midwest, 1949, 1952, 1956.*

Dennis S. Clark

RUPP, Adolph Frederick "Baron of Bluegrass" (b. September 2, 1901, Halstead, KS; d. December 10, 1977, Lexington, KY), college player and coach, was the son of Henry Rupp and Anna (Lichti) Rupp, who had immigrated to Halstead, Kansas, from Austria and Germany. Rupp had four brothers, Otto, Theodore, Henry, and Albert, and one sister, Elizabeth (Mrs. Paul Lawson). A baseball diamond on their 113-acre farm became a favorite playground for the neighborhood children, who also played some basketball. Rupp played basketball at Halstead High School from 1915 to 1919 and performed at guard for coach Forrest "Phog" Allen* at the University of Kansas from 1919 to 1923, supporting himself by waiting on tables at the Jayhawk Cafe.

Rupp, who substituted on Allen's first, undefeated 1922–1923 national championship team, learned how to win from a coach who triumphed in 771 games. He also learned from basketball's creator and University of Kansas faculty member, James Naismith*. Rupp's early coaching jobs at Burr Oak, Kansas (1923); Marshalltown, Iowa (1923–1926, including wrestling); and Freeport, Illinois (1926–1930) provided additional experience and an 82-16 basketball record. During summers, Rupp completed a Master's degree in education administration from Columbia University (New York). He married Esther Schmidt in August 1931 and had one son, Adolph F. Rupp Jr., known as "Herky."

This relative unknown with no college basketball coaching experience replaced John Maurer in 1930 at the University of Kentucky, where Rupp spent the next 42 years. His 67-19 victory over Georgetown (Washington, D.C.) University marked the first of 874 Kentucky victories for Rupp, eventually surpassing his mentor at the University of Kansas with the most wins in college basketball history. Rupp's first season's record of 15-3 set the pace for a career .825 winning percentage. Before being forced into retirement in 1972, Rupp established male coaching benchmarks surpassed only by Dean Smith*.

Rupp's teams won four NCAA championships (1948, 1949, 1951, and 1958) and finished second twice (1966 and 1975), appeared in 18 NCAA tournaments, and captured 27 SEC titles in 42 seasons. He developed 24 All-

Americas, seven Olympic gold medal–winners, and 28 professional players. Rupp was named SEC Coach of the Year twice, national Coach of the Year four times, and national runner-up twice. His other honors included selection to the HAF Hall of Fame (1944), Kentucky Hall of Fame (1945), and Naismith Memorial Basketball Hall of Fame (1969), being named Coach of the Century by the Columbus Touchdown Club (1967), and being chosen president of the NABC (1970–1971). The most games ever lost by a Rupp-coached University of Kentucky team (13) came in 1966–1967. The Wildcats averaged only four defeats per season during Rupp's reign. He also served as co-coach of the gold medal–winning 1948 U.S. Olympic team.

Contrary to popular opinion, Rupp did not bring an entirely new style of play to the University of Kentucky. Actually, he adopted the fast-break style of play used by predecessor Maurer. But Rupp's ability to popularize his program and intense desire to win attracted great players and large throngs of fans. The "Baron of Bluegrass" drove his athletes the same way he raised prize Hereford cattle and grew choice burlap tobacco: with an uncompromised devotion and discipline. He recruited "po' mountain boys" and transformed them into performers, who played the stickiest man-to-man defense and a relentless fast-break offense to wear down opponents.

From 1945 through 1954, Rupp produced more championship teams, All-Americas, and victories than any other coach. An NIT championship in 1945 (46-45 over the University of Rhode Island) was followed by a streak of NCAA championships in 1948 (58-42 over Baylor University), 1949 (43-36 over Oklahoma Agricultural and Mechnical University), and 1951 (68-58 over Kansas State University). Alex Groza* was named MVP on both the 1947–1948 and "the Fabulous Five" 1948–1949 squads, while Bill Spivey* won that honor in 1949–1950.

Rupp's spectacular career included some dark times. "The Baron" despised the "unhealthy" big-city atmosphere encroaching on the college game. New York Judge Saul Streit charged Rupp, the University of Kentucky, and its fans with overemphasizing the basketball program, leading players to accept bribes to influence the final outcome of games. "Gamblers couldn't get at our players with a 10-foot pole," Rupp once said. Five of his best players disproved their coach's claim by being implicated in point-shaving scandals that swept college basketball. When the NCAA placed Kentucky on one-year probation in fall 1952, the university cancelled its entire season. The Wildcats, however, rebounded in 1953 by winning all 25 games and earning the AP top ranking. Stars Cliff Hagan*, Frank Ramsay*, and Lou Tsioropoulos could not play in postseason competition because they had completed all degree requirements during their probation year. But they demonstrated their loyalty to brown-suited coach Rupp by bringing the program back into prominence.

Rupp's 1957–1958 squad, nicknamed the "Fiddlin' Five," topped Seattle University to give him his fourth and last NCAA championship. The 1965–1966 Wildcats, called "Rupp's Runts" because of their small stature, carried their 65-year-old coach into the NCAA Finals before losing to Texas Western University 72-65. Rupp's Coach of the Year award indicated sportswriters' respect for his second-place finish. An 81-73 victory over University of Notre Dame (Indiana) on December 26, 1967, marked his 772nd triumph, enabling him to surpass his mentor, Phog Allen. Rupp won many more games, but captured no more titles before being forced into retirement after the 1972 tournament. He coached longer and with greater success than any previous college basketball coach. He established a winning tradition at Kentucky rivaled later only by John Wooden* at UCLA and Smith at the University of North Carolina. Rupp Arena, whose 23,000 seats are filled for every game, stands as a monument for the coach who brought so much attention to the Commonwealth of Kentucky via his blue-and-white-clad Wildcats.

BIBLIOGRAPHY: "Baron's Runts," *Time* 87 (February 4, 1966), p. 60; "Bluegrass Sage," *Newsweek* 29 (January 6, 1947), pp. 62–63; Ron Cave, "Old Master Has a New Kind of Winner," *SI* 16 (February 19, 1962), pp. 52–53; Frank Deford, "Bravo for the Baron," *SI* 24

(March 7, 1966), pp. 20–23; V. A. Jackson, *Beyond the Baron* (Kuttawa, KY, 1998); *Kentucky Basketball Encyclopedia* (Champaign, IL, 2000); Curry Kirkpatrick, "E-Rupption in Wildcat Country," *SI* 31 (December 22, 1969), pp. 22–25; Herman L. Masin, "Old Rupp and Ready," *Scholastic* 52 (February 2, 1948), pp. 34–35; Barry McDermott, "Kaintuck-eee Jubilee," *SI* 45 (December 20, 1976), pp. 28–29; Bert Nelli, *The Winning Tradition: A History of Kentucky Wildcat Basketball* (Lexington, KY, 1984); *NYT*, December 12, 1977, p. 38; Billy Packer and Roland Lazenby, *College Basketball's 25 Greatest Teams* (St. Louis, MO, 1989); Sandy Padwe, *Basketball's Hall of Fame* (New York, 1971); Russell Rice, *Kentucky: Basketball's Big Blue Machine* (Huntsville, AL, 1976); Adolph Rupp file, Naismith Memorial Basketball Hall of Fame, Springfield, MA; Collie Small, "Craft Wizard of Lexington," *SEP* 219 (February 15, 1947), p. 23.

Gregory S. Sojka

RUSH, Catherine Ann Cowan "Cathy" (b. April 7, 1947, Atlantic City, NJ), college player and coach, is the daughter of John Cowan and Alice Cowan and has one sister. Her father was employed as an engineer for Atlantic City Electric Company, while her mother worked part-time as a convention recorder. An all-around tomboy, she participated in basketball, gymnastics, and cheerleading at Oakcrest (New Jersey) High School and graduated in 1964. At West Chester State College (Pennsylvania), she played basketball for two years. She then switched to gymnastics, a sport in which her compact physique was well suited. She received a Bachelor's degree in 1968 and a Master's degree in Education four years later. On June 1, 1968, she married Ed Rush, an NBA official, and has two sons, Eddie Jr. and Michael.

Rush taught physical education in secondary schools in the Philadelphia, Pennsylvania area until accepting a part-time position in 1970 as women's basketball coach at nearby Immaculata College. At the tiny Roman Catholic school, she initially received only a $500 annual salary. The Macs, as the team was called, compiled a 10-2 mark on a limited local schedule during her first season. Drawing from the tough girls' high school leagues of Philadelphia, Rush quickly assembled a powerful team. Immaculata lost only one game the next season and won the first AIAW's postseason tournament. Led by Teresa (Shank) Grentz*, the modern era's first dominant inside player, the Macs repeated as AIAW national champion in 1973 with a perfect 20-0 slate. Immaculata won a third consecutive AIAW title in 1974, establishing a college record that has not yet been broken. Rush directed her squads to the AIAW national finals again in 1974–1975 and 1975–1976, losing both championship matches to Delta State University (Mississippi). She resigned from Immaculata College after the 1976–1977 season with a seven-year, 145-13 college coaching record and a .918 winning percentage. Rush was honored as Coach of the Year by one organization or another in 1973, 1974, and 1975.

Rush's teams pioneered the running game for women and impressed others with their full-court press, poise, and frequent use of substitutes. During the winter of 1975, Immaculata participated in the first televised women's basketball game and in the initial college game between two women's teams at Madison Square Garden in New York before 12,000. Rush trained several future coaches, including Grentz, Rene (Muth) Portland*, and Marianne (Crawford) Stanley*. In the summer of 1975, she coached the U.S. national team in the World University and Pan American Games, where they won the championship with a 7-0 slate. She also was considered for the women's Olympic team coach in 1976, but women's basketball was not included as an Olympic sport until four years later.

Rush, her husband, and another couple started a summer basketball camp for girls in the Pocono Mountains of Pennsylvania in the early 1970s. Since then, this popular camp has grown from 45 to 3,000 participants and includes both boys and girls. Since leaving Immaculata, Catherine has helped promote the women's game throughout the United States. Rush co-authored a book on basketball techniques for women in 1976. She served as director of player personnel and promotions for the short-lived California Dreams (WPBL) during the summer of 1979. Rush resides in the Philadelphia area, where she still runs her sports camps, operates a college scouting service and an athletic equipment mail order business, and publishes a newsletter.

BIBLIOGRAPHY: Mike Douchant, *Encyclopedia of College Basketball* (Detroit, MI, 1995); Jim Haughton, "Hers," *Basketball Weekly* 7 (February 20, 1974), pp. 16ff.; Mike Mallowe, "The Game Gets Tougher for the Mighty Macs," *WomenSports* 2 (July 1975), pp. 36–39, 50–52; Cathy Rush and Laurie Mifflin, *Women's Basketball* (New York, 1976).

Dennis S. Clark

RUSSELL, Cazzie Lee, Jr. (b. June 7, 1944, Chicago, IL), college and professional player and coach, is the son of Cazzie Lee Russell, Sr., and participated in basketball on Chicago's South Side at Carver High School. He earned All-State honors and led his team to the city championship. Russell learned basketball skills from his high school coach, Larry Hawkins, and friendly janitors, who allowed him to play after hours. "If it weren't for them letting me practice," he commented, "I might have wound up driving a cab or working in the steel mills or pushing rocks on a construction gang."

Recruited by over 75 universities and colleges, Russell ultimately chose the University of Michigan over the University of Cincinnati (Ohio). He patterned his play after Oscar Robertson*, who advised him to attend Cincinnati. Russell selected Michigan because he "championed the underdog" and relished the "chance to be a star." With his quick moves and dazzling smile, he played with an exuberance and zest that delighted fans. At Michigan, Russell joined Bill Buntin, Oliver Darden, Larry Tregoning, and other premier players. The six-foot five-inch, 220-pound Russell electrified the crowd as a guard, leading the Wolverines to three BTC titles and three consecutive NCAA appearances.

During his sophomore year, Russell scored 670 points or 25 points per game to set a school record. He led the Wolverines to the NCAA semifinals, where Duke University (North Carolina) prevailed 91-80. Russell also was named to several All-Star teams. As a junior, he averaged 25.7 points to become a All-BTC and consensus All-America. In the New York Holiday Tournament against Princeton (New Jersey) University, Russell rallied the Wolverines from a 13-point deficit after Tigers star Bill Bradley* had fouled out. In the NCAA Finals, he scored 28 points against UCLA. Gail Goodrich*, however, netted 42 points for the victorious Bruins. Russell scored 800 points and averaged 30.8 points per game his senior year, as Michigan won the BTC title. The University of Kentucky ousted Michigan 84-77 in the Mideast regionals, but Russell was named MVP in the BTC and the third BTC National Player of the Year and became Michigan only three-time All-America. Russell established Wolverine career records with 2,164 points, a 27.1 scoring average 486 free throw, and an .828 free throw percentage.

The New York Knickerbockers (NBA) signed Russell for a salary and bonus exceeding $200,000. Although making the NBA All-Rookie Team and playing on the 1969–1970 NBA championship team, he never achieved his earlier stardom. Russell later played for the Golden State Warriors (NBA), Los Angeles Lakers (NBA), and Chicago Bulls (NBA), scoring 12,061 career points and averaging 15.4 points over 11 pro seasons. His best NBA season was 1971–1972, when he averaged 21.4 points per game for the Golden State Warriors. He served as head coach for Lancaster, Pennsylvania (CBA) from 1979 to 1988. The Atlanta Hawks (NBA) employed Russell as an assistant coach from 1988 to 1990. Russell coached a high school team in Columbus, Ohio, from 1990 to 1995 and NCAA Division III Savannah College of Art and Design in Savannah, Georgia since 1995. He married his wife, Myrna, a former Broadway dancer, in 1986 and serves as associate pastor at Happy Home Missionary Baptist Church in Savannah.

BIBLIOGRAPHY: Peter C. Bjarkman, *Big Ten Basketball* (Indianapolis, IN, 1994); Erik Brady, "Composition for Sports," *USA Today*, December 18, 2001, pp. 1C–2C; Jerry Brondfield and Kenneth L. Wilson, *The Big Ten* (Englewood Cliffs, NJ, 1967); Joe Gergen, *The Final Four* (St. Louis, MO, 1987); Merv Harris, ed., *On Court with the Superstars of the NBA* (New York, 1973); Zander Hollander, ed., *The Modern Encyclopedia of Basketball* (Garden City, NY, 1979); Jan Hubbard, ed., *The Official NBA Encyclopedia*, 3rd ed. (New York, 2000); Neil D. Isaacs, *All the Moves: A History of College Basketball* (Philadelphia, PA, 1975); Leonard Koppett, *Championship NBA—Official 25th Anniversary* (New York, 1970); Herman L. Masin, "Nothing But the Best," *Senior Scholastic* 87 (December 6, 1965), pp. 36–37; John D. McCallum, *College Basketball U.S.A. Since 1892* (Briarcliff Manor, NY, 1978); Robert Stern, *They Were Number One: A History of the NCAA Basketball Tournament* (New York, 1983); John Underwood, "His Hopes Hang by an Ankle," *SI* 20 (March 23, 1971), pp. 18–21.

Lawrence E. Ziewacz

RUSSELL, John "Honey" (b. May 3, 1903, Brooklyn, NY; d. November 15, 1973, Livingston, NJ), college and professional player and coach, was the son of John Russell and Helen (Keyes) Russell, both of Scotch-Irish descent. His father worked in the wholesale drug business. Russell graduated from Alexander Hamilton High School in Brooklyn, New York, and received a Bachelor of Arts degree from Seton Hall University (New Jersey) and a Master of Arts degree from NYU. He started his pro basketball career at age 16, gaining prominence with the Brooklyn Visitations (MeL). During the next three decades, Russell played in over 3,200 games for the era's most famous teams in almost every pro league. Regarded among the era's outstanding defensive players, he also performed well offensively and once held the professional scoring mark with 22 points in a game.

Russell starred from 1925 to 1931 in the first national professional league, the ABL. He finished second in ABL scoring with a 7.4 points average, and led the Cleveland Rosenblums to the ABL title during the initial 1925–1926 season. The six-foot one-inch, 175-pound Russell later performed for clubs for the Rochester Centrals (New York), Chicago Bruins, Brooklyn Visitations, and Paterson, New Jersey Whirlwinds; he was selected to the ABL's All-Star team four consecutive years (1926–1929). He also played minor league baseball for three seasons and pro football with George Halas' Chicago Bears (NFL). Russell married Charlotte Graf of Brooklyn in 1926 and had three children, John, Dorothy, and Peggy.

Russell began coaching basketball at Seton Hall University in 1936 and built the school's basketball program into one of the nation's strongest. From 1938 through 1941, his Seton Hall team won a then-national record 43 consecutive games. When Seton Hall dropped its basketball program during World War II, Russell returned to the professional ranks as an ABL player-coach and piloted the Brooklyn Indians, New York Americans, and Trenton (New Jersey) Tigers. During the 1945–1946 season, he coached both the Trenton Tigers and Manhattan (New York) College. In 1946, Russell was named coach of the Boston Celtics in the newly formed BAA. His teams won 22 games and lost 38 in 1946–1947 and finished 20-28 the next season to capture a playoff berth.

Russell returned to Seton Hall University in 1949 and remained there the next 11 seasons. His 1952–1953 team captured the NIT in New York, won 31 games—including 27 consecutive—and lost only two contests. During his two stints at the school, Russell compiled an overall record of 294 wins and only 129 losses and developed All-Americas Bob Davies*, Walter Dukes*, and Richie Regan. For 26 years, he served as a major league baseball scout for the Atlanta Braves (NL), Montreal Expos (NL), and Chicago White Sox (AL). Russell signed All-Star player and manager Joe Torre and 22 other major-leaguers. He also scouted pro football for the Cleveland Browns (NFL) and Los Angeles Rams (NFL) and promoted boxing, wrestling, rollerskating, and motorcycle events.

In 1964, Russell was elected as a player to the Naismith Memorial Basketball Hall of Fame. His basketball career represented a microcosm of the sport's development. As a professional, he performed during its barnstorming, dance-hall days and coached when the sport entered its modern phase in large big-city arenas. As a college coach, Russell remained in the mainstream of the sport's growth into the modern era of big-time basketball. During his entire career, he proved the consummate motivator and competitor.

BIBLIOGRAPHY: Peter C. Bjarkman, *Hoopla: A Century of College Basketball, 1896–1996* (Indianapolis, IN, 1996); Stanley Cohen, *The Game They Played* (New York, 1977); Larry Fox, *Illustrated History of Basketball* (New York, 1974); Neil D. Isaacs, *All the Moves: A History of College Basketball*

(Philadelphia, PA, 1975); Neil D. Isaacs, *Vintage NBA* (Silver Spring, MD, 1996); William Mokray, ed., *Ronald Encyclopedia of Basketball* (New York, 1963); *NYT*, 1925–1960; *NYT*, November 17, 1973; Robert W. Peterson, *Cages to Jump Shots Pro Basketball's Early Years* (New York, 1990); John Russell file, Naismith Memorial Basketball Hall of Fame, Springfield, MA; John D. Russell, *Honey Russell: Between Games, Between Halves* (Washington, 1986); Ken Shouler et al., *Total Basketball* (Wilmington, DE, 2003).

Karel de Veer

RUSSELL, William Felton "Bill" (b. February 12, 1934, Monroe, LA), college and professional player, coach, and executive, is the second son of Charles Russell and Katie Russell. To escape the vicious, humiliating racism of Monroe, Louisiana, the Russells moved to Oakland, California, when Bill was five years old. His father obtained a job at a war plant there, but family stability did not follow. Russell's parents separated when he was still in elementary school, and his mother died soon thereafter. He and his brother, Charles, largely were left on their own because their father rather unsuccessfully tried to both work full time and care for them. Russell attended Hoover Junior High School in Oakland and failed the tryout for the school basketball team. He barely made the McClymonds High School junior varsity team two years later. During high school, Russell progressively grew taller, stronger, and more coordinated. By his senior year, he played well enough to earn an athletic scholarship to a local Jesuit college with a dormant basketball program, the University of San Francisco (California).

With roommate K. C. Jones*, Russell transformed the dormant San Francisco basketball program into the nation's most exciting one. By his junior year, he had matured into an awesome player and a formidable six-foot nine-inch center playing aggressive defense and outstanding offense. Russell led San Francisco to 55 straight victories during the 1954–1955 and 1955–1956 seasons, two consecutive number-one rankings, and two NCAA championships. Although the nation's most sought-after college player when he graduated in 1956, he temporarily postponed pro commitments and helped the U.S. Olympic basketball team win a gold medal in the Summer Olympic games at Melbourne, Australia.

Russell signed in 1956 with the Boston Celtics (NBA) for $24,000 a year and provided just the impetus that the Celtics needed. Coach "Red" Auerbach's* Celtics had performed only mediocre on defense, preventing the team from fully exploiting the vast offensive talents of Bob Cousy*, Ed Macauley*, and Bill Sharman*. Russell's addition to the starting lineup in 1956, with his great skill at blocking shots and grabbing rebounds, turned the Celtics into a powerful machine capable of overwhelming opponents both defensively and offensively. Boston won both the Eastern Division title and the NBA championship during Russell's first year with the team. During the next nine seasons through 1965–1966, the Celtics won the Eastern Division title nine times and the NBA championship eight consecutive times.

At the start of the 1966–1967 season, Auerbach became the Celtics' general manager and named Russell as team coach. The first black to ever serve as head coach of a NBA team, Russell took over the Celtics when their NBA dominance was being challenged by the Philadelphia 76ers and seven-foot center Wilt Chamberlain*. The intense rivalry between the two teams produced some great on-court battles between player-coach Russell and Chamberlain. During these years, Boston captured the NBA championship two times out of three (in 1968 and 1969) and lost to Philadelphia in 1967. By the beginning of the 1969–1970 season, Russell saw his physical stamina and enthusiasm for playing begin to wane and retired with one year left on his contract.

During his 13 impressive years with the Celtics, Russell played in 963 games for 40,726 minutes; scored 14,522 points (averaging 15.1 points); grabbed 21,620 rebounds (the all-time Celtics leader); made 4,100 assists; shot 5,687 field goals in 12,930 attempts; and sunk 3,148 free throws in 5,614 attempts. He was named to the East All-Star Team 11 times and won the NBA's MVP Award five times (1958, 1961–1963, 1965). Russell made the All-NBA First Team in 1959, 1963, and 1965, and the All-NBA Second Team eight seasons. He was elected to the Naismith Memorial Basketball Hall of Fame in 1974, was selected to the NBA's 25th and 35th Anniversary All-Time Teams in 1970 and 1980, and chosen one of the 50 Greatest Players in NBA History in 1996. Although there is considerable debate, many basketball experts considered Russell the best player the game had ever seen until Michael Jordan*. In 1980 the PBWAA named Russell the "Greatest Player in the History of the NBA."

Later Russell made a few movies, appeared on television talk shows, provided color commentary for ABC Sports' *NBA Game of the Week*, and toured the college lecture circuit. At all times, he remained an outspoken and forthright advocate of civil rights and social justice and used his immense prestige to further the cause of black equality. Russell returned to professional basketball in 1973, signing a multiyear contract to become the coach and general manager of the Seattle SuperSonics (NBA). From the 1973–1974 through 1976–1977 seasons, his teams won 162 games and lost 166. He also led the SuperSonics into the NBA championship playoffs in 1975 and 1976, where they won six games and lost nine.

Russell, who married Rose Swisher in 1956 and has three children, worked as a sports announcer for the WTBS national cable television station in Atlanta, Georgia, wrote a syndicated newspaper column, offered news commentary for KABC TV in Los Angeles, and remained active in the civil rights movement. He has written two books, *Go Up for Glory* (1966) and *Second Wind: The Memoirs of an Opinionated Man* (1979) and a treatise *Russell Rules* (2001) on leadership. In April 1987, Russell signed a 10-year contract to coach the Sacramento Kings (NBA). Jerry Reynolds replaced Russell as head coach in March 1988 after the Kings struggled to an 18-41 mark, fourth worst in the NBA. Russell, who has compiled a 342-290 career NBA coaching mark, served as the Kings vice president through the 1989–1990 season and largely withdrew from the public limelight. He has served as a consultant for the Boston Celtics since 1999.

BIBLIOGRAPHY: Peter C. Bjarkman, *The Boston Celtics Encyclopedia* (Champaign, IL, 1998); Morgan G. Brenner, *College Basketball's National Championships* (Lanham, MD, 1999); John Capouya, "Bill Russell, Reconsidered," *Sport* 79 (January 1988), pp. 33–38; *CB* (1975), pp. 372–375; Jack Clary, *Basketball's Greatest Dynasties: The Celtics* (New York, 1992); Jay David, ed., *Growing Up Black* (New York, 1968); Roland Lazenby, *The NBA Finals* (Indianapolis, IN, 1996); *NYT*, 1956–1976; *NYT*, September 16, 1979; Bill Russell and Taylor Branch, *Second Wind: Memoirs of an Opinionated Man* (New York, 1979); Bill Russell, as told to William McSweeny, *Go Up for Glory* (New York, 1966); Bill Russell with David Falkner, *Russell Rules* (New York, 2001); Bill Russell file, Naismith Memorial Basketball Hall of Fame, Springfield, MA; Dan Shaughnessy, *Ever Green: The Boston Celtics* (New York, 1990); Ken Shouler et al., *Total Basketball* (Wilmington, DE, 2003).

Christopher E. Guthrie

S

SACHS, Leonard David (b. August 7, 1897, Chicago, IL; d. October 27, 1942, Chicago, IL), college basketball coach and professional football player, graduated in 1914 from Carl Schurz High School in Chicago, where he served as president of his senior class and earned 11 major letters in athletics. During World War 1, Sachs played on the Cleveland Naval Reserve basketball team. A 1923 graduate of the American College of Physical Education, he starred on the Illinois AC basketball team and helped them win the AAU title in 1918. Illinois triumphed by downing Brigham Young University (Utah) for its 32nd win in 33 games. In 1919, Sachs was named head football and basketball coach at Wendell Phillips High School in Chicago. He moved in 1921 to Marshall High School in Chicago and served as head basketball coach from 1925 to 1942 at Loyola University in Chicago. Between 1920 and 1926, the versatile five-foot eight-inch, 176-pound Sachs also played pro football as an end for the Chicago Cardinals (NFL) in 1920–1923 and 1925, the Milwaukee Badgers (NFL) in 1923–1924, and Hammond Pros (NFL) in 1924–1925, and as player-coach for the Louisville Colonels (NFL) in 1926.

Sachs used meager material to compile an impressive college basketball career coaching record of 224 victories and 129 defeats over 19 seasons. A proponent of the tall-man, fast-break style of play, he devised a system to make full use of the tall center. Sachs also developed an effective 2–2–1 zone defense with a goaltender, resulting in a new basketball rule that prohibited goaltending. Between 1927 and 1929, his Loyola University Ramblers won 32 consecutive games until Purdue University (Indiana) defeated them 25-20. Loyola captured 20 consecutive games in 1939, including a 51-40 victory over St. John's University (New York) in the NIT, but lost the championship game to Clair Bee's* undefeated Long Island (New York) University Blackbirds 44-32. Sachs coached All-Americas Marvin Colen, Mike Novak, and Wilbert Kautz. Sachs, who married Vera Blair and had one daughter, Anita Rose, died suddenly of a heart attack at age 44 while still active as a coach. Sachs, a member of the HAF Hall of Fame, was elected as a coach in 1961 to the Naismith Memorial Basketball Hall of Fame.

BIBLIOGRAPHY: *Chicago Daily Tribune*, October 28, 1942, pp. 25, 28; Ronald L. Mendell, *Who's Who in Basketball* (New Rochelle, NY, 1973); Leonard D. Sachs file, Naismith Memorial Basketball Hall of Fame, Springfield, MA.

John L. Evers

SADOWSKI, Edward Frank "Big Ed" (b. July 11, 1916, Johnstown, PA; d. September 18, 1990, Wall, NJ), college and professional player, was a strong, six-foot five-inch, 265-pound center and led North High School of Akron, Ohio to the state basketball championship in 1935, being named All-State. Sadowski matriculated at Seton Hall University (New Jersey), where coach John "Honey" Russell* lauded him as one of his greatest players. He scored 757 career points for Seton Hall, making the All-Eastern squad as a sophomore in 1938 and receiving All-America mention in 1940. Sadowski led Seton Hall to a 19-0 record in 1939–1940, the only undefeated season in the

Pirates' history, and played professional basketball for a Syracuse team under an assumed name. He participated in the first college All-Star Game in Chicago in 1941.

Sadowski declined a professional football contract with the New York Giants (NFL). The Detroit Eagles (NBL) drafted Sadowski, who averaged 10.7 points in 1940–1941. He played 24 games before entering the U.S. Army. After performing with the Wilmington (Delaware) Blue Bombers (ABL), Sadowski played with the Fort Wayne (Indiana) Zollner Pistons (NBL) in 1944–1945 and 1945–1946. He scored 592 points in 59 NBL games for a 10 points average.

With the formation of BAA, Sadowski split the 1946–1947 season between the Toronto (Canada) Huskies and the Cleveland Rebels. He led the Rebels with 877 points (16.5 points per game) and finished second among BAA scorers. In the 1947–1948 season, Sadowski joined the Boston Celtics (BAA) and scored 910 points in 47 contests for a career best 19.4 points average to place third among BAA scorers.

Sadowski, selected to the All-BAA First Team in 1948, spent the 1948–1949 season with the Philadelphia Warriors (NBA) and split the following year between Philadelphia and the Washington Bullets (NBA). In 229 BAA-NBA games, he scored 3,579 points (15.6 points average) and tallied 152 points in eight playoff games.

Sadowski retired from professional basketball in 1950, worked as a labor negotiator for the Cities Service Oil Company, and was employed by a beverage distributor. Sadowski, who married Charlotte K. O'Maro on February 2, 1942, and had two sons, Charles and Edward, resided in Wall, New Jersey.

BIBLIOGRAPHY: *Akron* (OH) *Beacon Journal*, September 19, 1990; Jan Hubbard, ed., *The Official NBA Basketball Encyclopedia*, 3rd ed. (New York, 2000); Neil D. Isaacs, *Vintage NBA* (Silver Spring, MD, 1996); David S. Neft and Richard M. Cohen, eds., *The Sports Encyclopedia: Pro Basketball*, 5th ed. (New York, 1992); *NYT*, September 19, 1990; Robert W. Peterson, *Cages to Jump Shots: Pro Basketball's Early Years* (New York, 1990); John D. Russell, *Between Games, Between Halves* (Washington, 1986); Robert Sadowski, brother, letter to Allan Hall, January 20, 1994; Seton Hall University Sports Information Department, South Orange, NJ; *TSN*, October 1, 1990, p. 49; Ken Shouler et al., *Total Basketball* (Wilmington, DE, 2003); Robert White, high school coach, letter to Allan Hall, January 7, 1994.

Allan Hall

SAILORS, Kenneth Lloyd "Kenny" (b. January 14, 1921, Bushnel, NE), college, amateur, and professional player, is the son of Edward Sailors and Corabell (Houtz) Sailors, and ranks among the greatest players in Wyoming basketball history. Sailors grew up on a ranch in Hillsdale, Wyoming and played basketball at Laramie High School, where he twice made the All-State team. At the Hillsdale ranch, he developed a one-handed jumpshot to become one of the real innovators in basketball history. According to Sailors, he learned the shot to compete against his oldest brother, Bud, a six-foot five-inch basketball All-Stater. The Sailors duo played one-on-one and used a hoop nailed to a windmill on their ranch.

Sailors in 1939 enrolled at the University of Wyoming (BSkC), where he made two-time basketball All-America under coach Ev Shelton*. His most memorable season came in 1942–1943, when the Cowboys won the NCAA title by defeating Georgetown (Washington, D.C.) University 46-34 at Madison Square Garden in New York. He led all players that game with 16 points. The NIT then still shared the college basketball spotlight with the NCAA as a test of college basketball excellence. Consequently, two nights after vanquishing Georgetown, the Cowboys returned to Madison Square Garden and edged NIT champion St. John's University in overtime 52-47 in a benefit game for the American Red Cross.

During their championship 1942–1943 season, the Cowboys compiled a 31-2 record. Sailors averaged 15 points and directed Wyoming on the floor. His style of play attracted the attention of fans and sportswriters. Although players possessed a limited offensive repertoire, he employed a unique jumpshot. Coaches marveled when Sailors dribbled the ball at a faster pace than most other players could run. Although the 195-pound Sailors stood only five-feet ten-inches tall, he possessed, as one commentator wrote, "wide shoulders and the biceps and long arms of a heavyweight-wrestler."

In close games, he delighted his fans by freezing the ball. Joe Commisky, sports editor of New York's *PM*, recalled this wizardry after the Georgetown game. "This Sailors," Commisky wrote, "can do everything with a basketball but tie a seaman's knot." Sailors began picking up recognition in 1943, when he was named First Team All-BSKC. To prepare for the NCAA tournament, the Cowboys entered the annual AAU basketball tournament in Denver, Colorado in mid-March. Wyoming lost to the Denver American Legion in the semifinals, but defeated the University of Denver for third place. Sailors, a First Team AAU All-America, was selected the most promising youngster of the tournament. In the regional basketball tournament at Kansas City, Missouri, the Cowboys overcame a nine-point deficit to edge University of Oklahoma 53-50, and a 13 points deficit to defeat the University of Texas 58-54. After defeating Georgetown University in the NCAA Final, Sailors won various All-America accolades and the Chuck Taylor Medal as the outstanding College Player of the Year.

Within a month, Sailors enlisted in the U.S. Marines. After two years in military service, he returned to the University of Wyoming for his last year of eligibility. Sailors made *True* magazine's First Team All-America in 1946 and played in the fledgling BAA-NBA for five seasons. He made the All-Rookie Team in 1947 with the Cleveland Rebels (BAA), averaging nine points a game. His 1947–1948 BAA campaign was split between the Chicago Stags, Philadelphia Warriors, and Providence Steamrollers. Sailors made the All-BAA Second Team in 1949, when he averaged 15.8 points with Providence. Sailors enjoyed his best year in 1949–1950, when he finished fourth in scoring while averaging 17.3 points for the Denver Nuggets (NBA). Sailors completed his NBA career in 1950–1951 with the Boston Celtics and Baltimore Bullets. He scored 3,480 points altogether and averaged 12.6 points for his BAA-NBA career.

After retiring from professional basketball, Sailors operated a dude ranch in Wyoming and pursued a career in politics. In 1965, he moved to Alaska and became a master guide for big game hunters and fishermen. Sailors and his wife, Marilynne, have two children, Dan and Linda, and divide their time between Alaska and Phoenix, Arizona. He was selected among the initial inductees to the Wyoming Athletics Hall of Fame.

BIBLIOGRAPHY: Peter C. Bjarkman, *The Biographical History of Basketball* (Chicago, IL, 2000); Morgan G. Brenner, *College Basketball's National Championships* (Lanham, MD, 1999); Jan Hubbard, ed., *The Official NBA Basketball Encyclopedia*, 3rd ed. (New York, 2000); Neil D. Isaacs, *Vintage NBA* (Silver Spring, MD, 1996); Kenneth Sailors file, University of Wyoming Department of Athletics, Laramie, WY; Alexander Weyand, *The Cavalcade of Basketball* (New York, 1960).

Adolph H. Grundman

ST. JOHN, Lynn Wilbur (b. November 18, 1876, Union City, PA; d. September 30, 1950, Columbus, OH), college football player, basketball coach, and athletic administrator, graduated from Ohio State University in 1900 and the College of Wooster in 1906. St. John became a major force in stabilizing basketball during those earliest transition years of the post–World War I era. As a member of the Joint Rules Committee from 1912 to 1937, he was praised as "a master in diplomacy" and performed an often monumental task of unifying various factions under a single acceptable playing code.

St. John began his athletic career at Monroe (Ohio) High School from 1892 to 1896 as a star in four sports, including basketball and football. At Ohio State University, he played only varsity football. St. John eventually made his true mark in the sport of basketball. At the outset of his lengthy and colorful career, he served as both basketball coach and athletic director at the College of Wooster (Ohio) and Ohio Wesleyan College. St. John returned to Ohio State University as basketball coach from 1912 to 1919 and as athletic director from 1915 to 1947. His contributions to the latter institution are permanently commemorated by the St. John Arena, basketball home of the Ohio State University Buckeyes.

St. John also demonstrated keen interest in formal codification of international basketball rules, helping form the NBCUS and chairing the group from 1933 to 1937. He also served as a member of the 1936 USOC and was responsible during the inaugural Olympic basketball competition for preventing potentially harmful splits among separate factions of U.S. amateur basketball. St. John, a giant among earliest administrators of the sport, entered the Naismith Memorial Basketball Hall of Fame as a contributor in 1962.

BIBLIOGRAPHY: Peter C. Bjarkman, *Big Ten Basketball* (Indianapolis, IN, 1994); Zander Hollander, ed., *The Pro Basketball Encyclopedia* (Los Angeles, CA, 1977); Ronald L. Mendell, *Who's Who in Basketball* (New Rochelle, NY, 1973); William G. Mokray, ed., *Ronald Encyclopedia of Basketball* (New York, 1963); Sandy Padwe, *Basketball's Hall of Fame* (Englewood Cliffs, NJ, 1970); Lynn St. John file, Naismith Memorial Basketball Hall of Fame, Springfield, MA.

Peter C. Bjarkman

SAITCH, Eyre "Ayers" "Bruiser" (b. February 22, 1902, New York, NY; d. November 28, 1985, Englewood, NJ), athlete, graduated in January 1921 from DeWitt Clinton High School in New York, where he starred in basketball. Saitch began playing professional basketball for the all-black New York Renaissance during the 1925–1926 season, when manager-coach Bob Douglas* acquired him.

Known for his outside shooting ability, Saitch played guard in professional basketball from 1926 to 1941. He participated on the seven-member 1932–1933 New York Renaissance team, winners of 88 consecutive basketball games. The 1932–1933 team was inducted into the Naismith Memorial Basketball Hall of Fame in 1963 and included teammates "Tarzan" Cooper*, William Smith*, Fats Jenkins*, Pappy Ricks, Casey Holt, and Bill Yancey*. Saitch also helped the 1939 Renaissance team defeat the Oshkosh All-Stars (NBL) to win the first-ever Professional Tournament in Chicago, IL. He was acknowledged as the player whom women came to see because of his handsome profile.

Saitch also excelled as a nationally ranked tennis player in the 1920s and 1930s. His several singles tennis titles included the 1928 and 1929 New York state championships and the 1930 New England Tennis Tournament. Saitch, equally impressive in doubles play, teamed with Dr. Sylvester Smith of New York to win the 1929 National Colored Doubles title and the 1930 New England Tennis championship. During the late 1920s and early 1930s, he ranked among the best African American tennis players in the United States. Although Saitch performed against white players on the basketball court, discrimination prevented him from playing against white athletes in tennis. Upon his death, he resided in Englewood, New Jersey.

BIBLIOGRAPHY: Ocania Chalk, *Pioneers of Black Sport* (New York, 1975); Glenn Dickey, *The History of Professional Basketball Since 1896* (New York, 1982); Bill Himmelman, Norwood, NJ, telephone conversation with Susan J. Rayl, October 1993; Zander Hollander, ed., *The Modern Encyclopedia of Basketball* (New York, 1993); *New York Amsterdam News*, August 31, 1929, p. 9; *New York Amsterdam News*, July 9, 1930, p. 13; New York Renaissance file, Naismith Basketball Hall of Fame, Springfield, MA; Robert W. Peterson, *From Cages to Jump Shots* (New York, 1990); Susan J. Rayl, *The New York Renaissance Professional Black Basketball Team, 1923–1950* (Syracuse, NY, 2001); Ken Shouler et al., *Total Basketball* (Wilmington, DE, 2003).

Susan J. Rayl

SALES, Nykesha Simone (b. May 10, 1976, Bloomfield, CT), college and professional player, is the daughter of Ray Sales and Kim Sales. She was taught to play basketball by her father, while her mother encouraged her to play as long as she maintained good grades. Sales honed her basketball skills on local courts and in high school. As a junior at Bloomfield (Connecticut) High School in 1992–1993, Sales played basketball on the East team at the U.S. Olympic Festival and was selected a *Parade* magazine All America. As a senior, she repeated *Parade*'s All America honors and was named *USA Today*'s national Female Player of the Year. Sales, who also excelled in the classroom and often appeared on the honor roll, and was named in 1994 by *Street and Smith* among the nation's top five scholastic recruits.

The heavily recruited Sales signed with the University of Connecticut Huskies, where she played from 1994 to 1998. She appeared in every game her freshman year, helping lead the Huskies in their perfect 35-0 season to the NCAA championship. Sales won Kodak All America honors and played on the All-BEaC

First Team her junior and senior seasons, averaging 16.4 points and 4.2 steals. She also set Connecticut records for most points in a single game with 46 and career with 2,178. Her senior year was marked with mononucleosis at the start of the season and a ruptured Achilles tendon later. Just shy of the all-time scoring record, Sales was allowed to score the opening lay-up of the last regular-season game against Villanova University, sparking a controversy. She graduated with a Bachelor's degree in business.

Sales took 1998 off from basketball to rehabilitate her Achilles tendon, but was drafted the next year by the Orlando Miracle (WNBA) and averaged 13.7 points her rookie season in 1999. Her game has remained through her first five WNBA seasons. During her four years with the Miracle from 1997 through 2002, she averaged 13.5 points. She averaged 16.1 points per game in 2003 and 15.2 points in 2004 with the Connecticut Sun (WNBA), leading the WNBA with 75 steals (2.2 average) the latter season. Sales set a WNBA Finals record with 32 points in Game 2, but the Seattle Storm defeated the Sun, two games to one, to take the 2004 title. During six WNBA seasons, she has netted 2,796 points, 846 rebounds, and 367 steals in 196 regular season games and 198 points, 65 rebounds, and 33 steals in 15 WNBA playoff games. Sales, a five time WNBA All-Star, hopes to open a clothing and shoe store for tall women.

BIBLIOGRAPHY: Peter C. Bjarkman, *The Biographical History of Basketball* (Chicago, IL, 2000); Dave Kindred, "The Sales Call," *TSN* (March 9, 1998), pp. 63; *TSN Official WNBA Guide and Register, 2004* (St. Louis, MO, 2004); Clifford Thompson, ed., "Nykesha, Sales," *CB Yearbook 1999*; WNBA website, www.wnba.com.

Lisa A. Ennis

SAMPSON, Kelvin (b. October 5, 1955, Laurinburg, NC), college athlete and basketball coach, is the son of John W. "Ned" Sampson and Eva Sampson. Sampson, a Native American of Lumbee Indian heritage, excelled academically and athletically and attended Pembroke, North Carolina High School, where his father coached. He captained the basketball team, quarterbacked the football squad, and played catcher-outfielder in baseball. Sampson won nine varsity letters in three sports before graduating in 1974. At Pembroke State University between 1975 and 1978, he earned Bachelors degrees in both health and physical education and political science. Sampson lettered four years in basketball and three years in baseball. Upon graduation in 1978, he received a graduate assistantship at Michigan State University, worked under head basketball coach Jud Heathcote, and completed work on his Master's degree.

Sampson's first coaching experience came in 1981, when he served as assistant basketball coach at Montana Tech University in Butte, Montana. From 1982 through 1985, he led the Orediggers to a 73-45 win-loss record in four seasons as head coach. Sampson was selected FrL Coach of the Year in 1984 and 1985. He joined Washington State University in 1986 as assistant basketball coach for two seasons before being named head coach of the Cougars for the 1987–1988 campaign. As head coach at Washington State for seven years, Sampson guided his 1991–1992 and 1993–1994 squads to 22 and 20 wins, respectively. Both units participated in postseason play, the first time for the Cougars since 1983. Sampson compiled a 103-103 win-loss coaching record between 1988 and 1994, being selected PTC Coach of the Year in 1992.

In April 1994, Sampson was named head basketball coach at the University of Oklahoma. In his first season at Oklahoma, the Sooners won 27 games to earn him BEC Coach of the Year honors. Sampson completed his eleventh year in 2004–2005, with his Sooners teams having recorded 260 victories and only 100 losses. In 21 years as a collegiate head coach, he has compiled a career record of 435 triumphs and 248 setbacks. Sampson directed the Sooners to seven consecutive 20-win seasons and nine consecutive NCAA tournament appearances through 2002–2003, advancing to the NCAA Sweet Sixteen in 1999 and the NCAA Final Four in 2002. His 2001 squad won 26 games and captured the BTwC tournament for the first time in 10 years. The Sooners posted a 31-5 record in 2001–2002, second most in school history, with Sampson being named NABC Coach of the Year.

Sampson has been involved with USA

basketball as the head coach of the 1993 U.S. Olympic Festival West team and the 1995 USA Junior World Championship team. He served as an assistant coach for the 1994 Goodwill Games Team and the 2002 World Championship team.

In 2002, Sampson received the Red Earth Ambassador of the Year Award for promoting pride in Native American heritage and making contributions in presenting a positive image of Native Americans. He was elected to the Montana Tech Hall of Fame in 1996 and the Pembroke State University Hall of Fame in 1998. He and his wife, Karen Lowery, have a daughter, Lauren, and a son, Kellen.

BIBLIOGRAPHY: *NCAA Men's Basketball Records, 2004* (Indianapolis, IN, 2003); Steve Richardson, *Kelvin Sampson—The OU Basketball Story* (Plano, TX, 2002); "Kelvin Sampson," *Profile*, http://www.soonersports.ocsn.com (2003); "Kelvin Sampson," *Red Earth Award*, http://www.redearth.com (2002); "Kelvin Sampson," *USA Basketball*, http:www.usabasketball.com (2003).

John L. Evers

SAMPSON, Ralph Lee, Jr. (b. July 7, 1960, Harrisonburg, VA), college and professional player, is the son of Ralph Lee Sampson, Sr., foreman of an aluminum window manufacturing plant, and Sarah (Blakey) Sampson. Sampson's basketball career began in the fourth grade at Waterman Elementary School in Harrisonburg, Virginia. Although very tall even as a youngster, he was not successful initially and had to work hard. Sampson was encouraged throughout this ordeal by his mother, who had played basketball in high school. He progressed well as a six-foot seven-inch freshman at Harrisonburg, played on the junior varsity team, and was promoted to the varsity during the playoffs. Under Coach Roger Bergey, Sampson led Harrisonburg High School to two Class AA state championships. During his sophomore year, he played in the state championship game that marked the first live televised high school basketball game in Virginia history. During his career at Harrisonburg, Sampson was recruited heavily by over 100 major colleges and universities. He narrowed his choices to the University of Kentucky, the University of North Carolina, Virginia Tech University, and the University of Virginia before choosing Virginia.

Sampson enrolled at Virginia in 1979 as a Speech Communications major and rewrote the Cavaliers record books, becoming the most dominant player in college basketball. During his playing career, Virginia produced a 112-23 record and .830 winning percentage. He led Virginia to the 1980 NIT title, 1981 NCAA East Regional title, and a 1981 Final Four appearance. With Sampson, Virginia won or shared the ACC championship in 1981, 1982, and 1983. Sampson set many Virginia career and seasonal records, including most games played (132) and field goals scored (899), best field goal percentage (.568), and most rebounds (1,511) and blocked shots (462). He ranks third on the all-time Cavaliers scoring list with 2,228 points and became only the sixth player in NCAA history to score over 2,000 points and collect more than 1,500 rebounds.

Sampson, one of the most dominant players in NCAA history, also received national recognition for his individual talents. He became only the third player to gain three successive National Player of the Year Awards, the first performer to win two straight Eastman Awards presented by Kodak, and the second player to win ACC Player of the Year three consecutive years. His other awards and honors included two John R. Wooden Awards, three Naismith Awards, and three straight UPI Player of the Year Awards. He also won three consecutive USBWA Player of the Year Awards, three straight Rupp Trophies as AP Player of the Year, and four consecutive All-America designations.

The seven-foot four-inch, 230-pound Sampson was the first player selected in the 1983 NBA draft. He was chosen by the Houston Rockets (NBA), who secured the number one pick by calling "heads" in a coin flip with the Indiana Pacers. Sampson's rookie season, 1983–1984, was an encore of his college career. Sampson led the Rockets in minutes played (2,693), scoring (1,722 points), rebounds (913), field goal percentage (.523), and blocked shots (197), and established records for blocked shots in a game (13 against the Chicago Bulls) and in a season. He was named to the All-Rookie team and unanimous winner of the Rookie of the Year award. The 1984–1985 season extended his personal success. With the acquisition of first-round pick Hakeem Olajuwon*, Sampson moved from center to forward and proved equal to the challenge of a new position. During the 1984–1985 season, he was named to the NBA All-Star team as a starter for the West squad. After leading his squad to victory, Sampson was named MVP of the thirtieth annual game. He closed out the season by leading his team into the NBA playoffs and by being named to the All-NBA Second Team.

In 1985–1986, Sampson compiled an 18.9 points scoring average, snared 879 rebounds during the regular season, and made the NBA All-Star Game West squad for the third consecutive time. His 20.0 points per game in the NBA playoffs helped the Rockets defeat the Los Angeles Lakers in the Western Conference Finals before losing to the Boston Celtics in the six-game championship series. Injuries limited Sampson to 43 games during the 1986–1987 regular season. He did not dominate in scoring or in any other aspect of the game. In December 1987, Houston traded Sampson and Steve Harris to the Golden State Warriors (NBA) for Joe Barry Carroll and Eric Floyd. Sampson missed 34 games in 1987–1988 and underwent surgery on his right knee in March 1988. He spent the 1988–1989 season with Golden State and was traded to the Sacramento Kings (NBA) in September 1989. Sampson had very limited action with Sacramento from 1989 to 1991, and ended his NBA career with the Washington Bullets (NBA) in 1991–1992. During his NBA career, Sampson scored 7,039 points (15.4 average), made 4,011 rebounds, and blocked 672 shots. He and his wife, Aleize, have one daughter.

BIBLIOGRAPHY: Peter C. Bjarkman, *ACC: Atlantic Coast Conference Basketball* (Indianapolis, IN, 1996); *Houston Rockets Official Press Radio-TV Guide, 1987–1988* (Houston, TX, 1987); Jan Hubbard, ed., *The Official NBA Encyclopedia*, 3rd ed. (New York, 2000); Roland Lazenby, *Sampson: A Life Above the Rim* (Roanoke, VA, 1984); Ron Morris, ed., *ACC Basketball: An Illustrated History* (Chapel Hill, NC, 1988); "Ralph and Magic Show Too Much for East Stars," *Houston Chronicle*, February 11, 1985; University of Virginia, Department of Sports Information, "Virginia's Ralph Sampson," *Cavalier Sport News*, Charlottesville, VA; "Unlike 1984, Sampson Is Refreshed After Leading West All-Stars to Win," *Houston Chronicle*, February 12, 1985; *TSN Official NBA Register, 1992–1993* (St. Louis, MO, 1992).

William A. Sutton

SAPERSTEIN, Abraham Michael "Abe" (b. July 4, 1902, London, England; d. March 15, 1966, Chicago, IL), professional player, coach, and executive, was the son of Louis Saperstein, a tailor, and Anna Saperstein, who migrated from Poland to England shortly after their marriage. In 1905, the Sapersteins moved to the U.S. and settled in Chicago, Illinois. Along with his eight surviving brothers and sisters (a ninth sibling died), he attended Graham Stewart and Ravenswood Elementary Schools. Saperstein graduated from Lake View High School in 1920 and attended the University of Illinois in 1922–1923. During his high school years, he won 15 letters in basketball, baseball, track and field, and wrestling. Saperstein became a U.S. citizen through his father's naturalization and married Sylvia Franklin of Chicago on May 5, 1934. The Sapersteins had two children, Gerald and Eloise (Saperstein) Berkley.

From 1920 through 1925, Saperstein helped augment his family's support by working for Schiller Florists in Chicago and spent his leisure time playing and coaching semipro basketball. He began coaching Negro basketball with the Giles Post American Legion Squad and the Savoy Big Five in 1926 and formed the Harlem Globetrotters as an outgrowth of these squads. The squad, whose name was chosen to indicate a Negro (Harlem) and traveling-barnstorming (Globetrotters) team, played its first game on January 7, 1927, at Hinckley, Illinois. The Globetrotters' historical highlights include their winning of the World's Basketball Championship in 1940, the coast-to-coast trips with the college All-Americas from 1950 to 1962, and their annual European summer tour since 1950.

Saperstein's main contribution came not as a basketball coach or strategist, but as a promoter and entertainer. His teams always fielded premier players, including Marques Haynes*, "Goose" Tatum*, and "Meadowlark" Lemon*.

Comedy became a natural offshoot of ball handling, which provoked laughter and enthusiasm from the fans when they watched clumsy attempts by the opposition to steal the ball from the Globetrotters. As this crowd response became more enthusiastic, Saperstein took more of an interest in comedy and spectator and player interaction to create laughter and involvement. The "Trotters" became almost pure entertainment, combining basketball skills and comedy in classic, designed, rehearsed routines.

Besides his interest in the Globetrotters, Saperstein participated in other sports enterprises. He was involved in the promotion of and had interests in Negro League baseball teams through the 1930s and 1940s. Saperstein owned stock in the St. Louis Browns (AL) and Cleveland Indians (AL) baseball clubs and an interest in the Philadelphia Warriors (NBA). He organized and served as commissioner of the unsuccessful ABL in 1961 and 1962. The Globetrotters became permanently linked with Saperstein. Although Saperstein died in 1966, they live on as his legacy. The Globetrotters have played over 16,500 games in 101 countries and territories before over 100 million spectators and have been the subject of several movies and television specials. The entertainment value of the Globetrotters is evidently as real as Saperstein perceived it to be. Saperstein was elected to the Naismith Memorial Basketball Hall of Fame in 1970 for his contributions to the sport.

BIBLIOGRAPHY: *Harlem Globetrotters 1976 50th Anniversary Issue* (Chicago, IL, 1975); Robert W. Peterson, *Cages to Jump Shots: Pro Basketball's Early Years* (New York, 1990); Abraham Saperstein file, Naismith Memorial Basketball Hall of Fame, Springfield, MA; George Vecsey, *The Harlem Globetrotters* (New York, 1973); Josh Wilker, *The Harlem Globetrotters* (New York, 1997).

William A. Sutton

SCHABINGER, Arthur August "Schabie" (b. August 6, 1889, Sabetha, KS; d. October 13, 1972, Atlanta, GA), college athlete, basketball coach, official and administrator, was the son of Karl Augustus Schabinger and Johanna (Pohl) Schabinger. Schabinger's father died before he was three years old, making the responsibility of leadership fall on his and an older brother's shoulders at an early age. He married Gladys Miriam Johnson and had three children, including twin daughters, Jane (Mrs. R. J. Le Favour) and Jean (Mrs. Lou Fockele). The Schabinger's son, Joe, was killed as a test pilot during World War II. Schabinger moved from tiny Sabetha, Kansas to Emporia, Kansas, where he lettered in four sports before graduating from high school in 1908. At the College of Emporia, "Schabie" was selected basketball All-Conference and team manager, led the basketball team in scoring his senior year, and captained the football and baseball squads. After earning his Bachelor of Arts degree from Emporia, Schabinger lettered in football and basketball at Springfield (Massachusetts) College and earned a Bachelor's degree physical education degree from there in 1915. During summers, he organized and coached baseball and basketball teams for children on the city playgrounds.

Schabinger began a 20-year basketball coaching career with five seasons at Ottawa (Kansas) University, interrupted by infantry service in World War I, and spent two years at Emporia Teachers College. After arriving as coach at Creighton University (Nebraska) in 1922, he compiled a 160-66 record against collegiate competition. In 13 seasons at Creighton, Schabinger suffered his only losing campaign in 1930–1931. Nevertheless, his 1930–1931 team finished in a three-way tie for the MVC championship. His overall 258-96 coaching record constituted one of the highest winning percentages (.800) for a college basketball coach. His Creighton Bluejays captured four NCC titles (1922–1923, 1923–1924, 1924–1925, 1926–1927) by utilizing an innovative fast-break attack for the time. His 1923–1924 championship team featured All-America forward Leonard Lovely and posted a 15-2 record. Edgar Hickey*, future Creighton coach, also played on this Bluejay squad.

In 1928 Schabinger moved Creighton to the MVC, where the Bluejays gained championships in 1929–1930, 1930–1931, 1931–1932, and 1934–1935. Creighton became the first undefeated MVC team since the conference's 1928 reorganization. Schabinger ended his coaching career to pursue other challenges. He moved to Chicago to promote the use and sale of the "last-bilt" basketball, developed by Milton Reach of Spalding Sporting Goods. This molded ball was manufactured with neither panels nor lacing and with perfect balance to allow for consistent performance.

Schabinger's impact on the sport extended far beyond his coaching success. He pioneered intersectional games, as his 1923–1924 squad lost to Marquette University and the University of Nebraska, but defeated Indiana University, the University of Iowa, and the University of Notre Dame among other Midwestern powers. Creighton was the first team to travel by air to accommodate the schedule. Schabinger and five other coaches organized the NABC when the CBRC threatened to reduce the dribble to one bounce in 1927 and served as NABC president in 1931–1932. In 1922, Marquette coach Frank Murray "froze" the ball during a 7-6 victory over Schabinger's squad. Schabinger's protests led to the establishment of the 10-second line, which required advancing the ball beyond a point inside half-court. He directed the Olympic Basketball Tournaments in 1936 and conducted the tryouts for this first U.S. Olympic team. Schabinger's experience as a major in the Special Services branch of the U.S. Air Force during World War II inspired him to capitalize on the educational possibilities of film. He founded the Official Sports Film Services in 1946 in Chicago, enabling uniform interpretation of rules through use of game footage. Officials across the nation could become more consistent in enforcing the rules of basketball, football, and baseball. These instructional films were translated into the language of every nation across Europe where those sports were played. Schabinger served on the NABC Rules Committee and chaired the AAU Basketball Committee for four years. In addition to officiating many football and basketball games played in the Midwest region, he served as BTC umpire, football scout, and baseball scout. For many years, he conducted coaching schools throughout the U.S.

The Naismith Memorial Basketball Hall of Fame in 1961 chose Schabinger as a contributor in recognition of his multifaceted contributions to basketball. His other honors include the Metropolitan IBA Award (1955), HAF Hall of Fame (1962), and Kansas Sports Hall of Fame (1963). Schabinger was a basketball pioneer and promoter when the game became formalized and developed on national and international levels.

BIBLIOGRAPHY: Bill Gutman, *The History of NCAA Basketball* (New York, 1993); John D. McCallum, *College Basketball, U.S.A Since 1892* (Briarcliff Manor, NY, 1978); Arthur Schabinger file, Naismith Memorial Basketball Hall of Fame, Springfield, MA; Alexander M. Weyand, *The Cavalcade of Basketball* (New York, 1960).

Gregory S. Sojka

SCHAYES, Adolph "Dolph" (b. May 19, 1928, New York, NY), college and professional player, coach, and executive, is the son of Carl Schayes and Tina Schayes. His father, who immigrated from Rumania and drove a linen truck, was a frustrated athlete and encouraged his sons to participate in sports. He persuaded Adolph to try out for the basketball team at DeWitt Clinton High School in the Bronx, New York. After initially being dropped from the basketball squad, Schayes eventually made the first team. Although not an outstanding basketball star in high school, he gradually improved. After graduation in January 1945, Schayes enrolled at NYU and immediately made the first team as a college freshman. He averaged only 10.2 points in 80 games during his NYU career. During his senior year in 1947–1948, NYU compiled a 22-4 record and played in the NIT.

On graduation, Schayes was drafted by the New York Knickerbockers (BAA) and the Syracuse (New York) Nationals (NBL). He chose Syracuse, which had offered more money. The next year, the BAA and NBL merged to form the NBA. Schayes' entire 16-year career as a player was spent with the Syracuse Nationals. On February 13, 1951, he married Naomi Gross and has four children. His son, Daniel, played basketball at Syracuse University and with seven NBA teams. Although many observers were not particularly impressed with Schayes when he first became a professional, dedication and constant practice resulted in the election of the six-foot eight-inch, 220-pound forward into the Naismith Memorial Basketball Hall of Fame in 1972. Despite his height, Schayes became a finesse player with various scoring moves. He took setshots from the corner and drove to the basket for three-point plays. One of the finest all-time free throw shooters, Schayes led the NBA in 1957–1958, 1959–1960, and 1961–1962 and converted .843 percent during his career. He consistently led Syracuse in scoring, averaging 18.2 points during his career. Schayes was a fine passer for his height and a good defensive player. He led the NBA in rebounding in 1951 and averaged over 10 rebounds in his career. His professional career included 19,247 points, 11,256 rebounds, and 6,979 foul shots. He led the franchise in all-time rebounds.

During Schayes' first NBA season in 1949–1950, Syracuse won the Eastern Division title and lost to the Minneapolis Lakers in the NBA Finals. The Nationals lost in the NBA Finals again to Minneapolis in 1954, but Schayes led Syracuse to an NBA championship the next year by defeating the Fort Wayne Pistons in seven games. Schayes' teams made the playoffs 15 of his 16 seasons. A durable athlete, Schayes played in 764 consecutive games from February 7, 1952, until December 27, 1961. He made NBA All-Star First Team six times (1952 through 1955, 1957 through 1958) and was voted to the All-NBA Second Team during six other seasons.

In 1963 the Syracuse Nationals became the Philadelphia 76ers, with Schayes as player-coach. During his last season as Philadelphia coach in 1965–1966, the 76ers finished first in the Eastern Division with a 55-25 record and Schayes was voted Coach of the Year. Because the 76ers performed poorly against the Boston Celtics in the playoffs, Schayes was fired at the end of the season. From 1966 until 1969, Schayes served as supervisor of NBA referees. In 1970–1971 he returned to coaching with the Buffalo Braves (NBA) and compiled a 22-60 record. Altogether, he compiled a 115-172 record as an NBA head coach. The lasting memory of Schayes is as a tenacious player, whose career began in the infancy of the NBA and concluded in the modern era. He made the NBAs 25th Anniversary All-Time Team in 1970 and was named one of the 50 Greatest Players in NBA History in 1996.

BIBLIOGRAPHY: Stanley Frank, "Basketball's Toughest War Horse," *SEP* 230 (December 28, 1957), pp. 24, 61–62; William Heuman, *Famous Pro Basketball Stars* (New York, 1970); Jan Hubbard, ed., *The Official NBA Encyclopedia*, 3rd ed. (New York, 2000); Neil D. Isaacs, *Vintage NBA* (Silver Spring, MD, 1996); Leonard Koppett, *24 Seconds to Shoot: An Informal History of the NBA* (New York, 1968); Roland Lazenby, *The NBA Finals* (Indianapolis, IN, 1996); *NYT*, April 11, 1955; *NYT*, May 3, 1966; *NYT*, October 14, 1971; Charles Salzberg, *From Set Shot to Slam Dunk* (New York, 1987); Adolph Schayes file, Naismith Memorial Basketball Hall of Fame, Springfield, MA; Joseph Siegman, *Jewish Sports Legends* (Washington, DC, 1999); William Simons, "Interview with Adolph Schayes," *American Jewish History* 74 (1985), pp. 287–307; Ken Shouler et al., *Total Basketball* (Wilmington DE, 2003); *TSN Official NBA Register, 2004–2005* (St. Louis, MO, 2004).

Jon S. Moran

SCHLUNDT, Donald (b. March 15, 1933, South Bend, IN; d. October 10, 1985, Indianapolis, IN), college player, was the son of Martin W. Schlundt, an auto plant worker, and Anna (Bodtke) Schlundt, a custodial employee at Washington Clay High School in South Bend, Indiana. Schlundt played basketball in junior high school and excelled as a softball pitcher in church and school leagues. At Washington Clay High School, he earned All-State basketball honors and was recruited by Indiana University (BTC) coach Branch McCracken*.

When someone asked if Schlundt was a good student, McCracken allegedly remarked that he must be since he was tall. The six-foot ten-inch, 210-pound Schlundt represented Indiana University's first big basketball player. The Korean War caused suspension of the prohibition on freshmen, enabling him to start all four years. In his sophomore season, the 1952–1953 Hoosiers won 23 games and lost only three. All losses came on last-second baskets. McCracken won his first outright BTC title and second NCAA crown, defeating the University of Kansas 69-68, as Schlundt tallied 30 points.

The 1953–1954 Hoosiers were favored to gain another NCAA title. The entire starting lineup returned, including Bob Leonard* and Dick Farley—both of whom later played professionally—Charles Kraak, and Burke Scott. Indiana repeated as BTC Champions, but was upset in the NCAA Tournament by the University of Notre Dame (Indiana). Indiana had crushed Notre Dame in the 1953 NCAA Tournament when Schlundt tallied 41 points to break George Mikan's* Chicago Stadium record. In these two years, the Hoosiers suffered only three BTC defeats.

Upon completing his senior year in 1955, Schlundt held 10 of the 14 recognized BTC records. These marks included 1,076 career rebounds and 2,192 career points (23.3 points per game). The latter remained the Indiana University standard until Steve Alford* broke it in 1987. Schlundt set the single-game Hoosier scoring record of 47 points twice, tallied 25 or more points in 40 games, and averaged 27.1 points in 1953–1954. He made All-BTC and All-America in his final three years, leading the BTC in scoring in all three campaigns and the Hoosiers in scoring for four years. His honors in 1954 included being chosen BTC MVP and the nation's Player of the Year. In 1989, Schlundt was named to the second squad of the "Dream Team" of Indiana's high school players.

The Syracuse Nationals (NBA) drafted Schlundt and offered him a $5,500 contract with a $1,000 bonus, but he declined a professional career to engage in insurance, his favorite college subject. An insurance career offered more money in an era long before the million dollar professional basketball contracts. He pursued an insurance career in Bloomington, Indiana, Indianapolis, Indiana, and Carmel, Indiana.

Schlundt wed his high school sweetheart, Gloria Blyton, on June 20, 1953, and had two children, Mark and Marylse. In 1981, a national magazine awarded him a cash prize for his barbecue sauce recipe. Schlundt, who played golf and enjoyed cooking, was collecting recipes for a cookbook when stricken by a terminal illness in 1983. The HAF College Basketball Hall of Fame enshrined him.

BIBLIOGRAPHY: Peter C. Bjarkman, *Big Ten Basketball* (Indianapolis, IN, 1994), Mike Douchant, *Encyclopedia of College Basketball* (Detroit, MI, 1995); Joe Gergen, *The Final Four: An Illustrated History* (St. Louis, MO, 1987); Bob Hammel et al., *Glory of Old IU* (Champaign, IL, 2000); Neil Isaacs, *All the Moves: A History of College Basketball* (Philadelphia, PA, 1975); Billy Packer and Roland Lazenby, *College Basketball's 25 Greatest Teams* (St. Louis, MO, 1989); Ken Rappoport, *The Classic* (Shawnee Mission, KS, 1978); Alexander Weyand, *The Cavalcade of Basketball* (New York, 1960).

Thomas P. Wolf

SCHMIDT, Ernest John "Ernie" "One Grand" (b. February 12, 1911, Nashville, KS; d. September 6, 1986, Goodland, KS), college player and official, performed on seven consecutive basketball championship teams in high school and college. Schmidt attended Winfield High School in Winfield, Kansas, where he started three years at center in varsity basketball. He was coached by Bill Martain and was named All-Arkansas Valley Conference three times. During those high school seasons, Schmidt led Winfield to three consecutive state championships and set all scoring records in conference and tournament play. He graduated from Winfield High School in 1929.

Schmidt matriculated at Kansas State College of Pittsburg and played basketball there four years. John F. Lance coached him at Kansas State, as the latter recorded four All-CeC seasons and helped the Wildcats win four straight CeC championships. He led Kansas State to 47 straight wins and managed exactly 1,000 career points. Schmidt, who became known as "One Grand Schmidt," was recognized as the nation's greatest college basketball player. He graduated from Kansas State in 1933, receiving his Bachelor of Science degree in physical education. Schmidt began to officiate for many BEC and MVC contests and remained loyal to basketball, attending several basketball tournaments. Schmidt was named to the HAF Hall of Fame for noteworthy achievement in basketball and in 1973 to the Naismith Memorial Basketball Hall of Fame as a player.

BIBLIOGRAPHY: *Pittsburg Sun*, 1932; Ernest Schmidt file, Naismith Memorial Basketball Hall of Fame, Springfield, Massachusetts.

Jeff Sanderson and Wayne Patterson

SCHOMMER, John Joseph (b. January 29, 1884, Chicago, IL; d. January 11, 1960, Chicago, IL), college athlete, coach, administrator, and official, worked his way through Central YMCA High School and the University of Chicago by selling leather belts he had designed. Schommer graduated from the University of Chicago in 1909. An All-Time All-America selection by the HAF, he from 1906 to 1909 became the first University of Chicago athlete to win 12 letters in four sports. On the Maroons basketball team, Schommer led all WC scorers for three consecutive seasons from 1906–1907 to 1908–1909. Only Indiana University's Don Schlundt* (1953–1955), Purdue University's Terry Dischinger* (1960–1962), and Rick Mount* (1968–1970) have equalled this feat. The four-time All-America made an eighty-foot field goal to give Chicago a last-second victory over the University of Pennsylvania for the national title in 1908. Chicago won the WC three consecutive years and was named HAF National Champions from 1907 to 1909. The captain of the 1909 Maroons, Schommer scored 19 field goals in a game against the University of Illinois. In one amazing defensive string covering nine games, he held the opposing centers to four field goals.

Under football coach Amos Alonzo Stagg, Schommer was selected as an All-WC end and played on WC championship teams in 1905, 1907, and 1908. At the University of Chicago, he participated in only seven losing basketball games and two losing football contests over four seasons. Schommer also excelled in track and field and was selected for the 1908 Olympic team, but declined the invitation to concentrate on his studies. During the 1910–1911 season, he served as basketball coach at the University of Chicago. In 1912, Schommer completed a postgraduate course in Chemistry and embarked on a longtime career as a professor of Chemical Engineering and Bacteriology, athletic director, and coach of all sports at the Illinois Institute of Technology. He later ranked among the nation's foremost football and basketball officials. After 32 years as a college official, Schommer worked NFL games from 1942 to 1944. During World War II, the federal government requested him to conduct a nationwide search for skilled mathematicians and scientists capable of engaging in atomic work. Congress awarded him a special medal for his services. After retiring from the faculty at Illinois Tech, he in 1949 became director of the new development program of the school's South Side campus. When Schommer died, he was survived by his widow, Jessie Hollecker Rogers, whom he had married in 1946. His first wife, Elsie Steffen, was the sister of Schommer's University of Chicago football teammate Walter Steffen and had died in 1945. Schommer, a member of the HAF Hall of Fame, was elected as a player to the Naismith Memorial Basketball Hall of Fame in 1959.

BIBLIOGRAPHY: Peter C. Bjarkman, *Big Ten Basketball* (Indianapolis, IN, 1994); *Chicago Daily Tribune*, January 12, 1960, Part 3, pp. 1–2; Zander Hollander, ed., *The Pro Basketball Encyclopedia* (Los Angeles, CA, 1977); John Schommer file, Naismith Memorial Basketball Hall of Fame, Springfield, Massachusetts.

John L. Evers

SCOLARI, Fred J. (b. March 1, 1922, San Francisco, CA; d. October 17, 2002, San Ramon, CA), college and professional player and coach, participated in basketball in the AAU and NBA in the 1940s and 1950s. The son of Italian immigrants, Scolari grew up in San Francisco, California's North Beach and graduated from Galileo High School. Galileo a few years earlier had produced Angelo "Hank" Luisetti*, the great Stanford University (California) basketball star. Too small to participate in varsity basketball in high school, Scolari played on Galileo's 130-pound basketball team. He made All-City as a senior and accepted a basketball scholarship at the University of San Francisco. Although leading the freshman team in scoring, Scolari left San Francisco in his sophomore year because of receiving little playing time. He never played college basketball again, but performed on several San Francisco AAU teams and competed in four National AAU basketball tournaments in Denver, Colorado between 1942 and 1946. Chet Nelson, who covered the national tournament for the *Rocky Mountain News*, described Scolari as "a carbon copy of Hank Luisetti" and "as loose as a feather bed and as full of fakes as a con man."

In 1946, the Washington Capitols (BAA)

drafted Scolari. Scolari led the BAA with a 81.1 free throw percentage in 1946–1947 and made the All-BAA Second Team in 1947 and 1948. The Capitols lost to the Minneapolis Lakers in the 1949 BAA championship series. After dividing the 1950–1951 season between Washington (NBA) and the Syracuse Nationals (NBA), Scolari spent two years with the Baltimore Bullets (NBA) and one each with the Fort Wayne Pistons (NBA) and Boston Celtics (NBA). He served as a playing coach for Baltimore in 1951–1952, compiling a 12-27 record, and played in the 1952 NBA All-Star Game. Scolari retired in 1955, having completed nine-years of professional basketball. A model of perseverance, he possessed limited vision in his left eye, was deaf in his right ear, and did not reach five-feet ten-inches and 165 pounds until after high school. Nonetheless, he played 534 regular-season NBA games, scoring 6,014 points for an 11.3 point average and averaging 2.7 rebounds and 2.6 assists.

From 1957 to 1988, Scolari directed the Salesian Boys and Girls Club in San Francisco. He had grown up playing basketball at the club, which profoundly impacted his life beyond basketball. In 1998, Scolari was inducted into the Bay Area Sports Hall of Fame. He and his wife, Gloria, had sons, Robert and Paul, and a daughter, Paulette.

BIBLIOGRAPHY: Jan Hubbard, ed., *The Official NBA Basketball Encyclopedia*, 3rd ed. (New York, 2000); Chet Nelson, "Sports this Morning," *Rocky Mountain News,* March 16, 1942 p. 11; Fred Scolari, interview, Walnut Creek, CA, June 25, 1997; Ken Shouler et al., *Total Basketball* (Wilmington, DE, 2003); "USF Hoop Great Fred Scolari Dies" USFDons.com.

Adolph H. Grundman

SCOTT, Charles Thomas "Charlie" (b. December 15, 1948, New York), college and professional player and coach, learned basketball on the streets of Harlem, New York. He attended Stuyvesant High School as a freshman and transferred to Laurinburg Prep School in North Carolina. Laurinburg lost only one game in his final two years, with Scott averaging 27 points as a senior.

In 1966, Scott became the first black scholarship athlete at the University of North Carolina (ACC). In three varsity seasons, he led the Tar Heels to two NCAA Final Four appearances. The lanky guard compiled a collegiate career scoring average of 22.1 points, being selected to the All-ACC team in 1968, 1969, and 1970 and having the ACC Athlete of the Year award in 1970. In 1969, Scott was named to the NCAA All-Tournament team. He also played on the gold-medal Olympic team in 1968.

The six-foot six-inch, 175-pound Scott signed professionally with the Washington Capitols (ABA), which soon became the Virginia Squires. He averaged 27.1 points his first ABA season and was named Co-Rookie of the Year. In the 1971–1972 season, Scott set an all-time ABA scoring record with 34.6 points per game. He played in two ABA All-Star Games and was named once each to the All-ABA First Team and All-ABA Second Team.

In March 1972, Scott jumped to the Phoenix Suns (NBA) after the Boston Celtics (NBA) traded his draft rights. He averaged over 24.8 points in his three full seasons with Phoenix and played in the NBA All-Star Game each year. In May 1975, Phoenix traded Scott to the Boston Celtics (NBA) for Paul Westphal*. Although his scoring decreased to 17.6 points per game, Scott won his only NBA championship ring in 1976 when the Celtics defeated the Suns. He set a record in that series by committing 35 fouls and fouling out of five of the six games.

Scott concluded his playing career in 1979–1980 after spending time with the Los Angeles Lakers (NBA) and the Denver Nuggets (NBA), compiling a 17.9 career NBA scoring average in 560 games. He is married to Trudy and most recently was employed by former Philadelphia 76ers (NBA) coach, Larry Brown*.

BIBLIOGRAPHY: Peter C. Bjarkman, *ACC: Atlantic Coast Conference Basketball* (Indianapolis, IN, 1996); Hal Bock and Ben Olan, *Basketball Stars of 1974* (New York, 1973); Mike Douchant, *Encyclopedia of College Basketball* (Detroit, MI, 1995); Joe Gilmartin, *The Little Team That Could . . . And Darn Near Did* (Phoenix, AZ, 1976); Raymond Hill, *Unsung Heroes of Pro Basketball* (New York 1973); Jan Hubbard, ed., *The Official NBA Encyclopedia*, 3rd ed. (New York, 2000); Neil D. Isaacs, *All the Moves: A History of College Basketball* (Philadelphia, PA,

1975); Bob Joseph, *Charlie Scott: Legend and Pioneer*, UNCbasketball.com; Ron Morris, *ACC Basketball: An Illustrated History* (Chapel Hill, NC, 1988); Ken Rappoport, *Tar Heel: North Carolina Basketball* (Huntsville, AL, 1976); Ken Rappoport, *Tales from the Tar Heel Locker Room* (Champaign, IL, 2002); Dean Smith, *A Coach's Life: My Forty Years in Basketball* (New York, 1999); *TSN Official NBA Guide, 1997–1998* (St. Louis, MO, 1997); *TSN Official NBA Register, 1980–1981* (St. Louis, MO, 1980).

Curtice R. Mang

SEDRAN, Bernard "Barney" "Mighty Mite of Basketball" (b. January 28, 1891, New York, NY; d. January 14, 1969, New York, NY), college and professional player and coach, began his basketball career in 1905 as player-coach of DeWitt Clinton High School in New York City. Although considered too small at five-feet four-inches and 115-pounds, Sedran still made the division championship team. He played basketball three years at the CCNY under coach Leonard Palmer and starred on numerous college All-Star teams. Sedran entered pro ranks in 1912 with the Newburgh Dizzy Izzies (HRL) and then starred with the Utica Indians (NYSL). He helped Utica win the World's Pro Title in 1913–1914, scoring a record 34 points in one game without a backboard. Other squads, on which Sedran excelled, included the New York Whirlwinds, the Carbondale (Pennsylvania) team (TCL), and the Philadelphia Jaspers (EL). Although statistics are incomplete, he scored at least 3,324 pro-career points.

Nicknamed the "Mighty Mite of Basketball," Sedran performed remarkably well professionally despite his small size. Paired with Marty Friedman* as the famous "Heavenly Twins," he led each of his leagues in scoring. Sedran and Friedman combined as a powerful backcourt combination for many seasons. After being enshrined in the Naismith Memorial Basketball Hall of Fame in 1962, he campaigned for Friedman to be similarly honored. The smallest Hall of Fame member, Sedran played on 15 teams in 13 pro seasons.

Sedran excelled as coach of six teams, including five pro squads. Besides guiding the Wilmington (Delaware) Bombers to ABL crowns in 1941 and 1942, he enjoyed considerable success with Kate Smith's Celtics, the Brooklyn (New York) Jewels, and New York Gothams. ABL president John J. O'Brien* later presented Sedran a scroll in recognition of his 35-year contribution to pro basketball. Sedran married Sadye Bodner and had two daughters, Doris Rosenberg and Rita Rose. A founder and contributor, he actively participated in the Naismith Memorial Basketball Hall of Fame functions. He took part in the first annual enshrinement ceremonies in 1959 and thereafter maintained a personal interest in the Hall of Fame. Sedran held the unique honor of receiving three Hall of Fame nominations, two as a player and one as a coach. Despite these noted honors, he primarily will be remembered as an outstanding player in the pioneering days of the All-American game.

BIBLIOGRAPHY: Murry R. Nelson, *The Originals: The New York Celtics Invent Modern Basketball* (Bowling Green, OH, 1999); Robert W. Peterson, *Cages to Jump Shots: Pro Basketball's Early Years* (New York, 1990); Bernard Sedran file, Naismith Memorial Basketball Hall of Fame, Springfield, MA; Ken Shouler et al., *Total Basketball* (Wilmington, DE, 2003).

Catherine M. Derrick

SELVY, Franklin Delano "Frank" (b. November 9, 1932, Corbin, KY), college and professional player, was born on the night of Franklin D. Roosevelt's election to the U.S. presidency and is the third of seven children of J. R. Selvy, a Corbin, Kentucky, coal miner and city worker. He could not make his high school basketball team until his junior year, but starred as a senior. Major college recruiters, including Adolph Rupp* of the University of Kentucky (SEC), ignored him. Selvy subsequently enrolled at Furman University (SC) in Greenville, South Carolina, where he became an honors student and president of his senior class, and set 21 different national scoring records in basketball.

National attention came to Selvy in his junior year in 1952–1953, as he tallied 738 points and averaged 29.5 points. Selvy's senior year in 1953–1954 saw him lead the nation in scoring and become the first player to surpass 1,000 points in a season. He tallied 1,209 points that season for a 41.7 point scoring average. His 355 free throws in 444 attempts remain national records. In three campaigns, he scored 2,538 career points and averaged 32.5 points to rank sixth best in all-time NCAA total point average. Selvy scored 100 points against Newberry (South Carolina) College on February 14, 1954, in the first game televised in South Carolina. A contingent from Corbin, including his parents (the only time they attended one of his games after high school), watched Selvy score 37 points by halftime, 25 points in the third quarter, and 38 points in the last quarter to reach the 100 mark. He made consensus Second Team All-America in 1953 and First Team All-America in 1954.

The Baltimore Bullets (NBA) selected Selvy first overall in the 1954 NBA draft. He scored 1,348 points as a rookie, averaging 19 points. He joined the Milwaukee Hawks (NBA) when the Baltimore franchise folded in November 1954. Selvy started the 1955–1956 season with the St. Louis Hawks (NBA) and rejoined them in 1957–1958 after a stint in military service. His other NBA teams included the Minneapolis Lakers (1957–1958, 1959–1960), New York Knickerbockers (1958–1959), and Syracuse Nationals (1959–1960). He finally found an NBA home with the Los Angeles Lakers (1960–1961 through 1963–1964), teaming with guard Jerry West*. Although overshadowed by other stars, Selvy scored 3,220 points with the Lakers and played in the 1955 and 1961 NBA All-Star Games. His NBA career featured 6,120 points in 565 regular-season games and 589 points in 512 playoff games.

The six-foot three-inch, 180-pound Selvy scored on lay-ups with either hand and possessed an outstanding jumpshot from outside the circle. He scored from anywhere on the court and made his final basket against Newberry from midcourt. Selvy, who retired from the NBA in 1964, currently resides in Greenville with his wife, a son, and a daughter and works in public relations with a local firm.

BIBLIOGRAPHY: Mike Douchant, *Encyclopedia of College Basketball* (Detroit, MI, 1995); Bill Fay, "All America in College Basketball," *Colliers* 133 (March 19, 1954), pp. 42–45; Larry Fox, *Illustrated History of Basketball* (New York, 1974); Zander Hollander, "He's Got His Points!" *Scholastic* 64 (February 17, 1954), p. 28; Jan Hubbard, ed., *The Official NBA Basketball Encyclopedia* (New York, 2000); Neil Isaacs, *All the Moves: A History of College Basketball* (Philadelphia, PA, 1975); Leonard Koppett, *24 Seconds to Shoot* (New York, 1968); *The NCAA Basketball Guide, 1953–1955* (New York, 1953–1955); NCAA Statistics Service, Mission, KS; Eddie Timanus, "50 years since Selvy's 100," *USA Today*, February 13, 2004, p. 7c.

Daniel R. Gilbert

SEYMOUR, Paul Norman (b. January 30, 1928, Toledo, OH; d. May 5, 1998, Jensen Beach, FL), college and professional player and coach, graduated from Woodward High School in Toledo, Ohio in 1945, and lettered in basketball for the 20-7 University of Toledo in 1945–1946. During the 1946–1947 season, the six-foot two-inch, 180-pound guard began his professional basketball career with the Toledo Jeeps (NBL). Seymour split the 1947–1948 campaign between the Baltimore Bullets (BAA) and Syracuse Nationals (NBL) and remained a reserve through the 1950–1951 season. Syracuse, the 1949–1950 Eastern Division titlists with a 51-53 mark, lost the NBA Finals in six games to the Minneapolis Lakers. He started with rookie George King* in 1951–1952, helping the 40-26 Eastern Division champions reach the NBA semifinals. Coach Al Cervi* employed a tenacious defense and disciplined offense.

Seymour's best NBA seasons came between 1952 and 1955, when he blossomed into a potent scorer. He unveiled an accurate two-handed set-shot to accompany his one-handers, nearly doubling his scoring production average. Seymour, an aggressive, hard-driving, scrappy defensive guard who collaborated effectively with star forward Dolph Schayes*, made the All-NBA Second Team in 1954 and 1955 and participated in the All-Star Games from 1953 through 1955. He averaged 14.2 points during 1952–1953, ranking fifth in NBA assists (294, 4.4 per game) and seventh in foul shooting percentage (.817 percent). Syracuse shared second place in the Eastern Division in 1953–1954, as Seymour finished fourth in NBA free throw percentage (.813 percent) and assists (364). The Minneapolis Lakers defeated the Nationals in the seven-game NBA Finals, but he tallied 14.9 points per game and shared the playoff lead in assists (60). Syracuse captured the Eastern Division crown with a 43-29 record in

1954–1955. Seymour attained career highs in points (1,050), scoring average (14.6 points), and assists (483), ranking second in NBA minutes played (2,950), fourth in assists (6.7 average), and eighth in free throw percentage (.811). The Nationals garnered their only NBA championship, defeating the Ft. Wayne Pistons in seven games. Seymour, who contributed 137 points (12.5-point average) and 75 assists in the playoffs, remained with Syracuse through the 1959–1960 campaign. During his NBL—NBA career, he scored 6,450 points (8.6-point average), converted .782 percent of his foul shots, and recorded 2,341 assists in 748 regular-season games and tallied 740 points (9.3-point average) and recorded 257 assists in 80 playoff games.

In November 1956, Syracuse appointed Seymour to replace Cervi as head coach. Under Seymour, the Nationals recorded second-place Eastern Division finishes in 1956–1957 and 1957–1958 and reached the NBA semifinals against the Boston Celtics in 1957 and 1959. Syracuse posted its best mark under Seymour in 1959–1960 at 45-30, but did not survive the first playoff round. The St. Louis Hawks (NBA) named Seymour to replace head coach Ed Macauley* in 1960. Seymour employed a running game, which vaulted St. Louis to a franchise record 51-28 mark and Western Division crown, but the Boston Celtics defeated the Hawks in the five-game NBA Finals. In December 1961, owner Ben Kerner fired him over strategy differences. Seymour briefly coached the Baltimore Bullets (NBA) to franchise-record second-place finish in 1965–1966 and the Detroit Pistons (NBA) to a 22-38 mark in 1968–1969. Altogether, he compiled a 271-241 regular-season coaching record in eight seasons and a 14-21 playoff mark.

Seymour, who married Doris Ann Hansen and had two sons, Shaun and Paul F., resided in Toledo and worked in the retail business from 1954 to 1990.

BIBLIOGRAPHY: Jan Hubbard ed., *The Official NBA Basketball Encyclopedia*, 3rd ed. (New York, 2000); Neil D. Isaacs, *Vintage NBA* (Silver Spring, MD, 1996); Leonard Koppett, *24 Seconds to Shoot: An Informal History of the National Basketball Association* (New York, 1968); Roland Lazenby, *The NBA Finals* (Indianapolis, IN, 1996); David S. Neft and Richard M. Cohen, eds., *The Sports Encyclopedia: Pro Basketball*, 5th ed. (New York, 1992); Wayne Patterson, Naismith Memorial Basketball Hall of Fame, Springfield, MA, letter to David L. Porter, February 8, 1994; Ken Shouler et al., *Total Basketball* (Wilmington, DE, 2003).

David L. Porter

SHANK, Theresa Marie. *See* Grentz, Theresa Shank

SHARMAN, William Walton "Bill" (b. May 25, 1926, Abilene, TX), college and professional athlete and basketball coach, and executive, grew up in Porterville, California and became the greatest athlete the small town ever produced. He initially attended Narbonne High School in Lomita, California. At Porterville High School, he captained the football and basketball teams, played on the baseball squad, and competed in championship tournament tennis. Sharman, who earned 15 letters, also competed as a shotputter, javelin thrower, hurdler, weight-lifter, and undefeated boxer. After graduating from high school in 1944, he married Ileana Bough and enlisted in the U.S. Navy.

In 1946 Sharman enrolled at the University of Southern California, where he participated in basketball, baseball, and tennis. He applied his disciplined and methodical style to both academics and sports, earning All-PCC basketball honors and twice being PCC MVP. Sharman set a PCC basketball scoring record with 239 points in 1949–1950 and made All-America in 1949 and 1950. Throughout college, he pursued a pro baseball career with various minor league clubs. After graduation from the University of Southern California in 1950, Sharman was drafted by the Washington Capitols (NBA) and signed a baseball contract with the Brooklyn Dodgers (NL). He spent a brief period in the Dodgers farm system before concentrating on basketball. After an impressive 1950–1951 season with Capitols, Sharman became Fort Wayne Pistons (NBA) property because the Washington club folded. Coach "Red" Auerbach* negotiated a deal in 1951, bringing him to the Boston Celtics (NBA) for the next decade.

The six-foot one-inch guard, one of the game's smallest players, ranked among the greatest scorers and helped make the pro game successful in Boston. Sharman, called "the best shooter from the backcourt ever" by Auerbach, teamed with Bob Cousy* to form among the greatest backcourt combinations in basketball history. His sure, deft touch enabled him to score 12,665 career points, make the All-NBA Second Team three times (1953, 1955, 1960) and be voted four times by the players to the All-NBA First Team (1956–1959). Sharman scored 102 points in eight All-Star Games and was selected MVP in the 1955 classic. He averaged 17.8 points during his career and led the Celtics in scoring during the 1955–1956 to 1958–1959 seasons. The NBA's greatest foul shooter, Sharman led the NBA in free throw percentage seven times. He averaged a record 93 percent of his free throws one season (1958–1959) and made 89 percent lifetime. In 1959, he set records of 56 straight free throws in the playoffs and another (broken in 1975) of 55 consecutive in regular-season competition.

In 1961, Sharman became the coach of the Los Angeles Jets (ABL). When the Jets folded halfway through the season, he guided the Cleveland Pipers (ABL) to a championship in 1962 before that team folded. Sharman coached the San Francisco Warriors (NBA) to a Western Division title in 1966–1967 and the Utah Stars to an ABA championship in 1970–1971. During the 1971–1972 season, he joined the Los Angeles Lakers (NBA) as head coach. Sharman became the only mentor to win championships in three pro leagues when the Lakers won the NBA crown in 1971–1972. His illustrious career brought him numerous accolades. In 1966, Sharman's number was retired at Boston Garden before his wife and four children. He was selected to the NBA's Silver Anniversary Team in 1970. He was named as a player in 1970 and a coach in 2004 to the Naismith Memorial Basketball Hall of Fame. In 1976, Sharman became general manager of the Los Angeles Lakers. He subsequently was elected vice president. Sharman, who then served as president of the Lakers from 1982 to 1990, chronicled his shooting philosophy in *Sharman on Basketball Shooting* (1965). In 1975, he co-authored with John Wooden* *The Wooden-Sharman Method: A Guide to Winning Basketball*. He has served as a consultant for the Lakers since 1990 and was named one of the 50 Greatest NBA Players in 1996. Sharman's career reflected his outstanding discipline, concentration, and will. A remarkable jumpshooter and foul shooter, he ignored conventional basketball wisdom and aimed at the back of the rim. His career shooting prowess verified the wisdom of his style.

BIBLIOGRAPHY: Arnold Auerbach and Paul Sann, *Red Auerbach: Winning the Hard Way* (Boston, MA, 1966); Peter C. Bjarkman, *The Boston Celtics Encyclopedia* (Champaign, IL, 1998); Joe Fitzgerald, *That Championship Feeling: The Story of the Boston Celtics* (New York, 1975); Jeff Greenfield, *The World's Greatest Team* (New York, 1976); Tom Henshaw, *Boston Celtics: A Championship Tradition* (Englewood Cliffs, NJ, 1974); Neil D. Isaacs, *Vintage NBA* (Silver Spring, MD, 1996); Roland Lazenby, *The NBA Finals* (Indianapolis, IN, 1996); Bill Libby, *The Coaches* (Chicago, IL, 1972); Charles Salzberg, *From Set Shot to Slam Dunk* (New York, 1987); Bill Sharman, *Bill Sharman on Basketball Shooting* (Englewood Cliffs, NJ, 1965); Bill Sharman file, Naismith Memorial Basketball Hall of Fame, Springfield, MA; Ken Shouler et al., *Total Basketball* (Wilmington, DE, 2003); George Sullivan, *The Picture History of the Boston Celtics* (New York, 1982); John Wooden and Bill Sharman, *The Wooden-Sharman Method: A Guide to Winning Basketball* (New York, 1975).

Daniel Frio

SHARP, Marsha (b. August 31, 1952, Washington, DC), college player, coach, and administrator, is the daughter of Charles Sharp and Mary (Dell) Sharp, graduated from Tulia (Texas) High School, and earned a Bachelor's degree in secondary education from Wayland Baptist University in Plainview, Texas in 1974 and a Master's Degree from West Texas State (now West Texas Agricultural and Mechanical) University in 1976. Sharp played high school basketball and aspired to play basketball for the Wayland Baptist University Flying Queens, a woman's basketball national power from the 1940s through the 1970s. Sharp, who began attending Wayland Baptist in the fall of 1971, failed to make the varsity squad. She played junior varsity for the Queen Bees and studied the game under legendary coach Harley Redin*. Sharp subsequently worked as a graduate assistant coach under both Redin and Wayland legend Dean Weese. She earned her Bachelor's degree in 1974 and became head basketball coach at Lockney High School for the 1975–1976 season. Although inheriting a 3-25 team, Sharp produced a winning record (15-13) in her first season. During six years with the Lockney, she finished 126-63 and captured district championships in 1976, 1977, 1979. Her success landed her an assistant basketball coaching position at Texas Tech University for the 1981–1982 campaign. When head coach Donna Wick resigned, Sharp became the Lady Raider's head coach.

During the early 1980s, Texas Tech University's program paled in comparison with SWC powerhouse University of Texas Lady Longhorns of Coach Jody Conradt*. Sharp's early squads enjoyed some success, finishing second in SWC play each year from 1982–1983 through 1985–1986 and third from 1986–1987 through 1990–1991, and making the NCAA tournament in 1984 and 1986. Texas Tech, however, still could not defeat Texas. The losing streak to Texas eventually stretched to 37 games. The "rivalry" finally became competitive in the 1991–1992 season, as the Lady Raiders scored their first ever win over Texas and their first SWC title. Between 1982–1983 and 2003–2004, the Lady Raiders under Sharp have become one of women's basketball elite programs. Their accomplishments include the 1993 NCAA national championship, 16 consecutive NCAA Women's Tournament appearances, 11 NCAA Sweet Sixteen appearances, and four NCAA Elite Eight appearances. In 2002–2003, the Lady Raiders reached the NCAA Elite Eight, being eliminated by Duke University.

Her numerous awards include being named National Coach of the Year in 1993 by the WBNS, the same honor in 1994 from the WBCA, and president of the NWBCA in 2001. She was inducted into the Texas Women's Hall of Fame in 1999, the Texas Sports Hall of Fame in 2000, and the Women's Basketball Hall of Fame in 2003. Sharp, who has served as Associate Athletic Director at Texas Tech University since 1995, recorded her 500th career win on February 19, 2003, as Texas Tech defeated the University of Oklahoma 59-48. Her overall record stands at 555-175 for a .760 winning percentage. Still, of all of her accomplishments, Sharp would argue that she is most proud of the 99 percent graduation rate for her players.

Sharp, who is single, remains very involved in the community. She participates in Women's Protective Services, the American Cancer Society's Coaches vs. Cancer Advisory Board, the Converse Coach of the Year Committee, the Kodak All American Selection Committee, and the Texas Girls Basketball Association Committee.

BIBLIOGRAPHY: Kent Best, "From Sharp's Mind," *Southwest Basketball: 1993–1993 Preview Magazine* 1, pp. 4–7; Patrick Gonzalez, "On Top of Her Game," *Lubbock Avalanche Journal*, November 10, 2002, pp. A1, A9; Patrick Gonzalez, "A Class Act," *Lubbock Avalanche Journal*, March 29, 2002, pp. C1, C2; Patrick Gonzalez, "Sharp's 500th," *Lubbock Avalanche Journal*, February 23, 2003, pp. 2–18; Ray Hawkes and John F. Seggar, *Celebrating Women Coaches: A Biographical Dictionary* (Westport, CT, 2000); Nancy Laine Price, *Courtly Love: A Profile of Coach Marsha Sharp* (Arlington, TX, 1994); Emily Sharp, "Marsha Madness: Reflections from an Unlikely Fan," *Lubbock Magazine*. (March 2000), pp. 44, 45; "Sharp Inducted into Hall," www.redraiders.com/stories/051103/wbb_051103015.shtml; "Sharp Prepares to Enter Hall," www.redraiders.com/stories/051003/wbb_051003011.shtml; Rosemarie Skaine, *Women College Basketball Coaches* (Jefferson, NC, 2001); Texas Tech University Women's Basketball, "Coach Bio: Marsha Sharp," www.texastech.ocsn.com/sports/w-baskbl/mtt/sharp_marsha00.html; Texas Tech University Women's Basketball, "Marsha Sharp to Be Inducted into Women's Basketball Hall of Fame," www.texastech.ocsn.com/sports/w-baskbl/spec-rel/111002aaa.html.

Jorge Iber

SHAVLIK, Ronald Dean (b. December 4, 1933, Denver, CO; d. June 27, 1983, Raleigh, NC), college and professional player, was the son of Ray Shavlik and excelled in basketball and baseball at East High School in Denver, Colorado, where he led his school to two state championships in basketball.

Shavlik attended North Carolina State University from 1952 to 1956. The agile six-foot eight-inch, 200-pounder proved an exceptional rebounder and versatile player, able to go outside and hit jumpers or drive to the basket. Shavlik averaged 22.1 points and 18.1 rebounds as a junior and 18.2 points and 19.5 rebounds as a senior, being named First Team All-ACC in 1955 and 1956 and ACC Player of the Year in 1956. He was selected Second Team All-America by the AP and UPI in 1955 and 1956 and led North Carolina State to three ACC titles. Shavlik played with a broken wrist as North Carolina State was upset by Canisius University (New York) in the 1956 NCAA tournament. He led the ACC in rebounding in 1956, setting a still standing conference record for highest rebounding average for a season. Shavlik, who averaged 18.5 points and 16.8 rebounds for his career, earned a Bachelor of Science degree in recreation.

The New York Knicks (NBA) selected Shavlik in the first round of the 1956 draft. His lack of bulk, however, limited him to a 1.1 point average in eight games over two seasons for the Knicks.

Shavlik later owned and operated Carolina Maintenance, a highly-successful Raleigh, North Carolina–based business that cleaned office buildings. He was heavily involved in area charities. The NCAA presented him with the 1980 Silver Anniversary Award. Shavlik married Beverly Anne Senna and had two children, Kim and Dean. He died of cancer.

BIBLIOGRAPHY: Peter C. Bjarkman, *ACC: Atlantic Coast Conference Basketball* (Indianapolis, IN, 1996); Douglas Herakovich, *Pack Pride: The History of N.C. State Basketball* (Cary, NC, 1994); Ron Morris, *ACC Basketball: An Illustrated History* (Chapel Hill, NC, 1988); Ken Shouler et al., *Total Basketball* (Wilmington, DE, 2003).

Jim L. Sumner

SHELTON, EVERETT F. "Ev" (b. May 12, 1898, Cunningham, KS; d. April 16, 1974, Sacramento, CA), college athlete and coach, starred as an all-around athlete at Cunningham (Kansas) High School and earned four letters each in basketball, football, and baseball. Following graduation in 1916, Shelton served in the U.S. Marine Corps during World War I and quarterbacked the S.O.S. football team in 38 games. After his discharge in 1919, he entered Phillips University in Enid, Oklahoma and earned four letters each in football, basketball, and baseball under Coach Ray Ballard. Shelton made All-Conference football quarterback and captained the basketball team as a senior before graduating with a Bachelor of Arts degree in Chemistry in 1923.

In the fall of 1923, Shelton began a 46 year coaching career as head coach for all sports at Claremore (Oklahoma) High School. A year later, he returned to his alma mater, Phillips University, as head coach in all sports. During the next three years, Phillips won 48 basketball games and lost only 29 contests. Shelton in 1927 moved to the AAU coaching ranks and guided the Sterling Milk Club for two seasons. He coached Cripes Bakery (1929–1930) and St. Joseph Boosters Club (1932–1933) in the AAU and all sports at Christian Brothers High School in Missouri from 1929 to 1933. He married Berniece Neal of Utica, Missouri in this period and had one son, Stephen. During the 1932–1933 season, Shelton developed the five-man weave. He coached the AAU Denver Safeways (1936–1937 to 1937–1938) and Antlers Hotel (1938–1939), guiding the former to the 1937 AAU National title.

In 1939, Shelton accepted coaching responsibilities for basketball, baseball, and golf at the University of Wyoming. As Cowboys' basketball coach for 20 seasons, he compiled a 328-201 win-loss mark, recorded a 221-13 mark in BSkC play, captured eight BSkC championships, appeared in nine NCAA tournaments, and won the NCAA championship in 1943. When World War II curtailed the 1943–1944 season, Shelton coached Dow Chemical in AAU play and then returned to Wyoming for the 1944–1945 season. He conducted basketball clinics for the U.S. Armed Forces in the Far East in 1951 and in Europe in 1953. He became treasurer of the NABC in 1955 and served in 1959–1960 as president, establishing the CNBRI.

In 1959, Shelton became head basketball and assistant baseball coach at Sacramento State College and was elected to the HAF Hall of Fame. At Sacramento State through 1968, he compiled a 188-188 win-loss record. Sacramento

State finished NCAA College Division runner-up in 1962. Shelton coached the West team in the 1967 NABC East-West All-Star Game and in 1969 received the Metropolitan Intercollegiate Basketball Award, the highest award voted by coaches. After retiring from coaching, he served as adviser to BCI in 1969 and as commissioner of the FWC from 1969 until his death. In 46 years of basketball coaching, Shelton achieved 850 victories against 437 losses. Additionally, he published articles on his specialty, "Team Offense and Defense," in *Coach and Athlete, Athletic Journal, Scholastic Coach*, and *Mentor*. Shelton, who took pride in guiding young men through sport in their total education, was elected in 1979 as a coach to the Naismith Memorial Basketball Hall of Fame.

BIBLIOGRAPHY: Mike Douchant, *Encyclopedia of College Basketball* (Detroit, MI, 1995); Zander Hollander, ed., *The Modern Encyclopedia of Basketball* (Garden City, NY, 1979); Ronald L. Mendell, *Who's Who in Basketball* (New York, 1973); *NCAA Men's Basketball Records, 2004* (Indianapolis, IN, 2003); Everett Shelton file, Naismith Memorial Basketball Hall of Fame, Springfield, MA.

Jerry Jaye Wright

SHIRLEY, James Dallas (b. June 7, 1913, Washington, DC; d. March 1, 1994, DuSoto, TX), college player and referee, ranks among the best all-time officials. A star basketball guard at Eastern High School, Shirley helped his team win the 1931 Washington, D.C., title as a senior. He later played basketball three years at Georgetown (Washington, D.C.) University and one year semiprofessionally with Washington, D.C. teams. Shirley's officiating career began as a student at Eastern High School and continued at Georgetown University. He officiated as an original member of the NBA crew, ECAC, SC, ACC, MDC, and the IABF. Shirley handled notable games in the NIT, NCAA Tournament, the 1959 Pan American Games in Chicago, and the 1960 Olympic Games in Rome, Italy, where he was the only American official.

Shirley, a teacher, coach, athletic director, and principal in the Washington, D.C., public school system for over 30 years, held many prestigious positions in basketball and other sports. As assistant commissioner of the SC, he recruited, trained, and assigned both basketball and football officials. Shirley served as president of the IAABO in 1952–1953, the CBOA in 1954, and the NABA. He chaired the ABAOC, the USOBOC in 1976, and the USPABOC in 1975.

Knowledgeable in all aspects of basketball, Shirley conducted clinics in at least nine countries, served as sports specialist to Libya, and coached the Libyan National team in 1961. He edited the officials manual and the IAABO Sportorial publication, and authored *Basic Basketball Skills for Coaches and Players*. The truly professional Shirley was well respected by coaches, players, and fellow officials. Besides discovering and training many top basketball officials, he implemented and perfected many officiating techniques used today. The recipient of numerous appreciation awards, he in 1979 was inducted into the Naismith Memorial Basketball Hall of Fame as a referee. He was survived by his wife, Peggy, and two children, Constance and James Dallas.

BIBLIOGRAPHY: James Dallas Shirley file, Naismith Memorial Basketball Hall of Fame, Springfield, MA.

Catherine M. Derrick

SHUE, Eugene William "Gene" (b. December 18, 1931, Baltimore, MD), college and professional player, coach, and executive, is the son of Michael Shue and Rose (Rice) Shue. Shue grew up in Baltimore, Maryland and attended Towson Catholic High School, where he was twice named All-State in basketball. Shue enrolled at nearby University of Maryland and became the best basketball player the Terrapins had yet produced. On graduation in 1952, he led the Terrapins in career points scored (1,397), field goals (504); and free throws (389) and averaged 18.6 points. An accurate shooter, he was named All-America his senior year.

The Philadelphia Warriors (NBA) in 1954 selected Shue first in the first round of the NBA draft, but sold him that November to the struggling New York Knickerbockers (NBA). In April 1956, he was traded to the shaky Fort Wayne Pistons (NBA) franchise for Ron Sophie. The Pistons moved to Detroit, where Shue became a standout player. During the 1959–1960 season, Shue scored a record 1,712 points for an NBA guard and recorded a career-high 22.8 points average. The next year, Shue scored 1,765 points and averaged 22.6 points. Shue made the All-NBA First Team in 1960 and All-NBA Second Team in 1961, but his performance fell short of the amazing Bob Cousy*, the wizard Oscar Robertson*, Bill Sharman*, and other pro guards of his era. He in 1963–1964 finished his playing career with the Baltimore Bullets (NBA) average having amassed 10,068 points in a 10-year career for a 14.4 points and playing on five All-Star teams (1958–1962).

Shue, who was named coach of the Baltimore Bullets in 1966, won Coach of the Year honors in 1969 by taking the once-lowly club to the NBA Eastern Division regular-season title. The well-disciplined 1970–1971 Bullets, led by Wes Unseld*, lost out in the NBA Finals to a Milwaukee Bucks team led by young Kareem Abdul-Jabbar*. In 1973, Shue became coach of the Philadelphia 76ers (NBA) and directed them to the NBA Finals behind the excellent play of Billy Cunningham*. After Philadelphia lost to the Portland Trail Blazers in the 1973–1974 NBA Finals and started slowly the next season, he joined the San Diego Clippers (NBA) as head coach and soon acquired Bill Walton*.

Shue rejoined the Bullets in 1980, this time directing an average team based in Washington, D.C. He earned NBA Coach of the Year honors again in 1981–1982, but was dismissed in March 1986 with his team struggling for a playoff berth. Altogether, Shue appeared in over 2,000 games as either a player or coach to establish an NBA record. He spent the 1986–1987 season as an analyst for Philadelphia 76ers telecasts. In May 1987, he replaced Don Chaney as head coach of the Los Angeles Clippers (NBA). The Clippers finished 17-65 in Shue's initial season and 10-28 in 1988–1989 before Don Casey replaced him in January 1989. Shue's 784 coaching victories rank twelfth on the all-time NBA list, but his overall performance with 861 losses (.477) is indifferent. He returned to the Philadelphia 76ers as General Manager from 1990 to 1992 and Director of Player Personnel from 1992 to 1997. Shue, a powerful franchise builder, has experienced sad misfortunes in the NBA playoffs, compiling a 30-47 record. He married Dorothea Maria Thisel on December 19, 1956, and has three children.

BIBLIOGRAPHY: Peter C. Bjarkman, *The Biographical History of Basketball* (Chicago, IL, 2000); Jan Hubbard, ed., *The Official NBA Encyclopedia*, 3rd ed. (New York, 2000); Neil B. Isaacs, *Vintage NBA* (Silver Spring, MD, 1996); Paul McMullen, *Maryland Basketball* (Baltimore, MD, 2002); *TSN Official NBA Register, 2004–2005* (St. Louis MO, 2004); *Washington Bullets Media Guide, 1984* (Washington, D.C., 1984); *Washington Post*, March 20, 1986; *WWA*, 43rd ed. (1984–1985).

John David Healy

SIKMA, Jack Wayles (b. November 14, 1955, Kankakee, IL), college and professional player and coach, grew up in the small Dutch village of Wichert, Illinois. During his first three years at St. Anne High School, Sikma played guard in basketball. During his senior year, he experienced a growth spurt to 6 feet 10 inches and played at the center position. Division I basketball schools, intrigued by his size, offered him basketball scholarship opportunities. He preferred to stay near home and attended Illinois Wesleyan University, a NAIA school with only 1,600 students. Although growing to be seven feet and 250 pounds, he did not exhibit a great leaping ability. Sikma worked with his college coach Dennis Bridges to establish the inside pivot move, which would create space for him to shoot his accurate jumpshot. During his four years at Illinois Wesleyan from 1973 to 1977, he averaged 13.1 rebounds and 21.2 points.

Sikma's size and stellar collegiate career led the Seattle SuperSonics (NBA) to make him their first round draft pick in 1977, although many fans questioned the wisdom of this choice. Sikma silenced his critics by averaging 10.7 points and 8.3 rebounds during his first NBA season and made the 1978 All-Rookie team, helping Seattle reach the NBA Finals against the Washington Bullets. During his second season, he grabbed over 1,000 rebounds and averaged 15.6 points. In the 1979 NBA Finals against the Washington Bullets, Sikma pounded the boards for 17 rebounds in Games 3, 4, and 5, leading the SuperSonics to a world title.

Seattle failed to attain another NBA championship, but Sikma's consistent rebounding and scoring helped the SuperSonics advance to the NBA playoffs in 1980, 1982, 1983, and 1984. After Seattle failed to reach the NBA playoffs in 1985 and 1986, the popular Sikma requested a trade to a contending club. The SuperSonics reluctantly honored Sikma's request on July 1, 1986 with a trade to the Milwaukee Bucks (NBA). Upon leaving Seattle with his wife, Shawna, and son, Jacob, Sikma possessed team career marks for rebounds (7,729), blocked shots (705), and free throws made (3,044). He also ranked second in Seattle history in points (12,034) and games played (715).

After joining Milwaukee, the durable Sikma continued averaging in double figures for scoring and rebounding and missed few games. During his tenure in Milwaukee from 1986–1987 to 1990–1991, the Bucks advanced to the NBA playoffs each season. Sikma announced his retirement after the 1990–1991 season. He scored 17,287 points and grabbed 10,816 rebounds, while averaging 15.6 points and 9.8 rebounds in 1,107 games. The seven-time All-Star was named to the NBA's All-Defensive Second Team in 1982.

Sikma, still beloved in Seattle for his long blond locks and rebounding prowess, saw his number 43 SuperSonics jersey retired during a November 21, 1992 game. He and his family relocated to Seattle and have operated a golf course management company.

BIBLIOGRAPHY: J. Fincher, "Aw-shucks Center of the Seattle SuperSonics," *Sport* 70 (January 1980), pp. 50–51; Jan Hubbard, ed., *The Official NBA Encyclopedia*, 3rd ed. (New York, 2000); "Jack Sikma, No. 43," SuperSonics.com http://www.nba.com/sonics/news/retired_Jerseys_sikmahtml (June 19, 2003); Roland Lazenby, *The NBA Finals* (Indianapolis, IN, 1996); Bruce Newman, "A Buck for a Change," *SI* 65 (November 3, 1986), pp. 70–72; *TSN Official NBA Register, 2004–2005* (St. Louis, MO, 2004).

Ron Briley

SILAS, Paul Theron (b. July 12, 1943, Prescott, AZ), college and professional player and coach, was a six-foot seven-inch, 230-pound rebounding and defensive specialist. A prototype of the modern power forward, he enjoyed a solid, and at times sparkling 16-year NBA career. The intelligent, articulate, concerned, and sensitive Silas, who possessed an intense desire to excel, was a product of the ghetto. On enrolling at Creighton University (Nebraska), he admitted being "hardly able to read and write." Silas learned how to study so well that, by his junior year, he had made Academic All-America, still one of his proudest achievements. His on-court record was equally impressive, as he holds the NCAA record for most rebounds (1,751) in a three-year career and remains one of only seven NCAA players to average over 20 points and 20 rebounds during their careers.

In the 1964 NBA draft, Silas was selected in the second round by the St. Louis Hawks (NBA) and the twelfth pick overall. He spent five years with that franchise, the first four in St. Louis and the final one at Atlanta. Silas proved a low-scoring, but increasingly useful and mature front-line player with his defending, rebounding, hustling, and learning. He was traded to the Phoenix Suns (NBA) in May 1969 for Gary Gregor, a pro journeyman. Silas kept improving his play, surpassing 1,000 rebounds during the 1970–1971 season and averaging around that total through the 1975–1976 campaign. Silas' improvement, however, took a quantum jump in the 1971–1972 season. He always had played at the rather heavy 240 to 245 pound range, but decided during the off-season to reduce his weight by 20 to 30 pounds to see if he could add quickness to his board strength. The results were nothing short of spectacular. His stamina, speed, mobility, self-assurance, and scoring increased while his defense and rebounding improved through his added versatility and control.

Crafty "Red" Auerbach*, the Boston Celtics permanent guidon bearer, picked Charlie Scott* in the seventh round of the 1970 NBA draft. Scott, a quicksilver guard and high-scoring machine with few defensive abilities and limited knowledge of team play, decided to play for the Virginia Squires of the ill-fated ABA. In 1972, however, the Phoenix Suns (NBA) signed Scott to a contract and thus committed themselves to compensate the Celtics, who held the original draft rights. Silas joined Boston in September 1972 and found a perfect niche in the Celtics system. He became the missing piece that Boston needed as the sixth man coming off the bench to add momentum. Silas provided a strong and coherent complement to center Dave Cowens'* exuberance and effectiveness under the boards. Silas helped the Celtics win two NBA championships (1974, 1976) with his alert play and finely tuned instincts, especially keeping the ball alive under the rim. His intangible contributions, including character, poise, discipline, and experience, were just as important as any set of statistics. After the 1975–1976 season, Silas was unable to reach an agreement with the Celtics and was sent in October 1976 to the Denver Nuggets (NBA) in a three-way trade. The Nuggets traded him to the Seattle SuperSonics (NBA) in May 1977. He played there for the next three years with considerably diminishing returns.

In 1,254 career NBA games, Silas made 12,357 rebounds, and 11,782 points. These statistics do not express the full reality of his commitment to the game and his sense of team play. Silas was named to the NBA-All Defensive First Team in 1975 and 1976 and to the NBA-All Defensive Second Team from 1971 to 1973. Twice selected to play in the NBA All-Star Game, he coached the hapless San Diego Clippers to 78 wins and 168 losses for a .317 average from 1980–1981 through 1982–1983. Silas spent 1988–1989 and 1992–1993 through 1994–1995 seasons as an assistant coach for the New Jersey Nets (NBA). He also served as assistant coach for the New York Knicks (NBA) from 1989–1990 through 1991–1992, the Phoenix Suns from 1995–1996 through 1996–1997, and the Charlotte Hornets (NBA) from 1997–1998 through March 1999, when he replaced Dave Cowens* as head coach. Silas guided the Hornets to five consecutive winning seasons and 208-155 mark in the regular-season and a 11-12 playoff mark. The Hornets moved to New Orleans after the 2001–2002 season. Tim Floyd replaced Silas as head coach following the 2002–2003 season. Silas, a father figure who developed Baron Davis and Jamaal Magloire, joined the Cleveland Cavaliers (NBA) as head coach in June 2003. Cleveland, led by much heralded rookie LeBron James* barely missed the playoffs with a 35-47 record in 2003–2004, more than doubling their victory total from the previous season. The Cavaliers slumped after the All-Star break in 2004–2005 and fired Silas in March 2005. Silas has compiled a 355-400 regular season record and 13–16 playoff mark in nine NBA seasons. Silas, a gentleman, tough competitor, and responsible citizen, is a model professional who performed well in his craft. He was a human being, who decided that well was not enough unless it meant to reach the top of his capabilities.

BIBLIOGRAPHY: Peter C. Bjarkman, *The Boston Celtics Encyclopedia* (Champaign, IL, 1998); *Cleveland Cavaliers Media Guide, 2004–2005* (Cleveland, OH, 2004); Tom Heinsohn, *The Boston Celtics: A Championship Tradition* (Englewood Cliffs, NJ, 1974); Bob Ryan, *Celtics Pride* (Boston, 1975); Bob Ryan, *The Pro Game* (New York, 1975); Ken Shouler et al., *Total Basketball* (Wilmington, DE, 2003); George Sullivan, *The Picture History of the Boston Celtics* (Indianapolis, IN, 1981); *TSN Official NBA Register, 2004–2005* (St. Louis, MO, 2004).

Gustavo N. Agrait

SIMMONS, Lionel James "Train" "L-Train" (b. November 14, 1968, Philadelphia, PA), college and professional player, excelled in basketball for the South Philadelphia (Pennsylvania) High School Rams. Following his senior season in 1986, he was named to the Philadelphia Public League Sports Hall of Fame.

The six-foot seven-inch, 250-pound forward attended LaSalle College between 1986–1987 and 1989–1990, establishing numerous Explorer records and receiving many individual accolades. In his freshman year in 1986–1987, Simmons scored 670 points, averaged of 20.3 points, and collected 322 rebounds in 33 games. The following season, he improved with 386 rebounds and 792 points in 34 games. Simmons enjoyed his best statistical season as a junior, scoring 908 points and averaging a career-high 28.4 points and 11.4 rebounds. In his final season, he scored 847 points and averaged 11.1 rebounds in 32 games. Simmons compiled 3,217 points in 131 regular-season games, ranking him third on the all-time NCAA scoring list and setting a school record with 24.6 points per game. He became a basketball legend in Pennsylvania and especially the Philadelphia area. Simmons led LaSalle to the NIT in 1988, but the Explorers lost in the third round. LaSalle qualified for the NCAA Tournament the following three seasons, but lost in the early rounds.

In 1987, Simmons was named MAAC Rookie of the Year. He became a four-time All-MAAC First Team selection, a three-time MAAC Player of the Year, and a Third Team All-America choice in 1988–1989. Simmons made First Team All-America, was named National Player of the Year, and won the Naismith Award and the Wooden Award in 1990.

Simmons ranks first among NCAA players with more than 3,000 points and 1,100 rebounds. He remains one of only four players in NCAA history to record at least 1,500 or more points, 500 rebounds, and 200 blocked shots, assists, and steals. Simmons completed his LaSalle career with 4,646 combined points and rebounds, only 17 behind the NCAA record held by Tom Gola* of LaSalle College between 1952 and 1957. Simmons once scored a career-high 56 points and in 1990 saw his jersey No. 22 retired by the college. In his four seasons at LaSalle, the Explorers, under coach Bill "Speedy" Morris, triumphed 131 times while losing only 31 games; the Explorers his senior season finished with a 30-2 win-loss record, the best in school history.

A 1990 LaSalle graduate, Simmons was selected in the first round as the seventh pick overall by the Sacramento Kings (NBA) in the 1990 NBA draft. He spent seven seasons with the Kings from 1990–1991 to 1996–1997, making the All-NBA Rookie Team in 1991. Simmons averaged 17.0 points and 7.9 rebounds in his first four NBA seasons, but averaged only 4.7 points and 2.9 rebounds in his last three seasons. Injuries eventually impaired his point production, rebounds number, and playing time. After two attempts of corrective surgery on his knees, Simmons retired as a professional basketball player on October 30, 1997.

Simmons scored 5,833 points, averaged 12.8 points, and recorded 2,833 rebounds, 1,498 assists, 514 steals, and 361 blocked shots in 434 regular-season NBA games. He played in four NBA playoff games in 1996, scoring 38 points while pulling down 12 rebounds.

BIBLIOGRAPHY: Peter C. Bjarkman, *The Biographical History of Basketball* (Chicago, IL, 2000); Jan Hubbard, ed., *The Official NBA Encyclopedia*, 3rd ed. (New York, 2000); Gary K. Johnson ed., *NCAA Men's Basketball's Finest* (Overland Park, KS, 1998); Gary K. Johnson ed., *The Official NCAA Men's College Basketball Record Book* (Overland Park, KS, 1998); "Lionel Simmons," *College Stats*, http://www.sportsstats.com (2004); "Lionel Simmons," *NBA Stats*, http://www.sportsstats.com (2004); "Lionel Simmons," *Statistics*, http://www.basketballdraft.com (2004); "Lionel Simmons," *Stats, History and Awards*, http://www.basketballreference.com (2003); Claudia Mitrol, ed., *Philadelphia's Greatest Sports Moments* (Champaign, IL, 2000); *TSN Official NBA Register*, 1997–1998 (St. Louis, MO, 1997).

John L. Evers

SLOAN, Gerald Eugene "Jerry" (b. March 28, 1942, McLeansboro, IL), college and professional player, coach, and scout, is the youngest of ten children born to Charles Ralph Sloan, a farmer, and Janie Sloan. When Jerry was four years old, his father died and his mother reared the children.

A 1960 graduate of McLeansboro (Illinois) High School, Sloan made All-State in basketball for the Foxes and remains the school's record holder in career scoring and rebounding. He enrolled at the University of Illinois without playing basketball and transferred to the University of Evansville (Indiana). In three varsity seasons, Sloan averaged 15.5 points and 12.4 rebounds. He led the Aces to the NCAA Division II national championships in 1964 and 1965 and was named MVP both years. Evansville finished undefeated (29-0) his senior year, as he was named to *TSN* Second Team All-America.

The Baltimore Bullets (NBA) drafted Sloan in 1965 as their third pick in the second round. He was selected in the NBA Expansion Draft the following year by the Chicago Bulls (NBA). A knee injury during the 1975–1976 season ended his playing career. In 11 NBA seasons, the six-foot five-inch, 200-pound Sloan compiled 10,571 points, 5,615 rebounds and 1,925 assists in 755 games. He played in two NBA All-Star Games and made the NBA All-Defensive First Team in 1969, 1972, 1974, and 1975, and the Second Team in 1970 and 1971. The Chicago franchise retired his number 4 jersey.

Sloan scouted for the Chicago Bulls in 1976–1977, served as assistant coach for Chicago the following season, and was promoted to the Bulls' head coaching position in 1979–1980. Chicago won only 19 of 51 games in the 1981–1982 season. He was dismissed after compiling a three year 94-121 win-loss record.

Out of basketball for one season, Sloan scouted for the Utah Jazz (NBA) in 1983–1984. He briefly served as head coach of the Evansville Thunder (CBA) in 1984, but resigned before coaching a game to become an assistant coach for the Utah Jazz. In December 9, 1988, Sloan replaced Frank Layden as head coach of the Jazz. Karl Malone* and John Stockton* spearheaded his offensive attack.

In 20 seasons as head coach from 1979–1980 through 2004–2005, Sloan has compiled a regular-season 943-617 win-loss record (eighth on the all time NBA list) for a .604 winning percentage (eighth). He coached the Jazz to 10 50-win seasons and 15 consecutive playoff appearances, posting 78 victories and 80 losses. The playoff streak ended in 2003–2004 after Malone departed for the Los Angeles Lakers and Stockton retired. With a franchise best record of 64 victories and 18 defeats in 1996–1997 and the following year with 62 wins and 20 losses, Sloan led the Jazz to the NBA Finals; Utah lost both times to Michael Jordan* and the Chicago Bulls in six games. In 1996, Sloan was named an assistant coach on the staff of the "Dream Team" that won the gold medal for the United States at the Summer Olympics in Atlanta, Georgia.

Sloan and his wife, Bobbye, have three children: two daughters, Kathy and Holly, and a son, Brian. Brian also played basketball for the Foxes of McLeansboro and led them to an undefeated season and the 1984 Class A Illinois state championship. He later played for coach Bob Knight* at Indiana University and practices medicine.

BIBLIOGRAPHY: Jack McCallum, "Getting Straight," *SI* 6 (February 11, 2002), pp. 48–51; "Jerry Sloan," *Coach*, http://www.utjazz.com (2003); "Jerry Sloan," *Coach Bio*, http://www.nba.com (2003); "Jerry Sloan," *Coaches*, http://www.hoopshype.com (2003); Ken Shouler et al., *Total Basketball* (Wilmington, DE, 2003); *TSN Official NBA Register, 2004–2005* (St. Louis, MO, 2004).

John L. Evers

SLOAN, Norman L. (b. June 25, 1926, Anderson, IN; d. December 9, 2003, Durham, NC), college player and coach, was the son of Norman L. Sloan Sr., a tool and dye worker, and Mary Sloan. Growing up in basketball-rich Indiana, Sloan decided to become a coach in the third grade. He met Joan Wildridge, a cheerleader, as a junior high student and married her in 1948. They had three children, Deborah, Michael, and Leslie. At Lawrence (Indiana) Central High School, he participated in basketball, football, baseball, and track and field. Sloan served in the U.S. Navy from 1944 to 1946. He declined an opportunity to attend the U.S. Naval Academy and instead selected North Carolina State University. There Sloan played point guard on Everett Case's* squads that won 80 games in three seasons and appeared in two NITs. He also earned two letters in football and one in track and field as the last triple-sport letterman there before graduating in 1951.

From 1951–1952 through 1954–1955 at tiny Presbyterian College in Clinton, South Carolina, Sloan compiled a 69-36 basketball record. After one season as an assistant at Memphis State University, he assumed the reigns of a woeful program at The Citadel in 1956. Sloan brought respectability to the Bulldogs in his first season and was named SC Coach of the Year. His four-year coaching slate of 57-38 still ranks third at The Citadel in career victories and second in winning percentage. Sloan moved to the University of Florida in 1960 and posted a cumulative 85-63 record over six campaigns. He returned to his alma mater at North Carolina State University in 1966, hoping to build a national basketball power. In 1969–1970 Sloan's squad of overachievers upset the highly favored University of South Carolina 42-39 in the ACC Finals and earned the coach his first NCAA Tournament appearance. North Carolina State, led by Tom Burleson and David Thompson*, went undefeated at 27-0 in 1972–1973, but watched UCLA win another NCAA title because of postseason probation. The next season, the Wolfpack lost only one early showdown in St. Louis, Missouri to the Bruins. In the NCAA semifinals, North Carolina State avenged that loss with an 80-77 double-overtime victory. An anticlimatic victory over Marquette University

(Wisconsin) gave Sloan an NCAA championship for 1973–1974. During 14 years through 1979–1980 at North Carolina State, Sloan compiled a 266-127 record with three ACC titles and five NCAA Tournament appearances.

In 1980 Sloan returned to the University of Florida to rebuild a faltering program. His Gators squads secured six straight postseason tournament bids, including their first-ever NCAA trip in 1986–1987. The 1986–1987 Gators, paced by guard Vernon Maxwell, finished 12-6 for second place in the SEC and notched a 23-11 overall mark. Florida defeated North Carolina State University and Purdue University (Indiana) before bowing to Syracuse (New York) University in the East Regional semifinals. In February 1988, Sloan became the eleventh NCAA Division I coach to win 600 games. In his final season in 1988–1989, he guided Florida to a 21-13 overall record and SEC title.

In 37 seasons as a head coach through 1988–1989, Sloan compiled a 627-395 career record. He held the unique distinction of being named Coach of the Year in three major conferences (SC, 1957; SEC, 1961; and ACC, 1970, 1973–1974) and was National Coach of the Year in 1974. He coached the 1980 British National Olympic team and belongs to the Indiana Basketball Hall of Fame.

BIBLIOGRAPHY: Peter C. Bjarkman, *ACC: Atlantic Coast Conference Basketball* (Indianapolis, IN, 1996); Peter C. Bjarkman, *The Biographical History of Basketball* (Chicago, IL, 2000); Morgan G. Brenner, *College Basketball's National Championships* (Lanham, MD, 1999); Chris Dortch, *String Music* (Washington, DC, 2002); Ronald L. Mendell, *Who's Who in Basketball* (New Rochelle, NY, 1973); Ron Morris, ed., *ACC Basketball: An Illustrated History* (Chapel Hill, NC, 1988); Billy Packer and Roland Lazenby, *College Basketball's 25 Greatest Teams* (St. Louis, MO, 1989); *University of Florida Basketball Guide, 1987–1988* (Gainesville, FL, 1987); Chris Wallace, ed., *Blue Ribbon College Basketball Yearbook for 1987* (Buckhannon, WV, 1986).

Dennis S. Clark

SMITH, Dean Edwards (b. February 28, 1931, Emporia, KS), college player and coach, guided the University of North Carolina 11 times to the NCAA Tournament's Final Four; achieving second place three times and winning the 1982 and 1993 NCAA championships. The basketball head coach at North Carolina from 1961–1962 to 1996–1997, Smith guided the Tar Heels to the ACC title 16 times and to second-place finishes several seasons. He twice was chosen National Coach of the Year (1976 by the NABC and 1979 by the USBWA) and six times was named ACC Coach of the Year (1967, 1968, 1972, 1976, 1977, and 1979). He won the Naismith Award in 1993. His teams achieved 27 consecutive 20-plus victory seasons and won 32 games twice. Smith produced 25 All-Americas, as his Tar Heels compiled a composite 879-254 (.776 percent) record in 36 seasons. Smith ranks first in career victories among NCAA Division I male coaches.

The son of Alfred Dillon Smith and Vesta Marie (Edwards) Smith, Smith starred in basketball three years at Emporia (Kansas) High School before entering the University of Kansas in 1949. During his junior and senior basketball seasons at Kansas, legendary coach Forrest "Phog" Allen* guided the Jayhawks to the 1952 NCAA Tournament championship and 1953 runner-up spot. Kansas, led by Clyde Lovellette*, triumphed 80-63 over St. John's University (New York) to take the 1952 title, but dropped a close 69-68 decision to Indiana University in the NCAA Finals the next year. Smith, a substitute throughout his basketball career at Kansas, observed the finer points of the game under the masterful Allen. He graduated in 1953 from Kansas with a Bachelor of Science degree in mathematics and physical education.

Smith served in the U.S. Air Force from 1954 to 1958 and was assigned the last two years to the newly established U.S. Air Force Academy as assistant basketball coach under head mentor Robert Spear. He helped direct the Falcons to two winning seasons and a combined 28-16 record. Smith returned to North Carolina in 1959 as assistant basketball coach under Frank McGuire*, and helped lead the Tar Heels the next three seasons to a composite 57-15 mark. When McGuire left North Carolina in 1962 to coach the Philadelphia Warriors (NBA), Smith succeeded him as Tar Heels' head coach.

After a point-shaving scandal the previous

year at the University of North Carolina, the NCAA restricted the Tar Heels to a 17-game schedule in 1961–1962 and allowed them only two out-of-state basketball scholarships. Smith, whose first team finished 8-9, took five years to overcome entirely the difficulties inherited at North Carolina. He was hung in effigy during his third season when the 12-12 Tar Heels placed fifth in the ACC. In 1966–1967, 26-6 North Carolina won its first of many ACC tournaments under Smith by defeating Duke University (North Carolina) 82-73 in the finals. That year North Carolina started a string of consecutive postseason tournament appearances, interrupted only in 1970 when they failed to qualify for either the NCAA or NITs. All-America Larry Miller and Charlie Scott* led the Tar Heels between 1967 and 1969. North Carolina lost twice in the NCAA Tournament semifinals (to the University of Dayton and Purdue University), and reached the NCAA Finals once before losing to UCLA. The Tar Heels won the NIT in 1971 with an 84-66 triumph over Georgia Institute of Technology in New York's Madison Square Garden. North Carolina subsequently was eliminated in the NCAA Tournament finals in 1977 (28-5 record) by Marquette University (Wisconsin) with All-America Butch Lee and in 1981 (29-8 record) by Indiana University. The Tar Heels were paced by All-America Phil Ford* and James Worthy*, respectively, against the Warriors and Hoosiers.

Smith is credited with originating the four-corner delay offense to protect a small lead in the final minutes of a contest. Critics of the tactic are reminded of the University of North Carolina's 85-point scoring average over a 10-year period, fifth highest in the nation. Smith used a pattern offense based on the shuffle. His players were well schooled in fundamentals, worked with weights at practice, and never were allowed to sit or kneel during workouts. Smith was one of the first coaches to realize the potential of the new rule permitting a team that has just scored to call a strategic time out to set up a defense against the inbounds pass. A compulsive detail man, he instituted player huddles before North Carolina free throws to set up defenses.

Smith guided the 32-2 University of North Carolina to the 1982 NCAA Tournament championship with a 63-62 triumph over Georgetown (Washington, D.C.) University. Worthy was joined that year by All-America Sam Perkins and Michael Jordan*, whose last second basket against the Hoyas decided the outcome. Georgetown, starring All-America Patrick Ewing* and Eric Floyd, stayed within two points of North Carolina throughout the championship game. Smith rallied North Carolina to 13 more seasons of at least 26 victories and appearances in the NCAA Tournament despite Worthy's and Jordan's early departures to the NBA. All-America Brad Daugherty* directed the North Carolina attack. The 1986–1987 Tar Heels, led by Kenny Smith, won the ACC regular-season title with a 14-0 mark and tied a school record with 32 victories, but did not take the ACC Tournament or make it to the NCAA Final Four for the fifth consecutive year. The 27-7 1987–1988 North Carolina squad, paced by J. R. Reid, was eliminated by the University of Arizona in the NCAA West regional finals. The Tar Heels finished 29–6 in 1990–1991, ending second in the ACC and reaching the NCAA semifinals. His 1992–1993 aggregate, featuring Eric Montross, fared 34-4, won the ACC, and defeated the University of Michigan 77-71 for the NCAA title. In 1994–1995, North Carolina featured Jerry Stackhouse, soared to a 28-6 record, shared the ACC title, and made the semifinals of the NCAA Tournament. Smith last coached in 1996–1997, guiding the Tar Heels to a 28-7 mark and the semifinal of the NCAA tournament with Antawn Jamison* and Vince Carter*. Smith was a member of the CBRC from 1967 to 1973 and head coach of the U.S. Olympic basketball team for the 1976 Montreal, Canada Games. He has lectured at basketball clinics in several European countries and the United States. In May 1976, Smith married Linnea Weblemoe, a physician specializing in Psychiatry. He has four children, Sharon, Sandy, Scott, and Kristen, from an earlier marriage.

BIBLIOGRAPHY: Smith Barrier, *On Tobacco Road: Basketball in North Carolina* (New York, 1983); Peter C. Bjarkman, *ACC: Atlantic Coast Conference Basketball* (Indianapolis, IN, 1996); Art Chansky, *The Dean's List: A Celebration of Tar Heel Basketball and Dean Smith* (New York, 1996); *Des Moines Register*, January 17, 1982; Mike Douchant,

Encyclopedia of College Basketball (Detroit, MI, 1995); Neil D. Isaacs, *All the Moves: A History of College Basketball* (Philadelphia, PA, 1975); Ron Morris, *ACC Basketball: An Illustrated History* (Chapel Hill, NC, 1988); *NCAA Men's Basketball Records, 2004* (Indianapolis, IN, 2003); Ken Rappoport, *The Classic: History of the NCAA Championship* (Mission, KS, 1979); Ken Rappoport, *Tales from the Tar Heel Locker Room* (Champaign, IL, 2002); Ken Rappoport, *Tar Heel: North Carolina Basketball* (Huntsville, AL, 1976); Ken Shouler et al., *Total Basketball* (Wilmington, DE, 2003); Dean Smith, *A Coach's Life: My Forty Years in Basketball* (New York, 1999); *Street and Smith's Official Basketball Yearbooks, 1983–1986*; *WWA*, 47th. ed. (1992–1993), p. 3140.

James D. Whalen

SMITH, Joseph Leynard "Joe" (b. July 26, 1975, Norfolk, VA), college and professional player, graduated from Maury High School in Norfolk, Virginia and attended the University of Maryland for two years. Smith was named National Freshman of the Year and College Player of the Year in 1995, becoming the first sophomore at the University of Maryland to score 1,000 points and the second to grab 500 rebounds. He garnered several awards as a sophomore, including First Team All-America, ACC Player of the Year, and the prestigious Naismith Award. Smith was named to the ACC Fiftieth Anniversary Basketball Team. At Maryland, he averaged 20.2 points and 10.7 rebounds in 64 games.

After enjoying a spectacular sophomore season, the 6-foot 10-inch, 225-pound center applied for early entry to the 1995 NBA draft and was selected as the number one draft pick by the Golden State Warriors (NBA). Smith was selected to the 1996 NBA Rookie All-Star Game and finished third in NBA Rookie of the Year voting, leading all rookies in blocked shots (134), rebounds (717), and games played (82). He was named Rookie of the Month twice and tallied a team-high 33 double-doubles. Smith was traded to the Philadelphia 76ers (NBA) in February 1998 and signed with the Minnesota Timberwolves (NBA) in January 1999. He was involved in a contract scandal with Minnesota and was forced to leave the team. Smith signed with the Detroit Pistons (NBA) as a free agent in November 2000 and returned to the Timberwolves in July 2001. The Milwaukee Bucks (NBA) acquired him in June 2003. Smith scored his 5000th point in March 2000 and grabbed his 2000th rebound in March 1999. During his NBA career, he has averaged 12.6 points, 7.2 rebounds, and 1.1 assists in 707 regular season games. He has appeared in 20 playoff games, tallying 125 points (6.3 point average). Smith, who portrayed Connie Hawkins* in the movie "Rebound," wears the number 32 in honor of his childhood hero, Magic Johnson*. He hosts a summer camp in his hometown for inner city youth. The youngest of seven children, he and his wife, Yolanda, have three children.

BIBLIOGRAPHY: http://www.hoopshype.com/players/joe_smith.htm?nav=page; http://www.inform.umd.edu/News/Diamondback/archives/2002/02/22/news2.html; http://www.nba.com/playerfile/joe_smith/bio.html; http://www.sportingnews.com/nba/players/3003/popup.html; http://www.startribune.com/stories/511/3726937.html; *TSN Official NBA Register, 2004–2005* (St. Louis, MO, 2004); Ken Shouler et al., *Total Basketball* (Wilmington, DE, 2003).

Maureen M. Smith

SMITH, Steven Delano "Steve" (b. March 31, 1969, Highland Park, MI), college and professional player, is the son of Donald Smith and Clara (Bell) Smith and graduated with honors from Pershing High School in Detroit, Michigan. He averaged 26 points, 12 rebounds, and 10 assists in basketball his senior year and made the All-City, All-Metro, and All-State basketball teams.

Smith attended Michigan State University (BTC) and starred in basketball under coach Jud Heathcote from 1987–1988 to 1990–1991. As a sophomore in 1988–1989, he led the Spartans in rebounds and scoring and tallied 34 points against Villanova University (Pennsylvania) in a 70-63 NIT semifinals win. In 1989–1990, Michigan State compiled a 26-8 record, won the BTC title, and attained an NCAA Sweet Sixteen berth, but suffered an 81-80 disputed overtime loss to Georgia Institute of Technology. Smith topped the Spartans in rebounding, scoring, and assists, made *TSN* First Team All-America and AP and UPI First Team All-BTC, and received the BTC Silver Basketball Award as its MVP. Although the Spartans fell to a 19-11 record in 1990–1991, the six-foot eight-inch, 221-pound senior guard averaged 25.1 points, 6.1 rebounds, and 3.6 assists, repeated as *TSN* First Team All-America, and made AP and UPI Second Team All-America and First Team BTC. Smith, the Spartans' second all-time leading scorer (2,263 points), ranks fourth in assists (453) and fifth in rebounds (704). Michigan State retired his number 21 in 1995 and uniform in 1999 and inducted him into its Hall of Fame in 2001.

The Miami Heat (NBA) made Smith the number-five pick in the 1991 NBA draft. In 1991–1992, he averaged 12.0 points, 3.1 rebounds, and 4.6 assists and garnered NBA All-Rookie First Team honors. Although missing the first 34 games in 1992–1993 due to a knee injury, Smith led the Heat with a career-high average of 5.6 assists and upped his scoring and rebound averages to 16.0 points and 4.1 rebounds. Although his offensive production steadily improved, Miami posted only one winning mark in six NBA seasons and never advanced beyond the first round of the playoffs.

In November 1994, Miami traded Smith and forward Grant Long to the Atlanta Hawks (NBA) for forward Kevin Willis. Smith enjoyed his best NBA seasons with the Hawks. From 1994–1995 through 1998–1999, he scored 6,332 points (18.6 per game) and dished out 1,213 assists (3.6 per game) in 341 games. Smith signed a seven-year $50.4 million contract in 1996 and in 1997–1998 scored a career-high 1,464 points (21.1-point average). Atlanta compiled a five-season 225-153 win-loss mark during Smith's tenure, but failed to win a Central Division title or advance beyond the Eastern Conference semifinals.

Atlanta traded Smith and guard Ed Gray in August 1999 to the Portland Trail Blazers (NBA) in exchange for guards Isaiah Rider and Jim Jackson. Smith's scoring average declined to 14.9 points in 1999–2000 and 13.6 points in 2000–2001. Portland finished second in the Pacific Division his first season there with a 59-23 mark, but lost four games to three to the eventual NBA champion Los Angeles Lakers in the Western Conference Finals. The Blazers finished fourth in their division the following season and were eliminated in the first round of the playoffs. In July 2001, Portland traded Smith to the San Antonio Spurs (NBA) for guards Derek Anderson and Steve Kerr. Although averaging only 11.6 points with the Spurs in 2001–2002, Smith led the NBA in three-point field goal percentage (.472). San Antonio won the Midwest Division title with a 58-24 record, but fell to the NBA champion Lakers in the second round of the playoffs. The Spurs won the NBA title in 2002–2003, defeating the New Jersey Nets in six games. Smith lost his starting position early that season and became a seldom-used $9.9 million reserve; San Antonio released him following the 2002–2003 campaign. The New Orleans Hornets (NBA) signed him as a free agent in October 2003. Through the 2004–2005 season, Smith compiled 13,898 points (14.4-point average), 2,993 assists (3.1-per-game average), and a .838 free throw percentage in 968 regular-season games. He appeared in 87 playoff games and recorded 1,338 points (15.4-point average), 195 assists (2.2 average), and a .858 free throw percentage. As a reserve in his only All-Star Game in 1998, Smith tallied 14 points and three rebounds in 16 minutes. He played on the gold medal–winning U.S. teams at the World University Games in 1989, the World Championship of Basketball in 1994, and the Sydney, Australia Olympic Games in 2000.

The well-liked Smith has long been recognized as one of the game's most charitable players. He donated $2.5 million to Michigan State University in 1997 to help build the Clara Bell Smith Student-Athletic Academic Support Center in honor of his late mother, and established a $600,000 scholarship program at Detroit Pershing High School for those students attending Michigan State. Smith won the 1998 J. Walter Kennedy Citizenship Award and the 2002 NBA Sportsmanship Award. He and his wife, Millie, have two sons, Brayden and Davis.

BIBLIOGRAPHY: John Ebling and John Farina, *Magic Moments: A Century of Spartan Basketball* (Chelsea, MI, 1998); Jan Hubbard, ed., *The Official NBA Encyclopedia*, 3rd ed. (New York, 2000); Roscoe Nance, "10-Year Vets Bide Time on Market: Steve Smith-types Sign Later at Bargain Prices," *USA Today*, July 31, 2003, p. 11c; Ken Shouler et al., *Total Basketball* (Wilmington, DE, 2003); *TSN Official NBA*

Guide, 2002–2003 (St. Louis, MO, 2002); *TSN Official NBA Register, 2004–2005* (St. Louis, MO, 2004).

Jack C. Braun

SMITH, William T. "Wee Willie" "Slim Green" (b. April 22, 1911, Montgomery, AL; d. March 14, 1992, Cleveland, OH), professional player, was the son of Isaac Smith and Mary Smith. The six-foot five-inch, 235-pounder married Estelle Taylor in 1937 and had three children: James, Faith and June.

Nicknamed "Wee Willie" due to his large frame and also "Slim Green," Smith played professional basketball in the 1930s and 1940s. He performed for Cleveland's Slaughter Brothers team prior to 1932, when he was spotted by New York Renaissance club owner Bob Douglas*. Douglas signed Smith to play center for the New York Renaissance team from 1932 through the 1941–1942 season. Smith became known for his defensive and rebounding skills and strong, aggressive play on the court. As an inside shooter, he ranked among the era's top players and starred on the superlative 1932–1933 Renaissance team. The Renaissance won 88 consecutive basketball games, breaking the professional record of 44 set by the Original Celtics. The Renaissance, consisting of just seven players, was elected to the Naismith Memorial Basketball Hall of Fame in 1963. Teammates included "Tarzan" Cooper*, "Fats" Jenkins*, Pappy Ricks, Eyre Saitch*, Casey Holt, and Bill Yancey*.

Smith also helped the Renaissance team win the first-ever Professional Tournament, held at Chicago Illinois in March 1939. He and his teammates frequently experienced discrimination and prejudice on the road and on one occasion became involved in a fight. The Renaissance team had to be escorted by police to leave town safely. After his tenure with the Renaissance, Smith played for the Allmen Transfers (NBL) and the Chase Brass (NBL) teams in Cleveland, Ohio in the early 1940s.

Following his basketball career, Smith worked for the Cleveland (Ohio) Public Transit System and the board of education. He was inducted into the Cleveland Sports Hall of Fame in the 1970s and resided in Cleveland until his death.

BIBLIOGRAPHY: Bijan C. Bayne, *Sky Kings* (New York, 1997); Ocania Chalk, *Pioneers of Black Sport* (New York, 1975); Glenn Dickey, *The History of Professional Basketball Since 1896* (New York, 1982); Faith Foster (daughter of William Smith), Cleveland Heights, OH, telephone conversation with Susan J. Rayl, December 1993; Nelson George, *Elevating the Game: Black Men and Basketball* (New York, 1992); Bill Himmelman, Norwood, NJ, telephone conversation with Susan J. Rayl, October 1993; Zander Hollander, ed., *The Modern Encyclopedia of Basketball* (New York, 1973); Wayne Patterson, Naismith Basketball Hall of Fame, Springfield, MA; Robert W. Peterson, *From Cages to Jump Shots* (New York, 1990); Susan J. Rayl, *The New York Renaissance Professional Black Basketball Team, 1923–1950* (Syracuse, NY, 2001); Ken Shouler et al., *Total Basketball* (Wilmington, DE, 2003).

Susan J. Rayl

SPENCER, Robert Lee "Bob" (b. September 10, 1932, Albia, IA), college coach, is the son of John Spencer and Wretha (Pence) Spencer. After graduating from Albia (Iowa) High School in 1951, Spencer earned a Bachelor's degree in physical education from Parsons College (Iowa) in 1957 and a Master's degree in physical education from Northern Colorado University in 1963. He and his wife, Pat, have one daughter, Lisa. In 1957 Carlisle (Iowa) High School appointed Spencer as girl's basketball coach. Under Spencer, Carlisle compiled a 100-57 win-loss record from 1957 to 1965.

Spencer pioneered women's athletic programs at John F. Kennedy College in Nebraska and Parsons College and William Penn College in Iowa. He became athletic director at John F. Kennedy College in 1965, guiding its women's basketball team to a 73-42 mark from 1966 to 1970. Parsons College designated Spencer as athletic director in 1970. He compiled a 67-39 mark as women's basketball coach at Parsons over three seasons. Spencer, who was appointed women's athletic director at William Penn College in 1973, coached the Lady Statesmen to an impressive 240-43 slate and to four seasons with at least 30 victories from 1973 to 1981. His Lady Statesmen captured seven Iowa state championships and six regional titles, advanced to the national tournaments six times, and received national ranking every year. His 43-3 1980–1981 squad established an AIAW collegiate single-season record for victories, was ranked first nationally, and captured the national championship. In 1981 Stayfree and the AWSF named Spencer Division II National Coach of the Year.

From 1981 until his retirement in 1993, Spencer achieved a 198-191 mark as women's basketball coach at Fresno (California) State University. Fresno State (BWC) had moved from NCAA Division III to Division I. His first losing collegiate season came in 1981–1982, but he was named NCAA Coach of the Year. The Bulldogs registered their first winning season ever in 1982–1983 and set five consecutive season records for victories, culminating with a 22-8 slate in 1986–1987. In March 1988, Spencer became the first NCAA women's basketball coach to achieve 500 career victories. He ranked second, behind Jody Conradt* of the University of Texas, among NCAA women's basketball coaches upon his retirement with a 578-274 mark in 27 seasons.

Nineteen All-Americas, including Jan Irby, Glenda Poock (who scored 2,007 career points), Becky King, Wendy Martell, Shannon McGee, and Yvette Roberts, played under Spencer. Besides serving on the Kodak and AWSF All-American selection committees, Spencer directed basketball camps for over 23,000 girls, conducted clinics for coaches and players in 27 states, Mexico, and Belgium, and sponsored the first training camps held in the United States for the World University Games. His players represented the United States in the World Tournament, the World Festival, the Pan American Games, and U.S. Olympic Festivals, participated on the U.S.-Russian Tour team, and played professional basketball in Europe. Spencer, a personable, caring, intense, and determined coach, instilled pride, a winning spirit, and academic excellence in his players.

BIBLIOGRAPHY: *Des Moines* (IA) *Register*, March 7, 1991, p. 45; Mike Douchant, *Encyclopedia of College Basketball* (Detroit, MI, 1995); *Fresno State University Women's Basketball Media Guide, 1992–1993* (Fresno, CA, 1992); *Oskaloosa* (IA) *Herald*, 1973–1981; Robert Spencer, letters to David L. Porter, January 24, 1985, March 5, 1990; *William Penn College Women's Basketball Media Guide, 1980–1981* (Oskaloosa, IA, 1980).

David L. Porter

SPIVEY, BILL (b. March 19, 1929, Lakeland, FL; d. May 8, 1995, Quepos, Costa Rica), college and professional player, grew up in Warner Robins, Georgia and excelled in basketball at Jordan High School in Macon, Georgia. As a high school sophomore, Spivey was six-feet eight-inches tall. He averaged 29.0 points as 6-foot 10½-inch, 179 pound senior. University of Kentucky coach Adolph Rupp* recruited him.

Following his graduation from high school in 1948, Spivey enrolled at Kentucky. He played 30 games as a sophomore in 1949–1950, scoring 578 points and averaging 19.3 points. Spivey registered 15 points in an NIT game in 1950. The following year, he recorded 635 points and averaged 19.3 points. In the 1951 NCAA championship game, Spivey led the Wildcats with 22 points and 21 rebounds in their 68-58 triumph over Kansas State University. He averaged 18.0 points and 13.8 rebounds in four NCAA games and was chosen consensus All-America in 1951. Spivey was selected the All-SEC First Team and the SEC All-Tournament Team. He did not play his senior year because of a knee injury and later was dropped from the squad because of his possible involvement in the 1950–1951 game-fixing scandals.

Spivey, who was indicted for perjury in the game fixing scandals, gave testimony conflicting with that of several teammates. He plead innocent, and his personal case ended in a 9-3 hung jury for his acquittal on all charges. The only apparent wrong committed by Spivey was not informing on his teammates. His professional status was left in the hands of NBA Commissioner Maurice Podoloff*, who banned Spivey and teammates Ralph Beard* and Alex Groza* from the NBA for life. "The scandal left him a broken man," his former wife, Audrey Spivey said.

The seven-foot Spivey spent the rest of his basketball career on minor professional teams. Between 1953 and 1957, he played for the Boston Whirlwinds, House of David, Washington Generals, New York Olympians, and Kentucky Colonels against the Harlem Globetrotters and Marques Haynes'* Harlem Magicians. Spivey returned to Kentucky in 1953 to complete work on his Bachelor's degree.

Spivey played 11 seasons with the Wilkes-Barre, Pennsylvania, Barons, Baltimore, Maryland, Long Beach, California, and Scranton, Pennsylvania, Miners in the EBL between 1957 and 1968 and with Los Angeles-Hawaii (ABL) in 1968–1969. In 12 minor league seasons, Spivey compiled 8,096 points and averaged 25.3 points in 320 games.

Spivey later operated Bill Spivey's Restaurant and Lounge in Lexington, Kentucky, sold insurance and real estate, served as deputy state insurance commissioner, and announced for Kentucky Lieutenant Governor in 1987. He had one son, Cashton, a doctor.

BIBLIOGRAPHY: "Adolph Rupp," *Great Teams*, http://www.tournamentfacts.com (1985); "Bill Spivey," *Career Statistics*, http://www.ukfans.net (2004); "Bill Spivey," *Final Tribute* (*Lexington-Herald Leader*, May 21, 1995), http://www.ukfans.net (2004); "Bill Spivey," *Obituary* (*Lexington-Herald Leader*, May 9, 1995), http://www.ukfans.net (2004); "Bill Spivey," *Professional Career Highlights*, http://www.members .aol.com (2003); Peter C. Bjarkman, *The Biographical History of Basketball* (Chicago, IL, 2000); Mike Douchant, *Encyclopedia of College Basketball* (Detroit, MI, 1995).

John L. Evers

SPREWELL, Latrell Fontaine (b. September 8, 1970, Milwaukee, WI), college and professional player, is one of three children born to Latoska Fields and Patricia Sprewell. His father left the family when Sprewell was only six years old and moved to Flint, Michigan. Sprewell split time between his mother's and father's homes until his father was jailed for a drug-related charge.

Sprewell attended Washington High School in Milwaukee, Wisconsin and was recruited during his senior year by coach James Gordon to play basketball. A natural athlete, Sprewell averaged 28 points and made the All-City team. His achievements earned him a basketball scholarship to Three Rivers JC in Popular Bluff, Missouri in 1988–1989 and 1989–1990. Although struggling academically and being suspended for shoplifting, Sprewell averaged over 20 points. He secured a basketball scholarship to the University of Alabama, where he played for two seasons in 1990–1991 and 1991–1992. In his senior year, Sprewell led the Crimson Tide in scoring, averaging 18.7 points. Alabama advanced to the second round of the NCAA Tournament.

The Golden State Warriors (NBA) selected Sprewell in the first round of the 1992 NBA draft. The six-foot five-inch, 190-pound guard-forward enjoyed an outstanding rookie campaign with the Warriors, averaging 15.4 points and making the NBA All-Rookie Second Team. During his second season, injuries to teammates caused coach Don Nelson* to play Sprewell more minutes than any other NBA player. The athlete responded to the challenge by leading the Warriors in scoring with 21 points a game.

During the 1994–1995 season, Sprewell earned a starting berth in the All-Star Game and was named to All-NBA First Team. He argued with coach Nelson and teammates, however, resulting in two suspensions. Tensions eased the next season when Rick Adelman* succeeded Nelson and named Sprewell team captain. Sprewell averaged 18.9 points and was awarded a $32 million multi-year contract. Adelman left the Warriors after one season and was replaced with disciplinarian P. J. Carlesimo, whose abusive style angered Sprewell. On December 1, 1997, Calesimo screamed at Sprewell, who physically attacked the coach until subdued by teammates. The Warriors terminated Sprewell's contract, the athletic-shoe company Converse cancelled his endorsement deal, and the NBA banned him for a year. Sprewell maintained that the NBA overreacted. On March 4, 1998, an arbitrator agreed, reduced the NBA suspension to six months, and ordered the Warriors to reinstate the terminated contract.

San Francisco traded Sprewell to the New York Knicks (NBA) in January 1999, resurrecting his career. He helped the Knicks reach the NBA Finals in 1999, averaging 20.7 points and 4.8 rebounds in 20 playoff games. In the 1999–2000 season, Sprewell led the Knicks to the Eastern Conference Finals against the Indiana Pacers. Although the Knicks lost in seven games, he won the support of New York fans by averaging 19.6 points in the series. Sprewell's rehabilitation in New York was also aided by his

$100,000 donation to a program for disadvantaged city youth. In July 2003, the Minnesota Timberwolves (NBA) acquired him in a three-team trade. He averaged 16.8 points to help Minnesota capture the top spot in the Western Conference with a 58-24 record in 2003–2004. Sprewell helped Minnesota past the first round of the NBA playoffs for the first time in 2004, but the Los Angeles Lakers ousted the Timberwolves in the Western Conference Finals. He enjoyed an outstanding playoffs, scoring 357 points in 18 playoff games and tallying at least 27 points five times. His scoring production dropped to a 12.8 point average in 2004–2005, as Minnesota missed the playoffs. The four-time All-Star played well with the Knicks and Timberwolves and has averaged 18.3 points, 4.1 rebounds, and 4.0 assists in 913 regular-season games through 2004–2005. He has averaged 19.7 points and 4.3 rebounds in 62 playoff games.

BIBLIOGRAPHY: R. Hoffer, "Back in the Game," *SI* 87 (October 22, 1997), pp. 70–72; Michael J. Pellowski, *Latrell Sprewell* (New York, 2002); Mark Starr and Allison Samuels, "Hoop Nightmare," *Newsweek* 130 (December 15, 1997), pp. 26–29; Ken Shouler et al., *Total Basketball* (Wilmington, DE, 2003); *TSN Official NBA Register, 2004–2005* (St. Louis, MO, 2004); Phil Taylor, "Center of the Storm," *SI* 87 (December 15, 1997), pp. 60–62.

Ron Briley

SPROUSE, Alline Banks (b. June 26, 1921, Manchester, TN), college player and coach, was the dominant women's basketball player of the 1940s. At Buchanan High School in Murfreesboro, Tennessee, Banks played varsity basketball for four years and was selected to the All-Regional team. There was no state tournament to test her skills further. She graduated in 1938 and then worked for Nashville Business College, which soon became the dominant power in women's amateur basketball. As a lanky 17-year-old participant in the national AAU tournament, Banks led Nashville Business College to a surprising upset of the then two-time defending champion team from Galveston, Texas. In 12 years of competition from 1939 through 1950, she made All-America 11 straight times and was chosen the captain or co-captain of that honors squad on nine occasions. Selection as captain symbolized being the best player in the AAU tournament, the highest level of competition then open to women. She played in nine championship games and led her team to victories with the Nashville Vultee Aircraft/Goldblumes (1943–1945), Atlanta (Georgia) Sports Arena Blues (1947), and Nashville Business College (1950).

The auburn-haired, five-foot ten-inch forward possessed an uncanny shooting touch, Banks, by far the top scorer of her era, consistently tallied in double figures during a time when an entire team might produce only 25–30 points a game. She led scorers in three consecutive championship triumphs by the Nashville Vultee/Goldblumes from 1943 to 1945. This squad, one of the all-time best, won 84 of 85 games during one stretch. The next season, Banks jumped to Atlanta and sparked the Blues to an AAU title. She scored 15 points in the championship match, including the winning basket in overtime. In her two seasons there, the Blues won 98 of 101 contests. Banks once scored 56 points in an All-Star Game held at Madison Square Garden in New York City. Back with Nashville Business College for the 1949 and 1950 seasons, she helped John Head* to his first national title by scoring 15 points in the 29-28 victory. After marrying during her last campaign she coached and worked in the Atlanta, Georgia area.

Sprouse, one of the first group of women basketball players selected to the HAF Hall of Fame in 1966, also has been inducted into the Georgia Sports Hall of Fame (1972) and Tennessee Sports Hall of Fame (1974). She was nominated for the Naismith Memorial Basketball Hall of Fame, which first considered women for membership in the mid-1980s.

BIBLIOGRAPHY: Joan S. Hult and Marianna Treskell, eds., *A Century of Women's Basketball* (Reston, VA, 1991); Alexander M. Weyand, *The Cavalcade of Basketball* (New York, 1960).

Dennis S. Clark and Wayne Patterson

STALEY, Dawn Michelle (b. May 4, 1970, Philadelphia, PA), college and professional player and coach, is the youngest of five children of Clarence Staley and Estelle Staley and learned to play basketball in the Raymond Rosen housing projects of north Philadelphia. She honed her passing skills on the playgrounds playing basketball with her three older brothers. At Dobbins Vocational Technical High School from 1986 to 1988, Staley averaged 33.1 points and led the Lady Mustangs to three Philadelphia Public League championships. During her senior year, she was named *USA Today's* National High School Player of the Year.

The heavily recruited, five-foot five-inch, 134-pound guard signed with the University of Virginia's Lady Cavaliers and played basketball there from 1988 to 1992. Staley led the Lady Cavaliers to four NCAA Tournaments, three NCAA Final Four appearances, three ACC Tournament titles, and an overall 110-12 win-loss record. Besides having a career average of 18.5 points, she earned the Naismith Award in 1991 and 1992 (one of five women to win the award multiple times), was named Player of the Year in 1991 and 1992, and was a three-time Kodak All America. In 1993, Staley became one of three Cavaliers to have their jersey retired. She graduated in 1992 with a Bachelor's degree in rhetoric and communications studies.

Staley began her professional career overseas with Segovia, Spain in 1992–1993. She played on four different teams in Italy, France, Brazil, and Spain during the 1993–1994 season and with Tarbes, France for the 1994–1995 season. Staley joined the U.S. National Team in 1994 and helped them win several gold medals, including in the 1996 Olympics and 2000 Olympics, and was named U.S. Basketball's Female Athlete of the Year in 1994.

Staley was drafted to play in the newly formed ABL for the Richmond Rage in 1997. She played there in 1997 and 1998, averaging 14 points. When the ABL folded, Staley signed with the Charlotte Sting (WNBA) in 1999. In her six seasons with the Sting, she has averaged 9.2 points and ranks third in career assists per game. She played on the 2004 U.S. Olympic Women's gold-medal winning basketball team.

In April 2000, Staley accepted the head basketball coaching position at Temple University (Pennsylvania). In just five seasons, the Lady Owls have won 104 games, lost just 51 contests, captured the program's first two ATC women's championships, and made the postseason three times. In her first coaching position, Staley has averaged nearly 21 wins per season. She was named the Philadelphia Big Five Coach of the Year in 2002. Staley also operates the Dawn Staley Foundation, which she created in 1996. The Foundation operates several programs in north Philadelphia for at-risk kids. In 1998 Staley was awarded the Cross Spectrum Award given by the American Red Cross to women who make outstanding contributions to their communities. She has authored four young adult books based loosely on her life and discussing the Challenges and joys of growing up.

BIBLIOGRAPHY: Peter C. Bjarkman, *The Biographical History of Basketball* (Chicago, IL, 2000); Vic Dorr Jr., "Philly Fanatic," *Richmond Times Dispatch*, February 23, 1997; Mike Douchant, *Encyclopedia of College Basketball* (Detroit, MI, 1995); Mel Greenberg, "The Staley Saga Continues," *Philadelphia Inquirer*, June 11, 2001; Donald Hunt, "Double Duty," *BskD* 30 (February 2003), pp. 64–66; Faye Hall Jackson, "Dawn Staley," *The Scribner Encyclopedia of American Lives: Sports Figures* (New York, 2002); Carol A. Oglesby, ed., "Dawn Staley," *Encyclopedia of Women and Sport in America* (Westport, CT, 1998); *TSN Official WNBA Guide and Register, 2004*; (St. Louis, MO, 2004); Temple University Athletics website, www.owlsports.com; WNBA website, www.wnba.com.

Lisa A. Ennis

STANLEY, Marianne Crawford (b. April 29, 1954, Philadelphia, PA), college player and coach, is the daughter of James Crawford and Marjorie Crawford. She graduated in 1972 from Archbishop Pendergast High School in Philadelphia, Pennsylvania, where she starred in basketball as a streetwise player. Crawford, recruited by Cathy Cowan Rush* to play for national champion Immaculata (Pennsylvania) College, became an important cog for the first national power of women's basketball in the modern era. The five-foot six-inch guard excelled as a playmaker and top defender on four teams that reached championship games of the AIAW's postseason tournament. Immaculata won AIAW national titles in 1973 and 1974 and finished second in 1975 and 1976. Crawford made consensus All-America her junior and senior years, despite generally scoring under 10 points a game. The catalyst and emotional leader of the "Macs," she enjoyed an exceptional AIAW national tournament in 1975. After leading Immaculata to a semifinal upset of Wayland Baptist University (Texas), Crawford almost single-handedly kept the team in the title game against Delta State University (Mississippi). After graduating with a Bachelor's degree in sociology in 1976, she worked one season as assistant basketball coach at Immaculata. She helped them to another AIAW national tournament, where they finished fourth.

The bespectacled coach secured her first basketball head coaching position at Old Dominion University (Virginia) the next year. She inherited an established primarily regionally based program and quickly turned it into a nationally recognized one. In her first season (1977–1978), the Lady Monarchs won the NWIT in Amarillo, Texas and finished with a 30-4 log. No other school besides Wayland Baptist University had won that tournament in its 10-year history. With All-Americas Nancy Lieberman-Cline* and Inge Nissen leading the way, Old Dominion University won AIAW national collegiate championships in 1978–1979 and 1979–1980 with 35-1 and 37-1 records. Stanley, Coach of the Year in 1979, helped make Old Dominion one of the nation's best fan-supported programs. In December 1979, a then–record crowd of 10,237 attended a women's game between Old Dominion and the Russian national team.

Stanley recruited 1979's top high school player, six-foot eight-inch Anne Donovan*, who became the focal point of the Lady Monarchs after the graduation of Lieberman-Cline and Nissen. Old Dominion University again reached the championship round, finishing third in 1981 and tied for third in 1983, when they hosted the first NCAA tournament for women. During this period, Old Dominion University set a record with 64 straight home victories, broke Louisiana Tech University's 54-game unbeaten string, and won the first SBC Tournament. In 1984 Old Dominion lost in the East Regional Finals, but the next season Medina Dixon and Tracy Claxton led them to their first NCAA championship title with a 70-65 victory over the University of Georgia. Old Dominion slumped to a 15-13 mark in an injury-plagued 1985–1986 season and compiled an 18-13 record in 1986–1987. Stanley's squad defeated North Carolina 76-58 in the second round of the Mideast Regional before losing to Auburn University (Alabama) 77-61.

During her first eight seasons, Stanley compiled a 236-33 record for a remarkable major college .877 winning percentage. In 15 years as a college player and coach, she has reached the national tournament Final Four 11 times. Stanley, who enjoyed a 297-59 composite mark at Old Dominion, was named head coach of the struggling University of Pennsylvania program in May 1987. Stanley's inexperienced Pennsylvania squads finished 6-20 in 1987–1988 and 5-21 in 1988–1989. She moved to the University of Southern California, compiling marks of 8-19 in 1989–1990, 18-12 in 1990–1991, 23-8 in 1991–1992, and 22-27 in 1992–1993. Stanley compiled a 71-46 overall mark, and 45-27 PTC mark, reaching the NCAA Regionals her last two seasons. She left Southern California in an equal play dispute and sued the institution. Stanford University (California) hired her to market women's basketball. As an intercollegiate coach. Stanley has compiled a 351-146 win-loss mark and a .706 winning percentage. A crusader for women's equality, she helped establish the Women's SpC of Tidewater to promote women's athletics. Stanley served as an assistant coach with the Los Angeles Sparks (WNBA) in 2000–2001 and the Washington Mystics (WNBA) in 2001–2002. In April 2002, the Mystics named her head coach. She won the 2002 WNBA Coach of the Year Award, guiding Washington to a 17-15 regular season record and a 2-0 sweep of the Charlotte Sting before losing to the New York Liberty in the Eastern Conference Finals. Stanley guided Washington to a 9-25 mark in 2003 and was replaced by Michael Adams. She served as an assistant coach for the New York Liberty (WNBA) in 2004. Marianne lives in the Palo Alto, California area with her daughter, Michelle, and enjoys golf, theater, music, and art.

BIBLIOGRAPHY: Mike Douchant, *Encyclopedia of College Basketball* (Detroit, MI, 1995); Nena Rey Hawkes and John F. Seggar, *Celebrating Women Coaches: A Biographical Dictionary* (Westport, CT, 2000); "Marianne C. Stanley—Head Coach," *Old*

Dominion University Press Guide, 1980–1981 (Norfolk, VA, 1980), pp. 2–3; Rosemarie Skaine, *Women College Basketball Coaches* (Jefferson, NC, 2001); University of Pennsylvania Department of Intercollegiate Athletics, Philadelphia, PA, to David L. Porter, May 19, 1988.

Dennis S. Clark

STARBIRD, Catherine Evelyn (b. July 30, 1975, West Point, NY), college and professional player, is one of five children of Ed Starbird, a retired Army Colonel, and Margaret Starbird, and began playing basketball at age seven. When her father was transferred to Fort Lewis in Tacoma, Washington, the weather made the gym across the street an appealing location. Starbird's shot became so accurate and quick that she was often invited to join the young privates' games.

Starbird excelled in basketball at Lakes High School in Lakewood, Washington, from 1989 to 1993, averaging 29.3 points and 7.7 rebounds. She was named Washington's Player of the Year in 1993 and ended her high school career as the state's all-time leading scorer with 2,753 points. She also excelled scholastically with a 3.95 grade point average and induction into the National Honor Society.

The ungainly six-foot two-inch, 153-pound Starbird accepted a scholarship to Stanford University (California) to play basketball for the Lady Cardinal from 1993 to 1997 and became one of the school's most distinguished players. During her four years, the Lady Cardinal won three consecutive PTC championships, made four NCAA Tournament appearances, and advanced to the NCAA Final Four three times. Her individual honors include being Naismith National Player of the Year in 1997, winning Kodak All-America honors for the 1995–1996 and 1996–1997 seasons, and being named Player of the Year by the WBCA and *TSN* in 1997. She also graduated in 1997 as Stanford's all-time leading scorer with 2,215 points in 131 games and a B.S. degree in computer science.

Starbird, recruited by both new women's leagues, the ABL and WNBA, chose the former. She played the 1997–1998 and 1998–1999 seasons for the Seattle Reign (ABL), ranking fourth in three-point shots and thirteenth in scoring. When the ABL folded, Starbird moved to the WNBA. She played one season with the Sacramento Monarchs (WNBA) in 1999 and almost three seasons with Utah Starzz (WNBA) from 2000 to 2002, before being traded in July 2002 to the Seattle Storm (WNBA). Starbird struggled in the WNBA, averaging less than 10 points. In May 2003, she was cut from the Storm. Since leaving basketball, Starbird has engaged in writing and the 3D graphics computer company, 3HC, which she helped to start.

BIBLIOGRAPHY: Filip Bondy, "Stanford's Starbird Walks a Thin Line, Gets Weighted Down," *Daily News*, March 29, 1997; Mark Kreidler, "The End of the Beginning," *TSN*, November 25, 1996; Kristina Lanier, "Kate Starbird Goes From College Heights to Pro Hoops 101," *Christian Science Monitor*, February 2, 1998; James Ponti, *WNBA* (New York, 1999); *TSN Official WNBA Guide and Register, 2003* (St. Louis, MO, 2003); "Starbird Kate," *Athletes and Coaches of Summer* (Detroit, MI, 2000); WNBA website, www.wnba.com.

Lisa A. Ennis

STEINMETZ, Christian "Chris" (b. June 28, 1882, Milwaukee, WI; d. June 11, 1963, Milwaukee, WI), college player, was the son of S. Christian Steinmetz and Frances (Hoya) Steinmetz. A two-sport star at Milwaukee (Wisconsin) South Division High School, he led his basketball team to the city and state titles as a senior in 1902. Steinmetz entered the University of Wisconsin and became college basketball's first scoring star. Although appearing in under 40 games in three seasons, he became the first player to surpass 1,000 career points. In 1905 Steinmetz scored 462 points, 23 more points than all opposing teams tallied against Wisconsin that season. His 25.7 points average remained a seasonal record until the early 1940s. He accomplished these remarkable scoring feats despite standing only five-feet nine and a half inches and weighing 137 pounds. Around 1900, however, one player was designated to shoot all his team's free throws. In 1905 Steinmetz made 238 of 317 free throw attempts. He scored 50 points in a game against Sparta College (Wisconsin), made 20 field goals against Beloit College (Wisconsin), and made 26 of 30 free throws in a single contest to set still-standing University of Wisconsin records.

Steinmetz captained the 10-8 Badgers squad of 1904–1905, which won the WC title and made an extended tour of the East Coast, then the center of college basketball. He reportedly suffered a fractured jaw in the Columbia University (New York) game, but no foul was called. Bob Zuppke, later a famous football coach at the University of Illinois, teamed with Steinmetz that year. The HAF Hall of Fame selected Steinmetz as its first Player of the Year for the 1904–1905 season. Steinmetz graduated from the University of Wisconsin in three years with a Law degree and was admitted to the Wisconsin bar. After marrying Bessie Engel on November 12 1908, he had four children, Christian, Ruth (Timm), Alan, and Don. Steinmetz proudly boasted that all three of his sons lettered athletically at the University of Wisconsin. For over 50 years, he practiced law in Milwaukee and represented several large insurance companies. Besides being active in many civic and political groups, Steinmetz coached and refereed basketball locally for 19 years and authored several articles in professional journals. Steinmetz, considered the "Father of Wisconsin basketball," was a charter member of the HAF, Naismith Memorial Basketball (1961) and Wisconsin halls of fame.

BIBLIOGRAPHY: Peter C. Bjarkman, *Big Ten Basketball* (Indianapolis, IN, 1994); *Converse Yearbook, 1963*; Ralph Hickok, *Who Was Who in American Sports* (New York, 1971); Don Kopriva et al., *On Wisconsin* (Champaign, IL, 1998); Ronald L. Mendell, *Who's Who in Basketball* (New Rochelle, NY, 1973); Sandy Padwe, *Basketball's Hall of Fame* (Englewood Cliffs, NJ, 1970); Christian Steinmetz file, Naismith Memorial Basketball Hall of Fame, Springfield, MA; *Who's Who in the Midwest, 1949, 1952*.

Dennis S. Clark

STEITZ, Edward Stephen "Ed" (b. November 7, 1920, Beacon, NY; d. May 21, 1990, East Longmeadow, MA), amateur basketball administrator and coach, was the son of insurance agent Charles Steitz and Magdaline (Esch) Steitz and graduated from Beacon (New York) High School in 1938. At Beacon High School, he won 12 letters in basketball, baseball, and cross country. Steitz earned a Bachelor of Science degree in 1943 from Cornell University (New York), where he captained the baseball squad and made the All-IvL Team. After serving in the U.S. Army from 1942 to 1946, he received a Master's degree in education in 1948 and a Doctoral degree in Physical Education in 1963 from Springfield (Massachusetts) College. Steitz married librarian June Harrison on January 18, 1946 and had three children, Stephen, Nancy, and Robert. In 1948, he began teaching physical education at Springfield College. Steitz became assistant director of the School of Physical Education in 1950, assistant director of athletics in 1954, and director of athletics in 1956. As head men's basketball coach from 1956 to 1966, he guided the Maroons to a 185-86 composite win-loss record and four NCAA championship appearances. During the summer of 1965, his basketball squad posted a 25-0 record while touring the world for the U.S. State Department.

Steitz, the world's leading authority on basketball rules, chaired the NCAA RRC from 1956 to 1966. He edited the annual NCAA *Basketball Rules of the United States and Canada* from 1966 until his death and co-edited the NFSHSAA *Basketball Case Book* from 1967 to 1979. The author or editor of 58 books and over 300 magazine and journal articles, he edited *Athletic Administration in Colleges and Universities* and wrote *Illustrated Basketball Rules* (1976) and *The Art of Officiating* (1976). Steitz conducted over 1,000 Basketball Rules Interpretation Clinics across the U.S. and 31 foreign countries since 1956. His major rules changes included originating the three-point shot, legalizing dunking during games, eliminating the air dribble, approving a wide out-of-bounds belt, requiring the ball to be inbounded within five seconds, tightening the definition of illegal use, of hands, widening the lane to 12 feet, instituting the one-and-one bonus rule on the seventh common team foul, awarding the ball out of bounds on common fouls until the bonus rule takes effect, permitting three officials, establishing the alternate possession rule on jump balls, and limiting player control to five seconds in the forecourt.

Steitz played a vital role in the establishment and growth of the Naismith Memorial Basketball

Hall of Fame as a member of its board of trustees and executive committee from 1959 to 1995. His organizational chairmanships included the NABC Research Committee (1954–1966), USOBOC, NEBCA Basketball Committee (1964–1970); NCAA College Division Basketball Tournament Selection Committee (1963–1965); and the ECAC Holiday Festival Tournament Selection Committee (1968–1972). Steitz presided over the ECBA (1969–1971, 1973–1975) and the NEBCA (1963–1965) and directed the Western Massachusetts High School Basketball Championships (1956–1971).

An international basketball promoter, Steitz chaired the USOBC for the 1984 Los Angeles Olympic Games; vice chaired USOBC for the 1972 Munich, West Germany Olympic Games; served on the USOBC for the 1964 Tokyo, Japan, 1968 Mexico City, Mexico, 1976 Montreal, Canada, and 1980 Moscow, USSR Olympic Games; and helped select players for the Tokyo and Mexico City Olympic Games. He played an active role on the USOC Executive Committee, chaired the NCAA Olympic Committee, and presided over BFUSA, pioneering in its formation. Steitz represented the BFUSA at FIBA meetings, thus gaining a broader impact for U.S. colleges, junior colleges, and high schools on the international basketball scene. From 1981 to 1984, he headed the ABAUSA, successor to the BFUSA. At Steitz's request, FIBA in July 1974 had granted the ABAUSA the right to serve as the U.S. governing body for international basketball. The AAU had governed American involvement in international basketball for the previous 40 years.

Steitz's contributions to New England, national, and international basketball have been recognized widely. In 1981, Springfield College designated Steitz as Buxton Professor of Physical Education. A member of both the Naismith Memorial Basketball Hall of Fame (1984) and Springfield College Hall of Fame (1981), he received the U.S. State Department Medallion and Citation (1972), Walter Brown Award (1973), NABC Metropolitan Award (1973), and Springfield College Distinguished Alumni Award (1974).

BIBLIOGRAPHY: *Contemporary Authors*, vols. 69–72, pp. 555–556; Robert W. Marx, "Dr. Edward S. Steitz," Springfield College, Springfield, MA, Sports Information Release, June 1982; Wayne Patterson to David L. Porter, February 29, 1988; Edward S. Steitz file, Naismith Memorial Basketball Hall of Fame, Springfield, MA.

David L. Porter

STERN, David Joel (b. September 22, 1942, New York City, NY), professional executive, is the son of William Stern, a delicatessen owner, and Anna (Bronstein) Stern. Stern received his Bachelor of Arts degree in history in 1963 at Rutgers University (New Jersey) and completed his Bachelor of Laws degree in 1966 from Columbia University (New York), both with honors. In 1966, he joined the law firm of Proskauer, Rose, Goetz, and Mendelsohn, which represented the NBA. At age 32, he became the firm's youngest partner. From 1974 to 1978, Stern worked on many cases that involved the NBA. The Oscar Robertson* settlement agreement ended nearly a decade of confrontation between the NBA and its players. He played a key role in working out the expansion agreement under which four of the strongest ABA teams were brought into the NBA.

In September 1978, Stern joined the NBA as its first general counsel. The next year, he negotiated the first NBA-wide cable network contract with the USA Cable Network, successor agreements with USA and ESPN, and a totally new contract with WTBS. This new contract with Turner Broadcasting System called for the televising of 75 games per year, giving the NBA access to more than 30 million homes. Through these cable agreements, the NBA gained additional exposure in the airing of a highlights show on ESPN coverage of the NBA draft, the NBA Award Special, and the All-Star Saturday events. In November 1980, Stern assumed the newly created position of executive vice president, business and legal affairs. To this position, he added the responsibilities of marketing, broadcasting, and public relations. In the marketing area, Stern has overseen the development of NBA properties, the video and publishing divisions, the sale of NBA-licensed merchandise, and the NBA's first direct-mail campaign.

On November 15, 1983, less than one week after Lawrence O'Brien* announced his retirement, Stern was elected unanimously by the NBA Board of Governors as the fourth NBA commissioner. As the NBA commissioner, he has expanded television exposure dramatically, substantially increased rights fees, and internationalized NBA telecasts to include 35 nations. Stern formulated a collective bargaining agreement that set a cap on team salaries while guaranteeing players a percentage of NBA revenues. He implemented an anti-drug program that provides help for those players who come forward seeking it, but also includes drug testing with cause and a lifetime ban of any player who fails such a test. Stern suspended Lewis Lloyd and Mitchell Wiggins of the Houston Rockets in January 1987 after they tested positive for cocaine and suspended other players subsequently. During his tenure as commissioner, the NBA has achieved several consecutive seasons of record attendance. Stern launched the Women's National Basketball Association (WNBA) with 8 franchises in 1997. Under Stern's direction, the NBA expanded from 23 to 30 teams and the WNBA to 13 teams. He sought to increase the NBA fan base with various contests and fan-selected All-Star teams. He also employed some of the greatest athletes in the world, the Charlotte Hornets and Miami Heat franchises joined the NBA before the 1988–1989 season, the Minnesota Timberwolves and Orlando Magic before the 1989–1990 season, the Toronto Raptors and Vancouver Grizzlies before the 1995–1996 season and the Charlotte Bobcats prior to 2004–2005. *Sport* magazine named him the best commissioner in organized sport in 1990 and the AP recognized him as Sports Executive of the Decade.

Stern was criticized in 1998 and 1999 when a labor struggle resulted in a 191-day lockout, canceling hundreds of games. He insisted the strike was necessary, but owners sought to adjust the salary cap and tighten rookie restrictions. Stern in November 2004 suspended Ron Artest of the Indiana Pacers 73 games, Stephen Jackson of Indiana 30 games, Jermaine O'Neal* of Indiana 25 games, Ben Wallace* of the Detroit Pistons six games, Anthony Johnson of Indiana five games, and four other players one game each for their roles in a melee that occurred on and off the court in an Indiana–Detroit game on November 19 at The Palace in Auburn Hills, Michigan. Stern denounced the ugly brawl involving players and fans "shocking, repulsive, and inexcusable." Jackson's suspension subsequently was reduced to 25 games. In May 2005, Stern fined Houston Rockets coach Jeff Van Gundy $100,000 for claiming that NBA officials were instructed to watch Yao Ming more closely for illegal moving screens.

Stern served on the adjunct faculty of Cardozo School of Law in New York, teaching a course in sports law. He is on the Professional Advisory Board of *Cardozo Arts and Entertainment Law Journal* and chairs the Committee on Entertainment and Sports Law of the Association of the Bar of the City of New York. Stern married Dianne Bock in November 1963. They reside in Scarsdale, New York, with their two sons, Andrew and Eric.

BIBLIOGRAPHY: David Halberstam, *Playing for Keeps* (New York, 1999); Jan Hubbard, ed., *The Official NBA Encyclopedia*, 3rd ed. (New York, 2000); NBA, Public Relations News Release; Ken Shouler, et al., *Total Basketball* (Wilmington, DE, 2003); *WWA*, 44th ed. (1986–1987), p. 2679.

James E. Welch

STEWART, Lusia Harris "Lucy" (b. February 10, 1955, Minter City, MS), college and professional player, is the daughter of Willie Harris and grew up on a vegetable farm near the Tallahatchie River. The seventh of 11 children, Harris initially learned basketball competing against her brothers and sisters on a makeshift court in the farmyard. At Amanda Elzy High School, she served as team captain, won MVP for three straight seasons (1971–1973), and made State All-Star.

After graduation, Harris selected nearby Delta State University (Mississippi). Delta State was resurrecting its women's basketball program after four decades. With the six-foot three-inch, 185-pound protypical center leading the way, the Lily Margaret Wade* coached Lady Statesmen compiled records of 16-2, 28-0, 33-1, and 32-3. Delta State won three consecutive AIAW national collegiate championships (1975–1977) her final three seasons, as Harris made All-America three times. She led the nation in scoring in 1976 with 1,060 points and a 31.2 points average. Against Tennessee Tech, she once scored 58 points. In one of the first women's games ever played in Madison Square Garden in

New York, Harris tallied 47 points. During her college career, she scored 2,981 points (then a college record) and grabbed 1,662 rebounds. Harris averaged 25.9 points and 14.5 rebounds. She was named the MVP of the national tournament twice and became the first recipient of the Broderick Cup for the 1976–1977 season.

Internationally, Harris played on the World University and Gold Medal Pan American Games teams of 1975 and on the U.S. Olympic Team in 1976. At Montreal, Canada, she led the silver medal–winning squad in scoring and rebounding and scored the first field goal in women's Olympic basketball history. She led the Olympians in scoring (15.0 average) and in rebounding (7.0 average). At Delta State, Harris was a good student and campus leader. She was the first black homecoming queen and graduated in 1977 with a Bachelor's degree in health, physical education, and recreation. Harris married George E. Stewart on February 4, 1977 and has one son, Eddie. She worked as an admissions counselor, an assistant basketball coach for four years, and earned a Master's degree in education in 1984 at Delta State University.

Stewart became the first woman ever drafted by a men's pro basketball team when selected in the seventh round by the New Orleans Jazz (NBA) in 1977. She was picked as the number one free agent by the Houston Angels (WPBL) in the summer of 1978 and played briefly for them in 1980. The first real name women's basketball player, Harris had her uniform placed in the Naismith Memorial Basketball Hall of Fame and is also a member of Delta State's Hall of Fame. She was elected to the Naismith Memorial Basketball Hall of Fame in 1992 and served as a high school teacher and coach in Ruleville, Mississippi.

BIBLIOGRAPHY: Barbara Damrosch, "Aces—Lucy Harris; First Woman in History to Sink an Olympic Basket," *WomenSports* 3 (November 1976), pp. 66–68ff.; Mike Douchant, *Encyclopedia of College Basketball* (Detroit, MI, 1995); Bernard Fernandez, "Everyone Loves Lucy," *Basketball Weekly* 9 (March 4, 1976), p. 5; Barbara McDowell and Hanna Umlauf, ed., "Harris: Basketball Star," *The Good Housekeeping Women's Almanac* (New York, 1977), pp. 438–439; Jim O'Brien, "Best Player," *Street and Smith's Basketball Yearbook, 1976–1977*, p. 139; Victoria Sherrow, *Encyclopedia of Women and Sports* (Santa Barbara, CA, 1996); Lusia Harris Stewart file, Naismith Memorial Basketball Hall of Fame, Springfield, MA; Nancy Williamson, "The Women," *SI* (December 1, 1975), p. 64.

Dennis S. Clark

STEWART, Norman B. "Norm" (b. January 20, 1935, Leonard, MO), college and professional athlete and coach, is the son of Kenneth Stewart and Leona Stewart and graduated in 1952 from Shelbyville (Missouri) High School, where he played football and earned All-State honors in basketball and baseball. In 1952, Stewart began a 39-year affiliation with the University of Missouri (BSC) as student athlete and coach. As a junior and senior, he captained coach Wilbur "Sparky" Stalcup's Tigers basketball team and earned All-BSC honors. His senior year featured a 24.7 points average and All-America honors. Besides scoring 1,124 career basketball points, he starred as a pitcher on coach John "Hi" Simmons's Missouri team that won the 1954 NCAA baseball championship.

After graduation from Missouri in 1956, Stewart signed professional contracts with the St. Louis Hawks (NBA) and baseball's Baltimore Orioles (AL). He appeared in only five games with the Hawks, averaging two points during the 1956–1957 season. He spent 1957 in the Orioles' farm system, but the limited playing time in both basketball and baseball caused him to leave professional sports. He completed a Master's degree at the University of Missouri while serving a four-year stint as assistant coach in basketball and baseball.

In 1961, the University of Northern Iowa (NCC) appointed Stewart head basketball coach. His first team posted 19 wins and five losses, sharing the NCC title and earning a regional berth in the NCAA College Division Tournament. Stewart's 1963–1964 Panthers triumphed in their first 10 games, captured the NCC championship, and finished fourth in the NCAA College Division Tournament. His six winning seasons at Northern Iowa featured a record of 97 wins and 43 losses and produced the first two All-Americas in the school's history. In 1967, he succeeded Bob Vanatta as head coach at the University of Missouri.

Stewart rejuvenated a slumping Missouri

program, which had recorded only six wins in 49 games over the previous two seasons. In his first season, his Tigers triumphed only 10 times while dropping 16 games. The 1967–1968 campaign marked the first of only five losing seasons during his 32-year coaching career at Missouri. Stewart's Missouri teams compiled 634 wins and 333 losses, took eight BEC titles, and made four NIT and 15 NCAA Tournament appearances. Stewart's 38-year career record included 731 wins and 375 losses. Six All-Americas and over two dozen NBA players came from Stewart's programs. He garnered BEC Coach of the Year honors four times and was named UPI National Coach of the Year in 1982 and 1994. Stewart, was the dean of BEC coaches upon his retirement, with only the legendary "Phog" Allen* having spent more time at a BEC school.

One of America's most respected coaches, Stewart served on the NBRC. The ABAUSA, America's basketball governing body, twice recognized Stewart. He coached the North team in the 1982 National Sports Festival and the U.S. squad in the 1983 World University Games, and co-authored a book, *Basketball: Building the Complete Program*. He married Virginia Zimmerley of Kansas City, Missouri, a Missouri graduate and former homecoming queen, and has three children, Jeffrey, Lindsey, and Laura.

BIBLIOGRAPHY: Peter C. Bjarkman, *The Biographical History of Basketball* (Chicago, IL, 2000); Mike Douchant, *Encyclopedia of College Basketball* (Detroit, MI, 1995); Jan Hubbard, ed., *The Official NBA Basketball Encyclopedia*, 3rd ed. (New York, 2000); Ronald L. Mendell, *Who's Who in Basketball* (New Rochelle, NY, 1973); *Missouri Basketball Media Guide, 1991–1992* (Columbia, MO, 1991); MIZZOU Tigers News Release, 1990 Sports Information Office, Columbia, MO; *NCAA Men's Basketball Records, 2004* (Indianapolis, IN, 2003); Norman Stewart and George Scholz, *Basketball: Building the Complete Program* (Marceline, MO, 1980).

Jerry Jaye Wright

STILES, Jackie Marie (b. December 21, 1978, Kansas City, KS), college and professional player, is the oldest of four children born to Patrick Stiles and Pamela Stiles. As a child, she attended basketball practices with her father, who took her through the drills. Stiles spent hours attempting to perfect the plays her father demonstrated for her. She played basketball for Claflin High School in Claflin, Kansas, where she became the greatest career scorer in Kansas high school history—among women and men—with 3,603 career points. Her high school performance in basketball became legendary. Stiles, regularly taking 1,000 shots per practice, averaged 29.9 points as a freshmen and 26.4 points as a sophomore. In the first game of her junior year, she scored 61 points in 17 minutes. Stiles averaged 38.5 points her junior year and 46.4 points as a senior. She was chosen for the U.S. Basketball Junior team and was named *Parade* All-America and *USA Today* First Team in 1997. She also starred in tennis, cross country, and track and field at Claflin.

Stiles, a five-foot eight-inch, 142-pound shooting guard, starred in basketball at Southwest Missouri State University, leading all freshmen women in the nation in scoring in 1997–1998. She topped the (MVC) in scoring four consecutive seasons and was named MVC First Team Scholar Athlete her sophomore, junior, and senior years. Her 27.8 points average led the nation in 1999–2000, with her 56 points being the highest single game output during the campaign. In 1999–2000, her 1,062 points made her the first NCAA Division I woman to score more than 1,000 points in a season. On March 1, 2001, Stiles established the NCAA Division I career scoring record with 30 points against Creighton University (Nebraska), breaking the mark of 3,132 points, held by Patricia Hoskins*. She finished her collegiate career with 3,371 points. Stiles was chosen by the WBCA and the NAGWS for the Wade Trophy as the nation's best player in 2001 and captured the Broderick Cup as the 2001 Collegiate Woman Athlete of the Year. She earned a Bachelor of Arts degree in sports and fitness promotion in 2001.

The Portland Fire (WNBA) drafted Stiles in the first round in 2001. Stiles, the first Portland player selected for the WNBA All-Star Game, was chosen 2001 WNBA Rookie of the Year. Injuries limited her to 21 games in 2002. She was drafted by the Los Angeles Sparks (WNBA) in the 2003 dispersal draft when Portland ceased operations. Stiles missed the entire 2003 season because of chronic bursitis in the heel; the effects of surgeries on her wrist, shooting hand, and foot; back pain; and lasik eye surgery. She gave numerous basketball camps for junior high school and high school athletes during the year. Stiles retired following the 2003 season. Her WNBA career totals include 733 points scored, 95 rebounds, and 75 assists in 53 games.

University of Kansas women's head basketball coach Bonnie Hendrickson had asked Stiles to serve as her assistant coach for the 2004–2005 season. She was engaged to Matthew Barrett, a Springfield, Missouri middle school coach, and plans to become a high school teacher and coach.

BIBLIOGRAPHY: AP, "Stiles Endures Rough Second WNBA Season," ESPN, *WNBA* (June 26, 2002), pp. 1–2; AP, "Stiles Named 2001 WNBA Rookie of the Year," *Dodge City* (KS) *Daily Globe* archives (2001), pp. 1–3; Antonya English, "Stiles Is Living a Dream," *St. Petersburg* (FL) *Times ONLINE*, Sports (March 29, 2001), pp. 1–6; Tony Hawley, "Injured Stiles Still Aspiring to Make Mark in Pro Basketball," *Jefferson City* (MO) *News Tribune* (April 11, 2004) archives pp. 1–3; *Lawrence* (KS) *Journal World* staff, "Stiles Mulls Joining KU Staff," *Lawrence Journal World* (April 6, 2004), p. 1; Mechelle Voepel, "Stiles Is Something Special," *ESPN.com* (March 7, 2001), pp. 1–4; WNBA, "Jackie Stiles," *WNBA Notes* (2002), pp. 1–7; WNBA, "Jackie Stiles Player Info," *WNBA.com* (2003), pp. 1–2.

Frank J. Olmsted

STOCKTON, John Houston, III (b. March 26, 1962, Spokane, WA), college and professional player, is the son of John H. Stockton, Jr., a tavern owner, and Clementine (Frey) Stockton, and was a surprise first-round selection (sixteenth pick overall) by the Utah Jazz in the 1984 NBA draft. The six-foot one-inch, 175-pound Stockton, who was twice All-WCAC and WCAC MVP at Gonzaga University (Washington) scored 1,340 points (12.5 average) in 107 career games. He combined uncanny "floor sense" and passing ability with hard-nosed competitiveness to become one of the top point guards in NBA history.

Stockton, who retired in May 2003, ranked first in NBA history in career assists 15,806 and first in average assists per game for both career (10.5) and season (14.5). In February 1995, he recorded his 9,922nd assist to break Magic Johnson's* career assist mark. The NBA leader in assists nine consecutive seasons (1988–1996), Stockton surpassed Naismith Memorial Basketball Hall-of-Famer Bob Cousy* in most seasons (9) and most consecutive seasons (9) pacing the NBA. The first NBA player to compile over 1,000 assists in more than one season, Stockton accomplished the feat seven times (1988–1994) and holds the NBA record for the most assists in a single season (1,164). In 1993 and 1994, he won the first Bausch and Lomb NBA Court Vision Awards as the NBA's assist leader. Stockton made 28 assists on January 15, 1991 against the San Antonio Spurs and 10 steals on December 9, 1993 against the Washington Bullets. The extremely accurate shooter, who consistently scored in double figures, compiled 19,711 career points (13.1 point scoring average) and .515 field goal and .826 free throw percentage marks. The tenacious Stockton, also an outstanding defensive player, led the NBA in steals twice (1989, 1992), ranks first in career steals (3,265), and was named five times to the NBA's All-Defensive Second Team (1989, 1991, 1992, 1995, 1997). He holds the Utah records in career assists (15,806) and career steals (3,265). Stockton averaged 13.4 points, 10.1 assists, and 1.85 steals in 182 NBA playoff games. Utah reached the NBA Finals in 1997 and 1998 against the Chicago Bulls, losing in six games both times.

In recognition of his all-around abilities, Stockton was voted six times All-NBA Second Team (1988–1990, 1992, 1993, 1996), twice All-NBA First Team (1994–1995), and three times All-NBA Third Team (1991, 1997, 1999). He was also elected to nine consecutive All-Star teams (1989–1997), another All-Star Game in 2000, and was named Co-MVP of the 1993 All-Star Game with teammate Karl Malone*. The member of "Dream Team I," which won the gold medal at the 1992 Summer Olympics in Barcelona Spain, missed the four preliminary games because of a hairline fracture of the right fibula, suffered during practice, and played sparingly in medal-round games. Stockton also played on Dream Team II, which won the gold medal in the 1994 World Championship of

Basketball in Toronto, Canada, and on the gold-winning U.S. Olympic team of Atlanta, Georgia in 1996. He was named to the NBA 50th Anniversary All-Time Team in 1996.

Former Miami Heat coach Pat Riley* stated Stockton's "ball-handling skills are second to none, his decision-making and running of the offense are flawless, and he [is] a productive shooter." Former Utah Jazz president Frank Layden asserted, "Many people say Magic [Johnson] was a point guard and a better player than John. But as for a pure point guard, I defy anyone to say there has been anyone better than John Stockton." Stockton, a private person who avoids the spotlight, married Nada Stepovich in 1986 and has four children.

BIBLIOGRAPHY: Chuck Daly and Alex Sachare, *America's Dream Team: The Quest for Olympic Gold* (Atlanta, GA, 1992); *Deseret News*, November 4, 1993; Mike Douchant, *Encyclopedia of College Basketball* (Detroit, MI, 1995), Larry R. Gerlach interview with John Stockton, December 7, 1993; Jan Hubbard, ed., *The Official NBA Encyclopedia*, 3rd ed. (New York, 2000); Roland Lazenby, *Stockton to Malone: The Rise of the Utah Jazz* (Lenexa, KS, 1998); Kurt Kragthorpe, "John Stockton's Stock Keeps Rising," *BskD* 15 (March 1988), pp.44–46; Jack McCallum, "The Assist Man," *SI* 76 (February 17, 1992), p.77; Brad Rock, "Jazz Maestro Stockton Plays a Quiet Tune," *BskD* 20 (March 1993), pp.44–48; Steve Rushin, "City of Stars," *SI* 77 (July 27, 1992), pp.62–74; Robert E. Schnakenberg, *Teammates: Karl Malone and John Stockton* (Brookfield, CT, 1998); Ken Shouler et al., *Total Basketball* (Wilmington, DE, 2003); *TSN Official NBA Guide, 2004–2005* (St. Louis, MO, 2004); *TSN Official NBA Register, 2004–2005* (St. Louis, MO, 2004); *Utah Jazz 2002–2003 Media Guide.* (Salt Lake City, UT).

Larry R. Gerlach

STOKES, Maurice "Mo" (b. June 17, 1933, Pittsburgh, PA; d. April 6, 1970, Cincinnati, OH), college and professional player, enjoyed a spectacular basketball career that prematurely ended after three NBA years with a disabling form of encephalitis, manifested by a heart attack from rehabilitative strain that actually took his life. The son of Tero Stokes from Pittsburgh, Pennsylvania's Homewood section, he launched his outstanding performances as a basketball player with Pittsburgh's Westinghouse High School and starred at tiny St. Francis College in Loretto, Pennsylvania. Stokes established numerous Frankies' game, season, and career records, as he led the team in scoring and rebounding all four years. Stokes combined speed and agility with size and strength to rank him among the greatest all-around players of his era. As a freshman, he averaged 16.7 points. Stokes compiled 2,282 career points, including 760 his senior year in 1954–1955, and 1,819 career rebounds (25.3 per game average), with 733 in 1954–1955. His best individual single-game performances included 43 points against the University of Dayton (Ohio) in the 1955 NIT and 35 rebounds versus John Carroll College in 1954–1955. Walter McLaughlin, NIT Selection Committee chairman, called Stokes's effort against Dayton, in which he also snared 19 rebounds, "the greatest performance I have ever seen." Stokes, the NIT MVP, nearly led St. Francis to the NIT Finals, dropping an overtime semifinal game to Dayton, 79-73. His small-school anonymity mitigated against All-America recognition, with the NIT visibility coming too late.

The six-foot seven-inch, 240-pound, broad-shouldered center, who rejected an offer from the Harlem Globetrotters, was drafted by the Rochester Royals (NBA) in 1955 and quickly became one of the NBA's top performers. Stokes ranked among the top three in rebounds and assists and averaged 16.3 points, compiling a 202-game career total of 1,251 field goals and 813 free throws for 3,315 points. His soft shooting touch and strength on the boards awed scouts and garnered him NBA Rookie of the Year honors in 1956. He appeared in the All-Star Game and made Second Team All-NBA all three NBA seasons.

The Rochester franchise was moved to Cincinnati for the 1957–1958 season. In his brief NBA tenure, Stokes became a friend of teammate Jack Twyman*. The friendship lasted the rest of the crippled player's life as Twyman, a great humanitarian, became his guardian. Following the 1957–1958 season, Stokes collapsed and spent several months in a coma. Encephalitis, a crippling brain disease, made him an invalid. He began a long, painful period of rehabilitation, but died at age 36 after a courageous battle. In 2004, he was inducted to the Naismith Memorial Basketball Hall of Fame.

BIBLIOGRAPHY: Peter C. Bjarkman, *The Biographical History of Basketball* (Chicago, IL, 2000); Mike Douchant, *Encyclopedia of College Basketball* (Detroit, MI, 1995); Zander Hollander, ed., *The Modern Encyclopedia of Basketball* (New York, 1973); Jan Hubbard, ed., *The Official NBA Basketball Encyclopedia*, 3rd ed. (New York, 2000); *St. Francis College Basketball Media Guides* 1951–1954 (Loretto, PA, 1951–1954); Chet Smith and Marty Wolfson, *Greater Pittsburgh History of Sports* (Pittsburgh, PA, 1969); Maurice Stokes file, Naismith Memorial Basketball Hall of Fame, Springfield, MA.

Robert B. Van Atta

STONER, C. Vivian. *See* Stringer, C. Vivian Stoner

STRINGER, C. Vivian Stoner (b. March 16, 1945, Edenborn, PA), college player and coach, is the daughter of Charles H. Stoner, a coal miner and musician, and Thelma Stoner. Stringer graduated in 1966 from German Township High School and in 1970 with a B.S. degree in health and physical education from Slippery Rock College, where she played for the nationally ranked basketball, tennis, field hockey, and softball teams. In 1974, she earned an M.S. degree in physical education from Slippery Rock.

In 1971 Cheyney (Pennsylvania) State College hired her as assistant professor of recreation, health, and physical education and head women's basketball coach. Stringer remained at Cheyney State 11 seasons, producing a 251-51 win-loss record. Her 28-3 1981–1982 squad, led by All-America Valerie Walker, made the first-ever NCAA Women's Final Four, losing the championship game 76-62 to Louisiana Tech University. In 1982, she was named Stayfree NCAA Division I Basketball Coach of the Year. Her other honors included being chosen Women's Basketball Coach of the Year by the PSWA twice and PAIAW once. *Ebony* magazine ranked her among the Outstanding Black Women in Sports in 1980.

In 1983, the University of Iowa (BTC) named her head women's basketball coach to revive its program. Through the 1994–1995 season, she compiled a 269-84 record for the Hawkeyes. Iowa finished 29-2 in 1987–1988, winning its first outright BTC title and ranking first nationally for eight consecutive weeks. Michelle Edwards was selected WBCA Player of the Year and Iowa's initial First Team All-America. The Hawkeyes fared 21-9 in 1990–1991, 27-4 in 1992–1993, and 21-7 in 1993–1994, ranking third nationally and sharing the BTC crown with Ohio State University in 1992–1993. Iowa reached the 1993 NCAA Final Four, losing the semifinals to Ohio State. The Hawkeyes made nine consecutive NCAA appearances until suffering an 11-17 mark in 1994–1995. BTC Player of the Year awards were earned by Hawkeye stars Franthea Price in 1990 and Toni Foster in 1993. Stringer was named WBCA Coach of the Year in 1988 and 1993 and BTC Women's Basketball Coach of the Year in 1991 and 1993. In 1993 she received the *SI* Women's Basketball Coach of the Year honors and the WBCA Carol Eckman Award for her coaching spirit, integrity, and courage. Stringer made women's basketball more exciting, boosting home attendance. In 1988, 22,157 spectators attended the Iowa–Ohio State game at Carver-Hawkeye Arena, shattering the single-game national women's basketball attendance record.

In July 1995, Rutgers University (New Jersey) named Stringer its new women's basketball coach. She has compiled a 171–103 record there through the 2003–2004 season. Rutgers finished 26-4, ranked seventh nationally, and reached the third round of the NCAA Tournament in 1998–1999; and fared 22-7, ranked eighth nationally and reached the NCAA semifinals before losing 64-54 to the University of Tennessee in 1999–2000.

Altogether, Stringer compiled a 695-239 record through 2003–2004. Her .744 winning percentage ranks as the nation's tenth best and third highest for coaches with over 600 victories. Only two active women's basketball coaches have recorded more victories. In January 1994, Stringer became only the third woman to achieve 500 career victories. No other NCAA Division I women's basketball coach has taken three different teams to the NCAA Final Four.

Stringer has promoted the development of women's basketball internationally and organizationally. She coached U.S. teams touring the People's Republic of China in 1981, at the 1985 World University Games, and at the 1989 World Championship zone qualifications. Her team won a bronze medal at the 1991 Pan-American Games in Havana, Cuba. Besides helping start the WBCA, she participates on the Kodak All-America Selection Committee and serves on the Advisory Board of the WSF, ABAUSA, and Nike Shoes.

Stringer married William D. Stringer, an exercise physiologist, in 1971 and has three children, David, Janine (who has meningitis), and Justin. She took a five-week leave of absence from coaching following her husband's sudden death of a heart attack at age 47 in November 1992. Her careful analysis of opposition game plans, meticulously planned practices, brilliant game plans, 97 percent player graduation rate, devotion to charitable organizations, and role as mother best exemplify her.

BIBLIOGRAPHY: Arthur R. Ashe, *A Hard Road to Glory: A History of the African-American Athlete Since 1946* (New York, 1988); Janice A. Beran, letter to David L. Porter, February 15, 1994; *Des Moines* (IA) *Register*, March 23, 1988, pp. S1, S4; *Des Moines Register*, November 28, 1992, pp. S1, S4; *Des Moines Register*, March 30, 1993, p. S1; *Des Moines Register*, April 3, 1993, pp., S1–S2; *Des Moines Register*, January 21, 1994, p. S1; *Des Moines Register*, January 29, 1994, p. S1; Mike Douchant, *Encyclopedia of College Basketball* (Detroit, MI, 1995); *ESPN Sports Almanacs*, 2000, 2001, 2004 (New York, 1999, 2000, 2003); Nena Ray Hawkes and John F. Seggar, *Celebrating Women Coaches: A Biographical Dictionary* (Westport, CT, 2000); Cheryl Levitt, Iowa Intercollegiate Athletics, Iowa City, IA, memorandum to David L. Porter, April 13, 1994; Rosemarie Skaine, *Women College Basketball Coaches* (Jefferson, NC, 2001); *Street & Smith's College Basketball Yearbooks*, 1982–1994.

David L. Porter

STROM, Earl "Yogi" "The Pied Piper" (b. December 15, 1927, Pottstown, PA; d. July 10, 1994, Pottstown, PA), college and professional referee, was the son of Max Strom, a foreman in a bakery, and Bessie Strom. He married Yvonne Trollinger in 1952 and had five children, Margie, Susan, Stephan, Eric, and Jonathan.

From 1940–1941 to 1944–1945, Strom participated in football, baseball, and basketball at Pottstown (Pennsylvania) High School. After graduating in 1945, he served two years in the U.S. Coast Guard. Upon his discharge from active duty, Strom began officiating. He enrolled in Pierce JC in Philadelphia, Pennsylvania, graduating in 1951. Strom refereed football and basketball games at this level for nine years and began working ECAC and other college games for three additional seasons, schools. His skill and talent in handling a game ranked him high in the evaluations conducted by NBA officials.

Strom began officiating NBA games in 1957, starting 29 years of service with the NBA and three years with the ABA. His tenure as an NBA official ended June 1990 when he called the fourth game of the championship series between the Detroit Pistons and the Portland Trail Blazers. He brought about respect and admiration from owners, players, fans, and game officials because of his sense of fairness and his ability to control the game and ranks among the best-ever NBA officials.

Between 1957–1958 and 1989–1990, Strom officiated 2,400 NBA regular-season games and 295 NBA playoff games. He called seven NBA All-Star Games and 29 NBA and ABA Finals. Strom joined Mendy Rudolph and refereed all seven games of the 1961 NBA Finals between the Boston Celtics and the St. Louis Hawks, the only time this happened in NBA history. In 1967 and 1968, Strom served as the NBA Crew Chief.

The six-foot, 180-pound Strom was named the top referee in the NBA in a poll taken in 1990 by *USA Today*. In 1995, a year after his death, he was inducted into the Naismith Memorial Basketball Hall of Fame. He was also elected to the Pottstown Sports Hall of Fame in 1984 and the Pennsylvania Sports Hall of Fame in 1987.

BIBLIOGRAPHY: "Earl Strom," *Career Highlights*, http://www.jewsinsports.org (2003); "Earl Strom," *Highlights and Bio*, http://www.hoopball.com (2003); Jan Hubbard, ed., *The Official NBA Encyclopedia*, 3rd ed. (New York, 2000); Earl Strom with Blaine Johnson, *Calling the Shots* (New York, 1990).

John L. Evers

STURDY, Denise Long. *See* Andre, Denise Long Sturdy

STUTZ, Stanley J. (b. Stanley J. Modzelewski, April 14, 1920, Worcester, MA; d. October 28, 1975, New Rochelle, NY), college and professional athlete and referee, was the son of Matthew Modzelewski and Cornelia Modzelewski and starred in three sports at Classical High School in Worcester, Massachusetts, becoming the all-time leading scorer in Western Massachusetts high school basketball. Stutz earned a Bachelor's degree in 1942 from Rhode Island State University (now the University of Rhode Island), the alma mater of his high school basketball coach Chet Jaworski. He played basketball under legendary, flamboyant coach Frank Keaney* from 1938 to 1942. Keaney countered the era's static zone defenses by developing a "firehouse," fast-break style of offense and relied extensively on Stutz as one of his most prolific scorers. Although only five-feet ten-inches and 170 pounds, Stutz scored 1,730 career points in 80 college games for a 21.6 point average. These represented significant figures in an era of relatively low-scoring contests. His honors included making consensus Second Team All-America in 1941 and 1942, HAF 1942 Player of the Year, and three NIT All-Tournament teams (at the time, the most prestigious postseason tournament). He also played baseball at Rhode Island State.

The Baltimore Bullets (ABL) professional basketball team signed Stutz, who led that team to the 1946 ABL championship. He joined the New York Knicks (BAA) later that year and returned to Baltimore (BAA) for the 1948–1949 season before retiring as an active player. During his BAA career, Stutz scored 1,181 points in 166 games and tallied another 104 points in 11 playoff games. He held the New York Knicks playoff scoring record by tallying 30 points against the Cleveland Rebels in April 1947. Willis Reed* broke the scoring mark in 1969. A right guard, Stutz also paced the Knicks in regular-season free throws from 1946 to 1948 and scored on fast breaks, from drives, and from the corner.

Subsequently, Stutz won acclaim as a collegiate and NBA basketball referee. He officiated over 1,000 professional games, including the 1953 NBA All-Star Game, retiring in 1959. Stutz also coached both high school and amateur basketball teams and served as an executive and sales representative with several corporations in the New York area. He died while playing golf at Wykagel Country Club in New Rochelle, New York, leaving a widow, two sons, and a daughter. His memberships included the HAF Basketball Hall of Fame and Rhode Island State Hall of Fame.

BIBLIOGRAPHY: Kyle Crichton, "Keaney's Courier, R. I. State Basketball Players," *Collier's* 109 (February 28, 1942), p. 17; Mike Douchant, *Encyclopedia of College Basketball* (Detroit, MI, 1995); Larry Fox, *The Illustrated History of Basketball* (New York, 1974); Jan Hubbard, ed., *The Official NBA Basketball Encyclopedia*, 3rd ed. (New York, 2000); Neil D. Isaacs, *All the Moves: A History of College Basketball* (Philadelphia, PA, 1975); Neil D. Isaacs, *Vintage NBA* (Silver Spring, MD, 1996); Leonard Koppett, *24 Seconds to Shoot* (New York, 1968); *The NCAA Basketball Guide, 1939–1943* (New York, 1939–1943); *NYT*, October 31, 1975; Robert W. Peterson, *Cages to Jump Shots: Pro Basketball's Early Years* (New York, 1990); University of Rhode Island Sports Information Office, Kingston, RI.

Daniel R. Gilbert

SUMMITT, Patricia Sue Head "Pat" (b. June 14, 1952, Clarksville, TN), college player and coach, is the daughter of James Richard Head, a self-employed businessman, and Hazel (Albright) Head. Head graduated from Cheatham County High School in Ashland City, Tennessee in 1970, the University of Tennessee at Martin with a Bachelor's degree in physical education in 1974, and the University of Tennessee with a Master's degree in physical education in 1975. She lives with her husband, R. B. Summitt II, in Seymour, Tennessee, and has no children. As an undergraduate, Summitt led the U.S. women's basketball team to a silver medal in the 1973 World University Games in her first international competition. In 1975, she helped the U.S. basketball squad take a gold medal in the Pan American Games and played on the world championship team. The zenith of her competitive career came in helping the U.S. win the silver medal in the 1976 Summer Olympic Games at Montreal, Canada.

Summitt began her illustrious coaching career at the University of Tennessee in 1974 and has compiled a career 882-172 record there through the 2004–2005 season. During 20 of the past 28 years, she has led Tennessee to the Final Four in the AIAW and NCAA national tournaments. Her squads finished first six times, second seven times, and third six times. In 1986–1987, the Lady Vols finished 28-6 during the regular season and won their first NCAA championship by routing Louisiana Tech 67-44 at Austin, Texas. Forward Bridgette Gordon averaged 16.8 points and 6.8 rebounds to pace Tennessee during the regular season, while guard Tonya Edwards was selected MVP of the NCAA championship. Gordon and Edwards paced the 1987–1988 Lady Vols to a 28-2 regular-season mark and a number one national ranking, as Tennessee recorded the nation's highest team scoring average of nearly 90 points a game. Tennessee won the East regional tournament, but Louisiana Tech snapped the Lady Vols' 22-game winning streak 68-59 in the NCAA national semifinals at Long Beach, California. In 1988–1989, Tennessee finished 35-2, 8-1 in the SEC, and defeated Auburn (Alabama) University 76–60 in the NCAA Finals, with Bridgette Gordon being named MVP. Two years later, the Lady Volunteers fared 30-5 and triumphed over the University of Virginia 70-67 in overtime for another national title. Tennessee, aided by Chamique Holdsclaw*, captured three consecutive NCAA titles: over the University of Georgia 83-65 in 1996, against Old Dominion University (Virginia) 68-59 in 1997, and over Louisiana Tech University 93-75 in 1998. Summitt also guided Tennessee to the NCAA championship finals in 1995, 2000, 2003 and 2004, and has surpassed Jody Conradt* of the University of Texas as the winningest coach in Division I women's basketball. During the 2005 NCAA tournament, she passed Dean Smith* as the career victory leader among all Division I coaches. Other notable players have included Tamika Catchings*, Daedra Charles, and La Toya Davis. In addition, Summitt has coached numerous U.S. basketball Olympians, All-Americas, and international athletes. She also serves as Player Personnel Consultant for the Washington Mystics (WNBA).

As a coach in international competition, Summitt won two gold medals in 1977 with the U.S. Junior Women's National Team. In 1979, she coached the Women's National Team to gold medals at the world championship and William R. Jones Cup Games and to a silver medal in the Pan American Games. The next year, Summitt served as assistant coach of the U.S. Olympic team in the pre-Olympic qualifying tournament. Named the 1984 U.S. Olympic coach, she directed the U.S. team in 1983 to a silver medal in the world championship. In pre-Olympic competition and throughout the 1984 Olympic Games at Los Angeles, her team handily defeated all opponents to capture the first gold medal for the U.S. in women's basketball. Her international coaching record remained a marvelous 63-4 through 1985.

Summitt has been recognized as Coach of the Year by the WSF (1980), the *Shreveport* (LA) *Journal* (1981), and by Converse (1983, 1995, 1998). For several years, she was listed among the Outstanding Young Women of America. Summitt was inducted to the Woman's Sports Foundation Hall of Fame in 1990 and the Naismith Memorial Basketball Hall of Fame in 2000. Besides being on the Board of Trustees of the Naismith Memorial Basketball Hall of Fame, Summitt served as vice president of the ABAUSA and on the Women's Games Committee of the ABAUSA. In 1990, she became the first woman to receive the John Bunn Award from the Naismith Memorial Basketball Hall of Fame. She remains in constant demand as a conference speaker and a basketball clinician. Summitt, the prototype player for the 1960s, began her basketball in the fourth grade. As a player, she developed great instincts for the game, became an awesome defensive performer, rebounded with authority, took the ball to the hoop and yet effectively defeated zone defenses with accurate shots from the perimeter, and took charge of the game. She coaches the same way, with her record verifying the devastating effects for opponents.

BIBLIOGRAPHY: Mike Douchant, *Encyclopedia of College Basketball* (Detroit, MI, 1995); Pat Head Summitt to Angela Lumpkin, January 15, 1985; Pat Summitt, *Raise the Roof* (New York, 1998); Pat Summitt file, Naismith Memorial Basketball Hall of Fame, Springfield, MA; Chamique Holdsclaw, *Chamique*

(New York, 2000); *Tennessee Lady Vols, Basketball Media Guide*, 2003–2004 (Knoxville, TN, 2003).

Angela Lumpkin

SUTTON, Eddie (b. March 12, 1936, Bucklin, KS), college player and coach, graduated from Bucklin High School in 1954 and from Oklahoma State University (BSC), where he earned both the Bachelor's (1958) and Master's (1959) degrees. Sutton played guard for the legendary Hank Iba* averaging 6.6 points in his three-year varsity career.

Sutton's basketball coaching career began as a graduate assistant at Oklahoma State, followed by a 119-51 record as head coach at Tulsa (Oklahoma) Central High School from 1960 to 1966. He coached basketball at Southern Idaho JC, starting its basketball program. His 83-14 record from 1967 to 1969 there led to his selection as Creighton University (Nebraska; MVC) basketball coach. Sutton's five years at Creighton featured an 82-50 overall record and 2-1 mark in the NCAA Tournament. The University of Arkansas (SWC) hired Sutton, who took over a mediocre basketball program averaging under 10 wins the previous decade. Sutton made Arkansas a consistent winner, guiding nine NCAA appearances in 11 years and notching a 260-75 overall mark and 10-9 NCAA record. By nearly tripling attendance to a 9,000 average, he turned Arkansas' home court, Barnhill Arena, into one of the toughest places for visitors to play. His Razorbacks lost only eight games there. During this period, he was named SWC Coach of the Year four times and won that honor nationally twice. Ten Razorbacks, including Sidney Moncrief*, made the NBA. Sutton completed his tenure at Arkansas with the highest winning percentage in SWC history.

Unlike the Creighton and Arkansas jobs, Sutton assumed one of the most successful college basketball programs when he joined the University of Kentucky (SEC) as head coach for the 1985–1986 season. He had followed the distinguished Kentucky program by radio as a lad. The Wildcats preeminence was created by fellow Kansan Adolph Rupp*. Rupp's successor, Joe B. Hall, continued Kentucky's winning tradition and garnered an NCAA title in 1978. At one of the most demanding posts in college basketball, Sutton enjoyed immediate success with a 32-4 mark his first year. The Wildcats won the SEC regular-season and tournament crowns and reached the NCAA Final Eight before losing to LSU. He was named both SEC and national Coach of the Year in 1986. Sutton coached four more years at Kentucky, winning both the 1988 SEC regular season and tournament, then resigning in 1989. His overall 88-39 Kentucky record included his first losing season in 1988–1989 and a 5-3 NCAA tournament mark.

After a one-year absence from basketball coaching, Sutton returned to his alma mater at Oklahoma State. He has compiled a 351-135 overall record there through 2004–2005 and a 21-13 record in the NCAA Tournament. In his first year, the Cowboys won the 1991 BEC title. He became the first coach to take teams from four different universities to the NCAA Tournament. The Cowboys, led by center Bryant Reeves, finished with a 24–10 mark, but were upset by the University of Tulsa in the second round of the NCAA tournament. Oklahoma State finished 23-9 in 1994–1995 and lost to UCLA 74-61 in the NCAA semifinals. Under Sutton, the Cowboys fared 24-6 and reached the NCAA Regional Finals in 1999–2000, and 23-8 in 2001–2002 with an NCAA Tournament berth. The Cowboys, led by guards Tony Allen and John Lucas Jr., ended 27-3 in 2003–2004, won the BTwC tournament, and lost to Georgia Institute of Technology in the NCAA tournament. During 35 seasons, Sutton has compiled a 781-299 overall record and 39-26 record in NCAA Tournaments.

Sutton married Patsy Wright and has three sons, Steve, Sean, and Scott. Scott played for his father at Oklahoma State, while Sean started for his father at Kentucky.

BIBLIOGRAPHY: Mike Douchant, *Encyclopedia of College Basketball* (Detroit, MI, 1995); *Kentucky Basketball Encyclopedia* (Champaign, IL, 2000); Alan Ross, *Wildcat Wisdom* (Nashville, TN, 1999); *NCAA Men's Basketball Record, 2004* (Indianapolis, IN, 2003); *Oklahoma State University Basketball Media Guide, 2004–2005* (Stillwater, OK, 2004); Russell Rice, *Kentucky Basketball's Big Blue Machine* (Huntsville, AL, 1987); Alexander Wolff, "For Now He's the Cat's Meow," *SI* 63 (December 16, 1985), pp. 30–32, 36.

Thomas P. Wolf

SWOOPES, Sheryl Denise "Texas Tornado" (b. March 25, 1971, Brownsfield, TX), college and professional player, is the daughter of Billy Swoopes and Louise Swoopes. Her father left the family before she was born, leaving her mother to support a family of five. Her brothers taught her to play basketball. She graduated from Brownsfield (Texas) High School in 1989 and enjoyed a spectacular scholastic basketball career, being named the state's Female High School Player of the Year as a senior. The heavily recruited Swoopes signed a letter of intent to attend the University of Texas. After a few days on campus, she became homesick and returned to Brownsfield. Swoopes enrolled at South Plains JC in nearby Levelland, Texas. Besides setting 28 school records, she was named junior college All-America in 1990 and 1991 and was selected JC Player of the Year in 1991. She averaged 21.5 points, 11.9 rebounds, 146 assists, and 4.7 steals.

After transferring to Texas Tech University for her last two years, Swoopes led the Red Raiders to a 58-8 win-loss record and two SWC titles. She led Texas Tech to the NCAA tournament in 1991–1992, but failed to win the title. In 1992–1993, she won the SWC Player of the Year Award for the second time. In the NCAA tournament, Swoopes scored 53 points in the Dallas, Texas Arena, registered 31 points against Vanderbilt University in the semifinals, and netted 47 points against Ohio State University in the NCAA championship game, leading the Red Raiders to their first NCAA title. In the finale against the Buckeyes, she broke Bill Walton's* record of 44 points for the championship game. She scored a record 177 points in five games and averaged of 35.4 points. Her 78 points in NCAA Final Four remains a record for the women. Swoopes was named Outstanding Player of the Year and the MVP of the NCAA Final Four. She finished the 1992–1993 season with a 28.1 points average and was named Player of the Year by nine different organizations. Her jersey number 22 has been retired.

In 1994, Swoopes joined the U.S. National Women's team preparing for the 1996 Olympics. At Atlanta, she averaged 13 points and helped the United States win a gold medal. In January 1997, Swoopes signed with the Houston Comets (WNBA). Swoopes, one of the WNBA's original signings, suddenly got married to Eric Jackson. She gave birth to her son, Jordan in June 1997. The six-foot, 145-pound point guard starred for the WNBA champion Houston Comets from 1997 through 2000 and missed the 2001 season because of injury.

During her career with the Comets, Swoopes averaged 16.8 points, 5.2 rebounds, and 2.32 steals in 195 regular-season games through 2004. She was named the WNBA MVP and Defensive Player of the Year in 2000, 2002 and 2003. Swoopes was named All-WNBA First Team four times (1998–2000, 2002) and All-WNBA Second Team in 2003 and led voting for the WNBA All-Star Game three times (1999, 2000, 2002). Swoopes led the WNBA in scoring (20.8 point average) and steals (2.81 average) in 2000 and paced the WNBA in steals (2.48 average) in 2003. She ranks first in Comets history in assists (634), and second in scoring (3,280 points), rebounds (1,015) and blocked shots (162). In 25 career WNBA playoff games, Swoopes has tallied 403 points for a 16.1 point average, 150 rebounds, 82 assists, and 56 steals. She played in four All-Star Games, scoring only 29 points. Swoopes also performed on the gold medal winning 2004 U.S. Olympic Women's basketball team.

Swoopes became the first woman to have her own NIKE basketball shoe, "Air Swoopes," named after her. She may be best remembered as the woman who once played one-on-one against Michael Jordan*.

BIBLIOGRAPHY: Peter C. Bjarkman, *The Biographical History of Basketball* (Chicago, IL, 2000); "Sheryl Swoopes," *Africa-America News*, http://www.aframenews.com (2003); "Sheryl Swoopes," *Background*, http://www.wnba.com (2003); "Sheryl Swoopes," *Basketball*, http://www.sportsillustrated.cnn.com (2003); "Sheryl Swoopes," *Bio*, http://www.usbasketball.com (2003); "Sheryl Swoopes," *Statistics*, http://www.nba.com (2003); "Sheryl Swoopes," *University of Texas*, http://www. gballmag.com (2003); *TSN Official WNBA Guide and Register, 2004* (St. Louis, MO, 2004).

John L. Evers

T

TANENBAUM, Sidney "Sid" (b. October 8, 1925, Brooklyn, NY; d. September 4, 1986, Far Rockaway, NY), college and professional player, made consensus All-America as an NYU guard in 1946 and 1947. His honors included making the All-Metropolitan New York City All-Star basketball team three times and winning the Frank Haggerty Award in 1946 and 1947 as the outstanding metropolitan area hoopster. He sparked NYU to the 1945 NCAA Basketball Tournament finals against victorious Oklahoma (State) Agricultural and Mechanical College, pacing Violet scorers with 34 points in three tournament games. Tanenbaum, a six-foot, 160-pound HAF Basketball Hall of Fame member, was named the outstanding 1947 Jewish Athlete.

Tanenbaum suffered a broken right hand when he was 13 years old. His parents purchased a basketball for him to use during his rehabilitation, igniting a lifetime competitive fire. He made the New York City All-Scholastic basketball team while at Thomas Jefferson High School in Brooklyn's Brownsville section. Tanenbaum, who developed an outstanding two-handed setshot, amassed 992 points in four varsity NYU seasons under coach Howard Cann* and averaged 12.9 points in an era of slower-paced, deliberate-style basketball. He suffered from rheumatic fever as a child and experienced difficulty breathing during basketball games, requiring him to have a sprinkle of water and whiff of oxygen during time-outs. Ray Lumpp, a former NYU teammate, observed, "Basketball was Sid's life. He was master of the give and go and the setshot . . . and the crowds loved him."

Tanenbaum averaged 10.1 points in 1947–1948 for the New York Knicks (NBA), second-place Eastern Division finishers. New York traded him during the 1948–1949 season to the Baltimore Bullets (NBA), as he finished with an 8.5 point average. He quit after two NBA campaigns stating, "I didn't like the road [travel], and I have no regrets." His 70-game NBA career saw him tally 633 points, average 9.0 points, and record 163 assists. Tanenbaum owned a metal-stamping shop in Far Rockaway, Queens, and helped the neighborhood homeless find medical and legal assistance. He was fatally stabbed at his store, leaving behind his wife, Barbara (Wolfson) Tanenbaum, and two sons, Michael and Steven.

BIBLIOGRAPHY: Peter C. Bjarkman, *The Biographical History of Basketball* (Chicago, IL, 2000); Morgan G. Brenner, *College Basketball's National Championships* (Lanham, MD, 1999); Mike Douchant, *Encyclopedia of College Basketball* (Detroit, MI, 1995); Jan Hubbard, ed., *The Official NBA Basketball Encyclopedia,* 3rd ed. (New York, 2000); William G. Mokray, ed., *Ronald Encyclopedia of Basketball* (New York, 1963); *NYT*, September 6, 1986; Ken Rappoport, *The Classic* (Mission, KS, 1979); Ken Shouler et al., *Total Basketball* (Wilmington, DE, 2003); Sidney Tanenbaum file, Naismith Memorial Basketball Hall of Fame, Springfield, MA.

James D. Whalen and Wayne Patterson

TARKANIAN, Jerry "Tark the Shark" (b. August 8, 1930, Euclid, OH), college basketball player and coach, came from a poor Armenian family Tarkanian, whose father died when he was 11, moved from Ohio to California in 1946 with his mother, stepfather, sister, and brother. He attended Pasadena (California) High School and Pasadena City College and graduated with a Bachelor's degree from Fresno (California) State University in 1956. Tarkanian played basketball at each school, but was used primarily as a reserve at Fresno State. He married Lois Huter on November 3, 1956 and has four children, Pamela, Jodie, Danny, and George. Tarkanian earned a Master's degree in educational management from Redlands (California) University, while his wife earned a Ph.D. degree in human behavior from U.S. International University (California).

Tarkanian coached five years in California high schools, including San Joaquin Memorial (1956, 1957), Antelope Valley (1958), and Redlands (1959, 1960). As head coach of Riverside (California) City College (1962–1966), he compiled a 145-22 win-loss record. Riverside won California JC Championships in 1964 with a 35-0 mark, 1965 with a 31-5 state, and 1966 with a 33-1 record. Tarkanian secured a record fourth consecutive JC title with Pasadena City College in 1967 at 35-1. After the next season, he moved to California State University at Long Beach. His composite junior college record was 212-26 for an impressive .891 winning percentage.

At California State University-Long Beach, Tarkanian transformed an obscure basketball program into a nationally recognized one. The Forty Niners won five straight PCAA titles and participated in four NCAA postseason tournaments, losing three times to eventual national champion UCLA. Over five seasons, his teams never lost a home game (winning 65 in a row) and finished with at least 23 victories each season. Eight Long Beach players, including Chuck Terry, Ed Ratleff, and Leonard Gray, later played professional basketball. His cumulative win-loss record there came to 122-20 for an .859 winning percentage. Additionally, Tarkanian was named Professor of the Year and Salesman of the Year for promoting the university.

His basketball success continued at the University of Nevada–Las Vegas from 1973–1974 to 1991–1992. Over 15 seasons, the Runnin' Rebels compiled a 509-105 slate and appeared in the NCAA tournament 12 times and the NIT twice. Tarkanian became the second youngest NCAA Division I basketball coach to reach the 400-victory plateau. After initially belonging to the WCAA and being WCAA champions in 1975, the University of Nevada-Las Vegas competed as an independent for seven seasons. They then joined the PCAA, winning PCAA titles from 1982–1983 through 1987–1988. Nevada–Las Vegas compiled an impressive 97-9 mark in the PCAA from 1982–1983 through 1987–1988.

UNLV joined the BWC in 1989 and won or shared titles four consecutive seasons. The Runnin' Rebels finished 35-5 and won the 1990 NCAA championship, defeating Duke University (North Carolina) 103-73 in the Final. UNLV returned to the NCAA Final Four in 1991, with a 34-1 record, losing to Duke 79-77 in the semifinals.

Although known as a zone coach in JC and an inside-power coach at California State University–Long Beach, the towel-chewing Tarkanian used a fast-break, wide-open style of play at Nevada–Las Vegas. The Runnin' Rebels led the nation in team scoring in 1975–1976, 1976–1977, 1978–1979, and 1986–1987, and established an NCAA record of 110.5 points per game for an entire season in 1975–1976. The 29-3 1976–1977 team, among his best, set 15 NCAA records and reached the NCAA Final Four. A record six members of that squad were drafted by the NBA. His 1986–1987 squad, paced by Armon Gilliam and Freddie Banks, became the PCAA's first undefeated champion in 13 years and led the AP and UPI polls at the end of the regular season. Nevada–Las Vegas made the NCAA Final Four and defeated PCAA opponents by over 20 points a game. His 1989–1990 squad featured Larry Johnson*, Stacey Augman, and Anderson Hunt. Over two dozen Nevada–Las Vegas Tarkanian-coached players, including Ricky Sobers, Eddie Owens, Sidney Green, Reggie Theus, Banks, and Gilliam, have been drafted by the NBA. His son, Danny, played point guard for him and twice was named an Academic All-America.

Tarkanian, UPI Coach of the Year in 1983 and winner of a similar honor from *Basketball Times* in 1984, was the winningest active Division I coach with a remarkable .823 percentage in his first 20 seasons. Only coaches Clair Bee*, Adolph Rupp*, John Wooden* and Roy Williams* have compiled career winning percentages over 80 percent. Yet he remained a controversial coach, as the NCAA placed his schools on probation in 1974, 1977, and 1991. Tarkanian was equally known for working with "difficult" players and active community involvement. The Los Angeles Lakers (NBA) sought to hire him as coach in 1978, but he stayed at Nevada–Las Vegas. He became assistant athletic director in 1983 and has written one book on basketball coaching. Tarkanian left UNLV following a 26-2 record in 1991–1992, with the Runnin' Rebels on probation. He coached the San Antonio Spurs (NBA) to a 9-11 mark at the start of the 1992–1993 season. He returned to Fresno State as head coach in 1995 and guided the Bulldogs to a 147-77 mark through the 2001–2002 season. Tarkanian ranks seventh in wins and sixth in winning percentage with a 778-202 mark and a .794 percentage in 31 seasons.

BIBLIOGRAPHY: Mike Douchant, *Encyclopedia of College Basketball* (Detroit, MI, 1995); Richard Harp and Joseph McCullough, *Tarkanian: Countdown of a Rebel* (New York, 1984); Ray Kennedy, "427: A Case in Point," *SI* 40 (June 10, 1974), pp. 86–100, and (June 17, 1974), pp. 24–30; Ronald L. Mendell, *Who's Who in Basketball* (New Rochelle, NY, 1973); *NCAA Men's Basketball Records, 2004* (Indianapolis, IN, 2003); *TSN Official NBA Register, 1991–1992* (St. Louis, MO, 1991); Alexander Wolff, "The Son Has Also Risen," *SI* 60 (February 20, 1984), pp. 30–40.

Dennis S. Clark

TATUM, Reece "Goose" (b. May 3, 1921, Calion, AR; d. January 18, 1967, El Paso, TX), professional player, performed with the Harlem Globetrotters and Harlem Magicians. The son of a traveling Methodist preacher, the gifted athlete starred in football, basketball, and baseball. His nickname "Goose" referred to how he looked when catching a football, but baseball proved Tatum's first love. Tatum originally signed with Abe Saperstein's* black baseball team in Minneapolis–St. Paul, Minnesota as an outfielder and first baseman in 1941. A colorful player, he enjoyed great rapport with the crowd and was moved by Saperstein to first base to be closer to the spectators. Tatum played first base in the Negro Leagues with the Birmingham Black Barons in 1941 and 1942, Cincinnati Clowns in 1943, and Indianapolis Clowns from 1946 to 1949 with mediocre results. Saperstein in 1942 made him part of his Harlem Globetrotters basketball team. Teamed with Marques Haynes*, the six-foot six-inch, 190-pound Tatum left his mark in the sport.

Tatum's greatest physical asset was the size of his hands, which enabled him essentially to play and control the ball with one hand. His contributions to the Globetrotters' routines included the "roll," where he would roll the ball to teammates instead of tossing or bouncing it. The "swing" was another Tatum contribution, whereby he would stand and swing the ball around his hips while opposing guards watched in bewilderment. He also pioneered holding the ball one-handed above his head whether passing or shooting a hookshot. This style was copied by Wilt Chamberlain*, Connie Hawkins*, and Kareem Abdul Jabbar* in the NBA. After his inaugural season with the Globetrotters, Tatum entered the armed services. For the next three years, he played basketball for the Lincoln (Nebraska) Army Air Base team. At the Air Base, Tatum perfected the overhead hookshot and made it one of his trademarks. Unfortunately, he disappeared from the Globetrotters periodically without permission or notice, leading to his eventual resignation in 1955. When Tatum played, he remained without question the greatest drawing card in basketball during the 1940s and early 1950s. Tatum's absence caused a similar absence of spectators.

Tatum proved the consummate showman and a gifted basketball player. Within the Globetrotters system, his enormous talents manifest themselves. He set individual-game scoring records in Chicago with 55 points and San Francisco with 64 points. A month-long suspension by owner Saperstein caused Tatum to leave the Globetrotters in August 1955 and form his own team called the Harlem Magicians. Tatum was joined in this venture by ex-Globetrotter Haynes. Tatum continued to play with the Magicians into the mid-1960s when a liver ailment often hospitalized him. He died of a heart attack.

BIBLIOGRAPHY: *Harlem Globetrotters, Souvenir Book, 1967*; *The Lincoln Library of Sports Champions*, vol. 12 (Columbus, OH, 1974); William Nack, "On the Road Again and Again," *SI* 62 (April 22, 1985), pp. 78–92; James R. Riley, *The Biographical Encyclopedia of the Negro Baseball Leagues*

(New York, 1994); Ken Shouler et al., *Total Basketball* (Wilmington, DE, 2003); George Vecsey, *The Harlem Globetrotters* (New York, 1973); Josh Wilker, *The Harlem Globetrotters* (New York, 1997).

William A. Sutton

TAURASI, Diana Lurena (b. June 11, 1982, Chino, CA), college player, is the daughter of Mario Taurasi, a machinist and former professional soccer goalie, and Liliana Taurasi, a part-time waitress, and started playing basketball in the second grade. At Don Lugo High School, she scored a school record 3,047 points in four years. In her senior year, Taurasi averaged 23.5 points, 8.4 rebounds, and 6.1 assists, won the Cheryl Miller Award, Naismith National High School Player of the Year, and *Parade magazine* National High School Player of the Year, and was named All-America First Team by *USA Today* and *Parade*. Upon graduation in 2000, she selected the University of Connecticut for its well-known basketball program.

Under coach Geno Auriemma's* direction, the Connecticut Huskies reached the NCAA Final Four in 2001. The six-foot, 170-pound Taurusi enjoyed an impressive rookie season as a guard-forward averaging 10.9 points, ranking second on the team in assists (109) and first in three-pointers (71) and free throw percentage (.878). She was the first rookie ever receiving the Most Outstanding Player award at the 2001 BEaC championship and was selected to the BEaC All-Rookie Team. Featuring four high-profile seniors and sophomore Taurasi, the Huskies captured another national championship in 2002 with a perfect 39-0 season. Taurasi averaged 14.5 points and 5.3 assists, was named 2001 Kodak All-America, and made the 2002 All-BEaC First Team and BEaC All-Tournament Team. In 2002–2003, Taurasi led the Huskies with 17.9 points, 6.1 rebounds, 4.4 assists and 1.2 blocks per game. Under her leadership, Connecticut achieved a 37-1 record, a record 70-game winning streak, and defeated archrival University of Tennessee 73-68 in the title game, in which Taurasi scored 28 points. The 2002–2003 Huskies became the first team to win the NCAA title without a senior on their roster. Taurasi was named the consensus National Player of the Year, All-America, 2003 BEaC Player of the Year, and the NCAA Final Four Most Outstanding Player. In 2003–2004, Taurasi again paced Connecticut with 15.5 points, 3.9 rebounds, and 4.9 assists per game. The Huskies finished 25-4 and again defeated Tennessee 70-61 in the national title game, in which Taurasi scored 17 points. Connecticut became just the second team in NCAA Women's Division I history with three consecutive national titles. Taurasi again was named consensus National Player of the Year, All-America, the 2004 BEaC Player of the Year, and the NCAA Final Four Most Outstanding Player, averaging 19.8 points. She won ESPY awards as the best College female athlete in 2003 and 2004 and as best female athlete in 2004.

The Phoenix Mercury (WNBA) selected Taurasi first overall in the April 2004 draft, making her just the second guard to be the top WNBA draft pick. She played on the gold-medal winning 2004 U.S. Olympic Team. Taurasi earned WNBA Rookie of the Year and All-WNBA First Team honors in 2004, finishing sixth in scoring (17.0 point average, and tenth in assists with 132 (3.9 average). She also averaged 4.4 rebounds and 1.2 steals, helping the Mercury improve by nine games over 2003 with a 17–17 record and nearly attain a playoff berth.

Nicknamed "Dee," Taurasi speaks Spanish fluently, has an older sister, Jessica, and earned a B.A. degree in communication science.

BIBLIOGRAPHY: Michael Bamberger and Kelli Anderson, "Driving Force," *SI* 98 (January 20, 2003), pp. 54–56; Dick Patrick, "Best to Come for Taurasi," *USA Today*, February 20, 2002, p. 8C; Kelly Whiteside, "Taurasi Takes Women's Game to a New Level," *USA Today*, April 7, 2004, pp. 1C–2C.

Di Su

TAYLOR, Charles "Chuck" (b. June 24, 1901, Brown County, IN; d. June 23, 1969, Indianapolis, IN), professional player and promoter, was an accomplished businessman and basketball equipment innovator. Taylor graduated in 1918 from Columbus (Indiana) High School, where he started four years in basketball and made All-State two years. Although never playing varsity college basketball, he enjoyed an 11-year career as a player in early pro leagues.

Taylor's special contribution, however, came as a basketball entrepreneur and salesman. He developed the first specialized basketball shoe in 1921 and spent the remainder of his active life expanding what had begun as a business venture into a career of promoting the game he so loved. In 1922, Taylor presented his first organized basketball clinic at the North Carolina State University. His instructional clinics took him to cities throughout the U.S. and abroad, including Hawaii, South America, Mexico, Puerto Rico, Canada, Africa, and Europe. Taylor continued specialized instruction in the roundball game by inaugurating the popular *Converse* (Rubber Company) *Basketball Yearbook* in 1922. He helped select All-America college basketball teams after 1932 and coached the U.S. Air Force All-Star basketball team during World War II. His U.S. Air Force tenure also featured continued presentation of his patented basketball clinics at bases through the U.S. and overseas, earning him a special military commendation. Taylor was elected into the Naismith Memorial Basketball Hall of Fame in 1968 in recognition of his early pioneering efforts in the popularizing and the promotion of America's national game.

BIBLIOGRAPHY: Peter C. Bjarkman, *The Biographical History of Basketball* (Chicago, IL, 2000); Zander Hollander, ed., *The Pro Basketball Encyclopedia* (Los Angeles, CA, 1977); Charles Taylor file, Naismith Memorial Basketball Hall of Fame, Springfield, MA.

Peter C. Bjarkman

TAYLOR, Fredrick Rankin "Fred" (b. December 3, 1924, Zanesville, OH; d. January 6, 2002, Columbus, OH), college and professional athlete and coach, won most recognition for his basketball coaching achievements. After graduating from Zanesville (Ohio) High School in 1943, Taylor excelled in basketball and baseball at Ohio State University. He lettered three years in both sports and played basketball under Coach William Dye. The six-foot three-inch, 201-pound Taylor started at forward on a BTC championship team that finished third in the NCAA national tournament. In 1950, he received All-America status as a baseball first baseman. Taylor played professional baseball for the Washington Senators (AL) organization from 1950 to 1954. He appeared in only 22 major league games, batting .191 and knocking in four runs.

Taylor accepted the Ohio State University head basketball coaching job in 1959 and directed the Buckeyes to numerous championships throughout the next 18 years. His successes began in his second season as head coach in 1959–1960, when Ohio State captured the BTC championship and claimed the NCAA title with a 75-55 victory over the University of California. Taylor's next two seasons (1960–1961 and 1961–1962) again brought him BTC championships and runner-up finishes at the NCAA Tournament. Taylor led the Buckeyes to Co-BTC championships in 1962–1963 and 1963–1964, giving him five straight BTC titles. He also coached the Buckeyes teams to BTC championships in 1967–1968 and 1970–1971. Taylor retired from coaching in 1976 after achieving a .653 winning percentage and a 297-158 win-loss record.

Taylor served on the USOBC from 1964 to 1972 and as president of the NABC in 1972–1973. He later managed a U.S. national team to a FIBA world championship in 1978 and a U.S. Pan American Gold Medal team in 1979. Taylor coached Naismith Memorial Basketball Hall-of-Famers John Havlicek* and Jerry Lucas* and 1984 Olympic Gold Medal coach Bob Knight* of Texas Tech University. Taylor twice was named Coach of the Year by the USBWA and UPI and was elected to the Naismith Memorial Basketball Hall of Fame in 1985.

BIBLIOGRAPHY: Peter C. Bjarkman, *Big Ten Basketball* (Indianapolis, IN, 1994); Mike Douchant, *Encyclopedia of College Basketball* (Detroit, MI, 1995); *NCAA Men's Basketball Records, 2004* (Indianapolis, IN, 2003); Ohio State University, Sports Information Department, Columbus, OH; Billy Packer and Roland Lazenby, *College Basketball's 25 Greatest Teams* (St. Louis, MO, 1989); Fred Taylor file, Naismith Memorial Basketball Hall of Fame, Springfield, MA.

Jeff Sanderson and Wayne Patterson

TEAGUE, Bertha Frank (b. September 17, 1906, Carthage, MO; d. June 13, 1991), high school basketball coach, was the daughter of John Frank, a road contractor. Her family soon moved to Amity, Arkansas, where she graduated from high school in 1923. On October 16, 1924, Frank married James E. Teague in Arkadelphia, Arkansas and moved to Oklahoma. As an elementary school teacher in Cairo, Oklahoma, she organized an outdoor girls team and taught them basketball fundamentals. Interestingly, Teague had never played the game. Teague taught first grade there for 39 years. She majored in Design and Art at East Central State University and Oklahoma State University, graduating in 1932 with a Bachelor's degree in education. She had one child, Geneva.

At Byng High School, Teague became the nation's most successful girls' basketball coach. Over 43 seasons from 1927 to 1969, her teams took 1,157 games and lost only 115 contests for a remarkable .910 winning percentage. The Lady Pirates won 38 conference titles, 40 district championships, and 22 regional crowns. Byng High School took eight state tournament championships and finished second on seven other occasions. Five of Bertha's teams recorded undefeated seasons, while 18 squads recorded 30-plus victories. Her *average* season mark was 27-3.

Teague's squads won 98 straight games between 1936 and 1939. During this glory period, Byng High School annexed four Oklahoma state titles (1936, 1937, 1938, and 1940) in five years. In 1938 Byng High School participated in the AAU's national tournament in Wichita, Kansas, where they competed against older, more experienced college and commercial teams. Byng High School lost in the first round, but won the consolation bracket trophy and the admiration of the spectators. Other outstanding squads included the 1950–1952 Lady Pirates that won three district and regional crowns and two state championships, the 1955–1957 group that posted a 97-8 mark but lost in the state championship game all three years, and the undefeated 27-0 1965 squad. In a storybook ending to a long coaching career, a short jumpshot at the buzzer gave her last team a 46-45 victory over Elk City High School in the 1969 state championship game.

Teague's book, *Basketball for Girls* (1962), outlined her philosophy and coaching methods. She believed the key elements of a good athlete were a strong desire to win and good physical conditioning. Teague's portrayal of competitive sport as a healthy activity for women was not a widely held view from the 1930s until the late 1960s, but is readily accepted today. She spread her ideas during summer clinics in the South and Midwest and served on the WNRC from 1949 to 1960. Teague also helped organize the OHSGBCA and founded the Bertha Teague Mid-America Girls Basketball Tournament, which annually brings together top girls' teams from several states for a holiday tournament. Her numerous honors have included being the first woman selected for the Oklahoma Athletic Hall of Fame (1971) and a Special Service Award from the NHSACA (1975). She remained active in local and state affairs and served on the Jim Thorpe Memorial Athletic Hall of Fame Commission. In 1985, Teague became one of the initial three women inducted into the Naismith Memorial Basketball Hall of Fame.

BIBLIOGRAPHY: Peter C. Bjarkman, *The Biographical History of Basketball* (Chicago, IL, 2000); Wallace R. Lord, ed., "Bertha Frank Teague Retires," *Converse Yearbook, 1969*, p. 51; Ken Shouler et al., *Total Basketball* (Wilmington, DE, 2003); Bertha Frank Teague, "Basketball for Girls," *Converse Yearbook, 1952*, p. 34; Bertha Frank Teague, *Basketball for Girls* (New York, 1962).

Dennis S. Clark

THOMAS, Isiah Lord, III (b. April 30, 1961, Chicago, IL), college and professional basketball player, coach, and executive, is the son of Isaiah Thomas II, an International Harvester plant supervisor, and Mary Thomas, a cook, housekeeper, and human services counselor, attended West-chester (Illinois) St. Joseph's Prep School, and was one of the flashiest ball handlers and best pure point guards ever to play basketball. The youngest of nine children from a ghetto family on Chicago's West Side, Thomas excelled as a high school honors student at suburban St. Joseph's School and won an athletic scholarship.

A childhood basketball prodigy, he already provided halftime displays of dribbling and shooting at neighborhood CYL games when three years old. Thomas was offered a basketball scholarship to Indiana University by coach Bobby Knight* after demonstrating the same sparkling ball-handling and offensive play in leading St. Joseph's to second place in the 1979 Illinois State High School Tournament and earning national high school All-America accolades. He was chosen an All-BTC his freshman season at Indiana University and made consensus All-America his sophomore campaign.

Two brilliant seasons at Indiana University were not, however, the happiest times of Thomas' basketball life because the All-America point guard repeatedly conflicted with fiery coach Knight. Although Thomas respected and admired Knight's basketball leadership, he objected to what often appeared as impolite and dehumanizing behavior toward players. Knight once grabbed him by the jersey to administer admonishment before national television cameras during a 1979 Pan-American Games contest. Despite flammable moments with coach Knight and poor early-season play by the 1980–1981 Hoosiers, the sophomore and team captain led his Indiana University squad to a national championship victory over the University of North Carolina in the NCAA Finals at Philadelphia. The dramatic victory and NCAA tournament MVP performance marked both the pinnacle and swansong of his brief collegiate basketball career. The first-round and second overall (after fellow Chicagoan Mark Aguirre*) hardship draft choice of the Detroit Pistons (NBA) in the 1981 NBA college draft, Thomas entered the NBA as a much-heralded but slightly undersized 20-year-old rookie in the fall of 1981. But skeptics were quickly answered, as his impact on the NBA was immediate.

Not since Bob Cousy* had any diminutive guard influenced playing styles and captured fan interest as had Thomas during his 13 NBA seasons in Detroit. Besides averaging 19.2 points from 1981–1994, Thomas ranked second only to Earvin "Magic" Johnson* as NBA leader in assists, and led the NBA in minutes played (3,093) his second season. He set an NBA single-season record for assists in 1984–1985 with 1,123, breaking the old mark of 1,099 assists set by Kevin Porter.* Thomas, known for his penetrating style of play and for accurate long-range shooting, ranked second in the NBA in three-point field goal percentage in 1982–1983. He also passed Dave Bing* as the Pistons all-time career leader in assists during only his third NBA year. Thomas, *TSN* NBA Rookie of the Year in 1982, was only the fourth rookie ever selected to start in an NBA All-Star Game. Thomas was an All-Star Game starter 11 NBA seasons and earned honors as the All-Star Game MVP of the 1984 game in Denver, posting 21 points, 15 assists, and four steals in 39 minutes. In 1986, he again was selected All-Star Game MVP, scoring 30 points and dishing out 10 assists at Dallas, Texas.

Thomas' finest all-around season came in the 1983–1984 campaign, when he averaged 21.3 points, 11.1 assists (second in the NBA), and 2.5 steals (also second), played over 3,000 minutes, and gained All-NBA First Team honors. Thomas averaged 24.1 points in leading Detroit to the 1986–1987 Eastern Conference Finals before the Pistons lost to the Boston Celtics. He also made the All-NBA First Team in 1985 and 1986 and the All-NBA Second Team in 1983 and 1987. His point production dropped to 19.5 points per game in 1987–1988, but he finished seventh in the NBA in assists (678) and led the 54-28 Pistons to the Central Division title. Detroit, paced by Thomas, upset the Boston Celtics in the Eastern Conference Finals to reach the NBA Finals for the first time. Thomas set an NBA playoff record for most points in one quarter by scoring 25 points in the third quarter of Game Six, but injured his ankle in the same contest. The Lakers defeated the Pistons four games to three in the hard-fought series. Thomas led Detroit to NBA championships in 1989 and 1990. In 1988–1989, the Pistons compiled a 63-19 record, triumphed over the Chicago Bulls the Eastern Conference Finals, and swept the Los Angeles Lakers in the NBA Finals. The Pistons followed with a 59-23 record in 1989–1990 and defeated the Portland Trail Blazers in the five-game NBA Finals. Thomas was named 1990

NBA Finals MVP, averaging 27.7 points, 7.0 assists, and 5.2 rebounds. Detroit made the NBA playoffs the next two seasons, but struggled in his final two campaigns. Thomas retired in 1994 as the greatest player in Pistons history after suffering a torn Achilles tendon. During 13 NBA seasons, he scored 18,822 points, recorded 9,061 assists, and made 1,861 steals in 979 games. In 111 playoff games, Thomas led the franchise with 2,261 points (20.4 average), 987 assists (8.9 average), and 234 steals. The Pistons retired his uniform number 11 jersey. Despite foregoing his final two years of collegiate eligibility for a lucrative pro career, Thomas continued studies at Indiana University in fulfilling a promise to his mother, Mary, to earn his college degree. He concentrated undergraduate studies on criminal justice in a prelaw curriculum, graduating in May 1987. He and his wife, Lyne Kendah, have two children, Joshua and Lauren.

In May 1994, Thomas became part owner, executive vice president of basketball operations, and general manager for the Toronto Raptors, Canada's first NBA expansion franchise. After his bid to buy the entire team was rejected in 1997, he broadcast for NBC Sports. Thomas served as a majority owner of the Continental Basketball Association in July 1999, but the league folded a year later. In July 2000, he became the head coach for the Indiana Pacers (NBA). The Pacers finished 41-41 in 2000–2001, 42-40 in 2001–2002, and 48-34 in 2002–2003, but were eliminated in the first round of the NBA playoffs each year. Thomas was fired as Pacers coach following the 2002–2003 season, having compiled a 131-115 regular-season and 5-10 playoff record. In January 2004, Thomas became president of the New York Knicks (NBA). He tried to rejuvenate the Knicks, replacing coach Don Chaney with Lenny Wilkens* and acquiring guards Stephen Marbury and Penny Hardaway* in a trade with the Phoenix Suns. The Knicks surged to seventh place in the Eastern Conference with a 39-43 record and made the playoffs, being swept by the New Jersey Nets in the first round. New York slipped to 33-49 in 2004–2005, switching coaches and missing the playoffs. Thomas was named to the NBA's 50th Anniversary All-Time Team in 1996 and to the Naismith Memorial Basketball Hall of Fame in 2000.

BIBLIOGRAPHY: Ira Berkow, "Isiah Thomas' Giant Step to the Pros," *The Complete Handbook of Pro Basketball* (New York, 1981); Barbara Bigelow, ed., *Contemporary Black Biography*, vol. 7 (Detroit, MI, 1994); David Bradley, "The Importance of Being Isiah," *Sport* 79 (May 1988), pp. 24–27 29; *TSN Official NBA Register, 2004–2005* (St. Louis, MO, 2004); Paul C. Challen, *The Book of Isiah: The Rise of a Basketball Legend* (Toronto, Canada, 1996); *Current Biography Yearbook* (New York, 1989); Jan Hubbard, *The Official NBA Encyclopedia*, 3rd ed. (New York, 2000); Isiah Thomas with Matt Dobek, *Bad Boys! An Inside Look at the Detroit Pistons 1988–89 Championship Season* (Indianapolis, IN, 1989); Isiah Thomas, *The Fundamentals: 8 Plays for Winning the Games of Business and Life* (New York, 2001); Isiah Thomas file, Naismith Memorial Basketball Hall of Fame, Springfield, MA.

Peter C. Bjarkman

THOMPSON, David O'Neil (b. July 13, 1954, Shelby, NC), college and professional player, is the son of Vellie Thompson and Ida Thompson. One of 11 children, Thompson became an outstanding basketball player at Crest High School in Shelby, North Carolina, and received a scholarship to play basketball at North Carolina State University. He starred for North Carolina State from 1971 until 1975, leading the Wolfpack to some of its finest basketball seasons. During his sophomore year, the six-foot four-inch, 195-pound swingman averaged 24.7 points and led his team to a 27-0 record. Since North Carolina State was on probation for recruiting violations involving Thompson, the Wolfpack could not play in the NCAA Tournament. The next year (1973–1974), however, his team ended the nine-year reign of John Wooden's* UCLA squads by defeating the Bruins 80-77 in two overtimes in the semifinal game of the NCAA Tournament. Despite a head injury suffered during a fall in the regional finals. Thompson scored 28 points in the game. In the final game, he scored 21 points and pulled down seven rebounds to help North Carolina State defeat Marquette University for the NCAA championship. Thompson, known for his extraordinary jumping ability and quickness, was chosen the NCAA Tournament's

MVP. Although the Wolfpack enjoyed less success during his senior year, he averaged 26.8 points over his college career and shot 546 from the field and .763 from the foul line. He was selected as an All-America in 1973, 1974, and 1975 and was chosen Player of the Year in his junior and senior years by several polls.

After graduation, Thompson was drafted by both the NBA and the ABA. In the 1975–1976 season, he played for the Denver Nuggets (ABA) in the final ABA year. Thompson, who averaged 26.0 points, was chosen MVP in the ABA All-Star Game and the ABA's Rookie of the Year. In 1976, Denver and three other ABA teams joined the NBA. Thompson came into the NBA as a potential superstar. A forward and guard, he possessed quickness and shooting ability that created problems for defenders. During his first five NBA years (from 1976–1977 to 1980–1981), Thompson averaged 25.2 points per game and made All-NBA First Team in 1977 and 1978. Denver made the playoffs during three of those seasons (1976–1977, 1977–1978, 1978–1979), with Thompson averaging 25.5 points in the playoffs.

Although Denver again made the playoffs in 1981–1982, Thompson lost his starting position and averaged only 14.9 points. He was traded to the Seattle SuperSonics (NBA) in 1982, but drug problems and injuries slowed him. During the 1983–1984 season, Thompson sustained a serious career-ending knee injury in a fall at a New York City nightclub. During his NBA career, he scored 11,264 points and averaged 22.1 points. He authored *Skywalker* (2003). In 1996, he was inducted into the Naismith Memorial Basketball Hall of Fame. Thompson married Cathy Barrow on January 31, 1979 and has two children, Erika and Brooke.

BIBLIOGRAPHY: Peter C. Bjarkman, *ACC: Atlantic Coast Conference Basketball* (Indianapolis, IN, 1996); Peter C. Bjarkman, *The Biographical History of Basketball* (Chicago, IL, 2000); Ron Morris, ed., *ACC Basketball: An Illustrated History* (Chapel Hill, NC, 1988); Bruce Newman, "Flying High Once More," *SI* 53 (November 17, 1980), pp. 36–39; *NYT*, March 24, 1974; *NYT*, March 26, 1974; *TSN Official NBA Register, 1984–1985* (St. Louis, MO, 1984); David Thompson et al., *Skywalker* (Champaign, IL, 2003); David Thompson file, Naismith Memorial Basketball Hall of Fame, Springfield, MA; *Washington Post*, March 7, 1978.

Jon S. Moran

THOMPSON, John (b. September 2, 1941, Washington, DC), college and professional player and college basketball coach, graduated from John Carroll High School in Washington, D.C. A high school All-America, Thompson led his team to 55 consecutive victories and two city championships. He attended Providence (Rhode Island) College, helping the Friars to two NITs (including one championship) and one NCAA Tournament. At Providence, Thompson majored in economics and received the Outstanding Senior Award on graduation in 1964. He also was named New England Player of the Year. Thompson was drafted in 1964 by the Boston Celtics (NBA) and sat on the bench for two straight world championship seasons as backup for the sensational Bill Russell*. In 74 games, he scored 262 points and averaged 3.5 points.

Thompson left the NBA to coach at St. Anthony's High School in Washington, D.C., and remained there from 1966 to 1972. His 128-22 record brought him in 1972 to Georgetown (Washington, D.C.) University, which was seeking to improve its basketball program from a dismal 3-23 record the previous season. By 1974–1975, he led the Hoyas to the NCAA Midwest Regionals. Thompson served as an assistant coach for the U.S. Olympic team in 1976 and took his Georgetown team to the NIT semifinals. Georgetown made it to the NCAA Tournament finals for the first time ever in 1982, and appeared in the Midwest Regionals the next year. His squad of Patrick Ewing*, David Wingate, Fred Brown, Gene Smith, Michael Graham, and Ralph Dalton defeated the University of Houston 84-75 to garner the 1984 NCAA championship. Georgetown's depth clearly wore down the opposition in that contest.

The championship marked a social phenomenon. Georgetown, the elite Roman Catholic school, became the center of attention through its star center, Ewing, and Thompson, both African Americans. When Georgetown's president was asked to comment on reaction of Georgetown's immediate Washington community to the NCAA victory, he replied, "Not much—most of the people next to us are into running with the hounds." It was a different story, however, in the rest of the predominantly black capital city. Ewing was popular and was named All-America as a junior, but Thompson predicted it would be difficult for his team to repeat as champions. The Georgetown University Hoyas lost out in the 1985 NCAA Finals to Villanova University (Pennsylvania) despite having a 35-3 record. In 1986–1987, Georgetown tied for first in the BEaC with a 12-4 mark and finished 29-5 overall, being paced by Reggie Williams. Thompson was named Big East Conference and UPI Coach of the Year. Thompson was named head coach of the 1988 U.S. Olympic Team, which finished third. All his teams except for the 1990–1991 aggregate won at least 21 games from 1988–1989 through 1996–1997. In 1988–1989, Georgetown finished 29-5, captured the BEaC title, and reached the fourth round of the NCAA tournament. His 1991–1992 squad fared 22-10, shared first in the BEaC, and split two NCAA Tournament games. Led by Allen Iverson,* the Hoyas finished 26-7, ranked fourth naturally, and reached the fourth round of the NCAA tournament. Thompson retired following the 1998–1999 season, having compiled a record of 596 wins and 239 losses and having guided the Hoyas to 17 NCAA and three NIT events. Thompson not only had exceeded expectations at Georgetown, but also, perhaps more important, played a dynamic role as leader for black student athletes. Thompson was elected to the Naismith Memorial Basketball Hall of Fame in 1999. His son, John III, coaches basketball at Georgetown University.

BIBLIOGRAPHY: Peter C. Bjarkman, *The Biographical History of Basketball* (Chicago, IL, 2000); Richard Coren, *Providence College Basketball* (Charleston, SC, 2002); Mike Douchant, *Encyclopedia of College Basketball* (Detroit, MI, 1995); *Georgetown Basketball Yearbook, 1988* (Washington, D.C., 1988); *NCAA Men's Basketball Records, 2004* (Indianapolis, IN, 2004); *NYT*, April 3, 4, 1984; Leonard Shapiro, *Big Man on Campus: John Thompson and the Georgetown Hoyas* (1991); John Thompson file, Naismith Memorial Basketball Hall of Fame, Springfield, MA.

John David Healy

THOMPSON, John A. "Cat" (b. February 10, 1906, St. George, UT; d. October 7, 1990, Idaho Falls, ID), college player and high school coach, grew up in St. George, Utah and enjoyed basketball, baseball, and farming. The 5-foot 10-inch, 160-pound guard attended Dixie High School from 1923 to 1926 and led his team to the Utah State High School title in 1925. That same year, Dixie High School captured second place at the national tournament in Chicago, Illinois by winning six times in five days. In one game Thompson made 56 points, an incredibly high number considering the era's low scores. After high school graduation, he attended Montana State University. The clever, quick, superbly conditioned Thompson earned his nickname there. During a practice session, Montana State coach G. Ott Romney said of him, "That isn't a human being—that's a treecat." The nickname always remained with him.

At Montana State, Thompson became one of the nation's best players. In 1927–1928, he led the Golden Bobcats to a 36-2 record, was selected to the All-RMC team and was named All-America. The team was nicknamed the "Wonder Five." Montana State continued its wondrous ways during the 1928–1929 season, even though Schubert R. Dyche replaced the highly successful Romney. Under Dyche, Montana State again compiled a 36-2 record. Thompson repeated as All-RMC and All-America, helping Montana State capture the RMC championship and become the HAF National Champions for 1928–1929. He was named Player of the Year.

Although Utah State University upset Montana State University by taking the RMC championship in 1929–1930, the Golden Bobcats enjoyed a memorable eastern trip by defeating Purdue University (Indiana), the University of Nebraska, Marquette University (Wisconsin), and Penn State University while losing to the University of Pittsburgh, Butler University (Indiana), and Loyola University of Chicago. Thompson remained one of the nation's top players and made All-America for the third consecutive season. During his three-year career, Thompson scored 1,539 points.

After his collegiate career, Thompson played one year of AAU basketball and became basketball coach at Idaho Falls (Idaho) High School. He coached there from 1931 to 1946 with two of his squads winning consecutive state titles. After his coaching career, Thompson entered the sporting goods business in Idaho Falls. Thompson, the first real "name" player from the Montana area, is a member of the HAF Hall of Fame and Naismith Memorial Basketball Hall of Fame (1962).

BIBLIOGRAPHY: Mike Douchant, *Encyclopedia of College Basketball* (Detroit, MI, 1995); Zander Hollander, ed., *The Pro Basketball Encyclopedia* (Los Angeles, CA, 1977); Ronald L. Mendell, *Who's Who in Basketball* (New Rochelle, NY, 1973); Paul Soderberg and Helen Washington, eds., *The Big Book of Halls of Fame in the United States and Canada* (New York, 1977); John Thompson file, Naismith Memorial Basketball Hall of Fame, Springfield, MA; Alexander M. Weyand, *The Cavalcade of Basketball* (New York, 1960).

Curtice R. Mang

THOMPSON, Tina Marie (b. February 10, 1975, Los Angeles, CA), college and professional player, has two brothers and one sister and attended Inglewood (California) Morningside High School, where she was named 1993 California AAA Player of the Year in basketball. The six-foot two-inch, 178-pound forward played four seasons from 1994 to 1997 at the University of Southern California, assisting her team to a 77-37 record, three NCAA tournaments, and one NCAA Final Eight. In 1993–1994, Thompson was named PTC Freshman of the Year and Freshman All-America by *BT*, and set the USC freshman rebounding record with a 10.5 rebounds average. Her other collegiate honors included making AP All-America Second Team in 1997, Kodak All-District VIII Regional Team in 1995 to 1997, a silver medal in the 1995 World University Games, a gold medal in the 1996 R. William Jones Cup, and All-PTC First Team in 1995, 1996 and 1997. Thompson graduated in 1997 with a B.S. degree in sociology and hoped to return for a law degree. She finished her college basketball career among USC's all-time leaders in scoring (2,248 points, fifth), rebounds (1,168, fifth), rebound average (10.2 per game, third), scoring average (19.7 points, fourth), field goal percentage (50.6 percent, eighth), and blocked shots (103, seventh).

Thompson was the first overall pick of the Houston Comets in the first round of the 1997 inaugural WNBA draft. As part of the "Big Three" with Cynthia Cooper* and Cheryl Swoopes*, she helped the Comets win the 1997, 1998, 1999, and 2000 WNBA championships. Thompson was named to the 1997 All-WNBA First Team. The trio was pictured on boxes of Special K cereal, making the Comets the first women's team to be featured on a Kellogg's box. She made the All-WNBA Second Team from 1999 to 2002, started in WNBA All-Star Games from 1999 to 2002, and was named WNBA Player of the Week on June 24, 2001. After eight WNBA seasons, she ranked as the league's second all time scorer, the second-ever WNBA athlete to post 1,000 rebounds, and the Comets' all-time leader in points (3,699), rebounds (1,599), blocked shots (197) and minutes played (7,911). Thompson, the seventh WNBA player to score 1,000 points, the fifth player in WNBA history to score 2,000 career points, and the third player in WNBA history to score 3,000 points works with several charities and events that help underprivileged children. She has averaged 12.7 points and 7.1 rebounds in 27 WNBA playoff games and played on the gold medal winning 2004 U.S. Olympic Women's basketball team. Thompson missed the start of the 2005 season becuse of pregnancy.

BIBLIOGRAPHY: Matt Maciero and Leigh Klein, eds., *My Favorite Moves: Shooting like the Stars* (Terre Haute, IN, 2003); David G. Oblender, ed., *Contemporary Black Biography*, vol. 25 (Farmington Hills, MI, 2000); *TSN Official WNBA Guide and Register, 2004* (St. Louis, MO, 2004); *USA Basketball: Tina Thompson,* http://www.usabasketball.com/bioswomen/tina_thompson_bio.html (2003); WNBA.com: Tina Thompson Player Info, http://www.wnba.com/playerfile/tina_thompson/index.html?nav=page (2003).

Jeannie P. Miller

THURMOND, Nathaniel "Nate" (b. July 25, 1941, Akron, OH), college and professional player, is the son of a Firestone rubber plant worker. Thurmond graduated from Akron (Ohio) Central High School, where he made the

All-City basketball team. He attended Bowling Green (Ohio) State University from 1959 to 1963 and was named All-America his final basketball season there. At Bowling Green, he scored 1,356 career points and averaged 17.8 points. Thurmond, who established a NCAA record for most rebounds in a game with 31, set a Falcons record with 488 rebounds in the 1962–1963 season and made 1,295 career rebounds in 76 games. From 1960 through 1963, he was selected to the All-MAC First Team.

Thurmond was selected by the San Francisco Warriors (NBA) as the third pick of the 1963 NBA draft. Always a team-oriented player, he was forced to play at forward during his first NBA seasons. When Wilt Chamberlain* was traded to the Philadelphia 76ers in 1965, the 6-foot 11-inch, 235-pound center returned to his natural position and developed into one of the truly great centers of his time. He ranked somewhat better defensively than Chamberlain and somewhat better offensively than Bill Russell*.

With quickness and long hands, a smooth outside shooting touch, effective rebounding, flow-reversing shot-blocking, and commitment to team play, Thurmond exhibited an outstanding offensive-defensive balance. His 14,437 lifetime points scored and 14,464 total rebounds—both for 15.0-per-game averages—verify his well-rounded skills. During his NBA career, he made 5,521 field goals (42 percent) and 3,395 free throws (66.7 percent) and was selected to the All-Star teams in 1965–1968, 1970, and 1973. Besides being chosen to the All-NBA Rookie Team (1964), Thurmond made the All-NBA Defensive First Team (1969, 1971) and All-NBA Defensive Second Team (1972, 1974). He also holds the NBA record for most rebounds in one quarter with 18 against Baltimore on February 28, 1965.

Thurmond's goal of playing for an NBA championship team, however, was not realized. Successive physical problems, including two back injuries, a broken hand, and two serious knee injuries, hampered him. A strained relationship with San Francisco Warriors owner Franklin J. Mieuli, who in 1970 made a particularly insensitive and shocking comment to a newspaperman questioning Thurmond's attitude for the game and commitment to the team, contributed to that. Thurmond was traded to the Chicago Bulls (NBA) in September 1974 and Cleveland Cavaliers (NBA) in November 1975. During his twilight NBA seasons before his retirement in 1977, he played a substantially diminished role. Thurmond, who was selected as a player to the Naismith Memorial Basketball Hall of Fame in 1985, always enjoyed the respect of his peers for his dignity and wit as a person and his intense, unselfish play throughout his career. Thurmond served as director of community relations for the Golden State Warriors (NBA) from 1981 to 1995 and as community relations ambassador since 1995.

BIBLIOGRAPHY: Mike Douchant, *Encyclopedia of College Basketball* (Detroit, MI, 1995); Merv Harris, *The Lonely Heroes* (New York, 1975); Jan Hubbard, ed., *The Official NBA Encyclopedia*, 3rd ed. (New York, 2000); Ken Shouler et al., *Total Basketball* (Wilmington, DE, 2003); *TSN Official NBA Register, 2004–2005* (St. Louis, MO, 2004); Nate Thurmond file, Naismith Memorial Basketball Hall of Fame, Springfield, MA.

Gustavo N. Agrait

TISDALE, Wayman Lawrence (b. June 6, 1964, Tulsa, OK), college and professional basketball player, is the son of L. L. Tisdale, a Baptist minister and Deborah Tisdale. At Booker T. Washington High School in Tulsa, Oklahoma Tisdale led his team to the Class 5A basketball title in 1980–1981. In his senior season, he was selected to virtually every high school All-America team. Converse Rubber Company named him its National Prep Player of the Year. He averaged 23.7 points and 11.8 rebounds.

The six-foot nine-inch, 250-pound, left-handed Tisdale attended the University of Oklahoma from 1982 to 1985 and led the Sooners to three appearances in the NCAA Tournament. In the 1985 event, Oklahoma made the finals of the Midwest Regional before losing 63-61 to Memphis (Tennessee) State University. The three-time BEC Player of the Year and three-time consensus All-America became the only player in college basketball history named to the first team as a freshman, sophomore, and junior.

On December 6, 1982, Tisdale scored 51 points against Abilene (Texas) Christian University for an NCAA single-game freshman scoring record. His performance also eclipsed the University of Oklahoma's single-game scoring mark of 43, set in 1975 by Alvan Adams. Named MVP of Hawaii's Rainbow Classic, he completed his first season with 810 points (24.5 points average) and 341 rebounds (10.3 rebounds average). Tisdale led Oklahoma his sophomore year to a 29-5 record and the most victories ever by a BEC squad. After establishing a BEC-record 61 points against the University of Texas–San Antonio on December 28, 1983 and shattering several BEC Tournament records, he earned the MVP award. Tisdale scored 919 points (27.0 points average) with 329 rebounds (9.7 rebounds average) as a sophomore and ranked second in scoring behind Michael Jordan* on the 1983 U.S. Pan-American Team.

The leading rebounder on the 1984 gold medal U.S. Olympic Basketball Team, Tisdale became the BEC career scoring leader as a junior against Northwestern Louisiana State University on January 12, 1985. He captured his third consecutive BEC scoring title and again was chosen MVP in the BEC Tournament. Tisdale became the University of Oklahoma's career rebounding leader with 1,048, placing him third best in BEC history. He became one of only three players in BEC history, along with Cliff Meely of the University of Colorado and Steve Stipanovich of the University of Missouri, to rank among the BEC's top 10 in both career scoring and rebounding.

Tisdale, known for his high-arching, left-handed, turn-around jumpshot, established a Sooners single-game record with 22 rebounds on November 26, 1984 against the University of Arkansas–Little Rock. Electrifying the crowds with his alley-oop slam dunks, he scored in double figures in 103 of the 104 games he played at the University of Oklahoma. Tisdale owned or shared 17 Sooners records and 12 BEC standards. He tallied 932 points for a single-season BEC mark and a 25.2 points average and collected 378 rebounds for a 10.2 rebounds average as a junior. During his three college seasons, Tisdale scored 2,661 points (twentieth in NCAA history) for a 25.6 points average. He recorded 1,048 rebounds for a 10.1 rebounds average, compiled a .578 field goal percentage and scored at least 30 points in 33 games.

Tisdale passed up his senior year to enter the 1985 NBA draft and was selected in the first round by the Indiana Pacers. Only Patrick Ewing* preceded him in the draft selections.

Tisdale spent 12 seasons in the NBA, performing for the Indiana Pacers (NBA) from 1985 until being traded in February 1989, the Sacramento Kings (NBA) from 1989 through August 1994, and the Phoenix Suns (NBA) from September 1994 through the 1996–1997 season. His best season came in 1989–1990 when he averaged a career-high 22.3 points. During 12 NBA seasons, Tisdale scored 12,878 points (15.3 point average) and made 5,117 rebounds (6.1 average) in 840 regular season games. He appeared in 22 playoff games, averaging 7.1 points. Tisdale and his wife, Regina, live on a 20-acre farm outside Tulsa. He is a left-handed bass player and jazz singer in a band and in 2004 recorded a CD, *Hang Time.*

BIBLIOGRAPHY: Mike Douchant, *Encyclopedia of College Basketball* (Detroit, MI, 1995); Jan Hubbard, ed., *The Official NBA Encyclopedia*, 3rd ed. (New York, 2000); *NCAA Men's Basketball Records, 2004* (Indianapolis, IN, 2003); *TSN Official NBA Register, 1997–1998* (St Louis, MO, 1997); Alexander Wolff, "A New Breed of Sooner Boomer," *SI* 58 (February 28, 1983), pp. 30–34; U.S. Olympic Basketball Trials brochure, 1984; *University of Oklahoma Media Guide, 1984–1985* (Norman, OK, 1984).

John L. Evers

TOBEY, David (b. May 1, 1898, New York, NY; d. January 25, 1988), college and professional player, coach, referee, and author, ranked among the best all-time officials. Tobey participated in baseball, basketball, and track and field at DeWitt Clinton High School from 1912 to 1916 and baseball, basketball, soccer, and track and field at Savage School for Physical Education from 1916 to 1918. During Savage's undefeated basketball seasons in 1917 and 1918, he led the squad in scoring. Tobey, who later earned Bachelor of Science (1935) and Master of Arts (1940) degrees from NYU, also starred on the University Settlement House Whirlwind Club team from 1910 to 1913 and captained the Glencoe AC squad from 1917 to 1920. Glencoe

AC won the city club championship in 1918 and finished runner-up in 1919, as Tobey scored 24 of his team's 26 points in the final game. Tobey played professionally from 1919 to 1926 with Peekskill, New York, Ebling, and the New York Knickerbockers. He retired as a player after scoring the winning basket for the Lou Gehrig All-Star Team to defeat the world champion Original Celtics of New York.

During his 24-year officiating career (1918–1938, 1942–1945), Tobey handled professional games in New York City through 1926 and then top Eastern college games until his retirement. He officiated the first game to experiment with the three-person referee system (Georgetown [Washington, D.C.] University against Columbia University [New York]), the initial East–West game, three Army-Navy battles, and many premier Madison Square Garden contests in New York. At the 1945 NIT, he finished his officiating career with the St. John's University–University of Rhode Island game. As a high school and college basketball coach, Tobey compiled an impressive 715-331 win-loss record. From 1927 to 1942, Tobey coached both St. Ann's Academy and the Savage School for Physical Education. St. Ann's captured eight divisional basketball titles, while his early Savage teams won 35 consecutive contests. Tobey in 1947 began his most challenging basketball coaching job with the Cooper Union (New York) College squad. Cooper Union offered no athletic scholarships, did not enjoy a home-court facility, and boasted the nation's highest academic entrance criteria. Tobey compiled a 112-116 win-loss record in 12 seasons there, despite having only eight players with any high school experience. In 1960, Cooper Union dropped its entire athletic program. He also coached baseball, football, track and field, soccer, golf, and cross-country at Kearny (New Jersey) and DeWitt Clinton High Schools.

Tobey conducted basketball clinics, delivered lectures, wrote numerous articles for *Scholastic Coach* magazine, and authored *Basketball Officiating* (1944). The first book written on the subject, *Basketball Officiating* discussed one- and two-person officiating systems and player-coach-referee relations. Tobey, who married Dorothy Langley of West Englewood, New Jersey, and had no children, was enshrined into the Naismith Memorial Basketball Hall of Fame as a referee in 1961.

BIBLIOGRAPHY: Peter C. Bjarkman, *The Biographical History of Basketball* (Chicago, IL, 2000); David Tobey file, Naismith Memorial Basketball Hall of Fame, Springfield, MA.

Catherine M. Derrick

TOMJANOVICH, Rudolph, Jr. "Rudy" (b. November 24, 1948, Hamtramck, MI), college and professional player and coach, was the oldest child of Rudolph Tomjanovich Sr. and Katherine Moditch. His father, an autoworker, shoemaker, and garbage collector, had a drinking problem, which his mother was employed as an autoworker. Of Croatian decent, he and his sister grew up in poverty. Tomjanovich, driven to prove he was good, took up basketball at age 12 after realizing he could not star in baseball. After being cut from the freshman basketball team, he challenged his coach to a game of one-on-one and was allowed on the team. Through hard work, Tomjanovich became a basketball star as a high school junior. As a senior, the six-foot eight-incher averaged 43 points. He compiled a 3.5 grade average and was given a basketball scholarship to the University of Michigan.

At Michigan, Tomjanovich was named All-BTC three-times, All-America twice, and team captain, and held seven Wolverine scoring and rebounding records. His jersey was retired in 2003. He was selected as the second pick in the 1970 NBA draft by the San Diego Rockets (NBA). The Rockets moved to Houston in 1971. He married his wife, Sophia, in 1970 and had two daughters.

Tomjanovich played his entire 11-year NBA-career with the Rockets, appearing in 768 games and making 631 starts. He enjoyed a career .501 field goal percentage, averaged more than 20 points in four seasons and 17.4 points altogether, led the 1976–1977 division championship team in scoring, and was selected NBA All-Star forward five times. Tomjanovich was injured by a punch on December 9, 1977 while trying to stop a fight. The injury resulted in five surgeries, adversely affecting his playing career and changing NBA policy regarding fighting and officiating.

Tomjanovich retired as an NBA player in October 1981 and became a Rockets' assistant coach in 1983. He was made head coach in February 1992 and led them to the franchise's only two NBA titles over the New York Knicks and Orlando Magic in 1994 and 1995, respectively. Tomjanovich coached the U.S.A. Basketball Senior National Team in 1998 and the undefeated, gold-medal U.S. Olympic Basketball Team in 2000. He was diagnosed with bladder cancer on February 18, 2003 and missed his first game in 11 years while undergoing surgery. Tomjanovich resigned after the 2002–2003 season, having compiled a 503-397 regular-season record and 57-39 playoff mark. In July 2004, he replaced Phil Jackson* as head coach of the Los Angeles Lakers (NBA). The stress of coaching the Lakers wore him down physically, leading to his resignation in February 2005. Tomjanovich guided the Lakers to a 24-19 mark, giving him 527 career victories and 416 losses.

BIBLIOGRAPHY: Peter C. Bjarkman, *Big Ten Basketball* (Indianapolis, IN, 1994); *Detroit (MI) Free Press*, March 27, 2003, p. 8G; John Feinstein, *The Punch: One Night, Two Lives and the Fight that Changed Basketball Forever,* (Boston, MA, 2002); Roland Lazenby, *The NBA Finals* (Indianapolis, IN, 1996); *NYT*, March 19, 2003, p. C22; *NYT*, March 27, 2003, p. C20; Ken Shouler et al., *Total Basketball* (Wilmington, DE, 2003); *TSN Official NBA Guide, 2004–2005* (St. Louis, MO, 2004); *TSN Official NBA Register, 2003–2004* (St. Louis, MO, 2003); Sports Information, University of Michigan, 2003; Rudolph Tomjanovich with Robert Falkoff Jr., *A Rocket at Heart* (New York, 1997).

Keith McClellan

TOWER, Oswald "Ossie" "Mr. Basketball" (b. November 23, 1883, North Adams, MA; d. May 28, 1968, West Caldwell, NJ), college player, coach, and referee, played a dominant role on the formation and development of the sport as a member from 1910 to 1960 of the NBRC. He succeeded George Hepbron* in 1915 as editor of the *Basketball Guide* and served as the official rules interpreter until his retirement in 1960. Tower, a prominent high school and college basketball and football referee for 35 years, was inducted as a charter member of the Naismith Memorial Basketball (1959) and HAF halls of fame as a contributor. Nicknamed "Mr. Basketball," in 1942 he received the Harold M. Gore Award at the sport's half-century celebration as the individual who did the most for basketball. The citation read: "The game was born in the mind of Dr. Naismith, but nourished in the mind of Oswald Tower."

The 5-foot 10½-inch, 145-pound Tower starred in football, basketball, and baseball at North Adams (Massachusetts) Drury High School and graduated from there in 1901. He was employed as an errand boy for two years with the local Windsor Print Works, earning sufficient money and a scholarship to enroll at Williams College in Massachusetts. Tower performed at guard for the Purple basketball squad and was named First Team All-America in 1907. A four-year star from 1903–1904 to 1906–1907 on teams that compiled a combined 62-14-1 record (the tie was a disputed game with Syracuse [New York] University in 1906), he captained and coached the Williams unit that captured the 1907 New England basketball championship. Tower, after graduation in 1907 from Williams College, taught English and mathematics and coached football, basketball, and baseball for three years at Wilbraham (Massachusetts) Academy. In 1910 he joined the faculty of Phillips Academy in Andover, Massachusetts as a coach and Mathematics instructor and remained there until 1949. He served as dean of the faculty the last five years.

Tower dressed neatly, stood erectly, had blue eyes and graying brown hair, and wore glasses. He was dignified, sincere, analytical, dedicated, and influential. Coaches and referees turned to him for the final word on basketball rules interpretation. Tower received volumes of mail and late-night telephone calls during the basketball season. No exceptions were taken to his rulings. He reversed the outcome in 1927 of a Swarthmore College–Muhlenberg College basketball game when the referee failed to hear the whistle ending the game as the winning shot was made. A man of vision, Tower favored elimination of the center jump and establishment in pro basketball of the 24-second shooting rule. He became one of the first boosters of the NBA and was awarded a lifetime pass to Boston Celtics games by founder Walter A. Brown*. Tower, who married Helen Boyle and had two sons and two daughters, wrote several textbooks and served as a member of the Pan-American Games Committee and secretary of the Board of Trustees of Lawrence Academy. Mrs. Tower once stated, "The weather was never too stormy or the journey too long to keep my husband from answering the call of basketball."

BIBLIOGRAPHY: Peter C. Bjarkman, *The Biographical History of Basketball* (Chicago, IL, 2000); Boston *Sunday Globe*, November 22, 1964; William G. Mokray, ed., *Ronald Encyclopedia of Basketball* (New York, 1963); *NYT*, May 30, 1968; Oswald Tower file, Naismith Memorial Basketball Hall of Fame, Springfield, MA; Alexander M. Weyand, *The Cavalcade of Basketball* (New York, 1960).

James D. Whalen and Wayne Patterson

TRESTER, Arthur L. (b. June 10, 1878, Pecksburg, IN; d. September 8, 1944, Indianapolis, IN), administrator, helped develop the IHSAA into the finest organization of its kind in the nation. He graduated from Plainfield Academy in 1897, Earlham College (Indiana) in 1904, and Columbia University (New York) in 1913. Trester's early career was devoted to public school instruction in Indiana, where he served as classroom teacher, coach, high school principal, and public school superintendent. In 1911, Trester organized the statewide tournament for determining an Indiana high school basketball champion. This tournament has come to be known fondly over the past half-century as "Hoosier Hysteria." His crucial role in statewide high school athletics commenced in earnest with his appointment as secretary to the struggling IHSAA in 1913. Under his guiding hand, the IHSAA grew to over 800 member schools by the time he ascended to the commissioner's office in 1922. Trester already had played a dominant role in freeing the IHSAA from both the specter of debt and the manipulations of local politicians. The IHSAA under Trester became a model for numerous other states establishing such governing bodies for public school athletics. From its earliest days, the showcase of the IHSAA remained its boys' state basketball tournament. Under Trester's administrative expertise, established political integrity, and magnetic personality, the tournament became a state showpiece and a recognized model of administrative efficiency. In recognition of his administrative and promotional support of high school basketball, Trester was inducted into the Naismith Memorial Basketball Hall of Fame as a contributor in 1961.

BIBLIOGRAPHY: Zander Hollander, ed., *The Pro Basketball Encyclopedia* (Los Angeles, CA, 1977); Ronald L. Mendell, *Who's Who in Basketball* (New Rochelle, NY, 1973); Herb Schwomeyer, *Hoosier Hysteria: A History of Indiana High School Boys Basketball*, 6th ed. (Greenfield, IN, 1970); Bob Williams, *Hoosier Hysteria: Indiana High School Basketball* (South Bend, IN, 1982).

Peter C. Bjarkman

TUBBS, Billy (b. March 5, 1935, St. Louis, MO), college athlete and coach, is the son of Oscar Tubbs and Bessie Tubbs and grew up in Ft. Smith, Arkansas. Oscar died when Billy was an infant, while his mother died just prior to his entrance into high school. Tubbs moved to Tulsa, Oklahoma, where he lived with the family of his married brother, Wayne. He graduated from Central High School in 1953 and played basketball at guard, performing "racehorse" style basketball with the "Firehouse Five." Wayne commented, "Getting Billy involved in athletics was the best thing to happen to him because he was a tough street kid, and he could have gone either way." Tubbs enrolled in 1953 at Lon Morris JC in Jacksonville, Texas, helping basketball coach O. D. Adams's fast break offense. He led Lon Morris to the 1955 national JC finals and made the 1955 JC All-America team at guard. In September 1955, Tubbs transferred to Lamar University (Texas), where he played guard two seasons for coach Jack Martin. He averaged 6.7 points, as the 1955–1956 Cardinals finished fourth in the LSC with a 12-12 win–loss record. In 1956–1957, Tubbs averaged seven points for the 14-11, fifth-place Lamar squad. He earned his Bachelor's degree in physical education from Lamar in 1958 and his Master's degree in physical education from Stephen F. Austin University in 1959. Crockett High School in Beaumont, Texas, appointed him in 1959 as a teacher and head basketball coach. His first season produced a 21-11 mark.

From 1960 to 1971, Tubbs served as Lamar assistant basketball coach under Jack Martin. The Cardinals finished at .500 or better in eight of those seasons. The 1962–1963 Lamar quintet compiled a 22-5 record and won its third consecutive LSC title, while the 1963–1964 and 1968–1969 Lamar teams won SoC titles. Lamar enjoyed its second-best season record with a 20-4 mark in 1968–1969. In 1971, Southwestern University in Georgetown, Texas, named Tubbs head basketball coach. Under Tubbs, Southwestern achieved a composite 31-24 win-loss record from 1971 to 1973. Tubbs returned to the assistant coach's level at NCAA Division I North Texas State University from 1973–1974 through 1975–1976.

Lamar University hired Tubbs in 1976 to revive its program after six consecutive losing seasons. After finishing 12-17 in 1976–1977, the Cardinals won three consecutive SoC titles with a 25-5 composite conference record and 63-29 overall record. The 1978–1979 Lamar team became the first Cardinal quintet to participate in the NCAA Division I basketball championships, defeating favored University of Detroit (Michigan). The 23-9 Cardinals set a new school record for season wins. The 22-11 1979–1980 Lamar team again represented the SoC in the NCAA tournament. Tubbs had built the Cardinals into a basketball power with a 75-46 overall record.

In 1980, the University of Oklahoma (BEC) selected Tubbs to build the Sooner basketball fortunes, providing him with a new arena, an ample budget, a school of national prominence, and several talented in-state high school players to recruit. The 1980–1981 Sooners struggled to an 8-19 seventh-place BEC finish. Tubbs became the all-time winningest Oklahoma basketball coach with a composite 333-132 win–loss record through 1993–1994. The Sooners won four BEC championships (1984, 1985, 1988–1989) and participated in eight consecutive NCAA Division I tournaments (1983–1990)—a BEC record—and another in 1992. The Sooners won 263 games and lost only 81 contests from 1983 to 1993, achieving at least 30 wins in the 1984–1985, 1987–1988, and 1988–1989 seasons. The 1987–1988 Oklahoma quintet, considered by many to be the most exciting collegiate team ever, averaged 102.9 points, compiled a 35-4 records, attained a Sooner record for season victories, and reached the 1988 NCAA Division I championship game, losing 83-79 to BEC foe the University of Kansas.

Al McGuire*, former NCAA championship coach at Marquette University, remarked, "Tubbs had been a pathfinder in the Big Eight, showing that a running team can win big, and Oklahoma will remain a dynasty as long as he stays." Tubbs had built the basketball program mostly around in-state talent. Wayman Tisdale* from Tulsa gained the most recognition for Sooners basketball. At Oklahoma from 1982–1983 through 1984–1985, Tisdale attained consensus All-America three times at forward. Oklahoma enjoyed 24-9, 29-5, and 31-6 marks, respectively, reaching the 1985 NCAA Tournament Final Eight. Tubbs's son, Tommy, was a Sooners letterman at guard in 1984 and 1985, and numerous other Sooners helped establish Oklahoma as a perennial national basketball power. The Oklahoma style, "the best defense is a good offense," sometimes was called "Billy Ball." The 1990–1991 team recorded Tubbs's tenth consecutive 20-victory season, losing to Stanford University (California) in the NIT Finals. The Sooners fared 21-9 in 1991–1992, sharing second in the BEC and making the NCAA Tournament.

Tubbs coached at Texas Christian University (WAC) from 1995 through 2002, compiling a 187-119 record. TCU enjoyed its best season in 1997–1998, finishing 27-6, winning the WAC title, and making the NCAA Tournament. Tubbs became athletic director at Lamar University (SoC) in 2002 and assumed head basketball coach duties in 2003 after Mike Deane departed, compiling an 11-18 record in 2003–2004 and 14-11 mark in 2004–2005. During 30 seasons, he boasts a 620-326 regular-season record and 18-12 NCAA Tournament record. Tubbs and his wife, Pat, also have a daughter, Taylor, another Sooner alumna, and reside in Beaumont, Texas.

BIBLIOGRAPHY: Mike Douchant, *Encyclopedia of College Basketball* (Detroit MI, 1995); *Lamar University Basketball Media Guide, 1979–1980, 2003–2004* (Beaumont, TX, 1979, 2003); *Lamar University Sports News*, May 15, 1990; *NCAA Men's Basketball Records, 2004* (Indianapolis, IN, 2003);

Hal Nuwer, "Call Him Mr. Tubbs," *Sport* 79 (December 1988), pp. 72–76; Mike Treps, interview with Robert Saunders, March 22, 1990; *University of Oklahoma Basketball Media Guide, 1993–1994* (Norman, OK, 1993); Rush Wood, interview with Robert Saunders, March 22, 1990.

Robert C. Saunders and Wayne Patterson

TUCKER, Gerald "Gerry" (b. March 14, 1922, Douglass, KS; d. May 1979, West Bloomfield Hills, MI), college and amateur player and coach, excelled as a six-foot four-inch, 210-pound center-forward. After leading Winfield High School to consecutive Kansas state basketball championships in 1939 and 1940, Tucker played basketball under coach Bruce Drake* at the University of Oklahoma. In 1942–1943, he earned consensus Second Team All-America honors and led the Sooners to the NCAA Tournament, where they lost in the first round to the University of Wyoming, the eventual champion. After serving three years in the U.S. Army, Tucker returned to Oklahoma for his senior year in 1946–1947. The Sooners finished 24-7 and lost to the College of Holy Cross (Massachusetts) in the championship game of the NCAA Tournament. Tucker led all scorers with 22 points and won All-America honors for the second time. In 69 games, he talled 864 points and averaged 12.8 points.

Tucker started the next three years for the Phillips 66ers, the best team in AAU basketball. In 1948 Phillips defeated the University of Kentucky in the Olympic basketball tournament, as Tucker was named an alternate on the 1948 Olympic team. In 1949 and 1950, he was selected to the AAU All-America teams.

Tucker retired as a player after 1950, but returned to the Phillips 66ers basketball program as an assistant basketball coach in 1953 and head basketball coach from 1954 through 1958. Tucker's teams won four NIBL championships and the 1955 AAU national tournament in Denver, Colorado. The highlight of his coaching career came in 1956, when Phillips defeated the College All-Star team, led by Bill Russell*, in the 1956 Olympic tournament. Tucker was named coach of the 1956 Olympic team, which included five Phillips 66ers and was led by the brilliant Russell. His pressing defense befuddled international teams, which could not come within 30 points of the Americans. The U.S. easily won the gold medal.

Tucker retired from coaching after the 1958 season, but continued to work for Phillips until his death. He and his wife, Deeon, had five children, Billy, Marty, Brooke, Lynne, and Treat.

BIBLIOGRAPHY: Tom Boyd and Daniel B. Oroege, *Phillips The First 66 Years* (Bartlesville, OK, 1983); Mike Douchant, *Encyclopedia of College Basketball* (Detroit, MI, 1995); Adolph M. Grundman, "Basketball Before It Was Big Business," unpublished manuscript in author's possession.

Adolph H. Grundman

TWYMAN, John Kennedy "Jack" (b. May 21, 1934, Pittsburgh, PA), college and professional player and broadcaster, graduated from Pittsburgh (Pennsylvania) Central Catholic High School in 1951 and the University of Cincinnati (Ohio) in 1955. The hardworking, six-foot six-inch Twyman became one of the best pure-shooting forwards in the first two decades of the NBA. He also became one of the most dedicated players in NBA history, practicing over 100 foul shots, 200 jumpshots, and 150 setshots per day during the off-season summer months. Twyman, a four-year starter at the University of Cincinnati, was the school's second all-time leading rebounder on graduation and earned several All-America honors in 1954–1955.

A second-round draft pick and the tenth player chosen overall by the Rochester Royals (NBA) in 1955, Twyman enjoyed an 11-year pro playing career with the Rochester-Cincinnati franchise and never averaged below double figures in scoring until his final campaign. In his three most outstanding seasons as one of the greatest cornermen in the pro game, he registered scoring averages of 25.8, 31.2, and 25.3 points between 1958–1959 and 1960–1961. His 31.2 scoring average in 1959–1960 stood second in the NBA to Wilt Chamberlain*. Further honors included All-NBA Second Team selections in 1960 and 1962 and six appearances in the NBA All-Star Game (1957–1963). Twyman finished his career among all-time leaders in several offensive categories with 15,840 points, 19.2 points scoring average, and 5,421 rebounds in 823 regular season games. He averaged 18.3 points and 7.5 rebounds in 34 playoff games. The Royals retired his uniform number 27. He enjoyed successful careers as an ABC-TV basketball color commentator and as vice president of A. W. Shell Insurance Company of Cincinnati. Twyman is perhaps best remembered, however, for his humanitarian acts on behalf of Royals teammate Maurice Stokes*, stricken with a crippling and ultimately fatal illness in 1958. For 27 years Twyman organized the NBA's Maurice Stokes Memorial Benefit Basketball game, held annually at Kutsher's Country Club in upstate New York to raise funds for needy ex-professional players from the game's earlier days. He was elected to the Naismith Memorial Basketball Hall of Fame in 1983.

BIBLIOGRAPHY: Peter C. Bjarkman, *The Biographical History of Basketball* (Chicago, IL, 2000); Mike Douchant, *Encyclopedia of College Basketball* (Detroit, MI, 1995); Jan Hubbard, ed., *The Official NBA Encyclopedia*, 3rd ed. (New York, 2000); Ronald L. Mendell, *Who's Who in Basketball* (New Rochelle, NY, 1973); *TSN Official NBA Register, 2004–2005* (St. Louis, MO, 2004); Jack Twyman file, Naismith Memorial Basketball Hall of Fame, Springfield, MA.

Peter C. Bjarkman

U

UNSELD, Westley Sissel "Wes" (b. March 14, 1946, Louisville, KY), college and professional player, coach, and executive, is the son of Charles D. Unseld and Cornelia Unseld. His father worked as an oiler for International Harvester, while his mother worked in a cafeteria at Newburg Elementary School in Louisville, Kentucky. Westley's emergence as a high caliber basketball performer began at Louisville's Seneca High School, where he led his team in the Kentucky state championship in both 1963 and 1964. The highly sought Unseld was the first black recruited by the University of Kentucky, but chose to attend the University of Louisville so his father could see him play. An All-America performer, he holds several Louisville records and remains the all-time Cardinals leader in scoring average (20.6 points) and rebounding average (18.9 rebounds). Unseld set Cardinals records for most points scored in a game (45) versus Georgetown (Washington, D.C.) University in 1967 and was one of only three Louisville players to attain over 1,000 points and 1,000 rebounds. Despite his commitment to basketball, he earned a Bachelor's degree in physical education and history in 1968.

Unseld's early career plans included becoming a teacher, but he was made the number-one draft choice and second overall pick in the draft by the then Baltimore Bullets (NBA). He in 1968–1969 became only the second NBA player to be named Rookie of the Year and MVP in the same season, the other being Wilt Chamberlain*. Unseld also made the NBA All-Rookie Team and All-NBA First Team in 1969 and led the NBA in rebounding (1,036) in 1974–1975. During his 13-year pro career, Unseld became the tenth all-time rebounder in NBA history (13,769 rebounds) and is one of only 29 players ever to score over 10,000 career points (10,624) and 10,000 rebounds (13,769). The five-time All-Star ranks as the all-time leader in Bullets' history in assists and rebounds. The pinnacle of Unseld's career came during the 1977–1978 season and playoffs, when he led Washington to the NBA championship and was named MVP of the championship series. Off the court, Unseld has generously volunteered his time to worthy public service activities. In 1975, he received the first NBA Walter Kennedy Citizenship Award for his off-the-court activities in the Baltimore, Maryland and Washington D.C. areas. Unseld retired as an active player in 1981 and served from 1981–1982 to 1995–1996 as vice president of the Capital Center and the Washington Bullets. He was named one of the 50 Greatest Players in NBA History in 1996. Unseld began the 1987–1988 season as Washington assistant coach and replaced Kevin Loughery as head coach in January 1988 after the Bullets struggled to an 8-19 start. He guided Washington to a 30-25 mark over the remainder of the 1987–1988 season, helping the Bullets make the playoffs. The Detroit Pistons, however, eliminated the Bullets in the first round of the NBA playoffs. Washington recorded its best record under Unseld in 1988–1989, finishing 40-42. Unseld coached the Bullets through 1993–1994, compiling a 202-345 record and .369 winning percentage. He served as executive vice president-general manager of the Washington

Bullets (renamed the Wizards) from 1996 to 2004 and headed professional scouting operations for them since 2004.

In 1988, Unseld was elected to the Naismith Memorial Basketball Hall of Fame. He resides in Baltimore with his wife, Connie, daughter, Kimberly, and son, Westley Jr.

BIBLIOGRAPHY: John Carrico, "In Louisville, They're Sold on Unseld," *TSN*, January 20, 1986; Mike Douchant, *Encyclopedia of College Basketball* (Detroit, MI, 1995); Dick Fenlon, "Louisville's Unseld Makes Run in All American Derby," *Louisville* (KY) *Courier Journal*, January 27, 1966; Jan Hubbard, ed., *The Official NBA Encyclopedia*, 3rd ed. (New York, 2000); "Information on All-American Candidate Westley Unseld," University of Louisville, Department of Athletics Release, Louisville, KY, 1966; Roland Lazenby, *The NBA Finals* (Indianapolis, IN, 1996); "One of U of L's Best: Westley Unseld," University of Louisville Game Program, 1967; Ken Shouler et al., *Total Basketball* (Wilmington, DE, 2003); *TSN Official NBA Register, 2004–2005* (St. Louis, MO, 2004); Wes Unseld file, Naismith Memorial Basketball Hall of Fame, Springfield, MA; *Washington Bullets Media Guide, 1993–1994* (Washington, D.C., 1993).

William A. Sutton

V

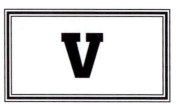

VAN ARSDALE, Richard Albert "Dick" (b. February 22, 1943, Indianapolis, IN), college and professional basketball player and announcer, is the son of Raymond Van Arsdale, a mathematics teacher and track and field coach and Hilda (Thomas) Van Arsdale. At Manual High School in Indianapolis, Indiana, he and his twin brother Tom* excelled scholastically and were selected All-State basketball performers. As co-winners of the Arthur L. Trester Award for Mental Attitude and state Mr. Basketball Award, they led the Redskins to the state championship title game before losing 68-66 to Kokomo High School in overtime.

A high school All-America in 1961, Van Arsdale attended Indiana University and graduated in 1965 with a Bachelor's degree in economics. In three varsity seasons under Branch McCracken*, the six-foot five-inch 219-pounds forward scored 1,240 points for a 17.2 points average and collected 719 rebounds for a 9.9 rebounds average in 72 games. He ranks high on Indiana's all-time scoring and career rebounding. An All-BTC selection and Academic All-America in 1964 and 1965, Van Arsdale placed fifth in BTC scoring and made the All-BTC First Team (1964–1965). As seniors, he and Tom both received the Hoosiers MVP award and helped the U.S. squad win a gold medal at the 1965 World University Games in Budapest, Hungary.

Van Arsdale was selected by the New York Knickerbockers (NBA) in the second round of the 1965 NBA draft and in 1966 made the All-NBA Rookie team. After the Phoenix Suns (NBA) made him their number-one choice in the 1968 expansion draft, he played nine seasons there. Possessing driving ability and strong defensive skills, Van Arsdale became a three-time NBA All-Star (1969–1971). His best season came in 1971, when he ranked twelfth in NBA scoring with 1,771 points for a 21.9 points average. Van Arsdale led the Suns in scoring (1970–1971, 1973–1974), field goal percentage (1973–1974), free throw percentage (1971–1972 to 1973–1974, 1976–1977), and assists (1973–1974). The Suns lost to the Boston Celtics in the 1976 NBA championship series. Van Arsdale retired after the 1976–1977 season. In 12 NBA seasons, he played in 921 games and scored 15,079 points for a 16.4 points average. Married to Barbara Irene Fenton on August 13, 1966, Van Arsdale has two children, Jill and Jason. He served as a radio and television commentator for the Phoenix Suns and is engaged in the real estate business with his brother, Tom. Van Arsdale replaced John MacLeod* as Phoenix interim head coach in February 1987 and guided the Suns to a 14-12 mark for the remainder of the season. He serves as senior vice president for player personnel for the Suns.

BIBLIOGRAPHY: Paul Adams, "The Vans—A Dynamic Duo," *Indiana-Minnesota Basketball Program*, February 5, 1983, pp. 54-55, 58; Peter C. Bjarkman, *Big Ten Basketball* (Indianapolis, IN, 1994); Mike Douchant, *Encyclopedia of College Basketball* (Detroit, MI, 1995); Bob Hammel et al., *Glory of Old IU* (Champaign, IL, 2000); Ken Shouler et al., *Total Basketball* (Wilmington, DE, 2003); *TSN Official NBA Guide, 1976–1977* (St. Louis, MO, 1976); Tom and Dick Van Arsdale, with Joel H. Cohen, *Our Basketball Lives* (New York 1973).

John L. Evers

VAN ARSDALE, Thomas Arthur "Tom" (b. February 22, 1943, Indianapolis, IN), college and professional player, is the son of Raymond Van Arsdale, a mathematics teacher and track and field coach, and Hilda (Thomas) Van Arsdale. At Manual High School in Indianapolis, Indiana, he and his twin brother Dick* excelled scholastically and were All-State basketball performers. As co-winners of the Arthur L. Trester Award for Mental Attitude and state Mr. Basketball Award, they led the Redskins to the state championship title game, before losing 68-66 to Kokomo High School in overtime.

A high school All-America in 1961, Van Arsdale attended Indiana University and graduated in 1965 with a Bachelor's degree in economics. In three varsity seasons under Branch McCracken*, the six-foot five-inch, 202-pounds forward scored 1,252 points for a 17.5 points average and collected 723 rebounds for a 10.0 rebounds average in 72 games. He ranks high on Indiana's all-time scoring and career rebounding lists. An All-BTC selection and Academic All-America in 1964–1965, Van Arsdale placed seventh in BTC scoring and made the All-BTC Second Team (1965). As seniors, he and Dick both received the Hoosiers' MVP Award and helped the U.S. squad win a gold medal at the 1965 World University Games in Budapest, Hungary.

Van Arsdale was selected by the Detroit Pistons (NBA) in the second round of the 1965 NBA draft and in 1966 made the All-NBA Rookie Team. After being traded to Cincinnati (NBA) 1968, he played six seasons with the Royals. The franchise was switched to Kansas City-Omaha at the beginning of the 1971–1972 season. Van Arsdale captained the team in 1972–1973. Van Arsdale performed for the Philadelphia 76ers (NBA; 1972–1973 to 1974–1975) and Atlanta Hawks (NBA; 1975–1976) before joining his brother with the Phoenix Suns (1976–1977) to complete their playing careers. An all-out competitor, he became a three-time NBA All-Star (1970–1972). His best season came in 1970–1971, when he ranked tenth in NBA scoring with 1,875 points (22.9 points average). Van Arsdale led Detroit in free throw percentage (1966–1967), Cincinnati in scoring (1970–1971), Philadelphia in free throw percentage (1972–1973, 1973–1974), and Atlanta in free throw percentage (1974–1975). In 12 NBA seasons, he played in 929 games and scored 14,232 points for a 15.3 points average. Van Arsdale married Jeannie Klise on May 10, 1968, and, since retiring as a player in 1977, has engaged in the real estate business in Phoenix, Arizona, with his brother, Dick.

BIBLIOGRAPHY: Paul Adams, "The Vans—A Dynamic Duo," *Indiana-Minnesota Basketball Program*, February 5, 1983, pp. 54–55, 58; Peter C. Bjarkman, *Big Ten Basketball* (Indianapolis, IN, 1994); Bob Hammel et al., *Glory of Old IU* (Champaign, IL, 2000); Ken Shouler, et al., *Total Basketball* (Wilmington, DE, 2003); *TSN Official NBA Guide, 1976–1977* (St. Louis, MO, 1976); Tom and Dick Van Arsdale, with Joel H. Cohen, *Our Basketball Lives* (New York, 1973).

John L. Evers

VAN BREDA KOLFF, Willem Hendrick "Bill" "Butch" (b. October 28, 1922, Glen Ridge, NJ), college and professional player and coach, coached Princeton University (IvL) to the 1965 NCAA Final Four and the Los Angeles Lakers to the NBA Finals in 1968 and 1969. Van Breda Kolff produced a 482-272 college record through 1993–1994 and a 308-354 record in 10 NBA campaigns.

Van Breda Kolff, the son of former Dutch Olympic soccer player and stockbroker Jan Van Breda Kolff, began playing basketball at home in Montclair, New Jersey. He played soccer and basketball in 1941 at Princeton (New Jersey) University before flunking out as a sophomore. Van Breda Kolff served 42 months in the U.S. Marines during World War II and returned to Princeton. He captained the 1946 Princeton basketball team and was named All-America in soccer before flunking out a second time. Van Breda Kolff finished his Bachelor's degree at NYU while playing guard for the New York Knicks (NBA). In four seasons from 1946 through 1950 under coach Joe Lapchick*, he played in 175 games and averaged 4.7 points for New York.

Van Breda Kolff began coaching basketball at Lafayette College (Pennsylvania) in 1951 and produced a 68-34 record in four seasons there, earning an NIT berth. He coached basketball at

Hofstra University (New York) from 1955 to 1962, compiling a 136-43 mark. His greatest success as a college basketball coach, however, came at Princeton University, where he won 103 games and four IvL titles in five years. His 1965 squad, featuring star Bill Bradley*, finished third in the NCAA Tournament. Van Breda Kolff's 17-year, 307-109 cumulative record made him the third winningest active college basketball coach behind Adolph Rupp*, and John Wooden*.

Van Breda Kolff in 1968 joined the Los Angeles Lakers (NBA), winners of only 36 games the previous year, as head basketball coach. His Lakers captured consecutive Western Conference titles, triumphing in 52 and 55 games, respectively, but lost in the NBA Finals both seasons to the Boston Celtics. With the Lakers, he coached stars Jerry West*, Elgin Baylor*, and Wilt Chamberlain*.

Friction with Chamberlain forced Van Breda Kolff to accept a head basketball coaching assignment with the Detroit Pistons (NBA) in 1969. He coached the Pistons two seasons, producing a then franchise-best 45-37 mark his second season, but left Detroit 12 games into the 1971 season. The Phoenix Suns (NBA) hired him in 1972 and quickly fired him eight games into that campaign. Van Breda Kolff coached the Memphis Tams (ABA) in 1973 and moved to the New Orleans Jazz (NBA) the following year. He produced a 93-135 record in three seasons with New Orleans until being fired in 1977. Star Pete Maravich* played under Van Breda Kolff at New Orleans.

After leaving the NBA ranks, Van Breda Kolff spent two years as basketball coach and athletic director at the University of New Orleans and two seasons as basketball coach with the New Orleans Pride (WPBL). He held several jobs out of basketball and coached high school basketball before returning to coach basketball at Lafeyette College (ECAC) in 1985. In 1989, Van Breda Kolff returned to coach basketball at Hofstra University (ECC) and retired after the 1993–1994 season. Upon returning to college coaching, he compiled a 119-107 record at New Orleans, Lafayette, and Hofstra through 1993–1994. He and his wife, Florence (Smith) Van Breda Kolff, have four children, Jan, who coached basketball at Vanderbilt University (Tennessee), and daughters Kaatje, Karen, and Kristina.

BIBLIOGRAPHY: Mike Douchant, *Encyclopedia of College Basketball* (Detroit, MI, 1995); Jan Hubbard, ed., *The Official NBA Encyclopedia*, 3rd ed. (New York, 2000); Roland Lazenby, *The Lakers: A Basketball Journal* (New York, 1993); Ronald L. Mendell, *Who's Who in Basketball* (New Rochelle, NY, 1973); William Nack, "I Made My Own Bed, I've Got to Lie in It," *SI* 60 (February 1984), pp. 60–76; *NCAA Men's Basketball Records, 2004* (Indianapolis, IN, 2003); David S. Neft and Richard M. Cohen, eds., *The Sports Encyclopedia: Pro Basketball*, 5th ed. (New York, 1992); Gary Nuhn, "ECC," *Street and Smith's College and Prep Basketball*, 1993–1994; Jack Olsen, "The Hedonist Prophet of the Spartan Game," *SI* 29 (September 23, 1968), pp. 28–39.

Brian L. Laughlin

VAN LIER, Norman Allen, III "Norm" "Stormin Normin" (b. April 1, 1947, Midland, PA), college and professional player and sportscaster, is the son of Norman Van Lier II and Helen Van Lier. He and his wife, Susan, have two daughters, Heidi and Hillary. Susan serves as his business manager and partner in Van Lier Productions.

Van Lier graduated in 1969 from Midland (Pennsylvania) Lincoln High School, where he excelled in basketball and football. He and teammate Simmie Hall led the Leopards to an undefeated (28-0) basketball season and the Pennsylvania state high school basketball championship in 1964–1965, ranking as the third best team in state history. Van Lier, coached by Henry J. Kuzma, won recognition as an All-Star quarterback in football and an All-State performer in basketball.

In 1965, Van Lier enrolled at St. Francis College in Loretto, Pennsylvania. He led the Red Flash in basketball scoring with an 18.8 point average as a junior and a 21.0 point average as a senior. Van Lier received honorable mention All-America honors by *TSN* his final two seasons and established a school record for most career assists. In 1969, he received a Bachelor's degree in history and special education.

The six-foot one-inch, 175-pound Van Lier was chosen in the third round by the Chicago Bulls (NBA) in the 1969 NBA draft. He was traded to the Cincinnati Royals (NBA) in October 1969. In his second season with the Royals, Van Lier was named to the All-NBA Defensive Team and led the NBA with 832 assists for an average of 10.1 assists. The Royals returned him to the Bulls in November 1971 for center Jay Fox. Van Lier played for the Bulls between 1971–1972 and 1977–1978 and finished his NBA career with the Milwaukee Bucks (NBA) in 1978–1979. He gave the Bulls a formidable lineup accompanying proven defensive players Jerry Sloan*, Chet Walker*, Bob Love*, and Tom Boerwinkle. The Bulls made the NBA playoffs five of Van Lier's seven seasons. Van Lier led the Bulls each year in assists, ranking among the top six NBA assist leaders six of seven years. In 10 NBA seasons, he scored 8,770 points (11.8 point average) and dished out 5,217 assists (7.0 assists average) in 746 regular season contests. In 38 NBA playoff games, Van Lier recorded 234 assists (6.2 assists average) and tallied 530 points (13.4 points average). He played in three NBA All-Star Games (1974, 1976–1977), was named to the All-NBA Second Team once and the NBA All-Defensive Team eight times, and served as team captain and playmaker of the Bulls.

Van Lier appears frequently around Chicago. He serves as the in-studio analyst for Fox Sports, broadcasts college basketball games, cohosts sports talk shows, and delivers numerous motivational speeches. He was awarded an Emmy for his television work during the 1995–1996 season.

BIBLIOGRAPHY: "Chicago Bulls," *Individual Honors*, http://www.angelfire.com (2003); Jan Hubbard, ed., *The Official NBA Encyclopedia*, 3rd ed. (New York, 2000); "Norm Van Lier," *Celebrities V*, http://www.summitevening.com (2003); "Norm Van Lier," *Hall of Fame Inductee*, http://www.louholtzhalloffame.com (1999); "Norm Van Lier," *Sponsors*, http://www.chicagochallenge.com (2003); "Norm Van Lier," *Statistics*, http://www.basketballreference.com (2003); "Norm Van Lier," *Statistics*, http://www.basketzone.com (2003).

John L. Evers

VANDERVEER, Tara (b. June 26, 1953, Melrose, MA), college player and coach, is the oldest of five children of Dunbar VanDerveer, a teacher and school administrator, and Rita VanDerveer, a speech teacher. VanDerveer was named for the planatation in the 1939 film, *Gone With the Wind*. Her grandfather, Edward Hannigan, served as a long time basketball coach and athletic director in western Massachusetts. VanDerveer attended Niagara Falls (New York) High School and graduated from Buffalo, (New York) Seminary High School in 1971. In high school, she read every available book on basketball. VanDerveer played basketball as a freshman at Albany College in New York and transferred to Indiana University, where she played the guard position three years. VanDerveer attended a coaching clinic with Indiana men's basketball head coach, Bobby Knight*, and regularly sat in on his practices to observe his coaching techniques and style. She received a Bachelor of Arts degree in sociology in 1975 from Indiana.

In 1978, VanDerveer became women's basketball head coach at the University of Idaho. In her two seasons there, the Lady Vandals won 42 of 56 contests. From the 1980–1981 season through the 1984–1985 campaign, she served as head coach for the Ohio State Lady Buckeyes, winning 110 of 147 games.

In her first season as head coach of the Stanford University (California) Cardinal women's basketball team in 1989–1990, VanDerveer compiled 32 victories in 33 games and won the NCAA championship. Stanford won 30 of 33 contests in 1991–1992 and captured a second NCAA championship. Cardinal teams have won 30 games six times under her leadership. A disciplined, methodical, and demanding coach who endlessly studies the game, VanDerveer has won 482 games and lost 120 contests in 19 seasons at Stanford. Through the 2004–2005 campaign, her overall women's collegiate basketball record includes 631 victories and 170 defeats. She has won 17 conference titles and has earned National Coach of the Year three times.

From 1986 to 1996, VanDerveer coached U.S. Women's Basketball teams in the Goodwill Games, World University Games, Olympic Festival, and Olympics and fashioned an incredible

88 wins in 96 games. In 1995 and 1996, she led the U.S. National team on a world tour to 52 consecutive victories in preparation for the Olympics. VanDerveer guided the USA to a gold medal at the 1996 Olympic Games in Atlanta, Georgia. In April 2002, she was inducted into the Women's Basketball Hall of Fame in Knoxville, Tennessee.

VanDerveer, who is single, lives in Menlo Park, California, and enjoys playing the piano, snow and water skiing, biking, and rowing.

BIBLIOGRAPHY: Peter C. Bjarkman, *The Biographical History of Basketball* (Chicago, IL, 2000); Sara Corbett, *Venus to the Hoop: A Gold Medal Year in Women's Basketball* (New York, 1997); Nena Ray Hawkes and John F. Seggar, *Celebrating Women Coaches: A Biographical Dictionary* (Westport, CT, 2000); Rosemarie Skaine, *Women College Basketball Coaches* (Jefferson, NC, 2001); Lisa Smith, ed., *Nike Is a Goddess: The History of Women in Sports* (New York, 1998); Stanford Women's Basketball, "Women's Basketball: Tara VanDerveer," *Stanford Cardinal Official Athletics Website* (September 6, 2003), pp. 1–4; Tara VanDerveer with Joan Ryan, *Shooting from the Outside: How a Coach and Her Olympic Team Transformed Women's Basketball* (New York, 1997).

Frank J. Olmsted

VANDEWEGHE, Earnest Maurice, III "Kiki" (b. August 1, 1958, Weisbaden, West Germany), college and professional player, coach, and executive, is the son of Earnest Vandeweghe, a former college and professional basketball player, and Colleen Vandeweghe. After graduating from Pacific Palisades High School in southern California, Vandeweghe attended the University of California at Los Angeles. He became a full time starter as a junior and averaged 19.5 points as a senior, leading the Bruins to the NCAA Finals before losing to the University of Louisville in 1980.

The Dallas Mavericks (NBA) chose the six-foot eight-inch, 220-pound Vandeweghe in the first round of the 1980 NBA draft. His rights were traded to the Denver Nuggets (NBA) in December 1980. In Denver, he combined with Alex English* to form one of the most potent scoring duos in NBA history. Vandeweghe enjoyed his best scoring season in 1983–1984, finishing third in the NBA in scoring with 29.4 points per game. He tallied a career-high 51 points that season in the highest scoring game in NBA history, a 186–184 loss to the Detroit Pistons.

Vandeweghe continued his scoring prowess after a June 1984 trade to the Portland Trail Blazers (NBA), averaging more than 20 points in each of his first four seasons there. Injuries began to limit his availability. In February 1989, he was traded to the New York Knicks (NBA), where his father had played during the 1950s. Injuries continued to plague Vandeweghe the remainder of his career, limiting him to under 70 games in five of his last six seasons.

Vandeweghe scored 15,980 points (19.7-point average) in 13 NBA seasons, including three seasons with over 2,000 points. He recorded a .525 field goal percentage and a .872 free throw percentage for his career, finishing among the top 10 in free throw percentage eight times. The two-time All-Star also participated in 68 playoff games, missing the playoffs only in his rookie season.

After spending two years as an assistant basketball coach with the Dallas Mavericks (NBA), Vandeweghe was named general manager of the Denver Nuggets (NBA) in 2001. He and his wife, Peggy, have one son, Earnest Maurice IV.

BIBLIOGRAPHY: *Denver Nuggets Media Guide, 2002–2003* (Denver, CO, 2002); Scott Howard-Cooper, *The Bruins 100* (Lenexa, KS, 1999); Jan Hubbard, ed., *The Official NBA Encyclopedia*, 3rd ed. (New York, 2000); *TSN Official NBA Guide, 1993–1994* (St. Louis, MO, 1993); *TSN Official NBA Register, 1993–1994* (St. Louis, MO, 1993): Martin Taragano, *Basketball Biographies* (Jefferson, NC, 1991).

Curtice R. Mang

VANDIVIER, Robert P. "Fuzzy" (b. December 26, 1903, Franklin, IN; d. July 30, 1983, Indianapolis, IN), college basketball player, was a celebrated All-Star high school hoopster and is a member of the Naismith Memorial Basketball Hall of Fame. Only five men were inducted into Indiana's Basketball Hall of Fame as charter members. The inaugural 1962 class of Hoosier greats consisted of Vandivier, John Wooden*, Ward "Piggy" Lambert*, "Griz" Wagner, and Homer Stonebraker. Three legendary basketball figures of the early decades of the current century—Vandivier, Stonebraker, and Wooden—are still considered by longtime observers to be unparalleled stars of the Indiana hardwood sport. Numerous supporters consider Vandivier as the finest of them all. In leading Franklin High School to the Indiana state championship an unparalleled three consecutive years (1920–1922), he was a three-time All-State performer. Vandivier captained the team, which became known in Indiana sports annals as the Franklin "Wonder Five".

All five starting members of the 1922 state championship team entered hometown Franklin College, leading the Grizzlies to their finest basketball achievements in school history between 1922 and 1926.

No school has ever matched the three consecutive Indiana high school championships achieved by the Franklin Wonder Five, coached by Griz Wagner and led oncourt by Vandivier. During Vandivier's three prep seasons, Franklin High School achieved miraculous winning records of 29-1, 30-3, and 30-4. Vandivier, the only returning starter on the 1921 team, attained the unique distinction of being named to the All-State tournament team for three consecutive years. When Coach Wagner transported his fabulous starting five of Vandivier, Carlyle Friddle, James Ross, Ike Ballard, and John Gant less than a mile to the Franklin College campus, the magic continued with a freshman-year 17-1 record against such highly touted opponents as the University of Notre Dame (Indiana), the University of Wisconsin, Marquette University (Wisconsin), and Purdue University (Indiana); the season's only loss was to Indiana University. During his sophomore and junior seasons, Franklin finished with 19-1 and 15-3 marks.

During the 1926 season, injuries and illness finally tarnished the magic of the fabled "Wonder Five." Vandivier's own career was cut short his senior season by a painful back ailment. He was honored, however, by selection to the All-Western college All-Star team with Noble Kizer of Notre Dame and Harry Kipkes of the University of Michigan. Vandivier later served as principal of Martinsville (Indiana) High School when that school won the 1934 state basketball championship. He eventually coached at his high school alma mater and achieved perhaps his finest coaching moments at the 1939 state championship finals, when Franklin was defeated by Everett Case's* Frankfort High School five. The star of that 1939 Franklin team was George Crowe, Indiana's first high school Mr. Basketball and later a major league baseball player with the Milwaukee (NL), St. Louis (NL), and Cincinnati (NL) clubs. During Vandivier's coaching tenure at Franklin (1926–1944), his teams won almost every sectional tournament until 1940 and twice entered the sub-state tournament round before achieving the championship game in 1939. Vandivier served as athletic director there for 18 more years after his retirement from active coaching and continued his teaching career until 1968.

Almost 50 years after the Franklin Wonder Five completed its unparalleled domination of Hoosier basketball, Vandivier achieved perhaps the finest honor ever awarded to an Indiana high school player. He was selected to coach Tony Hinkle's* All-Dream Team, which also included Oscar Robertson*, Wooden, George McGinnis*, and Stonebraker. In 1975, the most memorable member of the Franklin Wonder Five was inducted as a player into the Naismith Memorial Basketball Hall of Fame.

BIBLIOGRAPHY: Peter C. Bjarkman, *The Biographical History of Basketball* (Chicago, IL, 2000); Jan Hubbard, ed., *The Official NBA Encyclopedia*, 3rd ed. (New York, 2000); Herb Schwomeyer, *Hoosier Hysteria: A History of Indiana High School Boys Basketball*, 6th ed. (Greenfield, IN, 1970); Bob Williams, *Hoosier Hysteria: Indiana High School Basketball* (South Bend, IN, 1982).

Peter C. Bjarkman

VERGA, Robert Bruce "Bob" (b. September 7, 1945, Neptune, NJ), college and professional player, grew up in Sea Girt, New Jersey. Verga attended Duke University (North Carolina) from 1963 through 1967. The six-foot one-inch, 190-pound guard proved an exceptional scorer, noted for his shooting range. Verga scored 1,758 career points in 80 varsity games at Duke, averaging 22 points. He led the ACC with 705 points (26.1 point average) in 1966–1967, a mark that remains the best in Duke history.

Verga was named Most Outstanding Player in the 1966 NCAA Final Four. He played ineffectively in Duke's Final Four loss to the University of Kentucky, however, after contracting strep throat. Verga was named First Team All-ACC in 1965, 1966, and 1967, one of only five Duke players so honored three times. He was selected Second Team All-America by both the AP and UPI in 1966 and 1967.

Verga played for the Dallas Chaparrals (ABA) in 1967–1968, Denver Rockets (ABA), New York Nets (ABA), and Houston Mavericks (ABA) in 1968–1969, Carolina Cougars (ABA) from 1969 through 1972, and Pittsburgh Condors (ABA) in 1972. In 1970, he averaged 27.5 points, the ABA's third highest average, for Carolina and was selected First Team All-ABA. Verga averaged 21.2 points and 4.1 rebounds in 321 ABA games. He finished his professional career with the Portland Trail Blazers (NBA) in 1973–1974, averaging 5.0 points in 21 games.

Verga also excelled at tennis following his basketball career. He earned several number one rankings in New Jersey and the Middle Atlantic region in his age group in tennis singles competition. Verga ranked as high as fifteenth nationally in age 40-and-over singles in 1986. He became a head club pro in 1978 and has served as a club and teaching pro ever since. He coached the Seton Hall University (New Jersey) men's tennis team in 1978–1979 and the St. Peter's College (New Jersey) women's team in 2001–2002.

BIBLIOGRAPHY: Bill Brill, *An Illustrated History of Duke Basketball* (Dallas, TX, 1986); Ron Morris, *ACC Basketball: An Illustrated History* (Chapel Hill, NC, 1988); Terry Pluto, *Loose Balls* (New York, 1990); Ken Shouler et al., *Total Basketball* (Wilmington, DE, 2003).

Jim L. Sumner

W

WACHTER, Edward A. "Eddie" (b. June 30, 1883, Troy, NY; d. March 12, 1966, Troy, NY), professional player and college coach, ranks as the finest center in early basketball. Although never attending high school or college, Wachter compiled 1,800 points as a professional player from 1901 to 1924. He consistently led his professional leagues in scoring and participated on more championship teams than anyone in his generation. In 1904–1905, Wachter led the Schenectady (New York) Company E team to the championship in a three-game sweep over the Kansas City Blue Diamonds. His greatest contribution to the professional game came as a player with Troy, New York (NYSL). Wachter's team so dominated competition from 1909–1910 to 1914–1915 that the NYSL was forced to disband. Troy then toured the midwest and won 38 consecutive road games, a remarkable feat because they encountered different rules at each locality. The Troy team introduced many modern techniques, styles, and play patterns, including a tip-off tap generating a quick, driving lay-up. Other innovations included the bounce-, short- and long-passing game, fast break, legal block, five-man offense, and man-to-man switch defense. In 1911–1912, Wachter and his brother Lew of the Troy club introduced the current free throw rule, requiring the player fouled to shoot from the line. Before that time, any player on the floor could take the foul shot.

Wachter, who never married, later coached basketball 25 years at Albany (New York) State Teacher's College, Rensselaer Polytechnic Institute (New York), Williams College (Massachusetts), Harvard University (Massachusetts), and Lafayette College (Pennsylvania). Outspoken in many developmental facets of basketball, he proposed that all amateur, college, and pro organizations be governed by a single set of rules in 1918 and 1919. Besides chairing the RDC for the BBO in 1920, Wachter founded and presided over the NEBA in 1928 and 1929 and helped promote uniform rules there. He in 1927 opposed the rule limiting the dribble to just one bounce. A lanky, aggressive, versatile, quick center, Wachter possessed accurate long shots and free throws. He authored a brochure, *How to Play Basketball*, and published several lectures on *Basketball Pre-Season Training*.

Wachter was selected in 1928 to *Who's Who in Sports* and in 1961 to the Naismith Memorial Basketball Hall of Fame as a professional player.

BIBLIOGRAPHY: Robert W. Peterson, *Cages to Jump Shots: Pro Basketball's Early Years* (New York, 1990); Ken Shouler et al., *Total Basketball* (Wilmington, DE, 2003); Edward A. Wachter file, Naismith Memorial Basketball Hall of Fame, Springfield, MA.

Catherine M. Derrick

WADE, Lily Margaret (b. December 31, 1912, McCool, MS; d. February 16, 1995, Cleveland, MS), college player and coach, was the last of eight children born to Robert Miller Wade and Bittie (Veal) Wade and grew up in Cleveland, Mississippi, where she enjoyed all kinds of sports. After graduating from Cleveland High School in 1929, Wade followed her brother, Broughton, and enrolled at Delta State Teachers College in their hometown. At Delta State, she played basketball for three seasons and helped her school compile a combined 28-5-2 record. Wade captained Delta State her sophomore and junior years, but the school discontinued its women's program before the 1932–1933 season. The decision very much upset Wade and her teammates. She graduated in 1933 with a Bachelor's degree in health, physical education, and recreation and later earned a Master's degree from the University of Alabama.

Wade played semiprofessional basketball for two years with the Tupelo Redwaves, but a knee injury ended her playing career. She coached girls' high school basketball at Marietta (1934) and Belden (1935) in Georgia and Mississippi. At Cleveland High School, her squads forged an impressive 453-89-6 win-loss-tie record in 21 seasons. Wade, who never married, returned to Delta State Teachers College in 1959 as director of the Women's Physical Education Department and was primarily concerned the next 14 years with administrative affairs. In 1973, the 61-year-old resurrected the women's intercollegiate basketball program at Delta State. Wade immediately produced a 16-2 winning season in 1973–1974. Her first Lady Statesmen squad won the Mississippi state championship.

In a cool, deliberative manner resembling that of John Wooden*, Wade directed her teams to three national AIAW titles. Delta State finished undefeated (28-0) in 1974–1975 and won the AIAW tournament by triumphing over defending champion Immaculata (Pennsylvania) College. The Lady Statesmen extended their victory string to 51 games the next season before losing a regular-season contest. In the 1976 AIAW championship contest, Delta State avenged that defeat by defeating Immaculata again and finishing the season at 33-1. A third title came in 1976–1977 with a 32-3 slate. Wade's teams exhibited sound execution and court discipline and seldom used substitutes. Starters on the three consecutive AIAW championship squads included Lusia Harris (Stewart)*, Cornelia Ward, Ramona Von Boeckman, Debbie Brock, and Wanda Hairston. Wade retired from college coaching after two more seasons, having compiled a 157-23 record at Delta State.

Wade, whose combined high school and college coaching slate was an amazing 610-112-6, received many awards and became the first woman selected to the Mississippi Sports Hall of Fame. Wade's greatest honor perhaps is being the namesake for the award given every season to the outstanding junior or senior women's basketball player in the nation, stressing academics and community service as well as player performance. Wade continued teaching basketball coaching at Delta State until December 1982 and co-authored a book on basketball techniques with Delta State's men's coach Mel Hankinson. In 1985, she was named to the Naismith Memorial Basketball Hall of Fame as one of the first three female members.

BIBLIOGRAPHY: Mike Douchant, *Encyclopedia of College Basketball* (Detroit, MI, 1995); Nena Ray Hawkes and John F. Seggar, *Celebrity Women Coaches: A Biographical Dictionary* (Westport, CT, 2000); Langston Rogers, ed., "Margaret Wade, Head Coach," *Lady Statesmen Press Guide, 1977–1978* (Cleveland, MS, 1977), p. 8; Jacqui Salmon, "Margaret Wade: A Prize Coach," *Women's Sports* 4 (May 1982), pp. 40–42; Ken Shouler et al., *Total Basketball* (Wilmington, DE, 2003); Rosemarie Skaine, *Women College Basketball Coaches* (Jefferson, NC, 2001); Pat Tashima, "Delta State Rebounds for Glory," *Womensports* 2 (December 1975), pp. 34–35, 56; Margaret Wade file, Naismith Memorial Basketball Hall of Fame, Springfield, MA.

Dennis S. Clark

WALKER, Chester "Chet" "The Jet" (b. February 22, 1940, Benton Harbor, MI), college and professional player, was a talented six-foot seven-inch, 220-pound forward for 13 NBA seasons (1962–1975) with Syracuse, Philadelphia, and Chicago. Walker graduated from Benton Harbor (Michigan) High School and studied at Bradley University (Illinois) from 1958 to 1962. He finished his college career with 1,975 points for a 24.4 points average and 1,036 rebounds and was selected to *TSN* All-America First Team in 1962 and Second Team in 1961.

In the 1962 NBA draft, Walker was selected by the Syracuse Nationals (the franchise transferred to Philadelphia in 1963) in the second round as the fourteenth overall pick. The powerful, smooth, well-rounded, particularly effective one-on-one forward performed on the imposing front line with forward Luke Jackson and center

Wilt Chamberlain* to anchor the 1966–1967 Philadelphia 76ers championship team, among the greatest in NBA history. His lifetime NBA record includes 1,032 games played, 6,876 baskets, and 5,079 free throws for 18,831 points scored (18.2 points average), 7,314 rebounds, a .796 free throw percentage, and a .470 field goal percentage. He averaged in double figures during his 13 NBA seasons, recording consecutive 22.0 points averages during the 1970–1971 and 1971–1972 seasons. He led the NBA in free throw percentage in 1970–1971, played in seven All-Star Games (1964, 1966–1967, 1970–1971, 1973–1974), and scored a career-high 56 points in a game against the Cincinnati Royals in 1972. He was traded with Shaler Halimon to Chicago (NBA) in September 1969 and played for the Bulls until his retirement in 1975. Walker's teams notably reached the playoffs during all his 13 NBA seasons.

BIBLIOGRAPHY: Mike Douchant, *Encyclopedia of College Basketball* (Detroit, MI, 1995); Jan Hubbard, ed., *The Official NBA Encyclopedia*, 3rd ed. (New York, 2000); Leonard Koppett, *Championship NBA: Official 25th Anniversary* (New York, 1970); Wayne Lynch, *Season of the 76ers* (New York, 2002); Ronald L. Mendell, *Who's Who in Basketball* (New Rochelle, NY, 1973); *TSN Official NBA Register, 2004–2005* (St. Louis, MO, 2004).

Gustavo N. Agrait

WALKER, Hazel Leona. *See* Crutcher, Hazel Leona Walker

WALKER, James "Jimmy" (b. April 8, 1944, Amherst, VA), college and professional player, played nine NBA seasons following a spectacular career at Providence (Rhode Island) College. As a child, Walker moved with his family from Virginia to Boston, Massachusetts. His high school basketball coach discouraged his college aspirations. Boston Celtics (NBA) star Sam Jones*, who observed Walker's basketball ability on a Boston playground, secured him a prep school scholarship at Laurinburg, (North Carolina) Institute. At Providence College, the six-foot three-inch, 195-pound guard averaged over 20 points in each of his four seasons from 1963–1964 through 1966–1967 under coach Joe Mullaney. His freshman team enjoyed a 21–0 win–loss campaign, while his sophomore varsity squad won 19 games before suffering its first loss.

In three varsity seasons, Walker led Providence to a composite 67-14 record and three postseason tournament appearances. He scored 73 points in two 1967 NIT games and made the All-NIT team. His 24.5 point average as a junior included 50 points in an ECAC Tournament game at Madison Square Garden in New York, earning him a place on every major All-America team. As a senior, Walker averaged 30.4 points to edge UCLA's Lew Alcindor (Kareem Abdul Jahbar*) for the NCAA scoring title and repeated as consensus All-America. The Detroit Pistons (NBA) selected him first in the 1967 NBA draft and signed him to a four-year contract for about $300,000, making him for a time the second-highest-paid player in NBA history.

Some authorities believe that Walker failed professionally to fulfill his potential, but he blossomed into an NBA All-Star in the 1969–1970 campaign. The 1969–1970 through 1973–1974 seasons saw him average 19.4 points. In 1971–1972 Walker was named for the second time to the East All-Star squad and enjoyed his finest professional season, tallying 21.3 points per game. The strong free-throw shooter sank .829 percent of his foul shots during his NBA career and peaked at .884 percent in 1972–1973.

Detroit traded Walker to the Houston Rockets (NBA) in August 1972. During the 1973–1974 season, he was traded to the Kansas City–Omaha Royals (NBA). His playing career concluded there in 1976. In 698 NBA games spanning nine seasons, Walker tallied 11,655 points (16.7 points average) and recorded 2,429 assists.

BIBLIOGRAPHY: Richard Coren, *Providence College Basketball* (Charleston, SC, 2002); Frank Deford, "That Providence Cannonball," *SI* 26 (January 23, 1967), pp. 18–19; Mike Douchant, *Encyclopedia of College Basketball* (Detroit, MI, 1995); Jan Hubbard, ed., *The Official NBA Basketball Encyclopedia*, 3rd ed. (New York, 2000); Herman L. Masin, "An Act of Providence," *Senior Scholastic* 90 (March 17, 1967), p. 24; Ronald L. Mendell, *Who's Who in Basketball* (New Rochelle, NY, 1973); James Walker file, Naismith Memorial Basketball Hall of Fame, Springfield, MA.

Frederick Ivor-Campbell and Wayne Patterson

WALLACE, Ben (b. September 10, 1974, White Hall, AL), college and professional player, is the tenth of 11 children in his family. At Central High School in Alabama, the outstanding athlete earned All-State honors in football, basketball, and baseball and also competed in track and field.

Wallace's achievements at a small high school in Alabama failed to draw the attention of NCAA Division I college recruiters, but he was offered a basketball scholarship to Cuyahoga CC in Ohio. As a sophomore in 1993–1994, he averaged 24 points, 17 rebounds, and 7 blocked shots and earned a scholarship to Virginia Union University. During his senior year in 1995–1996, Wallace led Virginia Union to a 28-3 record and the NCAA Division II Final Four. He made the NCAA Division II All-America First Team, averaging 12.5 points, 10.5 rebounds, and 3.7 blocked shots.

As a NCAA Division II player, however, Wallace was not selected in the 1996 NBA draft. The six-foot-nine-inch, 240 pound center-forward was signed by the Washington Bullets (NBA) as a free agent and used primarily as a reserve during his rookie season. The franchise was renamed the Washington Wizards during the 1997–1998 season. His playing time increased in 1997–1998, as he blocked 72 shots and averaged 4.8 rebounds. Although primarily a shot blocker, rebounder, and strong defender, Wallace increased his scoring average to six points during the 1998–1999 season. The Wizards traded him to the Orlando Magic (NBA) in August 1999.

Wallace enjoyed a successful 1999–2000 campaign in Orlando with 1.6 blocked shots and 8.2 rebounds per game. Nevertheless, he was involved in a controversial trade to the Detroit Pistons (NBA) for Grant Hill* in August 2000. Injuries kept Hill from performing up to expectations in Orlando, but Wallace blossomed in Detroit.

During 2000–2001, Wallace averaged 6.4 points and 2.3 blocks and led the NBA with 13.2 rebounds per game. The following season, he led the Pistons to 50 wins and a berth in the NBA playoffs. After pacing the NBA in rebounding (13 per game) and blocked shots (3.5 per game), he overwhelmingly was chosen NBA Defensive Player of the Year.

Wallace retained his NBA Defensive Player of the Year Award in 2002–2003 while averaging 15.4 rebounds and making the All-NBA Second Team. The Pistons again won 50 games, but an early exit in the NBA playoffs led to Larry Brown* replacing Rick Carlisle as head coach. Wallace ranked third in the NBA with 1,006 rebounds and 246 blocked shots in 2003–2004, helping Detroit finish second in the Eastern Conference with 54 victories. His rebounding and blocked shots helped Detroit defeat the Milwaukee Bucks, four games to one, New Jersey Nets in seven games, and Indiana Pacers four games to two in the playoffs, and upset the heavily favored Los Angeles Lakers four games to one in the NBA Finals. Wallace tallied 20 points and 22 rebounds in the decisive game against Los Angeles. He again made the All-NBA Second Team and All-NBA Defensive Team. Under Brown, Wallace had the opportunity to improve his playoff performance. He led the Pistons with 902 rebounds, 176 blocked shots, and 106 steals in 74 games in 2004–2005, helping Detroit finish second in the Eastern Conference with 54 wins and played in the NBA Finals against the San Antonio Spurs. Through 2004–2005, he has 6,556 career rebounds (10.6 average) and 1,419 career blocked shots (2.3 average) in 616 regular-season games and has averaged 14.8 rebounds and 2.5 blocked shots in 68 playoff games through the 2005 Eastern Conference Finals. He appeared in three consecutive All-Star Games from 2003 through 2005, and made the All-NBA Defensive First Team from 2002 through 2005, being NBA Defensive Player of the Year the latter three seasons. He also earned All-NBA Third Team honors in 2005. Commissioner David Stern* suspended Wallace six games for his role in a melee that occurred on and off the court in a game with the Indiana Pacers on November 19, 2004 at The Palace in Auburn Hills, Michigan. Wallace attempted a dunk with about 45 seconds left with the Pacers safely in front when Ron Artest fouled him hard. Wallace responded with a two handed shove. He married his high school girlfriend, Chanda.

BIBLIOGRAPHY: "Ben Wallace," *USA Basketball*, http:www.usabasketball.com/biosmen/ben_wallace_bio.html (June 19, 2003); Ken Shouler et al., *Total Basketball* (Wilmington, DE, 2003); *TSN*, *Official NBA Register, 2004–2005* (St. Louis, MO, 2004); L. J. Wertheim, "Ben Wallace," *SI* 88 (March 9, 1998), p. 103.

Ron Briley

WALSH, DAVID H. (b. October 5, 1889, Hoboken, NJ; d. June 2, 1975, Boca Raton, FL), college and professional referee, ranked among the top six referees in the Eastern United States and worked the first game ever to use the three-referee system. Walsh graduated in 1907 from Hoboken (New Jersey) High School, where he played basketball and baseball. He then attended Montclair (New Jersey) Teacher's College from 1907 to 1911 and Sargent School of Physical Education in Cambridge, Massachusetts from 1912 to 1914. Montclair fielded no organized or formal sports teams during that era, but Walsh played semiprofessional basketball until suffering a compound fracture of his left ankle. Walsh coached basketball from 1911 to 1933 at Demarest (New Jersey) High School (formerly Hoboken High School), producing among the best teams in New Jersey. His 1924 squad won the state championship title after Passaic High School, winners of 157 consecutive games, refused to play favored Demarest in the semifinal game. Walsh also served as physical director at Demarest High School, supervisor of physical education for the city of Hoboken from 1920 to 1933, and principal of Boys Junior High School and Wallace Elementary School from 1933 to 1951.

His officiating career began in 1911, when he refereed games at the high school, college, and pro levels. Walsh was chosen to work the first game ever to use the three-referee system. In 1914 Walsh limited his officiating to college games and handled mainly EIBL games. He joined the IAABO in 1922 and served as its secretary-treasurer from 1948 to 1956. During his tenure, Walsh established uniformity in the judgment and application of basketball rules. He retired from officiating in 1941 and then served as associate director of the CBOA until 1956. As associate director, Walsh conducted basketball clinics and interpretation meetings in the East and trained and taught new officials. He also supervised officials for the ECAC. Walsh co-authored the first *Manual of Basketball Officiating*, a book used by high school and college referees throughout the world. His post-retirement honors included recognition by the NJAA for outstanding contributions and service to basketball in 1955, election as honorary executive secretary of the IAABO, and enshrinement into the Naismith Memorial Basketball Hall of Fame as a referee in 1961. Walsh married Marie V. Catoggia of Hoboken on June 14, 1924, and had no children.

BIBLIOGRAPHY: Zander Hollander, ed., *The NBA's Official Encyclopedia of Pro Basketball* (New York, 1981); David H. Walsh file, Naismith Memorial Basketball Hall of Fame, Springfield, MA.

Catherine M. Derrick and Wayne Patterson

WALTON, William Theodore, III "Bill" (b. November 5, 1952, La Mesa, CA), college and professional player and sportscaster, is the son of William Theodore Walton, a district chief of the San Diego Public Works Department, and librarian Gloria Walton. Walton attended Blessed Sacrament School and Helix High School in San Diego, California. In high school, he grew six inches one year and remained slender until his senior year. Walton led his team to a 33-0 record his senior year and to 49 consecutive victories over two seasons. He averaged 20 points and 22 rebounds and made 70 percent of his field goals in his senior year. The heavily recruited Walton chose UCLA for both its academic and athletic reputations.

At UCLA, Walton averaged 21.1 points and 15 rebounds his sophomore year and shot 64 percent from the field. Walton, whose team won all 30 games and the NCAA championship, already was favorably compared with recent UCLA graduate Lew Alcindor (Kareem Abdul-Jabbar*). He again led UCLA to an undefeated season and the NCAA championship his junior year, scoring 44 points and getting 13 rebounds in the championship game against Memphis (Tennessee) State University. UCLA won a record 88 consecutive games before losing to the University of Notre Dame (Indiana) in January 1974. In Walton's three seasons, UCLA compiled an 86-4 win-loss mark. He scored 1,767 points and made more rebounds (2,325) than Alcindor. Walton averaged over 20 points and made .651 of his field goals. For three consecutive years, he was chosen an All-America and Player of the Year by both the AP and UPI. In 1974, he won the James E. Sullivan Memorial Trophy as the nation's outstanding amateur athlete.

After his junior year at UCLA, 6 foot 11 inch Walton declined a huge pro contract offer from the Philadelphia 76ers (NBA). After his senior year, he accepted a five-year, $3 million offer from the Portland Trail Blazers (NBA). Health problems limited his effectiveness his first two pro seasons. His weight dropped from 220 to 205 pounds, while he suffered through the flu, tendinitis of the knees, a dislocated finger, and a bone spur on his ankle and missed over one-half of his team's games. The expansion Trail Blazers struggled through Walton's first two seasons to a combined 75-99 record. Walton underwent widespread criticism, as one who would not play with pain.

Elected Trail Blazers' captain for 1976–1977, a healthy Walton led Portland to its first NBA championship and was named MVP. Chronic injuries hampered his effectiveness the next season and caused him to miss the 1978–1979 year. In May 1979 Walton was traded to the San Diego Clippers (NBA), where his performance was spotty. Vestiges of this outstanding player sometimes were evident, but he seemed to lack the interest or ability to play on other occasions. The controversial Walton brought suit against Portland, charging that they caused him permanent injury by playing him with serious injury. In September 1985, the Clippers traded him to the Boston Celtics (NBA) for Cedric Maxwell, a 1986 first-round draft choice, and cash. Walton played a valuable reserve role, appearing in 80 games for the first time, making a career-high .562 percent of his shots, and averaging 7.6 points. Walton helped the Celtics win the Atlantic Division title and take the NBA championship over the Houston Rockets. He missed most of the 1986–1987 and the entire 1987–1988 season with a foot injury before retiring. During 10 seasons, he scored 6,215 points (13.3 points per game) in 468 games and made 4,923 rebounds. Walton was named All-NBA First Team in 1978, All-NBA Second Team in 1977, and NBA All-Defensive First Team in 1977 and 1978.

At UCLA, Walton had become part of the era's anti-war, student protest movement. He let his red hair grow long, became a vegetarian, and supported anti-war and pro-environment causes. His political and social commitments and unconventional appearance aroused spectator resentment during his first few NBA seasons, particularly when he failed to fulfill expectations on the court. Walton's identification with activist friend Jack Scott and the Patty Hearst affair contributed to his alienation from many fans, who viewed him as an unpatriotic radical. Spectators probably were more disappointed in his failure to fulfill their desire for a new white superstar to compete with numerous black stars who had emerged in recent years. Walton rejected the entire concept as racist. He was elected to the Naismith Memorial Basketball Hall of Fame in 1993 and designated one of the 50 Greatest Players in NBA History in 1996. *Street and Smith's* named him the second greatest college basketball player of all-time. Walton served as a broadcaster for NBC Sports from 1992 to 2002 and as an analyst for ABC and ESPN since 2002. He and his wife, Susan, have three sons. His son, Luke, played basketball for the University of Arizona and for the Los Angeles Lakers (NBA).

BIBLIOGRAPHY: *CB* (New York, 1977), pp. 421–424; Mike Douchant, *Encyclopedia of College Basketball* (Detroit, MI, 1995); Zander Hollander, ed., *The Modern Encyclopedia of Basketball* (Garden City, NY, 1979); Zander Hollander, ed., *The NBA's Official Encyclopedia of Professional Basketball* (New York, 1981); Scott Howard-Cooper, *The Bruins 100* (Lenexa, KS, 1999); Jan Hubbard, ed., *The Official NBA Encyclopedia*, 3rd ed. (New York, 2000); Curry Kirkpatrick, "Who Are Those Guys?" 38 (February 5, 1973); Roland Lazenby, *The NBA Finals* (Indianapolis, IN, 1996); Bill Libby, *The Walton Gang* (New York, 1981); Ken Shouler et al., *Total Basketball* (Wilmington, DE, 2003); *TSN Official NBA Register, 2004–2005* (St. Louis, MO, 2004); *Street and Smith's 100 Greatest College Basketball Players* (December, 2003); Bill Walton, *Nothing but Net* (New York, 1994); William Walton file, Naismith Memorial Basketball Hall of Fame, Springfield, MA; *WWA*, 42nd ed., (1982–1983), p. 3469; Grant Wohl, "My Three Sons," *SI* 94 (March 12, 2001).

Stephen D. Bodayla

WANZER, Robert Francis "Bobby" (b. June 4, 1921, New York, NY), college and professional player and coach, led his Benjamin Franklin High School basketball squad to New York City titles in 1939–1940 and 1940–1941 before entering Seton Hall University (New

Jersey) in 1941. A stint in the U.S. Marines and at Colgate University (New York) in the U.S. Navy's V-12 program interrupted his Seton Hall career. Wanzer returned to Seton Hall for the 1946–1947 basketball campaign, scoring 266 points in 23 games (11.6 points average), captaining the Pirates squad, and earning All-America honors. He and his wife, Nina (Penrose) Wanzer, have three children.

The Rochester Royals (NBL) drafted the six-foot, 172-pound guard in 1947. During his 10-year pro career from 1947–1948 to 1956–1957, Wanzer excelled as an outside shooter, playmaker, ball handler, and defender, and teamed effectively with guard Robert Davies*. In 1948–1949, Wanzer averaged 10.2 points to help 45-15 Rochester win the Western Division and led the Royals for the first of six consecutive seasons in free throw shooting. The Minneapolis Lakers, however, ousted Rochester from the NBL playoffs. Wanzer led the 1949–1950 Royals in shooting percentage, improved his scoring average to 11.8 points, and helped 51-17 Rochester to second place in the NBA Central Division behind Minneapolis. In 1950–1951, he averaged 10.8 points for the second-place Royals. Rochester upset the Lakers in the semifinals and defeated the New York Knickerbockers four games to three to win the NBA championship. Wanzer made the 1952 All-NBA Second Team, scoring a career-high 1,033 points (15.7 points-average). Besides pacing the Royals in field goal percentage, he led the NBA in free throw percentage by making 377 of 417 free throws for a stellar 904 mark. Rochester finished first in the Western Division with a 41-25 record before bowing to Minneapolis in the playoff semifinals.

Wanzer repeated as an All-NBA Second Team selection in 1952–1953, tallying 1,020 points (14.6 points average) for the second-place Royals and earning NBA MVP honors. In 1953–1954, he made the All-NBA Second Team for the third consecutive time and led Rochester for the first time in scoring with 958 points (13.3 points average) and for the third time in shooting percentage. The Lakers edged the Royals for the Western Division crown and again in the NBA semifinals. Rochester dropped to a 29-43 third-place finish in 1954–1955, as Wanzer again paced the Royals in scoring with 942 points and averaged 13.1 points. Wanzer retired after the 1956–1957 season, having tallied 7,091 career points (11.7 points per game) in 608 games. His honors included five All-Star Game appearances for the West squad from 1952 through 1956 and election to the Naismith Memorial Basketball Hall of Fame in 1987.

Wanzer became Rochester player-coach in 1955–1956 and guided the struggling Royals to two consecutive 31-41 marks and fourth-place finishes. Maurice Stokes* and Jack Twyman* paced Wanzer's club in scoring. The franchise moved to Cincinnati, Ohio, before the 1957–1958 season and improved slightly to a 33-39 second place record. Clyde Lovellette* paced the 1957–1958 Royals to the NBA playoffs. Tom Marshall replaced Wanzer as coach after Cincinnati's miserable 3-15 start in the 1958–1959 campaign. As Royals head coach, Wanzer compiled a lackluster 98-136 mark. Seton Hall University retired Wanzer's number 8 jersey in December 1987.

BIBLIOGRAPHY: Jan Hubbard, ed., *The Official NBA Encyclopedia*, 3rd ed. (New York, 2000); Neil P. Isaacs, *Vintage NBA* (Silver Spring, MD, 1996); Roland Lazenby, *The NBA Finals* (Indianapolis, IN, 1996); Wayne Patterson to David L. Porter, April 4, 1988; Seton Hall University Sports Information press release, South Orange, NJ, December 17, 1987; Ken Shouler et al., *Total Basketball* (Wilmington, DE, 2003); Robert Wanzer file, Naismith Memorial Basketball Hall of Fame, Springfield, MA.

David L. Porter

WASHINGTON, Kermit Alan (b. September 17, 1951, Washington, D.C.), college and professional player, is the second son of Alexander Washington, a medical technician, and Barbara Washington, a teacher who suffered from manic depression. After his parents divorced, he spent part of his childhood living with his great grandmother.

At Coolidge High School in Washington, D.C., Washington performed poorly on the basketball court and in the classroom. Tom Young, coach at American University, watched Washington try out for a city all-star team and offered him a scholarship. Washington starred in basketball at American University (Washington,

D.C.) from 1969 to 1973, eventually earning a Bachelor's degree in psychology. The six-foot nine-inch, 230-pounder led the nation in rebounding in 1971–1972 and 1972–1973, concluding his collegiate career with an average of over 20 points and 20 rebounds. The consensus Second Team All-America was selected by the Los Angeles Lakers (NBA) in the 1973 NBA draft with the fifth overall pick. Following the draft, Washington married Pat Carter.

Washington starred at power forward and teamed with Kareem Abdul Jabbar* to rejuvenate the Los Angeles Laker franchise. During the 1976–1977 season, the Lakers enjoyed the best regular-season NBA mark. Washington averaged 9.3 rebounds and 9.7 points in 53 games despite being slowed by a knee injury.

Washington's NBA career, however, was altered in a December 9, 1977 confrontation with the Houston Rockets. When Washington became embroiled in a scuffle with Kevin Kunnert, Rudy Tomjanovich* of the Rockets leaped off the bench and rushed onto the court. Washington turned and landed what has become known as "the punch." Tomjanovich was knocked to the floor, suffering from severe fractures to the face and skull. After reconstructive surgery, Tomjanovich continued his NBA career and coached the Rockets to world championships. He also won a $3.2 million lawsuit from the Lakers.

Washington was fined $10,000 and suspended for 60 days. After his reinstatement, the Lakers traded him to the Boston Celtics (NBA) in December 1977. In August 1978, the Celtics shipped Washington to the San Diego Clippers (NBA). He played with the Portland Trail Blazers from 1979 to 1982, but he left the NBA at age 30. Washington was heckled by crowds throughout the NBA, and his career was never the same after his altercation with Tomjanovich. In 1987–1988, he attempted an aborted comeback with the Golden State Warriors (NBA). In 10 NBA seasons, Washington averaged 8.3 rebounds and 9.2 points in 507 games.

Washington wanted to pursue coaching following his NBA playing career, but he blames "the punch" for blocking that avenue. He settled in Portland, Oregon, but went bankrupt in 1997 when his sports bar in Vancouver, Washington failed. That same year, his marriage, which produced two children, collapsed. He has reconciled with Tomjanovich and participates in "Project Contact," providing medical supplies for African nations.

BIBLIOGRAPHY: John Feinstein, *The Punch* (New York, 2002); Jan Hubbard, ed., *The Official NBA Encyclopedia*, 3rd ed. (New York, 2000); Roland Lazenby, *The Lakers: A Basketball Journey* (New York, 1993); Jim Van Vlict, "A Life Altering Punch," *Sacramento Bee*, January 27, 2002.

Ron Briley

WATTS, Stanley Howard "Stan" (b. August 30, 1911, Murray, UT; d. April 6, 2000, Provo, VT), college athlete, basketball coach, and administrator, is the seventh of 11 children born to William Eugene Watts and Ethel Gertrude (Park) Watts. Watts grew up on a small farm, where his father raised sugar beets and served as field representative for a sugar company. A highly competitive, all-around athlete, he played football, basketball, and baseball at Murray (Utah) High School. After graduation in 1928, Watts attended Henagar BC in Salt Lake City, Utah for one year and then worked as a service station attendant and truck farmer before entering Weber State JC in Ogden, Utah in 1934. At Weber, he made All-UIJCC for two years in both football and basketball and also lettered two years in track and field. Watts then played football, basketball, and baseball at Brigham Young University (Utah). In 1938, he graduated with a Bachelor's degree in physical education and minored in history and was named the outstanding senior scholar-athlete. Watts married Emily Kelly on August 21, 1939, and had four children, Susan Jo, Janice Kay, Judith Ann, and Howard Brent. He coached multiple sports in Utah at Millard High School in Fillmore from 1939 to 1941, Dixie JC in St. George from 1941 to 1945, and Jordan High School in Sandy from 1945 to 1947, before being named head baseball coach and freshman football and basketball coach at Brigham Young University in 1947. In 1949, Watts became head basketball coach and assistant athletic director there. He served as Brigham Young's athletic director from 1972 to 1976.

Watts quickly became one of the most successful, respected basketball coaches in the nation, winning the RMC title his first two years. The sixth coach to win more than 100 games in his first five seasons, he never experienced a losing season in the 1950s. Overall, he suffered only four losing seasons in 23 years in leading the Cougars to a 372-254 record (.594 winning percentage), eight RMC and WAC championships (1950, 1951, 1957, 1965, 1967, 1969, 1971, 1972), 11 postseason appearances, and two NIT titles (1951, 1966). His teams featured discipline and a fast-break offense. In 1964–1965 and 1965–1966, the Cougars scored over 100 points 21 times and tallied at least 95 points 34 times. Often named RMC or WAC and Regional Coach of the Year, he made great achievements, including creating a winning basketball tradition at Brigham Young University, establishing a national athletic identity for the Mormon Church school, and infecting the surrounding community with hoop fever. His tenure saw the Cougars play in every major holiday tournament and the construction of two new fieldhouses, including the then-largest college basketball arena (22,700 seats) in the nation. Brigham Young in 1971 set a NCAA record with an average attendance of 21,818. Although one of the first coaches actively to recruit European players, Watts could not recruit black athletes because of the then-racially discriminatory priesthood policy of the Mormon Church. The 1969–1970 squad, the target of frequent, often violent student protests, posted the worst record (8-18) of his career.

A master teacher, Watts enjoyed the esteem of fellow coaches. His book, *Developing an Offensive Attack in Basketball* (1958), became the standard treatise on the fast-break offense. He remained in constant demand at coaching clinics across the nation and in Europe, the Far East, and South Africa. His Cougar teams performed exhibitions in Brazil in 1950 and toured South America in 1965 and Asia and the South Pacific in 1968 under the People-to-People program. Watts served the NABC on numerous committees, on the board of directors for 11 years (1958–1968), and as president (1969–1970). He also served four years (1951–1955) on the NBRC. In 1972 Watts retired from coaching, was named to coach the West team in the College All-Star Game, elected to the HAF Hall of Fame, chosen NCAA Rocky Mountain Area Coach of the Year, and voted WAC Coach of the Decade. Subsequently, he served two years (1975–1976) as chairman of the USOC, four years (1973–1976) on the NCAA Division I Basketball Committee (chair, 1975–1976), and two years (1976–1978) as supervisor of WAC basketball officials. Watts was elected to the Athletic Directors Hall of Fame in 1977 and as a coach to the Naismith Memorial Basketball Hall of Fame in 1985.

BIBLIOGRAPHY: Richard Dahl, *Stan Watts: The Man and His Game* (Bountiful, UT, 1976); *Deseret News*, March 17, 1972; *Deseret News* March 23, 1976; Paul James, *Cougar Tales* (Sandy, UT, 1984); *NYT*, March 18, 1951; *NYT*, March 20, 1966; Brad Rock and Lee Warnick, *Greatest Moments in BYU Sports* (Salt Lake City, UT, 1984); Salt Lake City *Tribune*, May 4, 1986; Stan Watts, *Developing an Offensive Attack in Basketball* (Englewood Cliffs, NJ, 1958); Stan Watts file, Brigham Young University Athletic Department, Provo, UT; Stan Watts file, Naismith Memorial Basketball Hall of Fame, Springfield, MA.

Larry R. Gerlach

WEATHERSPOON, Teresa Gaye (b. December 8, 1965, Jasper, TX), college and professional player, is the daughter of Charles Weatherspoon Sr., a minor league baseball catcher in the Minnesota Twins (AL) organization, and Rowena Weatherspoon, a champion drum majorette, and has two brothers—Charles Jr. and Michael—and three sisters—Diana, Carolyn, and Denise. Weatherspoon developed terrific basketball handling ability at West Sabine High School in tiny Pineland, Texas, where she graduated as valedictorian. She twice made All-America at Louisiana Tech University, led them to the NCAA championship in 1988, and was named NCAA National Player of the Year. Weatherspoon earned the Kodak All-America Award in 1987 and 1988. She won a gold medal on the U.S. basketball team at the 1988 Summer Olympics in Seoul, South Korea and a bronze medal at the 1992 Summer Olympics in Barcelona, Spain.

With no professional opportunities in the United States, Weatherspoon spent eight seasons in Europe playing in Italian and Russian basketball leagues. In 1997, she signed with the New York Liberty (WNBA). Her aggressive, smothering defense as a guard confounded opponents and made her a fan favorite. Weatherspoon twice earned WNBA Defensive Player of the Year accolades. She took the Liberty to the championship game against the Houston Comets in her first professional season. Weatherspoon led the WNBA in steals in 1997 and 1998, recording 100 the latter season. The consummate team player paced the WNBA with 6.1 assists per game in 1997 and finished second with 6.4 assists per game the following season. Weatherspoon recorded a career high eight steals against the Charlotte Sting on July 10, 1997. The five-foot eight-inch, 160-pound guard made a career best 19 points on August 15, 1997 against Sacramento Monarchs.

She made the All-WNBA Second Team in 1997, 1998, 1999, and 2000. In February 2004, the Los Angeles Sparks (WNBA) signed her as a free agent. Weatherspoon's career statistics through 2004 include 1,338 assists, 779 rebounds, 465 steals, and 1,264 points in 254 games. She has averaged 5.4 points, 6.0 assists, 3.3 rebounds, and 1.45 steals in 31 WNBA playoff games. She has made five WNBA All-Star teams.

Weatherspoon, who is single, loves to work with children and participates in the WSF and anti-drug crusades. She enjoys bowling, tennis, karate, and reading and authored *Teresa Weatherspoon's Basketball for Girls*, in which she shares her insights on playing good fundamental basketball. She claims baseball is her best sport.

BIBLIOGRAPHY: James Ponti, *WNBA Stars of Women's Basketball* (New York, 1999); *TSN Official WNBA Guide and Register, 2004* (St. Louis, MO, 2004); Teresa Weatherspoon, *Teresa Weatherspoon's Basketball for Girls* (Chichester, England, 1999); WNBA Enterprises, *Teresa Weatherspoon Playerfile* (WNBA.com), pp. 1–2.

Frank J. Olmsted

WEBBER, Mayce Edward Christopher, III "Chris" (b. March 1, 1973, Detroit, MI), college and professional player, is the son of Mayce Webber and Doris Webber. His father worked on a General Motors assembly line, while his mother operated an in-home preschool program. His parents overruled his objections and sent him on scholarship to a private school in Birmingham, Michigan. When he struggled with being relatively poor in an upper-class environment, his father took him to Mississippi to show him where he had grown up under humble, "Jim Crow" conditions. It was a life-changing event for Webber, who led the Country Day High School basketball team to two state Class B championships and a Class C state title. He became Michigan high school's third highest all-time scorer with 2,628 points and was named the state's Mr. Basketball as a senior. He was considered the nation's top high school player in 1991.

Known for excellent hands, quick leaping ability, and ferocious low-post play, Webber enrolled at the University of Michigan as part of the "Fab Five" freshman group that took the Wolverines to the finals of the NCAA Tournament in 1992 and 1993. He was selected Freshman of the Year and Second Team All-BTC in 1992 and First Team BTC in 1993. Webber made the NCAA All-Tournament Team in 1992 and 1993 and All-America in 1993. He ranks second all-time at Michigan in field goal percentage (.588) and blocked shots (175). His illegal timeout in the 1993 NCAA championship game contributed to the University of North Carolina's win. His college career was clouded in 2002, when Ed Martin pleaded guilty to giving thousands of dollars to Michigan basketball players, and Webber was indicted on charges of lying to a federal grand jury. Michigan penalized itself by forfeiting all of the games in which the "Fab Five" played.

The six-foot ten-inch 245-pound Webber was selected the number-one NBA pick by the Orlando Magic (NBA) in 1993 and traded that day to the Golden State Warriors (NBA), where he was chosen 1994 NBA Rookie of the Year. He played for the Washington Bullets (NBA) from 1994–1995 to 1997–1998 and was traded to the Sacramento Kings (NBA) in May 1998. He has matured into a NBA All-Star power forward with the Kings, having appeared in five NBA All-Star Games (1997, 2000–2003), and made the All-NBA First Team in 2001, All-NBA Second Team in 1999, 2002, and 2003 and All-NBA Third Team in 2000. In March 2005, the

Philadelphia 76ers acquired him. Through 2004–2005, he scored 14,945 points (21.8 point average) and averaged 10.1 rebounds in 686 regular-season games. He has averaged 20.9 points and 9.3 rebounds in 64 playoff games.

Webber is not married.

BIBLIOGRAPHY: Mitch Albom, *Fab Five* (New York, 1993); Fahizah Alim, "A King's Treasure," *Sacramento Bee,* January 24, 2003, NBA.com.; "Ed Martin, Obituary," *NYT*, February 18, 2003, p. A25; Larry Platt, "The Chris Webber Nobody Knows," ESPN.com, May 9, 2002; Ken Shouler et al., *Total Basketball* (Wilmington, DE, 2003); *TSN Official NBA Guide, 2000–2001*, (St. Louis, MO, 2000); *TSN Official NBA Register, 2004–2005* (St. Louis, MO, 2004); University of Michigan Athletic Department, Sports Information Ann Arbor, MI.

Keith McClellan

WELLS, W. R. Clifford "Cliff" (b. March 17, 1896, Indianapolis, IN; d. August 15, 1977, Garland, TX), college coach, served as the first executive director of the Naismith Memorial Basketball Hall of Fame. A 1920 graduate of Indiana University, Wells enjoyed an illustrious career as high school basketball coach in Indiana. His high school coaching career spanned three decades, included tenures at Columbus, Bloomington, and Logansport, and featured state championships at Bloomington in 1919 and Logansport in 1934. Wells' Indiana high school teams won 617 games, punctuated by fifty regional, district, and invitational hoop titles. After World War II, Wells coached at Tulane University (Louisiana) from 1945 until his retirement in 1963, compiling a 250-155 win-loss record. His combined high school and college coaching record comprised an awesome 885 wins against only 418 losses, earning him election to the Naismith Memorial Basketball Hall of Fame in 1971 as one of the game's outstanding pioneer contributors.

Wells conducted countless clinics, wrote numerous articles on the techniques and strategies of the sport, and served on the NBRC. As one of many memorable Indiana high school coaches of the Depression and post-Depression eras of the 1930s and 1940s, he made his greatest impact on schoolboy basketball. Wells stood justifiably in the company of such truly monumental coaches as Everett Case*, Howard Sharpe, Glenn Curtis, and Marion L. Crawley, who contributed to the development of high school athletics in basketball-rich Indiana. His position as an Indiana coaching legend has been permanently immortalized with his induction to the Indiana Basketball Hall of Fame in Indianapolis. Wells, who served as executive director of the NABC for 12 years and as a director of the Naismith Memorial Basketball Hall of Fame, was survived by two daughters, Mrs. William Moore and Mrs. Clyde Black Jr., and two sons, Robert and Richard.

BIBLIOGRAPHY: Peter C. Bjarkman, *The Biographical History of Basketball* (Chicago, IL, 2000); Zander Hollander, ed., *The Pro Basketball Encyclopedia* (Los Angeles, CA, 1977); Ronald L. Mendell, *Who's Who in Basketball* (New Rochelle, NY, 1973); *NCAA Men's Basketball Records, 2004* (Indianapolis, IN, 2003); *NYT*, August 16, 1977, p. 38; Herb Schwomeyer, *Hoosier Hysteria: A History of Indiana High School Boys Basketball*, 6th ed. (Greenfield, IN, 1970); Cliff Wells file, Naismith Memorial Basketball Hall of Fame, Springfield, MA; Bob Williams, *Hoosier Hysteria: Indiana High School Basketball* (South Bend, IN, 1982).

Peter C. Bjarkman

WEST, Jerry Alan (b. May 28, 1938, Cheylan, WV), college and professional player, coach, and executive, is the son of Howard West and Cecil Sue (Creasey) West. His father worked as a machinist, gas station operator, and electrician. West attended East Bank High School, where he led the team his senior year to the state championship and became the first West Virginia schoolboy to score over 900 points in a season. By averaging 32.2 points-per-game, he helped his team to a 23-5 win-loss record. West, recruited by over 60 colleges, chose West Virginia University on his high school graduation in 1956. After his college freshman team finished 17-0, West started as a sophomore and averaged 17.8 points. As a junior, he scored 26.6 points-per-outing and led the Mountaineers to the NCAA Final. In his superlative senior season, he averaged 29.3 points, led the Mountaineers to their third consecutive SC Championship, and was selected consensus All-America. West also played on the U.S.

Olympic Team, which won the Gold Medal at the Rome, Italy, Olympic Games in 1960. That year, he also married Martha Jane Kane and was drafted by the Los Angeles Lakers (NBA). The Wests had three sons, David, Michael, and Mark. After their divorce, he married Karen Bua in May 1978 and has one son, Ryan.

West did not start his rookie season with the Lakers, but still averaged 17.6 points. That year, he was overshadowed by Cincinnati Royals rookie Oscar Robertson*, who averaged over 30 points. In 1961–1962, West matched Robertson by coincidentally averaging identical 30.8 points. Thereafter, he always averaged at least 20 points. Although playing forward in college, the six foot three inch, 185-pound West moved to guard as a pro. He battled with the bigger players, however, and suffered eight broken noses during his career. West played virtually his entire career with Elgin Baylor* and three years with Wilt Chamberlain*, but they could not bring the Lakers an NBA championship until the 1971–1972 season. Coached by Bill Sharman*, the Lakers won 33 consecutive games that year on their way to the NBA championship.

Besides being one of the greatest shooters in NBA history, West also was a great playmaker and ranked among the highest assist makers (6,238) in NBA history. He notched 63 points against the New York Knickerbockers in 1963, averaged over 30 points four seasons, and scored 25,192 career points (27.0 points per game). West, who made 3,160 career free throws (.814) and was selected 1972 All-Star Game MVP, led the NBA in scoring in 1969–1970 (2,309 points, 31.2 points average) and in assists in 1971–1972 (career-high 747), and converted the most free throws in one season (818 in 1965–1966). West made the All-NBA First Team 10 times (1962 through 1967 and 1970 through 1973) and the All-NBA Second Team in 1968 and 1969. He also was named to the All-NBA Defensive First Team from 1970 through 1973. West was the all-time playoff leader in free throws made (1,622) and scoring average (29.1 points).

West retired because of recurring injuries after the 1973–1974 season, but returned in 1976 as Lakers' coach. He compiled a 145-101 win-loss record with a .589 winning percentage and led Los Angeles to the playoffs for three consecutive years (1976–1977 through 1978–1979), yet found the NBA championship elusive.

West served as general manager of the Los Angeles Lakers, winners of five NBA championships in the 1980s, from 1982–1983 through 1993–1994. He was executive vice president of basketball operations for the Lakers from 1994–1995 through 1999–2000 and became president of basketball operations for the Memphis Grizzlies (NBA) in 2002.

In 1962, West was selected to the College Basketball Hall of Fame. He was named as a player to the Naismith Memorial Basketball Hall of Fame in 1979, to the NBA's 35th Anniversary All-Time Team in 1980, and one of the 50 Greatest Players in NBA History in 1996.

BIBLIOGRAPHY: Peter C. Bjarkman, *The Biographical History of Basketball* (Chicago, IL, 2000); Richard Hoffer, "Mister Clutch, Master Builder," *SI* 72 (April 23, 1990); Zander Hollander, ed., *The Modern Encyclopedia of Basketball* (Garden City, NY, 1979); Zander Hollander, ed., *The NBA's Official Encyclopedia of Professional Basketball* (New York, 1981); Jan Hubbard, ed., *The Official NBA Encyclopedia*, 3rd ed. (New York, 2000); Roland Lazenby, *The Lakers: A Basketball Journey* (New York, 1993); Charles Salzberg, *From Set Shot to Slam Dunk* (New York, 1987); Ken Shouler et al., *Total Basketball* (Wilmington, DE, 2003); *TSN Official NBA Register 2004–2005* (St. Louis MO, 2004); Jerry West with Bill Libby, *Mr. Clutch: The Jerry West Story* (Englewood Cliffs, NJ, 1969); Jerry West file, Naismith Memorial Basketball Hall of Fame, Springfield, MA; *WWA*, 44th ed. (1986–1987), p. 2947.

Stephen D. Bodayla

WESTPHAL, Paul Douglas (b. November 30, 1950, Torrence, CA), college and professional player and coach, learned basketball from his older brother, Bill. Westphal's father, Armin, a helicopter designer, drove him around the Los Angeles area to participate in many basketball leagues. Westphal graduated in 1968 from Aviation High School in Redondo Beach, California, averaging 32 points and becoming the first Southern California high school player to surpass 1,000 points in a season. As a senior, he was named CIF Player of the Year and an All-America. UCLA coach John Wooden* heavily recruited the six-foot four-inch, 195-pound guard. Westphal, however, followed his brother's footsteps at the University of Southern California and made the All-PEC First Team as a sophomore and a junior. He led the 1970–1971 Trojans to a school best 24-2 record. A knee injury limited him to 14 games in 1971–1972, but he still made the All-PEC Second Team and averaged 20.3 points.

The Boston Celtics (NBA) drafted Westphal in the 1972 first round as the tenth player selected. The valuable reserve participated on the 1974 Celtic championship team and averaged 7.3 points in three seasons with the Celtics. In May 1975, Boston traded him to the Phoenix Suns (NBA) for Charlie Scott*. Led by Westphal and 1976 Rookie of the Year Alvan Adams, Phoenix qualified for the 1976 NBA championship series against the Celtics. Westphal paced the Suns in scoring his first five years, averaging 25.2 points in 1977–1978 and 24.0 points in 1978–1979. On February 21, 1980, he scored a career-high 49 points against the Detroit Pistons.

Phoenix dealt Westphal to the Seattle SuperSonics (NBA) in a controversial June 1980 trade for Dennis Johnson*. A foot injury limited Westphal to only 36 games in 1980–1981, but he appeared in the 1981 All-Star Game. After Seattle released him, the New York Knicks (NBA) signed him in March 1982. The 1982–1983 campaign saw Westphal earn the NBA Comeback Player of the Year Award. He finished his NBA career at Phoenix in an injury-plagued 1982–1983 season. Westphal, who was named to the All-NBA First Team in 1977, 1979, and 1980 and the All-NBA Second Team in 1978, appeared in four All-Star Games with the Suns and one with the SuperSonics, and averaged 19.4 points in those contests. In 823 games, he scored 12,809 points (15.6 point average) and made 3,591 assists.

Westphal's basketball coaching career began at Southwestern Bible College in Phoenix, Arizona, in 1985, guiding the school to a 21-9 win-loss record and a national title. Under Westphal, Grand Canyon College (Arizona) finished 26-12 in 1986–1987 and 37-6 in 1987–1988 and won the 1988 NAIA national title. The Phoenix Suns employed Westphal an assistant coach from the 1988–1989 through 1991–1992 season.

Westphal served as head coach of the Phoenix Suns from 1992–1993 through January 1996, compiling a 191-88 record and finishing first in the Pacific Division in 1992–1993 and 1994–1995. In 1993, the Suns defeated the Seattle SuperSonics in the Western Conference Finals and lost to the Chicago Bulls, four games to two, in the NBA Finals. Westphal coached the Seattle SuperSonics from 1998 to December 2000, compiling a 76-71 record. Seattle enjoyed a 45-37 record in 1999–2000, and lost in the first round of the playoffs. During seven NBA seasons, Westphal boasted a 267-159 regular-season record and 27-22 playoff mark. Westphal coached Pepperdine University since 2001, guiding them to a 22-9 mark and share of the WCC title in 2001–2002. Pepperdine finished 15–13 in 2002–2003, 15-16 in 2003–2004, and 16-14 in 2004–2005. In seven years as a collegiate coach, he has notched a 130–70 record and .650 winning percentage. He and his wife, Cindy, have two children, Victoria and Michael Paul.

BIBLIOGRAPHY: Peter C. Bjarkman, *The Biographical History of Basketball* (Chicago, IL, 2000); Mike Douchant, *Encyclopedia of College Basketball* (Detroit, MI, 1990); Joe Gilmartin, *The Little Team That Could and Darn Near Did!* (Phoenix, AZ, 1976); *Phoenix Suns 1979–1980 Media Guide and Record Book* (Phoenix, AZ, 1979); *Phoenix Suns Fastbreak* 1 (1989); Ken Shouler et al., *Total Basketball* (Wilmington, DE, 2003); *TSN Official NBA Guide, 1984–1985* (St. Louis, MO, 1984); *TSN Official NBA Register, 2004–2005* (St. Louis, MO, 2004).

Curtice R. Mang

WHITE, Joseph Henry "Jo Jo" (b. November 16, 1946, St. Louis, MO), college and professional player, coach, and executive, is the youngest of seven children of George White, and Elizabeth White a minister. A natural athlete with excellent speed, White started playing basketball at age 11 in the St. Louis (Missouri) Buder Recreation Center. His high school basketball career began at Vashon High School as a freshman and sophomore and continued at McKinley High School as a junior and senior. He won All-State honors both years. At the University of Kansas, White played on two BEC championship basketball teams (1965–1966, 1966–1967), was selected three-time All-BEC, and was chosen two-time All-America (1968, 1969). For the Jayhawks, he scored 1,286 points, averaged 15.3 points, and made 42 percent of his field goal attempts. White represented the United States in the World University Games at Tokyo, Japan, in 1966; the Pan-American Games at Winnipeg, Canada, in 1967; and the Olympic Games at Mexico City, Mexico, in 1968. He played a key role in the gold medal–success of each of those teams. Because of his amateur success, White became one of the most sought after basketball players of his era.

In 1969, White became the first-round pick (ninth overall selection) of the Boston Celtics (NBA). Because he had to complete a six-month tour with the U.S. Marines, he did not join the Celtics until November 13. Even though the six-foot three-inch, 190-pound guard missed one-fourth of his rookie season, White played in 60 games, averaged 12.2 points, and earned a spot on the 1970 NBA All-Rookie Team. During 12 NBA seasons with the Boston Celtics (1969–1979), Golden State Warriors (1979–1980), and Kansas City Kings (1980–1981), he played on two NBA championship teams (1974, 1976) and in seven consecutive NBA All-Star Games (1971–1977) and twice was named to the All-NBA Second Team (1975, 1977). White was selected the 1976 NBA playoffs MVP, recording 408 points, 98 assists, 71 rebounds, and 23 steals. On April 9, 1982, his uniform number 10 was retired by the Boston Celtics. In July 1981, White joined the basketball coaching staff of Ted Owen at the University of Kansas. Larry Brown* succeeded Owen in April 1983 and dismissed White on July 14, 1983 because of "philosophical differences." White then moved to Rochester, New York and worked as a sports agent. At age 41 and desiring to return to the NBA, White played briefly with the Topeka Sizzlers (CBA) during the 1987–1988 season. Since 2000, he has served as director of special projects for the Boston Celtics.

During the latter part of the 1960s and throughout the 1970s, White possessed the physical and mental ability, determination, and dedication to become one of the nation's best basketball players.

BIBLIOGRAPHY: Peter C. Bjarkman, *The Boston Celtics Encyclopedia* (Champaign, IL, 1998); Boston Celtics, Public Relations Office, Boston, MA; *Des Moines* (IA) *Register*, November 5, 1987; Mike Douchant, *Encyclopedia of College Basketball* (Detroit, MI, 1995); Jack Etkin, "White Brings Celtics Legacy into Coaching," *Kansas City Times*, November 11, 1981; Joe Fitzgerald, "Jo Jo White, K.C. King, Calls It a Career," *Boston Herald American*, November 3, 1980; Merv Harris, "Jo Jo White," *On Court with the Superstars of the NBA* (New York, 1973); John Hendel, *Kansas Jayhawks* (Coal Valley, IL, 1991); *NBA Sports*, February 17, 1970; *NYT*, July 15, 1983; Bob Ryan, "Didn't Anyone Notice Jo Jo's Arrival?" *Boston Globe*, January 6, 1974; Bob Ryan, "Jo Jo White Superstar Finally," *Black Sports* (January 1977), pp. 23–25; Ken Shouler et al., *Total Basketball* (Wilmington, DE, 2003); *TSN NBA Register, 2003–2004* (St. Louis, MO, 2003).

James E. Welch

WHITE, Nera Dyson (b. November 15, 1935, Macon County, TN), college player, is the daughter of teacher Horace White and Lois (Fishburn) White and had three brothers and three sisters. At Macon County High School in Lafayette, Tennessee, White captained the basketball team for two years and participated in many school activities. After graduating in 1954, she attended George Peabody College for Teachers from 1954 to 1958 and was recruited by coach John Head* to play basketball for Nashville (Tennessee) BC. White quickly became a team leader at Nashville BC and won All-America honors in her first AAU Tournament. She received All-America honors fifteen consecutive times (1955 to 1969) for a women's basketball record. Nine times White was named the MVP of the national AAU Tournament. In the 1962 championship game, she scored 28 points in Nashville BC's 63-58 victory over Wayland Baptist College. White's 23 points in the 1966 title match secured another AAU championship and an undefeated season.

An all-around playmaker, rebounder, defender, and shooter, White was principally known as an unselfish player dedicated to team victory. Nashville BC won 85 percent of its games, including 10 AAU championships and three second-place AAU finishes, while she played. Nashville BC captured eight straight AAU titles and 91 of 92 games in one stretch before the team disbanded after the 1968–1969 season. White frequently participated on the U.S. international team from the mid-1950s to mid-1960s. In the 1957 World Championship Tournament, she led the American team to the gold medal in a close game over the Russians in Rio de Janeiro, Brazil. As a result, White was voted the Best Woman Player in the World.

The six-foot, 157-pound White also excelled at softball, being named to numerous state and regional All-Star teams, and being selected as All-World on the ASA Fast Pitch team in 1959 and 1965. A centerfielder, shortstop, and pitcher whose best asset was speed, she became the first woman to circle the bases in 10 seconds flat. White also won a softball-throwing contest by tossing the ball out of the stadium. She later played slow-pitch softball and was named an All-America in 1980. In 1984, she played for Universal Plastics Company of Cookeville, Tennessee.

Between 1960 and 1981, White worked at Nashville Auto-Diesel College and was promoted to printing department supervisor. She currently farms near Lafayette and has one son. The greatest female player of her era, White has been elected to the AAU Basketball (1959), HAF (1966), Tennessee Sports (1968), and Naismith Memorial Basketball (1992) halls of fame.

BIBLIOGRAPHY: Peter C. Bjarkman, *The Biographical History of Basketball* (Chicago, IL, 2000); Mike Douchant, *Encyclopedia of College Basketball* (Detroit, MI, 1995); Bill Isom, "AAU Women's Basketball Queen," *Amateur Athlete* (November 1969), pp. 6–8; Ken Shouler et al., *Total Basketball* (Wilmington, DE, 2003); Nora White file, Naismith Memorial Basketball Hall of Fame, Springfield, MA.

Dennis S. Clark

WHITE, Stephanie Joanne (b. June 20, 1977, Danville, IL), college and professional player, coach, and sportscaster, is the daughter of Kevin White and Jennie White and has two sisters, Shanda and Stacey, a forward on the Illinois State women's basketball team. At Seeger High School in West Lebanon, White averaged 36.9 points, 8.2 assists, 13.1 rebounds, and 7.0 steals her senior year to claim the Gatorade, *USA Today*, and *Parade* magazine National Prep Player of the Year accolades. She scored in double figures in 98 of 99 her varsity games during her high school career, amassing 2,869 total points (an Indiana state high school record), and averaging 29 points, 11.2 rebounds, 7 assists, and 6.5 steals. The Patriots won 92 of 99 games during her four campaigns.

White was selected two time All-America in basketball at Purdue University (Indiana), National Player of the Year runner-up, four time All-BTC Team, and three time All-BTC Academic Team. On January 22, 1999, she made the first triple-double in Purdue women's basketball history, scoring 22 points, making 11 assists, and grabbing 11 rebounds against Indiana University. White severely sprained her left ankle in the fourth quarter of the 1999 NCAA championship game, won by the Boilermakers 62-45 over Duke University. She established Purdue records with 127 consecutive starts and 707 points in a season. White scored 2,182 points in 127 career games at Purdue and earned a Bachelor of Arts degree in communications from Purdue in 1999.

White, a five-foot nine-inch, 155-pound guard was drafted in 1999 by the Charlotte Sting (WNBA) and played 30 games as a rookie, scoring 209 points with 52 assists. She was traded to the expansion Indiana Fever (WNBA) for Sandy Brondello and a first-round draft pick in December 1999. On a team loaded with forwards, she often came off the bench during the 2000 and 2001 seasons. Surgery on her right knee and left ankle forced her to sit out the 2002 campaign. White returned to the Fever in 2003 and led the team with a .938 free throw shooting percentage. She appeared in just 22 games in 2004, averaging 4.1 points. Her WNBA career totals through the 2004 season included 1,061 points scored, 233 rebounds, 277 assists, and 134 steals. She scored on .828 percent of her free throw attempts. She retired from the WNBA after the 2004 season.

White served as assistant girls basketball coach for Lafayette Jefferson High School in Lafayette, Indiana in 2001–2002 and Logansport (Indiana) High School during the 2002–2003 season. In May 2003, she was named assistant women's basketball coach at

Ball State University of Indiana. She has served as a sideline reporter for Fox Sports and operates Stephanie White Basketball Camps.

White married longtime boyfriend Brent McCarty in May 1998. She has played under the names White and McCarty at Purdue and in the WNBA and currently uses the name White.

BIBLIOGRAPHY: AP, "McCarty Bulked up for WNBA Season," Sports Illustrated.com (May 3, 2001), pp. 1–2; AP, "McCarty to Draw On On-Court Success," *Fort Wayne (IN) Journal Gazette* (September 26, 2002), website, pp. 1–2; Conrad Brunner, "Renewed Love of Game Fuels White's Comeback," WNBA Enterprises, WNBA.com, (May 7, 2003), pp. 1–2; Shari L. Finnell, "Stephanie McCarty Gets Feverish Hot Times ahead at Conseco Fieldhouse," *Indianapolis Woman* (June 2000); Clay Kallam, "What Did You expect? Superstars?," *WNBA fullcourt press* (December 15, 1999), pp. 1–2; Tom Schott, "Is There a Seamstress in the House?," *Student Advantage* (June 16, 1998), p. 1; "Stephanie McCarty Player profile," WNBA.com (2003), p. 1.

Frank J. Olmsted

WICKS, Sidney (b. September 19, 1949, Los Angeles, CA), college and professional player, is the son of divorced parents and has three brothers. His mother, Mrs. James Smiley, brought up the three children. Wicks, a skinny child with pipe-stem legs, developed into a fine basketball player at Hamilton High School in Los Angeles, California. He attended Santa Monica City College (California) one year, averaging 26.0 points and being named the MVP.

Coach John Wooden* recruited Wicks in 1968 for UCLA (PEC), a team that already had won four NCAA championships in five seasons. Wicks averaged 7.5 points as a sophomore reserve, helping UCLA capture the 1969 NCAA championship. As a junior, the six-foot nine-inch, 225-pound forward averaged 18.6 points and led the Bruins to an 80-69 victory over the Jacksonville University (Florida) in the memorable 1970 NCAA title game. Wicks, who was assigned to cover the much taller Artis Gilmore*, scored 17 points and grabbed 18 rebounds. His honors included being selected the NCAA Tournament's Most Outstanding Player and making the All-America Second Team as a junior, as well as being named to the All-America First Team and *TSN* College Player of the Year as a senior. He led UCLA to its fifth consecutive NCAA championship in 1971, averaging 21.3 points. The HAF College Basketball Hall of Fame enshrined him. The Portland Trailblazers (NBA) drafted Wicks in the first round in 1971. In his first season, Wicks paced Portland in scoring with a career-high 24.5 points average and attained NBA Rookie of the Year honors. He averaged at least 19 points in the next four seasons and appeared in four All-Star Games, but could not turn the Trail Blazers into a winning team. Portland sold Wicks to the Boston Celtics (NBA) in October 1976. He averaged 15.1 points in two seasons with the Celtics and scored 13.1 points in nine 1977 playoff games, his only postseason experience. Wicks completed his career with a three-year stint from 1978–1979 to 1980–1981 with the San Diego Clippers (NBA). Wicks averaged 16.8 points during 10 NBA campaigns, experiencing a decrease in scoring average in each successive season.

BIBLIOGRAPHY: Morgan G. Brenner, *College Basketball's National Championships* (Lanham, MD, 1999); Dwight Chapin and Jeff Prugh, *The Wizard of Westwood: Coach John Wooden and His UCLA Bruins* (Boston, MA, 1973); Mike Douchant, *Encyclopedia of College Basketball* (Detroit, MI, 1995); Jan Hubbard, ed., *The Official NBA Encyclopedia*, 3rd ed. (New York, 2000); Scott Howard-Cooper, *The Bruins 100* (Lenexa, KS, 1999); *Official NCAA Basketball Guide, 1971* (Phoenix, AZ, 1971); *TSN Official NBA Guide, 1971–1972* (St. Louis, MO, 1971); *TSN Official NBA Register, 1981–1982* (St. Louis, MO, 1981), John Wooden, *They Call Me Coach* (Waco, TX, 1972).

Curtis R. Mang

WILKE, Louis G. "Lou" (b. October 10, 1896, Chicago, IL; d. February 28, 1962, Chicago, IL), college player, coach, and administrator, graduated from Alva High School in Alva, Oklahoma, and then Northwestern (Oklahoma) State College in 1916. He coached all sports except basketball at Shattuck (Oklahoma) High School in 1916–1917 and earned a Bachelor of Arts degree from Phillips University in Bartlesville, Oklahoma in 1920. Wilke captained both the Northwestern and Phillips University basketball teams and served with the American Expeditionary Force in Europe during World War I. As a head coach at Nowata (Oklahoma) High School (1920–1926) and Bartlesville High School (1926–1928), he developed several excellent football, basketball, and track and field teams.

In 1928, Wilke became head football and basketball coach and athletic director at Phillips University. His football squads upset the University of Tulsa (Oklahoma) twice, while his basketball teams made two highly successful trips to the Pacific Coast. The Haymakers basketball squad also defeated the 1928 Kansas City, Missouri Cook Paints and the 1930 Wichita, Kansas Henrys, both National AAU champions, and reached the quarterfinals of the 1929 AAU Tournament. Wilke joined the marketing division of the Phillips Petroleum Company in 1929 and coached the Phillips 66ers basketball team to a composite 98-8 win-loss record during the 1929–1930 and 1930–1931 seasons. His coaching career ended when the depression forced Phillips to suspend its basketball program from 1931 to 1936.

Wilke promoted amateur athletics for the next three decades. His activities included being president of the Oklahoma and Rocky Mountain AAU Associations and a member of the Naismith Memorial Basketball Hall of Fame Executive and Selections Committees and the IBFRC. Wilke chaired the National AAU Basketball Committee and the USOBC and managed the 1948 U.S. Olympic Basketball Team, gold medal–winners at the London, England Summer Games. He also was vice chairman of the IABF and vice president of the PAFB.

During World War II, Wilke chaired the Committee for Joint Use of Oil Marketing Facilities in the Rocky Mountain area and directed the Supply and Marketing for District Number Four under the Petroleum Administration for War at Denver, Colorado. The very successful National AAU Basketball Tournaments, dominated by the Phillips 66ers during the 1940s, were conceived for Denver by Wilke. His expanding basketball assignments now included memberships on the IBC, the U.S. Olympic Executive Committee, and President Dwight D. Eisenhower's Citizen's Advisory Committee on Fitness of American Youth, chairmanship of the U.S. Olympic Policy Committee, and the presidency of the NIBL (two terms) and of the National AAU (1954–1955). In 1959, he presided over the U.S. delegation at the World Amateur Basketball Tournament in Santiago, Chile, and was technical director of the Pan American Games at Chicago. Wilke headed the administrative committees of the 1960 Winter Olympic Games at Squaw Valley, California and the 1960 Summer Olympic Games at Rome, Italy. Before his death, he helped the U.S. Olympic Board of Governors and the USOBC begin preparations for the 1964 Summer Olympic Games at Tokyo, Japan.

Wilke, who was elected to the HAF Hall of Fame and in 1983 to the Naismith Memorial Basketball Hall of Fame, retired as assistant sales manager of Phillips Petroleum Company in 1961 and continued to administer amateur athletic programs until his death. In November 1961, the IBF asked him to mediate differences between the NCAA and AAU over which group should represent the U.S. in international basketball competition. He and his wife, Maxine (Watson) Wilke, resided in Bartlesville and had two children. Wilke had promoted amateur basketball by building the Phillips 66ers outstanding hoop program and by exhibiting enormous leadership in AAU and Olympic activities.

BIBLIOGRAPHY: Tom Boyd and Daniel B. Droege, *Phillips: The First 66 Years* (Bartlesville, OK, 1983); Norman Lobsenz, *The Boots Adams Story* (Bartlesvilles OK, 1965); *NYT*, March 1, 1962; Wayne Patterson to David L. Porter, February 29, 1988; Louis G. Wilke file, Naismith Memorial Basketball Hall of Fame, Springfield, MA.

David L. Porter

WILKENS, Leonard Randolph "Lenny" (b. October 28, 1937, Brooklyn, NY), college and professional player, coach, and executive, is the son of Leonard R. Wilkens and Henrietta (Cross) Wilkens and grew up in the Bedford-Stuyvesant ghetto in Brooklyn New York. Wilkens began playing basketball in the early 1950s in the CYO. His friend, future major league baseball star Tommy Davis persuaded him to join his high school basketball team for the final semester of his senior year. Few colleges outside of New York had heard of Wilkens, but

CYO coach Father Thomas Mannion helped him receive a full scholarship to Providence (Rhode Island) College. The six-foot one-inch, 185-pound Wilkens was small by basketball standards, but made most All-America teams as a senior in 1960. He still ranks among the all-time leaders in points (1,193) and rebounds (583) at Providence.

In 1960, Wilkens was drafted in the first round by the St. Louis Hawks (NBA). Despite winning three consecutive Western Division titles, the Hawks possessed a weak backcourt. Wilkens became a starter midway through his rookie year and finished with an 11.9 points scoring average. With the Hawks, he became the annual team leader in assists and always ranked among the NBA leaders. During his eight seasons with the Hawks, Wilkens averaged 15.9 points and dished out 3,048 assists. After the 1967–1968 season, he was traded to the Seattle SuperSonics (NBA) for Walt Hazzard.* In his first season with Seattle, Wilkens recorded a career-high 22.4 points scoring average. He became the SuperSonics' player-coach in his second season. Under Wilkens, the young SuperSonics improved by winning 38 and 47 games in successive seasons. His stellar play continued, as he finished second in the NBA in assists in 1971–1972 while scoring 18.0 points per game.

Because the burden of being a player-coach had become increasingly difficult, Wilkens stepped down as SuperSonics coach in 1972 with a 121-125 composite mark. Seattle traded him in August 1972 to the Cleveland Cavaliers (NBA), where he enjoyed two more successful seasons. In 1974–1975, Wilkens became player-coach for the Portland Trail Blazers (NBA). This marked his final season as a player, as he averaged under 10 points for the first and only time in his career. He remained as Portland's coach for one more unsuccessful season with a 75-89 composite mark before being replaced by Jack Ramsay*. After the Seattle SuperSonics started the 1977–1978 season with a 5-17 record, he replaced Bob Hopkins as coach. Under Wilkens, the SuperSonics compiled a 42-18 standard for the remainder of the season. Seattle made the NBA Finals before losing to the Washington Bullets in seven games. He led the SuperSonics to the NBA Finals the next season and to their first NBA championship by defeating Washington in five games. Wilkens remained as Seattle coach through the 1984–1985 campaign for a 357-277 composite record and then became the team's general manager.

Wilkens joined the youthful Cleveland Cavaliers (NBA) as head coach and guided them to a 31-51 mark in 1986–1987. Cleveland, paced by Larry Nance and Brad Daugherty*, improved to a 42-40 mark in 1987–1988 and made the NBA playoffs. He coached Cleveland through the 1992–1993 season, compiling a 316-258 record and a 18-23 mark in five NBA playoffs. His best seasons came in 1988–1989 and 1991–1992, when the Cavaliers finished 57-25 and second in the Central Division. Wilkens coached the Atlanta Hawks (NBA) from 1993–1994 through 1999–2000, boasting a 310-232 mark. He guided Atlanta to a 57-25 mark and first place in the Central Division in 1993–1994, being named NBA Coach of the Year. Atlanta also finished 50-32 in 1996–1997 and 31-19 in 1998–1999, placing second in the Central Division. Wilkens coached the Toronto Raptors (NBA) to 47-35 in 2000–2001, 42-40 in 2001–2002, and 24-58 in 2002–2003, then joined the New York Knicks (NBA) as head coach in January 2004. He guided the Knicks to a 23-19 record and seventh-place finish in the Eastern Conference in 2004, but his club was swept by the New Jersey Nets in the first round of the playoffs. Wilkens resigned as Knicks coach in January 2005 after a disappointing 17–22 start. He coauthored *The Lenny Wilkens Story* (1974) and *Unguarded* (2000).

As an NBA player for 15 seasons, Wilkens scored 17,772 points, averaged 16.5 points, and recorded 7,211 career assists, ninth on the all-time list. He played nine All-Star Games and was named MVP in the 1971 game. Wilkens also coached for 32 seasons through 2005 and accumulated 1,332 wins and 1,159 regular-season losses, currently first on the NBA all-time list. His clubs finished 80-98 in 20 NBA playoffs. He was elected to the Naismith Memorial Basketball Hall of Fame as a player in 1988 and coach in 1998, joining John Wooden* and Bill Sharman as the only such inductees. He made the NBA's 50th Anniversary All-Time Team in 1996 and coached Team U.S.A. to a 8-0 record and gold medal at the 1996 Atlanta, Georgia Olympic games.

BIBLIOGRAPHY: Peter C. Bjarkman, *The Biographical History of Basketball* (Chicago, IL, 2000); Richard Coren, *Providence College Basketball* (Charleston SC, 2002); Raymond Hill, *Unsung Heroes of Pro Basketball* (New York, 1973); Jan Hubbard, ed., *The Official NBA Encyclopedia*, 3rd ed. (New York, 2000); *The Lincoln Library of Sports Champions*, vol. 13 (Columbus, OH, 1974); Ken Shouler et al., *Total Basketball* (Wilmington, DE, 2003); *TSN Official NBA Guide, 2004–2005 (St. Louis, MO, 2004); TSN Official NBA Register, 2004–2005* (St. Louis, MO, 2004); Lenny Wilkens, with Paul Erickson, *The Lenny Wilkens Story* (New York, 1974); Lenny Wilkens, with Terry Pluto, *Unguarded: My Forty Years Surviving the NBA* (New York, 2000); Lenny Wilkens file, Naismith Memorial Basketball Hall of Fame, Springfield, MA.

Curtice R. Mang

WILKES, Glenn Newton (b. November 28, 1928, Mansfield, GA), college player and coach, served as basketball coach at Stetson University (Florida) for 36 years and authored several books on basketball coaching. He compiled a career 551-436 record at Stetson from 1958 to 1993.

Wilkes, the son of Homer Wilkes and Dorothy Wilkes, attended Mansfield (Georgia), public schools and played basketball at Mercer University in Macon Georgia, where he graduated with a Bachelor of Arts in physical education in 1950.

Wilkes coached basketball at Brewton-Parker College in Mt. Vernon, Georgia in 1950 and 1951 and served in the U.S. Army from 1951 to 1953, attaining the rank of sergeant. After leaving the U.S. Army, he coached basketball at Baker County High School in Newton, Georgia, for one season. Wilkes returned to Brewton-Parker College as basketball coach in 1954 and remained there until 1957 while completing his M.A degree at Peabody College. In 1957, Stetson University in DeLand, Florida, hired him as head basketball coach. He married his wife, Jan, in 1957 and has five children.

Wilkes served 36 seasons as head basketball coach at Stetson from 1957 to 1993. His 551 wins ranked him thirty-ninth on the list of career major college basketball coaching victories. During the mid-1960s, Wilkes earned his Ph.D. in physical education from Stetson. He served as athletic director from 1965 to 1985. His teams competed in the NAIA until 1966, joined the NCAA Division II in 1966, and entered the NCAA Division I in 1973. Wilkes's first Division I squad, his single best team, produced a 22-4 record. His clubs remained independent until joining the TAAC in 1987. Wilkes produced two NAIA All-Americas, Joel Hancock and Lamar Deaver, and one NCAA Division II All-America, Earnest Killum. His teams reached the NAIA championship tournament five times (1953, 1957, 1960, 1962, 1963), made the NCAA Division II Tournament in 1967 and 1970, and captured third place in 1971.

Wilkes's longevity has earned him numerous distinctions among college basketball coaches. He coached 987 games, twentieth most in college basketball history. Only 16 mentors coached more years, but only 12, including Adolph Rupp*, Ray Meyer*, and Henry Iba*, remained as many or more years at one school. Only 61 coaches spanning all college classifications have surpassed him in career victories.

Wilkes wrote several books on basketball coaching, his first being *Winning Basketball Strategy* (1959). His third book, *Men's Basketball*, published in 1969, appeared in five editions. He also authored *The Basketball Coach's Complete Handbook* (1962) and *Fundamentals of Coaching Basketball* (1982). Besides writing several books and articles, Wilkes has produced motivational tapes for coaches and athletes. He taught physical education at Stetson and helped arrange exhibition games between college and foreign basketball teams.

BIBLIOGRAPHY: *CA* 17 (1986), p.483; Brian L. Laughlin, interview with Jim Jordan, Stetson University, January 4, 1994; *NCAA Men's Basketball Records, 2004* (Indianapolis, IN, 2003); Stetson University 1993–94 *Basketball Media Guide* (Deland, FL, 1993); *Who's Who in the South and Southwest*, 1980.

Brian L. Laughlin

WILKES, Jackson Keith. *See* Wilkes, Jamaal "Silk"

WILKES, Jamaal "Silk" (b. Jackson Keith Wilkes, May 2, 1953, Berkeley, CA), college and professional player, is the oldest son of Leander Wilkes and Thelma Wilkes. Wilkes attended Ventura (California) High School as a sophomore and junior and graduated from Santa

Barbara (California) High School in 1970. He made the CIF First Team from to 1968 to 1970 and was selected its 1970 Player of the Year. Coach John Wooden* of UCLA (PEC) recruited him. With the UCLA Bruins, Wilkes played for the 1972 and 1973 NCAA championship teams and the 1974 third-place team. He scored 1,349 career points for UCLA, averaging nearly 15.0 points and 7 rebounds and making consensus All-America in 1973 and 1974.

In 1974, the Golden State Warriors (NBA) chose Wilkes in the first round as the eleventh overall pick. The six-foot six-inch, 190-pound forward played 12 NBA seasons, performing for the Golden State Warriors (1974–1977), Los Angeles Lakers (1977–1985), and Los Angeles Clippers (1985–1986). In 1975, he attained NBA Rookie of the Year honors and made the NBA All-Rookie Team. The Los Angeles Lakers signed him as a free agent in July 1977. Wilkes's career saw him selected twice to the NBA All-Defensive Second Team (1976–1977) and three times to the NBA All-Star Team (1976, 1981, 1983). Wilkes appeared in six NBA championship series, including one with the Warriors (1975) and five with the Lakers (1980, 1982–1985), and performed on the 1975, 1980, 1982, and 1985 title teams. In September 1985, he joined the Los Angeles Clippers as a free agent. The consistent player averaged 17.7 points and 6.1 rebounds during 828 regular-season games and 16.1 points and 6.3 rebounds in 113 playoff games. He has operated a real estate firm, "Smooth as Silk," since 1986 and resides in the Los Angeles, California area with his wife, Valerie, and their three children.

BIBLIOGRAPHY: Mike Douchant, *Encyclopedia of College Basketball* (Detroit, MI, 1995); Scott Howard-Cooper, *The Bruins 100* (Lenexa, KS, 1999); Curry Kirkpatrick, "Who Are these Guys?," *SI* 38 (February 5, 1973); Roland Lazenby, *The Lakers: A Basketball Journey* (Indianapolis, IN, 1996); Bill Libby, *The Walton Gang* (New York, 1981); *Official NCAA Basketball Records, 1981* (Shawnee Mission, KS, 1981); Billy Packer and Roland Lazenby, *College Basketball's 25 Greatest Teams* (St. Louis, MO, 1989); Ken Shouler et al., *Total Basketball* (Wilmington, DE, 2003); *TSN Official NBA Register, 1986–1987* (St. Louis, MO, 1986); Bill Walton, *Nothing but Net* (New York, 1994); Jerry West, telephone interview with James E. Welch, November 29, 1990; Jamaal Wilkes, telephone interview with James E. Welch, December 5, 1990.

James E. Welch

WILKINS, Jacques Dominique "Dr. Dunk" "Nique" "Zoid" (b. January 12, 1960, Sorbonne, France), college and professional player and executive, is the second oldest of eight children born to John Wilkins and Gertrude Wilkins. His father served three years of U.S. Army duty in Paris, France. The Wilkins family then settled in Baltimore, Maryland, where his parents soon divorced. Wilkins spent summers with his grandparents in Washington, North Carolina, and attended Washington High School. The Washington squad, led by Wilkins, won 56 consecutive games, then the nation's longest streak, and two state titles. As a senior, he averaged 29 points and 16 rebounds and attained high school All-America.

An intense recruiting campaign and considerable indecision followed. The shy Wilkins enrolled at the University of Georgia (SEC), an unlikely institution to showcase his basketball skills. Under coach Hugh Durham*, he led the Bulldogs to the 1981 SEC Tournament as a sophomore and was selected tournament MVP. During his junior year, Wilkins became the all-time Georgia career scoring leader, averaged 21.6 points, and led his team in blocked shots. The three-time All-SEC choice and First-Team All-America sought early entry into the NBA. The financially struggling Utah Jazz (NBA) drafted him third overall and dispatched him in September 1982 to the Atlanta Hawks (NBA) for $1 million, All-Star forward John Drew, and Freeman Williams Jr*.

Wilkins quickly reached NBA stardom, averaging 17.5 points and being named Rookie of the Year in 1983. He was nicknamed the "Human Highlight Film" because of his acrobatic, powerful dunks. With his 48-inch vertical leap, 9.8 second speed in the 100 yard dash, and heavily muscled, six-foot eight-inch, 200-pound frame, Wilkins specialized in unstoppable tomahawk dunks. He won the NBA Slam Dunk title in 1985 and 1990 and finished second in 1986 and 1988. His dunking prowess enabled him to score a career- and NBA-high 30.7 points per game in the 1987–1988 season. However, critics labeled him a slam-dunking machine more interested in personal statistics than team performance. He won the NBA scoring title in 1985–1986 and finished second in scoring three times from 1987 to 1993.

In February 1994, the Hawks traded Wilkins to the Los Angeles Clippers (NBA) for Danny Manning*. Wilkens spent the 1994–1995 season with the Boston Celtics (NBA) and played with Panathinaikos in the Greek League in 1995–1996. His other clubs included the San Antonio Spurs (NBA) in 1996–1997, Teamsystem Balogna (ItL) in 1997–1998, and the Orlando Magic (NBA) in 1998–1999. He retired following the 1998–1999 season. The charges of being a one-dimensional player hurt Wilkins, who improved his defense and passing and diversified his shot selection. He developed into an all-around player who remained among the NBA's scoring leaders.

During 15 NBA seasons, Wilkins participated in eight All-Star Games and led the Hawks to a Central Division title in 1986–1987. In 1,074 games, he compiled 26,668 points (24.8-point average), 7,169 rebounds, and 378 steals. Wilkins, who twice scored 57 points in a game, holds Hawks records in scoring, field goals, free throws made, and scoring average. He holds the single-game record for most free throws without a miss with 23 against the Chicago Bulls in December 1992. Wilkins made the All-NBA First Team in 1986, All-NBA Second Team in 1987, 1988, 1991, and 1993, and All-NBA Third Team in 1989 and 1994. His career scoring average ranks tenth highest in NBA history. Wilkins relished competing against his younger brother, Gerald, who played guard for the New York Knicks (NBA) and three other teams. Wilkins, who enjoys playing tennis and listening to jazz music, has a daughter Aisha, who lives in Los Angeles, California. After serving as special assistant to the executive vice president of the Atlanta Hawks, he was promoted to vice president of basketball operations in 2004.

BIBLIOGRAPHY: *Atlanta Hawks Media Guide, 2004–2005* (Atlanta, GA, 2004); Steve Brunner, "Hawks Have Turned Wilkins' Direction," *Gwinnett* (GA) *Daily News*, March 15, 1985; Mike Douchant, *Encyclopedia of College Basketball* (Detroit, MI, 1995); Roy S. Johnson, "Flash: If You've Got It, Flaunt It," *NYT*, February 9, 1986; Jack McCallum, "Dominique Had Himself a Picnique," *SI* 59 (April 28, 1986), pp. 30–32, 37; Kenneth Richardson, "The Right Stuff Plus," *Seattle* (WA) *Post-Intelligencer*, February 8, 1986, pp. B1, B3; Ken Shouler et al., *Total Basketball* (Wilmington DE, 2003); *TSN Official NBA Register, 2004–2005* (St. Louis, MO, 2004); *USA Today*, April 23, 1991; Mark Whicker, "The Unique 'Nique," *BT* January 9, 1986; Jack White, "In North Carolina: The Strange Case of 'Dr. Dunk,'" *Time* 114 (December 24, 1979), pp. 4–5; "Wilkins to Enter Draft," *NYT*, April 4, 1982, p. S8.

Bruce J. Dierenfield

WILKINSON, Richard Warren "Buzzy" (b. 1932 or 1933, Welch, WV), college player and executive, grew up in the small town of Pineville, West Virginia, about 30 miles north of Welch. His father, a doctor, had moved from Hopewell, Virginia to southern West Virginia during the Depression to establish a maternity clinic. By the standards of his era, Wilkinson should have been nicknamed the "Springfield Rifle," but his grandmother named him "Buzzy" because she thought he resembled a character in the comic strip "About Buzzy."

Wilkinson played basketball at Pineville High School and enrolled at Greenbrier (West Virginia) Military High School, from where he graduated. The University of Kentucky, coached by Adolph Rupp*, offered Wilkinson a scholarship to play basketball for the Wildcats, but he opted for the the University of Virginia Cavaliers.

The formation of the premier ACC in 1954 brought together natural rivalries and excitement among the member schools. The magic of competitive basketball and the creation of a superstar further enhanced the popularity of basketball. Wilkinson began his exciting varsity career with the Virginia Cavaliers in 1952–1953. The Cavaliers played the type of basketball that excited the fans and sustained their interest. Wilkinson shot numerous times from anywhere on the floor with equal accuracy. On December 1, 1954, he scored a career-high 48 points against Hampden-Sydney (Virginia) College. He registered 40 or more points in a single game 10 times in his career. On March 4, 1954, Wilkinson shot 44 times against Duke University (North Carolina), still a Cavalier and ACC record. He possessed an incredible eye for the basket and was considered a "pure shooter." Wilkinson compiled 2,233 career points, still third on the school's all-time list behind Jeff Lamp and Bryant Stith, and 11th on the ACC list. He recorded 521 points as a sophomore, 814 points as a junior, and 898 points his final season. Wilkinson, team captain of the 1954–1955 Cavaliers, became the first collegian to average 30 or more points in consecutive seasons. He averaged 30.1 points as a junior and 36.1 points the following year. His 28.6 points career average ranks him among the Top 25 Division I players. His 36.1 point average as a senior remains a school and a ACC record. He also holds Virginia and ACC records in field goals attempted and made, free throws attempted and made, and consecutive free throws.

The six-foot two-inch Wilkinson was selected by the Boston Celtics (NBA) in the 1955 NBA draft and was offered a no-cut contract by the Celtic organization. He was travelling to seek advice from Boston Coach "Red" Auerbach* when he suffered an automobile accident that terminated his playing days. Wilkinson became the first Cavalier to earn All-America honors and saw his jersey number 14 retired. Wilkinson entered law school in 1962 and earned his law degree from the University of Virginia. He never practiced law and has served since then as president and Chief Executive Officer of the First Century Bank in Bluefield, West Virginia.

BIBLIOGRAPHY: Peter C. Bjarkman, *The Biographical History of Basketball* (Chicago, IL, 2000); "Richard "Buzzy" Wilkinson," *Ahead of the Time*, http://www.Roanoke.com (2003); "Richard "Buzzy" Wilkinson," *Archives*, http://virginiasports.com (2003); "Richard "Buzzy" Wilkinson," *Statistics and Records*, http://www.virginiasports.com (2003); "Richard "Buzzy" Wilkinson," *Where Are They Now?*, http://www.virginiasports.com (2003).

John L. Evers

WILLIAMS, Freeman, Jr. "Free" (b. May 15, 1956, Los Angeles, CA), college and professional player, led the nation in scoring in 1976–1977 and 1977–1978, averaging 38.8 and 35.9 points as a basketball guard at Portland (Oregon) State University. Williams finished second nationally in scoring in 1975–1976, compiling a 30.9 point average as a sophomore. Williams tallied 3,249 career points in four seasons with the Vikings, rating second highest in history behind Pete Maravich*. His honors included making the 1978 Coaches First and *TSN* Second All-America Teams and playing on the U.S. championship squad at the 1977 World University Games.

Williams, the six-foot four-inch, 195-pound son of Freeman Williams Sr. graduated from Los Angeles Manual Arts High School in 1974 and was named to the All-City basketball squad. The Portland State business major garnered 50 or more points six times. His best single game performances included 81 points against Rocky Mountain College (third highest in history), 71 versus Southern Oregon State College (sixth best), and 66 against George Fox College (Oregon; tenth highest). "He's an amazing pure shooter with eye-popping range," Jim Van Valkenburg of the NCAA Statistics Service declared. "Williams gets 10 more shots per game from the field than his competitors." Portland State, a major Pacific Coast independent, played nearly two-thirds of its games on the road under Coach Ken Edwards, compiling a combined 65-41 (.613 percent) win-loss record during Williams career.

Williams graduated with a Bachelor's degree from Portland State in 1978 and was drafted in the first round by the Boston Celtics (NBA) as the eighth player taken overall. Boston traded him in August 1978 to the San Diego Clippers (NBA). He made NBA All-Rookie Second Team and netted an NBA career personal high of 51 points against the Phoenix Suns in January 1980. The December 1980 NBA Player of the Month averaged 26.8 points that month. His 19.3 point average for the entire season led San Diego scorers. Williams, who is unmarried and whose hobbies are movies and music, was traded to the Atlanta Hawks (NBA) in January 1982 and the Utah Jazz (NBA) in September 1982. He left Utah following the 1982–1983 season and appeared briefly with the Washington Bullets (NBA) during the 1985–1986 campaign. In 323 NBA games, he tallied 4,738 points and averaged 14.7 points per contest.

BIBLIOGRAPHY: Mike Douchant, *Encyclopedia of College Basketball* (Detroit, MI, 1995); Jan Hubbard, ed., *The Official NBA Basketball Encyclopedia*, 3rd ed. (New York, 2000); *NCAA Official Collegiate Basketball Guides, 1976–1979* (Shawnee Mission, KS, 1976–1979); *NCAA Men's Basketball Records,*

2004 (Indianapolis, IN, 2003); *TSN Official Basketball Register, 1982–1983* (St. Louis, MO, 1982); Freeman Williams Jr. file, Naismith Memorial Basketball Hall of Fame, Springfield, MA.

James D. Whalen and Wayne Patterson

WILLIAMS, Gary (b. March 9, 1945, Collingswood, NJ), college player and coach, is the son of Bill Williams, a bank check sorter, and Shirley Williams. Williams lived a disorderly home life, with his parents divorcing when he was age 14. He resided with his father and two brothers, and his interest turned to participation in sports to fulfill his needs.

Williams graduated in 1964 from Collingswood (New Jersey) High School, where he lettered four years in baseball and basketball. He graduated from the University of Maryland in 1968 with a Bachelor's degree in business. A point guard on the Maryland basketball squad, Williams started for the Terrapins during the 1965–1966, 1966–1967, and 1967–1968 seasons and captained the team as a senior. He helped the Maryland capture the 1965 Sugar Bowl championship and established a school record in field goal percentage in 1966 when he made all eight shots from the field against the University of South Carolina. Williams was inducted into the University of Maryland Hall of Fame in 1999. He and his wife, Diane, were married in 1968 and had one daughter Kristen, a school teacher, before their 1990 divorce.

Williams began his basketball coaching career in 1969 as a graduate assistant at Maryland under freshman coach Tom Davis. He served one year as an assistant basketball coach at Woodrow Wilson High School in Camden, New Jersey before becoming head coach. Williams led his first team in 1971–1972 to a perfect 27-0 record and the state championship. After one more season in Camden, he joined Tom Davis in 1972 as his assistant at Lafayette College (Pennsylvania) and served as head soccer coach. Williams accompanied Davis to Boston (Massachusetts) College in 1978. After one year there, he was named head basketball coach at American University (Washington, D.C.) in 1979. Williams led the Eagles to a 72-42 win-loss record in four years as their coach from 1979 to 1983. His 1981 team established a school record with 26 victories and only four losses, won the ECC title, and made their first of two NIT appearances.

Williams replaced Davis as head coach at Boston College in 1983 and posted a four-year, 76-45 win-loss record. The Maroon and Gold responded to him in his first season with a 25-7 record, a BEaC title, and a berth in the NCAA Tournament Sweet Sixteen, an accomplishment Boston College repeated in 1985. In three seasons as head basketball coach at Ohio State University from 1987 to 1990, Williams led the Buckeyes to three postseason appearances and an overall 59-41 record.

Williams returned to his Maryland alma mater in 1990 as head basketball coach and completed his 15th year at the helm in 2005. He directed the Terrapins to their first NCAA national championship in school history in 2002, and to the first of two consecutive appearances in the NCAA Final Four in 2001. The national title team, led by Juan Dixon, Lonny Baxter, and Chris Wilcox, recorded the most victories (32-4) in the school's history, the first outright ACC crown in 22 years, and the first ever number one seed in the NCAA tournament. Williams, the 2002 National and ACC Coach of the Year, produced more than 20 victories seven consecutive years and eight of nine campaigns through 2002–2003, while establishing a school-record 11 consecutive NCAA Tournament appearances. Maryland reached the NIT semifinals in 2004–2005. From 1990–1991 through 2004–2005, Williams has directed the men's basketball team to a 334-178 win-loss record; he owns a 27-year career record of 541 victories and 306 defeats.

BIBLIOGRAPHY: "Gary Williams," *Profile*, http://www.fansonly.com (2003); "Men's Basketball," *Maryland's 2002–2003 Results*, http://www.umterp.ocsn.com (2003); *NCAA Men's Basketball Records, 2004* (Indianapolis, IN, 2003); Paul McMullan, *Maryland Basketball* (Baltimore, MD, 2002); Grant Wahl and Seth Davis, "A Staggering Achievement," *SI* 15 (April 8, 2002), pp. 36–42.

John L. Evers

WILLIAMS, Jason "Jay" (b. September 10, 1981, Plainfield, NJ) college and professional player, is the only child of David Williams, a computer executive, and Althea Williams, an educator. Williams attended St. Joseph's High

School in Plainfield, New Jersey, where he excelled in academics and athletics. He was named a *Parade* and McDonald's All-America in high school and won the Morgan Wooten Award, given to the nation's top prep player.

Williams attended Duke University (North Carolina) from 1999 through 2002. An unusually strong and quick six-foot two-inch guard, he proved a versatile scorer and playmaker. Williams was named Second-Team All-ACC as a freshman in 2000 and First-Team All-ACC in 2001 and 2002. *TSN* selected him National Freshman of the Year in 2000. In 2001, he averaged 21.6 points and teamed with Shane Battier* to lead Duke to the NCAA championship. Williams was selected to the 2001 NCAA All–Final Four team and was named Player of the Year by *TSN*. He averaged 21.3 points in 2002, won the Wooden and Naismith awards, and was named National Player of the Year by AP and *TSN*. Williams led the ACC in scoring in 2001 and 2002 and scored 2,079 career points at Duke, the only player to reach 2,000 points in three seasons in that school's history. He averaged 19.3 points and 6.0 assists at Duke, which retired his number 12 in 2003.

Williams graduated in three years with a Bachelor's in sociology. The Chicago Bulls (NBA) made him the second pick of the 2002 draft. He averaged 9.5 points and 4.7 assists for the Bulls and was named Second Team NBA All-Rookie in 2003.

Williams suffered serious injuries, including a broken left leg and a fractured pelvis, in June 2003, when he crashed his motorcycle in Chicago, Illinois. These injuries kept him out of the 2003–2004 NBA season. In February 2004, the Bulls agreed to a $3 million buyout of his contract.

BIBLIOGRAPHY: Bill Brill with Mike Krzyzewski, *A Season Is a Lifetime: The Inside Story of the Duke Blue Devils and Their Championship Season* (New York, 1993); *Duke Basketball Media Guide, 2002–2003* (Durham, NC, 2002); Jack McCallum, "Double Feature," *SI*, 94 (February 5, 2001); Ken Shouler et al., *Total Basketball* (Wilmington, DE, 2003); *TSN Official NBA Register, 2003–2004* (St. Louis, MO, 2003); Alexander Wolff, "The Road Not Taken," *SI*, 95 (November 19, 2001).

Jim L. Sumner

WILLIAMS, Natalie Jean (b. November 30, 1970, Taylorsville, UT), college and professional player, is the daughter of Nate Williams, former NBA power forward, and Robyn Barker Gray, and has one sister and one brother. She grew up with her mother in Taylorsville, Utah where she began playing basketball in seventh grade. Williams played volleyball and basketball at Taylorsville High School, helping her team win state championships in both sports her senior year. She also participated in softball and won the state long-jump championship.

Williams matriculated at UCLA on a volleyball scholarship, but also played basketball. She led the volleyball team to the NCAA Final Four all four years and was named NCAA Player of the Year, and Asics/*Volleyball Monthly* Player of the Year. After being red-shirted in basketball her freshman year, she played four years for the Bruins. She was the first woman named All-America in both sports at UCLA and remains the only athlete named PTC Player of the Week in both sports in (different weeks). She was selected a Kodak All-America in basketball in 1993–1994.

After graduating with a Bachelor's degree in sociology in 1994, Williams concentrated on volleyball. She did not make the 1996 Olympic volleyball team and turned to basketball. Williams played center with the Portland Power in the newly formed ABL in 1996–1997, lifting them from the cellar to Western Conference champions. She was named PTC Athlete of the Decade in 1996, Utah's Woman Athlete of the Decade in 1996, Utah's Woman Athlete of the Century in 1996, and All-ABL First Team, All-ABL All-Star Team, and ABL MVP in 1997–1998. After a brief stint with the Long Beach Sting Rays, Williams was the third pick by the Utah Starzz (WNBA) in the first round of the 1999 WNBA draft. She made All-WNBA First Team for three consecutive seasons from 1999 to 2001 with the Starzz and led the WNBA in rebounding in 2000 with 11.6 per game. In 1999, Williams played in the first WNBA All-Star Game and led the victorious Western Conference team in scoring. She also appeared in the 2000 All-Star Game. Williams played on the gold medal–winning teams in both the 1998 and 2000 World Championships and the 2000 Olympics in Sydney, Australia. Nell Fortner, Team U.S.A.

coach, credited Williams with resurrecting and perfecting the art of catch-and shoot and indicated that she was virtually unstoppable once she had control of the ball. Williams adopted twins, a girl, Sydney, and a boy, Turasi, and opened "Natalie's" sports bar and restaurant in Salt Lake City in February 2001. In May 2003, the six-foot one-inch, 210-pound power forward was traded to the Indiana Fever (WNBA). Through 2004, she had tallied 2,643 points (14.5 average) and made 1,646 rebounds (8.8 average) in 87 WNBA games.

BIBLIOGRAPHY: Conrad Brunner, "William's Arrival Signals High Expectations for Fever," *Fever*, http://www.wnba.com/fever/news/feature_williams_031516.html (2003); Michele Kort, "Natalie Williams: Bo Jackson of College Sports," *Women's Sports and Fitness* (September 1991), p. 56; "OK, You Pick the Olympic Team," *Full Court Press: The Women's Basketball Journal*, http://www.fullcourt.com/columns/clay41499.html (*April 14, 1998*); *TSN Official WNBA Guide and Register, 2004* (St. Louis, MO, 2004); "Who's That?: Current Starzz Players," *StarzzFan*, http://www.starzzfan.com/PlyNatalie.htm (July, 2003); *Who's Who Among African Americans*, 16th ed. (Detroit, MI, 2003).

Jeannie P. Miller

WILLIAMS, Roy (b. August 1, 1950, Spruce Pine, NC), college coach, is the son of Mack Clayton "Babe" Williams and Mimmie Williams. His father was an alcoholic and often abused his mother, and there was never a close relationship between Roy and his father.

Williams grew up in Biltmore, North Carolina, where he attended T.C. Roberson High School. A four-year letterman in basketball and baseball, he made the All-West Carolina basketball team and captained in the 1968 North Carolina blue and white All-Star Game. Williams played on the University of North Carolina freshman team, but his playing days ended when he did not make the varsity squad. He graduated from North Carolina in 1972 with a Bachelor's degree in physical education.

Williams began his coaching career in 1973 at Charles D. Owen Swannanoa (North Carolina) High School. He coached basketball and other sports for five years before returning to North Carolina as an assistant to head basketball coach Dean Smith*. Williams remained an assistant for 10 seasons, helping guide the Tar Heels to 10 NCAA Tournament appearances, an NCAA championship game loss to Indiana University in 1981, and a victory over Georgetown (Washington, D.C.) University the following year for the national title.

Williams accepted the head basketball coaching position at the University of Kansas prior to the 1988–1989 season. He led the Jayhawks for 15 seasons through the 2002–2003 campaign. His teams averaged 27 victories each year, won 417 games, and lost only 100 times for an .807 winning percentage. Williams owned a 34-14 win-loss record in NCAA Tournament play at Kansas. He guided Kansas to 14 straight 20-win seasons, 14 consecutive NCAA Tournament appearances, nine BTWC championships, four BTWC Tournament titles, and four NCAA Final Fours. His teams finished second to Duke University (North Carolina) in 1991 and Syracuse (New York) University in 2003 for the NCAA national championship. Williams' squads won all three preseason NITs in which they have participated. He became the fourth fastest coach in NCAA Division I to reach 400 victories. In his tenure at Kansas, Williams developed a numerous outstanding players including Jacque Vaughn, Scot Pollard, Jerod Haase, Raef LaFrentz, Paul Pierce*, Ryan Robertson, T.J. Pugh, Nick Collison, Drew Gooden, and Kirk Hinrich.

Internationally, Williams served in 1991 and 1992 as assistant basketball coach for the U.S. teams in the World University Games and for the Olympic Development Team, and as the head coach of the 1993 U.S. team qualifying for the World Championships.

Williams was named USBA National Coach of the Year in 1990, AP Coach of the Year in 1992, and the Naismith and *TSN* National Coach of the Year in 1997. He has earned BTWC Coach of the Year honors seven times in 1990, 1992, 1995, 1996, 1997, 2000, and 2003.

Williams and his wife, Wanda, have a son, Scott, a former guard for the University of North Carolina basketball team, and a daughter, Kimberly, a senior at North Carolina.

In April 2003, Williams resigned his coaching position at Kansas to become the head basketball coach at the University of North

Carolina. He guided the Tar Heels to an 19–11 mark in 2003–2004 and to the second round of the NCAA tournament. The Tar Heels, led by Sean May, compiled 33-4 record in 2004–2005 and defeated the University of Illinois, 75-70, in the NCAA Finals. Williams became just the third men's basketball coach to title two NCAA Division I teams to the title game. In 17 seasons, has compiled a 470-116 win-loss record and a 41-15 mark in NCAA tournament play.

BIBLIOGRAPHY: Mike Douchant, *Encyclopedia of College Basketball* (Detroit, MI, 1995), Gary K. Johnson, *NCAA Basketball's Men's Finest* (Overland Park, KS, 1998); John Hendel, *Kansas Jayhawks* (Coal Valley, IL, 1991); William Nack, "Home At Last," *SI* 10 (March 10, 1997), pp. 55–58, 60, 65–66; *NCAA Men's Basketball Records, 2004* (Indianapolis, IN, 2003); "Roy Williams," *Big 12 Coach of the Year*, http://www.cingular.com (2001); "Roy Williams," *One Great Ride*, http://www.cingular.com (2002); "Roy Williams," *Profile*, http://www.usabasketball.com (2001); "Roy Williams," *Roy Williams's Honors*, http://www.rockchalkzone.com (1999).

John L. Evers

WITTE, Leslie "Les" (b. April 2, 1911, Swanton, NE; d. December 23, 1973, Denver, CO), college player, was the son of A. S. Witte and grew up in Lincoln, Nebraska. Witte enrolled at the University of Wyoming (RMC) in 1930 when his brother, Willard, an all-around University of Nebraska athlete, became Cowboys head basketball coach. Under the Witte brothers, Wyoming compiled an exceptional 89-14 win-loss basketball record. The six-foot two-inch forward led the Cowboys in scoring from 1930–1931 to 1933–1934, averaging around 11.5 points and accounting for over 25 percent of his team's production.

The 1930–1931 Cowboys captured an RMC championship, as Witte and the three other starters earned First Team All-RMC honors. Witte's 274 points set a school single-season record, with his left-handed hookshot posing as a potent offensive weapon. Wyoming posted a 19-4 record, but dropped its last two games to the University of Utah.

The Cowboys also captured the next three RMC championships, establishing the University of Wyoming as a regional and national basketball power. "It's Wyoming against the world," noted one sportswriter. No previous Wyoming cager had scored 1,000 career points. Witte's illustrious career culminated during 1934 when Wyoming advanced to the National AAU Tournament Finals in Kansas City, Missouri. The Cowboys lost the AAU championship 29-19 to the Diamond X Oilers of Tulsa, Oklahoma a semiprofessional squad of older, more experienced players. Witte, along with teammates Eddie McGinty, Art Haman, John Kimball, and Haskell "Pete" Leuty, earned AAU All-America honors.

Witte became Wyoming's first and only three-time All-America. In 1958, the HAF inducted Witte, Bill Russell* of the University of San Francisco, and Ed Macauley* of St. Louis University into its College Basketball Hall of Fame. Wyoming's first sports hero truly had earned these honors. Witte worked for the Bureau of Reclamation in Denver, Colorado, and was survived by his wife, Esther, and sons, William and James.

BIBLIOGRAPHY: Larry Birleffi, "The Golden Years," *Wyoming Eagle*, January 28, 1973; Mike Douchant, *Encyclopedia of College Basketball* (Detroit, MI, 1995); Bob Hammond, "Les Witte, Former Poke Great Dies," *Laramie* (WY) *Boomerang*, December 20, 1973; Alexander Weyand, *The Cavalcade of Basketball* (New York, 1960); *Wyoming Cowboy Cage Fever* (1989), p. 72.

Gregory S. Sojka

WOODARD, Lynette (b. August 12, 1959, Wichita, KS), college and professional player, is the daughter of fireman Lugene Woodard and Dorothy (Jenkins) Woodard. Woodard graduated from Wichita (Kansas) North High School in 1977 and the University of Kansas in 1981 with a Bachelor's degree in speech communications and human relations. During her last two years at Kansas, she earned Academic All-America honors with her 3.04 grade point average. In 1982, she began working on her Master's degree at the University of Kansas and served as a volunteer assistant coach. The articulate, poised, and friendly star is single.

Woodard scored a Division I record with 3,649 career points and led the nation in steals her last three collegiate seasons. As a sophomore, she set all-time Kansas single-game (49 points) and single-season (1,177 points) scoring records and a single-game rebound mark with 33. A three-time (1979 to 1981) BEC Tournament MVP, Woodard established BEC Tournament records for most points scored in a game (38), year (94), and career (302), and for career rebounding (123). Named a Kodak All-America four consecutive years (1978–1981), Woodard in 1981 won the Wade Trophy Award as the nation's outstanding women's basketball player. In 1981, she also was recognized as the Outstanding Female of the Year by the BEC and became the second woman ever nominated for the NCAA Top Five Award. Woodard held the women's career college scoring mark with 3,649 points.

Woodard's basketball talents earned her selection to several national teams. She toured Asia in 1978 with the U.S. Select Team and played the next summer in the Spartakiade Games in the U.S.S.R. After graduation from the University of Kansas, Woodard played in Italy and led the league in scoring. A member of the 1980 and 1984 Olympic teams, she helped win the first gold medal for the U.S. women's basketball team in the 1984 Los Angeles Olympic Games. Woodard also captured gold medals in the 1979 World University Games and the 1983 Pan-American Games, a Silver Medal in the 1983 World University Games, and second place in the 1983 World Championships. In 1980 she became the first female athlete inducted into the University of Kansas Hall of Fame and has been selected for the Kansas State High School Activities Hall of Fame. The Wichita branch of the NAACP recognized her as Woman of the Year for her outstanding community service in 1982. She in October 1985 became the first woman basketball player for the Harlem Globetrotters and added special spirit and fan attraction to the Globetrotters before leaving them two years later because of a contractual dispute. Woodard later played professionally in Italy and Japan, served as an assistant coach at Kansas, and played for the Cleveland Rockers (WNBA) in 1997 and Detroit Shock (WNBA) in 1998. She notched 217 points and 116 rebounds in 28 games in 1997 and 95 points and 66 rebounds in 27 games in 1998. During two WNBA seasons, she recorded 312 points (5.7 average) and 182 rebounds (3.3 average) in 55 games. In 2004, she was elected to the Naismith Memorial Basketball Hall of Fame.

BIBLIOGRAPHY: Steve Beitler, "Basketball," *Women's Sports 5* (November 1983), p. 38; Peter C. Bjarkman, *The Biographical History of Basketball* (Chicago, IL, 2000); Mike Douchant, *Encyclopedia of College Basketball* (Detroit, MI, 1995); Anne Janette Johnson, *Great Women in Sports* (Detroit, MI, 1996); Matthew Newman and Howard Schroeder, *Lynette Woodard* (1986); Burt Rosenthal, *Lynette Woodard: The First Female Globetrotter* (Chicago, IL, 1986); *TSN Official WNBA Guide and Register, 2000* (St. Louis, MO, 2000); *University of Kansas Women's Basketball Media Guide, 1983–1984* (Lawrence, KS, 1983); Marian Washington to Angela Lumpkin, August 14, 1984; Lynette Woodard file, Naismith Memorial Basketball Hall of Fame, Springfield, MA; Barbara Zeff to Angela Lumpkin, July 17, 1984.

Angela Lumpkin

WOODEN, John Robert (b. October 14, 1910, Hall, IN), college player and coach, is the son of Joshua Wooden and Roxie Wooden, who owned a 60-acre farm near Centerville, Indiana. Wooden's parents brought him up in austere surroundings and instilled moral principles in all of their four sons. When the farm failed, the Woodens moved to Martinsville, Indiana. There, Wooden met his future wife, Nellie Riley, and joined the high school basketball team. At five feet ten inches, he quickly dominated the game in a state obsessed by basketball. Wooden lettered four times and was selected as an All-State player his last three years. Martinsville captured the state championship in his junior season and finished runner-up in his sophomore and senior years.

Wooden played basketball for Ward "Piggy" Lambert* at Purdue University (Indiana) and enjoyed an extraordinary college career. Called the "India rubber man" for his suicidal dives on the court, he twice co-captained the Boilermakers. As a guard, Wooden set a WC scoring record with 154 points in his senior year and averaged 12.8 points. He was named to the WC, Midwestern, and All-America teams for all three years of varsity play. Wooden also received a WC medal for proficiency in scholarship (English) and athletics. During his senior year in 1932, he was chosen college basketball's Player of the Year. These honors reflected the spectacular seasons enjoyed by the Boilermakers. With Wooden as the playmaking guard exhibiting aggressive defensive instincts, Purdue won WC championships in 1930 and 1932, and also earned the national championship in 1932.

After college graduation, Wooden pursued a basketball career. For the next two years, he taught English and coached basketball, baseball, and track and field at Dayton (Kentucky) High School. During his first year, Wooden suffered his only losing season as a coach. To maintain his own skills, he played semiprofessional basketball on weekends for Kautsky's AC, earning $50 a game and a bonus for winning. Wooden once sank a record 132 consecutive free throws in competition. In 1934, he accepted a better position at South Bend (Indiana) Central High School. Wooden captured the conference title several times in nine years there, but never took the state championship. After Pearl Harbor was attacked, he enlisted in the armed forces and served as a lieutenant from 1943 to 1946. Wooden returned to his coaching duties after World War II, disillusioned by the discrimination against war veterans and by the inflationary spiral that put comfortable housing out of his reach. He left secondary school coaching after amassing 218 wins and just 42 losses, an amazing .839 percent winning ratio.

When Wooden received an offer in 1946 to enter the college basketball coaching ranks, he welcomed the opportunity. At Indiana State University in Terre Haute, he served as athletic director, head basketball and baseball coach, and teacher in the Physical Education Department. During his first year, Indiana State captured the conference title with an 18-7 record. Wooden, however, rejected a NAIA invitation to compete in its postseason tournament. The NAIA invitation contained a whites-only provision, while Wooden wanted a black reserve to be included. The next year, Indiana State elevated its performance to 29-7. The NAIA lifted its racial ban, as Indiana State lost in the finals to the University of Louisville (Kentucky). During these two years, Wooden won 47 and lost 14 for a .771 percent winning record.

Wooden desired to coach basketball at a BTC school, but the University of Minnesota telephoned its decision to hire him two hours late because of a raging snowstorm. Unaware of the situation, he reluctantly agreed to a $6,000 offer to coach basketball at UCLA, which had an inferior gymnasium and poorly prepared players. Although UCLA was tabbed to finish last in the PCC, Wooden led the Bruins to a 22-7 season in 1948–1949 for the most basketball wins the Bruins had ever posted. UCLA also captured the PCC's southern division. His success formula was simple and largely derivative. He believed in lengthy practices for conditioning and endless drills to perfect fundamental skills. Wooden also utilized Coach Lambert's "controlled offense with free-lance aspects," which meant a disciplined fast break with options dependent on the defensive alignment.

Although Wooden always had winning and even championship seasons at UCLA, sustained success did not come easily, quickly, or without significant changes. He did not like recruiting, and prospective players sometimes blanched at the 2,500-seat gymnasium. Occasionally Wooden clashed with promising athletes, who resisted his Christian piety, emotional outbursts, and exacting standards. By the early 1960s, however, the UCLA basketball program matured. Wooden hired combative former player Jerry Norman to recruit and react quickly to strategic shifts in game situations. With Wooden's approval, Norman and later Denny Crum* brought in numerous superior players, especially African-American ones. His premier players included All-Americas Walt Hazzard*, Gail Goodrich*, Lew Alcindor (Kareem Abdul-Jabbar*), Lucius Allen*, Mike Warren, Sidney Wicks*, Curtis Rowe, Henry Bibby, Bill Walton*, Jamaal Wilkes*, Richard Washington, and Dave Meyers. Wooden also included key substitutes in scrimmages with the first team. Heretofore, inexperienced substitutes had performed erratically in crucial games. Under the guidance of new athletic director J. D. Morgan, UCLA built a first-class facility named Pauley Pavilion. The facility in 2003 was renamed in honor of Wooden and his wife. Morgan also scheduled second-rate non-conference opponents for the Bruins to augment their record. Finally, Wooden used a demanding 2-2-1 full-court zone press, which was designed to harass and force the opponent's guards to throw errant passes or dribble carelessly.

Once these building blocks were laid, Wooden's teams scaled unprecedented heights. Indeed, no future team is likely to approach his UCLA coaching accomplishments. His Bruins set all-time records with four perfect 30-0 seasons, the greatest average margin of victory in a season (33 points in 1971–1972), 88 consecutive NCAA victories, 16 PEC championships, 38 straight NCAA Tournament victories, and 10 NCAA championships, including seven consecutive. No other coach has won more than four NCAA crowns. He ranks fourth all-time among college coaches with 885 wins and 203 losses, including 620 wins and 147 setbacks at UCLA, for an unequalled overall .813 winning percentage.

As Wooden entered the 1970s, Wooden seemed hard pressed to accept the different mores of his players and needed to motivate them to win after achieving unparalleled success. Some of his incredibly gifted players eyed lucrative pro contracts and frequently put individual statistics ahead of team play. Others, including Walton and Greg Lee, dabbled in political dissent during the Vietnam War and openly embraced the counterculture. Wooden bent his standards for the most talented performers, but believed he had accomplished all that basketball could offer. After UCLA won the NCAA title in 1975, he retired following 27 years of coaching the Bruins.

Wooden's illustrious basketball career was amply rewarded. He was the first person to be inducted into the Naismith Memorial Basketball Hall of Fame as both a player (1960) and a coach (1972). He was named Coach of the Year six times (1964, 1967, 1969, 1970, 1972, 1973), *TSN* Sportsman of the Year in 1969–1970, and the First Annual Dr. James Naismith Peach Basket Award winner in 1974 for outstanding contributions to basketball. For his contributions away from the sport, Wooden received honors for humanitarianism, fatherhood (he has two children, Nancy and James), alumni activities, and Christian leadership. In 1973 Campbell College (North Carolina) bestowed an Honorary Doctor of Humanities on him.

BIBLIOGRAPHY: Peter C. Bjarkman, *The Biographical History of Basketball* (Chicago, IL, 2000); *CB* (New York, 1976), pp. 450–452; Dwight Chapin and Jeff Prugh, *The Wizard of Westwood: Coach John Wooden and His UCLA Bruins* (Boston, MA, 1973); Mike Douchant, *Encyclopedia of College Basketball* (Detroit, MI, 1975); David Halberstam, *The Breaks of the Game* (New York, 1981); Zander Hollander, ed., *The Modern Encyclopedia of Basketball* (Garden City, NY, 1979); Scott Howard-Cooper, *The Bruins 100* (Lenexa, KS, 1999); *Indianapolis Star*, March 8, 1932; Neil D. Isaacs, *All the Moves: A History of College Basketball* (Philadelphia, PA, 1975); Neville Johnson, *The John Wooden Pyramid of Success* (2000); Curry Kirkpatrick, "The Ball in Two Different Courts," *SI* 37 (December 25, 1972), pp. 29–33; Curry Kirkpatrick, "Oh, Johnny, Oh, Johnny, Oh!" *SI* 36 (April 3, 1972), pp. 31–37; Roland Lazenby, *Fifty Years of the Final Four* (St. Louis, MO, 1987); Bill Libby, *The Walton Gang* (New York, 1981); Purdue University, news releases, West Lafayette, IN; Ken Shouler et al., *Total Basketball* (Wilmington, DE, 2003); UCLA news release, Los Angeles, CA; Bill Walton, *Nothing but Net* (New York, 1994); John Wooden file, Naismith Memorial Basketball Hall of Fame, Springfield, MA; John Wooden, *They Call Me Coach* (Waco, TX, 1972); John Wooden with Steve Jamison, *Wooden: A Lifetime of Observations On and Off the Court* (Lincolnwood, IL, 1997).

Bruce J. Dierenfield

WOOLPERT, Philipp D. "Phil" "The Thin Man of the Hilltop" (b. December 19, 1915, Danville, KY; d. May 5, 1987, Sequim, WA), college and professional player and coach, graduated from Manual Arts High School in Los Angeles in 1933 and earned a Bachelor's degree in 1940 from Loyola University of Los Angeles, where he played basketball as a forward-center under coach James Needles. His teammates included later coaching rivals Pete Newell* and Scotty McDonald. Loyola combined a tight, aggressive defense with a disciplined, patterned offense. Woolpert, a tall, thin, nervous, serious-minded intellectual, coached basketball at St. Ignatius Prep School in San Francisco, California from 1940 to 1950.

In 1950 the University of San Francisco, a Jesuit school, named Woolpert to replace Newell as head basketball coach. The Dons did not have a full-time assistant coach or their own gymnasium, practicing at St. Ignatius and playing home games at the Cow Palace. Woolpert, an introverted defensive genius, employed a tight, aggressive press, disdaining frills, showmanship, and racehorse basketball. San Francisco struggled to a 30-41 mark during his first three seasons. He recruited several local African American prospects who could play pressure defense and perform well academically. Minimal budgets mandated that players be recruited from the San Francisco area, not noted for its prep basketball. African American recruits included Bill Russell* a tall, lanky center who had not started at McClymonds High School in Oakland, California K. C. Jones,* a football star at Commerce High School in San Francisco, and Hal Perry. Woolpert taught Russell how to rebound and block shots, Jones how to renew his confidence after a ruptured appendix, and Perry how to play tough defense. He produced his first winning season with a 14-7 mark in 1953–1954, Russell's sophomore campaign.

After losing the third game of the 1954–1955 season to UCLA 47-40, San Francisco charged through their remaining 26 games without defeat. The 28-1 Dons won the CaBA title and led the nation in defense for the second consecutive year. Russell tallied 622 points, grabbed 594 rebounds, and blocked many shots, vaulting San Francisco to first place AP and UP national rankings. In the 1955 NCAA Finals at Kansas City, Missouri, the Dons triumphed over LaSalle University 77-63. Russell, the tournament MVP, scored 118 points in five games and earned First Team All-America honors, while Jones sparkled defensively.

San Francisco repeated as NCAA champions in 1955–1956 with a 29-0 record, capturing the CIT and NYHF and overwhelming all CaBA rivals. The Dons defeated all opponents by at least seven points, leading the nation in scoring (87.3 points per game average) and ranking second defensively (55.5-point average). Russell grabbed 607 rebounds, blocked many shots, and scored 597 points, while Jones and Perry played stellar defense. San Francisco defeated the University of Iowa 83-71 to take the NCAA crown again at Evanston, Illinois, as Russell scored 26 points and snared 27 rebounds. The Dons had attained 55 consecutive victories, retaining first place AP and UP national rankings. "I can't imagine a better team," Woolpert acknowledged. "We had find balance, excellent shooting, and tremendous defense." Russell and Jones, both First Team All-Americas, made the victorious 1956 U.S. Olympic basketball team.

Woolpert guided San Francisco to a 21-7 mark in 1956–1957. The University of Illinois snapped the Dons' winning streak at 60 games, but San Francisco repeated as CaBA titlists and reached the NCAA semifinals at Kansas City. Led by All-America Mike Farmer,* the 24-4 Dons won another CaBA title in 1957–1958, led the nation defensively, and ranked among the top four. San Francisco slumped to a 6-20 mark in 1958–1959, causing Woolpert to resign as head coach. The pressures of coaching, big-time recruiting, noisy crowds, ticket hustlers, alumni, and zone defenses, along with a back injury, discouraged him.

Woolpert had guided the Dons to a 153-78 record, three NCAA Final Four appearances, and two NCAA championships in nine seasons. The Dons' 60-game consecutive winning streak stood until UCLA broke it in the 1970s. Woolpert, UP Coach of the Year in 1955 and 1956 and NABC president, dared to start African-American players when other coaches demurred. His innovative defense and textbook press were adopted successfully by Newell at the University of California and John Wooden* at UCLA.

After coaching the San Francisco Saints of the short-lived ABL in 1961–1962, Woolpert coached the University of San Diego to a 90-90 record from 1962 to 1968. Woolpert, who boasted a 243-168 composite coaching record, served as athletic director at San Francisco from 1951 to 1959 and San Diego from 1962 to 1972. He and his wife, Mary, had three daughters, Mary Ann, Teresa, and Lorraine, and settled in Sequim, Washington, where he grew vegetables and drove a local school bus. In 1992, the Naismith Memorial Basketball Hall of Fame posthumously enshrined him. He also was inducted into the University of San Francisco and University of San Diego halls of fame.

BIBLIOGRAPHY: Peter C. Bjarkman, *The Biographical History of Basketball* (Chicago, IL, 2000); Morgan G. Brenner, *College Basketball's National Championships* (Lanham, MD, 1999); Mike Douchant, *Encyclopedia of College Basketball* (Detroit, MI,

1995); Zander Hollander, *The Modern Encyclopedia of Basketball* (New York, 1973); Neil D. Isaacs, *All the Moves: A History of College Basketball* (Philadelphia, PA, 1975); John D. McCallum, *College Basketball, U.S.A.* (New York, 1978); *NCAA Men's Basketball Records, 2004* (Indianapolis, IN, 2003); Billy Packer and Roland Lazenby, *College Basketball's 25 Greatest Teams* (St. Louis, MO, 1989); Bill Russell as told to William McSweeny, *Go Up for Glory* (New York, 1966); Jim Scott, "Success Story at U.S.F.," *Sport* 25 (March 1958), pp. 28–29, 64–67; Ken Shouler et al., *Total Basketball* (Wilmington, DE, 2003); *TSN*, May 18, 1987, p. 51; Alexander M. Weyand, *The Cavalcade of Basketball* (New York, 1960); Phil Woolpert file, Naismith Memorial Basketball Hall of Fame, Springfield, MA.

David L. Porter

WOOTTEN, Morgan (b. April 21, 1931, Durham, NC), high school coach, attended Montgomery Blair High School in Silver Spring, Maryland, where he lettered three years in basketball. Wootten played basketball one season at Montgomery JC. After graduating with a Bachelor's degree from the University of Maryland in 1955, he was hired as junior varsity football and basketball coach by Joe Gallagher, head basketball coach at St. John's College High School, a military high school in Washington, D.C. In 1956, Wootten was named assistant baseball, football, and basketball coach, and world history teacher at then relatively new St. John De Matha Catholic High School in Hyattsville, Maryland. He taught five periods of history a day. In Wootten's early years, his basketball teams lost to Archbishop John Carroll High School of Washington, D.C. Archbishop John Carroll won 55 consecutive games in 1959 and 1960, being led by Tom Hoover and John Thompson*. In 1961, Wootten coached DeMatha to a 27-1 record and their first number one ranking in the Washington metro region. The following season, the Stags finished 29-3 and ranked number one nationally.

Wootten's most memorable victory came in February 1965, when DeMatha ended the 71-game winning streak of New York City's Power Memorial High School, which featured seven-foot one-inch Lew Alcindor (later known as Kareem Abdul-Jabbar*). The Stags won the game 46-43, holding Alcindor to 16 points. To prepare his players for shooting over Alcindor, Wootten had them practice shooting over teammates holding tennis rackets over their heads. A capacity crowd braved a snowstorm and filled the University of Maryland's Cole Field House to see the game.

Wootten's lengthy career was filled with momentous games. De Matha trailed nationally-ranked Long Island (New York) Lutheran by 23 points in the fourth quarter in 1968 and won the game 71-68, allowing only five points in the final eight minutes. In the 1969 Knights of Columbus Tournament, the Stags faced the nation's top-ranked team, Washington, D.C.'s McKinley Tech. De Matha played without All-America James Brown (now a Fox sportscaster), who had been hospitalized for exhaustion after a semifinal victory. Wootten draped Brown's warmup jacket over a chair to inspire his players, who defeated McKinley 95-69. In the 1991 city championship game, De Matha overcame an 18 point deficit to defeat Dunbar High 72-71, on a buzzer-beating basket by Vaughn Jones and preserve a perfect record of 30-0.

Wootten's teams won five national championships and were ranked number one in the Washington metro area 22 times. Under Wootten, De Matha won at least 20 games in 44 seasons and never had a losing record. He sent 150 players to college basketball and 20 to professional basketball in the United States or abroad. Every senior Wootten ever coached received a college basketball scholarship, regardless of whether he was a starting player or a reserve at De Matha. Some players he coached who became standout college or professional players were John Austin, Sid Catlett, Aubrey Nash, James Brown, Adrian Dantley*, Charles "Hawkeve" Whitney, Kenny Carr, Derek Whittenburg, Sidney Lowe, Adrian Branch, Danny Ferry*, Joseph Forte, and Keith Bogans. Perry Clark, Mike Brey, Whittenburg, and Lowe became college or NBA coaches. Wootten also coached football from 1956 to 1968, mentoring eventual professional football players Brendan McCarthy and Garrett Ford. He was considered for the head coaching job at the University of Maryland in 1969 before Lefty Driesell* took the position. Wootten declined the head coaching position at North Carolina State University in 1980. He taught his high school history class until 1990.

Wootten hovered near death during the summer of 1996 while working at his basketball camp. He returned to coaching that fall after receiving a liver transplant and became a vocal advocate for organ transplants.

In 2000, Wootten became just the third person elected to the Naismith Memorial Basketball Hall of Fame based on a high school coaching career. The same year, he was voted the Naismith High School Coach of the Century. Wootten announced his retirement in November 2002. *SI* named him one of the 50 greatest sports figures from Maryland. He recorded 1,274 wins and only 192 losses for an .868 winning percentage. He and his wife, Kathy, have one daughter, Carol (Paul).

BIBLIOGRAPHY: Morgan Wootten file, Naismith Memorial Basketball Hall of Fame, Springfield, MA; Morgan Wootten Invitational website, www.mwinvite.com; Naismith Memorial Basketball Hall of Fame website, www.hoophall.com; Morgan Wootten basketball camp website, www.coachwootten.com.

Bijan C. Bayne

WORTHY, James Ager (b. February 27, 1961, Gastonia, NC), college and professional player, is the youngest son of Ervin Worthy and Gladys Worthy and graduated from Ashbrook High School in 1979, where he averaged 21.5 points and 12 rebounds as a senior and made consensus High School All-America, University of North Carolina (ACC) Coach Dean Smith* recruited Worthy, who averaged 14.5 points and 7.4 rebounds over three seasons. His honors included being selected to the All-ACC Team twice and an All-America in 1982. Worthy led the Wolfpack to two consecutive NCAA Final Four appearances. North Carolina lost to Indiana University, 63-50, in the 1981 finals, but defeated Georgetown University 63-62 for the 1982 Championship. Worthy, the MVP of the 1982 NCAA Final Four, left North Carolina following his junior year and entered the 1982 NBA draft. The Los Angeles Lakers drafted him in the first round.

The six-foot nine-inch, 235-pound forward played 12 seasons with the Lakers through the 1993–1994 campaign. He has appeared in 926 regular season games, scoring 6,320 points, averaging 17.6 points, and making 4,708 rebounds. He ranked high on the all-time NBA list for field percentage (.521) and has performed in seven NBA Finals (1983–1985, 1987–1989, 1991), on three NBA Championship teams (1985, 1987–1988), and in seven consecutive All-Star games (1986–1992). In 1991 the Lakers played the Portland Trail Blazers in the Western Conference Finals. Worthy sprained an ankle in the fifth game of the series, limiting him to jump shooting thereafter and sidelining him in the last game of the NBA Finals against the Chicago Bulls. The Lakers sorely missed his ability to supplement Magic Johnson* and uncharacteristically losing three consecutive home games and the final series, four games to one. In 1991 Worthy made the All-NBA Third Team for the second time. During the 1982–1983 season, Worthy tallied 1,033 points in 77 games and made the 1983 All-NBA Rookie team. He was named the 1988 NBA Finals MVP, averaging 21.1 points and 5.8 rebounds. Worthy, named to the NBA's 50th Anniversary All-Time Team in 1996, resides in the Los Angeles area with his wife, Angela (Wilder), and daughter, Sable. He was inducted into the Naismith Memorial Basketball Hall of Fame in 2003.

BIBLIOGRAPHY: Peter C. Bjarkman, *ACC-Atlantic Coast Conference Basketball* (Indianapolis, IN, 1996); David Daly, *One to Remember* (Asheboro, NC, 1991); Roland Lazenby, *The Lakers: A Basketball Journey* (Indianapolis, IN, 1996); Jan Hubbard, ed., *The Official NBA Encyclopedia*, 3rd ed. (New York, 2000); Los Angeles Lakers Public Relations Office, telephone interview with James E. Welch, November 1990; Ron Morris, *ACC Basketball: An Illustrated History* (Chapel Hill, NC, 1988); Bruce Newman, "At the Head of the Class," *SI* 58 (February 21, 1983), pp. 36–38; Bruce Newman, "Trust Worthy, Praise Worthy," *SI* 64 (March 19, 1986), pp. 51–52; Ken Rappoport, *Tales from the Tar Heel Locker Room* (Champaign IL, 2002); Dean Smith, *A Coach's Life: My Forty Years in Basketball* (Random House, 1999), *North Carolina National Championship, 1982* (UMI Publications, 1982); Ken Shouler et al., *Total Basketball* (Wilmington, DE, 2003); *TSN Official, Basketball Register, 2003–2004;* James Worthy file, Naismith Memorial Basketball Hall of Fame, Springfield, MA.

James E. Welch

Y

YANCEY, William James "Bill" "Yank" (b. April 2, 1904, Philadelphia, PA; d. April 13, 1971, Moorestown, NJ), professional athlete and scout, was the son of Charles B. Yancey and Emma (Davis) Yancey. Yancey completed eight years at Logan Elementary School and three years at Central High School in Philadelphia, Pennsylvania and began his professional baseball career as an infielder with the Philadelphia Giants in 1924. He married Louise Warrick on June 28, 1928 and had no children. After several seasons with the Giants, Yancey played for the Philadelphia Hilldale Daisies (ECL) in 1927 and 1931, the Philadelphia Tigers in 1928, New York Lincoln Giants (ANL) in 1929–1930, New York Black Yankees (NNL) from 1932 to 1934, Brooklyn Eagles (NNL) in 1935, New York Cubans (NNL) in 1935, Atlantic City, New Jersey Bacharach Giants (ECL) in 1931, and Philadelphia Stars (NNL) in 1936. In 1945, he managed the Atlanta Black Crackers.

Yancey, a wide-ranging shortstop, possessed good speed, sure hands, a strong and accurate arm, and an even disposition, and was highly regarded as a team player and defensive spark plug. The right-handed hitter delivered the occasional timely blow. Like all black baseball players, Yancey relished successes against white major league barnstormers. He participated in victories over the powerful Philadelphia Athletics (AL) in 1927 and Dizzy Dean's Brooklyn Bushwicks of the 1930s. An All-Star aggregation won only one of seven doubleheaders against its African-American opponents. Yancey also enjoyed outstanding baseball success in Panama, where he prepared a national team for the 1936 Berlin, Germany Summer Olympic Games and helped establish the Atlantic Side and Pacific Side national teams. The game was welcomed so enthusiastically that nearly one dozen players later entered the Negro Leagues from Panama.

During most of his professional baseball career, Yancey also starred as a guard in pro basketball. After performing with a Philadelphia team, he graduated to the superlative New York Renaissance and teamed with Negro League outfielder Clarence "Fats" Jenkins*. Organized in 1922, the Renaissance played until the 1940s with a record of 2,588 wins and 529 losses for an .830 winning percentage. Yancey, one of the Magnificent Seven of the 1930s heyday, teamed with Jenkins to initiate the team's devastating fast break. Although only five-feet nine-inches and 165-pounds, he became a masterful playmaker with a sharp eye for teammates cutting toward the basket. Yancey provided outside shooting, although his accuracy often was impaired by flipping shots underhanded. The Renaissance team was elected to the Naismith Memorial Basketball Hall of Fame as a unit in 1963.

During World War II, Yancey toured the China-Burma-India theater with a USO group. Subsequently, he managed baseball teams in Latin America, worked as a beer salesman, and enjoyed success as a baseball scout. He discovered baseball player Billy Bruton for the Milwaukee Braves (NL) and Al Downing for the New York Yankees (AL). Although childless, he and his wife, Louise, formed close relationships with many young ballplayers.

BIBLIOGRAPHY: Bill Bruton, telephone interview with A. D. Suehsdorf, March 2, 1984; Edwin Bancroft Henderson, *The Negro in Sports,* rev. ed. (Washington, D.C., 1949); Zander Hollander, ed., *The Pro Basketball Encyclopedia* (Los Angeles, CA, 1977); John Holway, *Voices from the Great Black Baseball Leagues* (New York, 1975); Monte Irvin, telephone interview with A. D. Suehsdorf, August 29, 1983; September 20, 1983; William "Judy" Johnson, telephone interview with A. D. Suehsdorf, September 21, 1983; Walter "Buck" Leonard, telephone interview with A. D. Suehsdorf, September 21, 1983; Ted Page, telephone interview with A. D. Suehsdorf, October 3, 1983; Robert W. Peterson, *Cages to Jump Shots: Pro Basketball's Early Years* (New York, 1990); Robert W. Peterson, *Only the Ball Was White* (Englewood Cliffs, NJ, 1970); Susan J. Rayl, *The New York Renaissance Professional Black Basketball Team, 1923–1950* (Syracuse, NY, 2001); James A. Riley, *The All-Time All-Stars of Black Baseball* (Cocoa, FL, 1983); James A. Riley, *The Biographical Encyclopedia of the Negro Leagues* (New York, 1994); Donn Rogosin, *Invisible Men: Life in Baseball's Negro League* (New York, 1983); Eyre Saitch, telephone interview with A. D. Suehsdorf, April 18, 1983; April 23, 1983; and May 10; 1984; Ken Shouler et al., *Total Basketball* (Wilmington, DE, 2003); Normal C. "Tweed" Webb, telephone interview with A. D. Suehsdorfs, December 28, 1983; William Yancey file, National Baseball Library, National Baseball Hall of Fame and Museum, Cooperstown, NY.

A. D. Suehsdorf

YARDLEY, George Harry, III "The Bird" (b. November 23, 1928, Hollywood, CA; d. August 12, 2004, Newport Beach, CA), college and professional player, was the son of building contractor George Yardley II and Dorothy Yardley. His father was the first University of Chicago athlete to captain both the football and basketball teams. At Newport High School in Balboa, California, Yardley excelled in football, basketball, and tennis. Without an athletic scholarship, he earned a Bachelor's degree in civil engineering in 1950 at Stanford University (California). He played varsity basketball from 1947–1948 to 1949–1950, scoring 820 points and making All-America in 1948–1949 and 1949–1950. Nicknamed "The Bird" because of his six-foot five-inch, 190-pound frame, the bald Yardley possessed knobby knees, ran with a lope, and did not look like a basketball player. The Fort Wayne Pistons (NBA) selected him in the first round of the 1950 NBA draft, but Yardley refused their offer and entered AAU basketball instead. In 1951 and 1952, he led the San Francisco Stewart Chevrolets to the AAU title and earned the MVP award in the National AAU Tournament. Yardley spent the 1952–1953 season in the U.S. Navy, helping his Los Alamitos, California team win the All-Service championship and AAU crown.

After turning professional with Fort Wayne in 1953–1954, Yardley experienced a mediocre rookie season. Yardley, encouraged to develop his game, pioneered a shooting style that helped revolutionize basketball. He altered his shot in midair to offset any moves made by the defense. With the Pistons between 1953 and 1958 (the franchise was transferred to Detroit in 1957) and the Syracuse Nationals (NBA) in 1959 and 1959–1960, Yardley played in 472 games, scored 9,065 points, and averaged 19.2 points. He led the NBA in scoring in 1957–1958, becoming the first player to score over 2,000 points in one season. His 2,001 season points (27.8 points average) eclipsed the 1,932 mark set by George Mikan* in the 1951–1952 season. Besides leading the Pistons in scoring (1956–1957 to 1957–1958) and rebounds (1956–1957), Yardley made the All-NBA First Team in 1958 and the All-NBA Second Team in 1957. He played in 46 playoff games, scoring 933 points for a 20.3 point average and played in six NBA All-Star Games from 1955 to 1960. Yardley established NBA records for the most free throws (665) and most free throw attempts (808) and set 11 individual Pistons marks. Between seasons, he worked as a developmental engineer and specialized in missiles. He invented the liquid oxygen seal, which helped make the Titan intercontinenal ballistic missile operative.

After scoring 482 points during the 1961–1962 season for the Los Angeles Jets (ABL), Yardley retired and worked as a sales engineer in Newport Beach, California. Yardley, a member of the HAF Hall of Fame, was elected to the Naismith Memorial Basketball Hall of Fame in 1996. He married Diana Gibson in 1953 and had three children, Marilyn, and twin sons, Robert and Richard. He battled arteriolateral sclerosis for over a year before his death.

BIBLIOGRAPHY: Zander Hollander, ed., *The Modern Encyclopedia of Basketball* (Garden City, NY, 1979); Zander Hollander, ed., *The Pro Basketball Encyclopedia* (Los Angeles, CA, 1977); Jan Hubbard, ed., *The Official NBA Encyclopedia*, 3rd ed. (New York, 2000); Neil D. Isaacs, *Vintage NBA* (Silver Spring, MD, 1996); Charles Salzberg, *From Set Shot to Slam Dunk* (New York, 1987); Ken Shouler et al., *Total Basketball* (Wilmington, DE, 2003); *TSN Official NBA Register, 2004–2005* (St. Louis, MO, 2004); George Yardley file, Naismith Memorial Basketball Hall of Fame, Springfield, MA.

John L. Evers

YOUNG, Jewell (b. January 18, 1913, Hedrick, IN; d. April 16, 2003, Bradenton, FL), college and professional player, was the son of Russell Young, an automotive executive, and Hazel Young, and starred as a basketball forward and baseball centerfielder at Jefferson High School in Lafayette, Indiana. Young made First Team All-America and All-WC at forward for Purdue University (Indiana) in 1937 and 1938, averaging 14.3 points and 15.3 points respectively, to lead all WC scorers. The six-foot, 160-pounder, an HAF Basketball Hall of Fame member, starred for the Boilermakers under coach Ward "Piggy" Lambert*. Purdue compiled a 49-11 (.817 percent) win–loss record between 1936 and 1938, garnering one shared and one outright WC basketball championship.

Young teamed with Robert Kessler, Glenn Downey, and Gene Anderson in 1936, helping Purdue defeat national champion University of Notre Dame (Indiana) by 14 points and tie Indiana University for the WC title. Two years later, the Boilermakers defeated DePaul University (Illinois), Loyola University of Chicago, the University of Southern California, and UCLA in nonconference action and edged defending WC co-champion University of Minnesota for the WC crown.

After graduating with a Bachelor's degree from Purdue in 1938, Young joined Indianapolis (NBL) and led the Kautskys in scoring in 1938–1939 with a 10.2 point average. He performed with the Kautskys in the 1939–1940 and 1941–1942 campaigns. The Kautskys suspended operations in 1942 because several players were inducted into military service after the United States entered World War II. Illness forced Young to play an abbreviated 1942–1943 season with the Oshkosh (Wisconsin) All-Stars (NBL). His NBL professional basketball career ended in 1946, when he played in eight games for the reorganized Indianapolis Kautskys. During five NBL seasons, he tallied 683 points in 88 games as a guard forward and averaged 7.8 points.

After coaching and teaching school between 1938 and 1954, Young joined Waddell and Reed Company of Indianapolis, Indiana. He married in 1938, had one child, and retired in 1972 as division manager.

BIBLIOGRAPHY: Peter C. Bjarkman, *Big Ten Basketball* (Indianapolis, IN, 1994); Mike Douchant, *Encyclopedia of College Basketball* (Detroit, MI, 1995); Lafayette Journal and Courier Staff, *Most Memorable Moments in Purdue Basketball History* (Champaign, IL, 1998); William G. Mokray, ed., *Ronald Encyclopedia of Basketball* (New York, 1963); Robert W. Peterson, *Cages to Jump Shots: Pro Basketball's Early Years* (New York, 1990); Alexander Weyand, *The Cavalcade of Basketball* (New York, 1960); Jewell Young file, Naismith Memorial Basketball Hall of Fame, Springfield, MA; Jewell Young, letter to James D. Whalen, February 4, 1991.

James D. Whalen and Wayne Patterson

YOW, Sandra Kay (b. March 14, 1942, Gibsonville, NC), college coach, is the daughter of Hilton Yow, a retired machinist, and Elizabeth Yow and the sister of Susan Yow, women's basketball head coach at Providence (Rhode Island) College, Debbie Yow, Athletic Director at the University of Maryland, and Ron Yow, a historic homes restorer. Yow, who is five feet, nine inches tall, starred in basketball at Gibsonville, North Carolina High School and still holds the school single-game scoring record with 52 points. She received a Bachelor of Arts degree in English and library science from East Carolina State University in 1964, but played only intramural basketball because the university lacked a women's team. In 1970, Yow earned a Master's degree in physical education from the University of North Carolina-Greensboro. She taught English and coached women's basketball for Gibsonville High School in (1964–1965) and Allen Jay High School in High Point, North Carolina in 1965–1969, compiling a 92-27 win-loss record. She served as women's head basketball coach at Elon College from 1972 to 1975, winning 57 of 76 contests and capturing two North Carolina state titles

Yow became head basketball coach at North Carolina State University in 1976. Through the 2004–2005 season, she has won 617 and lost 288 contests at North Carolina State and has compiled a 674-307 career mark to make her fifth winningest active basketball coach. Yow became only the fifth women's basketball coach to surpass 600 victories and just the third to collect 500 wins at one university. Under Yow, North Carolina State has won five ACC regular-season titles and four ACC Championships. She has taken North Carolina State to the ACC Finals 12 times and to the NCAA Tournament 18 times, making 10 NCAA Sweet Sixteen appearances. Her teams have won 20 or more games 19 times.

Yow served as the assistant basketball coach for the 1984 United States Olympic team that captured the gold medal in the Los Angeles games, and was selected head coach for the 1988 Olympic team in Seoul, South Korea, piloting the women to a gold medal. She led U.S. teams to gold medals at the 1996 Goodwill Games and 1996 World Basketball Championships and coached U.S. teams in the Pan-American Games and World University Games.

Yow's accolades include being only the fifth woman inducted into the Naismith Basketball Hall of Fame in 2002, winning the Carol Eckman Award of the WBCA and earning *SI for Women* 2000 National Coach of the Year honors. She also was inducted into the Women's Basketball Hall of Fame in 2000, received the President and Mrs. Bush 1999 Community Impact Award from the Fellowship of Christian Athletes, earned the *College Sports News* 1998 Coach of the Year award, and was elected to the Women's Sports Hall of Fame in 1988.

Yow's greatest victory came against breast cancer. Since being diagnosed in 1987, she has raised well over $1,000,000 for cancer research. Yow, who is single, lives in Cary, North Carolina and cares for her father.

BIBLIOGRAPHY: Ned Barnett, "Kay Yow: 2002 Tar Heel of the Year," newsobserver.com, (2004), pp. 1–11; Nena Ray Hawkes and John F. Seggar, *Celebrity Women Coaches: A Biographical Dictionary* (Westport, CT, 2000); Tony Haynes, "Kay Yow Set to be Enshrined in Basketball Hall of Fame," *Student Advantage* (Sept. 26, 2002), pp. 1–3; Linda Morton, "ECU educated, NCSU employed Kay Yow is Olympic bound," *Joyner Library University Archives* (Greenville, NC, 2002); Rosemarie Skaine, *Women College Basketball Coaches* (Jefferson, NC, 2001); David Smale, "Kay Yow to go to Hall of Fame," *Victory Magazine* (Fellowship of Christian Athletes, 2002), pp. 1–2; Sandra Kay Yow file, Naismith Memorial Basketball Hall of Fame, Springfield, MA.

Frank J. Olmsted

Z

ZASLOFSKY, Max "Slats" (b. December 7, 1925, Brooklyn, NY; d. October 15, 1985, New York, NY), college and professional player and coach, was one of the leading formative pro stars. His first basketball experience came at Thomas Jefferson High School in Brooklyn, New York. After two years in military service, Zaslofsky enrolled at St. John's University. His coach was legendary early pro basketball star Joe Lapchick*. Zaslofsky played in only 18 college games, averaging an undistinguished 7.8 points. Nevertheless, the Chicago Stags (BAA) expressed interest in him

During his rookie 1946–1947 season, the six-foot two-inch, 175-pound forward was named All-BAA First Team. Zaslofsky made All-BAA—NBA First Team the next three seasons. He led the BAA in scoring in 1947–1948 and the NBA in free-throw shooting in 1949–1950. After averaging 14.4 points as a rookie to finish fifth in the BAA, Zaslofsky scored 21 points per game in 1947–1948 and won the scoring championship. The next year, he ranked third in scoring in the BAA. Before the 1949–1950 season, the war between the NBL and the BAA ended and the NBA was formed. The Chicago Stags, however, did not profit by the merger and folded after only one year in the new NBA. Zaslofsky's name was put into a pool from which existing teams drafted. He ended up with the New York Knickerbockers (NBA), who acquired his contract from the defunct Stags for $10,000. The price was considered a bargain because Zaslofsky had been chosen All-NBA First Team that season. The move was a good investment for the Knicks, as Zaslofsky averaged 67 games a year primarily as a starter and scored 13 points per game over the next three seasons with New York. He gave some stability to a club that traditionally had been weak.

Zaslofsky played only sporadically in his last year in New York. He was traded to the Baltimore Bullets (NBA) before the 1953–1954 season and spent only a short time there before being traded in November 1953 to the Milwaukee Hawks (NBA). The next month, Zaslofsky was traded to the Fort Wayne Pistons (NBA). Still, the travel did not interfere with his game. With the three teams in 1953–1954, Zaslofsky played in 65 games, shot nearly 37 percent from the field (three points above his lifetime average) and 72 percent from the free throw line, made a respectable 160 rebounds, and averaged 12.5 points for his three employers. He finished his career with the Fort Wayne Pistons (1953–1956), where he was used sparingly. Zaslofsky ended his career with 7,990 points and a 14.8 points average and 1,093 assists in 540 regular season games spanning 10 professional seasons and added another 899 points in 63 playoff games with the Stags, Knicks, and Pistons. He appeared in the first BAA All-Star Game in 1946–1947 and scored 11 points in his only appearance in an NBA All-Star Game in 1952.

Zaslofsky favored the old-style two-hand set shot over the jump shot and scored many of his points on shots from beyond the 30 foot mark. Although an aggressive, hard-playing athlete, he amazingly never fouled out of a pro game. Zaslofsky coached two years in the ABA, compiling a 36-42 record with the New Jersey Americans in 1967–1968 and a 17-61 mark with the New York Nets the next season. His death ended a five-year battle with leukemia.

BIBLIOGRAPHY: Peter C. Bjarkman, *The Biographical History of Basketball* (Chicago, IL, 2000); Zander Hollander, ed., *Modern Encyclopedia of Basketball* (Garden City, NY, 1979); Jan Hubbard, ed., *The Official NBA Encyclopedia*, 3rd ed. (New York, 2000); Neil D. Isaacs, *Vintage NBA* (Silver Spring, MD, 1996); Frank Menke, ed., *Encyclopedia of Sports* (New York, 1972); William G. Mokray, ed., *Ronald Encyclopedia of Basketball* (New York, 1963); *TSN*, November 11, 1985; *TSN Official NBA Register*, 2004–2005 (St. Louis, MO, 2004).

Jay Berman

ZOLLNER, Fred (b. October 1, 1899, Little Falls, MN; d. June 21, 1982, North Miami Beach, FL), executive, whose name appears on the NBA Western Conference championship trophy, was the son of Theodore Zollner and was elected to the Naismith Memorial Basketball Hall of Fame in 1999 as a contributor. His father started the Zollner Corporation in Duluth, Minnesota in 1912 and moved the company to Fort Wayne, Indiana, in 1931. Zollner joined the firm in 1926, the year before earning his Bachelor's degree in mechanical engineering from the University of Minnesota. He entered professional basketball modestly in Fort Wayne, Indiana in 1939 when his Zollner Pistons Company, sponsored a team in an industrial league. Two years later, the team joined the NBL as the Fort Wayne Zollner Pistons.

The Zollner Pistons topped the NBL standings in 1942–1943, but lost to the Oshkosh (Wisconsin) All-Stars in the playoffs. The Pistons won the NBL title the next three seasons and three World Professional Basketball Tournaments in Chicago from 1944 through 1946. They were officially employed by the company and received regular wages. Zollner put all of the team's income beyond expenses into a kitty, which was divided up by the players at season's end. Each share was worth several thousand dollars, making the Pistons by far the best paid players in pro basketball.

Zollner took his Pistons into the short-lived BAA in 1948 and helped lead the merger of the BAA with the older NBL to form the NBA in 1949. He presided over the Zollner Pistons Company, which manufactured up to 70 percent of the world's heavy-duty aluminum pistons for internal combustion engines. Zollner, probably the wealthiest of the infant NBA's owners, contributed generously to the NBA's survival.

Zollner strongly advocated changes to speed up the game and reduce fouling, including the 24-second shot clock, the six-foul rule, and widening the foul lane from nine to 12 feet to keep big men farther from the basket. He sold the Pistons in 1974 to a Detroit group. The team continues today as the Detroit Pistons.

BIBLIOGRAPHY: *Basketball* (November 1946), pp. 5–6; *Fort Wayne Journal-Gazette*, June 23, 1982, pp. 6A, 8A, 1B; *Fort Wayne (IN) News-Sentinel*, June 22, 1982, pp. 1A, 5A–6A, 1C–2C; Neil D. Isaacs, *Vintage NBA* (Silver Spring, MD, 1996); Robert W. Peterson, *Cages to Jump Shots: Pro Basketball's Early Years* (New York, 1990); Ken Shouler et al., *Total Basketball* (Wilmington, DE, 2003); Fred Zollner file, Naismith Memorial Basketball Hall of Fame, Springfield, MA.

David L. Porter

Appendix 1
Entries by Place of Birth

The following lists the entries alphabetically by their state or, in a few instances, foreign nation of birth.

ALABAMA (6)

Charles Barkley
Derrick Coleman
William Gates
Travis Grant
William Smith
Ben Wallace

ARIZONA (2)

Sean Elliott
Paul Silas

ARKANSAS (8)

Gordon Carpenter
Joan Crawford
Hazel Crutcher
Sidney Moncrief
Scottie Pippen
Glen Rice
Lurlyne Greer Rogers
Reece Tatum

CALIFORNIA (35)

Richard Adelman
Walter Allen
Don Barksdale
Denzil Crum
Denise Curry
Howard Dallmar
Ann Meyers Drysdale
Robert Feerick
Gale Goodrich Jr.
David Greenwood
Alexander Hannum
Melvin Hutchins
Dennis Johnson
Kevin Johnson
Jason Kidd
Lisa Leslie
Frank Lubin
Angelo Luisetti
Arvid Mikkelsen
Cheryl Miller
Reginald Miller
Michael Montgomery
Edward O'Bannon Jr.
Gary Payton
Paul Pierce
James Pollard
Fred Scolari
Diana Taurasi
Tina Thompson
William Walton Jr.
Paul Westphal
Sidney Wicks
Jamaal Wilkes
Freeman Williams Jr.
George Yardley III

COLORADO (1)

Ronald Shavlik

CONNECTICUT (6)

Marcus Camby
Howard Cann
James Kennedy
Rebecca Lobo
Calvin Murphy
Nykesha Sales

DELAWARE (1)

Charles T. Cooper

DISTRICT OF COLUMBIA (8)

Elgin Baylor
David Bing
Austin Carr
Adrian Dantley
Johnny Dawkins Jr.
Marsha Sharp
James Shirley
John Thompson

FLORIDA (9)

Vincent Baker
Otis Birdsong
Vincent Carter
John Chaney
Clifford Ellis
Artis Gilmore
Tracy McGrady Jr.
Mitchell Richmond
David Robinson

GEORGIA (6)

Teresa Edwards
Walter Frazier II
World Free
Norman Nixon
Bill Spivey
Glenn Wilkes

HAWAII (1)

Luther Gulick

IDAHO (1)

Clarence Edmundson

ILLINOIS (33)

Mark Aguirre
Lewis Andreas
Maurice Cheeks
Paul Collins
Cynthia Cooper
Thomas Eddleman
Michael Finley
Harry Gallatin
Yolanda Griffith
Robert Gruenig
Timothy Hardaway
Hersey Hawkins
Francis Hearn
Daniel Issel
John Kerr
Edward Krause
Michael Krzyzewski
Arthur Lonborg
Stephanie McCarty
Raymond Meyer
George Mikan
Donald Ohl
Harlan Page
Andrew Phillip
Henry Porter
Kevin Porter
Cazzie Russell
Leonard Sachs
John Schommer
Jack Sikma
Gerald Sloan
Isiah Thomas III
Louis Wilke

INDIANA (37)

Stephen Alford
Richard Barnett
Michael Benson
Larry Bird
Vincent Boryla
Victor Bubas
Everett Case
Calbert Cheaney
Robert Cummings
Louie Dampier
Everett Dean
Terry Dischinger
Leroy Edwards

Paul Hinkle
Shawn Kemp
William Leonard
Clyde Lovellette
John MacLeod
Emmett McCracken
Arad McCutchan
George McInnis
Richard Mount
Charles Murphy
Paul Nowak
Paul Popovich
Ruth Riley
Glenn Robinson Jr.
Donald Schlundt
Norman Sloan
Charles Taylor
Arthur Trester
Richard Van Arsdale
Thomas Van Arsdale
Robert Vandivier
W. R. Wells
John Wooden
Jewell Young

IOWA (6)

Denise Long Sturdy Andre
John Dee
William Fitch
Lynne Lorenzen
Olan Ruble
Robert Spencer

KANSAS (15)

Alva Duer
Paul Endacott
Harold Foster
Gene Keady
John McLendon
Ralph Miller
Adolph Rupp
Arthur Schabinger
Ernest Schmidt
Everett Shelton
Dean Smith
Jackie Stiles
Eddie Sutton
Gerald Tucker
Lynette Woodard

KENTUCKY (12)

David Cowens
Edgar Diddle Sr.
Hugh Durham
Joseph Fulks
Clarence Gaines
Darrell Griffith
Clifford Hagan
Frank Ramsey
Arnold Risen
Franklin Selvy
Westley Unseld
Philipp Woolpert

LOUISIANA (17)

Clara Baer
William Leon Barmore
Alana Beard
Frank Brian
Clyde Drexler
Joe Dumars III
Elvin Hayes
Antwan Jamison
Marques Johnson
James Jones
Pamela Kelly
Robert Love
Karl Malone
Robert Parish
Robert Pettit
Willis Reed Jr.
William Russell

MARYLAND (4)

Leonard Bias
Daniel Ferry
George Hepbron
Eugene Shue

MASSACHUSETTS (11)

Walter Brown
James Calhoun
Robert Carpenter
George Haggerty
George Hoyt
William Laimbeer
Anthony Lavelli Jr.
Lawrence O'Brien Jr.

Stanley Stutz
Oswald Tower
Tara VanDerveer

MICHIGAN (14)

Shane Battier
David DeBusshere
George Gervin
Thomas Izzo
Earvin Johnson Jr.
Daniel Majerle
Kenyon Martin
Donald Nelson
William Reid
Danny Roundfield
Steven Smith
Rudolph Tomjanovich Jr.
Chester Walker
Mayce Webber

MINNESOTA (7)

Fred Enke
Clifford Fagan
Richard Garmaker
Burette Haldorson
George Keogan
Kevin McHale
Fred Zollner

MISSISSIPPI (7)

Sue Gunter
Spencer Haywood
Patricia Hoskins
Janice Lawrence
Scott May
Lusia Harris Stewart
Lily Wade

MISSOURI (15)

Forrest Allen
Lucious Allen Jr.
Gene Bartow
Richard Boushka
William Bradley
Forrest DeBernardi
Lowell Fitzsimmons
Henry Iba
Robert Kurland
Edward Macauley
Billie Moore
Norman Stewart
Bertha Frank Teague
Billy Tubbs
Joseph White

NEBRASKA (3)

Edgar Hickey
Kenneth Sailors
Leslie Witte

NEW HAMPSHIRE (1)

Ernest Blood

NEW JERSEY (24)

Alvin Attles Jr.
Thomas Barlow
Richard Barry III
Carol Blazejowski
Bernhard Borgmann
Bernard Carnevale
Tamika Catchings
Anne Donovan
Fulvio Forte Jr.
Michael Fratello
Thomas Heinsohn
Matthew Kennedy
William Mokray
Frank Morganweck
John O'Brien
Shaquille O'Neal
Dennis Rodman
John Roosma
Catherine Cowan Rush
Willem Van Breda Kolff
Robert Verga
David Walsh
Gary Williams
Jason Williams

NEW MEXICO (2)

Bill Bridges
James Gardner

NEW YORK (74)

Kareem Abdul-Jabbar
Cermelo Anthony

Nathaniel Archibald
Arnold Auerbach
David Banks
John Beckman
Suzanne Bird
James Boeheim Jr.
Elton Brand
Carl Braun
Joseph Brennan
Lawrence Brown
Roger Brown
Luigi Carnesecca
Alfred Cervi
Lawrence Costello
Robert Cousy
William Cunningham
Henry Dehnert
Julius Erving
Harry Fisher
Lawrence Fleisher
James Freeman
Max Friedman
Sihugo Green
Richard Guerin
Victor Hanson
Lester Harrison
Cornelius Hawkins
Alfred Heerdt
Arthur Heyman
Chamique Holdsclaw
Nathan Holman
William Holzman
Charles Hyatt
Edward Irish
Michael Jordan
George Kaftan
Bernard King
Rudolph LaRusso
Christian Laettner
Robert Lanier Jr.
Joseph Lapchick
Christopher Leonard
Nancy Lieberman-Cline
Robert McDermott
Alfred McGuire
Frank McGuire
Richard McGuire
Christopher Mullin
Jeffrey Mullins
John Nucatola
John O'Brien
Richard Phelps
Richard Pitino
Ernest Reich
Patrick Riley
Elmer Ripley
Jennifer Rizzotti
Leonard Rosenbluth
John Russell
Eyre Saitch
Adolph Schayes
Charles Scott
Bernard Sedran
Catherine Starbird
Edward Steitz
David Stern
Sidney Tanenbaum
David Tobey
Edward Wachter
Robert Wanzer
Leonard Wilkens
Max Zaslofsky

NORTH CAROLINA (19)

Walter Bellamy
John Cobb
Melvin Daniels
Bradley Daugherty
Walter Davis
Phil Ford
Sylvia Hatchell
Ned Hemric
Louis Hudson
Samuel Jones
John Lucas Jr.
Robert McAdoo
Horace McKinney
Kelvin Sampson
David Thompson
Roy Williams
Morgan Wootten
James Worthy
Sandra Yow

NORTH DAKOTA (1)

Robert Luther Olson

OHIO (30)

William Anderson
Gary Bradds

John Bunn
Henry Carlson
Charles Chuckovits
Walter Dukes
Wayne Embry
Lawrence Foust
Clarence Francis
Robin Freeman
John Green
Alex Groza
John Havlicek
Edward Hickox
LeBron James
Gus Johnson Jr.
Donald Johnston
Eddie Jones
Robert Jones
Walter Jones
Robert Knight
Dwight Lamar
Jerry Lucas
Ramon Mears
Carl Neumann
Melvin Riebe
Alvin Robertson
Paul Seymour
Jerry Tarkanian
Nathaniel Thurmond

OKLAHOMA (10)

Ronald Boone
Donald Haskins
Marques Haynes
Louis Henson
William Johnson
A. E. Lemons
John McCracken
William Price
Joseph Reiff
Wayman Tisdale

OREGON (5)

Daniel Ainge
Cynthia Brown
Lauren Gale
Armony Gill
Howard Hobson

PENNSYLVANIA (40)

Mahdi Abdul-Rahmad
Paul Arizin
Kobe Bryant
Peter Carril
Wilton Chamberlain
Leonard Chappell
Claire Cribbs
Charles Daly
Charles Davies
Robert Davies
Eric Gathers
George Glamack
Thomas Gola
Theresa Shank Grentz
Richard Groat
Alvin Julian
George Karl
John Kundia
Kenneth Loeffler
Peter Maravich
Zigmund Mihalik
Lawrence Miller
Vernon Monroe
Ralph Morgan
Jameer Nelson
James Phelan
Rene Muth Portland
John Ramsay
Guy Rodgers
Edward Sadowski
Lynn St. John
Lionel Simmons
Dawn Staley
Marianne Crawford Stanley
Maurice Stokes
C. Vivian Stringer
Earl Strom
Jack Twyman
Norman Van Lier III
William Yancey

RHODE ISLAND (2)

Ernest Calverly
Frank Keaney

SOUTH CAROLINA (6)

Alexander English

Kevin Garnett
Meadow Lemon III
Katrina McClain
Jermaine O'Neal
Saudia Roundtree

SOUTH DAKOTA (2)

Justin Barry
Ward Lambert

TENNESSEE (12)

Jennifer Azzi
T. Wesley Bennett
Anfernee Hardaway
John Head
Bailey Howell
Andrew Landers
Nikkia McCray
Charles Newton
Oscar Robertson
Alline Banks Sprouse
Patricia Head Summitt
Nera White

TEXAS (20)

Don Baylor
Zelmo Beatty
Mack Calvin
Jody Conradt
Clarissa Davis-Wrightsil
Bruce Drake
Kamie Ethridge
Terrance Ford
Grant Hill
Larry Johnson
K. C. Jones
Guy Lewis
Slater Martin
William Naulls
Chukwuemeka Okafor
Harley Redin
Nolan Richardson Jr.
William Sharman
Sheryl Swoopes
Teresa Weatherspoon

UTAH (7)

Jerry Buss
Thomas Chambers
C. Arnold Ferrin Jr.
John Motta
John A. Thompson
Stanley Watts
Natalie Williams

VIRGINIA (9)

Robert Dandrige
Charles Driesell
Allen Iverson
Earl Lloyd
Moses Malone
Alonzo Mourning Jr.
Ralph Sampson Jr.
Joseph Smith
James Walker

WASHINGTON (2)

Marvin Harshman
John Stockton III

WEST VIRGINIA (9)

Clair Bee
Harold Greer
James Harrick Sr.
Eli Henderson
Robert Huggins
Rodney Hundley
George King Jr.
Jerry West
Richard Wilkinson

WISCONSIN (4)

Rick Majerus
Harold Olsen
Latrell Sprewell
Christian Steinmetz

FOREIGN NATIONS

AUSTRIA (1)

Harry Litwack

CANADA (4)

Robert Houbregs
James Naismith
Peter Newell
Ernest Quigley

ENGLAND (2)

Walter Meanwell
Abraham Saperstein

FRANCE (1)

Jacques Wilkins

GERMANY (2)

Dirk Nowitzki
Earnest Vandeweghe III

HUNGARY (1)

Frank Basloe

ITALY (2)

Geno Auriemma
Daniel Biasone

JAMAICA (1)

Patrick Ewing

LITHUANIA (1)

Senda Berenson Abbott

NIGERIA (1)

Hakeem Olajuwon

PANAMA (1)

Rolando Blackman

RUSSIA (2)

Edward Gottieb
Maurice Podoloff

SCOTLAND (1)

John Moir

VIRGIN ISLANDS (1)

Timothy Duncan

WEST INDIES (1)

Robert Douglas

ZAIRE (1)

Dikembo Mutombo

UNKNOWN (1)

James Furey

Appendix 2
Women Basketball Players and Coaches

Senda Berenson Abbott
Denise Long Sturdy Andre
Jennifer Azzi
Clara Baer
Alma Beard
Suzanne Bird
Carol Blazejowski
Janice Lawrence Braxton
Cindy Brown
Tamika Catchings
Jody Conradt
Cynthia Cooper
Joan Crawford
Hazel Walker Crutcher
Denise Curry
Clarissa Davis-Wrightsil
Anne Donovan
Ann Meyers Drysdale
Teresa Edwards
Kamie Ethridge
Theresa Shank Grentz
Yolanda Griffith
Sue Gunter
Sylvia Hatchell
Chamique Holdsclaw
Patricia Hoskins
Pamela Kelly
Lisa Leslie
Nancy Lieberman-Cline
Rebecca Lobo
Lynne Lorenzen
Katrina McClain
Nikki McCray
Cheryl Miller
Billie Moore
Rene Muth Portland
Ruth Riley
Jennifer Rizzotti
Lurlyne Greer Rogers
Saudia Roundtree
Catherine Cowan Rush
Nykesha Sales
Marsha Sharp
Alline Banks Sprouse
Dawn Staley
Marianne Crawford Stanley
Catherine Starbird
Lusia Harris Stewart
Jackie Stiles
C. Vivian Stringer
Patricia Head Summit
Sheryl Swoopes
Diana Taurasi
Bertha Frank Teague
Tina Thompson
Tara VanDerveer
Lily Margaret Wade
Teresa Weatherspoon
Nera White
Stephanie White
Natalle Williams
Lynette Woodard
Sandra Yow

Appendix 3

NAISMITH MEMORIAL BASKETBALL HALL OF FAME MEMBERS

PLAYERS (129)

Kareem Abdul-Jabbar
Nathaniel Archibald
Paul Arizin
Thomas Barlow
Richard Barry III
Elgin Baylor
John Beckman
Walter Bellamy
*Sergei Belov
David Bing
Larry Bird
Carol Blazejowski
Bernard Borgmann
William Bradley
Joseph Brennan
Alfred Cervi
Wilton Chamberlain
Charles Cooper
*Kresmir Cosic
Robert Cousy
David Cowens
Joan Crawford
William Cunningham
Denise Curry
*Drazen Dalipagic
Robert Davies
Forrest DeBernardi
David DeBusshere
Henry Dehnert
Anne Donovan
Clyde Drexler
Ann Meyers Drysdale
Paul Endacott
Alexander English
Julius Erving II
Harold Foster
Walter Frazier II
Max Friedman
Joseph Fulks
Lauren Gale
Harry Gallatin
William Gates
George Gervin
Thomas Gola
Gail Goodrich Jr.
Harold Greer
Robert Gruenig
Clifford Hagan
Victor Hanson
John Havlicek
Elvin Hayes
Marques Haynes
Thomas Heinsohn
Nathan Holman
Robert Houbregs
Bailey Howell
Charles Hyatt
Daniel Issel
Harry Jeannette
Earvin Johnson
William Johnson
Donald Johnston
K. C. Jones
Samuel Jones
Edward Krause
Robert Kurland
Robert Lanier Jr.

*members from foreign countries not included in this volume

Joseph Lapchick
Nancy Lieberman-Cline
Clyde Lovellette
Jerry Lucas
Angelo Luisetti
Edward Macauley
Robert McAdoo
Emmett McCracken
John McCracken
Robert McDermott
Richard McGuire
Kevin McHale
Moses Malone
Peter Maravich
*Hortencia Marcari
Slater Martin
*Dino Meneghin
George Mikan
Arild Mikkelsen
Cheryl Miller
Vernon Monroe
Calvin Murphy
Charles Murphy
Harlan Page
Robert Parish
*Drazen Petrovic
Robert Pettit
Andrew Phillip
James Pollard
Frank Ramsey
Willis Reed Jr.
Arnold Risen
Oscar Robertson
John Roosma
John Russell
William Russell
Adolph Schayes
Ernest Schmidt
John Schommer
Bernard Sedran
*Uljana Semanova
William Sharman
Christian Steinmetz
Lusia Harris Stewart
Maurice Stokes
Isiah Thomas III
David Thompson
John A. Thompson
Nathaniel Thurmond
John Twyman
Westley Unseld
Robert Vandivier
Edward Wachter
William Walton Jr.
Robert Wanzer
Jerry West
Nera White
Leonard Wilkens
Lynette Woodard
John Wooden
James Worthy
George Yardley

TEAMS (5)

Buffalo Germans
First Team
Harlem Globetrotters
New York Renaissance
Original Celtics

REFEREES (12)

James Enright
George Hepbron
George Hoyt
Matthew Kennedy
Lloyd Leith
Zigmund Mihalik
John Nucatola
Ernest Quigley
James Shirley
Earl Strom
David Tobey
David Walsh

COACHES (73)

Forrest Allen
William Anderson
Arnold Auerbach
William Barmore
Justin Barry
Ernest Blood
James Boeheim
Lawrence Brown
James Calhoun

*members from foreign countries not included in this volume

Howard Cann
Henry Carlson
Luigi Carnesecca
Bernard Carnevale
Peter Carril
Everett Case
John Chaney
Jody Conradt
Denzil Crum
Chuck Daly
Everett Dean
*Antonio Diaz-Miguel
Edgar Diddle Sr.
Bruce Drake
Clarence Gaines
James Gardner
Armony Gill
*Aleksandr Gomelsky
Sue Gunter
Alexander Hannum
Marvin Harshman
Donald Haskins
Edgar Hickey
Howard Hobson
William Holzman
Henry Iba
Alvin Julian
Frank Keaney
George Keogan
Robert Knight
Michael Krzyzewski
John Kundla
Ward Lambert
Harry Litwack
Kenneth Loeffler
Arthur Lonborg
Arad McCutchan
Alfred McGuire
Frank McGuire
John McLendon
Walter Meanwell
Raymond Meyer
Ralph Miller
Billie Moore
Peter Newell
*Aleksandar Nikolic
Robert Olson
John Ramsay
*Cesare Rubini
Adolph Rupp
Leonard Sachs
William Sharman
Everett Shelton
Dean Smith
Patricia Head Summitt
Fredrik Taylor
John Thompson
Lily Wade
Stanley Watts
Leonard Wilkens
John Wooden
Philipp Woolpert
Morgan Wootten
Sandra Yow

CONTRIBUTORS (50)

Senda Berenson Abbott
Clair Bee
Daniel Biasoni
***Hubie Brown
Walter Brown
John Bunn
***Jerry Colangelo
Robert Douglas
Alva Duer
Wayne Embry
Clifford Fagan
Harry Fisher
Lawrence Fleisher
Edward Gottlieb
Luther Gulick
Lester Harrison
Francis Hearn
*Ferenc Hepp
Edward Hickox
Paul Hinkle
Edward Irish
*R. William Jones
James Kennedy
Meadow Lemon III
Emil Liston
William Mokray
Ralph Morgan

*members from foreign countries not included in this volume
***member elected too late for inclusion in this volume

Frank Morganweck
James Naismith
Charles Newton
John J. O'Brien
Lawrence O'Brien Jr.
Harold Olsen
Maurice Podoloff
Henry Porter
William Reid Jr.
Elmer Ripley
Lynn St. John
Abraham Saperstein
Arthur Schabinger
**Amos Alonzo Stagg
*Boris Stankovic
Edward Steitz
Charles Taylor
Bertha Frank Teague
Oswald Tower
Arthur Trester
W. R. Wells
Louis Wilke
Fred Zollner

*members from foreign countries not included in this volume
**member in Football volume

Index

About the Editor and the Contributors

David L. Porter is Louis Tuttle Shangle Professor of History at William Penn University in Oskaloosa, Iowa. He has authored or edited 14 books on sports history and the U.S. Congress and specializes in sports biography and baseball history. His most recent books are *Latino and African American Athletes Today* (2004), *The San Diego Padres Encyclopedia* (co-authored, 2002), *Biographical Dictionary of American Sports: Baseball, Revised and Expanded Edition* (three volumes, 2000), and *African American Sports Greats* (1995). He served as associate editor of sports entries for the 24-volume *American National Biography* series. He and his wife, Marilyn, reside in Oskaloosa, Iowa and have two grown children.

The following people contributed basketball entries to one or more volumes. They are listed alphabetically with their official position at the time of their last contribution.

GUSTAVO N. AGRAIT, writer and communications consultant, San Juan, Puerto Rico.
MARK ALTSCHULER, professor, Department of American Studies, University of New Mexico, Albuquerque, New Mexico.
FREDERICK J. AUGUSTYN Jr., subject cataloger, economics and political science, Library of Congress, Washington, D.C.
BIJAN C. BAYNE, sports author and lecturer, Washington, D.C.
JAY BERMAN, professor, Department of Communications, California State University at Fullerton, Fullerton, California.
PETER C. BJARKMAN, sports author, Lafayette, Indiana.
**STEPHEN D. BODAYLA, head, Department of History and Pre-Law Coordinator, Marycrest College, Davenport, Iowa.
JACK C. BRAUN, associate professor, Edinboro University, Edinboro, Pennsylvania.
RON BRILEY, assistant headmaster, Sandia Preparatory School, Albuquerque, New Mexico.
ROBERT L. CANNON, lawyer and freelance writer, Santa Monica, California.
**STAN W. CARLSON, editor and publisher, Minneapolis, Minnesota.
DENNIS S. CLARK, instructor, Alternative Secondary Program, Lane Community College, Eugene, Oregon.
SCOTT A.G.M. CRAWFORD, associate professor, Department of Physical Education, Eastern Illinois University, Charleston, Illinois.
JUDITH A. DAVIDSON, director of intercollegiate athletics, Central Connecticut State University, New Britain, Connecticut.
CATHERINE M. DERRICK, former research specialist, Naismith Memorial Basketball Hall of Fame, Springfield, Massachusetts.
KAREL DE VEER, property manager, Santa Barbara, California.

**deceased

BRUCE J. DIERENFIELD, associate professor, Department of History, Canisius College, Buffalo, New York.
JOHN E. DIMEGLIO, Professor of History, Mankato State University, Mankato, Minnesota.
LISA A. ENNIS, coordinator of instruction and government documents, Georgia College and State University, Milledgeville, Georgia.
JOHN L. EVERS, high school teacher and administrator, Carmi, Illinois.
LEONARD H. FREY, professor, Department of Linguistics, San Diego State University, San Diego, California.
DANIEL FRIO, teacher, Wayland High School, Wayland, Massachusetts.
LARRY R. GERLACH, professor, Department of History, University of Utah, Salt Lake City, Utah.
DANIEL R. GILBERT, professor, Department of History, Moravian College, Bethlehem, Pennsylvania.
SARA-JANE GRIFFIN, professor, Department of Health and Physical Education, Pennsylvania State University, Wilkes-Barre Campus, Lehman, Pennsylvania.
ADOLPH H. GRUNDMAN, professor, Department of History, Metropolitan State College, Denver, Colorado.
WILLIAM A. GUDELUNAS, associate professor, Department of History, Pennsylvania State University, Schuylkill Campus, Schuylkill Haven, Pennsylvania.
MARY LOU GUST, professor, Department of Physical Education, Metropolitan State University, St. Paul, Minnesota.
CHRISTOPHER E. GUTHRIE, professor, Department of Social Sciences, Tarleton State University, Stephenville, Texas.
ALLAN HALL, athletic director, Department of Athletics, Ashland College, Ashland, Ohio.
JOHN DAVID HEALY, professor, Drew University, Madison, New Jersey.
JORGE IBER, professor, Department of History, Texas Tech University, Lubbock, Texas.
FREDERICK IVOR-CAMPBELL, freelance writer and historian, Warren, Rhode Island.
NJOKI-WA-KINYATTI, York College Library, City University of New York, Jamaica, New York.
TONY LADD, professor, Lifetime Fitness Center, Wheaton College, Wheaton, Illinois.
JAY LANGHAMMER, sales manager, Freeman Exhibit Company, sports editor of fraternity magazines, Fort Worth, Texas.
BRIAN L. LAUGHLIN, student, Creighton University Law School, Omaha, Nebraska.
ANGELA LUMPKIN, associate professor, Department of Physical Education, University of North Carolina at Chapel Hill, Chapel Hill, North Carolina.
BILL MALLON, physician and secretary general, international Society of Olympic Historians, Durham, North Carolina.
CURTICE R. MANG, insurance underwriter, Phoenix, Arizona.
GEORGE P. MANG, executive vice-president, Statewide Insurance Corporation, Phoenix, Arizona.
KEITH MCCLELLAN, editor and writer, Haworth Press, Oak Park, Michigan.
**ARTHUR F. MCCLURE, professor, Department of History, Central Missouri State University, Warrensburg, Missouri.
JEANNIE P. MILLER, director, Science and Engineering Services, Sterling C. Evans Library, Texas Agricultural and Mechanical University, College Station, Texas.
JON S. MORAN, associate professor, Department of Philosophy, Southwest Missouri State University, Springfield, Missouri.
JOHN G. MUNCIE, professor, Department of History, East Stroudsburg University, East Stroudsburg, Pennsylvania.
STEVE OLLOVE, freelance sportswriter and author of *Sportsbuff,* Hamilton, Massachusetts.
FRANK J. OLMSTED, Pastoral Department, De Smet Jesuit High School, St. Louis, Missouri.
KANT PATEL, associate professor, Department of Political Science, Southwest Missouri State University, Springfield, Missouri.
WAYNE PATTERSON, research specialist, Naismith Memorial Basketball Hall of Fame, Springfield, Massachusetts.
JOAN PAUL, professor and head, Department

**deceased

of Human Performance and Sport Studies, University of Tennessee, Knoxville, Tennessee.
ROBERT W. PETERSON, freelance writer and editor, Ramsey, New Jersey.
DAVID L. PORTER, Louis Tuttle Shangle Professor of History, William Penn University, and author, Oskaloosa, Iowa.
SUSAN J. RAYL, assistant professor, State University of New York at Cortland, Cortland, New York.
GEORGE ROBINSON, associate editor, *The Main Event*, and sportswriter, United Feature Syndicate and Newspaper Enterprise Association, New York, New York.
JEFF SANDERSON, former sports information director, William Penn University, Oskaloosa, Iowa.
ROBERT C. SAUNDERS, associate professor, Department of Physical Education, Marshall University, Huntington, West Virginia.
BARRY M. SCHUTZ, professor, Third World Studies, Defense Intelligence College, Washington, D.C.
FRED M. SHELLEY, professor, Department of Geography, University of Southern California, Los Angeles, California.
JOE LEE SMITH, public information director, Lamar University, Beaumont, Texas.
MAUREEN M. SMITH, associate professor, Department of Kinesiology, California State University-Sacramento, Sacramento, California.
*RONALD A. SMITH, professor, Department of Physical Education, Pennsylvania State University, University Park, Pennsylvania; and secretary-treasurer, North American Society for Sport History.
GREGORY S. SOJKA, academic dean, University of Wyoming/Casper College, Casper, Wyoming.
DI SU, York College Library, City University of New York, Jamaica, New York.
A. D. SUEHSDORF, writer and editor, Sonoma, California.
JIM L. SUMNER, historian, North Carolina State Historical Preservation Office, Raleigh, North Carolina.
WILLIAM A. SUTTON, professor, Department of Sports Management, Ohio State University, Columbus, Ohio.
FRANK W. THACKERAY, professor, Department of History, Indiana University Southeast, New Albany, Indiana.
ROBERT B. VAN ATTA, freelance writer and history editor, Greensburg *Tribune*, Greensburg, Pennsylvania.
JAMES E. WELCH, professor, Business Administration, Kentucky Wesleyan College, Owensboro, Kentucky.
JOEL WESTERHOLM, professor, Department of English, University of Connecticut, Storrs, Connecticut.
JAMES D. WHALEN, purchasing agent, credit union treasurer/manager, Federated Department Stores, Dayton, Ohio.
JOHN D. WINDHAUSEN, professor, Department of History, St. Anselm College, Manchester, New Hampshire.
THOMAS P. WOLF, professor, Department of Political Science, Indiana University Southeast, New Albany, Indiana.
JERRY JAYE WRIGHT, professor, Department of Physical Education, Pennsylvania State University, Altoona Campus, Altoona, Pennsylvania.
LAWRENCE E. ZIEWACZ, professor, Department of American Thought and Language, Michigan State University, East Lansing, Michigan.

**deceased